CONNECT

by experie...

Students will experience history in a variety of ways:

thinking about
SCIENCE & TECHNOLOGY

**Finding One's Way at Sea:
The Invention of Latitude and Longitude**

Long before the invention of global positioning system (GPS) devices, ancient mariners faced a nearly impossible task: finding their way when out of sight of land. To avoid disaster, sailors needed to be able to determine where they were in a vast ocean without any landmarks to guide them. But someone would first have to map and measure the earth before sailors would have the essential tools for calculating their location.

Hipparchus of Nicaea developed trigonometry, the mathematics of measuring angles, in the second century B.C.E. He used trigonometry to create an imaginary grid of latitude and longitude lines on the globe of the world (see **Figure 3.11**). Latitude (horizontal) lines measure the angle from the equator, and longitude (vertical) lines measure the angle from the prime meridian. All places on the earth have an address of sorts that we can express by their position on this grid, and because mathematics measures a circle in "degrees," we use this designation for the globe's address. Sicily, for example, is about 37 degrees north latitude and 14 degrees east longitude. This "address" is the same on Hipparchus's chart and in the GPS instruments we use today. Thus, with

trigonometry's invention, early sailors got the tools to compute their position on the global grid.

Yet mapping the earth and having the means to calculate one's position was just a first step. Mariners still had to determine their location on the global grid *while sailing on a vast, featureless*

FIGURE 3.11 Global Map Divided by Latitude and Longitude Lines

ocean. Calculating latitude was relatively easy, for that required only measuring the angle between the horizontal and a fixed location in the sky—either Polaris or the sun. Longitude was far more difficult to measure, because as the earth rotates during a 24-hour day, the

positions of Polaris and the sun move across the sky. One therefore has to know the exact time of day to calculate longitude. (For example, at the equator, a one-minute error in time causes about a 17-mile error in computing one's east-west position.)

Precise measurements of longitude while at sea would have to wait until the eighteenth century, when sophisticated clocks were invented that could compensate for the rough movements, caused by wind and waves, that had thrown off the accuracy of older clocks. Only then, with an accurate measure of the time of day, could a mariner calculate an exact reading of his longitude, just as we can do with our GPS devices.

Follow the development of navigation through the book. See, for example, the astrolabe in Figure 6.14 and the exploration of the world in Chapter 12.

Connecting Science & Society

1. How did Hipparchus's invention of trigonometry aid ancient sailors? What is the connection between measuring angles and finding one's way at sea?

2. What does the invention of latitude and longitude suggest about the relationships among science, people's practical needs, and inventions? What inventions (of new products or new processes) in your own lifetime show these relationships in action?

- With *Connect History*, students are no longer simply reading—they can also interact online with text activities, engaging in a visual, auditory, and hands-on experience.

- Through its narrative approach and its features, *The West in the World* emphasizes that history is not just a collection of facts but is created from the ongoing detective work of historians examining evidence from the past.

- "Thinking About" boxes—exploring primary source documents, geography, art, and (new to this edition) science and technology—involve students actively and analytically in the learning process, guiding them to approach documentary and material evidence in the ways that working historians do.

- *Connect History* helps students confirm what they know and learn what they don't know through interactive exercises and review questions.

- *Connect History* builds critical thinking skills by placing students in a "critical mission" and asking them to examine, evaluate, and analyze the data in order to support a point of view.

- *Connect History* includes tools for understanding maps and geography, exploring primary source documents, and writing a research paper (including how to document sources and avoid plagiarism).

THE WEST IN THE WORLD

Volume I: To 1715

THE WEST IN THE WORLD

Volume I: To 1715

FOURTH EDITION

Dennis Sherman
John Jay College
City University of New York

Joyce Salisbury
University of Wisconsin–Green Bay

The McGraw·Hill Companies

McGraw Hill
Connect
Learn
Succeed™

Published by McGraw-Hill, an imprint of The McGraw-Hill Companies, Inc., 1221 Avenue of the Americas,
New York, NY 10020. Copyright © 2011, 2008, 2006, 2004, 2001. All rights reserved. No part of this
publication may be reproduced or distributed in any form or by any means, or stored in a database or retrieval
system, without the prior written consent of The McGraw-Hill Companies, Inc., including, but not limited to,
in any network or other electronic storage or transmission, or broadcast for distance learning.

This book is printed on acid-free paper.

1 2 3 4 5 6 7 8 9 0 DOW/DOW 9 8 7 6 5 4 3 2 1 0

ISBN: 978-0-07736759-6
MHID: 0-07-736759-6

Vice President Editorial: *Michael Ryan*
Editorial Director: *William R. Glass*
Publisher: *Christopher Freitag*
Sponsoring Editor: *Matthew Busbridge*
Marketing Manager: *Stacy Best Ruel*
Director of Development: *Rhona Robbin*
Developmental Editors: *Arthur Pomponio, Sylvia Mallory*
Editorial Coordinators: *Briana Porco, Jaclyn Mautone*
Senior Production Editor: *Carey Eisner*
Art Editor: *Robin Mouat*
Illustrator: *Patti Isaacs*
Design Manager: *Laurie Entringer*
Interior Designer: *Maureen McCutcheon*
Cover Designers: *Laurie Entringer and David Carlson, Gearbox*
Lead Photo Research Coordinator: *Alexandra Ambrose*
Photo Researcher: *Judy Mason*
Buyer II: *Sherry L. Kane*
Composition: *10.5/12 Goudy Old Style by Laserwords Private Limited*
Printing: *45# New Era Matte Thin, R.R. Donnelley & Sons*

Cover: Top: © Mike Agliolo/Corbis; Middle: Detail from the Bayeux Tapestry, before 1082 (wool embroidery
on linen), / Musee de la Tapisserie, Bayeux, France / The Bridgeman Art Library; Bottom: Art Resource

Library of Congress Cataloging-in-Publication Data

Sherman, Dennis.
    The West in the world / Dennis Sherman, Joyce Salisbury. —4th ed.
        p. cm.
    Includes bibliographical references and index.
    ISBN-13: 978-0-07-736759-6 (v. 1 : alk. paper)
    ISBN-10: 0-07-736759-6 (v. 1 : alk. paper)
    1. Civilization, Western—History—Textbooks. I. Salisbury, Joyce E. II. Title.
CB245.S465 2011
909'.09821—dc22
                                                                                2010037319

The Internet addresses listed in the text were accurate at the time of publication. The inclusion of a Web site
does not indicate an endorsement by the authors or McGraw-Hill, and McGraw-Hill does not guarantee the
accuracy of the information presented at these sites.

www.mhhe.com

Dennis Sherman

DENNIS SHERMAN is Professor of History at John Jay College, the City University of New York. He received his B.A. (1962) and J.D. (1965) degrees from the University of California at Berkeley and his Ph.D. (1970) from the University of Michigan. He was Visiting Professor at the University of Paris (1978–1979, 1985). He received the Ford Foundation Prize Fellowship (1968–1969, 1969–1970), a fellowship from the Council for Research on Economic History (1971–1972), and fellowships from the National Endowment for the Humanities (1973–1976). His publications include *A Short History of Western Civilization*, Eighth Edition (coauthor), *Western Civilization: Sources, Images, and Interpretations*, Seventh Edition, *World History: Sources, Images, and Interpretations*, Fourth Edition, a series of introductions in the Garland Library of War and Peace, several articles and reviews on nineteenth-century French economic and social history in American and European journals, and several short stories in literary reviews. He is the recipient of John Jay College's *"Outstanding Teacher of the Year"* award.

Joyce Salisbury

JOYCE SALISBURY is Professor Emerita of History at the University of Wisconsin–Green Bay, where she taught history to undergraduates for more than twenty years. She received a Ph.D. in medieval history from Rutgers University in New Jersey. She is a respected historian who has published many articles and has written or edited more than ten books, including the critically acclaimed *Perpetua's Passion: Death and Memory of a Young Roman Woman*, *The Blood of Martyrs: Unintended Consequences of Ancient Violence*, *The Encyclopedia of Women in the Ancient World*, and *The Greenwood Encyclopedia of Daily Life*, which won many awards for its creative organization and timely presentation of the material. In 2010, Salisbury published a second edition of her classic work on the history of attitudes toward animals: *The Beast Within: Humans and Animals in the Middle Ages*. Salisbury is an award-winning teacher who was named *"Professor of the Year for Wisconsin in 1991"* by CASE (Council for Advancement and Support of Education), a prestigious national organization. Since retiring from the University of Wisconsin–Green Bay, Salisbury has taught twice on Semester at Sea, a program sponsored by the University of Virginia that teaches students as they circumnavigate the world. Salisbury brought a global perspective to the history of Western civilization while teaching abroad, and this edition of the book has benefited from her interaction with students as they make sense of our twenty-first-century global civilization.

ABOUT THE AUTHORS

What's the best way to write an interesting, accessible, and accurate account of the West's complex history? This question confronts everyone who approaches this huge and important task. On the one hand, we believed strongly that different authors' perspectives would give readers a sense of the richness of the past. On the other hand, we wanted a seamless narrative that read like a good story. We decided that a careful, two-author collaboration would best enable us to achieve both goals. We brought our different backgrounds, research interests, and teaching experiences to the table. We talked over our ideas and read and struggled with one another's words. Throughout, we never lost sight of our goal: to bring the compelling history of the West in the world to students of the twenty-first century.

A NOTE FROM THE AUTHORS

Dennis Sherman

I was in the twelfth grade in west Los Angeles when I first realized I had a flair for history. Our teacher wisely gave us much latitude in selecting topics for two lengthy papers. I chose ancient Egypt (I liked the National Geographic visuals) as my first topic and Tasmania as the second. (I was the only one who seemed to know that Tasmania was an island below Australia.) Assembling the material and writing the papers just came easily to me, as did any questions our history teacher posed in class (though I was an otherwise fading-into-the-background student). I more or less blundered into different majors in college and then slid through law school (which taught me how to be succinct) before returning to history. At the beginning of my first semester of graduate school, I met my advisor, who asked me what courses I wanted to take. I ticked off four selections: History of South Asia; Nineteenth-Century Europe; Twentieth-Century America; and European Intellectual History. "You're a generalist," he said. Indeed I was. He wisely counseled me to narrow my focus. However, throughout my studies and professional career I have found the big picture—the forest rather than the trees—the most interesting aspect of history.

A few years later I moved to the front of the classroom and, never forgetting what it was like to be a student, found my heart in teaching. Teaching and writing about the sweep of Western civilization within the broadest possible context has remained my greatest interest over the years. That is why I have written this book with Joyce.

Joyce Salisbury

I grew up in Latin America (ten years in Brazil and five in Mexico). Through those years, I attended American schools filled with expatriates. There I studied a curriculum of Western culture, which in those days was equated with European history. But even as a young girl, I knew I wasn't getting the whole story. After all, we celebrated Mardi Gras (a Christian holiday) to an African drumbeat, and the national museum of Mexico was bursting with Napoleonic artifacts. I knew that the history and culture of the West was intimately tied to that of the rest of the world.

In the more than twenty years that I've been teaching Western civilization, I've brought this global perspective to the classroom, and now Dennis and I have brought it to this book. It is very satisfying to me to work with my students as we trace the unfolding history of the West and to see that all my students—with their own rich and varied cultural backgrounds—recognize their stories within the larger narrative. In Spring 2007 and Spring 2009, I had the opportunity to implement intensively my commitment to the integration of Western and global history: I signed on to the University of Virginia's Semester at Sea and had the wonderful experience of teaching Western civilization (as well as other courses) to students as we cruised around the world. This was indeed the opportunity to teach the West in the world!

BRIEF CONTENTS

CONTENTS

LIST OF PRIMARY SOURCE DOCUMENTS

THINKING ABOUT GEOGRAPHY

LIST OF MAPS

Connect your students to history. Connect your students to the dramatic story of Western civilization. Connect your students to your course.

With *The West in the World,* Fourth Edition, students take an active, analytical approach to understanding history and historical change. They come to appreciate that history does not happen in isolation but rather is the consequence of a complex set of intersecting events, forces, and human actions among which there are cause-and-effect links that extend into the present day. As it compellingly tells the story of Western civilization, *The West in the World* encourages a critical examination and analysis of major events and themes, to promote student understanding and to uncover students' personal connections to the past.

HOW DOES *THE WEST IN THE WORLD,* FOURTH EDITION, ACHIEVE ITS PEDAGOGICAL GOALS?

The West in the World offers students broad and deep pedagogical support, including chapter previews, timelines, key dates boxes, margin notes, and critical thinking questions. In addition, the chapters feature a series of "Thinking About" selections with accompanying questions, focused on primary source documents, geography, science and technology, and works of art. The "Thinking About" examples encourage analytical thinking and active learning, as students read about, reflect on, and connect the events and themes of Western civilization to build an understanding of the past and an appreciation of history's influence on the present. In addition, new "Connect to Today" questions at the end of each chapter ask students to apply lessons from the past to today's issues.

With this edition, *The West in the World* also immerses students in *Connect History,* a new web-based assignment and assessment platform that includes a fully integrated e-book plus interactive quizzes and activities that make learning and studying both engaging and efficient.

HOW CAN *CONNECT HISTORY* HELP ENSURE THAT STUDENTS WILL COME TO CLASS PREPARED TO LEARN AND PREPARED FOR EXAMINATIONS?

A recent survey of professors by the *Chronicle of Higher Education* showed that 84 percent believe that their students are "unprepared" or only "somewhat prepared" to pursue a college degree. Through pre-tests and post-tests, map labeling, primary source activities, and a variety of question types, *Connect History* helps students determine what they know and do not yet know, guiding them to concentrate on their particular needs and to better prepare for class discussions, writing assignments, and examinations.

****

GOALS OF *THE WEST IN THE WORLD,* FOURTH EDITION

We have written the story of the West in a way that vividly reveals the complicated interactions and connections that distinguish it. Our primary goals have been to:

- *Tell the dramatic, diverse, and personal stories of Western Civilization.*

We showcase both the "art" and the "science" of history, as *The West and the World*'s engaging narrative of Western civilization (the "art") probes the events, individuals, ideas, and developments (the "science"). Students are drawn into the drama as they follow the evolution of Western culture from its earliest roots to the present day.

Building on a political framework, we integrate social history throughout the narrative. Our approach illuminates how individuals from *all* walks of life have shaped history—not just generals and political leaders or artistic and scientific geniuses.

- *Demonstrate the relationship between the West and the wider world.*

Historians use the term "Western civilization" to identify societies that seemed to share certain historical traditions and cultural traits. We present Western civilization as an ever-changing pattern of culture that originated in the ancient Middle East and spread westward through the Mediterranean lands, northward to Europe, and, in the sixteenth century, across the Atlantic.

To emphasize that the West did not progress in isolation, and to help students appreciate how the evolving West interacted with the rest of the world, we include **The World & the West** and **Global Connections** essays. What's more, throughout the narrative, we emphasize the importance of all interactions— economic, social, and cultural, as well as political— that have shaped Western civilization.

- *Create an accessible text of manageable length.*

The medium length of *The West in the World* is unusual for a history of Western civilization. Long accounts can overwhelm students in their level of detail and can make the assignment of supplementary readings difficult. Brief texts, while allowing time for additional reading, typically lack essential coverage and detail and make it a challenge for the authors to achieve the braided, nuanced narrative that history deserves. *The West in the World* is long enough to present a comprehensive, rich narrative but concise enough to give instructors the flexibility to use other sources and books as supplements.

A Note About the Dating System

The various civilizations across the world do not all use the same dating system. For example, the Hebrew calendar counts the Western year 3760 B.C.E. as year 1—which some consider to be when the world was created. Muslims use the date 622, the year that the Prophet fled from Mecca to Medina, as year 1 in their history. Furthermore, all cultures do not measure months on a solar calendar, which marks days based on the earth's revolution of the sun. Muslims, for instance, use a purely lunar calendar consisting of twelve lunar months in a year of 354 or 355 days. This tradition makes it particularly complicated to translate a date from the Islamic system to the Christian system.

Before the seventh century, people in the West (and in many other parts of the world) used dating systems based on rulers. That is, they might say "in the third year of the reign of Emperor Vespasian." Beginning in about the seventh century, many people in the West began to use a dating system that counts backward and forward from the birth of Christ, which Westerners consider year 1. Events that took place "Before Christ," designated as B.C., were counted backward from year 1. Thus something that happened 300 years before Christ's birth was dated 300 B.C. Events that took place after the birth of Christ were also dated from the hypothetical year 1 and were labeled A.D., which stands for the Latin *anno Domini*, meaning "in the year of our Lord."

In the twentieth century, many historians, scholars, and others who recognized that the West was not solely Christian wanted a dating designation that would apply more easily to non-Christians and that could be used more universally in a global context. They kept the same numerical system—counting backward and forward using the hypothetical date of Jesus' birth—but changed the designations. Now the common usage is "B.C.E.," which means "Before the Common Era," and "C.E.," meaning the "Common Era." We first adopted this system in the third edition of *The West in the World*, and we continue this practice in the fourth edition. The events described in the first four chapters all took place B.C.E. In Chapter 5, we have marked all dates with C.E., but because everything after that time is C.E., we then drop the designation.

Content changes for *The West in the World,* Fourth Edition

We have revised the narrative and the features throughout this fourth edition so as to keep the account up-to-date and in pace with the latest scholarly work. We have also made revisions in response to adopters' and reviewers' comments.

In all chapters, we have:

- Redesigned the maps and fine-tuned their content for enhanced clarity and pedagogical value.
- Rewritten and reformatted the critical thinking questions for the maps, biographies, and art to facilitate their use in the classroom and in individual study.
- Expanded and enriched the photo captions to increase their value as learning tools.
- Added a new section at the end of each chapter—"Connect to Today"—asking questions that help students connect what they have learned to current Western and world issues.
- Updated the suggested readings in the "Beyond the Classroom" section.

On a chapter-by-chapter basis, the significant changes include the following:

CHAPTER 1 THE ROOTS OF WESTERN CIVILIZATION: THE ANCIENT MIDDLE EAST TO THE SIXTH CENTURY B.C.E.

- New treatment of the lives and livelihoods of Paleolithic peoples
- New discussion of Paleolithic peoples' expression of symbolic thought through art, featuring a recent excavation of the earliest-known work of figurative sculpture
- New material on the Phoenicians' trade and industry and their impact on regional growth
- Expanded treatment of the Hittites' introduction of a new technology of warfare

CHAPTER 2 THE CONTEST FOR EXCELLENCE: GREECE, 2000–338 B.C.E.

- Extensive new material on the Greek architectural orders
- Expanded discussion of city-states beyond Athens and Sparta
- New information on Delos, shedding light on the growth of Athenian imperial ambitions

CHAPTER 3 THE POLEIS BECOME COSMOPOLITAN: THE HELLENISTIC WORLD, 336–150 B.C.E.

- Fresh discussion of the Greeks' achievements in applying theoretical science to practical applications
- New "Thinking About Science & Technology" feature on the invention of latitude and longitude

CHAPTER 4 PRIDE IN FAMILY AND CITY: ROME FROM ITS ORIGINS TO THE REPUBLIC, 753–44 B.C.E

- New material on the Etruscans, including a look at recent DNA studies of their origin
- Expanded examination of the government structure and social classes of the Roman Republic
- New account of Roman engineering genius as applied to the building of aqueducts across the Mediterranean world

CHAPTER 5 TERRITORIAL AND CHRISTIAN EMPIRES: THE ROMAN EMPIRE, 31 B.C.E.–410 C.E.

- New, extended treatment of the praetorian guard
- New information on the Roman imperial government's finances and its considerable reliance on philanthropy
- Extended treatment of the fall of the Roman Empire, including new discussion of the invasions of the Goths and Visigoths
- More on the Wailing Wall and its symbolic significance
- Expanded examination of Constantine and his support of Christians

CHAPTER 6 A WORLD DIVIDED: WESTERN KINGDOMS, BYZANTIUM, AND THE ISLAMIC WORLD, ca. 376–1000

- New information on the discovery of a hoard of Anglo-Saxon gold and silver objects, ca. 675, excavated in 2009 in Staffordshire, England, and its confirmation of the accuracy of the accounts in *Beowulf*
- Expanded narrative on Muslim science, featuring a look at the invention of the mariner's astrolabe

CHAPTER 8 ORDER RESTORED: THE HIGH MIDDLE AGES, 1000–1300

- Revised section on medieval European peasants' use of windmills, incorporating details on recent excavations of tidal mills
- New "Thinking About Science & Technology" feature on windmills
- Substantial new discussion of Byzantium's external threats and disintegration on the eve of the crusades
- Expanded coverage of the Fourth Crusade

CHAPTER 9 THE WEST STRUGGLES AND EASTERN EMPIRES FLOURISH: THE LATE MIDDLE AGES, ca. 1300–1500

- New information on the Black Death, taking into account recent DNA studies
- Extended treatment of the Ottoman Turks' expansion, including a new look at their military structure
- Additional material on eastern Europe and the fall of the Byzantine Empire
- Expanded analysis of Russia and the impact of the Mongol legacy

CHAPTER 10 A NEW SPIRIT IN THE WEST: THE RENAISSANCE, ca. 1300–1640

- Revised introduction establishing the chapter's key theme of the transformative ideas of the Renaissance
- Extended treatment of the aftermath of the Great Schism and the influence of Pope Martin V, including his development of Rome as a seat of papal power
- New information on the expansion of the popes' territorial power
- Substantial new discussion and analysis of Renaissance music and the popularization of music in this era

CHAPTER 11 "ALONE BEFORE GOD": RELIGIOUS REFORM AND WARFARE, 1500–1648

- Increased coverage of John Calvin and his influence
- New analysis of Scotland's adherence to the firm Calvinism preached by John Knox and of the Scots Confession of 1560
- Expanded discussion of warfare in the Thirty Years' War
- New "Thinking About Science & Technology" feature on the invention of gunpowder

CHAPTER 12 FAITH, FORTUNE, AND FAME: EUROPEAN EXPANSION, 1450–1700

- Continued discussion of the impact of gunpowder and cannons, focused on explorations in the New World
- In-depth new treatment of Native Americans in North America, with examination of the cultures and livelihoods of southwestern, Mississippi Valley, and eastern tribes
- New account of the first European contacts with North America and their impact on native peoples in the form of rampant disease and devastating depopulation

CHAPTER 13 THE STRUGGLE FOR SURVIVAL AND SOVEREIGNTY: EUROPE'S SOCIAL AND POLITICAL ORDER, 1600–1715

- New material on the Ottomans' military defeat at the hands of Leopold and Sobieski and the subsequent stagnation and deterioration of the once-powerful Ottoman Empire

CHAPTER 15 COMPETING FOR POWER AND WEALTH: THE OLD REGIME, 1715–1789

- New narrative and analysis on the Ottoman Empire and the Middle East, including an examination of the empire's continuing decline
- New material on the institution of the monarchy, focusing on the emergence of a public sphere where individuals and groups exchanged information and ideas
- New analysis of France's celebration of the American Revolution as a triumph in France's own competition with its British rivals

CHAPTER 16 OVERTURNING THE POLITICAL AND SOCIAL ORDER: THE FRENCH REVOLUTION AND NAPOLEON, 1789–1815

- Increased coverage of Napoleon's invasion of Egypt and the consequences

CHAPTER 17 FACTORIES, CITIES, AND FAMILIES IN THE INDUSTRIAL AGE: THE INDUSTRIAL REVOLUTION, 1780–1850

- Updated material on England's Industrial Revolution

CHAPTER 19 NATIONALISM AND STATEBUILDING: UNIFYING NATIONS, 1850–1870

- Expanded treatment of the Ottoman Empire's struggles with the divisive forces of nationalism, highlighting the Ottomans' troubles with their North African and Balkan provinces as well as with their Russian neighbors

CHAPTER 20 MASS POLITICS AND IMPERIAL DOMINATION: DEMOCRACY AND THE NEW IMPERIALISM, 1870–1914

- Revised account of Western imperialism in Asia and Africa, emphasizing the advantages conferred by new ships, weapons, and finances
- New information on the Russian expansion that influenced Britain's imperialist strategy and of tensions between Russia and Britain in the 1880s.
- Extensive new narrative on the opening of Japan to trade and foreign presences and on the subsequent collapse of the Tokugawa shogunate

- Concise analysis of Japan's transformation from a feudal society with a preindustrial economy to a modern industrialized nation

CHAPTER 21 MODERN LIFE AND THE CULTURE OF PROGRESS: WESTERN SOCIETY, 1850–1914

- New "Thinking About Science & Technology" feature on universities and the professionalism of science

CHAPTER 22 DESCENDING INTO THE TWENTIETH CENTURY: WORLD WAR AND REVOLUTION, 1914–1920

- Extended coverage of the Ottoman Empire's attempts to reverse its decline
- New information on the 1918 flu pandemic and its ravages
- New account of the events leading up to the establishment of the republic of Turkey
- New material on Arab outrage in areas of North Africa and the Middle East owing to decisions of the Allied powers.
- Revised treatment of the course and consequences of World War I
- New "Thinking About Science & Technology" feature on the invention of the tank

CHAPTER 23 DARKENING DECADES: RECOVERY, DICTATORS, AND DEPRESSION, 1920–1939

- New material on Turkey focusing on Atatürk and his reforms and dictatorship
- Revised analysis of the appeal of Nazism and Nazi doctrine

CHAPTER 24 INTO THE FIRE AGAIN: WORLD WAR II, 1939–1945

- Revised treatment of the Holocaust
- New material on German society during World War II and citizens' knowledge of Hitler's Final Solution
- New analysis of developments in Eastern Europe

CHAPTER 26 INTO THE TWENTY-FIRST CENTURY: THE PRESENT IN PERSPECTIVE

- New text on Europeans' concerns about welcoming Turkey into the European Union and on the 2009 ratification of the Lisbon Treaty
- New material updating developments in the Middle East
- Revised, updated account of the political situation in Afghanistan and Pakistan
- New material on the recent U.S. financial crisis and economic recession and their global impacts
- Updated look at Russia's leadership and its internal and external political status
- New material on Barack Obama's election as president of the United States and its potential wider political impact
- New information on economic growth in Asia and worldwide
- New "Thinking About Science & Technology" feature on CERN—the European Organization for Nuclear Research
- All-new documents looking respectively at the end of the Cold War, the war in Afghanistan, and the Copenhagen Accord on climate change

Teaching the Art and Science

The powerful pedagogy of *The West in the World* features easy-to-use critical thinking tools that involve students actively in the quest for understanding the Western past—and that forge vital connections to the present and future.

The Thinking About series of boxes focuses on four key areas: primary source documents, geography, art, and, new to this edition, science and technology. All include critical thinking questions to help students connect with, understand, and apply the material.

thinking about
DOCUMENTS

DOCUMENT 4.2

Hannibal Triumphs at the Battle of Cannae

The Battle of Cannae, 216 B.C.E.

Rome
→ Advance ■ Infantry
→ Retreat ■ Cavalry

Carthage
→ Advance ■ Infantry
→ Retreat ■ Cavalry

Cannae   Cannae

The Carthaginians, led by Hannibal, were able to inflict the single greatest defeat of the Romans in the history of their empire. By feigning retreat and convincing the Romans that they were abandoning Cannae, the Carthaginian army was able to surround the Romans and defeat them without mercy. This defeat caused great alarm to the citizens of Rome, as it left them nearly defenseless.

FIGURE 4.9 The Battle of Cannae, 216 B.C.E.

The Roman historian Florus (ca. 70–ca. 140 C.E.) wrote History of the Romans, *in which he recounted the long-remembered Battle of Cannae (216 B.C.E.), a turning point during the Second Punic War between Rome and Carthage. Military thinkers today still study Hannibal's winning battle strategy, but Florus notes Hannibal's mistake. Study* **Figure 4.9** *to understand Hannibal's winning strategy.*

The fourth and almost mortal wound of the Roman Empire was at Cannæ, an obscure village of Apulia; which, however, became famous by the greatness of the defeat, its celebrity being acquired by the slaughter of forty thousand men. Here the general, the ground, the face of heaven, the day, indeed, all nature conspired together for the destruction of the unfortunate army. For Hannibal, the most artful of generals, not content with sending pretended deserters among the Romans, who fell upon their rear as they were fighting, but having also noted the nature of the ground in those open plains, where the heat of the sun is extremely violent, the dust very great, and the wind blows constantly, and as it were statedly, from the east, drew up his army in such a position that, while the Romans were exposed to all these inconveniences, he himself, having heaven, as it were, on his side, fought with wind, dust, and sun in his favor. Two vast armies, in consequence, were slaughtered till the enemy were satiated, and till Hannibal said to his soldiers, "Put up your swords." Of the two commanders, one escaped, the other was slain; which of them showed the greater spirit is doubtful. Paulus was ashamed to survive; Varro did not despair. Of the greatness of the slaughter the following proofs may be noticed: that the Aufidus was for some time red with blood; that a bridge was made of dead bodies, by order of

Hannibal, over the torrent of Vergellus, and that two *modii* of rings were sent to Carthage, and the equestrian dignity estimated by measure.

It was afterward not doubted but that Rome might have seen its last day, and that Hannibal, within five days, might have feasted in the Capitol, if—as they say that Adherbal, the Carthaginian, the son of Bomilcar, observed—"he had known as well how to use his victory as how to gain it." But at that crisis, as is generally said, either the fate of the city that was to be empress of the world, or his own want of judgment, and the influence of deities unfavorable to Carthage, carried him in a different direction. When he might have taken advantage of his victory, he chose rather to seek enjoyment from it, and, leaving Rome, to march into Campania and to Tarentum, where both he and his army soon lost their vigor, so that it was justly remarked that "Capua proved a Cannæ to Hannibal"; since the sunshine of Campania and the warm springs of Baiæ subdued—who could have believed it?—him who had been unconquered by the Alps and unshaken in the field.

SOURCE: Florus, *History of the Romans*, in *The Great Events by Famous Historians*, vol. II, ed. Rossiter Johnson (The National Alumni, 1905), pp. 186–187.

Analyze the Document

1. What are the tactics of ancient battles, and in what ways is Hannibal particularly skilled?
2. How much devastation is caused

▲ Thinking About Documents

thinking about
GEOGRAPHY

Legend:
■ Habsburg Lands
■ Valois Lands
■ Ottoman Lands
← Ottoman Attacks
▭ Boundary of the Holy Roman Empire
✦ Battle Sites

SCOTLAND
North Sea
SWEDEN
DENMARK
Baltic Sea
IRELAND
ENGLAND
POLAND
ATLANTIC OCEAN
Bremen 1547
Ghent 1540 Minden 1546
Cambrai 1543 Magdeburg 1550
Luxemburg 1542; 43, 52
Toul 1552 Frankfurt 1552
Augsburg 1552 Budapest 1541
FRANCE Vienna 1529
MILAN Mohács 1526
Pavia 1525 HUNGARY
Nice 1524
PORTUGAL
SPAIN PAPAL STATES
Corsica Rome 1527 Belgrade 1521
Sardinia NAPLES Black Sea
Balearics Naples 1528, 1552 OTTOMAN EMPIRE
Mediterranean Sea Turkish Attack 1537
NORTH AFRICA Tunis 1535 SICILY

MAP 11.1

Europe in 1526—Habsburg-Valois Wars

This map illustrates the political division of Europe in 1526 and highlights the Habsburg lands inherited by Charles V. It also shows the Ottoman Empire on Charles's borders.

Explore the Map

1. Why did the French king feel threatened by his powerful neighbor?
2. Why was Charles so concerned about the proximity of the Ottoman Empire?
3. Notice all the battles Charles fought. What might have been the impact of this warfare both on the people and on the emperor's ability to rule?

Thinking About Geography ▶

Thinking About Art ▶

thinking about
ART

FIGURE 10.12
Raphael, *School of Athens*, 1510–1511

Pope Julius II commissioned the painter Raphael to create a fresco for his library. The artist portrayed famous ancient philosophers, such as Euclid, Pythagoras, and Socrates, along with Plato and Aristotle in the center. Plato (looking remarkably like Leonardo da Vinci) is on the left, with his hand pointing in the air to ... is speaking to ..., reminding ... nowledge. ... he right (in the black hat) and a depiction of a brooding Michelangelo sitting in the center foreground, leaning his head on his hand.

Connecting Art & Society

1. Identify the following characteristics of the Renaissance in this image: individualism, appreciation of the classics, and perspective.

2. Why would the pope find the content of this fresco suitable subject matter for the papal library?

3. Why do you think Raphael included portraits of his artist contemporaries in the company of the philosophers?

thinking about
SCIENCE & TECHNOLOGY

Destruction and Amusement: The Development and Uses of Gunpowder

By the tenth century, Chinese alchemists—recall that alchemy was the early practice of chemistry—were experimenting with mixing various substances for medicinal purposes. In the process, they invented an effective gunpowder. The formula was 75 percent saltpeter (potassium nitrate), which released chemically bound oxygen to support combustion; 15 percent charcoal to supply carbon to fuel the fire; and 10 percent sulfur to lower the temperature of ignition and speed up combustion.

Europeans adopted this recipe and began to use gunpowder on the battlefield in the fourteenth century. Then, in the fifteenth century, Western powder engineers developed a technique of binding the powder into small clumps called corned powder, which was easy to transport, to keep dry, and to load efficiently into guns and cannons. Importantly, the corned powder also was more stable; the corning technology prevented accidental dust explosions and detonation from static electricity and provided a more controlled burn rate.

With the enhanced stability and transportability of the improved powder, large, mobile cannons could be brought into the battlefields, whereas previously they could only be mounted on ships and forts. From this moment on, battlefield violence increased dramatically, and foot soldiers faced devastating explosions as they charged. Gunpowder's impact would become starkly evident in the violence of the early modern wars and in the sea battles that would bring Europeans to power across the world.

People throughout history have found ways to adapt technological innovations for entertainment purposes, and this ingenuity was true for gunpowder. As early as the late fifteenth century in the West,

gunpowder moved from wartime to peacetime uses as people set off gunpowder-powered fireworks to light up European night skies on special occasions. These displays were potentially hazardous, however; for example, the pyrotechnics that were lit during one of Shakespeare's productions ignited the fire that burned down the playwright's Globe Theatre in 1613. Even firemasters, individuals who made gunpowder, did not know exactly how gunpowder worked, and **Figure 11.1** shows the explosive results that often accompanied their experiments. This mystery stimulated scientific investigation for years to come, helping to move science from alchemy to chemistry as researchers finally identified the oxygen hidden in the saltpeter that fed the fires of what had long been believed to be a magic powder.

Remember the struggle for mastery of the chemistry of gunpowder so that when you learn about the Scientific Revolution in Chapter 14, you might consider again the relationship between practical utility and scientific theory.

Connecting Science & Society

1. Trace how the scientific experimentation behind the development and improvement of gunpowder led to the application of gunpowder technology for various purposes.

2. How did advances in the stability and transportability of gunpowder transform warfare?

3. Cite some instances in your lifetime where inventions of practical items or techniques have been later adapted for entertainment purposes.

INVENTIONS ILLUSTRES
La poudre

FIGURE 11.1 Experimenting with gunpowder.

◀ Thinking About Science & Technology

The **Biography** feature spotlights the lives of men and women who embody major themes. Accompanying **Connecting People & Society** questions draw students into each individual's life and help them to link this personal experience to larger developments.

Biography ▶

The text demonstrates the complex relationship between Western and world history through **The World & the West** and **Global Connections** essays.

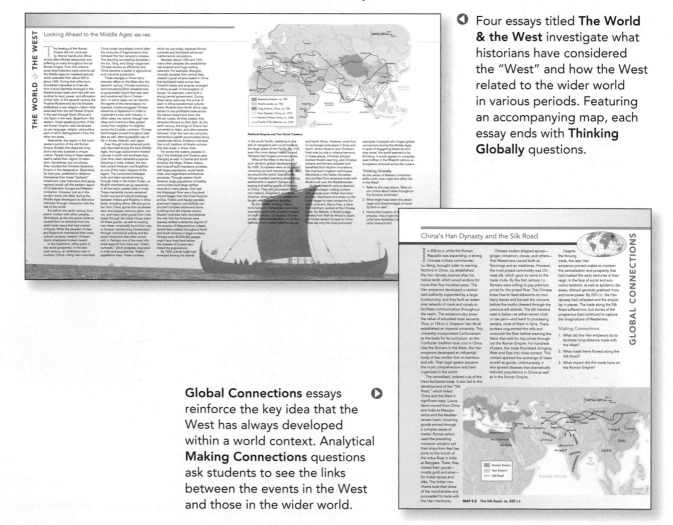

◀ Four essays titled **The World & the West** investigate what historians have considered the "West" and how the West related to the wider world in various periods. Featuring an accompanying map, each essay ends with **Thinking Globally** questions.

Global Connections essays reinforce the key idea that the West has always developed within a world context. Analytical **Making Connections** questions ask students to see the links between the events in the West and those in the wider world. ▶

The West in the World *ensures student success through* preview *and* review *features and an exciting* *digital program,* Connect History.

The Struggle for Survival and Sovereignty 13

Europe's Social and Political Order, 1600–1715

"This poor country is a horrible sight," wrote the abbess of a French town in January 1649. "[I]t is stripped of everything. The soldiers take possession of the farms . . . there are no more horses . . . the peasants are reduced to sleeping in the woods . . . and if they only had enough bread to half satisfy their hunger, they would indeed count themselves happy." France had just emerged a victor from the Thirty Years' War (discussed in Chapter 11), only to find itself embroiled in a series of internal revolts. These revolts, like many others erupting throughout Europe, signaled new strains on European society from the bottom to the top of the traditional order.

For the vast majority—peasants who worked the fields—pressures came from powers outside their control. The landowning aristocracy required service and obedience; governmental officials demanded ever more taxes and military service; and the impersonal forces that most people attributed to luck, fate, or God brought bad weather, failed harvests, and plagues. Sometimes peasants fled their aristocratic masters or turned violently against isolated governmental officials. However, against the fates and well-armed soldiers, they were powerless.

For those at the top of society, the pressures came from central governments and monarchs. Kings, struggling with the increasingly heavy burdens of war and governance, chipped away at aristocratic independence year after year. They argued that "the royal power is absolute. . . . The prince [king] need render account of his acts to no one." Elites insisted that "our privileges and liberties are our right and due inheritance, no less than our very lands and goods." This contention between monarch and aristocrat sometimes broke out in violence, at other times led to compromises, and often severely strained the elite order.

These two struggles—the first faced by the vast majority on the bottom, the second by the dominant elites on top—colored the West's social and political life during the seventeenth and early eighteenth centuries. This chapter follows these intertwined conflicts in four areas—France, eastern Europe, England, and the Netherlands—where the story took different turns.

TIMELINE

Romanov Dynasty in Russia 1613–1917

Civil War in England 1642–1649

Stuart Dynasty in England 1603–1714

Russia's Time of Troubles 1584–1613

Thirty Years' War 1618–1648

Commonwealth in England 1649–1660

Bourbon Dynasty of France 1589–1792

1600 1610 1620 1630 1640 1650 1660 1700 1800 1900

○ Each chapter begins with a high-interest **vignette** that forecasts the major themes and sets the historical stage. A **Timeline** covers the period as a whole and tracks the sequence of the events.

PREVIEW

STRESSES IN TRADITIONAL SOCIETY
Learn about the growing problems in both lower and upper orders.

ROYAL ABSOLUTISM IN FRANCE
Trace the rise of the French monarchy from Henry IV to Louis XIV.

THE STRUGGLE FOR SOVEREIGNTY IN EASTERN EUROPE
Study the political fortunes of Prussia, Austria, Russia, and Poland.

THE TRIUMPH OF CONSTITUTIONALISM
Learn about the English civil war and the Republic of the Netherlands.

△ The chapter **Preview** highlights the main topic headings and states the learning focus for each major section.

REVIEW, ANALYZE, & CONNECT TO TODAY

REVIEW THE PREVIOUS CHAPTERS

Chapter 12—"Faith, Fortune, and Fame"—told how several European powers expanded overseas during the fifteenth, sixteenth, and seventeenth centuries and grew rich from the commerce. Chapter 13—"The Struggle for Survival and Sovereignty"—focused on how kings and nobles battled for power, the resolutions of those struggles, and their impact on the millions of people outside the elite.

1. Analyze how the expansion of Europe might have stimulated scientific research.

2. In what ways did the effort of monarchs to increase their power and create stability relate to the promotion of science and the desire for greater intellectual certainty?

ANALYZE THIS CHAPTER

Chapter 14—"A New World of Reason and Reform"—examines the changing intellectual foundations of the West.

1. List and analyze the differences between the new scientific views of the world and traditional medieval views.

How did standards for ascertaining the "truth" differ between these two perspectives?

2. Analyze the beliefs and motives of three central figures in the Scientific Revolution. What barriers did they have to overcome to present their views?

3. Do you think the Enlightenment merely popularized the Scientific Revolution, or did it accomplish something more?

4. In what ways did the Enlightenment threaten traditional views and authorities?

CONNECT TO TODAY

Think about the meaning of the Scientific Revolution and the values underlying the Enlightenment.

1. In what ways are our present-day assumptions about the physical universe and the workings of nature based on the ideas and discoveries of the Scientific Revolution?

2. What aspects of world politics today reflect Enlightenment values? What asp[ects of] global politics seem to be oppo[sed]

◁ **Review, Analyze, & Connect to Today** questions at the end of each chapter ask students first to review the preceding chapters and to place the present chapter's history in the context of what has come before; second, to analyze developments in the current chapter; and third, to connect the ideas and developments discussed in the chapter at hand to present-day issues

Connect History provides students with ▷ a fully integrated e-book with highlighting and note-taking features, plus interactive quizzes and activities that make learning and studying engaging and efficient.

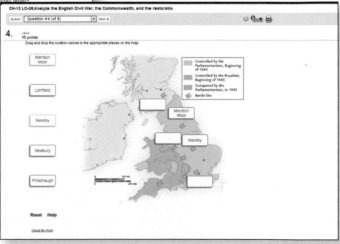

FOR STUDENTS

ONLINE LEARNING CENTER

The Online Learning Center, at www.mhhe.com /sherman4e, provides a wide range of tools that will help students test their understanding of the book. It includes chapter summaries, learning objectives, interactive maps and glossary, and multiple choice and essay quizzes, as well as matching and identifying games.

PRIMARY SOURCE INVESTIGATOR ONLINE

McGraw-Hill's Primary Source Investigator (PSI), available online at www.mhhe.com/psi, is designed to support and enrich the text discussion in *The West in the World*, 4e. PSI gives instructors and students access to more than 650 primary and secondary sources including documents, images, maps, and videos. Students can use these resources to formulate and defend their arguments as well as further their understanding of the topics discussed in each chapter. All assets are also indexed alphabetically as well as by type, subject, place, and time period, allowing students and instructors to locate resources quickly and easily.

INVESTIGATIONS

The Investigation activities give students an opportunity to try their hand at historical analysis. Based on sources found in PSI, the modules ask students to evaluate multiple sources and formulate their own interpretation of an historical event, providing valuable skills for their own research.

RESEARCH AND WRITING CENTER

The online Research and Writing Center offers a guide to college success, plus general assistance for writing college papers, as well as specific tips for history papers. Topics include research, paragraph and argument creation, a comparison of style guides, information on plagiarism and source citation, and much more.

FOR INSTRUCTORS

ONLINE LEARNING CENTER

The Online Learning Center, at www.mhhe.com /sherman4e, contains several instructor tools including a link to the faculty guide on Primary Source Investigator (www.mhhe.com/psi), PowerPoint presentations for each chapter, and the computerized test bank. The instructor side of the OLC is password protected to prevent tampering. Please contact your local McGraw-Hill representative for details.

CLASSROOM PERFORMANCE SYSTEM (CPS)

The Classroom Performance System brings ultimate interactivity to *The West in the World*. CPS is a wireless response system that gives you immediate feedback from every student in the class. With CPS you can ask subjective and objective questions during your lecture, prompting every student to respond with his or her individual, wireless response pad, and providing you with instant results. A complete CPS Tutorial is available at www.einstruction.com.

VIDEOS

Created and narrated by Joyce Salisbury, this three-video collection illuminates the author's lectures on the Middle Ages with the sculpture and fine art of the times. Available to adopters through your local McGraw-Hill representative, this unique series contains a video on each of the following topics: medieval women, medieval Judaism, and medieval life. A wide range of videos on classic and contemporary topics in history is available through the Films for the Humanities and Sciences collection. Instructors can illustrate classroom discussion and enhance lectures by selecting from a series of videos that are correlated to complement *The West in the World*. Contact your local McGraw-Hill sales representative for further information.

PRIMARY SOURCE INVESTIGATOR ONLINE FACULTY GUIDE

The annotated Faculty Guide provides easy reference to all learning assets, both in the text and on PSI, available to instructors and students. Each chapter is accompanied by a rich list of resources, including PowerPoint slides, image bank, outline maps, book maps, and test bank questions, all keyed to the chapter. Resources are organized within chapters by A-heads to streamline lecture and assignment preparation. Icons allow users to quickly differentiate between text and PSI sources. Each asset is listed by title and includes a brief annotation.

In addition to assets, the Faculty Guide also includes a chapter overview, a list of themes, lecture strategies, teaching suggestions, suggestions for further reading, and chapter-specific film recommendations. These, too, are organized by chapter and A-head to make classroom implementation simple.

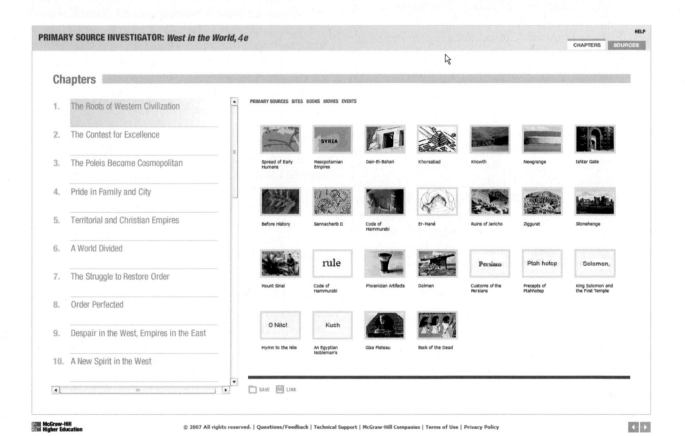

ACKNOWLEDGMENTS

We have nurtured this book through many drafts, and every page has benefited from the advice of numerous reviewers, some of whom we have gone back to several times. For their thoughtful comments and generous contribution of time and expertise, we would like to thank the following reviewers:

For the Fourth Edition

Karen A. Bartley, *University of Dayton*; Carl Boening, *Shelton State Community College*; Fred Boettcher, *Otero Junior College*; Robert Brennan, *Cape Fear Community College*; Robert J. Brown, *SUNY Finger Lakes Community College*; Tracy Nichols Busch, *Ferris State University*; Marie Therese Champagne, *University of West Florida*; Margaret Crowe, *Bridgewater State College*; Salvador Diaz, *Santa Rosa Junior College*; Martin F. Ederer, *Buffalo State College*; Natalie Kimbrough, *Community College of Baltimore County*; Janilyn Kocher, *Richland Community College*; Pamela Koenig, *Seminole State College*; Ilana Krug, *York College of Pennsylvania*; Mike Kugler, *Northwestern College*; Margaret H. Mahoney, *Bellarmine University*; Thomas Martin, *Sinclair Community College*; Ronald Palmer, *SUNY Jefferson Community College*; Elizabeth Propes, *Mesa State College*; Mark Edward Ruff, *Saint Louis University*; Steven Soper, *University of Georgia*; John F. Weinzierl, *Lyon College*; Steven Jay White, *Bluegrass Community and Technical College*; Julianna Wilson, *Pima Community College*; Sergei I. Zhuk, *Ball State University*

For the Third Edition

April Brooks, *South Dakota State University*; Daniel Patrick Brown, *Moorpark College*; Kathleen Carter, *High Point University*; Laura Cruz, *Western Carolina University*; Philip Daileader, *College of William and Mary*; Cassie Farrelly, *Fordham University*; Beth Fickling, *Coastal Carolina Community College*; Ginger Guardiola, *Colorado State University*; Jennifer Hedda, *Simpson College*; Barry Jackisch, *Gannon University*; Molly Johnson, *University of Alabama–Huntsville*; William Kinsella, *Northern Virginia Community College*; Todd Larson, *Xavier University*; Elizabeth Lehfeldt, *Cleveland State University*; William Lipkin, *Union County College*; Nancy Locklin, *Maryville College*; Karl Loewenstein, *University of Wisconsin–Oshkosh*; Michael Loughlin, *Ohio Northern University*; Jack Pesda, *Camden County College*; Penne Prigge, *Rockingham Community College*; Dana Sample, *University of Virginia's College at Wise*

For the Second Edition

Joseph Appiah, *Virginia Community College*; Douglas C. Baxter, *Ohio University*; Jonathan Bone, *William Paterson University*; Suzanne Bowles, *William Paterson University*; April Brooks, *South Dakota State University*; Katherine Clark, *University of Kansas*; Sandi Cooper, *City University of New York*; Florin Curta, *University of Florida*; Norman C. Delany, *Del Mar College*; David D. Flaten, *Plymouth State College*; Marsha L. Frey, *Kansas State University*; Bruce Garver, *University of Nebraska at Omaha*; Carla Hay, *Marquette University*; Holly Hurlburt, *Southern Illinois University*; Andrew Keitt, *University of Alabama at Birmingham*; Dave Kelly, *Colorado State University*; Jason Knirck, *Humboldt State University*; Mark W. McLeod, *University of Delaware*; Carol Menning, *University of Toledo*; Jeffrey Lee Meriwether, *Roger Williams University*; Zachary Morgan, *William Paterson University*; Michael Myers, *University of Illinois*; Max Okenfuss, *Washington University*; Jack Pesda, *Camden County College*; Dolores Davison Peterson, *Foothill College*; Paul Rempe, *Carroll College*; Harry Rosenberg, *Colorado State University*; Shawn Ross, *William Paterson University*; Glenn Sanders, *Oklahoma Baptist University*; Marc Schwarz, *University of New Hampshire*; David Stefanic, *Saint Mary's College*; Aliza Wong, *Texas Technical University*; Michael A. Zaccaria, *Cumberland County College*

For the First Edition

Edward Anson, *University of Arkansas*; William S. Arnett, *West Virginia University*; Richard Berthold, *University of New Mexico*; Robert Blackey, *California State University–San Bernardino*; Hugh Boyer, *Michigan Technical University*; Carol Bresnahan-Menning, *University of Toledo*; April Brooks, *South Dakota State University*; Nathan Brooks, *New Mexico State University*; Blaine T. Browne, *Broward Community College*; Donald Butts, *Gordon College*; Frederick Corney, *University of Florida*; Jeffrey Cox, *University of Iowa*; Florin Curta, *University of Florida*; Norman Delaney, *Del Mar College*; Robert Dise, *University of Northern Iowa*; Chris Drake, *Houston Community College–Northwest*; Lawrence G. Duggan, *University of Delaware*; Laird Easton, *California State University–Chico*; Gregory Elder, *Riverside Community College*; Nancy Erickson, *Erskine College*; Chiarella Esposito, *University of Mississippi*; Gary Ferngren, *Oregon State University*; Nancy Fitch, *California State University–Fullerton*; Elizabeth Lane Furdell, *University of North Florida*; Frank Garosi, *California State University–Sacramento*; Don Gawronski, *Mesa Community College*; Paul Goodwin, *University of Connecticut*; Anita Guerrini, *University of California–Santa Barbara*; Louis Haas, *Duquesne University*; Alice Henderson, *University of South Carolina–Spartanburg*; Jennifer Hevelone-Harper, *Gordon College*; Steven Hill, *Wake Technical Community College*; Laura J. Hilton, *Ohio State University*; Karen Holland, *Providence College*; David Hudson,

California State University–Fresno; Gary Johnson, University of Southern Maine; Jonathan G. Katz, Oregon State University; Andrew Keitt, University of Alabama–Birmingham; Charles Killinger, Valencia Community College; Lisa Lane, Mira Costa College; John Livingston, University of Denver; David Longfellow, Baylor University; Donna Maier, University of Northern Iowa; James I. Martin Sr., Campbell University; Carol Miller, Tallahassee Community College; Eileen Moore, University of Alabama–Birmingham; Frederick I. Murphy, Western Kentucky University; Max J. Okenfuss, Washington University; Michael Osborne, University of California–Santa Barbara; Jack Pesda, Camden County College; Russell Quinlan, Northern Arizona University; Patricia Ranft, Central Michigan University; Roger Reese, Texas A&M University; Harry Rosenberg, Colorado State University; Constance M. Rousseau, Providence College; Jay Rubenstein, University of New Mexico; Claire Sanders, Texas Christian College; Alan Schaffer, Clemson University; Daryl Schuster, University of Central Florida; Marc Schwarz, University of New Hampshire; David Shearer, University of Delaware; Arlene Sindelar, University of Central Arkansas; James Sisson, Central Texas College; Ronald D. Smith, Arizona State University; Saulius Suziedelis, Millersville University of Pennsylvania; Hunt Tooley, Austin College; Kevin Uhalde, Northern Illinois University; David Ulbrich, Kansas State University; Bruce Venarde, University of Pittsburgh; Charlotte Wells, University of Northern Iowa; Michael Wilson, University of Texas–Dallas; Robert Wise, University of Northern Iowa; Bill Wrightson, American River College

In addition to our reviewers and focus group participants, we would like to thank Matthew Busbridge, sponsoring editor; Rhona Robbin, director of development; Arthur Pomponio and Sylvia Mallory, developmental editors; Briana Porco, Carey Eisner, Robin Mouat, Laurie Entringer, Alexandra Ambrose, and the rest of the Fourth Edition team, whose efforts have made this a better book. Last, but certainly not least, we would like to thank the many professors who choose to use this text in their classrooms. It is they who will fulfill our hope for this text—that it will bring the past to life for many undergraduates and will perhaps awaken in them a love for history and an awareness that understanding the past is the key to our future.

TUTANKHAMEN'S GOLDEN THRONE, ca. 1322 B.C.E.

In this image from the burial of the boy-king Tutankhamen, the king sits on his throne as his wife, Akhsenamun, anoints him with scented unguent. Both bask in the rays of the holy sun-disk that they worshiped as a god. This colorful scene vividly captures the essential character of ancient Egypt and its people: the wealth and power of the god-kings; the importance of marriage and family ties; and the deep connection of the institutions of marriage and family with religion and longing for immortality. This image also reveals the power of written words—in this case, the hieroglyphs in the background—which allow us, millennia later, to read firsthand about the past and trace the developing story of the West.

The Roots of Western Civilization

The Ancient Middle East to the Sixth Century B.C.E.

"Since time immemorial, since the seedcorn first sprouted forth . . . [powerful men] have been in charge for their own benefit. The workingman was forced to beg for his bread; the youth was forced to work for others." In 2400 B.C.E., the Sumerian ruler Uruinimgina wrote these words as he took power in a Mesopotamian city. He claimed that his reforms freed citizens from usury, burdensome controls, hunger, theft, and murder—troubles that, in varying forms, have periodically plagued civilization since it first arose in cities. With his thoughtful policies and passionate sense of justice, Uruinimgina embodied another important characteristic of Western civilization: the occasional rise to power of people who strive to correct social injustice.

In the growing cities of Mesopotamia, Egypt, and the coast of the eastern Mediterranean Sea, other ideas developed that would also form the basis of civilization in the West. Societies practicing social stratification, sophisticated religious ideas, and concepts of law emerged in the same environment that spawned the social ills Uruinimgina briefly corrected. Perhaps most important, these early peoples invented writing, which preserved their cultures in the tablets and scrolls that reveal their world to us as we explore ancient cultures. The culture of the West was born in the Fertile Crescent of what we now know as the Middle East.

By the tenth century B.C.E., some states in the Fertile Crescent were able to create large, multinational empires, introducing a new political structure in the early history of the West. The Egyptians, Assyrians, Babylonians, and finally Persians established their rule over extensive areas and developed new ways of governing, as the concept of empire entered the Western consciousness.

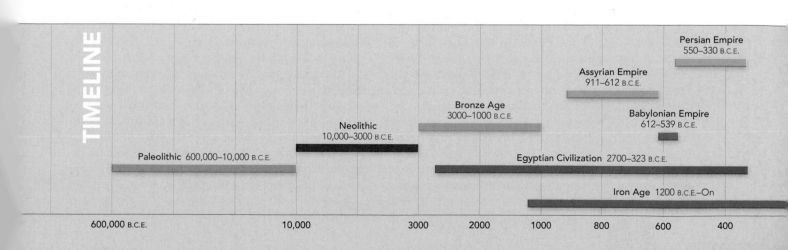

TIMELINE

Persian Empire 550–330 B.C.E.

Assyrian Empire 911–612 B.C.E.

Bronze Age 3000–1000 B.C.E.

Babylonian Empire 612–539 B.C.E.

Neolithic 10,000–3000 B.C.E.

Paleolithic 600,000–10,000 B.C.E.

Egyptian Civilization 2700–323 B.C.E.

Iron Age 1200 B.C.E.–On

600,000 B.C.E.   10,000   3000   2000   1000   800   600   400

PREVIEW

BEFORE WESTERN CIVILIZATION

In 2500 B.C.E., a Sumerian schoolboy wrote an essay about his struggles to learn reading and writing. He claimed in his essay that he practiced these skills in school all day, and he took his writing tablet home to his father, who praised the boy's progress. That night, the boy ate his dinner, washed his feet, and went to bed. The next day, however, he had a difficult time in school. He arrived late and was beaten for his tardiness and several other offenses, including poor handwriting. In despair, the boy invited the schoolmaster home to dinner. The father gave the teacher gifts, and the boy began having fewer problems in school.

This narrative, dating from 4,500 years ago, is perhaps most remarkable for its timeless themes. Tardy students, schools, and concerned parents are all a part of life for most of us today. Here, in the village of this young boy, we can find the roots of what we have come to call Western civilization (or "the West"). This term does not define one location but instead refers to a series of cultures that slowly evolved and spread to impact societies all over the world. Even 4,500 years ago, in the village of this Sumerian, we can identify certain characteristics that define Western civilization and that gave it an advantage—for better or worse—over competing cultures. Western civilization began in the Middle East, which enjoyed the striking advantage of having plants for agriculture and animals for domestication native to the region. Then large cities arose with attendant division of labor and social stratification based on relationships other than family. Another dramatic advantage was

the development of writing, which gave schoolboys so much difficulty but allowed the preservation and transmission of advantageous developments.

Finally, one of the hallmarks of Western civilization was that it never developed in isolation. Throughout its recorded history, the peoples of the Mediterranean basin traded with other societies, and the resulting cultural diffusion strengthened all the cultures involved. For example, crops from the ancient Middle East spread westward as far as Britain as early as about 4000 B.C.E., and by the second millennium B.C.E., wheat, barley, and horses from the Middle East reached as far east as China. In fact, the trade routes from the Middle East to India and China, and west and south to Africa and Europe, have a permanence that dwarfs the accomplishments of conquerors and empire builders. These constant and fruitful interactions with other cultures perhaps gave Western civilization its greatest advantage.

Yet, recorded history represents less than 1 percent of the time that humans have lived on the earth. Hundreds of thousands of years before this day in the life of a young, urban Sumerian, life for human beings was completely different. Before we begin the story of the development of Western civilization, we must explore the life of the first humans in the lush lands of sub-Saharan Africa.

Out of Africa: The Paleolithic Period, 600,000–10,000 B.C.E.

Human beings first appeared in sub-Saharan Africa hundreds of thousands of years ago. Archaeologists have classified the remains of these early humans into various species and subspecies, most of which were evolutionary dead ends. Modern humans belong to *Homo sapiens sapiens* ("thinking, thinking man"), a subspecies that migrated north and northeast from Africa. These earliest ancestors first appeared some 40,000 years ago and ultimately colonized the world. The first humans used tools made from materials at hand, including wood and bone, but the most useful tools were those made of stone. Initial stone tools were sharpened only roughly, but later humans crafted stones into finely finished flakes ideal for spearheads, arrowheads, and other blades. These tools have led archaeologists to name this long period of human prehistory the Old Stone Age, or the **Paleolithic.**

Throughout the Paleolithic, our ancestors were nomadic peoples living off the land as hunters and gatherers. This nomadic life involved small bands of people—about 30 to 40—who moved to follow the animals and the cycles of plant growth. A culture of hunters and gatherers prevents people from accumulating property, for whatever one owns must be portable, and that includes infants and small children. Anything extra is a burden, not a benefit. Paleolithic cultures also enjoyed a good deal of leisure time—indeed, estimates suggest that working four hours a day would usually generate enough food for a group. Of course, the ancient hunters and gatherers also faced famine if they exhausted the resources of a local area.

Our earliest human ancestors were also distinguished by their ability to use symbols to represent not only reality but also their hopes and fears. That is, the earliest humans created and appreciated what we call art. **Figure 1.1** shows a wonderful, tiny carving on mammoth tusk that was discovered in 2008 in Germany. Carbon dating places this figure between 35,000 and 40,000 years ago, making it the oldest piece of figurative sculpture in the world and demonstrating that art was one of the defining characteristics of humans. The 2.4-inch-tall carving shows a female figure that looks pregnant, and its creator seems to have designed it to be worn as a pendant. It was most likely intended as a sympathetic magic figurine to ensure fertility and perhaps safety in childbirth. This diminutive yet striking figure from the dawn of human history marks the beginning of symbolic thought expressed in sculpture, painting, and ultimately writing. These products of the human imagination serve to give us remarkably revealing windows on the past.

Paleolithic peoples developed their artistic skills over millennia, and the greatest expression of this ancient art survives in cave paintings from about 17,000 years ago. People returned seasonally to the same caves and painted new figures near, and sometimes over, earlier images. Some caves show evidence of repeated painting across an astonishing span of 10,000 years, revealing the preservation of traditions over lengths of time that are almost unimaginable today. These paintings probably coincided with the gathering of the small tribes of hunter-gatherers, and the movement of peoples and their goods shows that commerce joined art as a defining quality of early human societies.

Evidence from the late Paleolithic Age tells us that groups of humans returned seasonally to the same regions instead of wandering endlessly to new areas. As they traveled, kin groups **Trade networks** encountered other clans and traded goods as well as stories. Archaeological evidence indicates that shells and especially stone tools were often traded in places far from their

FIGURE 1.1 The World's Oldest Sculpture, ca. 33,000 B.C.E. This carving on mammoth tusk is the oldest figurative sculpture found to date. Showing a pregnant woman, it probably was a magic talisman for fertility.

original sites. For example, late Stone Age people living in what is now Scotland rowed small boats to an offshore island to bring back precious bloodstone that flaked accurately into strong tools. This bloodstone spread widely across northern Europe through trade with the original sailors. Commerce thus became established as an early human enterprise.

By the end of the Paleolithic Age (about 10,000 B.C.E.), the human population of Europe stood at about 20,000. These numbers may seem sparse by today's standards, but **Stone monuments** they suggest that *Homo sapiens sapiens* had gained a sturdy foothold on the European continent. By the late Stone Age, these early Europeans practiced agriculture and copper metallurgy, but their most enduring remains are huge stone monuments (called *megaliths*), of which Stonehenge in western England (shown in **Figure 1.2**) is probably the most famous. Stonehenge was built in stages over millennia beginning in about 7000 B.C.E., although most of the stones were erected about 3000 B.C.E. In its present form, it consists of about 160 massive rocks, some weighing up to 50 tons, which are arranged in concentric circles and semicircles. People moved the heavy stones long distances without using wheels, which were unknown in Europe at this time, and shaped many of them with only stone tools. Most scholars believe that the stones were carefully aligned to show the movements of the sun and moon. If this is so, the astonishing structure shows both a long tradition of studying the heavens and humans' impressive curiosity. Whatever the purpose of these stone structures that dot Europe, they all suggest highly organized societies that were able to marshal the labor

FIGURE 1.2 Stone Age Monuments from Stonehenge, Southern England, ca. 7000–1500 B.C.E. These huge structures of stone, carefully shaped and moved long distances, testify to early human technical skill. The alignment of the stones suggests knowledge of the heavens gained from many years of observations.

needed for such complex building projects. (**Map 1.1** shows the range of the megaliths.)

However, although these early Europeans displayed some characteristics that would mark Western civilization—agriculture, a curiosity about nature, and a highly developed political structure—these great builders in stone lacked a critical component: writing. Although wisdom transmitted solely through memory can be impressive, it is also fragile, and thus engineering skills and astronomical knowledge of the earliest Europeans were lost. The real origins of Western civilization lay in the Middle East, where an agricultural revolution occurred that changed the course of human history, and where writing preserved the story of the developing West.

The Neolithic Period:
The First Stirrings of Agriculture,
10,000–3000 B.C.E.

Sometime around 10,000 B.C.E., people living in what we call the Middle East learned how to plant and cultivate the grains that they and their ancestors had gathered for millennia. With this skill, humankind entered the **Neolithic** era, or the New Stone Age. Agriculture did not bring complete improvement in people's lives compared to hunting and gathering. Diets were often worse (with a reliance on fewer foods), sewage and animal wastes brought more health problems, and farming was a lot of work. People adopted this way of life because the environment changed, but once people learned how to plant crops instead of simply gathering what grew naturally, human society changed dramatically.

Just as people discovered how to control crops, they also began to domesticate animals instead of hunting them. Dogs had been domesticated as hunting partners during the Paleolithic, but around 8500 B.C.E., people first domesticated sheep as a source of food. Throughout the Middle East, some people lived off their herds as they traveled about looking for pasturage. Others lived as agriculturalists, keeping their herds near stationary villages.

| Domestic animals |

These two related developments—agriculture and animal domestication—fostered larger populations than hunting and gathering cultures, and gradually agricultural societies prevailed. In large part, the success of the Western civilization in eventually spreading throughout the world lay in its agricultural beginnings in the Middle East. Why were people in this region able to embrace agriculture so successfully? The main answer is luck—the Middle East was equipped with the necessary resources.

Of the wealth of plant species in the world—over 200,000 different varieties—humans eat only a few thousand. Of these, only a few hundred have been more or less domesticated, but almost 80 percent of the world's human diet is made up of about a dozen species (primarily cereals). The Middle East was home to the highest number of the world's prized grains, such as wheat and barley, which are easy to grow and contain the highest levels of protein. By contrast, people who independently domesticated local crops in other regions did not enjoy the same abundance.

| Middle East plants and animals |

The Middle East maintained the same advantage when it came to animals for domestication. Very few species yield to domestication; beyond the most common—dogs, sheep, goats, cows, pigs, and horses—there are only a few others—from camels to reindeer to water buffalo. Because domesticated animals provide so many benefits to humans—from food to labor—the distribution of animals fit for domestication helped determine which societies would flourish. Most of these animals were confined to Europe and Asia, and seven—including goats, sheep, and cattle—were native specifically to the Middle East. With these resources, the people of the Middle East created civilization, which quickly spread east and west (along with valuable crops and animals).

With the rise of agriculture, some small kin groups stopped wandering and instead slowly settled in permanent villages to cultivate the surrounding land. As early as 8000 B.C.E., Jericho (see **Map 1.1**) boasted about 2,000

| Population growth |

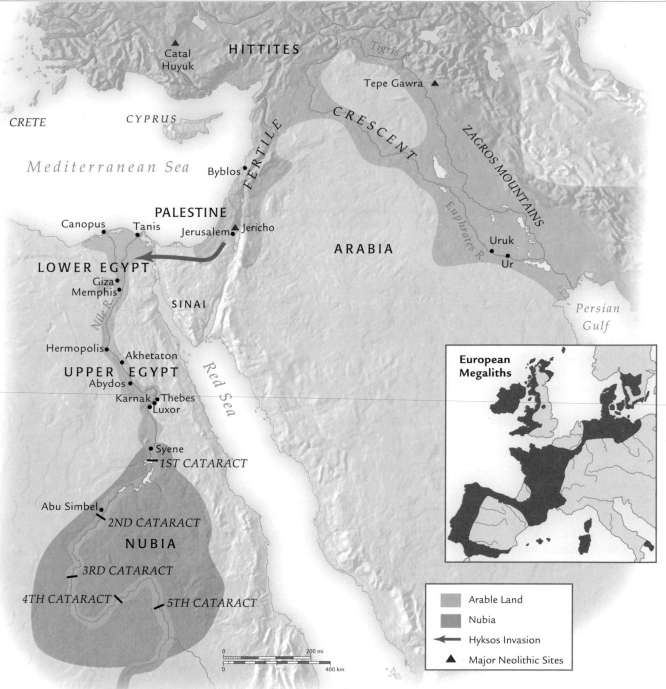

MAP 1.1

Mesopotamia and Egypt, ca. 2000 B.C.E.

This map illustrates the cradles of Western civilization in Mesopotamia (the Fertile Crescent), along the coast of the Mediterranean Sea, and in Egypt. It also identifies this region's major Neolithic sites, which may be contrasted with the locations of the European stone monuments (megaliths) in western Europe shown on the inset.

Explore the Map

1. What advantages did the locations of the rivers provide to the growing cultures?

2. How do the distances between the European megaliths (stone monuments) and Mesopotamia support the view that these cultures developed independently?

3. How did Nubia serve geographically to connect the Mediterranean world with sub-Saharan Africa?

people who lived in round huts scattered over about 12 acres. Human social forms broadened from small kin groups to include relative strangers. The schoolboy whom we met earlier had to make a point of introducing his teacher to his father. This effort would have been unheard of in the small hunting clans of the Paleolithic.

Agriculture also sparked a major change in values. Since people no longer had to carry everything they owned as they traveled, farming, animal husbandry, and fixed settlement led to the accumulation of goods, including domesticated animals. Consequently, a new social differentiation arose in agricultural villages as some people acquired more belongings than others.

The social stratification that arose in the earliest cities included slavery as part of what people thought of as the natural order of things. | **Slavery** | There were various ways to become a slave in ancient Middle Eastern society. Sometimes economic catastrophe caused parents to sell their children or even themselves into slavery to repay their debts, and children born to slaves were automatically enslaved. Although slavery was part of ancient societies, it was a slavery that could be fairly fluid—unlike the slavery of the early modern world, it was not a racial issue. Slaves could save money to purchase their freedom, and children born of a freewoman and a slave were free. Ancient slavery, while taken for granted, was based on an individual's bad luck or unfortunate birth, so a servile status did not hold the severe stigma it later would acquire.

The accumulation of goods also changed the nature of warfare. Although hunter-gatherers fought over territory at times, the skirmishes tended to be short-lived and small scale because the individuals involved were too valuable to waste through this sort of conflict. The agricultural revolution pushed warfare to a larger scale. With the population increase that the revolution fueled, there were more people to engage in conflict and more rewards for the winners, who could gain more goods and enslave the losers. Excavations have shown that the early settlement of Jericho was surrounded by a great stone wall about three yards thick—one of the earliest human-made defensive structures. Indeed, people must have greatly feared their neighbors to invest the labor needed to build such a wall with only stone hand tools. Settlements arose throughout the Neolithic in Europe and in Asia Minor (as well as in many regions in Asia), but the mainstream in the story of the West arose farther east in a river valley where writing preserved the details of the development of even larger and more sophisticated cities.

STRUGGLING WITH THE FORCES OF NATURE: MESOPOTAMIA, 3000–ca. 1000 B.C.E.

Between 3000 and 1000 B.C.E., people began to cultivate a broad curve of land that stretched from the Persian Gulf to the shores of the Mediterranean (**Map 1.1**). This arc, the Fertile Crescent, has been called the cradle or birthplace of Western civilization. It earned this appellation in part because of its lucky possession of essential plants and animals and its central location, which placed it at a crossroads, for mingling of ideas and peoples. The | **Bronze Age** | ancient Greeks called this region Mesopotamia, or "land between the rivers," emphasizing the importance of the great Tigris and Euphrates rivers to the life of the area. The earliest cities in which civilization took root were located in the southern part of Mesopotamia. During the late Neolithic period, people living in this region used agriculture; sometime after 3000 B.C.E., they learned to smelt metals to make tools and weapons. By smelting, they developed a process to combine copper and tin to make a much stronger metal, bronze. At last, there was a substance that improved on stone, and archaeologists note this innovation by calling this period the Bronze Age.

Life in southern Mesopotamia was harsh but manageable. Summer temperatures reached a sweltering 120 degrees Fahrenheit, and the region received a meager average rainfall of less than 10 inches a year. Yet the slow-running Euphrates created vast marshlands that stayed muddy and wet even during the dry season. Villagers living along the slightly higher ground near the marshes poled their boats through the shallow waters as they netted abundant river fish and shot waterfowl with their bows and arrows. Domesticated cattle and sheep grazed on the rich marsh grass while agriculturalists farmed the fertile high ground, which was actually made up of islands in the marshland. The villagers used the marsh reeds as fuel and as material to make sturdy baskets, and they fashioned the swamp mud into bricks and pottery.

The Origins of Western Civilization

In about 3000 B.C.E., a climate change occurred that forced the southern Mesopotamians to alter their way of life. As they did so, they created a more complex society that we call Sumerian—the earliest civilization. Starting around 3200 B.C.E., the region became drier. The rivers no longer flooded as much of the land as before, and more and more of the marshes evaporated. When the rivers flooded, they still deposited fertile soil in the former marshlands, but the floods came at the wrong times of the year for easy agriculture. Fed by the melting snows in the Zagros Mountains (see **Map 1.1**), the Tigris flooded between April and June—a time highly inconvenient for agriculture in a region where the growing season runs from autumn to early summer. Furthermore, the floods were unpredictable; they could wash away crops still ripening in the fields or come too early to leave residual moisture in the soil for planting. Men and women had to learn how to use the river water efficiently to maintain the population that had established itself during centuries of simpler marsh life. Now people began to dig channels to irrigate the dry land and save the water for when they needed it, but these efforts were never certain because the floods were unpredictable. Mesopotamians developed an intense pessimism that was shaped by the difficult natural environment of the land between the rivers, which could bring seemingly random abundance or disaster.

FIGURE 1.3 Ziggurat at Ur, ca. 2100 B.C.E. The great mud-brick temples known as ziggurats rose from the flat landscapes of Mesopotamia. The builder wrote that he was ordered to erect this ziggurat by his god Marduk. The structure shows both the power of religion and the skill of builders in this cradle of Western civilization.

To manage the complex irrigation projects and planning required to survive in this unpredictable environment, the Sumerians developed a highly organized society—they worked hard to bring order to the chaos that seemed to surround them. Their resourcefulness paid off; by 3000 B.C.E., the valley had become a rich food-producing area. The population of Uruk, shown on **Map 1.1**, had expanded to nearly 10,000 by about 2900 B.C.E. Neighbors no longer knew each other, and everyone looked to a centralized administration to organize daily life.

| Administration |

Priests and priestesses provided the needed organization. In exchange, these religious leaders claimed a percentage of the land's produce. With their new wealth, they built imposing temples that dominated the skylines of cities like Uruk and Ur. **Figure 1.3** is a modern-day photograph of one of those temples, which was built about 2100 B.C.E. The temple shown here consists of levels of steps that were designed to lead the faithful up toward heaven. Known as a **ziggurat,** the structure was intended to bridge the gap between gods and humans. These huge structures were located in a temple complex that spanned several acres. A statue of a god or goddess was placed in a sacred room at the top, and after priests and priestesses conducted a ritual dedication of the statue, people believed the deity dwelled symbolically within the temple, bringing blessings to the whole community. The scale and wealth committed to the ziggurat revealed the dominant role that religion played in the Sumerians' lives.

Ziggurats also served as administrative and economic centers of cities, with storehouses and administrative rooms housed in the lower levels. They were bustling places as people came to bring goods and socialize with neighbors. Just as religion was at the center of the Sumerian world, these buildings, rising like mountains out of the mud plains, served as the center of city life.

| Economic functions |

The labor and goods of the local men and women belonged to the deity who lived in the inner room at the top of the temple. In one temple dedicated to a goddess, attendants washed, clothed, and perfumed the statue every day, and servants burned incense and played music for the statue's pleasure. Meanwhile, temple administrators organized irrigation projects and tax collection in the cities to foster the abundance that allowed the great cities to flourish and serve their patron deities. Through these centralized religious organizations, ancient loyalties to family and clan were slowly replaced by political and religious ties that linked devoted followers to the city guarded by their favored deity. This was a crucial step in creating the large political units that were to become a hallmark of Western civilization.

Life in a Sumerian City

In the shadow of the ziggurats, people lived in mud-brick houses with thick walls that insulated them from heat, cold, and noise. Women and slaves prepared the family meals, which consisted mostly of barley (in the south) or wheat (in the north). Vegetables, cheese, fish, figs, and dates supplemented the Sumerian diet. A large portion of the calories people consumed came from ale. Forty percent of all the grain grown in the region was brewed for ale by women in their homes, not only for their family's consumption but also for sale.

Although Mesopotamia offered early settlements the significant advantage of indigenous plants and animals, the area had some severe

Trade shortages. The river valleys lacked metal and stone, which were essential for tools and weapons. The earliest settlements depended on long-distance trade for these essential items, and soon the wheel was invented to move cartloads of goods more easily. Materials came from Syria, the Arabian peninsula, and even India, and Mesopotamian traders produced goods for trade. The most lucrative products were textiles. Traders transported woven wool great distances in their quest for stone, metal, and, later, luxury goods. Mesopotamian goods, animals, and even plants moved slowly as far as China as the ancient cultures of the Eurasian land embarked on mass trade. The essential trade routes that marked the whole history of Western civilization appeared at the dawn of its inception.

In the bustling urban centers, families remained the central social tie. Parents arranged marriages for their sons and daughters and bound the contract with an exchange of goods that women brought to the marriage as their dowry. The earliest

Families written laws regulated married life in an attempt to preserve public peace through private ties. Adultery was a serious crime punished by death, but divorce was permitted. If a woman who was above reproach as a wife wished a divorce, she could keep her dowry. If, however, a wife neglected her home and acted foolishly in public, she would lose her dowry. Her husband could then insist that she remain as a servant in his house even when he remarried. The laws also recognized that men kept concubines in addition to their legal wives and provided ways for children of such informal unions to be considered legitimate. All these laws attempted to preserve the family as an economic unit and as the central social unit in a complex, changing society.

Sumerian women worked in many shops in the cities—as wine sellers, tavern keepers, and merchants. Some women were prosti-

Women's work tutes, although in time Sumerians came to view this profession as a threat to more traditional ties. Late in Mesopotamian history, laws arose that insisted on special clothing to distinguish "respectable" women from prostitutes. Ordinary women were expected to veil their heads in public, whereas prostitutes and slaves were forced to go about their day with bare heads. At the end of Mesopotamian ascendancy, these laws were made extremely strict—any slave woman who dared to wear a veil was punished by having her ears cut off. In this society, in which people did not know one another, city residents strove mightily to distinguish social ranks. City life came with increasing emphasis on social stratification as the cornerstone of urban order.

Gods and Goddesses of the River Valley

The men and women of the Tigris-Euphrates river valley believed that all parts of the natural world were invested with will. For example, if a river flooded, the event was interpreted as an act of the gods. People also viewed intercity warfare as a battle between each city's gods. On a broader level, the Sumerians saw themselves and their deities as combatants locked in a struggle against a mysterious chaos that could destroy the world at any moment—just as sometimes the unpredictable rivers flooded and brought destruction. People viewed themselves as slaves of the gods and provided the deities with everything they needed—from sacrifices to incense to music—to try to keep order in their uncertain world. In spite of their appeasements, however, when disorder appeared in the form of natural disasters or disease, the pessimistic Sumerians were not surprised.

In addition to venerating their city's patron, Sumerians in time invested their universe with a bewildering number of demons who needed placating. Demons caused illness, and magicians or priests—rather than physicians—were called on for cures. To understand the world, priests tried to read the future in the entrails of animals (a practice known as **augury**). Magic, omens, and amulets rounded out the Mesopotamian religious world, as people struggled to try to control what seemed to be a world in which people owed everything to capricious deities.

An anonymous Sumerian poem of despair expresses the anxiety that came with this view of religious responsibility. In this **Sumerian pessimism** poem, a once-prosperous man suffers a reversal of fortune. He laments:

> My ill luck has increased, and I do not find the right.
> I called to my god, but he did not show his face,
> I prayed to my goddess, but she did not raise her head.

The man seeks out diviners and dream priests, but no one can tell him the omission that brought about his downfall. In his despair, he can only hope that continued devotion to the gods will restore his prosperity, but his tone is not optimistic.

Neither the Sumerians nor their eventual conquerors envisioned an attractive afterlife. They believed that the spirits of the dead went to a shadowy, disagreeable place from where they might occasionally affect the living, usually for ill. Sumerians' only hope for happiness lay in the present life, and that happiness hinged on capricious deities who cared little for humans.

These beliefs prevailed in the Fertile Crescent from the fourth millennium B.C.E. up to the middle of the first millennium B.C.E., even as conquests changed the prevailing rulers. **Sargon** During that time, conquerors made a conscious effort to appease the local deities, and this

FIGURE 1.4 King Sargon and His Daughter, Enheduanna, ca. 2350 B.C.E. Sargon used religion to unite the people of his empire, and his daughter served as high priestess of both the Akkadian and the Sumerian goddesses. She is shown in the inset (second figure from the left) worshiping at an altar.

administration, sky gods became more crucial in the heavenly hierarchy. Fearsome war gods like Marduk sometimes demanded human sacrifices in exchange for victory over invading tribes. The heavenly hierarchy grew more elaborate and demanding.

By the third millennium B.C.E., earthly society in the ancient Middle East mirrored the hierarchical heavenly one. Kingship was universally accepted as the correct political order, and castes of nobles and priests were also deemed natural. Inequality among people was seen as normal and theologically justified, and people accepted their place in this highly ordered world with kings on top and slaves on the bottom. Individuals' longings for social justice and hopes for improving their situations all took place within a frame of reality that was very different from ours—one that assumed inequality was natural.

Sometime during the second millennium B.C.E., the Sumerians began to reflect on individuals' relationships with the gods. Instead of being content with a corporate association between a city and its guardian, some men and women looked to a more personal alliance, just as the despairing poet we met earlier cried out for a divine explanation of his plight. This longing led individuals to ponder the concept of immortality, wondering whether death was avoidable. In the celebrated poem *The Epic of Gilgamesh*, the poet articulates this search for meaning in death while telling an engaging story of a Sumerian hero and his fortunes. This is an early example of an important literary genre called the epic of quest. Gilgamesh (shown in **Figure 1.5**) was a king who ruled Uruk (see **Map 1.1**) in about 2700 B.C.E. Sometime after 2000 B.C.E., stories about the by-then semimythical king were collected and written down in the epic. In one version of Gilgamesh's adventures, his best friend, Enkidu, is killed and the reality of death strikes home. Gilgamesh refuses to bury Enkidu; in his grief he is unwilling to give up his friend. When the reality of decomposition confronts the king, he travels to find the secret of immortality. At the bottom of the sea he finds a plant that will give eternal life, only to see the magic herb stolen by a snake before he can bring it back to Enkidu. Gilgamesh is left facing the reality of death and the equally important reality of the value of finding joy in the present. This pessimistic epic once again reveals the Sumerian assumption that humans are doomed to struggle endlessly in a difficult universe.

The carving of Gilgamesh shown in **Figure 1.5** was made in the eighth century B.C.E. and shows the enduring popularity of the Sumerian legend. Here Gilgamesh is shown with the long curled beard of a king—which looks remarkably like Sargon's in **Figure 1.4.** The captured lion illustrates his hunting prowess. These characteristics of kings—power and strength—persist through the ancient world.

Individual longings

accommodation serves as a model for the continuing interchange of ideas that was one of the strengths of Western culture. For example, when the Akkadian ruler Sargon invaded Sumer in about 2350 B.C.E., he had to facilitate peace among the Akkadian northerners and the Sumerian southerners. The bronze head probably depicting Sargon shown in **Figure 1.4** was designed to show the power of this great king. His long beard, carefully curled, was a symbol of masculine strength, and he wears a band around his head showing his royal office.

Sargon chose religion as the key to uniting the people and appointed his daughter Enheduanna as high priestess of both the Akkadian and Sumerian goddesses. In the inset in **Figure 1.4,** the priestess (the second figure from the left) is shown wearing the elaborate clothing appropriate to her rank, surrounded by her attendants as she moves to the altar to worship. Enheduanna wrote beautiful hymns (which have survived to the present) in which she identified the Sumerian goddess Inanna with her Akkadian counterpart, Ishtar. She proved so successful in reconciling goddesses in this way that Sargon's successors continued the practice of making their daughters high priestesses, thus forging a link between the cultures of the region. As kings began to handle earthly

FIGURE 1.5. Gilgamesh, eighth century B.C.E. *The Epic of Gilgamesh*, preserved on cuneiform tablets, is the oldest surviving epic poem, ca. 2000 B.C.E. This image of Gilgamesh holding a conquered lion reveals how visual illustrations served to remind people of their treasured literature.

The Development of Writing

Although religion dominated Mesopotamian thought, the Sumerians' real impact on the future of Western civilization derived from their more practical inventions. As Mesopotamian cities expanded and grew wealthy, the need arose for a system of keeping records that would prove more enduring and accurate than the spoken word. In response, the Sumerians developed a system of writing. Some scholars believe that writing first emerged from a system of trade tokens. For example, if a merchant wanted to verify the number of sheep someone else was supposed to deliver, he would count out tokens to represent the sheep and seal them in a clay envelope that would be broken open upon delivery. The tokens left an imprint in the clay, and in time people realized that they could omit the tokens entirely and simply mark the clay.

At first, Sumerian writing consisted of stylized pictures of the objects represented—birds, sheep, or bowls to signify food. Soon the characters became more abstract and indicated sounds as well as objects. By 2800 B.C.E., the Sumerians had developed a sophisticated writing system called **cuneiform** (named from the Latin word that means "wedge"). Scribes imprinted wedge-shaped characters into wet clay tablets, which became highly durable when dried. **Figure 1.6** shows a tablet of cuneiform script made in about 2600 B.C.E., which lists quantities of various commodities.

<Cuneiform>

Scribes labored for many years to memorize the thousands of characters of cuneiform script. By 2500 B.C.E., scribal schools had been established to train the numerous clerks needed to serve the palaces and temples. Some surviving cuneiform tablets reveal that these students also studied mathematics and geometry. At first, girls attended these scribal schools, and records testify to a number of successful female scribes. Later, however, the occupation became exclusively male, but the reasons for this change have been lost. The schoolboy described at the beginning of this chapter was one of the lucky few who were trained to read and write. Anyone possessing these skills was assured a prosperous future.

Most of the Sumerian tablets that have been excavated refer to inventories, wills, contracts, payrolls, property transfers, and correspondence between monarchs. Such content reflects both the complexity of this civilization and the everyday necessity of tracking economic transactions. However, writing also let people record more abstract subject matter. *The Epic of Gilgamesh* and other myths preserved the dreams and hopes of these early civilizations, and the hymns of the priestess-poet Enheduanna attest to their spiritual longings and aesthetic sensibilities. However, beyond providing us a glimpse of this long-lost civilization, the invention of writing gave Western culture a distinct advantage over societies that depended only on human memory to recall their achievements. Writing enabled the transfer and dissemination of knowledge, which allowed people to build on previously acquired advancements instead of continually rediscovering and relearning the same material.

<Written records>

Laws and Justice

Writing also fostered the emergence of another element that would remain an essential component of Western civilization: a written law code. Recording laws in writing was an attempt to establish order in the land between the rivers that seemed so susceptible to chaos. But these laws also tried to express principles of justice that outlasted the ruler who issued them. As early as 2500 B.C.E., Uruinimgina tried to reform his society by passing laws that protected the powerless while preserving the socially stratified society that all took for granted. This tradition continued throughout Mesopotamian history and formed a powerful precedent for subsequent civilizations. In about 2100 B.C.E., Ur-Nammu, king of Ur, wrote laws to preserve "the principles of truth and equity."

The most famous and complete of the ancient law codes was that of the Babylonian king Hammurabi (ca. 1792–1750 B.C.E.), who ruled the southern Mesopotamian valley. In the prologue to his law code, which is preserved in cuneiform script on a stone column, the king expressed the

Code of Hammurabi

highest principles of justice: "I established law and justice in the language of the land and promoted the welfare of the people." Studying Hammurabi's code, which was a compilation of existing laws, opens a window into the lives of these ancient urban dwellers. It regulated everything from family life to physicians' fees to building requirements. The king seemed determined to order his society, for he introduced harsh penalties that had been absent from earlier laws. His code literally demanded an "eye for an eye"—one law stipulated that "should a man destroy another's eye, he shall lose his own." Another stated that a son who strikes his father shall have his hand cut off.

Hammurabi's code clearly expressed the strict social hierarchy that Mesopotamian society counted as natural. The laws specified different penalties for the three social orders: elites, freemen, and slaves. The elites included everyone from officials to priests and warriors. Beneath them were freemen, including artisans, merchants, professionals, and some farmers. Slaves occupied the bottom stratum, but they, too, had some rights under Hammurabi's laws—for example, they might own land and marry free persons. Many of the laws sought to protect the powerless so, as the prologue says, "that the strong may not oppress the weak."

Many laws tried to protect women and children from unfair treatment and limited the authority of husbands over their households. For

Women and children

example, women could practice various trades and hold public positions. Husbands could not accuse their wives of adultery without proof, for the penalty for proven adultery was harsh—the adulterous wife and her lover would be drowned. However, a woman could obtain a divorce from her husband. In spite of

FIGURE 1.6 Cuneiform Script, ca. 2600 B.C.E. Sumerian writing, made with wedge-shaped indentations in wet clay, revolutionized record keeping, allowing texts to long outlast memory. This tablet records lists of trade commodities.

these protections, women still remained largely the property of their husbands. For example, a woman could be put to death for entering—without her husband—a facility that served alcoholic beverages. Furthermore, a wife's fortunes were so dependent upon her husband that he could even sell her into slavery to pay his debts.

Perhaps one of the most significant things about Hammurabi's code was that the king intended his laws to outlast his own rule. On the tablet, he inscribed: "For all future time, may the king who is in the land observe the words of justice which I have written upon my monument!" Writing, and written law in particular, gave kings and reformers like Hammurabi hope for the establishment of timeless justice and a chance for a kind of personal immortality for the king.

Indo-Europeans: New Contributions in the Story of the West

While the people in the Fertile Crescent developed many of the elements that contributed to the formation of Western civilization—agriculture, writing, and law—the emerging culture remained subject to transformation. As we have seen, one of the advantages of the ancient Middle East was its location, which permitted it to benefit from influences from the far reaches of Asia. Of course, this geographic openness also contributed to instability—ideas often came with invaders and destruction. The region north of the Black Sea and the Caucasus Mountains (see **Map 1.4**) produced peoples living on the steppes who waged war on the peoples of the Fertile Crescent and developed a culture that eventually had a profound influence on the West.

Linguists, who analyze similarities in languages, have labeled these people Indo-European because their language served as the basis for virtually all subsequent European languages (except Finnish, Hungarian, and Basque). This language family sepa-

Indo-European languages

rates the Indo-Europeans from most of the original inhabitants of the Fertile Crescent, who spoke "Semitic" languages. The steady influx of Indo-European invaders (later called Celts, Latins, Greeks, or Germans) formed the dominant population of Europe. Other Indo-Europeans moved east and settled in India or traveled south into modern-day Turkey and Iran.

The Indo-Europeans were led by a warrior elite, who were buried in elaborate graves. Excavations of these graves have allowed scholars to analyze the prized possessions and weapons that were buried with these rulers, yielding many insights into this society. Some archaeologists refer to the Indo-Europeans as "battle-ax people" because of the many axes found in their burial sites. They also rode

Mounted warriors

horses, which they first domesticated for riding in about 2000 B.C.E. Riding on horseback gave Indo-European warriors the deadly advantages of speed, mobility, and reach over the Stone and Bronze Age archers they encountered in their travels.

The warrior elite of the Indo-Europeans excelled in battle and moved their families with them as they journeyed and fought. They carried their belongings in heavy carts outfitted with four solid, wooden wheels. The carts were a significant departure from the Sumerian two-wheeled chariots, which proved too unstable over long distances.

Contributions

The heavy carts traveled best over flat surfaces, and evidence indicates that as early as 2000 B.C.E. wooden roadways were built across boglands in northern Europe to accommodate the movement of people and their goods.

When the Indo-Europeans moved into the Fertile Crescent, they were not literate, but they preserved their values in oral traditions. Later, influenced by the literary traditions of those they conquered, Indo-Europeans developed their own written languages, and many of these tales were written down and preserved. Ideals of a warrior elite and worship of gods who lived in the sky instead of on the earth continued, as did the Indo-European language. These elements were among the Indo-European contributions

to Western civilization. In turn, early in the history of the Indo-Europeans (long before they acquired a written language), they adopted some things from the Mesopotamian cradle of civilization. They acquired many of the grains and other foods that were native to Mesopotamia and spread them widely. The successful culture of the Fertile Crescent was making its impact known far outside the river valleys that spawned it.

Hittites Establish Their Empire

In about 1650 B.C.E., an Indo-European people called the Hittites established a kingdom in Asia Minor (modern Turkey) and set up their capital at Hattusas (see **Map 1.2**). For the next three hundred years, the Hittite people planted crops on the fertile lands north of their capital, irrigated their fruit groves, and mined the ore-rich mountains. Throughout this time, they interacted with their neighbors in Mesopotamia and integrated much of Mesopotamian language, literature, law, and religion into their own Indo-European heritage. The interactions were often violent as the Hittites entered into the stormy politics of the ancient world.

The Hittites introduced a new technology of warfare into the West in the form of powerful—and deadly—war chariots. The oldest reference to chariot warfare in the ancient Near East comes from about the eighteenth century B.C.E., in a text that mentions

FIGURE 1.7. War Chariot, ca. 1299 B.C.E. The Hittites' war chariot was a fearsome military innovation that launched an arms race in the ancient world. The light wheels allowed rapid deployment that overwhelmed slower infantry.

forty teams of horses at one battle. The wheels of the Hittite chariots, lighter than those for any previous vehicle, made the chariots highly maneuverable, and the axle was set forward for stability. **Figure 1.7** shows a Hittite chariot with an archer trampling a fallen enemy. The Hittites' chariot-building prowess led to an arms race of sorts, culminating in the Battle of Kadesh in 1299 B.C.E., when some five thousand chariots participated in the struggle between Egyptians and Hittites.

Fortunately for historians, the Hittites learned the art of writing from the Mesopotamians. At Hattusas archaeologists have excavated about 10,000 cuneiform tablets, which shed much light on this culture that stood at the crossroads of the Middle East for such a long time.

A king whose military and administrative skill significantly changed the Hittite fortunes came to power in about 1380 B.C.E. Suppiluliuma I (r. ca. 1380–ca. 1345) thought of himself as both avenger and conqueror, and he launched the Hittites into building an empire. Within a century, he and his successors had built the most powerful state in the region. Suppiluliuma placed his sons in control of Syrian states and gained control of the lucrative trade along the Euphrates. Inevitably, Hittite armies clashed with the culture arising to the south and west—along the river valley of the magnificent Nile River.

RULE OF THE GOD-KING: ANCIENT EGYPT,
ca. 3100–1000 B.C.E.

The food crops that proved so successful in Mesopotamia spread to Egypt, stimulating another ancient civilization that arose on the banks of a great river—the roots of Western civilization moved farther west. The Nile River in Egypt flows more than 4,000 miles, from central Africa north to the Mediterranean Sea. Just as in Mesopotamia, a climate change forced dependence on the great river. In about 6000 B.C.E. the prevailing Atlantic rains shifted, changing great grassy plains into desert and forcing people to move closer to the Nile to use its waters.

Unlike the Tigris and Euphrates, the Nile reliably overflowed its banks every year at a time convenient for planting—flooding in June and receding by October. During this flood, the river deposited a layer of fertile black earth in time for a winter planting of cereal crops. In ancient times, the Nile also provided the Egyptians with an excellent communication and transportation system. The river flowed north, encouraging traffic in that direction, but the prevailing winds blew from north to south, helping ships to sail against the current.

Egypt was more isolated than the ancient civilizations to the northeast. The deserts to the Nile's east and west stymied most would-be invaders, and in the southern Sudan a vast marsh protected the area from encroachers. Potential invaders from the Mediterranean Sea confronted shallows that prevented ships from easily approaching the Egyptian coast. As a result, Egyptian civilization developed without the fear of conquest or the resultant blending and conflict among cultures that marked the Mesopotamian cities. By about 3100 B.C.E., a king from Upper Egypt (in the south), who according to tradition was named Menes, had consolidated his rule over the entire Egyptian land.

Prosperity and Order: The Old Kingdom, ca. 2700–2181 B.C.E.

Ancient Egyptians believed that the power of the gods was visible in the natural world—in the Nile and in the people and animals that benefited from its bounty. Consequently, they worshiped the divine spirit that was expressed through heavenly bodies, animals, and even insects. Over time, some gods were exalted over others, and deities were combined and blurred. However, through most of Egypt's history the most important deities were the sun god Re (or Amon) and the Nile spirits Isis, her husband-consort, Osiris, and their son, the falcon-god Horus. Unlike the Mesopotamians, the Egyptians were optimistic about their fortunes. They believed they were blessed by the gods, who brought such a regular and fertile flooding of the Nile, not cursed by their chaotic whims. This optimism infused Egyptian culture with extraordinary continuity—why change something that brought such blessings?

At the heart of their prosperity was the king, whom Egyptians considered the living embodiment of the deity, and this linking of political power with religion reinforced the stability of the Old Kingdom. While Mesopotamians believed their kings served as priests to their gods, Egyptians believed their rulers *were* gods, who had come to earth to bring truth, justice, and order—all summarized in the word **ma'at**. In return, the populace was obligated to observe a code of correct behavior that was included in the concept of *ma'at*. In about 2450 B.C.E., a high palace official named Ptah-hotep left a series of instructions for his son, in which he urged the boy to follow the precepts of *ma'at*: "He who departs from its laws is punished. . . . Evil may win riches, but it is the strength of *ma'at* that endures long." For millennia, kings and advisors like Ptah-hotep believed strongly that the importance of proper behavior brought prosperity to the land, and such beliefs contributed to a stable society. (The funeral inscription in Document 1.1 shows

DOCUMENTS

DOCUMENT 1.1

An Egyptian Nobleman Writes His Obituary

This document from second-millennium B.C.E. Egypt records the obituary inscribed on the tomb of an Egyptian nobleman named Ameni (or Amenemhet). This excerpt reveals what he counted as his greatest deeds in his years of service during Egypt's Middle Kingdom.

First Expedition

I followed my lord when he sailed southward to overthrow his enemies among the four barbarians. I sailed southward, as the son of a count, wearer of the royal seal, and commander in chief of the troops of the Oryx nome, as a man represents his old father, according to [his] favor in the palace and his love in the court. I passed Kush, sailing southward, I advanced the boundary of the land, I brought all gifts; my praise, it reached heaven. Then his majesty returned in safety, having overthrown his enemies in Kush the vile. I returned, following him, with ready face. There was no loss among my soldiers.

Second Expedition

I sailed southward, to bring gold ore for the majesty of the King of Upper and Lower Egypt, Kheperkere (Sesostris I), living forever and ever. I sailed southward together with the hereditary prince, count, oldest son of the king, of his body, Ameni. I sailed southward, with a number, 400 of all the choicest of my troops, who returned in safety, having suffered no loss. I brought the gold exacted of me; I was praised for it in the palace, the king's-son praised god for me.

Ameni's Able Administration

I was amiable, and greatly loved, a ruler beloved of his city. Now, I passed years as ruler in the Oryx nome. All the imposts of the king's house passed through my hand. The gang-overseers of the crown possessions of the shepherds of the Oryx nome gave to me 3,000 bulls in their yokes. I was praised on account of it in the palace each year of the loan-herds. I carried all their dues to the king's house; there were no arrears against me in any office of his. The entire Oryx nome labored for me.

Ameni's Impartiality and Benevolence

There was no citizen's daughter whom I misused, there was no widow whom I oppressed, there was no [peasant] whom I repulsed, there was no shepherd whom I repelled, there was no overseer of serf-laborers whose people I took for (unpaid) imposts, there was none wretched in my community, there was none hungry in my time. When years of famine came I plowed all the fields of the Oryx nome, as far as its southern and northern boundary, preserving its people alive and furnishing its food so that there was none hungry therein. I gave to the widow as (to) her who had a husband; I did not exalt the great above the small in all that I gave. Then came great Niles, possessors of grain and all things, [but] I did not collect the arrears of the field.

SOURCE: James Henry Breasted, *Ancient Records of Egypt*, vol. 1 (Chicago: University of Chicago Press, 1906), pp. 251–253.

Analyze the Document

1. Where did the nobleman travel in the course of his service, and what does this tell you about the global connections of the ancient world?

2. What kinds of accomplishments did he most want readers of this inscription to remember about him?

3. What does this inscription reveal about the values of ancient Egypt?

---

these enduring values.) This ordered society was ruled by a god-king later called **pharaoh** (great house), a term that referred to the general institution of the monarchy as well as the ruler.

The Old Kingdom period (ca. 2700–2181 B.C.E.) saw astonishing prosperity and peace, as farming and irrigation methods provided an abundance of crops and wealth to many. Unlike the Mesopotamian valley, Egypt had | Trade | ready access to mineral resources, most importantly copper, which was in great demand for tools. Egyptians refined copper ore at the site of the surface mines, and ingots of copper were transported by caravans of donkeys overland to the Nile. From there, the precious ores were manufactured or used to trade abroad. Egypt was also happily situated to capitalize on trade with Nubia, which gave access to the resources of sub-Saharan Africa. (See Global Connections on page 17.) From Nubia, Egyptians gained gold, ivory, ebony, gems, and aromatics in exchange for Egyptian cloth and manufactured goods. With the surpluses of metals and grains, Egyptians could import goods from the Middle East and beyond. In addition to textiles, Egyptians desperately needed wood to make large seagoing vessels for their trade and navy. All this industry generated prosperity for many people, and in the Old Kingdom, people used these resources to support close families.

Ptah-hotep advised his son to start a family as soon as he could afford to: "If you are prosperous you should establish a household and love your wife as is fitting. . . . | Family life | Make her heart glad as long as you live." The artwork of the time suggests that many Egyptians took Ptah-hotep's advice and established

Nubia: The Passage from the Mediterranean to the Heart of Africa

From the dawn of civilization, the history of the West and the history of Africa developed together through cultural interactions that unfolded along the Nubian corridor. And throughout history, diverse groups—who spoke languages different from Egyptian—mingled in ancient Nubia. At times these groups even managed to unite into large kingdoms—one of which would conquer Egypt itself. Late in ancient Egyptian history, Nubian kings even became Egyptian pharaohs.

Lush and flat, the northern Nile valley stimulated the ancient Egyptians' agriculture and settlement. But near Aswan, in the south, the land changed. Here sandstone cliffs dropped directly from the desert plateau to the riverbank, and the river churned as it descended through a succession of swift rapids. These rapids are the first of six cataracts that impeded navigation south along the great river. Early rulers of Egypt marked the First Cataract as a natural southern border of their kingdom. However, later Egyptians pushed south beyond the First Cataract into Nubia. Egyptians had strong motivation to do so: Nubia provided the only reliable route around the Sahara desert to the riches that lay deep within the interior of the African continent.

In Nubia, goods moved north to the Mediterranean and south from Egypt and Mesopotamia. From the beginning, both Nubians and northerners recognized the benefits of this trade. See **Figure 1.11** for an artistic portrayal of Nubian trade. As early as 3000 B.C.E., domestic goats and sheep that had originated in Mesopotamia showed up in Nubia. Sometime after that, Nubians began to cultivate the domestic grains from Mesopotamia along the valley of the southern Nile beyond the First Cataract.

As early as the Old Kingdom in Egypt, kings valued the goods that came through Nubia, and even the sparse records from this ancient time reveal the importance of the trade with the south. For example, the Egyptian princes who governed Aswan bore the title "Keeper of the Door of the South," and sometime around 2250 B.C.E., the pharaohs sent a prince of Aswan named Herkhuf (or Harkhuf) on three journeys into Nubia to trade and to recruit mercenary troops to fight in Egypt's armies. Herkhuf headed south on the Nile, his ships propelled against the current by the prevailing north winds. The skilled navigators he employed negotiated the roiling rapids. The proud records carved on Herkhuf's tomb do not indicate how far beyond the Second Cataract he traveled, for we cannot identify the names of the various tribes he encountered. Yet most scholars think he made it to the Third Cataract. Seven months later, Herkhuf returned from one journey with 300 donkeys laden with incense, ebony, oil, leopard skins, elephant tusks, boomerangs, and other goods. His bounty revealed that Nubia served as a trading hub for luxuries and staples far beyond the Nile. The lure of Nubia was only increased when rich gold mines were discovered there in about 1980 B.C.E.

During the Middle Kingdom under the reign of Senwosret I (ca. 1980 B.C.E.), Egyptians began to mine for gold in Nubia, and the rich mines brought Nubia into the politics as well as the trade of the north. (Indeed, "Nubia" means "gold" in Egyptian.) Egyptians began to fortify the Nile, and Nubia engaged in the wars of the north. The fall of the ancient Egyptian kingdom did not end the importance of Nubia, which remained the major passage to the heart of Africa.

Making Connections

1. What aspect of its geographic location made Nubia so important to the ancient world? What role did Nubia play in trade?

2. How did the presence of domestic animals in sub-Saharan Africa demonstrate ancient connections between this region and Mesopotamia?

3. What trade items stimulated the connections between Africa and the Mediterranean?

---

loving families during this prosperous era. **Figure 1.8** shows a limestone carving of one such family. Seneb, the man depicted in the portrait, was a dwarf who had made a successful career in the court. He headed the court's weaving mill and then became the priest of the dead for two kings. His success was acknowledged when he married a member of the royal house. Husband and wife are shown side by side, perhaps suggesting the woman's high status. In this sculpture, the couple embrace affectionately and smile with seeming self-satisfaction while they tower protectively over the children below. The two figures at the lower left are each placing a finger over their lips, the Egyptian sign for "child." Stylized portraits like these suggest the success, contentment, and prosperity of many Old Kingdom families—at least those with enough wealth to commission portraits.

FIGURE 1.8 Egyptian Family, ca. 2320–2250 B.C.E. This is the family portrait of Seneb, head of the royal weaving mill, who married a woman of the royal family. The two are shown with their children in this idealized view of Egyptian family life.

Hieroglyphs: Sacred Writing

Sometime around 3000 B.C.E., Egyptians developed a system of writing. Egyptian writing was not cuneiform, nor was it used primarily for accounting purposes. While Egyptian administrators surely had as much need for clear records as the Sumerians, they primarily used writing to forward religious and magical power. Every sign in their writing system represented a real or mythical object and was designed to express that object's power. The ancient Greeks saw these images on temples and named Egyptian script **hieroglyph,** meaning "sacred writing."

Hieroglyphs were more than a series of simple pictures. Each symbol could express one of three things: the object it portrayed, an abstract idea associated with the object, or one or more sounds of speech from the spoken Egyptian word for the object. (The technical terms for these three uses are *pictogram*, *ideogram*, and *phonogram*.) Because this writing had ceremonial religious use, it changed little over the centuries as

scribes carved it into stone monuments. An example of hieroglyphic writing can be seen in the background of **Figure 1.10** (p. 20).

However, hieroglyphs were too cumbersome for everyday use, so scribes learned two other simplified scripts—called Hieratic and Demotic—to keep records or write literature. Whereas many of the hieroglyphs were carved into stone, everyday records were more often written on papyrus, a kind of paper made from the Nile's abundant papyrus reeds. This versatile, sturdy reed could be reused—much like recycled paper today—and in the dry desert air was very durable. Often in Egypt's history, the lucrative export of papyrus increased the royal treasury.

Scribes studied for many years to master the complicated, varied Egyptian scripts. As in Mesopotamia, there are early records of women scribes, but the occupation later became restricted to men. On one surviving papyrus fragment, a scribe praised his occupation: "Writing for him who knows it is better than all other professions. It pleases more than bread and beer, more than clothing and ointment. It is worth more than an inheritance in Egypt, than a tomb in the west."

Scribes

Pyramids and the Afterlife

Scribes furthered the prosperity of the god-kings by carefully tracking the rulers' finances as they grew rich from state monopolies and taxes on all the products created in the fertile land. Whenever they had excess income, the kings proved their greatness by building pyramids, monuments to their glory that in some cases survive today. Imhotep, the chief advisor to the Egyptian king Djoser in about 2650 B.C.E., designed and built the first pyramid at Sakkara (near Memphis, shown on **Map 1.2,** on page 21). This early pyramid, depicted in **Figure 1.9a,** is called a step pyramid. It was intended to join heaven and earth. An inscription on one pyramid explains: "A staircase to heaven is laid for [the king] so that he may mount up to heaven thereby." Unlike the ziggurats, which were made of dried clay bricks, these pyramids were built of cut stone—a remarkable building innovation.

The Old Kingdom rulers made the pyramids the great symbol of Egyptian power and longevity. An anonymous architect refined the early pyramid design and built the Great Pyramid as a burial tomb for the Fourth Dynasty ruler, Khufu (also known as Kheops), in about 2590 B.C.E. This pyramid became the model for the later Old Kingdom tombs that were built in Giza, which continue to dominate the skyline there. **Figure 1.9b** shows the pyramids at Giza, with the Great Pyramid of Khufu on the left. The pyramid of Khufu's son is in the back; it appears taller because it is on

Pyramids

higher ground. Khufu's pyramid covers about 13 acres and is made of more than two million stone blocks. Peasants labored on these pyramids before planting season during the months when the Nile was in flood. Ancient Greek historians later claimed that the Great Pyramid of Giza took twenty years to build and required the labor of 100,000 workers. Modern estimates tend to agree with these calculations. The pyramids—so visible in the ancient skyline—proclaimed the god-king's immortality and the permanence of the order he brought to the land along the Nile.

Pyramids—and later mortuary temples—were built as tombs for the god-kings or, more precisely, as houses for their departed spirits. The departed's

Afterlife soul was sustained in the tomb by the same food and goods that had sustained the living body. The Egyptian notion of immortality marked an important contribution to the world of ideas, for the afterlife Egyptians conceived of was dramatically different from the dark world of the Mesopotamian dead. We do not have an exact idea of how the Egyptians visualized the afterlife, but it seems to have been an improved version of this world—a heavenly Nile valley. Some poets even wrote of death as a pleasant release:

Death is before me today
Like a man's longing to see his home
When he has spent many years in captivity.

Upon the death of a king, or in later years a nobleman who could afford a burial, the body was

Burial rituals embalmed. Embalmers removed the internal organs through an incision in the abdomen and placed them in a vessel filled with a salty preserving solution. The body cavity was then probably dried in a pile of natron crystals. Later in Egypt's history, embalmers used resin-soaked linen to pack the body cavity. Finally the embalmers wrapped the body in more linen with resin. The wrapped, embalmed body—the mummy—along with a box containing the internal organs, was then placed in a chamber deep within the pyramid. Stocking the tomb with an array of food, household goods, and precious jewels for the pharaoh to enjoy in the afterlife completed the burial process.

Pyramids from the Old Kingdom contained no images, but later artists painted the interior walls of tombs with scenes of activities that the deceased could expect to enjoy in the afterlife, and these scenes offer us a glimpse of how Egyptians viewed the next world. **Figure 1.10** shows a happy scene that was painted on the walls of a New Kingdom tomb. In this picture, the noble family frolics on a bird-hunting trip that yields far more abundance than any real-life trip ever could. Under their boat

FIGURE 1.9 Pyramids, ca. 2590 B.C.E. These burial places for the royal dead had a long history in the Old Kingdom. Figure 1.9a is the earliest such structure (ca. 2680 B.C.E.), a "step pyramid" intended to join heaven and earth. Figure 1.9b shows the later, most famous pyramids at Giza, with the Great Pyramid of Khufu on the left.

swims a fish so fat it belongs in a fisherman's paradise. A child grips her father's leg while he catches birds with the help of his hunting falcon. His well-dressed wife stands in the background. Even the family cat enjoys an abundant afterlife, catching three

ANCIENT EGYPT CIVILIZATION

ca. 2700–2181 B.C.E.	Old Kingdom
2181–2140 B.C.E.	First Intermediate Period
ca. 2060–1785 B.C.E.	Middle Kingdom
ca. 1785–1575 B.C.E.	Second Intermediate Period
1570–1085 B.C.E.	New Kingdom
ca. 1504–1482 B.C.E.	Pharaoh Hatshepsut
ca. 1377–1360 B.C.E.	Pharaoh Akhenaten
ca. 1279–1213 B.C.E.	Pharaoh Ramses II

KEY DATES

FIGURE 1.10 Egyptian Paradise, ca. 1400 B.C.E.   In this tomb painting of the New Kingdom, the deceased, a court official named Nebamun, is shown with his wife and daughter on a hunting trip in the afterlife. The depiction of scenes of daily life reveals the Egyptians' joy in earthly life, as well as their expectations of a pleasant existence beyond death.

birds at once. This illustration reveals how much the Egyptian "heaven" had changed from the dark Mesopotamian netherworld.

Changing Political Fortunes, ca. 2200–1570 B.C.E.

The order and prosperity promised by the pyramids proved less enduring than the Egyptians expected. At the end of the Old Kingdom period, the climate turned against the god-kings. As drought in Famine southern Nubia led to a series of low floods in Egypt, crops failed, and people pillaged the countryside in a desperate search for food. There was even one account of cannibalism. Under such pressure, Egypt needed a strong ruler to preserve *ma'at,* but one was not forthcoming. Near the end of the Old Kingdom, one king—Pepi II (ca. 2270–2180 B.C.E.)—reputedly ruled for more than 90 years,

which was an extraordinary feat in an age when a decade or two was considered a substantial rule and when 40 years of age was the normal life expectancy. However, the old king was unable to keep a strong rule; during his reign, authority broke down, and he outlived his heirs. After his death a succession of little-known kings with very short reigns followed—a clear indication that all was not well within Egypt. Sources indicate that one of these ephemeral rulers was a woman—Nitocris—who ruled for about two years. During these times of weak central authority, local nobles exerted power, and Egypt suffered a period of social and political instability called the First Intermediate Period (2181–2140 B.C.E.).

A text from the time articulated poignantly the widespread misery experienced during these hard years: "Everything is filthy: there is no such thing as clean linen these days. The dead are thrown into the river. . . . The ladies of the nobility exclaim: 'If only

The Ancient Near East, ca. 1450 B.C.E.

This map shows the growth of the Egyptian Empire along with the territories of its neighbors, the Hittite Empire and the Mesopotamian kingdoms.

Explore the Map

1. Compare this map with **Map 1.1**. What new territories has Egypt conquered?

2. How was Egyptian culture affected by the conquest of territories populated by peoples of different cultures?

3. How do you think the Egyptian presence in Palestine drew Egypt into the many wars of the Middle East?

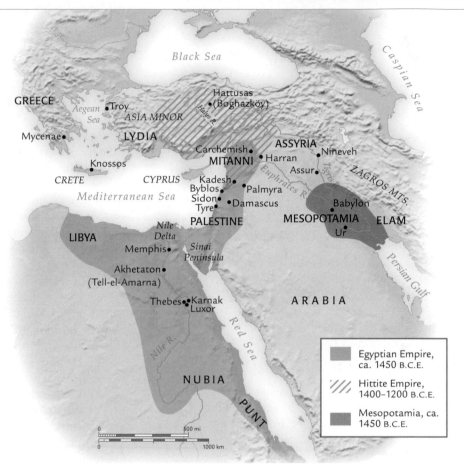

we had something to eat!' They are forced to prostitute their daughters. They are reduced to sleeping with men who were once too badly off to take a woman."

During these difficult times, people began to hope for a more pleasant afterlife, which many began to believe was possible for more than just the royal family. In the First Intermediate Period, anyone who could afford the appropriate burial rituals and magic spells could expect to achieve immortality. Still, prosperity continued to elude the Nile valley.

In about 2060 B.C.E., Amenemhat I of Thebes finally restored peace to the crippled valley and introduced what has come to be called the Middle Kingdom period (ca. 2060–1785 B.C.E.). **Middle Kingdom** Egypt prospered once again, and one pharaoh wrote: "None was hungry in my years, none thirsted then; men dwelled in peace." During these years, the kings conquered Nubia and grew rich on the gold of that kingdom. This conquest also brought sub-Saharan Africa into closer contact with the Mediterranean world, and continued trade with Nubia integrated African goods and elements of their culture into Egypt's and into the developing Western culture in general. The funeral

inscription in Document 1.1 testifies to the increased trade. Egypt's rulers also introduced impressive engineering projects that expanded Egypt's amount of irrigated land by more than 17,000 acres. The Egyptians also began engaging in lucrative trade with the peoples of the Fertile Crescent. This practice had a price, however: It drew Egypt into the volatile politics of the ancient Middle East.

In the eighteenth century B.C.E., trouble struck again. The kings at the end of the twelfth dynasty were weak, and local magnates began to claim autonomy. Without a strong central authority, the Nubians in the south revolted **Egypt conquered** and broke away from Egyptian control, taking their gold with them. In 1650 B.C.E., the Hyksos who had settled in the lowland where the Nile poured into the Mediterranean (the Delta) rose to power (see **Map 1.1**). The Hyksos brought with them a new technology of warfare. They fought with bronze weapons, chariots, and body armor against the nearly nude Egyptians, who used only javelins and light copper weapons. The Hyksos established a kingdom in the Delta and this uneasy time, the Second Intermediate Period, extended from about 1785 to 1575 B.C.E.

thinking about

ART

FIGURE 1.11

Egyptian Fresco, ca. 1295–1186 B.C.E.

A fresco is a kind of mural painted on plaster. This **fresco** from Thebes shows Nubians bearing gifts (tribute) of an exotic giraffe, an animal skin draped over a man's arm, a mound of ostrich eggs, and most valuable of all, highly bred cattle, valued for their coloring. All these were brought to the Egyptian pharaoh. Egyptian artists created this fresco to show the power of their ruler, and in the process they portrayed sub-Saharan Africans realistically, with dark skin, particular hairstyles, and woven clothing that we can use as historical evidence for Nubian society.

Connecting Art & Society

1. What does the fresco suggest about the value of Nubian trade to Egypt?

2. Which of the trade items that are depicted continue to be valued today? What makes them valuable?

3. How might this image, with its accurate portrayal of Nubians, be used as historical evidence for the imperial aspirations of the Egyptians?

Political Expansion: The New Kingdom, 1570–1085 B.C.E.

In about 1570 B.C.E., the Egyptians adopted the new technology of warfare. With bronze weapons and chariots of their own, they liberated themselves from the hated Hyksos and established a new dynasty that introduced what historians call the New Kingdom (1570–1085 B.C.E.). While these kings—now officially called pharaohs—intended to restore the conservative

glory of the Old Kingdom, they nevertheless remembered the lesson of the invasion from the north and no longer relied on Egypt's geographic isolation to protect their way of life. Instead, the newly militant god-kings embarked on a series of foreign wars to build an empire that would erect a territorial barrier between Egypt and any potential invaders. **Map 1.2** shows the extent of the Egyptian Empire by 1450 B.C.E.

As the Egyptian Empire expanded, it was in turn shaped by Fertile Crescent politics and culture. For example, the riches that poured into the Nile valley from foreign conquests often ended up in the hands of temple priests, who began rivaling the pharaohs in power. Slaves, captured abroad and brought to Egypt, introduced new languages, views, and religions to the valley. Not surprisingly, the lives of Egyptian soldiers, battling in foreign wars, changed for the worse. The scribe we met earlier, who praised his own occupation above all others, wrote about the grim life of a soldier of the New Kingdom: "He is called up for Syria. He may not rest. There are no clothes, no sandals. He drinks water every third day; it is smelly and tastes of salt. His body is ravaged by illness. He does not know what he is about. His body is weak, his legs fail him." As **Map 1.2** shows, the imperial expansion of Egypt encroached on the borders of the strong Hittite Empire, which soon threatened the restored New Kingdom.

Despite the challenges, the imperial pharaohs successfully built their empire and made Egypt prosperous again. However, such expansion always came with a cost. Rulers had to weigh placing resources into military expansion or into local projects. Hatshepsut's (ca. 1504–1482 B.C.E.) endeavors demonstrated this tension as she ruled the extended Egypt (see the Biography on pages 24–25). While protecting her borders, Hatshepsut concentrated her resources on domestic developments and commercial enterprises. Her inscriptions claim that she restored temples that had lain in ruins since the Second Intermediate Period, and she engaged in numerous public works, all achievements that made her popular among her people.

Hatshepsut's accomplishments were all the more remarkable since it was highly unusual for a woman to rule alone. Women in a pharaoh's family had always held the important position of consort to their brother-husbands. They joined them in being descended from gods, but the king had always been the incarnation of the principal deity. Hatshepsut used artistic representations to overcome this problem, ordering that all statues of her portray her as a man. In **Figure 1.13,** on page 25, a formal portrait, she is dressed in the traditional male royal style—bare-chested and wearing a short, stiff skirt. She even wears an artificial, ceremonial beard.

Hatshepsut's successors reversed her traditional politics and revived Egypt's imperial ambitions. The New Kingdom reached its apogee in expansion and prosperity under the reign of Amenhotep III (r. ca. 1412–ca. 1375 B.C.E.). This

Empire building

confident pharaoh built huge statues of himself and a spacious new temple. His luxurious lifestyle, however, took its toll on him. He died at age 38, and his mummified remains reveal a balding, overweight man with rotted teeth.

The Religious Experiment of Akhenaten, ca. 1377–1360 B.C.E.

During the New Kingdom, the traditional relationship between the god-king and his priests began to change. Priests of Amon became almost as powerful as the pharaohs in administering the kingdom. The priests of Osiris grew popular with wealthy people, to whom they offered the possibility of immortal life

in return for money. Within this increasingly tense environment arose a reformer who tried to create a religious revolution.

Amenhotep IV (r. ca. 1377–1360 B.C.E.), the son of Amenhotep III, tried to renounce the many divine principles worshiped in all the temples of Egypt and institute worship of a single god whom he called Aten, the sun-disk. The god-king changed his name from Amenhotep (Amon is satisfied) to Akhenaten (useful to Aten, the sun-disk). Then he withdrew his support from the old temples and tried to

Akhenaten's religion

dissolve the powerful priesthoods. Akhenaten also departed from tradition by introducing a new naturalism in art, in which he allowed himself to be portrayed realistically, protruding belly and all (see **Figure 1.12**). However, the artwork in Aten's new temples often featured portraits of Akhenaten's beautiful wife, Nefertiti, without the pharaoh, suggesting that the queen may have played a large role in planning the new cult.

FIGURE 1.12 Pharaoh Akhenaten and Family, ca. 1340 B.C.E. This limestone carving shows Akhenaten, his wife, Nefertiti, and three of their daughters relaxing in a family pose that departed from the usual formal depictions of the pharaoh. They bask in the rays of Aten, the sun-disk, the new deity they worshiped.

Hatshepsut & Thutmose
(r. 1473–1458 B.C.E.) (ca. 1482–1450 B.C.E.)

Powerful

Queen and

Vengeful

Son-in-Law

The Egyptian pharaoh Thutmose I had three children by his chief wife—two sons who died in their youths, and a daughter, Hatshepsut. In the complex households of the pharaohs, the succession to the throne was never clear; Thutmose I also had a son by a lesser wife. This son, Thutmose II, married his half-sister Hatshepsut and succeeded his father as pharaoh. Thutmose II apparently was sickly and died in 1504 B.C.E. after he and Hatshepsut had a daughter, Neferure. The succession again went to a son by a concubine. However, this next son, Thutmose III, was younger than 10 years old when his father died. The logical regent was his aunt/stepmother, Hatshepsut. Although it was customary for a man to rule,

Hatshepsut wanted to be pharaoh, not regent. To this end, she cultivated the support of the powerful priests of Amon, and of the army, and had herself declared pharaoh. Thutmose III had to accept a position of titular co-ruler with no actual authority. Hatshepsut seems to have treated her young charge well. Contemporaries praised his extraordinary skills in reading and writing and his study of military arts. He was also healthy and a strong athlete. His remains show that he escaped even the severe dental decay that appears in many royal mummies. Thutmose III was probably married to his aunt's daughter, Neferure, to guarantee his succession.

Hatshepsut grappled with two major challenges during her reign: how to forward her political vision for Egypt and how to ensure her credibility. She approached both tasks shrewdly, ever aware of the importance of appearances as well as policy. In her political vision, she focused attention on trade and peaceful pursuits, and she turned to art and building to validate her rule. Hatshepsut commissioned portraits that showed her dressed as a male king, and she built a magnificent funerary temple intended to stand forever and proclaim her passage into the land of the gods.

While Hatshepsut focused on internal building projects, she kept the army strong, because Egypt's neighbors did not feel powerful enough to threaten the borders. The accomplishments she seemed proudest of, however, were in trade. She commissioned a great carving that recounted her successful trade mission to "Punt," an African kingdom that we can no longer exactly identify, although some historians suggest it may be near modern-day Somalia (see **Map 1.2**). In any case, this wealthy sub-Saharan kingdom had been the destination of several trade

---

Figure 1.12 shows a casual family portrait of Akhenaten, Nefertiti, and three of their daughters. Husband and wife are shown the same size. Both wear regal headdresses that suggest an unusual equality, and Akhenaten affectionately kisses one of his daughters in a remarkably informal portrayal. The sun-disk is above and shines down on both, indicating not only that the family is blessed by the sun deity, but also that they can serve to bring the blessings of the sun to their people.

A beautiful hymn to Aten has survived, perhaps written by Akhenaten himself. In the hymn, the pharaoh praises Aten as the only god: "O sole god, like whom there is no other! Thou didst create the world according to thy desire." In a development remarkable for the ancient world, Akhenaten declares this god to be universal, belonging to all peoples: "Their tongues are separate in speech, and their natures as well; Their skins are distinguished, As thou distinguishest the foreign peoples. . . . The lord of all of them, . . . The lord of every land." In the ancient world, gods were associated with individual peoples and cities, so Akhenaten's praise of a universal god is extraordinary.

Many scholars have speculated about the motives behind this dramatic religious innovation. Had Akhenaten been influenced by Israelites living in Egypt? Was his declaration of a single god a political move to reduce the power of the priests of Amon? Or was the king a sickly dreamer who merely had a strange spiritual vision? We will never know Akhenaten's motives, but his reign caused turmoil in Egypt.

The Twilight of the Egyptian Empire, 1360–ca. 1000 B.C.E.

Akhenaten was succeeded by Tutankhaton (r. 1347–1338 B.C.E.), who was only 9 years old at the time of his succession. He is shown with his wife in the chapter opener on page 2. Compare the chapter opener with **Figure 1.12.** Notice that both feature the comfortable family grouping that marked the artwork of Akhenaten's reign and that both show the sun-disk—Aten—bestowing blessings. However, the young Tutankhaton was unable to carry on the unpopular religious reforms of his father-in-law. The priests of the old cults had grown increasingly resentful of Akhenaten—whom they called "the criminal"—and within three years the young king changed his name to Tutankh*amen* as he renounced the old pharaoh's

FIGURE 1.13 Hatshepsut, ca. 1460 B.C.E.

missions during the Middle Kingdom, and all knew of the wealth that was available. The carving depicts the pharaoh meeting with the Queen of Punt—an obese and powerful woman—and bringing back many luxury items of trade. Hatshepsut's ships were filled with incense, ebony, gold, ivory, animal skins, and even live baboons, sacred to Egyptian gods. The pharaoh brought these great luxuries back to Egypt and used much of the wealth in her monumental building projects.

When Thutmose III grew to manhood, he gained control of the army and seemed ready to rule without Hatshepsut's guidance. The early death of his wife, Neferure, weakened his ties to Hatshepsut, and sources hint that the woman pharaoh was murdered (or simply deposed) in 1458 B.C.E. Late in his reign, the pharaoh Thutmose III tried to eradicate all memory of Hatshepsut. He had her temples and most of her statues destroyed and her name scraped off stone monuments. Was he angry about his long regency? Did he object to Hatshepsut's gender? Did he disapprove of her popular political agenda, or was he trying to ensure a smooth succession for his son? We can never know the answers to these questions. Fortunately for students of history, Thutmose was unable to erase all the evidence that tells of his remarkable predecessor.

Thutmose III was a great leader, although his political vision for Egypt differed markedly from that of his aunt. Specifically, he believed that Egypt should be an imperial power. During his 54-year reign, he led military expeditions and established the empire that defined Egypt during the New Kingdom. In the story of Hatshepsut and Thutmose, we see two accomplished pharaohs with conflicting visions of Egypt—one looking backward to its Old Kingdom greatness, the other looking forward to the empire building of the future. Both rules embodied major, dramatic themes in Egyptian history.

Connecting People & Society

1. In what ways does the queen's life reveal the tensions between the New Kingdom's involvement with other regions and its desire for isolation?

2. How does the queen work to rule within the constraints of her gender? How successful is this strategy?

---

religious convictions. Tutankhamen died at just 18 years of age, and the general who succeeded him as pharaoh—Harmhab—destroyed Akhenaten's temples and restored the worship of the old gods.

Egypt showed a hint of its former greatness during the reign of Ramses II (1279–1213 B.C.E.), who reestablished the imperial frontiers in Syria and restored peace under Egypt's traditional gods. After the hard-fought battle at Kadesh in 1274 B.C.E., Ramses negotiated a treaty with the Hittites that is believed to be the first recorded nonaggression pact. Ramses' success in bringing peace allowed him to free resources for huge building projects, most notably a great temple carved out of the rocky cliffs along the Nile. The tribute portrayed in **Figure 1.11** testifies to the prosperity restored during the New Kingdom.

Subsequent pharaohs, through the end of the New Kingdom in 1085 B.C.E., tried to maintain the fragile empire. However, major challengers arose to confront the god-kings. Libyans to the west and Nubians from the south invaded the Nile valley and took power for a while. Eventually, greater empires to the east and north would conquer Egypt permanently, and the center of Western civilization would move to other lands. However, the advanced culture, ordered life, and intense spirituality of the rich land of the Nile would again exert a profound impact on the early peoples of the West, as we will see in Chapter 3.

PEOPLES OF THE MEDITERRANEAN COAST,
ca. 1300–500 B.C.E.

Along the eastern coast of the Mediterranean Sea, various civilizations arose and became part of the power struggles plaguing the Middle East. Most of these Mediterranean cultures eventually were absorbed by their neighbors and disappeared. However, two of them—the Phoenicians and the Hebrews—made a lasting impact as they vigorously expanded their fortunes and furthered the worship of their gods.

The Phoenicians: Traders on the Sea

The Phoenicians were successful traders whose culture was based in the coastal cities of Sidon, Tyre, and Byblos (see **Map 1.2**). These seagoing merchants made the most of their location by engaging in prosperous trade with Egypt and the lands in the Fertile Crescent. The Phoenicians controlled forests of cedar trees that were highly prized in both Mesopotamia and Egypt. They also had an even more lucrative monopoly on purple dye made from coastal shellfish. Purple dyes were so rare that cloth of this color was expensive, so it soon became identified with royalty. Phoenician weavers dyed cloth purple and sold it throughout the Middle East and western Mediterranean for huge profits. Throughout the ancient world, nobility was demonstrated by wearing purple clothing.

Explorers from the Phoenician cities traveled widely throughout the Mediterranean Sea. By 950 B.C.E., these remarkable sailors traded as far west as Spain, and even into the Atlantic down the west coast of Africa. Like all ancient sailors, they hugged the coast as they traveled so that they could stop each night to beach the ships and sleep. To guarantee safe harbors, Phoenician traders established merchant colonies all along the north coast of Africa; by some estimates there was a colony about every 30 miles. The most important colony was Carthage, which was founded about 800 B.C.E. and would become a significant power in the Mediterranean (see Chapter 4). Through these colonies, the Phoenicians spread the culture of the ancient Middle East—from their trading expertise to their gods and goddesses—around the Mediterranean all the way to Spain.

The enterprising Phoenician sailors left their mark on the Mediterranean world long after neighboring empires conquered the Phoenicians' home cities on the eastern coast. They began their early voyages in search of metals: tin, copper, iron for tools and weapons, and silver and gold for luxury items. This quest even led these intrepid sailors through the Strait of Gibraltar into the Atlantic, where they traded as far as the African coast and Britain. They were skilled at smelting metals—including the difficult-to-forge iron—and their metallurgy talents, along with the trade they fostered, stimulated growth throughout the region.

The Phoenicians' most important contribution to Western culture was their remarkable alphabet. In developing a writing system, the Phoenicians improved on the Sumerian script by creating a purely phonetic alphabet of only twenty-two letters. This system was simpler than the unwieldy cuneiform and hieroglyph that dominated the rest of the Middle East. The Phoenician alphabet spread rapidly and allowed later cultures to write without the long apprenticeships that characterized the proud scribes like the one shown at the beginning of this chapter. Through adopting a Phoenician-style alphabet, cultures of the West achieved a significant advantage over cultures whose written languages remained the exclusive province of the elite.

The People of the One God: Early Hebrew History, 1500–900 B.C.E.

Phoenician society in the Near East ultimately disappeared as an independent state, but not before it had performed an immense service as a transmitter of culture throughout the Mediterranean. The Phoenicians' neighbors, the Hebrews, followed an entirely different course. The Hebrews resiliently withstood both time and conquest and emerged from a difficult journey with their culture intact.

While the Sumerians and their successors in Mesopotamia developed complex civilizations based on irrigation and built ziggurats to their many deities, the seminomadic Hebrews moved their flocks from Mesopotamia into the land of Canaan, comprising much of the modern states of Israel, Lebanon, and western Syria. As they traveled, they shared many of the ancient stories of Mesopotamia, such as the tale of a great flood that destroyed the land (present in *The Epic of Gilgamesh*, described earlier) and a lost Garden of Eden. The Hebrews, perhaps seeing the Mesopotamian ziggurats from a distance, also viewed their neighbors as overly proud. The Hebrew story of the ill-fated Tower of Babel captures this theme of overweening pride.

Sometime before about 1700 B.C.E., the early leaders of the Hebrews, the patriarchs—Abraham, Isaac, and Jacob—led these seminomadic tribes that roamed the eastern Mediterranean and beyond. Jacob changed his name to Israel ("he who prevails with God"), and this name marked Jacob's followers as having a special relationship with one God. Consequently, historians refer to these tribes as the Israelites. Several clans traveled to Egypt, where Israelite texts claim they were enslaved by the Egyptians, although their status is not clear. They might simply have been employed in the labor-intensive Egyptian work projects, and their position may have changed over time to a more restrictive relationship. Some historians identify the Israelites with a group who helped build the huge projects of the Egyptian pharaoh Ramses II (r. ca. 1279–1213 B.C.E.). According to the Bible, Moses led this same group from Egypt. This Exodus (which means "journey out" in Greek) transformed them into a nation with a specific religious calling.

The details of the history of the Israelites are found in the Hebrew Scriptures (later called the Old Testament by Christians). Made up of writings from oral and written traditions and dating from about 1250 to 150 B.C.E., these Scriptures record laws, wisdom, legends, literature, and the history of the ancient Israelites. The first five books (known as the Pentateuch) constitute the **Torah,** or law code, which governed the people's lives. The Bible contains some information that is historically accurate and can be generally confirmed by archaeological evidence. For example, as early as 1208 B.C.E. the pharaoh Marneptah, the son of Ramses II, erected a victory stone recording his triumphs, including the conquest of Israel: "Israel is laid waste, his seed is no more. . . ." The Egyptian god-king would not have bothered to brag about the conquest of the Israelites if this accomplishment had not been fairly substantial, so we know that the Bible's descriptions of a strong Israelite kingdom in Palestine during the second millennium B.C.E. are well founded.

| Hebrew Scriptures |

Historians must be cautious when using the Bible as a source, because it is basically a religious book that reveals faith, not science. Archaeology and history can illuminate the events of the ancient Israelites, but these sciences can shed no light on the faith that underlies the text. Used carefully, though, the Bible is an important source of information on these early Israelites, for they made a point to record and remember their own history—they wove teachings and morality into a historical narrative. Thus, Hebrew religion was rooted in history rather than myth, and from this text we can begin to re-create the early history of this profoundly influential people.

According to the Bible, the Hebrews from Egypt eventually returned to ancient Palestine and slowly reconquered the land, uniting the other nearby Hebrew tribes in the process. During this period of settlement, between about 1200 and 1050 B.C.E., Israelites experienced a change in leadership. Instead of relying solely on tribal leaders, people turned to "judges"—charismatic leaders who helped unite the people against the threats of their neighbors. In time, the elders of the tribes felt they needed a king to lead the people, declaring, "then we shall be like other nations, with a king to govern us, to lead us out to war and fight our battles" (1 Sam. 8:20). The people insisted that Samuel, the last of the judges, anoint their first king, Saul (r. ca. 1024–ca. 1000 B.C.E.).

| Establishing a kingdom |

Saul's successor, David (r. ca. 1000–ca. 961 B.C.E.), began encouraging the tribes to settle in a fixed location, with their capital at Jerusalem. David's successor, Solomon (r. ca. 961–ca. 922 B.C.E.), brought Phoenician craftsmen to Jerusalem to build a great temple there. Now a territorial power like others in the Fertile Crescent, the Hebrews worshiped their God in the temple overlooking a majestic city. But the costs of the temple were exorbitant, causing increased taxes and the growth of an administrative structure to collect them.

Solomon was a king in the Mesopotamian style. If the biblical account is to be believed, he used marriage to forge political alliances, accumulating hundreds of wives and many hundreds more concubines, including the daughter of an Egyptian pharaoh. The biblical excerpts in Document 1.2 show Solomon's fame, long-distance trade, and the difficulties accompanying his many marriages. However, the unified kingdom of tribes barely outlasted Solomon's reign. After his death, the northern tribes—particularly angry about Solomon's taxation and administrative innovations—broke away to form the separate kingdom of Israel (**Map 1.3**). The southern state was called Judah, with its capital at Jerusalem, and at this time the southern Israelites began to be called Jews. Israel was the more prosperous of the two kingdoms and was tied more closely to Phoenicia by trade and other contacts. Judah adhered more rigorously to the old Hebrew laws. The two kingdoms often fought each other as they participated in the shifting alliances of their neighbors. Dominating all politics, however, was their commitment to their one God.

| Dividing a kingdom |

The authors of the Scriptures developed an overriding theme in Jewish history: the intimate relationship between obedience to God's laws and the unfolding of the history of the Jewish people. As these authors recorded their recollection of events, they told of periodic violations of the uncompromising covenant with God and the resulting punishments that God imposed.

A Jealous God, 1300–587 B.C.E.

When Moses led his people out of Egypt, they reportedly wandered for forty years in the wilderness of the Sinai Peninsula before returning to the land of Canaan (see **Map 1.3**). During that time, Moses bound his people to God in a special covenant, or agreement, through which the Jews would be God's "chosen people" in return for their undivided worship. The ancient Hebrews were not strictly monotheistic, for they believed in the existence of the many deities of their neighbors. For Moses' people, however, there was only one God, and this God demanded their exclusive worship. As the historian of the sixth century B.C.E. wrote in the Bible's Book of Deuteronomy, "He is the faithful God, keeping his covenant of love to a thousand generations of those who love him and keep his commands." This promise was a conditional one: God would care for his people only if they practiced his laws, and there were many laws.

| The covenant |

The core of the Hebrew legal tradition lay in the Ten Commandments that the Bible claims God gave to Moses during his exodus from Egypt, and these were supplemented by other requirements listed in the Scriptures. Adhering to these laws defined one as a Jew. While the laws bound the Jewish people together—to "love thy neighbor as thyself"—they also set the Jews apart from their neighbors. For

| Hebrew laws |

DOCUMENT 1.2

King Solomon Secures His Realm's Fortune

These passages from the Book of Kings in the Bible show that King Solomon, like other ancient leaders, tried to secure the fortunes of his kingdom through marriages with neighboring peoples. They tell of King Solomon's fame and his relationship with women. The first passage describes the wealthy queen of Sheba (modern Yemen), and the second passage describes Solomon's many marriages.

Now when the queen of Sheba heard of the fame of Solomon concerning the name of the Lord, she came to test him with hard questions. She came to Jerusalem with a very great retinue, with camels bearing spices, and very much gold, and precious stones; and when she came to Solomon, she told him all that was on her mind. And Solomon answered all her questions; there was nothing hidden from the king which he could not explain to her. And when the queen of Sheba had seen all the wisdom of Solomon, the house that he had built, the food of his table, the seating of his officials, and the attendance of his servants, their clothing, his cupbearers, and his burnt offerings which he offered at the house of the Lord, there was no more spirit in her.

And she said to the king, "The report was true which I heard in my own land of your affairs and of your wisdom, but I did not believe the reports until I came and my own eyes had seen it; and behold, the half was not told me; your wisdom and prosperity surpass the report which I heard . . . then she gave the king a hundred and twenty talents of gold, and a very great quantity of spices, and precious stones; never again came such an abundance of spices as these which the queen of Sheba gave to King Solomon (1 Kings 10:1–7, 10).

Now King Solomon loved many foreign women: the daughter of Pharaoh, and Moabite, Ammomite, Edomite, Sidonian, and Hittite women, from the nations concerning which the Lord had said to the people of Israel, "You shall not enter into marriage with them, neither shall they with you, for surely they will turn away your heart after their gods"; Solomon clung to these in love. He had seven hundred wives, princesses, and three hundred concubines; and his wives turned away his heart. For when Solomon was old his wives turned away his heart after other gods; and his heart was not wholly true to the Lord his God, as was the heart of David his father. For Solomon went after Ashtoreth the goddess of the Sidonians and after Milcom the abomination of the Ammonites. So Solomon did what was evil in the sight of the Lord, and did not wholly follow the Lord as David his father had done. Then Solomon built a high place for Chemosh the abomination of Moab, and for Molech the abomination of the Ammonites, on the mountain east of Jerusalem. And so he did for all his foreign wives, who burned incense and sacrificed to their gods. And the Lord was angry with Solomon . . . (1 Kings 11:1–9).

SOURCE: Bible. 1 Kings 10:1–13; 1 Kings 11:1–13 (*New Oxford Annotated Bible with the Apocrypha.* New York: Oxford University Press, 1973).

Analyze the Document

1. How do the two passages, in different ways, reveal the importance of women during Solomon's reign?

2. What goods does the queen bring from Arabia? How does her gift of these materials illustrate the importance of long-distance trade to the Hebrew state?

3. What particular challenges do monotheistic Jews face in dealing with their neighbors?

KEY DATES

HEBREWS

2000–1700 B.C.E.	Patriarchs
ca. 1250 B.C.E.	Moses exodus from Egypt
ca. 1200–1050 B.C.E.	Judges
ca. 1024–ca. 1000 B.C.E.	King Saul
ca. 1000–ca. 961 B.C.E.	King David
ca. 961–ca. 922 B.C.E.	King Solomon
ca. 800 B.C.E.	Prophets
587 B.C.E.	Babylonian Captivity
515 B.C.E.	Second Temple built

example, boys were circumcised as a mark of the covenant between God and his people. In addition, Jews observed strict dietary laws that separated them from others—for example, they could eat no pork nor any animal that had been improperly slaughtered. But the fundamental commandment that allowed for no compromise with non-Jews was the injunction against worshiping the idols, or deities, of their neighbors.

Around the eighth century B.C.E., Jews were called to even higher ethical standards by a remarkable series of charismatic men—the prophets. These men, such as Amos, Micah, Hosea, Jeremiah, and Isaiah, were neither kings nor priests nor soldiers. Instead, they were common people—shepherds or tradesmen—who cared nothing for power or glory. They were brave men

Prophets

MAP 1.3

Mediterranean Coast in the First Millennium B.C.E.

This map shows the major kingdoms of the Mediterranean coast, together called the Land of Canaan in the Bible. The kingdoms include those of the Philistines, Hebrews, and Phoenicians.

Explore the Map

1. Look at the scale of the map. How close were these kingdoms? How might that proximity have contributed to increased warfare in the region?

2. Based on the map, why do you think there were so many battles between the Philistines and the Hebrews?

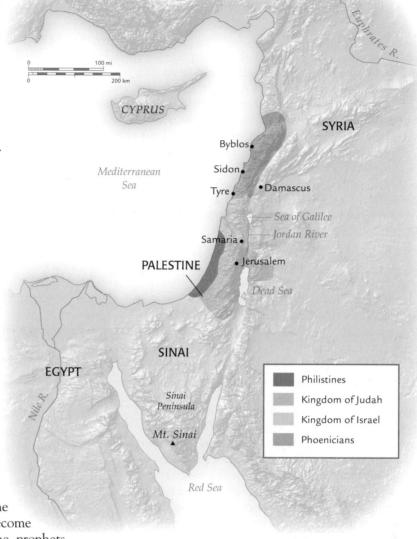

who urged their people to return to the covenant and traditional Hebrew law. In times of social distress, they became the conscience of Israel, and in turn they helped shape the social conscience that was to become part of Western civilization. The prophets reminded the Jews to care for the poor: "Seek justice, relieve the oppressed, Judge the fatherless, plead for the widow" (Isa. 1:17). In doing so, they emphasized the direct ethical responsibility of every individual. Unlike the other religions of the ancient Middle East, Judaism called individuals to follow their consciences to create a more ethical world. Religion was no longer a matter of rituals of the temple, but a matter of people's hearts and minds. The prophets preached a religion that would be able to withstand turmoil and political destruction, and it is fortunate that they did so, for the Hebrews would suffer much adversity, which they believed was a form of testing by their God.

According to the Bible, King Solomon had a weakness that stemmed from his polygamy. (See Document 1.2.) Not only did he violate the biblical command not to take foreign wives, but to please them he allowed the worship of other deities (especially the fertility goddess Astarte), even in the holy city of Jerusalem. Prophets claimed that it was

his impiety that had divided the kingdom against itself. Later events showed a similar theme. Ahab (r. 869–850 B.C.E.), king of the northern kingdom of Israel, married a Phoenician princess, Jezebel, and erected an altar to her god Baal in order to please her. When Israel was conquered in 721 B.C.E. by the Assyrians, prophets who had predicted its downfall pointed to Ahab's breach of the covenant as the cause of the misfortune. The southern kingdom of Judah fared little better than Israel in trying to escape the aggressions of its neighbors. In 587 B.C.E., the Babylonians captured Jerusalem and destroyed Solomon's magnificent temple. Many Jews were exiled and enslaved in Babylon, and the "chosen people" were once more without a country or a religious center. From then on, there would be substantial numbers of Jews who lived outside Israel or Judah, and they later would be collectively known

"God's punishments"

as the **Diaspora.** Instead of renouncing their God, however, the Jews reaffirmed their covenant in a different way.

Judaism in Exile

Hebrew priests in exile worried that Diaspora Jews living among non-Jews would forget the old traditions and be assimilated into the cultures of their neighbors. Therefore, they carefully compiled and edited the Scriptures to preserve their unique view of religion and history. These written accounts helped Judaism survive without a geographic center. The authors of the Scriptures arranged the history of the Jews to show that, despite hardships, God had always cared for his people. The priests believed that the destruction of the two Hebrew kingdoms had come because people either did not know the laws or had failed to obey them. As a result, Hebrew teachers emphasized the study of and strict adherence to the purity laws to keep their people separate from others even when they lived in close proximity as neighbors.

Without the temple in Jerusalem to serve as the center of worship, Jewish worship began to convene in more local establishments—synagogues and the home itself. This movement had an important impact on the status of women in Jewish culture. The emphasis on details of purity law to keep the chosen people separate reduced women's roles in formal prayer because the law stressed that anyone worshiping God had to be "clean." Women, seen as sometimes unclean because of menstrual blood or childbirth, were excluded from participating in the formal worship rituals. On the other hand, the experience of exile strengthened the family as a social and religious unit, a change that improved women's lives in other ways. For example, concubinage disappeared and women presided over the household, upholding the dietary laws and household rituals that preserved the Jewish culture wherever they lived.

In time, however, the Hebrews were able to reestablish their religious center in Jerusalem. After ruling Judah for forty-eight years, the Babylonians were, in turn, conquered by new peoples, the Persians. The Persians proved much more tolerant than the Babylonians of the varied beliefs of their subject peoples. In 538 B.C.E., the Persian king Cyrus let the Jewish exiles return to Jerusalem. The Jews built a new temple in 515 B.C.E., an event that introduced the "Second Temple" period. Again, the Jews had a temple and center of worship like other Mesopotamian peoples. However, all Jews did not return to Israel, and the question of the relationship between Diaspora Jews and the cultures in which they lived would reemerge periodically throughout history as followers of this old covenant interacted with their neighbors.

"Second Temple" period

The ancient Hebrews made a tremendous impact on the future of Western civilization. They believed that God created the world at a specific point in time, and this notion set them apart dramatically from their neighbors, such as the Egyptians, who believed in the eternity of the world. The Hebrews' view of history as a series of purposeful, morally significant events was unprecedented in the ancient world. Their concept of ethical monotheism, in which a single God of justice interacted with humans in a personal and spiritual way, offered a vision of religion that eventually dominated in the West. The many deities and demons that ruled the Mesopotamian and Egyptian worlds would in time be rendered insignificant by the God of the Hebrews, who transcended nature. The Hebrews believed that there was a profound distance between people and God, and thus individuals took more responsibility for the events of this world even as they worshiped and held in awe the deity who had made a deep and abiding covenant with the Jewish people.

Hebrew contributions

TERROR AND BENEVOLENCE: THE GROWTH OF EMPIRES, 1200–500 B.C.E.

By the second millennium B.C.E., many people could see the value of centralized control over larger territories. The Egyptians were establishing an empire, and the Hebrews had united into a kingdom. Not only did size offer the potential for larger armies, but expansion westward also secured access to valuable seaborne trade (which was making the Phoenicians wealthy) and would secure the strategically important region of Syria and Palestine. Perhaps most important, people wanted to expand their territories to acquire the metals so necessary for military and economic success. These impulses led to the growth of a new political form in the West—huge empires based on a new technology, iron.

The Age of Iron

Before the eleventh century B.C.E., ancient civilizations depended on bronze, an alloy of copper and tin. All across Europe and the Middle East, people used bronze plows to cultivate the land and employed bronze-tipped weapons to make war. While agriculture remained the most important enterprise, the economies of these civilizations were fueled by trade in copper and tin. Initially, these essential metals came largely from Asia Minor (see **Map 1.2**), Arabia, and India. Later, sources of these metals were also found in the western Mediterranean.

In about 1200 B.C.E., warfare disrupted the usual trade routes, making tin scarce. Pure copper is a soft

MAP 1.4

The Assyrian Empire, ca. 662 B.C.E.

This map shows the homeland of the Assyrians and their expansion as they conquered the older centers of Western civilization. Compare this map with **Maps 1.1, 1.2,** and **1.3.**

Explore the Map

1. How many cultures were included in this large empire?

2. What problems would you expect to arise in the governance of such a diverse empire?

3. How might the location of the Assyrians' homeland have facilitated their expansion?

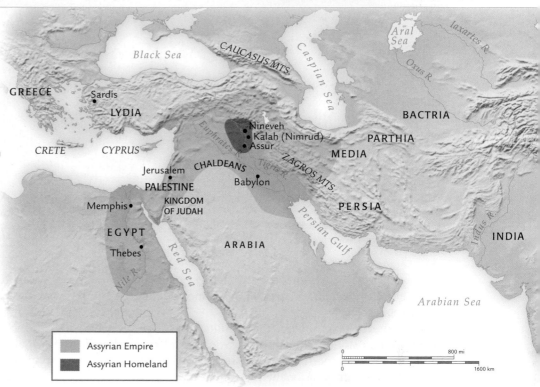

Assyrian Empire
Assyrian Homeland

metal, and without the tin needed to make bronze, smiths could not produce effective tools and weapons.

| Iron Age | To overcome the tin shortage, Hittite metalworkers in Asia Minor first began to employ iron, an abundant mineral in that region. Unforged iron is not much stronger than copper. However, when it is repeatedly heated in a hot charcoal furnace, carbon molecules combine with iron molecules to form a very reliable metal known as carbon steel. Even low-carbon steel is stronger than bronze, and when it is cold hammered, the strength more than doubles. People—and particularly soldiers—gained a huge advantage by using the new metal.

The technology used to create the superior forged iron spread rapidly throughout the Mediterranean world, and from about 1000 B.C.E. on it was used in tools, cookware, and weapons. The use of iron spread to sub-Saharan Africa through Nubia, and ironworking became prominent throughout much of that continent, which was rich in iron ore. Soldiers wielding iron weapons easily vanquished those armed with bronze. The Age of Iron had dawned, and it dominated the world until the late nineteenth century when metalsmiths developed new ways to make iron into steel without the carbon method (Bessemer steel). Iron Age kings in Mesopotamia forged enough weapons and fielded armies so large, their extensive conquests introduced multiethnic empires that dwarfed all that had gone before.

Rule by Terror: The Assyrians, 911–612 B.C.E.

The Assyrians, a people living originally in the northern Tigris-Euphrates valley, had traded profitably with their neighbors for centuries. In the early tenth century B.C.E., they began arming themselves with iron weapons and following the one command of their god Assur: Expand the frontiers of Assyria so that Assur finally rules over all. **Map 1.4** shows the striking success of the Assyrians as they cut a swath through the civilizations of the ancient Near East.

The Assyrians' success stemmed from the skill of their armies and their willingness to engage in almost constant warfare to follow the command of Assur. Assyrian histories recounting their military campaigns were written as propaganda pieces to instill fear in their enemies. The historians accomplished their goal, and the cold-blooded details cemented the Assyrians' reputation for ruthlessness. King Sargon II's (r. 722–706 B.C.E.) description of his conquest of Babylon is one chilling example of these accounts: "I blew like the onrush of a hurricane and enveloped the city like a fog. . . . I did not spare his mighty warriors, young or old, but filled the city square with their corpses."

Beyond sheer brutality, the Assyrians relied on some of the most advanced military techniques that the ancient world had seen. They employed a corps of military engineers to build bridges, tunnels, and efficient siege weapons capable of penetrating strongly

FIGURE 1.14 Escaping a Battle The Assyrians were fearsome warriors. Their art frequently memorialized their accomplishments, as in the case of this image of fugitives escaping from Assyrian archers. This depiction shows an ancient technique of swimming underwater with air-filled pigskins.

fortified cities. Furthermore, they had a highly trained and well-rewarded officer corps who became the elite in Assyrian society.

The Assyrians portrayed their military achievements in their art as well as in their writings. But along with interminable portrayals of destruction and carnage, Assyrian art occasionally reveals unusual details of experience during the ninth century B.C.E. The carving shown in **Figure 1.14** depicts three men fleeing Assyrian archers as they swim the river toward the fortified town on the right. Two of the swimmers hold pigskins filled with air to breathe underwater, offering a surprising glimpse of an underwater swimming technique. This carving captures an incident that may have been particularly memorable due to the fugitives' creative escape. However, although the fugitives eluded the archers, the Assyrians conquered the town.

The Assyrians were first both to acquire such a large territory and to try to govern it cohesively. In many ways, they proved to be skilled administrators. For example, they built roads to unify their holdings, and kings appointed governors and tax collectors to serve as their representatives in the more distant territories. One of the elements that facilitated governing and trade over large areas was the Assyrians' use of Aramaic as a common language. This was a Semitic language originally spoken by the Aramaeans, successful merchants who lived in Mesopotamia in about 1100 B.C.E. Aramaic remained the official language of subsequent empires—it was even spoken by Jesus. In spite of the Assyrians' reputation for violence, the Greek historian Herodotus (ca. 484–ca. 424 B.C.E.) recalled the peaceful accomplishments of Queen Semiramis, who built "magnificent embankments to retain the river [Euphrates], which till then used to overflow and flood the whole country around Babylon."

Governing an empire

Many Assyrian rulers also appreciated the wealth of knowledge and culture that had accumulated in these lands for centuries. The great Assyrian king Ashurbanipal (669–627 B.C.E.) collected a huge library from which 20,000 clay tablets have survived. Within this collection, the king preserved the best of Mesopotamian literature, including *The Epic of Gilgamesh*. The highly educated Ashurbanipal took pride in his accomplishments: "I acquired the hidden treasure of all scribal knowledge, the signs of the heaven and the earth. . . . I have solved the laborious problems of division and multiplication. . . . I have read the artistic script of Sumer and the obscure Akkadian." This quotation offers an excellent example of how a written language served to preserve and disseminate the culture developing in the ancient Middle East.

Preserving learning

Although the Assyrians were skilled in making both war and peace, they still faced the problem that confronted all empire builders: how to keep the empire together when subject peoples resisted. The Assyrians used terror to control their far-flung territories. When individuals dissented, they were publicly tortured; when cities revolted, they were razed to serve as examples to others. To break up local loyalties, Assyrian commanders uprooted and moved entire populations. These methods worked for a while; eventually, however, they catalyzed effective opposition.

Fall of Assyrians

Ashurbanipal ruled from his capital in Nineveh—reputedly so well fortified that three chariots could ride abreast along the top of the walls surrounding the city. However, even those great walls could not save the king's successors. A coalition including Babylonians from southern Mesopotamia; Medes, an Indo-European tribe from western Iran; and Egyptians gathered against the Assyrian domination. Because the empire was so large it overextended the Assyrians' resources, and the provinces gave way quickly. Nineveh itself finally collapsed in 612 B.C.E. after a brutal two-year siege. In an ironic turn of events, the great city was defeated by the very river that had sustained it for so long—the Tigris flooded higher than normal and eroded Nineveh's defensive wall. Assyrian rule came to an ignominious end. However, the Assyrians left an enduring legacy for Western civilization: centralized empires that ruled over extended lands and different peoples.

Babylonian Rule, 612–539 B.C.E.

After vanquishing the Assyrians, the Medes left Mesopotamia and returned to their homeland near the Zagros Mountains (see **Map 1.4**). The Babylonians (also called Chaldeans, or Neo-Babylonians, to distinguish them from the earlier kingdom of Hammurabi) remained and ruled the lands of the former Assyrian Empire. The new rulers emulated the Assyrian use of terror to enforce their will on subject peoples. King Nebuchadrezzar (r. 605–561 B.C.E.) kept penalties similar to those in the Code of Hammurabi for civil crimes, but introduced extreme punishments for enemy rulers and their followers. When captured, these people were often flayed or burned alive. It was this severity that led Nebuchadrezzar to destroy Jerusalem in 587 B.C.E. and lead the Jews into captivity. This incident was the formative "Babylonian Captivity" discussed earlier that shaped much of subsequent Jewish history.

The Babylonians also continued the Assyrian passion for art and education. The king rebuilt his capital city of Babylon in such splendor that it was admired throughout the ancient world. His architects constructed huge ziggurats in praise of the Babylonian god Marduk and fortified the structures with walls more impressive than even Nineveh's had been. Under Nebuchadrezzar, Babylon blossomed into an impressive city graced by gardens, palaces, and temples.

Culture and commerce

The magnificent architecture that marked Babylon cost a fortune, and the Babylonian kings obtained these funds largely through fostering the commerce that often guided their military policies. One king, for example, besieged Tyre for thirteen years, hoping to win control over the Phoenicians' far-reaching trade. Another king established himself in Arabia in an attempt to control a new trade—in incense—that came from southern Arabia to the Mediterranean Sea.

Kings used their new wealth not only to decorate their cities, but also to foster learning. Within the cosmopolitan city, Babylonian priests excelled in astronomy and mathematics. They observed the heavens

in an effort to understand the will of the gods, and in the process they charted the skies with impressive accuracy; they could predict solstices, equinoxes, and other heavenly phenomena. Their passion for predictions led them to develop another innovation with which they sought to foretell the future for individuals: astrology. By the fifth century B.C.E., Babylonian astrologers had divided the heavens into twelve signs—including the familiar Gemini, Scorpio, Virgo, and others—and began to cast horoscopes to predict people's futures based on their birth dates. The earliest surviving example of a horoscope was for a child born in 410 B.C.E. and marks the beginning of a long-standing practice.

Astronomy and mathematics

As part of their astronomical calculations, Babylonians developed advanced mathematics. Their tablets show that they regularly used multiplication, division, calculations of square and cube roots, algebra, and other operations. In addition, they based their numerical system on the number 60, working out an elaborate method of keeping time that led to the division of hours and minutes that we use today. The benefits of the Babylonians' impressive intellectual achievements were not spread widely through society. More subjects resented Babylonian rule than benefited from its accomplishments.

Rule by Tolerance: The Persian Empire, ca. 550–330 B.C.E.

In 553 B.C.E., the fortunes of the Babylonian Empire changed. The Persians, a people from east of the Zagros Mountains, overran the land of their Indo-European relatives, the Medes. Under their wise king, Cyrus the Great (r. 559–530 B.C.E.), the Persians expanded westward to establish an empire even larger than that of the Assyrians (**Map 1.5**). They quickly conquered the kingdom of Lydia in Asia Minor and then turned southeast to the Babylonian Empire. The Babylonian rulers found few supporters against the invaders even among their own people, and in 539 B.C.E. Babylon fell to the Persians virtually without a struggle.

Cyrus rejected the Assyrian policies of terror and sought to hold his vast empire together by tolerating differences among his many subject peoples. As mentioned earlier, in 538 B.C.E. he allowed the Jewish captives in Babylon to return to Jerusalem and rebuild their temple. At the same time, he appeased Babylonians by claiming he was "friend and companion" to their god Marduk. In the conquered provinces—or satrapies—Cyrus retained local officials but installed Persian governors called **satraps.** He controlled the satraps' power by appointing additional officials who were directly responsible to the king. The Persians required subject peoples to pay

Persian administration

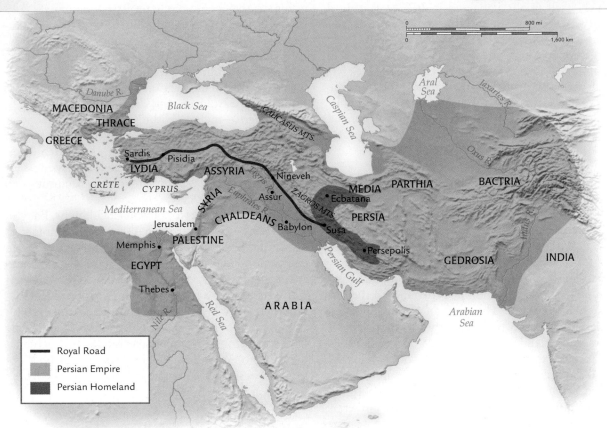

MAP 1.5

The Persian Empire, ca. 500 B.C.E.

This map illustrates the Persian Empire that replaced and greatly expanded the previous Assyrian domain and highlights the Royal Road, which spanned a large portion of the territory. It also shows the capital of the empire, Persepolis. Compare the extent of this empire with that of the Assyrians shown in **Map 1.4.**

Explore the Map

1. What problems do you think the Persians encountered due to the empire's vast expanse and diverse cultures?

2. How might the Royal Road have helped the Persian rulers to deal with the challenges of administering such a large empire?

3. Given that the Persian homeland and capital were so far east, what might the impact have been on Western culture?

reasonable taxes and serve in their armies, but Cyrus's system prevented local officials from abusing their power excessively. Conquered peoples could worship their own gods and follow their own customs, and under Cyrus's reign, the ancient civilizations enjoyed a long period of peace. The great king (as his subjects called him) was seen as a semidivine figure who ruled benignly from his golden throne.

After Cyrus's death in 530 B.C.E., his son Cambyses II (r. 529–522 B.C.E.) inherited the throne and continued the expansion his father had begun so effectively. The new king extended Persian control to the eastern Mediterranean by conquering Egypt and the Phoenician port cities. (See Document 1.3 for a description of Cambyses' military expansion.)

Cambyses was succeeded by Darius (r. 521–486 B.C.E.), a brilliant ruler who was able to consolidate and further organize what Cyrus and Cambyses had hastily conquered. Darius built a new capital city at Persepolis (see **Map 1.5**), moving the center of his empire east, but he also realized how important it was to facilitate travel throughout his empire. To accomplish this, he built and carefully maintained a complex system of roads, and the most famous was the Royal Road, between Susa in the east (in modern Iran) and Sardis (in modern Turkey) in the west. This impressive road, almost 1,700 miles long, fostered the economic life of the empire.

A unified empire allowed the Persians to adopt ideas that had proven successful in the civilizations

DOCUMENT 1.3

Cambyses Conquers Egypt

This passage from the fifth-century B.C.E. Greek historian Herodotus describes the Persian king Cambyses' conquest of Egypt in 525 B.C.E. and his treatment of the pharaoh who had opposed his conquest. Cambyses was a controversial king, known for his "madness" (perhaps caused by alcoholism), yet even his reign was marked by policies that helped make the Persian Empire so successful.

After their defeat, the Egyptians fled in disorder and shut themselves up in Memphis. Cambyses called upon them to come to terms, sending a Persian herald up the river to the town in a Mytilenean vessel; but directly they saw the ship coming into the town, they rushed out from the walls in a body, smashed up the ship, tore everyone on board limb from limb, and carried the bits back inside the walls. They then stood a siege, but after a time surrendered. The neighbouring Libyans were alarmed by the fate of Egypt and gave themselves up without a battle, agreeing to pay tribute and sending presents. . . . Ten days passed, and Cambyses, wishing to see what stuff the Egyptian king Psammenitus was made of—he had been but six months on the throne—forced him with other Egyptians, to witness from a seat in the city outskirts a spectacle deliberately devised to humiliate him. . . .

[Cambyses was pleased at the young king's reactions.] They brought Psammenitus to Cambyses, at whose court he lived from that time onward. Here he was well treated; and indeed, if he had only had the sense to keep out of mischief, he might have recovered Egypt and ruled it as governor; for the Persians are in the habit of treating the sons of kings with honour, and even of restoring to their sons the thrones of those who have rebelled against them. There are many instances from which one may infer that this sort of generosity is usual in Persia. . . . Psammenitus, however, did not refrain from stirring up trouble, and paid for it. He was caught trying to raise a revolt amongst the Egyptians, and as soon as his guilt was known by Cambyses, he drank bull's blood and died on the spot. And that was the end of Psammenitus.

SOURCE: Herodotus, *The Histories*, trans. Aubrey de Sélincourt (New York: Penguin, 1996), pp. 159–160.

Analyze the Document

1. Why do you think the document emphasizes the treatment of Cambyses' enemies?

2. What persuades the Libyans to surrender? Is this strategy effective? Explain.

3. How does Herodotus expect Cambyses to treat the defeated Egyptian king? What actually happens to the king?

---

that preceded them. For example, Persians retained Aramaic as the common language of commerce, making communication easier across many cultures, and they fostered the trade routes that had brought so much wealth to the Babylonians. Persian astrologers learned from their Babylonian predecessors as well. These wise men, or magi, became celebrated for their knowledge of the heavens.

Of all the conventions the Persians borrowed from the inhabitants of their diverse empire, the adoption of coinage had the greatest long-term impact. The Lydians seem to have invented the use of coins in the seventh century B.C.E. Before this time, traders either bartered or used cumbersome bars of precious metals to purchase goods. For example, in Egypt in 1170 B.C.E., a burial vault that was priced at 5 pounds of copper might have been bought with 2½ pounds of copper, one hog, two goats, and two trees. By minting coins with precise, identifiable values, kingdoms greatly facilitated trade. The kings of Lydia were said to have grown fabulously rich after their invention, and the Persians rapidly spread the use of coins throughout their far-flung lands.

Coins

While the Persians adopted many novelties of their predecessors, they also made a unique contribution of their own: a new movement in religious thought initiated by the talented prophet Zoroaster (ca. 628–551 B.C.E.). One of the most important religious reformers of the ancient world, Zoroaster founded a new religion (later called **Zoroastrianism**) that contained the seeds of many modern belief systems. Zoroaster experienced a revelation given to him by the one god, Ahura Mazda, the Lord of Light. In this revelation, recorded in a holy book called the Avesta, Zoroaster was called to reform Persian religion by eliminating polytheism and animal sacrifice. In the tradition of Uruinimgina, Hebrew prophets, and others throughout the early history of Western civilization who called for social justice, Zoroaster also urged people to live ethical lives and to show care for others. Finally, the prophet believed that the history of the world was one of ongoing conflict between Ahura Mazda and the forces of the evil god Ahriman. Zoroaster also felt confident that Ahura Mazda would ultimately prevail over evil and that eventually the dead would be resurrected. Believers would go to paradise, while evildoers would fall into a hell of perpetual torture.

Zoroastrianism

Beginning with the pious Zoroastrian Darius, the Persian kings claimed to rule the earth as Ahura Mazda's viceroys, but slowly the old nature worship returned and became incorporated into Zoroastrian beliefs. For example, people began to venerate Mithra, the ancient sun god, as an assistant to Ahura Mazda. Zoroaster's ideas had an influence that far outlasted the Persian rulers. During the Roman Empire, the worship of Mithra would be an important cult (see Chapter 5). Furthermore, followers of Zoroastrianism still exist today, and even in the ancient world many of the prophet's ideas influenced other religions as well. Over time, some believers transformed Zoroaster's monotheism into a dualistic belief in two gods, one good and one evil. Judaism—and, later, Christianity—seem to have been influenced by his vision, for Jewish texts began to write of the power of a devil and of a final struggle between good and evil. Zoroaster was the first prophet whose ideas would spread throughout a large political empire, but he would not be the last.

LOOKING BACK & MOVING FORWARD

Summary   In the 3,000 years that make up the history of the ancient Middle East, many elements that characterize Western civilization emerged. Great cities sprang up, introducing commerce, excitement, diversity, and extremes of wealth and poverty that the West both values and struggles with even today. Tyranny and oppression arose, as did the laws and principles designed to hold them in check. Sophisticated religions provided vehicles for metaphysical reflection, and artists expressed those hopes and dreams in beautiful forms. Perhaps most important, writing systems evolved to let people preserve their accumulated knowledge for future generations, including ours. Finally, these early centuries established a pattern of interaction and cross-fertilization of goods and ideas that would mark Western civilization from its beginnings through today.

The great civilizations of the Nile and Tigris-Euphrates valleys—the Egyptians, Sumerians, Akkadians, Babylonians, and others—were ultimately absorbed by larger empires. Yet their contributions endured as a result of the mutual influence that always occurs when cultures mingle. The Hebrews, too, contributed much to the growing body of Western ideas and values. By 500 B.C.E., the Persian kings had united the region, creating an empire rich with the diversity of many peoples and thousands of years of history. The Persian Empire marks a culmination of the first stirrings of Western civilization in the ancient Middle East. The next developments in the story of the West would come from different peoples: the Greeks.

KEY TERMS

Paleolithic, *p. 4*
Neolithic, *p. 6*
ziggurat, *p. 9*
augury, *p. 10*
cuneiform, *p. 12*
ma'at, *p. 15*
pharaoh, *p. 16*
hieroglyph, *p. 18*
fresco, *p. 22*
Torah, *p. 26*
Diaspora, *p. 30*
satraps, *p. 33*
Zoroastrianism, *p. 35*

REVIEW, ANALYZE, & CONNECT TO TODAY

REVIEW AND ANALYZE THIS CHAPTER

Chapter 1 traces the development of Western civilization from its earliest beginnings in the cities of the ancient Middle East through the establishment of great empires. One of the significant themes throughout this chapter is the interaction among the various cultures that allowed each to assimilate and build on the innovations of the others.

1. What environmental advantages did the ancient Middle East have that permitted the growth of agriculture and cities? What disadvantages did the Middle East have? How did environmental conditions affect the various cultures?

2. Review the long-standing contributions of the Sumerians, Egyptians, Nubians, Phoenicians, and Hebrews.

3. How were the Jews able to maintain their integrity while being part of the Diaspora?

4. Review the empires—Assyrian, Babylonian, Persian—that arose in the ancient Middle East, and note the strengths and weaknesses of each.

CONNECT TO TODAY

Think about the changes in agriculture and animal husbandry discussed in this chapter.

1. How did the development of agriculture affect ancient societies? In what ways might advances in agriculture in more recent times have stimulated changes similar to those that occurred in the ancient world? Consider modern innovations such as the development of

drought-resistant grains and genetically modified foods. What other modern agricultural advances can you think of?

2. Ancient diseases moved from domesticated animals to humans, creating waves of pandemics followed by the development of immunities. What related situations do we face in our own times?

BEYOND THE CLASSROOM

BEFORE WESTERN CIVILIZATION

Diamond, Jared. *Guns, Germs, and Steel.* New York: W.W. Norton, 1997. A brilliant Pulitzer Prize–winning global analysis of the natural advantages that gave Western civilization its head start.

STRUGGLING WITH THE FORCES OF NATURE: MESOPOTAMIA, 3000–ca. 1000 B.C.E.

Binford, Lewis R. *In Pursuit of the Past.* New York: Thames & Hudson, 1988. An archaeological study of the transformation of human society.

Bryce, Trevor. *The Kingdom of the Hittites.* New York: Oxford University Press, 2006. A work that describes the rise and fall of the Hittites and includes the latest archaeology and translations of primary sources.

Crawford, Harriet. *Sumer and the Sumerians.* New York: Cambridge University Press, 1991. A summary of the historical and archaeological evidence that offers a solid survey of the field.

Hawkes, Jacquetta. *The Atlas of Early Man.* New York: St. Martin's Press, 1993. An accessible study of human thought.

Hooker, Jeremy T. *Reading the Past: Ancient Writing from Cuneiform to the Alphabet.* Berkeley: University of California Press, 1991. An exploration of the stages of the ancient scripts of past civilizations.

Postgate, Nicholas. *Early Mesopotamia: Society and Economy at the Dawn of History.* New York: Routledge, Chapman and Hall, 1992. A narrative depiction of the life of the peoples of early Mesopotamia.

Roux, Georges. *Ancient Iraq.* New York: Penguin, 1993. An excellent overview of the ancient world—from Mesopotamia to the Hellenistic conquests—that incorporates archaeological finds through 1992.

RULE OF THE GOD-KING: ANCIENT EGYPT, ca. 3100–1000 B.C.E.

Capel, A.X., and G.E. Markoe. *Mistress of the House, Mistress of Heaven: Women in Ancient Egypt.* New York: Hudson Hills Press, 1996. A beautifully illustrated study of the roles of women in ancient Egypt.

Grimal, N. *A History of Ancient Egypt.* Oxford: Oxford University Press, 1994. An insight into the essence of Egyptian culture and its relations with outsiders throughout its history.

Hornung, Erik. *History of Ancient Egypt: An Introduction.* Translated by David Lorton. Ithaca, NY: Cornell University Press, 1999. A concise and accessible summary of history that incorporates an excellent discussion of daily life in ancient times.

Tyldesley, Joyce. *Daughters of Isis: Women of Ancient Egypt.* New York: Penguin, 1995. A highly readable, illustrated account of women in Egypt.

PEOPLES OF THE MEDITERRANEAN COAST, ca. 1300–500 B.C.E.

Smith, Mark K. *Early History of God: Yahweh and the Other Deities in Ancient Israel.* San Francisco: Harper, 1990. A controversial look at the convergence and differentiation of deities toward monotheism in Israel.

Walton, John. *Ancient Near Eastern Thought and the Old Testament: Introducing the Conceptual World of the Hebrew Bible.* Grand Rapids, MI: Baker Academic, 2006. Balanced introductory look at the ideas in the Hebrew Bible, with excellent comparative dimensions.

TERROR AND BENEVOLENCE: THE GROWTH OF EMPIRES, 1200–500 B.C.E.

Curtis, J.E., and N. Tallis, eds. *Forgotten Empire: The World of Ancient Persia.* Berkeley: University of California Press, 2005. Comprehensive and scholarly view of the Persian Empire, beautifully illustrated with new archaeological finds.

Holland, Tom. *Persian Fire: The First World Empire and the Battle for the West.* New York: Anchor, 2007. Bold and engaging retelling of the Greek-Persian conflict, with a new emphasis on the Persian background.

Kuhrt, Amelie. *The Ancient Near East, ca. 3000–330 B.C.* New York: Routledge, 1997. A definitive account of ancient history, including the Israelites, that incorporates current scholarship and bibliography.

GLOBAL CONNECTIONS

Adams, William Y. *Nubia: Corridor to Africa.* Princeton, NJ: Princeton University Press, 1977. A comprehensive history of Nubia from prehistory through the nineteenth century.

The Ancient World, 700 B.C.E.–400 C.E.

By 700 B.C.E., the roots of Western civilization had been firmly planted in the great civilizations that arose in the Fertile Crescent from Mesopotamia to Egypt. Skilled farmers cultivated diverse crops and domesticated animals. A bustling commerce connected traders from far Asia with merchants operating around the Mediterranean basin, through Egypt, and into sub-Saharan Africa. A developing sense of law and a new tradition of writing fostered growing communities, even as leaders regularly launched armies at one another in hopes of expanding their power.

Although the peoples of the Eurasian landmass did not know it, successful cultures were also developing in the extensive lands far to the west across the Atlantic ocean. While scholars are still thinking about how the Americas were settled, it is clear that humans arrived at least 20,000 years ago. Studies of blood type, teeth, and language suggest a direct link between humans in the Americas and those in northern China and northeastern Siberia. Therefore, most scholars still argue that people walked across a land bridge from Siberia to Alaska before it disappeared about 14,000 years ago under floods caused by melting glaciers. Other scholars argue that people may have migrated by boats along the coasts from Siberia down the Pacific coasts of the Americas. Whatever their origin, groups of successful hunters began to spread through this vast north-south landmass.

By 5000 B.C.E., many of the peoples of the Americas had developed maize (corn) as a domesticated crop that cannot grow on its own without human intervention. The abundance of this kind of agriculture allowed agricultural societies to spread throughout Meso-america. Toward the end of the second millennium B.C.E., large ceremonial centers began to appear, similar to the great centers of Egypt. Recent studies even suggest that indigenous peoples in the Amazon basin successfully began to build thriving populations in the rainforests. Certainly, there were flourishing communities from Alaska to Chile while Europe was still virtually unpopulated.

Advanced civilizations in the great river valleys of Asia—the Yellow River in China and the Indus and Ganges valleys in India—had characteristics in common with the agricultural societies in the West. They, too, cultivated crops, raised animals, and valued a bustling trade. Western civilization took a different course as Greece, and later Rome, rose to prominence and the civilization's center moved farther west.

If the agricultural roots of the West lay in the Fertile Crescent, its philosophical roots lay in Greece. This society planted the seeds for many of the West's values—from its praise of democracy and rational inquiry and its aesthetic tastes to its appreciation for individual human accomplishment. These ideas spread all the way to India with the conquests of Alexander the Great, the Macedonian military genius, in the fourth century B.C.E. However, the ideas also changed as they spread. For example, after Alexander's conquests, Greek artists began to infuse more emotion into their works, and philosophers thought less about abstract concepts of truth and justice, and more about how an individual might live a tranquil life. Indeed, when East and West met in the kingdoms that arose after Alexander's death, each transformed the other.

By the first century B.C.E., the center of Western civilization had shifted still farther west as the Romans built a powerful empire that endured for centuries. In this thriving realm, Westerners solidified their love of law, duty, and engineering (among other things). As we will see, the Roman Empire was counted among the most diverse empires of the ancient world, rivaling even the Persian Empire in its ability to bring together people from many cultures. As just one example, Roman soldiers hailing from sub-Saharan Africa helped guard Hadrian's Wall in Scotland, the northern reaches of the empire.

Of course, as these centuries unfolded, the rest of the world did not sit idle. In China, successive dynasties of rulers unified the centers of civilization along the Yellow River. Later dynasties then spread Chinese unification well beyond the Yellow River—into central Asia and south to the South China Sea. The Qin dynasty (221–207 B.C.E.) began joining culturally distinct regions into a larger Chinese society, a process that continued during the Han dynasty (206 B.C.E.–220 C.E.). Han China then spread its cultural accomplishments to neighbors in Korea, Vietnam, and central Asia and fostered the prosperous Silk Road, by which merchants in the East traded with the Roman Empire in the West.

In India, a complex society grew up in the valley of the great Indus River. Archaeologists call this culture Harappan, named after Harappa, one of its two chief cities. Scholars have not yet deciphered Harappan written records, so the details of this culture remain obscure. But thanks to archaeological remains, we do know that people living in this early society conducted long-distance trade with Mesopotamians and Egyptians.

During the second millennium B.C.E., roving bands of peoples from the north swept into India, replacing a declining Harappan society. Scholars have determined that these new arrivals, who later established the Mauryan dynasty, had connections with the West because the invaders spoke an Indo-European language similar to those that later appeared in western lands. Linguists have identified similarities between words in English, German, Greek, Latin, and Indian Sanskrit, and these commonalities testify to ancient cross-cultural contacts throughout the Eurasian landmass.

Inspired by the imperial successes of Alexander the Great in the West,

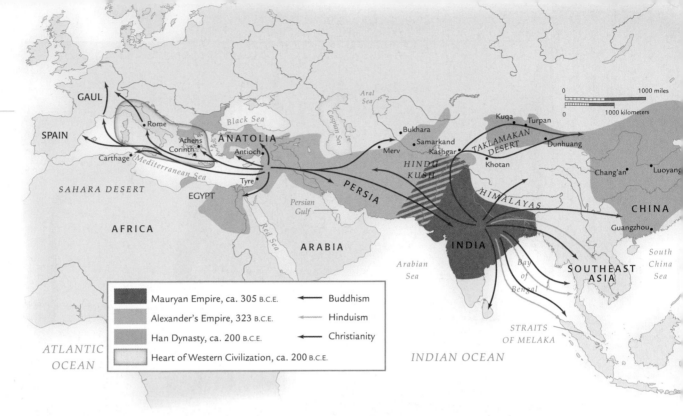

Ancient Empires and the Spread of Religion

Legend:
- Mauryan Empire, ca. 305 B.C.E.
- Alexander's Empire, 323 B.C.E.
- Han Dynasty, ca. 200 B.C.E.
- Heart of Western Civilization, ca. 200 B.C.E.
- ← Buddhism
- ← Hinduism
- ← Christianity

leaders of the Mauryan dynasty unified diverse Indian peoples under one ruler in the fourth century B.C.E. When the Mauryan dynasty broke apart in the second century B.C.E., later rulers who remembered its accomplishments tried to re-create a single India. In the fourth century C.E., a new leader once again unified the northern Indian lands and established the Gupta dynasty, which endured until the end of the fifth century C.E. The idea of one India may have come initially from the West. But with the establishment of the successful Gupta dynasty, the new India served as a conduit by which goods and ideas flowed from east to west.

Thanks to such interactions, civilizations around the world flourished. The empires that expanded during the ancient world embraced and fostered profitable trade, even as rulers changed. The famous Silk Road, stretching from China to the Mediterranean, conveyed goods and peoples from realm to realm. Meanwhile, trade in India stretched northwest through the Hindu Kush mountains to Persia, east along the Silk Road, and overseas in the Indian Ocean basin, where sailors learned to predict the prevailing

winds. Archaeologists working in southern India have unearthed hoards of Roman coins that offer silent testimony to the dynamic trade between east and west in the ancient world.

As always, movements of goods and peoples spurred exchanges of ideas both within and across civilizations. For example, during the ancient era, civilizations all over the Eurasian landmass experienced striking revolutions in religious thought. In China, the great philosopher Confucius (551–479 B.C.E.) urged Chinese leaders to adopt new moral and ethical principles and implored ordinary people to be kind and humane. At roughly the same time, a prince in India, Siddhartha Gautama (563–483 B.C.E.), struggled to understand and solve the problem of human suffering. Once he became "enlightened," he was called Buddha, and he initiated a movement that spread out from India during the Mauryan dynasty and influenced societies all over the world.

Westerners, too, experienced a wave of religious innovation during approximately the same time. In about the eighth century B.C.E., the ancient Hebrews were called to a higher ethical

standard by prophets who maintained that worship of God belonged as much in people's hearts as in Temple rituals. Four centuries later, Socrates and his student Plato argued for a philosophy that recognized and sought transcendent moral truths.

The most influential religious transformation in the ancient West came with the life of Jesus, a Jew born in the Roman Empire. Christian apostles and missionaries traveling through the empire slowly spread Jesus' teachings even as far as India. Eventually the Roman Empire adopted Christianity as its official faith. This transformation gave the West the last attribute it acquired from the ancient world over the next millennium and beyond: The West would be equated with Judeo-Christian beliefs.

Thinking Globally

1. What empires had begun to dominate the Eurasian landmass in this period?

2. How would these empires foster global interactions?

3. What examples of the spread of cultures do you notice on the map?

ATHENA *PARTHENOS*, REPRODUCTION IN NASHVILLE, TN, 2002

Athena *Parthenos*, a magnificent cult statue of the Greek goddess Athena, was unveiled in the temple known as the Parthenon, in Athens, in about 438 B.C.E. Built by the famous sculptor Phideas, the 41-foot-tall statue was made with skin of ivory and dressed in more than a ton of gold. In Phideas's interpretation, Athena held a 6-foot-high *Nike* (victory) statue in her hand. As Athenians looked with pride and awe at their patron goddess, who splendidly portrayed wisdom, wealth, and victory, they recognized their city at the height of its power. The original statue was destroyed after a millennium but was long remembered as a paragon of beauty. This carefully researched reproduction, completed in Nashville, Tennessee, in 2002, is the largest indoor statue in the West. The re-creation reveals our debt to the glory that was Greece.

The Contest for Excellence

"It is the greatest good every day to discuss virtue . . . for life without enquiry is not worth living for a man. . . ." The Greek philosopher Socrates reputedly spoke these words, and they have become a famous articulation of the value of the spirit of inquiry. But the society that produced Socrates was also one that spawned an often-violent competition among men and among cities. Violence even swept up Socrates' voice of rationalism, for his memorable words were spoken at his trial as his neighbors accused him of undermining their way of life. Yet the philosopher/stonemason claimed he would rather die than give up challenging his neighbors to think about everything from truth and beauty to life and death. Because he refused to be silent, he was condemned to die. Fortunately his call for rational inquiry did not die with him but flourished in the contentious city-states of Greece, ultimately to become a fundamental characteristic of Western civilization.

The Greeks grappled with other challenges in addition to new philosophical approaches. Two brilliant Aegean civilizations, the Minoans and the Mycenaeans, rose and fell. In city-states such as Athens and Sparta, Greek citizens battled powerful neighbors such as the Persians, fought over spheres of influence, and invented unprecedented forms of participatory government. The individualistic Greeks also created magnificent works of art that set the standard of beauty for millennia and literature that inspires readers even in modern times. Ancient Greeks believed that in a heroic search for excellence, a man could accomplish anything. In some cases, they were almost right. However, in their quest for excellence—whether in war or peace—they also planted the seeds of their own downfall by valuing competition over cooperation.

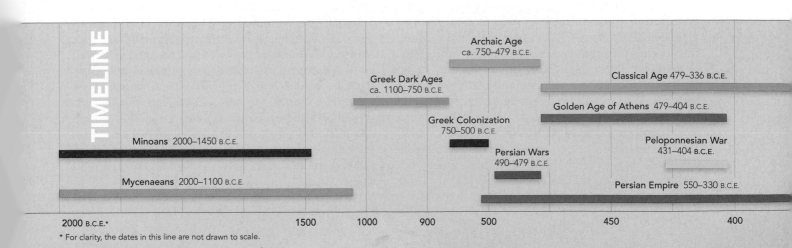

TIMELINE

Archaic Age
ca. 750–479 B.C.E.

Greek Dark Ages
ca. 1100–750 B.C.E.

Classical Age 479–336 B.C.E.

Golden Age of Athens 479–404 B.C.E.

Greek Colonization
750–500 B.C.E.

Minoans 2000–1450 B.C.E.

Peloponnesian War
431–404 B.C.E.

Persian Wars
490–479 B.C.E.

Mycenaeans 2000–1100 B.C.E.

Persian Empire 550–330 B.C.E.

| 2000 B.C.E.* | 1500 | 1000 | 900 | 500 | 450 | 400 |

* For clarity, the dates in this line are not drawn to scale.

THE RISE AND FALL OF ANCIENT HEROES,
2000–800 B.C.E.

Ancient Greek men and boys gathered in the household hall in the evenings to enjoy songs of heroic deeds recited by skilled performers. (Literary texts also show that women and girls listened from the seclusion of their own rooms.) For centuries, poets recited accounts that later were gathered together to form the epic poem the *Iliad*. This work, by the eighth-century poet Homer, told of 50 days in the 10-year war between the Greeks and the Trojans, a people living on the coast of Asia Minor. The *Iliad* was also a story of the Greek mythic hero Achilles, whose prowess in battle overcame great odds. Despite his successes, Achilles was subject to outbursts of monumental anger—a trait that, as Homer wrote, "brought the Greeks so much suffering." The leader of the Greeks, King Agamemnon, provoked a quarrel with Achilles. When exerting his right to take the booty seized in war, he took Briseis, a woman who first had been allotted to Achilles. In protest, the wrathful warrior sat in his tent and refused to fight while many of his compatriots died under the Trojan onslaught. As one Greek leader in the story said, "Now look at Achilles. He is a brave man, yet who but he will profit by that bravery?"

Modern historians understandably have questioned the accuracy of certain details in Homer's epics, but the ancient Greeks saw these poems differently. For centuries, people believed that the epics portrayed Achilles' actions accurately. Indeed, many aspiring heroes strove to emulate the mythical soldier whose mere presence or absence on the battlefield could change the course of the war. By reading or listening to these accounts of a lost age, young men learned about heroism and about the destructiveness of human weakness. The tension between heroic aspirations and dangerous individual pride became a prominent theme throughout the history of the ancient Greeks as they built their civilization on a rocky peninsula in the Aegean Sea.

The Greek Peninsula

The Greek peninsula is dominated by striking mountain ranges. Lacking large rivers that would have provided natural communication links, the ancient Greek civilization consisted of separate communities scattered throughout the peninsula and the numerous Aegean islands. The mountain ranges protected the Greeks from large-scale invasions, but the rocky soil made agriculture difficult. The Greeks had to grow their wheat and barley on the scarce lowland, and in time they came to depend on imports for the grain they needed. The Greek historian Herodotus summed up the difficulties of agriculture when he wrote, "Greece has always poverty as her companion." As **Map 2.1** indicates, most places in Greece enjoyed a close proximity to the sea, which allowed overseas trade to become an essential part of ancient Greek society. This orientation toward the sea stimulated the many cultural contacts that marked the development of Western civilization (as discussed in Chapter 1). In fact, the earliest advanced civilization that arose in this region originated on an island that lay at the heart of the eastern Mediterranean.

The Minoans,
2000–1450 B.C.E.

By 2000 B.C.E., the islanders living on Crete boasted the wealthiest, most advanced civilization in the Mediterranean. They were not Greek—nor Indo-European—but were probably a Semitic people related to those living in the eastern and southern Mediterranean. At the height of its economic and political power, Crete consisted of a number of principalities, each dominated by a great palace. Knossos (see **Map 2.1**) is the best excavated and thus the most well known of the palaces. Early Greek historians identify the ruler of Crete as King Minos, and thus modern excavators named Minoan society after this legendary king. Minoan prosperity permitted the growth of a relatively large, peaceful population. During the golden age of this culture, the population of Crete reached an impressive 250,000, with 40,000 living in Knossos alone.

MAP 2.1

The World of the Greeks

This map shows the Greek peninsula with the surrounding seas. Notice the locations of Asia Minor and the islands of Crete and the Cyclades. Locate the important cities of Troy (in Asia Minor), Athens, and Sparta.

Explore the Map

1. How would sea travelers best proceed from the Greek mainland to Asia Minor and back? What does this route suggest about the importance of the islands in the Aegean Sea?

2. Where is Troy? What does its location at the entrance of the Hellespont (the narrow strait that allows access to the Black Sea and the interior of Asia) indicate about its strategic importance?

3. How did the location of Crete allow the island's people to control the trade in the region?

By trading with the peoples of the Fertile Crescent, the Minoans learned much of the best of early Western civilization. They learned to make bronze from the Sumerians, and their foundries produced a steady stream of valuable bronze tools and weapons. Minoan ships were the best made in the region. With their heavy construction and high front prows, these vessels cut effortlessly through rough seas and proved reliable in conditions that the islanders' shore-hugging contemporaries deemed impossible.

Centers of economic as well as political power, Minoan palaces comprised vast mazes of storerooms, workrooms, and living quarters. These structures were markedly different from the huge buildings in Sumeria and Egypt, where architects of pyramids

> Economic power

and ziggurats valued symmetry. Minoan architects preferred to build palace rooms of different sizes that wandered without any apparent design. The Greeks later called these palaces labyrinths. Kings controlling the trade through which wealth poured into Crete stashed goods away in the huge palace storerooms. One room in the palace at Knossos contained clay jars for olive oil that totaled a remarkable capacity of 60,000 gallons.

Like many maritime civilizations, the Minoans learned much from their encounters with other peoples. For example, their artwork reveals the influence of Egyptian colors and styles. The Minoans also learned writing from the Sumerians, and their script (called Linear A) was also a pictographic script written on clay tablets. As in Sumer, archaeologists have excavated clay tablets in Crete that seem to have been used for accounting and for tracking the movement of merchandise. So far, the symbols of Linear A have not been translated, so to learn about Minoan society, we must rely on archaeological remains, including their riveting artwork.

The Minoans decorated their palaces with magnificent frescoes, created by mixing paint with plaster and crafting the image as part of the wall. These paintings portrayed many of the everyday objects and activities that Minoans held dear, including religious rituals. Many statuettes from Crete showing goddesses holding snakes suggest that the predominant Minoan deity was a fertility goddess. The fresco in **Figure 2.1** shows a ritual in which men and women performed gymnastic activities with a wild bull. In this painting, one woman grabs the bull's horns to prepare to vault over it, while a man is already at the apex of his leap. Another woman waits to guide the jumper's descent. Some scholars suggest that this dangerous event may have been a religious ritual that culminated with the sacrifice of the bull and an opulent banquet at which men and women feasted on the meat and celebrated the goddess's generosity in bringing abundance to the society.

`Religious ritual`

In the centuries after the Minoans, the ancient Greeks often told their history in the form of myths that recounted heroic acts from the Greek past. Some of these myths recalled the eventual destruction of Minoan society. In their myths, Greeks remembered a time when Greece owed tribute to Crete, including young people to be sacrificed to the Minotaur—a

`Minoan destruction`

FIGURE 2.1 Minoan Acrobats, ca. 1500 B.C.E.   This fresco from Knossos, Crete, depicts what was probably a religious ritual in which women (shown with pale skin) and a man leap over a charging bull.

creature that was half human and half bull. The king of Knossos may have worn the head of a bull on ceremonial occasions, and perhaps it was this tradition that gave rise to the legend of the Minotaur. One mythical Greek hero, Theseus, joined the sacrificial group, killed the Minotaur, and escaped the palace labyrinth by following a thread he had unraveled as he entered. (See Document 2.1, page 56, for more on the myth of Theseus.) This myth may hold a core of truth, for archaeological evidence shows that Minoan society was toppled by invaders. The great Minoan palaces apparently were burned by invaders who destroyed the unfortified cities. A man named Theseus may not have killed a minotaur, but it seems that Greeks killed the king of Crete.

Historians have looked further for the cause of the Minoans' downfall. Some suggest that a natural disaster contributed to their decline. In about 1450 B.C.E., a volcanic explosion on the nearby island of Thera (today known as Santorini) caused a tidal wave that may have destroyed the Minoans' protective fleet. However, this explanation is uncertain because other scholars question the date of the eruption, placing it two centuries earlier than the burning of Crete. Whatever the cause, the center of Aegean civilization passed to the earliest Greeks, whom we call the Mycenaeans.

Mycenaean Civilization: The First Greeks, 2000–1100 B.C.E.

Sometime after 2000 B.C.E., Indo-European Greek-speaking people settled on the mountainous Greek peninsula. By 1600 B.C.E., they were increasingly influenced by the Minoans and had developed a wealthy, hierarchic society centered in the city of Mycenae (see **Map 2.1**). Excavations of their shaft graves have yielded golden crowns and masks and, as with other Indo-European burials, many weapons, perhaps confirming ancient writers' characterizations of these people as the "war-mad Greeks." Yet, these early Greeks were also traders, and much of their wealth came from the growing commerce in the Aegean. As the Mycenaeans traded with wealthy Minoans, they learned much from them, evidenced by the strong Minoan influences in Mycenaean artwork. Mycenaean Greeks even learned to write from the Minoans, and their script is called Linear B for its similarity to the Minoan script. Because Linear B recorded an early form of the spoken Greek language, linguists have been able to translate Mycenaean tablets.

After Minoan society was destroyed in about 1450 B.C.E., the Mycenaeans took over as the commercial masters of the Mediterranean. As their wealth increased, so did the complexity of their governing system, which had a hierarchy of kings, nobles, and slaves. Powerful kings built palaces of stone so large that later Greeks thought they must have been constructed by giants. Unlike Minoan palaces, these structures were walled, indicating to archaeologists that there was a great deal of warfare, necessitating defensive fortifications. This conclusion is reinforced by written sources claiming that the kings surrounded themselves with soldiers.

Mycenaean states were not self-sufficient. Like the civilizations of the ancient Middle East, they depended on trade for many essentials. For example, there was little **Trade** copper and no tin on the peninsula, so they had to trade for ore to make bronze weapons and tools. The vast expanse of Mycenaean trade is clear. Mycenaean pottery has been found on the coast of Italy, and after the destruction of Crete, Mycenaean pottery replaced Minoan pottery in Egypt, Syria, Palestine, and Cyprus. These pottery remnants testify to the beginnings of the trade that linked the fortunes of the ancient Greeks intimately with those of their neighbors.

In about 1200 B.C.E., violence and a wide-ranging movement of peoples disrupted the eastern Mediterranean. A scarcity of sources does not allow historians to detail the exact causes of the upheaval, but we can see the effects **Violence and** on kingdoms and individuals. The **disruption** Egyptian Empire was besieged and lost territory as Syria and cities all along the coast confronted invaders. A letter from the king of the island of Cyprus urged the king of a city in Syria to hold firm against invaders: "You have written to me: enemy ships have been seen at sea. . . . Where are your troops and chariots? . . . Await the enemy steadfastly." Archaeological evidence shows towns sacked and burned throughout the region during these times of trouble. The important trade in copper from Cyprus was interrupted, and as we saw in Chapter 1, this violent era stimulated the dawning of the Iron Age.

The Mycenaeans were surely involved in these invasions that disrupted the ancient civilizations. According to later Greek myths, part of this violence included the Mycenaean invasion of Troy (see **Map 2.1**) in about 1250 B.C.E. The Trojan War became the basis of Homer's influential epics. Greek mythology attributes the conflict to a rivalry over a beautiful Greek woman, Helen, who was seduced by the Trojan prince Paris. Less-romantic historians believe the war stemmed primarily from the intensifying economic competition and growing violence in the eastern Mediterranean. Either way, the fighting was relentless and devastating—Homer claimed that the Greeks besieged Troy for ten years. At the end of this ordeal, Troy was destroyed (demonstrated by evidence from archaeological excavations).

Sometime after 1200 B.C.E., Mycenaean civilization itself dissolved. Later Greeks attributed this downfall to the Trojan War, which supposedly kept the Mycenaean leaders and soldiers away from home for so long. Archaeological evidence, however, shows that during and shortly after the Trojan War, the highly structured life on the Greek mainland broke down. Amid crop failures due to drought and internal instability, more Greek invaders from the north (later called Dorian Greeks) moved into the peninsula, especially the southern part, the Peloponnese. Population dropped dramatically. Excavations in one region reveal thirteen villages during the Mycenaean period; by 1100 B.C.E. only three remained. We do not know exactly what happened, but the flourishing Bronze Age Mycenaean society came to such a complete end that even the valuable art of writing was lost. All the great Mycenaean centers except Athens were destroyed. Life on the Greek mainland now consisted of a smattering of small villages, where people survived largely through subsistence farming.

From Dark Ages to Colonies

The period after the fall of Mycenae is called the Dark Ages (which extend from about 1100 B.C.E. to about 750 B.C.E.), because with the loss of writing, we have no texts that illuminate life during this time. For three centuries, life went on in the small villages, and people told tales that preserved their values. At the end of the Dark Ages, in about 800 B.C.E., Homer brilliantly recast some of these oral tales. The details he included offer glimpses into life during the previous three centuries. For example, Homer's descriptions of the cremation of the dead, which had not been practiced in Mycenaean civilization, suggest that cremation was developed after the fall of the early Greeks. As tantalizing as these bits of literary evidence are, most of our information for this period nevertheless must come from archaeology.

Excavations show that during these years, bronze gave way to iron as the primary metal used in weapons and tools. Archaeological findings also reveal that near the end of the Dark Ages, trade of wine, olive oil, and other goods began to flourish again all over the Mediterranean. By tracing

Founding colonies the movement of Greek goods through the remnants of pottery and other artifacts excavated around the Mediterranean, archaeologists have discovered that Greek culture spread through the many colonies Greeks established in the region. At first, Greeks fled the disasters on the peninsula by settling on the numerous islands of the Aegean and the coast of Asia Minor (called Ionia) (see Global Connections on page 50). Later, colonists may have left the peninsula to escape overpopulation and seek new land and prosperity. Some aristocrats in Greek cities used the founding of

new colonies as a way to diffuse social unrest by sending the dissatisfied elsewhere. **Map 2.2** shows the extent of the Greek colonies along the coast of the Mediterranean Sea. They were rivaled in number only by the Phoenicians, the master colonists we met in Chapter 1. Greek colonies were very different from modern colonial efforts because Greeks in the new settlements arranged themselves in cities that were just as independent as the mother city. The ties to the original cities were ones of emotion, not of colonial control.

For a time, Greeks in the new colonies remained independent from the other civilizations around them—the neighboring Phoenicians and the Babylonian and Persian Empires. However, while trading with their neighbors, the Greeks participated in the growth of Western civilization by adopting much that had gone before. For example, they derived their systems of weight from Babylonia and Phoenicia and adopted the practice of making coins from the Lydians (see Chapter 1). Societies transform acquired innovations, and the Greeks were no exception. For their coins, they minted silver (instead of the Lydian white gold) and usually placed secular images on them—sometimes illustrating their exports, like grapes or fish, and sometimes using emblems of civic pride. However, when describing Greek use of others' inventions, the Greek philosopher Plato (428–348 B.C.E.) characteristically gave the Greeks undue praise, boasting, "Whatever the Greeks have acquired from foreigners, they have in the end turned into something finer."

EMERGING FROM THE DARK: HEROIC BELIEFS AND VALUES

Through their trade with the Phoenicians, the Greeks acquired and adapted the Phoenician alphabet, and writing reemerged among the Greeks around 800 B.C.E. Once more Greek society was illuminated for historians. The Greeks did not use writing only for trade and contractual agreements—the Phoenician alphabet was simpler than other scripts, so it lent itself to a wider use. Talented Greeks used writing to record and transmit powerful and inspiring poetry that had been preserved for centuries only through human memory, and the ideas of the ancient Greeks once more came to light; the Dark Ages were over.

Heroic Values Preserved

The earliest of this Greek literature preserved a series of values that define what historians call a heroic society, in which individuals seek fame through great deeds and advocate values such as honor, reputation, and prowess.

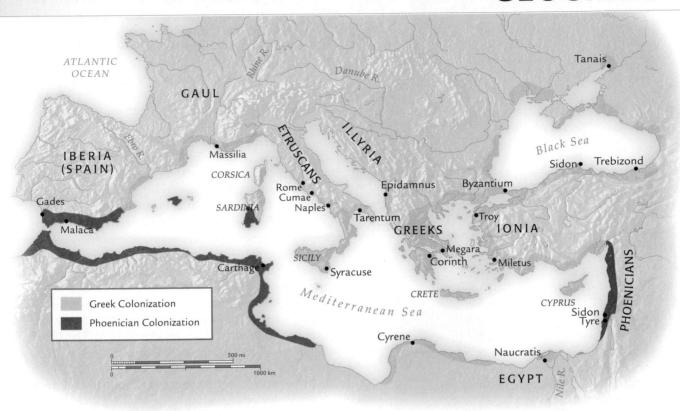

MAP 2.2

The Greek Colonies in About 500 B.C.E.

This map shows the locations of the Greek and Phoenician colonies. Because ancient ships could not navigate at night, these colonies provided essential stopping points for long-distance trade.

Explore the Map

1. What spheres of influence are implied by the locations for the respective colonies?

2. Based on the map, in what regions would the Greeks most likely come in conflict with other powers?

3. How did the fall of Troy allow for Greek colonization around the Black Sea?

As we saw in the opening account of Achilles, the most influential Greek poet was Homer, who historians believe lived in the early eighth century B.C.E. Homer's two greatest epics were the *Iliad*, the tale of Achilles' heroic wrath, and the *Odyssey*, the story of the Greek warrior Odysseus's ten-year travels to return home from Troy. The *Iliad* became a seminal text for later ancient Greeks—schoolchildren and adults never tired of this tale of heroic deeds that captured details from Homer's times and preserved many Mycenaean values.

Homer

The highest virtue for Homer (and subsequent Greeks) was **arête**—manliness, courage, and excellence. *Arête* was best revealed in a "contest," whether sporting, warfare, or activities extending into many other areas of life and recreation. The ancient Greeks believed that striving for individual supremacy enhanced one's family honor, and the hero's name would live in poetic memory. Such beliefs and values helped fuel the greatness of ancient Greece. However, this striving for excellence—for heroism—was not always beneficial. At times it created a self-centered competitiveness that caused much suffering—just as Achilles' heroic-scale rage was said to have caused his companions' deaths. Harboring such intense competitive spirit, Greeks also held a deep disregard for all cultures other than their own (and they even had disdain for neighboring Greeks from different cities). Greeks distinguished themselves from "barbarians"

FIGURE 2.2 Perfecting the Human Form, ca. 530 B.C.E.
Greek artists glorified humanity by carving monumental, realistic life-size statues. Sculptors revealed their interest in the human form by depicting the males—called *kouros* (pl. *kouroi*), a word that is Greek for "boy"—without clothing. The females—called *kore* (pl. *korai*), the Greek word for "girl"—are always portrayed modestly clothed. Yet the female humanity is indicated by a smile on the female's face, referred to as the *archaic smile*.

who "spoke other languages" and felt it demeaned them to work alongside such foreigners. Individuals adhering to "heroic" values brought a combination of good and bad results, and the best of the Greeks from Homer on recognized this ambiguity.

Visual artists in the archaic age also glorified humanity in their increasingly realistic portrayal of the human figure. **Figures 2.2a** and **b** show two typical sculptures from the sixth century B.C.E. Both portray adolescent youths, called **kouros** (male) and **kore** (female). Such figures begin an aesthetic that will dominate ancient Greece—the male body is portrayed nude as the ideal of human perfection and beauty; the female is modestly clothed.

In literature, too, poets praised human accomplishments. Hesiod, an early Greek poet who wrote around 750 B.C.E., left almost as important a mark as Homer. His *Works and Days* describes farm life, wisdom, and values near the end of the Greek Dark Ages. Like social critics who had come before him, Hesiod complained of the powerful who cheat and exploit the poor and strive only for riches. Deploring the selfish "age of iron" in which he lived, Hesiod lamented the loss of what he believed were more virtuous heroic ages of "gold" and "bronze." He was no doubt wrong in assuming that the leaders of the Mycenaean age were less corrupt than those in his time, but his vision reveals the desire to imagine better times.

Hesiod lived in poverty—cheated out of his inheritance by a greedy brother and corrupt officials—yet he still articulated the ideals of heroic individualism. However, he clearly saw that the pursuit of excellence was a two-sided coin. At the end of *Works and Days*, he wrote of two kinds of "strife." One was good—a healthy spirit of competitiveness that Hesiod believed made people work and achieve their best. The other kind of strife, however, was bad and led to some people exploiting others, as happened in Hesiod's own life. This tension within heroic values marked Greek life and values and even their gods and goddesses.

The Family of the Gods

The ancient Greek historian Herodotus (482–425 B.C.E.) claimed that Homer and Hesiod powerfully shaped subsequent Greek religious beliefs. As Herodotus observed, these early poets "gave the gods their epithets, divided out offices and functions among them and described their appearance." The poems of Homer's and Hesiod's day were indeed populated by an extended family of gods and goddesses, loosely ruled by Zeus and his wife, Hera. This family included ten other main deities, among them Aphrodite, goddess of love; Athena, goddess of wisdom and war; Poseidon, god of the sea; Apollo, god of music, divination, and healing; and Demeter, goddess of fertility. These gods lived on Mount Olympus and periodically interfered in human affairs.

The Greek gods and goddesses resembled humans so much that one Greek critic from the sixth century B.C.E. observed that "Homer and Hesiod ascribed to the gods everything that among men is a shame and disgrace: theft, adultery, and deceiving one another." It is true that the gods shared human flaws, but they also shared admirable human qualities. Like the Greeks themselves, they loved beauty, banquets, processions, athletic competitions, music, and theater. The Greeks therefore infused all these activities with a feeling of worship. Religious rituals, for example, had an intensely festive air, and ancient Greek writings characterize religious activities as "sacrificing and having a good time."

As with the ancient religions of the Middle East, proper worship for the Greeks involved sacrificing a portion of human production to the gods. In contrast to the Mesopotamians, Greeks sacrificed things of relatively little value—the fat-wrapped thigh bones or internal organs of sacrificial animals—while keeping the best parts for themselves. Families, magistrates, and citizen assemblies were primarily responsible for observing proper respect for the gods. As a result, unlike in Egypt and Mesopotamia, powerful religious institutions never developed in ancient Greek society. Each temple had a priest or priestess, but their duties were usually part-time activities requiring little training.

The real religious professionals were oracles— people who interpreted divine will. Among these, the Delphic oracle, a woman who reputedly could enter into a trance and receive cryptic

| Oracles | messages from Apollo, was the most famous. **Figure 2.3** shows the Delphic oracle sitting on a tripod under which vapors emerge from the earth, sending her into a trance. The latest scientific speculation suggests that the vapors were ethane, a gas that can be used as an anesthetic. The oracle consults a bowl in which float herbs or animal entrails to help stimulate her vision so that she might advise the man (here, Theseus's father) seeking advice.

Oracle messages were received in the form of ambiguous riddles and had to be interpreted by humans, so a central role for human agency remained in Greek religion. Perhaps the most famous inquiry at Delphi was made by King Croesus of Lydia in about 546 B.C.E. Croesus was worried about the Persian king Cyrus, who was threatening his kingdom (see Chapter 1), and asked the oracle whether he should wage war against Persia. The priests of Delphi returned with the answer: If Croesus were to make war on the Persians, he would destroy a mighty empire. Croesus was elated, but he had misinterpreted the oracle: The mighty empire that fell was that of Croesus as Cyrus defeated the Lydians. Messages from oracles needed to be interpreted very carefully, indeed.

Just as they envisioned their gods with all the qualities and foibles of humans, the Greeks embraced all facets of human behavior, even the irrational. To Homer's list of Olympians, subsequent Greeks added the worship of Dionysus, the god of wine and fertility.

| Worship of Dionysus | Men worshiped this god during lavish banquets, but the cult had special appeal to women. During worship of Dionysus, women temporarily escaped their domestic confinement and engaged in drinking, ecstatic dancing, and sometimes sexual license as part of the ritual.

FIGURE 2.3 Foretelling the Future, ca. fifth century B.C.E. This pottery depicts the famous Delphic oracle sitting on a tripod where vapors from the earth sent her into a trance. Here she is shown recovered from her trance and reading the future in the bowl she holds.

Greek religious thought marked a significant departure from the forms of worship of the ancient Middle East. In Greece, the gods were so much like humans that worshiping them encouraged people to aspire to the greatest in human accomplishments and to acknowledge the worst in human frailties. It was this view, for instance, that | Impact of religious ideas | caused them to count Achilles as a flawed, yet powerful, hero. The Greeks did add a cautionary warning in their praise of humanity. If people exhibited excessive pride or arrogance as they tried to become godlike (called **hubris**), the gods would destroy them. Yet they still had a great deal of room to celebrate human accomplishments. As Greek thinkers placed humans rather than gods at the center of their understanding of the world, and as they studied reality from a human perspective, they began to transform the Mesopotamian view that had contributed so much to Western civilization. Humans were no longer impotent before a chaotic world ruled by arbitrary deities; instead, they were encouraged to understand and master their world.

Studying the Material World

The Greeks had great confidence in their ability to learn everything about the world. They rejected many earlier explanations and began an objective, almost scientific, approach to comprehending nature. This special search for knowledge was termed

Transforming Science in Asia Minor

In 585 B.C.E., Asia Minor—the turbulent crossroads where Eastern empires met Western Greeks—once again became embroiled in warfare. Lydians (in Asia Minor) and Medes (Persians) had skirmished over land and power for five years, when suddenly, amid a battle, the sun darkened. Frightened by this apparent message from the gods, the two armies laid down their weapons and negotiated peace. Not far away, the Ionian Greeks interpreted the darkening sun differently. One of their own, the esteemed teacher Thales of Miletus (ca. 642–ca. 548 B.C.E.), had predicted this solar eclipse well in advance of that day. Based on his studies of the heavens, he knew eclipses were natural occurrences, not messages of divine anger. This kind of thinking gave birth to a new, rational approach to understanding previously mysterious events.

How did this new view of natural occurrences appear in Ionia on the coast of Asia Minor? (See **Map 2.1** for the locations of Lydia and Ionia.) Miletus was a cosmopolitan city on the coast of the Aegean Sea (see **Maps 2.1** and **2.2**). In this bustling urban center, travelers from the New Babylonian Empire, Egypt, and Greece mingled and shared ideas. By the seventh century B.C.E., these Ionian Greeks had already learned much from their Asian neighbors. For example, they were using the Phoenician alphabet, a Babylonian system of weights, and Phrygian structures of music, called modes. Soon they would also begin using coins invented by the Lydians. But as Thales' knowledge of eclipses demonstrated, these practical tools were only a few of the important ideas that spread from the East to Greece.

Thales himself probably came from a distinguished family of mixed Greek and Phoenician background. He took an interest in everything from Greek myths to Babylonian science, and his unconventional, cross-cultural background proved fertile soil for sprouting new ideas. Fortunately for him, he had access to the sophisticated learning of the Babylonians.

The Babylonian king Nebuchadrezzar (r. 605–561 B.C.E.), though he destroyed Jerusalem in 587 B.C.E. and led the Jews into the Babylonian Captivity, was also a builder. He made Babylon the greatest city in the world. Covering 2,100 acres—far more than the 135 acres of the typical Sumerian city—Babylon amazed the Ionian Greeks who visited the city to trade or simply tour. They returned home with captivating stories of grand palaces and temples aglow with brightly colored glazed bricks. These architectural wonders only underscored the considerable skill of the Babylonian engineers.

The greatest Babylonian accomplishments, however, came in the fields of astronomy and mathematics. For thousands of years, Mesopotamians had studied the night sky, and Babylonians perfected this art. Starting in 747 B.C.E., Babylonian court astronomers kept monthly tables on which they recorded all planetary movements together with reports of earthly affairs. These efforts gave birth to the pseudoscience of astrology, through which Babylonians tried to understand the effect of heavenly objects on earthly events. Their observations set the stage for astronomical science in the Greek world and beyond.

The Babylonians also made great strides in mathematics. Using their base-60 number system, Babylonian mathematicians pioneered detailed calculations such as square and cube roots, as well as many other impressive reckonings. To demonstrate the complexity of solving mathematical problems using a base-60 system, **Figure 2.4** shows a calculation to obtain the square of 147 (or 147 times 147). Using our number system, multiplying 147 by itself is fairly simple and yields the result of 21,609. In the cuneiform calculation shown in the figure, the number 147 is indicated as 2,27, and squaring gives the answer of 6,0,9. The location of these digits refers to a position of a number on a complex chart containing six columns, each of which had ten numbers. Only specialists had access to such charts.

The difficulties of these early mathematics makes Thales' ability to apply their principles even more impressive. He purportedly mastered mathematics and geometry so thoroughly that he could determine the height of a pyramid by measuring the length of its shadow at the time of day when the length of a person's shadow equaled his or her height. Thales' skill made him a much-sought-after teacher who could explain the Babylonians' arcane mathematical wisdom to ordinary people and extend that learning to a new generation.

In 539 B.C.E., the Persians finally conquered Asia Minor. One of Thales' students, Pythagoras, fled the violence in Ionia to settle in Croton in southern Italy. There he continued his studies of mathematics and geometry, spreading the mix of Asian and Greek science farther west. His work would leave a lasting influence on Western science.

Making Connections

1. Why was Ionia well placed to serve as a crossroads between East and West?

2. How did Thales help make mathematics and astronomy relevant to the Greeks?

3. How difficult would it have been to use Babylonian mathematics? Can *you* figure the system out?

4. How did this fruitful combination of Eastern and Western science influence our science today?

FIGURE 2.4 147 squared = 21,609. Babylonian: 2,27 squared is 6,0,9.

philosophy (love of wisdom) and would become the Greeks' most important intellectual invention. The earliest known scholar of this kind was Thales of Miletus (ca. 624–ca. 548 B.C.E.). The location of Miletus on the Ionian coast (see **Map 2.2,** on page 47) shows how Greek culture and its tremendous influence had moved beyond the Greek mainland itself.

Thales reputedly studied Egyptian and Babylonian astronomy and geometry and brought this knowledge to practical use by measuring pyramids, based on the length of their shadows, and predicting a solar eclipse. (See Global Connections on page 50.) Departing from most of his Egyptian and Mesopotamian predecessors, Thales believed in an orderly cosmos that was accessible to human reason. This formed the heart of much subsequent Greek (and Western) inquiry. He sought a single primal element that would explain a cosmic unity and believed that element was water. Although Thales' conclusion was wrong, his assumption of an orderly universe accessible to human inquiry was pivotal to the future of Western thought.

Thales and Democritus

Thales was followed by others who continued the rational approach to the natural world. Democritus (ca. 460–ca. 370 B.C.E.), for example, posited an infinite universe of tiny atoms with spaces between them. Although his ideas were not widely supported in ancient Greece, they were proven by early-twentieth-century physicists.

Pythagoras (ca. 582–507 B.C.E.), who fled from Ionia to Italy, made even greater discoveries in the fields of mathematics and astronomy. He believed that order in the universe was based on numbers (not water), and that mathematics was the key to understanding reality. Pythagoras is credited with being the first to suggest that the number 13 is unlucky, but his mathematics extended far beyond such attempts to quantify fortune. He developed the Pythagorean Theorem, the geometrical statement that the square of the hypotenuse of a right triangle is equal to the sum of the squares of the other two sides. He went on to explore additional theories of proportion that have contributed to much modern mathematics. Pythagoras was also among the first to claim that the earth and other heavenly bodies were spherical and that they rotated on their axes. The mathematician was so respected that his followers later developed a religious cult in his name.

Pythagoras

These philosophers, in a dramatic way, changed the direction of thinking about the world. They rejected the mythopoeic approach to understanding the world and made the first attempts to understand and explain the world in a scientific and philosophical way. Because they had little experimental equipment and no prior knowledge to draw upon, their ideas were not necessarily accurate by our standards, but we would not be who we are without them.

Men like Thales, Democritus, and Pythagoras operated on an abstract level of almost pure science. Yet the Greeks also practiced an applied technology, with results that continue to astound us. The sixth-century B.C.E. engineer Eupalinus, for example, constructed a 3,000-foot-long tunnel through a mountain in order to bring water from a spring into a city. To accomplish this feat, he used only hand tools, and he had to work in the dark because he lacked a light source. Most extraordinary, he dug from both sides of the mountain—and the two parts of the tunnel met in the middle with only a slight adjustment needed. Pythagoras was on Eupalinus's island of Samos at about the time the tunnel was dug, so some scholars speculate that the mathematician helped in the process. Others have suggested that Eupalinus used a system of mirrors to line up the halves of the tunnel and illuminate the interior as he excavated. However he managed this feat, he counts among the most accomplished Greeks who applied reason to practical matters.

Practical applications

While modern scholars admire these early Greek thinkers, many contemporaries looked with suspicion on those who studied the world while seemingly ignoring the gods. Even though the Greeks worshiped humanlike gods and goddesses, they still revered them, and accusations of impiety always hovered on the borders of scientific inquiry. In 432 B.C.E., the democratic assembly of Athens made it a crime to "deny the gods, or disseminate teachings about the things that take place in the heavens." This law was precipitated by the teachings of Anaxagoras (ca. 500–ca. 428 B.C.E.), who claimed that the sun was a white-hot stone instead of a god. Even in the field of rational inquiry, in which the Greeks made such impressive strides, the ambiguities that marked this dynamic society are evident. The same culture that produced impressive thinkers like Anaxagoras and Socrates (whom we met at the beginning of this chapter) sometimes recoiled from the results of their studies. Nevertheless, Greek intellectual accomplishments formed one of their central contributions to Western civilization.

Fears of "impiety"

LIFE IN THE GREEK POLEIS

As we saw in Chapter 1, ancient societies had taken for granted a natural order of society that placed kings and priests in charge, and the Mycenaean Greeks had shared this view. With the brisk trade that comes so naturally to sea peoples, however, a new prosperity based on commercial expansion emerged, creating

thinking about

ART

FIGURE 2.5

Ezekias, Suicide of Ajax, Athenian Vase, ca. 450 B.C.E.

The famous vase painter Ezekias has portrayed a significant moment in the Trojan War. After the death of Achilles, the hero Ajax expected to be named to lead the army. Instead, the Greeks chose Odysseus. In his humiliation, Ajax commits suicide. The artist shows him preparing for his death, burying the hilt of his sword in the earth so that he can fall on his sword. On the right, the artist shows the all-important hoplite weaponry: the great shield with the head of the mythological monster Gorgon emblazoned on the front, the helmet, and the long spear. Yet, in this contest for excellence the pride of the individual was more important than the strength of the army, and the artist shows this in the vase.

Connecting Art & Society

1. Would the Greeks have considered this act heroic or cowardly?

2. Is Ajax showing the same kind of individualistic pride as Achilles did in the incident described at the beginning of this chapter, when he refused to fight?

3. What would our society think of this act?

an urban middle class of merchants and artisans who owed no loyalty to aristocratic landowners.

By 700 B.C.E., changes in warfare brought about in part by the growth of Greek trade also made aristocratic warriors less important. First, the growing commercial classes became wealthier, and at the same time the increased | **Hoplite armies** | trade brought down the price of metals. Now more men could afford to arm themselves and go to war. New armies of infantrymen (called **hoplites**) dominated the art of making war. Common citizens armed with swords, shields, and long thrusting spears formed a **phalanx**—a tight formation about eight men deep and as wide as the number of troops available. As long as these soldiers stayed tightly pressed together, they were virtually impenetrable. Elite warriors once could rely on their own heroism and on their monopoly of horses and cavalry to ensure victory on the battlefield. Now that a hoplite phalanx could withstand cavalry charges, the aristocracy no longer maintained a privileged position; they needed the support of citizen armies. This dependence further weakened aristocratic rule. **Figure 2.5** shows the tension between the traditional values of heroic pride on the one hand and the needs of the phalanx-dependent hoplite army on the other hand. Even as the artist immortalized the hero's prideful suicide, he also highlighted the hoplite weaponry that made the phalanx invincible.

The Invention of Politics

Between 650 and 550 B.C.E., civil war broke out in many cities as the lower classes rose to overthrow the aristocracy. This violence led to the rule of men who became rulers by | **Tyrants** | physical force. Although kingship had a long-standing tradition in the West, this was a new form of authority—based on power, not hereditary right. The Greeks called such rulers *tyrants* to distinguish them from more traditional kings. At first the term had no pejorative connotation—one could easily be a kind tyrant, and indeed some were sincere reformers seeking to end aristocratic exploitation. For example, some tyrants gained popular support by such reforms as freeing slaves, eliminating debts, redistributing land. Later, however, as these rulers relied on force to hold power, the term *tyrant* acquired the negative meaning it holds today. Tyrants often favored the commercial classes to try to hold on to power, but such alliances proved insubstantial. In some city-states, tyrants were replaced by various forms of participatory governments.

Greek citizens—especially those who controlled the lucrative trade and fought in the successful phalanxes—thus began to take charge of the political life of their cities. A Greek city-state was called a **polis** (pl. *poleis*). It was a small but autonomous political unit that generated intense loyalty from its citizens, who conducted their political, social, and religious activities in | **City-states** | its heart. The poleis frequently included a fortified high ground—called an *acropolis*, the most famous of which is in Athens. They also had a central place of assembly and market, called the **agora** (pl. *agorae*). Surrounding villages began to consolidate and share a political identity, and the word *polis* came to mean the city-state itself and its surrounding countryside. Each city-state was an independent governing entity, but in the view of its residents, a polis was also a state of mind. Unlike in Mesopotamia, Egypt, and Mycenae, polis inhabitants did not think of themselves as subjects of a king or as owing obedience to a priesthood. Instead, they were "citizens" who were actively responsible for guiding their poleis. Aristotle (384–322 B.C.E.) even characterized humans by their participation in politics (the word *politics* is derived from the word *polis*), arguing that "man is a political animal" (although a more accurate translation is "man is an animal of the polis").

Although Greece's rocky terrain separated the land into many small city-states, they shared certain characteristics. They all developed self-government by male citizens, with variations as to the exact form. For example, Corinth and many other small poleis had an **oligarchy** (rule by a few), whereas Athens developed an early form of democracy that was strikingly new in the West and in the world. All the states relied on hoplite armies, and all used slavery to run their small-scale industries and farming. In all the city-states as well, Greek men who fought together in the hoplite armies gathered daily in the agorae to discuss matters of life and politics.

The Heart of the Polis

The heart of the polis was the household, which consisted of a male citizen, his wife and children, and their slaves. This configuration formed the basis for both the rural and urban economies. In the villages outside the walls of the city itself, household members herded sheep and goats, worked in the vineyards and olive groves, and struggled to plant crops in the rocky ground. Olive trees yielded abundant fruit, but harvesting required a good deal of labor.

Olive harvesting was well worth the effort, however, for the olives and their precious oil brought much wealth into some of the city-states. Athens's economy in particular depended upon its olive oil exports. A well-known story about the philosopher Thales illustrates the economic importance of olives to the Greeks. His neighbors mocked him, saying, "If you are smart, why aren't you rich?" In response, he purchased the use of all the local olive presses cheaply during the off season. Then, when everyone was trying to press their olives after the harvest, they had to buy the use of the presses from Thales. He made a fortune and silenced his neighbors. As his final retort, Thales pointed out that philosophers could easily become rich, but they loved the life of the mind more than money.

In addition to olive harvesting, craftsmanship and trade completed the polis economy. Artisans in the polis labored at their crafts or sold their merchandise in the open market during the mornings. After a large afternoon meal, they napped and then either returned to their shops or (more likely) went to the gymnasium to exercise and talk with other citizens. The gymnasium grew in part out of the Greek belief in cultivating perfection in all things; thus a skilled artisan or philosopher also needed to cultivate his physical prowess as part of his pursuit of excellence. The gymnasium proved an enduring feature of life in the Mediterranean city-states. This was a highly public life for male citizens; work, exercise, and talk were all central activities of the masculine life.

Men's and women's roles

In most city-states, women's lives were more restricted than men's—at least in the ideal. Wealthy, upper-class women were married at puberty and were supposed to stay indoors. A text from the early fourth century B.C.E. describes how a husband educated his 15-year-old wife on domestic responsibilities. He told her that men belonged outdoors: "For a man to remain indoors . . . is a thing discreditable." Women, on the other hand, should stay inside, teaching female slaves necessary skills, managing the goods brought into the household, and presiding over the spinning and weaving. When men entertained their peers at dinner parties or visited, "respectable" women stayed home and out of sight along with their female slaves and children. (As we will see, life for women in Sparta marked an exception to this pattern.)

Of course, real life seldom measures up to the extremes of the ideal. Even in Athens, many women were visible in the marketplace: Slaves went to the fountains to carry water, prostitutes offered their services, and priestesses served in more than forty religious cults of the city. Between these extremes, there were many women of the poorer classes who sold their wares—cloth or garden produce—in market stalls as they worked hard to supplement the family income.

In addition to having defined gender roles, Greek society depended heavily on slave labor; virtually every household had a few slaves. In the earliest years of the poleis, just as elsewhere in the ancient Middle East, slaves were either captives of war or debtors. By the sixth century B.C.E., debt slavery had been virtually banned throughout the Greek world, but slavery itself remained a central institution. However, in many ways slaves' lives resembled those of their owners. Numerous slaves worked alongside free men and women in almost every occupation. (There were even slave policemen in Athens.) Slaves frequently lived in their own residences, worked in a trade, and earned their own money. Sometimes called "pay-bringers," they owed their owners a portion of their income but could retain some of the money they earned. With this revenue, some slaves in turn bought slaves for themselves or purchased their own freedom. Many Greek cities even had benefit clubs that lent slaves

Slave labor

enough money to buy their freedom and repay the loan later. Numerous bright, ambitious slaves gained their freedom and became quite prosperous.

All slaves did not enjoy this relatively easy life. Some slaves had brutal masters and suffered all forms of abuse; in Athens, some slaves who tried to flee their condition bore the brand of a runaway on their foreheads. Slaves who lived under the worst conditions were those who had the misfortune to work in the silver mines, an essential source of income for Athens. In these mines, they were fed just enough to stay strong and were beaten regularly to keep them working in the mines that produced immense wealth for free Greeks. For the most part, however, slavery was treated as a simple fact of life—an essential tool for getting necessary work done.

Fears and Attachments in Greek Emotional Life

The extreme separation of men and women seems to have contributed to a wide range of insecurities and emotional attachments in Greek society. Many Greek writers expressed a great suspicion of women. As one poet, Semonides of Amorgos, wrote: "God made the mind of women a thing apart." The strict segregation of men and women through their lives may have contributed to misunderstandings. Men with little experience with women believed that virtuous women were scarce. Many husbands feared that their wives would escape their seclusion and take lovers, and thereby raise questions about the paternity of their children. These fears permeate many writings by Greek men.

Perhaps as part of their overall praise of masculinity, many ancient Greeks accepted bisexuality, at least among wealthy urban dwellers. The ideal of such a relationship took the form of a mentoring arrangement between a well-connected older man and a "beardless youth" (although school-aged, free-born boys were protected from such liaisons). As the pair matured, the elder man would marry and take up his family responsibilities, and the younger would serve as a mentor to a new youth. Such relationships were seen as a natural part of a world in which men often feared female sexuality, spent all their time together, exercised nude in the gymnasia, and praised the male body as the ideal of beauty. Indeed, many Greeks believed that the male-male relationship offered the highest possibility for love and that such ties usually brought out the best in each partner, making both braver and nobler.

Bisexual relations

We have fewer examples of women engaging in homosexual behavior, probably because their lives were conducted in privacy and were not recorded in as many historical documents. However, one sixth-century B.C.E. poet, Sappho from the island of Lesbos,

expressed passionate love for the young women in her social circle. Her poetry has since been both highly respected for its beauty and severely criticized for its content. The philosopher Plato admired Sappho so much that he referred to her as a goddess of poetry, but some Greek playwrights dismissed and ridiculed her as an ugly woman who could not attract a man. Nevertheless, Sappho's poetry was so influential that the word *Lesbian*, meaning a resident of Sappho's island of Lesbos, has become synonymous with female homosexuality.

Sappho of Lesbos

Not all women were confined to the home. While respectable women stayed carefully indoors, some women—slaves or foreigners—who had no economic resources or family ties became prostitutes and courtesans who shared men's public lives at dinners and drinking parties. Prostitutes were even registered and taxed in many Greek city-states and thereby became a legitimate part of social and economic life. Men and prostitutes drank freely together from the wine bowls abundantly filled at banquets. These bowls were decorated inside and out with appropriate themes. **Figure 2.6** shows a prostitute dressed in loose, seductive clothing who holds a wine bowl in each hand as she plays a Greek drinking game in which the participant twirls the drinking vessel until the dregs go flying. Such exuberant images not only portrayed scenes from the parties but also were intended to spur people on to greater abandon. Women in ancient Greece, particularly Athens, were thus placed in the peculiar situation of being invisible if they were "respectable," and mingling with and influencing powerful men only if they were not.

Courtesans

All the city-states shared many of these elements of urban life, from work to pleasure. However, each polis had its own distinctive character, as citizens structured their political lives to suit themselves. The two best-documented Greek cities were Athens and Sparta, and yet most of the cities did not match the extremes in art and austerity that marked these two influential states.

Athens: City of Democracy

Theseus, whose father was portrayed consulting the Delphic oracle in **Figure 2.3,** founded Athens. Document 2.1 relates the city's founding myth and suggests that participatory democracy was at the heart of its origins. The reality of a developing democratic form of government was more complicated. By 700 B.C.E., Athenian aristocrats had established a form of government that allowed them to run and control the growing city. Three (and later nine) administrators—called *archons*—were elected by an assembly of male

Oligarchy

FIGURE 2.6 A Drinking Game, ca. fifth century B.C.E. This pottery cup shows a courtesan swirling a wine bowl until the dregs fly out. It reminds us that although respectable women stayed home, prostitutes were a regular part of Athenian social life.

citizens (the *Ecclesia*) and ran the business of the city. They served for only one year, and after their tenure they permanently entered a council called the Areopagus (eventually numbering 300 men), which held the real power because it was composed of senior men who could not be removed from office. This government, in which the wealthy effectively controlled power, proved unable to respond to changing economic fortunes, which had profound political consequences.

By about 600 B.C.E., the weaknesses in the Athenian economy had become apparent. Small farmers could not produce enough to feed the growing population, and many fell into debt and even slavery by offering themselves as security in exchange for food. At about the same time, the hoplite armies caused the aristocracy to lose its monopoly over the military. A social crisis was in the making, but it was resolved by a far-sighted Athenian aristocrat, Solon, who was elected as sole archon in 594 B.C.E. Like so many men in the West who periodically tried to alleviate social ills, Solon introduced reforms intended to appease these lower classes while keeping aristocrats in power.

Solon first addressed the alarming debt crisis by introducing reforms—called the Shaking Off of Burdens—that canceled (or limited) existing debts and banned debt slavery altogether. Solon also introduced some agricultural reforms, striking at the

> Solon's reforms

economic heart of the problem. He ordered that no agricultural product could be exported except olive oil, thus stimulating the cultivation of the valuable olives that would become the basis of Athens's prosperity. He also standardized the weights used by the Athenians, making it easier for them to trade with other poleis. With the economic reforms in place, Solon turned to the political structures that had proved inadequate to prevent civil strife.

Solon did not try to eliminate the old families from power; instead, he paved the way for men growing wealthy from the export trade to participate in government. He first divided up all citizens into four groups based on wealth (instead of birth), and only members of the top two groups were eligible to become archons (and subsequently members of the Areopagus). While this preserved some privilege of rank, it nevertheless appeased the newly wealthy, who were now permitted to aspire to the highest offices. Solon then revitalized the assembly of citizens, and to further weaken the power of the Areopagus, he created a Council of 400 to set the agenda for the Ecclesia. To round out the reforms, Solon tried to ensure justice for everyone by establishing a special people's court of appeal intended to offer protection against the abuse of power by archons.

> Increased democracy

Solon's reforms were balanced and attempted to provide a compromise among the contentious social groups in Athens. However, his attempts to placate the various factions were unsuccessful because each party tried to gain more privileges. During the resulting civil strife, Athens turned to tyranny, bringing Peisistratus to power in 560 B.C.E. He ruled (between periods of exile) until 527 B.C.E., when his son Hippias tried to continue the rule. He was to be the last of Athens's tyrants. He fell to a coalition of aristocrats and Greeks from other city-states hoping to gain some political advantage for themselves. The period of tyranny broke the power of the aristocrats and paved the way for full democracy.

> Tyranny

The people rallied to Cleisthenes, a nobleman who stood for popular interests. In 508 B.C.E., Athens adopted the Constitution of Cleisthenes, which refined Solon's reforms and brought a remarkable degree of direct democracy to the city. Cleisthenes kept Solon's basic structure, but his major innovation (which has earned him the credit for establishing democracy in Athens) was to redistrict the city in a way that old alliances of geography and clan were broken and could no longer control the city offices. Everyone was divided up into ten tribal units, and this was how they were represented in the Assembly. Furthermore, Solon's old Council of 400 was increased to 500—each tribal unit could select 50 members by lot. By breaking the old alliance system, Cleisthenes

thinking about

DOCUMENTS

DOCUMENT 2.1

Theseus Founds the City of Athens

The famous ancient biographer Plutarch (46–120 C.E.) related Athens's founding myth, in which the hero Theseus defeated the Minotaur of Crete and returned to establish a city that would be unlike any that had gone before.

After the death of Ægeus, Theseus conceived a great and important design. He gathered together all the inhabitants of Attica and made them citizens of one city, whereas before they had lived dispersed, so as to be hard to assemble together for the common weal, and at times even fighting with one another.

He visited all the villages and tribes, and won their consent, the poor and lower classes gladly accepting his proposals, while he gained over the more powerful by promising that the new constitution should not include a king, but that it should be a pure commonwealth, with himself merely acting as general of its army and guardian of its laws, while in other respects it would allow perfect freedom and equality to every one. By these arguments he convinced some of them, and the rest knowing his power and courage chose rather to be persuaded than forced into compliance.

He therefore destroyed the prytanea, the senate house, and the magistracy of each individual township, built one common prytaneum and senate house for them all on the site of the present acropolis, called the city Athens, and instituted the Panathenaic festival common to all of them. He also instituted a festival for the resident aliens, on the sixteenth of the month, Hecatombaion, which is still kept up. And having, according to his promise, laid down his sovereign power, he arranged the new constitution under the auspices of the gods. . . .

Wishing still further to increase the number of his citizens, he invited all strangers to come and share equal privileges, and they say that the worlds now used, "Come hither all ye peoples," was the proclamation then used by Theseus, establishing as it were a commonwealth of all nations. But he did not permit his state to fall into the disorder which this influx of all kinds of people would probably have produced, but divided the people into three classes, of Eupatridæ or nobles, Geomori or farmers, Demiurgi or artisans.

To the Eupatridæ he assigned the care of religious rites, the supply of magistrates for the city, and the interpretation of the laws and customs sacred or profane; yet he placed them on an equality with the other citizens, thinking that the nobles would always excel in dignity, the farmers in usefulness, and the artisans in numbers. Aristotle tells us that he was the first who inclined to democracy, and gave up the title of king; and Homer seems to confirm this view by speaking of the people of the Athenians alone of all the states mentioned in his catalogue of ships.

SOURCE: Plutarch, "Life of Theseus," in *The Great Events by Famous Historians*, vol. I, ed. Rossiter Johnson (The National Alumni, 1905), pp. 50–51.

Analyze the Document

1. What was unusual about Theseus's vision for the city?

2. How might this myth have influenced the development of Athenian democracy?

3. Might the myth have been created after Athens had adopted a democratic constitution?

secured a remarkable form of direct democracy for Athens with provisions to curb the power of any group that might become too strong.

Although the Ecclesia offered a new level of participation to the men of the ancient world and a model of representation that has been praised since, it was not a perfect democracy. It still represented only about 20 percent of the population of Athens, for it excluded women and slaves. Also excluded were the *metics*, resident foreigners who lived and worked in Athens in manufacturing and commerce and who represented nearly one-third of the free population of Athens. Furthermore, recent scholarship shows that only a minority of the qualified citizens could attend the assembly at any given time—only about 6,000 can fit into the meeting place, a small sloping hillside. It seems that when the meeting place was full, no one else could enter and a quorum was declared. Thus, probably many of the same people (those living nearby) attended the Ecclesia regularly.

Assessing democracy

However, other parts of the Athenian government made sure the principle of egalitarian democracy prevailed. The Council of 500 was chosen annually by lot from male citizens over age 30, and citizens could not repeat tenure. Choosing representatives by lot (instead of by election or other device) removed much of the influence of wealth and personal power from the political process. The Council set the agenda for the Ecclesia, preparing forms of legislation for the assembly's action. Its influence was enormous, but the full governing power remained in the direct democracy of the Ecclesia. These practices assumed that all citizens could fulfill the duties of government, and this egalitarian assumption is astonishing for the ancient world (and perhaps for the modern one as well). The great leader of Athens Pericles, in a famous funeral oration preserved (or paraphrased) by the historian Thucydides, rightly observed: "Our constitution is called a democracy because it is in the hands not of the few but of the many."

The people did recognize that sometimes individuals could threaten the rule of the many, and to protect the democracy, Cleisthenes instituted an unusual procedure early in the sixth century B.C.E.: ostracism. Once a year, Athenians could vote for the man they considered most dangerous to the state by inscribing his name on a scrap of pottery (called an *ostracon*). If a man received 6,000 votes, he was sent into exile for ten years. **Figure 2.7** shows examples of these pottery shards. The scrap on the lower left votes to exile a man named Hippocrates, while the other three cast votes for "Themistocles, son of Neocles." It appears that Themistocles was well on his way to exile! Although Athenian democracy was not perfect, it was an extraordinary new chapter in the history of the West, and one that has held long-standing appeal.

Sparta: Model Military State

Sparta's development led to the emergence of a state thoroughly different from Athens, with a markedly different set of values. Whereas Athenians were creative, artistic, and eloquent, Spartans were militaristic, strict, and sparing of words (our word *laconic* comes from the Greek word for "Spartans" or the region they inhabited). The nature of their state was shaped by an early solution to their land hunger.

FIGURE 2.7 Pottery Voting Ballots Once a year, Athenians were able to vote for someone whom they believed should be exiled for ten years. They inscribed his name on pottery scraps called *ostraca*, such as the ones shown here. That Greek word is the source of the English word *ostracize*, meaning "to ban from the group."

Instead of sending out colonists or negotiating partnerships with the peoples in their vicinity (as the Athenians had done), the Spartans conquered their neighboring districts and enslaved the local populations. The slaves, called **helots,** were treated harshly. As one Spartan poet observed, they were like "donkeys worn down by intolerable labor." Sparta's helots greatly outnumbered free citizens and always seemed to threaten rebellion. To keep the helots in slavery, the Spartans virtually enslaved themselves in a military state of perpetual watchfulness. They consoled themselves by observing that at least they had chosen their harsh life, whereas their helots had not.

The Spartan constitution—reputedly introduced by the semilegendary Lycurgus in about 600 B.C.E.—reflected their deep conservatism and made a minimal concession to democracy. Authority was carefully kept in the hands of the elders. In this oligarchy, citizen representation was firmly guided by age and experience, and many outsiders admired Sparta's "mixed constitution," which seemed to balance democracy with oligarchy.

Life in Sparta was harsh, although it was much admired by many Greeks who appreciated the Spartans' powers of self-denial. At birth, each child was examined by elders, and if deemed physically deficient, the child would be exposed— left outdoors to die. At the age of 7, boys were turned over to the state and spent the next thirteen years in training to learn military skills, endurance, and loyalty to the polis. At 20, young men entered the army and lived the next ten years in barracks. They could marry but could visit their wives only by eluding the barracks guards. At 30, men became full citizens and could live at home. Nevertheless, they were expected to take all meals in the military dining hall, where food was sparse and plain.

While their men lived isolated in the barracks, Spartan women had far more freedom than Greek women of other city-states. Because men concentrated on their military activities, women handled most of the household arrangements and had wide economic powers. They attended contests to cheer the brave and mock the losers, but they were not simply spectators. Women, too, trained in athletic endurance, and the fierceness of Spartan women was said to match that of their men. The Greek biographer Plutarch (46?–120? C.E.) recorded a series of quotations that were supposedly the words of Spartan women. The most famous is from a woman who tells her son to come back from war either with his shield (victorious) or on it (dead). Such resolve made the armies of Sparta the best in Greece, and though the Spartans created no works of art, they probably would have said that their own lives were masterpiece enough.

Ostracism

Spartan life

The Love of the Contest: Olympic Games

Athens and Sparta were only two examples of the many varieties of city-states that developed with fierce independence on the Greek mainland and in the colonies throughout the Mediterranean. But, although there was much rivalry among the poleis, they still shared a certain sense of identity. They spoke the same language, worshiped the same gods, cherished Homer's poetry, and had a passionate love for individual competition. They recognized these affinities, calling themselves *Hellenes* (the Romans later called them "Greek" after a Greek colony), and they considered all Hellenes to be better than other peoples. Their love of contest caused Hellenes to gather at many local competitions that included drama as well as sport. The largest and most famous of these events was a religious festival dedicated to Zeus, and Hellenes even stopped their almost interminable warfare to come together and compete.

The first pan-Hellenic Olympic Games were held in 776 B.C.E. At first, the event consisted only of a footrace, but soon the games | Olympic Games | expanded to include boxing, wrestling, chariot racing, and the grueling pentathlon, which consisted of long jumping, discus and javelin throwing, wrestling, and the 200-meter sprint. Olympic victors brought glory to their home cities and were richly rewarded there with honor and free meals.

The Olympics were so popular that they served as an inspiration to many artists. The athletes shown in **Figure 2.8** demonstrate the perfection that people expected from their athletic heroes. The scene portrays several of the contests: the footrace, the javelin throw, and, in the center of the relief, the most difficult event, wrestling. The athletes tense all their muscles as they begin the contest that virtually defined Greek life. Critics, such as the playwright Euripides (485–406 B.C.E.), chided Greeks for their adulation of athletes. "We ought rather to crown the good man and the wise man," he scolded. Nevertheless, spectators flocked to the games.

Olympic planners prohibited women from attending the contest, although they could purchase a chariot and horses with which men would compete in their names. One woman defied the convention and dressed as a trainer so that she could watch her son compete. After he | Women at Olympics | won, she jumped over a fence in her excitement and accidentally revealed her gender. Olympic officials promptly passed a law requiring all future trainers to attend the games in the nude to prevent further disguises.

Some women conducted games of their own separately from the men's. These games, dedicated to Zeus's wife, Hera, involved footraces run by unmarried women of various ages. Women judged and sponsored the games and awarded the fastest competitors crowns of olive branches. However, these winners did not receive the high level of acclaim or wealth accorded to male victors, who brought prestige to their cities and fame for themselves through their athletic prowess. Although the Olympic Games offered a safe outlet for the Greeks' love of competition, Greek history was shaped by more devastating strife in which city-states tried to outdo each other on the battlefields.

The Persian Wars, 490–479 B.C.E.

Greek colonists who settled in Asia Minor built their city-states in lands that the Persian Empire had claimed by 500 B.C.E. As we saw in Chapter 1, the

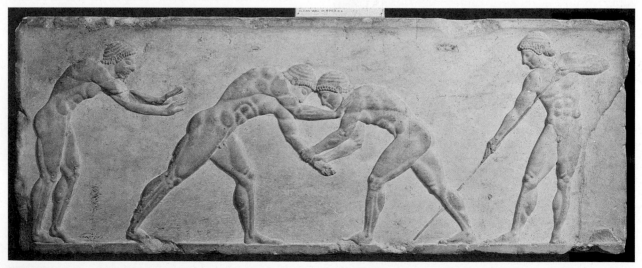

FIGURE 2.8 The Olympic Games, late sixth century B.C.E. As part of their ongoing contest for excellence, the Greeks developed the Olympic Games in honor of Zeus. Here, athletes participate in the footrace, wrestling, and the javelin throw.

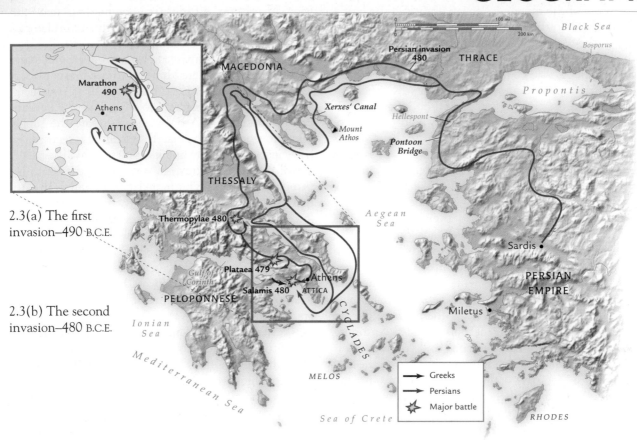

2.3(a) The first
invasion—490 B.C.E.

2.3(b) The second
invasion—480 B.C.E.

MAP 2.3A & B

The Persian Wars,
490–479 B.C.E.

This map shows the routes of invasions and the major
battles of the wars between Persia and the Greek poleis.
Map 2.3a traces the first invasion by sea in 490 B.C.E.,
and Map 2.3b illustrates the routes of the second invasion, during which armies marched by land, supported
by accompanying ships.

Explore the Map

1. What might have been the particular advantages and
   disadvantages posed by the land and sea routes?

2. How did the topography of Greece, with its narrow
   passes, serve as a disadvantage to the more numerous Persian forces?

3. Why did the Persian land route require engineering marvels such as the Pontoon Bridge and Xerxes'
   canal? How might these have served as models for
   future military expeditions?

Persians were tolerant of the various subject peoples
within their territories, so they did not object to the
growing spirit of independence that accompanied the
prosperity of these successful commercial cities. However, open revolt was another matter.

In 499 B.C.E., the Greek tyrant ruling in the city of
Miletus (**Map 2.3**) offended the Persian rulers. Hoping to avoid retribution, he staged a
revolt against Persian rule and
asked for help from his compatriots
on the Greek mainland. Sparta refused, but Athens
sent twenty ships—enough only to anger the Persians

Causes of war

but not to save Miletus. The Greek city was sacked,
and the Persians turned their attention to the Greek
peninsula. They planned an invasion in part to punish Athens for its involvement in the Miletus
uprising.

Any forces seeking to invade the Greek mainland
had to negotiate the mountainous terrain and the
narrow passes that afforded the only access to the
interior. Furthermore, an invading land army had to
be supplied by a shore-hugging fleet that backed up
the infantry while navigating the narrow straits of
the Aegean shoreline. In 490 B.C.E., the Persian king

Darius I (r. 522–486 B.C.E.), therefore, sailed across the Aegean and landed near Athens. **Map 2.3a** depicts the route of the invading Persian army and the battle site located on the plain of Marathon.

At the Battle of Marathon, the Athenians and their allies were far outmatched by the numerous Persians. The worried Athenians asked their Spartan compatriots for reinforcements, but the Spartans replied that they had to complete their religious festival first—then it would be too late

Battle of Marathon

to repel the Persians. Athens and its allies had to stand alone. In spite of being outnumbered, the Athenians decided to march from Athens to meet the Persians near their landing site on the plain of Marathon. Confident of an easy victory, the Persians launched their attack. Things did not go as expected for the Persians, however. The Athenian general, Miltiades, developed a clever strategy that helped the Greeks outwit the lightly armed Persians. Weakening the center of their line and strengthening the two wings, the Athenians outflanked the advancing Persian force and inflicted severe damage. The Greeks also made a running advance, a novelty that surprised and confused their enemy. Athenian innovation and energy won the day, bringing a decisive and stunning victory to the Greeks. According to the texts, 6,400 Persians perished in the battle, compared with only 192 Athenians. This unexpected victory of the polis over the huge empire of Persia earned Athens great prestige, and the Athenian victory also inspired confidence in the newly emerging democracy itself.

One of the heroes of Marathon was a fast runner, Philippides, who ran approximately 150 miles in two days to request the help of the Spartans. However, he is more remembered for a probably untrue story that claims he ran to Athens to deliver the news of victory to the polis and then died on the spot from his exertions. Modern-day races are called *marathons* in commemoration of Philippides' legendary 26-mile run from the plain of Marathon to Athens.

Athens had fended off the invaders, but the humiliated Persians were determined to try again. Ten years after the disaster at Marathon, Darius's successor, Xerxes (r. 486–465 B.C.E.), plotted a full-scale invasion of the Greek mainland. Xerxes brought the best

A second invasion

of ancient engineering to the invasion to try to avoid the disaster of the first war. To move a large infantry force, he built a pontoon bridge across the Hellespont and marched 180,000 soldiers to Greece. Even more impressive, he ordered his men to build a canal a mile and a quarter long through a peninsula in northern Greece so that his fleet could supply the ground force. Historians have debated for decades about whether the canal existed, but recently, scientists from Britain and Greece proved conclusively

that the canal was built. It spanned about 100 feet at the surface, just wide enough for two war galleys to pass. It was an astonishing engineering feat and showed Xerxes' determination. (Both the bridge and the canal are shown on **Map 2.3b**.)

As the Persians invaded, several Greek city-states in the north surrendered quickly to the Persian Great King. Meanwhile, Athens had readied its own fleet, assuming that the best way to withstand the Persians was to control the Aegean and therefore the supply routes to troops on the march. Athens also secured the participation of Sparta and its allies to aid in the battle.

For the Persian army, the gateway to the south lay through the pass at Thermopylae (see **Map 2.3b**). Yet the narrow pass, held by a small coalition of Greeks led by Spartans, turned the Persians' greater numbers into a liability. The Greeks held the pass for days against repeated

Thermopylae

assaults by the best Persian forces. In the end, however, they were betrayed by a Greek who expected to enrich himself by aiding the attackers. The traitor led the Persians around the defended pass, where they could fight the Greeks from the rear. Only the Spartans stayed to fight to the death. Defending themselves from front and back, the Spartans fought fiercely in a long-remembered feat of bravery, and all died with sword in hand. An inscription placed on their graves immortalized their heroic stand: "Tell them the news in Sparta, passer by. That here, obedient to their words, we lie."

The Persians' success at Thermopylae opened a route for them to march south to Athens itself. The outmatched Athenians consulted the Delphic oracle (shown in **Figure 2.3**), who told them to trust in wooden walls. The Athenian leader, Themistocles, persuaded the people that the oracle meant the wooden "walls" of their ships, not the walls of Athens, so the Athenians scattered, taking refuge in their fleet and abandoning the polis for nearby islands. Many horrified Greeks were close enough to watch as the Persians plundered Athens and burned the temples on the Acropolis as an act of revenge for their previous losses. Yet, as in Marathon, the tide again turned against the mighty Persians, this time in the bay of Salamis (see **Map 2.3b**).

Artemisia, queen of Caria in Persia and commander of a squadron of Xerxes' fleet, immediately saw that the Persians would lose their advantage in numbers fighting in a narrow bay and strongly advised the Persian king against it. Her military wisdom proved well founded;

Greek naval victory

the swift Greek vessels rallied and crushed almost the entire Persian fleet. Artemisia managed to escape through her remarkable strategy and bravery. Xerxes withdrew from the melee after sending his children home to safety on Artemisia's ship. The despondent emperor, watching Artemesia's success and the destruction of the rest of his fleet, lamented: "My men have become women, and my women men." The next year, the Spartans led a coalition that defeated the remnants of the Persian army at Plataea (see **Map 2.3b**). The individualistic, dispersed Greeks had triumphed once more over the vast, unified Persian Empire.

Herodotus: The Father of History

In a famous work called simply *The History*, the Greek historian Herodotus recorded the great deeds of the Persian Wars with a combination of a broad perspective and an attention to detail. This monumental work—some 600 pages long—was so pathbreaking that he is universally considered the father of Western history. With his first sentence, Herodotus placed himself within the Greek heroic tradition, claiming to have written in order "that the deeds of men may not be forgotten, and that the great and noble actions of the Greeks and Asiatics may not lose their fame." While immortalizing these warriors, Herodotus did not take the traditional approach of converting heroic deeds into godlike myths. Instead, he drew from oral traditions acquired during his extensive travels— the things he had "seen and been told"—and wrote what he intended to be a total picture of the known world. This was an account not simply of a war but of a heroic-scale conflict between two types of societies, the poleis and the Asian empire—or, for Herodotus, between freedom and despotism.

Herodotus did much for the discipline of history by striving to record historical events as accurately as possible and separating fact from fable, but his efforts marked only a beginning in the quest for historical objectivity. He clearly shared the Greeks' belief that their culture was far superior to that of the "barbarians," and these preconceptions biased his conclusions.

Although Herodotus wrote a lively, fascinating history, as we will see, he was wrong in identifying the Persians as the Greeks' worst enemies. Just as a Greek had betrayed the Spartans at Thermopylae, the Greeks themselves would one day bring about their own downfall. But for the time being, they gloried in their astounding victory over Persia, the great power of Asia.

GREECE ENTERS ITS CLASSICAL AGE, 479–336 B.C.E.

Victory over the mighty Persian Empire launched the Greeks into a vigorous, creative period that later historians and art critics admired so much they named it the classical age. This period was marked by stunning accomplishments in art, architecture, literature, philosophy, and representative democracy in Athens. This same age that saw such impressive artistic innovations ended as the contest for excellence among the city-states plunged them into devastating wars. At the beginning of the period, however, Athens, which took the lead in guarding Greece from Persian incursions, began to flex its muscles.

Athens Builds an Empire, 477–431 B.C.E.

The Greeks' defeat of the Persians, though sweet, presented the fiercely independent poleis with a new dilemma. The Persian Empire was still powerful. How would the Greek city-states work together to remain vigilant in the face of this threat, and who would lead them? The most effective defense of Greece lay in controlling the Aegean, and the Athenians possessed the strongest fleet.

In 477 B.C.E., most maritime poleis on the coasts and the islands of the Aegean finally decided to form a defensive league. Each member of the league contributed money to maintain a large fleet for the defense of them all. The island of Delos (near modern Mykonos) is | Delian League | small and rocky, only about 2 miles long and less than a mile wide, but its importance was disproportionate to its size (see **Map 2.1**, on page 43). Its location was perfect; as the halfway point between mainland Greece and Ionia, it capitalized on the trade through the Aegean. Furthermore, it was reputed to be the birthplace of Apollo, so its sanctuary to that god brought pilgrims (and wealth) from all over the Greek world. Even Homer mentioned Delos as a religious center for Ionian Greeks. Because people thought the sanctuary was sacred and protected by the god, the alliance decided to establish their treasury on Delos. The coalition was thus called the Delian League. Theoretically, all league members were entitled to an equal voice in decision making, but Athens was the strongest member and began to dominate league policy.

As early as the 470s B.C.E., some members took offense at Athens's prominent role and sought to withdraw from the arrangement. But the Athenians swiftly made the situation clear: This was not a league of independent states after all, but an Athenian empire with subject cities. In 454 B.C.E., the Athenians dropped any pretense of the member states' autonomy and moved the league's treasury from Delos to Athens. It is hard to imagine how deeply the Athenian actions horrified the Greek world, but consider that it was a sacrilege to raid the shrine that had been safe under Apollo's protection for centuries. It is also hard to grasp how vast were the stores of money on Delos. The Athenians would use this wealth to rebuild the Acropolis and to fund Athens's Golden Age, which included dressing the cult statue of Athena in astonishing amounts of gold (see the chapter-opening photo on page 40).

One critic of Athenian policy complained that, because the smaller Aegean states depended on seaborne imports and exports for their survival, they did not dare to defy the Athenian "rulers of the sea." Nevertheless, the Athenian Empire did succeed in protecting the mainland from further Persian assaults and conferred other benefits: The poleis of the Aegean and Asia Minor were free to trade safely under the protection of the Greek ships. They received peace in exchange for autonomy.

During the Persian Wars, the Athenian military commanders had understandably acquired a good deal of power. Officials called **strategoi** (sing. *strategos*) were elected as commanders of the tribal army units, and during Athens's imperial age, a particularly strong strategos came to wield consider-

| Pericles |

able power for a time. The political architect of Athens's Golden Age was the statesman Pericles (495–429 B.C.E.), who was elected strategos every year from 443 B.C.E. to his death in 429 B.C.E. He so dominated Athenian affairs that many compared him to a tyrant, yet this powerful aristocrat eloquently championed democracy in the assembly of Athens and encouraged democratic principles within the states of the league. However, he did not permit independent action by subject states. Thus, Pericles supported Athens's removal of the league treasury. As he pointed out, it was only right that Athenians enjoy the money, given that they had led the victory over Persia in the first place and their city had been burned in the process. Pericles followed up this argument by playing an instrumental role in plans for spending the money.

Pericles' closest companion and most influential advisor was the talented courtesan Aspasia, who headed an establishment that boasted the most cultured young courtesans in Athens, and in the mid-440s B.C.E., she became Pericles' mistress. Despite her status with Pericles, Aspasia drew intense criticism for her "undue" influence over Athens's great leader. For example, the Athenians suspected her of persuading Pericles to involve Athens in military alliances advantageous to her native city of Miletus. Rumors also circulated that she helped write the orator's speeches. The ever-loyal Pericles ignored all these complaints, however, and maintained his close relationship with Aspasia until his death.

Pericles forwarded democracy within Athens by trying to ensure that even poor citizens could participate fully in Athenian politics and cul-

| Pericles' democracy |

ture. His most significant contribution was to pay the people who served as jurors or on the Council of 500. Now all male citizens—not just the rich—could participate in the democracy. Equally important, he used much of the treasury to employ citizens on a project designed to beautify the public spaces of Athens. He organized armies of talented artists and artisans and paid thousands of workers to participate in the project. Finally, he put about 20,000 Athenians on the municipal payroll, a move that stimulated widespread involvement in the democratic proceedings of the city.

Artistic Athens

Pericles' leadership made Athens the political and cultural jewel of Greece. At the heart of the reconstruction program lay a plan to rebuild the Acropolis, which the Persians had destroyed. The restored Acropolis consisted of several temples and related buildings. As they designed the buildings, architects drew from the best of Greek tradition to make a political as well as an artistic statement. Design came first: Greek temples had always been constructed of *post and lintel* form, in which columns supported the roof. By 600 B.C.E., Greeks had developed "orders" of architecture to describe the various designs of the columns (and buildings), and these orders have influenced architecture down to the modern day. There were three orders of classic Greek buildings—Doric, Ionic, and Corinthian. **Doric,** the oldest order, developed on the Greek mainline, has a simple capital on top of a fluted column. The **Ionic** order, developed in Ionia on the eastern Mediterranean (see **Map 2.2**), features taller, more slender columns topped with elegant scroll shapes. The **Corinthian** order was a later development (probably from the fifth century B.C.E.) and was not used on the Acropolis, but its columns, topped with an acanthus-leaf capital, were extremely popular in later architecture. **Figure 2.9** shows a sketch of the major elements of these three

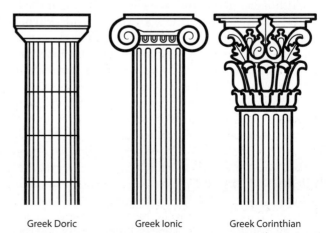

Greek Doric   Greek Ionic   Greek Corinthian

FIGURE 2.9 Architectural Orders The magnificent Greek architects developed *orders*, conventional architectural styles most readily identified by the tops of the columns. The Doric, Ionic, and Corinthian orders are shown here. The Greeks' orders have influenced architecture into modern times.

FIGURE 2.10 Acropolis of Athens, 448–432 B.C.E. After raiding the treasury of Delos, Athenians rebuilt their Acropolis with temples to the deities. The greatest temple was the Parthenon, featured here, which continues to be a model of architectural perfection.

orders that make them recognizable. The architects of the buildings on the Acropolis used both Doric and Ionic columns in the temples, as you can see in **Figure 2.10.** Specifically, the Doric style was featured on the magnificent Parthenon, and the Ionic on the Temple of Athena Nike.

In effect, these structures were nothing less than a political statement. Indeed, visitors to the Acropolis could see the empire's might in the majestic columns, which proclaimed Athenian control over the mainland to the Ionian coast. Although people would forget that political statement over time, the architectural elements would constantly be duplicated.

Builders designed all the temples with extraordinary care, constructing them according to principles of mathematical proportion, which the Greeks (following in the footsteps of Pythagoras) believed underlay the beauty of the universe. At the same time, the architects knew that human beings cannot visually perceive absolute, mathematical perfection, so they compensated by creating an optical illusion, curving some of the temples' lines to make them appear straight to the human eye. In other words, Greek architects used practical means to strive for abstract perfection. In this longing, the buildings of the Acropolis mirrored the Greeks' pursuit of excellence.

The largest temple in the Acropolis was the Parthenon (shown in the center in **Figure 2.10**), located on the highest point and dedicated to Athena, the patron goddess of the city. The temple had a magnificent statue of the goddess (now lost) created by Phidias, the greatest sculptor of the day, whose reputation for excellence continues today. The reproduction of this statue is on page 40.

The Athenians adorned the Parthenon with many sculptures and statues of both gods and humans. (Today, few statues remain in Athens—most are in museums elsewhere.) These statues, which all bear a strong resemblance to one another, echo the Greek belief that gods and humans had much in common.

Figures 2.11 and **2.12,** photos of sculptures from the Parthenon, depict both gods and ordinary Athenians. The gods and goddess in **Figure 2.11** are seated, waiting for the procession of the Athenians to begin. They are shown posed and dressed as Athenian citizens. At the same time, the Athenian youths in **Figure 2.12** who ride in the procession are as beautifully formed and as serenely confident as gods. By blurring humanity and divinity in their visual arts in this way, the Greeks explored the highest potential of humanity in their artwork. Their sculpture represented an idealized humanity, not real people.

FIGURE 2.11 Gods on the Parthenon, ca. 440 B.C.E. Every four years, Athenians staged a major festival, the Panathenaic procession. The frieze along the Parthenon's inner colonnade memorializes the event. In this detail, the humanlike gods are shown reclining and enjoying their tribute.

FIGURE 2.12 Athenians on the Parthenon, ca. 440 B.C.E. The human riders in this detail from the frieze along the Parthenon's inner colonnade look godlike as they take part in the Panathenaic procession. The artist, Phidias, carved the horses' legs in deeper relief to cast shadows on the lower part of the frieze and thereby to increase the optical illusion of movement.

Greek Theater: Exploring Complex Moral Problems

In addition to their architecture and sculpture, the Athenians' theatrical achievements set new standards for Greek culture. Greek theater grew as part of the religious celebration of Dionysus, held in the late spring. Every year, Athens's leaders chose eight playwrights to present serious and comic plays at the festival in a competition as fierce as the Olympics. The plays were performed in open-air theaters with simple staging. Men played both male and female parts, and all actors wore stylized masks. The themes of these plays centered on weighty matters such as religion, politics, and the deep dilemmas that arose as people grappled with their fates. During Athens's Golden Age, playwrights reminded the Athenians that, even at the height of their power, they faced complex moral problems.

One of Athens's most accomplished playwrights was Aeschylus (ca. 525–456 B.C.E.), who had fought at the Battle of Marathon. His earliest play, *The Persians*, added thoughtful nuance to the celebrations that the Athenians had enjoyed after their victory. Instead of simply praising Athenian success, Aeschylus studied Persian loss, attributing it to Xerxes' hubris at trying to upset the established international order. This also subtly warned the Athenians not to let their own arrogant pride bring about their own destruction.

Aeschylus and Sophocles

The most revered playwright of this period, however, was Sophocles (ca. 496–406 B.C.E.), who is best known for *The Theban Plays*, a great series about the mythological figure Oedipus and his family. All Athenians would have known the story of Oedipus, an ill-fated man whose family was told by a soothsayer at his birth that he was doomed to kill his father and marry his mother. The family exposed the baby to die, but he was rescued by a shepherd and raised as a prince in a faraway land. When he was grown, a soothsayer in his new land repeated the prediction, and when Oedipus fled to avoid killing the man he believed was his father, he returned to his original home, where he unintentionally fulfilled the prophecy. In Sophocles' hands, the play became a study in the range of human emotions measured by how man responds to tragic fates. As Document 2.2 shows, Oedipus moves from pride in his own position as king to deep agony and humility as he discovers the horrifying truth of his life. The play concludes with a reminder to all spectators not to feel complacent in their own lives.

DESTRUCTION, DISILLUSION, AND A SEARCH FOR MEANING

Sadly for the Athenians, they failed to heed Sophocles' warnings about pride and impiety. Their era of prosperity came to a violent end with the onset of the Peloponnesian War, a long, destructive conflict between Athens and Sparta and their respective allies. Like the Persian Wars, this new contest generated its own historian. Thucydides (460–400 B.C.E.), an even more objective historian than Herodotus, wrote: "I began my history at the very outbreak of the war, in

Thucydides

DOCUMENT 2.2

A Playwright Reflects on the Meaning of Life

The tragic playwright Sophocles wrote Oedipus the King *in about 429* B.C.E. *at the beginning of the Peloponnesian War and at the height of Athenian power. The two passages included here express two Greek views of life. In the first, Oedipus has just learned of his adoptive father, Polybus's, death, which seemed to make a lie of the prophecy that Oedipus would kill his father and marry his mother. Oedipus's wife, Jocasta, urges him to the heroic values of fearlessness and boldness. The final speech, given by the chorus, reminds all of Athens never to be prideful and complacent. Notice the contrast between these two speeches.*

Oedipus: It was sickness, then [that killed Polybus]?

Messenger: Yes, and his many years.

Oedipus: Ah! Why should a man respect the Pythian hearth, or give heed to the birds that jangle above his head? They prophesied that I should kill Polybus, kill my own father; but he is dead and buried, and I am here—I never touched him, never, unless he died of grief for my departure, and thus, in a sense, through me. No. Polybus has packed the oracles off with him underground. They are empty words.

Jocasta: Had I not told you so?

Oedipus: You had; it was my faint heart that betrayed me.

Jocasta: From now on never think of those things again.

Oedipus: And yet—must I not fear my mother's bed?

Jocasta: Why should anyone in this world be afraid? Since Fate rules us and nothing can be foreseen? A man should live only for the present day. Have no more fear of sleeping with your mother: How many men, in dreams, have lain with their mothers! No reasonable man is troubled by such things.

. . . .

Chorus: Men of Thebes: look upon Oedipus. This is the king who solved the famous riddle and towered up, most powerful of men. No mortal eyes but looked on him with envy. Yet in the end ruin swept over him. Let every man in mankind's frailty consider his last day; and let none presume on his good fortune until he find life, at his death, a memory without pain.

SOURCE: Dudley Fitts and Robert Fitzgerald, *The Oedipus Rex of Sophocles: An English Version* (New York: Harcourt Brace, 1977) in Lamm, *The Humanities in Western Culture* (New York: McGraw-Hill, 2003), p. 13.

Analyze the Document

1. Which of the two speeches—by Jocasta or the chorus—better represents the Greek heroic ideal? Why?

2. What are Jocasta's and Oedipus's views on prophecies and auguries? Why do you think the playwright included these skeptical opinions?

3. How do you think the Athenian audience would have reacted to Sophocles' warning against pride just as Athens was beginning a war against Sparta?

---

the belief that it was going to be a great war. . . . My belief was based on the fact that the two sides were at the very height of their power and preparedness. . . ." Historians today share his desire for intellectual analysis of the facts but might come to different conclusions about the results. In any case, as a result of Thucydides' *History of the Peloponnesian War*, we now have the earliest, most carefully detailed record of a war—and of the destruction of a way of life.

The Peloponnesian War, 431–404 B.C.E.

To counter growing Athenian power, Sparta gathered together allies—the Peloponnesian League—to challenge the power of the Athenian Empire. While the flash point of the conflict was a dispute between two poleis, Thucydides recorded the Spartan viewpoint: "What made war inevitable was the growth of Athenian power and the fear which this caused in Sparta." At its core, this was a war to preserve the independence of each city-state and the unique brand of competitiveness among all the poleis. Athens had grown too strong, and the contest too uneven. Sparta felt compelled to take action when Athens increased its imperial ambitions.

The actual fighting proved awkward and difficult, for Athens and Sparta each had differing strengths and military styles. Athens was surrounded by long walls that extended to the shore (see inset in **Map 2.4**). Therefore, as long as the Athenian navy controlled the sea, Athens could not be successfully besieged. Thus Athens preferred to conduct battle with its navy and harried Spartan and allied territories from the sea. Sparta, on the other hand, put its trust in its formidable infantry. Bolstering their individual strengths, Athens's allies surrounded the Aegean Sea, while Sparta's allies were largely land based, as **Map 2.4** shows. As the Spartans marched across the isthmus near Megara to burn Athens's crops and fields, Athenians watched safely from behind their walls and supplied their needs with their massive fleet. However, there were bloody clashes as young Athenians tried to stop the Spartans, who were ravaging

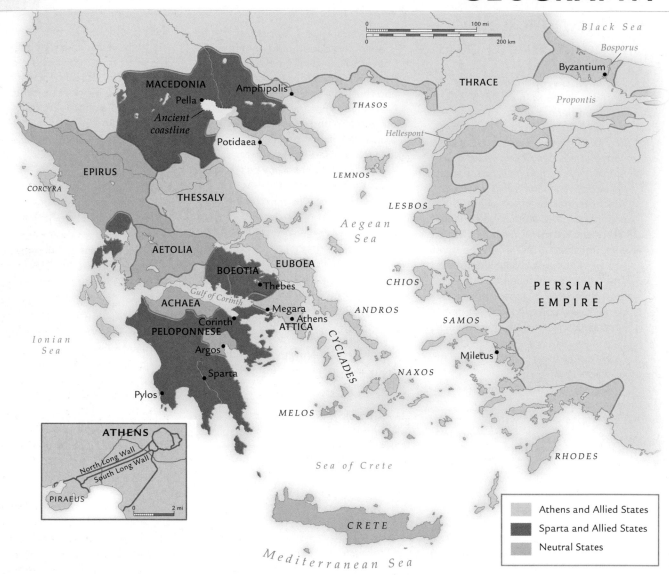

MAP 2.4

The Peloponnesian War, 431–404 B.C.E.

This map shows Athens and Sparta and their allies during the Peloponnesian War. The inset illustrates the "long walls" that joined Athens to the sea at its port of Piraeus.

Explore the Map

1. What evidence for the importance of Athens's fleet can you draw from the map?

2. Which city-state's allies were closest to Persia? Given the proximity of these allies, which side might Persia be disposed to support in this war? Why?

the countryside, and Athenians suffered inside the city, which was overcrowded with refugees. Under these conditions, plague struck the city in 430–429 B.C.E. Even Pericles succumbed, along with about one-quarter of the population. Athenian leadership fell to

lesser men, whom contemporaries denounced as selfish and impulsive (such as Alcibiades, featured in the Biography on page 67).

The realities of war caused Athenian ethics to deteriorate further with the city-state's shameful

BIOGRAPHY

Alcibiades
(ca. 450–404 B.C.E.)

Alcibiades was born to a well-placed family in Athens, but his father died when the boy was only about three. The child was then raised in the house of Pericles, the talented leader of Athens, who was his mother's cousin. Tall, handsome, wealthy, charming, and a skilled orator (in spite of a lisp), Alcibiades had all the advantages of a privileged Athenian youth. The philosopher Socrates took a personal interest in the promising young man and spent a great deal of time teaching him. Alcibiades was perfectly positioned to succeed Pericles as a leader in Athens. However, he lacked his foster father's integrity and his teacher's sense of virtue. Instead, he seems to have been overly proud and impulsive and placed his own interests above those of his polis.

The outbreak of the Peloponnesian War in 431 B.C.E. gave the young man the opportunity to win the admiration of his countrymen. At one point in the war, Alcibiades shared a tent with Socrates, who saved his life during a skirmish but allowed the youth to take credit for heroism. Alcibiades' political career was launched on the battlefield, where Athenian men traditionally proved their manhood.

Alcibiades married a well-born woman, Hipparete, with whom he had a son. Hipparete quickly learned of Alcibiades' character flaws and licentiousness and tried to divorce him. Family ties and political expedience were against her, however, and she was forced to remain a dutiful wife. She chose to ignore her husband's philandering, while he built his reputation in public life.

When the war against Sparta subsided temporarily after 421 B.C.E., Alcibiades turned to other means to buttress his fame. In 416 B.C.E., he entered seven four-horse teams in the chariot races of the Olympics and won the top prizes. Except for one Greek king, no one had ever before spent so much money on the races, and no one had won so much. Yet Alcibiades saw war as the real path to glory. He maneuvered to revive the conflict with Sparta and urged Athens to request a deputation from Sicily, which wanted Athens's assistance against Syracuse. Alcibiades saw in this alliance an opportunity to win riches and land, and he persuaded the Athenians to send a large expedition to Sicily.

Before the expedition could depart, however, the Athenians were shocked by a display of impiety that seemed to bring a bad omen. The statues of Hermes that adorned the city had been smashed and mutilated. During an investigation into this desecration, which struck at the very heart of Athenian pride, the citizens heard testimony that implicated Alcibiades himself. In addition, one of his own slaves accused Alcibiades of ridiculing the sacred "mysteries" of Demeter by drunkenly mocking the goddess's religious rituals at a dinner party. The charge seems to have been true and shows the tension between those Athenians who had little fear of the gods and those who found impiety terrifying.

As the proceedings against Alcibiades dragged on, the summer sailing season began to wane. The Athenian expedition left for Sicily with Alcibiades in the lead. However, the fleet had not even reached Sicily when Alcibiades was recalled to answer the mounting charges against him.

The Sicilian expedition ended in disaster, but Alcibiades was not there to see it.

Instead of returning to Athens, Alcibiades fled to Sparta, offering advice and leadership to his traditional enemy. He impressed the Spartans with his obvious talents and with his seeming ability to live with no luxuries. He stayed in Sparta for two years, helping his newfound allies plot against Athens.

Alcibiades' luck evaporated when he reputedly seduced the Spartan king's wife. To escape the king's ire, he fled to Persia, the enemy of both Sparta and Athens. The Persians, too, were impressed with Alcibiades' talents. He negotiated an alliance with the Persians that would prove damaging to Sparta and then returned triumphant to Athens. When war broke out again between Sparta and Athens, Alcibiades was given command of the Athenian fleet and the opportunity to assume the kind of power that Pericles had held. However, the Spartan commander Lysander won a spectacular victory. The loss was not Alcibiades' fault, but the Athenians blamed him and he was again forced to flee. In 404 B.C.E., the Spartans and Persians arranged the assassination of Alcibiades. In an ironic twist, the heroic opportunist who chose personal glory over allegiance to his polis died at the hands of his former partners in treachery.

Hero, Military Genius, and Traitor

Connecting People & Society

1. How did Alcibiades' life illustrate the concept of the drive for excellence and personal greatness at any expense?

2. How might Alcibiades' relationship to Socrates have contributed to the philosopher's condemnation?

treatment of Melos, an island that sought neutrality in 416 B.C.E. in the conflict between Athens and Sparta. Athens argued that its supe-

Melos destroyed rior strength gave it the right to force Melos into serving as its ally. Maintaining that they had the right to make their own choices, the Melians held their ground. The furious Athenians struck back, killing every last man on Melos and enslaving the women and children. Dismayed by this atrocity, Thucydides observed that the ravages of war had reduced "men's characters to a level with their fortunes." By this he meant that, under the relentless pressure of war, the Athenians had sacrificed their ideals of justice in favor of expediency.

A significant event in the war came when Alcibiades, one of the new leaders of Athens, persuaded residents of the polis to meddle in a

Athens loses dispute between two Greek city-states in Sicily. Alcibiades saw this involvement as a way to gain glory for himself, and perhaps as a ploy by which Athens could extend its control outside the Aegean Sea. It may have worked, for if Athens could control the sea trade between Greece and Italy (the Ionian Sea), Sparta's commercial allies would have been ruined. However, the venture ended in disaster: Athens lost as many as 200 ships and 40,000 men. Its fleet severely weakened, Athens could no longer rule the Aegean, and its reluctant "allies" began to fall away. Although eight years would elapse between the Sicilian disaster and Athens's final defeat, the city-state could not recover enough to prevail. The Peloponnesian League's fleet, partially financed by a Persia eager to help weaken Athens, destroyed the remnants of the Athenian fleet. Cut off from the trade that would have let them survive a siege, the Athenians were forced to surrender in 404 B.C.E. Their defeat would have profound political and philosophic ramifications.

Philosophical Musings: Athens Contemplates Defeat

During the devastating war, some Athenians started asking themselves sobering questions about justice and the meaning of life. The answers they came up with led them down new pathways of thought—pathways that would permanently alter the direction of Western philosophy. Athenian politicians like Alcibiades and the architects of the Melos atrocity had promulgated the principle of moral relativism—whatever was good for them was right. At the time, some philosophers in Athens shared this belief. These Sophists (or "wise ones") doubted the existence of universal truths and, instead, taught their followers how to influence public opinion and how to forward their own fortunes. Rather than seeking truth, the Sophists argued that "man is the measure of all things" and that people should therefore act in accordance with their own needs and desires—exactly what Alcibiades had done during the Peloponnesian conflict.

Socrates (ca. 470–399 B.C.E.), the first great philosopher of the West, developed his ideas as a reaction against the Sophists' moral relativism. Supposedly, the Delphic oracle had reported that there was "no man wiser than Socrates."

After this revelation, the philoso- **Socrates** pher spent the rest of his life roaming the streets of Athens, questioning his fellow citizens in an effort to find someone wiser than he. His questions took the form of dialogues that forced people to examine their beliefs critically and confront the logical consequences of their ideas. Socrates came to the conclusion that, indeed, he was the wisest man because he alone understood that he knew nothing, and that wisdom lies in the endless search for knowledge. Athenians came to know the rather homely man, whose father worked as a stonemason and whose mother was a midwife. Socrates, who saw himself as giving birth to ideas, claimed to have followed his mother's occupation more closely than his father's.

Socrates left no writings, so we know of his ideas only from the words of one of his students, Plato. According to these texts, Socrates expressed the idea that there were absolutes of truth and justice and excellence, and that a dormant knowledge of these absolutes rested within all people. In these inquiries, Socrates departed not only from the Sophists but from the early philosophers like Thales who wanted to know the nature of the world—Socrates wanted to explore the nature of right action. The method he employed was that of questioning and refuting students' answers, and with this method—now called the **Socratic method**—he brought students to see the truth.

Socrates called himself a gadfly for his efforts to goad other Athenians into examining their opinions—but gadflies that sting painfully are seldom appreciated. Socrates began his inquiries in the dynamic period before the Peloponnesian War, but in the times of disillusionment after the war, Athenian jurors were suspicious of anyone who seemed to oppose the democracy—even by pointing out humankind's inadequacies. Socrates was brought to trial and accused of impiety and corruption of the young. The latter charge was no doubt forwarded by the reprehensible behavior of Alcibiades, who had been Socrates' student, but the former charge had no basis. Socrates was found guilty, even though he shrewdly refuted the charges during his trial. His friends urged him to stop questioning others and to simply flee, to which he replied with the famous words that began this chapter: "Life without enquiry is not worth living." He received the death penalty and drank a cup of the deadly poison hemlock.

Socrates' ideas, however, did not die with him but lived on in his students. Plato, his best-known follower, wrote many dialogues in Plato which he seems to have preserved his teacher's ideas, although historians are uncertain where Socrates' teachings end and Plato's begin. Plato believed that truth and justice existed only as ideal models, or forms, but that humans could apprehend those realities only to a limited degree. Real people, he argued, lived in the imperfect world of the senses, a world that revealed only shadows of reality. This was his answer to the relativist Sophists, who saw the imperfect world as the true measure of right and wrong. For Plato, the goal of philosophical inquiry was to find the abstract and perfect "right" that was so elusive in this world. He established a school in Athens called the Academy to educate young Greek men in the tenets of virtue, for he believed that only through long training in philosophy could one learn to understand the ideal forms that exist outside the human world.

Plato was disillusioned with the democracy that had killed his teacher, Socrates, and admired Sparta's rigorous way of life. This political affinity shaped what is perhaps Plato's best-known work, *The Republic*, in which he outlined the ideal form of government. Instead of encouraging democracy, he explained, states should be ruled autocratically by philosopher-kings. In this way, the world might exhibit almost perfect justice. In some respects, this work expresses an articulate disillusionment with the failure of Athenian democracy to conduct a long war with honor or to tolerate a decent man pointing out citizens' shortcomings.

Plato's perfect state was never founded, but his ideas nevertheless had an enduring impact on Western civilization. Subsequent philosophers would confront his theory of ideal forms as they created other philosophic systems. His call for introspection and an awareness of self as the way to true knowledge would also have profound intellectual and religious implications.

Plato's ideas were not accepted universally in the Greek world. The career of his student Aristotle is one example. The son of a physician, Aristotle studied at Plato's Academy and then spent another twenty years refining his thinking, debating his ideas, and writing. As much as Aristotle valued his teacher, he departed from Plato's theory of "perfect forms"

and declared that ideas cannot exist outside their physical manifestations. Therefore, he concluded, to study anything—from plants to poetics to politics—one had to observe and study actual entities. Through his practical observations, Aristotle divided knowledge into categories, which remained the organizing principle of learning for over a thousand years. He said there were three categories of knowledge: ethics, or the principles of social life; natural history, the study of nature; and metaphysics, the study of the primary laws of the universe. He approached these studies through logic, which, in his hands, became a primary tool of philosophy and science. Aristotle's approach represented a major departure from the perspective of Plato, who argued that one should think about ideals instead of studying the imperfect nature of this world.

Aristotle also departed from his teacher on the subject of politics. As was his custom, the philosopher studied the different kinds of governments—monarchies, aristocracies, and republics—and discussed how each style could degenerate into corruption. He thought the ideal state was a small polis with a mixed constitution and a powerful middle class to prevent extremes. Aristotle recoiled from extremes in all aspects of life and argued for a balance—in his famous phrase, a "golden mean"—that would bring happiness. The philosopher extended his idea of moderation to the realm of ethics, arguing that the lack of excess would yield virtue.

Tragedy and Comedy: Innovations in Greek Theater

Athens's disillusioning war with Sparta had prompted philosophers to explore challenging questions of justice and virtue. Athenian theater, too, underwent change during the conflict. The playwright Euripides (485–406 B.C.E.) wrote tragedies in which people grappled with anguish Euripides on a heroic scale. In these plays, he expressed an intense pessimism and the lack of a divine moral order that marked Athens after the Peloponnesian War. In *Women of Troy*, written in the year of Alcibiades' expedition against Sicily, Euripides explored the pain of a small group of captured Trojan women. Though set in the era of the war immortalized by Homer, *Women of Troy* also had a strong contemporary message. In part, it represented a criticism of Athens's treatment of Melos and of the enslavement of Greek women and children. When a character in *Women of Troy* mused, "Strange how intolerable the indignity of slavery is to those born free," Euripides was really asking the Athenians to reflect on their own actions. In foretelling destruction to the Greeks who abused the women of Troy, Euripides predicted the eventual downfall of Athens.

Tragedy was not the only way to challenge contemporary society; talented playwrights also used comedy. As Greeks laughed at the crudest of sexual jokes and bathroom humor, they criticized public figures and conquered their own anxieties. These plays appeal less to modern audiences than do the Greek tragedies, for in their intense fascination with human nature, Greeks embraced even our basest inclinations. The comedies of this era also reveal much about Greek perceptions of the human body; just as their character flaws became the subject of tragedies, their bodies were often the focus of comedies.

The vase in **Figure 2.13** portrays a typical scene from Greek comedy. In this rendering, each actor sports a long, artificial phallus hanging well below his tunic, and padded buttocks to increase the comic effect. The actors also wear highly stylized masks. In the window is a man wearing a woman's mask. The scene portrays Zeus trying to seduce the woman in the window, and the extreme costuming highlights the bawdy and disrespectful subject matter. Although we often find such graphic portrayals tasteless at best, Greek society was surrounded with them, and we cannot fully understand the Greeks without recognizing the way they accepted their humanity in its fullest sense.

Aristophanes

While people laughed at these comic portrayals, the greatest of the comic playwrights also used humor for serious purposes. Aristophanes (455–385 B.C.E.), for example, used costumes and crude humor to deliver biting political satire. This esteemed Athenian playwright delivered a ruthless criticism of contemporary

FIGURE 2.13 Greek Comedy, fourth century B.C.E. This urn depicts a scene from a comedy with all the typical features: artificial phallus, stylized masks, and simple staging. Bawdy comedies reveal the Greeks' love of everything human, even tasteless jokes.

Athens. Like many citizens, Aristophanes longed for peace. In 411 B.C.E.—at the height of the Peloponnesian War—he wrote *Lysistrata*, a hilarious antiwar play in which the women of Athens force their men to make peace by refusing to have sexual intercourse with them until they comply. With *Lysistrata*, Aristophanes reminded people that life and sex are more important than death and war.

Hippocrates and Medicine

While philosophers and playwrights mulled over abstract notions of life and human nature, Greek physicians turned to a practical study of the human body, influencing subsequent opinions of medicine. Previous ancient societies had made a number of strides in medical knowledge—the Babylonians and Assyrians kept catalogs of healing herbs, and the Egyptians were famed for medical treatments such as setting fractures, amputating limbs, and even opening skulls to relieve pressure on head injuries. However, most of the medical knowledge that influenced the West for centuries came from the Greeks, whose systematic treatises really began to separate medicine from the supernatural. Hippocrates (ca. 460–ca. 377 B.C.E.), considered the father of modern Western medicine, supposedly claimed that "every disease has a natural cause, and without natural causes nothing ever happens." With this statement Hippocrates rejected the ancient belief that spirits were responsible for human ailments.

KEY DATES

GREEK HISTORY AND CULTURE

ca. 1250 B.C.E.	Trojan War
ca. 750 B.C.E.	Homer composes *Iliad* and *Odyssey*
490 B.C.E.	First Persian invasion repelled
495–429 B.C.E.	Pericles leads Athens, builds Acropolis temples
480–479 B.C.E.	Second Persian invasion repelled
431–404 B.C.E.	Peloponnesian War—Athens vs. Sparta
399 B.C.E.	Death of Socrates
399–347 B.C.E.	Plato flourishes
322 B.C.E.	Death of Aristotle

Hippocrates was a highly respected physician and gave his name to a body of medical writing known as the *Hippocratic Collection*, compiled between the fifth and third centuries B.C.E. The *Collection* established medicine on a rational basis devoid of supernatural explanations of disease—a major innovation in Western culture. Consistent with other Greek thinkers from Thucydides to Aristotle, Hippocrates also emphasized careful observation. This body of writings contains more than four hundred short observations about health and disease—for example, "People who are excessively overweight are far more apt to die suddenly than those of average weight," or "Extremes in diet must be avoided." Overall, this new approach to medicine put human beings, rather than the gods, at the center of study. The human-centered outlook of Greek medicine culminated in a long-standing idea expressed in the Hippocratic Oath. Modern physicians still take this oath, in which they vow first to do no harm to their patients.

Though Athens suffered some dark days of war and disillusionment, this difficult era also witnessed the rise of geniuses who used the hard times as a backdrop for exploring the complex nature of humanity. Greek philosophers, playwrights, and physicians created brilliant works and conceived of ideas that transcended their time despite the turmoil of the age.

The Aftermath of War, 404–338 B.C.E.

As a condition of its surrender at the end of the Peloponnesian War, Athens agreed to break down its defensive walls and reduce its fleet to only twelve ships. These harsh measures not only ended the Athenian Empire but also erased any possibility for a politically united Greece. The Spartans left a garrison in Athens and sent the rest of their troops home to their barrack state to guard their slaves. Sparta's subsequent attempts to assemble a political coalition foundered on its high-handed and inept foreign policy. Sparta's major allies, especially Corinth, opposed the Peloponnesian peace treaty, accusing Sparta of grabbing all the tribute and objecting to what they saw as lenience toward Athens. The generous treaty also stipulated that the Greek states in Asia Minor be given to Persia as the price for Persia's aid to Sparta, further eroding Greek unity.

All these postwar developments heightened competition among the poleis in the years after Athens's loss. For example, Corinth and Thebes fought wars to earn control of other Greek city-states, while Sparta ineptly struggled to preserve some leadership. Persia remained involved in Greek affairs, shrewdly offering money to one side and then

Power struggles

another so that the Greeks would continue to fight one another. In this way, Persia kept the poleis from marshaling their strength against their longtime imperial enemy.

These wars among the poleis only aggravated serious weaknesses within each city. Democracy in Athens as a political form, for example, had been deeply threatened by the long, devastating war, especially since decisions made by the citizens led to failure. Antidemocratic feelings expressed in the works of Plato erupted as Athens fell. As Thucydides had noted, democracy was not safe during turbulent times. As the war came to an end in 404 B.C.E., Sparta imposed an oligarchy of 30 men over Athens, a brutal tyranny that tried to stamp out the vestiges of democracy. Fifteen hundred democratic leaders were killed in the coup, and 5,000 more were exiled. This oligarchy lasted only eight months before democracy was restored, but the revived government had only a shadow of its former vigor. Fed by an involved citizenry, democracy had flourished in Athens. Now, without its empire and large fleet, fewer citizens became wealthy, and political involvement waned.

Traditional participatory government in all the poleis unraveled further with innovations in military tactics. Under skillful generals, lightly armed javelin throwers, slingers, and archers began to defeat the heavily armed citizen hoplite armies that had once been the glory of Greece. Moreover, in the century following the Peloponnesian War, more and more Greeks served as mercenaries. See Document 2.3 for a famous account of Greek mercenaries fighting in Persia. These paid soldiers, owing allegiance to no city, added further disruption to an already unstable time, finally breaking the link between the poleis and the citizen-soldiers who defended them. In this period of growing unrest, every major Greek polis endured at least one war or revolution every ten years.

The nascent collective power of the Greek city-states also deteriorated during the postwar era. None of the poleis had succeeded in forging a lasting Hellenic coalition. The sovereignty of each city remained the defining idea in Greek politics. With this principle as a backdrop, individualism and loyalty to one's own city overrode any notions of a larger civic discipline. This competitive attitude had fueled the greatest of the Greeks' accomplishments in the arts, athletics, and politics, but it also gave rise to men like Alcibiades, who could not see beyond their own self-interests. In the midst of the troubled fourth century B.C.E., many Greeks feared that Persia would return to conquer a weakened Greece. As we will see in the next chapter, they should have worried about the "backward" people to the north instead.

DOCUMENT 2.3

Ten Thousand Greek Mercenaries Return Home

After the Peloponnesian War ended (404 B.C.E.), many Greek soldiers served as mercenaries in the Persian armies. This account written by the Greek historian Xenophon (ca. 434–ca. 355 B.C.E.), who traveled with the expedition, tells of a famous incident in which some mercenaries struggled to return home to Greece.

It was thought necessary to march away as fast as possible, before the enemy's force should be reassembled, and get possession of the pass.

Collecting their baggage at once, therefore, they set forward through a deep snow, taking with them several guides, and, having the same day passed the height on which Tiribazus had intended to attack them, they encamped. Hence they proceeded three days' journey through a desert tract of country, a distance of fifteen parasangs, to the river Euphrates, and passed it without being wet higher than the middle. The sources of the river were said not to be far off. From hence they advanced three days' march, through much snow and a level plain, a distance of fifteen parasang; the third day's march was extremely troublesome, as the north wind blew full in their faces, completely parching up everything and benumbing the men. One of the augurs, in consequence, advised that they should sacrifice to the wind, and a sacrifice was accordingly offered, when the vehemence of the wind appeared to everyone manifestly to abate. The depth of the snow was a fathom, so that many of the baggage cattle and slaves perished, with about a third of the soldiers.

They continued to burn fires through the whole night, for there was plenty of wood at the place of encampment. But those who came up late could get no wood; those, therefore, who had arrived before and had kindled fires would not admit the late comers to the fire unless they gave them a share of the corn or other provisions that they had brought. Thus they shared with each other what they respectively had. In the places where the fires were made, as the snow melted, there were formed large pits that reached down to the ground, and here there was accordingly opportunity to measure the depth of the snow.

From hence they marched through snow the whole of the following day, and many of the men contracted the *bulimia*. Xenophon, who commanded in the rear, finding in his way such of the men as had fallen down with it, knew not what disease it was. But as one of these acquainted with it told him that they were evidently affected with bulimia, and that they would get up if they had something to eat, he went round among the baggage and wherever he saw anything eatable he gave it out, and sent such as were able to run to distribute it among those diseased, who, as soon as they had eaten, rose up and continued their march. . . . Some of the enemy too, who had collected themselves into a body, pursued our rear, and seized any of the baggage-cattle that were unable to proceed, fighting with one another for the possession of them. Such of the soldiers also as had lost their sight from the effects of the snow, or had their toes mortified by the cold, were left behind. It was found to be a relief to the eyes against the snow, if the soldiers kept something black before them on the march, and to the feet, if they kept constantly in motion, and allowed themselves no

rest, and if they took off their shoes in the night. But as to such as slept with their shoes on, the straps worked into their feet, and the soles were frozen about them, for when their old shoes had failed them, shoes of raw hides had been made by the men themselves from the newly skinned oxen.

From such unavoidable sufferings some of the soldiers were left behind, who, seeing a piece of ground of a black appearance, from the snow having disappeared there, conjectured that it must have melted, and it had in fact melted in the spot from the effect of a fountain, which was sending up vapor in a wooded hollow close at hand. Turning aside thither, they sat down and refused to proceed farther. Xenophon, who was with the rear-guard, as soon as he heard this tried to prevail on them by every art and means not to be left behind, telling them, at the same time, that the enemy were collected and pursuing them in great numbers. At last he grew angry, and they told him to kill them, as they were quite unable to go forward. He then thought it the best course to strike a terror, if possible, into the enemy that were behind, lest they should fall upon the exhausted soldiers [so he urged the tired Greeks to rise and make noise to frighten the Persians following them].

SOURCE: *The Great Events by Famous Historians*, vol. II, ed. Rossiter Johnson (The National Alumni, 1905), pp. 70–71.

Analyze the Document

1. What kinds of hardships do the Greeks face, and what do we learn about ancient travel?

2. What is the Greek view of augurs and sacrifices? How does this perspective contrast with the ideas of Jocasta in Document 2.2?

3. Why do you think this account became so inspiring and influential to future Greek armies?

LOOKING BACK & MOVING FORWARD

Summary   Small city-states nestled in the mountains of the Greek peninsula rerouted the course of Western civilization. These fiercely independent cities developed participatory forms of government that encouraged men to take active roles in all aspects of their cities. Through their vigorous involvement in the life of their poleis, the men of ancient Greece created magnificent works of art, theater, and architecture that came to define Western aesthetics. These men also developed a rational approach to inquiry that has enriched Westerners' understanding of life, history, philosophy, and medicine even in modern times.

But the pride in individual accomplishment that catalyzed such extraordinary accomplishments also contained the seeds of Greece's own political destruction. The future leadership of the eastern Mediterranean would come from a people who could set aside their heroic individualism to support a larger unity. However, this influx of new ideas did not erase the legacy of Greek achievement. The newcomers would ultimately spread the accomplishments of this complex culture as far east as India as they forged a new empire.

KEY TERMS

arête, *p. 47*
kouros, *p. 48*
kore, *p. 48*
hubris, *p. 49*
hoplites, *p. 52*
phalanx, *p. 52*
polis, *p. 52*
agora, *p. 52*
oligarchy, *p. 53*
helots, *p. 57*
strategoi, *p. 62*
Doric order, *p. 62*
Ionic order, *p. 62*
Corinthian order, *p. 62*
Socratic method, *p. 68*

REVIEW, ANALYZE, & CONNECT TO TODAY

REVIEW THE PREVIOUS CHAPTER

Chapter 1—"The Roots of Western Civilization"—described the growth and development of the civilizations of Mesopotamia, Egypt, and the eastern Mediterranean coast, highlighting their contributions to the future of Western civilization. It also described the growth of empires in that region.

1. Review the growth of empires in the ancient Middle East and contrast that process with the political development of Greece.

2. Review the characteristics of Phoenician society discussed in Chapter 1. Consider what qualities the Phoenicians had in common with the early Greeks that might have led both peoples to be such successful colonizers.

ANALYZE THIS CHAPTER

Chapter 2—"The Contest for Excellence"—looks at the rise and fall of the civilizations in the Aegean region culminating in the growth of classic Greek civilization. It describes life in ancient Greece, the political fortunes of the city-states, and the dramatic accomplishments in culture and science that influenced the future.

1. Review the causes of the decline of the Minoans, the Mycenaeans, and the Athenian Empire.

2. Review the economic life of the Greek city-states, and consider the impact of geography on their economic

choices. Also consider how the Greek economy influenced political decisions.

3. Compare and contrast Athens and Sparta and their political and social systems. Why did Spartan women play a more meaningful role in society than did Athenian women?

4. Consider the Greeks' views on religion and review how these views influenced their approach to other aspects of their lives, like science and medicine.

5. Review Greek accomplishments in the arts, sciences, and political life, and consider why they would be so influential on future societies.

CONNECT TO TODAY

Think about the tensions in the ancient Greek world between individualism and society, as discussed in this chapter.

1. In what ways do societies today have to struggle with the same issues? Give some examples.

2. The trial of Socrates has remained a reference point for discussions of freedom of speech and thought. How do you think his trial might apply to contemporary issues such as hate speech and political postings on Internet sites such as Facebook and YouTube? For what other present-day issues is Socrates' trial relevant?

Morris, Ian, and B.B. Powell. *The Greeks: History, Culture, and Society.* Upper Saddle River, NJ: Prentice Hall, 2005. A comprehensive and up-to-date work that integrates art, architecture, literature, and political history.

THE RISE AND FALL OF ANCIENT HEROES, 2000–800 B.C.E.

Burkert, Walter. *Greek Religion.* Cambridge, MA: Harvard University Press, 1985. A masterful reconstruction of Greek festival activities that addresses the problem of rituals of animal sacrifice.

Fitton, J. Lesley. *The Discovery of the Greek Bronze Age.* Cambridge, MA: Harvard University Press, 1996. An informed and elegantly written account of the history of archaeological investigations.

Graves, Robert. *The Greek Myths: Complete Edition.* New York: Viking Penguin, 1993. An in-depth study of the major Greek myths.

Larson, Jennifer. *Greek Heroine Cults.* Madison: University of Wisconsin Press, 1995. A solid study of an unusual and little explored phenomenon: women venerated as heroes.

LIFE IN THE GREEK POLEIS

Cartledge, Paul. *The Spartans: The World of Warrior Heroes of Ancient Greece.* New York: Vintage, 2004. A detailed description of Spartan life, arguing that the Spartans contributed discipline and self-sacrifice to the ideals of Western civilization.

Dodds, Eric R. *The Greeks and the Irrational.* Berkeley: University of California Press, 1968. A classic study of human experience through the Greek mind.

Dover, Kenneth J. *Greek Homosexuality.* Cambridge, MA: Harvard University Press, 1978. A description of homosexual behavior and sentiment in Greek art and literature between the eighth and second centuries B.C.E.

Fantham, E., H.P. Foley, N.B. Hampen, S.B. Pomeroy, and H.A. Shapiro. *Women in the Classical World.* New York: Oxford University Press, 1995. A readable, illustrated, chronological survey of Greek and Roman women's lives, focusing on vivid cultural and social history.

Garland, Robert. *Daily Life of the Ancient Greeks.* Westport, CT: Greenwood Press, 2008. An exploration of the daily lives of ordinary people, illuminating every aspect of ancient Greece life.

Miller, Stephen G. *Arete: Greek Sports from Ancient Sources,* enl. ed. Berkeley: University of California Press, 2004. A study of all aspects of ancient sports, including male and female athletes and athletic festivals.

Sealey, R. *Athenian Democracy.* University Park: Pennsylvania State University Press, 1987. An interpretation of Athenian constitutional history.

GREECE ENTERS ITS CLASSICAL AGE, 479–336 B.C.E.

Herodotus. *The History of Herodotus,* trans. D. Grene. Chicago: University of Chicago Press, 1987. The primary source for the Persian Wars by the acknowledged father of history.

McGregor, Malcolm F. *The Athenians and Their Empire.* Vancouver: University of British Columbia Press, 1987. The standard brief history of the Athenian Empire.

Pedley, John Griffiths. *Greek Art and Archaeology.* New York: H.N. Abrams, 1993. A study of the architecture, sculpture, pottery, and wall paintings of ancient Greece.

Wood, Ellen M. *Peasant-Citizen and Slave: The Foundations of Athenian Democracy.* New York: Routledge, Chapman and Hall, 1988. Controversial piece disputing two modern myths—that of the idle mob and that of slavery—as the basis of Athenian democracy.

DESTRUCTION, DISILLUSION, AND A SEARCH FOR MEANING

Lindberg, David C. *The Beginnings of Western Science: The European Scientific Tradition in Philosophical, Religious, and Institutional Context, 600 B.C. to A.D. 1450.* Chicago: University of Chicago Press, 1992. An accessible and comprehensive study showing scientific advances and offering the benefits of a broad historical view.

Roochnik, David. *Retrieving the Ancients: An Introduction to Greek Philosophy.* Oxford: Wiley-Blackwell, 2004. Highly accessible narrative surveying Greek thought—a perfect introduction to the subject.

Sutton, D. *Self and Society in Aristophanes.* Washington, DC: University Press of America, 1980. A sophisticated analysis of the portrayal of Greek society in the plays of Aristophanes.

Thucydides. *The Peloponnesian War,* trans. J.H. Finley. New York: The Modern Library, 1951. The great primary source on the Peloponnesian War, which forms the starting point for any study.

OLD MARKET WOMAN, third or second century B.C.E.
In the great cosmopolitan cities of the Hellenistic world, many people lived in poverty and struggled all their lives just to survive. Artists began to portray these people in realistic images that were much less heroic than those favored by earlier Greek artists. Change was afoot in the Greek world.

The Poleis Become Cosmopolitan 3

The Hellenistic World, 336–150 B.C.E.

Alexander "conducted himself as he did out of a desire to subject all the races in the world to one rule and one form of government making all mankind a single people." The Greek biographer Plutarch (46–119 C.E.) wrote these words four hundred years after the death of the Macedonian king Alexander the Great (356–323 B.C.E.). In his description of Alexander, Plutarch attributed high ideals to the young conqueror that Alexander himself may not have held. However, the biographer's glowing portrayal captured the reality of Alexander's conquests, whereby he joined the great civilizations of the ancient Middle East and classical Greece in a way that transformed them both.

This new world that began in 336 B.C.E. with Alexander's conquest of Persia was described as "Hellenistic" (meaning "Greek-like") by nineteenth-century historians. During this time, the ideal Greek poleis changed from scattered, independent city-states into large, multiethnic urban centers—what the Greeks called "world cities," or cosmopolitan sites—firmly anchored within substantial kingdoms. Greek colonists achieved high status in the new cities springing up far from the Greek mainland, making the Greek language and culture the ruling ideal from Egypt to India. In this Hellenistic age, classical Greek culture was in turn altered through the influences of the subject peoples, and the new world left the old world of the Greek mainland behind. Society, economy, and politics all played out on a larger scale, and kings, rather than citizens, now ruled. Royal patronage stimulated intellectual and cultural achievement among the privileged classes, while ordinary people struggled to find their place in a new world.

The Hellenistic culture continued even as these kingdoms were conquered by Rome, the next power to rise in the West. In this chapter, we will see the origins and characteristics of this cosmopolitan culture that endured for so long.

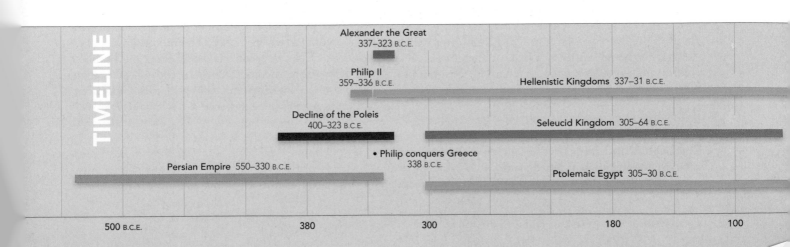

TIMELINE

Alexander the Great
337–323 B.C.E.

Philip II
359–336 B.C.E.

Hellenistic Kingdoms 337–31 B.C.E.

Decline of the Poleis
400–323 B.C.E.

Seleucid Kingdom 305–64 B.C.E.

• Philip conquers Greece
338 B.C.E.

Persian Empire 550–330 B.C.E.

Ptolemaic Egypt 305–30 B.C.E.

500 B.C.E.   380   300   180   100

THE CONQUEST OF THE POLEIS

In 220 B.C.E., an Egyptian father appealed to the Greek king to help him resolve a domestic dispute. He claimed that his daughter, Nice, had abandoned him in his old age. According to the father, Nice had promised to get a job and pay him a pension out of her wages every month. To his dismay, she instead became involved with a comic actor and neglected her filial duties. The father implored the king, Ptolemy IV, to force Nice to care for him, pleading, "I beg you O king, not to suffer me to be wronged by my daughter and Dionysus the comedian who has corrupted her."

This request—one of many sent to the king during this period—reveals several interesting points about Mediterranean life in the Hellenistic era. For example, it suggests that women worked and earned money instead of staying carefully guarded within the home. It also shows a loosening of the tight family ties that had marked the Greek poleis and the ancient Middle East civilizations—a father could no longer exert authority over his rebellious daughter and could no longer count on his children to care for him in his old age. Finally, it indicates people's view of their king as the highest authority in redressing personal problems. These were dramatic changes, and to trace their origins, we must look to Macedonia, a province on the northeast border of Greece. There, in a land traditionally ruled by strong monarchs, a king arose who would redefine life in the ancient world.

Tribal Macedonia

Although Macedonia was inhabited by Greek-speaking people, it had not developed the poleis that marked Greek civilization on the peninsula. Instead, it had retained a tribal structure in which aristocrats selected a king and served in his army bound by ties of loyalty and kinship. The southern Greek poleis—populated by self-described "civilized" Greeks—had disdain for the Macedonians, whom they saw as backward because they did not embrace the political life of the city-states.

The Macedonian territory consisted of two distinct parts: the coastal plain to the south and east, and the mountainous interior. The plain offered fertile land for farming and lush pastures in which fine warhorses grazed along | Geography | with sheep and oxen. The level land of the coastline bordered two bays that afforded access to the Aegean Sea. The Macedonian interior, by contrast, was mountainous and remote and posed the same problems for rulers that the Greek landscape presented. Kings struggled to exert even a little authority over the fierce tribes in the hills. Yet, concealed within the mountains were precious reserves of timber and metals, including abundant veins of gold and silver in the more remote locations.

For centuries, the weak Macedonian kings failed to take full advantage of such treasures, in large part because they could not control the remote tribes. Repeated invasions of Macedonia by its neighbors to the north only | Uniting the tribes | added to the problem. Throughout this turbulent period, the southern Greeks thought of Macedonia only as an area to exploit for its natural resources. The Greeks neither helped nor feared their beleaguered relatives to the north and instead focused on keeping their old enemy, Persia, at bay. Nevertheless, eventually a Macedonian king arose who not only succeeded in marshaling the resources of his land but also rerouted the direction of Greek history.

This great king, Philip II (r. 359–336 B.C.E.), had participated in some of the many wars that disrupted Greece during the fourth century B.C.E. (see Chapter 2) and, as a result, had been held hostage as a young man in the Greek city-state of Thebes for three years. During his captivity, he learned much about the strengths and weaknesses of Greek politics and warfare. When he returned to Macedonia, he used his new knowledge to educate his people. As his son Alexander later reminded the Macedonians: "Philip took you over when you were helpless vagabonds mostly clothed in skins, feeding a few animals on the mountains. . . . He gave you cloaks to wear instead of skins, he brought you down from the mountains to the plains. . . . He made you city dwellers and established the order that comes from good laws and customs."

Philip II: Military Genius

The pride of the Macedonian army was the cavalry, led by the king himself and made up of his nobles, known as "companions." Yet Philip showed his military genius in the way he reorganized the supporting forces. The shrewd monarch changed the traditional Greek phalanx, already threatened by a new fighting style that favored lightly armed—and therefore more mobile—foot soldiers. Philip strengthened the phalanx by arming his soldiers with pikes 13 feet long or longer instead of the standard 9-foot weapons. Then he instructed the infantry to arrange themselves in a more open formation, which let them take full advantage of the longer pikes. Philip also hired lightly armed, mobile mercenaries who could augment the Macedonian phalanx with arrows, javelins, and slings.

In battle, the long Macedonian pikes kept opponents at a distance, while the cavalry made the decisive difference in almost every | **Military innovations** | battle. The mounted warriors surrounded the enemy and struck at their flank, leaving the lightly armed mercenaries to move in to deliver the final blow. This strategy, which combined traditional heavily armed foot soldiers with the mobility of cavalry and light troops, would prove virtually invincible.

Philip also developed weapons for besieging walled cities. During the Peloponnesian War, even mighty Sparta's only strategy against the sturdy walls of Athens had been to starve the inhabitants to death—a slow and uncertain method. Philip is credited with using a torsion catapult that twisted launching ropes to gain more force than the older models that used counterweights could exert. With this new device, his forces could fire rocks at city walls with deadly force. Although Philip is credited with developing these siege weapons, his son would be the one to successfully use them against many fortified cities.

With his forces reorganized and equipped with the latest weapons, Philip readied himself to expand his kingdom. First, he consolidated his own highlands and the lands to the north and east. These conquests allowed him to exploit the gold and silver mines in the hills, which yielded the riches he needed to finance his campaigns. With his northern flank secure and his treasury full, the conqueror then turned his attention to the warring Greek cities to the south.

Philip dreamed of uniting the Greek city-states under his leadership. Some southern Greeks shared this dream, looking to the Macedonian king to save them from their own intercity violence. Isocrates (436–338 B.C.E.), an | **Greek responses** | Athenian orator and educator, made eloquent speeches in which he supported Philip's expansionist aims. Expressing a prevalent disillusionment with democracy, Isocrates argued that the Greeks were incapable of forming a cohesive union without a leader like Philip. In his view, this form of participatory governance had become so corrupt that "violence is regarded as democracy, lawlessness as liberty, impudence of speech as equality." Isocrates believed that only Philip could unify the Greeks and empower them to face Asia as one people finally to vanquish their ancient enemy, Persia.

Isocrates' words were compelling. But Athens had another great orator who opposed Philip and who proved more convincing than Isocrates. Demosthenes (384–322 B.C.E.) argued brilliantly for a position that rejected union under a tyrant like Philip in order to preserve Athens's traditional freedom and the self-government of the polis. As we saw in Chapter 2, the classic polis had eroded in the aftermath of the Peloponnesian War, but the orator was looking backward to a more golden age of democracy. Historians have characterized Demosthenes as everything from a stubborn, old-fashioned orator to the last champion of the lost cause of Athenian freedom. Ultimately, however, the spirited debate about Philip became moot. The question of freedom was answered not in the marketplace of Athens but on the battlefield.

In 338 B.C.E., Philip and his armies marched south toward the peninsula, where they confronted a Greek coalition led by Athens and Thebes, longtime rivals who at last joined in | **Greece conquered** | cooperation. The belated cooperation among the Greeks came too late. At the Battle of Chaeronea near Thebes, the powerful left wing of Philip's phalanx enveloped the approaching Greeks. The Macedonian cavalry, led by Philip's talented son, Alexander, slaughtered the surrounded Greeks. The victory paved the way for Philip to take control of the Greek city-states (except Sparta).

Philip proved a lenient conqueror; he charged the Greeks no tribute, but instead united them in a league under his command, so they were technically allies with Macedonia. No longer allowed to wage war against one another, the poleis joined the combined army of Greeks and Macedonians. Isocrates' hope was fulfilled, and the Greeks reluctantly renounced internal warfare. Now they prepared to follow Philip to attack the Persian Empire, which extended far beyond the borders of the Persian homeland into Asia.

Death of the King

Philip's brilliance on the battlefield exceeded his judgment in domestic matters. In the tradition of Macedonian kings, Philip had taken at least six wives. The most important was Olympias, daughter of the king of Epirus (which was southwest of Macedonia and bordered the Greek city-states) and mother of Alexander. According to Plutarch, who drew from earlier sources, Olympias and Alexander were highly insulted when Philip, in his forties, took a young bride, Cleopatra. At the wedding, Cleopatra's uncle made a toast implying that he hoped Philip would disinherit Alexander.

Political and personal resentments came to a head in 336 B.C.E. at the wedding of Alexander's sister, also named Cleopatra. On the morning of the festivities,

Philip murdered

members of the court attended the theater. Philip was escorted by his son, the bridegroom, and his bodyguards. As the little group separated to enter the theater, Pausanias, one of Philip's jilted companions, saw his opportunity. He stepped in and mortally stabbed the king. Pursued by the guards, Pausanias ran outside but tripped and fell. A guard drew his sword and killed him on the spot.

Alexander, suspecting a conspiracy behind the assassination, vigorously investigated the murder. He tried and executed the diviner who had predicted good omens for the day, and he put to death anyone who he thought had even a remote claim to the Macedonian throne. Later, even Philip's wife Cleopatra and their infant child were killed, an act that finally eliminated Alexander's rivals. Because of insufficient evidence, historians have never ascertained the full reasons for Philip's assassination. Some ancient sources accused Olympias of organizing the murder; others blame a conspiracy of nobles; still others consider the killing the solitary act of a jealous courtier. Whatever the cause, Alexander was now king.

Alexander's Conquests

The brilliant king was dead, but Philip's son, Alexander, would make an even greater mark on the world than his father had. Alexander (r. 337–323 B.C.E.) was born in 356 B.C.E. and raised by his parents expressly to rule. Philip diligently taught the young boy the arts of Macedonian warfare, including horsemanship, an essential skill for service in the cavalry. Philip and Olympias also encouraged Alexander's intellectual development. They appreciated the accomplishments of the classical Greeks and hired the revered philosopher Aristotle (384–322 B.C.E.) to tutor their

promising heir. We cannot know the exact influence of the philosopher on his young student, but Aristotle certainly imparted a love of Greek culture and literature to Alexander. Moreover, he may well have cultivated Alexander's curiosity about the world, which would fuel the young man's later urge to explore. However, Alexander seems to have rejected Aristotle's prejudice against non-Greek "barbarians." Philip's son imagined a world much wider than that of Aristotle's ideal, small city-state.

As soon as Alexander ascended the Macedonian throne, he needed to be recognized as the legitimate king, so he consolidated his rule in the region with a decisive ruthlessness that marked all his subsequent campaigns. For example, when the Greeks revolted after hearing false rumors of Alexander's death, the king promptly marched south, sacked the city of Thebes, and

Military exploits

slaughtered or enslaved the inhabitants. With the Greeks subdued, he then turned to implementing Philip's planned war against the Persian Empire. In 334 B.C.E., Alexander advanced into Asia Minor with a large army of hoplites and cavalry. He was joined by Callisthenes, Aristotle's nephew, who later wrote the history of Alexander's campaigns. Although this text has been lost, it served as a pro-Macedonian, but carefully detailed source for Alexander's early campaigns, and subsequent chroniclers who had access to the work have passed elements of it on to us.

After several decisive victories in Asia Minor, Alexander engaged the full power of Persia at the Battle of Issus (**Map 3.1**), where he matched with Persian forces and Greek mercenaries led by the Persian Great King Darius III. Through skillful deployment and swift action, Alexander's armies defeated a force more than twice as large as their own. Darius fled the battle, leaving his mother, wife, and children. The young king captured Darius's family but treated them with respect and courtesy. In this way, he showed his belief that savagery should be reserved for the battlefield.

Before driving deeper into Asia, Alexander turned south along the Phoenician coast, shrewdly recognizing the problem of the superior Persian fleet, which was reinforced by Phoenician vessels. He captured the great coastal cities of Sidon, Tyre, and finally Gaza, thus rendering the fleet useless without ever engaging it. The brilliant young strategist also perfected the art of siege warfare, improving on Philip's catapults and adding siege towers erected next to the defensive walls that allowed attackers to penetrate the fortresses. As the proud cities fell one by one, Alexander gained a reputation for brutal warfare but generosity to subject peoples. Subsequent cities surrendered quickly and joined the rapidly growing Macedonian Empire.

KEY DATES

POLITICAL EVENTS

359–336 B.C.E.	Philip II rules Macedonia
338 B.C.E.	Philip conquers Greece
337–323 B.C.E.	Alexander rules
333 B.C.E.	Battle of Issus
332 B.C.E.	Alexander conquers Egypt
331 B.C.E.	Battle of Gaugamela
330 B.C.E.	Alexander destroys Persepolis
323 B.C.E.	Successor kingdoms established
ca. 166–164 B.C.E.	Maccabean Revolt

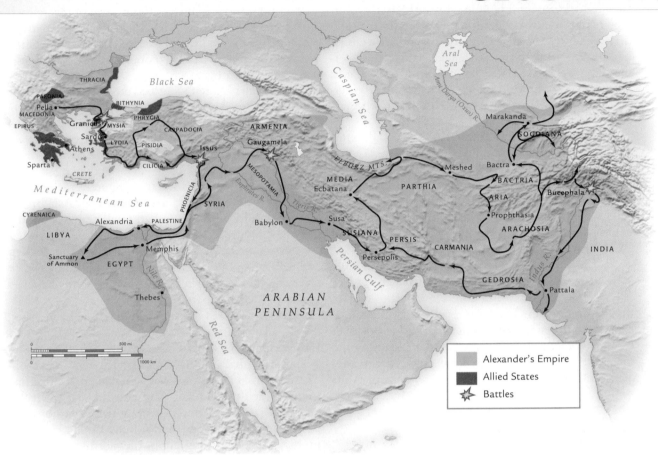

MAP 3.1

Alexander's Empire

This map shows the vast territory Alexander conquered, the route he took, and the major battle sites. Using the scale on the map, calculate the distance Alexander traveled. Consider the difficulties of supplying an army over this distance.

Explore the Map

1. Compare this map with **Map 1.5,** of the Persian Empire. What additional lands did Alexander conquer?

2. Based on the map and what you have learned from the text, what effects might Alexander's expansion have on the old Persian Empire?

3. What effects might his conquests have on Egypt?

After conquering Gaza, Alexander swept into Egypt virtually unopposed in 332 B.C.E. The Egyptian priests declared Alexander the incarnation of their god Amon, treating him as pharaoh. Now the god-king of Egypt, the young Macedonian founded a new city, Alexandria, on the Delta. This development brought Egypt more fully into Mediterranean economy and culture than it had ever been before, as the new northern, coastal capital encouraged trade and attracted colonists from elsewhere—a cosmopolitan center was founded in Egypt. With his western flank thus secured, Alexander once again headed for Asia to revive his pursuit of the Persian Great King, Darius.

After crossing the Euphrates and Tigris rivers, Alexander encountered Darius at Gaugamela in 331 B.C.E. The Persian ruler had fitted chariots with sharp scythes to cut down the Macedonian infantry, and his forces far outnumbered Alexander's army—by about 250,000 to 47,000 (although these figures are certainly exaggerated). Despite the Persian strength, Alexander's superior strategy vanquished the Persian warriors yet again. He forced the Persians to turn to confront his wheeling formation and thus opened fatal gaps in the long Persian line. His cavalry set upon the trapped Persian infantry. In the ensuing slaughter, a reputed 50,000 Persians died. Alexander entered Babylon and was welcomed as a liberator. He then turned southeast to Persepolis, the Persian capital. Despite fierce resistance, in 330 B.C.E. Alexander captured the city and plundered it ruthlessly, acquiring enough wealth to fund his future military ambitions. Then he burned it to the ground. Alexander never met Darius on the battlefield again, for the Persian king was assassinated by one of his own guards. After this, no one could doubt that the mighty Persian Empire had a new master—Alexander, who was crowned Great King.

Alexander thought of himself as a powerful, semidivine Greek hero; he claimed descent from Achilles through his mother and from Heracles (whom we remember by the Roman name Hercules) through his father. The shrewd conqueror was also a skilled propagandist, and his identification with ancient heroes helped consolidate his authority in the minds of Greeks raised on the stories of Homer. **Figure 3.1** shows a portion of a beautifully carved sarcophagus from the city of Sidon, on the Phoenician coast of the Mediterranean. The local royalty buried here had commissioned a scene of Alexander's victory over Darius to grace the side of the coffin, recognizing the moment that the Sidonian king changed his allegiance from Persia to Macedonia. Alexander sits

| The Greek hero |

astride a rearing horse at the left, while the defeated Persians fall before him. The conqueror wears a lion skin on his head, in a typical portrayal of Heracles. It is highly unlikely that Alexander fought in anything other than the traditional Macedonian armor, but the artistic license reveals the popular view of Alexander as a true Greek hero.

Alexander himself identified most strongly with the hero Achilles. According to Plutarch, Alexander slept with a copy of Homer's *Iliad*, edited by Aristotle, under his pillow and "esteemed it a perfect portable treasure of all military virtue and knowledge." Through Alexander, then, the heroic values of the Greek world endured and spread, and as Plutarch maintained, "thanks to Alexander, Homer was read in Asia. . . ."

The war against Persia had finally ended, but the young conqueror was still not satisfied. Having studied world geography as documented by the ancient Greeks, Alexander yearned to push his conquests to the edge of the known world. He mistakenly believed that this enticing frontier lay just beyond the Indus River in India. A last major battle against an Indian

| India |

king eliminated opposition in northern India, and Alexander made plans to press farther into the subcontinent. However, his Macedonian troops had had enough and refused to go on. Alexander wept in his tent for days at the mutiny of his beloved troops, but he finally conceded and turned back. However, instead of returning along the northern route, he led his troops south to explore the barren lands at the edge of the Arabian Sea (see **Map 3.1**). His exhausted, parched army finally reached the prosperous lands of Mesopotamia. Yet their relief was marred by an ironic tragedy: Alexander, seriously weakened by ever-growing alcohol abuse, caught a fever and died in Babylon in 323 B.C.E. He was just 32 years old. Others would have to rule the lands conquered by Alexander the Great.

A Young Ruler's Legacy

Was Plutarch right in thinking that Alexander wanted to make "all mankind a single people"? This ideal, which marked a radical departure from traditional Greek attitudes, has provoked intense historical debate virtually from the time of Alexander's life to the present. The Macedonian conqueror implemented several policies that some have interpreted as his desire to rule over a unified rather than a conquered people. One such policy, and certainly the most influential, was his founding of cities. In all his conquered territories, Alexander established an array of new cities. He intended these urban centers in part to recreate the Greek city life that he and his father had so admired. To this end, the conqueror helped settle numerous Greek and Macedonian

FIGURE 3.1 Alexander in Battle, fourth century B.C.E
This magnificent marble sarcophagus (burial casket) found in Sidon (present-day Lebanon) shows a victorious Alexander defeating the Persians at the Battle of Issus. Originally painted in brilliant colors, the coffin reveals the tremendous influence of classic Greek art.

DOCUMENT 3.1

Alexander Restores Greek Exiles

In 324 B.C.E., Alexander issued a proclamation that all Greek exiles should be allowed to return to their homes, even though many had been gone for generations. This policy pleased the exiles, but it also offended many residents who resented Alexander's high-handed interference in their affairs—in stark contrast to Philip's promise to give the Greeks a measure of autonomy. The Sicilian historian Diodorus describes the decree and its reception. Alexander died less than a year after this decree, and his successors rescinded it.

A short time before his death, Alexander decided to restore all the exiles in the Greek cities, partly for the sake of gaining fame and partly wishing to secure many devoted personal followers in each city to counter the revolutionary movements and seditions of the Greeks. Therefore, the Olympic games being at hand, he sent Nicanor of Strageira to Greece, giving him a decree about

the restoration, which he ordered him to have proclaimed by the victorious herald to the crowds at the festival. Nicanor carried out his instructions, and the herald received and read the following message: "King Alexander to the exiles from the Greek cities. We have not been the cause of your exile, but, save for those of you who are under a curse, we shall be the cause of your return to your own native cities. We have written to Antipater about this to the end that if any cities are not willing to restore you, he may constrain them." When the herald had announced this, the crowd showed its approval with loud applause; for those at the festival welcomed the favour of the king with cries of joy, and repaid his good deed with praises. All the exiles had come together at the festival, being more than twenty thousand in number.

Now people in general welcomed the restoration of the exiles as a good thing, but the Aetolians and the Athenians took offence at the action and were angry. The reason for this was that the Aetolians had exiled the Oeniadae from their native

city and expected the punishment appropriate to their wrongdoing; for the king himself had threatened that no sons of the Oeniadae, but he himself would punish them. Likewise, the Athenians who had distributed [the island of] Samos in allotments to their citizens, were by no means willing to abandon that island.

SOURCE: R.M. Greer, trans., *Diodorus of Sicily* 18.8, vol. 8 of Loeb Classical Library (Cambridge, MA: Harvard University Press, 1969).

Analyze the Document

1. Why was the problem of displaced Greeks so significant during this period? (Consider this in the light of Document 2.3.)

2. Why do you think Alexander made the announcement at the Olympic Games?

3. What were Alexander's motives according to Diodorus?

4. Who supported and opposed the decree?

5. Why do you think the decree was rescinded?

---

colonists in the new cities. Hundreds of thousands of Greeks emigrated to the newly claimed lands in Asia, taking privileged positions. We will see that as they introduced their culture into Asia, these colonists inevitably influenced and were changed by the subject peoples. These culturally rich cities rank among Alexander's most enduring legacies.

The movement of Greeks to cities far into Asia raised questions about exiles' continued ties with their cities of origin, and Alexander's royal power raised questions about the traditional autonomy of the Greek poleis. Document 3.1 reproduces an edict issued by Alexander near the end of his life that intended to address these lingering issues.

Meanwhile, in Asia, Alexander strongly supported the intermarriage of Greeks and Macedonians with Asians. He himself married the daughter of Darius and Roxane, the daughter of an Asian tribal king who ruled near modern-day Afghanistan. Alexander also presided over the weddings of hundreds of his generals to highborn Persian women. As Plutarch said, he "joined together the greatest and most powerful

peoples into one community by wedlock." Ten thousand more of Alexander's soldiers also married Asian women. Alexander might well have imagined that the offspring of these marriages would help seal the union of the two populations.

Finally, Alexander had a constant need for additional soldiers to support his campaigns, and he obtained these men from the conquered peoples. He accepted both Persian soldiers and commanders into his companies. Preparing for the future, he also chose about 30,000 Asian boys whom he slated to learn the Greek language and the Macedonian fighting style. These boys would become the next generation of soldiers to fight for the king in a combined army.

Alexander's cultural blending disturbed those upper-crust Greeks and Macedonians who saw themselves as conquerors rather than as equals among the subject peoples. Indeed, while in Persia, Alexander adopted Persian robes and courtly ceremonies, including having his subjects prostrate themselves on the ground in his presence. Without a doubt, this ritual helped Persians accept their new king—but it also

Intercultural marriages

Resentments

offended the proud Macedonians. Alexander's inclusion of Asians in the military elite only intensified Macedonian resentment. At one point, an outcry arose among Alexander's soldiers when the king apparently sought to replace some of them with Asians. Alexander squelched these objections decisively, executing 13 leaders and suggesting that the rest of them go home so that he could lead the Asian troops to victory. The Macedonians backed down, pleading for their king's forgiveness. Alexander resolved the incident with a lavish banquet of reconciliation, at which Asians and Macedonians drank together and Alexander prayed for harmony (sometimes mistranslated as "brotherhood") between them.

Alexander died too soon for historians to be certain of his exact plans for ruling his vast, multiethnic empire. For all we know, he might well have intended that Greeks and Macedonians would remain a ruling elite. The cities and colonies guaranteed a continued Greek presence, as did the invaders' weddings to local women. The conqueror's inclusive army might have been simply a practical means of ensuring a large enough force to fulfill his ambitions. Whatever his intentions, Alexander created a fertile combination by joining the cultures of the ancient Middle East and classical Greece.

Alexander's legacy included more than his political conquests—which in some regions hardly outlasted the young king himself. The memory of his accomplishments has endured in an embellished way far beyond even his most impressive victories. For example, Plutarch's interpretation

Alexander's memory

of Alexander's desire for a blending of peoples made this notion a foundational characteristic of Western culture, regardless of whether the king truly held this ideal. Moreover, a highly imaginative version of Alexander's accomplishments, titled *The Alexander Romance*, was translated into twenty-four languages and found its way from Iran to China to Malaysia. The idea of a great empire ruled by one king may have exerted an influence as far as the Han dynasty in China. It certainly shaped Mediterranean thinking, where would-be conquerors reverently visited Alexander's tomb in the spectacular Egyptian city of Alexandria that he founded.

THE SUCCESSOR KINGDOMS, 323–ca. 100 B.C.E.

Admirers across the world may have romanticized Alexander's supposed dream of a unified kingdom. In reality, however, brutal politics sullied the picture soon after the Great King's death. Legends preserve the probably false tale that as Alexander lay dying, he told his comrades that the kingdom should go "to the strongest." Even if Alexander never said this, the story reflects the reality of the violent fighting that broke out among the Macedonian generals shortly after the king died. Alexander's wife, Roxane, was pregnant when he succumbed, and presumably the empire should have gone to his infant son, Alexander IV. But within thirteen years of Alexander's death, both Roxane and her young son had been murdered. Moreover, the Macedonian generals had carved up the great empire into new, smaller kingdoms that became the successors to Alexander's conquests. **Map 3.2** shows the successor kingdoms.

Egypt Under the Ptolemies

Upon Alexander's death, one of his cavalry "companions," Ptolemy, moved toward Egypt with his own loyal troops to take control of that wealthy region. Ptolemy diverted the king's corpse, which was being returned to Macedonia for burial, and took it to Alexandria, where he erected an imposing tomb for Alexander. It seems that Ptolemy believed the presence of the conqueror's remains would help legitimize his own rule. Fending off attempts by Alexander's other generals to snatch the rich land of the Nile, Ptolemy and his successors ruled as the god-kings of Egypt for the next three hundred years.

The **Ptolemies** inherited a land with a long tradition of obedience to authority. Accordingly, the new kings wisely struck a bargain with the Egyptian priests, promising to fulfill the traditional duty of the pharaohs to care for the temples (and the priests) in exchange for protection of their legitimacy. Through most of their

Continuity of life

history, the Ptolemies lived in luxury in Alexandria, conducting official business in Greek while Egyptian peasants continued to obey the age-old dictates of the Nile, the priests, and the tax collectors. Life away from the court under the new order changed very little, which made it easier for the new dynasty to rule. The parallel practicing of both Egyptian and Greek ways continued throughout most of the Ptolemaic rule. In fact, the majority of these Greek kings rarely carried out traditional ritual functions, and some were probably not even formally crowned. For their part, the priests honored the Ptolemies while still governing in the traditional way.

However, in one significant way the Hellenistic rulers departed from their Egyptian predecessors—their queens took a more prominent role. Many of the Ptolemaic rulers engaged in brother-sister marriages as the ancient Egyptians had done, but many women were able to exert considerable power. Hellenistic

Hellenistic queens

queens derived much of their authority from controlling substantial wealth and spending it on public works (and on hiring large armies). The height of the

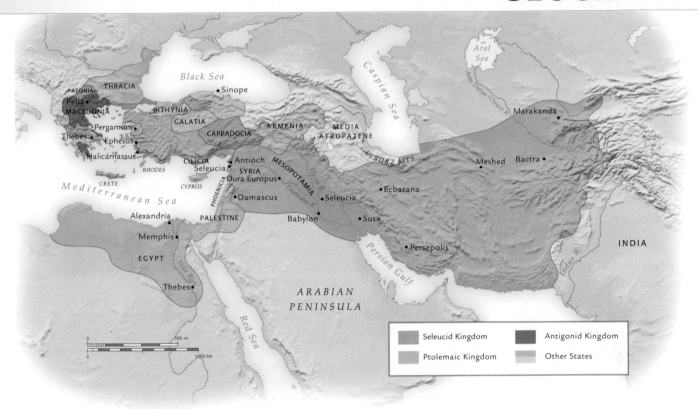

MAP 3.2

The Successor States After the Death of Alexander, ca. 240 B.C.E.

This map shows the breakup of Alexander's empire into three states and illustrates the relative sizes of the successor kingdoms.

Explore the Map

1. Based on your analysis of previous maps, as well as the information in the text, what were the historical and geographic reasons for the differing sizes of the successor kingdoms?

2. How might the movement of the Egyptian capital from Thebes to Alexandria have affected Egypt?

Hellenistic queens of Egypt came with the last one—Cleopatra VII—who challenged the growing power of Rome (discussed in Chapter 4).

Under the Ptolemies, the port city of Alexandria became the premier city of the Hellenistic world. It was a dynamic cosmopolitan city that by the end of the first century B.C.E. boasted almost one million inhabitants. Alexandria was a bustling port city where the main enterprise was the pursuit of wealth. The harbors were busy and the markets thronging, and international banks grew up to serve the people. To make sure ships could enter the port safely, Hellenistic scientists built a huge lighthouse on an island (Pharos) outside the harbor. The structure was 440 feet high, and the light from the lantern at the top was intensified by a system of reflectors. Ships approaching the harbor were guided by the beam of the lantern. This lighthouse came to be regarded as one of the seven wonders of the ancient world.

For all its commercial value, Alexandria under the Ptolemies also became an intellectual and cultural center. The rulers established a world-famous museum (the word *museum* means "temple to the muses," the Greek goddesses who served as inspiration to creativity). At the museum, scholars from around the Mediterranean and Asia gathered to study texts and discuss ideas. The Greek rulers founded a great library as part of this museum and ambitiously designed it to stand as the West's first complete collection of published works. Well established by 280 B.C.E., the library boasted more than 700,000 volumes just one century later, making it the largest collection the ancient world had seen.

BIOGRAPHY

Arsinoë II
(315–ca. 270 B.C.E.)

Brilliant

and Ruthless

Queen of

Egypt

The Hellenistic dynasties created by the successor states to Alexander's empire (see **Map 3.2**) set new precedents for the ancient world by bringing strong women to power. These queens of all three dynasties (Seleucid, Antigonid, and Ptolemaic) derived their power from two main things: their descent from the original founders of the dynasties and their great wealth.

Many of these women strongly influenced the great events of the day. The story of Arsinoë II, queen of Egypt, reveals the violent world of Hellenistic politics and shows the fierce will for power that both men and women leaders often needed to rule effectively.

Arsinoë was the daughter of the first Ptolemy, Alexander's successor who took over Egypt. Like most Hellenistic princesses, she was well educated and raised to rule. She was married at age 15 to the king of Thrace, Lysimachus, an old companion-in-arms of Ptolemy. Lysimachus renounced his first wife in favor of the young, and very beautiful, Arsinoë. By the time Arsinoë was 30, she had borne three sons and had begun to plan for their (and her) future. To position her sons to inherit the throne, she accused Lysimachus's son by his first wife of treason and perhaps had him poisoned.

Yet despite Arsinoë's plans, her family became ensnared in one of the seemingly endless Hellenistic wars of power. First, Seleucus marched from Asia to Thrace to conquer Lysimachus. Amid the combat, Arsinoë's husband (now almost 80 years old) died. Then as Arsinoë fled with her children to Greece, her half-brother Ceraunus seized control of her old realm. Ceraunus well understood the benefits of legitimacy that Arsinoë's bloodline could provide, and the advantages of her great wealth. He offered to marry her and make her children his heirs. She agreed, but he betrayed her, killing her two youngest children in order to secure the kingdom for his own progeny. She and her eldest son managed to escape to Egypt to seek the protection of her brother, Ptolemy II.

Safe in Egypt, Arsinoë moved to rebuild her power. Not content to be simply sister to the king, she had Ptolemy's wife exiled and married him herself to assure herself the title of queen. From then on, she and her brother were known as "sibling-lovers" (*philadelphus*). If we are to believe the poets of the period, the couple genuinely loved each other. One poet wrote, "No more splendid wife than she ever clasped in bridal chamber her bridegroom, loving him from her heart, her brother and her lord." Satisfied with her newly secured position as the head of Egypt's ruling family, Arsinoë ignored her husband's many mistresses, although purportedly she quickly killed any political rivals who tried to reduce her authority.

The sibling marriage not only gave Arsinoë the power she craved but also helped consolidate the power of the dynasty by bringing the Ptolemies closer to traditional Egyptian practices; sometimes Egyptian pharaohs had married their sisters. However, the Greek Macedonians decried the practice as incest and forbade it. In marrying each other, Arsinoë and Ptolemy reclaimed an older form of legitimacy that had shaped the Egyptian ruling families. Artistic portrayals of Queen Arsinoë depict this movement toward traditional Egyptian practices. **Figure 3.2a** shows her in the traditional Macedonian fashion, crowned only by the slim band that

---

Eventually, however, the Ptolemies encountered both internal and external pressure to change. Under the reign of Ptolemy V (r. ca. 205–ca. 183 B.C.E.), a boy not yet in his teens, priests began demanding that the young king be more involved in religious rituals. The boy-king's problems only worsened when sub-Saharan Nubians (see Global Connections, Chapter 1), detecting his weakness, clamored for their own pharaoh. In addition, the armies of Alexander's successor in Asia were threatening Egypt's borders. Pressured on all sides, Ptolemy offered concessions to the powerful priests in return for their support in rallying the Egyptians to his cause. The young ruler reduced taxes on the peasants and increased payments to the priests. In return for his cooperation, the priests brought Ptolemy to Memphis, the traditional capital of the pharaohs, where they placed the great double crown of Egypt—the sign of royalty—on his head. Finally, they ordered that Ptolemy V be worshiped in every Egyptian shrine. To make good on this policy, they demanded that scribes write all the accomplishments of Ptolemy V "on a slab of hard stone, in the writing of the words of god, the writing of documents and the letters of the Northerners, and set it up in all the temples. . . ."

Figure 3.3 shows the **Rosetta Stone,** the tablet that resulted from this decree, which was unearthed in 1799. Demonstrating the presence of both Greeks and Egyptians in the kingdom of the Ptolemies, | Rosetta Stone | the stone records Ptolemy's deeds in three written versions: the sacred hieroglyphics at the top, Egyptian cursive administrative script at the center, and Greek ("the letters of the Northerners") at the bottom.

FIGURE 3.2a Arsinoë

marked their rulers. **Figure 3.2b,** on the other hand, shows Arsinoë wearing the traditional headdress of the Egyptian rulers. The Macedonian queen had become an Egyptian one. During the next centuries, the Ptolemies in Egypt followed the precedent set by Arsinoë and Ptolemy. They preserved much of their Macedonian ways while adopting enough Egyptian traditions to let them rule the ancient country effectively. Historians have argued over how much political influence Arsinoë wielded. However, we should perhaps believe the ancient historian Memnon, when he wrote, "Arsinoë was one to get her own way."

FIGURE 3.2b Arsinoë

In addition, in a decree after her death, Ptolemy wrote that he followed the "policy of his ancestors and of his sister in his zeal for the freedom of the Greeks." Arsinoë's zeal for freedom stemmed more from her hostility to the Seleucid rulers (who had driven her from her lands in Thrace) than from any abstract ideals of independence. The queen wanted to be sure her Egyptian dynasty would be free from intrusion from the successors of Alexander coming from the north, so she even traveled to the front to survey the defenses. Furthermore, she and Ptolemy knew that their safety in Egypt would hinge on sea power,

so they expanded the Egyptian fleet significantly.

Even while securing the independence of Egypt, the Ptolemies did not forget the Greek love of learning that marked all the successor kingdoms. As their greatest accomplishment, they constructed an immense library in Alexandria, which served as the center of learning in the Mediterranean world for almost the next thousand years.

Egyptian priests followed Ptolemy's lead in worshiping Arsinoë as a goddess, and following her death in about 270 B.C.E., Ptolemy issued edicts and built shrines to stimulate her cult. Poets described Arsinoë as a special patron of sailors, claiming, "She will give fair voyages and will smooth the sea even in midwinter in answer to prayer." The veneration of Queen Arsinoë by Egyptians and Greeks alike ensured that the cultural blending that emerged during her lifetime continued long after her death.

Connecting People & Society

1. How did the reign of Arsinoë II contribute to the blending of Greek and Egyptian culture that marked the Ptolemaic dynasty?

2. How do the portrayals of the queen in art reflect the transformation of the Macedonian kingship?

In the hieroglyphic section the king's name is enclosed in circles, which supposedly protected his name and, because the names of pharaohs had always been so encircled, also signaled to all who saw it that Ptolemy was indeed the rightful god-king. Equally significant, the Rosetta Stone provided the key that finally let nineteenth-century scholars decipher hieroglyphic writing. Without the stone, the meaning embedded in the great carvings of the ancient Egyptians might still remain a mystery.

The Seleucids Rule Asia

In the violent political jockeying that broke out after the death of Alexander, one of Ptolemy's lieutenants, Seleucus, entered Babylon in 311 B.C.E. and captured the imperial treasure there. With this money,

Seleucus laid claim to the old heartland of the Persian Empire. Yet the extensive eastern lands that Alexander had conquered eluded his grasp. As early as 310 B.C.E. Seleucus gave northwest India back to its native rulers in return for five hundred war elephants, and by the third century B.C.E., eastern Asia Minor had fallen away. Nevertheless, Seleucus founded a long-standing kingdom that continued the Hellenizing process begun by Alexander.

Like Alexander, the **Seleucids** founded cities and populated them with imported Greek and Macedonian bureaucrats and colonists. Seleucia, about fifty miles north of Babylon, was established as the new | Commercial cities capital of the kingdom, and Dura Europus, near the midpoint of the Euphrates River, was another important center. Their locations reveal that the Seleucid

FIGURE 3.3 Rosetta Stone, 197 B.C.E. Greek-speaking Macedonian rulers had to communicate with Egyptians. Fortunately, the Macedonians wrote an edict in Greek and translated it into two Egyptian scripts on this famous stone. This translation provided the key to scholars' ability to read Egyptian hieroglyphs.

were exempt from paying taxes and even received free food until their first crops could be harvested. These colonists did not expect to work the land themselves; instead, resident dependent laborers farmed the land for their foreign conquerors. Again, as in Egypt, the resident peasantry served their Greek-speaking masters. Not surprisingly, the Seleucid kings gained a loyal following among the elite with these allocations of land.

Although Greek sovereignty faded quickly in the easternmost edges of the Seleucid lands, evidence remains of the impact of the Greek presence there. To illustrate, consider the great king of northern India Aśoka (r. ca. 268–ca. 233 B.C.E.). Aśoka is perhaps most remembered for spreading the ideals of Buddhism through inscriptions on stones. Like the Rosetta Stone, these Rock Edicts testify to the Hellenic presence in India, because Aśoka's sayings were preserved both in the Indian language of Prakrit and in Greek. In wise phrases such as "Let them neither praise themselves nor disparage their neighbors, for that is vain," the ideas of Buddhism met the language of Hellenism in the farthest lands of Alexander.

Antigonids in Greece

The Seleucid kings concentrated on ruling the western portions of their Asian provinces, ever watchful for opportunities to gain advantage over the Ptolemies or the Macedonian leaders who now ruled in Macedonia and Greece. These kings, known as the **Antigonids,** were descended from Antigonus the One-Eyed (382–ca. 301 B.C.E.), a general who had joined in the struggle for succession after Alexander's death. Antigonus failed to score a decisive military victory, however, and died on the battlefield at the venerable age of 80, still trying to win control of the entire Macedonian Empire. Nevertheless, his descendants eventually took power in Macedonia and Greece and introduced the Antigonid dynasty.

In the short run, Alexander's conquests profoundly affected Macedonian society and economy. At first, wealth poured from the east into the young | Life in Macedonia king's homeland. Indeed, near the end of his life, Alexander sent home one shipment of booty that proved so large that 110 warships were needed to escort the merchant vessels on their return journey. Numismatic evidence also confirms the volume of wealth that initially flowed into Macedonia, for its mint churned out about 13 million silver coins immediately after Alexander's reign. Much of this coinage came into wide circulation, for officials used it to pay troops and provide stipends for veterans' widows and orphans. Yet the money did not profoundly alter Macedonian society. By the reign of Antigonus's

kings recognized the crucial role of eastern trade in the prosperity of their kingdom. These cities controlled the trade routes through the Tigris-Euphrates valley and the caravan trails that crossed the desert from Damascus and, along with Antioch, became vital political and economic centers within the former Persian lands (see **Map 3.2**).

While the Ptolemies could depend on an established Egyptian priesthood to facilitate their control of their kingdom, the Seleucids had | Seleucid colonists | no such ready-made institution. Instead, they relied in part on Macedonian and Greek colonists to secure their hold on their Asian lands. After Alexander's death, the Seleucids settled at least 20,000 Macedonian colonists in Syria and Asia Minor. This number was supplemented by others from Macedonia who came looking for riches and privileges.

The Macedonian settlers viewed themselves as world conquerors and expected to maintain their high-status positions in the new lands. The Seleucid kings, who saw the colonists as the backbone of their armies, granted them considerable farmlands. Some charters from this time show that certain colonists great-grandson, Demetrius II (r. 239–229 B.C.E.), life in Macedonia had changed little from even as far back as Philip II's time. The army still consisted mainly of Macedonian nobles, who fought as companions to their king. Invaders from the north still threatened; indeed, in the 280s B.C.E. the Gauls, a tribe on the Macedonians' northern border, launched an attack that cost Macedonia dearly. To make matters worse, the Greeks to the south, who had never really accepted Macedonian rule, kept revolting.

The Greek city-states experienced more change than Macedonia did, for the traditional democracy of Athens and the other poleis had

Changes in Greece evaporated. The poleis relaxed their notions of citizenship, so many immigrants and freed slaves became citizens, but at the same time people had less attachment to their cities. Many jobs—from soldier to athlete—became the province of specialists, not citizens, and thus international professionals replaced the native competitors who brought glory and wealth to their cities. Furthermore, the new economy of the Hellenistic world widened the gulf between rich and poor, and the disparity undermined participatory government: Rich Greeks took over governance and frequently forgot that they had any responsibility to the poor.

Despite these tensions, outright revolution never materialized. The relentless warfare plaguing the poleis simply proved too distracting. In addition, Greeks from all walks of life continued emigrating to the other Hellenistic kingdoms in search of a better life, and this exodus helped ease population pressures at home. Bureaucrats and scientists headed for the Greek colonies to take advantage of the tempting opportunities there—for example, a talented mathematician, Apollonius, first worked in Alexandria, Egypt, and then was lured to the Seleucid kingdom in the east. The poleis, which in the old days had claimed people's loyalty, had given way to cosmopolitan cities. Now individuals sought to enhance their own fortunes in a wider world.

EAST MEETS WEST IN THE SUCCESSOR KINGDOMS

The vast breadth of the Hellenistic kingdoms stimulated the West's economy to new heights. Trade rhythms quickened, and merchants raked in unprecedented wealth. Under Alexander and his successors in the various kingdoms, Greek became the universal language of business. Now traders could exchange goods across large distances without confronting confusing language barriers. The Greeks also advanced credit, a business practice that let merchants ply their trade without having to transport unwieldy quantities of hard currency.

FIGURE 3.4 Hellenistic Coins Standardized currency facilitated trade among all the Hellenistic kingdoms and serves as fine historical evidence. Coin (a) is an eight-drachma coin of Ptolemy II of Egypt (r. ca. 284–ca. 247 B.C.E.). Coin (b) is a silver coin of King Orophernes (2nd century B.C.E.) from Cappadocia in the Seleucid kingdom.

Money in the New Cosmopolitan Economies

The Hellenistic kings standardized currency as well, another boon for trade. There were two weights of coins in the Hellenistic world: One was based on Alexander's standard, **Coinage and trade** in which one drachma contained 4.3 grams of silver. The Ptolemies in Egypt abided by a different standard, using only 3.5 grams of silver in the drachma. Despite the dual standards, the consistency of both helped merchants buy and sell with ease throughout the extensive region. **Figure 3.4** shows two coins from this era. The gold coin from Egypt in **Figure 3.4a** is worth eight drachmas. It shows Ptolemy II with his wife Arsinoë II (featured in the Biography) on the front and Ptolemy's parents, Ptolemy I and Berenice, on the reverse. By showing two generations of royalty, the coin is proclaiming a dynastic succession that was traditionally important in Egypt. The silver coin in **Figure 3.4b** is a "tetradrachma," from Cappadocia in Asia Minor (modern Turkey). It shows King Orophernes, with the Greek goddess Athena on the reverse. These coins show that the Hellenistic kingdoms had much in common. Both coins show the monarchs in the style of Macedonian rulers, wearing the simple diadem that since Philip II's time had marked Macedonian kingship, and both are based on the drachma. They also graphically represent both the wealth that the Macedonian conquests generated and the spread of Greek cultural influence throughout the region as trade intensified.

Goods moved briskly through the Hellenistic kingdoms, reshaping old patterns of trade and consumption. Athens initially benefited from the widespread demand for Greek goods like pottery and weapons, but a century after the death of Alexander, Alexandria had replaced Athens as the commercial capital of the eastern Mediterranean. The small islands of Rhodes and Delos also rose to prominence because of their advantageous locations along the routes that connected the north and southeast areas of the Mediterranean with Greece and Italy.

Heightened trade led to new approaches to agriculture as people rushed to develop and sell novel delicacies. As one example, Greek farmers began planting their precious olive trees and grapevines in the eastern kingdoms, permanently altering the ecosystems in those regions. In turn, eastern spices transformed cooking on the Greek mainland and in Egypt. Agricultural crossbreeding also became common, though it failed in some cases—even seeds imported from Rhodes to cross with Egypt's bitter cabbage could not sweeten that pungent vegetable of the Nile valley.

While commerce made countless merchants rich, the individual kingdoms also benefited—mainly by taking control of economic activity. In Egypt, where pharaohs traditionally controlled much trade and industry—a system called a command economy—the Ptolemies increased their controls to funnel the riches of the Nile valley into the royal treasury. They converted the most successful industries into royal monopolies, controlling such essentials as sesame oil, salt, perfumes, and incense. Their most successful venture, however, was the beer industry, which had been a royal monopoly since the Old Kingdom. The Ptolemies insisted that the millions of gallons of beer consumed each year in Egypt be manufactured in the royal breweries, though many women doubtless continued to brew the beverage for household consumption as they had always done.

Command economies

Kings also levied taxes on imports and exports, such as grain, papyrus, cosmetics, timber, metals, and horses. These policies required a complex administrative system, which in turn led to the proliferation of Greek-speaking bureaucrats. Equally important, the kings used their new riches not only to live lavishly, but also to fund the expensive wars that ravaged the Hellenistic world.

Armies of the Hellenistic World

One of the most famous statues of the Hellenistic world, shown in **Figure 3.5**, is the Nike of Samothrace—called Winged Victory because Nike was the Greek goddess of victory—and it is a perfect

FIGURE 3.5 Statue of Nike (Winged Victory), ca. 190 B.C.E. This 8-foot-tall marble sculpture shows the goddess Nike descending through the wind to celebrate a victory at sea. The blowing draperies mark the Hellenistic style of flowing movement.

symbol of the war-dominated Hellenistic age. Originally part of a sculptural group that included a war galley, Nike strides confidently into the wind, certain of victory. However, the battles of the Hellenistic world seemed to bring endless suffering more often than clear victory.

The Macedonian kings thought of themselves as conquerors and derived their legitimacy in large part from their military successes. Like Alexander, whom they strove to emulate, these monarchs fully expected to participate in the hardships of battle and the dangers of combat. Consequently, they regularly made war on one another in hopes of gaining land or power. The ideal of conquest thus persisted after Alexander's death. However, the scale of warfare had broadened.

This broadening occurred partly because of the larger territories in dispute. Some boundaries now far surpassed the dimensions of the earlier Greek poleis. To cover these daunting distances, monarchs accumulated vast armies. Philip had conquered Greece with a force of about 30,000 men, and Alexander had increased the

Mercenary armies

numbers significantly as he moved east. Alexander's force in India may have exceeded 100,000—exceptional for ancient armies. The Hellenistic kings, however, regularly fielded armies of between 60,000 and 80,000 troops. These large armies consisted no longer primarily of citizen-soldiers but of mercenaries—who were loyal only to their paymaster and who switched sides with impunity. Tellingly, Hellenistic theater often featured mercenary soldiers who returned home with lots of money to spend and a newly cynical outlook.

The Macedonian armies were also influenced by their contact with the far eastern provinces. For example, in these distant lands they encountered war elephants for the first time. Just as horses had offered mounted warriors advantages of | War elephants | mobility and reach over foot soldiers, soldiers mounted on elephants had an even greater military advantage. Furthermore, elephants participated in the fray, trampling men and using their trunks as weapons. As mentioned previously, the earliest Seleucids had exchanged territory in India for the prized elephants, and these formidable animals eventually became part of the Hellenistic armory. The Seleucids tried to breed elephants in Syria but had to keep trading with India for more elephants when their efforts failed. To retain their advantage, the Seleucid kings cut off the Ptolemies' trade in Asian elephants, forcing the Egyptians to rely on the smaller, less effective African breed. The Greek historian Polybius (ca. 200–ca. 118 B.C.E.) described a confrontation between the two classes of pachyderms: The African elephants, "unable to stand the smell and trumpeting of the Indian elephants and terrified, I suppose, also by their great size and strength, . . . at once turn tail and take to flight." As impressive as the Asian elephants were, foot soldiers learned to dodge the beasts and stab or hamstring them. However, the massive animals remained a valuable tool for moving heavy siege engines to walled cities and attacking fortified positions.

Large, wealthy, and well-equipped armies now routinely toppled defensive walls, and kings followed Alexander's ruthless model of wiping out any city that showed even a hint of defiance. Mercenaries, too, cared little for civilians, and historical sources describe soldiers drunkenly looting private homes after a conquest. The countryside also suffered from the warfare, and peasants repeatedly petitioned kings to ease their burdens. Peasants faced increased taxes levied to fund expensive wars and then frequently confronted violence from marauding mercenaries. To an unprecedented level, civilians became casualties in wars waged between kings.

The incessant warfare also changed the nature of slavery in the Greek world. As we have seen, during the classical Greek period—as throughout the ancient world—slavery was taken for granted. Every household had one or two domestic slaves, and most manufacturing and | Slavery | other labor was done by slaves. Alexander's immediate successors generally avoided mass enslavement of prisoners, but traditionally it was customary to enslave losers in battle. Therefore, by the late third century B.C.E., prisoners began to be enslaved in huge numbers. This changed the scale of the institution of slavery and, ultimately, the treatment of the slaves themselves. By 167 B.C.E., the island of Delos in the Aegean Sea housed a huge slave market. Claiming that 10,000 slaves could arrive and be sold in a day on Delos, the Greek historian Strabo quoted a contemporary saying about the slave markets that suggested how quickly the slave-traders sold their human cargo: "Merchant, put in, unload—all's sold." Although these large numbers are surely an exaggeration, they testify to the huge increase in numbers of slaves that began to be moved around the eastern Mediterranean. Wealthy households now could have hundreds of slaves, and others worked in gangs in agriculture and mining. This new scale of slavery further dehumanized those who had been taken, and slaves joined civilians as a population suffering under the new kingdoms.

A True Cultural Blending?

Whether or not Alexander had envisioned a complete uniting of east and west, in reality a full blending of peoples never occurred in the lands he conquered. The Hellenistic kingdoms in Egypt and Asia consisted of local native populations ruled by a Greek/Macedonian elite who made up less than 10 percent of the population. However, this elite was not limited to people of direct Macedonian descent; it also included those who acquired Greek language and culture through formal or informal education. Alexander's conquests opened opportunities for people from many ethnic backgrounds to join the elite—a development that inevitably transfigured Greek culture itself.

The intermingling of East and West intensified with the movement of travelers, which the common use of the Greek language and the size of the kingdoms facilitated. Travelers included merchants and mercenaries and diplomats seeking political and economic advantages | Travelers | or opportunities to spy. Perhaps most instrumental in blending cultures were the artists and artisans who journeyed widely in search of patrons and prizes.

In this new, cosmopolitan world, even women traveled with a freedom unheard of in the classical Greek poleis. Female musicians, writers, and artists embarked on quests for honors and literary awards. One inscription on a commemorative stone recalls

"Aristodama, daughter of Amyntas of Smyrna, an epic poetess, who came to the city and gave several readings of her own poems." The citizens were so pleased with this poet's work that they granted her citizenship. During such readings, authors shared experiences from one part of the world with the people of another, enhancing the diversity that marked this vibrant time.

Such diversity showed up vividly in the art of the period. For example, classical Greek artists had sometimes depicted black Africans in their works. In the Hellenistic age such portrayals grew more frequent. **Figure 3.6** exemplifies the cultural blending that occurred in the visual arts of this period. This bronze figure was cast in the Greek style, yet | Diverse art | it shows a youth from sub-Saharan Africa, possibly Nubia, which partook in continued close interaction with Egypt (discussed in Global Connections in Chapter 1). The subject's pose suggests that he may have once held a lyre, a traditional Greek (not African) musical instrument. The young man might well have been a slave, given that the Hellenistic kingdoms traded heavily in slaves of all ethnic backgrounds. Or he might have been one of the many traveling performers who earned a living by entertaining newly wealthy, cosmopolitan audiences.

All travelers left some evidence of their visits in the farthest reaches of the Hellenistic world. In the third century B.C.E., for example, the Greek philosopher Clearchus discovered a Greek-style city, complete with a gymnasium at the center, on the northern frontier of modern Afghanistan. In the gymnasium, Clearchus erected a column inscribed with 140 moral maxims taken from a similar pillar near the shrine of Apollo at Delphi. Like the Rock Edicts of Aśoka, the pillar of Clearchus preserves in stone the mingling of ideas at the fringes of the Hellenistic world.

Struggles and Successes: Life in the Cosmopolitan Cities

The new cities founded by Alexander and his successors were in many ways artificial structures—they did not grow up in response to local manufacturing or commercial needs. Instead, they were simply created by rulers as showcases of their wealth and power. Expensive to maintain, these cities burdened local peasants with extra taxes and produced little wealth of their own. However, they played a crucial role as cultural and administrative centers, and they became a distinctive feature of Hellenistic life. Modeled on the Greek city-states, these cities still differed markedly from the poleis in several important ways, including the opportunities for women.

The travelers and the diversity of the cities helped break down the tight family life and female seclusion

FIGURE 3.6 African Musician, second century B.C.E. The Hellenistic kingdoms were characterized by a movement of peoples and a resulting cultural blending, exemplified by this African musician playing a Greek musical instrument.

that had marked traditional Greek cities. Women were more free to move about in public. Furthermore, many texts indicate that Hellenistic women had more independence of | Women | action than their Greek counterparts. For example, a marriage contract explicitly insists that a couple will make joint decisions: "We shall live together in whatever place seems best to Leptines and Heraclides, deciding together." These new opportunities for independence made possible the situation at the opening of this chapter, when the young working woman ran off with her lover.

The Hellenistic cities also differed from their Greek counterparts in that they owed allegiance to larger political entities, the kingdoms. Now Greek monarchies had | Cities and kings |

DOCUMENT 3.2

Cities Celebrate Professional Women

Throughout the Hellenistic age, there is evidence of women whose public service brought them to the attention of their communities. The following three inscriptions commemorate women who served as a physician, a public official, and a musician. Notice that the inscription for the public official indicates that she was the first woman to serve, so this reflects a change from previous practice.

1. Physician and Midwife: Phanostrate of Athens, fourth century [B.C.E.] Funeral inscription

Phanostrate . . . , the wife of Melitos, midwife and doctor, lies here. In life she caused no one pain, in death she is regretted by all.

2. Public Servant: Phile of Priene, first century [B.C.E.] Public inscription

Phile daughter of Apollonius and wife of Thessalus, the son of Polydectes, having held the office of stephanephoros, the first woman [to do so], constructed at her own expense the reservoir for water and the city aqueduct.

3. Harpist: Polygnota of Thebes, Delphi, 86 [B.C.E.] Public inscription

Since Polygnota, daughter of Sokrates, a harpist from Thebes, was staying at Delphi at the time the Pythian games were to be held, but because of the present war, the games were not held, on that same day she performed without charge and contributed her services for the day; and having been asked by the magistrates and the citizens, she played for three days and earned great distinction in a manner worthy of the god and of the Theban people and of our city, and we rewarded her also with five hundred drachmas; with good fortune, the city shall praise Polygnota, daughter of Sokrates, a Theban for her reverent attitude toward the god and her piety and her conduct with regard to her manner of life and art; and there shall be given by our city to her and to her descendants the status of a proxenos, priority in consulting the oracle, priority of trial, inviolability, exemption from taxes, a front seat at the contests which the city holds, and the right to own land and a house. . . .

SOURCES:

1. *Inscriptiones Graecae* 2.3(2), 6873, in *The Ancient World: Readings in Social and Cultural History*, ed. D. Brendan Nagle (Englewood Cliffs, NJ: Prentice Hall, 1995), p. 174.

2. *Die Inschriften von Priene*, 208, in *Women in the Classical World*, ed. Elaine Fantham et al. (New York: Oxford University Press, 1994), p. 156.

3. *Sylloge Inscriptionum Graecarum* (3) 738, in ed. D. Brendan Nagle, p. 174.

Analyze the Document

1. What are the contributions of each woman, and how do their communities recognize their contributions (money, acclaim, and so on)?

2. What evidence do you see for the continued importance of families in the Hellenistic world?

3. What aspects of Hellenistic cities allow women to become prominent?

---

replaced Greek city-states as the influential political form in the developing history of the West. The relationship between the Hellenistic kings and the new cities derived from both Macedonian and Greek traditions. For example, during and after Alexander's reign, monarchs advocated democracy within the cities they founded. Cities were governed by magistrates and councils, and popular assemblies handled internal affairs. In return, the kings demanded tribute and special taxes during times of war. However, these taxes were not onerous, and a king might even exempt a city from taxation. In response, many cities introduced a civic religious cult honoring their kings. As one example, to show this dual allegiance to both their king and city, citizens of the city of Cos had to swear the following oath: "I will abide by the established democracy . . . and the ancestral laws of Cos, . . . and I will also abide by the friendship and alliance with King Ptolemy."

These cities flourished under the patronage of their kings, but they also struggled with all the problems endemic in any urban area. To feed the townspeople, city officials often

Urban problems

had to import supplies from distant sources. Following Hellenistic ideas of a command economy, these urban leaders set grain prices and sometimes subsidized food to keep the costs manageable. They also regulated millers and bakers to prevent them from making large profits from cheap grain. Finally, the cities suffered the unavoidable problems of what to do about sewerage and water drainage; the largest urban centers had drainpipes under the streets for these purposes. Gangs of slaves owned by the city maintained the drainage system and cleared the streets.

City leaders gave little attention to public safety. They hired a few night watchmen to guard some public spaces, but for the most part, they considered safety a personal matter. Consequently, people mingling in the crowded markets or venturing out at night were often victims of robberies, or worse. Danger lurked everywhere, but especially in the many fires that broke out from residents' use of open flames to cook and heat their wooden homes. Despite the perils of fire, crime, and lack of sanitation, however, cities still offered the best hope of success for enterprising people.

The greatest of the new cities—Alexandria, Antioch, Seleucia—drew people from around the world. No longer connected to the original Greek city-states, such newcomers felt little obligation to participate in democratic politics or to profess loyalty to a clan or polis. Greeks, Phoenicians, Jews, Babylonians, Arabs, and others gathered in the cosmopolitan centers to make their fortunes. As the most ambitious among them took Greek names, the old divisions between Greek and "barbarian" blurred. Traditional family ties dissolved, too, as we saw in the story that opened this chapter.

City dwellers improved their lot in several ways, some of them advancing through successful military activities. The Greek Scopas, for example, unable to find work in his home city, "turned **New opportunities** his hopes toward Alexandria," where he got a job in the army. Within three years, Scopas had risen to command the armies of Ptolemy V. Women, too, had opportunities to participate in the public sphere. Document 3.2 offers examples of women who were remembered for their contributions to their cities.

Though cities opened up new opportunities, they also spawned miseries. Many poor people were forced to continue working well into their old age; indeed, the elderly market woman shown at the beginning of the chapter would have been a common sight in the Hellenistic period. The father in the chapter's opening story looked to his king to spare him an impoverished old age. His pleas probably went unheard, however; cities and their royal patrons tended to ignore the mounting problems of poverty. Slums cropped up, becoming just as characteristic of Hellenistic cities as the palaces of the wealthy and the libraries of the wise.

In some cities, destitute people designed institutions to help themselves. Artisans' guilds, for example, offered a sense of social connection to people bewildered by the large, anonymous cosmopolitan cities. Some people organized burial clubs, in which members contributed money to ensure themselves a decent interment at the end of lives that had little material security. Historical evidence suggests that some rich city dwellers worried about the possibility of social revolution. As one illustration of this fear, the citizens of a city in Crete were required to include the following statement in their oath of citizenship: "I will not initiate a redistribution of land or of houses or a cancellation of debts."

Patronage, Planning, and Passion: Hellenistic Art

The monarchs who were becoming fabulously wealthy did not spend much money on the urban poor. What did they do with the mounds of coins that filled their coffers? In part, they spent fortunes as patrons of the arts, commissioning magnificent pieces that continue to be treasured today. However, not all critics have admired the products of the Hellenistic artists. For example, early in the first century C.E., the prolific Roman commentator Pliny the Elder (23–79 C.E.) energetically discussed Greek art. A passionate admirer of classical Athenian art, Pliny claimed that after the accomplishments of Lysippus (ca. 380–ca. 318 B.C.E.), "art stopped." His dismissal of the Hellenistic world's artistic contributions has since been shared by many observers who admire the idealized poses of classical Greek works. But art did not stop with Lysippus; it merely changed as its center migrated from Athens to the great cosmopolitan centers of the East.

Classical Greek artists had been supported by public funding by democratic poleis. By contrast, Hellenistic artists received their funding from wealthy kings seeking to build **Royal patrons** and decorate their new cities. Royal patronage began with monarchs who wanted their newly established cities to reflect the highest ideals of Greek aesthetics. At the same time, this policy served the political agenda of promoting Greek culture. These rulers hired architects to design cities conducive to traditional Greek life, with its outdoor markets and meeting places, and employed artists to decorate the public spaces. Pergamum (see **Map 3.2**) posed a special challenge to architects: Its center was perched on a high hill, so city planners had to take the steep slopes into account in designing the city. In the end, they arranged the royal palaces at the top of the hill—visibly proclaiming the king's ascendancy—and the markets at the bottom. The layout of this magnificent city is typical of many Hellenistic urban centers.

Citizens in Pergamum shopped in the colonnaded building shown at the lower left corner of **Figure 3.7**. Higher up the hill was an altar to Zeus and higher still, a temple to Athena that served as the entrance to the library. The heights were dominated by the royal palaces and barracks. (The temple shown at the center of the hilltop was built later by Roman conquerors.) On the left side of the model, there are theater seats built into the hillside, where some 10,000 spectators could gather to watch the latest dramatic productions. The city preserved the gracious outdoor life of the classical Greek cities, yet was dominated by the majesty and power of the new kings.

After cities were designed, kings commissioned sculptors to decorate the great public buildings, especially temples. Throughout the Hellenistic period, sculptors also found a **Sculpture** market in the newly wealthy, who hired these artists to create works of beauty to decorate their homes. Hellenistic sculpture built on classical models in the skill with which artists depicted the human form and in the themes that harked back to the age of Greek heroes and the Trojan War. Still, Hellenistic artists departed from the classical style in significant ways. Classical Greek sculptors sought to portray the ideal—that is, they depicted scenes and subjects that were above the tumult and passion of this world. By contrast, Hellenistic artists faced passion and emotion head-on. Their works exhibit a striking expressiveness, violence, and sense of movement, along with contorted poses that demonstrate these artists' talents for capturing human emotion in marble.

Hellenistic artists also portrayed themes that the classical artists in Athens would have considered undignified or even demeaning. These themes included realistic portrayals of everyday life. For example, classical artists, in their search for ideal beauty instead of imperfect reality, would have ignored subjects such as the market woman shown at the beginning of the chapter. The boxer in **Figure 3.8** also exemplifies the contrast to the Olympic heroism that we saw in Chapter 2. Here the artist shows his knowledge of Greek idealism in the perfectly crafted hair and musculature of the bronze figure. Yet this boxer is tired, not heroic. He rests his taped hands on his knees and his shoulders sag in exhaustion, or perhaps defeat. The marks of his contest show clearly on his face—his cheek bleeds, his nose is broken, and his ear is deformed from too many blows. Many art critics, like Pliny, who mourned the "death of art," have condemned Hellenistic artists for not striving to portray perfection. Nonetheless, they had remarkable courage in showing the flawed reality of cosmopolitan life.

Resistance to Hellenism: Judaism, 323–76 B.C.E.

Much of Hellenistic art and life in the cosmopolitan cities reflected a deep and, in many ways, successful blending of classical Greek culture with that of the ancient Middle East and Egypt. Yet Alexander's desire to make "all mankind a single people" did not appeal to everyone in the Hellenistic world. Throughout their history, Jews had worked to preserve their distinctive identity, and this desire came directly into conflict with spreading Hellenism (ancient Greek culture). Although Judea remained an independent political unit under Alexander and the Ptolemies, the successor kingdoms offered opportunities for Jews from Palestine to trade and settle throughout the Hellenistic world. In the new multiethnic areas, urban Jews struggled to clarify and sustain their sense of identity. The most pious among them lived together in Jewish quarters where they could observe the old laws and maintain a sense of separate community. Alexandria and Antioch had substantial Jewish quarters, and most large cities had a strong Jewish presence.

Some Jews compromised with Hellenism, learning Greek and taking advantage of the opportunities available to those | **Hellenized Jews** who at least had the appearance of Hellenism. As they learned to speak and write in Greek and studied the classical texts, some of their

FIGURE 3.7 Restored Model of Pergamum Hellenistic rulers built great new cities such as Pergamum in what today is the country of Turkey. The city spread over a high hill, from the royal palace at the top to markets at the bottom. A new style of life developed in the royal cities.

FIGURE 3.8 Seated Boxer, second century B.C.E. This bronze sculpture reveals much about the Hellenistic world. Hellenistic peoples still praised the Greek sports contests, but they recognized and documented emotions other than the joy of victory. This boxer, for example, appears to be dejected, tired, and bruised.

them that God would exact vengeance for their impiety. In an ironic twist, his text was translated into Greek by his grandson.

These uncertainties within the Jewish community came to a head when the Seleucid kings wrested Palestine from the Ptolemies in 200 B.C.E. The pace of Hellenization quickened after this pivotal event. Both Jewish and pagan historical sources claim that the Seleucid king Antiochus IV (r. 175–163 B.C.E.) intended to change Jewish observance in order to "combine the peoples"—that is, to Hellenize the Jews. According to an early Jewish text, even the high priest of Jerusalem supported the king and "exercised his influence in order to bring over his fellow-countrymen to the Greek ways of life." Antiochus established Greek schools in Jerusalem and went so far as to enter Jewish contestants in the Greek-style athletic games celebrated at Tyre. In 168 B.C.E., he ordered an altar to Zeus to be erected in the Temple of Jerusalem and sacrifices to be offered to the Greek god. The Roman historian Josephus (75 C.E.) later described the sacrilege: "He sacrificed swine upon the altars and bespattered the temple with their grease, thus perverting the rites of the Jews and the piety of their fathers."

Antiochus's policies proved too much for pious Jews, and in ca. 166 B.C.E., Judas Maccabeus (Judas the Hammer) led an armed revolt against the Seleucids. (See Document 3.3.) The account of the **Maccabean Revolt** is preserved in a text titled *The First Book of the Maccabees*, probably written in 140 B.C.E. by a Jew in Judea. The author articulated the goal of Antiochus clearly: "Then the king wrote to his whole kingdom that all should be one people, and that each should give up his customs." This decree of Antiochus is reminiscent of Plutarch's praise of Alexander quoted at the beginning of this chapter, and it confirms the differing, intensely felt opinions that people often have about cultural blending.

> Maccabean Revolt

In the end, the Maccabeans prevailed. In 164 B.C.E. the Jewish priests rededicated the Temple, and the Jews celebrated the restoration of their separate identity. The historian of *First Maccabees* wrote that "Judas and his brothers and all the assembly of Israel determined that every year at that season the days of the dedication of the altar should be observed with gladness and joy for eight days." This declaration instituted the feast of Hanukkah, which Jews continue to celebrate today.

The Maccabean revolutionaries established a new theocratic state of Judea, which the Seleucids were too busy with war on their eastern borders to challenge. The reinvigorated Jewish state continued its conquests of neighboring states, including Greek cities in Galilee, and by 76 B.C.E. the Jews had established a kingdom almost as extensive as

> Independent Judea

traditional beliefs changed, especially where they sought to reconcile Judaism with Hellenism. Sometime in the third century B.C.E., the Hebrew Scriptures were translated into Greek, in the influential document known as the **Septuagint.** (The name derives from the Latin word for "seventy," recalling the legendary group of 72 translators who were credited with the accomplishment.) In great cities like Alexandria, Jews gathered in synagogues to pray in a traditional fashion, but in many of these centers of worship, the Scriptures were read in Greek.

In Palestine, too, Jews and Gentiles, or non-Jews, met and mingled. Palestine had many Greek settlements, and even in Jerusalem Jews faced the question of what it meant for them to compromise with Hellenism. Jesus Ben Sirach, a Jewish scribe and teacher in Jerusalem, wrote a text called *Ecclesiasticus* (ca. 180 B.C.E.) in which he scolded believers who had turned away from the traditional Jewish Law of Moses and warned

DOCUMENT 3.3

Judas Maccabeus Liberates Jerusalem

In the first century C.E., the Jewish historian Josephus wrote a history of the Jews in which he described the revolt of Judas Maccabeus against the Hellenistic king Antiochus in ca. 166 B.C.E. As part of his desire to bring together his diverse peoples, Antiochus erected an altar to Zeus in the Temple at Jerusalem.

[Judas Maccabeus] overthrew the idol altar and cried out, "If," said he, "anyone be zealous for the laws of his country and for the worship of God, let him follow me"; and when he had said this he made haste into the desert with his sons, and left all his substance in the village. Many others did the same also, and fled with their children and wives into the desert and dwelt in caves; but when the King's generals heard this, they took all the forces they then had in the citadel at Jerusalem, and pursued the Jews into the desert; and when they had overtaken them, they in the

first place endeavored to persuade them to repent, and to choose what was most for their advantage and not put them to the necessity of using them according to the law of war; but when they would not comply with their persuasions, but continued to be of a different mind, they fought against them on the Sabbath day, and they burned them as they were in the caves, without resistance, and without so much as stopping up the entrances of the caves. And they avoided to defend themselves on that day because they were not willing to break in upon the honor they owed the Sabbath, even in such distresses; for our law requires that we rest upon that day.

There were about a thousand, with their wives and children, who were smothered and died in these caves; but many of those that escaped joined themselves to Mattathias and appointed him to be their ruler, who taught them to fight even on the Sabbath day, and told them that unless they would do so they would

become their own enemies by observing the law [so rigorously] while their adversaries would still assault them on this day, and they would not then defend themselves; and that nothing could then hinder but they must all perish without fighting. This speech persuaded them, and this rule continues among us to this day, that if there be a necessity we may fight on Sabbath days.

SOURCE: Josephus, "The Jewish Wars," in *The Great Events by Famous Historians*, vol. II, ed. Rossiter Johnson (The National Alumni, 1905), p. 247.

Analyze the Document

1. What religious motivations undergirded this war?

2. How did the Maccabees compromise their own religious beliefs to fight the war?

3. How did this conflict resemble modern controversies regarding fighting during Ramadan or Christmas?

---

that of Solomon (r. 970–931 B.C.E.) (see Chapter 1). Though they had revolted to preserve their cultural and religious purity, the new rulers proved intolerant of their Gentile subjects, forcing many to convert and insisting that non-Jewish infant boys be circumcised. These practices worsened the instability already plaguing the region.

THE SEARCH FOR TRUTH: HELLENISTIC THOUGHT, RELIGION, AND SCIENCE

Hellenistic rulers from Alexander on consciously spread Greek ideas and learning. To do this, they vigorously supported education, which they saw as key to the preservation of Greek ideals and the training ground for new Hellenized civil servants. Within these educated circles occurred most of the intellectual and cultural blending that created the brilliance of Hellenistic art as well as the struggles of cultural identity. However, these communities of the educated also proved a fertile ground for intellectual inquiry in which great minds eagerly sought truth about the world, religion, and the meaning of life.

A Life of Learning

Great speculations, however, began first in the schoolrooms. Families who wanted their boys to succeed invested heavily in education. At the age of 7, boys attended privately funded schools and practiced Greek and writing. The parchment samples of their

INTELLECTUAL LIFE	
ca. 400–ca. 325 B.C.E.	Diogenes advocates Cynicism
ca. 342–ca. 292 B.C.E.	Life of playwright Menander
ca. 335–ca. 280 B.C.E.	Life of physician Herophilus
ca. 312 B.C.E.	Zeno founds Stoicism
ca. 310–ca. 230 B.C.E.	Life of Aristarchus, who posited heliocentric universe
ca. 306 B.C.E.	Epicurus founds school of philosophy
ca. 300 B.C.E.	Euclid publishes *Elements* on mathematics
ca. 220 B.C.E.	Archimedes advances engineering

KEY DATES

assignments reveal a strong anti-"barbarian" prejudice in which the culture of all non-Greeks was dismissed. Thus, even early schooling aimed to inculcate Greek values among non-Greek peoples. This indoctrination was reinforced by an emphasis on Homer's works as the primary literary texts.

At 14, boys expanded their education to include literary exercises, geography, and advanced studies of Homer. Successful students then continued their studies in the gymnasium, the heart of Hellenistic education and culture. Most cities boasted splendid gymnasia as their central educational institutions. Often the most beautiful building in the city, the gymnasium sported a running track, an area for discus and javelin throwing, a wrestling pit, and baths, lecture halls, and libraries. Here Greek-speaking boys of all ethnic backgrounds gathered, exercised naked, and finished an education that allowed them to enter the Greek ruling class.

Hellenistic kings cultivated education just as they served as patrons of the arts. They competed fiercely to hire sought-after tutors for their families and schools and to purchase texts for their libraries. The best texts were copied by hand on Egyptian papyrus or carefully prepared animal hide called parchment. (The word parchment derives from Pergamena charta, or "Pergamum paper," which refers to where the best-quality parchment was made.) Texts were prepared in scrolls rather than bound in books and were designed to be unrolled and read aloud.

This advocacy of education yielded diverse results. Many scholars produced nothing more than rather shallow literary criticism; others created literature that captured the superficial values of much of Hellenistic life; and some created highly sophisticated philosophy and science. The range of these works, however, contributed important threads to the tapestry of Western civilization.

Theater and Literature

The tragedies and comedies of classical Greek theater had illuminated profound public and heroic themes ranging from fate and responsibility to politics and ethics. Theater proved extremely popular in the Hellenistic cities as well. Though some cosmopolitan playwrights wrote tragedies, few of these works have survived. We do have many comedies from this era, which contrast so starkly with the classic Greek examples of this genre that this body of work is called New Comedy. Hellenistic plays were almost devoid of political satire and focused instead on the plights of individuals.

The best-known playwright of New Comedy is Menander (ca. 342–ca. 292 B.C.E.), whose works often centered on young men who fell in love with women who were unattainable for some reason. Most of these

plots ended happily with the couples overcoming all obstacles. In general, New Comedy characters were preoccupied with making money or indulging themselves in other ways. This focus on individual concerns reflected the realities of cosmopolitan life—ruled by powerful and distant kings, individuals had limited personal power. Menander and the other playwrights of the age shed light on this impotence by focusing on the personal rather than on larger questions of good and evil.

New comedies

A new genre of escapist literature—the Hellenistic novel—also emerged in this environment. The themes in these novels echo those of the plays: Very young men and women fall in love (usually at first sight), but circumstances separate them. They must endure hardships and surmount obstacles before they can be reunited. Surprisingly, most of these novels portray young women as resourceful and outspoken individuals. For example, a remarkable heroine in the novel Ninos dresses in gender-ambiguous clothing and leads a band of Assyrians to capture a fortified city. Although wounded, she makes a brave escape while elephants trample her soldiers.

Hellenistic novels

Both the New Comedy and the Hellenistic novel sought to provide an escape from the realities of cosmopolitan life. Yet they also reflected new ideals in this society that often looked to the personal rather than to the polis for meaning. For example, unlike the writings of classical Greece, Hellenistic texts expressed an ideal of affection within marriage. The philosopher Antipater of Tarsus wrote, "The man who has had no experience of a married woman and children has not tasted true and noble happiness." The literature of the day also revealed an increased freedom of Hellenistic women to choose their partners. While families still arranged most marriages, some women (and men) began to follow their hearts in choosing a spouse. Woman also gained more freedom in divorce laws. Like men, they could seek divorce if their husbands committed adultery. One marriage contract from as early as 311 B.C.E. included clauses forbidding the husband to "insult" his wife with another woman. Taken together, all these themes expressed a new emphasis on love within the family.

Cynics, Epicureans, and Stoics: Cosmopolitan Philosophy

Like their literary counterparts, Hellenistic philosophers also narrowed the focus of their inquiry. Most of them no longer tackled the lofty questions of truth and justice that had preoccupied Socrates and Plato. Instead, they considered how an individual could achieve happiness in an age in which vast, impersonal kingdoms produced the kind of pain and weariness embodied by the market woman pictured at the beginning of the chapter.

The sensibilities of the Hellenistic age had been first foreshadowed by Diogenes (ca. 400–ca. 325 B.C.E.), an early proponent of the philosophic school called **Cynicism.** Diogenes was disgusted with the hypocrisy and materialism emerging around him in the transformed life of Athens as traditional polis life deteriorated. Diogenes and his followers believed that the only way for people to live happily in a fundamentally evil world was to involve themselves as little as possible in that world. The Cynics therefore claimed that the more people rejected the goods and connections of this world—property, marriage, religion, luxury—the more they would achieve spiritual happiness.

To demonstrate his rejection of all material things, Diogenes reputedly lived in a large tub. The carving in **Figure 3.9** shows him in the tub, oblivious to the lavish villa behind him. He is talking to Alexander the Great, enacting a likely apocryphal story in which Alexander offers the famous philosopher anything in the world. Diogenes simply asks Alexander to "stand out of my light and let me see the sun." The dog perched on top of the tub symbolizes Cynicism. (The word *cynic* derives from the Greek word *kunos,* which means "of a dog," or "doglike," because Cynics supposedly lived as simply and as filthily as dogs.)

Although Plato had dismissed Diogenes as "Socrates gone mad," Cynicism became popular during the Hellenistic period as people searched for meaning in their personal lives, rather than justice for their polis. Some men and women chose to live an ascetic life of the mind instead of involving themselves in the day-to-day activities of the Hellenistic cities. However, most found it difficult to reject material goods completely.

Other Hellenistic philosophies offered more practical solutions to the question of where to find personal happiness in an impersonal world. Epicurus (ca. 342–ca. 270 B.C.E.), for example, founded a school of philosophy that built on Democritus's (460–370 B.C.E.) theory of a universe made of atoms (described in Chapter 2). Envisioning a purposeless world of randomly colliding atoms, Epicurus proclaimed that happiness came from seeking pleasure while being free from pain in both body and mind. From a practical standpoint, this search for happiness involved pursuing pleasures that did not bring pain. Activities such as overeating or overdrinking, which ended in pain, should thus be avoided. In Epicurus's view, the ideal life was one of moderation, which consisted of being surrounded by friends and free of the burdens of the public sphere. His circle of followers included women and slaves. The Roman **Epicurean** Lucretius Carus (ca. 99–ca. 55 B.C.E.) articulated Epicurus's ideal: "This is the greatest joy of all: to stand aloof in a quiet citadel, stoutly fortified by the teaching of the wise, and to gaze down from that elevation on others wandering aimlessly in a vain search for the way of life." Of course, this "greatest joy" required money with which to purchase the pain-free pleasures that Epicurus advocated. His was not a philosophy that everyone could afford.

While Epicurus honed his philosophy in his private garden, the public marketplace of Athens gave rise to a third great Hellenistic philosophy: **Stoicism.** Named after *stoa,* the covered walkways surrounding the marketplace, the school of Stoicism was founded by Zeno (ca. 335–ca. 261 B.C.E.). Zeno exemplified the cosmopolitan citizen of the Hellenistic world, for he was born in Cyprus of non-Greek ancestry and spent most of his life in Athens.

At age 22, Zeno was a follower of Crates the Cynic, but later he abandoned his early connection to Cynicism, arguing that people could possess material goods as long as they were not emotionally attached to them. Indeed, the Stoic philosophers advocated indifference to external things. While this attitude paralleled Epicurus's desire to avoid pain, Zeno and

Cynics

Epicurus

Stoics

FIGURE 3.9 Diogenes and Alexander Diogenes argued that people should live a simple life, much like the dog shown sitting on the barrel in which the great philosopher lived. The artist included in this scene Alexander the Great, who reputedly admired the simple lifestyle that was so rare in the Hellenistic kingdoms.

the Stoics did not frame their philosophy in terms of the materialism of an atomic universe. Instead, they argued for the existence of a Universal Reason or God that governed the universe. As they explained, seeds of the Universal Reason lay within each individual, so everyone was linked in a universal brotherhood. In quasi-religious terms, this belief validated Alexander's supposed goal of unifying diverse peoples.

The Stoics' belief in a Universal Reason led them to explain the apparent turbulence of the world differently than the Epicureans. Stoics did not believe in random events but instead posited a rational world with laws and structures—an idea that would have a long history in the West. While individuals could not control this universe, they could control their own responses to the apparent vagaries of the world. Followers were implored to pursue virtue in a way that kept them in harmony with rational nature, not fighting it. The ideal Stoic renounced passions (including anger) even while enduring the pain and suffering that inevitably accompany life. Through self-control, Stoics might achieve the tranquillity that Epicureans and Cynics desired.

Cynicism, Epicureanism, and Stoicism had many things in common. Arising in settings where individuals felt unable to influence their world, they all emphasized control of the self and personal tranquility. Whereas the classical Greeks had found meaning through participation in the public life of their poleis, Hellenistic philosophers claimed that individuals could find contentment through some form of withdrawal from the turbulent life of the impersonal cosmopolitan cities. Moreover, all three philosophies appealed primarily to people with some measure of wealth. The indifferent, pain-free life of both the Epicureans and the Stoics required money, and the self-denial of the Cynics seldom appealed to really destitute people.

New Religions of Hope

For most ordinary people, the philosophies of the Hellenistic age had little relevance. These people looked instead to new religious ideas for a sense of meaning and hope. During this period, the gods and goddesses of the poleis gave way to deities that had international appeal and that were accessible to ordinary individuals—two features that marked a dramatic departure from previous religions of the West. Furthermore, the new religions offered hope in an afterlife that provided an escape from the alienation of the Hellenistic world. The international component paved the way for a blending of religious ideas—syncretism—and individuals felt a deeply passionate spiritual connection to their deities. The most popular new cults were known as **mystery religions**

because initiates swore not to reveal the insights they received during the highest ceremonies. The historical roots of these cults stretched back to early Greece, Egypt, and Syria, but they acquired a new relevance throughout the Hellenistic era.

Mystery cults included worship of fertility goddesses like Demeter and Cybele, and a revitalized cult of Dionysus. However, the most popular was that of the Egyptian goddess Isis, who achieved a remarkable universality. Inscription stones offering her prayers claim that Isis ruled the world and credited her with inventing writing and cultivation of grain, ruling the heavenly bodies, and even transcending fate itself—the overarching destiny that even the old Homeric gods could not escape. Isis reputedly declared: "I am she who is called Lawgiver. . . . I conquer Fate. Fate heeds me." In other inscriptions, worshipers claimed that Isis was the same goddess that other peoples called by different names: "In your person alone you are all the other goddesses named by the peoples."

Figure 3.10, a marble relief from Athens, demonstrates religious syncretism in action. The piece was carved in the classical technique showing an apparently traditional Greek family worshiping at an altar. At the right of the altar, standing before the veil of mystery, is the Egyptian goddess Isis, depicted in traditional Greek style. The god seated at the right resembles Zeus, but he is Isis's brother/husband Osiris, the traditional Egyptian consort of the goddess-queen. This figure shows the syncretic nature of the new Hellenistic religions, in which patron deities of particular cities acquired international appeal. In their worship of these mysteries, the people of the Hellenistic kingdoms may have almost achieved Alexander's rumored ideal of universalism.

Men and women who wanted to experience the mysteries of these new religions believed that they had been summoned by a dream or other supernatural call. They took part in a purification ritual and an elaborate public celebration, including a procession filled with music and, sometimes, ecstatic dance in which people acted as if possessed by the goddess or god. Finally, the procession left the public spaces and entered the sacred space of the deity, where the initiate experienced a profound connection with the god or goddess. Many mysteries involved sacred meals through which people became godlike by eating the flesh of the deity. Such believers emerged from this experience expecting to participate in an afterlife. Here lay the heart of the new religious impulses: the hope for another, better world after death. The mystery religions would continue to draw converts for centuries, and perhaps paved the way for Christianity—the most successful mystery religion of all.

Hellenistic Science

The philosophic and religious long-ings of the Hellenistic world bred long-standing consequences for the future. People living in later large, impersonal cities turned to the philosophies of indif-ference and religions of hope. Equally impressive were the improvements on classical Greek science and technology that emerged in the Hellenistic learn-ing centers. This flourish of intellectual activity was fostered in part by the gen-erous royal patronage that made Alexan-dria and Pergamum scholastic centers, and in part by the creative blending of ideas from old centers of learning.

One scholar who benefited from the new Hellenistic world of learning was Herophilus (ca. 335–ca. 280 B.C.E.), who traveled to Alexandria from the Seleu-cid lands near the Black Sea to study medicine. The first

Medical advances physician to break the strong Greek taboo against cutting open a corpse, Herophi-lus performed dissections that led him to spectacular discoveries about human anatomy. (His curiosity even reputedly led him to perform vivisections on con-victed criminals to learn about the motion of living organs.) His careful studies yielded pathbreaking knowledge: He was the first to recognize the brain as the seat of intelligence and to describe accurately the female anatomy, including the ovaries and fallopian tubes. However, all physicians were not as willing as Herophilus to treat the human body as an object of scientific study. Even in intellectually advanced Alex-andria, dissection became unpopular, and subsequent physicians focused on techniques of clinical treat-ment rather than on anatomy. However, they made major strides in pharmacology, carefully studying the influence of drugs and toxins on the body.

In spite of these noteworthy advances, the most important achievements of the Hellenistic scientists occurred in the field of mathematics. Euclid (335–270 B.C.E.), who studied in Alexandria, is considered one of the most accomplished mathematicians of all time. In his most famous work, *Elements* (ca. 300 B.C.E.), Euclid presented a geometry based on increasingly complex axioms and postulates. When

Mathematics and astronomy Euclid's patron, King Ptolemy, asked the mathematician whether there was an easier way to learn geometry than by struggling through these proofs, Euclid replied that there was no "royal road" (or shortcut) to under-standing geometry. Euclid's work became the standard

FIGURE 3.10 Isis and Osiris, later second century B.C.E. This sculpture is a votive relief, a carving that would have been placed in a temple and dedicated to fulfill a vow to a deity. Commissioned in Athens, it shows a family worshiping the Egyptian deities Isis and Osiris, who both look remarkably Greek in this rendering. The work illustrates the blending of religions that occurred in the Hellenistic world.

text on the subject, and, even today, students find his intricate proofs both challenging and vexing.

Euclid's mathematical work laid the foundation for Hellenistic astronomy. Eratosthenes of Cyrene (ca. 275–ca. 195 B.C.E.), for example, used Euclid's theorems to calculate the circumference of the earth with remarkable accuracy—he erred only by about 200 miles. Aristarchus of Samos (ca. 310–ca. 230 B.C.E.) posited a heliocentric, or sun-centered, universe (against prevailing Greek tradition) and attempted to use Euclidean geometry to calculate the size and distance of the moon and sun. Although Aristarchus's contemporaries rejected his work, he and other astronomers introduced a striking change into the study of the heavens: They eliminated superstition and instead approached their work with mathematics.

Many Greek thinkers combined theoretical sci-ence with practical applications. One of the most influential in this regard was Hipparchus of Nicaea (160–125 B.C.E.). A brilliant mathematician, Hip-parchus invented trigonometry—the mathematics of measuring angles—and applied these insights to measuring the heavens and the earth. His accom-plishments demonstrated once again the benefits of cultural blending, for he introduced into Greece the Babylonian mathematical convention of measur-ing the circle in terms of 360 degrees (see Global Connections, Chapter 1), the method by which we

thinking about SCIENCE & TECHNOLOGY

Finding One's Way at Sea: The Invention of Latitude and Longitude

Long before the invention of global positioning system (GPS) devices, ancient mariners faced a nearly impossible task: finding their way when out of sight of land. To avoid disaster, sailors needed to be able to determine where they were in a vast ocean without any landmarks to guide them. But someone would first have to map and measure the earth before sailors would have the essential tools for calculating their location.

Hipparchus of Nicaea developed trigonometry, the mathematics of measuring angles, in the second century B.C.E. He used trigonometry to create an imaginary grid of latitude and longitude lines on the globe of the world (see **Figure 3.11**). Latitude (horizontal) lines measure the angle from the equator, and longitude (vertical) lines measure the angle from the prime meridian. All places on the earth have an address of sorts that we can express by their position on this grid, and because mathematics measures a circle in "degrees," we use this designation for the globe's address. Sicily, for example, is about 37 degrees north latitude and 14 degrees east longitude. This "address" is the same on Hipparchus's chart and in the GPS instruments we use today. Thus, with

trigonometry's invention, early sailors got the tools to compute their position on the global grid.

Yet mapping the earth and having the means to calculate one's position was just a first step. Mariners still had to determine their location on the global grid *while sailing on a vast, featureless*

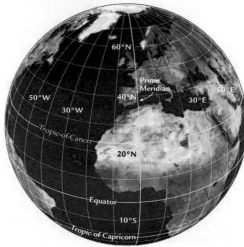

FIGURE 3.11 Global Map Divided by Latitude and Longitude Lines

ocean. Calculating latitude was relatively easy, for that required only measuring the angle between the horizontal and a fixed location in the sky—either Polaris or the sun. Longitude was far more difficult to measure, because as the earth rotates during a 24-hour day, the

positions of Polaris and the sun move across the sky. One therefore has to know the exact time of day to calculate longitude. (For example, at the equator, a one-minute error in time causes about a 17-mile error in computing one's east-west position.)

Precise measurements of longitude while at sea would have to wait until the eighteenth century, when sophisticated clocks were invented that could compensate for the rough movements, caused by wind and waves, that had thrown off the accuracy of older clocks. Only then, with an accurate measure of the time of day, could a mariner calculate an exact reading of his longitude, just as we can do with our GPS devices.

Follow the development of navigation through the book. See, for example, the astrolabe in Figure 6.14 and the exploration of the world in Chapter 12.

Connecting Science & Society

1. How did Hipparchus's invention of trigonometry aid ancient sailors? What is the connection between measuring angles and finding one's way at sea?

2. What does the invention of latitude and longitude suggest about the relationships among science, people's practical needs, and inventions? What inventions (of new products or new processes) in your own lifetime show these relationships in action?

---

continue to measure the globe. Among Hipparchus's other practical applications were measuring the length of the lunar month within an error of one second, a stunning achievement, and being the first to use the ideas of latitude and longitude consistently to measure the earth. The map in Thinking About Science and Technology illustrates this significant application of trigonometry to empirical observation.

Another beneficiary of Greek mathematics was Archimedes (ca. 287–ca. 212 B.C.E.), often considered the greatest inventor of antiquity. Like so many cos-

Archimedes

mopolitan scholars, Archimedes, who was born in Syracuse, traveled

to Alexandria to study. He later returned to Syracuse, where he worked on both abstract and practical problems. He built further on Euclid's geometry, applying the theorems to cones and spheres. In the process, he became the first to determine the value of pi—essential in calculating the area of a circle. He also applied geometry to the study of levers, proving that no weight was too heavy to move. He reportedly coined the optimistic declaration "Give me a place to stand, a long enough lever, and I will move the earth."

Archimedes did more than advance theoretical mathematics: He also had a creative, practical streak. For example, he invented the compound pulley, a valuable device for moving heavy weights. His real challenge, however, came at the end of his life. As we will see in Chapter 4, Syracuse, the city of Archimedes' birth, was besieged by Rome, a rising power in the Mediterranean. Throughout the siege, Syracuse used both offensive and defensive weapons that Archimedes had invented. Yet the great man's inventions could not save the Sicilian city. The Romans ultimately prevailed, and in 212 B.C.E. Archimedes was struck down by a Roman soldier as he was drawing a figure in the sand.

Archimedes serves as an apt symbol for the Hellenistic world that produced him. He was educated with the best of Greek learning and combined it with the rich diversity of Asia and the Mediterranean lands— a blending that gave Western civilization dramatic impetus. The Hellenistic scientist died at the hands of a new people—the Romans—who embraced the practical applications of men like Archimedes and who next took up the torch of Western culture.

LOOKING BACK & MOVING FORWARD

Summary The Macedonian kings Philip and Alexander permanently transformed the life of the polis that had marked the glory of Greece. Their conquests of Greece, and then Egypt and the Asian portion of the Persian Empire, created a unique blend of these ancient civilizations. By establishing a ruling elite of Greeks and Macedonians in cities from the Mediterranean to India, Alexander and his successors spread key elements of Greek civilization. Yet they also reshaped the culture of the polis. Political and cultural centers moved from the Greek city-states to bustling cosmopolitan areas, where people from all over the Hellenistic world mingled. Some benefited greatly from the new opportunities for personal enrichment that cosmopolitan life offered; many more sank to unprecedented levels of poverty. Some peoples embraced the cultural blending; others rejected it.

Though the armies of the Hellenistic kings competed endlessly for land and power, kings still had the resources to support culture and learning. Scientists, artisans, and scholars of this complex age made impressive advances. However, a new force was gathering momentum in the West, one that would profoundly impact the fate of Hellenistic civilizations.

KEY TERMS

Ptolemies, *p. 84*
Rosetta Stone, *p. 86*
Seleucids, *p. 87*
Antigonids, *p. 88*
Septuagint, *p. 96*
Maccabean Revolt, *p. 96*
Cynicism, *p. 99*
Epicurean, *p. 99*
Stoicism, *p. 99*
mystery religions, *p. 100*

REVIEW, ANALYZE, & CONNECT TO TODAY

REVIEW THE PREVIOUS CHAPTERS

In Chapter 1—"The Roots of Western Civilization"—we explored the beginnings of city life in Mesopotamia. Chapter 2—"The Contest for Excellence"—looked at the life, culture, and political fortunes of the classical Greek city-states.

1. Contrast the culture of classical Athens with artistic and philosophic ideas of the Hellenistic world, and consider what contributed to the transformation in ideas.

2. Review the urban experiences of Mesopotamia and Greece, and compare and contrast them with those of people in the cosmopolitan cities of the Hellenistic world. What do you think are the most significant differences, and what elements of urban life remained constant?

3. Chapter 1 summarized the early history of the Jews. Consider how their past contributed to the Maccabean Revolt under the Seleucids.

ANALYZE THIS CHAPTER

Chapter 3—"The Poleis Become Cosmopolitan"—describes the conquest of Greece by Macedonia and traces the spread of Greek culture as far east as India, as vibrant new monarchies combined Greek culture with the diversity of many other peoples to create the Hellenistic world.

1. What contributed to the conquest of the Greek city-states by Macedonia? Consider both the weaknesses of the poleis and the strengths of Macedonia.

2. What elements of Hellenic culture were most transformed, and in what ways were the cultures of the Persian Empire changed by contact with Greek culture?

3. Describe the changes in economics and warfare that were introduced in the Hellenistic world.

4. How did the opportunities for women change under the Hellenistic monarchies?

CONNECT TO TODAY

Think about some of the major issues the Hellenistic kingdoms faced—for example, cultural diversity, urban problems, and people's struggles to find meaning.

1. Does the United States, as a society, share some of these problems today? If so, how have the American people responded?

2. Do religious struggles such as those experienced by the Jews in Hellenistic times have parallels in the contemporary world? If so, how have countries responded?

BEYOND THE CLASSROOM

THE CONQUEST OF THE POLEIS

Borza, Eugene N. *In the Shadow of Olympus: The Emergence of Macedon*. Princeton, NJ: Princeton University Press, 1992. A chronological survey seeking to trace the emergence of Macedonia as a major force in the political affairs of the fourth-century B.C.E. Balkans.

Cartledge, Paul. *Alexander the Great*. Woodstock, NY: Overlook Hardcover, 2004. A riveting narrative of the life of Alexander that argues he was more concerned with his own glory than with a spread of Hellenism.

Harding, Philip. *From the End of the Peloponnesian Wars to the Battle of Ipsus*. New York: Cambridge University Press, 1985. A sophisticated analysis of the late Greek world before its conversion into the Hellenistic world by Alexander's conquest.

Worthington, Ian. *Philip II of Macedonia*. New Haven, CT: Yale University Press, 2008. Detailed biographical account, nicely illustrated with maps, offering a compelling argument that Philip is to be credited with the military innovations that Alexander put so effectively to use.

THE SUCCESSOR KINGDOMS, 323–ca.100 B.C.E.

Chaniotis, Angelos. *War in the Hellenistic World: A Social and Cultural History*. Hoboken, NJ: Wiley-Blackwell, 2005. Excellent discussion of military history and the ways almost-constant warfare shaped the Hellenistic world.

Grant, M. *From Alexander to Cleopatra: The Hellenistic World*. New York: Scribner, 1982. A general survey of the Hellenistic world.

Green, Peter. *From Alexander to Actium*. Berkeley: University of California Press, 1990. A complex analysis of the Hellenistic world's politics, literature, art, philosophy, and science.

EAST MEETS WEST IN THE SUCCESSOR KINGDOMS

Bartlett, John. *Jews in the Hellenistic and Roman Cities*. London: Routledge, 2002. A collection of essays offering a wide-ranging analysis of Jews in the classical world.

Billows, Richard A. *Kings and Colonists: Aspects of Macedonian Imperialism*. New York: E.J. Brill, 1995. An in-depth study of the problems of Macedonian imperial rule.

Cohen, Getzel M. *The Hellenistic Settlements in Europe, the Islands and Asia Minor*. Berkeley: University of California Press, 1995. A good general history of Hellenistic settlement—its founders, early history, and organization.

Dmitriev, Sviatoslav. *City Government in Hellenistic and Roman Asia Minor*. Oxford: Oxford University Press, 2005. An examination of city governments in the Hellenistic world and of the social and administrative transformation of Greek society.

Laks, Andre, and Malcolm Schofield. *Justice and Generosity: Studies in Hellenistic Social and Political Philosophy*. New York: Cambridge University Press, 1995. A comprehensive guide to the social and political philosophies in a period of increasing interest to classicists, philosophers, and cultural and intellectual historians.

Stewart, Andrew. *Faces of Power: Alexander's Image and Hellenistic Politics*. Berkeley: University of California Press, 1993. A remarkable look at art as a legitimate source of historical evidence.

THE SEARCH FOR TRUTH: HELLENISTIC THOUGHT, RELIGION, AND SCIENCE

Clauss, James. *Companion to Hellenistic Literature*. Malden, MA: Blackwell, 2009. Essays exploring the social and intellectual context of literature from the Hellenistic period.

Hicks, R.D., trans. *Diogenes Laertius: Lives of the Eminent Philosophers*. Cambridge: Loeb Classical Library, 1922. An excellent primary source on the giants of speculative thought in Greece.

Martin, Luther H. *Hellenistic Religions: An Introduction*. New York: Oxford University Press, 1987. A well-written survey of Hellenistic religions, their characteristic forms and expressions, differences and relationships, and their place in the Hellenistic system of thought.

Pollitt, J.J. *Art in the Hellenistic Age*. New York: Cambridge University Press, 1986. An accessible and well-illustrated look at Hellenistic art as an expression of cultural experience and aspirations of the Hellenistic age.

Sharples, R.W. *Stoics, Epicureans and Sceptics*. New York: Routledge, 1996. A readable account of the principal doctrines of these Hellenistic philosophies.

ORATOR ADDRESSING THE ROMAN PEOPLE

Romans lived public lives in which men were encouraged to serve their city in public office.
This calling required rhetorical skills to gain the support of Roman crowds, who gathered in the
Forum to listen to speeches and shout for their favorite speakers. Since the crowds were so large,
orators had to rely on broad gestures to sway masses outside the range of the human voice.
Rome grew great served by men such as Aulus Metellus, the orator depicted here in a life-size
bronze statue from the first century B.C.E.

Pride in Family and City

Rome from Its Origins Through the Republic, 753–44 B.C.E.

4

"No country has ever been greater or purer than ours or richer in good citizens and noble deeds; . . . nowhere have thrift and plain living been for so long held in such esteem." The Roman historian Livy (59 B.C.E.–17 C.E.) wrote a long history of Rome, in which he wanted to show how the heroic citizens of a small city-state became the masters of the world. He attributed their success to their upright character. At the same time Greek civilization was flourishing, a people had settled in the center of Italy, on the hills surrounding what would become the city of Rome. They were a serious, hardworking people who placed loyalty to family and city above all else. In time, this small group conquered the Italian peninsula, forging a coalition of peoples that enjoyed the benefits of peace and prosperity while relentlessly expanding through military conquest.

After overthrowing the monarchy, Rome developed a republican form of government, in which rich and poor citizens alike participated in a highly public legislative process. Within the city, men worked, relaxed, and talked in public spaces while noble women directed the household. Both nonnoble men and women worked in many areas of the city and contributed to an increasingly prosperous urban life.

Roman experience conquering and ruling the tribes of Italy prepared Roman armies to face foes farther afield. As Rome became a great power in the Mediterranean, it came into conflict with Carthage in North Africa. The two powers fought three wars—the Punic Wars—which destroyed Carthage. Rome was then drawn into wars in the eastern Mediterranean, in Greece, and into Asia Minor. These wars transformed Roman identity as Rome became a world power, in which an orator speaking in the Forum could hardly address the problems of the far-flung lands, and the republican form of government was no longer effective. Conquests funneled untold wealth and numerous slaves into Rome, and contact with Hellenistic civilization brought new culture, ideas, and values—causing Livy to lament the decline of "plain living" that he believed had made the Romans great.

At the end of this period, the stresses would prove too great, and the Roman Republic would end in civil war and murder. Yet despite its troubled demise, the Republic left a lasting legacy. Throughout the Mediterranean world, everyone knew of the proud city and its old families who had established laws, technology, and a way of life that exerted a continuing influence.

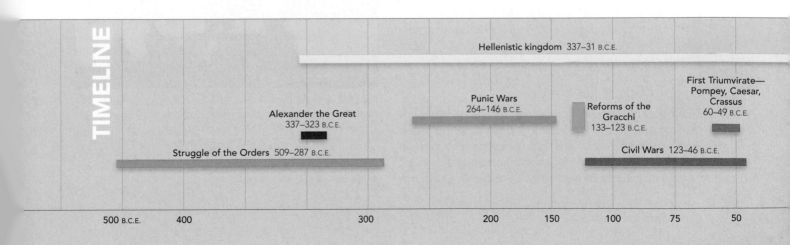

TIMELINE

Hellenistic kingdom 337–31 B.C.E.

Punic Wars 264–146 B.C.E.

First Triumvirate—Pompey, Caesar, Crassus 60–49 B.C.E.

Alexander the Great 337–323 B.C.E.

Reforms of the Gracchi 133–123 B.C.E.

Struggle of the Orders 509–287 B.C.E.

Civil Wars 123–46 B.C.E.

500 B.C.E. 400 300 200 150 100 75 50

THE RISE OF ROME,

753–265 B.C.E.

On a warm spring day in 458 B.C.E., a Roman farmer
was plowing the land adjacent to his small, round hut
when the Senate recognized an imminent threat from
a nearby tribe. In the face of such emergencies, the
Roman Senate could offer one man supreme power
for the duration of the crisis, giving him the title
"dictator." The Senate offered the dictatorship to the
farmer, Cincinnatus. He accepted the task and successfully led his armies to defeat the invaders. His grateful
fellow villagers asked him to continue his leadership
after the crisis, but he refused, preferring to return to
his plow. Throughout the next centuries, this story of
the strong, unassuming farmer Cincinnatus was told
and retold by conservative Romans who looked back
to the "ways of the fathers," *mos maiorum*, for models of
virtue. (The American city Cincinnati was so named
to honor George Washington—another savior farmer-
general.) Romans preserved stories like this to remember their heroes and transmit their values to their
families. Though they exist on the border between
history and legend, these stories offer a glimpse of the
origins of the greatness that would become Rome.

A Great City Is Founded

The historian Livy did not mind mixing history with
myth, for he said: "There is no reason to object when
antiquity draws no hard line between the human
and the supernatural; it adds dignity to the past."
Romans regularly remembered their history in terms
of legends. Perhaps the most beloved of these stories
told Romans how their city was founded. Like the
story of Cincinnatus, the tale of the birth of Rome
is filled with drama, conflict, heroes, and values. The
tale begins with Aeneas, a Trojan hero who escaped
from the destruction of his city after the Trojan War
(described in Chapter 2). A royal female descendant
of Aeneas decided to dedicate her life to serving the
gods. She became pregnant by the god Mars and bore
twin boys, Romulus and Remus. The princess's uncle
did not believe in the miraculous conception, nor did
he want her sons to threaten his rule, so he threw the
infant boys in the Tiber River. Soon a shepherd found
them being suckled by a wolf and raised them as his
own sons. Many years later, after the boys had grown
up, Romulus killed his brother during a quarrel and
became the first king of the newly founded city of
Rome. The traditional date of the founding of the city
is 753 B.C.E., and archaeological evidence confirms the
existence of a settlement there by this time.

Figure 4.1 shows a well-known statue from the
fifth century B.C.E. that depicts the two brothers,
Romulus and Remus, being suckled by the wolf that
saved them. The age of the original statue—which
was only of the nursing wolf—reveals how much the
Romans treasured this myth of their city's founding.
The twins were added about 2,000 years later, during
the Renaissance, showing the continued attraction of
the myth. Images like this helped Romans remember
and carry on their valued traditions from generation
to generation. Reflecting this sense of destiny and
heroic action, Livy concluded that "with reason did
gods and men choose this site for our city—all its
advantages make it of all places in the world the best
for a city destined to grow great."

FIGURE 4.1 Wolf of Rome, fifth century B.C.E. The
Romans often looked back to their founding myth, in which
a wolf nursed the brothers Romulus and Remus. This Roman
statue celebrates that myth, though the nursing infants were a
Renaissance addition. In ancient Rome, a live wolf was kept on
the Capitoline Hill to remind Romans always to venerate their
ancestors' history and ways.

Rome was located on hills overlooking a fertile, low-lying plain and the Tiber River, which afforded access to the Mediterranean Sea and to the inland regions. The geography of the surrounding Italian peninsula offered a number of advantages that would ultimately favor the growth of the young city. In contrast to Greece, whose mountainous terrain discouraged political unification, the large plains along Italy's western and eastern shores fostered trade, communication, and agriculture. The Apennine mountain range that marches down through the peninsula also creates abundant rainfall on the western plain. Therefore, Rome's fields were better situated for large-scale agriculture than had been possible for the Greek city-states. In addition, calm, accessible harbors along the western coast opened avenues for trade throughout the Mediterranean, which was further enhanced by Italy's central location in that important sea.

Geography

The initial settlers of Rome, like many of the other tribes in the region, were Indo-Europeans, those ubiquitous migrants from near the Black Sea whom we first saw in Chapter 1. They farmed, living in round huts and plowing their land. Cato the Elder (234–149 B.C.E.), a Roman political leader known for expressing traditional Roman values, summarized the Romans' pride in this way of life: "From farmers come the bravest men and sturdiest soldiers." Yet Rome also grew stronger through absorbing some of the culture and ways of its particularly talented neighbors. Greek colonies were well established in southern Italy and Sicily; Phoenician colonies prospered along the coast of North Africa. Most influential, however, were the Romans' immediate neighbors to the north, the Etruscans.

The Etruscan Influence

The Etruscans had appeared in Italy by 800 B.C.E., and for millennia historians argued about the origin of these peoples who did not speak an Indo-European language. Did they come from northern Europe, Italy, or North Africa? Modern DNA testing has confirmed the ancient historian Herodotus's claim that they arrived from Lydia in Asia Minor. The DNA evidence demonstrates that not only did the people come from modern Turkey, but they also brought their own cattle, setting that breed apart from the indigenous Italian cattle. The Etruscans settled the land and prospered. They traded all over the Mediterranean, importing luxury items and enjoying a good life.

Scholars have not yet deciphered all the Etruscan writings, so our best source of information about their daily life is their surviving artwork. **Figure 4.2** shows an Etruscan sarcophagus, or stone coffin, adorned by

FIGURE 4.2 Etruscan Sarcophagus, ca. 520 B.C.E. This sarcophagus (stone burial casket) was designed to hold cremated remains. The decoration celebrates the couple's life. They are shown reclining at dinner, an activity in which the wife and husband shared equal status.

a carving of a married couple. The couple recline together as they would have at dinner, and their poses suggest much affection between them. Indeed, women's active participation in this society surprised many of the Etruscans' contemporaries. The famous Greek philosopher Aristotle (384–322 B.C.E.), writing centuries later, described with some shock how even respectable Etruscan women joined in banquets with men.

Etruscan kings ruled Rome for a time, and the Romans learned a good deal from their civilization; indeed, much that we define as Roman was in fact Etruscan. For example, the Romans adopted Etruscan engineering and used their newfound skills to drain their lowland marsh, which formed the center of the growing city of Rome, and to build the great sewers that drained water from the city. They also adopted Etruscan architectural features—among them, the arch and vault construction—and modeled their temples on those of the Etruscans. Inside the temples, Romans learned to rely on divination—interpreting the will of the gods in the entrails of sacrificial animals—from Etruscan priests. Romans also adopted the toga, the white woolen robe worn by citizens, as well as the *fasces*, a bundle of rods surrounding an ax that was the powerful emblem of Roman authority.

Finally, the Romans acquired the Etruscan alphabet and began using it to write in their own Latin language. Note the statue of the orator shown at the beginning of this chapter. This perfect model of Roman life has his Roman name written in Etruscan letters on the bottom of his Etruscan-style toga. The Italian region of Tuscany is named after this early people who exerted an enduring influence on the growing culture of Rome.

The Roman Monarchy, ca. 753–509 B.C.E.

Like other ancient civilizations, the early Romans were ruled by kings, but to work out the details of the monarchy, historians have to struggle with combinations of history and legend. Romulus (ca. 753–ca. 715 B.C.E.) was the first king, and more unverifiable legends claim he was followed by four more monarchs. By the seventh century B.C.E., it seems, Rome was ruled by an Etruscan dynasty that governed for almost a century, from about 616 to about 509 B.C.E.

By the end of the sixth century B.C.E., the Roman aristocracy had come to chafe against the Etruscan kings' authority. Roman tradition holds that rebellion against the Etruscans erupted in response to the violation of Lucretia, a virtuous Roman matron. According to Livy, Sextus, son of the Etruscan king Tarquin the Proud, raped Lucretia at knifepoint. Her husband, Collatinus, told her not to blame herself, but

Overthrow of Etruscans

after extracting her husband's promise to exact vengeance, she committed suicide. She was remembered as a chaste, heroic woman who chose death over dishonor. After her death, Romans rallied around the leadership of an Etruscan nobleman—Brutus—who joined Collatinus in a revolt that toppled the monarchy. The story of Lucretia illuminates the values of bravery and chastity held by early Roman men and women, but it also became a symbol of Romans' revulsion against kings, which would be a continuing theme throughout their history.

The legend accurately concluded that the Etruscan monarchy was overthrown, but the historical reality was more complex. All Romans did not support the overthrow of the monarchy—many in the lower classes relied on the monarchy to control the power of the noble families (the **patricians**), and some patricians who were related to kings also supported the monarchy. With these competing social forces, simply overthrowing a monarchy would not resolve social issues. However, just as the Greek poleis had overthrown their own kings and replaced them with oligarchies of nobles during their early history, the situation was repeated in Rome. The erection of a stable governmental form would require time and struggle.

Governing an Emerging Republic, 509–287 B.C.E.

With the overthrow of the Etruscan monarchy, the Romans established a republic, a Latin word that meant "public matter" (often rendered "public realm" or "commonwealth" in English), which they distinguished from the "private realm" of the Etruscan kings. For Romans, this meant that power rested with the people assembled together and that magistrates served the state. This influential vision of government was in striking contrast to that of the Hellenistic kings, who generally viewed their kingdoms as their own property, their spoils of war, their private realm.

In practice, the Republic consisted of three parts—consuls, the Senate, and the assemblies. Executive authority rested with two male **consuls** who were elected annually by an Assembly of Centuries organized by army groupings of 100 men, or "centuries." The consuls were advised by a body of elder statesmen, the **Senate.** Finally, adult male citizens met in **assemblies,** outdoor public gatherings in which the participants voted—by group, not as individuals—on issues that had previously been presented to them by leading statesmen. Beyond this governmental structure, the Roman people were separated by two general social distinctions into groups called patricians and plebeians. The patricians, old families who composed about 6 percent of the population, were recognized as socially and legally superior to everyone else. The **plebeians,** who made up the majority of the population, were the Republic's working people; their numbers, however, did not include slaves. Although the republican system seemed to offer a balance of power, in reality authority rested with the patricians, who sat in the Senate, and with the wealthy men who dominated the Assembly of Centuries.

Perhaps not surprisingly given that so few dominated the many, some individual patricians found ways to enrich themselves and their families. Many abused their power and oppressed the commoners in their charge, even enslaving many because of debts they incurred. By the fifth century B.C.E., social relations between patrician and plebeian had deteriorated enough that a social revolution occurred, which historians have called the **Struggle of the Orders.** Two main issues fueled this controversy: First, the poor wanted guarantees against the abuses of the powerful, and second, the wealthy plebeians wanted a role in government. This struggle was not a civil war, but instead a series of political reforms forced on the aristocracy from about 509 to 287 B.C.E.

Struggle of the Orders

Plebeians began their revolution by establishing themselves as a political alternative to the patricians. They withdrew from the city, held their own assemblies, established their own temple to counter the patrician cults, and even elected their own leaders, called **tribunes,** who were to represent plebeian interests. Tribunes could veto unfavorable laws and represent plebeians in law courts, for example. Patricians also had a practical reason to listen to the voice of the people through their tribunes, because they needed the plebeians to fight in the infantry. Just as Greek citizens forced concessions from aristocrats who needed armies, Roman citizen-soldiers threatened to refuse military service unless some of their demands were met. This was an effective threat; slowly, plebeians gained in political skill and, through the pressure of their tribunes, extracted meaningful concessions.

Plebeians won a number of important rights: First they gained a written law code that could be consistently enforced. Between 451 and 449 B.C.E., the laws were written down and displayed in a form called the **Twelve Tables.** Subsequent Romans looked back proudly to this accomplishment, which established a Roman commitment to law that became one of Rome's most enduring contributions to Western culture. To mark the importance of the establishment of written law, Roman children continued to memorize the Twelve Tables for up to four centuries later. Plebeians also won the right to hold sacred and political offices. Although, in practice, offices more readily went to the wealthy, upward mobility was possible. Perhaps the greatest concession the plebeians eventually won was the right to marry patricians. This removed birth as the most serious impediment to the rise of talented and wealthy plebeians.

The plebeian struggle for representation culminated in 287 B.C.E., when the Tribal Assembly became the principal legislative body. **Figure 4.3** shows this new republican structure. This group was named because the assembly was organized in "tribes" or regions, urban and rural, where plebeians lived. Laws passed by the Tribal Assembly did not need Senate approval, but bound everyone—rich or poor. The resulting society in Rome contained three main social classes: patricians, wealthy plebeians—later called **equestrians** (or knights) because they could afford to be in the cavalry—and the poorer plebeians. Money and connections dominated Roman politics as patricians and equestrians fought to increase their power. In spite of these problems, Polybius believed the people retained important powers, as Document 4.1 describes.

Governing the Republic

As **Figure 4.3** shows, the Roman constitution was complex, but logical. All citizens participated in the two Assemblies that elected the magistrates who served the state. Roman men with money and influence could move through the *cursus honorum,* the career path of a successful public official. A man would be elected to each office for one year, and then (through the late Republic) automatically become a member of the Senate—that venerable institution which by now had no actual constitutional power but a great deal of influence. The Roman system probably worked in part because most of the political life took place within a more informal system.

Informal Governance: Patrons and Clients

From the earliest years of the Republic, Romans relied on semiformal ties to smooth social and even political intercourse. Powerful members of society, called patrons, surrounded themselves with less powerful people—clients—in a relationship based on informal yet profoundly important ties. Patrons provided clients with what they called "kindnesses," such as food, occasional financial support, and help in legal disputes. Clients consisted of people from all walks of life: aristocratic youths who looked to powerful patrons for help in their careers (or hoped to be remembered in a rich patron's will), businessmen who wanted to use a patron's political influence to profit in their enterprises, poets who needed money, or freed slaves who remained attached to their former owners. Because Rome remained overwhelmingly an agricultural society, the largest group of clients was small farmers, who depended on their patrons to help them survive in a land that was becoming dominated by powerful aristocratic landowners. Clients owed their patrons duties, such as financial and political support.

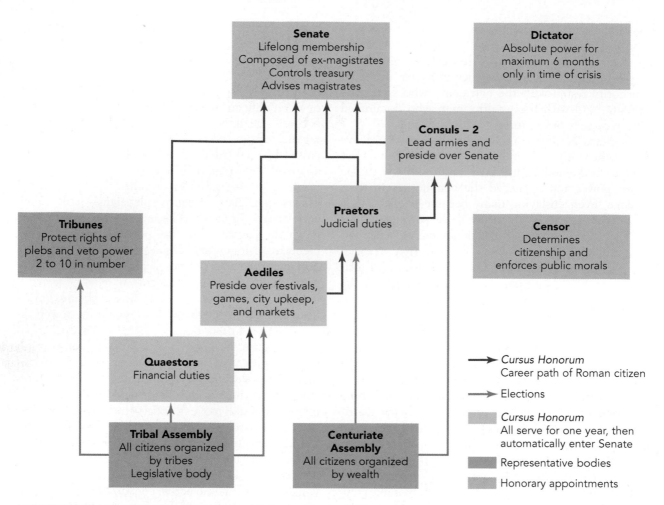

FIGURE 4.3 The Roman Republic   The Republic had a complex political structure that still influences governments today. This chart illustrates both the representative bodies and the positions the Roman assemblies elected. It also shows the *cursus honorum*, that is, the expected political path of a Roman man as he rose in public office.

Many clients gathered at their patrons' doors every morning as the cock crowed—failure to appear would jeopardize one's tie of clientage. This mixed crowd numbering in the tens to hundreds received ritual gifts, ensuring that the poorest would eat and the richest were remembered, and everyone was invited into the patron's home to greet him. The patron was supposed to exert a moral authority over his clients, helping them to be good citizens. As the Roman poet Horace (65–8 B.C.E.) wrote, "A wealthy patron governs you as a good mother might do and requires of you more wisdom and virtue than he possesses himself."

In the public world of Mediterranean society, clients provided patrons visible proof of their authority. After the morning greeting, clients accompanied their patron to the center of the city, where the day's business took place. A patrician surrounded by hundreds of clients was a man to be reckoned with. Political life of the Republic was conducted in the **Forum,** a large gathering area surrounded by temples and other public buildings. The Forum included the Senate chamber, the people's assembly, and a speaker's platform—called the Rostra—where politicians addressed the Roman people. **Map 4.1** shows the City of Rome with its important public spaces, including the Rostra and the Senate chamber. Clients would cheer their patron, shout down his opponents, and offer their votes to his agenda. An aristocrat who abandoned this public life that gave him stature and dignity was described sadly: "He will have no more entourage, no escort for his sedan chair, no visitors in his antechamber."

The Struggle of the Orders created a republic in which rich and poor both had a voice. In fact, it was a system dominated by wealth and an aristocracy that used its influence in the Senate and the Forum to preserve traditional privileges. However, the wealthy never forgot they needed the support of the Roman clients who gathered at their doors in the morning, shouted their support in the Forum, and manned Rome's armies.

Dominating the Italian Peninsula

As the Republic gathered strength, territorial wars between Rome and its neighbors broke out almost

Clients' role

The Power of Public Opinion

The Greek historian Polybius (ca. 200–ca. 118 B.C.E.) was a great admirer of the Roman constitution, which he described in his Histories. *He thought the republican constitution would ensure a stable government. After he described the roles of the Senate and all the officers of the state, he turned to the more informal power of the people of Rome.*

After this one would naturally be inclined to ask what part is left for the people in the constitution, when the Senate has these various functions, especially the control of the receipts and expenditure of the exchequer; and when the Consuls, again, have absolute power over the details of military preparation, and an absolute authority in the field? There is, however, a part left for the people, and it is a most important one. For the people is the sole fountain of

honour and of punishment; and it is by these two things and these alone that dynasties and constitutions and, in a word, human society are held together: for where the distinction between them is not sharply drawn both in theory and practice, there no undertaking can be properly administered,—as indeed we might expect when good and bad are held in exactly the same honour. The people then are the only court to decide matters of life and death; and even in cases where the penalty is money, if the sum to be assessed is sufficiently serious, and especially when the accused have held the higher magistracies. . . .

Again, it is the people who bestow offices on the deserving, which are the most honourable rewards of virtue. It has also the absolute power of passing or repealing laws; and most important of all, it is the people

who deliberate on the question of peace or war. And when provisional terms are made for alliance, suspension of hostilities, or treaties, it is the people who ratify them or the reverse. These considerations again would lead one to say that the chief power in the state was the people's, and that the constitution was a democracy.

SOURCE: Polybius, *The Histories of Polybius* (London: Macmillan, 1889), in eds. Brian Tierney and Joan W. Scott, *Western Societies: A Documentary History*, vol. I, 2nd ed. (New York: McGraw-Hill, 2000), pp. 102–103 (page citations are to second edition).

Analyze the Document

1. What powers does Polybius describe as belonging to the Senate and consuls?

2. What powers does he attribute to the people? Do you think he's right that these powers are substantial?

---

annually. What led Rome into these repeated struggles? Romans themselves claimed that they responded only to acts of aggression, so their expansion was self-defensive. The reality, however, was more complicated. Rome felt a continual land hunger and was ever eager to acquire land to establish colonies of its plebeians. Roman leaders also had a hunger for glory and plunder that would let them acquire and reward clients—victorious generals were well placed to dominate Rome's political life. Thus, farmers often had to drop their plows, as Cincinnatus did, to fight.

By the beginning of the fourth century B.C.E., Rome was increasingly involved in wars in the Italian peninsula. From an early period, Romans identified themselves with fellow Latin tribes as they fought together against surrounding hillside tribes. By the early Republic, this alliance was known as the Latin League. Under Rome's leadership, | Italian wars | the Latin League successfully defended its borders during the fifth and fourth centuries B.C.E. However, Rome's allies became increasingly resentful of Rome's leadership and revolted in 340 B.C.E. Two years later, Rome decisively defeated the rebellious allies and dissolved the League. Here, however, Rome showed its genius for administration. Instead of crushing the rebellious states, Rome extended varying degrees of citizenship

to the Latins. Some received the rights of full Roman citizenship, while others became partial citizens who could earn full citizenship by moving to Rome. This benign policy allowed Rome with its allies to confront and conquer other peoples of the peninsula.

As **Map 4.2** shows, Rome acquired territories to the south and north. This was not a time of endless victories, however. In 390 B.C.E., the Gauls of northern Italy (a Celtic tribe) sacked much of the city before being bribed to leave with a large tribute payment, but it would be another eight hundred years before a foreign army once more set foot in the city. However, their invasion had weakened the Etruscan cities of the north, so by 295 B.C.E., Roman armies controlled the north of the peninsula. By the middle of the third century B.C.E., Rome dominated most of the Italian peninsula.

The Romans' successful expansion in part stemmed from their renowned courage and tenacity in battle. Most of their success, however, came from their generosity in vic- | Foreign policy | tory. Although in **Map 4.2** it looks as if Rome had "united" Italy, in fact, the peninsula remained a patchwork of diverse states allied to Rome by separate treaties. These treaties were varied, but all were generous to conquered peoples. Romans allowed all the tribes to retain full autonomy in their own

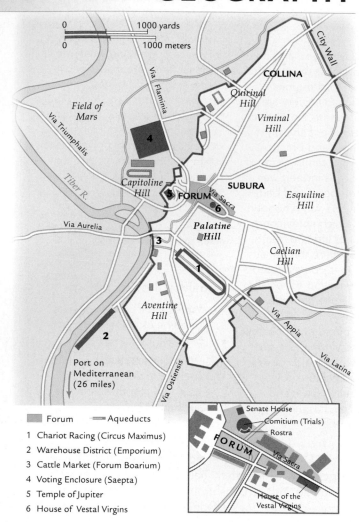

MAP 4.1 scale: 0–1000 yards / 0–1000 meters

Legend:
- ■ Forum
- ═ Aqueducts
- 1 Chariot Racing (Circus Maximus)
- 2 Warehouse District (Emporium)
- 3 Cattle Market (Forum Boarium)
- 4 Voting Enclosure (Saepta)
- 5 Temple of Jupiter
- 6 House of Vestal Virgins

MAP 4.1

Rome During the Republic

This map shows the city of Rome during the late Republic. The inset pinpoints the locations of the important features of the Forum.

Explore the Map

1. Which elements in the Forum and at the center of the city show how political life and religious institutions dominated life in Rome?

2. What were the political implications of the fact that the famous slum district, the Subura, was located so near the Forum and the Palatine Hill, where the wealthiest Romans lived?

territories and to elect their own officials, keep their own laws, and collect their own taxes. These peoples were required to supply troops for Rome's armies and to avoid pursuing independent foreign policy. Many

of the conquered peoples did have to give up some territory for Rome to use as colonies to feed their land hunger, but the colonies served to help Rome watch over and control its ever-widening borders of influence. As a result of Rome's leadership, the conquered territories at times enjoyed more peace and freedom than they ever had. Rome's sensible policy toward the territories bought the loyalty of many states and created a relatively cohesive unit that would fuel further imperial expansion.

FAMILY LIFE AND CITY LIFE

The great Roman orator Cicero (106–43 B.C.E.) wrote that the Romans were like other peoples except in their religious fervor: "In reverence for the gods, we are far superior." Perhaps more than other ancient civilizations, the Romans saw the world as infused with spirits; in their view, almost every space was governed by some divinity. Rome itself was guarded by three deities that protected the state—Jupiter, Juno, and Minerva—but there were gods for even smaller spaces. There were goddesses for the countryside, for the hills, and for the valleys. There were three gods to guard entrances—one for the door, another for the hinges, and a third for the lintel, the door's upper supporting beam. The remaining spaces within the home were equally inhabited by spirits that demanded worship and sacrifice.

A Pious, Practical People

Formal worship of the many gods and goddesses took place at the temples, where priests presided over sacrifices and divination officials looked for favorable omens in the entrails of sacrificial animals. The Vestal Virgins, six priestesses who presided over the temple of Vesta, goddess of the hearth, kept the sacred fire of the state hearth burning. (See the major Temple of Jupiter and the House of the Vestal Virgins in **Map 4.1.**)

According to the Roman people, their success hinged on proper worship, which meant offering sacrifices. Sacrifices could be as small as a drop of wine or a honeycake, or as large as an ox, but the Romans believed their destiny was deeply tied to their proper observation of religious rituals. When Rome was sacked by the Gauls in 390 B.C.E., Livy reported, one Roman general supposedly said, "All things went well when we obeyed the gods, but badly when we disobeyed them."

In addition to piety, Romans valued moral seriousness. These hardworking men and women prized duty to family, clients, patrons, and the Republic itself. They rejected the individualism of the Greeks and would have found the idea of Achilles sulking in his tent while his compatriots died incomprehensible.

Legend:
- Territory of Roman Citizens
- Roman Territorial Conquests
- Carthaginian Territories
- Greek Territories

MAP 4.2

Italy, 265 B.C.E.

This map shows the tribes of the Italian peninsula who were conquered by the Romans, the dates of the conquests, and the nearby Carthaginian territories.

Explore the Map

1. How would the location of the Tiber River yield advantages for Rome's developing trade?

2. How would Rome's expansion in the western Mediterranean begin to intrude on Carthaginian holdings?

3. Why would Messana's location (where Rome and Carthage would first clash) be strategically important?

These serious men and women, who stressed collective responsibility and obedience to both secular and religious authority, would one day rule the entire Mediterranean world.

Loyalty to the Family

Roman religion, duty, and loyalty began in the family. A father, in theory, had complete authority over everyone in his household, including his wife, children, slaves, and even ex-slaves. The father served as guardian of the family's well-being and shared with his wife the responsibility for venerating the household gods. In addition to recognizing all the spirits who guarded the home, families worshiped their ancestors, whom they considered the original source of their prosperity. The best families displayed busts of their important ancestors in niches in the home. **Figure 4.4** shows a Roman man holding the busts of his forefathers, revealing the piety and ancestor worship so vital to Romans at that time.

Marriages in early Rome were arranged, to make politically advantageous alliances between families and ensure the continuation of the family through children. A woman could be given

Marriage patterns

in marriage in two ways. Her family of origin might transfer her to her husband's control, in which case she became part of his family and participated in the worship of his ancestors. Or she might remain under her father's "hand," never becoming a full part of her husband's family. In this case, the woman's family of origin kept more political and financial control of her resources. **Figure 4.5** shows a modest, serious Roman couple with their child. They do not touch, and they stand together looking into the distance. The couple in this gravestone contrasts strikingly with the affectionate Etruscan couple shown in **Figure 4.2** and suggests that Romans considered marriage a serious duty.

Despite the authority of husbands, women still played an important role in the family. They instilled the values of Rome in their children and raised them to be responsible and obedient citizens. Historical evidence such as letters indicate that mothers exerted as much stern authority as fathers and therefore wielded some political power through their sons.

The Challenges of Childhood

Birth in a Roman home always involved great risk to the newborn. When a child was born, the midwife inspected it, even before the umbilical cord was cut, to judge whether it was physically perfect. If it was not, she would likely cut the cord too closely, thus killing the child. A healthy newborn was placed at the father's feet. If he accepted the infant, picking

FIGURE 4.4 Roman Patrician, first century C.E. The conservative Romans took great pride in their ancestors, whose lives, they believed, gave legitimacy to their descendants. Romans venerated busts of their ancestors, as this statue of a Roman holding two busts of his forebears shows.

up a boy or acknowledging a girl, then the child was raised. If he did not, the baby would be "exposed"—placed outside to die or to be taken in and raised as a slave. Roman law required the father to raise one daughter, but he could choose to raise all his daughters, as many families did. However, it is impossible to know how many children were exposed and how many died as a result. In one chilling letter, a soldier matter-of-factly instructs his pregnant wife to keep the child if it is a boy and to expose it if it is a girl. We can only conclude that the practice of exposure was not considered extraordinary.

When the child was accepted, however, he or she received endless attention. Influential physicians like Soranus and Galen (second century C.E.) detailed explicit instructions on how to raise an infant, and all the child-rearing advice focused on molding the baby to be shapely, disciplined, and obedient. Newborns were tightly bound in strips of cloth for two months to ensure that their limbs would grow straight. Once a day they were unwrapped to be bathed in a tepid bath. Parents would then stretch, massage, and shape the screaming babies before tightly wrapping them again. Noble children were usually breast-fed by a wet nurse (a slave woman who had recently had a child), and many physicians recommended that children begin to drink sweet wine at 6 months. Infant mortality was high despite the recommendations of physicians and the attentions of loving parents—fewer than half of the newborns raised reached puberty.

Child-rearing practices

At the age of 6 or 7, children were put in the care of tutors, and their formal education began. Patrician children of both genders were expected to receive an education so as to transmit Roman culture to the next generations. Girls also learned to spin and weave wool, activities that consumed much of their time in their adult years.

By age 12, boys had graduated to higher schooling, learning literature, arithmetic, geometry, music, astronomy, and logic. This general education prepared boys for public life—the honorable and expected course for a wealthy boy. If a boy was talented, at age 16 he began an advanced study of rhetoric. This skill would help him later to speak persuasively to the crowds that had so much influence on the political life of the Republic.

Life in the City

By the late Republic (ca. 50 B.C.E.), the population of Rome had reached an astounding 1,000,000. The richest lived on the hills (shown on **Map 4.1**), aloof from the bustle of the crowds and the smells of the lower city. They surrounded themselves with elegance and beauty and often decorated their houses with wall paintings called frescoes.

The painting in **Figure 4.6** adorned the inner wall of a house of a wealthy Roman and shows an urban scene where attractive houses range up the hills. This view not only gives us a sense of what the ideal city looked like but also reveals the degree to which Romans praised the urban life that formed the heart of Roman culture. The decorated door at the front of the painting demonstrates how separate the noble Roman's private space was from the public space of the colonnaded temple at the top of the illustration. At this front door, clients gathered in the hopes of

FIGURE 4.5 Family Gravestone, first century B.C.E. This memorial stone of Lucius Vibius and his wife and child captures the qualities of the ideal republican Roman family: serious and modest, with no visible emotion.

being welcomed in. Even in this urban life, Romans did not forget their affection for the land—notice the potted plants near the door. The houses of the wealthy featured elaborate, well-tended pleasure gardens and fountains. Even landless renters kept potted plants on the terraces and balconies of their apartment buildings.

Below the hills, most city dwellers lived in small houses or crowded, multistoried tenements. The region of the city called Subura was the most notorious, and as **Map 4.1** shows, it was near the Forum and at the foot of the most prestigious house on the Palatine Hill. People brought water from the public fountains and heated their homes with open flames or burning charcoal. Waste ran down sewers and washed out of the city, but never with the efficiency that modern hygiene requires. Townspeople dumped garbage just outside city walls near the cemetery for the poor, where shallowly buried corpses rotted and carrion crows circled endlessly. Wealthy urban men and women carried little bouquets of fragrant flowers that they held to their noses to protect themselves from the smells of the city.

In addition to being the political center of Rome, the Forum was the economic and social center. Two rows of shops lined the large square, and merchants shouted, hawking their wares as slaves shopped for the household needs. In the afternoon, work ceased and the men headed for the baths. (Women, too, probably had public bathing time set aside for them as *Life in the Forum* well, but the historical evidence for the Republic does not explicitly discuss it.) The baths served much as a

Family Life and City Life 117

FIGURE 4.6 Urban Scene Fresco, ca. 45 B.C.E. When Mount Vesuvius erupted in 79 C.E., it buried a beautiful villa at Boscoreale, near Pompeii. Excavations have uncovered magnificent frescoes such as this urban scene that was painted on a wall to give the illusion of looking out a window at the urban spaces the Romans designed and built so well.

modern health club. People exercised or played ball, swam, took steam baths, had massages, got their body hair plucked, and socialized. Then, in the late afternoon and evening, it was time for leisure. The crowds in the Forum strolled, chatted, and gossiped. Romans always included a political dimension in this informal talk, for here politicians gained nicknames like "knock-knees" or more obscene appellations. In the course of passing on rumors and jokes, Romans helped set future political fortunes.

In the afternoon and at home, men abandoned their togas (a huge length of unbleached wool, carefully wrapped around the wearer) and wore their undergarments: usually a tunic that came down to the thighs. Men who wore sleeves or long tunics were considered effeminate. Women, on the other hand, covered themselves with long, sleeved tunics that they wore under their dresses.

As in cities today, life in the urban heart of Rome was a mixture of ease and hardship, and of excitement, fellowship, and danger. Yet this complex, vibrant center marked the ideal of the Republic: a place where citizens met and mingled in a public setting, and where political and economic dramas unfolded. Unfortunately for the Romans, this appealing way of life could not last. As Rome expanded, its spectacular military successes brought changes that undermined the Roman civic ideal.

EXPANSION AND TRANSFORMATION,
265–133 B.C.E.

The Romans who enjoyed and contributed so much to the good life of the city represented only a part of the population. Rome's success derived primarily from its army. Over time, the army began to define the very structure of what was becoming an empire. As we saw in the example of Cincinnatus, the army of the Republic was made up of citizen-soldiers who set aside their work to fight for a season. When Rome's leaders believed they were threatened by foreign invaders, the consuls raised a red flag in the Forum. Then free householders throughout the territory—that is, tax-paying men between the ages of 17 and 46—had to report to the capitol within thirty days. From this large group, the consuls and military tribunes chose their army.

Weapons and discipline

The Romans' Victorious Army

By the early Republic, the army was organized in legions of about 4,000 men—about 40 companies of 100 men each, although the actual numbers that constituted a legion or a company varied over time. These were mostly foot soldiers fighting bare-legged in their tunics. All soldiers took an oath binding themselves to the army until death or the end of the war. The remarkable strength of this citizen army lay in its unequaled discipline. For example, commanders practiced decimation, in which one soldier in ten was killed if a unit disobeyed an order or failed badly. Traditionally, warfare in the Mediterranean was governed by informal rules that allowed surrender before either side suffered extensive losses. The Roman soldier, however, hated to return home defeated. The shame of it would prevent him from resuming his life in the city where everyone met face-to-face in the Forum.

The Roman army was an obedient, iron-willed fighting machine under the strict command of its leaders. Roman soldiers ate only wheat bread and drank only water while at war. In hot weather, they added some vinegar. Sometimes during campaigns in which the wheat ran out, the soldiers had to eat meat, but they feared the meat would "soften" them and erode their invincibility. They sneered at their opponents who slept heavily on wine and food, and this attitude probably gave them confidence in the heat of battles. The iron discipline extended to camp life, because soldiers could not rest until they had fortified their camp to make them impregnable to surprise attack. **Figure 4.7a** shows soldiers building such a camp after a long day's march.

The victorious republican soldier returned after a season of fighting with only a few gold coins in his

FIGURE 4.7(a)

Trajan's Column

This relief carving (a) is a detail of one of the winding panels from Trajan's Column, which was dedicated in 113 C.E. to celebrate the emperor Trajan's victories in war. The full column is shown on the right (b). Even though this column is from later than the republican period, it remains one of the important historical sources for Roman military life. The scene highlighted here depicts soldiers, dressed in battle armor (except

FIGURE 4.7(b)

their helmets), building a camp—a common daily activity for soldiers while they were on campaign.

Connecting Art & Society

1. What specific tasks are the soldiers performing?

2. Why do you think the artists included these tasks on a column celebrating a military victory?

3. How did these activities contribute to the might of the Roman army?

---

hand and the pride of victory in his heart. Through a relentless series of such victories, by 265 B.C.E. Rome had unified virtually the whole Italian peninsula (see **Map 4.2**). However, the Republic's growing wealth and power clashed with new foes outside the peninsula. These contests would transform the army, the Republic, and the Romans.

Wars of the Mediterranean

As we saw in **Map 4.2,** after Rome consolidated its hold on the Italian peninsula, it confronted Carthage, the other great power in the western Mediterranean. Carthage was founded around the same time as the city of Rome (ca. 800 B.C.E.) by a group of colonists from Phoenicia. The colony profited from its trade, prospered, and became a diverse and cosmopolitan

city as great as those of the Hellenistic kingdoms. At the height of its power, the population of Phoenician Carthage probably approached 400,000, of whom no more than 100,000 were of fairly pure Phoenician heritage. In the busy shops, merchants spoke Greek and many other languages of the Mediterranean as they sold wares drawn from the farthest reaches of the Hellenistic kingdoms.

The skillful Phoenician sailors even ventured outside the Mediterranean basin, trading along the western coast of Africa. The Greek historian Herodotus (ca. 484–ca. 424 B.C.E.) described how Carthaginian merchants traded with African tribes, relying on mutual trust instead of language skills. The merchants unloaded their cargo on the African shore, summoned local tribesmen by smoke signals, and then returned to their ships. The Africans approached and laid out what they thought would be a fair amount for the goods and then withdrew without taking the goods until the Carthaginians indicated their agreement on the price. As Herodotus wrote, "They say that thus neither party is ill-used; for the Carthaginians do not take the gold until they have the worth of their merchandise, nor do the natives touch the merchandise until the Carthaginians have taken the gold." By the third century B.C.E., the wealthy, enterprising Carthaginians had gained control of many territories in the western Mediterranean (see **Map 4.2**) and confronted the growing power of the Roman Republic.

Rome's expansion and growing alliances began to encroach upon the Carthaginians, who had controlled the western Mediterranean for so long, and it was only a matter of time before tensions came to a head. Rome's clash with Carthage began over who would control the Sicilian city of Messana, an area that the Romans saw as strategically vital to the security of southern Italy because it was on the straits between the island and the mainland (see **Map 4.2**). Carthage, for its part, resented the idea of Rome as a presence in Sicily. In 264 B.C.E., both sides sent troops in an effort to conquer the disputed island. This confrontation began the first of three hostile encounters between Rome and Carthage, called the Punic Wars. *Punic* meant "Phoenician," by which the Romans recalled the origins of the Carthaginians.

> First Punic War

But to broaden their military efforts beyond Italy, the Romans needed ships. The city managed to raise some money and build a fleet, yet it had trouble finding admirals who had any solid seafaring experience. The Romans nevertheless demonstrated their famous tenacity and designed a new warship that would change the nature of naval battles. Before the Romans, the basic tactic at sea was ramming one ship into another, thus sinking the second. Sometimes sailors would board the opposing ship to engage the enemy, but not very often. The Romans changed this. They developed a new vessel that featured a special platform that allowed many infantrymen on board. When they approached an opposing ship, Roman soldiers could then board the enemy vessel and fight hand to hand, a style that was their specialty. In the Punic Wars, Carthaginian naval commanders did what usually brought them success—they rammed the Roman ships. Before the Carthaginian vessel could pull away, however, a platform descended and Roman troops swept across, taking the lightly manned Carthaginian ship. The Romans would then simply scuttle their own destroyed ship and seize the Carthaginian one. **Figure 4.8** shows one of these impressive warships with infantrymen poised to fight.

> New Roman navy

FIGURE 4.8 Roman Warship The Roman infantry was unbeatable, but when Romans challenged Carthage, they had to learn to fight at sea. Instead of ramming an opponent's ship, Romans lowered a gangplank so that their infantry, shown here, could board the enemy ship and fight by hand.

In 241 B.C.E., Rome finally won a decisive sea battle against Carthage, and the First Punic War ended with a Roman victory. The Republic received control of Sicily and a large financial indemnity from the Carthaginians. But the larger question of who would control the western Mediterranean remained unresolved. A second contest seems to have been inevitable.

The Second Punic War (218–201 B.C.E.) began in Spain, where Rome and Carthage had signed a treaty dividing the spheres of influence at the Ebro River (see **Map 4.3**). However, the treaty left one issue unresolved: Who would control the city of Saguntum, which lay south of the Ebro? Under the terms of the treaty it was in Carthaginian territory, but Rome had an alliance with Saguntum that predated the treaty. The Carthaginian general, Hannibal Barca, attacked Saguntum and in the process began the Second Punic War. This war was different from the first one, for when war was declared, the Romans had control of the sea, so Carthaginians knew victory would come only if they brought war to Rome itself.

> Second Punic War

The Carthaginians may have lacked a fleet, but in their general Hannibal they possessed one of the greatest military strategists in history. The confident general surprised the Romans by taking the war to Italy, moving his large Hellenistic-style army overland from Spain into the peninsula. Now Roman legions had to confront the military power of armies that included war elephants. Crossing the Alps with 30,000 to 40,000 men, 6,000 horses, and about 35 elephants was a difficult feat; many men and elephants fell and died in the dangerous passes. However, Hannibal emerged in northern Italy with enough of an army (complete with a dozen or so elephants) to shock the local population and win many victories.

Hannibal expected Rome's subject peoples to rise up in his support, and while some did, the inner

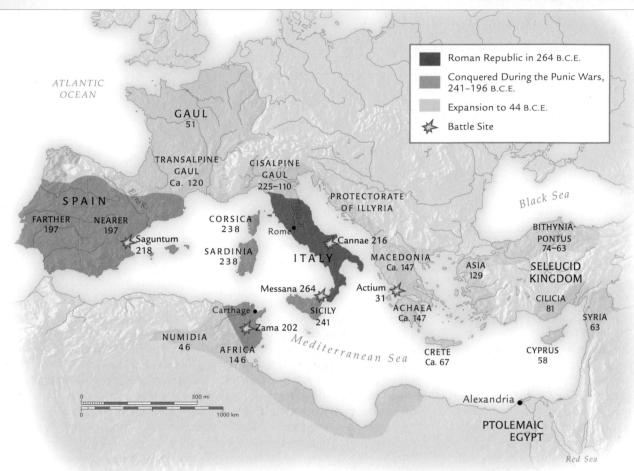

MAP 4.3

Expansion of the Roman Republic, 264–44 B.C.E.

This map shows the expansion of the Republic as it fought victorious wars against Carthage and the Macedonian and Seleucid kingdoms in the East. Notice the scale for distances.

Explore the Map

1. How hard would it have been for the Carthaginian general Hannibal to transport his army and elephants across the distances from Spain to Italy? Why?

2. Given Rome's expansion, how likely was it that the Hellenistic kingdoms of the Seleucids and Ptolemies would come into conflict with Rome?

3. How would Romans become influenced by Hellenistic culture in these conquests?

---

core of central Italy stayed loyal. The strong alliance system that Rome had built gave it a huge advantage. Nevertheless, the astonishing general handed Rome its worst defeat ever at the Battle of Cannae in 216 B.C.E., in which approximately 30,000 Romans died (see **Map 4.3**). Document 4.2 describes this significant battle and shows Hannibal's battle plan. Romans were shocked and frightened—for years Roman mothers would scare naughty children with the threat "Hannibal will get you"—and yet the Romans would not surrender. They adopted a defensive attitude of

delay and refusal to fight while the Carthaginian forces marched up and down Italy for almost seventeen years—wreaking havoc along the way.

Finally, Rome produced a general who could match Hannibal's skill. Publius Cornelius Scipio (236–183 B.C.E.) had studied Carthaginian battlefield tactics and had the skill to improve on them. Scipio took Carthage's Spanish lands and then sailed to North Africa, bringing the war to Carthage. Hannibal had to leave Italy to defend his homeland, and he had to face the Romans virtually unaided. The

thinking about
DOCUMENTS

DOCUMENT 4.2

Hannibal Triumphs at the Battle of Cannae

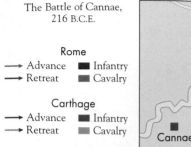
The Battle of Cannae, 216 B.C.E.

Rome
→ Advance   ■ Infantry
→ Retreat   ■ Cavalry

Carthage
→ Advance   ■ Infantry
→ Retreat   ■ Cavalry

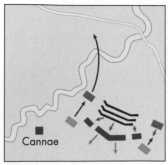
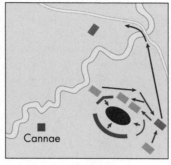

The Carthaginians, led by Hannibal, were able to inflict the single greatest defeat of the Romans in the history of their empire. By feigning retreat and convincing the Romans that they were abandoning Cannae, the Carthaginian army was able to surround the Romans and defeat them without mercy. This defeat caused great alarm to the citizens of Rome, as it left them nearly defenseless.

FIGURE 4.9 The Battle of Cannae, 216 B.C.E.

The Roman historian Florus (ca. 70–ca. 140 C.E.) wrote History of the Romans, *in which he recounted the long-remembered Battle of Cannae (216 B.C.E.), a turning point during the Second Punic War between Rome and Carthage. Military thinkers today still study Hannibal's winning battle strategy, but Florus notes Hannibal's mistake. Study* **Figure 4.9** *to understand Hannibal's winning strategy.*

The fourth and almost mortal wound of the Roman Empire was at Cannæ, an obscure village of Apulia; which, however, became famous by the greatness of the defeat, its celebrity being acquired by the slaughter of forty thousand men. Here the general, the ground, the face of heaven, the day, indeed, all nature conspired together for the destruction of the unfortunate army. For Hannibal, the most artful of generals, not content with sending pretended deserters among the Romans, who fell upon their rear as they were fighting, but having also noted the nature of the ground in those open plains, where the heat of the sun is extremely violent, the dust very great, and the wind blows constantly, and as it were statedly, from the east, drew up his army in such a position that, while the Romans were exposed to all these inconveniences, he himself, having heaven, as it were, on his side, fought with wind, dust, and sun in his favor. Two vast armies, in consequence, were slaughtered till the enemy were satiated, and till Hannibal said to his soldiers, "Put up your swords." Of the two commanders, one escaped, the other was slain; which of them showed the greater spirit is doubtful. Paulus was ashamed to survive; Varro did not despair. Of the greatness of the slaughter the following proofs may be noticed: that the Aufidus was for some time red with blood; that a bridge was made of dead bodies, by order of Hannibal, over the torrent of Vergellus, and that two *modii* of rings were sent to Carthage, and the equestrian dignity estimated by measure.

It was afterward not doubted but that Rome might have seen its last day, and that Hannibal, within five days, might have feasted in the Capitol, if—as they say that Adherbal, the Carthaginian, the son of Bomilcar, observed—"he had known as well how to use his victory as how to gain it." But at that crisis, as is generally said, either the fate of the city that was to be empress of the world, or his own want of judgment, and the influence of deities unfavorable to Carthage, carried him in a different direction. When he might have taken advantage of his victory, he chose rather to seek enjoyment from it, and, leaving Rome, to march into Campania and to Tarentum, where both he and his army soon lost their vigor, so that it was justly remarked that "Capua proved a Cannæ to Hannibal"; since the sunshine of Campania and the warm springs of Baiæ subdued—who could have believed it?—him who had been unconquered by the Alps and unshaken in the field.

SOURCE: Florus, *History of the Romans,* in *The Great Events by Famous Historians,* vol. II, ed. Rossiter Johnson (The National Alumni, 1905), pp. 186–187.

Analyze the Document

1. What are the tactics of ancient battles, and in what ways is Hannibal particularly skilled?

2. How much devastation is caused by the Battle of Cannae? Why does this destruction make the battle so traumatic to Romans?

3. Why does Hannibal not follow up with a decisive victory?

Roman control of the sea prevented the Carthaginian ally Philip V of Macedonia (of the Hellenistic Macedonian kingdom discussed in Chapter 3) from helping, and Carthaginian support in North Africa was weak. Scipio decisively defeated Hannibal at the Battle of Zama in 202 B.C.E. (see **Map 4.3**) and won the surname "Africanus" to commemorate his great victory that saved Rome. Carthage again sued for peace—giving up Spain and promising not to wage war without Rome's permission. But peace would prove temporary.

Carthage was placed in a difficult position, for Numidia, one of Rome's allies in North Africa, was encroaching on its territory. Yet Carthage could not wage war against Numidia without Rome's permission, and Rome withheld it. The Senate was led by Cato the Elder (234–149 B.C.E.), who was

Third Punic War

virulently anti-Carthaginian. Plutarch recorded his famous rousing speech in 150 B.C.E. as he tried to spur his countrymen to resume the fighting against Carthage. He reminded the Senate that Carthage was "only three days' sail from Rome," and he ended all his speeches with the phrase "Carthage must be destroyed." Cato spoke for many Romans who wanted to take on their old enemy again. The inflammatory language worked, and the Third Punic War began. After a long siege of the citadel at the top of the hill overlooking the town, Rome crushed the city of Carthage in 146 B.C.E. The Carthaginian general surrendered, and his wife, accusing him of cowardice, committed suicide by leaping with her two children into the flames of the burning city. The Roman general—another Scipio called Aemilianus—reputedly shed tears at the sight of the ruin of the great city. The once-shining city of Carthage would lie in ruins for a century until Rome itself recolonized it.

The wars against Carthage drew the Romans into battling in the eastern Mediterranean, leading to three wars against Macedonia between 215 and ca. 168 B.C.E. Romans felt drawn into the first war because the Macedonian king, Philip V (221–179 B.C.E.), had allied with Hannibal after the Roman defeat at Cannae. Following this indecisive war, Rome was again drawn into eastern affairs as some of the Greek poleis solicited Rome's help against a coalition between the Macedonian and Seleucid kings. | Macedonia and Greece | This time Rome won decisively and Macedonia agreed to stay out of Greek affairs. The third war arose when Macedonia again tried to reassert control over Greece. As a result of this war, Rome ruthlessly divided up Macedonia and eliminated any opposition.

At first, Rome left the Greeks "free," but there quickly arose a difference of opinion about the meaning of this term. The Greeks believed freedom meant to do as they liked; Romans believed it meant to act as obedient Roman clients. The Roman Senate finally ran out of patience and decided to annex the Greek mainland. To set an example to the recalcitrant Greeks, a Roman commander burned the city of Corinth, enslaved its inhabitants, and brought rich plunder back to Rome. The expansion eastward had begun, and it continued with the establishment of the province of Asia in 137 B.C.E., when the last king of Pergamum died, willing his land to Rome. Money, art, and slaves now flowed from the east to Rome, and the Republic had to decide how to govern its new far-flung conquests (see **Map 4.3**).

Historians still disagree about Rome's motives for continuing the warfare. Rome often marched to protect its allies—waging what they called "just wars." At the same time, some Romans were becoming rich in these enterprises, and Roman generals saw war as the road to upward mobility. Now the path to success for an ambitious Roman lay not in impressing his fellow citizens in the Forum, but in leading victorious armies.

Rome did not always annex territories outright. Sometimes it operated through client states, leaving local rulers in place. Sometimes victorious Romans established the conquered territories as provinces— one in Africa, one in Asia, and later across the Alps in Gaul (southern France) in an area that is still called Provence. | Administering provinces | Within the provinces, people lived as they had in the past, but Rome's leaders expected these states to conform to their wishes (which at times caused friction). Governors were appointed by the Roman Senate to preserve peace and administer justice to Roman citizens. Other duties were given to private individuals, who could make fortunes performing administrative duties. For example, tax collectors received a contract to collect a certain amount of taxes, and they could legally keep some profits they squeezed from local populations. The governors were supposed to make sure tax collectors did not abuse their privilege, but, not surprisingly, many of them took full advantage of this system and extracted huge amounts of money from helpless residents. The conquests in Italy had yielded most profits from land. In the provinces, on the other hand, people made money from land, slaves, and graft. In the process, the Roman Republic itself was transformed in various ways by its military success abroad.

An Influx of Slaves

In the ancient world, successful military campaigning earned a victor not just new territory and riches but also slaves. As Rome expanded, it accumulated more and more bondsmen and -women. After the Second Punic War, more than 200,000 men and women were captured as prisoners of war and brought to Italy as slaves. Numbers like these changed the nature of Roman society. Now, instead of each small householder having one to three slaves (as we saw was the pattern in

EXPANSION OF ROME

340 B.C.E.	Revolt of Latin allies
264–241 B.C.E.	First Punic War
263 B.C.E.	Rome rules Italian peninsula
218–203 B.C.E.	Hannibal fights in Italy
218–201 B.C.E.	Second Punic War
215–ca. 168 B.C.E.	Wars of Macedonia
149–146 B.C.E.	Third Punic War
148–146 B.C.E.	Macedonia and Greece become provinces

KEY DATES

ancient Greece), rich households might have hundreds of domestic slaves. By the end of the Republic, there were between two and three million slaves in Italy, an astounding 35 to 40 percent of the population.

Thousands of slaves labored in agriculture or mining, working in large anonymous gangs. However, in the cities, slaves and citizens often worked in the same occupations, and all could earn money through their labor. The most undesirable jobs—garbage collection, mining, acting, and prostitution—were generally reserved for slaves, although freed men and women, while technically citizens, were willing to do the most lucrative of these jobs. Often slaves dominated some of the higher-status jobs. After Rome's conquest of Greece (ca. 148 B.C.E.), most of the tutors and teachers to Roman children were Greek slaves. The Biography on page 125 describes the successful career of a playwright who had been a slave. Most physicians were either Greek or trained in Greece, and it was not unusual for physicians to be succeeded by their Greek slaves, whom they had trained and then freed to take their place.

Slave occupations

Perhaps not surprisingly, Romans often feared their slaves. The Stoic philosopher Seneca (4 B.C.E.–65 C.E.) wrote that "the least of your slaves holds over you the power of life or death." As the numbers of slaves increased, Romans had more and more reason to worry, and they passed laws to try to protect themselves. For example, the punishment for murdering one's master was severe—all the slaves in the household were to be executed. The Roman historian Tacitus (ca. 56–ca. 120 C.E.) recorded an incident when an ex-consul was murdered by a slave. A senator arguing that the state should enforce the harsh law and kill the whole household said: "Whom will a large number of slaves keep safe, when four hundred could not protect Pedanius Secundus? . . . In every wholesale punishment there is some injustice to individuals, which is compensated by the advantage to the state." Not only did individual instances of slave treachery crop up, but large-scale slave rebellions broke out as well.

Slave revolts

Three great slave uprisings disrupted Italy and Sicily between 135 and 71 B.C.E. The most famous was led by the gladiator Spartacus between 73 and 71 B.C.E. Spartacus escaped his master with 70 of his fellow gladiators. Many others joined them as the army of almost 70,000 slaves ravaged portions of Italy. They succeeded in defeating many of the soldiers sent after them. Some sources suggest that Spartacus even tried to take his army to Sicily to rally the slaves there but could not gather enough ships to cross the sea. Spartacus was finally killed and the rebellion crushed. Six thousand of Spartacus's followers were crucified—the brutal form of execution reserved for slaves. This revolt was suppressed, but Rome did not forget the potential

for violence that simmered within the many men and women they had enslaved in their imperial expansion.

Economic Disparity and Social Unrest

Just as the expansion of Rome altered the nature of slavery, it transformed many other aspects of life in the Republic. These changes were noted sadly by many conservative Romans who watched their traditional way of life fade. One Roman (Silius Italicus) lamented the aftermath of Rome's victory in the Punic Wars: "[I]f it was fated that the Roman character should change when Carthage fell, would that Carthage was still standing." But such qualms were too late; the Republic was transmuting into something else entirely, even as some Romans mourned it.

One of the most noticeable changes came in the form of increasing disparity between rich and poor. Many of the upper classes had grown very rich indeed. Governors of provinces had the opportunity to make fortunes undreamed of in the Republic's earlier years. Other enterprising Romans made fortunes in shipbuilding contracts, banking, slave trading, and many other high-profit occupations. Rome had become a Hellenistic state like the successor states of Alexander the Great (see Chapter 3), with a growing distance between the rich and the poor.

While some Romans amassed great fortunes, others suffered a worsening of their economic situations. The example of Cincinnatus, who fought for only one season and then returned to his plow, was impossible to repeat when foes were far away and wars long. During the Punic Wars, military time was extended. As a result, more than 50 percent of adult males spent over seven years in the army, and some spent as long as twenty years. Throughout most of the Republic, the army was not formally paid, and this caused both some hardship and a particularly strong relationship between soldiers and their generals. By right, generals controlled all booty taken in war, and they distributed some of it to their troops. Thus generals acted as patrons to their client soldiers, who increasingly owed loyalty to their general rather than to Rome itself. Meanwhile, as soldiers stayed longer in the army, their family fields remained unplowed. Numerous farmers went bankrupt, and soldiers returned to their homes to find them sold and their wives and children turned out of the family farm.

Newly rich men and women eagerly purchased these neglected lands, and small landholders were replaced by large plantations worked by gangs of new slaves. Fields that had cultivated wheat were slowly transformed to produce olives and wine grapes, much more lucrative crops. Other great landowners in Italy grew rich on ranches that raised animals for meat, milk, or wool. Now Romans had to import their wheat from abroad, particularly North Africa.

BIOGRAPHY

Publius Terentius Afer (Terence) (ca. 190–159 B.C.E.)

During the peaceful interlude between the First and Second Punic Wars, a slave trader in Carthage purchased a young man named Terence. We have no idea how Terence came into the hands of a slave dealer; we do know he was not a prisoner of war. However, many North Africans were enslaved by the Carthaginians; Terence may have come from one such slave family. His surname, Afer, meaning "the African," suggests that he was not originally from Carthage. He was described as being "of medium stature, graceful in person, and of dark complexion," and some scholars have suggested that he was from a black sub-Saharan family. The ambiguity of Terence's background points to the cosmopolitan, highly diverse nature of the city of Carthage. It was one of the jewels of the Mediterranean—a bustling city where people mingled from all over and shared in a dynamic cultural life. Terence's early experience in the cosmopolitan city no doubt prepared him to contribute to Rome's growing interest in Hellenistic literature.

The young slave was brought to Rome and sold to a senator, M. Terentius Lucanus, who must have recognized the youth's promise. The senator had him educated as a freeman and then granted him his freedom. This is but one example of many talented slaves who were freed by their owners during the optimistic years of the Republic. Terence then pursued a literary career.

The intellectual gifts that had won Terence his freedom earned him the acceptance of an aristocratic circle of young men who were interested in literature. These educated youths were actively involved in fostering Greek literature, and such literary circles had much influence in Hellenizing Roman society.

At first, Terence was outside the guild of poets and the working playwrights. He made his artistic breakthrough when he got a chance to submit one of his plays for production to the aging but well-established poet Caecilius. Terence found out where the poet was dining and approached him as he reclined on his couch eating with friends. Because Terence was a stranger and plainly dressed, Caecilius invited him only to sit on a stool and recite from his work. After a few verses, however, the old poet was so impressed with Terence's talent that he invited him to join him on the couch and share the festive dinner. The budding playwright's career was launched.

Terence wrote six plays based on traditional Greek models, even specifying that they be performed in Greek dress. These plays show Terence's talent and understanding of both human nature and the social realities in Rome. Yet he received mixed reactions from the Romans. During his short lifetime, Terence was much criticized by other playwrights, and like so much else in Rome, these critiques were conducted publicly. Terence addressed his critics (and attacked other playwrights) in the prologues to the plays. These public debates tell us much about the openly competitive nature of the artistic world during the Republic.

Terence was accused first of plagiarism, meaning that someone else claimed to have been the first to translate Greek plays into Latin. In a prologue, Terence flatly denies "any knowledge of the play's previous Latinization." Terence was also charged with being "untraditional"—a serious insult to Romans. According to his accusers, he did not remain true to the Greek originals. Terence admitted that he combined plots and created interesting works of art rather than translations. As he put it, precise translations often turned "the best Greek plays . . . into Latin flops." These criticisms reveal a people struggling to discover a new art form and to determine the rules with which to judge it.

Terence challenged his audiences to judge his works on their own merits. Not surprisingly, many of his contemporaries appreciated his talent, for he did more than reproduce classic plays—he gave them his own stamp. For example, instead of simply relying on slapstick humor (as Plautus did), Terence developed a clever use of language to provide humor. He also used suspense as a dynamic device that would have a long history in the theater. His fame long outlasted him. Long after Terence's death, Cicero and Caesar, both known for their eloquence, praised his work as a model of elegant language. Audiences ever since have found his plays brilliant.

A Talented

Slave

Unfortunately, Terence died while still in his prime. In 159 B.C.E., the 31-year-old undertook a journey to Greece, possibly to study theater or to escape the jealous rumors of his rivals. He died on the way, from either illness or shipwreck. He left a revered body of work that people still enjoy and appreciate today. Perhaps equally important, Terence exemplified the kind of upward mobility available to educated slaves during an age when Rome fell in love with Greek intellectual life.

Connecting People & Society

1. How does Terence's life demonstrate the Hellenizing of the Republic after the North African conquests?

2. What does this life reveal about the nature of Roman slavery?

3. What problems does Terence face, and what do they reveal about Roman culture?

Spurred by economic hardship, the displaced citizens flocked to the city. The population swelled with a new class of people—propertyless day laborers who were unconnected to the structures of patronage and land that had defined the early Republic. These mobs created more and more problems for the nobility because they always represented a potentially revolutionary force in the Forum. Aristocrats tried to keep them happy and harmless by subsidizing food, but this short-term solution could not solve the deeper problem of lost jobs taken by newly captured slaves and land seized by the newly rich. The situation had become volatile indeed.

New poverty

THE HELLENIZING OF THE REPUBLIC

As if these social tensions were not disruptive enough, new intellectual influences further modified Rome's traditional value system. As the Republican armies conquered some of the great centers of Hellenistic culture from Greece to North Africa, Romans became deeply attracted to many of the Hellenistic ways. As the Roman poet Horace (65–8 B.C.E.) observed: "Captive Greece took her Captor Captive." With the capture of slaves from Greece, Greek art, literature, and learning came to Rome, and many in the Roman aristocracy became bilingual, adding Greek to their native Latin. Rome became a Hellenized city, with extremes of wealth and poverty and a growing emphasis on individualism over obedience to the family.

Cato the Elder (234–149 B.C.E.)—the anti-Carthaginian orator—was one Roman who feared the changes that came with the increasing wealth and love of things Greek, and when he held the office of censor (see **Figure 4.3**), he tried to stem the tide of Hellenization. The office of censor had come to be an influential one. During the early Republic, censors had made lists of citizens and their property qualifications, but in time the censors became so powerful that they revised the lists of senators, deleting those whose behavior they deemed objectionable. To preserve the old values, Cato tried taxing luxury goods and charging fines to those who neglected their farms, but his efforts were in vain. Romans had added an appreciation of Greek beauty to their own practical skills, and they adopted a new love of luxury and power that seemed to erode the moral strength of old Rome. To men like Cato, the Republic was becoming unrecognizable.

Resisting change

Roman Engineering: Fusing Utility and Beauty

Most of the great building projects that so characterize Rome arose in the building boom during the early years of the empire, as we will see in the next chapter. However, the techniques that led to those projects were developed during the Republic and were refined by the influx of Greek ideas and artists during the wars of expansion in the third and second centuries B.C.E. During these years Rome developed a new aesthetic sense that combined its traditional love of utility with the Hellenistic ideals of beauty.

As we have seen, the Romans had learned much about engineering from the Etruscans, especially techniques for draining swamps and building conduits to move water. The early Romans had a strong practical side themselves and greatly admired feats of science and engineering. The Roman orator Cicero revealed this admiration when he traveled to Syracuse in 75 B.C.E. to visit the grave of Archimedes, the esteemed engineer we met in Chapter 3. When Cicero discovered that Archimedes' countrymen had forgotten him, he found the old engineer's grave and restored it.

Engineering

Rome's military success stemmed in part from the engineering achievements that supported the legions. For example, armies had to forge many rivers, and the Roman engineers invented ingenious devices to help them. General Julius Caesar (100–44 B.C.E.), in his account of one military campaign, described how he had to sink heavy timbers into the fast-moving Rhine River to build a bridge. The task was completed in ten days, and the army crossed. Engineers could build pontoon bridges even faster by floating flat-bottomed boats down the river and anchoring them at the intended crossing.

Perhaps Rome's greatest military engineering lay in the area of siege engines. Caesar described how the Romans patiently built a tall, fortified mound and tower next to a city they were besieging. As some soldiers fought from the top of the tower, they protected others who were beneath sturdy beams below. These hidden soldiers were then able to dismantle the bottom of the wall, causing it to collapse so the army could enter and take the city. Some Roman siege engines were so impressive that even Chinese sources documented them.

Engineering skills also brought many benefits to civilian life. The arch is a key example. The Greeks used post and lintel construction, which limited the variety of structures they could build. By using arches, Romans enhanced the size, range, and flexibility of their constructions. The use of the arch can most readily be seen in the aqueducts—perhaps the greatest examples of Roman civil engineering. Aqueducts brought water from rivers or springs into cities.

Romans had a huge thirst for water. The first aqueduct, the Aqua Appia, was built as early as 312 B.C.E., and it brought water through underground pipes from about 8 miles

Aqueducts

outside Rome. Later aqueducts used both subterranean pipes and overhead pipes mounted on arches, which allowed the engineers to adjust the height of the aqueduct to regulate the rate of the water flowing through the channel at the top. The more than 46-mile-long Claudian aqueduct, finished in 52 C.E., cost a fortune, what would be millions of dollars today. By the end of the first century C.E., nine aqueducts directed an astonishing 22,237,000 gallons of water into the city each day. (**Map 4.1** shows the locations of Rome's aqueducts.)

Rome exported these marvels of engineering to cities throughout the Mediterranean world, and some of the best-preserved aqueducts are outside Rome itself. **Figure 4.10** shows the most spectacular surviving aqueduct, the Pont du Gard outside Nîmes in southern France, which spans the River Gard and its valley. The water flows through an enclosed channel on the top, and a roadway runs over the lowest row of arches. Structures like these were marvels of Roman engineering, featuring solid design, practical application, visual appeal, and durability.

FIGURE 4.10 Pont du Gard Aqueduct, late first century B.C.E. Roman engineers built monumental aqueducts to carry water over great distances into their cities. This aqueduct in southern France brought water from springs 30 miles away to serve the city of Nîmes. The careful engineering maintains a constant decline, allowing the water to flow freely and gently.

Concrete: A New Building Material

In the late third century B.C.E., Roman architects discovered a new building material that opened even more architectural possibilities than the perfection of the arch. Masons found that mixing volcanic brick-earth with lime and water resulted in a strong, waterproof building material—concrete. With this new substance, architects could design large, heavy buildings in a variety of shapes.

Combining concrete construction with the knowledge of the arch allowed for even more flexibility than before. After they had mastered the arch, Romans built with barrel vaults, a row of arches spanning a large space. As early as 193 B.C.E., builders constructed a gigantic warehouse in Rome using this technique. Concrete and barrel vaults also made possible the design of large bathhouses, for the concrete was strong enough to withstand the heat of steam rooms. Finally, the new technology permitted the design of the oval amphitheaters that so characterized Rome.

Of course, people as religious as the Romans applied their architectural skills to their temples as well. Although most structures in Rome were made of brick or concrete covered with stucco, the growing Hellenization began to influence architectural tastes. Marble columns would soon grace the traditional buildings. In this new architecture, we can see the degree of the Greek slaves' influence on the Romans and Rome's own growing appreciation of Hellenistic art.

The fullest development of this temple construction took place early in the empire. The outstanding example of Roman religious architecture is the **Pantheon,** a temple dedicated to all the gods, shown in **Figure 4.11.** It was built in 125 C.E. on the site of a previous temple that had been constructed during the late Republic. The structure is a perfect combination of Roman and Hellenistic styles and thus embodies the transformation of republican Rome imposed by Hellenistic influences. The front of the temple has a classical rectangular porch with Corinthian columns (see **Figure 2.9,** on page 62) and a pediment, the triangular structure on top of the columns. From the front, the Pantheon resembles the Greek temples we saw in Chapter 2. Inside the temple, however, any resemblance to Hellenistic architecture disappears.

The interior of the Pantheon consists of a massive round space (visible in **Figure 4.11**) covered by a high dome, revealing the Romans' engineering skills. A heavy concrete base supports the weight of the whole, while the upper walls are constructed of a lighter mix of concrete. The center of the dome has an opening

Pantheon

FIGURE 4.11 The Pantheon, 125 c.e. The Romans' use of concrete permitted the construction of stunning, enduring structures such as the Pantheon, a temple devoted to all the gods. The dome's circular hole, called the *oculus* (eye), reminded visitors of the eye of Jupiter that watched them continuously.

have laughed at the play on words associating a punch with food, as well as the suggestion that the nobles were not really charitable to the starving. The plays included all types of Roman characters, from smart, scheming slaves to boastful soldiers and clever prostitutes, to many clients and patrons. Thus, Romans who watched these plays recognized and laughed at all the types of people that populated their world.

The Latin prose literature of the Republic emphasized the serious side of Roman character. The best of the prose writers were men who combined literary talent with public service—for example, Cicero and Julius Caesar.

Latin literature was shaped—indeed defined—by the writings of Cicero, whose career coincided with the decline of the Republic. His skillful oratory and strong opinions about Roman values placed him in the center of public life, but his long-standing influence derived from his prose, not his political involvement. His writings cover an extraordinary range of topics, from poetry to formal orations to deeply personal letters. From his more than nine hundred letters, we get a revealing picture of the personality of this influential man. He was deeply concerned about public affairs and political morality, writing, "our leaders ought to protect civil peace with honor and defend it even at the risk of life itself." At the same time, his letters reveal him to be vindictive, mercurial of mood, and utterly self-centered. Although scholars are ambivalent about the character of this complex man, there is no doubt about his influence. Cicero's writings defined the best use of Latin language, and his works were used as textbooks of how to construct elegant prose.

> Cicero

Julius Caesar's literary legacy also grew out of his active political life. As Caesar rose to power, he used literature to enhance his reputation in Rome. His accounts of his dazzling military campaigns in Gaul (across the Alps in modern France), vividly told in his *Commentaries*, intensified his popularity and have fascinated generations ever since. His Latin is clear and accessible, and his narrative vivid and exciting.

> Caesar's writings

that lets in natural light—and rain, though drainpipes beneath the ground (which still function today) took care of flooding problems.

Latin Comedy and the Great Prose Writers, 240–44 b.c.e.

In the third century b.c.e., Roman literature emerged. Written in Latin, it reflected the elements we have discussed throughout this chapter: Roman values, society, and the influence of Hellenistic culture. The earliest surviving examples of Roman literature are comic plays. Latin comedy flowered with the works of Plautus (205–185 b.c.e.) and Terence (190–159 b.c.e.), who wrote plays based on Hellenistic models but modified them for their Italian audience. Plautus and Terence wrote in verse, but unlike their Greek predecessors, they added a good deal of music, with flutes and cymbals accompanying the productions.

Like the Hellenistic plays, most comedies involved the triumph of love over obstacles. In Plautus's works particularly, the humor centered on jokes and elaborate puns within the stories and the plays were marked by slapstick, bawdy humor. For example, in one play Plautus described a confrontation in which a man threatened to beat a slave. The man said: "Whoever comes here eats my fists." The slave responded: "I do not eat at night, and I have dined; Pray give your supper to those who starve." The audience would

By the middle of the second century b.c.e., the Roman Republic had reached a crucial threshold. Vibrant, wealthy, and victorious in war, the Republic had established political and social structures that steadily fueled its success. But in crafting their society, the Romans had unwittingly planted the seeds of their own undoing. Their much-loved precepts, established in a simpler age, would prove unsustainable in a future where Rome boldly sought to extend its reach farther than ever before.

THE TWILIGHT OF THE REPUBLIC, 133–44 B.C.E.

In the mid-second century B.C.E., Rome suffered a sudden economic downturn. The wars of expansion had brought vast riches into Rome, and this wealth drove prices up. When the wars ended, the influx of slaves and wealth subsided. Furthermore, an unfortunate grain shortage made grain prices skyrocket. This shortage worsened in 135 B.C.E. with the revolt of the slaves in Sicily. Half of Rome's grain supply came from Sicily, so the interruption of grain flow threatened to starve the masses of people who had fled to Rome when their own small farms had been taken over. To stave off disaster, two tribunes of the plebeians, Tiberius and Gaius Gracchus, proposed reforms. (The brothers were known as the Gracchi, which is the plural form of their name in Latin.)

The Reforms of the Gracchi, 133–123 B.C.E.

The Gracchi brothers came from a noble family, yet they devoted their lives to helping the Roman poor. They credited their mother, Cornelia, with giving them the education and motivation they needed to use their privilege for the good of the Roman people. The Gracchi seemed to many Romans to represent the best of republican men—devoted to a public life. Of course, many modern historians have observed that helping the poor would increase their own clients and prestige. Regardless of the motivations of the brothers, they set themselves apart from many aristocrats who no longer obeyed the rigorous demands of public service, preferring private pleasures instead. There were too few nobles willing to sacrifice their own interests for those of Rome when Tiberius became tribune of the plebeians in 133 B.C.E.

In Tiberius's view, Rome's problems came from the decline of the small farmer, which in turn prompted migrations into the city and a shift to large-scale and cash-crop agriculture. Tiberius compassionately expressed the plight of the displaced soldier-farmers: "They are styled masters of the world, and have not a clod of earth they can call their own." Tiberius recognized an additional problem with the growing landlessness— Rome did not have a pool of soldiers, for men had to meet a property qualification to enter the army. Thus,

Tiberius's reforms

the newly poor could neither farm nor serve in the army—Rome had moved a long way from the days of the farmer-soldier Cincinnatus.

Tiberius proposed an agrarian law that would redistribute public land to landless Romans. The idea may have made a difference, but it alarmed greedy landlords. The law passed, but the Senate appropriated only a tiny sum to help Tiberius administer the law. Many senators were particularly worried when Tiberius announced he was running for reelection. Although in the distant past, tribunes had run for a second term, that had not been done for a long time, and Tiberius's opponents argued that it was illegal. In the ensuing turmoil, a riot occurred at an assembly meeting, and some senators with their followers beat Tiberius and 300 of his followers to death. With one stroke, a new element emerged in Roman political life: political murder.

Tiberius's land law continued to operate for a time, but not very effectively. In 123 B.C.E. Tiberius's brother Gaius became tribune in an effort to continue his brother's work, and he wisely appealed to a broad sector of the Roman people. He built granaries, roads, and bridges to improve the distribution of grain into the city, and these projects created jobs for many Romans. Gaius also tried to fix the price of grain to keep it affordable, and he appealed to the equestrian order by giving them more influence in the wealthy provinces. Gaius opened the new Asian provinces to equestrian tax collectors and placed equestrians in the courts that tried provincial governors accused of abusing their powers. Many senators believed these reforms were politically motivated to destroy the Senate (which had destroyed Tiberius), and it was true that cheap grain might weaken the patron-client relationship that represented the backbone of senatorial power. The Senate moved to undo his reforms as soon as Gaius was out of office, and he and some 250 supporters were murdered in 122 B.C.E.—their deaths were arranged by one of the consuls supporting the Senate.

Gaius's reforms

The Gracchi's sacrifices did not solve the Republic's problems. Their careers focused Rome's attention on its worries, but the brothers had also established a new style of republican government. From their time on, a struggle unfolded in Rome between men like the Gracchi, who enjoyed popular support (*populares*), and *optimates,* who intended to save the Republic by keeping power in the Senate. The old image of a nobility surrounded by and caring for its clients became supplanted by a much more confrontational model. The Gracchi were only the first to die in this struggle, and perhaps the greatest legacy of the Gracchi was the subsequent violence that descended upon the political arena. Roman public life would not be the same again.

Populares vs. Optimates: The Eruption of Civil Wars, 123–46 B.C.E.

Even as Rome experienced violence in its political life, life in the provinces, too, seemed threatened. In North Africa, Rome's old ally Numidia caused trouble, and the Gauls threatened Italy from the north. Just as the military emerged as a primary instrument of political power, the generals, especially, had new opportunities to play a role in internal politics. The political struggle between the *populares* and the *optimates* catalyzed by the Gracchi was continued by popular generals.

The first general to come to power based on the support of the army was Gaius Marius (ca. 157–86 B.C.E.). An equestrian tribune, Marius took up the cause of the *populares*. To address the problem of the African wars and the shortage of soldiers

| Marius |

noted by Tiberius, Marius initiated a way of enlisting new soldiers that would redefine the Roman military. He created a professional army, eliminating the previous requirement that soldiers own property. In addition, he formally put the soldiers on the payroll, making official the previous informal patron-client relationship between generals and their troops. Marius also promised them land after their term of service. In this way, he cultivated an army with many rootless and desperate men who were loyal only to him. Although Marius could not foresee the results, his policies established a dangerous pattern that continued through the rest of Roman history. With his new army at his back, the victorious general decisively defeated first the Numidians in Africa and then the Celts to the north. In his battles against Africans and Celts, Marius was accompanied by a brilliant young second-in-command, Lucius Cornelius Sulla (ca. 138–78 B.C.E.). In these wars that brought Marius so much power, Sulla felt that his brave exploits deserved some of the credit that Marius took, and he seethed with resentment.

New crises paved the way for the *optimates* to restore their own power under the aristocrat Sulla, who had learned warfare and resentment from Marius. The first threat to Rome's safety came from within Italy itself—the Italian allies who had first been conquered wanted a greater share in the prosperity that Rome's conquests were bringing. The violent fighting that took place between 90 and 88 B.C.E. finally forced Rome to give full citizenship to the Italian allies. This revolt by the Italian allies is called the "Social War" (from the Latin word *socii*, which means "allies"). The violence that devastated much of the countryside further weakened the Republic. As one of the consuls for 88 B.C.E., Sulla commanded six legions in the final stages of the Italian wars, and his successes earned him a governorship in Asia, where he was given the command

| Sulla |

to lead the armies against a second threat to Rome—Mithridates (120–63 B.C.E.), a king in Asia Minor who was threatening Rome's borders. However, fearing Sulla's growing strength, the assembly called Marius out of retirement and tried to give him control of Sulla's army. Perhaps Sulla's most dramatic moment came when he marched his army directly into Rome to confront Marius. The hostilities between the two generals made a permanent mark on the city, changing the peaceful Forum into a war zone. After defeating Mithridates, Sulla returned to Rome in 83 B.C.E. to take up the cause of the *optimates*.

Sulla assumed the long-dormant office of dictator (see **Figure 4.3**) but violated tradition by making the term unlimited. He also repealed laws that favored equestrians, and he killed off his political opponents. He buttressed the power of the Senate by passing laws to guarantee it, instead of allowing the tradition of Senate leadership to suffice. The venerable Roman constitutional system was becoming changed, and power politics began to fill the vacuum.

With the wars of Marius and Sulla, a new question confronted Roman politicians: how to protect the citizens from people seeking power and personal gain. Clearly, the old system of checks and balances no longer worked. The next group of popular leaders bypassed most of the formal structures and made a private alliance to share power. Modern historians have called this agreement the First **Triumvirate,** or the rule by three men. A contemporary called it a "three-headed monster."

The First Triumvirate (60–49 B.C.E.) was made up of three men who appealed to various sectors of Roman society. Pompey, beloved of the *optimates*, was a brilliant general who had won striking battles in the east against Sulla's old enemy, Mithridates, and Mediterranean pirates.

| First Triumvirate |

Julius Caesar was probably an even more talented general and brilliant orator, who won wars in Gaul and Britain and had the support of the

KEY DATES

RISE AND FALL OF THE REPUBLIC

509 B.C.E.	Defeat of Etruscan monarchy
509–287 B.C.E.	Struggle of the Orders
451 B.C.E.	Twelve Tables published
133–123 B.C.E.	Reforms of the Gracchi
90–88 B.C.E.	Social Wars—Rome vs. Italian allies
60–49 B.C.E.	First Triumvirate
49–ca. 46 B.C.E.	Civil war—Caesar vs. Pompey
44 B.C.E.	Julius Caesar murdered

populares. The third man was Crassus, a fabulously rich leader of the business community who had also led armies (including defeating the rebel slave Spartacus). In keeping with tradition in Roman society, the political alliance was sealed by marriage between Pompey and Caesar's daughter, Julia. Instead of bringing peace, however, the triumvirate simply became an arena in which the three powerful figures jockeyed for control.

Events soon came to a head. Crassus perished leading armies to confront a new threat in Rome's eastern frontier. Julia died in childbirth, along with her infant. With her death, little remained to hold Caesar and Pompey together. *Optimates* in the Senate co-opted Pompey in their desire to weaken the popular Caesar, and they declared Pompey sole consul in Rome. Pompey accepted this command from the Senate, breaking his agreement with Caesar, ensuring retribution from the popular general. Caesar defied the Senate, which had forbidden him to bring his army into Italy, and in 49 B.C.E. marched across the Rubicon River into Italy. There was no retreating from this defiant act—a new civil war had erupted.

Julius Caesar, 100–44 B.C.E.

Julius Caesar came from one of the oldest noble families of Rome. As with the Gracchi, his family associated itself with the *populares*. In the civil wars to come, Caesar enjoyed a high degree of support from the plebeians, but before he could take power, he needed the backing of an army. This he achieved in his wars of conquest in Gaul. Both his military successes and his captivating literary accounts of them won him broad popularity. According to the ancient writers, this accomplished general was tall with a fair complexion and piercing black eyes. The bust of Caesar shown in **Figure 4.12** reveals his memorable strength of character. Clearly a brilliant man in all fields, he enthralls historians today much as he fascinated his contemporaries.

The civil war between Caesar and Pompey that began in 49 B.C.E. was not limited to Italy; battles broke out throughout the Roman world. Caesar's and Pompey's armies clashed in Greece, North Africa, and Spain. After losing a decisive battle in Greece in 48 B.C.E., Pompey fled to Egypt, where he was assassinated. When Caesar followed Pompey to Egypt, he became involved with Queen Cleopatra VII (r. 51–30 B.C.E.) (also discussed in Chapter 5), who was engaged in a dynastic struggle with her brother. Caesar supported her claims with his army, spent the winter with her, and fathered her child; then he left in the spring to continue the wars that consolidated his victory over Pompey's supporters. In 46 B.C.E., Caesar returned to Rome.

Civil war

FIGURE 4.12 Julius Caesar One of the most controversial figures from the late Republic was Julius Caesar. As was customary with old patrician families, his family commissioned this bust after his death so that they and others would remember his deeds.

Cleopatra joined Caesar in Rome as he took up a task harder than winning the civil war: governing the Republic. The new leader faced two major challenges. First, he had to untangle the economic problems that had plagued the Republic since before the Gracchi attempted reform. Second, Rome needed a form of government that would restore stability to the factions that had burdened the city with so much violence.

Caesar applied his genius for organization to these practical tasks. He reformed the grain dole and established an ambitious program of public works to create jobs for the unemployed. To help displaced peasants, he launched a program of colonization all around the Mediterranean. Caesar's policies extended widely. With the help of an Egyptian astronomer who had accompanied Cleopatra to Rome, Caesar even reformed the calendar. The new "Julian calendar" introduced the solar year of 365 days and added an extra day every four years (the prototype of the "leap year"). With modifications made in 1582, the Julian calendar has remained in use throughout the West.

DOCUMENT 4.3

Conspirators Assassinate Julius Caesar

The ancient biographer Plutarch (46–120 C.E.) carefully chronicled the lives and deaths of ancient heroes, and his account of the assassination of Julius Caesar remains an important one. As Julius Caesar, the dictator for life, walked to the Senate building, he was surrounded by conspirators who stabbed him to death. After the murder, chaos reigned.

When Cæsar entered the house, the senate rose to do him honor. Some of Brutus' accomplices came up behind his chair, and others before it, pretending to intercede, along with Metillius Cimber, for the recall of his brother from exile. They continued their instances till he came to his seat. When he was seated he gave them a positive denial; and as they continued their importunities with an air of compulsion, he grew angry. Cimber, then, with both hands, pulled his gown off his neck, which was the signal for the attack. Casca gave him the first blow. It was a stroke upon the neck with his sword, but the wound was not dangerous; for in the beginning of so tremendous an enterprise he was probably in some disorder. Cæsar therefore turned upon him and laid hold of his sword. At the same time they both cried out, the one in Latin, "Villain! Casca! what dost thou mean?" and the other in Greek, to his brother, "Brother, help!"

After such a beginning, those who knew nothing of the conspiracy were seized with consternation and horror, insomuch that they durst neither fly nor assist, nor even utter a word. All the conspirators now drew their swords, and surrounded him in such a manner that, whatever way he turned, he saw nothing but steel gleaming in his face, and met nothing but wounds. Like some savage beast attacked by the hunters, he found every hand lifted against him, for they all agreed to have a share in the sacrifice and a taste of his blood. Therefore Brutus himself gave him a stroke in the groin. Some say he opposed the rest, and continued struggling and crying out till he perceived the sword of Brutus; then he drew his robe over his face and yielded to his fate. . . .

Cæsar thus despatched, Brutus advanced to speak to the senate and to assign his reasons for what he had done, but they could not bear to hear him; they fled out of the house and filled the people with inexpressible horror and dismay. Some shut up their houses; others left their shops and counters. All were in motion; one was running to see the spectacle; another running back. Antony and Lepidus, Cæsar's principal friends, withdrew, and hid themselves in other people's houses. Meantime Brutus and his confederates, yet warm from the slaughter, marched in a body with their bloody swords in their hands, from the senate house to the Capitol, not like men that fled, but with an air of gayety and confidence, calling the people to liberty, and stopping to talk with every man of consequence whom they met. There were some who even joined them and mingled with their train, desirous of appearing to have had a share in the action and hoping for one in the glory. . . .

Next day Brutus and the rest of the conspirators came down from the Capitol and addressed the people, who attended to their discourse without expressing either dislike or approbation of what was done. But by their silence it appeared that they pitied Cæsar, at the same time that they revered Brutus. The senate passed a general amnesty; and, to reconcile all parties, they decreed Cæsar divine honors and confirmed all the acts of his dictatorship; while on Brutus and his friends they bestowed governments and such honors as were suitable; so that it was generally imagined the Commonwealth was firmly established again, and all brought into the best order.

But when, upon the opening of Cæsar's will, it was found that he had left every Roman citizen a considerable legacy, and they beheld the body, as it was carried through the Forum, all mangled with wounds, the multitude could no longer be kept within bounds. They stopped the procession, and, tearing up the benches, with the doors and tables, heaped them into a pile, and burned the corpse there. Then snatching flaming brands from the pile, some ran to burn the houses of the assassins, while others ranged the city to find the conspirators themselves and tear them in pieces; but they had taken such care to secure themselves that they could not meet with one of them. . . .

SOURCE: Plutarch, "Lives," in *The Great Events by Famous Historians*, vol. II, ed. Rossiter Johnson (The National Alumni, 1905), pp. 328–329.

Analyze the Document

1. How did the chaos and confusion after Caesar's death contribute to Rome's instability?

2. What caused the Romans first to support Brutus and then to reject him?

Despite his organizational skill, Caesar could not solve the problem of how to govern the Republic. In 48 B.C.E., he accepted the title of dictator, the venerable title Romans reserved for those who stepped in during a crisis. Unlike Cincinnatus (the Roman with whom we began this chapter), Caesar did not renounce the title when the emergency was over, but ultimately proclaimed himself dictator for life, a shocking departure from the traditional six-month tenure. He reportedly refused the title of king to avoid offending the republicans, yet he took on many of the trappings of a monarch. He wore royal regalia and established a priesthood to offer sacrifice to his "genius"—what the Romans called each person's spirit. In 44 B.C.E., Caesar had his image placed on coins—perhaps the first time a living Roman was so honored. (Some historians believe Pompey may have beat Caesar to that distinction.) Some people began to question whether the Republic of Rome was changing too radically.

Political titles

The Roman Republic Ends

The peace and order that Caesar brought to Rome pleased many, particularly the *populares* whose support had lifted Caesar to power. However, many Romans, even among his supporters, were outraged by the honors Caesar took for himself. He had shrunken the role of the *optimates*, and peace seemed to come at the price of the traditional Republic and at the expense of the old power structure. Some conspirators were simply self-serving, hoping to increase their own power. Sixty senators with various motives entered into a conspiracy to murder their leader. Even Brutus, a friend and protégé of Caesar, joined in the plot. He would be like the Brutus of early Rome who had avenged Lucretia and freed Rome from the Etruscan kings. This Brutus would save Rome from a new king—Caesar.

Conspiracy

Caesar was planning a military campaign for March 18, 44 B.C.E., so the assassins had to move quickly. On March 15, the date the Romans called the "ides," or middle of the month, they surrounded the unwary dictator as he approached the Senate meeting place. Suddenly they drew knives from the

Caesar's murder

FIGURE 4.13 Commemorative Coin Coins were struck to memorialize famous people and important events. Caesar's assassins produced this coin, marked with the Ides of March, the date of Caesar's murder, as well as the dagger that killed him.

folds of their togas and plunged them into his body. He died at the foot of the statue of Pompey, his old enemy. Most of the killers seem to have genuinely believed they had done what was best for Rome. They saw themselves as "liberators" who had freed Rome from a dictator and who would restore the Republic. In 43 B.C.E., they issued the coin shown in **Figure 4.13.** The coin depicts the assassins' daggers and reads "Ides of March." On the other side of the coin is a portrait of Brutus.

This attempt to celebrate a great victory on the coin was mere propaganda. The conspirators had no real plan beyond the murder. They apparently had made no provision for control of the army, nor for ensuring peace in the city. In the end, their claim to "save the Republic" rang hollow. Document 4.3 reveals the chaos that followed the assassination. After Caesar's death, one of his friends supposedly lamented, "If Caesar for all his genius, could not find a way out, who is going to find one now?" The republican form of government so carefully forged during the Struggle of the Orders crumbled under the stress of civil wars and murder.

LOOKING BACK & MOVING FORWARD

Summary   The Republic of Rome, with its emphasis on family and city, rose to great power from 509 B.C.E. to the death of Caesar in 44 B.C.E. By that year, Rome controlled much of the Mediterranean world, and a system of wealthy slave owners and a large standing army had replaced the citizen farmer-soldier who had laid the foundation for the Republic's success. Whereas the early Romans had emphasized the ties between citizens, now violent power struggles tore at the social fabric. A people who had preserved stories of serious Roman heroes began to treasure Greek models of beauty and individualism.

Julius Caesar became a central figure in Rome's transformation from republic to empire. Since Caesar's death, historians have argued about his qualities. Was he a great man who detected the inability of the republican form of government—designed to govern a city-state—to adapt to the changed circumstances of empire and social unrest? Or was he a power-hungry politician who craved control and blocked his fellow citizens from having any political involvement in the Republic? The truth no doubt falls somewhere between these extremes. One thing is certain: Despite the assassins' confident claims, Caesar's murder did not solve anything. More violence would ensue until a leader arose who could establish a new form of government that would endure even longer than the Republic.

KEY TERMS

patricians, *p. 110*
consuls, *p. 110*
Senate, *p. 110*
assemblies, *p. 110*
plebeians, *p. 110*
Struggle of the Orders, *p. 111*
tribunes, *p. 111*
Twelve Tables, *p. 111*
equestrians, *p. 111*
Forum, *p. 112*
Pantheon, *p. 127*
populares, *p. 129*
optimates, *p. 129*
Triumvirate, *p. 130*

REVIEW, ANALYZE, & CONNECT TO TODAY

REVIEW THE PREVIOUS CHAPTERS

Chapter 1—"The Roots of Western Civilization"—discussed the rise of the first empires of the West, the Assyrian and the Persian. In Chapter 3—"The Poleis Become Cosmopolitan"—we saw the rise of large Hellenistic monarchies throughout the old empires of the ancient world. Rome inherited much from these empires.

1. Review the Persians' and the Assyrians' treatment of conquered peoples and consider which most closely resembled the Romans' approach. To what degree did the Romans' treatment of their subjects contribute to their success as an imperial power?

2. Compare and contrast Roman and Greek governments.

3. In what ways do you think Rome came to resemble the great Hellenistic cities, and what problems did they share?

ANALYZE THIS CHAPTER

This chapter—"Pride in Family and City"—traces the rise of the small city of Rome to a Hellenistic power whose territory extended throughout the Mediterranean world. In the course of this expansion, the old values of Rome were transformed and new constructs were slowly and violently implemented.

1. Review these changes in early Roman life and values as the armies successfully expanded Roman influence. How did Romans struggle with their changing identity as Rome moved from city to empire?

2. Review the political structure of the Roman Republic. What were its strengths and weaknesses? How did the patron-client system contribute to the strengths and weaknesses of the political system?

3. What were the strengths of the Roman army? Consider how and why Rome expanded its territories so extensively.

4. What were Rome's contributions to the fields of art and technology?

CONNECT TO TODAY

The government of the United States looks back to the Roman Republic as its model of representative democracy.

1. Compare the power of the people in ancient Rome with that of Americans today. In which system do you think the people have exerted the most authority? Support your answer.

2. Romans found it impossible to maintain their republican form of government during their expansion. What similar stresses can you identify in world democracies today? Consider, for example, the flow of immigrants into European countries that has changed the face of traditionally homogeneous European populations, or the feeling among some U.S. citizens that the United States has grown so large, they have little say about what their legislators do in Washington, D.C. In what other ways might people feel disconnected from their government?

THE RISE OF ROME, 753–265 B.C.E.

Bell, Sinclair, and Helen Nagy, eds. *New Perspectives on Etruria and Early Rome.* Madison: University of Wisconsin Press, 2009. Collection of essays exploring the latest archaeological discoveries yielding insights into early Italy; enhanced with maps and illustrations.

Garland, Lynda, and Matthew Dillon. *Ancient Rome: From the Early Republic to the Assassination of Julius Caesar.* London: Routledge, 2005. An accessible yet comprehensive summary that includes translations of documents and spotlights social and political developments during the Republic.

Meyer, J.C. *Pre-Republican Rome.* Odense, Denmark: Odense University Press, 1983. A highly illustrated archaeological look at pre-republican Rome.

Mitchell, Richard E. *Patricians and Plebeians: The Origin of the Roman State.* New York: Cornell University Press, 1990. A description of the separate patrician and plebeian systems.

FAMILY LIFE AND CITY LIFE

Aldrete, Gregory S. *Gestures and Acclamations in Ancient Rome.* Baltimore: Johns Hopkins University Press, 1999. An accessible, nicely illustrated, and fascinating discussion on the verbal and nonverbal communications between Roman crowds and their leaders.

Bradley, Keith R. *Discovering the Roman Family: Studies in Roman Social History.* New York: Oxford University Press, 1991. Essays that study the composition of the Roman family and household-central features of the Roman state.

De Albentiis, Emidio. *Secrets of Pompeii: Everyday Life in Ancient Rome.* Los Angeles: Getty Publications, 2009. A survey of how ancient Romans interacted in their public squares and marketplaces, decorated their homes, and spent their leisure time, as well as how they worshiped.

Gardner, J.F. *Women in Roman Law and Society.* Bloomington: Indiana University Press, 1986. An interesting look at the ways in which the practice of law affected women in various aspects of their lives.

Orlin, Eric M. *Temples, Religion and Politics in the Roman Republic.* New York: E.J. Brill U.S.A., 1996. An exploration into the relationship between the individual and the community.

Robinson, O.F. *Ancient Rome: City Planning and Administration.* New York: Routledge, 1994. A remarkable study of the level of organization, laws, and local governmental arrangements made to allow a large population to live together in the ancient world.

EXPANSION AND TRANSFORMATION, 265–133 B.C.E.

Bagnall, Nigel. *The Punic Wars.* London: Hutchinson, 1990. A detailed, chronological study of the different campaigns, studying them strategically, operationally, and tactically.

Goldsworthy, Adrian. *The Complete Roman Army.* New York: Thames & Hudson, 2003. A wonderfully comprehensive study of the development of the army from its days as a citizen's militia to the highly professional army that was the wonder of the Mediterranean world.

Mayor, Adrienne. *Greek Fire, Poison Arrows, and Scorpion Bombs: Biological and Chemical Warfare in the Ancient World.* Woodstock, NY: Overlook TP, 2008. A fascinating look at ancient weapons of mass destruction.

Ostenberg, Ida. *Staging the World: Spoils, Captives, and Representations in the Roman Triumphal Procession.* Oxford: Oxford University Press, 2009. Study of how Rome presented and perceived the defeated on parade, discussing what was displayed, how it was paraded, and observers' responses.

THE HELLENIZING OF THE REPUBLIC

Ogilvie, R.M. *Roman Literature and Society.* Harmondsworth, England: Penguin, 1980. A brief introduction to and fresh opinion of major Latin writers.

Rawson, Elizabeth. *Intellectual Life in the Late Roman Republic.* Baltimore: Johns Hopkins University Press, 1985. A summary intending to capture the full range of intellectual activity in the Republic.

THE TWILIGHT OF THE REPUBLIC, 133–44 B.C.E.

Lacey, W.K. *Cicero and the Fall of the Republic.* New York: Barnes and Noble, 1978. An in-depth study of all aspects of the man—speaker, author, philosopher—that shows how elements of Cicero's character developed over time in reaction to the social conditions of his age.

Langguth, A.J. *A Noise of War: Caesar, Octavian and the Struggle for Rome.* New York: Simon & Schuster, 1994. A chronologically organized focus on the personalities of these influential men.

Meier, Christian. *Caesar.* New York: Basic Books, 1997. A fine study that places Caesar, a remarkable individual, within his cultural context and encourages us to consider the relationship between the man and his times.

Shotter, David. *The Fall of the Roman Republic.* New York: Routledge, 1994. A brief survey of the elements surrounding the fall of the Roman Republic—a good introductory survey.

THE GEM OF AUGUSTUS (GEMMA AUGUSTEA), SARDONYX CAMEO, ca. 14 C.E.

This beautiful cameo was carved to praise a new order in Rome. At the top, Augustus is holding the staff of emperor while he is crowned as a god by other deities. At the left, his heir, Tiberius, descends from a chariot that he has ridden in triumph to celebrate his military victory in Germany. In the lower level, the army raises a trophy of victory while watched by defeated Germans. This piece shows how Rome had been transformed: No longer a republic, Rome was now led by a living god whose family expected to succeed him, and the greatness of the empire depended on soldiers and far-flung conquests.

Territorial and Christian Empires

The Roman Empire, 31 B.C.E.–410 C.E.

" . . . **[T]**he newborn babe shall end that age of iron, [and] bid a golden dawn upon the broad world. . . ." With these words, the Roman poet Virgil foretold the birth of a child who would save the world from the civil wars plaguing the late Roman Republic. For many Romans, that child arrived in the person of Caesar Augustus, a talented leader whose political and economic policies introduced almost two hundred years of internal peace. But this *Pax Romana* was no cure-all. The Romans still faced the challenges of unifying a multiethnic empire while ensuring a succession of capable emperors. They also struggled to preserve their concept of private morality, and they grappled with the complexity of people's political involvement under an imperial system. In the third century C.E., economic and political hardship nearly wiped out the empire, as soldiers created military emperors who battled each other, often leaving Rome's borders at risk. In the fourth century, the reforms of two great rulers—Diocletian and Constantine—temporarily held Rome's extensive dominions together.

Meanwhile, another child born in the time of Caesar Augustus inspired a new creed that seemed to offer salvation. Followers of Jesus grew steadily in numbers through the first centuries C.E. At first, the empire ignored them and occasionally persecuted them, but it later adopted Christianity as its own. This fusion of Roman and Christian ideas created a new Christian empire that many ancient Romans believed fulfilled the promise of the child Virgil praised. Both empires—Roman and Christian—contributed a great deal to the continuing development of the West.

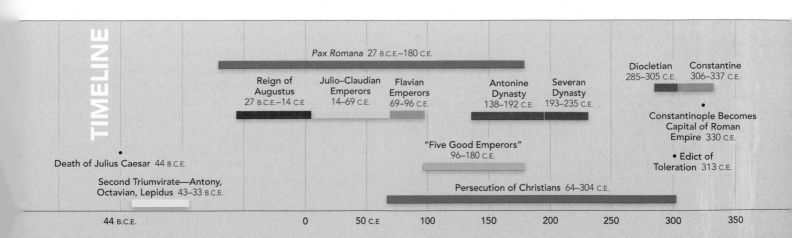

TIMELINE

Pax Romana 27 B.C.E.–180 C.E.

Diocletian 285–305 C.E.   Constantine 306–337 C.E.

Reign of Augustus 27 B.C.E.–14 C.E.

Julio–Claudian Emperors 14–69 C.E.

Flavian Emperors 69–96 C.E.

Antonine Dynasty 138–192 C.E.

Severan Dynasty 193–235 C.E.

Constantinople Becomes Capital of Roman Empire 330 C.E.

"Five Good Emperors" 96–180 C.E.

Edict of Toleration 313 C.E.

Death of Julius Caesar 44 B.C.E.

Second Triumvirate—Antony, Octavian, Lepidus 43–33 B.C.E.

Persecution of Christians 64–304 C.E.

44 B.C.E.   0   50 C.E   100   150   200   250   300   350

FIGURE 5.1 Cleopatra VII, ca. 30 B.C.E. This bust portrays the famous Egyptian queen who bore Julius Caesar a child and seduced Mark Antony. Although Cleopatra was a Hellenistic ruler, the sculptor portrayed her face in the Roman manner.

THE *PAX ROMANA*,
27 B.C.E.–180 C.E.

On the eve of their wedding, a young Roman couple, Vespillo and Turia, paused during the celebration to reflect on a sad memory. Turia's parents had perished in the civil war that had elevated Julius Caesar to power, but the troubled times were not over for the young couple. During new civil wars, Turia had to sell her jewelry to help her husband escape the political strife in the city and even had to beg for a pardon for Vespillo. Finally, the wars were over, and the couple "enjoyed quiet and happy days" through forty-one years of marriage, although sadly they produced no children. They were representative of many Romans who struggled through the violence after Julius Caesar's death finally to enjoy a long *Pax Romana,* or Roman Peace, that was introduced by his successor.

Augustus Takes Power

In 43 B.C.E., three powerful men emerged who established a new triumvirate to rule the Republic. Unlike the first, the Senate legitimized this Second Triumvirate, which ruled from 43 to 33 B.C.E. and seemed to offer a way to bring peace to the turbulent land.

Marc Antony, who managed Caesar's vast fortune, was a strong general who seemed to challenge senatorial power. To balance his power, the Senate turned to Julius Caesar's grandnephew and adopted son, Octavian—a remarkably talented 19-year-old who played on popular sympathy for the murdered dictator by calling himself Caesar. The young Octavian offered respect to the Senate as he jockeyed for position against Marc Antony. The two brought into their partnership one of Julius Caesar's loyal governors and generals, Lepidus. At first, the three men controlled various parts of the empire: Octavian based his power in Italy and the provinces to the west; Lepidus held North Africa; and Marc Antony governed Egypt, Greece, and the provinces to the east. However, like the First Triumvirate, the second soon deteriorated into a power struggle among the three rulers. Octavian forced Lepidus into retirement in 36 B.C.E., and he and Antony vied for sole control of the empire.

As was traditional in Rome, politics was intimately bound up with family and with the women who, through childbearing, held the key to future family alliances. Not surprisingly, the political struggles between Octavian and Antony were to some degree played out in the bedroom. Having lost Julius Caesar, Cleopatra sought to continue her ruling dynasty through a new alliance with a new ruler of Rome. **Figure 5.1** is a portrait bust of Queen Cleopatra showing her regal bearing and her fairly ordinary looks. She seduced Antony with the wit and charm that had so impressed the ancient biographers and bore him twins. Antony, however, was not yet committed to an alliance with Egypt's ruling house. Octavian's popularity in Rome was too high for Antony to risk offending the Roman people. Rumors already circulated in Rome's Forum that Antony wanted to move the Roman capital to Alexandria, so Antony had to negotiate a marriage that would be more acceptable to the public.

Antony and Octavian finally negotiated a peace that was to be secured by Antony's marriage to Octavian's sister, the young, beautiful Octavia. Octavia soon became pregnant, so the two families had the opportunity to seal their agreement permanently. But Antony left Octavia and traveled to Egypt. It is uncertain whether he decided that a strong political ally like Cleopatra afforded better security against Octavian than marriage to his rival's sister, or whether he was driven by the Egyptian queen's allure. In either case, the alliance bound through marriage dissolved. Octavian and Antony resumed their battle over who would rule all of Rome.

| Civil war |

The war between the two leaders finally came to a head in 31 B.C.E., when Antony and Cleopatra, surrounded by Octavian's forces, risked all on a sea battle near the city of Actium, off the western coast of Greece. During this famous battle, Cleopatra and Antony proved less determined than Octavian, for Cleopatra's squadron left for Egypt in the course of the battle, and Antony followed her. They abandoned their navy and about twenty legions of their troops. Octavian's navy destroyed the Egyptian fleet, and his land forces quickly occupied Egypt.

Antony committed suicide, and Octavian personally inspected his corpse to be sure his rival was dead. Cleopatra refused to be taken prisoner and, according to legend, ordered her servant to bring her a poisonous snake. She committed suicide by its bite. Although robbed of an imprisoned Egyptian queen, Octavian stood as sole ruler of Rome. With Cleopatra's death in 31 B.C.E., the last Macedonian kingdom fell, ending the Hellenistic age that had begun with the empire of Alexander the Great. Now the new empire of Rome dominated the Mediterranean world.

A New Form of Governing

Unlike his uncle, Julius Caesar, Octavian successfully established a form of government that let him rule without offending the traditions of conservative Romans. This delicate balance between his leadership style and the old ways earned him widespread popularity. On January 1, 27 B.C.E., the young general appeared before the Senate and claimed that he had brought peace and was thus returning the rule of the state to the Senate and the people of Rome. Octavian acted in the spirit of Cincinnatus (see Chapter 4), the general who gave up rule to return to his plow, and the tradition-loving Romans appreciated his gesture. The Senate showed its gratitude by giving him the title Augustus, a name that implied majesty and holiness. It is by this informal title that his people addressed him and historians remember him. Augustus, however, modestly referred to himself as the *princeps*—that is, the "first citizen." The government he established was in turn called the **principate,** after the first citizen upon whom everyone depended.

| The principate |

The principate transformed the republican form of government, and historians roughly date the beginning of the Roman Empire from 27 B.C.E.—the date of Augustus's famous renunciation and acceptance of power. Under this new imperial form, the traditional representatives of government—the Senate and the Roman people—continued to exist and appoint the traditional magistrates to carry out their public business. The Senate continued to make disbursements from the traditional treasury and, in fact, slowly increased its power as it began to take over elections from the popular assemblies. The Senate also maintained control over some of the provinces—the older ones that did not require so many soldiers to guard the borders. In these ways, Augustus avoided offending the senators as Julius Caesar had done.

| Governmental structure |

However, the vast extent of the empire and the increased complication of public affairs required a special magistrate—the princeps—to coordinate the administration of the empire and, more importantly, to control the army. By 70 C.E., the princeps was more often called emperor, a title with which troops had customarily hailed their generals. Building further on military precedent, Augustus established an imperial legion in Rome as his personal bodyguard. Known as the **praetorian guard,** this new body was named after the headquarters of the legion, or the *praetorium*. Roman generals had always had their own elite bodyguard, but because of its close association with the emperor, the praetorian guard, led by the praetorian prefect, became a powerful force on its own. The guard was unquestionably loyal to Augustus and worked to avert civil war such as the strife that had torn apart the Republic, but after his death a new political force had been created in Rome.

With these efforts, Augustus created a new structure on the remnants of the traditional Republic. Document 5.1 relates in Augustus's own words how

DOCUMENT 5.1

Augustus Tallies His Accomplishments

Shortly before he died in 14 C.E., Augustus left a number of state papers with the Vestal Virgins, including an account of his accomplishments that he wanted inscribed on bronze pillars to be installed in front of his mausoleum. Excerpts of this document give us a glimpse into this early period of the principate, which set the stage for subsequent imperial success.

3. I waged many wars throughout the whole world by land and by sea, both civil and foreign, and when victorious I spared all citizens who sought pardon. Foreign peoples who could safely be pardoned I preferred to spare rather than to extirpate. About 500,000 Roman citizens were under military oath to me. Of these, when their terms of service were ended, I settled in colonies or sent back to their own municipalities a little more than 300,000, and to all of these I allotted lands or granted money as rewards for military service. I captured 600 ships, exclusive of those which were of smaller class than triremes.

4. Twice I celebrated ovations, three times curule triumphs, and I was acclaimed *imperator* twenty-nine times. When the senate decreed additional triumphs to me, I declined them on four occasions. . . .

5. The dictatorship offered to me in the consulship of Marcus Marcellus and Lucius Arruntius by the people and by the senate, both in my absence and in my presence, I refused to accept. In the midst of a critical scarcity of grain I did not decline the supervision of the grain supply, which I so administered that within a few days I freed the whole people from imminent panic and danger by my expenditures and efforts. The consulship, too, which was offered to me at that time as an annual office for life, I refused to accept.

6. In the consulship of Marcus Vinicius and Quintus Lucretius, and again in that of Publius Lentulus and Gnaeus Lentulus, and a third time in that of Paullus Fabius Maximus and Quintus Tubero, though the Roman senate and people unitedly agreed that I should be elected sole guardian of the laws and morals with supreme authority, I refused to accept any office offered me which was contrary to the traditions of our ancestors. The measures which the senate desired at that time to be taken by me I carried out by virtue of the tribunician power. In this power I five times voluntarily requested and was given a colleague by the senate. . . .

15. To the Roman plebs I paid 300 sesterces apiece in accordance with the will of my father; and in my fifth consulship I gave each 400 sesterces in my own name out of the spoils of war; and a second time in my tenth consulship I paid out of my own patrimony a largess of 400 sesterces to every individual. . . . These largesses of mine reached never less than 250,000 persons.

17. Four times I came to the assistance of the treasury with my own money, transferring to those in charge of the treasury 150,000,000 sesterces. And in the consulship of Marcus Lepidus and Lucius Arruntius I transferred out of my own patrimony 170,000,000 sesterces to the soldiers' bonus fund, which was established on my advice for the purpose of providing bonuses for soldiers who had completed twenty or more years of service. . . .

22. I gave a gladiatorial show three times in my own name, and five times in the names of my sons or grandsons; at these shows about 10,000 fought. Twice I presented to the people in my own name an exhibition of athletes invited from all parts of the world, and a third time in the name of my grandson. I presented games in my own name four times, and in addition twenty-three times in the place of other magistrates. . . . Twenty-six times I provided for the people, in my own name or in the names of my sons or grandsons, hunting spectacles of African wild beasts in the circus or in the Forum or in the amphitheaters; in these exhibitions about 3,500 animals were killed. . . .

34. In my sixth and seventh consulships, after I had put an end to the civil wars, having attained supreme power by universal consent, I transferred the state from my own power to the control of the Roman senate and people. For this service of mine I received the title of Augustus by decree of the senate, and the doorposts of my house were publicly decked with laurels, the civic crown was affixed over my doorway, and a golden shield was set up in the Julian senate house, which, as the inscription on this shield testifies, the Roman senate and people gave me in recognition of my valor, clemency, justice, and devotion. After that time I excelled all in authority, but I possessed no more power than the others who were my colleagues in each magistracy.

35. When I held my thirteenth consulship, the senate, the equestrian order, and the entire Roman people gave me the title of "father of the country" and decreed that this title should be inscribed in the vestibule of my house, in the Julian senate house, and in the Augustan Forum on the pedestal of the chariot which was set up in my honor by decree of the senate. At the time I write this document I was in my seventy-sixth year.

SOURCE: Naphtali Lewis and Meyer Reinhold, *Roman Civilization: Sourcebook II: The Empire* (New York: Harper Torchbooks, 1966), pp. 10, 11, 14, 16, 19.

Analyze the Document

1. Why was Augustus so popular with the Roman people?

2. Which offices did he accept and which did he refuse? How did this help him avoid Julius Caesar's fate?

3. Notice the blurring of private and public funds. How do you think that blending contributed to Rome's stability and Augustus's office?

he balanced traditional offices with new demands. The document shows how he used his enormous personal wealth to balance the national treasury, to rebuild Rome, and to fund gladiator shows and other popular spectacles. In 2 B.C.E., the Senate awarded Augustus the title Father of the Fatherland. In a culture that depended on the father to guard his family's prosperity and honor, perhaps no other title could convey greater respect.

Of course, all these titles and honors, though significant, had little to do with the day-to-day practical problems of managing a large empire. Like any good father, Augustus ran the empire as one would run a household. He kept authority for himself, but the everyday business was handled by freedmen and slaves in his household. Although Rome itself remained governed largely by the traditional forms, Augustus made dramatic changes in governing the provinces.

| Administering an empire |

Augustus kept about half of the provinces—including wealthy Egypt—under his direct control, sending out representatives to govern there in his name. He began to create a foreign service drawn from the equestrian class (wealthy, upwardly mobile nonnobles), whose advancement depended upon their performance. This reform eliminated some of the worst provincial abuses that had gone on during the late Republic—for example, Augustus began eliminating private tax collectors. To keep the peace on the borders, Augustus stationed troops permanently in the provinces; the empire began to maintain fixed borders with military camps along the frontiers. Document 5.1 includes Augustus's own assessment of his accomplishments.

For all these reforms, even by ancient standards, the empire was astonishingly undermanaged—a few thousand individuals controlled some 50 million people. The genius of the system lay in a combination of limited goals on top—maintain peace, collect taxes, and prevent power from accumulating—with actual power exerted at the local level. Through its relative simplicity, the principate established by Augustus continued to function efficiently even during years of remarkably decadent rulers. The Roman people recognized Augustus's accomplishments by according him a level of respect almost suiting a god, and this veneration would dramatically shape the future of the principate.

Figure 5.2 reveals the Romans' love of this strong, wise leader. This famous statue—named for the villa of Augustus's wife, Livia, where the sculpture stood—captures the people's hopes for Augustus. In the statue, Augustus holds his right arm up in the fashion of a traditional republican orator. Compare this sculpture with the image at the beginning of Chapter 4, on page 106.

FIGURE 5.2 Augustus of Prima Porta, ca. 20 B.C.E. This idealized portrait of Augustus shows the first Roman emperor as a divine guardian of Rome.

The sculptor's interpretation of Augustus shows that the Republic had been transformed. Instead of a toga, Augustus wears the armor of a soldier, and in his left hand he holds the staff of an emperor, traditionally the commander of the army and now the leader of the state. He is also shown as more than a mortal hero. His bare feet indicate that he is a hero, perhaps even semidivine. The cupid astride the dolphin refers to the claim that Augustus's family was descended from the goddess Venus, mother of Cupid. The symbols on Augustus's breastplate—a victorious general and a generous Mother Earth—promise divine aid and prosperity. Although Augustus refused to let himself be portrayed explicitly as a god, these associations left no doubt about his near-divine status. Augustus allowed altars in his name to be erected in the provinces, but he refused to allow Romans to worship their "first citizen." His formal deification would come after his death.

This image of Augustus as a divine being was reinforced in the great literature produced under his patronage. Virgil's famous epic, the *Aeneid* (ca. 29–19 B.C.E.), is a mythological tale of the wandering of the Trojan hero Aeneas, who founded the city of Rome. However, in spite of the book's echoes of Homer, Aeneas was a kind of hero different from Achilles, and in this portrayal, Virgil was able to show that the virtues of the past could work in the new age of the principate. Aeneas refuses to yield to his weaknesses or his passions and is rewarded with a vision of the future in which his descendants will extend Rome's rule "to the ends of the earth." In his epic, Virgil promises:

Virgil's Aeneid

> . . . *yours will be the rulership of nations. Remember Roman, these will be your arts: to teach the ways of peace to those you conquer, to spare defeated peoples, tame the proud.*

The *Aeneid* did for Rome what Homer had done for classical Greece: It defined the Roman Empire and its values for subsequent generations, and in the process it contributed to the deification of Augustus. It was also a fine example of Augustus's talent for propaganda.

What Virgil did for Roman literature, Livy (59 B.C.E.–17 C.E.) did for the empire's recorded history. In his long, detailed work, *The History of Rome* (ca. 26 B.C.E.–15 C.E.), Livy recounted the development of his city from the earliest times to the principate, and he included many speeches that brought the past to life. Like Virgil, Livy emphasized Roman religion and morality, looking nostalgically back to republican values. And again like Virgil, the historian recognized that the future lay with the new imperial form of government. His history strongly influenced subsequent ancient historians and has remained a central source of information today.

Livy's Historia

The system established by Augustus was not perfect, but Augustus lived for so long that the principate became tradition. The Roman historian Tacitus (56–120 C.E.) wrote that by Augustus's death in 14 C.E., no one left alive could remember any other way to govern. For the next two centuries his successors ruled with the benefits of the imperial system that Augustus had established. But they also inherited major problems he left unresolved—Who should succeed the "first citizen"? How should one best govern such a large empire, and how would rulers handle such power?

Challenges to the Principate, 69–193 C.E.

Augustus's long tenure as emperor postponed the problem of imperial succession, but this weakness in the principate showed up soon after his death. The next four emperors all ascended the throne based on their ties to Augustus's family, and this succession showed how flimsy the concept of "first citizen" really was. An imperial dynasty had been established, and it did not matter that the rulers lacked the moral stature of Augustus or traditional republican virtues. During the Republic, leaders regularly confronted the Roman people in the Forum and yielded to the pressure of scorn or applause. However, the new rulers of the empire experienced no such corrective public scrutiny, and the successors of Augustus immediately proved that power corrupted. The historian Suetonius (69–130 C.E.) recorded the popular scandalous rumors that circulated about the decline of Augustus's successor, his stepson Tiberius (r. 14–37), shown celebrating his victory over the Germans in the chapter-opening art on page 136: "No longer feeling himself under public scrutiny, he rapidly succumbed to all the vicious passions which he had for a long time tried, not very successfully, to disguise." Tiberius "made himself a private sporting house where sexual extravagances were practiced for his secret pleasure," and in his isolation, Suetonius claimed, his paranoia grew. He even executed people for insulting his stepfather's memory if they carried a coin bearing Augustus's image into a lavatory or brothel. The Roman people believed that such excesses continued throughout the dynasty of Augustus's heirs.

Augustus's successors

One of the heirs in this dynasty was Caligula (r. 37–41), an irrational—if not insane—ruler who wanted to be worshiped as a god. The praetorian guard took matters into its own hands and assassinated Caligula. The guard then found Claudius, a retiring, neglected relative of Augustus, hiding in the palace and promptly declared him emperor. Claudius (r. 41–54) was regarded by many Romans as an imbecile subject to the whims of his wives, but the power of the connection to the family of Augustus prevailed to solidify his rule. The cameo in **Figure 5.3** is a beautiful piece of propaganda as well as art. It shows Claudius and his wife, Agrippina the Younger, in the foreground superimposed on Germanicus—Caligula's father—and his wife, Agrippina the Elder (the Younger's mother). The superimposition on the cameo emphasizes the family connections that gave Claudius the right to rule as "first citizen," and the horns of plenty on the front allude to the prosperity this dynasty promised to bring to the Romans. However, in contrast to the calm portrayal on the cameo, the dynasty only brought more family feuds.

FIGURE 5.3 Claudius and Agrippina the Younger This cameo gem depicts the emperor Claudius with his wife, Agrippina. In the background are his ancestors Germanicus and Agrippina the Elder. The design includes horns of plenty, symbolizing the prosperity the emperors were to bring to Rome.

Suetonius's history of those years tells of a series of murders within the family as members vied for the power of the princeps. Nero (r. 54–68) marked the most excessive of the murderers, for he killed many of his family members, mostly using his favorite means, poison. He even killed his mother, although it was not easy. He poisoned her three times, but she had taken a preventive antidote. Nero then tried to arrange for the ceiling of her room to collapse on her and for her boat to sink. When all these techniques failed, he simply sent an assassin to kill her and make it appear that she had committed suicide.

Nero was so despised that even his personal guard deserted him, and to avoid being captured and publicly executed, Nero commanded his slave to slit his throat, saying, "How ugly and vulgar my life has become!" It is not surprising that there were no more members of Augustus's family left to

| A new dynasty | claim the succession, and the armies and the praetorian guard fought a

bloody civil war to see which family would succeed to the imperial throne. Fortunately for Rome, Vespasian took power in 69 C.E. and restored some order to the empire, but even so fine an emperor could not ensure that his son would be equally competent. Each subsequent dynasty would eventually end through the weakness or corruption of one of the rulers, and the flaws in the succession policy were repeatedly highlighted. The assassination of Vespasian's murderous son Domitian (r. 81–96) introduced a new period, that of the "Five Good Emperors" (96–180). These rulers increasingly centralized their power at the expense of the Senate, but they ruled with a long-remembered

integrity. From Nerva (r. 96–98) to Marcus Aurelius (r. 161–180), these emperors established a tone of modest simplicity and adherence to republican values.

Marcus Aurelius represented the highest expression of a ruler whose political life was shaped by moral philosophy. He was highly educated in law, poetry, and philosophy, but the latter was his greatest love. When he was only 11, he adopted the coarse dress and sparse life of Stoic philosophers (discussed in Chapter 3), and when he became emperor, he continued to act based on the self-containment embodied in Stoic principles. His ideas have been preserved in a collection of his contemplative notes, called his *Meditations* (171–ca. 180). Within these notes he wrote a caution that should have been followed by all who rose to great power: When one is seduced by fame and flattery, one should remember how flatterers are frequently wrong on other occasions, so one should remain humble. Unfortunately, too many emperors did not share Marcus's wise self-containment.

Through these years, the City of Rome was transformed from a center of republican power to a glorification of imperial power. As **Map 5.1** shows, the entertainment centers—baths, games—offered by the emperors began to dominate the city, and temples to divine emperors sprang up.

Throughout the reigns of emperors good and bad, the borders had to be guarded. Armies fought in the east and as far away as Britain. Centuries of Roman military presence along the frontiers had brought Roman-style cities and agriculture— indeed, Roman civilization—to the | Provincial defense | edges of the empire. This long-term presence of Rome in lands far from Italy served to add Roman culture to the growing Western civilization in the north of Europe as well as the Mediterranean.

However, holding such extensive lands caused many of these soldier-emperors to be away from Rome for extended periods. Hadrian (r. 117–138) spent twelve of his twenty-one ruling years traveling around the provinces, establishing fortifications and checking on provincial administration. However, it was one thing to establish definite borders and quite another to hold them. The Stoic emperor Marcus Aurelius spent the better part of thirteen years in fierce campaigns to keep the border tribes out of the empire and he died while on campaign. His death brought an end to the era of the "good emperors," caused once again by a decadent son.

The long rule by good emperors may have been more the result of biological accident than anything else: Four of the emperors had no sons, so each of them adopted as his successor a man he thought best able to rule. However, Marcus Aurelius fathered a son, Commodus (r. 180–192), who unfortunately brought the age of the Five Good Emperors and the *Pax Romana* to an ignoble end through his cruel reign. Commodus

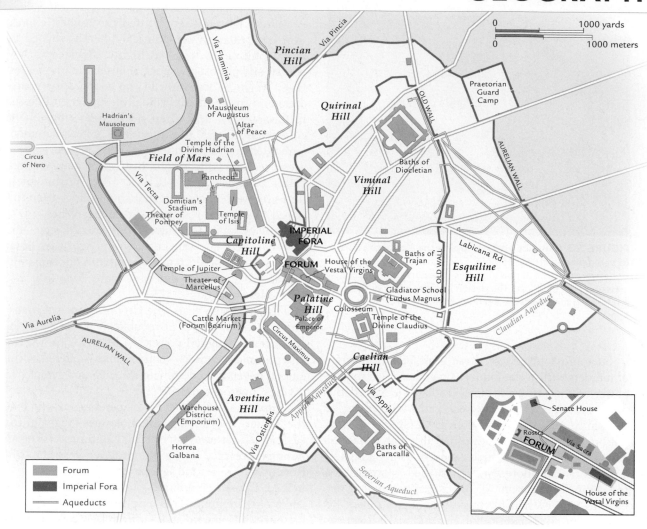

0   1000 yards

0   1000 meters

Legend:
- Forum
- Imperial Fora
- Aqueducts

MAP 5.1

City of Rome During the Empire

This map shows the city of Rome during the empire and identifies the new buildings constructed by the emperors. Compare this map with **Map 4.1,** of Rome during the Republic. Notice how monuments of imperial power and establishments for entertainment dominated the city during the empire.

Explore the Map

1. What new buildings dominated the city? What were their functions? What do these buildings reveal about the cultural focus of the Roman people under the empire?

2. Where were the new fora (plural of *forum*) built by the emperors? Where was the imperial palace? In what ways do these features demonstrate how the emperors displaced old republican centers of power?

seems to have been a simpleminded man who loved the games. He even shocked Rome by fighting in the arena as a gladiator. With Commodus's murder (he was strangled by his wrestling partner), peace ended in Rome in a fresh outbreak of civil war.

A Vibrant, Far-Flung Empire

One must credit the genius of Augustus's political system and the steadfastness of the Roman administrators for the empire's ability to flourish even during

China's Han Dynasty and the Silk Road

In 206 B.C.E, while the Roman Republic was expanding, a strong Chinese military commander, Liu Bang, brought order to warring factions in China. Liu established the Han dynasty (named after his native land), which would endure for more than four hundred years. The Han emperors developed a centralized authority supported by a large bureaucracy, and they built an extensive network of roads and canals to facilitate communication throughout the realm. The emperors also knew the value of educated royal servants. Thus, in 124 B.C.E, Emperor Han Wudi established an imperial university. This university incorporated Confucianism as the basis for its curriculum, so the Confucian tradition took root in China. Like the Romans in the West, the Han emperors developed an influential body of law, written first on bamboo and silk. Their legal system became the most comprehensive and best organized in the world.

The centralized, ordered rule of the Hans facilitated trade. It also led to the development of the "Silk Road," which linked China and the West in significant ways. Luxury items moved from China and India to Mesopotamia and the Mediterranean basin. Incoming goods arrived through a complex series of trades. Roman sailors used the prevailing monsoon winds to sail their ships from Red Sea ports to the mouth of the Indus River in India at Barygaza. There, they traded their goods—mostly gold and silver—for Indian spices and silks. The Indian merchants took their share of the merchandise and proceeded to trade with the Han merchants.

Chinese traders shipped spices—ginger, cinnamon, cloves, and others—that Westerners craved both as flavorings and as medicines. However, the most prized commodity was Chinese silk, which gave its name to the trade route. By the first century C.E., Romans were willing to pay premium prices for the prized fiber. The Chinese knew how to feed silkworms on mulberry leaves and harvest the cocoons before the moths chewed through the precious silk strands. The silk traveled west in bales—as either woven cloth or raw yarn—and went to processing centers, most of them in Syria. There workers ungummed the rolls and unwound the fiber before weaving the fabric that sold for top prices throughout the Roman Empire. For hundreds of years, the trade flourished, bringing West and East into close contact. This contact sparked the exchange of ideas as well as goods. Unfortunately, it also spread diseases that dramatically reduced populations in China as well as in the Roman Empire.

Despite the thriving trade, the later Han emperors proved unable to maintain the centralization and prosperity that had marked the early centuries of their reign. In the face of social and economic tensions, as well as epidemic diseases, disloyal generals grabbed more and more power. By 200 C.E., the Han dynasty had collapsed and the empire lay in pieces. The trade along the Silk Road suffered too, but stories of the prosperous East continued to capture the imaginations of Westerners.

Making Connections

1. What did the Han emperors do to facilitate long-distance trade with the West?

2. What trade items flowed along the Silk Road?

3. What impact did this trade have on the Roman Empire?

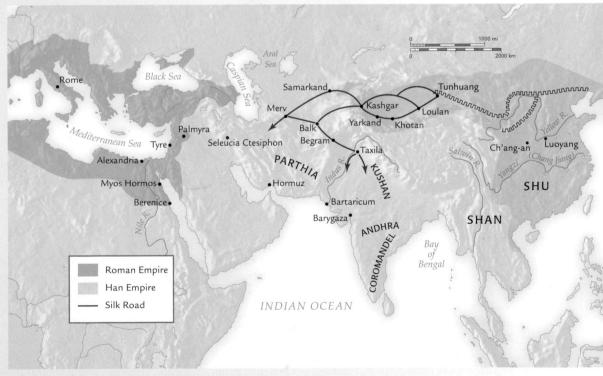

MAP 5.2 The Silk Road, ca. 200 C.E.

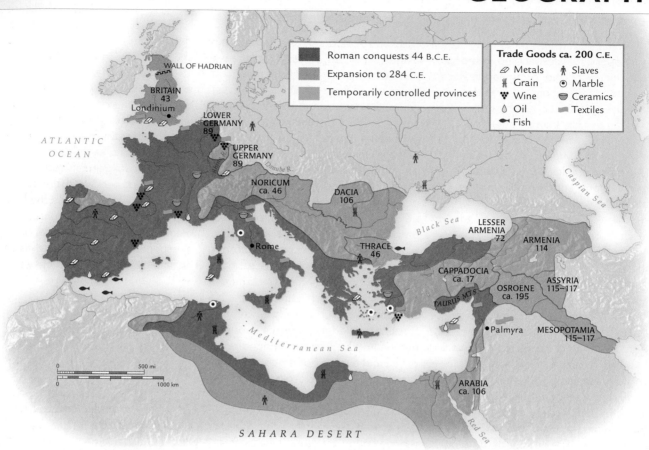

MAP 5.3

The Roman Empire, 44 B.C.E.–284 C.E.

This map shows the greatest extent of the Roman Empire. Notice how much of this territory was acquired during the Republic, before Augustus's rule. The key also shows the major trade goods from the various parts of the empire.

Explore the Map

1. How long did it take for a rapid message to go from Rome to the farthest reaches of the empire? (The most rapid travel time was about 90 miles a day; average travel was 20 miles a day.) What difficulties did such vast distances create?

2. Which territories brought the most essential or expensive trade goods?

3. Which territories might the empire have first abandoned when under pressure? Why?

years of imperial decadence. In our age of rapid communication and many levels of administrators and financial managers, it is difficult to imagine how hard it must have been to govern, with a small bureaucracy, an area as large as the Roman Empire. **Map 5.3** shows the extent of the empire through 284 C.E. Although this map looks impressive, it still requires some imagination to understand the meaning of these distances in the third century. For example, in good sailing weather, it took three weeks to sail from one end of the Mediterranean Sea to the other, and travel overland was even harder. Hauling goods by wagon train with escorts armed against bandits took so much time and manpower that it was cheaper to send a load of grain all the way across the Mediterranean than to send it 75 miles overland. Information moved almost as slowly as goods. What could hold the empire together against the centrifugal force of these distances?

The empire found a partial answer in Romanization. From the time of the Republic, Romans had established colonies for military veterans in the provinces, and such colonial expansion continued under the empire. Furthermore, to boost the strength of his army, Augustus recruited auxiliary troops from the noncitizen population all over the empire. After serving twenty-four years, these veterans were awarded with citizenship and land in the colonies. These auxiliary troops also served to spread Roman culture. Colonies became the cities that grew up in Britain, North Africa, Germany, and the East, bringing Roman culture to the most distant corners of the empire. The cities boasted all the amenities that Romans had come to expect: theaters, baths, a colosseum, roads, and townhouses. These urban communities had so much in common that they seemed to erase the huge distances that separated them.

Colonies

In these scattered, Romanized centers, local officials ruled. Town councils, for example, collected taxes and maintained public works, such as water systems and food markets. To collect taxes, officials maintained census figures on both the human population and agricultural produce and reported all to their superiors in Rome. This combination of local rule, Romanization, and some accountability to the central authority helped hold the fabric of the huge empire together.

Provincial administration

The provinces depended not only on the administrative skills of local officials but also on their philanthropy. In the best tradition of ancient Rome, men and women used their private resources for the public good. Inscriptions recalling private contributions survive in towns and cities all over the empire and reveal how essential such charity was to the maintenance of the Roman Peace. One woman in central Italy bequeathed one million coins in her will for the town to use to provide monthly child-assistance payments for all children until boys reached 16 years of age and girls 14. In another instance, the governor of the Asian city of Troy observed that the city was "ill-supplied with baths and that the inhabitants drew muddy water from their wells." The governor persuaded Emperor Hadrian to contribute three million coins to build an aqueduct, but when costs rose to seven million the governor paid for the difference from his own pocket. Philanthropists ensured that Roman life prospered all over the empire by contributing funds for baths, libraries, poor relief, and even public banquets.

The empire also remained unified through the marvels of Roman engineering. Fifty thousand miles of roads supplemented the great rivers as primary means of transportation. As is true today, the upkeep of roads posed a constant challenge and expense, and the empire used public and private means to fund them. The government collected tolls on goods in transit to fund road maintenance, but the toll payments seldom generated enough income. When in need, the empire turned to traditional philanthropy to make up the difference, asking local individuals and businesses to sponsor the upkeep of a particular portion of the road and erecting stones acknowledging their contribution. Such stones remain today in silent testimony to the philanthropy and organization that helped tie together the vast imperial lands.

Roman authorities also established a transportation system that provided travelers with horses and carriages and that monitored the movement of heavy goods. Regulations established maximum loads but were frequently ignored by inspectors, who often took bribes. With these elaborate networks of roads, lightly burdened travelers could cover an astonishing 90 miles a day—an extraordinary feat in ancient times.

Roads and transportation

During the early centuries of the empire, goods moved over great distances not only along the road network, for there was also a great deal of shipping. For the first time in the ancient world, the Roman navy kept the Mediterranean Sea relatively free of pirates, so shipping flourished. The sea had become a virtual Roman lake, and the Romans confidently called it Mare Nostrum (our sea) to show the degree to which the Mediterranean world was united under Rome.

The peace and unity of the empire allowed merchants to increase trade with the farthest reaches of Asia. The fabulous Silk Road brought spices and silks from as far away as China and only whetted the appetite of wealthy Romans for exotic goods from the East. Global Connections on page 145 discusses the Chinese empire that also profited from trade between the West and East.

Finally, the movement of people and armies also held the empire together. The Roman Empire boasted a remarkably multiethnic and multicultural population. Many educated provincials, for example, spoke at least three languages: Greek, Latin, and a local dialect. The imperial lands included a bewildering array of climates and geological features as well. **Figure 5.4** shows the 80-mile-long wall of Hadrian, the northern outpost of the empire in Britain built in the early second century. Here, Roman forts dotted the wall at 1-mile intervals. Roman soldiers peered into the damp fog, on alert against the fierce northern

Imperial diversity

FIGURE 5.4 Hadrian's Wall This photo shows the remains of the wall that marked the northern boundary of the Roman Empire on the British Isles. Ancient writers described the mist that hung on the wall through which soldiers watched for invaders from the wild north.

tribes who threatened to swarm across the imperial boundary. By contrast, **Figure 5.5** shows the forum of the ruins of Dougga, a Roman city in North Africa. You can see in the background the desert that marked the southern border of the empire. Beyond the great groves of olive trees that, together with abundant fields of grain, produced much of the agricultural wealth of North Africa, Roman legions stood watch against the Bedouin tribesmen who came galloping out of the desert to menace the edge of the empire.

With this remarkable diversity came the constant movement of people. Merchants traveled with their goods, and just as in the Hellenistic world, enterprising people moved about to seek their fortunes. Furthermore, to defend the empire's 6,000 miles of border, Roman authorities moved approximately 300,000 soldiers to wherever they were needed. The armies usually did not patrol their own regions. A garrison of black sub-Saharan Africans, for example, was stationed in the foggy north along Hadrian's Wall, and Germans from the north patrolled the desert. At the height of the *Pax Romana*, this flexible system seemed to ensure peace within Rome's borders.

As we will see, in time the centrifugal forces began to work against the ability of such a far-flung empire to hold together. The expense and difficulties of long-distance trade caused more and more provinces to produce their goods locally. Outside the empire itself, more tribes wanted to enter and share Rome's prosperity, and the borders would become all too permeable. But for the first two hundred years of the empire, it seemed as if the promise of a glorious new age had been fulfilled.

LIFE DURING THE PEACE OF ROME

Just as Augustus wanted to return politics to the traditional morality of the Roman Republic, he also tried to revive the old morality in the private lives of Rome's citizens. However, the new wealth that poured into the pockets of well-placed Romans made the old morality seem quaint and antiquated.

A New Decadence

Although the growing separation between rich and poor that began under the Republic continued through the empire, those getting more wealthy began to flaunt their riches. Silks and embroidery replaced the rough wool of republican virtue, and satirists wrote

FIGURE 5.5 Roman Ruins The southern boundary of Rome was marked by a desert. These Roman ruins in the city of Dougga in modern Tunisia show how Roman culture extended to the dry southern lands.

scathingly of women sporting makeup, high heels, elaborate hairstyles, and lots of jewelry. Men, too, indulged in similar excesses to ensure their appearance reflected their wealth and status. Augustus and subsequent moralists would fight a losing battle against such decadent displays.

The new wealth from trade and peace extended beyond Rome itself to people living in other growing urban areas. **Figure 5.6** is a painting from the wall of a baker's shop in the city of Pompeii (about 150 miles south of Rome, near Naples). Pompeii was a prosperous city that was buried in 79 C.E. under the ash of a violently erupting volcano, Mount Vesuvius. The rain of ash froze the city and its people in time, allowing modern excavators to see individuals engaged in many activities of daily life. The image in **Figure 5.6** offers insights into the Italian peninsula's urban life, in which both men and women participated and grew wealthy in commerce.

The Problem with Population

During the Republic, marriage and family ties were central values of the Roman people, and Augustus used his power to support those values. The princeps promoted legislation that assessed penalties on people who remained unmarried and instituted strong laws against adultery. These laws, though intended to strengthen the family, fell far short of their mark. Morality is singularly hard to legislate, and the Roman historian Tacitus observed that many people simply ignored the laws. Augustus himself experienced this phenomenon firsthand: Unable to control his own daughter's behavior (which he perceived as inappropriate), he ended up exiling her.

At heart, however, the laws were probably as much about children as about morality. The future of Rome, like the succession of the emperor, depended on offspring to carry on the family and other cultural traditions. Yet, throughout the empire, Romans had a particularly hard | Birthrates | time reproducing. Augustus even promoted a law that exempted women from male guardianship if they bore three children (four children for a freed slave). These numbers are a far cry from those in earlier times; Cornelia, mother of the Gracchi, earned praise for bearing 12 children! Fecundity in the empire certainly had plummeted to alarmingly low levels.

This phenomenon had cultural as well as physical causes. Wealthy Roman men and women often wanted few children, so as to preserve their inheritance intact. Yet, Augustus's law specifically tried to influence women. This law is particularly interesting in its assumptions: It recognized women's desire for freedom, and it assumed that women controlled their own fecundity. The former assumption may have been accurate, but the latter was only partially so. Sometimes women used birth-control methods based on herbs, spermicidal drugs, or douches. The texts also refer to abortion, although drugs strong enough to abort a fetus often endangered the life of the mother.

thinking about

ART

FIGURE 5.6

Wall Painting from a Baker's Shop in Pompeii, ca. 70 C.E.

This painting is from a baker's shop in the city of Pompeii, which was destroyed by the volcano Vesuvius in 70 C.E. Pompeii's preservation of small elements of Roman daily life makes it an important source of information about the past. The painting shows a prosperous, middle-class couple; the woman holds writing implements—a stylus and wax tablet—and the man holds a scroll (equivalent to an ancient book) with a label that identifies its contents. Notice how realistically the couple is portrayed.

Connecting Art & Society

1. Why might the couple have chosen to have themselves portrayed so realistically? What does the image indicate about what the couple valued?

2. What does this image suggest about the importance of literacy to a prosperous urban economy?

3. What does the image suggest about the woman's role in business, and in urban economy more generally?

The causes of Roman infertility lay in a full complex of medical misunderstandings combined with cultural practices.

Sexual and Medical Misunderstandings

Despite the scandalized commentary lamenting the sexual excess of "loose" women and decadent emperors, Romans in fact were very circumspect about sex. Medical wisdom warned men against the fatiguing effects of sexual activity, which they thought deprived the body of vital spirit. Roman physicians believed semen was made of brain fluid, and urged men to conserve it carefully.

By contrast, physicians did not believe that sexual intercourse weakened females. Indeed, medical advice for women focused on helping them to bear as many children as possible. Yet, medical misinformation actually contributed to Rome's falling birthrate. Physicians concluded, incorrectly, that women were most fertile soon after their menstrual periods, so they recommended reserving intercourse for that time. Furthermore, some doctors thought that women had to have intercourse before puberty in order to mature correctly. Medical misunderstanding about women's bodies and children's health care contributed to a low birthrate. These factors combined with other cultural issues—the desire to restrict children to keep from reducing inheritances, for example—help explain why Rome had so much trouble maintaining its population.

Despite the confusion regarding human reproduction, Roman medicine proved highly influential for the next 1,500 years. In particular, the physician Galen (131–201) popularized views that have prevailed even into modern times. Galen used some modern scientific techniques—for example, he performed vivisections on pigs to see the process of digestion—but his conclusions were strongly rooted in the classical world. He embraced the notion of moderation that was so central to ancient thought (recall Aristotle's "golden mean," discussed in Chapter 2) and therefore saw disease as the result of an imbalance, or excess. Galen believed that good health resulted from a balance among the four "humors,"

Galen

or bodily fluids—blood, bile, urine, and phlegm. He argued that each of these humors had its own properties—warm, cold, dry, and moist—and when a person was out of balance—that is, when one humor dominated—the cure was to restore an appropriate equilibrium. For example, if a person was feverish and flushed, he or she was considered to have an excess of blood. An application of blood-sucking leeches or the initiation of bleeding would reduce the blood and restore the balance. These ideas may not have improved people's health, but they formed the subsequent basis for medical treatment.

The Games

Families may have formed the basis of Roman society, but as we saw in Chapter 4, during the Republic, men forged critical ties in the world of civic affairs centered in the Roman Forum. Under the empire this focus changed; real power moved from the Forum to the emperor's household. Yet the Roman people still needed a public place to gather and express their collective will. Over time, they began satisfying this need at the great games and spectacles held in the amphitheaters across the empire. During the late Republic, wealthy men who craved the admiration of the people, and politicians who sought the loyalty of the crowd, spent fortunes producing chariot races in the Circus Maximus and hunts and gladiator games. After the time of Augustus, the emperors had a virtual monopoly on providing entertainment in Rome, although in the provinces others could produce spectacles. These games always had a religious significance to the Roman people, ritualizing Roman power and authority.

Figure 5.7 shows the Roman Colosseum, built by Emperor Vespasian (r. 69–79) as a gift to his subjects. **Map 5.1** shows its location within the city. This structure was the largest of its kind in the Roman world and held about 50,000 people. The photograph on the right (see **Figure 5.7**) shows what remains of the interior, including subterranean passages that held animals and prisoners. The photograph on the left shows the exterior, which dominated the skyline of Rome. Men and women flocked to the arena in the mornings to watch men hunt exotic animals that had been transported to Rome from the farthest reaches of the empire. Augustus proudly claimed to have provided a total of 3,500 animals in these hunts; other emperors were equally lavish in their displays.

From Forum to arena

The crowds then witnessed the public executions of criminals who were either set aflame or put in the path of deadly wild animals. Through such rituals, Rome displayed its power over its enemies. **Figure 5.8** shows a criminal being attacked by a leopard in the arena. This horrifying scene suggests that it was not easy to make animals attack humans; the victims had to be immobilized and the animals goaded into aggression. The very existence of the mosaic, however, which was displayed in a private home, reveals the Romans' pride in the empire's dominance over its perceived enemies. As we will see, these enemies would eventually include Christians.

Afternoons at the Colosseum were reserved for the main event, the gladiator contests. Gladiators were condemned criminals who were trained in the gladiator school near the Colosseum (see **Map 5.1**). They then received the right to live a while longer by fighting against each other in the arena. In time, the gladiatorial ranks were increased by slaves who were specifically bought and trained for this purpose. Gladiators armed with weapons were paired to fight until one was killed, and the winner won the right to live until his next fight. At first, gladiator contests were part of funeral rites, and the death blood of the losers was seen as an offering to the recently departed. Later, however, emperors sponsored contests featuring hundreds of gladiators. At the end of a gladiator contest,

Gladiators

FIGURE 5.7 The Colosseum This magnificent building was inaugurated in 80 C.E. The concrete foundations were 25 feet deep to support the structure of concrete and marble. More than 50,000 spectators entered through numbered gates to their seats.

FIGURE 5.8 Condemned to the Beasts, ca. second century C.E. During the mid-afternoon at the games in the amphitheaters, criminals sentenced to death were attacked by beasts. This mosaic from a private home was designed to celebrate Rome's victory over its enemies.

the man who had been overpowered was supposed to bare his throat unflinchingly to the killing blade of the victor. Not all defeated gladiators were killed; those who had fought with extreme bravery and showed a willingness to die could be freed by the emperor's clemency.

It is easy to judge these activities as wanton displays of brutality. Yet, from the Roman perspective, these rituals actually exemplified and perpetuated Roman virtue. In the arenas, private honor and public good intersected: The private generosity that funded the games served the community's need for ritual, and the emperor's sponsorship strengthened the community's loyalty to its leaders. Finally, individuals learned to face death bravely by watching people die; as the historian Livy (59 B.C.E.–17 C.E.) wrote: "There was no better schooling against pain and death." Nevertheless, all these demonstrations of Roman largesse, prowess, and courage could not stave off the threats to the empire that came at the end of the *Pax Romana*.

CRISIS AND TRANSFORMATION, 192–ca. 400 C.E.

The violence that accompanied the assassination of Marcus Aurelius's decadent son Commodus in 192 transformed Augustus's principate. The armies had grown strong under the military policy of the Five Good Emperors, so armies even beyond the praetorian guard became the king makers. Septimius Severus (r. 193–211) was a new kind of emperor—a North African general who came to power because of his army's support. A military man to the core, he also embodied

the multicultural elements of the empire. He spoke Latin with a North African accent and seemed to feel more at home among provincials than among the old, wealthy families of Rome.

The Military Monarchy

Septimius transformed the political base for Roman rule. Under the principate as established by Augustus, the empire was ruled by a partnership between the emperor and the Senate; Septimius and his successors ruled with the support of the army, | Severan dynasty | creating a military dictatorship. Septimius enlarged the army until it contained several legions more than the army of Augustus. He also raised soldiers' pay, ensuring their loyalty. Septimius militarized the civil government as well, by making extensive use of generals in positions of power. With these changes, the route to high office lay through the emperor's army instead of the *cursus honorum* (described in **Figure 4.3**). Rome had changed indeed.

Septimius established a dynasty (the Severan) that uneasily held power until 235. His son Caracalla (r. 211–217) was ruthless and was murdered while on campaign. Strong women in the Severan family—Julia Maesa, Caracalla's aunt, and her two daughters—managed to ensure that two more incompetent boys took the throne, but both Elagabalus (r. 218–222) and Alexander (r. 222–235) were murdered.

In the fifty years that followed Alexander's death, Rome was beset with chaos. During this period, legions in various parts of the empire put forth their own claimants to the throne. This era of conflict—from 235 to 285—was dominated by what has come to be called "barrack-room emperors," men who had little allegiance to the ancient values of the city of Rome. From 235 to 285, the number of claimants to the throne exploded. In one nine-year period, the emperor Gallienus fought off as many as 18 challengers. A unit whose general became emperor increased its own status, so armies fought for the throne.

While armies were busy trying to create emperors, Rome's borders were threatened on all fronts. In the north, Germanic tribes (discussed more fully in Chapter 6) began to penetrate across the Rhine and Danube defenses. Soldiers and resources had to be moved north to try to stem the tide. Meanwhile in the east, Rome seemed so weakened that Zenobia, a powerful queen of Palmyra (a city in Syria), declared | Border wars | independence from Rome and led armies against the legions. Emperor Aurelian (r. 270–275) crushed Palmyra after two wars and brought Queen Zenobia in chains to Rome. The resourceful queen ended up living out her life in an extravagant villa near Tivoli in

Italy, but her city was destroyed. Rome was not as successful in other eastern campaigns, as the Persian Empire encroached on Rome's eastern provinces. A Persian rock inscription celebrates a Persian victory and indicates the stress on the empire during these dark days: "We attacked the Roman Empire and annihilated . . . a Roman force of 60,000."

This whole military era demonstrates the centrifugal force that had marked Rome's growth from the beginning. Emperors were created in barracks far from Rome, and territories on the edges of the empire were slipping from centralized control. As if these internal and external pressures were not enough, a severe economic downturn loomed.

Ravaged by Recession, Inflation, and Plague

At the height of the empire, certain families accumulated astonishing wealth. Even though they gave some of it back to the public in the form of monuments or games, they still lived lavishly. Not only did they buy jewels and fine silks, but they gave banquets featuring exotic (and expensive) imported foods. One menu from a Roman cookbook recommends rare dishes from the far reaches of the empire: sow's udders stuffed with salted sea urchins, Jericho dates, boiled ostrich, roast parrot, boiled flamingo, and African sweet cakes.

Economic recession

This kind of luxury spending seriously damaged an already weakening economy for two reasons: It drained hard currency from the West and transferred it to the Far East, which supplied many of the luxuries; and it kept money from circulating, thus limiting the avenues for the growth of a prosperous middle class. As the poor in Rome received more and more food subsidies, the city had to spend more money on imported grain, further reducing the treasury. With the increase in imports from the East, the western centers of the empire began to suffer a shortage of hard currency, as money flowed to the great eastern centers that supplied most of the imports. As we will see, this shifting of wealth to the East had profound ramifications for the governing of the empire.

There was a further inherent weakness in the imperial economy: When territorial expansion stopped, there was little to bring new wealth into the empire. Instead, a growing bureaucracy, increased military expenses, and costly military rivalries served to drain money. The economy stagnated while expenses increased.

Emperors throughout the centuries tried to address the problem of a shortage of hard currency by debasing the coinage, which meant that plenty of money still circulated, but it was not worth as much as it had been before. Gold coins virtually disappeared from circulation, and by the mid-third century the silver content of coins had dropped to a negligible 1 percent. Not surprisingly, inflation struck. The price of grain climbed so much that a measure that cost two coins in 200 C.E. cost 330 coins just a century later. Inflation always hits the poor hardest, and many people turned to banditry out of desperation. The resulting fear and unrest further rocked life in the empire.

Inflation

To worsen matters, plague from China spread through the empire along with the luxury goods that came along the Silk Road. (See Global Connections, page 145.) Just as in China, the disease caused intense suffering and depleted the already low Roman population. Labor became as scarce as hard currency. The Roman government turned to the tribes outside its borders to replenish its armies. Mercenaries crossed the borders to fight for Rome, and the legions of Rome increasingly came to resemble the "barbarians" from the outside. Structures like Hadrian's Wall no longer clearly separated the "civilized" from the "uncivilized."

All the problems of the late second and third centuries demonstrated that the Roman Peace was over. The borders between Roman and non-Roman had dissolved, and hungry, restless residents agitated within the empire. Medical knowledge was helpless in the face of pandemics like the mid-third-century plague, and Roman families could no longer populate the empire. The empire seemed to teeter on the brink of collapse.

The Reforms of Diocletian, 285–305 C.E.

Considering the many disasters facing the empire in the mid-third century, it is a wonder that the empire did not fall then. In fact, it was the dramatic measures of Diocletian, an autocratic new emperor, that helped Rome avert ultimate disaster—at least for the time being. Diocletian (r. 285–305) was a general who rose from the ranks to wear the imperial purple. Not content to be called emperor, he assumed the title "lord" and demanded that his subjects worship him as a living god. (See Document 5.2.) The change in title marked the formal end of the principate founded by Augustus—from then on, emperors were no longer "first citizens." Diocletian had a shrewd, practical side and used his considerable administrative talents to address the problems plaguing the empire. The new Roman lord was up to the task and stopped the decline.

Turning to the problems of communication, administration, and succession, Diocletian organized the government into a **tetrarchy,** or rule by four men. Diocletian ruled in the wealthier eastern region of the empire, while assigning his partner, Maximian, to

Tetrarchy

DOCUMENT 5.2

Diocletian Becomes "Lord"

The Roman historian Aurelius Victor in the middle of the fourth century wrote a brief work titled Lives of the Emperors *in which he described the transformation of Diocletian from a "first citizen" like Augustus to a more aloof, godlike figure.*

By decision of the generals and [military] tribunes, Valerius Diocletian, commander of the palace guards, was chosen emperor because of his wisdom. A mighty man he was, and the following were characteristics of his: he was the first to wear a cloak embroidered in gold and to covet shoes of silk and purple decorated with a great number of gems. Though this went beyond what befitted a citizen and was characteristic of an arrogant and lavish spirit, it was nevertheless of small consequence in comparison with the rest. Indeed, he was the first after Caligula and Domitian to allow himself to be publicly called "lord," and to be named "god," and to be rendered homage as such. . . . But Diocletian's faults were counterbalanced by good qualities; for even if he took the title of "lord," he did act [toward the Romans] as a father.

SOURCE: Aurelius Victor, *Lives of the Emperors*, in *Roman Civilization: Sourcebook II: The Empire*, eds. Naphtali Lewis and Meyer Reinhold (New York: Harper Torchbooks, 1966), p. 456.

Analyze the Document

1. How did Diocletian present himself to the Roman public?

2. What innovations does Aurelius Victor describe? Did this historian approve of Diocletian's actions?

3. Contrast this view of leadership with that of Augustus shown in Document 5.1. Why do you think the Romans were prepared to accept such a kinglike demeanor in Diocletian?

---

rule in the West. To address the issue of succession, each of these "augusti" adopted a "caesar" who would succeed him. In the Roman tradition dating back to Octavian, each caesar married his augustus's daughter, sealing the alliance through family bonds. **Figure 5.9** depicts the ideals behind the tetrarchy. The four emperors—all military men—rest their hands on their swords. They also embrace one another. The overall arrangement of their figures conveys the concept of a unified rule by four men. **Map 5.4** shows the territorial division of the tetrarchy.

Diocletian then turned his administrative talents to problems other than succession. He recognized that the military that had created so many emperors from the time of Septimius Severus onward was a threat to political stability. He brought the army under control in part by reversing Septimius's policy of uniting civil and military offices. He separated the two so that provincial governors could not command armies, thus making it harder for generals to aspire to the purple. To address the problem of incursions along the imperial frontiers, Diocletian rearranged the armies. Instead of placing his greatest martial strength along the borders, he stationed mobile legions deep inside the empire. That way, they could move quickly to meet a threat rather than just react as outsiders encroached. The Germanic tribes on the northern borders were particularly eager to enter the empire, looking for wealth. Diocletian recruited many of these Germans to serve in this new army, further diluting its traditional Roman character even as he made it more effective.

Military reforms

FIGURE 5.9 Tetrarchs, ca. 305 C.E. Diocletian's division of the Roman Empire's administration among four men might have seemed to some to fragment it. This statue from Venice shows the four tetrarchs embracing and thus strongly linked as one, assuring the viewer that the empire still stood united.

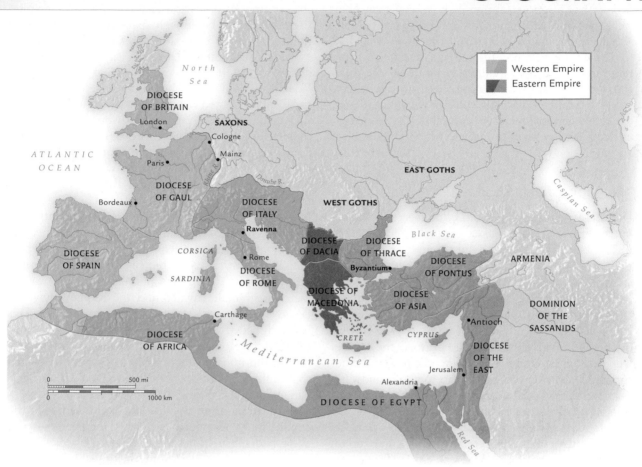

MAP 5.4

Diocletian's Division of the Empire, 304 C.E.

This map shows Diocletian's administrative reform of the empire and its division into four parts that would be governed by a tetrarchy (four men). Notice the primary division into east and west, with each unit ruled by an augustus.

Explore the Map

1. What geographic advantage led Diocletian to take the eastern portion of the empire?

2. Ravenna and Byzantium became the two new capitals of the empire, replacing Rome. What advantages did each city's location offer for trade and defense?

Finally, Diocletian turned to the severe economic problems troubling the empire. In the same way Augustus had tried to improve morality by decree, Diocletian issued economic edicts. He addressed the rampant inflation by freezing prices and wages, but these policies simply led merchants to withdraw goods from the open market to participate in informal black market exchanges. The emperor also raised taxes to pay for an expanding army, but he reformed the tax

Economic reforms

system so that it was partially based on payment in goods instead of in the inflated, scarce coins. This kind of authoritarian approach could not solve the empire's most deep-seated economic troubles, but it kept the economy from collapsing altogether.

The last problem that Diocletian addressed was the simple shortage of people to perform the tasks needed to keep the empire running. Again, he sought solutions in decrees. He identified "essential" occupations—ranging from soldier to farmer, baker,

Crisis and Transformation, 192–ca. 400 C.E.   155

and tax collector—and froze people in these jobs. Furthermore, he made these occupations hereditary. His decrees had a serious unintended consequence: They weakened the willingness of well-off locals to contribute to the public works and the games that had so defined imperial life. Instead, great estates became more self-contained, pulling away from the central authority and maintaining their own mercenary armies. People increasingly complained about the tax collectors and the central government that seemed to ask more and more of its citizens while providing less and less.

The Capital Moves East

Diocletian's attempts to stabilize the succession barely outlasted him. He and his co-augustus stepped down in 305 as planned, leaving the empire to be ruled by their two caesars, but Diocletian's hopes for a smooth transition proved overly optimistic. There were years of intrigue and civil war as several rulers fought for the throne. Finally, one of the caesars was succeeded by an ambitious son, Constantine (r. 306–337), who defeated his rivals to assume sole control of the empire. The new emperor finally disbanded the powerful praetorian guards, who had backed his rival. Beyond that, he kept Diocletian's economic and military reforms but put his own unique stamp on the empire.

In 330, Constantine made a momentous decision for the future of the empire: He built a new urban center on the site of the old Greek city of Byzantium. Later the city would be called Constantinople, after its founder, and become a second capital to the empire, eclipsing Rome itself in

| Constantinople |

power and grandeur. Rome was no longer a practical site for the capital of the empire because it was too far from the center of the military actions on the borders, and the conservative old Roman nobility made it very difficult for emperors to implement vigorous new ideas. Constantine could not have chosen a better site for a new capital city, which he called his "new Rome." It was easily defended and located along the rich eastern trade routes. Since Diocletian, when emperors ruled autocratically based in cities away from Rome, the great Roman Senate that had governed in concert with Augustus had shrunk to no more than a city council. The Roman Empire seemed to have little to do with Rome anymore and bore scant resemblance to the principate created by Augustus.

As the capital moved east, the western provinces came under increasing pressure from the Germanic tribes outside the empire. Great estates in the provinces—called *latifundia*—became more self-sufficient, needing nothing from the central authority.

After the death of Constantine in 337, emperors reacted to Germanic invaders by inviting some tribes into the empire to settle and become allies. The borders had already proved permeable, and with the continued population decline within the empire, there seemed to be enough space for everyone. This influx, however, carried the seeds of the empire's eventual disintegration. The Visigoths (more fully described in Chapter 6) were one of the tribes the Romans invited across the border to settle. However, the Romans treated them abysmally, giving them land they could not farm, raping their women, and forcing them to sell their children into slavery in return for food. The warlike tribe went on a rampage.

In 378, Romans under Emperor Valens (r. 364–378) confronted Gothic troops, and the resulting battle marked a change in military tactics. The Goths were heavily outnumbered by the heavy Roman infantry that had always seemed invincible. The Romans pushed the Goths back to their circled wagons, and defeat seemed imminent. Just then, Gothic cavalry dashed from the hills, smashing the Roman line. The infantry was no match for mobile cavalry, and the Roman army was destroyed. Emperor Valens was killed on the field. This battle dispelled the aura of invincibility that had surrounded the Roman legions for centuries and demonstrated the military importance of cavalry. It seemed that military might now lay in the hands of the "barbarians" rapidly pouring through the borders.

Even Rome itself was no longer the center of the empire, for by the fourth century, the emperors in the West had made Milan their capital. Then, in 402, Emperor Honorius fled from the invading Visigoths to create a new capital in Ravenna, behind defensible marshes. Ravenna was safe, but Rome was not, and in 410, the Visigoths plundered the "eternal city," Rome itself. Masses of panicked Romans (like Melania in the Biography on page 170) fled to Africa and the East.

It seemed that an era had passed and that the empire had finally fallen—but the end had not come quite yet. The Visigoths left Italy and settled in Spain as allies of the empire, just as many other tribes had done in other provinces. An emperor remained in the west, ruling from Italy, and a co-ruler continued to govern in the east, from Constanti-

| Twilight of the empire |

nople. But by 410 the western region had disintegrated so much that there seemed to be no point in referring to a Roman Empire in the West at all.

For the last few centuries, historians have spent a great deal of thought (and paper) exploring what has come to be known as the "fall" of the Roman Empire that began in the turmoil of the third century. Historians point to dwindling population, economic problems, reliance on slave labor, civil warfare, and moral decay as the causes of the decline. All of these

| Rome's "fall" |

factors contributed to the transformation of the old Roman world, but perhaps more important than anything else was the great influx of peoples from the north who invaded the empire. These invasions (which we will explore in more detail in Chapter 6) caused the breakup of the huge empire that had dominated the Mediterranean world since the time of Augustus. The territorial empire was ending, but throughout these years of power and turmoil a religion arose that would give a new source of unity to the Mediterranean world.

THE LONGING FOR RELIGIOUS FULFILLMENT

As we saw in Chapter 4, the Romans were a deeply religious people who carefully linked their deities to cherished spaces. As the empire controlled more and more land, its subjects seemed increasingly distanced from their traditional gods. In part, worship of the emperor served as a unifying religious cult. By the middle of the third century, some twenty festival days honored deified emperors or their families each year. However, for all the reverence given to the emperors, a spiritual dissatisfaction still gnawed at the Roman people. Many Romans seemed to long for a closer relationship to a truly transcendent divinity, and Romans expressed this longing through a rise in various philosophic and religious movements.

We can see this attempt to bring the gods a little closer to earth in the increasing numbers of spells and charms that Roman men and women purchased. People tried everything from healing and love charms to curses placed on chariot racers. Prophets, magicians, and charlatans also proliferated. One late-second-century writer described a man who made a fortune by pretending to prophesy through a giant serpent that he wrapped around himself. However, all the religious movements of the Roman world were not as superficial as magical curses and false prophets.

Stoicism and Platonism

The Hellenistic philosophies (Chapter 3) all continued to offer religious satisfaction to some educated Romans. The great Roman Stoic Seneca (ca. 4 B.C.E.–65 C.E.) wrote that by focusing on their own ethical behavior, people could locate the divinity that dwells within each person. As mentioned earlier, the Stoic emperor Marcus Aurelius used this philosophy to bring meaning to the challenges of his life. Like the reflective emperor, many people found in Stoicism ethical principles to help guide their lives, and Stoicism exerted an important influence on both Christianity and Western ideas in general.

The most influential philosophical system, however, came with a new form of Platonism, **Neoplatonism,** that emerged during the late empire. In the third century, these Neoplatonists created a complex system that offered an explanation for the link between the divine and the human.

Like Stoics, Neoplatonists believed that each person contained a spark | Neoplatonism | of divinity that longed to join the divinity that had created it. Through study, contemplation, and proper living, people could cultivate that bit of divinity within themselves and thereby reduce the distance between the human and the divine.

These philosophies, though intriguing, had limited appeal. Just as they had in the earlier Hellenistic kingdoms, they attracted people with leisure, education, and a respectable income. Most people instead tried to satisfy their spiritual desires through one or more of the mystery cults that gained popularity in the second century.

Mystery Cults

The mystery cults that had become popular during the Hellenistic world (Chapter 3) had an even stronger appeal in the difficult times of the late empire. These cults had always offered hope to individuals seeking meaning in their lives and ecstatic celebrations that seemed to transport individuals outside themselves into the world of the gods. Some cults claimed to offer a universality lacking in many of the Roman deities, and many offered hopes of a better afterlife to people disenchanted with their current existence.

The ancient Greek cult of Dionysus is one example of a cult that promised all these things. In this popular worship, men and women celebrated the mysteries of the god of | Cult of Dionysus | wine and rebirth by drinking, engaging in sex acts, and ritually eating the raw flesh of beasts. **Figure 5.10** shows a painting discovered in Pompeii that probably depicts the worship of Dionysus. The young woman on the left is being whipped, probably to bring about an ecstatic state. The woman on the right dances in naked ecstasy with a cymbal while the woman before her prepares to hand her the staff marking her entrance into the mysteries. Such ceremonies appealed to people's need to feel personally connected with the divine.

The cult of Isis, the Egyptian goddess of fertility, enjoyed remarkable popularity throughout the empire. Septimius Severus and his wife portrayed themselves as Isis | Cult of Isis | and her consort, Serapis. As we saw in Chapter 1, the ancient Egyptians called Isis's husband Osiris, but in the Hellenistic period, when many of the Egyptian deities were assimilated into the Greek pantheon, Osiris began to be called Serapis. As the noted Greek biographer Plutarch (ca. 46–ca. 120 C.E.) explained, "Serapis received this name at the time when he changed his nature. For this reason

FIGURE 5.10 Mystery Religions, first century C.E.   This fresco is from the Villa of the Mysteries near Pompeii, a site that was preserved by its burial in volcanic ash from the eruption of Mount Vesuvius. The image shows women participating in a sacred ritual, probably for the god Bacchus.

Serapis is a god of all peoples in common." In his new form as Serapis, the old god Osiris left his traditional home of the Nile and brought protection to wide areas of the empire. Thus, Serapis was an appropriate incarnation for Septimius, a North African emperor who wanted to combine imperial worship with that of a popular mystery religion to try to overcome Rome's lack of a single, unifying religion.

While some cults, like that of Serapis, strove for universal appeal, the worship of other deities was not intended to be for everyone. Instead, initiates prided themselves on participating in an exclusive and difficult worship. For example, some men and women celebrated the mystery of the Great Mother, the female goddess who brought fertility and comfort. In frenzied rituals, celebrants flogged themselves until their blood flowed, and some men castrated themselves as an ultimate sacrifice to the goddess. In another example, imperial soldiers felt particularly drawn to the mysteries of Mithraism, whose followers were exclusively men, and the religion's emphasis on

self-discipline and courage made it very popular with the armies of Rome. These soldiers gathered in special buildings, ritualistically ate bread and water, and awaited salvation.

These different mysteries practiced throughout the Roman world reflected the multicultural nature of the empire. People were willing to partake in mysteries of any origin, whether Egyptian, Syrian, or Persian. All these practices emphasized the irrational at the expense of the rational, in contrast to the Stoic or Platonist approaches. But in the ancient world, people did not feel compelled to choose only one path to spiritual fulfillment. The famous second-century author Apuleius, for example, was a magician, a Platonist, and an initiate into the mysteries of Isis.

The Four Faces of Judaism

Although Palestine had struggled for religious purity while under the Hellenistic kings, the Jews under Roman rule were not exempt from the religious angst

MAP 5.5

Israel at the Time of Jesus

This map shows the kingdom of Herod under the rule of Rome. It also illustrates how this kingdom reunited Judah and Israel and at the same time how much smaller it was than the old empire of King David.

Explore the Map

1. Where do the trade route lines go? What diverse influences did Judaism experience from the countless travelers who passed through the small kingdom?

2. Where were the major sites of Jesus' ministry? How close together were they? (Consult the scale.) How might these distances have contributed to the ministry?

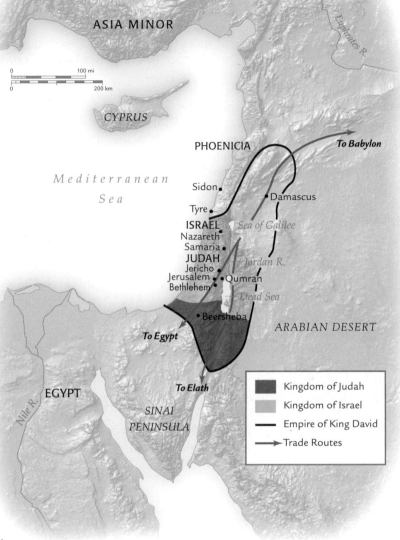

that swept the empire. At the time of Julius Caesar, the kingdom of Judah had been ruled by descendants of Judas Maccabes (see Chapter 3), but the kingdom was swept into the turmoil of Rome's civil wars following the death of Julius Caesar. Finally, Herod, a member of a prominent family in Hebron, south of Jerusalem, rose to power and, with the support of Octavian, was made king of Judea and subject to Rome by the Senate of Rome. **Map 5.5** shows the kingdom of Herod and illustrates its central location in the trade of the Middle East. Herod was unpopular with the Jews, and during this kingdom, controversies grew. The struggles of four main Jewish groups shaped the religious and political future of this region and beyond.

The **Sadducees** largely comprised members of priestly families. They emphasized Jewish worship at the Temple in Jerusalem, which they saw as the cult center of the Israelites. (In Chapter 3 we saw that the Temple had been rebuilt in the sixth century B.C.E., and this structure—which had been further rebuilt in 19 B.C.E.—is known as the Second Temple.) The Sadducees were religious conservatives who rejected any "new" ideas that they did not find in the Torah—the first five books of the Bible.

Sadducees and Pharisees

These innovations included the ideas of angels and resurrection of the dead, both of which began to win more adherents. The Sadducees were also willing to compromise with the Hellenized world and the Roman rulers as long as the Temple cult remained secure. However, the Sadducees would not continue as a viable force after Titus destroyed the Temple in 70 C.E.

The **Pharisees,** on the other hand, emphasized Jewish purity laws. They refused all compromise with the Hellenized world and adhered strictly to dietary rules and rituals to reinforce their separateness from all non-Jews. However, the Pharisees did accept new ideas such as the resurrection of the just and the existence of angels. For Pharisees, Judaism centered not on public worship in the Temple but on the private observances of Jews all over the Roman world. The Pharisees also supported sayings and interpretations of Jewish scholars, such as the influential Hillel the Elder (ca. 30 B.C.E.–ca. 10 C.E.), that later became part of the Jewish tradition. It was the work of the Pharisees that would ultimately lead to the expanded writings that updated the practice of the Torah.

Although the Pharisees believed strongly in separating themselves from the surrounding non-Jewish world, they avoided political revolution. Another group in Palestine, the **Zealots,** took a different approach. This group looked back to the successful revolt of the Maccabees against Seleucid rule and urged political revolt against Roman rule as a way to restore Israel to an independent state. Not surprisingly, clashes between the Zealots and Roman troops broke out throughout the early first century C.E.

Despite their differences, all these groups were struggling in some way with the same question that had plagued Jews since the first Hellenistic conquest: how to maintain a separate identity within the Roman world. A fourth group, the **Essenes,** tried to avoid the problem altogether by withdrawing from the social world. The Essenes moved to separate communities and attempted to live pure lives, seemingly alienating themselves from the Temple cult. The Essenes have drawn much scholarly attention because they probably authored one of the most exciting archaeological finds in biblical history, the Dead Sea Scrolls.

| Essenes |

In 1947, a shepherd boy discovered a deep cave containing ancient pottery jars holding hundreds of scrolls of texts dating from as early as 250 B.C.E. The scrolls include such valuable works as the oldest version of portions of the Hebrew Bible and other documents revealing the historical context of the biblical texts. Most of the works are severely damaged and have been reconstructed from hundreds of tiny fragments, which leaves lots of room for differing interpretations. Although many of the texts have been studied since the 1950s, there is still no scholarly consensus surrounding these precious scrolls.

Most scholars believe these texts were produced by the Essenes in their mountain retreat in Qumran (see **Map 5.5**)—a desert community fifteen miles from Jerusalem, near the Dead Sea—and hidden in the cave during the turbulent times when Rome was exerting its dominance in the region. All the writings were completed before 68 C.E., when the Romans destroyed the settlement at Qumran. Some scholars believe the writings came from a large library of various Hebrew documents, and thus they may reveal the origins of the many strains of Judaism, perhaps even the early Jesus movement. It is certain that continued analysis of these texts will shed a good deal of light on these early centuries that were so fertile to spiritual impulses.

In this time of spiritual longing, many Jews believed that a savior—a Messiah—would come to liberate them. Some believed that he would be a political figure who would liberate the Jews from foreign domination, and people like the Zealots were poised to fight for this political leader. Others, however, expected a spiritual savior—a Chosen One who would bring a kingdom of righteousness to earth. The Essenes may have withdrawn to the desert community to wait for the spiritual Messiah—their "Teacher of Righteousness." It was into this volatile religious time that Jesus of Nazareth was born.

| The Messiah |

The Jesus Movement

During the reign of Augustus (r. 27 B.C.E.–14 C.E.), at the beginning of the empire, a child named Jesus was born in about 4 B.C.E., possibly in Bethlehem (about 10 miles southeast of Jerusalem, shown on **Map 5.5**). This event dramatically influenced the empire by the fourth century. Thus, we must return to the time of Augustus to trace the fortunes of a small religious sect in Judea that would ultimately conquer Rome itself.

The information we have on Jesus' life and teachings is drawn largely from the Gospels of the New Testament of the Bible, which were written sometime after his death, probably by people who never knew him. (Estimates on the time of the composition of the Gospels range from thirty to ninety years after Jesus' death.) The Gospels offer little information about the first thirty years of Jesus' life. They do tell us that he was the son of a woman named Mary and a carpenter named Joseph and that he excelled in his religious studies, for he confounded the priests of the Temple with his knowledge of matters of faith.

According to the limited historical information available, Jesus drew from the rich religious environment in the Jewish lands. Like the Pharisees, he appealed to the poor, and many of his sayings resembled those of Hillel the Elder. His teachings also had some qualities in common with those of the Essenes, who had written of a coming Teacher of Righteousness. Unlike the Zealots, Jesus spoke of a heavenly kingdom rather than a violent revolution and attracted a large following of those who longed for a better life. Jesus began his ministry after being baptized by John the Baptist, and the Gospels tell the story of his activities after this defining event in some detail. For many, Jesus was the awaited Messiah who would save and transform the world. Many called him Christ—the Lord's Anointed, the Messiah.

| Jesus' ideas |

While Jesus' ideas resembled those of some of his contemporaries, the totality of his message was strikingly new and changed the course of Western civilization. For about three years, Jesus preached in Judea and Galilee, drawing huge crowds to listen to his message of peace, love, and care for the poor and suffering. He was accompanied by a small group of devoted followers—the apostles—who carried on his message after his death. Many people also believed that he performed miracles and cures. His growing popularity alarmed both Jewish leaders and Roman authorities, who constantly watched for uprisings in Judea. In about 29 C.E., the Roman governor, Pontius Pilate, sentenced Jesus to crucifixion, the cruel death reserved for many of Rome's enemies. The Romans nailed a sign on Jesus' cross identifying him as the "king of the Jews," perhaps mistranslating the powerful notion of Messiah as king, and certainly underestimating the nature and appeal of Jesus and his message.

Jesus' brief, three-year ministry had come to an end. However, three days later, Jesus' followers believed they saw him risen from the dead and subsequently taken into heaven. They believed this proof of Jesus' divinity promised a resurrection for his followers, and the apostles wanted to spread this good news to other Jews.

A small group of Jesus' followers led by the apostles Peter and James formed a Jewish sect that modern historians call the Jesus movement to identify the period when followers of Jesus continued to identify themselves as Jews. The apostles appealed to other Jews by preaching and praying at the Temple and at small gatherings of the Jewish faithful. The earliest history of this Jesus movement is recorded in Acts in what Christians call the New Testament of the Bible. Like others throughout the Roman world, these Jews believed that prophecy and miracles marked the presence of the divine. Thus, the apostles, the followers who had known Jesus personally, began traveling to bring his message to others. They spoke in prophetic tongues and appeared to work miracles. They also began preaching in Jewish communities around the Mediterranean world.

| Apostles |

The early Jesus movement could have taken various different directions. Would Jesus' followers withdraw from society like the Essenes and John the Baptist had done? The apostle James moved to Jerusalem and centered his leadership of the church there, thus choosing not to lead a sect in the wilderness. A more thorny issue was the question of accepting Gentiles—non-Jews—into the new religion. James took a position of conservative Judaism, insisting that Christianity required its adherents to follow the circumcision and strict dietary laws that had marked the Jewish people. The apostle Peter seems to have been more willing to preach to Gentiles, particularly "God-fearing" Greeks who were interested in the ethical monotheism of the Jews. Peter believed they would not have to be circumcised or keep all the Jewish festivals, but they would have to follow the dietary restrictions.

However, the man who would be remembered as the Apostle to the Gentiles had not known Jesus before his crucifixion. Saul of Tarsus (ca. 5–64 C.E.), whom we remember by the name of Paul, was a Hellenized Jew and a Roman citizen who had at first harassed Christians. After he experienced a vision of the risen Jesus, he converted and took up the mission of bringing the Christian message beyond the particularity of the Jewish communities to the wider world of the Roman Empire and beyond. He moved beyond Peter by eliminating all dietary restrictions on Christians, and he traveled widely through the eastern portion of the empire establishing new Christian communities. **Map 5.6** shows where Paul journeyed and how the Christian message slowly spread throughout the Roman world. Paul's influence on the young church was immense, and his letters became part of the Christian Scriptures.

| Paul of Tarsus |

Religious tensions between Jews and Roman authorities in Palestine culminated shortly after the deaths of Peter and Paul. Rome finally decided to take strong action against those in Judea, including Zealots, who were rebelling against Roman rule. In the course of the suppression, the Essene community at Qumran was destroyed (but not before they had buried their precious scrolls, which we call the Dead Sea Scrolls), and then the armies proceeded against Jerusalem. In 70 C.E., the son of Emperor Vespasian, Titus (who later became emperor in his own right), led Roman legions into Jerusalem, burned the city, and destroyed the Second Temple. All that seems to have remained of Herod's great

| Destruction of the Temple |

FIGURE 5.11 Western Wall, ca. 19 B.C.E. When the Romans destroyed the Jewish Temple in Jerusalem, all that was left standing was the western wall. This architectural remnant was called the Wailing Wall for centuries as Jews visited the site and lamented the loss of the Temple. Now people often refer to it simply as the Wall.

The destruction of the Temple inadvertently resolved the tensions within Judaism. The Sadducees, Essenes, and Zealots were all destroyed, and the Pharisees made peace with the Romans and recentered Judaism on synagogue worship. An emphasis on prayer and the law replaced sacrifices at the Temple. After 70 C.E., the Hebrew canon of scriptures came to be closed and the Hebrew Bible—what the Christians would call the Old Testament—was completed. Followers of the great teacher Hillel reached a compromise with the authority of Rome that let Jews maintain an identity within the empire, and future rabbis would study scripture and interpret the ways Jews should act while living among Gentiles.

`Dispersion of Jews`

The conquest of Jerusalem also settled any question about whether Christianity was to be centered in Jerusalem. Early Christianity, like Diaspora Judaism, was to be a religion that was not bound to one city, and it began to claim universality. The Jesus movement within Judaism was transformed and was now more accurately called the early Christian church.

Early Christian Communities

The spread of Christianity was slow. Small groups of converts in the major cities of the empire gathered in one another's houses because there were no designated churches for the new movement. When members of the small communities met together at least once a week, people took turns reading scripture, praying, and offering other forms of worship. As Paul wrote: "When you come together, each one has a hymn, a lesson, a revelation, a tongue, or an interpretation" (1 Cor. 14:26). "Tongue" and "interpretation" refer to speaking prophetically, which people in the communities believed proved the presence of God in their midst. The culmination of the service was the Eucharist—the commemoration of Jesus' last supper—in which the faithful shared cups of wine and pieces of bread. Members then offered prayers of thanksgiving for Christ's sacrifice and death, which the faithful believed offered them salvation and eternal life.

temple was the western wall. **Figure 5.11** shows this location, which has become an important symbol of Jewish faith and a location for prayer. For many years it was called the Wailing Wall, so designated to mark it as a mourning space for the destruction of the Temple. In the twenty-first century, it is more often called the Western Wall, and in Hebrew, it is simply called the Wall. (See Document 5.3.)

Titus returned to Rome in a triumphal procession and built a great arch celebrating his accomplishment. **Figure 5.12** shows a marble relief from that arch, in which Titus's troops return victorious from Jerusalem clutching spoils from the Temple. This figure shows soldiers carrying an important symbol of Judaism, the great menorah—a candelabra that held seven candles—which had been sacked from the holy place. The Temple was never rebuilt. Many Jews were scattered from Judea all over the Mediterranean after this devastation, and with them traveled numerous followers of the Jesus movement.

The relatively small numbers of Christians grew consistently throughout the first few centuries after the death of Jesus. Some estimates suggest that the total number of Christians at the beginning of the third century C.E. was about 200,000, or less than 0.5 percent of the total population. Although this is a small percentage, the actual number is significant—Christians were slowly becoming more visible. The church father Tertullian (ca. 160–ca. 217) wrote that there were thousands of Christians in Carthage in about 200, and he was probably accurate—a few thousand Christians in a population of about 500,000. This small but growing number would periodically come into conflict with the power of Rome.

FIGURE 5.12 Marble Relief Depicting the Sack of Jerusalem, ca. 81 C.E. The Romans erected a triumphal arch to commemorate Emperor Titus's victory in Jerusalem. The scenes depict the treasures—which the Romans described as a "river of gold and silver"—that flowed from their conquest. They were most impressed, however, by the huge golden menorah from the Temple, shown prominently in this detail from the arch.

FROM CHRISTIAN PERSECUTION TO THE CITY OF GOD,

64–410 C.E.

Conservative Romans looked askance at any innovations, particularly religious novelties. It was one thing for Christians to worship someone who had died within living memory as a divinity, but it was quite another for them to reject the traditional Roman assortment of gods. Furthermore, early Christians seemed to violate the traditional Roman social order by including the poor, slaves, and women as equals in their congregations.

Christians, who gathered unobtrusively in communities, differed significantly from Pagan Romans in their views of what happened after the faithful died. They expected their bodies to be resurrected after death. This new attitude toward the dead transformed traditional Roman attitudes and practices toward corpses. Roman graves were considered polluting and were dug outside the walls of the city. We have seen (Chapter 4) that the bodies of the poor received little respect as they were buried shallowly by garbage. Christians wanted to keep their dead close to the community, and the **catacombs** dug under the city in about the second century to bury the Christian dead are one of the visible reminders of this dramatic change. **Figure 5.13** shows the burial spaces in a catacomb. Here, rich and poor alike were interred to await resurrection together.

Looking for Christian Scapegoats

To quell accusations that he was responsible for a devastating fire in Rome, Emperor Nero looked for scapegoats and implemented the first large-scale persecution of Christians in Rome in 64 C.E. He executed hundreds of Roman Christians, possibly including the apostles Peter and Paul, and set a precedent that would be repeated periodically over the next two centuries. During the contentious years, provincial officials played a leading role in the persecutions. Some of these authorities chose to harass Christians; others ignored the new religion. Whatever their policy, however, the texts make it clear that when Christian men and women were brought to the arena, many died so bravely that some Roman spectators promptly converted.

During the third century when the empire confronted many internal and external problems, its policy toward Christians grew harsher. Under Emperor Decius (r. 249–251) and then again under Emperor Diocletian (r. 285–305), all imperial residents were to sacrifice to the emperor and receive a document recording their compliance. Diocletian, the autocratic emperor who legislated wages, prices, and military matters, thought he could decree religious beliefs as

Titus Destroys Jerusalem

In the first century C.E., the Jewish historian Josephus wrote a history of the Jews in which he described the violent destruction of Jerusalem in 70 C.E. by Titus. Josephus was an eyewitness who first fought against the Romans, then fled to the Roman camp and flourished in Rome after the war. In this excerpt, Josephus describes first the internal dissensions among the Jews (whom he calls the "seditious") and then relates the destruction that burnt the Second Temple.

The legions had orders to encamp at the distance of six furlongs from Jerusalem, at the mount called the Mount of Olives, which lies over against the city on the east side, and is parted from it by a deep valley, interposed between them, which is named Cedron.

Now, when hitherto the several parties in the city had been dashing one against another perpetually, this foreign war, now suddenly come upon them after a violent manner, put the first stop to their contentions one against another; and as the seditious now saw with astonishment the Romans pitching three several camps, they began to think of an awkward sort of concord, and said one to another: "What do we here, and what do we mean, when we suffer three fortified walls to be built to coop us in, that we shall not be able to breathe freely? While the enemy is securely building a kind of city in opposition to us, and while we sit still within our own walls and become spectators only of what they are doing, with our hands idle, and our armor laid by, as if they were about somewhat that was for our good and advantage. We are, it seems (so did they cry out), only courageous against ourselves [in mutual argument], while the Romans are likely to gain the city without bloodshed by our sedition." Thus did they encourage one another when they were gotten together and took their armor immediately and ran out upon the Tenth legion and fell upon the Romans with great eagerness, and with a prodigious shout, as they were fortifying their camp. . . . [After a long and bloody siege, the Romans finally entered the city.]

Now the number of those that were carried captive during this whole war was collected to be ninety-seven thousand; as was the number of those that perished during the whole siege eleven hundred thousand, the greater part of whom was indeed of the same nation [with the citizens of Jerusalem], but not belonging to the city itself. . . .

Now this vast multitude is indeed collected out of remote places, but the entire nation was now shut up by fate as in prison, and the Roman army encompassed the city when it was crowded with inhabitants. Accordingly the multitude of those that therein perished exceeded all the destructions that either men or God ever brought upon the world; for, to speak only of what was publicly known, the Romans slew some of them, some they carried captives, and others they made a search for underground, and when they found where they were they broke up the ground and slew all they met with. There were also found slain there above two thousand persons, partly by their own hands and partly by one another, but chiefly destroyed by the famine. . . . And now the Romans set fire to the extreme parts of the city, and burned them down, and entirely demolished its walls.

SOURCE: Josephus, *The Jewish Wars*, in *The Great Events by Famous Historians*, vol. III, ed. Rossiter Johnson (The National Alumni, 1905), pp. 151, 205–206.

Analyze the Document

1. How do the Jews' internal problems impede their defense of Jerusalem?

2. Why does Titus so thoroughly destroy the city?

3. How do you think the dissension among the Jews might have affected them after their dispersion?

---

well. But this wide-scale demand for conformity only provoked many more Christians to die for their beliefs. **Map 5.6** reflects the extent of Christian strength after the persecutions of Diocletian had ended.

Constantine: The Tolerant Emperor

In the long tradition of Roman emperors, Constantine looked for supernatural help in his wars with his rivals. According to the Greek historian Eusebius (ca. 260–ca. 340), as Constantine prepared for a crucial battle he saw in the sky a vision of a cross with Greek writing reading, "In this sign, conquer." That night he had a prophetic dream explaining that soldiers would triumph only if they fought under Christian symbols. He obeyed the dream and won a decisive victory. To the Romans, dreams and omens carried crucial religious messages, and Constantine's nighttime message convinced him of the power of the Christian God. In 313, he issued a decree of toleration (the Edict of Milan) for all the religions of the empire, including Christianity, and the martyrdoms ended.

Constantine did more than simply tolerate Christians. He actively supported the church. He returned property to Christians who had been persecuted, gave tax advantages to Christian priests, and let Christian advisors play a role in his court's inner circle. Constantine's support of Christians probably derived in part from his military victory under

> Constantine supports church

FIGURE 5.13 Christian Catacombs, ca. second century C.E. Unlike pagan Romans, who buried their dead outside the city, Christians longed to keep their "holy dead" close to the worship sites of the living. These catacombs were underground burial spaces for early Christians in Rome.

and state that moved Christianity in a new direction: It would continue to flourish and grow in the shadow of the imperial throne. It seems that the emperor finally committed to the new religion on his deathbed; he was baptized a Christian. His delay, however, has provoked much historical speculation. Had Constantine judged it politically unwise to become a Christian as he ruled, or had he not yet made up his mind? We do not know for sure, but we do know that subsequent emperors expanded his policies, moving from toleration toward a commitment to sole Christian worship.

The Empire Adopts Christianity

Theodosius I (r. 379–395) put the final cap on the movement toward Christianity by forbidding the public worship of the old Roman cults. With this mandate, Christianity became the official religion of the Roman Empire. Of course, everyone did not immediately convert to Christianity; Judaism remained strong, and those who clung to traditional Roman religious beliefs came to be called pagans. This word came from *pagani*, a derogatory term for backward peasants, and its etymology shows how Christianity spread first from urban centers.

This merging of a political and Christian empire irrevocably changed both Rome and Christianity. After the fourth century, Christian communities looked very different from those of two centuries earlier. Instead of gathering secretly in one another's homes, Christians met publicly in churches that boasted the trappings of astounding wealth. Indeed, where once people converted to Christianity in spite of the danger of persecution, the influential church father Augustine (354–430) complained, some people now converted only to impress the rich and powerful.

Figures 5.14 and **5.15** illustrate this shift in the status of Christianity. In **Figure 5.14,** a second-century statue of Christ depicts him as the Good Shepherd. He appears as an unpretentious peasant, wearing the typical shepherd costume of the day. The Good Shepherd was the most popular portrayal of Christ in the early, simple centuries of Christianity. **Figure 5.15** shows a very different Good Shepherd. In this fifth-century mosaic, Christ wears the royal purple cloth of emperors. Now the Lord, he watches over his flock rather than working to convert nonbelievers. The gold in the mosaic demonstrates the new wealth of

> Christianity changes

the sign of the cross. The women in his family exerted a strong influence on him as well. His half-sister Constantia and his mother, Helena, were both Christians. Whatever religious motives Constantine had for his support of Christianity, the emperor remained a shrewd politician. In fact, his support of the new religion included a practical political basis. For one thing, there were so many Christians in the empire that it would have been unwise to continue to marginalize them. Furthermore, Constantine's withdrawal of support for traditional pagan shrines permitted him to confiscate their gold to help standardize his currency.

Under Constantine's patronage, the Christian movement grew rich and powerful, and the emperor built beautiful churches in support of the religion. As part of the emperor's respect for Christianity, he decided to restore the Holy Places at Jerusalem and Palestine to Christian worship. Helena toured the region to identify the sacred spaces, but this was quite a feat, for since the destruction of the Temple, Jerusalem had become a Roman city that had lost all identification with its Jewish past. Nevertheless, Helena located what she believed were key sites in the life of Jesus, building great churches where he was born and where he died. With the backing of Constantine and his family, Jerusalem was revived as a holy place, and Christians began to make pilgrimages there. These journeys began a tradition of Christian claim on that land that would continue throughout the Middle Ages.

Constantine's support of Christianity throughout his life established a relationship between church

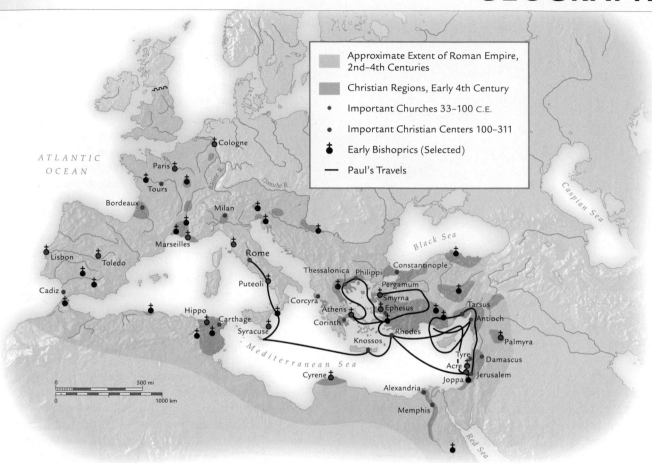

MAP 5.6

The Spread of Christianity to 311 C.E.

This map shows the areas of Christian strength by the fourth century and traces Paul's journey as he conducted his missionary work.

Explore the Map

1. Where were the areas of greatest Christian concentration? What might this clustering reveal about how influential Greek and Eastern thought was for the future development of the church?

2. Why did many of the Christian locations coincide with regions of commerce?

3. Why did Christianity spread mostly within the borders of the Roman Empire?

---

the church, as the image of Christ is transformed from that of a simple man to Lord of the universe.

As the empire embraced Christianity, the organization of the church began to duplicate the civil order of Rome. The emperor Diocletian had clustered provinces into larger units, called dioceses, for ease of administration. The church retained these divisions and placed bishops in charge of the major communities. Bishops were in charge of all aspects of church life, from finances to spiritual guidance, and as early as the third century in most regions they were paid by a church depending increasingly on

Christian organization

their administrative skills. For example, by 245 C.E. the province of North Africa had 90 bishops, and each was served by a well-developed hierarchy of priests and deacons. The ecclesiastical structure of the dioceses was divided into parishes, presided over by priests who reported to the bishops.

With Constantine's support, the church had become powerful. In the political world, power meant the ability to impose a uniformity of practice and even belief. Emperor Constantine tried to guide the church toward this kind of unity, and the church fathers began looking to authority figures to help them resolve differences. Prophecy—so important to the

FIGURE 5.14 Christ as the Good Shepherd, second century C.E. The earliest centuries of Christianity were marked by slow missionary work to gather new converts. The predominant image for this time and initiative was that of Christ the Good Shepherd gathering his flock.

In the eastern part of the empire, the relationship between bishops and emperor took a different turn. Beginning with Constantine, emperors in the East had involved themselves directly in religious disputes. Since the early third century, for example, Christians had quarreled over the nature of Christ. "Had he always existed," they asked themselves, "or did God bring him forth at a particular time?" In about 320, Arius, bishop of Alexandria, raised a furor when he argued that Jesus had been created by God. Arius's teachings polarized believers all over the empire, and Constantine did not want such a dispute raging in his lands. Therefore, he called a meeting that was the first "ecumenical" council—purportedly with representatives of the whole inhabited world. In 325, Constantine vigorously presided over the bishops he had summoned to the Council of Nicaea to resolve Arius's dispute over the nature of Christ. With the formulation of the Nicene Creed, which stated that Christ had always existed, Constantine and his bishops hoped to put that controversy to rest. However, as we shall see in Chapter 6, Arius's beliefs had already spread, and the church would have to face the problem of **Arianism** again. The council also set the precedent that orthodox Christians could exert their authority over those who believed otherwise.

Religious disagreements

Similarly in North Africa, Christians split over what to do about bishops and others who had "lapsed" during the years of persecution. This controversy was called the Donatist heresy, named after one of the protesting bishops. Church leaders believed it was essential to protect the notion that sacraments—like baptism and the Eucharist—were valid regardless of the behavior of the presiding priest, so they declared that bishops who had proven weak when threatened by torture could continue to hold their offices. The Donatists disagreed, saying that lapsed priests could *not* conduct the sacraments. Yet, passions had run so high over this issue that Donatists separated and tried to start a new church. The dispute catalyzed much violence in North Africa for centuries until the barbarian invasions created enough turmoil to move this issue to the background.

These and many other religious quarrels that spilled into secular politics raised the question of the relationship between church and state. In the early church, the relationship had been simple—Christianity focused on the next world while enduring an antagonistic earthly relationship with an unsympathetic state. Now, with church and state combined, the situation had become exceedingly complex. Many Christians felt ill at ease with all the resulting uncertainty. In his influential work *City of God* (413–427), Augustine tried to address these very complexities. Writing after the Visigoths had sacked Rome and terrified Romans had fled the city in waves, he explained that Christians

City of God

early church—became suspect, replaced by obedience to authority. As leaders began to look to a hierarchical organization for guidance in religious matters, it was perhaps inevitable that questions would arise over who should lead—religious or secular leaders. Ambrose (r. 374–397), the bishop of Milan in Italy, was one of the earliest bishops to challenge the power of the emperors and set a precedent for later bishops. In 390, Ambrose reprimanded Emperor Theodosius for massacring some rebellious citizens: The bishop excommunicated the emperor, forbidding him to participate in church services until he repented. Theodosius acceded to the bishop's demands, and later bishops of Rome (who came to be called popes) looked to this example of the church leading the state.

FIGURE 5.15 Christ as the Good Shepherd, ca. 450 C.E. After the Roman Empire became Christian, artists began to portray Christ with more imperial majesty. Here, Christ the Good Shepherd is shown clothed in gold and royal purple and presiding over his flock rather than working with his hands.

should not look at the current disasters with despair, nor see in them divine punishment. Instead, the church father drew from his strong background in Neoplatonism to explain worldly pain much as Plato had (described in Chapter 2), but with a Christian understanding. Augustine claimed that the world—and worldly cities—were made up of individuals who were constantly in struggle between their spiritual and earthly selves. Those people in whom the spiritual dominated belonged to a City of God, and those in whom the earthly dominated belonged to an earthly city. The perfect community of the faithful—the City of God—could exist only outside this world and would dominate at the end of time. In the meantime, all communities were mixed with members of both cities. Therefore, people ought to obey the political order and focus on the worthiness of their own souls rather than the purity of the reigning political institutions. They need not worry even when the city of Rome was sacked.

For Augustine and other religious thinkers, church and state were not incompatible. In fact, these men believed that the state should play an active role in ensuring the health of the church. In the early centuries of Christianity, **heresy** (expressing opinions that differed from official church doctrine) could be considered treason punishable by civil sanctions. Augustine, for example, suggested confiscating the property of the Donatists to persuade them to conform. However, in the late fourth century, a Christian heretic (Priscillian) was sentenced to death. As the ultimate power of the empire was brought to issues of conscience in these ways, church members learned that the path to salvation lay in obedience. Inevitably, there were Christians who objected to this direction, but the majority saw in this Christian order a fulfillment of God's plan—a victory for the earthly church.

The New Roman

Like political institutions and the church itself, everyday Roman life was also transformed with the burgeoning strength of Christianity. As church fathers in many regions of the empire wrote on matters of religion, they also addressed the larger question of how the new Christian Roman was to behave. In some areas of life it was easy simply to prohibit certain behaviors. For example, the church fathers wrote that Christians should not attend gladiator shows or arena games. Over time, the great amphitheaters fell out of use. Instead, Christian Romans satisfied their appetite for spectacle with chariot races, which remained hugely popular for centuries. In other areas, religious leaders and the populace reached a compromise—Christians could read the beloved traditional literature, such as Virgil or Homer (even though it praised pagan gods and suspect morality), but they were to try to extract a Christian message from it. (This is a major reason why such literature has survived.)

Christians also reshaped the social fabric of Roman life. For example, they did not believe in exposing unwanted children. Indeed, through the early centuries, they actively rescued foundling infants and raised them as Christian. Furthermore, they placed enormous priority on caring for the poor and needy. By the middle of the third century, church records show, in Rome alone the bishop provided charity for more than 1,500 widows and others in need.

Views on sexuality also shifted with the influence of the church fathers. As we have seen, although the Romans showed a certain cautiousness in their sexual lives, they also passionately believed that people had a duty to marry and procreate. Some Christian leaders, on the contrary, strongly advocated celibacy as the ideal life. Numerous Roman men complied with this recommendation, and many women used Christian celibacy as a way to free themselves from the expectations that they would marry and bear children. The influential church father Jerome (ca. 348–420) surrounded himself with chaste women who studied and traveled with him and founded monasteries. The Biography featuring Melania the Younger tells of one such fourth-century woman who was famous and admired during her lifetime and who spent her vast wealth establishing enduring religious institutions.

Christian sexuality

The most influential writer on sexuality was Augustine. In his widely read work *The Confessions*, he described his inability to give up his mistress and his "habit" of lust. As he explained, only with God's help was he able to summon the resolve to renounce these vices. This experience convinced Augustine that human beings were born with original sin and that this sin was passed to subsequent generations through semen during sexual intercourse. Because of original sin, Augustine concluded, people had to keep constant vigil against the force of lust—even marital intercourse was somewhat suspect. Through this kind of thinking, religious leaders involved themselves in people's private lives, and this watchfulness continued for centuries through a growing body of church law. Hardly any aspect of Roman life was left untouched by the Christianization of the empire.

THE HOLY LIFE

For early Christians, the path to God came through community; congregations of the faithful gathered together to help each other withstand the pressure of a hostile society. By the fourth century, some Christians were choosing another path to spiritual perfection. Men and women by the thousands left society to live alone in the deserts of Egypt and Syria, and their experiences profoundly influenced Christian life and thought.

Some Christians fled into the desert to escape the persecutions and chaos of the mid-third century. Others left during the fourth and fifth centuries because they objected to the union of church and state that developed after Constantine's rule. Still others fled the tax collectors. Whatever the reasons, the popularity of this movement reached enormous proportions. Historians estimate that by 325, as many as 5,000 men and women lived as hermits along the banks of the Nile, each in his or her own small cell. The fame of these holy people spread. Jerome advocated an ascetic life even for urban people and persuaded numerous wealthy Roman women to join him. Romans were scandalized when one of Jerome's young charges starved herself to death in her zeal for asceticism, but such was the passion for what many perceived was a holy life.

Flight to the desert

Many of these holy men and women survived extraordinary feats of self-denial—enduring lack of food, sleep, and other basic necessities. Some people insisted on living for decades on platforms perched high on poles. Women in particular sealed themselves into tombs that had only a tiny opening through which they could receive a small loaf of bread, and they eked out their lives in cramped, filthy solitude. These people's contemporaries found their behaviors so unusual that they concluded that to endure such hardships, the holy men and women must be recipients of God's power.

Of course, the extreme deprivation of heroic abstinence was not for everyone. Some people wanted simply to withdraw from the distractions of the world so as to worship God without enduring the rigors of the desert hermits. Communal monasticism developed as a parallel movement to the hermit life and offered an appealing alternative to life in the thick of Roman society. Discipline was strict in these pious oases, but participants had contact with other people, and conditions were not as harsh as those in the desert. In time, communal monasteries were brought into the overall structure of the church. Monks and nuns took vows of obedience to the monastery head (the abbot or abbess), and the monastic leader answered to the local bishop.

Monastic communities

The Influence of Holy People

The earliest holy people had been the Christian martyrs. Faithful observers witnessing their brave deaths concluded that God had invested their

BIOGRAPHY

Melania the Younger
(385–ca. 439)

FIGURE 5.16 Melania the Younger Icon.

Melania was born in 385, the daughter of a rich Roman patrician. By the time of her birth, Christianity was the official religion of the empire, and as a young girl she experienced the conflict of values that confronted so many Christian Roman families. Starting in her youth, Melania longed to follow a life of ascetic chastity like that of earlier holy women. As a daughter of Rome, however, she was expected to marry and bear children. As was the custom in a society in which women married young, when Melania was 14 years old her family arranged for her to marry Pinian.

A Model of Holiness

The young bride begged her new husband to live chastely with her so they could better worship God. Pinian wanted first to ensure the worldly succession of his family, so he told Melania she must bear two children before he would consider her request. A daughter was born to the young couple. Melania became pregnant again, but during this pregnancy she practiced many austerities in her search for a holy life. For example, she repeatedly prayed on her knees all night against the advice of her physician and the pleas of her mother. Furthermore, as a symbol of her commitment, she began to wear rough wool under the smooth silk clothing of the upper class. It is ironic that this return to republican simplicity was seen as rebellion by her family.

Melania's father tried to exert his paternal authority and make her care for herself and her unborn child in the traditional ways, but Christian beliefs introduced competing loyalties into family life. The young woman disobeyed her father, and her son was born prematurely. The infant boy died shortly after being baptized. Melania and Pinian's daughter died soon after that. Like so many Roman families, this young couple was unable to produce heirs. They saw the will of God in their children's deaths, however, and at age 20, Melania persuaded Pinian to join her in a vow of chastity.

As her first demonstration of religious commitment, she sought to liquidate her property. Her biographer's description of the problems involved in this task suggest the scale of wealth that many imperial Roman families had accumulated. For example, Melania owned thousands of slaves that she could not free without contributing adversely to Rome's unemployment problem. Furthermore, her house was so expensive even the emperor could not afford to buy it. However, the turmoil of the times helped resolve the difficulties of disposing of her property. The Visigoths who sacked Rome burned Melania's home, and she was able to sell the ruined property easily. As she and Pinian fled to Africa in the wake of the invasion, Melania used her money to ransom captives and buy islands for fellow ascetics to use as holy retreats.

After liquidating most of her wealth, Melania escalated her personal renunciations. She began to fast regularly, eating only some moldy bread twice a week. Beyond that, she spent her days reading and writing. She knew both Latin and Greek and studied the scriptures and the writings of church leaders. As her reputation for holiness grew, people began to come to her to listen to her teach.

Melania and Pinian then traveled from North Africa to Jerusalem to tour the holy places that Constantine had identified. From there, they visited the holy men and women living in the deserts of Egypt. Finally, Melania decided to found monasteries in Jerusalem, where she and Pinian could embark on a communal life dedicated to spirituality. Joined by 90 virgins and some reformed prostitutes, Melania spent the rest of her life studying, teaching, and traveling to holy sites. Shortly after her death, the faithful began to venerate her burial place, where miracles reputedly took place.

Melania's life exemplifies the Roman world transformed. She began as a well-off young girl, wearing silk and expecting to carry on the traditions of an upper-class Roman. After the disastrous barbarian invasions, she settled in the Holy Land, wearing rough wool and embodying the new values of the Christian world.

Connecting People & Society

1. How does Melania's life reveal the conflict of values between pagan and Christian Rome?

2. How did the Visigoths' invasions affect Melania and her family?

3. Where did Melania settle, and what did she do? How might she have served as a model for others?

bodies with the power to withstand torture. People believed that martyrs' remains contained sacred power and saved and venerated their bones, or **relics.** One woman in North Africa was reprimanded by her bishop for bringing a sacred bone to church and kissing it repeatedly. This kind of veneration strengthened the notion of resurrection of the flesh, in which the tortured flesh itself would receive its reward. Christianity thus became a religion that accepted the body. Believers wanted the holy dead to be buried near them, and by the fourth century, most altars included relics. In a very short time, the faithful and the enterprising began to engage in a brisk trade in relics that would be lucrative and influential throughout the Middle Ages. Historians have uncovered letters in which people solicit relics to help increase the power of their churches, and some of the correspondence is quite poignant. Bishop Braulio in seventh-century Spain responded to one such request, writing that he had many valuable relics, but all the labels had been lost. He could no longer identify the bones, but asked if the correspondent wanted them anyway.

Relics were preserved, treasured, and displayed in reliquaries—containers, often covered in precious metals and jewels, that displayed the precious bones that lay within. These reliquaries spread all over Europe and became a visible feature of the growing religion. Exquisite jeweled containers were supposed to express both the power of the relic and the incorruptibility of heaven, where people believed the saint dwelled.

Saints' cults

The desert fathers and mothers eventually supplanted the martyrs. They, too, seemed to embody holiness physically, and their *Sayings* reinforced the idea that people could not find spirituality without somehow sanctifying the flesh itself. Ironically, these holy people had traveled to the desert to find God and instead discovered their own humanity. They learned about the hunger that could drive one mad and about sexual urges that could relentlessly haunt their dreams. They even discussed nocturnal emissions and reflected on how to overcome boredom. The thinking of these spiritual people gave Christianity a profoundly human touch.

Like the martyrs, many of these holy people became venerated upon their deaths. The cult of saints became a strong part of Christian faith. Just as people believed that martyrs could intercede for them with God, so they felt convinced that prayer to a holy man or woman might also help them attain their desires. Holy men

Ascetic influence

and women who had learned so much about their humanity by transcending it seemed accessible even to the most ordinary of people. Saints gained reputations for doing everything from raising the dead and healing the sick to extending a too-short wooden beam so an overworked carpenter would not have to cut another. The conversion of the northern European countryside was inspired largely by living and dead holy people who had brought God's power down to the community.

The ascetic practices of the monasteries also shaped the lives of everyday Christians. Even for people who did not adhere to the strict rules of the monasteries, the luxuries of the Roman world seemed shameful when compared with the purity of the monasteries. Over time, people concluded that the ideal Christian life should be simple, and some Christians looked with disdain at those who surrounded themselves with comfort and pleasure. This tendency of monastic rigor to influence Christian life continued throughout the Middle Ages.

Monasteries always served both as havens during stormy political times and as outlets for those who sought a highly spiritual life. For centuries, these communities rejuvenated the Christian world and helped the church meet people's changing spiritual needs. Men and women in search of personal spiritual perfection would ultimately become powerful social forces for the medieval world.

LOOKING BACK & MOVING FORWARD

Summary   The conservative Romans who mourned the death of Julius Caesar and celebrated the victory of his young nephew Octavian (Augustus) would hardly have recognized the world of Augustine or of the late-fourth-century emperor Theodosius. The great territorial empire governed four hundred years earlier by Augustus and his successors in the name of the Senate and the people of Rome was still impressive. However, it was now a Christian empire ruled from Constantinople by an emperor who governed in the name of God and was advised by bishops.

KEY TERMS

Pax Romana,   *p. 138*

principate,   *p. 139*

praetorian guard,   *p. 139*

tetrarchy,   *p. 153*

Neoplatonism,   *p. 157*

Sadducees,   *p. 159*

Pharisees,   *p. 159*

The huge borders of the "civilized" world were still guarded by Roman legions, but by the fourth century these borders had become porous. The guarding legions more often than not wore the trousers of the Germanic peoples and rode horses instead of marching in the disciplined ranks of the tunic-clad Romans.

Sadly for Rome, the centrifugal forces pulling this radically transformed empire apart would prevail. As we will see in Chapter 6, the Roman Empire eventually split into three parts: Byzantium in the east, the Muslim world in the south, and the Germanic kingdoms in the west. However, the glory and accomplishments of Rome would remain in the West's memory and periodically inspire people to try reviving its greatness.

REVIEW, ANALYZE, & CONNECT TO TODAY

REVIEW THE PREVIOUS CHAPTER

Chapter 4—"Pride in Family and City"—described the rise and fall of the Roman Republic and the way expansion changed Roman life and values.

1. Review the "twilight of the Republic" that led to the civil wars and the murder of Julius Caesar. How did Augustus avoid the fate of Julius Caesar? What reforms did Augustus make to help the new empire endure?

2. Review the strengths and virtues that made the early Roman Republic so successful. Which of those were lost through the fourth-century reforms of Diocletian and Constantine? To what degree did these reforms contribute both to the decline of the empire and to its preservation?

ANALYZE THIS CHAPTER

Chapter 5—"Territorial and Christian Empires"—continues the story of the Roman Empire as it dominated the Mediterranean region for hundreds of years. The empire survived many crises and in turn was dramatically transformed by Christianity.

1. Consider the economic advantages of the great territorial empire of the Romans. Who benefited most from the Mediterranean trade? Who benefited least? What central weakness did the economy have during the empire?

2. What was the Silk Road? What goods traveled along it, and why was it so important to both the Roman and Han empires?

3. Describe the social, cultural, and medical ideas that contributed to Rome's declining population.

4. Review the situation in Judea and the various ideas within Judaism during the time of Jesus. How did the political and cultural environment in Judea affect the growth of Christianity?

5. Review the relationship between the early Christians and the Roman authorities. How did Christianity move from a persecuted sect to the religion of the Roman Empire?

6. The adoption of Christianity by the Roman Empire created profound transformations in both the early Christian church and the empire itself. Review these changes and consider which might have the longest-standing impact on the future of Western culture.

CONNECT TO TODAY

Think about the impact of the imperial Romans in establishing a multicultural empire, long-distance trade, and a revolution in religious life.

1. What similar issues is U.S. society struggling with today? In what ways might the study of the Roman Empire help citizens of the twenty-first century sort out and address public issues? In other words, what can we learn from the past?

2. What places in the world today are wrestling with changes in religion and with questions about the church-state relationship such as those that marked the late Roman Empire? How might people of opposing religious views avoid the violent religious struggles experienced by imperial Romans?

BEYOND THE CLASSROOM

THE *PAX ROMANA,*
27 B.C.E.–180 C.E.

Eck, Werner, et al. *The Age of Augustus,* 2nd ed. Cambridge, MA: Blackwell, 2007. A concise biography using varied sources to explain this revolution in the structure of Rome.

LeBohec, Yann. *The Imperial Roman Army.* New York: Hippocrene Books, 1994. A good description of the all-important Roman military.

LIFE DURING THE PEACE OF ROME

August, Roland. *Cruelty and Civilization: The Roman Games*. New York: Routledge, 1994. An exciting history of gladiators, chariot racing, and other games that offers an explanation of their appeal and function within society.

Dupont, Florence. *Daily Life in Ancient Rome*. Oxford: Blackwell, 1993. An informative interpretation of ancient Rome that describes and analyzes the everyday experiences of the Romans.

Jackson, Ralph. *Doctors and Diseases in the Roman Empire*. Norman: University of Oklahoma Press, 1988. A broad and concise account of classical medicine as it culminated in the Roman Empire.

Weidmann, Thomas. *Adults and Children in the Roman Empire*. New Haven, CT: Yale University Press, 1989. An interpretative analysis that traces changes in adult attitudes toward childhood.

CRISIS AND TRANSFORMATION, 192–ca. 400 C.E.

Gamsey, Peter D. *Famine and Food Supply in the Graeco-Roman World: Response to Risk and Crisis*. New York: Cambridge University Press, 1988. A study of the concerns and responses of both urban and rural dwellers to food crises, actual or anticipated.

Jones, A.H.M. *The Later Roman Empire, 284–602*, 2 vols. London: Blackwell, 1964. The most comprehensive classic study on the subject by a master historian.

Williams, S. *Diocletian and the Roman Recovery*. New York: Routledge, 1996. A vivid work that brings the emperor and his times to life and clearly explains Diocletian's military and civil reforms.

THE LONGING FOR RELIGIOUS FULFILLMENT

Riches, John. *The World of Jesus: First-Century Judaism in Crisis*. New York: Cambridge University Press, 1990. An examination of the ways in which Jewish figures and groups of the first century—including Jesus—reacted to the basic social, economic, and political realities of the time.

Turcan, Robert. *The Cults of the Roman Empire*. Cambridge, MA: Blackwell, 1996. A sound study of the cults during the Roman period.

FROM CHRISTIAN PERSECUTION TO THE CITY OF GOD, 64–410 C.E.

Brown, Peter. *Power and Persuasion in Late Antiquity: Toward a Christian Empire*. Madison: University of Wisconsin Press, 1992. Reopens the question of how the empire's transformation from paganism to Christianity affected its civic culture.

Carroll, James. *Constantine's Sword: The Church and the Jews*. Boston: Houghton Mifflin, 2002. An award-winning book that explores the relationship between Constantine's conversion, the adoption of the cross as a Christian symbol, and growing anti-Semitism. Provocative and fascinating reading.

Ehrman, Bart D. *Lost Christianities: The Battles for Scripture and the Faiths We Never Knew*. New York: Oxford University Press, 2003. A well-researched and clearly written look at the various early forms of Christianity that shows how they came to be suppressed or forgotten.

Frend, W.H.C. *The Rise of Christianity*. Philadelphia: Fortress Press, 1984. A comprehensive summary of the growth of Christianity, which includes the major figures and controversies of the movement.

Pagels, Elaine. *Beyond Belief: The Secret Gospel of Thomas*. New York: Vintage, 2004. An award-winning scholar of Gnosticism shows the diversity of the beliefs circulating in the early Christian communities.

Salisbury, J.E. *The Blood of Martyrs: Unintended Consequences of Ancient Violence*. New York: Routledge, 2004. A book that explores the ancient Christian martyrdoms that transformed many modern Western ideas, including images of the body, sacrifice, anti-Semitism, motherhood, suicide, and others.

Salisbury, J.E. *Perpetua's Passion: The Death and Memory of a Young Roman Woman*. New York: Routledge, 1997. A description of the cultural, social, and religious environment of early-third-century Carthage told through the story of a young martyr.

Stark, Rodney. *The Rise of Christianity: A Sociologist Reconsiders History*. Princeton, NJ: Princeton University Press, 1996. A controversial but influential analysis of how Christianity spread.

THE HOLY LIFE

Brown, Peter R.L. *The Body and Society: Men, Women, and Sexual Renunciation in Early Christianity*. New York: Columbia University Press, 1988. A classic study of the ascetic movements and their impact by the major scholar of late antiquity.

Bynum, Caroline Walker. *The Resurrection of the Body in Western Christianity, 200–1336*. New York: Columbia University Press, 1995. A fascinating look at the impact of martyrs and saints on ideas of the body and the afterlife.

GLOBAL CONNECTIONS

Wood, Frances. *The Silk Road: Two Thousand Years in the Heart of Asia*. Berkeley: University of California Press, 2004. A comprehensive and beautifully illustrated account that demonstrates the tremendous impact of the Silk Road in spite of relatively light traffic.

Looking Ahead to the Middle Ages, 400–1400

The breakup of the Roman Empire did not come easily. Warrior bands and official armies alike inflicted destruction and suffering on many throughout the old Roman Empire. From this violence arose what historians have come to call the Middle Ages (or medieval period), which extended from about 400 to about 1400. During that millennium, bloodshed intensified as three distinct cultural identities emerged in the Mediterranean basin and vied with one another for land, power, and affirmation of their faith. In the seventh century, the Prophet Muhammad and his followers established a new religion—Islam—that extended from the old Persian Empire in the east through North Africa and into Spain in the west. Byzantium—the eastern, Greek-speaking portion of the old Roman Empire—also developed its own language, religion, and politics, each of which distinguished it from the other two areas.

Meanwhile, the region in the northwestern portion of the old Roman Empire divided into disparate kingdoms that also boasted a unique culture. People living in these western realms called their region Christendom. Sometimes, but not always, they included the Christian Byzantine Empire in this designation. Byzantines, for their part, preferred to distance themselves from these "barbaric" westerners. Later historians (and geographers) would call the western region of Christendom Europe and Western civilization. However, just as in the ancient world, the West during the Middle Ages developed its distinctive character through interaction with the rest of the world.

But before the tenth century, Europeans' contact with other peoples diminished, as the disruptive violence caused them to withdraw from the great trade nexus that had marked antiquity. While the peoples of Islam and Byzantium maintained their cross-cultural contacts, western Christendom's inhabitants looked inward.

In the meantime, other parts of the world prospered. In the late sixth century, an ambitious ruler in northern China—Yang Jian—reunited China under centralized control after the centuries of fragmentation that followed the Han dynasty's collapse. The resulting succeeding dynasties—the Sui, Tang, and Song—organized Chinese society so efficiently that China became a leader in agricultural and industrial production.

These changes in China had a dramatic effect on the West after the eleventh century. Chinese inventions and innovations (from wheelbarrows to gunpowder) found their way west and transformed life in Christendom. In some cases, we can identify the agents of this transmission; for example, monks smuggled Chinese silkworms to Byzantium in order to implement a new cloth industry. In other cases, we cannot, though new ideas and inventions likely spread slowly from neighbor to neighbor across the Eurasian continent. Chinese technologies moved throughout east Asia as well, altering people's way of life in Korea, Vietnam, and Japan.

Even though India remained politically disunited during the early Middle Ages, the huge subcontinent molded cultures in south and southeast Asia. Over time, Islam attracted a popular following in India. Indeed, the new faith joined Hinduism and Buddhism as one of the major religions of the region. The connections between India and Islam remained strong through trade in the Indian Ocean, as Muslim merchants set up operations in all the major coastal cities in India. These mercantile centers remained fruitful sources of cultural exchange between Indians and Muslims in other lands, including Africa. Silk and porcelain from China; spices from southeast Asia; and pepper, precious gems, cotton, and many other goods from India swept through the Indian Ocean basin. All these goods—as well as exciting new ideas—eventually found their way to Europe, transforming Christendom through commercial activity and the social interaction that often comes with it. Perhaps one of the most influential exports from India was "Arabic numerals," which probably originated in India and acquired the "Arabic" appellation later. These numbers, which we use today, replaced Roman numerals and facilitated advanced mathematical calculations.

Between about 1000 and 1450, many other peoples also established vast empires and huge trading networks. For example, Mongols, nomadic peoples from central Asia, created a great empire based in China that facilitated trade across Asia. Powerful states and empires emerged in Africa as well. In the kingdom of Kongo, for example, rulers built a strong central government. During these same centuries, the arrival of Islam in Africa transformed cultures there. Muslims from North Africa capitalized on the profitable trade across the Sahara Desert and down the African coasts. As they traded, they attracted Africans to their faith. By the tenth century, the kings of Ghana had converted to Islam, and other peoples followed. Over the next two centuries, tremendous wealth accumulated along coastal east Africa. Evidence indicates that a rich tradition of Muslim scholarship also arose in these cities.

Far across the oceans, peoples living in the Americas and Oceania were changing as well. In Central and South America, the Maya, Toltecs, Aztecs, and Incas all built impressive societies, with large populations, social hierarchies, and magnificent architectural structures. Through eastern North America, large populations of healthy communities built large earthen mounds in many places. One near the Mississippi River was a four-level mound bigger than the Great Pyramid at Giza. Pueblo and Navajo peoples practiced irrigation and skillfully constructed complex adobe and stone buildings that still

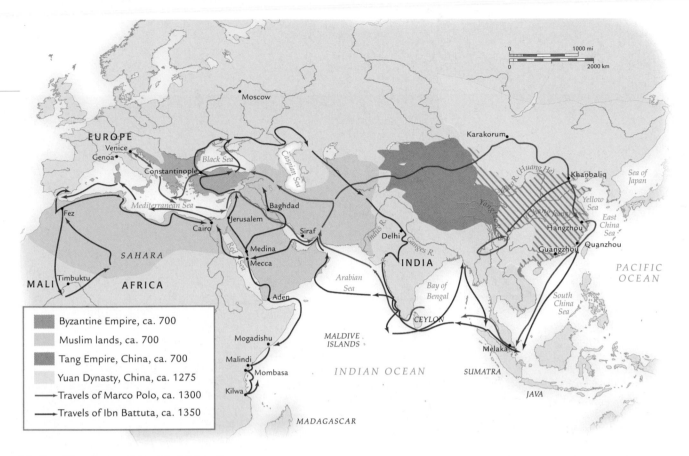

Medieval Empires and Two World Travelers

impress visitors. Modern scientists have reconsidered the view that the Americas were sparsely settled outside the regions of the empires of Meso-america; indeed, Amerindians settled throughout North and South America in large numbers. Perhaps even 40,000,000 people might have lived here before the diseases of Eurasia decimated the populations.

By 1000, a brisk trade had emerged among the islands in the south Pacific, testifying to the skill of navigators who could traverse the large spans of the Pacific. By 1100, even the more distant Hawai'ins and Tahitians had forged commercial ties.

What of the West in the face of such dynamic global developments? By 1000, Europeans were once again venturing out and interacting with others around the world. Scandinavian Vikings traveled overland, establishing settlements in eastern Europe and buying and selling goods all the way to China. They also journeyed west into Iceland, Greenland, and North

America, where they both traded and fought with indigenous peoples.

By the twelfth century, interactions between Christendom and Islam exerted a particularly powerful impact on both cultures. Crusading Christian armies confronted Muslims on the battlefields of the eastern Mediterranean and North Africa. However, more fruitful exchanges took place in Sicily and Spain, where Muslims and Christians lived side by side in relative harmony. In these places, Christian scholars studied Muslim learning, and Christian artisans and farmers adopted and benefited from Muslim innovations, like improved irrigation techniques. Merchants in the Italian city-states also profited from extensive trade with Muslims all over the Mediterranean.

As the thirteenth century dawned, Europeans began making contact with peoples even farther from their borders. Merchants and others on the move began to roam across the Eurasian continent. Marco Polo, a Venetian merchant, worked at the Chinese

court. Ibn Battuta, a Muslim judge, traveled from Mali (in Africa) to Spain, and across eastern Europe to China. These are only the most prominent examples of people who forged global connections during the Middle Ages. In spite of staggering distances and slow travel, the world seemed to be shrinking. It would appear to compress even further in the fifteenth century as Europeans ventured across the oceans.

Thinking Globally

As the center of Western civilization shifts north, how might this affect life in the West?

1. Refer to the map above. What do you notice about trade throughout the Eurasian landmass?

2. What might have been the advantages and disadvantages of travel by land or sea?

3. Notice the location of the large empires. How might these political units have facilitated trade and other interactions?

175

THE DOME OF THE ROCK, JERUSALEM, ca. 691

This Muslim pilgrimage site is located on the holiest place in Jerusalem. Jews revere the site as
the place where they believe Abraham was told to sacrifice his son, Isaac. Muslims believe that
the prophet Muhammad ascended to heaven from this spot. Christians respect it as the location
of the Temple where Jesus walked. This building symbolizes the dramatic cultural transformations
that unfolded as the Roman Empire dissolved, and it stands on one of the most contested pieces
of land in history.

A World Divided

Western Kingdoms, Byzantium, and the Islamic World, ca. 376–1000

"The harsh nature of war! The malevolent fate of all things! How proud kingdoms fall, suddenly in ruins! Blissful housetops that held up for long ages now lie torched, consumed beneath a huge devastation." These lines, written by Radegund, a nun living in sixth-century Gaul, poignantly express the turbulent world in which she lived. The Roman Empire was no longer a political unit that people could rely on for peace within its borders. The once mighty empire had fragmented into three culturally distinct parts separated by religion, language, and loyalties.

In the west, Germanic invaders established new kingdoms and converted to Christianity. Popes in Rome slowly became a force to be acknowledged in the West. In the East, the political form of the Roman Empire continued at least nominally for another thousand years. However, centered in the great city founded by Constantine, and separated from Rome, Byzantium began developing its own distinct character. The language of government changed to Greek, and people began to mingle more with the Slavic tribes to the north than with the Latins in the West. Finally, the desert of Arabia produced a prophet, Muhammad, who profoundly influenced the religious beliefs of millions. Followers of the new religion of Islam swept out of the desert and conquered the eastern and southern shores of the Mediterranean, as well as most of Spain. These three civilizations—the heirs of Rome—existed in uneasy, sometimes violent, proximity. Their differences and conflicts would remake the map of the Mediterranean basin and shatter the Roman unity that had graced the land for so long.

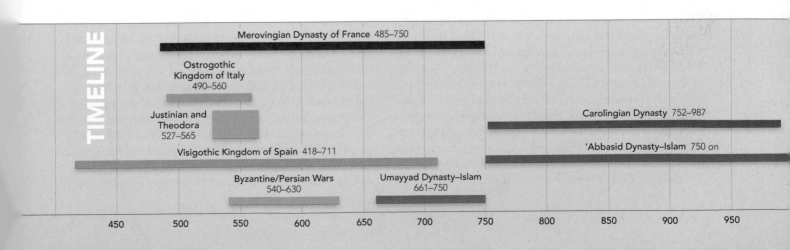

TIMELINE

Merovingian Dynasty of France 485–750

Ostrogothic Kingdom of Italy 490–560

Justinian and Theodora 527–565

Carolingian Dynasty 752–987

'Abbasid Dynasty–Islam 750 on

Visigothic Kingdom of Spain 418–711

Byzantine/Persian Wars 540–630

Umayyad Dynasty–Islam 661–750

450   500   550   600   650   700   750   800   850   900   950

THE MAKING OF THE WESTERN KINGDOMS,

ca. 376–750

Sidonius Apollinaris (ca. 431–ca. 480) was a Roman nobleman living in Gaul. He received a classical Roman education and wrote letters to his friends that brimmed with stories of the gracious life of a provincial Roman. In his missives, he described a lifestyle blessed by culture, ease, and luxury. Yet, Sidonius also witnessed much turmoil in his lifetime. In one letter he wrote, "Our town lives in terror of a sea of tribes which find in it an obstacle to their expansion and surge in arms all round it." He defended the walls of his town against the invading Visigoths and was imprisoned by the attackers. Later his captors released him, and he lived out the rest of his days tranquilly, serving as bishop in a town now governed by Visigoths. His Roman world had been reshaped, but not obliterated. To understand the changes that Sidonius experienced, we must first meet the Germans, who played such a major role in the remaking of the Roman Empire.

Life in a German Clan and Family

Who were these "Germani" that the Romans called "barbarians"? In about 500 B.C.E., when the earliest Romans were settling on the seven hills of their city and beginning their republic, groups of Indo-European Scandinavian people began to migrate south into the Baltic states and Germany and east into Ukraine. As they fanned out across the land, their tribes took on a bewildering array of separate names: East Goths (Ostrogoths), West Goths (Visigoths), Burgundians, Franks, Saxons, and so forth. These tribes traded with Rome and sometimes threatened its northern borders throughout the history of the empire. Whereas Chapter 5 focused on life within the empire, here we will move back in time to describe the culture of the early Germans and follow the fortunes of the tribes as they entered the empire.

Because the Germanic tribes had originally come from a small region in Scandinavia, they shared many cultural similarities. Their settlements were based on clans—families joined in kinship groups. A whole tribe made up of many clans might number no more than 100,000 people, including only about 20,000 warriors. Historians studying their early history are hampered by the fact that they did not write and thus left no written records. Instead, we must piece together their history from archaeology, Roman descriptions of the tribes, and texts based on imperfect memories written centuries later.

The earliest descriptions by Romans are not objective. Some Roman accounts depict the Germans as "barbarians" (outsiders) whose language sounded like babbling and whose personal hygiene was objectionable. One Roman wrote, "Happy [is] the nose that cannot smell a barbarian." However, the earliest and most famous text, Tacitus's *Germania*, written at the end of the first century, praises the Germans in order to criticize Roman society by contrast. Therefore, Tacitus portrays the Germans as strong and brave people who cared for their families and raised sturdy children. He writes: "With them good customs are of more avail than good laws elsewhere." However, readers must be cautious not to accept his descriptions uncritically—he was no objective reporter, and he was interested in urging Romans to adopt more virtuous customs. Nevertheless, by carefully using these imperfect sources in conjunction with archaeological finds, we can piece together a picture of the lives of the early Germanic peoples.

Roman sources

Tacitus praised the Germans' devotion to marriage—"This they consider their strongest bond"—and the children it produced. Although Tacitus somewhat romanticized the marriage bonds, without a doubt they forged the essential ties that bound society together. Within marriages, men and women had clearly defined and equally essential roles. Men cared for the cattle (a clan's greatest measure of wealth) and took primary responsibility for crop

Marriage patterns

tending, iron working, and war making. Women owned property and received a share of their husbands' wealth upon marriage. Women also performed agricultural labor, but they were mainly responsible for pottery and textile production and household care. In addition, they brewed the all-important alcoholic beverages—honey-sweetened ale and mead, a fermented concoction of honey and water—that provided much of the caloric intake needed for survival. Preserving knowledge of herb lore, women also cared for the sick and injured members of the clan. Perhaps in part because of their knowledge of brewing and healing, women were reputed to have a gift for prophecy, so men often consulted their wise female elders regarding important forthcoming enterprises.

Women were considered "peace-weavers," for through their arranged marriages they were supposed to bring peace between two families. However, family feuds often transcended family ties. Because the purpose of marriage was to join families, men were not limited to one wife. On the contrary, the more wives a man had, the larger his kin network became. The meager sources suggest that many pre-Christian Germans were polygynous; men had as many wives and concubines as they could support. Under these polygynous marriages, husbands and wives did not necessarily live in the same household, so women had a good deal of independence and maintained close ties with their birth families. Although Tacitus claimed adultery was rare, anthropological studies indicate that polygyny may encourage infidelity among women, and there is no reason to doubt that adultery occurred among these tribes. Adultery, however, deeply threatened the strong kinship ties that marriage forged and was severely punished.

Figure 6.1 shows the corpse of a 14-year-old girl who was executed in the first century C.E. by drowning, probably for committing adultery. Such bodies—well preserved by the northern European bogs—offer a wealth of information about the lives of these early Germanic peoples. This young girl's head was shaved, and she was blindfolded before her death. Her right hand is frozen in an obscene gesture—perhaps her last act of defiance toward her executioners. This find offers eloquent, though silent, testimony to the importance of the marriage ties holding Germanic communities together, and the gruesome penalty for violation.

Germanic Clothing and Food

Germanic peoples differed from the more southerly Romans in more ways than family traditions. Their clothing styles and diets also set them dramatically apart. Germanic men wore trousers, a long-sleeved jacket, and a flowing wool or fur cape secured by a large brooch or pin (or even a thorn if the wearer was impoverished). With their elaborate, luxurious detail, some of these brooches signified wealth and prestige. **Figure 6.2** shows six examples of Germanic jewelry from the sixth century C.E. There are clasps (also called fibulae) to secure the capes and clothing and a

FIGURE 6.1 Germanic Girl's Corpse, first century C.E. In the peat bogs of the north, corpses were mummified. The well-preserved bodies provide detailed information about ancient life. When this girl was killed, her right hand was frozen in an obscene gesture toward her executioners.

silver belt buckle. The valuable gold pieces are inlaid with precious stones; the fibula at upper right is less valuable because it is partially made of silver. As the pieces show, most of the design work of the ancient tribes utilized patterns rather than representations, a preference believed to demonstrate the Germans' awareness of the complex patterns symbolizing how fate wove together people's destinies.

Germanic women wore ankle-length dresses of linen or woven wool, which they colored with vegetable dyes. Like the men, they wore capes for warmth. They also dressed their hair with elaborate combs and hairpins and wore patterned jewelry as marks of wealth and prestige.

The Germans' diets were not as elaborate as their fashion accessories. The German peoples raised cattle but seldom ate the meat—the animals were too valuable for the milk and labor they provided. Instead, most of the clans were primarily agricultural. They apparently invented a large, wheeled plow that only a team of six to eight oxen had the strength to pull. Unlike the small plows of the south that merely scratched the surface of the sandier land there, this plow could turn over the heavy clay soils of the north. Furthermore, it encouraged cooperation—for to use a plow of this size, members of the community had to work together. But even this technology did not yield enough grain for a healthy diet, for the northern growing season was short. In addition, the disruptions of wars—even raids—upset agriculture and led to frequent hunger.

Agriculture and diet

FIGURE 6.2 Germanic Jewelry, ca. sixth century C.E.
Gold jewelry was a mark of pride among the ancient Germanic tribes. These finely wrought pieces display the creative skills of the artisans.

Due to malnutrition, the average Germanic woman stood just under five feet; the average man, five feet six inches.

Heroic Society

Like the ancient Greeks, the Germanic tribes of the north cherished the heroic ideals. Warfare played a central role in this society. The Roman historian Tacitus remarked on the German preference for war over work when he wrote: "They think it tame and stupid to acquire by their sweat what they can purchase by their blood." Although Tacitus understated the agricultural productivity of the tribes, these warriors did prefer raiding and plundering. Through such adventures, they acquired both wealth and fame. In the evening gatherings after a day of war making, a poet might praise a particularly heroic deed, and the warrior's name would be permanently preserved in the "word-hoard" or poetry of his people.

Just as Homer had recorded the dramatic deeds of Achilles and Odysseus, anonymous Germanic poets composed works remembering the heroes of the north. The Anglo-Saxon poem *Beowulf* is a written version of one such heroic account. *Beowulf* not only tells of the accomplishments of the monster-killing hero but also gives us a glimpse into traditional Germanic society: The warriors gather in the hall to boast,

drink, and prepare for their military feats; the women serve in the hall but also speak their minds; and the king takes responsibility for guarding his people and doling out gifts to ensure their loyalty.

A stunning hoard of Anglo-Saxon gold and silver objects dating from about 675 was excavated in 2009 in Staffordshire, England. This collection offers a recent confirmation of the accuracy of the accounts of the heroic society in *Beowulf*. The huge size of the collection—the gold alone weighs 11 pounds—suggests that Anglo-Saxon England was extremely wealthy. Most of the artifacts are war gear such as sword fittings, pommels, and helmets, and they may represent a victory hoard of the kind *Beowulf* refers to in documenting how warriors stripped the weapons of the defeated. The gold was probably buried to hide it from competing tribes and subsequently lost for over a millennium. Future archaeological finds will continue to fill in the gaps in the history of these elusive tribes who fought for gold and glory.

Each clan within the larger tribe was led by its own chieftain, who served as priest, main judge, and war leader. However, this was no absolute ruler, for the warrior elite (comitatus) was continually consulted in the decisions made for the whole clan. At times, small groups of warrior bands (usually less than 35 strong) set out to raid neighboring villages and bring back booty and tales of bravery. Sometimes the whole tribe decided to move, bringing along all the related clans and escorting their women and children. According to Tacitus, women traveling with these fighting tribes stayed behind the battle lines, probably within a protective circle of ox carts. If their men seemed to be losing, the women goaded the warriors to victory by baring their breasts behind the battle lines to remind them of their responsibility to protect their dependents.

Warrior bands

Infiltrating the Roman Empire, 376–476

While there was periodic, fierce fighting on the borders of the empire between the German tribes and the Romans, there was also a growing relationship based on mutual advantage. After the third century, Rome relied more and more on mercenaries to guard the empire's borders (described in Chapter 5). By the late fourth century, then, many tribes had a great deal of contact with the empire. Numerous young Germanic warriors no longer farmed but instead used Roman pay to support their families. Nearby tribes had learned to value Roman coins as much as cattle and jewelry (their traditional forms of wealth), and Rome had come to depend on the Germans' impressive skill in war.

This mutually satisfying relationship changed in the late fourth century when a Mongolian tribe

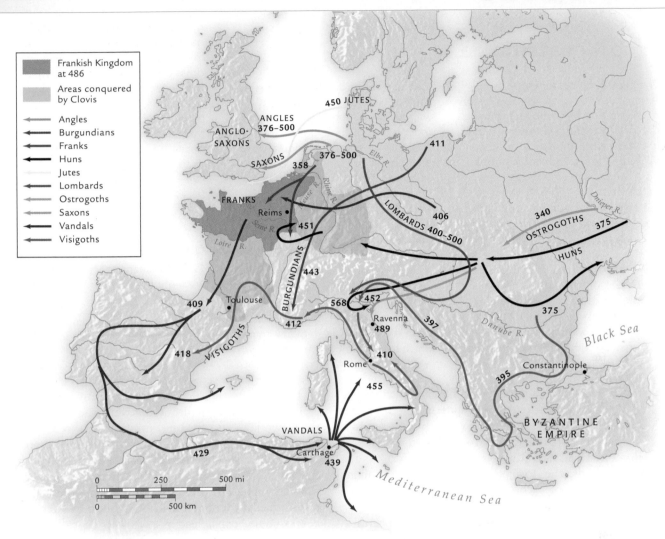

MAP 6.1

Germanic Invasions, Fifth Century

This map shows the routes of the various Germanic tribes as they invaded the Roman Empire and gives the dates of their invasions.

Explore the Map

1. Which tribes entered the empire, and where did they settle?

2. What regions might continue to be areas of contention following the invasions?

3. Notice the strategic location of Constantinople, whose walls protected it from invasion. Why would this city be able to control the important trade with the East?

originating in northern China came sweeping out of the steppes of Asia. These Huns (known as Hsiung-hu in their homeland) struck terror in the hearts of the Germanic tribes in their path. **Map 6.1** shows the route of the Huns as they galloped out of the east beginning in about 375. The Huns were a fierce people (even by Germanic standards) who charged across the continent

The Huns

on small ponies that seemingly needed no rest. Contemporary descriptions of the Huns reveal the dread and disgust generated by this wild and remarkably successful people. For example, the Roman historian Ammianus Marcellinus (ca. 354) wrote: They "are so prodigiously ugly and bent that they might be two-legged animals. Their shape, however disagreeable, is human." See Document 6.1 for an excerpt

DOCUMENTS

The Huns Menace Rome

The mid-fourth-century historian Ammianus Marcellinus wrote a history of the later Roman Empire, including the invasions of the Germanic tribes. In this excerpt, Ammianus describes the fearful Huns, a nomadic people from central Asia who drove many of the Germanic tribes to flee into the empire. The historian pointedly describes the Huns as strikingly different from the "civilized" Romans.

At the very moment of their birth the cheeks of their infant children are deeply marked by an iron, in order that the usual vigor of their hair, instead of growing at the proper season, may be withered by the wrinkled scars; and accordingly they grow up without beards, and consequently without any beauty, like eunuchs, though they all have closely knit and strong limbs and plump necks; they are of great size, and bow-legged, so that you might fancy them two-legged beasts, or the stout figures which are hewn out in a rude manner with an axe on the posts at the end of bridges.

They are certainly in the shape of men, however uncouth, but so hardy that they neither require fire nor well-flavored food, but live on the roots of such herbs as they get in the fields, or on the half-raw flesh of any animal, which they merely warm rapidly by placing it between their own thighs and the back of their horses.

They wear linen clothes, or else garments made of the skins of field-mice; nor do they wear a different dress out of doors from that which they wear at home; but after a tunic is once put round their necks, however much it becomes worn, it is never taken off or changed till, from long decay, it becomes actually so ragged as to fall to pieces.

SOURCE: Ammianus Marcellinus, "History," in *The Great Events by Famous Historians*, vol. III, ed. Rossiter Johnson (The National Alumni, 1905), pp. 353–354.

Analyze the Document

1. Which characteristics of the Huns might the Romans have found most frightening?

2. How might this description have shaped Roman policy toward the Huns?

of this influential source. Some Germanic tribes fled across the boundaries of the empire in search of safer territory. One such tribe, the Visigoths, crossed into the empire looking for land and ended up sacking Rome itself in 410 (discussed in Chapter 5). As the map reveals, the Visigoths were only one of many Germanic peoples who crossed into the empire in the early fifth century.

As we saw in Chapter 5, by the late third century, the Romans faced severe economic problems that kept them from successfully defending their borders against these new encroachments. They could not even afford to pay for the minimum defense, for the empire spent about thirty gold pieces a year for each soldier. An army of only 30,000 would have cost the entire annual budget of the western empire, so the Romans had to develop a new, less expensive way to defend its borders. To address this need, the Romans offered some encroaching tribes a treaty that made them **federates,** or allies, of Rome. Through this treaty, the warrior tribes received permission to live within the borders of the empire, and in exchange, they agreed to fight the enemies of Rome. The Visigoths became federates for enough grain to feed their warriors and families; in return they agreed to fight their traditional enemies, the Germanic Vandals. The Visigoths were later called north to protect the Italian borders. As more tribes were awarded federate status, the western empire began to be transformed by the blending of peoples.

| Federate treaties |

The federate treaties allowed the Germanic tribes to live within the empire and govern themselves by their own laws and customs, using their own leaders. This model of separate, coexisting cultures almost immediately proved to be utopian. In most of the territories, such as Spain or North Africa, the Germans were very much in the minority, so their culture was transformed by contact with neighboring Romans. For example, tribal leaders began to be called and treated as kings, although competing German noblemen consistently resorted to assassination to maintain their traditional voice in tribal affairs.

In many cases, two religions also existed side by side. Some pagan tribes (Anglo-Saxons, for example) restored paganism to parts of the nominally Christian empire. Other tribes (Visigoths and Ostrogoths) were Christian but had been converted by a missionary named Ulfila (ca. 310–ca. 381), whose Christian ideas had been shaped before Arius's teachings had been condemned at the Council of Nicaea in 325 (see Chapter 5). Ulfila's parents had been captured by Goths, and he grew up speaking the early Germanic language, so he was the natural candidate to convert the Germans. By the fifth-century settlements, the Arian tribes associated their religious beliefs with their ethnic identity, and this impeded their relationship with the orthodox Catholics living in the disintegrating empire.

| Arian Christianity |

A fifth-century North African Catholic (Victor of Vita) chronicled the invasion of the Vandals, and he particularly lamented the religious strife that erupted. He wrote that the Vandals "gave vent to their wicked ferocity . . . against the churches, . . . cemeteries and monasteries, so that they burned houses of prayer with fires greater than those used against cities." Although Victor probably exaggerated the villainy of the Vandals, his description pointed to the disintegration of the empire. When the emperor could not protect his Catholic subjects from his Arian ones, the religious differences further splintered an already weakened central authority.

In addition to having disputes with the federate tribes, the empire lost some provinces altogether. In about 407, Rome recalled legions **Loss of provinces** from Britain to help defend Italy against invaders. This left the Celtic Britons, who were Christian and lived in the Roman manner, alone to defend themselves against invaders from Scotland and from the Scandinavian countries. As **Map 6.1** shows, tribes of Angles, Saxons, and Jutes entered and settled the eastern portions of Britain, pushing most of the Celtic Britons to Wales and Ireland, the western edges of the British Isles. In the midst of these invasions, one British war chief won a great victory at the Battle of Badon (about the late fifth century) over the Anglo-Saxons. This victory stemmed the tide of the invasions, but only for a while. The deeds of this war chief, Arthur of Britain, were nevertheless remembered in the western Celtic lands and formed the basis for the famous Arthurian romances composed in the twelfth century (see Chapter 8). Britain was lost to Rome and became a mosaic of small Germanic kingdoms.

North Africa also fell away from the empire. At first the Vandals were settled as federates in the northern lands of Africa, but they soon broke off their allegiance to Rome and created a separate kingdom with their capital in Carthage. By the middle of the fifth century, Rome had lost the rich tax shipments of grain and oil that had come in a steady stream from North Africa. Struggling with this and other territorial losses, the empire in the West was slowly disintegrating.

Did Rome "Fall"?

By the fifth century, the provincial armies in the West were dominated by Germans, so it is not surprising that many rose to military power in Rome itself. When the Visigoths invaded Italy, the Roman defense was led by a Vandal general, which shows how ineffective the Roman emperors in the West had become. During the invasion, the Visigoths' leader even captured Emperor Honorius's (r. 395–423) sister, Galla Placidia, and took her with him as he sacked Rome itself.

Finally, in 476, the military leader Odovacar deposed the last western emperor (who, ironically, was named Romulus Augustulus after Romulus, the founder of the city of Rome, and Augustulus, "little Augustus," after Augustus, the first Roman emperor). Odovacar disdained the practice of dual emperorship that the Romans had established and shipped the imperial regalia off to the east. He then appointed himself regent in Italy.

The western empire did not fall with a cataclysmic crash. People like Sidonius in Gaul probably did not even use words such as "fall" to describe the times. After all, the eastern regions still had an emperor to whom people could give their allegiance if they wished, and in fact, many in the east celebrated the fact that there was once again one emperor **Transformation, not "fall"** who ruled the Mediterranean world. However, Sidonius and his contemporaries knew that the Roman Empire overall had undergone a major shift. Historians frequently use the term "late antique" to describe this period during which there was so much continuity with the Roman world. But this world was changed.

The empire's declining population played a key part in this transformation. The shrinking populace left plenty of room for the Germanic tribes to settle without severely dislocating residents. Even after the Germanic settlements, as much as 20 percent of the arable land was abandoned in some areas of the empire. As we saw in Chapter 5, economic and social problems had also eaten away at the empire for centuries. Finally, plagues and warfare had decimated the already fragile population. The empire, therefore, did not fall; instead, it was transformed as new people moved into the territory that the Romans failed to populate.

The urban life that had so characterized Roman culture was the first thing to go. The violence of the times crippled the towns, and the Germanic preference for rural living shifted attention to the countryside. The urban tax base shriveled as powerful Romans began to refuse to pay taxes to Rome. The Germans, for their part, were not often vigilant in collecting them. The roads and bridges that connected the empire fell into disrepair, and people's focus narrowed to the local level.

There were always Romans like Sidonius who continued their correspondence with Romans elsewhere, but they became fewer and fewer. Even Roman clothing changed; the toga that had symbolized the civilized life of the city was abandoned in favor of trousers more suited to country life. (Churchmen continued to wear more traditional Roman robes. Indeed, to this day, Catholic vestments resemble the clothing of the ancient Roman upper class.)

Of course, change happens in both directions when different peoples intermingle. The Germans were as much influenced by the Romans as the Romans were by Germanic culture. Slowly, the Germanic pagans

FIGURE 6.3 Illustration from the Gospel of Matthew, ca. 660 This manuscript illustration of Matthew, Jesus' disciple, was probably created in Ireland. It reveals the Germanic love of intricate patterning, as well as discomfort with portraying the human form.

cloak resembles the gold work on the jewelry in **Figure 6.2.** The Germans and the Romans, through their mutual influence, were creating a whole new culture—that of the medieval west—and this illustration reveals the blending of the two ways of life. After invading, the Germanic tribes settled down and created new political entities—kingdoms instead of tribal units. These new entities formed the basis for the medieval kingdoms that defined the West in the centuries to come.

Rise and Fall of a Frankish Dynasty, ca. 485–750

In the sixth century, the Germanic Franks established a powerful kingdom in the old Roman province of Gaul (see **Map 6.1**). The Franks were ruled by the Merovingian family (named after a legendary ancestor, Merovech). The most famous Merovingian was Clovis (r. 485–511), a brutal man who murdered many of his own relatives to consolidate his rule. Clovis's descendants were no less brutal, and the accounts of subsequent reigns tell of feuds and assassinations involving Merovingian princesses as well as princes.

Clovis is significant not only because he unified large portions of the Frankish kingdom but also because he converted to Roman Christianity. According to Gregory, Clovis's wife, Clotilda, was a Christian and was influential in persuading the king to convert. In the tradition of Constantine before him, Clovis reputedly vowed to convert if he won a significant battle. He won and fulfilled his vow | **Christian Merovingians** around the year 500 (although the date is controversial). Unlike the Visigoths and other Germans, Clovis converted to orthodox, not Arian, Christianity, and this began a long relationship between the popes and the Frankish kings. As was traditional with the German tribes, the conversion of the king meant the conversion of his people, which paved the way for the slow transformation of Germanic culture through the influence of the Roman church.

Figure 6.4 shows the baptism of Clovis—the defining moment during which the Frankish people (on the right) joined with the church hierarchy (on the left). In the center, an uncharacteristically innocent-looking Clovis is blessed by the dove of the Holy Spirit hovering above him. This illustration captures the king's central role in uniting the various groups in his society. The dove symbolized the Franks' belief that God had guided Clovis in his consolidation and conversion. This conversion also brought papal support to the Frankish kingdom. Like the manuscript illustration in **Figure 6.3,** this image testifies to the blending of Roman, Christian, and Germanic cultures that would characterize the early Middle Ages.

and Arians converted to orthodox Christianity and began to intermarry with resident Romans. In southern Europe, Germans began to speak the | **Germans transformed** | local Latin-derived dialects instead of their native Gothic. This is why the southern European languages (French, Spanish, Portuguese, Italian, Romanian) are called Romance languages—they are based on the language of the Romans. The Germans also became literate and began to produce written texts.

Figure 6.3 shows a page depicting the beginning of the Gospel of Matthew, from a manuscript made probably in Ireland in about the seventh century. Whereas the theme of the image is Christian, the aesthetics resemble those of the Germanic tribes, which were shared by the Celtic inhabitants of Ireland. The beautiful patterning in the border and in the man's

In the Merovingian territory, Christianity made significant strides through the efforts of a number of royal women who founded monasteries and supported education. Radegund, whose poetry opened this chapter, is one example. This Merovingian queen, one of the several wives of King Clothar (d. 562), left her husband to found a convent. With her royal family ties, her financial independence, and the force of her personality, she overcame the anger of both her husband and the local bishop and established a house for women who wanted to dedicate themselves to God. She and her ladies spent their days praying, reading, copying manuscripts, and helping the sick and poor in the neighborhood. The king may have declared his people Christian, but leaders like Radegund did much more to win individual hearts to the new religion.

Although Clovis had been highly skilled in forging a Christian kingdom from the ashes of the Roman Empire in Gaul, the subsequent Merovingians were not as competent. By the seventh century, the authority of these kings had deteriorated—frequently, children inherited the throne and in turn died young, leaving the throne to another child. Real power began to be exerted by the "mayors of the palace," an office controlled by another noble family, the Carolingians. This enterprising family included a number of skilled leaders, and as we will see, the Carolingian Charles Martel won a great victory in 732 to save the land. His son, Pepin the Short (r. 747–768), forwarded the fortunes of the family. Pepin wanted more than just to rule; in fact, he craved the royal title as well. Just as Clovis had enhanced his authority through Christian ritual, Pepin looked to the spiritual leader of Christendom for help. The shrewd Carolingian wrote to Pope Zachary (r. 741–752), asking him who should hold the title of king: he who actually exercised the power or he who had the name of king but no actual authority. The pope favored Pepin, and the mayor of the palace then gathered all the Frankish bishops and nobles, who promptly proclaimed him their king. The last of the ineffectual Merovingian kings was forced to cut his long hair (a symbol of his power) and lived out his days in a monastery. Armed with the support of the church, the vigorous new dynasty was now in a position to bring centralized order to western Europe. We will follow the fortunes of the Carolingians in Chapter 7.

Fall of Merovingians

Accomplishments and Destruction in Italy, ca. 490–750

As the Franks established their kingdom in the sixth century, another Germanic kingdom took shape on the

FIGURE 6.4 King Clovis The violent Merovingian king Clovis is shown here as a model of piety at the moment of his baptism, which drew together church and state in the lands of the Franks.

Italian peninsula. The story began when Theodoric (r. 493–526), an Ostrogothic leader, ousted Odovacar (who had deposed the last Roman emperor) and declared himself ruler of Italy. Theodoric had received a Roman education and proved a talented and balanced ruler—at first. The Ostrogoths were Arian Christians, so Theodoric had difficulty uniting Goths and Romans in Italy. Nevertheless, he seems to have exhibited a surprising religious toleration in an age that had little.

Theodoric fostered learning at his court and supported a number of scholars who had a profound influence on Western culture. Boethius, for example—a high official in Theodoric's court—was a man of great education. He translated works of Aristotle from Greek to Latin, and these translations became the basis for the study of logic for centuries. He also had an inventive streak and built a water clock for his patron. But Theodoric's court was plagued with intrigue, and Boethius was unjustly accused of treason and jailed. He wrote his most influential work, *The Consolation of Philosophy*, while in prison. In *The Consolation*, Boethius thought about the injustices of life and found comfort in philosophy. This profound and sensitive work remains much studied today. However, it did not save Boethius, for Theodoric had him executed.

Dionysius Exiguus, a Greek-speaking monk, was another respected scholar in Theodoric's Italy. A skilled mathematician, the monk calculated the date of Easter (which changes each year) and was apparently the first to suggest that calendars be dated from

Fostering learning

his estimation of when the Incarnation of Christ occurred (originally the B.C./A.D. system, which has turned into B.C.E./C.E.). Although modern scholarship shows that his dates were slightly wrong—Christ was probably born about 4 B.C.E.—Dionysius's dating system remains the basis of our Western dates. His student Cassiodorus (490–585) succeeded Boethius in the king's court, and his name is remembered much more than Dionysius's.

Thoroughly trained in Roman writings like the *Aeneid* and Livy's *History* (both discussed in Chapter 5), Cassiodorus seems to have recognized the power of historical writing to create and preserve a people's identity. Consequently, he wrote a historical chronicle, the *Origin of the Goths*, that was designed to show that the Goths had as impressive and ancient a history as the Romans. By showing that the history of the Goths resembled the epic scope of the Roman past, Cassiodorus helped assimilate the histories of both peoples. Although the original of this seminal work is lost, excerpts survive in the quotations of later historical writings. Through this work and its subsequent emulators, the history of the Germans was incorporated into the history of the Roman Empire—the Germanic tribes were slowly but surely merging with the peoples of the old empire they had inhabited.

| Historical writing |

Theodoric was succeeded by his daughter, Amalasuintha, who ruled at first as regent for her young son and then as queen after the boy's death. She was well educated and well suited to rule, but the unruly Germans were unused to being governed by a woman. Amalasuintha corresponded with the Byzantine emperor Justinian to gain support for her rule, writing: "We hope that the peaceful relations that you maintain toward us . . . may be extended." However, all her diplomatic skills could not save her from internal intrigue. In 535, she was murdered—according to Gregory of Tours, locked in an overheated steam bath where she was scalded to death.

| Fall of Ostrogoths |

Justinian used her death as an excuse to begin his reconquest of Italy as part of his ambitious plan to retake the western portions of the empire. The emperor's forces crushed the Ostrogothic kingdom. The scholar Boethius's widow seems to have received some satisfaction after the reconquest, for the emperor gave her permission to destroy statues of Theodoric as revenge for her husband's death. But few others celebrated the conquest that brought down the religiously tolerant and impressive rule of the Ostrogoths.

Justinian had overextended his resources, and the reconquest of Italy did not last long. A Germanic tribe that had fought as allies of the Byzantine army learned about the riches of Italy during the campaign against the Ostrogoths. In 568, these Lombards (longbeards) moved south and took over most of the peninsula (see **Map 6.1,** on page 181). Italy would now be ruled by a tribe much less Romanized than the Ostrogoths, and the slow struggle to achieve a synthesis between Germans and Romans began again. The fierce Lombards ruled the northern part of the peninsula until they confronted the growing power of the Franks in the north. Pepin conquered the Lombards in the mid-eighth century, and northern Italy came under the rule of the Frankish Carolingians.

| Lombards |

Pepin did not forget his debt to the papacy that had supported his coronation, and when the Byzantines demanded that he return the Italian conquests to them, Pepin angrily refused. He said he had fought his war for St. Peter, and it was to Peter (that is, the papacy) that he would hand over his conquests. From this time onward, the pope ruled in central Italy as an independent monarch, and the "Donation of Pepin" marked the beginning of the Papal States, which endured until the nineteenth century.

The Visigoths in Spain, 418–711

The history of the Visigoths in Spain resembles that of the other growing kingdoms. Like the Ostrogoths, Visigoths were Arian Christians when they became federates of Rome, and the two cultures, Roman and Goth, lived separate though parallel lives in Spain. However, in the 580s the Visigothic kings converted to Roman Christianity and paved the way for a close church and state rule. Like the Ostrogoths, Visigothic kings fostered learning in their land. The most famous Visigothic writer was Isidore of Seville (ca. 560–636), who compiled collections of Roman works that preserved classical knowledge for subsequent generations.

Two flaws marred Visigothic civilization, however. The first was a delight in political assassination, which even the violent Franks called the "Visigothic curse." Church and state repeatedly condemned people who "turned their hand against the king," but the assassinations continued, weakening the kingdom. The second problem was Visigothic persecution of Jews. Kings passed strict laws against the many Jews living in Spain, undermining their communities and dampening their loyalty.

| Visigothic weaknesses |

The Visigothic kingdom was ultimately destroyed by invasions of Muslims from North Africa. As we will see later, followers of the new religion of Islam swept across North Africa, crossed the narrow straits known as the Pillars of Hercules (now the Straits of Gibraltar), and in 711 conquered most of the Iberian Peninsula.

Figure 6.5 shows Iberian Christians taken into slavery by the victorious Muslims. The conquerors include the mounted leaders in the background towering over their bound captives and the African foot soldiers in the foreground guarding the new slaves. The mules, cattle, and long-haired sheep on the right represent the great wealth of the Visigothic kingdom that now came into the hands of the Muslims. The only remaining Christian territory on the peninsula lay in the northwest hills. From there the Iberians would spend the next seven hundred years reconquering their land. The invasion, the interaction between Christians and Muslims, and the long era of reconquest left the Visigothic kingdom in ruins and shaped the subsequent history and culture of Spain.

The Growing Power of the Popes

As central authority fell away in western Europe, some people—especially in the cities—looked to their local bishops to handle things previously left to secular authorities. Bishops sometimes organized aqueduct repair or food relief, and perhaps not surprisingly, the bishop of the most prestigious city—Rome—began slowly to come to the fore. In these tumultuous centuries, the bishops of Rome began to claim earthly as well as spiritual authority and, in doing so, established precedents that would reach well into the future.

All Christian bishops were believed to be the successors of the original apostles and as such held the authority to guide the faithful. However, as early as the fourth century, the bishops of Rome began to assert their supremacy over all the other bishops. Many bishops during the early church period were called popes, based on the Latin word for "father," but the bishops of Rome slowly began to claim exclusive use of that title to set themselves apart from other bishops. On what did the popes base their claims of leadership? In part, the early-fourth-century popes claimed primacy because Rome had been the capital of the empire. However, as the imperial city faded in importance, the popes began pointing to biblical writings to justify their leadership of the church. They based their claim mainly on a passage from the Book of Matthew (Matt. 16:18–19) in which Christ said: "And I tell you, you are Peter, and on this rock I will build my church. . . . I will give you the keys of the kingdom of heaven. . . ." The early popes had claimed that Peter was the first bishop of Rome, so each subsequent pope claimed to be the spiritual descendant of Peter—thus also controlling heaven's keys.

Figure 6.6, an illustration from an early-eleventh-century manuscript, portrays Christ giving Peter the keys to heaven. A crowd of people stand behind Peter, suggesting their | Petrine doctrine | dependency on him. The claim that the supremacy of the pope is based on Christ's words to Peter is called the **Petrine doctrine** of papal

FIGURE 6.5 Enslaved Christians   As Muslims conquered the Iberian Peninsula, they amassed wealth in the form of sheep and mules, but they also took many Christian slaves, such as those shown bound at the front of the image.

supremacy. Not surprisingly, some people—especially the emperors in the east and some other bishops—disagreed with this interpretation of the Bible.

Since the fourth century, some popes had involved themselves in politics. As we saw in Chapter 5, Bishop Ambrose had forced Emperor Theodosius to bend to his will, and in the following century, Pope Leo I (r. 440–461) successfully negotiated with invading Huns and Vandals to spare Rome. At the end of the fifth century, Pope Gelasius (r. 492–496) tried to resolve this issue of who had power by describing authority on earth as two swords: one wielded by kings and the other by the church. In Gelasius's view, the church's sword was the greater because it was spiritual—popes were responsible for the souls of kings. In a metaphorical sense, then, Gelasius converted St. Peter's keys to heaven into an earthly blade.

However, these early popes could exert only sporadic authority, and they had little real power. It was Pope Gregory the Great (r. 590–604) who dramatically forwarded the case for papal supremacy, as much through his | Gregory the Great | actions as with his words. A talented, energetic administrator, he defined the role of the pope in broad terms. For example, he took over the day-to-day administration of Rome, reorganizing estates and managing them in such a way as to generate extra revenue to feed the poor. When the Lombards invaded the peninsula, Gregory directed the defense of the city and negotiated the truce. Acting the part of a territorial ruler, he even exerted his authority outside Italy, writing letters to settle disputes

FIGURE 6.6 Papal Supremacy, ca. 1007 To argue for the supremacy of the popes over other bishops, some Christians looked to the biblical account of Christ giving the keys of heaven to his apostle Peter, an event that is shown in this colorful manuscript illustration.

and offering financial assistance to distant churches. Gregory's influence extended far beyond sixth-century Italy: In the ninth century, when the Anglo-Saxon king Alfred (see Chapter 7) selected seminal works to translate from Latin to Anglo-Saxon, Gregory's writings were prominently featured. With Gregory's precedent, popes of the eighth century and beyond were prepared to claim influence throughout western Christendom, although it would take until the thirteenth century for them to fully wield such authority over a Christian world.

Monasteries: Peaceful Havens

As the Germanic tribes were spreading into the western empire, many men and women sought refuge from the chaotic times in monasteries, where they could concentrate on their spiritual growth. As we saw in Chapter 5, communal monasticism began to appeal to many Christians throughout the empire. In the west, the most influential founder of communal monasticism was the Italian Benedict of Nursia (ca. 480–543). His twin sister, Scholastica, shared his calling and

| Benedict of Nursia |

founded monasteries for women. Like many other churchmen, Benedict disapproved of people who lived independently like the holy ascetics we met in Chapter 5. He feared that without guidance, such individuals might go astray, and he complained of wandering holy men, saying: "Whatever they think of or choose to do, that they call holy; what they do not like, that they regard as illicit." Instead, Benedict wrote a book of instruction—a *rule*—to guide monks and nuns in their communal lives.

Benedict eschewed the extreme fasts and bodily mortifications that had marked the eastern holy men and women, writing: "We hope to ordain nothing that is harsh or heavy to bear." Benedict's *Rule* required that people spend a balanced day divided into work and prayer, with moderate and regular meals. The requirement to work encouraged monks and nuns to study and copy the precious manuscripts that preserved classical learning. Benedict himself called his monastery a "schoolhouse for the Lord," which was an apt description for an institution that served a central role in education throughout the Middle Ages.

Although Benedict did not require heroic asceticism, the monk insisted that individuals ignore their own desires—whether for extra food, different work, or even extra hardships—and live in strict obedience to the head monk or nun. These monastic leaders, called abbots or abbesses, eventually became powerful figures in medieval life, extending their influence far outside monastery walls. By requiring a vow of obedience from monks and nuns, Benedict created an effective mechanism for bringing otherwise independent religious people into the Christian hierarchy.

Monasteries formed an effective avenue through which Christianity spread to the pagan outposts. In the early fifth century, a Romano-British Christian named Patrick (ca. 390–461) was kidnapped by

| Irish Christianity |

Irish raiders and enslaved in Ireland. He later escaped to Britain, where he became a bishop. However, he decided his calling was to return to Ireland to convert the pagan Irish. He established monasteries in Ireland, and the Irish consider him the founder of Irish Christianity. The strong monastic tradition in Ireland created monks who made great strides in preserving learning and stimulating ideals of asceticism in the West. Furthermore, some Irish monks became missionaries to the pagan Anglo-Saxons in Britain. In fact, scholars give the Irish monks a great deal of credit for preserving the classical wisdom and transmitting it on to subsequent civilizations of the West.

Pope Gregory the Great—a monk himself—was also interested in converting the Anglo-Saxons and bringing them into the orbit of Roman Christianity. The pope sent monks to Britain in 597 to convert the natives—a task they slowly, but successfully, achieved. However, the monks sent from Rome came in contact with those sent from Ireland, and it became clear that the two strands of Christianity had developed differing opinions on certain points (the most important was the date of Easter). In 664, the Anglo-Saxon king called a council in Whitby to resolve the discrepancy. After ascertaining that all the monks agreed on the primacy of the apostle Peter, the king decreed that Peter's heir in Rome should prevail. Thus, the practices of Roman—instead of Irish—Christianity prevailed throughout Europe.

Conversion of Britain

Beyond their missionary roles, monasteries served as quiet havens from a tempestuous world. In these retreats, men and women worked, prayed, and studied—keeping ancient texts alive for a time when learning could again emerge from behind monastery walls.

THE BYZANTINE EMPIRE,
ca. 400–1000

As early as the beginning of the fourth century, Roman emperors had recognized the unique strategic and economic advantages of the eastern portion of the empire. During the turbulent fifth and sixth centuries, the eastern Roman Empire with its capital in Constantinople held firm as the western provinces fell away to the Germanic tribes. However, the eastern empire did not remain unchanged; instead, Constantine planted seeds that would later flower into a dramatically different empire. By the eighth century, the eastern Roman Empire had changed so much that historians call it the Byzantine Empire, or Byzantium, to distinguish it from the Latin Roman Empire that it succeeded. As with the emergence of the western Germanic kingdoms, the rise of the Byzantine Empire represented not a sudden break from the past but simply another aspect of the Roman Empire's transformation.

When the Visigoths sacked Rome in 410, the eastern emperor, Theodosius II, began to build a great wall to protect Constantinople from a similar fate. This structure stood firm even during the violent fifth and sixth centuries—inhabitants of Constantinople watched from the safety of the top of the wall as smoke rose from villages set aflame by the Germanic tribes and the Huns surging westward. The wall continued to protect the new capital for almost a thousand years.

The wave of invasions separated the eastern and western portions of the old Roman Empire. While the western portion adopted some aspects of Germanic culture, the easterners consciously rejected such changes. For example, at the end of the fourth century, residents of Constantinople were forbidden to wear Germanic clothing, such as pants and anything made from furs. Between 400 and 1000 C.E., the Byzantine

A separate empire

Empire distanced itself more and more from the concerns of the west and turned its focus north and east instead. One eastern emperor stood out as an exception to this tendency and turned his attention again to the west.

Justinian and Theodora, r. 527–565

Justinian was born in 483 to peasant parents living in a province near Macedonia. A promising youth, he was adopted by an uncle in the royal court. His uncle became emperor, which paved the way for Justinian to take the crown at his uncle's death in 527. The most influential person in Justinian's court was his wife, Theodora. She, too, had come from a humble background. She had been an actress, and according to the Byzantine historian Procopius (d. 562) (whose *Secret History* is biased against Justinian, so it may not be fully accurate), Theodora won the emperor's heart with her skill as an erotic dancer.

Early in Justinian's reign, Theodora established her role in the emperor's court when a violent riot (remembered as the Nika riot for the rioters' rallying cry "Nika" which means "victory") broke out in Constantinople between two rival political factions who supported different chariot racing teams. In an uncommon alliance, they joined forces to try to oust Justinian. When the rest of his advisors urged Justinian to flee the city, Theodora insisted that Justinian confront the rioters, saying, "For one who has been an emperor it is intolerable to be a fugitive." Justinian's forces brutally squelched the riot—probably 30,000 were killed—and this victory broke any political opposition.

Nika riot

During the Nika riot, much of Constantinople was burned, so Justinian and Theodora embarked on an ambitious reconstruction plan. The most impressive outcome of this effort was the design and construction of a massive church, the Hagia Sophia (Holy Wisdom). **Figures 6.7** and **6.8** show the great church that still dominates the city and awes visitors. The central dome, with its diameter of 101 feet, is the largest such structure in the world. Two half-domes double the interior length of the church to 200 feet. After the Muslims captured the city in 1453, the church became a mosque, and the spheres with the Arabic calligraphy date from the Muslim years. Today the magnificent structure is a museum, but it still showcases the impressive Byzantine engineering along with the blend of cultures that marks this region.

Rebuilding the city

Besides the Hagia Sophia, Justinian left another enduring contribution: the codification of Roman law. From the earliest codification—the Twelve Tables (Chapter 4)—Roman law continued growing and changing. Emperors and senators had passed decrees,

FIGURE 6.7 Hagia Sophia, 537 The Byzantine emperor Justinian commissioned this huge church in Constantinople. The structure's expansive domes and flowing lines long remained the wonder of the world. Builders added the four minarets in 1453 when they converted Hagia Sophia into a mosque.

FIGURE 6.8 Hagia Sophia, Interior, 537 Hagia Sophia's awe-inspiring interior prompted Justinian to declare that he was a greater temple builder than the biblical king Solomon. Others argued that the church's splendor demonstrated that Constantinople was superior to Rome. Buildings were key symbols in ancient power struggles.

judges had made precedent-setting decisions, and jurists had written complicated legal interpretations.

By Justinian's time, the collections

Legal codification   were full of obscurities and internal contradictions, and the emperor wanted them organized and clarified. The enterprise was immense, as Justinian himself noted: "We turned our attention to the great mass of venerable jurisprudence and, as if crossing the open sea, we completed a nearly hopeless task." The results of this formidable project were published in fifty books called the *Corpus Iuris Civilis* (the *Body of Civil Law*) (ca. 533). In this form, Roman law survived and was revived in western Europe in about the thirteenth century. From there it has influenced Western legal codes through today.

Finally, as we have seen, after the murder of the Ostrogothic queen Amalasuintha, Justinian tried to reconquer the western territories that had fallen to

Germanic tribes. In part, he wanted

Reconquering   to recapture lost tax revenues, but
the west   probably the ambitious emperor also hoped to resurrect the Roman Empire to its past glory. However, he succeeded only in taking North Africa from the Vandals and Italy from the Ostrogoths.

Under the newly established control of Justinian, a great church was built in the imperial capital of Ravenna, in the north of Italy. **Figures 6.9a** and **b,** in Thinking About Art, are sixth-century mosaics of Justinian and Theodora that adorned this Church of San Vitale, and they reveal much about how people perceived the royal couple. The mosaics were a worthy celebration of the victorious conquest of Italy, but the accomplishment proved more ephemeral than the magnificent mosaics.

Map 6.2 shows the extent of Justinian's reconquest. As impressive as it looked, it was destructive and costly. While the North Africans welcomed the rule of the orthodox emperor over the Arian Vandals, the Italians, who were governed by the tolerant Ostrogoths, were less thrilled. The new regime brought more violence and taxation. Worse, Justinian had to rely on German mercenaries to win these battles. As noted on page 186, this strategy paved the way for the Lombards to conquer Italy in 568. Although Justinian temporarily accomplished some of his goals, the reconquest led only to failure in the long run. He could not maintain a firm grip on the western provinces, and the constant battling drained the eastern empire of needed resources. Justinian's dream of reuniting and reconnecting with the empire's old homeland in Rome would vanish forever.

Constantinople: The Vibrant City

Constantinople not only was the administrative and cultural center of the east but also served as the economic hub. The great city's wealth stemmed in part from commerce: Trade routes to the Far East all passed through Constantinople, so spices, silks, rare woods, and perfumes poured into the Byzantine capital. These luxury items brought a fine profit to the men and women who resold them. Streets thronged with shopkeepers displaying their wares: goldsmiths, silversmiths, furniture makers, textile merchants, and so on. Shoppers bargained at the booths, and the sounds of commerce rang through the streets.

The Byzantine Empire also grew rich producing luxury items. Artisans in Constantinople and the other major cities of the east crafted expensive fabrics, fine jewelry, glass-   Lucrative industries
ware, and ivory works. The empire imported silkworms from China in the sixth century, which opened a new, lucrative industry. The royal court held a monopoly on silk production, and the finest silk was made in the emperor's palace itself. The court also controlled the profitable industry of purple dye, which was produced from mounds of shellfish left to rot on the shores of the eastern Mediterranean. As we saw in Chapter 1, everyone, from east to west, who wanted to demonstrate their nobility or royalty had to have purple dye. The long purple robes worn by Justinian and Theodora in **Figures 6.9a** and **b** testify to more riches than the couple's gold and jewels.

While great wealth was available in the bustling city, it came to only a few. The Byzantines had abandoned the ancient Roman tradition of offering free food to the urban poor, but officials offered food to those who worked in imperial bakeries or on aqueduct repair. The palace also established a number of charitable institutions for the needy, including poorhouses, hospitals, and the first orphanages recorded in Western tradition.

Prosperity brought temptation, and emperors and other highly placed officials began to favor eunuchs (castrated men) as a way to control corruption. Easterners from the time of the ancient Persian Empire believed that eunuchs were less prone to corruption than other men. Because eunuchs had no children, they were expected to have little motivation to acquire wealth to pass along to subsequent generations. As eunuchs gained favor in high places, some poor families even had a son castrated to prepare him for a prosperous career. In addition to the emperor's closest aides, highly placed bureaucrats, some army and navy commanders, and some high church officials were eunuchs. Doctors who were eunuchs were allowed to treat women, though some women's hospitals insisted on letting only female doctors attend to their patients.

A society and economy that so prominently featured eunuchs would have been unthinkable in the

FIGURE 6.9(A)

Mosaics in San Vitale, Ravenna, Italy, 548

In 540, Emperor Justinian's troops conquered Ostrogothic Italy, restoring the peninsula and its capital, Ravenna, to Byzantine control. As part of the celebration of this victory, the mosaics shown here were added to the Church of San Vitale in time for its consecration in 548. The images depict Emperor Justinian with his attendants (a) and his wife, Theodora, similarly accompanied (b). These works of art were brilliant propaganda pieces, intended to show the faithful a new order—one

FIGURE 6.9(B)

in which church and state were combined, with the imperial family at the head.

Connecting Art & Society

1. What elements in the images show the wealth and power of the royal family?

2. What might the halos around their heads indicate?

3. Why are Justinian and Theodora shown bringing gifts to the church? He carries a golden plate for communion wafers, and she brings a golden cup for the wine.

Roman Empire of Augustus. Yet, the Byzantines did retain some Roman characteristics. For example, the Roman tradition of public political involvement continued in Constantinople, as Justinian and Theodora discovered during the riots. In this vibrant city, people argued about the great religious questions, political issues, and the ever-intriguing chariot races. In Rome, men and women had gathered in the Forum or the Colosseum to express their collective opinion; in Constantinople they flocked to see the chariot races. The great race track—the hippodrome—could seat 40,000 people, and the emperor frequently addressed his people there. The two chariot teams, the Blues and the Greens, signified much more than simply a love of sports. People aligned themselves with the teams as we do with political parties—by wealth, religion, social class, and political inclination.

Chariot races

Military Might and Diplomatic Dealings

Constantinople's walls kept the empire safe from the Germanic tribes heading west, but external enemies still posed a threat. The Byzantines clashed regularly with the powerful Persians and kept a vigilant eye on the tribes to the north. As we will see, the Muslim people to the south also represented a constant danger. To withstand these challenges, the Byzantines carefully considered both military and diplomatic science.

While the emperors kept the administration of Constantinople in civilian hands, they entrusted the care of the provinces to military men. Rulers divided up their empire into about twenty-five provinces, called **themes,** governed by military commanders. (See **Map 6.3,** on page 194, for the theme divisions.) Assemblies composed of "heads of households" empowered to make judicial and financial decisions

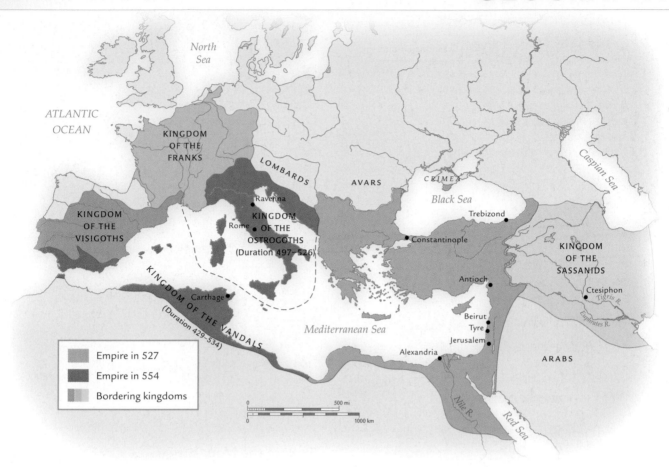

MAP 6.2

Justinian's Conquests, 554

This map shows the size of the Roman Empire in 527 C.E. after the western provinces had fallen away, and it illustrates the extent of Justinian's reconquest.

Explore the Map

1. What was the extent of Justinian's conquest? How expensive do you think it was to control all that territory? Why?

2. What factors might contribute to the loss of these lands again? Compare this map with **Map 6.3** to see how fragile this reconquest proved to be.

administered the villages within each theme. Governors designated most village families as "military households," which meant they owed one fully equipped man to the empire's army. In this way, the provinces were guarded by armies made up of local residents who had a strong stake in the protection of their homes.

Provincial organization

The Byzantine army was disciplined, well paid, and thoroughly armed. Its backbone, the heavy cavalry, provided the army with extraordinary flexibility. Protected by mail armor and outfitted with lances and swords as well as bows and arrows, these fighters could shoot from a distance as archers or do battle at close range while heavily armed. The cavalry in turn was supported by an efficient infantry. Though only about 120,000 men at its height, this standing army was supplemented by a large number of camp followers. Slaves and engineers accompanied the infantry everywhere. Unlike the Roman legions, who constructed their own camps every night, the Byzantines depended on camp slaves to carry out such tasks. The army also developed a finely tuned medical corps, complete with ambulance carts that moved the wounded to safety.

The army

In addition to its land army, the empire continued the Roman tradition of maintaining a strong navy. In the seventh century, Byzantine scientists invented "Greek fire," a deadly new weapon that gave the navy

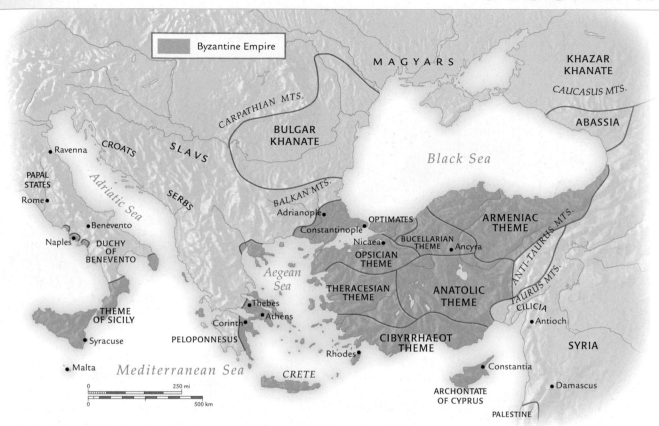

MAP 6.3

The Byzantine Empire, Eighth Century

This map shows the extent and the organization of the Byzantine Empire in the eighth century and identifies the peoples who surrounded the empire. The map also indicates the internal structure of the empire—its division into themes.

Explore the Map

1. Why might the theme organization have been an effective way to manage the decentralized provinces?

2. Locate the many peoples of the Balkan region—Bulgars, Serbs, Croats, Slavs, and others. Do you think it was difficult for the Byzantines to withstand pressure from all those peoples? Explain.

3. What might be the long-term implications of the diversity of the peoples inhabiting the Balkans?

a crucial competitive edge. **Figure 6.10** shows a manuscript illustration of the use of Greek fire in a naval battle. The substance was made of combustible oil that was pumped through tubes or placed in containers to be launched from a catapult. The liquid then burst into flames on contact with the target. This weapon proved particularly effective at sea; because the oil floated, it kept burning on the water. Not surprisingly, the Byzantines closely guarded the secrets of Greek fire.

The Byzantines' military success stemmed from more than strategic and technical innovations. Unlike their western counterparts, the easterners continued

and improved the ancient Romans' highly developed diplomatic techniques to protect their empire. Many Byzantine emperors considered diplomacy as important as war, and therefore worthy of just as much investment. As a matter of policy, these rulers used spies, lies, and money to weaken their enemies, and sometimes even turned their enemies against each other. Indeed, today the term *Byzantine diplomacy* still connotes expedient and tricky negotiations. However, such complex diplomacy needed money to succeed. As long as the empire was wealthy enough to keep funding bribes, spies, and counterintelligence efforts,

Diplomacy

FIGURE 6.10 Greek Fire The Greeks invented a combustible liquid that they pumped through tubes onto enemy ships. The liquid ignited the wooden hulls on contact and also floated on the water, killing sailors who attempted to escape. One enemy observed that the Greeks possessed lightning from the heavens to burn their enemies.

it stood firm. Later in the Middle Ages, the empire's diplomatic powers faded after an economic downturn. Nevertheless, the world learned much from the Byzantines about using diplomacy instead of war as a way to resolve conflict.

Breaking Away from the West

Emperors in the east saw themselves as heirs to the Roman Empire and frequently used images to demonstrate this continuity. However, it soon became apparent that the east was moving ever farther from the west.

Justinian was the last eastern emperor to use Latin as the official language. After the seventh century, the language of the Byzantine bureaucracy changed to Greek. This made sense given that the native language of most educated people in the east was Greek rather than Latin, but it accelerated the east's drift away from the west. The split became even more pronounced after people living in the Germanic kingdoms gradually forgot how to speak and read Greek. Men and women living in the two sections of the old Roman Empire could no longer converse except through interpreters.

During the late Roman Empire, Christianity had linked the faithful of many regions and backgrounds together in one worship. Greek was the language of scripture and worship in earliest Christianity, and as Christianity spread, people worshiped in their local languages. Usually that meant Latin in the west, and Greek, Syriac, Coptic, Armenian, and other languages in the east.

As people in the western portion of the old empire forgot how to speak Greek, the western church began to use Latin exclusively in worship services, while in the east church services continued to be conducted in local languages. Over time, these language differences drove the churches apart.

The question of who should lead the church posed another problem. As we have seen, the power vacuum caused by the invasions allowed the popes to emerge as independent political leaders. In the east, however, the self-styled sacred emperors

> Religious controversy

were **Caesaropapist;** that is, they led both church and state. Note, for example, how the images of Justinian and Theodora in **Figures 6.9a** and **b** include religious symbols in addition to emblems of their secular offices. Emperors led the church, appointed the patriarchs (the eastern equivalents of the highest-ranking archbishops), led church councils, and involved themselves in theological controversies.

Just as Constantine had called the Council of Nicaea in 325 to discuss the origin of Christ (see Chapter 5), the Byzantine emperor Marcian called the Council of Chalcedon in 451 to resolve questions about the human and divine natures of Christ. The council decided that Jesus was both fully human and fully divine. This position seemed eminently logical to the pope in the west. Yet some men and women in portions of the east were shocked by this conclusion. In their view, this statement seemed to reduce the power of God by acknowledging that Jesus remained human. The anger catalyzed by this resolution further separated portions of the eastern empire from the west.

In the eighth century, another religious controversy convulsed the east and brought the growing differences between the Latin and Greek churches to the forefront. From the fifth through the sixth centuries, the worship of the faithful in the eastern church had focused on icons—images of Jesus, Mary, and the saints. People viewed these depictions as more than simple portrayals; they believed that the images contained spirituality that had become material and thus could bring divine help. Byzantine monasteries in particular had amassed huge wealth by painting and selling icons. In the west, men and women also venerated images of saints, but not to the same degree.

Iconoclasm

The Byzantine emperor Leo III (r. 717–741) ordered all icons destroyed, and in an autocratic style, he intended for his decree to apply to all of Christendom, east and west. In part this dictate represented a belief common in the Asiatic provinces, that veneration of icons amounted to worshiping idols. Leo's policy also had a political side. The eastern emperors wanted to challenge the growing power of the monasteries that were producing most of the icons. This **iconoclasm** (icon breaking) controversy raged for a century in the east, during which time many mosaics in Constantinople and Asia Minor were destroyed, leaving Ravenna as the most important repository of the old mosaics. Finally, less controversial emperors withdrew their support from the iconoclasts (icon destroyers). In the meantime, however, the western popes did not acknowledge the emperor's authority, and Pope Gregory II (r. 715–731) defied Leo's edict. The tensions resulting from this struggle strained relations between the eastern and western churches even further.

Orthodox church

Over the centuries, two branches of Christianity grew more and more apart until they became two separate churches—the Catholic west and the Orthodox east. The Orthodox church rejected the concept of papal supremacy that was growing in the west and preserved the idea that the church should be led by five bishops (called patriarchs) who presided in the five major cities: Rome, Constantinople, Jerusalem, Alexandria, and Antioch. Each of the five patriarchs—called the Pentarchs—exerted jurisdiction in his own area and met with the other patriarchs in council to regulate matters of dogma and church discipline. Over time, they rejected decisions made outside these councils by the popes alone. Questions of language, theology, hierarchy, and the wording of the creeds finally severed ties between east and west.

In 1054, the two churches broke apart. The pope and the patriarch of Constantinople excommunicated each other, and the unified Christian church became two. (The mutual excommunications were finally withdrawn, but not until 1965.) Both the Roman Catholic and Greek Orthodox churches would grow and find adherents all over the world into the twenty-first century.

Converting the Slavs, 560–ca. 1000

Starting in the sixth century, the several Slavic groups settling along the Danube River, which had once formed the northeastern boundary of the Roman Empire, represented yet another challenge to Byzantine unity. These pagan tribes included Serbs, Croats, and Avars. In 679, the Bulgars, a Turko-Mongolian people, came out of the steppes of Russia and built a powerful kingdom just north of the Danube. **Map 6.3** shows generally where these peoples settled. In the ninth century, Scandinavian traders (and raiders) established a kingdom in Kiev (modern Ukraine) made up of Slavic people ruled by Scandinavian princes. (This principality, called Kievan Rus, became the origin of the name "Russia.") All these peoples alternately raided and traded with the eastern empire and personally experienced the famed Byzantine diplomacy. Some tribes were bribed into peace, some kings were offered Byzantine brides, and occasionally tribes were tricked into fighting each other.

The Byzantines sought a way to bring these peoples within the eastern empire's influence by converting them to Christianity. In 863, the Byzantine emperor Michael III (r. 842–867) sent two missionaries, Cyril and Methodius, to the Slavs. The missionaries realized that conversion depended in part on literacy. The Slavs, who had no written language, could not read the church services. Therefore, Cyril and Methodius developed a Slavonic written language based on the Greek alphabet.

Cyril and Methodius

Their mission was successful. Serbs and Russians embraced Greek Christianity, and the alphabet that Cyril and Methodius developed to transmit the religion became known as the **Cyrillic alphabet** (named after St. Cyril). It is still used in Russia and in portions of the Balkan peninsula today. The Bulgar leader also converted to Othodox Christianity in the 890s and adopted the Cyrillic alphabet.

Conversion of Russia

The state of Kievan Rus was brought to Christianity by a bargain struck between the reputedly ruthless prince of Kiev, Vladimir (r. 978–1015), and the Byzantine emperor Basil II (r. 976–1025). Basil wanted to secure Vladimir's military assistance and bring the growing eastern Slavic state into Byzantium's sphere of influence. Vladimir agreed to convert to Greek Orthodox Christianity and help Basil if the emperor would give his own sister, Anna—a princess "born to the purple"—as Vladimir's bride. The Kievan prince already had several wives, but

Basil had little choice. Anna went north and Vladimir established churches along the Byzantine model. Vladimir's "conversion" in 989 marks the traditional date for the beginning of Christianity in Russia.

Like its Byzantine counterparts, the Catholic church also sent missionaries who successfully converted tribes in portions of the east. The Poles, Bohemians, Hungarians, and Croats adopted Catholic Christianity and the Latin alphabet that came with it. These divisions in religion, loyalty, and alphabet divided eastern Europe, and, indeed, cultural divisions established during this period have continued to color the politics of the region into the twenty-first century.

By the tenth century, the Byzantine Empire had entered a sort of golden age. It had occupied and assimilated the strong Bulgarian kingdom, and the eastern emperor exerted his authority from the Adriatic to the Black Sea. The empire was prosperous and secure. The Byzantine culture and the western kingdoms would interact for centuries, during which time the West gained a great deal from Byzantium. The western legal system owed much to Justinian's codification, western scholars would gain from the Greek texts preserved in the east, and western kingdoms owed their survival to Byzantium's serving as a buffer state against incursions from the east. The eastern empire and the Orthodox church left an enduring cultural influence in eastern Europe that continues to affect political life today. In the seventh century, the Mediterranean world grew even more complex: A third great power was rising in the south and this new civilization would come to challenge both the west and Byzantium.

| Golden age |

ISLAM,
600–1000

In the early seventh century, the Arabian peninsula was part of neither the Byzantine nor the Persian Empire. The region contained both oases with settled populations and great reaches of desert. In the desert, nomadic Bedouin tribes roamed, living on milk, meat, and cheese from camels and goats; dates; and some grain from the oases. These tribes emphasized family and clan loyalty and fought, raided, and feuded with one another to protect their honor and their possessions. The Arabs were pagan, worshiping natural objects such as stones, springs, and a large ancient meteor that had fallen into the Arabian desert long before human memory.

The success of Bedouin life stemmed in large part from the use of domesticated camels. These magnificent desert animals could carry heavy loads for many miles without water and proved a speedy form of transportation in the raids of desert warfare. The Bedouins sold camels to the Arabs of the oases, who in turn used them for the long-distance trade that brought prosperity to the small cities of the oases.

During the wars between Byzantium and Persia (540–ca. 630), the land route to the Far East through Mesopotamia became dangerous. For safety's sake, some traders from Constantinople and Egypt decided to travel through Mecca in Arabia to reach a water route through the Red Sea. Others crossed the Arabian peninsula to leave by sea from the Persian Gulf. This trade brought even more wealth to the thriving oasis cities, the most important of which was Mecca. Mecca housed an important pagan shrine, the Ka'bah, containing the ancient meteorite, which drew Bedouins and other Arabs to gather in peace for trade. But trading had another consequence beyond stimulating commerce: It brought Arabs in contact with Christians and Jews, and, as a result, new ideas filtered into the Arabian peninsula.

The Prophet

The new ideas generated by Arab, Christian, and Jewish interaction came to be embodied in the person of a man named Muhammad. Muhammad (570–632) was an orphan who grew up in Mecca in the care of his uncle. He became a merchant and made an excellent marriage to a wealthy widow and businesswoman, Khadijah. The couple had seven children and lived a prosperous life. As a merchant, Muhammad earned a reputation for being a good and honest man. His nickname was "al-Amin"—"the trustworthy."

In his fortieth year, Muhammad began to have visions. First an angel appeared to him while he was sleeping and said: "Recite! Thy Lord . . . taught by the pen, taught that which they knew not unto men." When Muhammad

| The Qur'an |

GROWTH OF ISLAM

570	Muhammad born in Mecca
622	Hijra
628	Yemen converted to Islam
632	Muhammad dies in Medina
661	Murder of 'Ali
661–750	Umayyad dynasty rules from Damascus
ca. 691	Dome of the Rock built in Jerusalem
711	Muslims conquer Spain
732	Charles Martel wins Battle of Tours
750	'Abbasid dynasty begins
786–809	Harun al-Rashid rules

KEY DATES

awoke from this vision, he saw a huge man with his feet astride the horizon. This man claimed to be the angel Gabriel and told Muhammad to be the apostle to his people. According to Islamic tradition, Muhammad received an additional 114 revelations over the next twenty years. These revelations were recorded as the word of Allah (God) given in the Arabic language. Accounts of the revelations were collected after Muhammad's death and became the book of inspired scripture of the new religion. This scripture is called the Qur'an (sometimes written in English as "Koran").

Muhammad believed the God who spoke through him was the same God worshiped by Jews and Christians. Muhammad said that five major prophets had come before him: Adam, Noah, Abraham, Moses, and Jesus. Muhammad said each had brought truth, but Christians and Jews had departed from the prophets' messages—the Jews had ignored Jesus, and Christians had embellished the simple message of the Gospels by adding theological complexities. Therefore, Allah had decided to speak through Muhammad, who is known simply as the Prophet. The religion he founded is called Islam, and its followers are known as Muslims.

The Religion

The nature of Islam is as clear and stark as the Arabian desert itself. *Islam* means "surrender to God," and this idea lies at the heart of the religion, for a follower of the religion is called a Muslim—"one who submits." Christians had to study for years before converting and had to understand the subtlety of various creeds. For a man or woman to convert to Islam, he or she merely needed to testify, "There is no God but Allah and Muhammad is his prophet." Whenever children were born in Muslim lands, midwives and parents whispered this creed into their ears so that they would grow immediately into faith. After this simple creed, Muslims were to follow the Five Pillars of Faith.

The first pillar of faith is the profession of faith itself. Believers adhere to a strict monotheism. (For example, Muslims believe that the Christian belief in the Trinity of the Father, Son, and Holy Spirit signaled a departure from the command to have only one God.) Further, Muslims believe that **Faith** the Qur'an represents the word of God. The power of the spoken and written word had come to light in Muhammad's first vision, which emphasized the importance of God's words brought through the Prophet. Many of the faithful memorize and recite the entire Qur'an (which is about as long as the Christian New Testament).

Figure 6.11 shows a page from the Qur'an. The beautiful calligraphy of the Arabic letters and the gold leaf make precious manuscripts like this one as much

FIGURE 6.11 The Qur'an Because images are forbidden to Muslims, writing became the most honored art in the Islamic world. Muslims considered beautiful calligraphy to be part of the revealed word of God, as shown in this manuscript page from the Qur'an.

works of art as religious objects. Muslims believe that the Qur'an must not be translated from the original language, so all the manuscripts are copied in Arabic. This figure shows how strikingly different the Arabic alphabet is from the Greek and Latin scripts that dominated in the West. This visual signal points to the language barrier that would separate Muslim from Christian lands.

The first pillar concerned private behavior, indicating the faith within, but the next four reinforced the first through public actions of all believers. The second pillar of faith **Public rituals** is prayer, an activity that the faithful perform five times a day. In addition, every Friday, Muslims gather to pray together at the local mosque, called there by a human voice beckoning from the mosque towers, or minarets. (Christians are called by bells, and Jews by horns. Muslims believe the angel Gabriel told Muhammad to use the human voice to call his followers to prayer.)

Unlike Christian churches, mosques display no images of God. Muslims take the biblical prohibition against the idolatry of graven images literally. It may be that the Byzantine iconoclast movement was influenced by the example of the strict interpretation of the Muslims. Instead of images of God, mosques are decorated with beautiful geometric patterns. These designs are intended to help the faithful in their prayers by focusing their attention on the divine pattern of the universe. An example of mosaic patterning appears on the photograph of the Dome of the Rock shown at the opening of this chapter.

The third pillar of faith is almsgiving. Muslims are to donate a portion of what they earn to the needy, and this giving purifies the rest of their earnings. The fourth pillar of faith is fasting. All Muslims fast during the month of Ramadan, a time based on the lunar calendar that comes at a different point every year, which commemorates the month Allah revealed the Qur'an to Muhammad. During this month, the faithful ingest no food or drink and do not engage in sexual relations during the day, but eat and celebrate every night after sundown. This month is much loved by Muslims because it lets them attend to spiritual matters and family in a concentrated way.

The last pillar of faith is pilgrimage. All Muslims try to make a journey to Muhammad's holy city of Mecca once in their lifetime. This trip—called the *Haj*—is made during a designated pilgrimage month, so the city throngs with Muslims from all over the world during this special time. Muslims today continue to follow all the pillars of faith, including the Haj.

The Spread of Islam

When Muhammad began to speak of his visions, his wife Khadijah became his first convert. However, aside from her and some close friends, few people living in the market city of Mecca paid any attention to his message. This city had grown prosperous in part because of pilgrims coming to worship at the pagan shrine of the Ka'bah, so the city leaders had little interest in the words of a new prophet.

In 622, Muhammad and his small group of followers fled Mecca to another city 250 miles to the north. This city was later named Medina, *Hijra* which simply means "the city." Muslims consider this flight, called the *Hijra* (or *Hegira*), the turning point in the acceptance of the new religion. Just as Christians mark the birth of Christ as a turning point by dating the calendar from that year, Muslims remember the Hijra by using the year 622 as the year 1 in their calendar. The dating system uses A.H. (*anno Hijrah*) instead of C.E. (common era).

From his new base in Medina, Muhammad spread his ideas to the desert Bedouins. Tribe by tribe, the Arabians converted and began to focus their warfare on "unbelievers" instead of on each other, eventually coalescing into a unified group. In 628, Muhammad returned victorious to Mecca, where the large numbers of his followers persuaded the urban dwellers that his message was true. He kept the great shrine at the Ka'bah, convinced that the large meteor within it was sacred to Allah. Pilgrims still journey to this holy place and it is the focal point of the prayer of Muslims worldwide.

Map 6.4 shows the extent of Islam at the death of the Prophet in 632. At first, Muhammad's closest followers proclaimed themselves **caliphs** ("deputies" or "successors") of the Prophet. The map shows how rapidly the first four caliphs spread the new religion. These successes continued, and only a century after Muhammad's death, Islam held sway in an area stretching from India to Spain. After this remarkable spread, many people who were not Arabs became Muslims, and although all learned to speak Arabic so they could read the Qur'an, sometimes tensions emerged between Arab and non-Arab believers. Nevertheless, the spectacular growth of this new creed obliterated the Persian Empire, shrank the Byzantine Empire, and conquered the Vandal and Visigothic kingdoms.

In the summer of 732, the forces of Islam drove through the passes of the Pyrenees into the Merovingian kingdom of the Franks. The army was made up of a large body of light cavalry and was a formidable force. Muslim generals **Battle of Tours** were confident of their ability to conquer the less-organized Franks. They easily swept through the southern lands, destroying the opposition and taking great plunder. As the Arab chronicler relates, "All the nations of the Franks trembled at that terrible army." The retreating forces approached the Merovingian household for help, and the great general Charles Martel (Charles the Hammer) led a force to a large grassy plain near Tours (see **Map 6.4**). The Arab chronicler recognized the momentous nature of this meeting: "The two great hosts of the two languages and the two creeds were set in array against each other." The battle was fierce and tens of thousands died, but Charles won a decisive victory. The remaining Muslim force retreated across the Pyrenees, and the storm of Islamic conquests in the west was halted.

In spite of Charles's victory, the Islamic conquests were impressive. Why did Islam spread so quickly? There are a number of reasons. In part, its success came from the military strength of the recently unified Bedouin and oasis Arabs. Forming a new "tribe" based on religion, these **Reasons for** formerly separate groups now made **success** an effective fighting unit. Islamic armies also benefited from believing that God supported their military expansion, for the Qur'an urged warriors to fight vigorously in the cause of monotheism: "Fight in the path of God with those who fight with you . . . kill them; such is the reward of the infidels. . . . Fight them till there be no dissent, and the worship be only to God." As Muslim armies swept to victory in what they believed was a holy war, or *jihad,* they may have forced pagans to convert or be killed.

The concept of jihad is a complicated one because the word has several meanings that have allowed for different interpretations and emphases over time.

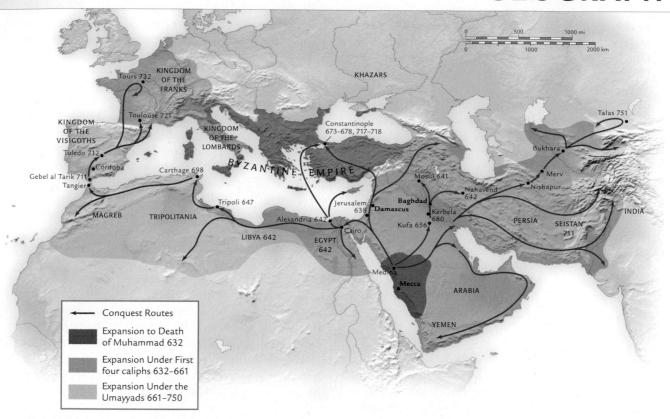

MAP 6.4

The Expansion of Islam to 750

This map shows the expansion of Islam from the Arabian peninsula to the southern and eastern Mediterranean, with the dates of the expansion. It includes the cities of Mecca, Damascus, and Baghdad—each of which, in turn, would become the capital of the Muslim world.

Explore the Map

1. Which sections of the Byzantine Empire were lost to the Muslims?

2. Which regions might be most influenced by the changes in the capitals? Why?

3. Where were the Islamic rulers most likely to focus their efforts while based in each of the capital cities?

From the beginning, Muslims identified two kinds of jihad: The "greater jihad" is the ongoing struggle within each individual to strive against base desires. This inner struggle is more meritorious than warfare, and many scholars emphasize this greater jihad when discussing the concept. The "lesser jihad" is a military struggle conducted against infidels.

Jihad

In the early Islamic expansion, the jihad against polytheism established Islamic territories, which were called the House of Islam. In theory, non-Muslim states were called a House of War that existed until they were subjugated or converted. Under early Muslim laws, jihad was to be a constant state of war against the infidels, but as we will see, this idea would change over time.

The expansion of Islam also drew strength from the relatively benign attitude of the Muslim conquerors.

Christians and Jews, whom Muslims called "people of the Book" because they all shared the same scriptural tradition and worshiped the same God that Muslims venerated, had only to pay taxes to the Muslim rulers. In one of the earliest political documents of Islam, Muhammad wrote a "constitution" for Medina in 622 outlining the policies of the new religion. In this document, he laid out the principle of toleration and mutual aid: "The Jews must bear their expenses and the Muslims their expenses. Each must help the other against anyone who attacks the people of this document." However, such toleration did not mean equality; it came with conditions, as shown in Document 6.2.

Many Christians, especially in Syria, Egypt, and North Africa, had rejected the policies of the Byzantine emperors and tolerated Islam. Within Byzantium, men and women whose beliefs had been declared

DOCUMENT 6.2

Christians Accept Caliph Umar's Terms

The caliph Umar I (r. 634–644) made an agreement with Christians in Syria, offering religious toleration. The following letter from the Christians outlines the agreed-upon terms and indicates what kinds of things Christians were forbidden.

We shall not build, in our cities or in their neighborhood, new monasteries, churches, convents, or monks' cells, nor shall we repair, by day or night, such of them as fall in ruins or are situated in the quarters of the Muslims. We shall not give shelter in our churches or in our dwellings to any spy, nor hide him from the Muslims. We shall teach the Qur'an to our children. We shall not manifest our religion publicly nor convert anyone to it. We shall not prevent any of our kin from entering Islam if they wish it. We shall show respect toward the Muslims, and we shall rise from our seats when they wish to sit. We shall not seek to resemble the Muslims by imitating any of their garments, the headgear, the turban, footwear, or the parting of the hair. We shall not mount our saddles, nor shall we gird swords nor bear any kind of arms nor carry them on our persons. We shall not engrave Arabic inscriptions on our seals. We shall not sell fermented drinks. We shall not display our crosses or our books in the roads or markets of the Muslims. We shall only use clappers in our churches very softly. We shall not raise our voices in our church services or in the presence of Muslims, nor shall we raise our voices when following our dead (in funeral processions). . . . We shall not bury our dead near the Muslims. . . . We shall not build houses overtopping the houses of the Muslims. We accept these conditions for ourselves and for the people in our community, and in return we receive safe-conduct. . . .

SOURCE: *Islam: From the Prophet Muhammad to the Capture of Constantinople*, vol. 2: *Religion and Society*, ed. Bernard Lewis (New York: Oxford University Press, 1987).

Analyze the Document

1. How were these prohibitions more lenient than what Christian heretics faced under Christian emperors? (Compare with Chapter 5.)

2. Why do you think Muslims chose these prohibitions?

3. What prohibitions do you think might have eventually encouraged many Christians to convert to Islam?

---

heretical had been forbidden to continue in their beliefs. Under the Muslims, who cared little about the subtleties of Christian theology, they could believe as they liked as long as they submitted to the conquerors. Jews, too, were free to practice their religion without the pressure they had experienced before, particularly under the Visigoths. In time, many Christians converted to Islam. The rise of Islam had created a whole new culture in the Mediterranean world.

Creating an Islamic Unity

The Muslim armies not only conquered large expanses of land but also quickly transformed the society and culture of these territories. Anyone traveling in the Mediterranean world today can see immediately that life in Algeria is strikingly different from life in Italy. This was not so during Roman times.

What was it about Muslim rule that made Islamic culture take root so powerfully in these formerly Christian regions? Language played a large role. Because the Qur'an was not to be translated, believers of Islam had to learn Arabic. Therefore, Arabic became the language of business, government, and literature in Islamic strongholds. Prayer and pilgrimage also served to solidify the Muslim world. As the faithful all looked to Mecca five times a day during prayer and made pilgrimages to the holy places, men and women broadened their attention and loyalties beyond their local kingdoms. Over time, they began to think of themselves as part of a larger group.

Law was another important unifying force. The Islamic governments were ruled by Muslim law based on the Qur'an and the Sunna, which is a collection of cultural traditions based on the life of the Prophet. These laws, administered by Muslim judges, governed most aspects of Islamic life. Uniform enforcement of the laws contributed to a growing cultural homogeneity.

Finally, the great Muslim trade network that extended from India to the Mediterranean powerfully united the Islamic world. The freedom that Muslim rulers allowed merchants and artisans fueled economic development. Arabic coins, dinars, began to replace Byzantine or Persian coins as the main trade medium, and the Muslims developed advanced banking techniques to facilitate trade. For example, they initiated the use of bank checks, which would not be employed in the West for another eight hundred years.

The Gracious Life

With large-scale trade came dramatic changes in Muslim society. The conquerors adopted the best of both the Persian and Hellenistic worlds and created a way of

Unifying elements

Yemen: Monotheism Spreads to Southern Arabia

Trade is the greatest stimulant to human interaction. Throughout history, men and women have willingly journeyed vast distances to sell or acquire luxury items like jewelry, fine clothing, and spices, as well as to trade everyday, useful objects like pots, knives, and basic ingredients for meals. But as merchants and entrepreneurs talked business and conducted deals along the major trade routes, they transported ideas in addition to merchandise. The ancient trade between the Mediterranean world and the southernmost tip of Arabia brought together peoples separated by immense deserts and exposed them to one another's religious ideas and controversies. As notions of religion spread, the lives of peoples from these two markedly different worlds began to be inextricably connected. Of course, the shifting sands of southern Arabia's deserts and the monsoon winds that whipped across the Red Sea posed daunting obstacles to people seeking to travel from southern Arabia, or Yemen, to the Mediterranean. Yet, these enterprising individuals found ways to interact with their counterparts in the eastern Mediterranean.

Some scholars suggest that after Africa, Yemen was the area of earliest human migration out of the African continent. Bold Africans crossed the Arabian Sea at the narrow straits separating the Red Sea from the Gulf of Aden, and the human expansion out of Africa had begun. The fertile plateaus of Yemen's highlands and the abundant seacoasts allowed early villages to flourish. As far back as 1,000 B.C.E., several wealthy kingdoms cropped up in this promising new land. Historians of technology are particularly impressed by the ruins of the ancient Marib Dam that settlers built in about 500 B.C.E. This astonishing structure allowed the ancient residents of the City of Saba (the Sabeans) to irrigate about 25,000 acres of land—and secure their food supply for the next thousand years.

But Yemen's real wealth came from trade. The region grows rare, brush-like trees that produce strong-smelling resins from which ancient peoples produced frankincense and myrrh. These resins—used in perfumes, medicines, and religious ceremonies—were prized throughout the ancient Mediterranean world. By 1,000 B.C.E., domestication of the camel enabled merchants to trade extensively across the Arabian desert. As one result, demand for frankincense and myrrh spread widely in the northern parts of Arabia and throughout the Mediterranean basin. One ancient writer described a caravan of three thousand camels that would have extended over 25 miles as it arrived at Mediterranean ports laden with the precious incenses. Certainly the best-known caravan of cherished goods from Saba was brought by the queen of Sheba (Saba) to the court of the Jewish king Solomon (see Document 1.2). This trade mission is described in both the Bible (1 Kings 10:1–13) and the Qur'an (27:16–44). For centuries, people throughout the ancient world continued to value frankincense and myrrh: The Roman scholar Pliny the Elder noted that Emperor Nero burned an entire year's harvest of frankincense to mark his mother's funeral. Indeed, southern Arabia prospered so much during this earliest era that the Romans called it Arabia Felix, which translates to "Happy Arabia."

life that was comfortable and pleasant, at least for the wealthy. Muslim households built on traditions drawn from the Bedouin tribes combined with practices from the Persian Empire. Previously, men had been allowed to have an unlimited number of wives, as in the Persian harems. However, the Qur'an limited a man to four wives, and this only if he could demonstrate that he had enough money to provide each wife with her own quarters and her own slaves. If husbands and wives did not get along, they could appeal to a judge who acted as an arbiter. If arbitration failed to resolve a conflict, either the man or the woman could obtain a divorce. Women's status under Islam improved in other ways as well: They were no longer treated strictly as property as they had been in pagan Arabic tribal society, and under Islamic law, Muslim women could inherit and keep their property even after marriage.

Within the household, women were separated from the company of men, and this seclusion continued when they went outdoors. Muslim women continued an age-old Middle Eastern practice of wearing heavy veils to cover themselves, and this practice continues in many Muslim countries today. Within

But even Happy Arabia was swept into the religious turmoil that raged through the Mediterranean world in the centuries after the birth of Christ. During the fourth and fifth centuries C.E., missionaries traveling the caravan routes began converting the southern Arabian tribes to monotheism. Their efforts spawned tensions. For example, in the early sixth century C.E., the Sabean king ordered all Christians in his realm to convert to Judaism. When twenty thousand of them refused, he ordered them executed. The Christian king of Ethiopia retaliated by seizing Yemen in 525 C.E. However, the Christian reign he initiated lasted just fifty years, crumbling when the Persians conquered the Yemeni kingdoms in 575. In 628, the Persian governor of Yemen embraced Islam, and the new religion spread quickly through the tribes of southern Arabia. As early as 630 (before the death of the Prophet), the first mosques rose in Yemen's cities. Still, the conversion of the Yemenis to Islam could not heal the religious divisions that had long plagued the region.

When the Muslim faithful split into factions (Sunni and Shi'ite) over the question of who should rule after the death of Muhammad, the faithful in Yemen also eventually took sides in the dispute. In the early eighth century, Shi'ites argued that the succession went to the grandsons of Husayn. Most of the Shi'ites recognized Husayn's elder son, Muhammad al-Baqir, as the fifth Imam. But some dissidents recognized the younger son, Zayd, as the legitimate successor. Both Zayd and his son were killed in subsequent battles and so could not fulfill their supposed destiny. However, many Shi'ites contended that while the next Imam must be a descendant of Husayn or his brother, Husan, he need not be the eldest of the siblings. This became one of several points of difference among the Shi'ite communities. Holding firm to their positions, a number of Zaydi sects emerged and formed a separate branch of the Shi'ite movement. In the late eighth century, some Zaydis fled to the mountainous region of Yemen. There, in 901, they established a Zaydi state. This long-standing branch of Shi'ism remains a significant minority in Yemen today.

As the centuries have unfolded, Yemen has continued to take part in the political and religious struggles marking interactions between the Western and Islamic worlds—from its conquest by the Ottoman Empire in the sixteenth century, to its engagement in Cold War politics during the mid-twentieth century. Religious tensions within Yemen have continued to affect interactions with the West: In 2000, extremists almost sank the U.S. battleship *Cole*, which was docked in one of its harbors, and in 2009, training camps in Yemen sent a 23-year-old Nigerian man to try to ignite an explosive on a U.S. airliner on Christmas Day. Fortunately the attack failed. In ancient times the trade in precious resins brought this land into close contact with the Mediterranean world, and its fortunes have remained intertwined with those of the West ever since.

Making Connections

1. What trade items brought Yemen into continuous contact with the Mediterranean world?

2. What religious ideas and controversies spread to Yemen?

3. How did the Shi'ite Muslims in Yemen split in disagreement?

the households, women presided over the many slaves generated from the conquests and subsequent trade and created a lifestyle that was the envy of many in the Mediterranean world.

Persians taught the Arabian Muslims to play chess and backgammon; from Syria, Muslims learned to wear wide trousers instead of the traditional Arab robes. They also began to eat at tables instead of sitting cross-legged on the floor. These seemingly small matters, when taken together, reflected a prosperous, relatively homogeneous society.

Daily life

Figure 6.12 reveals several unique aspects of Islamic society. In this illustration, two wealthy Muslim men are served wine by a Christian slave probably captured in Spain. (Islamic society depended heavily on slavery, just as the Persian and Roman cultures had.) This picture also captures Muslim attitudes toward alcohol. The Qur'an forbids drinking of wine, but many Muslims routinely violated this prohibition. Indeed, some beautiful Arabic poetry even extols the pleasures of good wine. As this illustration indicates, Muslim culture was developing into something very different from life in western Europe and Byzantium.

FIGURE 6.12 Spanish Muslims Muslim life included the enjoyment of many things, including a good game of chess. The game was probably developed in India and spread rapidly through Muslim lands into the West, where it was much beloved in the courts of Europe.

Forces of Disunity

For all its cultural commonalities, the Muslim world was not without strife. Two related problems led to conflict within the Muslim territories. One problem centered on ethnicity—specifically, relations between Arabs and other Muslim peoples. The other involved a pressing political question: Who would rule after the death of the Prophet?

Some Muslims believed that the caliphs should be spiritual leaders who based their authority on the Prophet's family. In the mid-seventh century, amid much controversy over the succession, the Prophet's son-in-law and cousin, 'Ali, became the caliph. 'Ali promoted the idea of equality for all believers, rather than privileged status for Arabs who had initially spread the Prophet's message. Although he hoped to serve less as a governor and tax collector than as a spiritual leader, 'Ali had to devote much of his reign to fighting political rivals.

Shi'ite Muslims

In 661, as 'Ali was entering a mosque to pray, an assassin supporting another political faction plunged a dagger into the caliph, but 'Ali's notion of the caliphate remained alive. Men and women who followed his ideal were called **Shi'ites.** They continue to believe that the Islamic world should be ruled by **imams,** men descended from 'Ali who act as true spiritual heads of the community. The Shi'ite faithful proclaimed 'Ali's two sons, Hasan and Husayn, the second and third Imams. Husayn is particularly revered by Shi'ites today because followers of the caliph killed him and his infant son. Although Shi'ites look upon the usurpation of 'Ali's rights to rule as the beginning of their movement, Husayn's death—which they saw as a martyrdom—served as the emotional rallying point

for the Shi'ites. To this day, the death of Husayn is the most fervently celebrated event in the Shi'ite calendar. From these early centuries on, Shi'ites have believed that imams are endowed with the Divine Light Wisdom, which enables them to interpret complicated passages in the Qur'an. Shi'ites today are a significant minority in the Muslim world and continue to disagree with the Sunnis, who advocate a political, rather than purely spiritual, caliphate. The Global Connections on pages 202–203 shows how this struggle influenced events in southern Arabia (modern Yemen).

After the murder of 'Ali, the caliphate was taken over by the Umayyad family, who established a dynasty that lasted almost a century. The Umayyads located their capital in Damascus and created a government that favored Arabs. This

Umayyad caliphate

dynasty represented the traditional military and economic leaders of the Arabs. Nevertheless, dissent stirred even within the Umayyad caliphate. The Dome of the Rock (shown at the beginning of this chapter) was built by an Umayyad caliph in 691 who wanted to de-emphasize Mecca. He encouraged the faithful to visit the rock in Jerusalem from where Muslims believed Muhammad had ascended to heaven. He was successful; the Dome of the Rock today is a much-loved shrine. Unfortunately, it stands on land that Jews and Christians also venerate, and the site continues to generate controversy.

In 750, the 'Abbasids overthrew the Umayyad caliphate. They intended to restore more spiritual authority to the caliphate and to broaden authority from the Arabs to other believers, but most important, they moved the capital from Damascus to Baghdad. This newly built city, located on the banks of the Tigris River, was perfectly suited to take advantage of the rich trade from the Far East. Its land was rich, and the caliph was particularly impressed with its cool nights and freedom from mosquitoes. The founder claimed, "It will surely be the most flourishing city in the world," and

'Abbasid caliphate

he was not wrong. The great city, fortified by three concentric round walls, was the administrative center of Islam and by the tenth century had a population of about 1.5 million people. This extraordinary city helped the Muslim world focus toward the old Persian provinces, with their rich trade routes to the east. Seen from this magnificent cosmopolitan city, rivaled only by Constantinople, western Europe seemed very primitive indeed. (See Global Connections in Chapter 7, on page 224.) However, the move to the east did not help the

Christians:
- Belonging to the Roman Catholic Church
- Belonging to the Greek Orthodox Church

Muslims:
- Under the Caliph of Baghdad ('Abbasid)
- Under the Caliph of Cairo (Fatimite)
- Under the Caliph of the Almoravids
- Under the Caliph of the Hammadites

(Stripes indicate blended religious groups)

MAP 6.5

Islam, ca. 1000

This map shows how the world of Islam was divided under the leadership of various rulers.

Explore the Map

1. What caliphate controlled the capital of Baghdad?

2. What caliphate focused on the East and the wealthy trade from India and China?

3. Given the distances involved, how difficult was it for the caliphate of Baghdad to exert authority over the Almoravids?

4. How might these divisions have weakened Islamic unity?

'Abbasids eliminate political dissension. The Umayyads continued to hold power in Spain, and the Shi'ites refused to support the 'Abbasids.

Beyond the disunity percolating within the ruling dynasties, there was the ever-present tendency toward local control. Caliphs in Baghdad growing rich on eastern trade had little authority over commanders as far away as Spain, and by the tenth century (fourth century of the Islamic calendar), military commanders, called **emirs,** were taking power in their local areas. Although they theoretically followed the rule of the caliphs, they frequently acted with a good deal of autonomy. As **Map 6.5** shows, the huge Muslim world, which formed a strong cultural unity, suffered

BIOGRAPHY

Avicenna (Ibn Sina)
(980–1037)

Avicenna was born in 980, the son of a wealthy governor of an outlying province in modern-day Afghanistan. His father was Turkish and his mother Iranian. Because education played an important role in Muslim families, Avicenna and his younger brother Mahmud had tutors from a young age. Avicenna showed great intellectual curiosity and talent, and by the age of 10, he had memorized the entire Qur'an. Within his home, he also explored philosophy, theology, and mathematics. For a while, the avid scholar studied with an Indian surveyor, from whom he learned Indian mathematics.

A turning point came in Avicenna's life when his father hired a well-known philosopher to live with the family and tutor him. Avicenna learned so quickly that the tutor was stunned. The young man found medicine and natural science so easy that by the age of 16 he was practicing medicine and teaching other physicians. However, it was logic and geometry that captured the young man's imagination. After much struggle, Avicenna mastered Aristotle's logic and was so grateful for this new knowledge that he gave extra alms to the poor as a way to thank Allah. The young man so voraciously consumed all the works of the great thinkers that by the age of 18, he claimed he had mastered all knowledge. He accomplished this prodigious feat of learning without renouncing the pastimes that engaged other young men: He was well known for satisfying his passions for wine and women as well as for knowledge.

The young scholar became a court physician to a sultan when he was only 18, and he began his prolific writing career during these years. He wrote on subjects ranging from ethics to the law to the Qur'an. However, this happy time in his life came to a tragic end at age 22, when Avicenna's father died. Forced to earn a more substantial living, he entered government service, moving among the courts of various emirs. While he was still in his early twenties, Avicenna began to teach Abu 'Ubaid al-Juzjani, who stayed with him throughout much of the remainder of his life and who wrote Avicenna's biography. Al-Juzjani moved with the philosopher as he went from court to court, negotiating the complex Islamic political scene. He had resisted his father's attraction to Shi'ism and was imprisoned only once, for corresponding with an emir who was seen as a rival to the man he served.

---

from the centrifugal forces that separated all the ancient empires.

The many divisions within the House of Islam that had emerged by the tenth century led to a transformation of the idea of jihad. During the early expansion years, there had been a clear, twofold division of the world—the House of War and the House of Islam. Now, complex realities of political alignments caused some Muslims to argue for an intermediate area—a House of Peace—in which non-Muslim states could be exempt from attack. This legal device permitted travel and trade between Muslim and non-Muslim regions, and through the tenth century there was often a relationship of mutual tolerance established between the Muslim world and regions outside its borders.

Heirs to Hellenistic Learning

Despite all the political tensions, the Muslim world still managed to make astonishing gains in the arts and sciences, and in fact remained the intellectual center of the Mediterranean world for centuries. By the eighth century, the caliphs had collected Persian, Greek, and Syriac scientific and philosophical works and had them translated into Arabic. In the ninth century, the 'Abbasids ruling in Baghdad maintained this support of science. They built the House of Wisdom in Baghdad, which included a library, a translation center, and a school. This careful cultivation of learning and the blending of so many traditions led to remarkable accomplishments. Muslim scientists and physicians were by far the best in the Western world.

Muslim doctors did not slavishly follow the great classical physicians Hippocrates and Galen, even though the works of these men circulated widely. Instead, they combined this ancient wisdom with practical and empirical observation. Islamic rulers required doctors to be licensed, so the practice of medicine was well regulated. Some Islamic physicians wrote extensively and exerted a profound influence on Western medicine. Razi (865–925) (called Rhazes in the West) authored more than one hundred books on medicine. He was the first to diagnose smallpox and prescribe an effective treatment for it. Ibn Sina (980–1037) (known as Avicenna in the West) wrote *Canon of*

Medicine

FIGURE 6.13 Avicenna

Occupied with public affairs during the day, Avicenna at night continued his studies and writings. He composed treatises on arithmetic, music, and language and invented a unique form of rhythmic poetry that was emulated by subsequent poets. However, his most significant contributions came in the fields of medicine and philosophy.

When the Western universities recovered the works of Aristotle in the twelfth century, the texts included Avicenna's commentaries. In this way, the Muslim scholar's interpretations of Aristotle's ideas influenced the West's intellectual revival. Furthermore, Avicenna's *Canon of Medicine* served as the main medical text for more than six centuries and was copied throughout the Mediterranean world. In the West, the *Canon* was probably second only to the Christian Bible in the number of times it was reproduced. Some scholars suggest that his techniques of experimentation and observation gave birth to the modern scientific method.

In 1037 Avicenna fell ill. In hopes of stealing his money, one of his slaves tried to kill him by contaminating his food with opium. The scholar survived this attempt by treating himself. However, his illness killed him shortly thereafter. Nevertheless, Avicenna represented the best of the Muslim world that valued education and applied science. His theories on the sources of infectious diseases, his explanation of sight, his invention of longitude, and his use of the astrolabe have all caused modern scientists to praise his genius. The scholar accomplished all this while negotiating the hazards of a world dependent on uncertain politics and disloyal slaves. To this day, the outstanding body of work that he left behind continues to earn wide admiration and respect.

Connecting People & Society

1. How does Avicenna's life reveal the high respect for learning in the Muslim world?

2. How did the divisions within Islam affect Avicenna?

3. Why have some credited Avicenna with beginning the modern scientific method?

Medicine, an encyclopedia of medicine that laid the foundation for experimental science.

Muslim surgeons performed remarkably complex operations. They practiced vascular and cancer surgery and developed a sophisticated technique for operating on cataracts of the eyes that involved using a tube to drain the fluid from the cataract. This technique was employed even in modern times, until physicians developed procedures for removing the cataracts completely. A wide range of anesthetics, from opium mixed in wine to more sophisticated drugs, made surgery tolerable for Muslim patients. Hospitals, too, sprang up throughout the Muslim world and included outpatient treatment centers and dispensaries for the many medicines being developed. Thanks to the careful sharing of knowledge and the development of advanced procedures and study, Muslim physicians provided outstanding medical care between the seventh and twelfth centuries.

Scientists made dramatic progress in other areas as well. Mathematicians brought the use of "Arabic" numerals from India, and these replaced the Roman numerals that

Mathematics

FIGURE 6.14 Mariner's Astrolabe Advances in Muslim mathematics allowed for the invention of the astrolabe, a device for measuring the angles of heavenly bodies. This new tool allowed navigators to calculate latitude more precisely in finding their way at sea.

had been used throughout the former empire. The major advantage of Arabic numerals was that they included the zero, which makes complex calculations

DOCUMENT 6.3

Shahrazád Mollifies a Murderous King

In the West, the best-known Muslim literary work is The Arabian Nights, *also called* The Thousand and One Nights, *which is set in the ninth-century court of Harun al-Rashid. This collection of tales circulated for centuries and was probably recorded in its present form in the fifteenth century. The story tells of a jealous king who marries a virgin each night and kills her in the morning so that his wives can never be unfaithful. The lovely Shahrazád escapes this fate by weaving a compelling story for the king every evening for a thousand and one nights. This excerpt explains what happened to Shahrazád after her years of storytelling.*

SHAHRAZÁD, during this period, had borne the King three male children; and when she had ended these tales, she rose upon her feet, and kissed the ground before the King, and said to him, O King of the time, and incomparable one of the age and period, verily I am thy slave, and during a thousand and one nights I have related to thee the history of the preceding generations, and the admonitions of the people of former times:

then have I any claim upon thy majesty so that I may request of thee to grant me a wish? And the King answered her, Request: thou shalt receive, O Shahrazád. So thereupon she called out to the nurses and the eunuchs, and said to them, Bring ye my children. According they brought them to her quickly; and they were three male children: one of them walked, and one crawled, and one was at the breast.

And when they brought them, she took them and placed them before the King, and, having kissed the ground, said, O King of the age, these are thy children, and I request of thee that thou exempt me from slaughter, as a favour to these infants; for if thou slay me, these infants will become without a mother, and will not find among women one who will rear them well. And thereupon the King wept, and pressed his children to his bosom, and said, O Shahrazád, by Allah, I pardoned thee before the coming of these children, because I saw thee to be chaste, pure, ingenuous, pious. May God bless thee, and thy father and thy mother, and thy root and thy branch! I call God to witness against me that I have exempted thee from every thing

that might injure thee.—So she kissed his hands and his feet, and rejoiced with exceeding joy; and she said to him, May God prolong thy life, and increase thy dignity and majesty! . . .

So they decorated the city in a magnificent manner, the like of which had not been seen before, and the drums were beaten and the pipes were sounded, and all the performers of sports exhibited their arts, and the King rewarded them munificently with gifts and presents. He bestowed alms also upon the poor and needy, and extended his generosity to all his subjects, and all the people of his dominions. And he and the people of his empire continued in prosperity and joy and delight and happiness until they were visited by the terminator of delights and the separator of companions.

SOURCE: Edward William Lane, trans., *The Arabian Nights' Entertainments—or The Thousand and One Nights* (New York: Tudor Publishing, 1927), pp. 962–963.

Analyze the Document

1. How might works of literature not only entertain but also reveal the values of the society that produce them?

2. What does this text say about early Muslim views of women?

3. What light does the story shed on the household of the caliph?

---

manageable. By the tenth century, Muslim mathematicians had perfected the use of decimals and fractions and had invented algebra. The word *algebra* comes from Arabic and means "the art of bringing together unknowns to match a known quantity." Today students all over the world continue to learn this art.

The mathematics of algebra allowed Muslim astronomers to calculate more precisely the angles of the sun and stars at different times of the year. Through algebraic computation, they made progress on the difficult challenge of finding their way at sea using the latitude portion of the grid of the world. (See Thinking About Science & Technology in Chapter 3.) With their new knowledge, they invented the mariner's **astrolabe**, shown in **Figure 6.14**, a heavy brass ring marked with degrees for measuring the angles of celestial bodies. The spread of this instrument to

Christian Europe in the twelfth century would transform navigation.

The accomplishments of Muslim society ranged far beyond science. The Qur'an is written in beautiful Arabic rhymed prose, and its study contributed to a lively appreciation for literature. Muslim writers throughout the Middle Ages would pen magnificent poetry that celebrated beauty, love, and the sensual | Literature | life. Perhaps the most famous literary work was *The Arabian Nights*. This widely admired collection of stories was set in Baghdad in the court of the most famous 'Abbasid caliph, Harun al-Rashid (r. 786–809), and has delighted readers in the East and West for centuries. Read Document 6.3 for an excerpt of this engaging work that reveals social attitudes of the early Muslim world.

Even the religious architecture developed by the Muslims put a unique imprint on the appearance of the southern Mediterranean cities. Whereas Christians emphasized religious images based on the human form, Muslims developed exquisite patterning designs. Domes and minarets gracing impressive mosques gave the skylines of eastern and southern cities their own distinct character.

Islam and the West

Before the seventh century, the story of the West unfolded rather organically from the Fertile Crescent around the Mediterranean basin and into northern Europe. Throughout these millennia, Western culture developed with contact from as far away as east Asia, until during the Roman Empire people identified themselves as participating in one empire—albeit a diverse, multicultural one. After Muhammad's visions and the spread of Islam, that experience changed. The Mediterranean world was split into two separate cultures. Historians have argued over the degree to which trade and travel were interrupted by the division, but none questions the cultural divide. From the seventh century on, Islam and the West would take two different paths, always interacting at some level, but always conscious of the difference between them.

LOOKING BACK & MOVING FORWARD

Summary   After the sixth century, the Mediterranean world of the old Roman Empire underwent a dramatic transformation. The Roman Empire in the west dissolved in the face of the rising Germanic kingdoms. The empire persisted in the east, but in a drastically changed form known as the Byzantine Empire. In the south, armies of the new religion of Islam conquered vast territories to create a new society and culture. Islam arose in part as a reaction to the Byzantine Empire and Christianity. Although they worshiped the same God as Christians and Jews, Muslims worshiped in a different way. Consequently, they developed a new way of life that led to a vigorous synthesis of the cultures of the many lands they conquered.

The emergence of this third culture in the lands of the old Roman Empire brought warfare, suffering, and religious tensions, but also a rejuvenated intellectual life. The West and Byzantium did not adopt Islamic religion, but they learned much from Muslim philosophers, scientists, and poets. From this time forward, the interactions among these three great cultures—western European, Byzantine, and Muslim—would profoundly shape the history of the West.

KEY TERMS

federates, p. 182
Petrine doctrine, p. 187
theme, p. 192
Caesaropapist, p. 195
iconoclasm, p. 196
Cyrillic alphabet, p. 196
Haj, p. 199
Hijra, p. 199
caliphs, p. 199
jihad, p. 199
Shi'ites, p. 204
imams, p. 204
emirs, p. 205
astrolabe, p. 208

REVIEW, ANALYZE, & CONNECT TO TODAY

REVIEW THE PREVIOUS CHAPTER

Chapter 5—"Territorial and Christian Empires"—followed the difficulties of the late Roman Empire and studied Diocletian's reforms, in which he tried to reorganize and preserve the empire, and Constantine's movement of the capital to the east.

1. What elements of Diocletian's reforms did the Byzantine emperors continue? Why did many of these reforms endure more in the east than in the west?

2. Review the reasons Constantine moved his capital. In what ways did his decision prove to be sound in the face of the events of the fifth and sixth centuries?

ANALYZE THIS CHAPTER

Chapter 6—"A World Divided"—shows how three distinct cultures emerged in the old territory of the Roman Empire.

1. Review the various characteristics of the societies of the Byzantine Empire, the Muslim lands, and the

western kingdoms. What are the strengths and weaknesses of each?

2. Compare and contrast the beliefs of Christianity, Judaism, and Islam.

3. What accounted for the rapid expansion of Islam?

4. As the Slavs converted to Christianity, they established cultural patterns that would affect Europe for millennia. Review the Slavic settlements and their conversion to Christianity.

5. Review the main elements of Muslim culture, including the forces of unity and disunity that helped shape the lands of Islam.

CONNECT TO TODAY

Think about the divisions of various cultures and religions that were described in this chapter.

1. How do the divisions within Islam, as traced in this chapter, continue to affect the world today?

2. How do you think the misunderstandings in this region might reflect the fragmentation that separated the Byzantine Empire from the West? Consider, for example, the split in the Christian churches and the use of differing alphabets by Greek and Latin speakers, as described in this chapter.

BEYOND THE CLASSROOM

THE MAKING OF THE WESTERN KINGDOMS, ca. 376–750

Brown, Peter. *The Rise of Western Christendom: Triumph and Diversity, A.D. 200–1000*. Boston: Blackwell, 1997. A highly readable narrative with a breadth of coverage presented by a master historian. Includes the Persian Empire and the differing development of the eastern and western church.

Glob, P.V. *The Bog People: Iron Age Man Preserved*. Translated by R. Bruce-Mitford. Ithaca, NY: Cornell University Press, 1969. A fascinating archaeological study of Iron Age people and their culture, based on the excavations of corpses from the bogs.

Heather, Peter. *The Fall of the Roman Empire*. New York: Oxford University Press, 2006. A convincing and elegant argument that Rome did not just fall but was dismantled by the German tribes, who had learned much in their centuries of living in Rome's shadow.

Noble, T.F.X. *The Republic of St. Peter: The Birth of the Papal State, 680–825*. Philadelphia: University of Pennsylvania Press, 1984. A clear study of the growth of the papacy in these early, little-studied centuries.

Russell, James C. *The Germanization of Early Medieval Christianity: A Sociohistorical Approach to Religious Transformation*. New York: Oxford University Press, 1994. An inquiry into Christianization efforts among the German peoples that considers the influence of the Germans on Christianity.

Wells, Peter S. *Barbarians to Angels: The Dark Ages Reconsidered*. New York: W.W. Norton, 2008. An examination of European culture after Rome's collapse, providing archaeological evidence to demonstrate the existence of a vigorous economic life during the early Middle Ages.

THE BYZANTINE EMPIRE, ca. 400–1000

Conte, Francis. *The Slavs*. New York: Columbia University Press, 1995. Summarizes the ancient Slavic world—its characteristics, internal and external contacts, and the influences that shaped its development.

Gregory, Timothy E. *A History of Byzantium*, 2nd rev. ed. Hoboken, NJ: Wiley-Blackwell, 2009. An extensively revised edition of a classic study that covers the empire from Constantine through the fall of Constantinople.

Hussey, Joan M. *The Orthodox Church in the Byzantine Empire*. New York: Oxford University Press, 1990. Explores the development of the church in the Byzantine Empire from the reshaping of the policies in the post-Justinian period of the seventh century to the fall of Byzantium in the fifteenth century.

Rodley, Lyn. *Byzantine Art and Architecture*. New York: Cambridge University Press, 1996. A well-illustrated introduction to the material culture of the Byzantine Empire.

ISLAM, 600–1000

Ansary, Tamim. *Destiny Disrupted: A History of the World Through Islamic Eyes*. New York: PublicAffairs, 2009. A lively survey of the history of Islam, showing how the relationship between Islam and the West has been mutually transforming.

Bidwell, Robin. *The Two Yemens*. Boulder, CO: Westview Press, 1983. An engaging history of Yemen from ancient to present times.

Esposito, John L. *The Oxford History of Islam*. New York: Oxford University Press, 2002. A collection of essays on various topics, from philosophy to history to art, that together offer a fine introduction to Islamic history.

Hillenbrand, Carole. *The Crusades: Islamic Perspectives.* New York: Routledge, 2000. A comprehensive, beautifully illustrated discussion of the Islamic sources, showing the changing idea of jihad, warfare, and life during the crusading period.

Momen, Moojan. *An Introduction to Shi'i Islam.* Oxford: George Ronald, 1985. A clear explanation of this branch of Islam written by a practicing Shi'ite.

Roberts, Robert. *The Social Laws of the Qur'an.* Atlantic Highlands, NJ: Humanities Press, 1990. A fine analysis of the laws in the Qur'an and how they impact society.

Stowasser, Barbara. *Women in the Qur'an: Traditions and Commentaries.* New York: Oxford University Press, 1994. A scripture-based examination of differing women's status in family and society.

FOUR EVANGELISTS, early ninth century

In the eighth century, after the waning of violence in the West, kings slowly began to restore order. In doing so, they looked to the learning of the past. This illustration of Matthew, Mark, Luke, and John comes from a Gospel book made in the palace chapel school at Emperor Charlemagne's court. The gracious folds of the tunics and the sparse but elegant landscape display classic artistry. At the top of the image, the artist shows the dawn breaking, promising a new order in the West that will be built on the literacy and the precious texts of the past.

The Struggle to Bring Order

The Early Middle Ages, ca. 750–1000

"Since I had not wherewith to feed and clothe myself, I wish to commend myself to you and to put myself under your protection. I have done so, . . . and as long as I live I shall never have the right to withdraw from your power and protection." With these words, drawn from a legal document, eighth-century noblemen placed themselves in a mutually binding contract with their superior. After the disruptions of the fifth, sixth, and seventh centuries, western Europeans struggled to restore order to their society, and they did it by trying to join all members of society in ties of law and loyalty. From the eighth to the tenth century, rulers worked to organize their kingdoms, and in doing so, they created a new culture that combined elements of the old Germanic tribes, the Roman Empire they inherited, and the Christian beliefs they embraced.

As kings worked to establish frameworks for their fragile new kingdoms, they discovered that written law codes and highly organized social structures gave their lands a relative peace that brought a growing prosperity. As law codes regulated people's behavior, nobles and peasants alike defined their relationships in terms of personal and contractual ties that stabilized day-to-day life for everyone. Kings also encouraged intellectual and cultural growth, which had stalled during the previous volatile centuries. Western civilization seemed poised to flourish again in a new form.

Anglo-Saxon England developed traditions of local government and law that planted the early seeds of constitutional government. However, the most successful combination of Germanic and Roman culture took place on the Continent, where Frankish rulers slowly consolidated an empire. With the peace brought by these new strong kings, the church, too, began to reassert its authority and its role in maintaining the Christian order. Although a new series of invasions in the tenth century undermined all these efforts, we can still find in them the roots of ideas and institutions that would shape the lives of men and women in the West for centuries.

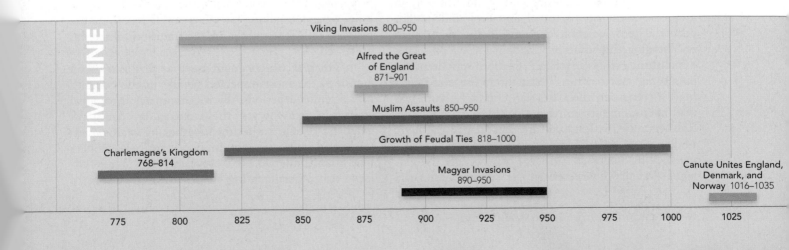

TIMELINE

Viking Invasions 800–950

Alfred the Great
of England
871–901

Muslim Assaults 850–950

Growth of Feudal Ties 818–1000

Charlemagne's Kingdom
768–814

Magyar Invasions
890–950

Canute Unites England,
Denmark, and
Norway 1016–1035

775   800   825   850   875   900   925   950   975   1000   1025

BRINGING ORDER WITH LAWS AND LEADERSHIP

Early in the eighth century, in the northern England town of York, a small child was sent to the newly founded school at the church. As the young boy grew, he became an accomplished scholar who corresponded with Latin-speaking scholars all over western Europe. In time, his Anglo-Saxon name, probably Alhwini, changed to the Latin form of Alcuin, and it is by this name that he is remembered today. In 766, when Alcuin was about 30 years old, he became headmaster of the church school, and he never lost his commitment to education. The illustration that opens this chapter portrays scholars similar to Alcuin, writing with quill pens on parchment books.

As we will see, Alcuin's career did not end in York—he went on to travel and profoundly influence the most celebrated courts of the time, even encouraging the emperor Charlemagne to pass laws establishing schools for all freeborn children. In preserving and teaching Latin literature and working to strengthen the Christian church, Alcuin was instrumental in furthering the synthesis of Germanic, Roman, and Christian culture that shaped the early Middle Ages. Alcuin's career and dedication to learning were made possible in large part because the violence that had characterized the centuries after the fall of the Roman Empire was slowly being brought under control by talented kings.

The Rule of Law

Long before their penetration into the Roman Empire (see Chapter 6), the Germanic tribes had valued the force of law. Laws were not written down, however, nor legislated by king or council. Instead, laws constituted the customs of the past enforced by individuals and families. Traditionally, kings could arbitrate between conflicting parties, but people believed the law transcended any individual ruler, and law was administered by assemblies of the people. The German assemblies had developed some unusual means to help determine the truth in disputed cases. For example, they might consider the character (or value to the community) of the accused, and in a practice called **compurgation,** 12 honorable men testified to the character of the accused (without any necessary knowledge of the facts of the incidents under discussion). Or the assembly might appeal to the supernatural, in a process called **ordeal** (the word originally meant "judgment"). In an ordeal, the accused might pick up a red-hot iron or immerse his hand in boiling water. If the hand was not severely burned, the accused was judged innocent. Later in the Middle Ages, ordeals by battle would also be used to determine guilt, and in late witchcraft trials, women were thrown into the water to see if they sank. Floating—an indication that the water rejected the woman—was seen as a sign of guilt.

In the late fifth century, the kings from the western Germanic kingdoms—who inherited the Roman traditions of the lands they held—began to codify their people's laws, and they were helped by their Roman subjects trained in classical law. The ancient laws of the Germanic peoples began to be written down in Latin and began to incorporate some of the principles of Roman law. The laws of the land became yet another example of the slow blending of cultures that shaped the medieval world. The codes of the Franks, Lombards, Visigoths, and Anglo-Saxons offer historians important insights into these early kingdoms. The prologues of these codes continued to insist that the kings were not making laws, but simply recording the people's will—the old Germanic tradition of law was preserved.

Legal codes

In villages (which might have as few as a dozen families), the most respected people in the community assembled periodically to administer their local affairs. In many ways, these day-to-day decisions, made by people gathering together at a crossroads in the village, were more important to these people's lives than the larger policies set by kings. These villagers were participating in an ancient custom of self-governance at the most local level. Document 7.1 gives examples of rural legislation in the Visigothic code.

Like the villagers, the nobles of the Germanic tribes also had traditions for resolving disputes; they depended upon private vengeance for justice. According to the recorded laws, the principal preoccupation was to find ways to stop the bitter feuds that broke out between extended families who cherished their ability to protect their people and their honor above all else. The written law codes became a first step toward regularizing and perhaps controlling the violence to bring order to the growing kingdoms.

Feuding was slowly regulated by placing limits on the occasions where vengeance was allowed. For example, a family was not permitted to seek revenge if one of their number was killed while committing a crime. Nor could a family strike back before an offender from another family was proven guilty. However, the most important mechanism for regulating violence was persuading family groups to accept compensation (in money or goods) instead of vengeance. If a member of one's kin was killed or injured, for example, the guilty party had to restore the victim's monetary worth to his or her family. This amount of money was called **wergeld,** or "man gold"—in other words, the worth of a man. A free peasant was worth about 200 shillings; a nobleman, six times that. The Germanic laws used the techniques of ordeal and compurgation to determine who should pay wergeld.

| Wergeld |

The written Germanic law codes reveal rulers' hopes that wergeld would compensate peacefully for the various injustices that inevitably cropped up as people—especially heavily armed men who spent a lot of time drinking—lived together. Wergeld covered quarrels—offenders had to pay 30 shillings for cutting off an ear, 60 shillings for removing a nose, and 8 shillings for knocking out a front tooth—as well as damaged reputations. For slandering an earl, the penalty was 60 shillings; for cutting his hair to insult him, 10 shillings; for damaging his beard—his symbol of masculinity—20 shillings.

This intricate system of fines included outrages committed against all members of the tribe, from women and children to livestock. Wergeld was assessed for the rape of young women or nuns, for adultery committed with a married woman, and even for crimes as specific as watching a woman who was modestly hiding behind a bush to urinate. The early laws of the Franks penalized anyone who hit a pregnant woman, and the penalty was increased if the woman died, thus killing the unborn child. The laws recognized that part of a woman's value included her potential for bearing children; if someone killed a postmenopausal woman, he had to pay one-third of the fine for killing a woman during her childbearing years.

These law codes that so precisely reveal the details of life in the early Germanic kingdoms may appear strange to us because they put a price on everything from an insult to a toe injury. However, they represented an important step in the emerging synthesis between Germanic and Roman societies, as kings began to record the customs of the people. These records were intended to bring peace and order to the kingdoms, but in this they were only partially successful: The early medieval kings never succeeded in weaning their subjects completely from their need for vengeance. In spite of the efforts of kings, the eighth and ninth centuries remained an era of rampant lawlessness, largely because these laws were too difficult to enforce. However, important seeds were planted in the legal traditions that we have come to identify with Western civilization.

The eighth-century monarchs slowly insinuated themselves and their royal officers between feuding families, and written law codes became an instrument by which royal power could be slowly increased. Wergeld, compurgation, and trial by ordeal became major legal pillars of the early Middle Ages, adding to the judicial tradition left by the Romans. The Germanic custom of trial by assemblies became an important base for the growth of representative institutions that would emerge in the Middle Ages. The concept of the rule of law—in which law superseded individual inclination and played a central role in keeping order—proved highly resilient and helped consolidate these early monarchies.

ANGLO-SAXON ENGLAND: FORWARDING LEARNING AND LAW

As the eighth century opened, Anglo-Saxon England consisted of several kingdoms (shown on **Map 7.1**). The most powerful were Northumbria, Mercia, and Wessex. At this time, these kingdoms were separate and struggling to integrate their new Christianity and the new learning they inherited from the Roman texts that Christian leaders brought to the island.

The Anglo-Saxons had been converted to Christianity in the seventh century, and after the Synod of Whitby in 664 (discussed in Chapter 6), the English church began to be organized along the Roman model— with a clearer hierarchy of bishops and priests—instead of as a monastic, missionary organization. In 669, Pope Vitalian sent Theodore of Tarsus to be the archbishop of Canterbury, and this erudite man from the eastern Roman Empire significantly forwarded learning in Britain. He established a school at Canterbury and brought other scholars with him who founded Benedictine monasteries in the north of England— at Wearmouth-Jarrow—that also became centers of

DOCUMENTS

The Visigoths Lay Down the Laws

In about the seventh century, Visigoths began to write down their customary laws, which are excellent sources of information about ancient village life. The laws use the principle of wergeld, monetary compensation, to resolve conflicts between neighbors.

I. Where a Horse, or Any Other Animal, Which Has Been Tied Up, Is Removed, or Injured, in Any Way, Without the Consent of the Owner.

If any person should free a horse, or any other animal belonging to another, from its halter, or from its hobbles, without the knowledge of the owner, he shall pay him a *solidus*. If said horse, or other animal, should die, in consequence, said person shall give its owner another of equal value. If he should use said animal to travel, or to work with elsewhere, without the knowledge of the owner, he shall be compelled to give him another of equal value; provided the owner should find him on that day, or on the following one. If said animal should not be found by the third day, the person who took it shall be deemed guilty of theft.

III. Where the Mane or Tail of a Horse, or of Any Other Animal, Is Cut Off by Anyone.

Anyone who disfigures the mane of a horse belonging to another, or cuts off its tail, must at once give to the owner of the same another animal of equal value. Should any other animal be mutilated in this manner, the third part of a *solidus* must be paid for every one so mutilated.

IV. Where Anyone Castrates an Animal Belonging to Another.

Whoever castrates any quadruped used for racing purposes, without the knowledge or consent of the owner; or castrates any animal which ought not to be castrated; shall be compelled to pay double the value of said animal to the owner of the same, who has been damaged on account of his malice.

V. Where Anyone Produces an Abortion upon a Beast of Burden Belonging to Another.

Whoever produces an abortion upon a mare, shall give to the owner of the same a foal, one year old, by way of compensation.

XIX. Where a Dog That Has Been Irritated, Whether the Provocation Was Wanton or Not, Is Proved to Have Injured or Killed Anyone.

Where a dog bites another person not his owner, and said person is known to have been crippled or killed, in consequence thereof, no responsibility shall attach to the owner of the dog, unless it shall be proved that he caused said dog to make the attack. If, however, he should encourage his dog to seize a thief, or any other criminal, and the latter should be bitten while in flight, and should be crippled, or die from the effects of the bite, the owner of said dog shall incur no liability therefor. But if he should cause said dog to injure an innocent person, he must render satisfaction according to law, in the same manner as if he himself had inflicted the wound.

SOURCE: S.P. Scott, trans., *The Visigothic Code (Forum Judicum)* (Boston: The Boston Book Co., 1910), pp. 284, 285, 286, 291.

Analyze the Document

1. What kinds of animals did the villagers have?

2. What kinds of problems arose among neighbors?

3. How were these problems resolved?

---

learning. By the end of the seventh century, England was poised to be a center of intellectual activity.

The illustration in **Figure 7.1** was produced at Jarrow and shows the intellectual skill that had grown in this island outpost of Christianity. *Beowulf*, the most famous Old English poem that has immortalized the heroic values of the Germanic tribes (described in Chapter 6), was probably written down during this period of monastic scholarship. Although the English monastic schools created valuable manuscripts, their proudest creation was probably the greatest scholar since the decline of the Roman world: the Venerable Bede (ca. 672–735).

The Venerable Bede:
Recording Science and History

In the early eighth century, Bede studied in Jarrow, and the young scholar mastered all the texts available to him. His writings interpreted the ancient works and made them accessible to his contemporaries. As a product of the monasteries, he wrote in Latin—the language of the church and of the educated—and his writings became essential to generations of subsequent Latin scholars. Bede was primarily a teacher who wrote a number of works intended as educational tracts. In these works he drew from previous scholars, thus preserving and expanding upon knowledge from previous centuries. For example, in an influential text—*The Nature of Things*—Bede incorporated much from the Roman encyclopedist Pliny the Elder (23–79) and the Visigothic scholar Isidore of Seville (ca. 560–636), but he added his own interpretations. For example, *The Nature of Things* attempted to explain the orbits of the earth, heavens, stars, and planets. In this widely copied and read work, Bede described the earth as a globe and discussed its geography, and this tract was counted among the most important scientific texts of the early Middle Ages.

Bede's *History*

Bede's most famous work, however, is the *Ecclesiastical History of the English People*, in which he tells the history of early Anglo-Saxon England to ca. 731. This enterprise was pathbreaking in that he took as his canvas an entire nation—not just a local region, as was customary. This was all the more remarkable from a man who probably never went farther than 7 miles from the place where he was born. But his vision helped shape the English into a cohesive entity. Bede drew from sources that are now lost, so his work is invaluable to our understanding of this early period of the Middle Ages. Further, Bede was careful to distinguish between knowledge and rumor, so he established principles of historical writing that had been virtually forgotten since the Roman historians. Perhaps the most influential aspect of Bede's history was that he adopted Dionysius Exiguus's B.C./A.D. (now B.C.E./C.E.) dating system (described in Chapter 6). Not many people had read Dionysius's tract, but Bede's was read and translated for centuries, and our adoption of Dionysius's historical dating system can be largely attributed to Bede.

Centuries of readers were not captivated by these technical details. Instead, they were drawn to his powerful prose that brought to life the centuries in which the Germanic tribes seemed very foreign to Roman Christian missionaries. He wrote of how the first missionaries ordered to go to England in 596 by Pope Gregory recoiled at the prospect: "For they were appalled at the idea of going to a barbarous, fierce, and pagan nation, of whose very language they were ignorant." Readers followed these timid missionaries as they slowly converted the Anglo-Saxon kings and established monasteries that by the late seventh century could spawn a scholar of Bede's stature. The missionaries had done their work so well that when royal courts were ready, learning could leave the monasteries and enter secular life.

Governing the Kingdom

Like the other Germanic kings, the Anglo-Saxon kings developed detailed law codes that combined wergeld with some principles of Roman jurisprudence. Indeed, the small island developed an enduring legal tradition that has become known as **common law,** which differs from the **statutory law** that is based on mandates passed by a legislative body. The common-law tradition preserves a vestige of the Germanic tradition in which the customs of the people are law.

The Christian kings claimed to rule by the grace of God, but they did so with the approval and advice of the powerful men in their court. A king could succeed to the throne only with the approval of the witan,

Witan

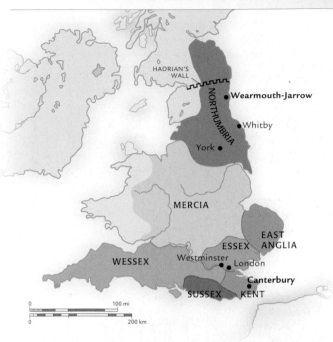

MAP 7.1

Anglo-Saxon Kingdoms, ca. 700

This map shows the seven Anglo-Saxon kingdoms that had emerged by the eighth century. It also locates the major intellectual centers—Canterbury and the monasteries at Wearmouth-Jarrow.

Explore the Map

1. Which of the three largest kingdoms was most vulnerable to invasion from Scandinavians from the north?

2. Which kingdoms were most likely to unite? Why?

3. What advantage was there to the location of the major intellectual centers at the northern and southern ends of the kingdoms?

or circle of wise men of the realm. (The full assembly was called the Witenagemot.) In addition, the king periodically called the Witenagemot to meet with him and discuss matters important to the governing of the realm. Like the laws themselves, the assembly had arisen through custom and tradition rather than from any constitutional authority. Moreover, its power ebbed and flowed in accordance with the king's power. For example, if a monarch were weak

thinking about
ART

FIGURE 7.1

Saint Matthew, from a Gospel Book, ca. 700

Medieval patrons from western European courts and monasteries commissioned colorfully decorated Gospel books. This illustration of Saint Matthew was part of a Gospel book made in Anglo-Saxon England in about 700. The work exemplifies how art could reveal the new synthesis of Germanic, Roman, and Christian elements that was forged in this era.

Connecting Art & Society

1. Compare the decorative design on the bench and in Matthew's robe's border with the Germanic gold filigree work in **Figure 6.2**, on page 180. What similarities do you find?

2. What elements of the image resemble Greco-Roman works of art?

3. How effective is this work in showing the synthesis of Germanic, Roman, and Christian culture that marked the Middle Ages?

(or young), the witan exerted a great deal of influence. A strong monarch, on the other hand, might call his lords together merely to confirm his decision. Over

time, however, all kings governed with the assistance of this body of powerful men.

In an age of slow communication, kings depended on other officials as well to govern their realms. Monarchs divided their kingdoms into shires (roughly the size of modern counties) and appointed royal representatives to govern in their name. These aristocratic earls had many responsibilities, including mustering the local men into armies if the king needed them and leading warriors into battle. Earls also served as the principal judges, presiding over shire courts and executing royal commands.

> Royal offices

Some earls amassed so much power that they governed several shires. This tendency might have weakened royal authority and essentially created new kingdoms had not the Anglo-Saxon monarchs moved to name additional royal officials. For example, kings appointed shire reeves (who later were called sheriffs) to help the earls fulfill their duties, but the sheriffs answered only to the kings, not to the earls. In this way, rulers kept a firm grip on power, even down to the shire level.

Yet, in this preindustrial world, in which people had no mail system or telephone network to connect them, kings had to do more than just appoint earls and sheriffs to keep order. For instance, collecting taxes and resolving legal disputes were matters for face-to-face contact. These emerging kingdoms struggled to provide the means for such contact and the ways by which to control it. The Anglo-Saxons accomplished this feat not only by assigning royal representatives to govern at the shire level, but also by recognizing that some tasks were best handled at the local village level. Village laws enforced by community elders formed the basic level of administrative order, and parish priests and local tax collectors joined sheriffs and earls in structuring a network that could govern the new kingdoms.

Alfred the Great: King and Scholar

The administrative organization and the patronage of the arts flourished in England under the reign of King Alfred the Great (r. 871–901) of Wessex. Alfred is the only English king who has been called "the Great," in memory of his military victories and his support of learning and culture in his realm.

Alfred's contemporary biographer, Asser, offered an engaging picture of the young prince and emphasized his early love of learning: "As he passed through his childhood and boyhood he appeared fairer in form than all his brothers, and more pleasing in his looks, his words and his ways. . . . From his cradle, Alfred had been drawn to wisdom." Despite his intelligence, Alfred did not learn to read until he was 12 years old. In adulthood, he would make up for lost time.

MAP 7.2

England in 886

This map shows the division of England between Alfred the Great and Guthrum the Dane in the treaty of 886. Compare this map with **Map 7.1.**

Explore the Map

1. How many of the old Anglo-Saxon kingdoms were united by Alfred? Which were taken by the Danes?

2. What advantage might Alfred's southern kingdoms have had because of their proximity to the Continent?

He studied Latin, collected books, and invited scholars to his court. His interests extended to the arts, for he encouraged singers to fill his court with sacred music and traditional folk songs.

By the time Alfred became king, the political divisions shown in **Map 7.1** had been shaken by a wave of outside invaders—the Danes from across the North Sea. As early as the late eighth century, raiders from the Scandinavian countries had begun raiding northern England. The great monastery of Jarrow had been looted and destroyed, and the intellectual flowering in the north that had produced Bede came to an end. A Danish raid with some 350 ships plundered London, and it looked as if the Anglo-Saxon kingdoms would all fall to the Northmen.

However, King Alfred had reorganized the military to confront the invaders, and he built the first English navy to patrol the coast against the

Danelaw

raiders. After some English victories, the Danes and the English signed a treaty in 886. Under its terms, Alfred and the Danish king Guthrum agreed to divide England between them. **Map 7.2** shows the division the two leaders agreed upon. The northern lands later became known as the Danelaw to recognize that they were governed by laws different from those in the southern parts of the land. As part of this settlement, Guthrum agreed to convert to Christianity (which would

ultimately make it easier for the peoples to share the land). The treaty also paved the way for Alfred to forge a unified kingdom in the south and to focus on the laws and learning that were his passions.

Alfred worked to bring southern England into the intellectual world of wider Europe through literature. From his own educational experience, Alfred knew that Latin texts were not

Alfred's translations

accessible to many inquiring minds. In a letter to one of his bishops, Alfred expressed the opinion (highly unusual in his time) that intellectual ideas should be available to everyone. He wrote, "It seems better to me for us also to translate some of the books which are most needful for all men to know into the language which we can all understand." The wise king followed his own advice and translated, or helped to translate, some of the great books of literature into

Old English so his own people could read them. Among other works, he translated Boethius's *The Consolation of Philosophy* (discussed in Chapter 6). Although Alfred valued the classical texts, he never lost his central interest in his own people, so his literary patronage extended to recording the history of their deeds. He translated Bede's *Ecclesiastical History of the English People* and initiated the writing of the *Anglo-Saxon Chronicle*, a history of England that continued Bede's effort to narrate the story of the English.

The rule of Alfred the Great marked the high point of the accomplishments of Anglo-Saxon England. Much of the southern portion of the island was ruled by this skilled king who brought the benefits of law and learning to his land. However, a century before Alfred's reign, across the English Channel, comparable developments had taken place on the Continent, where an even more powerful king had unified the lands of western Europe and established an empire that shone even more brightly than that of Alfred.

CHARLEMAGNE AND THE CAROLINGIANS: A NEW EUROPEAN EMPIRE

The Carolingian king Charles (later known as Charles the Great, or Charlemagne) earned that accolade by the force of his personality and the breadth of his talents. About six feet tall and physically powerful, Charlemagne boasted a full head of red hair and a prominent belly. Charlemagne the man has generated a lively debate among historians. His contemporary biographer, Einhard, left us with tantalizing bits of information about this man, who dominated the late eighth and early ninth centuries in western Europe, and who restored the centralized order that had disappeared with the fall of Rome. Charlemagne represented the high point in the process of the combining of classical, Germanic, and Christian cultural elements that we saw beginning in Chapter 6. **Figure 7.2** shows a ninth-century bronze statue that reputedly portrays this powerful ruler. In a conscious link with the classical past, the statue depicts him in the pose of the Roman emperor Marcus Aurelius—riding with no stirrups, as the Romans did, even though by Charlemagne's time the Germans did use stirrups. However, the rider also wears a Germanic cloak, a style that Einhard insists Charlemagne refused to abandon. In addition, he carries an orb representing his empire and wears a crown adorned with the symbol of office bestowed on him by the pope. In all these ways, this statue symbolizes the synthesis of cultures that restored a new kind of order to western Europe.

FIGURE 7.2 Charlemagne This bronze statue of the emperor portrays him in the pose of ancient Roman emperors, crowned and holding the orb of empire. The artist's intent was to communicate boldly that a new emperor reigned in the West.

Charlemagne's Kingdom

This impressive warrior undertook fifty-three campaigns throughout his reign—and won most of them. A pious man as well, Charlemagne established himself as a leader and reformer of the church. Finally, he had a deeply curious intellect. He knew the importance of education, recognized the worth of scholars like Alcuin, and energetically sponsored learning by establishing schools and hiring scholars. The political, ecclesiastical, and intellectual order that Charlemagne brought to the Continent has been called the Carolingian Renaissance, to emphasize the rebirth of learning that he initiated. As was the case in England, publicly fostered intellectual life depended upon a relatively ordered society, and in the early Middle Ages, this stability was purchased by military victories.

The map of Charlemagne's realm (**Map 7.3**) shows the vast span of territory—from northern Spain to the North Sea, from the English Channel well into Germany, and across the Alps into northern Italy—that this accomplished leader brought under his control. If we contrast this area with the smaller Anglo-Saxon kingdoms shown on

Administering the realm

MAP 7.3

The Empire of Charlemagne, ca. 800

This map shows the impressive kingdom of Charlemagne, with the dates of his conquests. Compare the size of this empire with that of the kingdom of Alfred shown in **Map 7.2.**

Explore the Map

1. What were the advantages and disadvantages of administering the two realms of such different sizes?

2. What aspect of Saxony's location might have given Charlemagne particular difficulties in administering that region?

3. What strategic advantage did the tributary peoples on Charlemagne's eastern border offer to the emperor?

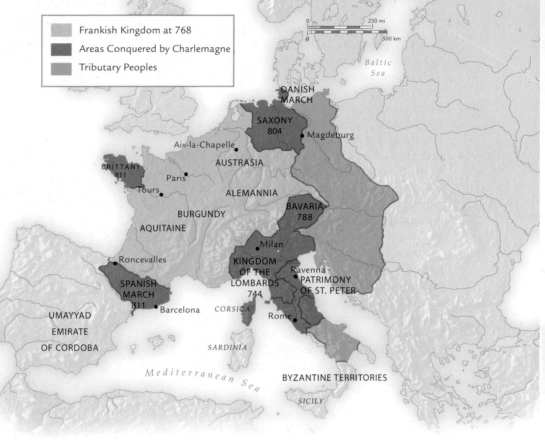

Frankish Kingdom at 768
Areas Conquered by Charlemagne
Tributary Peoples

Maps 7.1 and **7.2,** we can imagine the challenges Charlemagne faced in administering this territory.

Like his English counterparts, Charlemagne put noblemen in charge of the various provinces he controlled and tried to use laws to bring order to his lands. However, his approach differed from that of the Anglo-Saxons in that, instead of having fixed sheriffs at his command, Charlemagne sent traveling agents (called *missi dominici*) throughout his territory to examine conditions in his name and to redress certain abuses. These royal representatives traveled in pairs—a bishop and a nobleman, representing both the secular and religious arms of Charlemagne's realm. An edict issued by Charlemagne in 802 describes the high expectations he had for his officials, who were sent "throughout his whole kingdom, and through them he would have all the various classes of persons . . . live in accordance with the correct law . . . and let no one, through his cleverness or craft, dare to oppose or thwart the written law, as many are wont to do." The king knew that his rule depended upon his subjects obeying his laws.

Charlemagne enhanced his authority further by requiring his nobles to attend two assemblies a year. As the men gathered in the outdoor meeting fields, they listened to the emperor's latest decrees and

offered some opinions—but then went home and obeyed their ruler. In this way, Charlemagne moved from the original Germanic legal practice of the king simply recording the customs of the people; the Frankish king actually issued legal commands, and these carefully recorded capitularies serve as rich historical sources of his times.

In all these ways, Charlemagne departed from the Anglo-Saxon model and, in a strikingly new departure from traditional Germanic practice, sought to maintain a personal, centralized control over his unwieldy kingdom without appointing local administrators. Of course, personal rule hinges on the ruler's physical presence. Charlemagne met this requirement by traveling frequently throughout his lands, enjoying the hospitality of his noblemen. It is to Charlemagne's credit that this system worked as well as it did during his lifetime. As we will see, his administrative structure would not survive the loss of his personal attention.

Linking Politics and Religion

Charlemagne's political order had close links to his religious policies. He followed his father's lead in ensuring that his success as emperor was firmly tied to the fortunes of the church. This religious policy manifested itself in his treatment of the Saxons, a fierce people living on the northern borders of the empire. The Saxons had raided Frankish territory for generations. Charlemagne marched north in 772 and again in 775 and won decisive victories against the ferocious Saxons, but each time he left, they rose in revolt again. The emperor surmised that only by forcibly Christianizing the Saxons could he make them permanent members of his kingdom. In 785, after a particularly punitive campaign in which Charlemagne crushed the Saxon armies, the emperor forced the Saxon leader to convert to Christianity. Then Charlemagne established priests and monks in the conquered lands and punished relapses into paganism or other religious disobedience as treason. After some thirty years of religious coercion (which the scholar Alcuin opposed), Charlemagne's program worked—Christian Saxony no longer rebelled, again demonstrating how the church could serve his political ends.

As Charlemagne grew more powerful in the West, perhaps inevitably the question came up about his relationship with the Byzantine emperor in the East, and the two powers jockeyed for position. Charlemagne began to enter into many diplomatic contacts with the Byzantine court—he and Empress Irene of Byzantium engaged in ultimately unsuccessful negotiations to arrange a marriage between Charlemagne's daughter and Irene's son, the future emperor Constantine VI. However, in 797 Irene blinded and deposed her son Constantine, an act that made her the sole ruler. Charlemagne reputedly then proposed marrying Irene, thereby becoming the emperor himself, but these negotiations bore no fruit either. Instead, many wondered if Irene, a woman, could rule as emperor. If not, perhaps there was no emperor at all, and a new one should be named.

The turmoil in Byzantium contributed to one of the pivotal incidents in Charlemagne's reign, which showed his penchant for joining church and state. The event took place on Christmas Day in the year 800. The Carolingian king was in Rome; he had journeyed there at the request of Pope Leo III (r. 795–816), who had been attacked and brutally beaten while he conducted a procession through the streets of Rome. Charlemagne's armies restored the pope to power and calmed the violence in the city. While Charlemagne was in Rome, he must have visited Pope Leo's newly redecorated palace and seen the mosaics that the pope had commissioned, which had been completed in about 798, before the local rebellion.

One of those mosaics, shown in **Figure 7.3,** depicts the relationship between Pope Leo (on the left) and "King Charles" (on the right). Both kneel at the feet of Saint Peter, who was considered the founder and

Charlemagne's coronation

FIGURE 7.3 Pope and Emperor Charlemagne's crown did not resolve the question of who was superior: pope or emperor. This image tries to strike a balance, showing the two as equals as they kneel before Saint Peter.

guardian of the church of Rome. Peter hands Leo a priest's garment that marks his papal power and hands Charlemagne a spear with a banner of battle. The inscription on the bottom reads, "Blessed Peter, you give life to Pope Leo and you give victory to King Charles." Although the inscription was heavily restored in the eighteenth century, historians believe the original message was substantially the same. The mosaic offers a rough preview of the rebellion that threatened Leo's life, and of Charlemagne's subsequent military victory, but more than that it shows a certain relationship between the two men—they are separate, of equal stature, and both guided by religious principles.

When Charlemagne went to church in Rome on Christmas Day in 800, the relationship between pope and king was dramatically transformed. As the king of the Franks rose from prayer, the pope produced a crown and set it on Charlemagne's head. The watching crowds jubilantly proclaimed Charlemagne emperor. This event was of immense importance, for once again, a Roman emperor ruled in the West (independent of Byzantium), and he reigned by the might of his armies and with the blessing of God. The coronation reaffirmed the central alliance between the papacy and the Frankish kings, just as had been depicted on Leo's mosaic. A new prominence of the northern kingdom had begun. In his political activities and his personal life, the Frankish emperor personified the artful integration of God and politics.

Negotiating with Byzantium and Islam

As Charlemagne forged a new empire out of the fragmented kingdoms in the West, he naturally attracted the notice of the neighboring Byzantine and Islamic leaders. Not surprisingly, his taking the title of emperor irked the Byzantine court, but Irene ran out of time to object strenuously. She was overthrown in 802 by Nicephorus, a Byzantine aristocrat, who continued the diplomatic negotiations over the status of the Frankish ruler's title. Finally, in 813, both parties agreed that Charlemagne could be emperor of the Franks and the Byzantine emperor would be emperor of the Romans. This decision solved the immediate dispute, but the political split between east and west continued to widen. Einhard, friend and biographer of Charlemagne, summarized the uneasy relations between east and west by repeating a proverb he said was used in the east: "It is better that a Frank be your friend than your neighbor."

Charlemagne had more promising relations with the Islamic caliph in Baghdad, Harun al-Rashid (r. 786–809). Einhard said, "Charlemagne was on such friendly terms that Harun valued his goodwill more than the approval of all the other kings in the entire world." There were many diplomatic exchanges between the two courts, as it was in both their interests to forge a friendly bond against their mutual enemy, the Byzantine Empire. The Frankish sources say Harun even gave Charlemagne jurisdiction over the Christian holy places in Palestine, certainly a gracious, though empty, diplomatic gesture—Harun reportedly said, the holy land is "so far away that [Charlemagne] cannot defend it from the barbarians. . . . [Therefore] I myself will rule over it as his representative." Nevertheless, the two rulers exchanged many more tangible gifts to seal their friendship—among them an elephant that Harun gave Charlemagne in 802. The elephant lived eight more years and traveled with Charlemagne as he patrolled his kingdom, causing quite a stir among his subjects who had never seen such a beast. The Global Connections describes this relationship from the Muslim point of view.

Charlemagne's negotiations and the relative peace that came within his lands (in spite of almost incessant warfare on the borders) served to stimulate trade, which had declined during the previous tumultuous centuries. Through the ninth century, Venice,

in Italy, had assumed a leading role in the southern Mediterranean trade. Venetian merchants sent grain, wine, and timber to Constantinople in exchange for silk cloth and other luxury goods. Other Italian cities also joined in the growing trade, and the Mediterranean trade that had been one of the hallmarks of the West continued to link the region and its varied peoples. More trade brought increased prosperity into Charlemagne's lands, and the great emperor used a portion of it to forward intellectual endeavors.

An Intellectual Rebirth

As memorable as Charlemagne's political and diplomatic victories were, his most enduring impact came in the area of intellectual achievement. Although Charlemagne himself had never learned to write, he had always shown a wide-ranging intellectual curiosity that as a powerful ruler he was able to indulge. Like the Anglo-Saxon cultural revival, the Carolingian rebirth built upon learning that had been preserved in monasteries. Furthermore, the cultural revivals in England and on the Continent were directly linked in the person of the scholar Alcuin.

In the late eighth century, Alcuin, the head of the library at York and a product of the same training that had encouraged the genius of Bede, sailed across the English Channel to visit the pope in Rome. On his way home, he met the young Frankish king, Charlemagne, who was so impressed by the English scholar that he asked Alcuin to visit his court and help him reform the education there. The 50-year-old Alcuin readily agreed to come, and he guided the revival of learning on the Continent under Charlemagne's patronage.

Charlemagne's motivation for fostering learning stemmed primarily from his concern for the religious health of his kingdom. (Charlemagne's letter in Document 7.2 tells of his motives in his own words.) The emperor had observed that even many of the priests serving in his parishes could not read well enough to recite the proper form of the liturgy. Nor were they sufficiently educated to guide their parishioners to what the emperor considered the correct understanding of a Christian life. To address these matters, Charlemagne issued an edict ordering that "In the villages and townships the priests shall open schools," and that the clergy must accept all interested children without charging them fees—although he did allow teachers to accept "the small gifts offered by the parents." From this pool of literate children, Charlemagne expected to produce a clergy educated, as one of his edicts said, "in the psalms, musical notation, chant, the computation of years and season, and in grammar."

Providing schools was not enough; Charlemagne noted that this education depended upon the proper

The 'Abbasid Caliphate and Charlemagne

Chroniclers during Charlemagne's reign proudly wrote about diplomatic contacts between the Carolingian king and the Muslim caliph Harun al-Rashid that took place between 797 and 802. This diplomacy was stimulated by the exchange of kind words and gifts, including the famous elephant, named Abulabbas, that the caliph presented to Charlemagne. Chroniclers of the 'Abbasid caliphate, on the other hand, never mentioned these interactions. To the sophisticated Muslims, Charlemagne must have ranked among the minor rulers who exchanged goods with Harun al-Rashid, whose name means "the well guided."

When the 'Abbasids conquered the previous caliphate, the Umayyads, they moved their capital from Damascus (in modern-day Syria) to a new city, Baghdad (in modern-day Iraq). (See **Map 6.5.**) Thus the heart of Islam moved east, away from the Mediterranean basin. The capital blossomed into a cosmopolitan city. One Muslim poet did not exaggerate when he described the magnificent city: "Baghdad, in the heart of Islam, is the city of well-being; in it are elegance and courtesy. Its winds are balmy and its science penetrating. In it are to be found the best of

everything and all that is beautiful." Harun al-Rashid (r. 786–809) guided the 'Abbasid caliphate at the height of its success. Another Muslim poet praised the leader, writing, "Did you not see how the sun came out of hiding on Harun's accession and flooded the world with light?" Indeed, the revered caliph fostered prosperity, science, and poetry throughout his lands.

By the late ninth century, the Persian Gulf had become the main trade route to the Indian Ocean and the East. Muslim traders grew immensely wealthy. Their ships sailed to Ceylon and other southeast Asian ports and brought jewels, spices, and even elephants back to Baghdad. So many spices became available through the trade that Islamic cookbooks recommended using liberal quantities of pepper, nutmeg, cinnamon, musk, ginger, and cloves for the sophisticated palates of Baghdad. According to the famous fictional account *The Thousand and One Nights* (see Document 6.3, on page 208), even Harun was a skilled cook. Considering the delicacies that graced Eastern tables and households, it is perhaps not surprising that Charlemagne's gifts of hunting dogs caused little stir among Muslim chroniclers.

Why did Harun al-Rashid bother to engage in diplomatic relations with Charlemagne at all? The answer probably lay in the Byzantine Empire, which bordered the 'Abbasid lands. As a teenager leading his father's armies, Harun had won some glorious victories over the Byzantine forces, and as ruler, he planned to continue his encroachments on the weakening Byzantine territory. Charlemagne, too, had provoked tensions among the Byzantines, particularly after he took the title of emperor. (The Byzantine emperor felt that he alone could claim that title.) Despite deep differences in religion and culture, Harun al-Rashid discovered that he had something in common with the Carolingian emperor: a shared enemy. Politics can create unlikely allies.

Making Connections

1. Whose court was more prosperous and sophisticated—Charlemagne's or Harun al-Rashid's? Explain.

2. Why did Harun al-Rashid engage in diplomatic relations with Charlemagne?

3. Why didn't the Muslim chroniclers mention the interactions between the two men?

---

books, ordering "all books used shall be carefully corrected." To accomplish this, the emperor gathered scholars from all over Europe to assemble a canon of corrected readings. When he invited Alcuin to his court, he was not disappointed, for Alcuin drew scholars from throughout the continent to visit the emperor and to share their wisdom. The scholars took up residence in the emperor's court and were very well paid for their labors—Alcuin, for example, ended his life an extremely wealthy man.

These scholars revived a curriculum (originally proposed by fifth-century scholars) that would dominate medieval universities and profoundly influence modern liberal-arts education. To create this course of study, they divided knowledge into seven liberal arts. The most basic of these were the **trivium,** in which students learned grammar, rhetoric, and logic. With these tools, students could read texts, explain them, and understand the way to think about them. Next came the more advanced curriculum, the **quadrivium:** arithmetic, music, geometry, and astronomy. Whereas to us these four subjects may not seem obviously related, to medieval thinkers they all shared one characteristic: They involved the patterns by which God organized the world. Because scholars of the Middle Ages saw this organization as consistent, they believed they could study music, for example, to understand mathematics or the movement of the heavens.

DOCUMENT 7.2

Charlemagne Promotes Educational Reforms

Charlemagne (here identified as Karl the Great) wrote many letters, which are preserved in large collections. In this letter written ca. 790, he describes how he valued education.

Karl, by the aid of God king of the Franks and Lombards and patricius of the Romans, to the clergy of his realm. . . . Now since we are very desirous that the condition of our churches should constantly improve, we are endeavoring by diligent study to restore the knowledge of letters which has been almost lost through the negligence of our ancestors, and by our example we are encouraging those who are able to do so to engage in the study of the liberal arts. In this undertaking we have already, with the aid of God, corrected all the books of the Old and New Testament, whose texts had been corrupted through the ignorance of copyists. Moreover, inspired by the example of our father, Pippin, of blessed memory, who introduced the Roman chants into the churches of his realm, we are now trying to supply the churches with good reading lessons. Finally, since we have found that many of the lessons to be read in the nightly service have been badly compiled and that the texts of these readings are full of mistakes, and the names of their authors omitted, and since we could not bear to listen to such gross errors in the sacred lessons, we have diligently studied how the character of these readings might be improved. Accordingly we have commanded Paul the Deacon, our beloved subject, to undertake this work; that is, to go through the writings of the fathers carefully, and to make selections of the most helpful things from them and put them together into a book, as one gathers occasional flowers from a broad meadow to make a bouquet. And he, wishing to obey us, has read through the treatises and sermons of the various catholic fathers and has picked out the best things. These selections he has copied clearly without mistakes and has arranged in two volumes, providing readings suitable for every feast day throughout the whole year. We have tested the texts of all these readings by our own knowledge, and now authorize these volumes and commend them to all of you to be read in the churches of Christ.

SOURCE: *Bibliotheca rerum Germanicarum*, IV, p. 372, in Oliver J. Thatcher and Edgar H. McNeal, *A Source Book for Mediaeval History* (New York: Charles Scribner's Sons, 1905), pp. 56–57.

Analyze the Document

1. What major problems does Charlemagne identify in this letter?

2. What steps did he take to correct the problems?

3. What role did Paul the Deacon play in the reform efforts?

4. How effective do you think these reforms would have been in achieving his goals?

The scholars also contributed much to text reform.

| Correcting texts |

Before the invention of the printing press, scribes copied books laboriously by hand onto animal skins (called parchment or vellum) with quill pens and ink. (The illustration on page 212 portrays such scribal activity.) Copyists sometimes needed a full day to copy just six to ten manuscript pages. Moreover, there was a shortage of these scribes. Today, we learn to read and write at the same time. During the Middle Ages, however, these two skills were considered separate. Although many people could read, not so many could write.

The problems associated with handwriting only compounded these difficulties. Handwriting was not standardized, and copyists ran words together and employed contractions in an effort to use as little of the precious parchment as possible. Copyists not fluent in Latin (as few were) also made many mistakes. By the eighth century, these errors had been multiplying for several hundred years. The sample manuscript presented in **Figure 7.4a** shows how difficult this script was to read—words are connected and each small mark above the words means that one or more letters were deleted.

The scholars who gathered at Charlemagne's court school attacked these problems in two ways. First, they compared many versions of the same text to prepare a correct rendition. Second, they developed a standardized handwriting so that future copyists could accurately preserve the corrected text. **Figure 7.4b** shows a sample of Carolingian handwriting. Notice that the letters are well formed and the words more clearly spaced than in the Anglo-Saxon sample. This reformed handwriting style reduced errors, thus saving much wisdom for future generations. Moreover, the Carolingian handwriting style formed the basis for our own lowercase letters and the printing-press letters invented 600 years later. The scholars carefully working on texts played a crucial role in preserving the intellectual contributions of the classical world.

STRUGGLE FOR ORDER IN THE CHURCH

Established long before the Roman Empire disintegrated, the church had adopted the Roman administrative system in which bishops presided in dioceses (see Chapter 5). At the local level, priests in parishes cared for their flocks in manorial villages. Parish priests were accountable to their bishops, who in turn were accountable to archbishops, ruling in the largest urban center of the region. Archbishops called their subordinates together periodically to discuss church issues. During these meetings, bishops also learned about new church rules or ideas, which they then took back to their dioceses and communicated to their priests. This whole structure was designed to weave the Christian world and its administrators into a tight fabric of personal ties.

However, this structure sounds better on paper than it worked in practice during these tumultuous early medieval centuries. Communication among churchmen was always disrupted during warfare, and there was no certainty that competent priests and bishops would be appointed when a church office became vacant. Nor did the theoretical structure mean that the church operated independently of local warlords. Even during the years of relative peace under strong Carolingian kings such as Charlemagne, the church was dominated by monarchs, who felt responsible for bringing order to their churches. Nevertheless, during the eighth and ninth centuries, the church planted seeds of order that would fully flower in the High Middle Ages (see Chapter 8).

Monasteries Contribute to an Ordered World

Bringing structure to the ecclesiastical order was not limited to priests, bishops, popes, and kings. As we saw in Chapter 6, Benedict of Nursia (ca. 480–543) had established a monastic rule that brought men and women into obedience to their monastic leader, who in turn obeyed the local bishop. This kind of monastic structure had proved immensely popular. By the late seventh century, monasteries had sprung up throughout the northern regions of Europe, including Anglo-Saxon England. Monasteries for men and women provided one of the few avenues for social mobility for promising individuals, and for women, the monastic life offered the possibility of a voice in church affairs.

Monasteries performed an essential service in copying and preserving texts and learning. Bede and Alcuin were only two of numerous men and women who excelled in scholarship in an age that valued warfare more. The manuscript painting in **Figure 7.5** emphasizes the importance of this monastic learning. The illustration, taken from a Bible copied in a monastery, depicts the abbess (identified as Hitda in the image) offering a manuscript to the woman who commissioned its creation (identified as Saint Walburga).

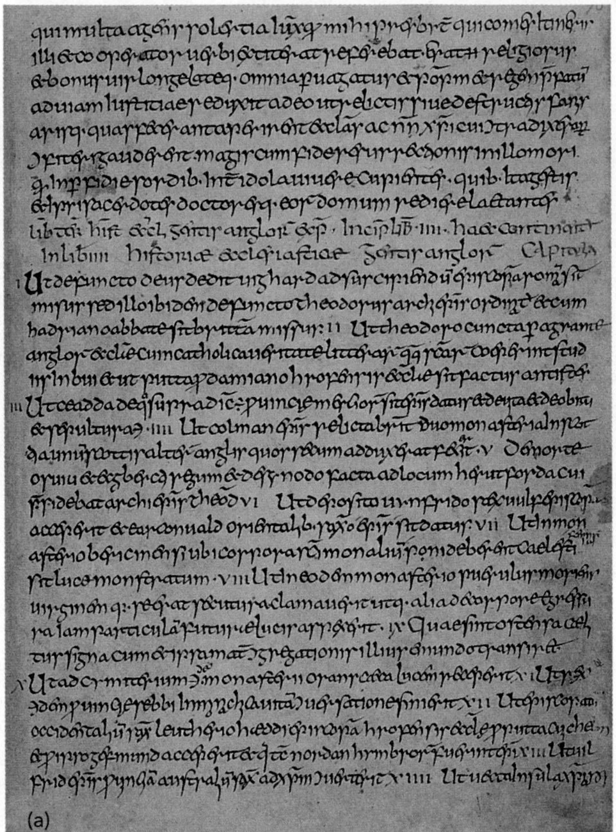

(a)

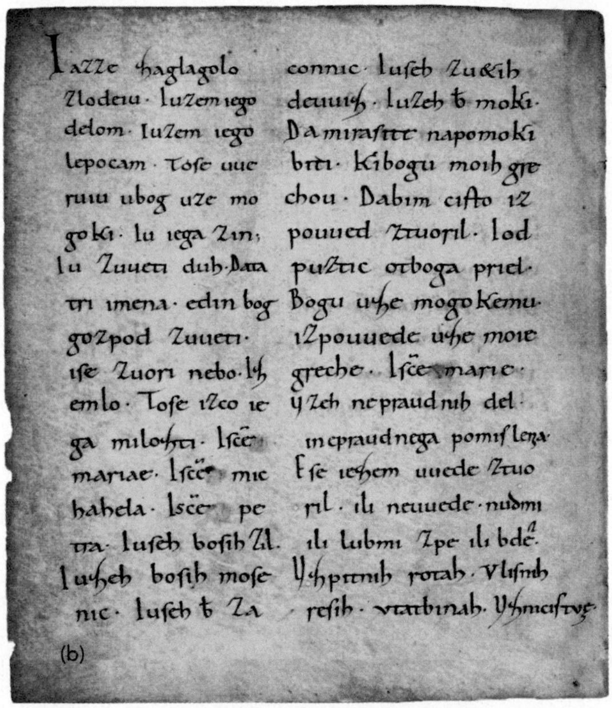

(b)

FIGURE 7.4 Early Medieval Handwriting (a) Merovingian minuscule. (b) Carolingian minuscule. These two samples illustrate how important Charlemagne's handwriting reforms were to make texts legible. In the earlier one from the Merovingian era, each mark above a work indicates a contraction, making it difficult to translate. The Carolingian is more clear and easier to copy without mistakes.

FIGURE 7.5 Literate Nuns Women played a vital role in the preservation of learning in the monasteries as they copied precious manuscripts. Women's valuable contribution is shown in this illustration of Abbess Hitda presenting a manuscript to Saint Walburga.

Walburga was an eighth-century Anglo-Saxon nun who traveled to Germany to establish a monastery to carry out missionary work among the Germans, and this image emphasizes the importance of both monastic missions and the careful transmission of texts from one house to another.

Monasteries also became involved in the growing political issues of the day. As we have seen, nobles and kings exerted control over priests and bishops in their lands, and they believed they could exert the same authority over mon-

Cluniac reform

asteries. To many spiritual reformers this seemed to subordinate spiritual values to secular politics, and in the early tenth century, reformers took a step to correct this imbalance.

In 910, a group of monks persuaded a duke in southern France to found a new monastery at Cluny. The Cluniac founding charter refined the Benedictine rule by insisting that the monastery was exempt from local control—owing only prayers for the donor and, as Duke William wrote in the founding charter, "subject neither to our yoke, nor to that of our

relatives, nor to the sway of royal might, nor to that of any earthly power." To do this, Cluny was established to be directly subordinate to the pope, and all subsequent Cluniac foundations were to be accountable to the abbot at Cluny and, through him, the pope. This tenth-century movement established a strong, reinvigorated monasticism that helped increase papal authority (as we will see in Chapter 8). However, all these developments establishing order and hierarchy in the church would be shaken—and almost destroyed—by a new cycle of violence that engulfed western Europe.

ORDER INTERRUPTED: VIKINGS AND OTHER INVADERS

Although Charlemagne valued much of classical culture, such as education and even the title of emperor, his imperial rule was different from that of an early Roman emperor. His sense of empire remained highly personal. Like the innumerable German kings before him, he saw his kingdom as consisting of subjects loyal to him and to his family, not to an abstract political entity. He viewed his realm as his to divide up among his sons, not as an entity separate from himself and his family. This perception put him firmly in the Germanic tradition. However, in the end it undermined the order that he had built, as the emperor's descendants vied for control of the lands he bequeathed them.

Competing for the Realm: Charlemagne's Descendants

Charlemagne's only son, Louis the Pious (r. 814–840), inherited the empire, but during the course of his reign problems began to appear. Document 7.3 shows a contemporary witness's perception of the growing difficulties. However, the final disintegration of Charlemagne's empire took place after Louis' death, when his kingdom was divided among his surviving three sons: Charles the Bald (r. 843–877), Lothair I (r. 840–855), and Louis the German (r. 843–876). The three

Treaty of Verdun

brothers succumbed to the Germanic tendency toward civil war, each seeking to increase his power at the expense of the others. Their violent clashes struck at the foundation of what Charlemagne had constructed, and they brought untold hardship to the subjects of the once-unified kingdom (see Biography on page 233). **Map 7.4** shows the division of the lands established in the Treaty of Verdun in 843, which effectively destroyed Charlemagne's creation of a united western Europe.

The Treaty of Verdun anticipated some important nationalistic developments in western Europe,

DOCUMENT 7.3

A Comet Predicts Disaster

The collection of letters of the Carolingian dynasty includes correspondence to Charlemagne's son Louis the Pious. This letter, written in 837 to Louis, mentions the devastating raids that eroded his land's security and describes a comet that the author interpreted as a forewarning.

It is believed by almost all the ancient authorities that the appearance of new and unknown heavenly bodies portends to wretched mortals direful and disastrous events, rather than pleasant and propitious ones. The sacred scriptures alone tell of the propitious appearance of a new star; that is, that star which the wise men of the Chaldæans are said to have seen when, conjecturing from its most brilliant light the recent birth of the eternal king, they brought with veneration gifts worthy [of] the acceptance of so great a lord. But the appearance of this star which has lately arisen is reported by all who have seen it to be terrible and malignant. And indeed I believe it presages evils which we have deserved, and foretells a coming destruction of which we are worthy. For what difference does it make whether this coming danger is foretold to the human race by man or angel or star? The important thing is to understand that this appearance of a new body in the heavens is not without significance, but that it is meant to forewarn mortals that they may avert the future evil by repentance and prayers. Thus by the preaching of the prophet Jonah the destruction of the city, which had been threatened by him, was deferred because the inhabitants turned from their iniquities and evil lives. . . . So we trust that merciful God will turn this threatened evil from us also, if we like them repent with our whole hearts. Would that the destruction which the fleet of the Northmen is said to have inflicted upon this realm recently might be regarded as the sufficient occasion for the appearance of this comet, but I fear that it is rather some new distress still to come that is foretold by this terrible omen.

SOURCE: *Bibliotheca rerum Germanicarum*, IV, p. 459, in Oliver J. Thatcher and Edgar H. McNeal, *A Source Book for Mediaeval History* (New York: Charles Scribner's Sons, 1905), pp. 59–60.

Analyze the Document

1. What evidence does the author use to demonstrate that the comet reveals terrestrial events? What does the author conclude about the relationship between the comet and the Northmen's raids?

2. What do you learn about medieval attitudes from this letter?

---

because for the first time, linguistic differences that would divide the lands seemed to be solidifying. When Charles the Bald and Louis the German took oaths (called the Strasbourg Oaths) to support each other in this division, the oaths were recorded in two languages so that the subjects of each would understand them—Charles pledged in a Romance (Latin-derived) language, and Louis spoke in an early Germanic tongue. This showed how the two sections of Charlemagne's empire were already separating culturally and linguistically.

Map 7.4 further suggests how vulnerable the central lands were, because by 870, Charles the Bald and Louis the German had divided up the middle kingdom between them. These central lands—the modern regions of Alsace and Lorraine—remained in dispute off and on into the twentieth century.

Battered by the disruptions of war, the already local economy became even more isolated. The long-distance trade that had begun to enrich the Italian cities as well as the Carolingian kings virtually evaporated, and money went out of circulation. If it had even a brief respite from this dynastic turmoil, the Carolingian Empire might have recovered from mismanagement by Charlemagne's grandsons—but this was not to be. Instead, the weakened empire would succumb to new invaders from the north, south, and east.

Map 7.5 shows the impact of these invasions on Europe. Part of the pressure came from the south, as Muslim maritime raiders sailed across the Mediterranean Sea and penetrated most of the southern coasts of Europe. Sicily fell to the forces of Islam, as did the islands in the western Mediterranean. In spite of Charlemagne's foresight in establishing protective tributary peoples on his eastern flank, eastern Europe reeled from a serious blow with the invasion of the Magyars (now known as Hungarians, a name derived from one group of Magyars). Magyar warlords led their people in raids across Germany, France, and Italy before they settled down and established the kingdom of Hungary. The influx of Muslims and Magyars left an indelible imprint on Europe. However, the invaders who wreaked the most violence, and ultimately settled the most widely, came from the north—bands of Scandinavian warriors known as Vikings.

New invaders

"The Wrath of the Northmen": Scandinavian Life and Values

Back when Charlemagne had forcefully converted the Saxons to Christianity, the people living farther north, in what we know as Denmark, Norway,

Sweden, and Finland, remained pagan. For the most part, these Scandinavians lived on farms rather than in communal villages; they grew crops and kept cows and sheep. The short growing seasons of the north made agriculture especially challenging, and the people supplemented their produce by fishing in the cold, stormy waters of the North Sea. Over time they became skilled seamen and even engaged in long-distance commerce. They traded furs, amber, and honey for finely wrought jewelry, glass, cloth, and weapons. These rugged seamen from the north drew a fine line between trading and pirating and crossed it often. Still, their activities prompted the spread of goods from all over Europe to Scandinavian farms.

Who were these northern peoples? The Scandinavians were Germanic, so their way of life resembled that of the Germanic tribes who had earlier invaded the Roman Empire. The Scandinavians cherished heroic values and sought fame in notable deeds and through the works of poets who recorded those deeds. In their literature—both the poetry and the old Norse prose narratives called **sagas** that preserve their history—we can detect a people who valued words and wit as much as strength and courage. They worshiped gods similar in function to those of the ancient Greeks and Romans, but with different names—Wodin, Thor, and Freya are three deities whose names have been preserved in the English days of the week: Wodin's Day (Wednesday), Thor's Day (Thursday), and Freya's Day (Friday).

The powerful and violent Scandinavians shared another trait with the early Germanic people: a passion for revenge. Although these northerners tried to control their feuding through a system of compensation involving wergeld, they had much less success stemming their tendency toward violence than even the Anglo-Saxons had. A saying from Viking literature succinctly expresses how violent Scandinavian life could be: "A man should never move an inch from his weapons when out in the fields for he never knows when he will need his spear." The sagas, too, recount many a bloody feud. Indeed, it may have been this very violence that prompted numerous Vikings to leave Scandinavia in search of new, more peaceful lands overseas. Some may have left to avoid feuds, and the sagas suggest that others emigrated to escape the growing power of kings who tried to impose peace on many violent men who did not want to submit to authority.

All Northmen did not emigrate to avoid or seek violence. Many were drawn by the wealth that had accumulated in Europe during the prosperous years of the Carolingians and Anglo-Saxons. All . these movements during the ninth and tenth centuries— raids, trading, and settlements—left a deep impact on European life.

Viking ships

MAP 7.4

Partition of the Carolingian Empire, 843—Treaty of Verdun

This map shows the division of Charlemagne's lands under his grandsons.

Explore the Map

1. Which of the three lands was most vulnerable to external attack? Why?

2. Which brother's lands were most susceptible to encroachment from the other kings? Explain.

3. Which of the lands was most desirable? Why?

Map 7.5 shows the Northmen's movements to the western and eastern edges of Europe. Their success in these campaigns stemmed largely from their innovative ships and their skill in navigating them. The Viking ships, one of which is shown in **Figure 7.6,** were marvels of engineering. They were highly valued possessions, guarded with honor and praised in

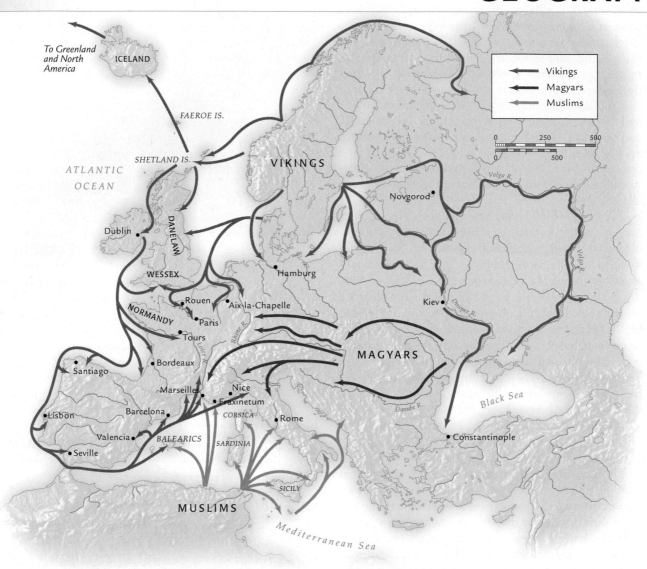

MAP 7.5

Invasions of Europe, Ninth and Tenth Centuries

The arrows on this map show the invasion routes of the major peoples who threatened Europe during the ninth and tenth centuries, along with the dates of their invasions.

Explore the Map

1. Which of the kingdoms shown on **Map 7.4** might have been most destabilized by the invasions?

2. Which rivers did the Vikings use for their invasions? How important was it for the Vikings to have ships that could easily navigate shallow rivers?

3. Based on the invasions (and subsequent settlements), where would you expect Muslim culture to influence the West?

Scandinavian poetry. Often built of oak and designed to flex with the rough waters of the North Atlantic, the vessels each carried between 50 and 100 men who manned oars on either side. A large sail, usually decorated in bright colors, completed the propulsion system.

Figure 7.6 also shows another unique feature of these ships: a shallow keel, the long timber that extended the length of the ship and supported the frame. This feature allowed the Vikings to pilot their ships up rivers during raids. It also let them beach the crafts easily and launch them back out to sea before their surprised victims could mount an effective counterattack. The ships and the ferocity and bravery of the men who sailed them earned the Scandinavians a widespread, fearsome reputation. A ninth-century chronicler wrote how Northmen "inflicted much harm," and he sharply captures the suffering: "The steel of the heathen glistened; excessive heat; a famine followed," as too many were dead to bring in a good crop. Many a European repeated the oft-quoted Anglo-Saxon prayer for God to "save us from the wrath of the Northmen."

Viking Travels and Conquests

As **Map 7.5** suggests, the unmatched navigational skills of the Vikings gave them access to many parts of Europe. Some Northmen traveled east down the Dnieper River to the Black Sea and the rich city of Constantinople, at times settling along this rich trade route. The oldest Russian chronicle contains the story of an invitation to the Northmen to come and rule, for there was no order in their land. As we saw in Chapter 6, the Scandinavians established a strong state centered in Kiev. Other Vikings traveled to Constantinople and served as soldiers of fortune in the Byzantine emperor's service. Throughout the tenth century, the emperor's personal guard—the Varangians—was composed entirely of Scandinavians. The most famous of these—Harald Sigurdson of Norway (r. 1046–1066)—grew so wealthy while serving in Constantinople that when he returned to Norway he became a great king. Archaeologists have discovered early-eleventh-century Byzantine coins in Norway that may have come from the hoard that Harald shipped home.

Harald's hoard of coins was not unique. Archaeologists have found some 1,700 treasure hoards, each containing on average about three hundred coins. These (primarily silver) coins were mostly eastern—Byzantine or Islamic. Great piles of treasure like these continue to draw our imagination, but the fact that so many were simply buried tells us that the Scandinavian eastern trade in the eighth and ninth centuries did not contribute much to the overall European economy. Most gold was not circulated; it was either hidden during the violence that dominated the age or used as jewelry to show status. For example, the coins shown in **Figure 7.7** on page 234 were joined to hooks so that the coins could be worn as jewelry instead of circulated as currency. This hoard of solid gold also indicates the volume of wealth that was plundered by the Vikings in their raids. However, great wealth like this may have contributed to the status of kings like Harald, but it did not improve the plight of hardworking Scandinavian farmers. Trade needs peace to benefit more people, and peace would have to wait.

Still other Scandinavians sailed west across the North Atlantic, seeking other lands and wealth. Although some Europeans may have imagined the world as flat, people who sailed westward out of sight of land and who watched ships return from the eastern horizon knew better. Like many ancients, Scandinavian sailors perceived the world as round. With these views, Scandinavians sailed confidently into the open seas in their sturdy, versatile ships. They established permanent settlements in Iceland and a settlement in Greenland that lasted for centuries. In the late tenth century, an expedition led by the Norwegian Leif Erikson (970–1035) traveled all the way to North America, which Erikson dubbed Vinland. Although the Vikings did not establish a permanent settlement there, their arrival on this distant coast counts as one of history's most extraordinary feats of sailing, and the difficult passage earned the captain the name "Leif the Lucky."

As the Vikings explored Greenland and North America, they naturally encountered peoples who already lived there. Because they considered these natives inferior, they called them by the contemptuous term *Skraelings*, which defies exact translation. They used this term to refer to Eskimos in northern Greenland and tribes they encountered in North America. The Scandinavians who settled in southern

Western explorations

FIGURE 7.6 Oseberg Viking Ship, ca. 800 This splendid, sleek Viking ship was buried as part of a funeral ceremony. Two women were interred with the ship, along with their precious goods. They must have been highborn to have been buried in such lavish style.

Greenland mostly ignored their neighbors to the north. In North America, the encounter proved more dramatic. At first, these tribes and the Scandinavians engaged in some trading. Amerindians especially valued the Vikings' red cloth and milk. They also coveted the Scandinavians' weapons, but the newcomers refused to give them up.

Relations between the two peoples soon soured. Several confrontations occurred in which parties on both sides were killed. The sagas described one incident in which Amerindians in skin-covered boats and armed with arrows and catapults attacked. In another case, only the courage of a pregnant Scandinavian woman saved the day for the Vikings. According to the story, the woman picked up a sword and slapped it on her bare breast as the natives charged her. Unnerved by this odd sight, the attackers fled, and the woman won praise for her bravery. After this confrontation, the Vikings concluded that, although the North American land was bountiful, they could not live there safely because of the ferocity of its inhabitants. They abandoned North America and returned to Greenland, Iceland, and other areas where they could settle more easily.

Within western Europe, Vikings (or their descendants) made permanent conquests in northern France (Normandy), Sicily, and England. As previously mentioned, one group of Vikings, the Danes, had conquered most of northeast England by the middle of the ninth century, until they were stopped by Alfred the Great in 886. However, the British Isles remained a tempting target for the Northmen. In the summer of 1016, a great fleet led by King Swein of Denmark and his son Canute sailed for England. The Anglo-Saxon king Edmund Ironside (r. 1016) was beaten, and Canute became king of a united England. He was an able ruler and was one of many who demonstrated that the Northmen were effective administrators as well as skilled warriors. In 1066, the Norwegian king Harald Sigurdson—the enterprising Varangian who brought a fortune back from Constantinople—set himself a final goal of conquering all of England. He died in the attempt, and the sources say that the only English land he claimed was the "seven feet of soil" required to bury this tall warrior.

European settlements

An Age of Invasions: Assessing the Legacy

The invasions from the north, south, and east brought sporadic violence to western Europe for about two hundred years. With this kind of pressure, Viking, Magyar, and Muslim conquests all disrupted the newly established order that had reigned in Europe for more than a century. In Charlemagne's Frankish Empire, the onslaughts from many foreign fronts accelerated the disintegration initiated by the emperor's feuding

descendants, and the central authority envisioned by Charlemagne could not hold.

Learning also suffered as people devoted more and more attention and resources to war. Charlemagne's great palace school in Aachen, which had drawn scholars from all over Europe, ceased functioning. Again, learning took place primarily behind monastery walls. However, this time monks and nuns had the benefit of texts that had been corrected during Charlemagne's rule. In time, these carefully preserved sources of knowledge would once more play a role in centers of learning, but not until peace returned to western Europe.

Finally, order in the church crumbled under the tenth-century turmoil. In Ireland and on the western coasts of Britain, the magnificent Celtic monasteries were almost completely destroyed by Vikings looking for plunder. The invaders damaged monasteries in France as well. This violence took a massive personal toll on men and women seeking God. As just one example, texts tell of houses of women who feared that the Vikings would rape them and thus violate their vows of virginity. To avert this disaster, the women cut off their noses and lips as the Vikings approached their gates and greeted the invaders with mutilated faces.

The church structure of parishes and bishops under the control of the pope also deteriorated. Bishops and priests placed themselves under the protection of local lords instead of looking to Rome for help. Sometimes lords simply took over church lands, as a Frankish law declared: "because of threats of war and the invasions of some of the border tribes, we shall . . . take possession of a part of the land belonging to the church . . . for the support of our army." The church itself became fragmented in the service of

THE EARLY MIDDLE AGES

ca. 731	Bede, *Ecclesiastical History of the English People*
786–809	Harun al-Rashid caliph in Baghdad
800	Charlemagne crowned emperor in Rome
814	Death of Charlemagne
814–840	Louis the Pious rules
843	Treaty of Verdun divides Carolingian Empire
871–901	Alfred the Great rules England
910	Monastery at Cluny founded
ca. 1000	Leif Erikson travels to North America
1016–1035	Canute rules Denmark and England
1060	Norwegians convert to Christianity

KEY DATES

BIOGRAPHY

Dhuoda, Bernard, & William
(ca. 840)

The political turmoil that marked the breakup of the empire assembled by Charlemagne destroyed the family of an educated, pious, remarkable woman named Dhuoda. This young woman was married at the palace of Emperor Louis the Pious in 824 to Bernard of Septimania, a relative of the emperor who served as a knight in Louis' court. Although marriage to such a high-born man seemed a good match, it was not to be a happy companionship. At first, Dhuoda joined her husband in his travels, but then Bernard sent her away to live in a small town in the south of France. The sources do not explain his reasoning—it could have been anything from personal to political. Nevertheless, he visited her periodically. In the meantime, Dhuoda spent her days quietly, immersed in books and prayer. She also followed the fortunes of her husband avidly, writing, "I rejoice in his campaigns." Dhuoda and Bernard had two sons: William, born in 826, and Bernard Jr., born in 841.

In spite of Louis the Pious's advocacy of marriage and his opposition to concubinage, his kinsman Bernard was one of many nobles who took it as their right to have many lovers. Bernard was not a loyal husband to Dhuoda during his absences, and he was particularly indiscreet in his choice of a companion. Accused of committing adultery with Louis' wife and of other treasonous conspiracy against his king, he lost the position of governor of Septimania. His relatives, too,

paid dearly for his transgressions. Bernard's sister, a nun, was accused of sorcery, sealed in a wine cask, and thrown into the river to drown. His brother was blinded and imprisoned after being accused of participating in Bernard's treason. In the Middle Ages, families were considered linked together in innocence and guilt, and even the life of a nun could be jeopardized by the misbehavior of her brother.

Bernard's fall from grace foretold his inability to negotiate the civil wars that erupted among Charlemagne's grandsons after Louis' death in 840. Just as Bernard's sister had paid the highest price for his infidelity, so Dhuoda and her sons would suffer because of Bernard's actions. In 841, Bernard returned to Dhuoda to attend the birth of their second son, Bernard Jr. He then took both boys from her and left. To curry favor with his new overlord, Charles the Bald, Bernard gave his 14-year-old son, William, to Charles as a hostage.

Dhuoda missed her boys acutely, especially William. In 841 she began writing a book of instructions for him, which she completed in 843. The book not only reveals her love for William but also reflects the central values of the ninth century. Dhuoda's writings urged her son to have faith in God and in the feudal ties that bound men together. She warned him, "Never let the idea of disloyalty against your lord be born or thrive in your heart." She also encouraged him to read, to give it the "same attention and zeal that others give to . . . a game of backgammon."

Yet all of Dhuoda's care and advice could not save this family caught in the crossfire of feudal conflict. Bernard shifted his allegiance from his own lord, Charles, to Pepin and was captured as he tried to leave for Pepin's army. Charles accused Bernard of treason and had him publicly beheaded. Fulfilling Germanic ideas of vengeance, young William tried to avenge his father's death, but Charles executed the 24-year-old youth. Like so many noble Carolingian families, Bernard, William, and Dhuoda were damaged by the jockeying for power wrought by the fall of Charlemagne's empire. In medieval families, political developments profoundly influenced personal matters. Even by devoting oneself to God, as Bernard's sister did, or studying and writing in solitude, as Dhuoda did, women could not escape political storms when their lives were joined to men who allied themselves with the wrong lord. Dhuoda's tender care and eloquent missives tell us of both the hopes and the tragedies of a typical Carolingian family. It is only through her love and thoroughness in writing to William that we have such a poignant glimpse of medieval life.

A Carolingian Family Tragedy

Connecting People & Society

1. How was Dhuoda's life affected by the turmoil of the breakdown of Charlemagne's central authority?

2. How important were marriage and family ties to medieval people, for both good and ill?

3. What does this life suggest about women's literacy?

---

war. In the end, the notion of a Christian Europe with both a pope and an emperor at its head disappeared into the wreckage of lives and property as the invasions dragged on.

In the eleventh century, the violence at last spent itself. The traditional Scandinavian farming and trading life was easier to conduct in peace than in war.

And as the invaders settled in newly conquered territories, they absorbed some of the structures already in place there. The Scandinavians also eventually converted to Christianity and thus became fully integrated into Christian Europe. Harald Sigurdson's brother, Olaf (r. 1016–1030), for example, converted the

Vikings convert

FIGURE 7.7 Viking Jewelry For a long time the Vikings, like the Germanic tribes, treasured precious metals like gold and silver and wore them as signs of status. This hoard reveals that even when the Vikings acquired gold and silver coins, they fitted them with clasps and wore, rather than spending, them.

together in personal relationships. In a modified version of the ties that bound the Germanic tribes, these structures were personal, tying each person to a superior. In the modern West, we often judge a society in terms of the freedom of its citizens, but in the Middle Ages, social order was defined by connections rather than degree of freedom. All men and women—from the peasantry all the way up to the king—were connected to someone above or below them in a contractual system of mutual obligations. The obligations did not fall equally on everyone, but each person had explicitly defined commitments to someone else. Everyone in society expected to live within a hierarchy that ordered nature, the church, and society. This social order was not a product of rational planning but instead developed slowly over centuries—and the chaos of the tenth century escalated the development.

Peasants and Lords: Mutual Obligations on the Medieval Manor

Manors developed from the agricultural estates of the old Roman Empire (described in Chapter 5) and the new divisions of the land made by early medieval kings. In various forms, manors existed throughout the Mediterranean world, including the Byzantine and Islamic empires. In western Europe during the Carolingian Empire, manors developed a characteristic pattern of **serfs** and lords that marked the medieval West for almost the next millennium. Virtually all manors consisted of the lord's home and outbuildings (barn, mill, etc.) and at least one village in which the peasants resided and worked.

Figure 7.8 shows the layout of a typical manor. Notice that unlike in today's farm communities, where farmers live on their cropland and travel into the village, medieval | Manor layout | peasants lived close together in the village and traveled out to their fields. The fields were organized in strips, with each peasant family using some and the lord owning a large number himself. The church, too, owned some strips for the priest's support. However, the pasture, woodlands, and water were as important as the cultivated land, because they supported the village's animals.

The survival of the peasants depended not only on the crops they grew on their plowed strips but also on their wise use of the other spaces identified in **Figure 7.8**. Serfs grazed their oxen and working horses, as well as their sheep and goats, on the common pastureland. They relied on the large draft animals to help with the hard labor of plowing, especially in the heavy, clay soils of northern Europe. The animals also provided essential leather and wool for clothing and other uses. In our age of cotton and synthetic fabrics, it is easy to forget how important animals were for medieval clothing. Farm animals supplemented a grain diet

Norwegians by force of arms and his own charisma in the early eleventh century. Leif Erikson "the Lucky" introduced Christianity to Iceland and Greenland around the same time. Canute, who ruled England, Denmark, and Norway, converted to Christianity and brought priests from England to complete the conversion of the Northmen.

The Vikings may have settled down, but the centralization that had unraveled through the centuries of chaos would not be restored easily. However, throughout this time people had created another kind of order—one that was not imposed by royal officials, like Charlemagne's *missi dominici,* traveling through the land. Instead, people bound themselves to each other in solemn contracts like the one quoted at the beginning of this chapter. These local ties formed a new order from which the medieval world would build again.

MANORS AND FEUDAL TIES: ORDER EMERGING FROM CHAOS

As early as the eighth century, Carolingian nobles began to develop mutual contracts that bound people as well, with milk and cheese (especially from goats) and some meat. Peasants ate very little meat because their animals were too valuable to be disposed of in this way. However, sometimes the lord gave the peasants his unwanted portions of meat (tails, hooves, or entrails) to make soup.

The forests of the manor also played a key role in village life. Although the trees and the game animals belonged to the lord, peasants were allowed to gather fallen branches as firewood. Pigs could browse in the forest as long as the lord got a share of the pork. Finally, in times of hunger, villagers gathered acorns in the oak forests and ground them into flour to make bread.

Medieval European peasants were at the bottom of the social order in that they had obligations to people above them, but no one below them owed them any commitments. Most medieval peasants were personally free (that is, they were not slaves), but they were bound to the land. When a lord received a land grant from the king, he also gained the service of the peasants who worked the land. Peasants who were semifree in this way—that is, personally free yet not free to move from their village—were called serfs.

Beyond their obligation to remain on the land, serfs owed their lords many other things—roughly divided into goods

Serfs' obligations and labor. For example, they had to give the lord a percentage of their crops or whatever livestock they raised—perhaps a tenth of their grain, a piglet, a number of eggs from their hens, or some of the cheese made from the milk of their goats. They also owed him their labor. On some manors, serfs had to work as many as three days a week on the lord's demesne lands, those set aside for his own consumption and use. Serfs had to plant his crops, build roads, erect walls or buildings, dig ditches, and do anything else the lord ordered. Serfs did not owe military service—fighting was the privilege of the nobility.

Peasant women worked as hard as the men. They did all the domestic chores, toiled in the fields, tended vegetable gardens, and fed the animals. In addition, they performed the time-consuming task of producing cloth. Women sheared the sheep, cleaned and prepared the wool, spun it into thread, and wove it into cloth. As serfs, women also shared the labor obligations of their husbands. They, too, owed the lord a portion of what they produced (from cloth to garden vegetables) and owed the lord and lady of the manor a certain amount of their labor for domestic chores, spinning, and weaving. Peasant children

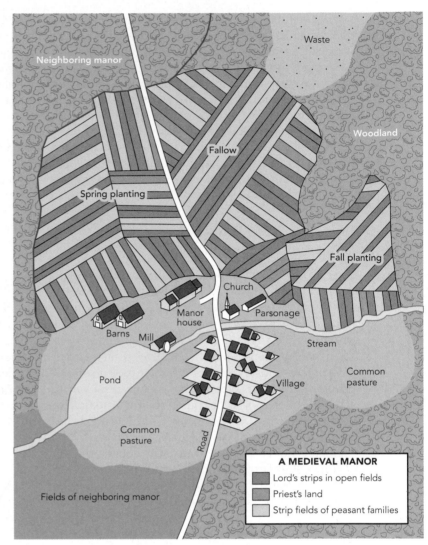

FIGURE 7.8 Medieval Manor This drawing of a hypothetical medieval manor shows how peasants lived in villages and worked strips of cultivated land. Notice all the important features of the manor, including pastures, mill, church, and woodlands.

bore obligations as well. Children as young as 6 were responsible for the care of their younger siblings, and older children worked in the fields alongside their parents.

In exchange for peasant services, lords provided things that required a large investment of capital: mills, barns, ovens, large draft animals, and the like. However, the lords primarily offered justice and protection to their serfs. In times of war, for example, the presence of a well-armed warrior and his followers could make the difference between a village's survival and its destruction. When an attacking army neared the vicinity, peasants with their flocks rushed inside the armed fortress of the lord to stay until the battle ended. However, they often had to watch as their crops and villages were raided and burned, and when the war ended they were left to begin again.

All serfs did not enter voluntarily into this contract in which they exchanged their labor for safety (especially since safety was never absolutely ensured). Sometimes armed lords who needed their lands cultivated forced peasants into servitude on their estates. Late in the Middle Ages, as we will see in Chapter 9, many serfs decided the benefits of protection were not worth the price. However, the newly restored order that established the medieval structure was built on the labor of peasants bound to work the land, which was divided up into manors—agricultural estates under the control of a lord.

Noble Warriors: Feudal Obligations Among the Elite

The medieval manors were structured and organized to provide food for everyone. However, in the medieval mind these manors served an additional function: They were the economic and agricultural base which supported the fighting forces that allowed rulers like Charlemagne and Alfred to conduct their campaigns. Armies were expensive. It took about ten peasant families to support one mounted soldier, so an efficient manorial organization was essential to produce an army. However, the Carolingians developed a way to organize the fighting men as well. Like the serfs, noble warriors were also bound to their lord in a system of mutual obligation. The legal formula that opened this chapter bound a noble fighting man. This system was a fluid one—each contract could be different, and some men might be bound to more than one lord. Nevertheless, a general system

slowly developed that was based on the exchange of land for military service. In its most general sense, this system—which historians in the sixteenth century called feudalism—formed the political structure of the elites in medieval society. Many historians today prefer to avoid the term *feudalism* because it seems to suggest a clearly organized structure instead of the loose system that varied from place to place. Regardless of modern disagreements, it is clear that medieval people saw themselves linked in a chain of mutual obligation; only the forms of those obligations were varied.

As we saw in Chapter 6, men in the Germanic tribes saw themselves as linked in loyalty to their chief. This was a personal tie that bound fighting men together. Charlemagne's grandfather, Charles Martel (r. 714–741) (who defeated the Muslims at the Battle of Tours, as we described in Chapter 6), seems to have at times joined these personal ties to the land that people occupied. Charles had seen the virtues of having an army made up of heavily armed men on horseback to replace the more lightly armed citizen foot soldiers that made up the Anglo-Saxon armies, for example. But armed, mounted knights were expensive. Instead of trying to raise money to support an army of this kind, Charles drew from what he had in abundance: land. He granted huge tracts of land, including the serfs who lived on them, to his followers in exchange for their military service. This process laid the foundation for a complex system that later brought order to the fighting men of the land.

The feudal system that grew out of Charles Martel's innovation bound men together in a series of mutual obligations, but what set it apart from other bonds of loyalty was the linking of loyal service with land. When a nobleman bound himself in service to a lord, he swore a solemn oath of fealty (that is, to be faithful to his vows and his lord) by placing his hands between those of his lord. The nobleman now became the lord's **vassal**—bound to him for life. In return, the vassal would receive his **fief**—usually land, but it might be something else that would generate enough income to support the vassal. The illustration in **Figure 7.9** cleverly portrays

Lords and vassals

FIGURE 7.9 Vassal Receiving Fief This intricate drawing captures the complexities of the relationship between vassals and lords. The vassal points to the grain as a symbol of the land he receives in exchange for his loyalty, which he demonstrates by placing his hands between his lord's palms.

the solemn bonds. The standing vassal, shown with four arms, simultaneously places his hands between those of his lord and points to the stalks of wheat that stand for his fief.

The lord (who could be a king or any other man with land to bestow) gave away enough land to support the lifestyle of his noble vassals. These nobles' main function was warfare; they did not work the land as serfs did. Later, vassals took on other titles, like baron or duke, that showed their position relative to other greater or lesser vassals, but the word *vassal* remained a general term that applied to all noblemen bound in contract and loyalty to a lord. Theoretically, a vassal only held his fief as long as he was able to fight for his lord, but in fact, by the ninth century, vassals expected to be able to pass their fiefs on to their sons. A son was expected to place his hands between those of his lord and renew his father's vows before he took full possession of the fief, but as fiefs became hereditary possessions, the lord's control over his fiefs was reduced.

Each party owed something to the other. Lords owed their vassals "maintenance" (usually land) and military protection. In recalling the old Germanic legal principle of compurgation, the lord was also to act as his vassals' advocate in public court. Vassals owed lords "aid and counsel." The primary aid took the form of military service. Just as serfs owed their own lords labor, nobles owed their superiors specified periods of fighting time; these varied, but an average length of service might be forty days a year. Vassals also owed monetary aid. When a lord incurred certain expenses, such as for his daughter's wedding or his son's knighting, the vassals paid extra taxes to fund the event. In addition, vassals owed their lord counsel, or advice at the lord's command. This obligation, along with the witenagemot, paved the way for the parliamentary system that developed later in the Middle Ages (see Chapter 8). Both parties owed the other fealty—that is, good faith to do the other no harm—and this was granted by a solemn kiss that sealed the pact.

Because this was a system of mutual obligation, if either party breached the contract, the arrangement could be rendered null. For instance, if a vassal failed to fight or give counsel, the lord could declare his land forfeit and give it to someone else. Of course, enforcement became complicated when armies of men were involved, but the system did establish the idea of the primacy of contract law that bound people together in a more ordered society. However, because the feudal system varied from place to place and across time, historians disagree on exactly how formal or influential these contractual bonds were. Nevertheless, in the most general sense, feudal ties joined older kinship bonds in linking medieval warriors and their families together.

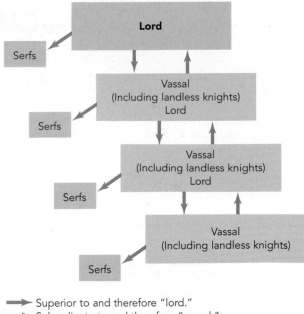

> → Superior to and therefore "lord."
> → Subordinate to and therefore "vassal."
> The same man can be both lord and vassal.

FIGURE 7.10 Feudal Organization Medieval society was tied together by mutual obligations. This chart shows how vassals could be both lord and vassal, while serfs owed allegiance to only one master.

In this system, a nobleman could be both a vassal to someone over him and a lord to someone under him. A powerful vassal who had received large tracts of land from his overlord might offer portions of it to other nobles who, in turn, would become his vassals. The lowest vassal in this structure was still a lord to the serfs who worked the land (who were lords to no one). Medieval people did not find ambiguity in these flexible terms, because the words *lord* and *vassal* were not absolute—they expressed a legal condition that defined one person's relationship with another. The chart in **Figure 7.10** outlines the complexities of this relationship of superior and subordinate.

Feudal complexities

These feudal bonds were remarkably flexible because they were adapted to each place, time, and individual. Furthermore, the feudal ties kept society from disintegrating altogether in the face of the invasions and decentralization of the ninth century. In spite of these benefits, feudal ties also had features that further decentralized society, and even contributed to increased violence. In most cases, the vow of fealty was not necessarily exclusive, and in time the notion of personal loyalty became secondary to the idea of acquiring more property. Many vassals would serve different lords in exchange for different fiefs. Several sources showing the obligations and growing ambiguities of the feudal ties are excerpted in Document 7.4.

DOCUMENT 7.4

Feudal Relationships Grow Complex

The following documents describe some legal contracts that created feudal ties. The first presents a legal form that arose in the mid-eighth century and that shows the establishment of the feudal relationship. The second and third entries from the early fourteenth century describe the later stages of the relationship: The second explains the mutual obligations established in the ritual of homage, and the third reveals that the vassal in this case held lands from four different lords, showing the increasing complexity of the feudal relationship.

1. To my great lord, (name), I, (name). Since, as was well known, I had not wherewith to feed and clothe myself, I came to you and told you my wish, to commend myself to you and to put myself under your protection. I have now done so, on the condition that you shall supply me with food and clothing as far as I shall merit by my services, and that as long as I live I shall perform such services for you as are becoming to a freeman, and shall never have the right to withdraw from your power and protection, but shall remain under them all the days of my life. It is agreed that if either of us shall try to break this compact he shall pay—solidi, and the compact shall still hold.

2. The tenant [vassal] should place his clasped hands between the hands of the lord; by this is signified, on the part of the lord, protection, defense, and guarantee; on the part of the vassal, reverence and subjection.

3. I, John of Toul, make known that I am the liege man of the lady Beatrice, countess of Troyes, and of her son, Theobald, count of Champagne, against every creature, living or dead, saving my allegiance to lord Enjorand of Coucy, lord John of Arcis, and the count of Grandpré. If it should happen that the count of Grandpré should be at war with the countess and count of Champagne on his own quarrel, I will aid the count of Grandpré in my own person, and will send to the count and the countess of Champagne the knights whose service I owe to them for the fief which I hold of them. But if the count of Grandpré shall make war on the countess and the count of Champagne on behalf of his friends and not in his own quarrel, I will aid in my own person the countess and count of Champagne, and will send one knight to the count of Grandpré for the service which I owe him for the fief which I hold of him, but I will not go myself into the territory of the count of Grandpré to make war on him.

SOURCE: *Formulae Turonenses*, no. 43; *De legibus et consuetudinibus Angliae*, 35; *Tabularium Campaniae*, in Oliver J. Thatcher and Edgar H. McNeal, *A Source Book for Mediaeval History* (New York: Charles Scribner's Sons, 1905), pp. 343–344, 364–365.

Analyze the Document

1. What were the mutually binding obligations that joined the parties to the relationship?

2. What responsibilities did each party have?

3. How did the vassal in the third document resolve potentially competing conflicts of interest?

The chart in **Figure 7.11** shows the complexities of vassals who served several masters. Of course, one can readily see the potential for divided loyalties built into this structure. What if both lords of one vassal were at war? Sometimes—very practically—a vassal followed the lord who gave him the largest fief. At other times, the vassal's first vow was the one that bound. Other vassals probably just tried to back the lord most likely to win the engagement. Beginning in the eleventh century in France and spreading from there over the next centuries, kings tried to establish the concept of **liege lord**—that is, the lord who could claim unreserved loyalty. Kings were able to enforce this with mixed success—the kings in England were successful, but in Germany they were less so. These systems of divided loyalty strained attempts to exert central authority in western Europe, so while feudal ties reduced the chaos, they still preserved some measure of violence. No doubt most people did not reflect upon these abstract considerations as they lived their lives. Feudal ties became simply one more reality of life in the Middle Ages.

Merriment, Marriage, and Medicine: A Noble's Life

The daily life of the nobility revealed the sense of community engendered by the feudal system. The feudal lords with their wives and children lived together with crowds of their own vassals and their servants. All ate together at long tables in the common hall of the manor house. The nobles amused themselves with music, dance, and games like backgammon, chess, and dice. Archaeologists have even found loaded dice in an Anglo-Saxon excavation, so cheating at such games is not a modern invention. In times of peace, both noblemen and noblewomen indulged their passion for hunting with hawks, horses, and hounds. Hunting was intended to keep their skills sharp for their real purpose: warfare.

Just as in the Germanic tribes, noble families in the feudal system were bound to each other by the important ties of marriage. Yet, the institution of marriage changed during the Carolingian years. In the tradition of the Germanic tribes, Charlemagne had taken a number of wives—

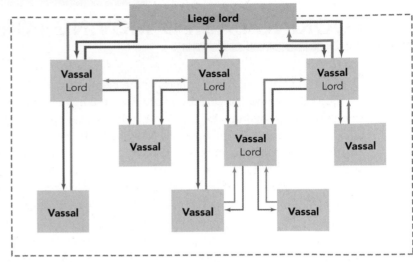

Superior to and therefore "lord."
Subordinate to and therefore "vassal."
Theoretically superior to all.

The same man can be both lord and vassal.

FIGURE 7.11 Feudal Complexities The chart in **Figure 7.10** illustrates the ideal feudal relationship. In reality, however, as this figure shows, vassals often had several masters and multiple vassals of their own. All were to owe allegiance to the liege lord. But the system's complexities, in the form of competing alliances, tended to promote violence and instability.

Marriage ties renouncing the marriage ties with one in order to marry another—and he even kept a number of concubines at the same time. However, under his religious son Louis the Pious, churchmen began to regulate the marriage bond, emphasizing monogamy and urging married men to give up their concubines. Although the church intruded more and more into the marriage relationship, it never persuaded all noblemen to make this sacrifice. Nonetheless, the church's interventions enhanced the status of the legal wife and made it essential that she, and only she, produce an heir. As a new bride came to the wedding with great ceremony, and as she emerged from the nuptial bedroom in the morning, crowds cheered the consummation of a marriage that everyone hoped would produce offspring. As highly placed wives, noblewomen exerted a significant degree of autonomy. Many texts suggest that such women were responsible for managing the royal treasury. Furthermore, when their husbands were away on military campaigns, noblewomen managed all the affairs of the manors—including defending the castles from hostile invaders when necessary.

Noble girls married young, many of them between the ages of 12 and 14, if not younger. A girl who was betrothed early might be raised in the household of her fiancé's family until she was deemed old enough for the marriage to be consummated. As they awaited their wedding day, girls learned household management, cloth making, and often reading and writing. Women could also inherit and hold land, but they still owed the feudal obligations that structured this society. If an unmarried girl's father died, she was placed under the wardship of the lord her father had served, because her future husband would become that lord's vassal. Widows, too, became wards until their lord arranged another marriage for them, but lords at times relinquished their rights of wardship in exchange for money, so wealthy widows might well control their own lives. Orphans were under the lord's control until they grew old enough to take their place in the lord's army or marry someone who could do so.

Germanic women had traditionally been responsible for medical care, and this continued through the early medieval period. Medicines consisted primarily **Medicine** of herbs, as suggested by the manuscripts from this era that preserve what are probably long-treasured medical recipes. Nasturtium, for example, was recommended for indigestion, wormwood for sleep disorders, and frankincense and oil for sore hands and fingers.

Even food was considered medicinal if prepared properly; therefore, women were also in charge of designing a healthful diet. Just as our notion of a balanced diet changes with the latest research, early medieval ideas about nutritious eating relied on contemporary understanding of health. For example, people during this period continued to hold the classical idea that health depended on a balance between the body's "humors": wet, dry, cold, and hot. A proper diet must be "tempered"—that is, feature a balance of foods in each category of humor. For example, beans were considered "cold," so they were supplemented by "hot" spices to balance them. Likewise, illness was treated by correcting an imbalance of the humors. For example, if a person was considered too hot, the patient was given predominantly "cold" foods to bring his or her humors back into balance. This system also applied to the preparation of food. Charlemagne's biographer tells about the emperor's growing "dislike" of his physician after Charlemagne was forced to forgo his beloved roast meat in favor of boiled fare. Food and medicine were considered interchangeable in this era, and knowledgeable men and women alike prescribed medicinal diets.

LOOKING BACK & MOVING FORWARD

Summary   At the beginning of the eighth century, the Germanic tribes that had precipitated the collapse of the Roman Empire in the West established kingdoms and converted to Christianity. Monasteries revealed the intellectual treasures from the classical world that they had painstakingly preserved in their libraries. Kings began to forge an effective synthesis between Germanic, Roman, and Christian cultures and create vigorous new societies governed by the rule of law. The culmination of these developments was Charlemagne's assumption of the imperial crown; it seemed as if a unified empire would exist again in western Europe.

However, the ninth- and tenth-century invasions by Scandinavians, Muslims, and Magyars broke down this progress, introducing another dark period of violence and retreat to local authority. Yet, the settlement of the Northmen and their conversion to Christianity paved the way for a new restoration of European order. This time, rulers did not have to reinvent the political and economic structures of Europe; they simply had to restore them. They built on a decentralized order that had flourished in the dark days after the fall of the Carolingian Empire. This included a manorial system that secured effective agricultural production and a feudal system that supplied a political organization uniting people in law and loyalty. In the late eleventh century, it remained for kings, emperors, and popes to take charge and bring about the high point of medieval culture in western Europe.

KEY TERMS

compurgation,   *p. 214*

ordeal,   *p. 214*

wergeld,   *p. 215*

common law,   *p. 217*

statutory law,   *p. 217*

trivium,   *p. 224*

quadrivium,   *p. 224*

sagas,   *p. 229*

serfs,   *p. 234*

vassal,   *p. 236*

fief,   *p. 236*

liege lord,   *p. 238*

REVIEW, ANALYZE, & CONNECT TO TODAY

REVIEW THE PREVIOUS CHAPTER

Chapter 6—"A World Divided"—described the breakup of the Roman Empire into western kingdoms, the Byzantine Empire, and the Muslim world. It also described the three cultures as the old Mediterranean world split.

1. Review Germanic culture and values. Which elements did Charlemagne, Alfred the Great, and the Vikings retain?

2. Compare the illustration on page 212 with that in Figure 6.3. Both portray Saint Matthew, but in very different ways. Explain how the differences reflect Germanic and Roman culture.

ANALYZE THIS CHAPTER

Chapter 7—"The Struggle to Bring Order"—traces the slow establishment of order in Europe as kings instituted laws for their kingdoms and as Charlemagne forged a new empire in western Europe. It also describes new destruction as migrating tribes again wreaked havoc on the continent.

1. How did Alfred the Great and Charlemagne structure the administration of their respective kingdoms? How did the large size of Charlemagne's empire pose particular challenges for the ruler?

2. Review Charlemagne's diplomatic negotiations with the Byzantine Empire and the 'Abbasid caliphate. Why did each ruler act the way he/she did?

3. What was the basis for papal claims of supremacy over the church? What helped the church exert an order over its organization, and what forces prevented it from doing so?

4. Review the intellectual accomplishments of the Anglo-Saxon and Carolingian kingdoms.

5. Review the invasions of the ninth and tenth centuries. Who invaded? Where did they go, and what impact did they have on European society?

CONNECT TO TODAY

Think about the ways in which wars disrupt societies and the ways in which societies are once again reordered following warfare.

1. What similarities are there between the turmoil described in this chapter and the disruptions of war experienced by present-day countries such as Iraq, Afghanistan, and the Balkan nations? What differences are there?

2. What lessons can we learn from the past as we compare and contrast attempts to reorder societies today with the parallel efforts of the early Middle Ages?

BEYOND THE CLASSROOM

BRINGING ORDER WITH LAWS AND LEADERSHIP

McCormick, Michael. *Origins of the European Economy: Communications and Commerce,* A.D. *300–900.* Cambridge: Cambridge University Press, 2002. A comprehensive book on international trade that examines the patterns of Mediterranean commerce. Well written and engrossing—a brilliant piece of scholarship.

Meyers, Henry A., and H. Wolfram. *Medieval Kingship.* Chicago: University of Chicago Press, 1982. A solid study of the institution of kingship as it changed over time in western Europe.

Rio, Alice. *Legal Practice and the Written Word in the Early Middle Ages: Frankish Formulae, ca. 500–1000.* Cambridge: Cambridge University Press, 2009. A creative and fascinating study that uses legal formularies (model legal documents) to explore daily life in early medieval Europe.

ANGLO-SAXON ENGLAND: FORWARDING LEARNING AND LAW

Alexander, Jonathan J.G. *Medieval Illuminators and Their Methods of Work.* New Haven, CT: Yale University Press, 1993. A clear description of the techniques of manuscript illuminations with beautiful illustrations.

Bassett, Steven. *The Anglo-Saxon Kingdoms.* New York: St. Martin's Press, 1989. A clear and fascinating study of the origins of the Anglo-Saxon kingdoms and kingship.

Mayr-Harting, Henry. *The Coming of Christianity to Anglo-Saxon England.* University Park: Pennsylvania State University Press, 1991. A work that attempts to show how Christianity itself was changed in Anglo-Saxon society.

Smyth, Alfred P. *King Alfred the Great.* Oxford: Oxford University Press, 1995. A controversial look at the life and times of Alfred the Great that argues against the historical value of Asser's life of the king.

CHARLEMAGNE AND THE CAROLINGIANS: A NEW EUROPEAN EMPIRE

Barbero, Alessandro. *Charlemagne: Father of a Continent.* Berkeley: University of California Press, 2004. Engaging study that demonstrates Charlemagne's pivotal role in shaping medieval Europe and re-creates the details of the Carolingian world.

Bullough, David. *Carolingian Renewal: Sources and Heritage.* New York: St. Martin's Press, 1992. A clear and interesting study of the spirit of the age with a solid analysis of the sources.

Butzer, Paul L. *Science in Western and Eastern Civilization in Carolingian Times.* Boston: Birkhäuser Verlag, 1993. Skillfully juxtaposes the heritage of classical science in western Europe with the Byzantine and Arab traditions of astronomy and mathematics.

Dhuoda. *Handbook for William: A Carolingian Woman's Counsel for Her Son.* Translated by Carol Neel. Lincoln: University of Nebraska Press, 1991. A good translation with commentary on the letter by Dhuoda featured in the Biography.

GLOBAL CONNECTIONS

Clot, André. *Harun al-Rashid.* Translated by John Howe. New York: New Amsterdam, 1989. An easy-to-read biography based on the Muslim sources that ranges more widely than just the caliph's life to discuss the political, economic, social, and cultural times of the caliphate centered in Baghdad.

STRUGGLE FOR ORDER IN THE CHURCH

Knowles, David. *Christian Monasticism.* New York: McGraw-Hill, 1969. A short and clear look at monastic life and its literature—a classic.

Lawrence, Christopher Nugent. *The Age of the Cloister: The Story of Monastic Life in the Middle Ages.* Mahwah, NJ: HiddenSpring, 2003. Comprehensive study of monastic ways, including details of daily life and an examination of the monastic world's impact on Western culture.

ORDER INTERRUPTED: VIKINGS AND OTHER INVADERS

Clark, Helen. *Towns in the Viking Age.* New York: St. Martin's Press, 1994. An insightful archaeological investigation of early medieval towns in northern Europe.

Hall, Richard. *The World of the Vikings.* London: Thames & Hudson, 2007. A thorough and up-to-date overview of knowledge about the Vikings, with many illustrations.

MANORS AND FEUDAL TIES: ORDER EMERGING FROM CHAOS

Bloch, Marc. *Feudal Society.* Translated by L.A. Manyon. Chicago: University of Chicago Press, 1961. A classic study of the growth and nature of feudalism in its broad social context, but see Reynolds for a revised view.

Collins, Roger. *Early Medieval Europe, 300–1000.* New York: St. Martin's Press, 1991. A study of the people, politics, and religion of early medieval Europe.

Reynolds, Susan. *Fiefs and Vassals: The Medieval Evidence Reinterpreted.* Oxford: Oxford University Press, 1994. An important work that revises traditional approaches and considers whether the terms *fiefs* and *vassals* were used in the early Middle Ages as they are by modern scholars.

Strayer, J.R. *Feudalism.* Princeton, NJ: Princeton University Press, 1985. This work revises and refines the classic study of Bloch.

KING OSWALD WITH HIS BISHOP AIDEN, ca. 1200

This illustration shows the hierarchy of medieval society: The king and his bishop talk at the table while the poor laborers sit at the great men's feet, soliciting charity. A fortified castle frames the whole picture and represents the structure of the medieval order in which some fight (kings), others pray (bishops), and the rest work (laborers).

Order Restored

The High Middle Ages, 1000–1300

"From the beginning, mankind has been divided into three parts—men of prayer, farmers, and men of war. . . ." These words written by Bishop Gerard of Cambrai in the eleventh century capture the social order as the people of the High Middle Ages understood it. In this highly organized world, everyone was expected to keep his or her place, or "order." And these orders were arranged by their function—prayer, warfare, and labor on the land. This understanding of the world ignored the important role of commerce in the growing cities.

After the year 1000, medieval society began to expand in all respects. Agricultural advances spurred population growth; commerce quickened in thriving cities; fortified houses for the nobility sprang up across Europe. After the devastation of the tenth century, kings again tried to consolidate their rule, and nobles resisted their incursion. Intellectual life also flourished with the new prosperity of the age, and philosophers, poets, and artists created works that still inspire us today.

The church, too, grew stronger, and popes began to exert their authority over secular matters. Church leaders called for crusades against Islam, luring western Europeans far from their homelands. Finally, the church's growing role in secular life ignited criticism from some people, who felt that it had forgotten its true purpose. In the face of such criticism, religious leaders responded by both reforming some church policies and repressing those who complained. It was indeed a dynamic age.

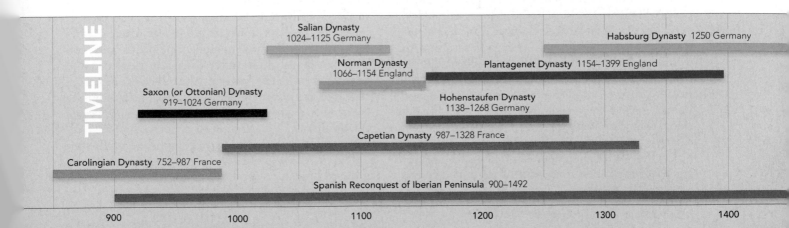

TIMELINE

Salian Dynasty
1024–1125 Germany

Habsburg Dynasty 1250 Germany

Norman Dynasty
1066–1154 England

Plantagenet Dynasty 1154–1399 England

Saxon (or Ottonian) Dynasty
919–1024 Germany

Hohenstaufen Dynasty
1138–1268 Germany

Capetian Dynasty 987–1328 France

Carolingian Dynasty 752–987 France

Spanish Reconquest of Iberian Peninsula 900–1492

900   1000   1100   1200   1300   1400

PREVIEW

THOSE WHO WORK: AGRICULTURAL LABOR

In the late twelfth century, a noble knight, William
Marshall, rested in the woods while on a journey
accompanied only by his squire. He was awakened
from his sleep by the sound of a woman's voice saying, "Ah, God, how weary I am." Opening his eyes,
William saw a well-dressed couple riding along. William quickly mounted and rode to introduce himself
and offer help, but the man was not pleased to see the
knight. As the stranger drew his sword, his hood fell
off and William saw by his tonsured hair that he was
a monk—the handsomest one that he had ever seen.
Filled with shame, the monk confessed he had run
from his monastery with his lady love: "I have carried
her off from her own country." William reprimanded
the young woman and offered to escort her back to
her brother so she would avoid the shame of the path
she had chosen. She refused, and William did not
persist. However, the knight did show continued concern, asking them how they would live. The monk
showed a belt bulging with coins and said that they
would lend money and live off the interest. The good
knight William was horrified. "Upon usury? By God's
sword, you shall not." He told his squire to take the
money to save the couple from falling into the additional shame of moneylending. He sent the couple on
their way (penniless) and took the money to the local
inn, where William generously treated his friends to
abundant food and drink with the purloined coins.

In this story of a noble knight—preserved in a long
poem written by his son—we can see the Middle Ages
coming into full flower. Knights acted with courtesy
to help women who may have been in distress, and
they were generous with money (that may not even
have been their own). Wealth and love were to be
had, and some people—even monks and women—
began to explore new ways to live their lives. All this
was stimulated by a technological and agricultural
boom.

Harnessing the Power of Water and Wind

After 1000, Europeans used more mechanical power
than any previous society had; and this power helped
fuel the expansion of population, commerce, and
political power in western Europe. Water mills provided the major source of mechanical power. In
England in 1086, there were often as many as three
mills for every mile of river. Water mills ground grain
with extraordinary efficiency, and their technology spread rapidly across Europe. **Figure 8.1** shows
two women bringing sacks of grain to a mill. The
women must cross a bridge over the river that powers the great waterwheel. The nearby buildings reveal
the prosperity of the mill owner—prosperity he has
acquired by charging a fee for the use of the mill. In
the picture, the man at the left stands ready to collect
the women's fees.

How did the mills actually work? A cam, project-
ing from the axle of the waterwheel, converted rotary
motion to vertical motion, which let mill workers
accomplish tasks from forging iron to softening wool
cloth to making beer and paper. By the twelfth century, creative builders had developed ways to bring
mechanical power to regions without rivers to drive
water mills.

In many parts of Europe, medieval peasants used
windmills to generate power from wind. Although
people had harnessed the wind much earlier in
Asia and the Middle East, European engineers evidently invented these mills based on water mills.
See **Figure 8.2** to analyze the independence of the
invention. In addition, enterprising engineers managed to tap power from tides. As evidence, in 2009,
archaeologists excavated a well-preserved tidal mill
in Greenwich, near London, that had been built of
huge oak trees cut down in 1194. The wheel diameter of this monumental engineering project is 16 feet.
This huge mill drew water in as the tide rose and
released it as it fell, powering the adjacent mill. This
new find, which supplements excavations around the
North Sea, demonstrates an early and wide use of
tidal mills.

Harnessing all this power accomplished what technology in the ancient world had never achieved: It
released human power for other uses.

New Agricultural Techniques

Peasants supplemented water power with effective use of animal muscle. In the early Middle Ages, as in the ancient world, people harnessed horses with the same kind of yoke they used on oxen. This device was highly inefficient on horses, however, because the yoke rested on their necks and impeded their breathing when they lowered their heads to pull. By the eleventh century, a new padded horse collar that had been developed in China appeared in western Europe. This harness rested on the animal's shoulders, making it possible for people to use horses for heavy plowing and pulling. Because horses can work 50 percent faster and two hours a day longer than oxen, the advantages were huge. Of course, now the peasant walking behind the team of horses also had to work longer and harder. Not surprisingly, the improvement was not as popular with workers as it was with their lords. Nevertheless, the amount of land under cultivation expanded dramatically with increased use of the horse.

The increased use of animal power required peasants to cultivate more land for fodder and hay. Traditionally—since Roman times—most peasants had used what is called a two-field system, in which half the land was left fallow (unplanted) while half was planted. The fertility of the fallow land was restored to yield more crops the following year. However, to accommodate the need to cultivate more land, manors slowly adopted a three-field system that further increased agricultural yields. In this system, plots of land were divided into thirds: One-third was planted in the spring and another in the fall, and the remaining third was left fallow. The three-field system also stimulated the growth of new crops that boosted production. Villagers began to plant legumes, such as peas and beans, which add nitrogen to the soil, thus fertilizing the subsequent grain crop. Legumes also provided an excellent source of protein, which vastly improved the villagers' diets.

Three-field cultivation

The Population Doubles

These agricultural improvements (and the declining violence after the ninth- and tenth-century invasions ended) led to unprecedented population growth. Although it is impossible to get exact figures, estimates of population growth indicate that from the eleventh through the thirteenth century, the population of Europe approximately doubled—from about 37 million to 74 million. Women in particular benefited from the addition of legumes to their diet because the iron in these foods helped replenish blood lost through menstruation and childbirth, and

FIGURE 8.1 Water Mill, 1470 The peoples of the Middle Ages saw the advantage of harnessing the power of running water. Over time, every community along a waterway had a mill. Women such as these brought their grain to be ground instead of grinding it by hand. Lords grew richer charging for the privilege.

it enabled healthy women to have fewer miscarriages and nurse stronger babies. With such improvements, women began outnumbering men during these centuries, and even some medieval commentators noted this disparity, considering it a "problem."

Throughout this period, infant and child deaths remained high due to diseases and accidents, and the overall mortality rates were much higher than in modern times. But anyone surviving past the years normally devoted to warfare or childbearing could expect to live as long as people do today. Indeed, the Biography on pages 256–257 features a man who was vigorous well into his 80s. And in 1204, one 97-year-old representative of the pope participated in the Crusades. There were plenty of gray heads and seasoned minds in the villages, castles, and churches of the Middle Ages.

Life span

To accommodate the ballooning population, western Europeans expanded their settlements. Hardworking villagers on the northwest coast (later the Low Countries) built dikes to hold back the ocean itself to expand their agricultural lands. Sometimes groups of villagers left an overcrowded area and cultivated new land, a process called assarting. The resulting "assart" was great open fields that the peasants divided into strips as they established new villages and manors. Primarily they moved eastward. Probably as many as three thousand new villages were established in lands east of the Elbe River in modern-day northern Germany. As they migrated east, settlers spread western European culture into the lands of the

FIGURE 8.2(A) Vertical-Design Persian Windmill, ca. eleventh century

FIGURE 8.2(B) Horizontal-Design European Windmill on a Pivot, ca. thirteenth century

Catching the Wind: The Development of Windmills

The search today for alternative sources of energy has reawakened interest in wind power. It so happens that before the use of fossil fuels, people depended on the wind to power essential machines. The earliest windmills, developed in Persia and China, relied on a vertical rotating shaft; the wind turned a pole that was fitted directly into a stone or a pump to grind grain or to pump water (see **Figure 8.2a**). In contrast, in the West, engineers built windmills that employed a horizontal shaft with a propeller-like structure to catch the wind and turn the shaft (**Figure 8.2b**). In this method, gears were used to transfer the power from the horizontal shaft (to which the windmill's wind-catching panels, or "sails," were attached) to a vertical shaft. This gearing matched the familiar structure of the watermills that had earlier transformed power in Europe.

In one sense, the vertical-shafted windmill of Eastern design was easier to operate, because it could catch wind from any direction, whereas northern Europeans had to rotate their horizontal-model windmill so that the sails would catch the shifting winds. Notice in **Figure 8.2b** that the European windmill is on a pivot so that it may be turned to face the wind. In the case of windmills, Europeans favored a familiar design over an import that was simpler and might have been more efficient.

Connecting Science & Society

1. What factors, existing knowledge, and/or prior experiences might have entered into the decision of Westerners to develop a horizontal shaft for their windmills instead of adopting one of the vertical-shafted models that they had observed in their travels to the East?

2. Today engineers are attempting to design the best and most efficient windmills as alternative energy sources. What factors—social, economic, and/or other—do you think might influence the decision to use wind power as opposed to other power-generating technologies, such as steam and nuclear, in the present day?

3. How do you think the shift to and use of wind power influenced medieval society? How might an increased reliance on wind power influence the lives of people in the twenty-first century?

Slavs. **Map 8.1** shows some of the eastern settlements that were founded as western Europeans relentlessly sought new lands.

Why would peasants leave their established villages to go east and do the hard work needed to clear new agricultural lands? The texts show that people had two motivations: the possibility of better lands and more freedom. The twelfth-century chronicler Helmod of Bosau described how Count Adolf II of Holstein (1128–1164) attracted settlers to his new lands: He insisted that "whoever might be in difficult straits because of a shortage of fields should come with their families to accept land which was excellent, spacious, fertile with fruits, abounding in fish and meat, and favorable to pastures." Still, the peasants drove a hard bargain—many surviving charters show that the new settlers gained many freedoms from the feudal obligations of serfdom. For example, the charter of the twelfth-century village of Lorris read: "No man shall pay a tax upon his food. Nor for measuring the grain which he obtains from his own labor or that of his animals. Nor shall he pay any tax on the wine which he obtains from his own vineyards." With such incentives, the spread to new lands blossomed, and western European culture flourished.

> New freedoms

Few expansions offer unmixed blessings, and the population growth had dire environmental consequences. To build their new settlements, people clearcut huge swaths of forest, often using slash-and-burn techniques that left clouds of smoke and ash hanging in the air. The settlers also dumped human waste and the remains of slaughtered animals in the rivers. In the cities, coal burning poured clouds of dangerous pollutants into the air. Still, the population kept expanding, and more and more people appreciated being freed from the land to populate the burgeoning cities and towns.

> Environmental consequences

THOSE OUTSIDE THE ORDER: TOWN LIFE

As we saw in the quotation that began this chapter, when medieval writers identified an ordered world of "those who work," they imagined agricultural laborers providing for the lords who ruled and the clergy who prayed. Yet, there were others who labored outside this well-defined hierarchy who did not fit medieval understandings based on a rural society. It was in these towns that people forged the real future of modern urban western European culture.

The few towns of the early Middle Ages were primarily administrative centers, serving as the residences of bishops or occasionally of a nobleman. These towns were walled for protection from

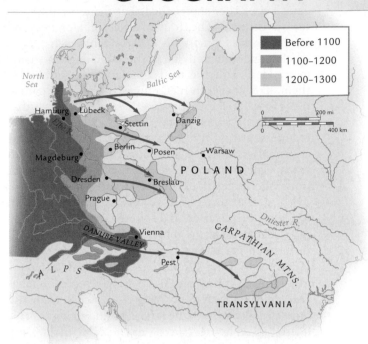

thinking about
GEOGRAPHY

MAP 8.1

German Migration Eastward

This map focuses on the new eastern settlements from about 1000 to 1300. It shows a steady progress of migrants eastward over a long time period in search of promising agricultural lands.

Explore the Map

1. Where did the major cities grow?

2. What might be the impact of these cities on trade routes around the Baltic?

3. What do these settlements suggest about population growth in western Europe?

the surrounding violence of the feudal world. After 1000, more cities grew up and began to take on more commercial roles. In the process, they grew not only larger, but wealthier, and they developed new ways to govern their increasingly prosperous lives.

Communes and Guilds: Life in a Medieval Town

People moved to towns that offered work in a thriving trade and a lively demand for goods. By present-day standards, most medieval towns were small. For example, of the 3,000 identified "towns" in late medieval Germany, 2,800 had populations of only about

1,000. Europe did have a few great cities, however. Cologne was home to some 40,000 people, and London's population approached that figure by the fourteenth century. The Italian cities of Florence and Venice boasted almost 100,000 residents each.

Men and women living in these small towns shared many ideas with the feudal society that surrounded them, like a belief in hierarchy and a sense of mutual ties. However, they expressed these ideas in ways that dramatically shaped urban life. To escape the many requirements imposed on village serfs, towns negotiated charters with the lords on whose lands the town stood. These charters granted townspeople freedom from labor obligations and freedom to travel at will. They also protected the growing town profits from unreasonable taxation and seizure, and some charters allowed the towns to run their own law courts. All these rights made towns islands of freedom in a tightly ordered world, and in return, the lords received money from the prosperous burgs. Towns also served as magnets drawing those who wished to escape from the ordered constraints of the feudal world. In most towns, if a serf could live for "a year and a day" without being caught, he had earned his freedom to stay in the town.

Sometimes townspeople could not peacefully obtain the liberties they desired, and they joined together in sworn associations called **communes** and staged violent revolutions to take communal liberties that they believed came with urban life. The communes elected their own officials, regulated taxation within the town, and generally conducted the business of running the urban centers. These communes were not democratic, for most people accepted it as natural that the rich citizens would govern the town. In Italy, the communes became so strong that the cities developed into independent city-states. In the French and English lands, by contrast, all the towns remained subject to the political authority of the king. In all cases, however, towns encouraged people to develop their skills, learn a trade, and make money.

Tradesmen within towns formed **guilds,** or organizations to protect their interests and control the trade and manufacturing within the towns. These guilds regulated the quality of such products as gold work, shoes, bread, and so forth; they managed their own membership and set prices. In part because urban women outnumbered men, they participated in the guilds, and families arranged marriages to cement bonds of loyalty and control of commerce. Widows in particular ran businesses and took their husbands' places in the trade organizations. Boys and girls served as apprentices in the shops until they learned their trade. Then they could work as "journeymen"—paid employees under the guidance of a master. Finally, journeymen would present a sample of their best work—whether a gold piece or a loaf of bread—to the guild masters to see if this "masterpiece" would qualify them to become full guild masters. In these ways, the guild could control both the quality of the products and the number of guild members involved in the trade.

For other groups, town life offered a more mixed set of opportunities and limits. Since the time of the Roman Empire, many medieval towns had a significant population of Jews. For centuries, Jews had played a vital role in town life as merchants, artisans, and members of many other professions. By the eleventh and twelfth centuries, however, Christian merchants and craftspeople began to view the Jewish community as competition. Slowly, they excluded Jews from guilds and, in some places, kept them from owning land. However, Jews still engaged in commerce and many Christians found them valuable—although separate—members of the town. For example, a late-eleventh-century charter was granted by a bishop (Rudgar) to Jews who were willing to settle in the German town of Speyer. He wrote that he thought "it would greatly add to its [Speyer's] honor if I should establish some Jews in it." He gave them a section of the city for their use (and walled it off to provide protection from less-enlightened Christians) and offered them special concessions for trading.

The bishop of Speyer also gave Jews the right to freely change coins, and, slowly, urban Jews such as those in Speyer began to enter into moneylending, which is essential to commercial enterprises. The Christian religion forbad its followers to collect interest on loans, for they believed that it was unseemly to make money from time, which belonged to God. While many Christians continued to engage in the lucrative practice of moneylending, slowly through the late Middle Ages, Jewish bankers increasingly began to take over the practice because Judaic practice contained no such strictures against lending money. The two urban groups thus depended on each other in an uneasy coexistence throughout most of the Middle Ages.

The Widening Web of Trade

The impetus for the growth of towns and wealth in the Middle Ages came not from manufacturing but from trade. Therefore, the most important towns were those that served as bustling centers for moving goods—throughout the Middle Ages most of the trade centered on luxury goods. Northern Italy, especially, became a significant nexus in southern Europe, and Venice, Pisa, and Genoa took the lead. As early as 998, Venetians had received charters from the Byzantine emperor that gave them complete freedom in Byzantine waters, and Pisa and Genoa had negotiated treaties with Muslim rulers that opened new markets. Thus, the way was paved for merchants to sail

Communes and guilds

Urban Jews

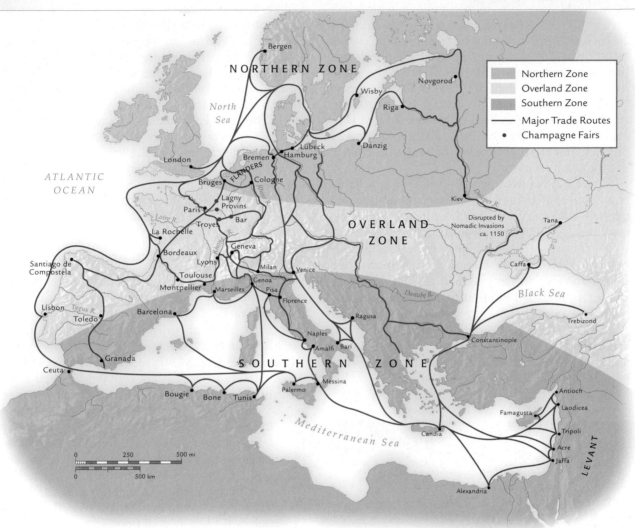

MAP 8.2

Trade Routes, Twelfth and Thirteenth Centuries

This map illustrates the major trading areas of the High Middle Ages, including the three principal zones of trade. It also shows the importance of sea and river routes and the Champagne fairs.

Explore the Map

1. Why were the Italian cities particularly well suited to take advantage of the southern trade?

2. What northern cities were well placed for sea and river trade?

3. In what respects were the Champagne fairs favorably located to bring together the northern and southern trade zones?

to the eastern Mediterranean and buy silks and spices passing through the great Muslim bazaars in Baghdad. They then brought the goods westward to Spain and southern France. Whereas the Mediterranean trade had been the commercial center during the Roman Empire, the medieval world opened a new trading hub in the north.

Cities in Flanders (particularly Bruges and Ghent) joined the Italian cities as commercial centers. They supplied fine wool cloth to all of northern Europe and

acted as a supply center for Scandinavian products—particularly furs and hunting hawks—that were in demand all over Europe. The growth of the cloth industry, and the handsome profits to be made, led many northern men to replace at the looms the women who had dominated the industry. **Map 8.2** shows the three major trade zones, northern, southern, and the central overland route that distributed goods. However, through the eleventh century, there was no easy mechanism for joining the three zones.

Early in the twelfth century, the French count of Champagne saw an opportunity to make a large profit by hosting fairs in his lands at which merchants could sell goods from the three zones. He granted the right to various towns in his county to organize such gatherings. (**Map 8.2** shows the major towns of the Champagne fairs.) The counts of Champagne provided the space, set up booths, arranged for police to keep order, and invited moneylenders. Each day, the trade featured a different product, and the counts collected a sales tax from all the transactions made.

Champagne fairs

Figure 8.3 depicts one such medieval fair. At the booths, people gather to purchase animals, bolts of cloth, and fine artifacts. At the center of the illustration, the bishop of Paris opens the fair by bestowing God's blessing on the enterprise. The fairs featured products from all over Europe: leather from Spain, iron from Germany, copper and tin from Bohemia, and smoked fish and furs from Scandinavia. They also offered an outlet for local products such as cheeses and wines. The fairs also drew people from the medieval underbelly of society; thieves, con artists, actors, and prostitutes plied their trade among the bustling crowds.

FIGURE 8.3 Medieval Fair in France Merchants gathered at periodic fairs to sell their wares, and these fairs stimulated long-distance trade. Local people found goods and excitement at the fairs' temporary stalls.

In the late thirteenth century, many cities in northern Germany united to create the Hanseatic League, an association to capitalize on the prosperous northern trade. The cities formed a political as well as an economic power, and they were able to acquire a monopoly on the Baltic trade, replacing Flanders as the center of the northern trading zone. At its height, the Hanseatic League included seventy or eighty cities, led by Lubeck, Bremen, Cologne, and Hamburg. By the fourteenth century, they offered their own great fairs, which replaced the French fairs. By looking at **Maps 8.1** and **8.2,** we can see that the eastward settlements around the Baltic Sea helped spawn prosperous trade regions that brought centers of wealth ever northward from the Mediterranean Sea.

Hanseatic League

The Glory of God: Church Architecture

With the wealth that came pouring into the cities, townspeople built great churches to celebrate the glory of God and express their pride in their own towns. From about the tenth century until the twelfth, church architecture was dominated by the **Romanesque** style. Mostly monastic structures, these buildings were large and dark with long, central aisles made of barrel vaults and round arches. They seemed so solid and formidable, people often called them "fortresses of God."

Figure 8.4a shows the interior of the monastery church of La Madeleine at Vézeley in Burgundy. Built in the early twelfth century, this structure represents the highest achievement of Romanesque architecture. Because the barrel vault was high, it could not support the heavy stone roof by itself, so builders made the walls extra thick and the windows small. As a result, the church, and others like it, was dark inside.

In about 1140, Abbot Suger of the Church of St. Denis near Paris decided to change all this. He envisioned a majestic church built in a new style—a church that reached up toward the heavens and that was filled with light. Architects and builders set about making this vision a reality, and to do so, they adopted innovative techniques that came to be called the **Gothic** style. Instead of round arches, they used pointed ones, as shown in **Figure 8.4b.** Some scholars believe the use of the pointed arch originated in India and found its way through the trade networks to France. Regardless of its origin, the new arch style directed the weight of the roof down the building's massive columns instead of its walls. But such tall walls were vulnerable to cracking under the pressure of high winds. To guard against this danger, architects developed

Gothic architecture

FIGURE 8.4 Romanesque and Gothic Architecture Medieval church architecture reflected two main styles. (a) Romanesque design, with thick walls and round arches like those in La Madeleine at Vézeley (ca. 1104), shown here, was the earlier style. (b) Gothic style, featuring pointed arches and soaring heights as exemplified in Cologne Cathedral (begun in 1248), shown in this photograph, came later.

"flying buttresses," large braces that supported the outside of the building.

With these innovations, the walls no longer needed to be thick to provide the support for the church. Builders could therefore add large windows that let light fill the interior. Glassmakers gathered in nearby forests to burn the hardwood needed to blow glass, and they added metallic oxides to make rich primary colors. Artists fitted the colored glass into intricate lead webs to form magnificent pictures showing everything from biblical stories to scenes of medieval life. Abbot Suger himself contracted the stained-glass windows for his new church. Delighted with the result, he wrote, "The entire sanctuary is pervaded by a wonderful and continuous light." The thirteenth-century

Stained glass

royal chapel in Paris shown in **Figure 8.5** contains some of the most remarkable examples of stained glass. The windows make up three-quarters of the wall surface.

Beginning in the mid-twelfth century, these immense Gothic cathedrals, with their pointed arches, stained-glass windows, and flying buttresses, began appearing in all the great cities of Europe. Designed to accommodate the entire population of a city (some can hold as many as 10,000 people standing during mass), they were also designed to attract admiring pilgrims. The cathedrals vied to acquire and feature relics of famous saints (see Chapter 5) that drew the faithful seeking solace and miracles. These pilgrims brought money to both the church and the city and helped stimulate movement throughout

FIGURE 8.5 Stained-Glass Windows, ca. 1245 In the Gothic style, strong stone columns supported the weight of the cathedral's roof, thus freeing the walls from weight-bearing function. Skilled artisans installed stained-glass windows into those walls, such as these examples from the magnificent Sainte-Chapelle, Paris.

medieval Europe. The skylines of medieval Europe were reshaped by the towers of these striking new cathedrals.

The Rise of Universities

The cathedrals became more than just centers of worship and pilgrimage; they began serving as places of learning. Scholars and students gathered at cathedrals to study, and these cathedral schools became vibrant centers. It soon became clear that the informal organization of these schools was inadequate. Document 8.1 describes the drawbacks of some educators in the noble households. Townspeople frequently protested to the bishop against the students, who were often rowdy and sometimes violent. Students, on their part, resented the high prices that townspeople charged for rooms, food, and drink, and they needed protection against incompetent teachers. By the twelfth century, new structures were emerging to address some of these problems, establishing the beginnings of universities.

Just as townspeople founded guilds and used charters to protect their interests, students and scholars did the same. In some places (like Paris), masters grouped themselves into guilds, and in other cities (like Bologna), students organized themselves. These organizations were called universities—from the Latin word *universitas,* which means "guild." These universities received charters that confirmed the guild's autonomy and authority to license teachers.

Young men (some only 14 years old) from all social classes attended universities; wealthy younger sons of the nobility and promising young village boys could eventually hope for lucrative jobs in the church or courts. (Women were not permitted to attend universities.) Students completed the traditional course of study that had been established centuries before at Charlemagne's (r. 768–814) court. They studied the trivium—grammar, rhetoric, and logic—first and then the quadrivium—arithmetic, geometry, music, and astronomy. Upon completion, they would receive first a bachelor's degree and then a master's degree.

Advanced students interested in focusing on a specialized course of study could continue their studies and receive a doctorate degree. Students might study medicine in **Advanced degrees** Salerno, where masters taught Arabic medicine and sometimes dissected human cadavers. Others might go to Bologna to study law based on Justinian's *Corpus* (discussed in Chapter 6) or study theology—the "queen of all the sciences"—in Paris. The many medieval universities of Europe are shown in **Map 8.3.** This map gives some idea of the potential for students to move from school to school as they sought different masters and different curricula. It also suggests how these institutes of learning served to link the intellectual life of such a broad geographic area.

The universities gave rise to a new kind of life for the young men who attended them. Many students eagerly devoured the ideas and knowledge that percolated at these centers of learning. The classroom pictured in **Figure 8.6** shows students with differing degrees of enthusiasm—those in the front listen attentively, while some in the back talk during the lecture and another in the foreground sleeps. The less serious students deeply enjoyed the freedom of university life, drinking in the local bars and brawling in the streets, raising the townspeople's ire. In Paris, a law was passed forbidding students to gamble with dice on the altar of the cathedral while mass was being said! All this freedom cost money; many letters in which students ask their parents to send more cash survive from this era. Yet, despite the occasional disruptions and distractions of life in the universities, students and teachers managed to engage in stimulating dialogues that led to exciting new ideas.

DOCUMENT 8.1

Guibert of Nogent Describes His Education

In the early twelfth century, Guibert, the abbot of Nogent in France, wrote a remarkable autobiography that offers an intimate glimpse into twelfth-century life. His parents had promised him to the church at his birth and raised him to become a monk. In this account, he gives a rare description of child-rearing practices.

There was a little before that time, and in a measure there is still in my time, such a scarcity of grammarians that in the towns hardly anyone, and in the cities very few, could be found, and those who by good hap could be discovered, had but slight knowledge and could not be compared with the itinerant clerks of these days. And so the man in whose charge my mother decided to put me, had begun to learn grammar late in life and was the more unskilled in the art through having imbibed little of it when young. Yet of such sobriety was he, that what he wanted in letters, he made up for in honesty.

Placed under him I was taught with such purity and checked with such honesty in the excesses which are wont to spring up in my youth, that I was

kept well-guarded from the common wolves and never allowed to leave his company, or to eat anywhere than at home, or to accept gifts from anyone without his leave; in everything I had to show self-control in word, look or act, so that he seemed to require of me the conduct of a monk rather than a clerk. For whereas others of my age wandered everywhere at will and were unchecked in the indulgence of such inclinations to their age, I, hedged in with constant restraints, would sit and look on in my clerical chasuble at the troops of players like a beast awaiting sacrifice.

Although, therefore, he crushed me by such severity, yet in other ways he made it quite plain that he loved me as well as he did himself. With such watchful care did he devote himself to me, with such foresight did he secure my welfare against the spite of others and teach me on what authority I should beware of the dissolute manners of some who paid court to me, and so long did he argue with my mother about the elaborate richness of my dress, that he was regarded as exercising the guardianship not

of a master, but of a parent, and not over my body only, but my soul, too. As for me, considering the dull sensibility of my age and my littleness, great was the love I conceived for him in response, in spite of the many weals with which he marked my tender skin so that not through fear, as is common in those of my age, but through a sort of love deeply implanted in my heart, I obeyed him in utter forgetfulness of his severity.

SOURCE: Guibert de Nogent, *The Autobiography of Guibert, Abbot of Nogent-Sous-Coucy.* Translated by C.C. Swinton Bland (London: George Routledge & Sons, Ltd., and E.P. Dutton & Co., New York, 1926), p. 32.

Analyze the Document

1. Why did Guibert's mother have to settle for a mediocre tutor?

2. What methods of instruction did the tutor use?

3. What did Guibert think of his tutor?

4. How did medieval ideas of education differ from modern notions?

Scholasticism: The Height of Medieval Philosophy

The main goal of medieval philosophy was to reconcile faith with reason—that is, to understand with one's mind what one believed in one's heart. This philosophy was called **scholasticism.** The medieval thinkers applied a particular form of logic, called dialectic, which involves using logic to explore various sides of an issue, and these writings often take the form of questioning. The greatest thinkers drawn to the new universities in the twelfth century wrestled constantly with this problem and, in doing so, shaped both knowledge and faith.

The earliest medieval philosopher to explore the religious applications of dialectic was Anselm of Canterbury (1033–1109). Anselm's motto was "faith seeking understanding," and his most famous effort involved showing a logical connection between the belief that God is a perfect

Anselm and Abelard

being and a proof (by the rules of logic) that God exists. He argued that because God was perfect he *must* exist, or else he would not be perfect (for Anselm, perfection demonstrated a real existence). Anselm wrote a number of works on logic, and his treatise *Why God Became Man* became the most important explanation of the central Christian mystery. Anselm established the exciting possibility that human reason could be brought to study the deep mysteries of Creation.

One of the most esteemed scholastic scholars was Peter Abelard (1079–1142), who taught in Paris. In his mid-thirties, Abelard was hired to tutor Heloise (ca. 1100–1163), the talented 17-year-old niece of a local church official. Teacher and student were soon lovers, and Heloise became pregnant. The couple married secretly because Heloise feared that a traditional marriage would hurt Abelard's reputation as a teacher, but her infuriated uncle had Abelard castrated. Leaving their child to be raised by relatives, both Heloise and

St. Andrews 1412

North Sea

Dublin 1312

0 ____ 250 mi
0 ____ 250 km

Rostock 1419

Kulm 1366

Oxford 12th cent.   Cambridge 1209

ATLANTIC OCEAN

Cologne 1388   Leipzig 1409

Louvain 1425

Erfurt 1379

Caen 1432

Cracow 1364

Paris 12th cent.   Heidelberg 1385   Würzburg 1402   Prague 1348

Angers 1229   Orléans 1309

Poitiers 1432   Gray 1291   Vienna 1365

Dôle 1422   Pavia 1361   Piacenza 1248   Ofen 1389
Mantua 1433

Bordeaux 1441   Geneva 1365   Verona 1339

Grenoble 1339   Vercelli 1228   Vicenza 1204   Cividale 1353

Cahors 1332   Turin 1405   Treviso 1318   Fünfkirchen 1367
Padua 1222

Palencia 1212   Toulouse 1229   Orange 1365   Reggio 12th cent.   Ferrara 1391

Coimbra 1308   Valladolid 1346   Ramiers 1295   Montpellier 12th cent.   Avignon 1303   Aix 1409   Bologna 12th cent.

Huesca 1354   Lucca 1369   Florence 1349

Salamanca 1227   Perpignan 1350   Pisa 1343   Arezzo 1215

Alcalá de Henares 1293   Lérida 1300   Gerona 1446   Siena 1246   Perugia 1308

Lisbon 1290   Barcelona 1430   Fermo 1398

Calatayud 1415   Orvieto 1377

Valencia 1245   Rome 1303

Seville 1254   Naples 1224

Mediterranean Sea   Salerno 12th cent.

Catania 1444

MAP 8.3

Medieval Universities

This map shows the numerous universities that were founded throughout the Middle Ages, as well as the years in which they were founded, where known.

Explore the Map

1. Which universities were founded earliest?

2. As time went on, how easy would it have been for students to move from school to school as they sought different programs of study? Explain.

3. Which region had the most universities? How might this clustering have affected the overall culture of that region?

Abelard entered monasteries, where they each continued brilliant careers of learning and influence.

Abelard established a method of applying critical reason to even sacred texts. His most famous work, *Yes and No* (*Sic et Non*), assembled a variety of authoritative sources, from the Bible to church fathers, that seemed to contradict one an other. From these, the scholar compiled 150 theological questions and the passages relevant to each question, which allowed scholars to consider the full range of the questions. Although his book has such provocative chapters as "Is God the Author of Evil, or No?" Abelard had no desire to undermine faith; on the contrary, he believed that this kind of inquiry would strengthen

FIGURE 8.6 Medieval Universities Universities were first founded in the Middle Ages. Scholars gathered at these new institutions to listen to lectures from famed masters. This image shows the students' diversity, as well as the youthfulness of many of them.

faith through the discovery of truth. This was an academic exercise in which students were expected to reconcile apparent contradictions.

Throughout the Middle Ages, there had always been people who believed that it was not possible or even desirable to reach God through reason. Abelard's adversary Bernard of Clairvaux (1090–1153) condemned many of Abelard's writings, primarily because he disapproved of the process of inquiry. Bernard wrote passionately: "I thought it unfitting that the grounds of the faith should be handed over to human reasonings for discussion." Although Bernard approved of rational inquiry in nonreligious areas, he firmly believed the way to God lay in faith and love—in other words, in emotion, not intellect. He wrote beautiful tracts on the mystic approach to God through feeling and faith, and many men and women chose to seek God through this mystic path rather than through logic.

Through the twelfth century, Islamic scholars also continued the great intellectual strides that had been begun by scholars like Avicenna (980–1037) (in Biography, Chapter 6). Muslim scholars from centers as far apart as Baghdad in the east and Toledo in Spain studied the classical works of Aristotle and others with a sophistication lacking in the western kingdoms. The Muslim scholar Averroës (1126–1198) and the eminent Jewish scholar Maimonides (1135–1204) interpreted Aristotle's works and left extensive commentaries on the sophisticated ideas. These texts were discovered in Arabic libraries in Spain as Christians slowly reconquered Muslim territory, and the emergence of these commentaries along with the advanced logic of Aristotle generated much intellectual excitement in the university communities of western Europe.

Some of Aristotle's ideas as interpreted by these non-Christian commentators (such as his belief in the eternity of the world) seemed to contradict Christian faith. In spite of some controversy, many readers thrilled at the intellectual possibilities contained in such texts and felt confident that faith and reason could be reconciled. The Biography of Ramón Lull

BIOGRAPHY

Ramón Lull
(ca.1232–1316)

Troubadour,

Scholar, and

Missionary

to the

Muslims

Ramón Lull was born in about 1232 on Majorca, one of the Balearic islands off the east coast of Spain. As a young man, Ramón was deeply drawn to the love poetry of the troubadours. He composed songs and poems of love and the life of luxury. However, at about age 30, he had a transforming experience. One night, as he crafted a love song for his lady, he beheld a vision of Jesus hanging on the cross. After a few more such visions, Ramón decided to renounce his frivolous life and turn his efforts to religion. In his view, God had called him to convert the Muslims to Christianity. Ramón began to train for his new vocation. To learn Arabic so he could preach to the Muslims, he bought a Muslim slave.

FIGURE 8.7 Ramón Lull, Balearic Islands, Mallorca

He studied with the slave for nine years and became fluent in Arabic. Toward the end of his studies, the slave tried to murder Ramón, perhaps to keep him from preaching Christianity to Muslims. The scholar survived the attack and had the slave arrested, but he felt torn about what to do with him. He did not want to order him killed, because that seemed un-Christian. At the same time, he felt unsafe freeing him. As he wrestled with this problem, the slave committed suicide in prison. Ramón interpreted the suicide as God's way of releasing him from his dilemma. He concluded that the death of his Muslim slave confirmed the correctness of his own desire to convert the followers of Islam.

Ramón then set out to build the skills he saw as essential for carrying the Christian message to the Muslim world. He attended the university at Paris to study theology and honed his skill in the formal logic practiced by the scholastics. All this preparation revealed Ramón's passion for education. He founded a school in Majorca

---

(see above) tells of one remarkable man's expression of this passion for reason.

The scholastic enterprise reached its height in the thirteenth century with the works of Thomas Aquinas (1225–1274), an Italian churchman whom many regard as the greatest scholar of the Middle Ages. Aquinas wrote many works, from commentaries on biblical books and Aristotelian texts to essays on philosophical problems and the *Summa Contra Gentiles*, a work probably intended for missionary use in converting heretics, Muslims, and Jews. However, his most important work was the *Summa Theologiae* (*Summary of Theology*), which was intended to offer a comprehensive summary of all knowledge available at the time.

Aquinas taught that faith and reason were compatible paths to a single truth, but that the mind by itself could grasp only the truth of the physical world. Faith (given by God's grace), however, could help reason grasp spiritual truths such as the Trinity. This central understanding—that faith and nature cannot contradict each other and that each can inform the other—has remained one

Thomas Aquinas

of Aquinas's most important contributions. The scholar wrote, "Our intellect is led by our senses to divine knowledge."

The most famous examples of his use of nature to yield divine truth were his "proofs" of God's existence, in which, like Anselm, he wanted to use logic available in the physical world to understand the mysteries of God. For instance, he showed that we can observe motion on earth and that all earthly motion is caused by some other motion. When we trace back all the motion that is caused, our logical mind leads us to the first mover that originated all other motion—the "unmoved mover"—who is God. Thus, our understanding of the physical world of motion, combined with faith, leads us to an understanding of one of the elements of God.

Aquinas's *Summa* remains one of the masterpieces of philosophy, but not all medieval thinkers found it satisfying. For some, it was too speculative and abstract. For all Aquinas's emphasis on using the natural world as a path to truth, he did not study the natural world very much. Instead, he read Aristotle's views on the natural world. Yet some of the great minds of the age turned directly to matters of the physical and wrote many books intended to bring knowledge to the faithful. His influential work, *The Order of Chivalry*, set forth a call for an educated and virtuous knightly class. However, Ramón still believed that his real calling was to educate the Muslims. In 1292, when he was a ripe 60 years old, he traveled to North Africa to begin his missionary work. Mallorca proudly claims Ramón as a native and erected the statue shown in **Figure 8.7** to remind people of his accomplishments. The long beard testifies to his longevity and the open book to his scholarship. He gazes toward Africa, where he spent so much time preaching.

In Tunis, a bustling Muslim city near Carthage, Ramón invited all the local Muslim scholars to debate with him the merits of the two religions. He stood by the scholastic idea that one could "prove" the truth of the Trinity over the truth of Muhammad through the power of Aristotelian logic. One Muslim scholar warned his fellows: "Beware ye! . . . He will bring such arguments against our law that it will be impossible to answer them."

Ramón eventually realized that logic alone could not make people change their views on matters of faith, but he never abandoned his belief in dialectic as a missionary tool. At the time, the great scholastics from Anselm to Aquinas already knew this. They saw scholasticism primarily as a way for the faithful to understand with their minds what they already knew in their hearts. It is not surprising that Ramón made few converts.

The rest of Ramón's life proved just as dramatic as his early and middle years. Tired of his preaching, the Muslims imprisoned Ramón for a time and then placed him on a ship to Italy, but a great storm sank the ship. The robust 76-year-old lost all his books and clothes but managed to swim ashore and survive the adventure. He again resumed his efforts to convert the Muslims. In 1311, he even implored the pope to call another crusade, but his request was ignored. Ramón Lull returned to Tunis when he was 83 years old, where he roamed the streets striking up conversations with anyone who would listen to

his advocacy of Christianity. Tunisian authorities finally lost patience with him in 1316 and executed him. Throughout his life, Ramón expressed the major medieval passions and accomplishments. From a love of poetry, chivalry, and philosophy to a single-minded desire to transform the Muslim world at his doorstep, Ramón's interests paralleled those of his greatest contemporaries. But few pursued so many of them as relentlessly as this vigorous, long-lived man.

Connecting People & Society

1. How was Ramón shaped by the main intellectual currents of the time, from poetry to chivalry to philosophy?

2. What was the relationship between Christians and Muslims, as shown by Lull's life?

3. How did Lull's behavior contribute to continuing animosity between people of the two religions?

---

world. In this area, they would find plenty to think about.

Discovering the Physical World

The passion with which university scholars read Aristotle and the other ancient writers led them to adhere to classical views of physics and medicine. The educated man or woman of the thirteenth century held the same view of the physical universe as the ancient Greeks had: a motionless world made of earth, water, air, and fire. In the east, Muslim astronomers made huge strides in building upon classical wisdom in studying the heavens. The Muslim astronomer/mathematician al-Tusi (born 1201) recalculated ancient Greek understandings of planetary orbits with a precision that would not be matched in western Europe until the sixteenth century.

In the west, scientific advances came (albeit slowly) in the fields of medicine as physicians built on the works of Galen and Avicenna. Physicians studying at the medical school in Salerno learned Galen's theory of the four "humors" (discussed in Chapter 5) and studied how to bring the body back into balance.

Since classical times, the study of women's health had been limited by the fact that midwives did not write medical texts. Yet, male physicians, who did write the texts, frequently misunderstood women's bodies. In the Middle Ages, a few

> Hildegard of Bingen

women wrote books that in part corrected this problem and thus contributed much to the field of women's health. The best known was Hildegard of Bingen (1098–1179), an abbess and mystic in Germany. She wrote compelling accounts of her visions, which showed the same blend of faith and scholarly knowledge that marked the university-trained scholastics. Perhaps most interesting, however, Hildegard authored a medical tract, *Of Causes and Cures*. In this important work, she took the classical view of human beings as consisting of either hot, cold, wet, or dry "humors", and applied it to women's health. In addition, she included in her text the popular cures she practiced as she ministered to the sick in the community, and she gave German and Latin names for drugs—all things that were not part of traditional scholarly writings. Hildegard's work pointed to the possibility of combining women's practical wisdom about women's health with traditional medical knowledge.

Despite such contributions, by the thirteenth century women began to be excluded from medicine, as universities gained exclusive right to train physicians. In doing so, they prevented many charlatans from practicing medicine, but they were also slowly moving women out of healing occupations that for centuries they had shared informally with men. This exclusion sometimes severely damaged the careers of women healers. In the early fourteenth century, for example, there was a famous case of a female Jewish physician (Jacoba Felicie) who had a thriving practice in Paris. She was prosecuted for practicing medicine without a university license, but so many of her patients testified to her skill that the action against her was withdrawn. Nevertheless, Jacoba was ordered to stop practicing medicine.

Some scholars noticed the loss in wisdom that accompanied the separation of practical experience from the universities. One Oxford master, Robert Grosseteste (1168–1253), challenged his students to develop an experimental method to question the ancients. His most famous student, Roger Bacon (ca. 1214–1292), continued Grosseteste's work and is usually credited with popularizing his teacher's movement toward a scientific method. Bacon's greatest practical contribution came in the field of optics, when he discovered how to make glasses by grinding lenses. Perhaps more important than any specific invention, Grosseteste and Bacon demonstrated the value of experimentation over pure logic, thus challenging the ancient scholars who formed the core of the traditional courses of study at the universities. In the centuries to come, the major discoveries in the physical world would come from people like Bacon, who had the courage to think for themselves instead of simply looking to ancient experts.

> Experimental science

This intellectual expansion was one of many measures of the vitality of medieval life. The cities and the universities were growing in ways the medieval world hardly understood, much less expected, but this was not the only expansion of the Middle Ages. The world of "those who fight" began to see a dramatic growth.

THOSE WHO FIGHT: NOBLES AND KNIGHTS

The multiplication of the population of Europe in the eleventh century prompted a surge of construction of homes for the nobility. The aristocracy required fortresses and towers to "keep the peace" (and to collect the taxes paid by the peasantry). The characteristic defensive structure of the nobility was the castle, which came to define the landscape of the medieval world.

Castles: Medieval Homes and Havens

In the tenth century, castles were actually private fortresses made of timber and earth that were built on mounds. By the thirteenth century, they had become large, defensive structures of wood and stone and were virtually impregnable. Many castles consisted of a large exterior wall surrounded by a moat filled with water, and an interior fortified structure that served as the noble family's home and an extra line of defense should invaders breach the outer wall. The inner fortress contained a deep well, for the castle's ability to endure a long siege depended on the availability of food and water as well as a strong defense. The Welsh castle in **Figure 8.8** shows the varied circles of defense that protected the interior. Instead of having a moat, this castle was actually built on an island in a lake, and the exterior wall in the foreground stood on the outer shore of the lake. Invaders who made it through this formidable outer wall would find themselves confronted by a lake and further walls. Protected by such features, a few people could withstand the assault of many.

> Living quarters

The main household of a castle consisted of a large public hall where the castle residents ate, played games, and entertained themselves while gathered around the open hearth in the center of the room. There were also smaller, private chambers where the lord and lady slept, the women of the household did the weaving and sewing, and children were born. In such a private chamber, the lord also stored a strongbox filled with coins and other valuables. In an age with no banking, most nobles guarded their wealth themselves.

By the thirteenth century, these living quarters were designed for comfort as well as safety. Noble families lived in high towers, where it was safe to have glass windows, and the open hearth was moved to the wall as a fireplace to reduce the smoke in the room. Latrines were built into the walls of adjacent rooms, and pipes brought water to the upper floors. The tower inhabitants decorated—and warmed—the stone walls by hanging intricate tapestries from ceiling to floor.

Thirteenth-century castles stood as marvels of engineering, and those who designed them were much in demand. One English architect designed and supervised the building of ten castles over a thirty-year period. However, these structures also took their toll on the environment. More great forests were cleared for timber to shore up the stones and build scaffolds as the workers rushed to complete the castles, and defenders wanted the surrounding area clear-cut so they could see approaching foes. The Castle of Windsor, for example, required the wood of more than four thousand oak trees in its construction. As the castle rose, its stone towers replaced the forests as the prominent feature of the landscape.

The Ideals of Chivalry

The contractual form of feudalism (see Chapter 7) persisted throughout the Middle Ages as a way to provide armies for lords and kings. However, the mutual contract did nothing to reduce the violence that continually plagued medieval society. Early in the eleventh century, churchmen meeting in councils tried to reduce the violence by advocating a Peace of God, which would impose rules of war—for example, exempting the poor and the clergy from the violence. In the middle of the eleventh century, churchmen tried to add a related concept, the Truce of God, which forbad fighting on Sundays and other holy days. Neither of these worthy movements fully quelled the violence.

By the twelfth century, the feudal tie had become interwoven with an elaborate code of values and symbolic rituals that served somewhat to tame the violent world of warriors. This code and culture of the ruling class was called **chivalry,** and its values became evident in church writings, romantic literature, and treatises. Ramón Lull, whose life was described in the Biography on pages 256–257, wrote *The Order of Chivalry,* one of the most famous of such treatises.

According to the texts, a knight should be strong and disciplined yet use his power to defend the church, the poor, and women in need. Knights were expected to possess the virtue of military prowess, but they also had to be loyal, generous, courteous, and "of noble bearing." In reality, knights probably violated these ethics as often as they adhered to them; the code of chivalry provided only a veneer of symbols and ceremonies that overlay the violence at the heart of "those who fight."

One activity required of chivalrous knights was participation in mock battles called jousts or tournaments. **Figure 8.9** shows a joust, which involved single encounters between two knights. (Tournaments were mock battles between teams of knights.) In this painted illustration, the knights display heraldic figures on their horses and shields that reveal their noble lineage and suggest the importance of noble blood to the ideals of chivalry. Women watch the contest and incite the men on to greater deeds of valor.

FIGURE 8.8 Caerphilly Castle, Wales Medieval warfare was largely defensive: Armor protected knights, and castle walls defended homes and borders. Wales was a frontier area, dotted with many castles built in the thirteenth century.

These were only mock battles, yet many combatants came away from them with debilitating—and sometimes fatal—injuries. The church repeatedly tried to ban tournaments, but the code of chivalry proved too powerful. Tournaments and jousts not only satisfied a profound social need but also provided a practical way for young men to win horses and armor—the victors in these contests took the equipment of the losers.

The very vehemence with which the aristocracy clung to demanding rituals of behavior points to a weakness in their rule. As the Middle Ages wore on, the public role of the nobility—defending and administering Europe—was weakening. Merchants had more wealth, so chivalry was in part a way to hold on to privileges that were eroding. Yet, the nobility convinced itself of its special place in the world through elaborate ceremonies, proper dress, staged battles, and a mania for genealogy. And in the evenings, members of the warrior class entertained one another with stories celebrating the chivalric ideals.

The Literature of Chivalry

During many of the evening gatherings, people listened to *chansons de geste,* or "songs of deeds," which celebrated the ideals of Christian knighthood in the eleventh and twelfth centuries. The most famous of these literary works are the French *Song of Roland* and the Spanish *Poem of the Cid.* Both poems extol the virtues of feudal heroes—Roland, a perfect vassal of Charlemagne; and Rodrigo Díaz de Vivar, known as El Cid (my lord), the perfect vassal of King Alfonso VI (r. 1065–1109) of Aragon. In both accounts, the knights embody the values of prowess and loyalty to a fault. Roland was too brave to call for help in the face

Jousts and tournaments

FIGURE 8.9 Joust Knights honed their skill in warfare by fighting in periodic mock battles such as the joust shown here. Elaborate heraldic markings conveyed the knights' noble lineage. The ladies who watched served as an admiring audience spurring on the combatants.

of overwhelming forces, and El Cid showed perfect fidelity to an unworthy lord. Both stories feature specific details of battle and bloody victories designed to delight an audience of warriors.

These poems also show another side of the chivalric ideal—men's strong emotional ties with one another. The loyalty and camaraderie formed on the battlefield pervaded many aspects of warriors' lives. Roland, for example, wept and swooned at the death of his friend Oliver. In these works, as in the many handbooks on chivalry, women played a peripheral role. They were expected only to incite men to greater deeds and existed mainly to be protected and to provide noble heirs. With the emergence of a new form of literature and a new social code, however, these attitudes shifted somewhat.

In Praise of Romantic Love

In the twelfth century, a new kind of poetry appeared in southern France that changed the social code between men and women—the poetry of the **troubadours,** or court poets. Historians are divided on why this new sensibility emerged at this time. Some postulate an influence of Arabic love poetry from Spain; others emphasize the patronage of wealthy noblewomen. Whatever its origin, the new poetry was highly influential in shaping people's ideas of love. In these works, the poets praised love between men and women as an ennobling idea worthy of being cultivated. Troubadour poetry is diverse, but from it we can distill some basic characteristics of this new romantic love. The ideal love was one in which a man grew more noble by loving and serving a highborn woman (not necessarily his wife and often somebody else's). As they complimented highborn ladies, poets wrote lines promising complete obedience: "And there's no task that's burdensome to me / If it should please my lady master." Knights who pledged this kind of service hoped to be rewarded ultimately with sexual favors: "Surely there'll some day be a time, / My lady beautiful and good / When you can pass me secretly / The sweet reward of a little kiss." This kind of love was meant to be difficult to attain, secret, and highly exciting.

In the twelfth century, Andrew the Chaplain wrote a book titled *The Art of Courtly Love* that paralleled earlier treatises on knightly chivalry. In this work, Andrew described | Courtly love | how lovers must always turn pale in the presence of the beloved and stressed that secrecy and jealousy were essential for intensifying feelings of love. The ideal of courtly love was as much the exclusive property of the nobility as the ideals of chivalry had been. For example, Andrew wrote that if a nobleman fell in love with a mere peasant woman, "do not hesitate to take what you seek and to embrace her by force." Andrew and his noble patrons believed that only the nobility could love properly—that is, possess the leisure and money to engage in this elaborate game. Andrew warned of the consequence if peasants enjoyed romantic love: Their "farms may through lack of cultivation prove useless to us."

Historians have argued about whether the ideal of courtly love improved the actual treatment of women, given that men supposedly bettered themselves in order to win women's hearts. Certainly Andrew's advice about raping peasant women helps answer this question. The poetry written by women troubadours also reveals something about women's experience of this kind of love. Some of this poetry describes the tension between women and the men who claimed to love them but then left to embark on great deeds. The women's poetry shows a desire to have men remain present and attentive. As one poet wrote: "Handsome friend, as a lover true / I loved you, for you pleased me / but now I see I was a fool / for I've barely seen you since."

At least in the literature of courtly love, women occupied the center of the narrative. **Figure 8.10** shows a lady and her knight out hawking together. Unlike in **Figure 8.9,** the woman is in the forefront of the image. She holds the hawk and is courted by the

FIGURE 8.10 Noble Couple Hunting   The nobility loved the hunt, which was one of their prerogatives. Here, a noble couple hunts with a trained hawk. Note how the artist incorporated elements demonstrating the couple's high status, including heraldic symbols at the top and the dapple-gray horse ridden by the woman.

attentive lover. The nobility of each is shown by the coats of arms above them. The artist also enhanced the woman's prestige by showing her on a dappled horse, the most expensive of the breed.

Troubadour poetry spread beyond France to other areas of Europe. Poets also wrote long romances describing the courtly love tradition. The earliest of these writers, Chrétien de Troyes, penned a number of romances set in the court of the imagined hero King Arthur. (The historical Arthur was the Celtic Roman general described in Chapter 6.) These works told of love, loyalty, and great deeds, and served to entertain a nobility that was as enthralled with courtly love as it was with chivalry. These stories and the ideal of romantic love profoundly influenced modern notions of the nature of love between men and women.

THE RISE OF CENTRALIZED MONARCHIES

While noblemen and noblewomen cultivated ideals of war and love, real warfare struck with relentless regularity. Kings were constantly trying to reestablish control over provinces that had drifted away during the turbulent tenth century. At the same time, nobles struggled to keep and even increase their own power. The repeated conflicts between monarch and aristocrat transformed the political map of Europe.

England: From Conquest to Parliament

In the early eleventh century, England had been ruled by the able Danish king Canute (r. 1016–1035) (see Chapter 7), but after his death his Scandinavian empire did not hold together. Before his death, Canute and the English nobility turned to a surviving member of the family of the Anglo-Saxon king Alfred. Thus, Edward the Confessor (r. 1042–1066) reestablished the Anglo-Saxon monarchy. However, a dynasty requires heirs to be stable, and Edward did not have any children. A new succession crisis would lead to the conquest of England.

In 1066, when Edward the Confessor died without an heir, the Anglo-Saxon witan crowned one of their own—Harold Godwinson—as king, and the Anglo-Saxon kingdom was poised to continue as it had before. However, two men believed they had better claims on the English crown. First, Harold Hardradi of Norway landed in the north of England. Harold Godwinson defeated him at the Battle of Stamford Bridge, but that was to be the last battle won by an Anglo-Saxon king. As Halley's comet streaked across the skies that year, seeming to predict disaster, the other claimant, Duke William of Normandy, prepared to sail. William was Edward the Confessor's cousin, and he also claimed that the Anglo-Saxon king had promised him the throne; he aimed to take what he believed was his right. William sailed a fleet across the English Channel and engineered the last successful large-scale invasion of England. The Anglo-Saxon king was killed at the Battle of Hastings and henceforth Duke William reigned as William the Conqueror (r. 1066–1087).

William brought a highly controlled feudal system to the island as he redistributed the Anglo-Saxon nobles' lands to his Norman followers. Although he allowed them to have subvassals, he required everyone to take an oath to him as liege lord (see Chapter 7), so the future Anglo-Norman kings could avoid some of the decentralization implicit in feudalism. William wanted to know exactly what lands he ruled, so he sent out royal officials to make a record of his holdings. The resulting text—the *Domesday Book*—is an invaluable historical record of the times. While William kept the local officials (like sheriffs) that had been so effective in Anglo-Saxon times, he replaced the Anglo-Saxon witan with his own assembly of vassals—the *curia regis*. In this assembly, or Great

Conquest of England

Council, vassals satisfied their feudal obligations to give the king advice and help him pass judgment. This advisory council would become one of the precedents for the growth of Parliament.

William's court spoke only ancient French, and the long coexistence of the two languages led to the incorporation of many French words into what became the modern English language. For example, the Anglo-Saxon words *pig* and *cow* turned into the French-derived *pork* and *beef* as they came to the table of the conquerors. Over the next centuries, however, the hybrid language that emerged was closer to Old English than to French.

The Norman conquest of England had implications for the French monarchy as well, for now the king of England held lands in France—Normandy—as vassal to the king of France. However, this English vassal was stronger than the French kings, and this ambiguous situation would lead to repeated tensions between the English and French royalty over these possessions in France (see Chapter 9).

Henry I (r. 1100–1135) was as able an administrator as William I. To make the *curia regis* more efficient, Henry created separate departments.

Henry I and II The financial department—known as the exchequer—with a chancellor at its head, became extremely important in making sure the crown remained fiscally solvent. Wealth remained the mainstay of power for the medieval monarchies; the other source was the law. Henry I used the law courts to maintain royal control over his vassals. However, a civil war over succession erupted after Henry's death, and during this time of troubles, the monarchy was weakened at the expense of strong nobles. It would take another strong monarch to restore the power of the kings. England found this monarch in Henry II (r. 1154–1189).

Henry II (who introduced the Angevin dynasty of English kings) left a permanent impact on the government and law of England. He continued Henry I's fiscal policies and expanded royal control of justice in the land. He sent traveling justices (called Justices in Eyre) empowered with royal authority around the countryside. They traveled regularly to the courts of the shire investigating and punishing crimes. Henry's legal reforms led to controversies with church courts (described later in this chapter), but they strengthened the power of the king.

Primarily through his marriage, Henry II greatly increased the English holdings in France. In 1152, Henry married Eleanor of Aquitaine, a great heiress (whose first marriage, to the king of France, had been annulled). She brought to the marriage her extensive family estates in France, and **Map 8.4** shows how much of France was under English control. This great English empire was increasingly threatening to the French kings, and it would have been even more so, but Henry and Eleanor's sons dissipated much of the royal wealth and power.

Henry's eldest son, Richard I (r. 1189–1199)—known as "the Lion-Hearted"—much preferred fighting to administering the land, and he spent all but ten months of his reign on campaign outside England. He died from a neglected wound received when he was besieging a castle, and the crown went to his younger brother, John.

The reign of John (r. 1199–1216) was marked by a series of humiliations. He fought costly wars in Normandy to try to defend his possessions against the French king's intrusions. To raise money, John departed from feudal custom in many regards; for example, he married heiresses to the highest bidders and even extorted money from his subjects.

Finally, in the spring of 1215, the barons, disgusted by John's high-handed behavior, staged a rebellion. They even took over London, forcing the king to retreat to a broad **Magna Carta** field south of the city. There, under duress, John signed the **Magna Carta** (the Great Charter), which asserted that kings were not above the law. Beyond establishing this general principle, the charter was a feudal document that promised the king would not impinge on noblemen's traditional rights. However, the charter also included two principles that shaped the future of English (and North American) law: The king would impose no new taxes without the consent of the governed and would not violate the due process of law. This document is treasured as one of the precedents of constitutional law.

Another central institution that arose in the Middle Ages with special implications for England was **Parliament.** As part of their feudal obligations, nobles were to give **Parliament** advice to their lords, and kings all over Europe gathered their vassals and wealthy townspeople in councils—called parliaments—to discuss matters of the realm, which included everything from justice to collecting new taxes. In England in

RISE OF PARLIAMENT IN ENGLAND

	1066	William of Normandy conquers England
	1066–ca. 1086	*Domesday Book* surveys English lands
	1154–1189	Henry II strengthens royal laws
	1170	Thomas Becket killed in Canterbury
	1215	John signs Magna Carta; king not above law
	1295	Edward I's Model Parliament

KEY DATES

MAP 8.4

Medieval France, England, and Germany, Tenth through Fourteenth Centuries

This map shows England, with the major cities and battles of the eleventh century, and the patchwork of lands that made up France and Germany. It also traces the slow centralization of royal control in France.

Explore the Map

1. How did the French royal domain expand over the centuries? What do the fragmented acquisitions suggest about how the lands were acquired?

2. Where is Flanders? What geographic advantages made it a profitable outlet for English wool?

3. Why might it have been difficult to centralize the Holy Roman Empire?

Lands of the French and English Kings
- 987
- 987–1180
- 1180–1328
- English Holdings in France 1180
- English and its French Lands 1328
- Holy Roman Empire ca. 1200
- ✦ Battle Sites

400 mi
800 km

the thirteenth century, this council took a significant turn and became an institution that was able to restrict the power of the king.

The English king Edward I (r. 1272–1307) desperately needed new taxes to finance his wars. Ordinarily English kings asked their nobles in parliament to give additional aid and then sent their agents to cities throughout the land asking for additional money from wealthy merchants. Edward simplified this process by calling for two knights from every county and two burgesses, or townsmen, from every city "to be elected without delay, and to . . . come to us at the aforesaid time and place."

This body with its expanded representation was called the Model Parliament, and it became precedent setting. As they gathered, the knights and the lower nobility sat with the burgesses and began to act together for their mutual benefit, while the clergy sat with the upper nobility. In time, the nobles would become the House of Lords, and the burgesses with the lower nobility, the House of Commons. At first, the House of Commons did little more than approve

the rulings of the lords, but in time this institution came to rule England.

The Spanish Reconquer Their Lands

On the Iberian Peninsula, kings and nobles still fought over the issue of centralization, but a larger political problem—the reconquest of Muslim lands—overshadowed this concern. Land that in other countries might have been held by the nobility emerged as small individual kingdoms—Aragon, Leon-Castile, and Navarre (see **Map 8.5**). These kingdoms sometimes presented a united front to the Muslims and other times fought each other to increase their power. With the threat of the Muslims constantly lurking on their borders, they simply could not afford to focus on unifying the Iberian kingdoms. In the twelfth century, Portugal continued the forces of decentralization

MAP 8.5

Christian Expansion in Iberia

This map shows the location of the Christian kingdoms on the Iberian Peninsula, tracing their expansion southward into the Muslim territories, with dates.

Explore the Map

1. Why was Toledo so important strategically to the Iberians?

2. Where is Santiago de Compostela, an important pilgrimage site? How might its location have stimulated the reconquest?

3. Where is Majorca, the birthplace of Ramón Lull, who is profiled in this chapter's Biography? How does this location help to explain why Lull was drawn to North Africa?

	Christian Territory, ca. 900
	Reconquista, ca. 900–1150
	Reconquista, ca. 1150–1250
	Muslim Holdings, ca. 1250

when it emerged as a separate kingdom. Portugal had once been part of Leon, but King Alfonso VI (r. 1065–1109) gave it as an independent country to his illegitimate daughter and her crusader husband.

Map 8.5 shows the Iberians' slow reconquest of the peninsula from the Muslims. As the map indicates, each Iberian kingdom pursued its

| The reconquest |

expansion southward at the expense of the Muslims. Kings then consolidated their hold on the new lands by establishing Christian settlers and building castles on the border lands. To encourage town settlements, which brought in profitable taxation, kings often gave privileges to Muslim and Jewish artisans and merchants. With this policy, the Iberian Peninsula became a hub for the fertile exchange of ideas among the three religious cultures.

The miraculous tenth-century discovery of the bones of Saint James the Elder stepped up the crusading zeal of the Iberian Christians. A peasant discovered the relics after a vision of brilliant stars shining over a field revealed their location to him. A great shrine—Santiago de Compostela (St. James of the Starry Field)—was built to house the bones. This shrine became a renowned pilgrimage site, attracting the faithful from as far away as Scandinavia. Such pilgrims brought both money and arms, which supported

the Iberians' battle against the Muslims. Visitors to the shrine also brought artistic talent, and traveling builders designed and built great Gothic churches along the pilgrimage route. Christian warriors believed that Saint James appeared on a white horse at the front of Christian armies. Their faith seems to have spurred on their efforts.

The Iberian armies fighting in the culturally diverse land made a significant contribution to the intellectual life of western Europe, for in 1085, King Alfonso VI retook the important city of Toledo, which dominated the peninsula's central plateau. There, churchmen following Alfonso's army recovered the precious manuscripts of Aristotle and the Muslim and Jewish scholars (discussed earlier) that made such an impact on the universities of Europe. As **Map 8.5** shows, by the late thirteenth century, the Muslim lands had dwindled to the city of Granada in the south and the surrounding countryside.

France and Its Patient Kings

Late in the tenth century, the Carolingian family finally lost the royal title west of the Rhine. The descendants of Charlemagne had not exercised effective control of the great feudal princes for a hundred years, yet the title of king still brought some measure of prestige. In 987, Hugh Capet, the lord of the Île-de-France (the region surrounding Paris), was elected by the nobles to the French throne. The church legitimized his rule and a new dynasty was in place in France (see **Map 8.4,** on page 263). The rule of the Capetians involved a long history of slowly reasserting control over the great nobles of their lands. As **Map 8.4** also shows, the kings had to wrestle with the problem of the extensive English holdings in France.

The history of France from the tenth through the fourteenth century suggests the patience of the French kings. **Map 8.4** shows how they gained control over one province after another. These monarchs seldom resorted to war and conquest, but used the means provided under feudal contract law to bring regions back under their control. They also made prudent marriages with wealthy heiresses who brought their inheritances back into royal control. Perhaps most important, the Capetians were fortunate enough to produce sons to inherit their throne.

Philip II Augustus (r. 1180–1223) made great strides in centralizing his lands by directly addressing the English holdings. In wars against the English, Philip finally defeated King John and took over the English lands of Normandy, Maine, and Anjou (see **Map 8.4**). Through these conquests, Philip quadrupled the income of the French monarchy. This talented king recognized the need to develop new ways to maintain his control over the widely dispersed patchwork that was France. Instead of relying on the feudal hierarchy to govern locally, he appointed salaried officials—bailiffs—to collect taxes and represent his interests. These ambitious men, most well educated at the University of Paris, did much to strengthen royal power at the expense of the feudal nobility.

Capetian dynasty

The fortunes of the Capetians were dramatically forwarded by Louis IX (r. 1226–1270), whom many consider the greatest of the medieval kings. He was a pious man who went to church at least twice a day and cared for the poor and sick, and he achieved a distinction highly unusual for a king: he was proclaimed a saint by the church.

Louis IX

For all his piety, Louis did not neglect matters of the realm. Although he did not try to extend the royal domain, he nevertheless expected his nobles to be good vassals. He also took an interest in law and justice and wanted royal justice to be available to all his subjects. The king himself liked to sit in the open under a great oak to receive petitions. **Figure 8.11** shows Louis listening to the pleas of his humble

FIGURE 8.11 King Louis in Judgment The French king Louis IX was known for the fairness of his personal judgments. In this two-part illustration, the guilty receive swift capital punishment by hanging (left), and Louis' subjects bring petitions to the king (right).

subjects—a monk and women. On the left, hanged criminals dangle from trees, demonstrating that the saintly king kept good order in his land. However, Louis did more than dispense personal justice; his advisors began to codify the laws of France, and he was the first king to legislate for all of France. Finally, Louis confirmed the Parlement of Paris—a court, not a representative assembly—as the highest court in France. (It held this position until 1789.) Saint Louis died while on crusade, and his successors continued to ride the Capetian momentum, slowly centralizing their authority.

King Philip IV "the Fair" (r. 1285–1314) believed that the greatest obstacle to his power was Edward I of England and his extensive French fief of Gascony (see **Map 8.4**). Philip engaged in intermittent wars against Edward from 1294 to 1302 and even tried to attack the important English wool industry by blocking importation of English wool into Flanders, but the Flemish towns revolted against him. All these wars were expensive and drove Philip to look for additional funds. The king tried to collect money from the church, which led to a protracted struggle with Pope Boniface VIII (described fully in Chapter 9).

Philip IV

In 1302, Philip needed the support of the realm in his struggles against the pope and to raise money, so he summoned representatives from church, nobility, and towns to the first meeting of the **Estates General.** As these men gathered to advise their king, they sat according to the medieval order—those who prayed, fought, and worked (including townsmen) deliberated separately. This triple arrangement, so different from the two houses of Parliament that grew up in England, helped diffuse each group's power, allowing kings to maintain tight control. This had dramatic consequences for the future of France.

By the end of the thirteenth century, the French monarchy was the best governed and wealthiest in Europe. It was a power to be reckoned with, but there were clouds on the horizon. The Flemish towns remained defiant, England continued to hold and contest lands in France, and the religious struggles had just begun. Philip's successors would face great difficulties.

The Myth of Universal Rule: The Holy Roman Empire

Map 8.4 depicts a large, seemingly powerful neighbor—the Holy Roman Empire—looming to the east of France. But that empire was not as potent as its size might suggest. Early in the tenth century, the last direct descendant of Charlemagne died. The German dukes recognized the need for a leader and, in 919, elected one of their number (Henry of Saxony) to be king. His descendants held the German monarchy until 1024.

The most powerful of this line of kings was Otto I (r. 936–973), who restored the title of emperor. Otto in many ways resembled Charlemagne. He was a warrior king who stopped the advance of the Magyars in 955 and won further conquests in northern Italy.

Saxon dynasty

Also like Charlemagne, Otto fostered a revival of learning in Germany in which literature and art flourished. (Otto had married a Byzantine princess, and she brought artists from Byzantium to enhance the German court.) Finally, the German king marched into Rome to receive the crown of the Roman emperor from Pope John XII, much as Charlemagne had done a century and a half earlier. For hundreds of years after this ceremony, an emperor would be proclaimed in German lands—later to be called the Holy Roman Empire. However, it is one thing to claim a far-flung empire and quite another to exert consistent control over it. Like other rulers in the west, Otto and his successors faced repeated challenges from the strength of the independent nobles within their lands. (**Map 8.4** shows many of the principalities within the empire.)

The Ottonian dynasty ended in 1024, and the German nobles selected Henry III (r. 1039–1056) from another branch of the Saxon family. Henry began the Salian dynasty of Germany. He was an able king who looked for ways to exert more control in his lands, and he increasingly used bishops and abbots that he appointed as his administrators. When his son Henry IV (r. 1056–1106) tried to continue that

Salian dynasty

policy, he ignited a firestorm of debate called the investiture controversy (see page 267).

The Emperor Frederick I (r. 1152–1190), known as Barbarossa, or "red-beard," elected from the house of Hohenstaufen, came close to establishing a consolidated German empire. He planned to exert tight control over three contiguous regions that could form the core of royal lands. He had inherited Burgundy (see **Map 8.4**) and Swabia and invaded Italy to subdue Lombardy in the north. However, while this policy was theoretically sound, it proved ill conceived, and the German emperors were weakened by their continued involvement in Italian politics. Italy's city-states and a strong papacy refused to submit to German rule. The resulting, almost incessant, wars in Italy drained rather than strengthened the emperors' resources.

Hohenstaufen dynasty

The rule of Emperor Frederick II Hohenstaufen (r. 1215–1250) effectively ended any chance of a unified German monarchy. Frederick was a brilliant ruler and patron of the arts, who had been raised in Sicily and had come to love the diverse Muslim and Christian cultures that coexisted in that sunny land. His policy was to confer upon the German princes and nobility virtual sovereignty within their own territories—he retained only the right to set the foreign policy of the empire. His goal was to take as much profit as possible from the German lands but focus his rule in Italy—particularly the Kingdom of the Two Sicilies in the south.

In southern Italy, he rigorously centralized his administration and imposed a monetary tax on all his subjects. He used Muslims as soldiers and was reputed to have a harem of Muslim women. He turned Sicily into a highly organized and culturally exciting monarchy, guided by his firm rule. Although many historians praise Frederick as the first modern ruler—highly organized and practically calculating—the pope and the northern Italian towns feared his expanding policies in Italy. Their fears were well founded, for Frederick led a campaign against the cities of northern Italy (the Lombard League) and scored some victories in 1237. The popes and the towns feared Frederick's encirclement. The pope excommunicated Frederick, and both sides conducted public relations campaigns to discredit the other. Frederick's attempts to unify Italy ended with his death in 1250.

The German princes wanted to preserve the freedoms they had acquired under Frederick II, so they elected a man they considered a weak prince—Rudolph of Habsburg—as emperor. Eventually, the Habsburgs acquired the duchies of Austria, which became the chief foundation for the powerful Habsburg dynasty (see Chapter 11). Burdened by independent nobles and worn down by political

Habsburg dynasty

trouble in Italy, medieval German emperors had little hope of holding their so-called empire together.

THOSE WHO PRAY: IMPERIAL POPES AND EXPANDING CHRISTENDOM

Like the monarchies that had seen their political power fragment during the tumultuous tenth century, the church, too, had decentralized. Local lords saw the churches on their manors as their own property and priests as their own vassals. Nobles sometimes treated bishoprics as rewards for loyal subjects rather than as religious positions. Critics of these practices began to voice demands for reform; and reformers sought an authentic leader who could preside over a universal Christendom.

A Call for Church Reform

One obvious candidate to reform the church was the Holy Roman Emperor. In 1046, when the German Henry III (r. 1039–1056) traveled to Rome to receive the imperial crown, he found the papacy dominated by Roman aristocrats and interfamilial disputes. When he arrived, three rival popes were vying for power. He deposed them all and established a pope (Clement II) loyal to Henry and a strengthened papal court. In the search for order in the Christian world, it seemed that the German emperors might preside over a unified Christendom.

But the eleventh-century popes also began to step forward as a force for reform. Pope Nicholas II (r. 1058–1061) began to free the papacy from military dependence on the German emperor by allying himself with the Normans in southern Italy. However, he also recognized that the church as a whole needed to be free from lay intervention. He was the first pope who expressly condemned the practice of lay investiture: Popes disapproved of a layperson (a secular ruler) giving a churchman the symbols of spiritual office (the ring and staff) because it appeared that the ruler was the source of spiritual authority. Nicholas was not able to stop that long-standing practice, but his voice would not be the last on this subject. However, he was able to move the selection of popes from lay interference, for he called a Roman council in 1059, which defined the principles by which popes were chosen by a college of cardinals, a practice that continues today. It seemed as if the popes might be able to preside over a unified Christendom.

Calls for church reform also came from another source: The ecclesiastical network of Cluniac monasteries that had been established in the early tenth century (see Chapter 7) began to raise its voice. From their foundation, Cluniacs had supported a strong papacy, and their influence increased even further when a cardinal highly sympathetic to the Cluniac order became Pope Gregory VII (r. 1073–1085). Gregory decided that popes, not kings or emperors, should guide Christendom. This outlook led him directly into conflict with the Holy Roman emperor Henry IV (r. 1056–1106).

The Investiture Controversy

The controversy between Gregory and Henry was triggered by the question of who should appoint or invest bishops in Germany, a matter that was as much political as religious. As we have seen, the emperors had used their right to choose bishops to appoint men to act as royal representatives throughout the lands of their independence-hungry nobles. The pope also understood the importance of having allies in distant lands, and he wanted his loyal men in the German churches. This controversy arose out of the dual allegiances bishops faced—to whom did they owe their principal loyalty, pope or king? Through the struggle, the two sides liberally wielded their weapons: Henry sent his armies marching into Italy; Gregory threatened to excommunicate the emperor (and indeed later did so), claiming that this action could free the ever-rebellious vassals from their feudal obligations. Gregory also had the support of a powerful patron, Matilda, Countess of Tuscany. This skilled tactician promptly challenged Henry's military strength, leading her own armies into battle against him.

Figure 8.12 shows a crucial incident in the investiture controversy. Henry IV kneels at Matilda's feet, while she is shown framed by her strong castle of Canossa. He begs her and Abbot Hugh of Cluny to intercede for him so that he may receive forgiveness from the pope, which Henry desperately needed to control his princes who saw this dispute as a way to gain more independence. This illustration also reveals the important roles both Matilda and the monks of Cluny played in the controversy, but the question of the independence of the church would not be easily solved. In a dramatic incident at Canossa, Henry waited three days in the snow dressed in the sackcloth of a penitent begging the pope's forgiveness. Gregory as a priest was obliged to forgive a sinner professing sorrow, so the two temporarily made peace.

Within three years, pope and king were again locked in combat. This time, however, when Henry invaded Italy, Gregory's Norman mercenaries caused so much damage in Rome that the outraged citizens forced the pope to abandon the city. He died in exile in 1085, bitterly convinced he had failed in forwarding papal authority. But Henry was unable to secure a decisive victory, either, and spent the remainder of his life trying to recover his authority in Germany. The issue of investiture was left for a later king and pope to resolve.

In 1122 the new emperor, Henry V, negotiated a compromise in the investiture controversy, the Concordat of Worms. Pope and emperor decided the pope could present new bishops with their symbols of office, indicating the priority of the church over its churchmen. However, the emperor could be present at and influence the elections of bishops. This compromise actually represented a victory for the popes, who now had an opening for exerting authority within the rising national monarchies all over Europe. But the papal victory would not come easily or unopposed.

Concordat of Worms

Such tensions persisted between clergy and lay rulers who wanted to strengthen their own rule in their home territories. In England, the struggle took the form of a deadly clash between King Henry II (r. 1154–1189) and his archbishop and once best friend, Thomas Becket. Becket wanted to preserve the church's right to be exempt from the legal authority Henry was using to consolidate his power over his land. One day, a small group of knights seeking to please their king surprised Becket in his church at Canterbury and split his head with their swords. Becket died on the altar he had served so well. Their plan to eliminate the influence of the archbishop backfired, however: Becket quickly became a martyr in the battle for church autonomy. In the face of popular revulsion for the crime, Henry was forced to compromise with the pope to gain forgiveness for his archbishop's murder. Henry had to allow the papacy to be the court of appeal from English ecclesiastical courts, and this concession brought the English church more closely into the sphere of Rome.

Thomas Becket

FIGURE 8.12 Henry IV and Matilda of Tuscany, twelfth century This image captures the importance of the noblewoman Matilda of Tuscany in the investiture controversy, for it shows Holy Roman emperor Henry IV being forced to kneel before her and ask for her intercession. The stylized castle surrounding Matilda symbolizes her power.

The power of the popes grew; the example of Becket showed that their weapons of excommunication and spiritual leadership were impossible to fight with swords. As church power grew, the papacy developed structures that increasingly resembled the powerful medieval monarchies. Just as monarchs began to rely on bureaucracy, court systems, and money to consolidate their power, the pope created a papal curia—an administrative unit—to handle financial matters. He also created a branch to handle legal appeals with the growing body of canon law, which was the compilations of religious laws that slowly came to govern much of medieval life.

By the beginning of the thirteenth century, popes could with some accuracy claim that they presided over a universal Christendom, and one of the most powerful was Innocent III (r. 1198–1216). Innocent was able to exert leadership over princes of Europe: He reprimanded the kings of England, Aragon, Portugal, France, Poland, and Norway and insisted that they obey him. He vigorously fought heretics and wanted to clarify Christian belief. To accomplish the latter, he called the Fourth Lateran Council, which met in 1215. Among other things, this council identified exactly seven sacraments and reaffirmed their

Innocent III

essential role in reaching salvation. The council also pronounced on many other matters, from qualifications for the priesthood to monastic life and veneration of relics. With the clarity expressed by the council, the medieval church was firmly defined. In effect, the church had become an empire that superseded all other empires.

The Byzantine Empire Struggles

The Byzantine Empire had reached the height of its expansion and power in 1056, but in the late eleventh century troubles flared up. The Byzantine army, once built so firmly on the theme system (see **Map 6.3**), had deteriorated, and the emperors had begun to use mercenary soldiers, who were expensive to maintain. When the empire became vulnerable on several fronts in the late eleventh century, neither the army nor the treasury was prepared. The Normans threatened Byzantine provinces in southern Italy, and the Muslims menaced in the east.

Islam had gained strength from the movement of the Seljuk Turks, a fierce central Asian tribe whose members had converted to Islam and reinforced the Muslim armies threatening Byzantium. In the midst of succession problems, Byzantium elected a strong soldier—Ramonos Diogenes (r. 1068–1071)—as emperor. Diogenes led an army east in 1071 and challenged the Turks. However, he experienced a crushing defeat at the Battle of Manzikert, and this loss triggered another succession crisis in the capital. Meanwhile, the victorious Turks drove deeper into the empire, capturing all of Asia Minor and taking control of some of the Byzantines' richest lands.

In Byzantium's darkest days, a strong new emperor, Alexius Komnenus (r. 1081–1118), emerged and managed to halt the imperial disintegration. (See Document 8.2 for Princess Anna Komnene's description of the problems her father faced when he took power.) Alexius built a new army based on feudal ties, raised taxes, and desperately cast about for ways to check the Turkish advance. Remembering the skilled knights whom his forces had fought in Sicily, Alexius looked to the West for help. His appeal found fertile ground with a papacy looking for a cause.

Christians on the March: The Crusades, 1096–1291

From as early as the fourth century, Christians had begun to visit holy places, and with the prosperity of the eleventh century, these pilgrimages became even more popular. One of the favorite pilgrimage destinations (along with Santiago de Compostela, described earlier) was Palestine, where Jesus had lived. Sometimes bands of thousands traveled, and when they journeyed to the Holy Land, they passed through Byzantine lands to reach the Muslim territories that included the holy places. For centuries, these trips—albeit hazardous—were possible.

The Turks, who now controlled Jerusalem, did not consciously stop the pilgrim traffic, but they did impose taxes on travelers, and to many Christians it seemed that the Holy Land should not be controlled by these Turks. When Emperor Alexius sent an appeal to Pope Urban II (r. 1088–1099) pleading for help to supplement his forces, the pope was ready to respond. In 1095, Urban called for Christians to begin a holy war against the newly strengthened Muslims.

The text of Urban's speech was preserved by several (sometimes conflicting) chroniclers, yet all agree that it shows a clear perception of the needs of the West and the motives of crusaders. Urban reminds his audience that | Pope Urban's call | western Europe is becoming too confining: "For this land which you inhabit, . . . is too narrow for your large population; nor does it abound in wealth; and it furnishes scarcely food enough for its cultivators." He further promised crusaders remission of sins if they undertook this journey. Urban's call was spectacularly successful, and members of the aristocracy began to plan the journey to the Holy Land.

Urban told departing soldiers to wear the sign of the cross on their breasts and encouraged them to earn the right to wear the symbol on their back when they returned, a symbol proving they had successfully fulfilled their vow to fight in this holy cause. The series of military engagements against the Muslims that continued for two hundred years are called the **Crusades,** named for the cross under which the Christians fought. People went on crusade for a number of reasons. Many were driven by sincere religious motivation, although their lofty purposes frequently deteriorated in the heat of battle. Some propertyless nobles hoped to find some land of their own, and other people sought wealth to bring home.

People responded to Urban's call with a fervor that surprised even the planners of the crusade. The first to respond included large numbers of peasants who followed two self-appointed leaders—Peter the Hermit and Walter the Penniless—to the east to free the Holy Land. Long before they reached the Holy Land, their zeal led them to violence in the West. They terrorized local people, looting for food and supplies to take on their way. A contemporary chronicler also told how their religious fervor led to other violence: "Led by their zeal for Christianity, they persecuted the hated race of the Jews wherever they were found and strove either to destroy them completely or to compel them to become Christians." These early excesses would mark many of the subsequent crusades. When these peasants arrived in Constantinople, the emperor quickly shipped them over to Asia Minor, where they were massacred by the Turks.

DOCUMENT 8.2

Princess Anna Komnene Writes of Byzantium's Troubles

The Byzantine emperor Alexius's daughter Anna was a highly educated, skilled writer. In the twelfth century, she wrote The Alexiad, *a history of her father's reign. Anna was a valuable eyewitness to the First Crusade and to the growing animosity between western Europeans (whom she called Franks) and the Byzantines. In these excerpts, she offers a clear assessment of the weaknesses of the Byzantine Empire that led Alexius to seek help from the West.*

Book 3: IX   Alexius saw that the Empire was nearly at its last gasp, for in the East the Turks were grievously harassing the frontiers whilst in the West things were very bad. . . . Consequently the young and brave Emperor was desperate, and did not know which way to turn first, as each of his enemies seemed to be trying to begin war before the other, and thus he grew sorely vexed and disturbed. For the Roman Empire possessed only a very insufficient army (not more than the 300 soldiers from Coma cowardly and inexperienced in war, besides just a few very barbarian troops, accustomed to carry their swords on their right shoulder). And further there was no large reserve of money in the imperial treasury with which to hire allied troops from foreign countries. For the preceding Emperors had been very inefficient in all military and warlike matters and had thus driven the State of Rome into very dire straits. . . .

Book 3: X   Before he had enjoyed even a short rest, he heard a report of the approach of innumerable Frankish armies. Now he dreaded their arrival for he knew their irresistible manner of attack, their unstable and mobile character and all the peculiar natural and concomitant characteristics which the Frank retains throughout; and he also knew that they were always agape for money, and seemed to disregard their truces readily for any reason that cropped up. For he had always heard this reported of them, and found it very true. However, he did not lose heart, but prepared himself in every way so that, when the occasion called, he would be ready for battle. And indeed the actual facts were far greater and more terrible than rumor made them. For the whole of the West and all the barbarian tribes which dwell between the further side of the Adriatic and the pillars of Heracles, had all migrated in a body and were marching into Asia through the intervening Europe, and were making the journey with all their household. The reason of this upheaval was more or less the following. A certain Frank, Peter by name, nicknamed Cucupeter [Peter of the Cowl], had gone to worship at the Holy Sepulchre and after suffering many things at the hands of the Turks and Saracens who were ravaging Asia, he got back to his own country with difficulty. But he was angry at having failed in his object, and wanted to undertake the same journey again. However, he saw that he ought not to make the journey to the Holy Sepulchre alone again, lest worse things befall him, so he worked out a cunning plan. This was to preach in all the Latin countries that "the voice of God bids me announce to all the Counts in France that they should all leave their homes and set out to worship at the Holy Sepulchre, and to endeavor wholeheartedly with hand and mind to deliver Jerusalem from the hand of the Hagarenes [Muslims]." And he really succeeded. For after inspiring the souls of all with this quasi-divine command he contrived to assemble the Franks from all sides, one after the other, with arms, horses and all the other paraphernalia of war. And they were all so zealous and eager that every highroad was full of them. And those Frankish soldiers were accompanied by an unarmed host more numerous than the sand or the stars, carrying palms and crosses on their shoulders; women and children, too, came away from their countries. And the sight of them was like many rivers streaming from all sides, and they were advancing towards us through Dacia generally with all their hosts.

SOURCE: Anna Comnena (Komnene), *The Alexiad,* ed. and trans. Elizabeth A. Dawes (London: Routledge, Kegan, Paul, 1928).

Analyze the Document

1. What weaknesses in the Byzantine Empire does Anna Komnene describe?

2. Why, according to Anna, did the Franks come to crusade? Why do you think she does not attribute their arrival to Alexius's summons?

3. What characteristics does she attribute to the Franks?

4. How might a Western observer have described the same events?

The earliest crusaders were vividly described by the Byzantine emperor's daughter Anna Komnene in *The Alexiad,* a history of her father's reign. In addition to offering a first-person account of the crusaders, Anna sheds light on the mutual suspicion and ill will that divided Byzantines from westerners (whom she called Franks) and forecasts a future deterioration of the crusading ideal. In contrast to Komnene, western sources describe the crusaders as fulfilling a high purpose: "The Franks straightway began to sew the cross on the right shoulders of their garments, saying that they would all with one accord follow in the footsteps of Christ." These contrasting accounts underscored the widening split between East and West, which was fueled by a fundamental misunderstanding: The crusaders wanted land in exchange for their military

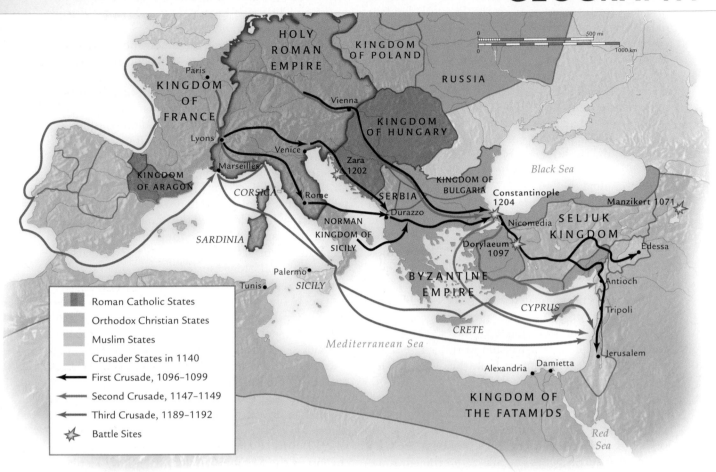

MAP 8.6

The Early Crusades, 1096–1192

This map shows the dates, routes, and major battles of the first three crusades.

Explore the Map

1. What were the advantages and disadvantages of the two routes to the Holy Land—by land and by sea?

2. How difficult would it have been to reinforce the crusader states and to hold that outpost given that it took the earliest crusaders about nine months to reach the Holy Land?

3. Which of the crusader states might have been the most vulnerable and first to fall? Why?

---

service (western-style feudalism), but Alexius just wanted to pay them and have them turn over the land to him. The Muslims wanted them all to stay away from their lands.

Anna Komnene's "soldiers of fortune" were highly skilled and successful warriors, and they relentlessly swept the Muslim forces out of the Holy Land. In 1099, when they took Jerusalem after a five-week siege, the carnage was brutal. The eyewitness Fulcher of Chartres tells of the bloodshed: "Within Solomon's Temple, about ten thousand were beheaded. If you had been there, your feet would have been stained up to the ankles with the blood of the slain." When the

violence died down, the crusaders took the Holy Land and established kingdoms there. **Map 8.6** shows the routes of the Crusades and the locations of the crusader states.

The crusader principalities served as outposts of western European culture in the East. They entertained pilgrims, fought skirmishes on their borders, and learned about life in the eastern Mediterranean. Generations of western Europeans living in proximity with Muslims were changed somewhat by the interactions. They learned to eat different foods, began to value bathing, and acquired a taste for urban life,

Crusader states

unlike their rural cousins at home. Even a Muslim chronicler noticed the transformation: "Everyone who is a fresh emigrant from the Frankish lands is ruder in character than those who have become acclimatized and have held long association with Muslims."

However, the official relationship between crusader and Muslim was not friendly. On the Muslim side, the appearance of Christian soldiers reawakened the spirit of jihad that had receded from political policy. (See Chapter 6.) For example, a Syrian legal scholar in the twelfth century wrote a work called the *Book of Holy War,* in which he argued that it was the neglect of jihad that allowed the crusaders to conquer Jerusalem and surrounding areas. His solution was to call for a moral and military resurgence to respond to the crusading movement. But this work was not widely circulated; it established an ideal, but it took until later in the twelfth century for Muslims to rally against crusaders in the spirit of jihad.

The most important determinant of the relations between the two groups was probably geographic. **Map 8.6** shows the precarious location of the crusader states, surrounded by the Muslim world. These states would need constant support from the West to keep them from being retaken by the Muslims.

As early as the 1120s, the Muslims had begun to strike back, and Edessa fell in 1144. Christians in the west mounted further Crusades to support their fellows in the Holy Land, but the subsequent crusades were not as successful as the first, even though some illustrious western kings participated.

Map 8.6 shows the routes and dates of the two subsequent crusades. The Second Crusade was urged on by Bernard of Clairveaux (Peter Abelard's foe, described earlier), but the two leaders—King Louis VII of France and Emperor Conrad III of Germany—could not coordinate their efforts enough to make any difference.

Things became worse for the crusader states: The Muslims of Syria produced a vigorous leader named Saladin, who controlled Syria and Egypt. Using the newly invigorated spirit of jihad, Saladin conducted a coordinated force that retook Jerusalem in 1187. Saladin did not permit a massacre of civilians, and he even tolerated a continuation of Christian services, but the West was ablaze with calls for a new crusade. Three major monarchs responded: Emperor Frederick Barbarossa, Richard the Lion-Hearted of England, and Philip II of France. Everyone thought these pillars of chivalry could retake the Holy City, but they, too, had problems coordinating their efforts. After some stunning successes, Frederick Barbarossa drowned while swimming and his army went home. The French king also retreated after some losses, leaving Richard and Saladin to negotiate a settlement whereby Christian pilgrims could have free access to Jerusalem. However, these concessions seemed humiliating to Christians in the West who unrealistically hoped for a decisive victory.

The Crusades spurred the emergence of new religious orders that followed a monastic rule and that served as a crucial part of the permanent garrison guarding the Holy Land. Their principal function was to serve God by fighting Muslims, and Muslims and Christians alike respected their military accomplishments. The Knights Templars, the most famous of these orders, protected pilgrims and served as bankers for those traveling to the Holy Land, but they grew so powerful that many began to resent their strength and organization. Saladin hated the Templars, saying, "Let us rid the earth of the air they breathe," but they remained a central force in the Holy Land. Again, the medieval social order blurred, as one group of those who prayed also began to specialize in warfare.

The noble ideal of crusading deteriorated over time as Christians began to focus less on the Holy Land itself and more on Christendom's perceived enemies. For example, crusading fervor led Christians in Europe to conduct more pogroms (massacres) against Jews in Europe.

Crusading armies also turned on Byzantine Christians as relations between them had continued to deteriorate. In 1182, the man who would become the Byzantine emperor Andronikos (r. 1183–1185), the last of the Komnenian dynasty, allowed a massacre of Latins in Constantinople. Westerners reacted to the slaughter with rage. Andronikos's death ended the strong Komnenian dynasty, and the Byzantine royalty once again was roiled by family feuding, negligence, and corruption. As you can see from **Map 8.7,** in 1204, crusaders were drawn into Byzantine politics and took advantage of the Byzantine disarray. The Fourth Crusade, short of money, first attacked the Christian city of Zara for the Venetians in exchange for their passage to the Holy Land. Then a pretender to the Byzantine throne offered crusaders money to place him in power, and crusaders attacked Byzantium itself. Successful in their mission, they sacked the great city, raping women (some of them nuns) and defiling altars. Despite the pope's condemnation, the westerners divided the empire among themselves and abandoned their plan to go to Jerusalem. They held Byzantium for fifty-seven years—until the Byzantines managed to retake it—but this interim badly weakened the empire, as well as the crusading ideal.

You can follow the continued fortunes of the subsequent crusades on **Map 8.7.** The Seventh and Eighth crusades, led by the saintly French king Louis IX (r. 1226–1270), went to North Africa, where the crusaders failed miserably. Louis died in Tunis.

Knights Templars

Subsequent crusades

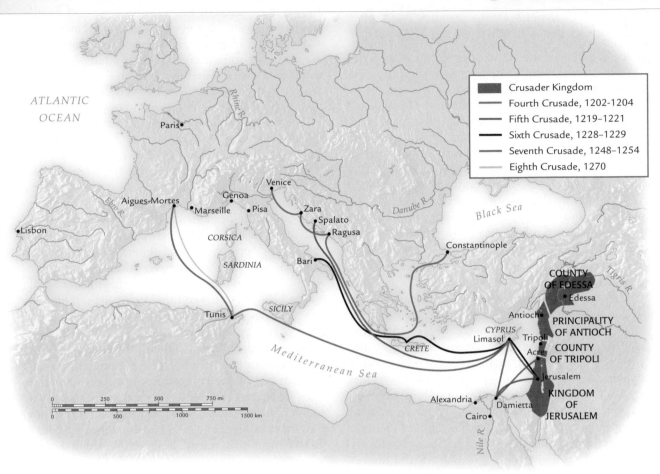

ATLANTIC
OCEAN

Legend:
- **Crusader Kingdom**
- Fourth Crusade, 1202-1204
- Fifth Crusade, 1219-1221
- Sixth Crusade, 1228-1229
- Seventh Crusade, 1248-1254
- Eighth Crusade, 1270

MAP 8.7

The Late Crusades, 1202–1270

This map shows the routes and destinations of the Fourth through the Eighth Crusades.

Explore the Map

1. Why were the county of Edessa and the city of Acre the first and last areas to fall back to the Muslims?

2. Why did several of these crusades never reach the Holy Land?

3. All of these crusades took the sea route to the east. What does this fact suggest about Venice's growth as a sea power?

Perhaps the height of misplaced religious zeal took place during the Children's Crusade (1212–1213), when some preachers argued that crusaders had lost God's help through their misdeeds, and only the innocent might save the Holy Land. The sources say thousands of innocent children died or were sold into slavery during this fiasco. (Some modern historians question whether this appalling incident really occurred.)

Finally, in 1291, the Muslims seized the last crusader outpost on the Asian mainland when the fortified city of Acre fell. This was a terrible military disaster for the West, and the last frightened Christians in the Holy Land paid ship masters fortunes for passage out of the doomed city. Knights Templars died courageously while guarding the evacuation of Christians from the burning city. Two centuries of Christian expansion into the eastern Mediterranean ended with few concrete results. Islam was as strong as ever; Byzantium had only weakened further. For centuries, however, the image of knights galloping across Europe to reclaim the Holy Land from the Muslims continued to captivate Christians throughout the West. The church lost prestige as crusaders lost the Holy Land, but

Crusaders expelled

even more devastating criticism emerged in western Christendom itself.

Criticism of the Church

In the West under the guidance of many skilled popes, the church had established a strong organization and wielded much authority. Yet some Christians, called heretics by the orthodox, disagreed with established doctrine and criticized the direction the church had taken. Some of these people believed that the church had erred in becoming rich as early as the reign of the Roman emperor Constantine (r. 306–337) (discussed in Chapter 5). These critics wanted to follow the example of the apostles described in the Bible and live a simple life by being poor, preaching, and reading the sacred text. This criticism also reflected a new reality in the West—there now existed a richer and increasingly urban world with the kind of visible inequities that seemed worth rejecting.

The best-known proponent of the simple life was Valdes of Lyons. (Later he became incorrectly called Peter Waldo, and he is often remembered by that name.) A rich mer-

| Waldensians |

chant in his younger years, Valdes gave up all his material possessions in order to wander, beg, and preach. Many ordinary Christians were drawn to the holy simplicity of his life, but churchmen were threatened by his implicit criticism of churches decorated with gold. The pope condemned Valdes and his followers as heretics in 1181, but many of his supporters, called Waldensians, stayed loyal to their beliefs, and in fact, Waldensian churches exist today.

Several similar sects arose that advocated the apostolic life (called *vita apostolica*). Indeed, numerous men and women throughout the Middle Ages continued to consider wealth and Christianity incompatible. Taken together, such movements represented a growing discomfort with a church that seemed too powerful and too embroiled in the gritty details of the physical world to fulfill the spiritual needs of men and women. The thirteenth-century church met these criticisms with both accommodation and repression.

The Church Accommodates: Franciscans and Dominicans

New monastic movements had always been a source of reform for the church and an outlet for men and women who sought different ways of expressing their religious impulses. In the thirteenth century, popes approved two such movements, the Franciscans and the Dominicans, that promised to address the criticism that had arisen so strongly against the church. In previous monastic movements, men and women isolated themselves behind great walls to devote themselves to God. By contrast, the new religious impulses called for holy men and women to mingle among the people in the growing towns of Europe and help alleviate the new problems of urban poverty and suffering. Therefore, Franciscans and Dominicans did not retire from society as monks but were called **mendicant orders** (literally "begging orders," which alludes to their poverty) and served God by helping the needy within their villages and towns.

The Franciscan movement was founded by Francis of Assisi (1182–1226), the son of a wealthy Italian merchant. Like Valdes of Lyon, Francis had a conversion experience

| Francis of Assisi |

that inspired him to give up all his earthly goods to live in poverty. He survived by begging, and he helped care for the poor people of Assisi and other nearby towns. His gentle demeanor and charismatic preaching had broad appeal. Francis attracted a number of followers among the young in Assisi. One young woman, Clare, heard him speak, and in 1212 she followed him into a religious life. She established a mendicant order for women and presided over a group of women dedicated to the same ideals she had embraced. These Poor Ladies of Assisi, sometimes called Poor Clares, became the female counterparts of the Franciscans, but soon their lives were structured differently from that of their male counterparts: Instead of wandering and preaching, they lived in silence in enclosed convents. In spite of this change, this spiritual life still attracted many followers.

Although Franciscans in some ways resembled the Waldensians, who had been condemned as heretics, they differed in one significant respect: They believed in obedience to the pope. Because of this humility, Francis received papal dispensation to establish a new order of "friars," who would live in poverty and preach.

The Franciscans appealed to those who believed in a poor and humble church, but their work did not satisfy all the critics. Many people thought that the church had fallen into error because of ignorance.

| Dominican order |

Another new mendicant order, the Dominicans, arose to address this problem. The Dominicans were led by the Spanish priest Dominic de Guzmán (1170–1221), an intellectual who believed that heresy could be fought through preaching. In 1215, Pope Honorius approved the Order of Preachers, or the Dominicans, who, like the Franciscans, took an oath of poverty and lived among the townspeople instead of in monasteries. However, they emphasized preaching rather than poverty and stressed study at universities to ensure that their preaching was strictly orthodox. The Dominicans thus appealed to people's minds, whereas the Franciscans spoke to their hearts.

Through permitting both of these orders, the church had responded to the spiritual needs of its followers by authorizing dedicated men and women to teach and practice among the people. Christians hungering for a more profound sense of spiritual connectedness welcomed the lessons they received from these pious teachers.

The Church Suppresses: The Albigensian Crusade and the Inquisition

The church did not always prove so accommodating in the face of criticism. In the late twelfth century, a heretical movement became very popular, particularly in southern France. This movement, called Catharism (from the Greek word for "pure"), was similar to Zoroastrianism (described in Chapter 1) in that it professed a system of two principles (or two deities)—light and darkness—fighting for supremacy. Adherents identified the god of darkness with the Old Testament deity who created the world and the god of light with the New Testament and spiritual salvation. They believed that people had to struggle to help the good principle trapped in everyone escape the evil world of the flesh. Because a center of this group was in Albi in southern France, they are also commonly known as Albigensians.

Albigensians were particularly threatening to the church because their ideas struck at the very heart of Christian belief, which considered the material world as good. Pope Innocent III first sent preachers to Albi to show people the error of their ways. However, in 1209, after some violence against papal representatives, the pope lost patience and called a crusade against the heretics. Northern French nobles, eager to break the power of the strong southern lords, participated avidly in the savage campaign. **Figure 8.13** shows Albigensians being expelled from one of the major heretical strongholds of Carcassone. This illustration contrasts the simplicity of the men and women heretics with the fierce crusaders, perhaps revealing some compassion for the heretics, because during the crusade's twenty years, thousands of people were massacred. In one especially tragic example, 7,000 men, women, and children of the town of Béziers took refuge from the crusaders in the local cathedral. When soldiers asked the papal representative how they could distinguish between heretics and the faithful, he reportedly replied, "Kill them all; God will know his own." All 7,000 of the townspeople—heretic and orthodox alike—died that day in the church's attempt to stamp out heresy.

Even after such brutal displays of power, church leaders still felt endangered by diversity of beliefs.

Albigensian Crusade

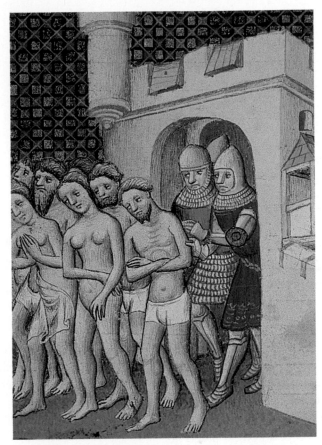

FIGURE 8.13 Albigensian Crusade The church turned the power of crusade against heretics in southern France, centered in Albi. This illustration documents the expulsion of the Albigensians from the town of Carcassone in 1209; their nudity symbolizes how they lost all their goods.

In the mid-thirteenth century, the church established a new court—the **inquisition**—designed to ferret out and eradicate threatening ideas. Unlike secular courts, which determined the guilt or innocence of actions, the inquisition aimed to detect wrong beliefs. The court recognized the difficulty in examining people's ideas and developed special means by which to determine what people were thinking. Often it relied on the Dominicans, with their training in understanding heresy, to serve as the inquisitor generals. These generals used questioning, starvation, and other forms of torture to force people to reveal their beliefs. Many unfortunate victims "confessed" to escape further torture or execution, and although they were released, many faced extreme "penances," such as renunciation of property or imprisonment. All self-confessed heretics faced severe social repercussions from their neighbors, who no longer wanted to associate with the "guilty." Those who were deemed guilty and unrepentant were turned over to the secular authority to be executed, usually by burning.

The inquisition

The inquisition swept through much of Europe, inflicting more damage in some communities than in others. Perhaps the only way to understand this phenomenon is to remember that people in the Middle Ages were deeply concerned about the state of their souls and their own salvation. They believed that exposure to incorrect religious ideas could jeopardize that salvation, and this was a risk they simply could not take. In their emphasis on community over the individual, they did not share modern beliefs that efforts to save one another from "wrong" ideas potentially put all ideas in peril.

By 1300, many in medieval Europe were convinced that order was established in the world. Bishop Gerard of Cambrai, whose quotation opened this chapter, elaborated on the three-part structure of this perfectly ordered society: Those who pray are able to enjoy this "holy leisure" because of the efforts of those who fight, who guarantee their security. Both of these groups are able to fill their functions because those who work see to the needs of their bodies. The world seemed perfectly appointed.

LOOKING BACK & MOVING FORWARD

Summary   At the turn of the first millennium C.E., agricultural innovations sparked a dramatic surge in the European population. This growth fueled an expansion of western European civilization that represented the high point of the Middle Ages. During this time of expansion, western Europeans made great intellectual innovations—philosophical systems, engineering wonders, and creative literature. Kings slowly changed their feudal lands into national monarchies—sometimes by exerting their legal rights and sometimes by violent confrontations with their nobles. The church, too, increased its central power, ultimately claiming to rule over a Europe united in faith, although it had to resort to extreme measures to preserve this fiction.

Finally, the West was strong enough to expand its horizons and again confront the great cultures on its borders and beyond. With the violent Crusades in the eastern Mediterranean, Christians challenged the power of Islam and lost; with the reconquest of Spain, however, Christians prevailed over the Muslims. More significantly, Christians learned much about science, technology, and life from the Muslims. However, this ordered, prosperous age would confront dramatic challenges in the fourteenth century, when disasters would strike. Would medieval structures prove resilient enough to withstand the pressure?

KEY TERMS

communes, *p. 248*

guilds, *p. 248*

Romanesque, *p. 250*

Gothic, *p. 250*

scholasticism, *p. 253*

chivalry, *p. 259*

troubadous, *p. 260*

Magna Carta, *p. 262*

Parliament, *p. 262*

Estates General, *p. 265*

Crusades, *p. 269*

mendicant orders, *p. 274*

inquisition, *p. 275*

REVIEW, ANALYZE, & CONNECT TO TODAY

REVIEW THE PREVIOUS CHAPTER

Chapter 7—"The Struggle to Bring Order"—described manorialism and the feudal contract as the organizing structures of medieval life. It also described the invasions of the ninth and tenth centuries that undermined the developing order in the West.

1. Review the obligations of peasants and the nature of village life described in Chapter 7 and consider the strengths of these structures that allowed for the agricultural boom in the eleventh century.

2. Review the invasions by Vikings and others that caused a decentralization of power and the weakening of kings.

How did this decentralization influence the growth of England and France from the eleventh through the thirteenth century?

ANALYZE THIS CHAPTER

Chapter 8—"Order Restored"—traces the High Middle Ages and follows the fortunes of the social groups and political entities that made up the West.

1. Consider the growth of towns and the related developments of trade. How did towns govern themselves? How was the prevalence of Gothic cathedrals and pilgrimages related to the growing prosperity of towns?

2. One of the themes of this chapter is the struggle between popes and emperors or kings to decide who should lead a Christian Europe. Review these struggles and consider the advantages and disadvantages of each party's position.

3. Review the Crusades. Why did the crusaders go to the Holy Land, and what did they accomplish?

CONNECT TO TODAY

Think about the revolution in technology that fueled the West's growth in the Middle Ages.

1. Are there parallels in recent times with the medieval technological revolution? Explain.

2. What can we learn from the past about how to manage swift technological change?

Think about the long series of Crusades that the West initiated against Islam.

1. What world events today do you think reflect the long-standing Muslim–Western animosity fostered by the Crusades?

2. How do we use the word *crusade* today? How do you think that usage might contribute to mutual misunderstandings between Christians and Muslims?

BEYOND THE CLASSROOM

THOSE WHO WORK: AGRICULTURAL LABOR

Hanawalt, B. *The Ties That Bind: Peasant Families in Medieval England.* New York: Oxford University Press, 1986. An eminent historian provides a vivid and engaging picture of peasant life.

Schofield, Phillip R. *Peasant and Community in Medieval England, 1200–1500.* New York: Palgrave Macmillan, 2002. A study of peasant life, with an emphasis on interactions between the village and the outside world.

THOSE OUTSIDE THE ORDER: TOWN LIFE

Bennet, Judith M. *Ale, Beer, and Brewsters in England: Women's Work in a Changing World.* Oxford: Oxford University Press, 1999. An excellent discussion of the changing economic roles of women as the medieval economy grew.

Evans, G.R. *Philosophy and Theology in the Middle Ages.* New York: Routledge, 1993. A sound, comprehensive survey of intellectual thought, showing the ties between philosophy and theology.

Pounds, Norman. *The Medieval City,* 2nd ed. Westport, CT: Greenwood Press, 2005. An introduction to medieval towns emphasizing their historical development and functions.

Ridder-Symoens, Hilde de. *A History of the University in Europe: Universities in the Middle Ages.* New York: Cambridge University Press, 1991. Remains the only comprehensive history of medieval universities that includes their social and political context.

Wigelsworth, Jeffrey R. *Science and Technology in Medieval European Life.* Westport, CT: Greenwood Press, 2006. A discussion of the ideas and inventions that made a large impact on all facets of medieval daily life.

THOSE WHO FIGHT: NOBLES AND KNIGHTS

Bartlett, Robert. *The Hanged Man: A Story of Miracle, Memory, and Colonialism in the Middle Ages.* Princeton, NJ: Princeton University Press, 2004. A brief, brilliantly written account of the examination of a purported thirteenth-century miracle in which a hanged rebel was restored to life.

Gies, J., and F. Gies. *Life in a Medieval Castle.* New York: Harper & Row, 1974. A popular, illustrated work that offers a summary of noble life. Although not scholarly, it is nevertheless accurate and engaging.

Poly, Jean-Pierre, and Eric Bournazel. *The Feudal Trans-formation, 900–1200.* New York: Holmes & Meier, 1991. A scholarly and provocative detailed analysis of French sources to explore ideas of social hierarchy, war and peace, and medieval ideas.

Sanchez, Jose. *Medieval Knights: The Age of Chivalry.* Havertown, PA: Andrea Press, 2008. Beautifully illustrated and comprehensive account of medieval knights—their customs, military strategy, tactics, and social life.

THE RISE OF CENTRALIZED MONARCHIES

Fletcher, Richard. *Moorish Spain.* New York: H. Holt, 1992. A concise survey of the Iberian Peninsula from the Muslim invasion to the fall of Granada that shows the significant impact of the reconquest.

Furman, Horst. *Germany in the High Middle Ages, c. 1050–1200.* Translated by T. Reuter. New York: Cambridge University Press, 1986. A clear and engaging survey of a complex time.

Haines, Roy Martin. *King Edward II: Edward of Carnarfon, His Life, His Reign and Its Aftermath, 1284–1330.* Montreal:

McGill–Queen's University Press, 2006. A comprehensive narrative, backed by careful scholarship, that should remain the definitive work on this important period of English history.

Hallam, Elizabeth M. *Capetian France, 987–1328.* New York: Longman, 1980. A chronicle of the slow consolidation of these French kings as they expanded their power.

THOSE WHO PRAY: IMPERIAL POPES AND EXPANDING CHRISTENDOM

Ladurie, LeRoy. *Montaillou: The Promised Land of Error.* Translated by Barbara Brey. New York: Vintage Books, 1979. A classic study of the inquisition records of Albigensian villagers in southern France that reads like a novel with the insights of a master historian.

Lyons, Malcolm C. *Saladin: The Politics of Holy War.* New York: Cambridge University Press, 1985. A fine study of one of the most remarkable figures involved in the Crusades.

Maalouf, Amin. *The Crusades Through Arab Eyes.* New York: Schocken, 1989. An intriguing work using contemporary Arab sources to illuminate a perspective on crusading seldom discussed, with insights into today's controversies.

Madden, Thomas F. *The New Concise History of the Crusades,* 2nd ed. New York: Rowman & Littlefield, 2005. A thorough yet succinct history of the Crusades, with special attention on their impact on Islam and Byzantium.

Morris, Colin. *The Papal Monarchy: The Western Church from 1050–1250.* New York: Oxford University Press, 1991. Offers a balanced interpretation of the whole structure of the church in the formative central Middle Ages as the popes rose in power.

Peters, Edward. *Inquisition.* Berkeley: University of California Press, 1989. Traces the evolution of the concept of inquisition as represented in modern literature, art, and political theory.

Roach, Andrew. *The Devil's World: Heresy and Society 1100–1300 (The Medieval World).* New York: Longman, 2005. A thorough examination of heresy that argues for a relationship between ideas and social and economic realities.

Sayers, Jane. *Innocent III: Leader of Europe, 1198–1216.* New York: Longman, 1994. Examines all aspects of this influential pontiff.

FOUR HORSEMEN OF THE APOCALYPSE, BEATO DE LIEBANA

MANUSCRIPT, ca. eighth century

In the fourteenth century, Europeans were struck with a series of disasters that seemed to foretell the end of the world, causing many to look to the images of the Four Horsemen of the Apocalypse, described in the Book of Revelation in the New Testament. The rider on the white horse with the bow brought conquest; the second, with a sword, brought war. The rider on the black horse with the scale brought famine and plague, and the final rider, on a pale horse, brought death, which followed close behind him. Survivors at the end of the fourteenth century lived through all these calamities that changed medieval society forever.

The West Struggles and Eastern Empires Flourish

9

The Late Middle Ages, ca. 1300–1500

"In the year of the Lord 1315, shall begin a great famine on earth. . . . Also the Church shall totter and the line of Saint Peter shall be execrated. Also the blood of many shall be poured out on the ground." A fourteenth-century priest, Jean de Venette, told of this prophecy that appeared in a dream, and it came all too true as the century brought a series of disasters that would break down the medieval order that had seemed so secure a century before.

At the beginning of the century, bad weather ruined harvests and introduced years of famine, which drove many people from their lands to search for food. This misery was compounded when a terrible plague swept in from east Asia and raged through western Europe, killing over a third of the population and bringing fear and despair to many survivors. Peasants in the countryside and urban workers responded by staging revolts that further seemed to attack the social order itself. In the High Middle Ages, people looked to the church and the pope to bring comfort and order, but in the fourteenth century the church too was split by controversy as disputed papal elections brought several popes to power at once. As these disasters swept over Europe, England and France engaged in a violent war—the Hundred Years' War—that brought destruction to civilians and mounted knights alike. In eastern Europe and beyond, new empires threatened western Europe from the outside.

At the end of a century and a half of devastation, the feudal, the manorial, and many of the intellectual structures of the medieval world had been undermined. Many people believed these disasters heralded the end of the world; instead, western Europe was transformed by the horrors that swept over it and moved in exciting new directions.

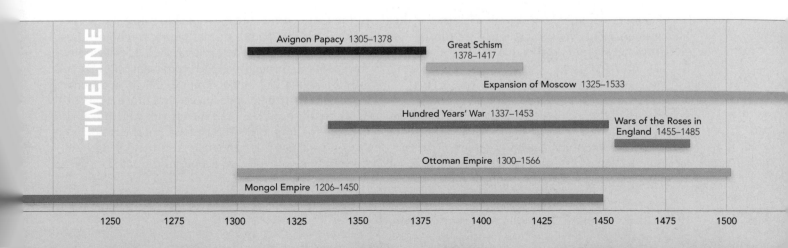

TIMELINE

Avignon Papacy 1305–1378

Great Schism 1378–1417

Expansion of Moscow 1325–1533

Hundred Years' War 1337–1453

Wars of the Roses in England 1455–1485

Ottoman Empire 1300–1566

Mongol Empire 1206–1450

| 1250 | 1275 | 1300 | 1325 | 1350 | 1375 | 1400 | 1425 | 1450 | 1475 | 1500 |

ECONOMIC AND SOCIAL MISERY

The town of Douai in medieval Flanders (now in France) was a prosperous place, where men and women produced woolen cloth in a booming cottage industry that made many merchants rich. Some people spun the wool, others wove it, and still others dyed the cloth. Then they turned it over to the merchants with whom they held their labor contracts. In prosperous times, there were good wages to be had, but early in the fourteenth century, hard times suddenly came. Years of bad harvests began in 1315, and the shops in Douai no longer had enough food to satisfy the town's needs. Tensions erupted in 1322, when rumors spread that the rich merchants were hoarding grain. Many of the cloth workers took to the streets, and in the legal records of the town, we learn that 18 workers—including two women—were arrested in the turmoil. The workers "in the full marketplace" had urged an assault on grain merchants to take the needed food from their warehouses. The two women were charged with being especially vocal, and in punishment they had their tongues cut off before being banished from the city for life. This was only one small incident in a century that brought suffering and despair to many in Europe.

Famine

The growth of European society stemmed mostly from agricultural innovations that had generated the boom of the eleventh century. By 1300, however, the burgeoning population began to put a strain on medieval technology. People were cultivating poorer lands, and crop yields were dwindling; on some marginal lands, farmers might harvest only three bushels for every one planted. After setting aside one bushel to plant the following year, the remainder was hardly enough to maintain a fixed population.

As the population grew, people tried to bring more and more lands into cultivation to make up for the scarcities, and this often resulted in plowing the common fields on which villagers grazed their animals. Unable to feed their livestock, people were forced to kill many of their animals—from one-quarter to one-third of their animals were slaughtered. This significant reduction of livestock also reduced the amount of manure for fertilizer, and yields fell again. By the beginning of the fourteenth century, farmers faced increasing difficulties accumulating a surplus of food—and then the weather worsened.

A series of years with too much rain began in 1310; lands were drenched. Chroniclers all over Europe wrote that the rains—with unusually deafening thunder and terrible lightning—were steady from April throughout the summer. The winds and overcast skies made the whole growing season abnormally cool. The rains came when the seed had just been scattered—washing much of it away—and continued to fall through the summer, flooding the lower croplands. When farmers tried to harvest the meager crops, the rains came again. Rivers flooded, bridges were swept away, and the crops, with previously low yields, failed.

> Bad weather

Famine began in 1315 and, in some parts of Europe, lasted until 1322. During these years, cold winters followed by cool and extraordinarily wet summers brought disastrous harvests. Aching hunger drove peasants from their lands in search of food, and according to some reports, starving farmers at times even resorted to cannibalism. Still, the disasters of this century were only beginning. Many who did not starve suffered from malnutrition and were susceptible to infection. Respiratory illnesses and intestinal ailments reached epidemic proportions in this century, but an even greater threat appeared.

The Black Death: A Pandemic Strikes

In the fourteenth century, a horrible pandemic swept in from the east and devastated Europe. The disease spread over vast areas, helped by increased trade from ships moving through the Mediterranean and by the expansion of the Mongol Empire. There is general agreement that the plague arrived in Europe in about 1348 on ships of Genoese merchants who traveled between Sicily and the Middle East, but the historical consensus about this pandemic ends here. What was this terrifying disease that people in the Middle Ages called the **Black Death?**

MAP 9.1

The Spread of the Black Death

This map tracks the progress of the plague as it spread gradually northward. It also shows how long it took the plague to travel north.

Explore the Map

1. How might weather and travel conditions have delayed the progress of the disease?

2. Compare this map with **Map 8.2.** What relationship do you think there was between trade routes and the plague's progress?

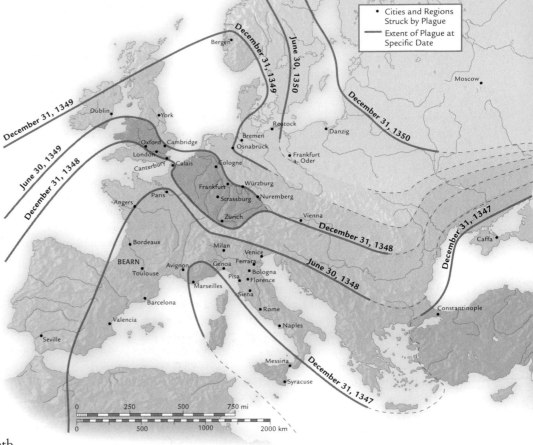

Medieval descriptions of the disease were vivid: Boccaccio, a fourteenth-century observer, described the symptoms, which included armpit and groin swellings that turned black. Once skin darkened in spots, death was virtually certain. This description causes most historians to identify the disease as bubonic plague, caused by a virulent bacillus (*Yersinia pesta*) that infected rodents in Manchuria, then spread to black rats. As we saw in Chapter 1, some of the most devastating diseases have been those that move from animals to humans, and this rodent disease was passed to humans from the bites of infected fleas. Bubonic plague can also reach a person's lungs, becoming pneumonic plague, which spreads rapidly through sneezing and coughing. Estimates are that between 30 and 70 percent of people who catch bubonic plague die, but almost 100 percent of those with pneumonic plague die.

The disease

In modern times, bubonic plague does not spread quickly, which causes some historians to question whether it was indeed the Black Death that brought such destruction. Some argue that this virulent form spread quickly to the lungs, becoming the deadly pneumonic form. Others suggest that several diseases—like smallpox—might have joined bubonic plague in sweeping through a population already weakened from famine. However, recent DNA studies confirm the presence of *Yersinia pestis* in plague cemeteries; so, although other diseases may have joined

forces with the plague in killing a weakened population, the Black Death did cause the devastation.

Whatever the exact disease, the pandemic raced through Europe. It spread quickly in the summer and declined in the winter months—the cold, wet summers helped the plague spread. **Map 9.1** shows the progress of the plague and the dates that the disease moved north from Italy to Scandinavia. The pandemic killed a shocking one-third to one-half of the population, but historians are uncertain of the exact numbers of the dead. Modern estimates agree that one-third of the population died, but they disagree on what that fraction means in actual numbers—estimates range from 20,000,000 to 35,000,000 dead. Disease hit the crowded cities hardest: Paris may have lost half its population and Florence as much as four-fifths. The eyewitness account in Document 9.1 describes the devastation in hard-hit Siena. These staggering numbers mean that everyone—especially in the cities where death rates were highest—saw neighbors, friends, and family members die.

The psychological impact of so great a plague was perhaps even more important than the actual loss of

DOCUMENT 9.1

Agnolo the Fat Survives the Plague

Agnolo di Tura del Grasso lived in Siena, Italy, when the plague struck in 1348. He wrote a chronicle of events from 1300 to 1351 that provides an eyewitness account of the horror. His description of the disease helped historians to identify it with bubonic plague.

The mortality began in Siena in May (1348). It was a cruel and horrible thing; and I do not know where to begin to tell of the cruelty and the pitiless ways. It seemed to almost everyone that one became stupefied by seeing the pain. And it is impossible for the human tongue to recount the awful thing. Indeed one who did not see such horribleness can be called blessed. And the victims died almost immediately. They would swell beneath their armpits and in their groins, and fall over dead while talking. Father abandoned child, wife husband, one brother another; for this illness seemed to strike through the breath and sight. And so they died. And none could be found to bury the dead for money or friendship. Members of a household brought their dead to a ditch as best they could, without priest, without divine offices. Nor did the death bell sound. And in many places in Siena great pits were dug and piled deep with the multitude of dead. And they died by the hundreds both day and night, and all were thrown in those ditches and covered over with earth. And as soon as those ditches were filled more were dug.

And I, Agnolo di Tura, called the Fat, buried my five children with my own hands. And there were also those who were so sparsely covered with earth that the dogs dragged them forth and devoured many bodies throughout the city. There was no one who wept for any death, for all awaited death. And so many died that all believed that it was the end of the world. And no medicine or any other defense availed. . . . This situation continued until September, and it would take too long to write of it. And it is found that at this time there died in Siena 36,000 persons twenty years of age or less, and the aged and other people [died], to a total of 52,000 in all in Siena. And in the suburbs of Siena 28,000 persons died; so that in all it is found that in the city and suburbs of Siena 80,000 persons died. Thus at this time Siena and its suburbs had more than 30,000 men, and there remained in Siena (alone) less than 10,000 men. And those that survived were like persons distraught and almost without feeling. And many walls and other things were abandoned, and all the mines of silver and gold and copper that existed in Sienese territory were abandoned as is seen; for in the countryside . . . many more people died, many lands and villages were abandoned, and no one remained there. I will not write of the cruelty that there was in the countryside, of the wolves and wild beasts that ate the poorly buried corpses, and of other cruelties that would be too painful to those who read of them. . . .

The city of Siena seemed almost uninhabited for almost no one was found in the city. And then, when the pestilence abated, all who survived gave themselves over to pleasures: monks, priests, nuns, and lay men and women all enjoyed themselves, and none worried about spending and gambling. And everyone thought himself rich because he had escaped and regained the world, and no one knew how to allow himself to do nothing. . . .

1349. After the great pestilence of the past year each person lived according to his own caprice, and everyone tended to seek pleasure in eating and drinking, hunting, catching birds and gaming. And all money had fallen into the hands of nouveaux riches.

SOURCE: Agnolo di Tura del Grasso, "Plague in Siena: An Italian Chronicle," *Cronica Maggiore* in *Black Death: A Turning Point in History?*, ed. William M. Bowsky (New York: Holt, Rinehart & Winston, 1971), pp. 13–14.

Analyze the Document

1. How did the devastation break down traditional social ties and rituals?

2. How did people react to all the deaths?

3. How did the survivors react?

4. How did the plague contribute to the breakdown of medieval society?

---

life. Law and tradition broke down, and many survivors saw no point in trying to preserve medieval customs. Boccaccio wrote: "In this sore affliction and misery of our city, the authority of the laws, both human and divine, was all dissolved and fell into decay," and he described how many sick died untended in the streets.

Reaction

At the time, people did not realize that the disease was caused by bacteria and transmitted by fleas. Theories of the Black Death's etiology ranged from punishment by God to "bad air." Victims could expect only traditional treatments from physicians. In **Figure 9.1**, an ill king is attended by his doctors. One holds his nose to indicate the belief that the disease left an offensive smell owing to the buildup of bad "humors." The physicians have applied leeches, used on previous patients, to the king to remove excessive blood—a lethal practice that is equivalent to sharing needles between patients who have a blood-borne disease.

As medicine failed to offer solace for this horrifying disease, many could only conclude that God's wrath brought the devastation. Responding to this notion, some people resorted to extreme measures to try to bring God's aid against the plague. One group—the

Flagellants

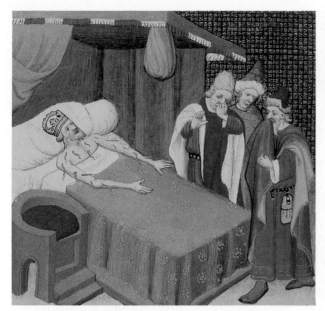

FIGURE 9.1 Curing the Plague This illustration reflects popular attitudes about the Black Death. A physician holds his nose, expressing the general belief that one of the ways the plague spread was through bad air. Physicians have applied leeches to the king to draw his blood and reduce his fever.

FIGURE 9.2 Flagellants, fifteenth century Many people of the time believed that the plague was caused by the wrath of an angry God. Flagellants—individuals who beat themselves—tried to appease God by staging ritual parades of self-punishment.

flagellants—thought that by inflicting pain on themselves, they could ask God to relieve the suffering of others. **Figure 9.2** shows a group of flagellants banded together in a procession. In this image, the procession is led by men carrying a cross and a dragon as a mark of their brotherhood. Flagellants beat themselves three times a day with leather thongs tipped in lead. They marched from town to town "splashing the church walls with their blood," according to contemporary witnesses. This movement reflected the desperation of people searching for ways to appease a seemingly angry God.

In their fear, some people turned against their neighbors, and in many cities, Jews were accused of bringing the plague by poisoning wells. The persecutions fell particularly heavily on Jewish communities in Germany because periodically throughout the thirteenth century, the English and French kings had forced Jews out of their lands and many had moved eastward. Because there was a larger presence of Jews in Germany, their Christian neighbors used them as a focus of their fears. A contemporary chronicler (Jacob von Konigshofen) described a pogrom in Strasbourg that killed thousands of Jews accused of causing the plague: "On Saturday . . . they burnt the Jews on a wooden platform in their cemetery. There were about two thousand people of them. Many small children were taken out of the fire and baptized against the will of their fathers and mothers." In a practical aside, Jacob noted that the persecutors also had money on their minds, because they confiscated the property of

Attacking Jews

the Jews: "The money was indeed the thing that killed the Jews. If they had been poor and if the feudal lords had not been in debt to them, they would not have been burnt. . . ."

In spite of the foolishness of blaming people who were also dying from the plague, anti-Jewish persecutions spread. More than sixty major Jewish communities in Germany had been destroyed by 1351. Many Jews fled to eastern Europe—to Russia and Poland—where they received protection, and slowly many Jewish communities moved their homes even farther east. Popes would later condemn this irrational persecution.

The plague continued to ravage Europe in waves into the seventeenth and even early eighteenth centuries. These subsequent visitations of the disease also took a large toll on the population. It seems that the plague finally abated when the larger, meaner Norwegian brown rat (today's urban rat) displaced the European black rats. The brown rats had thicker fur, which resisted the flea bites of the black rat fleas, so the disease bacillus slowly lost its host pool. Even though the disease eventually disappeared, it left a legacy of fear and despair that haunted Europe for centuries.

Peasants and Townspeople Revolt

As an immediate result of the plague, the European countryside suffered a disabling shortage of labor. Desperate lords tried to increase their customary—and

FIGURE 9.3 Peasants' Revolt, 1381 The English preacher John Ball, shown on horseback, led peasants and knights in a revolt for better conditions for the peasantry. Although the uprising failed, rural conditions nevertheless improved.

already excessive—labor requirements in an effort to farm their lands. Free laborers, detecting an opportunity, began to demand higher wages, prompting some countries to pass laws freezing earnings. For example, a statute of laborers passed in England in 1351 said, "No one shall pay or promise to pay to anyone more wages . . . or salary than was accustomed." This policy enraged peasants across Europe. Determined to resist, they roamed the countryside, burning manor houses and slaughtering the occupants.

In some of these uprisings, popular preachers arose as leaders who combined social reform with religious hopes. Living in an age crippled by plague and famine, many believed that these "times of troubles" presaged a better world in which Christ would return. (See the Four Horsemen in the chapter opener on page 280.) The most famous of | John Ball | these preachers was John Ball of England, who rallied listeners by calling for the overthrow of the social order: "Oh good people, things . . . will not go well until everything is held in common and there are no more serfs or lords." His most famous couplet attacked the very hierarchical privilege that had marked the three orders of medieval society. He said simply: "When Adam delved and Eve span, where then were all the gentlemen?" When Adam and Eve lived in the Garden of Eden, both worked the soil and no one was a noble "gentleman."

The illustration in **Figure 9.3** shows a confrontation between English peasants and the king's forces in 1381. John Ball rides the horse, and another popular preacher—Wat Tyler—stands in the foreground, holding a banner with the English coat of arms. This illustration shows two main things: First, the peasants had the support of well-armed and disciplined soldiers who had been trained to defend the English coast. Second, both sides hold the same royal banners, indicating that the peasants did not blame the king for their misery but remained loyal to the teenaged Richard II (r. 1377–1399). They blamed his advisors and the local nobility for their misery. Their loyalty made no difference in the outcome—the king joined in repressing the revolt.

French peasants, too, rose up against their lords, in a revolt called the **Jacquerie.** French chroniclers told in horror of peasants storming manor houses and brutally killing noblemen and their families. English peasants burned houses of aristocrats, lawyers, and government officials, at times burning the records that they believed contributed to their oppression. However, the peasants in all regions could not hold out for long against the aristocracy and its superior arms. Eventually, all the revolts were suppressed, with many peasants and their leaders massacred. Yet the violence, the labor shortages, and the prevailing belief that things were changing had begun to erode the old medieval manorial system. Over time, peasants who owed only rent gradually replaced serfs who had owed labor as well as rent. For these new peasants, their labor was now their own, giving them more freedom and opportunities to work for their own profit. Although the condition of many peasants improved, the trend was not uniform throughout Europe. The situation of peasants in western Europe improved more quickly than that of those in eastern Europe.

As the anecdote about the town of Douai that opened this chapter indicates, the unrest was not limited to the countryside. As population dropped, the declining demand for goods led to falling prices, and some industries suffered. Merchants and manufacturers responded by trying to limit competition and reduce the freedoms of the lower classes in the | Urban revolts | towns. Revolts broke out in many towns throughout Europe. In addition to Douai, violence erupted in Ghent, Rouen, and Florence. (This last was the famous Ciompi revolt in 1378—named for the wooden shoes worn by wool workers who rioted.) While some of these revolts led to short-term gains, most were crushed. Improvements for urban workers would eventually come with the labor shortages caused by the high death rates. But the rural and urban revolts of the fourteenth century set off social conflicts that periodically resurfaced throughout Western history.

IMPERIAL PAPACY BESIEGED

Throughout these troubled times, many medieval men and women looked to the church, especially the papacy, to guide them. Yet the popes were grappling with their own problems, and these very troubles undermined people's confidence in the church. Early in the fourteenth century, the issue of the relative sovereignty of kings and popes resurfaced once more over the taxation of church lands and the clergy's claim to immunity from royal courts. This time, the French king proved stronger than the popes. In the course of this dispute, the French king, Philip IV (r. 1285–1314), ordered his troops to arrest Pope Boniface VIII (r. 1294–1303). Although the elderly pope was quickly freed by his supporters, he died soon afterward as a result of the rough treatment. Unlike Henry II of England after the death of Becket (described in Chapter 8), Philip IV was able to capitalize on the violence against the church. He brought pressure on the college of cardinals—which had elected popes since 1059—and they elected his favored French cardinal as pope.

Popes Move to Avignon

Philip expected this pope to support French interests, and to forward this aim, the king persuaded the pope to rule from Avignon, on the east bank of the Rhône River. Although the city was in the Holy Roman Empire, the French influence there was strong. The new pope, Clement V (r. 1304–1314), complied and set up his court in Avignon. The popes never again tried to exert authority of taxation and legal immunity over the French kings. However, the pope's absence from Rome raised serious issues. After all, the pope was the bishop of Rome and was obligated to be there to guide the faithful in his charge.

For seventy-two years after the election of Clement V, the popes ruled from Avignon—in the shadow of the French king. Many Christians objected to this **"Babylonian Captivity,"** as the Italian Petrarch (1304–1374) called it. Some people believed this shocking breach of tradition contributed to the subsequent plague, famine, and violence that accompanied the popes' residence in Avignon, and they urged the popes to resume ruling from Rome. The Avignon popes also expanded their administration, and they streamlined and made more efficient their collection of ecclesiastical taxes because they could not depend on the income from their lands in Rome. To many, it seemed that the church had become all too secular when the world was in desperate need of spiritual leadership.

FIGURE 9.4 Catherine of Siena, ca. 1447 This lavish painting by Paolo di Giovanni Fei documents the significant moment in the papal history when Saint Catherine of Siena persuaded Pope Gregory XI to leave his exile in Avignon and return to Rome.

An influential mystic, Catherine of Siena (1347–1380), felt called by God to intervene in this situation. Catherine had experienced a number of visions and was highly respected in her home city in the mountains south of Florence, in Italy. Catherine wrote a series of letters to Pope Gregory XI (r. 1370–1378) in which she urged him to return to Rome, and in 1376 she traveled to Avignon to urge him in person. The painting in **Figure 9.4** shows this emotion-charged meeting. Catherine kneels before the pope, pleading with him to once more take up his duties in Rome. He was persuaded, and in that year he tried to correct the decline in the papal prestige by returning to Rome. But the church's problems only increased.

Return to Rome

Things Get Worse: The Great Schism

Gregory XI died in Rome in 1378, and the situation was volatile. The citizens of Rome feared that the college of cardinals would choose another French pope who would return to Avignon. Indeed, the guard of the cardinals warned them that they "ran the risk of being torn in pieces" if they did not elect an Italian. The fearful cardinals elected an Italian,

MAP 9.2

The Great Schism, 1378–1417

This map shows how countries' loyalties were divided between the competing popes in Rome and Avignon.

Explore the Map

1. What regions supported which pope?

2. What political advantage might each country have achieved by its alliance?

3. Do the shifting alliances of the Holy Roman Empire demonstrate the lack of unity in that region? Explain.

Pope Urban VI (r. 1378–1389). Urban almost immediately indicated his plans to reduce the French influence in the college of cardinals, and, not surprisingly, the French cardinals—claiming that the election of Urban VI was invalid because they had been coerced by the Roman mob—left Rome. The dissenting cardinals elected a Frenchman—Pope Clement VII (r. 1378–1394)—who took up residence in the papal palace in Avignon. Now there were two popes, initiating what has been called the **Great Schism** of the church. (This is not to be confused with the schism

of 1054, which divided the church into the Latin west and the Greek Orthodox east. See Chapter 6.)

Many people chose to follow one pope over the other based on political rather than religious motivations, and **Map 9.2** shows the respective alliances. Each pope denounced the other as the anti-Christ, and each tried to increase the revenues that now were split in half as Christians were divided in their loyalties. Many people began to criticize the church for its seeming concern for money over spiritual matters, and they advocated restoring a unified leadership to the divided Christendom. As the Black Death plundered Europe, the papacy lost its moral authority as the ruler of a united Christendom. Who could restore unity?

The Conciliar Movement

Church theorists had long speculated on who might rule the church if the pope should become incompetent. Some suggested the college of cardinals would be the logical body, but the college was split in two, so some theologians suggested that a general council of bishops might be able to restore the order and reform the abuses of the church. There was ample precedent for church councils to meet to resolve controversies, for as early as the fourth century, Emperor Constantine had called the bishops together at Nicaea (see Chapter 5). However, these new "conciliarists" wanted to convert the church to a kind of constitutional monarchy in which the power of the popes would be limited. This would be a dramatic step, but the times seemed to call for radical measures.

The first test of the **Conciliar movement** came at the Council of Pisa, convened in 1409 by cardinals of both Rome and Avignon. This council asserted its supremacy by deposing the two reigning popes and electing a new pope. Although this should have solved the problem, it only exacerbated it—the two previous popes would not step down, so now *three* popes reigned.

Finally, a second council was called. Some 400 churchmen assembled at the Council of Constance (1414–1418), which was the greatest international gathering in the Middle Ages. This august body deposed all three of the popes and elected a Roman cardinal—Martin V (r. 1417–1431). The Great Schism was finally over and the Western church was once more united under a single head. However, never again did the popes have the power that the medieval popes had, and church councils gathered periodically to address changes in the church.

New Critics of the Church

Not surprisingly, as men and women became disenchanted with the established church, they sought new ways to approach God so as to address the pressing challenges of the age. Criticisms of the church that had been expressed periodically throughout the Middle Ages appeared with more urgency in this age of crisis. The preacher John Ball was simply one of many who offered a different view of religion, and even the dreaded inquisition could not silence the new critics.

The Englishman and Oxford theologian John Wycliffe (ca. 1320–1384) offered a serious critique that struck at the heart of the organized church. Wycliffe argued that there was no scriptural basis for papal claims of earthly power and that the Bible should be a Christian's sole authority. In the course of his writings, he attacked many of the practices of the medieval church (such as pilgrimages, the veneration of saints, and many of the rituals that had grown up over the centuries). Furthermore, Wycliffe argued that the church (and the popes in particular) should renounce earthly power, leaving it to kings. As he put it, "the pope [should] leave his worldly lordship to worldly lords." Wycliffe wanted a more simple church, led by a clergy that rejected all wealth. This would have been a major renunciation because the church was by far the greatest landlord in Europe. There was a great deal at stake.

John Wycliffe

Though Wycliffe's ideas were profoundly threatening to the established church, he had powerful protectors in the English court, who kept him unharmed until he died. Many of his followers (called **Lollards**) were condemned, but not until the early 1400s, when his ideas seemed to stimulate treasonous acts. One of the most famous proponents of some of Wycliffe's ideas was Jan Hus (ca. 1373–1415), a popular preacher and rector of the university in Prague. Hus and his followers demanded a reform of the church, and his ideas were joined to a desire for Bohemian freedom from German dominance. Hus was certain that his beliefs were correct and defended them before the influential Council of Constance. However, the Czech scholar was found guilty of heresy and was burned. An eyewitness to the execution wrote that Hus died bravely with the words of the Lord's Prayer on his lips. Many Czechs remembered Hus as a martyr both to conscience and to a growing desire for Czech independence. While the council could silence Hus, it could not silence the growing numbers of voices calling for a significant transformation of the medieval church. As we will see in Chapter 11, these calls for reform would eventually be heard.

Jan Hus

MORE DESTRUCTION: THE HUNDRED YEARS' WAR, 1337–1453

As if famine, plague, revolts, and religious controversy weren't enough, England and France entered into the **Hundred Years' War**—a century-long conflict that became the closing chapter in an age in which long-standing traditions and social contracts crumbled. The issue that triggered the conflict was the succession to the throne of France—the Capetians' good luck in producing male heirs finally ran out in 1328, when the last Capetian died. The nearest male relative was King Edward III of England, son of a Capetian king's (Philip IV) daughter (Isabel). The Parlement of Paris (the supreme court of France) claimed that a woman could not transmit a claim to the crown, so Philip VI of Valois, a first cousin of the previous ruler, became king. Edward at first did not dispute this decision, but he soon found cause to do so.

England vs. France

There were two other reasons for the two kings to clash: one was economic—urban revolts in Flanders gave Philip VI an excuse to interfere in the lucrative wool trade between England and Flanders. The Flemish asked Edward to assert his claim to the French crown so the rich trade could continue unimpeded. The second cause was feudal—the French king wanted to claim the status of liege lord over the lands in southern France held by Edward III. (See Chapter 8 to review how the English kings came to hold land in France as vassals to the king of France.) Edward, as a king himself, did not believe he should accept Philip as his liege lord. In response, Philip declared Edward's lands forfeit and Edward decided to exert his dynastic claim to be king of both England and France.

The long struggle began with some stunning English victories. The English first secured their communications across the channel with a naval victory at Sluys in 1340 (see **Map 9.3**); they then could turn to a land invasion of France. Although the French outnumbered the English, the English skillfully used new tactics and new weapons to supplement their mounted knights. In their wars against the Scots in the thirteenth century, the English learned of the effectiveness of the Welsh longbow and brought archers to fight against the French cavalry. The longbow was a simple yet highly effective device that had a greater range than the crossbow and could be fired with unprecedented speed. A longbowman could loose up to ten arrows a minute, compared with the crossbowman's two.

New weapons

The English armies also took advantage of the pike—a weapon developed in Switzerland and used to good effect against the mounted armies of the Holy Roman Emperor. Foot soldiers wielded the long spears and braced them on the ground to fend off the charge of mounted knights. Some English foot soldiers brought pikes to France to support England's horsemen, who were outnumbered by the French cavalry.

While longbows and pikes challenged the ascendancy of mounted knights, their obsolescence was sealed with the spread of gunpowder from China. Iron shot appeared in England as early as 1346 and Italy in 1341, but the powder was unstable and did not explode immediately. Throughout the war, desperate soldiers used new (and frequently unreliable) guns to bring down knights, and equally desperate armorers tried to make plate armor stronger and curved so it could deflect bullets. However, the mounted knights simply grew too expensive and ineffective for the new warfare; the future lay with the infantry.

The English, led by Edward III, forged across the channel to confront the superior force of French mounted knights. Edward brought a strong infantry, loud guns, and lethal longbows, which eyewitness accounts of the Battle of Crécy in 1346 described as blackening the sky with English arrows. By the end of the battle, the flower of French knighthood lay crushed, which struck a blow against feudalism itself when "those who fought" lost. In this victory, the English had secured Flanders and the important port of Calais. The strategy was repeated at Poitiers in 1356, and the exhausted French were forced to sue for peace (the Peace of Bretigny) in 1360. By the terms of this peace, King Edward renounced his claim to the French throne in exchange for Calais and enlarged holdings in Aquitaine.

English victories

The French were not willing to allow so much of their land to remain in English hands, so the war was reopened in 1369 under the French king Charles V (r. 1364–1380). He introduced a wise strategy of avoiding major military confrontation and, instead, wearing down the English forces on the Continent. During this phase of the war, soldiers on both sides devastated the countryside, plundering villages and ruining crops and vineyards. The illustration in **Figure 9.5** shows soldiers pillaging a house during the Hundred Years' War. They carry out chests and barrels, and some search for valuables hidden in pots and jars while others break open wine casks. This sort of civilian destruction contributed to the misery of the fourteenth century.

Edward III died in 1377, and Charles V in 1380. At this point, the English had almost been pushed out of France—they held only Calais and a small strip of land between Bordeaux and Bayonne. At first no formal peace was signed, but in 1396 a long truce ended this phase of the Hundred Years' War, and the monarchs turned their attention to internal affairs for a while.

Henry V (r. 1413–1422), who succeeded to the English throne in 1413, was an able soldier, eager to reopen the long-suspended war against France. His timing was good, because the powerful duke of Burgundy had used the turmoil to increase his own land at the expense of the French kings (see **Map 9.3**). The Burgundians leapt into the fray on the side of the English, and with this new ally, Henry reasserted his claims to the French throne. In August 1415, he landed in Normandy with a substantial force of knights and about 6,000 archers, but his men were soon exhausted by casualties and dysentery. The bold king heard that the French army was marching against him, and he had to prepare for battle. Henry chose a troop formation in

Agincourt

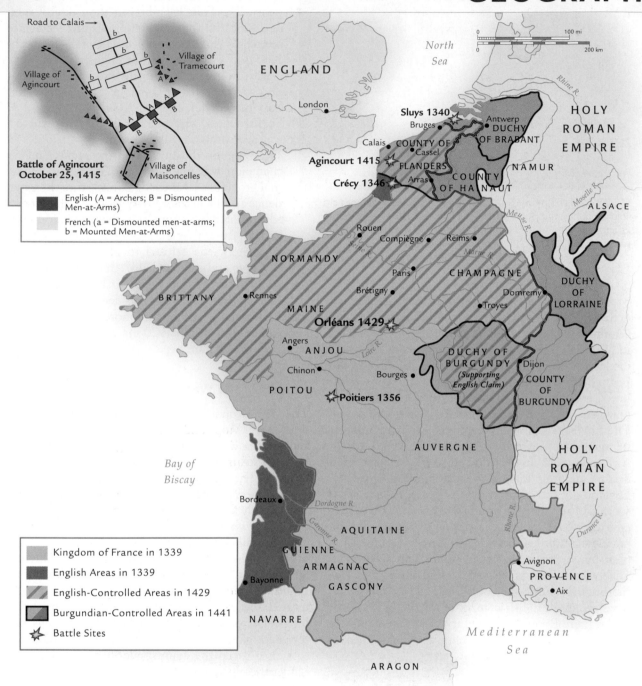

Battle of Agincourt
October 25, 1415

English (A = Archers; B = Dismounted Men-at-Arms)

French (a = Dismounted men-at-arms; b = Mounted Men-at-Arms)

Kingdom of France in 1339

English Areas in 1339

English-Controlled Areas in 1429

Burgundian-Controlled Areas in 1441

Battle Sites

MAP 9.3

The Hundred Years' War, 1337–1453

This map illustrates the Hundred Years' War between England and France. It shows that the major battle sites and areas of combat were in the north, even though the English claims in France lay in the south. The inset traces the Battle of Agincourt.

Explore the Map

1. What does the pattern of warfare (emphasizing the north) suggest about the significance of the various causes of the war?

2. What mistakes did the French make in the significant Battle of Agincourt?

3. Why do you think the location of Orléans (along the Loire River), where Joan of Arc made her decisive victory, proved to be strategically significant?

FIGURE 9.5 Pillaging Soldiers This illustration of rampaging soldiers during the Hundred Years' War shows them searching for valuables in a home and carrying them off. The war and its attendant plunder contributed to the woes of a society that was already beset by famine, plague, revolts, and religious controversy.

which the flanks were protected by gardens and orchards of two villages, and he arranged his men forming solid blocks flanked by the archers. (See inset in **Map 9.3.**) The French knights repeated the same tactics that had failed at Poitiers in 1356—a small body of dismounted men-at-arms took the center, followed by mounted knights and supported by crossbowmen, who were placed too far back to be useful. The English slaughtered the French knights in great numbers.

The French king was forced to sue for peace and declare his heir (called the **Dauphin**) illegitimate. England got direct control of northern France as far south as the Loire River and the promise that Henry's son would inherit the throne of France. For all practical purposes, France was defeated. The Dauphin could not accept these terms, but he seemed unable to rally any systematic resistance. In 1428, the English laid siege to Orléans, and its fall would have ensured English control of all the lands north of the Loire River. It seemed it would take a miracle to restore the French monarchy, and, many people believed they got one.

Joan of Arc

During these darkest days of France, a young peasant girl—Joan of Arc (1412–1431)—believed she saw visions in which angels urged her to lead the French troops to victory. She persuaded the Dauphin of the authenticity of her mission, and he gave her command of an army. Joan donned armor and almost miraculously stirred the determination of France's armies and lifted the siege at Orléans. Some accounts attribute her success to a skill in placing artillery, the new weapon of warfare. After this victory, she escorted the Dauphin to Reims—the city where French kings were traditionally crowned—where he received the crown of France, thus renouncing the previous treaty. The French embraced the cause of their new king and the new national spirit seemed to revitalize the French armies. They rallied, and by 1453 only Calais was left in English hands.

However, Joan did not live to see the victory. She was captured in 1431 by the Burgundians, who turned her over to their English allies, who put her on trial for witchcraft and heresy. The Dauphin did not try to intervene, and his champion was put on trial. The record of her trial provides a fascinating glimpse into the experience of this extraordinary woman. She repeatedly restated her conviction that her voices were from God and that she was following a just cause. Ultimately, she refused to abandon her men's clothing and acknowledge that she had been wrong, so she was condemned to be burned at the stake. Document 9.2 reveals this deeply poignant episode in her trial. The French honored Joan of Arc as a savior of France, and in 1920 she was declared a saint of the Catholic Church.

[Joan executed]

Results of the War

The new weaponry that was used during the Hundred Years' War set European armies on a new course. Indeed, the weaponry and violence against civilians have caused many scholars to call this the first modern war. The feudal system that demanded knights' military service began to break down, and lords increasingly accepted money (called scutage) instead of military service. Now lords could hire professional armies—called **free companies** because they had no feudal ties and sold their services to the highest bidder—which were becoming more effective than traditional knights. (The knights continued to fight in their beloved tournaments long after they were less welcome on the battlefields.) Many kings had repeated difficulties paying their free companies, and soldiers ravaged the countryside in lieu of their pay. Under these pressures, the deterioration of the feudal system accelerated into what is sometimes called bastard feudalism, in which the old ties of loyalty were replaced with cash payments. Nobles, like kings, simply hired soldiers, dressed them in elaborate uniforms sporting the special colors of the noble families, and created their own private armies.

As a result of the Hundred Years' War, the English were expelled from French soil; the French king emerged more powerful than all his vassals, and the slow consolidation of royal rule was effectively complete. The monarchy had a permanent army, a strong tax base, and a great deal of prestige among people who were coming to see themselves as "French."

thinking about
DOCUMENTS

Joan of Arc Is Defiant

The record of Joan of Arc's trial offers a fascinating glimpse into both the inquisitorial proceedings of the late Middle Ages and the psychology of the accused. Earlier in her trial, Joan is found guilty and agrees to recant and renounce the voices that guided her in her battle against the English. This section begins with her recantation, which she later renounces.

Then, in the presence of all the aforenamed, in presence of an immense number of people and Clergy, she did make and utter her recantation and abjuration, following a formula written in French, which was read to her; . . .

". . . I, Jeanne, commonly called the Maid, a miserable sinner, after that I had recognized the snares of error in the which I was held, and [after] that, by the grace of God, I had returned to our Holy Mother Church, in order that it may be seen that, not pretending but with a good heart and good will, I have returned thereto; I confess that I have most grievously sinned, in pretending untruthfully to have had revelations and apparitions from God, from the Angels, and Saint Catherine and Saint Margaret; in seducing others; in believing foolishly and lightly; in making superstitious divinations; in blaspheming God and His Saints; in breaking the Divine Law, Holy Scripture, and the lawful Canons; in wearing a dissolute habit, misshapen and immodest and against the propriety of nature, and hair clipped 'en ronde' in the style of a man, against all the modesty of the feminine sex; . . ."

And the same day, **Thursday, May 24th, in the afternoon,** We [the judges] did repair to the place in the prison where Jeanne was to be found. . . . We told her to leave off her man's dress and to take a woman's garments, as the Church had ordered her. In all our observations Jeanne did reply that she would willingly take woman's garments, and that in all things she would obey the Church. Woman's garments having been offered to her, she at once dressed herself in them, after

having taken off the man's dress she was wearing; and her hair, which up to this time had been cut "en ronde" above her ears, she desired and permitted them to shave and take away.

Monday, May 28th, the day following Trinity Sunday.

We, the aforesaid Judges, repaired to the place of Jeanne's prison, to learn the state and disposition of her soul. . . .

And because Jeanne was dressed in the dress of a man—that is to say, a short mantle, a hood, a doublet and other effects used by men—although, by our orders, she had, several days before, consented to give up these garments, we asked her when and for what reason she had resumed this dress.

She answered us:

"I have but now resumed the dress of a man and put off the woman's dress."

"Why did you take it, and who made you take it?"

"I took it of my own free will, and with no constraint: I prefer a man's dress to a woman's dress."

"You promised and swore not to resume a man's dress."

"I never meant to swear that I would not resume it."

"Why have you resumed it?"

"Because it is more lawful and suitable for me to resume it and to wear man's dress, being with men, than to have a woman's dress. . . ."

And as We, the Judges, heard from several persons that she had returned to her old illusions on the subject of her pretended revelations. We put to her this question:

"Since last Thursday [the day of her abjuration] have you heard your Voices at all?"

"Yes, I have heard them."

"What did they say to you?"

"They said to me: . . . 'God had sent me word by St. Catherine and St. Margaret of the great pity it is, this treason to which I have consented, to abjure and recant in order to save my life! I have damned myself to save my life!' . . ."

"Do you believe that your Voices are Saint Catherine and Saint Margaret?"

"Yes, I believe it, and that they come from God."

"Tell us the truth on the subject of this crown which is mentioned in your Trial."

"In everything, I told you the truth about it in my Trial, as well as I know."

. . . After hearing this. We retired from her, to act and proceed later according to law and reason.

Wednesday, May 30th, towards 9 o'clock in the morning, . . .

We, the Bishop and Vicar aforesaid, having regard to all that has gone before, in which it is shown that this woman had never truly abandoned her errors, her obstinate temerity, nor her unheard-of crimes; . . . We have at last proceeded to the Final Sentence on these terms:

For the causes, declaring thee fallen again into your old errors, and under the sentence of excommunication which you have formerly incurred. WE DECREE THAT YOU ART A RELAPSED HERETIC, by our present sentence which, seated in tribunal, we utter and pronounce in this writing; we denounce thee as a rotten member, and that you may not vitiate others, as cast out from the unity of the Church, separate from her Body, abandoned to the secular power as, indeed, by these presents, we do cast thee off, separate and abandon thee:—praying this same secular power, so far as concerns death and the mutilation of the limbs, to moderate its judgment towards thee, and, if true signs of penitence should appear in thee, [to permit] that the Sacrament of Penance be administered to thee.

SOURCE: Saint Joan of Arc Center, Albuquerque, NM, "The Relapse, the final adjudication and the sentence of death," www.stjoan-center.com.

Analyze the Document

1. How did clothing—symbol of gender roles and obedience—play a significant part in the proceedings?

2. Why did Joan take back her confession?

3. What was the church's sentence?

4. What do you think of these events?

5. How might Joan have been treated today?

England had a longer struggle after its loss in the war. England's monarchy was seriously weakened as Parliament took more control of the purse strings after the wartime excesses. During the turmoil, the Lancaster and York families unleashed a civil war as they competed for the throne. Each family had a different color rose as its emblem, so this sporadic conflict was called the Wars of the Roses (1455–1485). The fighting perpetuated the worst aspects of feudal life as it degenerated into local skirmishes orchestrated by the nobility. The situation was made worse by mercenary soldiers unemployed after the end of the Hundred Years' War, who returned to England and sold their services to feuding families. Many old noble families were decimated in the course of this war.

Wars of the Roses

Richard III (r. 1483–1485) took the throne from his 12-year-old nephew, Edward V, and had the young king and his brother imprisoned in the Tower of London, where they were murdered. This long-remembered act of cruelty stimulated a final resistance. Nobles rallied to the banner of Henry Tudor, a Lancastrian, and he finally vanquished Richard III at the Battle of Bosworth Field in 1485. He was crowned Henry VII (r. 1485–1509). To try to heal the breach between the noble factions, he married Elizabeth of York; at last the civil war was officially ended, but Henry needed all his skill to restore solid centralized control. He confiscated the lands of rebellious nobles and prohibited private armies. At the end of his reign, England was strengthened; and by the time of his granddaughter's rule, it was poised to expand beyond the seas (see Chapter 12).

RESPONSES TO THE DISRUPTION OF MEDIEVAL ORDER

As war and revolt have shown, one of the ways people responded to the fourteenth-century disasters was to consider new approaches to old problems. Wycliffe and Hus questioned church practices; Edward III of England thought of new battle strategies to confront French knights. These are only three of many famous and anonymous people who changed their world with creative new ideas. Philosophers, writers, and artists, too, produced works that dramatically changed the direction of Western thought.

William of Ockham Reconsiders Scholasticism

Within a century after Thomas Aquinas's synthesis (described in Chapter 8), a new breed of thinkers challenged the premises of scholasticism and questioned the ties between faith and reason. William of Ockham (ca. 1285–1349) was the most prominent of these thinkers. Scholasticism was based on the idea that thinkers could extract general truths (or universals) from individual cases. Ockham was an English philosopher who argued that universals had no connection with reality, and this philosophy was called New Nominalism. (Ockham used **nominalism,** derived from the Latin word for "name," because he said that universals, or categories, were only convenient names for things.) New Nominalists believed that it was impossible to know God or prove his existence through reason—because God was all-powerful, he did not have to act logically.

So what should philosophers do? Ockham's studies spawned a decline in abstract logic, but a rise in interest in scientific observation that would bear much fruit in later generations. Ockham also discovered a fundamental principle that remained the basis of much scientific analysis. Called **Ockham's razor,** this principle says that between alternative explanations for the same phenomenon, the simpler is always to be preferred. People who have studied the material world ever since have looked to simple, elegant explanations to satisfy Ockham's razor. New Nominalism became popular in universities, and Ockhamite philosophy became known as the *via moderna* (modern way). Indeed, intellectuals were beginning to reject the old and look at the world in a new way.

New Literary Giants

In the fourteenth century, more authors began to write in the vernacular, their national languages, instead of Latin, which had been the language of great literature

KEY DATES

A CENTURY OF DISASTERS FOR THE WEST

1305–1378	Babylonian Captivity of papacy
1315–1322	Famine
ca. 1320–1384	John Wycliffe
1337–1453	Hundred Years' War
1348	Arrival of Black Death in Europe
1358	Jacquerie revolt in France
ca. 1373–1415	Jan Hus
1378–1417	Great Schism
1378–1385	Urban revolts
1381	Peasant revolt in England
1414–1418	Council of Constance
1415	Battle of Agincourt
1431	Death of Joan of Arc
1455–1485	Wars of the Roses in England

FIGURE 9.6 Domenico di Michelino, *Dante and His Poem, the Divine Comedy* This illustration of the Italian poet Dante's famous *Divine Comedy* was painted on the walls of Florence's cathedral. In addition to depicting Dante, it shows hell (on the left), a mountain of purgatory, and a celestial heaven.

throughout the Middle Ages. (Latin still remained the language of the church and of official government documents.) In the Middle Ages, romances and other poetry had been written in the vernacular (see Chapter 8), but in fourteenth-century Italy in particular, a new kind of literature emerged that explored people's place in the world. Italian poets from Tuscany made Italian a literary language and composed some of the greatest literature of all time.

The first of these writers was Dante Alighieri (1265–1321), who was born in Florence. In 1302, he became embroiled in the turbulent political situation of his city and was exiled. He always hoped to return to his beloved city but never succeeded, and he grew to be a bitter, disillusioned man wandering from city to city until he died in 1321. While in exile, he composed his masterpiece, now called the *Divine Comedy*. The work became so popular that a century after his death, Florence recognized his genius and commissioned the painting shown in **Figure 9.6** to honor the man they had exiled. He stands in the center holding

Dante

the book that brought such posthumous fame to the man and the city that spawned him.

The *Divine Comedy* is a magnificent allegory of a soul's journey through despair to salvation. The lengthy work is divided into three sections—Hell, Purgatory, and Paradise—and the poet journeys through them all. He is first led through Hell by Virgil, the Roman poet whose works still formed the basis of a good education. Dante described the punishments of the damned in gruesome detail: In one location he saw "long lines of people in a river of excrement that seemed the overflow of the world's latrines," and in these pits Dante placed his contemporaries (as well as historical figures) who deserved punishment. The damned are shown in **Figure 9.6** on the lower left descending into Hell. Dante then leaves Hell and climbs the mountain of Purgatory (shown in the background of **Figure 9.6**), where sinners who would ultimately be saved were doing penance for their sins. Finally, Dante was led into Paradise by a mysterious woman—Beatrice—who was reputed to be the love of the poet's life.

thinking about ART

FIGURE 9.7

Illumination from a Book of Hours, Fifteenth Century

This image is an illumination—an illustration within a hand-decorated, hand-colored manuscript—from a fifteenth-century Book of Hours. This work was commissioned by the wealthy Duke of Burgundy and used as a prayer book. The image is strictly hierarchic in structure: The castle is at the highest point, supported by hardworking peasants peacefully working a well-tended landscape and tending their flock. The whole scene unfolds under a well-ordered heaven.

Connecting Art & Society

1. Given the disasters of the fourteenth and fifteenth centuries, does the world that is depicted look realistic? Explain.

2. Why would this image have been particularly appealing to a noble patron?

3. What might this image indicate about one sort of human response to disasters and hardship?

Some scholars consider the *Divine Comedy* a perfect medieval work: It incorporates Aquinas's theology and Aristotle's science, and the whole work has the complexity of a Gothic cathedral or a *Summa Theologiae* (the philosophic summaries described in Chapter 8). Other scholars see in the work something new—a departure from the medieval world that shaped the poet. Dante, after all, was a layman who presumed to express theology of salvation. Furthermore, he articulated the growing criticism of the medieval church by placing many popes in Hell. Finally, his beloved guide through Hell and Purgatory was a classic poet—Virgil, who represented reason. His final tour through heaven was conducted by Beatrice, who was an allegory of faith. As we will see in Chapter 10, many thinkers who like Dante struggled with the despair of the age would find solace in pagan classics and faith in God's grace.

Another Florentine who had a profound impact on literature was Giovanni Boccaccio (1313–1375), who witnessed the devastating plague as it swept through his city. In his most famous work, *The Decameron*, Boccaccio offers a poignant eyewitness description of the plague, with insights into how various people responded to catastrophe, for he said some shut themselves off from everyone else, others prayed diligently in hopes of avoiding early death, and still others denied themselves nothing, "drinking and reveling incessantly from tavern to tavern." This description sets the stage for the heart of the book, in which ten young people escape to a villa outside Florence and decide to amuse themselves by telling stories. *The Decameron* is the collection of the stories they tell, and most are highly entertaining.

Boccaccio

The stories reflect a new, permissive attitude that arose in the wake of the plague, for the stories talk frankly of sex, lies, and ordinary people. The heroes are not knights or philosophers, but clever men and women who live by their wits, and their stories were intended more to amuse than to teach moral lessons. In his later years, Boccaccio became uneasy with his lighthearted works, and in a letter written in 1373 he urged someone to not let women read his stories, warning, "You know how much in them is less than decent and opposed to modesty." However, there was no return to a more modest, conservative age—the fourteenth century had disrupted much that was traditional, and many people welcomed a new way to look at life. In these dark times, many found a lighthearted tribute to pleasure particularly satisfying.

One typical way to react to disaster is to look back longingly to a "golden age"—in this case, to an imagined tightly ordered medieval world. **Figure 9.7** shows one such idealized world.

One of the world's most gifted poets—the Englishman Geoffrey Chaucer (ca. 1340–1400)—also looked longingly backward. Chaucer drew from tales like

Boccaccio's to offer a different view of the turbulent fourteenth century. His most famous work, *The Canterbury Tales*, was written in English and tells of a group of 29 pilgrims who journey from Southwark (outside London) to Canterbury to the shrine of Thomas Becket. Like Boccaccio's youths, Chaucer's pilgrims tell tales to pass the time on their journey, but unlike Boccaccio, Chaucer draws each pilgrim vividly, with a clear personality so each stands out as an individual. The stories are varied, from knightly romances to bawdy tales, and they still delight readers today.

> Chaucer

Chaucer's descriptions of the pilgrims offer a subtle, yet revealing, look at fourteenth-century society. He criticized corruption in the church by commenting on monks who would rather hunt than pray, or friars who were not interested in the poor: "He knew the taverns well in every town. / The barmaids and innkeepers pleased his mind / Better than beggars and lepers and their kind." However, Chaucer was also a medieval man who looked back to what he imagined was a golden age when knights were virtuous crusaders, priests cared nothing for money, and scholars loved only knowledge. If that golden age ever existed, it was gone by the fourteenth century—money was rapidly becoming the measure of success, and the future belonged to bright individuals with as much character as Chaucer's pilgrims.

A New View: Jan van Eyck

Just as Chaucer carefully and precisely created his pilgrims with words on a page, painters in Flanders began to re-create their world in paint with a precision that continues to astonish the viewer. One of the most famous of the Flemish artists is Jan van Eyck (ca. 1395–1441), who was among the first to use oil paint—a medium that allowed the artist to capture realistic details. In the painting of a husband and his bride shown in **Figure 9.8,** van Eyck portrays the scene with amazing realism, down to the witnesses to the marriage who are reflected in the mirror on the wall in the background. Both the new medium and the technical skill of the artist point to the new directions that European culture took in this period.

Like Chaucer and Dante, van Eyck was breaking new ground in the arts, but he also looked back to the Middle Ages and preserved much of their ideals. In the medieval world, people looked to intense and detailed symbolism to both reveal and explain their world, and van Eyck filled the painting shown in **Figure 9.8** with symbolism. The dog is a symbol of fidelity, and the carving on the bedpost is of Saint Margaret, the patron saint of childbirth. The

> Realism and symbolism

FIGURE 9.8 Jan van Eyck, *Giovanni Arnolfini and His Bride,* 1434 Painters who worked in Flanders in the fifteenth century were more innovative than their Italian contemporaries. Whereas the Italians favored tempera, a water-based paint, artists in Flanders preferred oil paint, which allowed them to depict highly lifelike details. Note the realistic qualities of this famous portrait, which is also brimming with symbolism.

single lighted candle indicates God's presence and blessing of the couple's wedding night. The combination of realism infused with symbolic meaning is characteristic of the late Middle Ages, and the Flemish painter captured this spirit perfectly.

The disasters of the long fourteenth century had caused many to question their traditional views and values. As the ordered world they had known was crumbling, however, room was being made for new ideas and new approaches. As we will see in the next chapter, the West would take a fresh and exciting path.

EMPIRES IN THE EAST

As the West struggled with disasters that fractured the medieval order, winds of change also blew from the Far East into Europe. New empires were forming

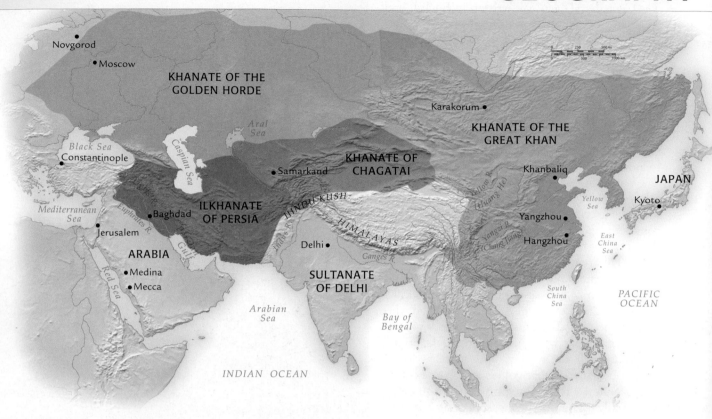

MAP 9.4

The Mongol Empire, ca. 1300

This map shows the greatest expanse of the Mongol Empire as it extended from the Pacific Ocean to the Black Sea. The scale indicates the vast distances of the empire.

Explore the Map

1. What problems did the Mongols face in governing an empire that encompassed so many cultures and religion?

2. How did the Mongolian conquests stimulate cross-cultural contacts between the West and non-West?

3. Locate Constantinople and Novgorod. Why were the Byzantine Empire and the Russian state threatened by the proximity of the Mongol Empire?

in the East that dominated the political landscapes of the regions for the next few centuries, and the West was brought into a new global relationship with lands as far away as east Asia.

Eastern Universalism: The Mongols

As early as the thirteenth century, while the West struggled between localism and centralization, dynamic conquerors swept out of Mongolia and established a new, unified empire extending from eastern Europe across Asia to the Pacific Ocean. In 1206, Genghis Khan (r. 1206–1227) united diverse nomadic groups and forged a formidable army that he led with consummate skill. He was an extraordinary figure who is remembered for his appalling cruelty as well as for his wisdom and talent as a leader, for after the violence of his initial conquest, he established a peaceful, tolerant rule. He implemented the first Mongol written language and promulgated the first law code for his nomadic people. His grandson, Kublai Khan (r. 1260–1294), was an equally powerful ruler, whose wealthy empire, centered in China, offered a tantalizing lure to travelers from the West.

Map 9.4 shows the remarkable extent of the Mongol Empire in about 1300—from China and Korea in the east to Moscow and Ukraine in the west. The rulers of the Scandinavian/Slavic state centered in Kiev had already moved their capital to the far north in

Mongol Empire

A Franciscan Missionary Goes to China

John of Monte Corvino (1247–1328) was a Franciscan priest sent to convert the Mongols in China (called Cathay here). He wrote this letter in January 1305, asking for support from his fellow Franciscans in Italy, and the letter gives an idea of the difficulties of his assignment and of his successes.

I proceeded on my further journey and made my way to Cathay, the realm of the Emperor of the Tartars who is called the Great Khan. To him I presented the letter of our lord the Pope, and invited him to adopt the Catholic Faith of our Lord Jesus Christ, but he had grown too old in idolatry. However he bestows many kindnesses upon the Christians, and these two years past I am abiding with him. . . . In this mission I abode alone and without any associate for eleven years; but it is now going on for two years since I was joined by Friar Arnold, a German of the province of Cologne.

I have built a church in the city of Khanbaliq, in which the king has his chief residence. This I completed six years ago; and I have built a bell-tower to it, and put three bells in it. I have baptized there, as well as I can estimate, up to this time some 6000 persons; . . . And I am often still engaged in baptizing.

Also I have gradually bought one hundred and fifty boys, the children of pagan parents, and of ages varying from seven to eleven, who had never learned any religion. These boys I have baptized, and I have taught them Greek and Latin after our manner. Also I have written out Psalters for them, with thirty Hymnals and two Breviaries. By help of these, eleven of the boys already know our service, and form a choir and take their weekly turn of duty as they do in convents, whether I am there or not. Many of the boys are also employed in writing out Psalters and other things suitable. His Majesty the Emperor moreover delights much to hear them chanting. I have the bells rung at all the canonical hours, and with my congregation of babes and sucklings I perform divine service, and the chanting we do by ear because I have no service book with the notes.

Indeed if I had but two or three comrades to aid me 'tis possible that the Emperor Khan would have been baptized by this time! I ask then for such brethren to come, if any are willing to come, such I mean as will make it their great business to lead exemplary lives. . . .

I have myself grown old and grey, more with toil and trouble than with years; for I am not more than fifty-eight. I have got a competent knowledge of the language and character which is most generally used by the Tartars. And I have already translated into that language and character the New Testament and the Psalter, and have caused them to be written out in the fairest penmanship they have; and so by writing, reading, and preaching, I bear open and public testimony to the Law of Christ. . . .

As far as I ever saw or heard tell, I do not believe that any king or prince in the world can be compared to his majesty the Khan in respect of the extent of his dominions, the vastness of their population, or the amount of his wealth. Here I stop.

SOURCE: John Monte Corvino, "Letter of John Monte Corvino," in *Cathay and the Way Thither,* trans. and ed. Sir Henry Yule, 2nd ed. revised by Henri Cordier (London: Hakluyt Society, 1914), vol. III, second series, vol. 37, pp. 45–51, passim. Slightly abridged and reprinted in Leon Barnard and Theodore B. Hodges, *Readings in European History* (New York: Macmillan, 1958), pp. 107–108 (some spelling modernized). See also http:www.fordham.edu/halsal/source/corvino1.html.

Analyze the Document

1. Why do you think the pope was so eager to convert the Mongol khan?

2. How did the khan treat the Christians? Why did he treat them so?

3. What techniques did John use to convert the Chinese?

4. Do you think that the arrival of more Franciscans would have ensured the conversion of the khan?

5. Why do you think John argued this?

Novgorod, and this Russian state had to pay tribute to the Mongol Empire to its south. This empire encompassed an extraordinary diversity of peoples and religions—from Muslims to Christians to Buddhists—and it accommodated them seemingly without conflict. The popes were eager to convert the Mongols to Christianity and sent missionaries to China. Document 9.3 describes the trip of one such missionary.

This unified empire also created a huge trade area through which goods and ideas traveled easily. It is likely that Europeans learned the recipe for gunpowder from travelers through the Mongol Empire. (See Thinking About Science & Technology, Chapter 11.)

As we saw in Chapter 8, the Venetians in particular were well placed to take advantage of this trade. By the fourteenth century, the Venetians had established many trading posts where they could engage in a lucrative commerce. **Figure 9.9** on page 303 shows Venetian merchants trading cloth for oriental products—possibly spices—with traders who had landed in a Mediterranean port.

Certainly the most famous western Europeans who took advantage of the Venetian experience in trade were the Venetians Marco Polo (1254–1324) and his father and uncle, who traveled to the far reaches of

Marco Polo

FIGURE 9.9 Venetian Traders With the rise of the Mongol Empire came the facilitation of trade across the old Silk Road. Venetians such as Marco Polo and his family were well placed to take advantage of this lucrative business. Here, Venetian merchants trade cloth for spices.

the Mongol Empire. During several trading journeys, the Polos traveled all the way to the court of the great Kublai Khan in Khanbaliq. The journey took them three and a half years by horseback. The Polos stayed at the khan's court for seventeen years, and Marco apparently served as an emissary of the khan himself. When the Polos returned home to Venice, they brought back a wealth of spices, silks, and other luxurious curiosities. The extravagant items were so impressive that other merchants followed; by 1300 there was even a community of Italians living in China.

Perhaps Marco Polo's most important contribution was a book about his voyages, which has been translated into English as *The Travels of Marco Polo.* His writings told of things that people in the West found unbelievable. For example, the merchants found it extraordinary that the Chinese used paper money; as Marco wrote: "The coinage of this paper money is authenticated with as much form and ceremony as if it were actually of pure gold and silver." Even more astonishing, Marco described "a sort of black stone, which they dig out of the mountains. When lighted it burns like charcoal." The Chinese had been burning coal since about 100 B.C.E., but in the West such a feat seemed implausible. Few believed the exotic tales of the traveler, but the book did excite the imaginations of adventurers. It fueled the great age of exploration that followed—Christopher Columbus carried a well-marked copy of the book through his voyages.

The Ottoman Empire, 1300–1566

The political situation in eastern Europe changed permanently with the establishment of a new empire

at its borders. In the thirteenth century, a group of Asiatic nomads (later called Ottoman Turks) migrated westward from the expansive Asian steppes. Along the way, they converted to Islam and brought new vigor to Muslim expansion. The Turks were ruled by sultans, who were supposedly the successors of Muhammad and therefore empowered to interpret Muslim law. In this way, the sultans drew on seven hundred years of history to legitimize their authority.

As **Map 9.5** shows, the Ottoman Turks expanded slowly but steadily around the eastern Mediterranean. As they moved through the Balkans, the conquerors added to the diversity of the region's population. Even before the arrival of Muslim conquerors, the Balkans had been divided by culture and religion. Some countries, among them Hungary, were Catholic and used the Latin alphabet. Others, such as Serbia, were Greek Orthodox and used a Cyrillic alphabet. The Muslim invaders brought a new religion and a new alphabet into the already culturally diverse region, thus setting the stage for problems that would continue into the twentieth century. The Biography of Vlad III (1431–1476), king of Wallachia in what today is the country of Romania, sheds light on how the ongoing Muslim invasions destabilized the Balkans by causing a continually shifting balance of power.

The Ottoman expansion was powered by a formidable military at whose heart was an elite force called the janissaries. The janissaries were slaves who had been raised from boyhood and trained to fight for the sultan. As the Turks took over the Balkans, they forced the occupied peoples to pay a tribute of boys. These youths would be enslaved, converted to Islam, and trained to fight using the latest weapons, including artillery and guns.

By 1355, the Ottomans had effectively surrounded the Byzantine Empire, which had stood for so long as a powerful state and a buffer for the West. Finally, a powerful sultan, Mehmed II (r. 1451–1481), committed his government to a policy of conquest. The sultan turned to new technology to breach the walls surrounding Constantinople; he commissioned a gunner to craft an oversized cannon and smelted smaller weapons for the metal. The barrel, 26 feet long, could launch a stone ball weighing more than 1,000 pounds. Fifty yokes of oxen were needed to move the gun, and 700 men manned it. Constantinople's massive walls shook with the impact of the bombardment. The heavy stones that had provided an impregnable defense for so many centuries cracked. The city fell in 1453, and the last emperor, Constantine XI Palaeologus, died in the battle. Mehmed, now known as the "conqueror," made

> Conquest of Constantinople

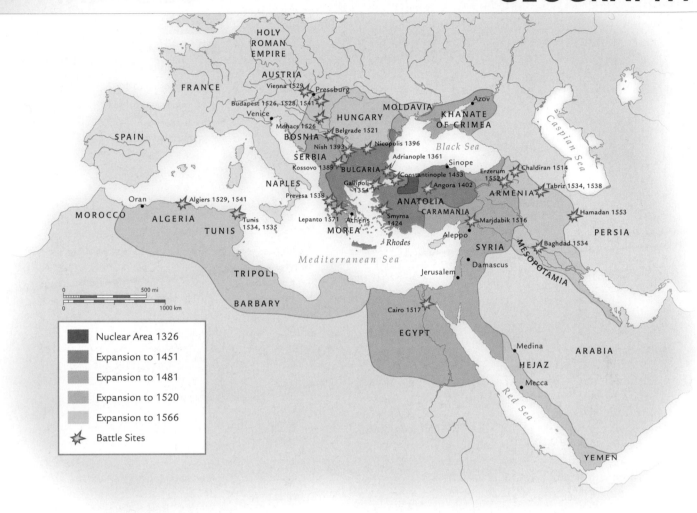

MAP 9.5

The Ottoman Empire, 1300–1566

This map shows the spread of the Ottoman Empire and identifies the major battles that marked its expansion.

Explore the Map

1. How did the nuclear area of the Turks in 1326 help them expand into the Byzantine Empire?

2. Notice how Constantinople had been surrounded long before its fall. Was there any chance that it could have avoided capture, even with external help? Explain.

3. How might western Europeans have felt threatened by the invigorated empire that extended well into the Balkans?

Constantinople his capital under the name of Istanbul, by which it is known today. (The name was not formally changed until 1930.) Mehmed extended his power around the Black Sea.

Almost a century later, the sultan Suleiman I the Magnificent (r. 1520–1566) brought the Ottoman Empire to the height of its power. As **Map 9.5** shows, the Ottoman Empire extended throughout the Middle East and into North Africa. In order to secure his holdings in the eastern Mediterranean, Suleiman made the Ottomans into a major naval power. Suleiman's newly expanded navy had to confront the last Christian outpost in an otherwise Ottoman sea—the island of Rhodes (shown on **Map 9.5**), a highly fortified location held by the crusading order Knights of Saint John. The sultan lost many men in repeated assaults on the fortified island, but eventually his

Suleiman I

Map legend:
- Nuclear Area 1325
- Expansion to 1389
- Expansion to 1462
- Expansion to 1533
- ✦ Battle Site

MAP 9.6

The Rise of Moscow, 1325–1533

This map shows the expansion of the principality of Moscow as it grew from a small state in 1325 to a large empire in 1533. It also identifies the Mongol Khanate of the Golden Horde.

Explore the Map

1. In what ways was Russia well placed to take advantage of the Mongols' retreat from their westernmost province?

2. Compare this map with **Map 9.5.** Why would Russia have considered itself the logical heir to the Byzantine Empire as guardian of Christianity in the face of a growing Muslim threat?

artillery prevailed and the knights surrendered. They were allowed to leave the island with their weapons and they moved to the island of Malta in the central Mediterranean, where they continued to fight against Muslim expansion. However, Suleiman's victory consolidated his hold in the East, and Christian merchants seeking to capitalize on the rich trade with the East found themselves confronted by the sultan's ships and tax collectors. As we will see in Chapter 12, westerners became highly motivated to find new routes to the rich lands of east Asia.

With the sea secure, Suleiman turned his attention northward, and in 1529 he even threatened Vienna, in the heartland of Europe. From now on, the new monarchies of western Europe would have to conduct their diplomatic and military escapades with the Turks in mind, and, as we will see in the next chapters, the Turkish presence posed a significant threat to the West.

Russia: The Third Rome

At the beginning of the fourteenth century, Russia was divided into many principalities, each self-sufficient and independent. All of them, however, were subject to the Mongol khan of the Golden Horde, to whom they owed tribute and loyalty. The Mongols did not like the forested land of Russia, so they did not occupy it directly. Instead, they stayed in the steppes north of the Black Sea and simply collected tribute. One of the small principalities, the Duchy of Moscow, was able to take advantage of the Mongol overlords' absence to rise to a great empire. **Map 9.6** shows the small nuclear area of Moscow in 1325—three years before an enterprising prince, Ivan I (r. 1328–1341), came to power.

Ivan cultivated a relationship with the Mongol khan, offering loyalty and gifts. In return, Ivan received the right to collect the Mongol tribute within Russia. He grew so rich in the process (probably by withholding most of the money due the Mongols) that he earned the nickname Moneybags. This money fostered the growth of the Russian Empire in the fifteenth century, when the Mongols' fortunes declined. The khanate's hold on the territories of Russia and Ukraine loosened, and the Duchy of Moscow took the lead in overthrowing the last of Mongol rule.

Ivan I also wisely cultivated the Orthodox Church, gaining the support of that venerable institution. The Orthodox Church had flourished in Russia with the support of the Mongols, who gave the church immunity from taxation. Ivan I encouraged the Metropolitan Bishop of the Russian Church to make Moscow his permanent residence, so that city was well placed to lead the Orthodox Church when Constantinople fell in 1453.

Ivan III ("the Great") (r. 1462–1505) pushed back the final Mongol advance on Moscow in 1480 and established himself as the first ruler of the new Russian state. Ivan had married a niece of the last Byzantine emperor, so the Russian declared himself the heir to the Byzantine Empire—he proclaimed Moscow the Third Rome and took the title caesar, or tsar. The tsar strove to reestablish the greatness of the Byzantine Empire, and like the Byzantines, he closely allied with the Orthodox Church in his land. In 1589, the bishop of Moscow was proclaimed a patriarch—one of the five who presided over the eastern Orthodox Church. (See Chapter 6 for the origins of this church.) The Orthodox Church supported the tsar's claim that Moscow was the spiritual heir to Constantinople. Thus, religion and tradition supported the tsar's claim for absolute and universal authority.

Russia's empire stretched from Europe into the steppes of Asia, creating what would be a long-standing question in Russia: Where does its identity lie? Is it Western, Asian, or something else? Ivan III did not resolve this question by claiming the mantle of the Byzantine Emperor, and future Russian leaders would continue the discussion as they ruled the new conservative empire that had arisen in the East.

Ivan III

EASTERN EMPIRES FLOURISH

1206–1227	Mongol Genghis Khan
1260–1294	Mongol Kublai Khan
1328–1341	Russian tsar Ivan I
1451–1481	Ottoman Mehmed II
1453	Ottoman conquest of Constantinople
1462–1505	Russian tsar Ivan III the Great
1520–1566	Ottoman Suleiman I

KEY DATES

BIOGRAPHY

Vlad III Dracula (the Impaler), King of Wallachia

(1431–1476)

A Vicious, Controversial King

In the fifteenth century, eastern Europe was a region of complex and shifting loyalties. Then, as now, three religions—Greek Orthodox, Catholic, and Muslim—coexisted uneasily. The balance of power was changing as the armies of the powerful Ottoman Empire swept through the Balkans. The political situation took a shocking turn in 1453, when the Ottoman sultan Mehmed II conquered the ancient city of Constantinople, which had stood as a bulwark of orthodoxy against Islam. The fall of the Byzantine Empire and the rise of a strengthened Islam provoked Christian rulers to call for new crusading armies to protect Europe, but the political situation on the ground was never so simple, as Christians sometimes allied with Muslims to forward their own political aims. These tumultuous times brought to power one of the cruelest and most controversial kings of Europe, Vlad III, whose nickname, Dracula, would become linked in the nineteenth century with folklore accounts of a bloodthirsty vampire.

Vlad's father, Vlad II, was king of Wallachia, a region in what today is southern Romania. In the fifteenth century, Wallachia lay dangerously between two powerful neighbors—Hungary and the expanding Ottoman Empire. In 1410, during the height (and twilight) of chivalry, the king of Hungary founded a secret order of knights called the Order of the Dragon, whose members vowed to defend Christendom against the Turks. Vlad II was admitted to the order, and he proudly displayed its dragon emblem on his crest and his coins. *Dragon* in Romanian is *Drac*, so Vlad II was called Vlad Drac—Vlad the Dragon. His son, Vlad III, born in the neighboring region of Transylvania, was called Son of the Dragon, or Dracula, the name that would become so infamously linked with vampires.

Vlad Dracula did not hold his throne easily; throughout his life, he shifted alliances as unpredictably as the Balkan winds changed direction. In fact, he reigned three different times. He ruled first in 1448 with the support of the Turks, but he lasted only two months before a rival, supported by Hungary, drove him out. After the fall of Constantinople in 1453, Vlad made an alliance with Hungary, and he came to power again in 1456, promising to fight his former allies, the Turks. This time, he ruled until 1462, when invading Turks forced him to flee to Hungary, where he was imprisoned for years. Finally, he converted from orthodoxy to Catholicism, pleasing his Hungarian captors, who then supported his restoration to power in 1476. Throughout his turbulent reign, Vlad Dracula had to fear the threat posed by the local nobles—the *boyars*—who were themselves kingmakers and power brokers. He also had to deal with some powerful German merchants who seemed to be exploiting local Wallachians. How did Vlad respond to all these pressures in his brief rule? With terror and cruelty.

Indeed, Vlad Dracula developed a horrifying method of torturing and executing his enemies. He drove sharp stakes through the full length of their bodies and then erected the stakes in the ground, leaving the suffering victims to die slowly, some for hours and some for days. He often placed large rings of staked victims outside towns, where the decaying corpses served to terrify and appall his opponents. For his horrifying execution method, he won the infamous nickname Vlad the Impaler. Even the intrepid conqueror of Constantinople, Mehmed II, reputedly was sickened by the sight of 20,000 impaled Turkish prisoners outside the city of Tirgoviste, a spectacle that observers dubbed the Forest of the Impaled.

Vlad Dracula used his brutal execution technique against various enemies. Of course, he impaled military foes, from Turks to Hungarians. He also impaled Wallachians who violated his own ideas of justice: The *boyars*, for example, were frequent targets of his cruelty, and he kept them under control by his terror campaign. He also tortured thieves and merchants who cheated customers, in so doing earning the gratitude of peasants and others who longed for law and order. Vlad reputedly had strong ideas about the proper behavior of women, as he also impaled those whom he deemed unchaste or poor wives. Accounts indicating that Vlad Dracula impaled tens of thousands of people during his brief reign seem exaggerated—

indeed, the numbers are logistically improbable—but there is no doubt that he used this savage technique many, many times.

Evidently, Vlad did not practice torture simply as a political tool. Even Russian sources, which were generally favorable to him, describe how, when he was imprisoned, Vlad captured mice and birds, impaling their small bodies and watching them die in pain. Modern psychologists would surely identify him as a psychopath.

In 1476, when the Hungarians supported his return to power, Dracula invaded Wallachia with Transylvanian forces and took back his throne. However, the Transylvanians quickly went home, and Dracula was left with only a small army of supporters. When the Turks invaded to replace Vlad with a ruler of their choice, he was able to gather only about 4,000 troops, and he was killed near Bucharest in December 1476. There are conflicting reports of his death. Some suggest that he was slain by his own *boyars*; others maintain that he fell during a Turkish advance. We will probably never know the truth. The Turks took the king's head to Istanbul and displayed it on a stake to prove that Vlad the Impaler was dead. His body is reputedly buried at Snagov, an island monastery near Bucharest.

The historical sources describing Vlad Dracula vary in their assessment. German pamphleteers from the late fifteenth century describe him as a "monster" who tortured German merchants; **Figure 9.10,** from a German pamphlet, shows Dracula calmly eating while surrounded by a forest of the impaled. The Russians, whose czars were struggling to curb

FIGURE 9.10 Vlad III Dracula German pamphlet, Nuremberg, 1499.

the power of their own *boyars*, called him a cruel but just prince who cared about his people. The Romanian folk tradition has embraced him as a national hero who defended his land from invading Turks and exploitative Germans. However, the characterization of Vlad that is most remembered, owing to the Irish writer Brad Stoker's novel *Dracula* (1897), is that of a vicious impaler. Most scholars of Stoker's work of fiction, which opens in Transylvania, believe that although the author drew from eastern European folktales on vampires, he based his character on the bloodthirsty Vlad Dracula the Impaler. These differing accounts show how historical records are shaped by the

political opinions of the writers and how, in a complex world of shifting alliances, a sadistic king can become a folk hero.

Connecting People & Society

1. How did the expansion of the Turks lead to instability in the Balkans?

2. How might such instability have contributed to the rise to power of a ruthless king?

3. Why might historians and other writers have come to different conclusions as they assessed Vlad Dracula's rule?

LOOKING BACK & MOVING FORWARD

Summary The fourteenth century brought with it a series of disasters in the West that broke down the medieval order that had prevailed before. Famine and plague killed millions, depopulating villages and towns. Revolts broke out in towns and across the countryside, not only bringing more violence but also raising the shocking specter of people attacking the very order of society. The manorial system in which serfs labored for their lords slowly broke down under the pressure, leaving a monetary system of rents and labor for hire. If one survived the disasters, life (at least in western Europe) might be better—higher wages and more opportunities awaited.

The papacy, too, fell prey to disasters. After new struggles with the kings of France, the popes lost prestige as they left Rome to live in Avignon and, subsequently, precipitated the Great Schism when disputed elections left two, then three, popes ruling at the same time. The medieval imperial papacy could not recover from such blows. Feudalism with its knights in shining armor also proved to be inadequate in the new age. During the devastating Hundred Years' War, infantry armed with bows and arrows, pikes, and later guns proved more effective than knights, and kings slowly began to prefer money to military service from their vassals.

In eastern Europe, new empires arose with strong, autocratic rulers, and with the strengthening of these empires East and West grew further apart. The tensions that emerged between the two profoundly influenced European life in the future. However, these eastern empires would soon face a western Europe with ideas and values dramatically different from those of the medieval West. What form would this new sensibility take?

KEY TERMS

Black Death, *p. 282*

Jacquerie, *p. 286*

Babylonian Captivity, *p. 287*

Great Schism, *p. 288*

Conciliar movement, *p. 289*

Lollards, *p. 289*

Hundred Years' War, *p. 289*

Dauphin, *p. 292*

free companies, *p. 292*

nominalism, *p. 294*

Ockham's razor, *p. 294*

REVIEW, ANALYZE, & CONNECT TO TODAY

REVIEW THE PREVIOUS CHAPTER

Chapter 8—"Order Restored"—described the three orders of the High Middle Ages and traced the fortunes of the social groups and the kings who ruled them. It also looked at the intellectual and religious accomplishments of that vigorous age.

1. Review the agricultural innovations that allowed for expansion during the High Middle Ages and consider why these no longer proved adequate in the fourteenth century.

2. Review the development of England and France in the High Middle Ages to see how they came to the violent confrontation of the Hundred Years' War in the fourteenth century.

ANALYZE THIS CHAPTER

Chapter 9—"The West Struggles and Eastern Empires Flourish"—traces the disasters of the fourteenth century that undermined the medieval structures, and it also shows the growth of empires in eastern Europe.

1. In the struggle between popes and kings over who should lead a Christian Europe, popes had dominated

in the thirteenth century. When the struggle reopened in the fourteenth century, the kings prevailed. Review the events that led to the Great Schism and its resolution.

2. How did the disasters of the fourteenth century undermine the feudal and manorial systems?

3. What were the eastern empires that came to power by the end of the fifteenth century, and what were their relative strengths?

CONNECT TO TODAY

Think about the chapter's discussion of the disruptions caused by natural disasters and disease. Also consider the growth of the Russian Empire and the spread of Islam into the Balkans.

1. What are some recent instances in which pandemics have disrupted (or have threatened to disrupt) societies? How have people responded to such threats?

2. The United States was involved in warfare in the Balkans during World War I and also later in the twentieth century. How might the events described in this chapter have contributed to the United States' involvement?

BEYOND THE CLASSROOM

ECONOMIC AND SOCIAL MISERY

Hilton, Rodney. *Bond Men Made Free*. New York: Methuen, 1973. A classic, highly sympathetic study of peasant unrest in the late Middle Ages.

Jordan, William Chester. *The Great Famine*. Princeton, NJ: Princeton University Press, 1996. A comprehensive study of this devastating event that looks at the causes, impact, and responses to the famine—certain to remain the classic work on the subject.

Kelly, John. *The Great Mortality: An Intimate History of the Black Death, the Most Devastating Plague of All Time*. New York: Harper Perennial, 2006. An extremely detailed and readable account of the plague that incorporates the latest findings.

IMPERIAL PAPACY BESIEGED

Blumenfeld-Kosinski, Renate. *Poets, Saints, and Visionaries of the Great Schism, 1378–1417*. Pittsburgh: Penn State University Press, 2006. A discussion of the calamity of the Great Schism in a wide sense, including an examination of artistic, visionary, and literary texts.

Swanson R.N. *Universities, Academics, and the Great Schism*. Cambridge Studies in Medieval Life and Thought, Third Series. Cambridge: Cambridge University Press, 2002. Analysis of the schism from the viewpoint of the academics who were prominent in the university rivalries, concluding with a look at their contribution to the Conciliar movement.

MORE DESTRUCTION: THE HUNDRED YEARS' WAR, 1337–1453

Allmand, Christopher. *The Hundred Years' War: England and France at War, ca. 1300–ca. 1450*. Cambridge: Cambridge University Press, 2008. A brief account that remains the best summary of this conflict.

Gillingham, John. *The Wars of the Roses: Peace and Conflict in Fifteenth-Century England*. Baton Rouge: Louisiana State University Press, 1981. A political and military history of this influential conflict.

Warner, Marina. *Joan of Arc: The Image of Female Heroism*. New York: Knopf, 1981. Examines Joan's life and legend.

RESPONSES TO THE DISRUPTION OF MEDIEVAL ORDER

Bergin, Thomas Goddard. *Boccaccio*. New York: Viking Press, 1981. A scholarly study of the life and thought of this influential writer.

Hicks, Michael. *Bastard Feudalism*. New York: Longman, 1995. A careful work that revisits the development of "bastard feudalism" in England, particularly in the fifteenth century, and shows that it is an acceleration of previous trends.

Huizinga, Johan. *The Waning of the Middle Ages*. New York: St. Martin's Press, 1967. A brilliant study of the mentality of the people in the late Middle Ages, including art, literature, and general outlook.

Lambert, Malcolm. *Medieval Heresy: Popular Movements from the Gregorian Reform to the Reformation*, 3rd ed. Oxford: Blackwell, 2002. A general explanation of the Hussite and Lollard movements placed within the larger context of other heresies.

Leff, Gordon. *William of Ockham*. Manchester, England: Manchester University Press, 1975. An authoritative study that makes the ideas of this difficult philosopher accessible.

EMPIRES IN THE EAST

Imber, Colin. *The Ottoman Empire, 1300–1650: The Structure of Power*. New York: Palgrave Macmillan, 2004. A detailed chronological survey that both introduces and summarizes the period.

Martin, Janet. *Medieval Russia, 980–1584*. New York: Cambridge University Press, 1995. A well-written, accessible account of the growth of Russia.

Morgan, David. *The Mongols*, 2nd ed. New York: Blackwell, 2007. A survey that stresses the impact of the Mongol Empire on eastern Europe.

PEDRO BERRUGUETE, *FEDERICO DA MONTEFELTRO AND HIS SON GUIDOBALDO*, ca. 1476

This portrait shows the founder of the dynasty of Urbino—a soldier of fortune who was made duke by the pope in 1474. The artist used oil paint and a new sense of realism to depict the duke with everything that mattered to him: the armor of a soldier, the book of a scholar, the support of the papacy, shown by the tiara in the upper left corner, and the presence of his son, an heir to perpetuate his dynasty. Strong, well-rounded individuals such as this brought a dramatic new spirit to the West.

A New Spirit in the West

The Renaissance, ca. 1300–1640

"This age is dominated by great men [who] labored much to aggrandize themselves and to acquire glory. And yet, would it not have been better if they had undertaken fewer enterprises and been more afraid of offending God and of persecuting their subjects and neighbors?" With these words, a contemporary biographer of Louis the Spider, king of France during the Renaissance, pinpointed both the strengths and weaknesses of this new age: Talented individuals accomplished much, yet often to the neglect of those in their care.

This rise of new talent first became evident in Italy during the disastrous fourteenth century, when some individuals responded to the troubled times with a clear-eyed realism that let them see opportunity amid the chaos. The transforming ideas of the era have been dubbed the Renaissance (meaning "rebirth"), and they promised a return to the spirit of ancient Greece and Rome that might restore the glory of the Roman Empire.

Political turbulence in the Italian city-states led visionary rulers to govern in new ways, developing innovative military strategies and novel diplomacy. This individual achievement in politics generated similar accomplishments in literature, architecture, and the visual arts as rulers became patrons supporting artists who mirrored their values. Just as these patrons stimulated artistic expression, intellectuals created a cultural movement that emphasized the study of Greek and Roman classics and praised realism and individual accomplishments. Perhaps the true greatness of the Renaissance lay in the application of these abstract ideas to real life. The innovative ideas that emerged in Italy subsequently spread throughout Europe as the ravages of the fourteenth century broke down old medieval structures and institutions.

Although these new ideas brought wealth and power to some, everyone did not benefit equally. Indeed, public policies in these centuries often worsened the lot of the poor and the powerless. Nevertheless, the Renaissance was an exciting, vibrant time that ushered Europe from the medieval world toward modern life.

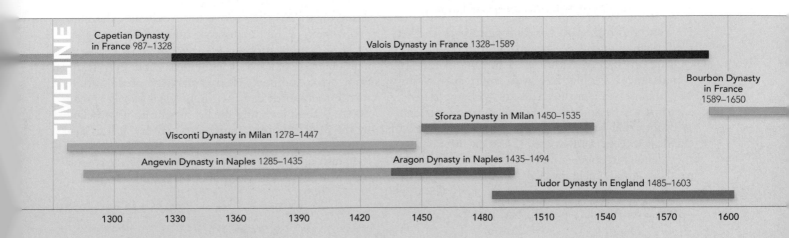

TIMELINE

Capetian Dynasty in France 987–1328

Valois Dynasty in France 1328–1589

Bourbon Dynasty in France 1589–1650

Sforza Dynasty in Milan 1450–1535

Visconti Dynasty in Milan 1278–1447

Angevin Dynasty in Naples 1285–1435

Aragon Dynasty in Naples 1435–1494

Tudor Dynasty in England 1485–1603

1300 1330 1360 1390 1420 1450 1480 1510 1540 1570 1600

PREVIEW

A NEW SPIRIT EMERGES: INDIVIDUALISM, REALISM, AND ACTIVISM

In the late thirteenth century, Cimabue, an important painter from the Italian city-state of Florence, was walking in the countryside and saw a young shepherd boy drawing sheep on a rock. The painter recognized the boy's talent and took him on as an apprentice. The young shepherd, Giotto (ca. 1267–1337), flourished under his master's tutelage, and stories arose about the youth's talent for realistic painting—and his independent spirit. He was said to have once painted a fly on the nose of a face that Cimabue was painting, and the fly was so lifelike that the master tried to brush it off several times before he grasped his student's joke. Giotto grew up to vastly surpass his master and create paintings of such realism and emotional honesty that they helped change the direction of painting. As the new century dawned, there would be others like Giotto who creatively broke new ground.

The Renaissance: A Controversial Idea

For centuries historians have struggled with the very idea of whether this age beginning in the fourteenth century in Italy constituted a turning point—the **Renaissance.** People living in fourteenth-century Italy themselves identified this era as characterized by a return to the sources of knowledge and standards of beauty that had created the great civilizations of classical Greece and Rome. (Classical literature, as they defined it, covered a period from about 800 B.C.E. to about 400 C.E.) Francesco Petrarch (1304–1374),

an Italian writer who studied the classics and wrote poetry, was an early proponent of Renaissance ideas. Petrarch lamented that he could find no one in his own time who could serve as a model of virtuous behavior—he mirrored the example of many in the fourteenth century who despaired of their time (see Chapter 9). However, through his studies, he came to revere figures from antiquity who seemed to understand proper values and follow them regardless of worldly distractions. Petrarch even wrote letters to ancient figures, and in one such letter to the Roman historian Livy, he wrote: "I only wish, that I had been born in your time or you in ours. . . . I have to thank you . . . because you have so often helped me forget the evils of today." Later Renaissance thinkers would follow Petrarch's example and see in ancient Greece and Rome the models to shape a new world.

Yet, they overstated their case—medieval scholars had never lost touch with the Latin texts, and no one gazing at the Gothic cathedrals and the magnificent illuminated manuscripts of the Middle Ages can doubt that medieval people had an exquisite sense of beauty. Indeed, most of the qualities that we identify with the Renaissance had existed in some form throughout the Middle Ages. For this reason, some modern scholars have suggested that the Renaissance should not be considered a separate historical era. Some see this era as part of a succession of "renaissances" that spurred the intellectual history of the West. Others argue that a different spirit clearly emerged during the period that we have come to call the Renaissance.

In its simplest sense, the Renaissance was an age of accelerated change that began in Italy and that spread new ideas more rapidly than ever before. Many people, especially urban dwellers, questioned medieval values of hierarchy, community, and reliance on authority and replaced them with a focus on ambitious individualism and realism (both of which had to some extent existed in the Middle Ages but received new emphasis). Some no longer used the classic texts to reinforce the status quo, as had become common in the medieval universities; instead, they studied to transform themselves. Petrarch eagerly noted that the texts "sow into our hearts love of the best and eager desire for it." As they strove for excellence, the men and women of the Renaissance ushered in a new age.

Thus, many historians identify the Renaissance as a unique state of mind or set of ideas about everything from art to politics. Having first sprouted in Italy in the fourteenth century, these ideas slowly spread north as the prevailing medieval culture was rocked by the disasters of the fourteenth century. Just as historians disagree about the nature of the Renaissance, they also differ on exactly why these new ideas took root in Italy. What was it about the Italian situation

> Medieval antecedents

in the early fourteenth century that made that land ripe for fresh ideas about individualism and realism and that fostered the rise of enterprising people?

Why Italy?

Because the people of the Renaissance themselves believed the heart of their rebirth was a recovery of the spirit of classical Greece and Rome, the ancient ruins provided a continuing stimulus for such reflections. As Petrarch mapped the ruins, he said the pastime was wonderfully pleasant "not so much because of what I actually saw, as from the recollection of our ancestors, who left such illustrious memorials of Roman virtue. . . ." For Petrarch and others, these ruins were an ever-present reminder of an age that they believed was dramatically different from their own—an age they sought to recapture.

The new appreciation of classical authors caused a resurgence of interest in the Greek classics that had been neglected in the West for so long. In 1396, the Florentines invited a Greek scholar from Byzantium to lecture at the University of Florence, but this first step received a huge impetus in the mid-fifteenth century when Constantinople fell to the Turks (see Chapter 9). Many eastern scholars fled to Italy, bringing their language skills and Greek manuscripts with them. Over the next decades, new translations of some of the greatest Greek works became fully integrated into Western culture. The study of Greek texts would make a dramatic impact on religious studies, as we will see in Chapter 11.

A fresh reading of the classics certainly stimulated in some literate Italians a desire to recover a spirit of classical greatness, but were readings alone enough to change a culture's sensibilities so dramatically? Some historians argue instead that the tumultuous politics of the Italian city-states particularly favored the growth of new ideas. Incessant warfare among the states opened the door for skilled, innovative leaders to come forward. These leaders in turn surrounded themselves with talented courtiers who willingly broke from tradition to forward their own careers as they pleased their princes. A new spirit found fertile ground in these ambitious, upwardly mobile men.

Others point to the Black Death, which entered Italy in 1348, as the catalyst that transformed the old order (see Chapter 9). The plague's drastic reduction of the population engendered huge economic changes. Prices plummeted, and trade in luxuries such as silk, jewelry, spices, and glass quickened. Italy was ideally placed to profit from this commerce, for throughout the Middle Ages, the Italian city-states had dominated trade in the eastern Mediterranean. During the fourteenth century, individuals, families, and institutions accumulated a good deal of capital, and

Plague disruptions

men and women used some of this money to support the arts. Some have vividly suggested that the Renaissance became one long shopping spree that supported the talented artists whose vision helped define this controversial era—the bridge that began to move Western history from the Middle Ages to modernity.

A Multifaceted Movement

At its core, the Renaissance emphasized and celebrated humans and their achievements. It thus revived an advocacy of individualism that the West had not seen since the time of the ancients. As the Italian writer Giovanni Pico della Mirandola (1463–1494) optimistically wrote in his *Oration on the Dignity of Man*, "Man is rightly . . . considered a great miracle and a truly marvelous creature," and in addition to this, Pico said that people could determine their own destiny. This optimistic faith in the human potential was an exciting new idea. Renaissance thinkers asserted a powerful belief in the human ability to choose right and wrong and to act on these choices.

Individualism

During the Renaissance, Europeans favored a biblical verse from Genesis that described humans as being created in God's "image and likeness." **Figure 10.1** shows one portion of the Italian artist Michelangelo's (1475–1564) revered painting on the ceiling of the Sistine Chapel. In this image, the realistic and beautifully proportioned figure of Adam mirrors the physical beauty of the Creator. Michelangelo also portrayed Adam as more than a piece of inert clay waiting for the divine spark to bring him life. Instead, Adam reaches up to God, meeting him halfway in the act of Creation. For Michelangelo and many other artists of the time, man was indeed created in God's image—not merely spiritually and morally, but also as a creator himself, shaping his own destiny. Here Michelangelo echoes Pico in expressing this idea that was the essence of Renaissance thought.

Renaissance men and women also prided themselves on their accurate view of the world. This form of realism appears vividly in the art of the period. Throughout the rest of this chapter, the various examples of artwork from these centuries show a realistic portrayal of the world.

Realism

Another prevailing theme in the Renaissance came with the emergence of activism. Petrarch himself succinctly expressed the energetic spirit of the age, writing, "It is better to will the good than to know the truth." In other words, being wise was not enough; one had to exert one's will actively in the world to make a difference. Leon Battista Alberti (1404–1472) expressed the same sentiment: "Men can do all things if they will." As we see, Michelangelo's

Activism

FIGURE 10.1 Michelangelo, *Creation of Adam*, 1508–1512 Michelangelo was commissioned to paint frescoes on the ceiling of the Sistine Chapel, the pope's personal chapel in the Vatican, Rome. This famous scene depicts God's work, with the shaping of Adam in His image.

Adam in **Figure 10.1** participates in his own creation by reaching up to receive the spark of life, and people were encouraged to imitate this active involvement.

A final characteristic of this new spirit was that it was secular—that is, it did not take place in the churches, monasteries, or universities that were dominated by religious thought. That is not to say Renaissance thinkers were antireligious, for they were not—Petrarch explained quite clearly: "Christ is my God; Cicero is the prince of the language I use." While most believed deeply in God and many worked in the church, their vocation was to apply the new spirit to this world, not the next.

A secular spirit

Renaissance thinkers felt that the spirit of the classical worlds of Greece and Rome had been reborn before their very eyes. In part, they were right. This vital new age witnessed a renewed belief in human beings' capacity to perfect themselves, to assess the world realistically, and to act vigorously to make an impact on their society. The key to this transformation was education.

Humanism: The Path to Self-Improvement

The urban dwellers of the Italian cities knew that education was the key to success. Men entering business had to be trained at least in reading, writing, and mathematics. In Florence at the beginning of the fourteenth century, the number of students enrolled in private schools testifies to the value practical Florentines placed on education: Out of a total population of about 100,000, some 10,000 youths attended private schools to obtain a basic education.

Of those, about 1,000 went to special schools to learn advanced business mathematics. However, another 500 pursued a more general liberal education. From these latter emerged an educational movement that defined and perpetuated the Renaissance spirit and changed the course of Western thought.

Petrarch departed from the traditional medieval course of study and from his father's desire that he prepare for a career in law. Instead, he pursued a general study of classical literature. The cities of Italy spawned many young men like Petrarch, who wanted an education separated from the church-dominated universities that had monopolized learning for centuries. Such students sought to understand the causes of human actions through the writings of the ancients, and in turn improve themselves. After all, if they believed they were created in God's image, they had a responsibility to cultivate their capabilities. The humanities—literature, history, and philosophy—thus formed the core of the ideal Renaissance education, which aimed to shape students so that they could excel in anything. Proponents of this teaching method were called **humanists.**

Humanist curriculum

Humanists stressed grammar (particularly Latin and Greek so that students could read the classics), poetry, history, and ethics. Following the ancient Roman model, humanists capped off their education with rhetoric, the art of persuasive speaking, which prepared men to serve in a public capacity. Although this course of study may not appear revolutionary, it proved to be.

The early humanists' passion for classical texts led them to search out manuscripts that might yield even greater wisdom from the ancients. As they read and compared manuscripts, they discovered that mistakes had crept into texts that had been painstakingly copied over and over in the medieval monasteries. So the early humanists carefully pored over the many copies of texts to compile accurate versions. These techniques established standards for historical and literary criticism that continue today. Our debt to these literary scholars is incalculable as we enjoy accurate editions of works written thousands of years ago.

The Renaissance emphasis on study inspired some writers to comment on educational theory. Christine of Pizan (1365–ca. 1430) was a professional writer who worked in the French court. She supported herself and

Educational theory her children through her works of poetry and prose. Reflecting the interests of the times, she also wrote several pedagogical treatises: one instructing women on their roles in society (*The Book of Three Virtues*), a manual of good government for the French Dauphin (*The Book of Deeds of King Charles V*), and even a military handbook (*The Book of Feats of Arms and of Chivalry*).

In the same vein, many others authored books to help people learn to cultivate their talents. The best known of these is *The Book of the Courtier*, by the Italian author Baldassare Castiglione (1478–1529). In this popular work, the author summarizes the expected behavior of men of the court. For Castiglione, native endowments were only the beginning—a courtier had to cultivate military skills, a classical education, and an appreciation of art through music, drawing, and painting. Castiglione turned the Renaissance ideal of an active, well-developed individual into a social ideal of the aristocracy.

Other humanists proposed more formal educational settings. One educator (Guarino da Verona) established a model secondary school at Mantua, in Italy, called the Happy House, which taught humanities, religion, mathematics, and physical education. The school even included lessons on diet and dress; no facet of the whole human was neglected in the effort at improvement.

Urban families who prized education for their sons also expected their daughters to be educated, but not to the same degree. The eminent Italian humanist Leonardo Bruni (1374–1444) wrote an oft-quoted letter praising a humanist—but not a

Women humanists full—education for women. For example, he argued that rhetoric in particular was inappropriate for women: "For why exhaust a woman with the concerns of . . . [rhetoric] when she will never be seen in the forum?" His comments reveal the crux of the matter: Women could be educated, but they were not to use their education in a public way, and since rhetoric was central to the humanists, educated Renaissance women were caught in a paradox.

As one example, Isotta Nogarola (1418–1466) earned much recognition from her family and some family friends for her learning. However, as soon as she tried to engage in a public dialogue (through letters), male humanists reprimanded her and deemed her immoral for her public display. She retired into the seclusion of her study, just as other women took refuge in convents to pursue their research.

Rulers, of course, were exempt from such prohibitions of public use of education, and royal women made good use of the latest Renaissance notions of study. Queens such as Elizabeth I of England (r. 1558–1603) and Isabella of Castile (r. 1474–1504) employed their education to rule effectively, support the arts, and encourage the new educational methods. The Biography of Isabella d'Este (on page 314) describes the life of one Italian woman who possessed so much political authority that she became a renowned patron of the arts and of education.

Humanists applied their skills in many areas of life. Some—called **civic humanists**—involved themselves in politics, treating the public arena as their artistic canvas. Others applied their skills at literary criticism to the Bible and other Christian texts. The most influential of these **Christian humanists** came from outside Italy. As we will see in Chapter 11, men such as the Spanish cardinal Ximénez de Cisneros (1436–1517) and the Dutchman Desiderius Erasmus (ca. 1466–1536) transformed the study of the Bible and paved the way for dramatic changes in religious sensibilities.

Humanist scholarship was crucial in shaping the new spirit of the Renaissance, but it was not sufficient in itself. Scholars and artists and talented young men would have made little impact without the generosity of patrons such as Isabella, who supported the new talent and assiduously purchased their productions. The spirit of the Renaissance thrived on the money that flowed abundantly (albeit unevenly, as we will see) in the Italian cities.

The Generosity of Patrons: Supporting New Ideas

The talented writers and artists of the Renaissance depended on generous patrons to support them. During the early Renaissance, cities themselves served as artistic patrons, stimulating the creation of art by offering prizes and subsidies for their talented citizens. Guilds, too, served as artistic patrons, commissioning great public monuments to enhance the spaces of their cities. The public art that graced the streets and squares enhanced the reputation of the city itself and in turn forwarded the new ideas of the gifted artists.

In time, warfare and internal strife caused cities to have less money to use in support of art, and patronage was taken over by wealthy individuals. In addition to Isabella d'Este, many other rulers, such as the Medici

BIOGRAPHY

Isabella d'Este
(1474–1539)

FIGURE 10.2 Isabella d'Este

Duchess

of Mantua,

Diplomat,

and Patron

of the Arts

Isabella d'Este was born the daughter of a duke in 1474 in the small Duchy of Ferrara, just south of Venice. She grew up in a court that both appreciated Renaissance education and art and succumbed to the violence that marked fifteenth-century Italy.

When Isabella was only 2, her father's nephew attacked the palace in an effort to seize power from the duke. Before Isabella was 8 years old, Venetian armies had invaded Ferrara to try to dominate the small duchy. Yet Isabella's father was a skillful diplomat and withstood these and many other challenges. In the process, his daughter began learning about Renaissance diplomacy.

The young girl was educated in the best humanist tradition. Her tutors taught her to read the great classics of the Roman world in the original Latin. She learned quickly and spoke Latin fluently at an early age. She also was an accomplished musician and excelled at singing and playing the lute.

When she was 6 years old, Isabella's parents began searching for a suitable future husband for her. They approached the family of the nearby Duke of Mantua to discuss a betrothal between Isabella and their eldest son, Francesco. When representatives of Francesco's family interviewed the young child, they wrote back to the prospective in-laws that they were astonished at her precocious intelligence. They sent Francesco's parents a portrait of the lovely black-eyed, blond child but assured them that "her marvelous knowledge and intelligence are far more worthy of admiration [than her beauty]." A betrothal was arranged that would unite the two houses trying to maintain independence from their powerful neighbors, Milan and Venice.

Isabella and Francesco were married in 1490, when she was 15. An elaborate ceremony joined the two families, and in her old age, Isabella proudly wrote of her memories of the gifts, decorations, and lavish banquet that marked this turning point of her life.

Under the skillful rule of Francesco and Isabella, Mantua rose to the foremost rank of the smaller Italian city-states. Isabella involved herself in the art of diplomacy throughout the couple's reign. She wrote more than two thousand letters—many of them to popes, kings, and other Italian rulers. In one letter to her husband, Isabella assured him that he could concentrate completely on military matters, for "I intend to govern the State . . . in such a manner that you will suffer no wrong, and all that is possible will be done for the good of your subjects." This talented woman was as good as her word, for when Francesco was captured in 1509 and imprisoned, Isabella ruled in his stead and valiantly saved the city from invasion.

Like other Italians influenced by Renaissance pseudoscience, Isabella avidly believed in astrology. She embarked on no important venture without consulting her astrologers. But she also took an interest in the real-world findings of the time. She received correspondence about Columbus's discovery of America and the "intelligent and gentle" natives he found there.

Yet the educated duchess is most remembered as a patron of the arts. She wrote explicit instructions for the works she commissioned: One painting prompted her to pen as many as forty letters. Recognizing excellence, she wanted to commission a work from Leonardo da Vinci, but the artist never found the time to oblige her. (See Document 10.1.)

With a love of literature nurtured since her youth, Isabella accumulated a library that became one of the best in Italy. She took advantage of the new printing industry to acquire the first editions of the great classics as well as the contemporary works of Petrarch and Dante. Her requests for these editions show her appreciation of beauty even in her search for literature: She asked for books printed on parchment (instead of paper) and bound in leather.

When Isabella was 64 years old, Francesco died. The aging duchess turned to her many children and grandchildren for comfort and companionship. She took particular delight in one grandchild who could recite Virgil at the age of only 5. Isabella died in 1539, a year after losing her husband. In the last months of her life, a great scholar of the age called her "the wisest and most fortunate of women"—an apt epitaph for someone who so personified the Renaissance spirit.

Connecting People & Society

1. What conclusions can you draw from this life about the importance of family ties in the Renaissance?

2. What opportunities did a wealthy woman have to participate in the intellectual life of the Renaissance?

3. What can you learn from this life about the importance of patronage to the arts?

DOCUMENT 10.1

Isabella d'Este Implores Leonardo da Vinci to Paint for Her

In 1504, Isabella d'Este of Mantua (see Biography in this chapter) wrote letters to Leonardo da Vinci soliciting a painting. Although she never received her painting, these letters show the tensions that often arose between purchasers' desires and artists' aesthetic inclinations and shed light on the all-important process of patronage.

Letter 1. "To Master Leonardo Vinci, the painter. M. Leonardo,—Hearing that you are settled at Florence, we have begun to hope that our cherished desire to obtain a work by your hand may be at length realised. When you were in this city, and drew our portrait in carbon, you promised us that you would some day paint it in colours. But because this would be almost impossible, since you are unable to come here, we beg you to keep your promise by converting our portrait into another figure, which would be still more acceptable to us; that is to say, a youthful Christ of about twelve years, which would be the age He had attained when He disputed with the doctors in the temple, executed with all that sweetness and charm of atmosphere which is the peculiar excellence of your art. If you will consent to gratify this our great desire, remember that apart from the payment, which you shall fix yourself, we shall remain so deeply obliged to you that our sole desire will be to do what you wish, and from this time forth we are ready to do your service and pleasure, hoping to receive an answer in the affirmative." Mantua, May 14, 1504.

Letter 2. On the 27th of May, Angelo del Tovaglia replied:—"I received the letter of Your Highness, together with the one for Leonardo da Vinci, to whom I presented it, and at the same time tried to persuade and induce him, with powerful reasons, to oblige Your Excellency by painting the little figure of Christ, according to your request. He has promised me without fail to paint it in such times and hours as he can snatch from the work on which he is engaged for this Signory. I will not fail to entreat Leonardo, and also Perugino, as to the other subject. Both make liberal promises, and seem to have the greatest wish to serve Your Highness. Nevertheless, I think it will be a race between them which is the slower! I hardly know which of the two is likely to win, but expect Leonardo will be the conqueror. All the same, I will do my utmost."

SOURCE: Julia Cartwright, *Isabella d'Este: Marchioness of Mantua, 1474–1539*, vol. 1 (New York: E. P. Dutton, 1903), pp. 324–327.

Analyze the Document

1. What painting does Isabella want? How do you think modern artists would react to getting such specific instructions? Why?

2. Letter #2 is from Leonardo's uncle. What does this fact indicate about the relationship among family ties, art, and patronage in the Renaissance?

---

in Florence and the Sforza in Milan, used their wealth to stimulate the creation of spectacular works of art. In return, patrons gained social and political status by surrounding themselves with objects of beauty or intellect.

Cosimo de Medici (1389–1464) offers a perfect model for the impact of patrons in the Renaissance. Cosimo supported intellectuals and artists and personally financed the acquisition of manuscripts. His fascination with the Greek philosopher Plato led him to make perhaps his greatest contribution to the intellectual life of the West: He founded the Platonic Academy, hiring the famous Neoplatonic scholar Marsilio Ficino (1433–1499) to guide the studies. Ficino translated the works of Plato and wrote works that demonstrated that Platonism and Christianity shared a belief that humans were permeated with divine love and that the goal of humanity was to rise upward toward the Divinity. These studies shaped the glorification of human accomplishments that were to be the hallmark of the Renaissance, and they were made possible by the powerful patronage of Cosimo and other leaders.

Not only rulers, but rising bourgeoisie could enhance their social status by owning works of art, and this activity served to spur the production of art. Document 10.1 describes Isabella d'Este trying to contract a painting.

The church also supported the arts. Religious fraternities commissioned many paintings, and popes financially backed numerous artists. Like cities and individuals, churches gained status through their patronage, but churches also recognized a religious purpose of art. Many people attributed miraculous power to visual portrayals of religious themes, and churchmen supported this belief. For example, the Florentines customarily brought an image of the Virgin Mary (called the *Madonna of Impruneta*) down from the hills to Florence in times of crisis, and in 1483, a procession of the Madonna was credited with stopping a destructive, monthlong rainfall.

> Religious patronage

Such ceremonies also served the civic purpose of bringing the faithful together in a public way. The painting in **Figure 10.3** shows a religious procession

FIGURE 10.3 Gentile Bellini, *Procession of Eucharist,* 1496 This painting shows the importance of religious festivals in the great St. Mark's Square of Venice, where pilgrims gathered to visit the relics of the famous saint.

in Venice, in which the sacred Eucharist was paraded through the square encased in a magnificently ornate carrier. The painting reinforces the way these religious festivities united the residents and indeed celebrated the beautiful public spaces of the city itself.

Thus, dynamic city life and a new emphasis on education stimulated new ideas, and generous patronage helped them grow. However, the new spirit spread rapidly by the late Renaissance owing to a revolutionary advance in technology.

The Invention of the Printing Press: Spreading New Ideas

Throughout the Middle Ages, precious texts had to be laboriously copied by hand, making books relatively scarce and expensive. As we saw in Chapter 1, one of the significant advantages to the growth of civilization is the ability for more people to read and have access to the written word. In Asia (China and Korea), inventors had developed a way to reproduce texts and pictures more quickly—wood-block printing. With this technique, images and some text were carved into wooden blocks and then could be mass-produced by printing. This technique had spread to the West by the late fourteenth century. By the early fifteenth century, Asian printers had replaced wooden type with bronze type, which was much more durable and offered a more consistent print. This method, too, rapidly spread to the West.

In the 1440s, these early printing techniques reached their culmination with the development of movable type and the adaptation of an oil press to print pages more rapidly. A German silversmith named Johannes Gutenberg (ca. 1400–1470) is credited with bringing all these innovations together to produce the first printed Bible in 1455. Suddenly, literature became more available, thereby ultimately affecting all of Western civilization.

The development and proliferation of the printing press were a testimony to the growing confidence that there was a market for books. In addition to a demand for their product, print shops also needed something to print on. Paper technology gave them the necessary cheap medium to replace the expensive parchment used during the Middle Ages. The technique of papermaking came to Europe from China through the Muslim world. By the fourteenth century, Italian paper mills were using old rags to make inexpensive, yet high-quality, paper. Although some wealthy patrons, such as Isabella d'Este, often preferred the more traditional parchment, the future lay with the new paper.

Printing presses spread rapidly through Europe—by the 1480s many Italian cities had established their own presses, and by 1500 there were about a thousand presses all over the continent. Previously, valuable books, painstakingly copied by hand, belonged to the patron who paid for the copy. Now the literary world looked to a broader reading public for support, consequently igniting a rapid spread of ideas that carried the new spirit throughout Europe. Subsequent notions—from the excitement of international discoveries to intellectual challenges to religious ideology—also spread rapidly. The pace of change in Western civilization quickened as the European presses circulated ideas with unprecedented speed.

All the elements were in place for the transformation of thought that we have come to know as the

MAP 10.1

Italy in 1454

This map shows the political divisions of Italy in the fifteenth century. It also includes the locations of the major city-states of the north.

Explore the Map

1. Which of the city-states was most likely to be threatened by the expansion of the Papal States? Why?

2. Why was Venice so well placed to dominate trade in the eastern Mediterranean?

3. Which states were threatened by Venice's expansion into the peninsula?

4. What contributed to Naples's relative isolation from the politics of the northern states?

Renaissance. The study of classical texts had helped change people's views of themselves and their approach to the world. Money flowed in support of talented and enterprising individuals, and technology helped spread the ideas rapidly. Finally, men actively implemented these ideas in many fields, from art to business to politics.

THE POLITICS OF INDIVIDUAL EFFORT

The medieval power struggle between emperors and popes left an enormous power vacuum in northern Italy. This vacuum allowed small city-states, or cities that controlled the surrounding countryside, to become used to independence. As the fourteenth century opened, most of the northern cities were free communes (see Chapter 8) with republican forms of government, but as the fourteenth century progressed, changes occurred.

The Italian City-States

These city-states engaged in almost constant warfare over their borders and commercial interests, and within the cities, classes and political factions fought for control of the government. In such unstable times,

most of the republican governments were under pressure, and strong men with dictatorial power took over. As we saw in Chapter 9, mercenary armies had become a significant feature of warfare, and they also became a force in Italian politics as city-states hired army captains (called *condottieri*) with their armies to come fight their wars. These mercenaries frequently ravaged the countryside, bringing more misery than protection to the population. Through the fourteenth and fifteenth centuries, city-states would see repeated internal and external strife as they wrestled with their neighbors and with internal governing. These turbulent times brought misery to many but opportunity to others. Sometimes strong, talented individuals rose to positions of authority without constitutional or hereditary legitimacy. The Duke of Urbino, portrayed in the chapter-opening illustration, was one such successful mercenary captain. These rulers introduced a new kind of politics and perhaps inadvertently stimulated the new spirit of the Renaissance.

Map 10.1 shows Italy in 1454. Notice that the northern areas consisted of a patchwork quilt of city-states. Among these, Venice, Milan, and Florence were the largest and most powerful. Popes controlled the large, central strip of the peninsula, and the Kingdom of Naples dominated the south. It was the competition among the northern states that fueled the politics of individual effort that so influenced Renaissance ideas such as individualism and activism.

The Italian city-states fell into two general categories: republics and principalities. Republics featured the institutions of the medieval city communes, in which an urban elite governed. For the most part, Venice and Florence preserved the republican form of government during most of the Renaissance. Principalities, on the other hand, were ruled by one dynasty. Milan and Naples were the most notable examples of this form of government.

Florence: Birthplace of the Renaissance

Florence at the beginning of the fourteenth century was a vibrant republic where Renaissance ideas seem to have been first fostered. Florence prided itself on its republican form of government, in which eligible men held office by random selection. But the city was an uneasy republic indeed, fragmented by local rivalries that always threatened to break out into violence within the urban spaces themselves. Only guild members could participate in the government, and an oligarchy of the leading families was frequently able to control it. Florence was badly hit by the plague—in 1348 alone, almost 40 percent of its population was killed, and its economy, too, was badly damaged as cloth production declined. Warfare with Milan in the early fifteenth century bankrupted many of the city's leading commercial families and created a massive public debt. In their troubles, the Florentines turned to the wealthiest banking family in Europe—the Medici. The republic got more than it bargained for.

In 1434, Cosimo de' Medici took control of the Florentine oligarchy and exiled his rivals. In the tradition of Caesar Augustus, whom he admired, Cosimo concentrated power in his household while ostensibly keeping a republican form of government. Under this shrewd family, Florence and the arts flourished. Cosimo's grandson, Lorenzo the Magnificent (r. 1469–1492), epitomized the ideal Renaissance ruler. A great statesman, he was also a patron of the arts, a poet, and an athlete.

| The Medici |

Yet even Lorenzo could not bring peace to the contentious Florentine people. During his life he faced intrigue and assassination attempts and had to use all his diplomatic skills to preserve Florence from foreign foes. Late in his tenure, voices began to be raised against the Renaissance ideals that he so actively supported. Shortly after Lorenzo's death, the rule of the Medici could not withstand the growing pressures from outside and within the city.

In 1494, French armies invaded the countryside around Florence, and the city-state was again buffeted with financial and material woes. The French armies found an ally within the city in the person of a fiery preacher who had objected to the rule of the Medici and to the passionate acquisition of money and art that had dominated the early Renaissance.

| Savonarola |

Girolamo Savonarola (1452–1498) was a courageous, yet uncompromising, man who had resented the rule of the Medici and accused the clergy of corruption from the papacy on down. He argued vigorously against the lust for money that motivated citizens in the high-tempo Florentine economy. Perhaps most of all, he despised humanism, which he believed poisoned everything from art to religion by placing humans in the spotlight. The passionate preacher clearly recognized the changing times, but he advocated a different response to these changes.

Helped by the disruptions caused by the French invasions, Savonarola was able to arrange for the Medici to be expelled from the city and for a republic to be reintroduced. But Savonarola also wanted to return people's sensibilities to those of what he perceived to be a more pious age. He preached against nude paintings and sculptures and in 1497 presided over a public "burning of the vanities"—a huge bonfire into which people tossed ornaments, pictures, cards, and other "frivolous" items. This event is described by an eyewitness in Document 10.2.

Eventually, the monk's zeal sparked opposition. The pope chafed at Savonarola's attacks and finally excommunicated him and forbad him to preach. Savonarola himself came to an ironic, fiery end: He was condemned and hung, and his body was burned in the public square of Florence—exactly where the "vanities" had been burned.

Like the other great figures of the age, Savonarola was a product of the Renaissance—he felt the same civic pride and shared the same love of education. But, instead of responding to these forces with a sense of humanism and realism, he looked for a spiritual reaction, a religious renewal that he believed should shape the future. In time, northern Europeans picked up Savonarola's call for religious renewal, but not yet. In Florence the Medici were restored in the sixteenth century, and the republic was formally dissolved in 1530.

At first glance, it may seem incongruous that the stormy political history of Florence spawned the creative ideas that we have come to identify with the Renaissance. However, the very environment that made people feel they had to be actively involved in their city and fight for their own interests stimulated the driving individualism that characterized this age. Politicians vied to prove themselves superior to

DOCUMENT 10.2

Friar Savonarola Ignites a "Bonfire of the Vanities"

Luca Landucci ran a small apothecary shop in Florence and kept a diary chronicling these turbulent times. This excerpt from 1497 describes the notorious incident in which the reforming friar Savonarola (whom Landucci calls Fra Girolamo) ordered his followers— young boys—to collect Florentine artworks and burn them in the square.

27th February (the Carnival). There was made on the *Piazza de' Signori* a pile of vain things, nude statues and playing-boards, heretic books, Morganti [poems], mirrors, and many other vain things, of great value, estimated at thousands of florins. Although some lukewarm people gave trouble, throwing dead cats and other dirt upon it, the boys nevertheless set it on fire and burnt everything, for there was plenty of small brushwood. And it is to be

observed that the pile was not made by children; there was a rectangular woodwork measuring more than *12 braccia* [about 23 feet] each way, which had taken the carpenters several days to make, with many workmen, so that it was necessary for many armed men to keep guard the night before, as certain lukewarm persons, specially certain young men called *Compagnacci* wanted to destroy it. The *Frate* was held in such veneration by those who had faith in him, that this morning, although it was Carnival, Fra Girolamo said mass in *San Marco*, and gave the Sacrament with his hands to all his friars, and afterwards to several thousand men and women; and then he came on to a pulpit outside the door of the church with the Host, and showing it to the people, blessed them, with many prayers: *Fac*

salvum populum tuum Domine, etc. There was a great crowd, who had come in the expectation of seeing signs; the lukewarm laughed and mocked, saying: "He is excommunicated, and he gives the Communion to others." And certainly it seemed a mistake to me, although I had faith in him; but I never wished to endanger myself by going to hear him, since he was excommunicated.

SOURCE: Luca Landucci, *A Florentine Diary from 1450 to 1516,* trans. Alice de Rosen Jervice (London: Dent, 1927), pp. 130–131.

Analyze the Document

1. What kinds of objects did the friar's followers collect?

2. Who supported the friar?

3. Was Landucci sympathetic to Savonarola?

4. Why was Florence a particularly appropriate place for this act?

---

their rivals, often by supporting artists whose products contributed to their own status. In the republican turmoil, the Renaissance was born.

Venice: The Serene Republic?

Venice preserved its republic with much less turmoil than Florence, although there, too, an oligarchy ruled. Venice's constitution called for only its aristocratic merchant families—numbering about 2,000— to serve in its Great Council. From among this number, they chose one man to serve as the council leader, or **doge,** for life, but most men were in their 70s before being elected to this office. This rule by the elders made political life in Venice remarkably stable—indeed, the city called itself the "Most Serene Republic." This title underplayed the ever-present factional strife that plagued the Italian cities, but Venetians were able to suppress the strife, and many believed their self-proclaimed myth of serenity.

This peace also stemmed from the prosperity generated by overseas trade, which Venice dominated owing to its advantageous location on the Adriatic Sea. **Map 10.2** shows how Venice's location perfectly situated it to take advantage of the lucrative

| Overseas trade |

trade in the eastern Mediterranean. From Venice's earliest history, it enjoyed a privileged position in the trade with Byzantium, and as we saw in Chapter 8, during the Fourth Crusade in 1204, the Venetians led in the conquest of Constantinople itself. Not only does the painting of St. Mark's Square in **Figure 10.3** show the wealth of Venice, but the domed church in the background reveals the continuing influence of Byzantium on the aesthetics of the city that was formed by interactions with the East. The end of the crusader kingdoms did not end the Venetian dominance of trade, and at the beginning of the Renaissance, wealth continued to pour into the Serene Republic. To consolidate its hold on the eastern Mediterranean, Venice built an empire of coastal cities and islands—as shown on **Map 10.2.**

Venice was built on a collection of islands in a lagoon, and the Grand Canal that continues to mark its main thoroughfare is a perfect representation of the city's maritime orientation. Of the city-state's total population of about 150,000 people, more than 30,000 were sailors. Venice's navy boasted forty-five galleys—large warships with sails and oars—and three hundred hefty sailing ships.

In the beginning of the fifteenth century, Venice began to engage in a policy of expanding into the

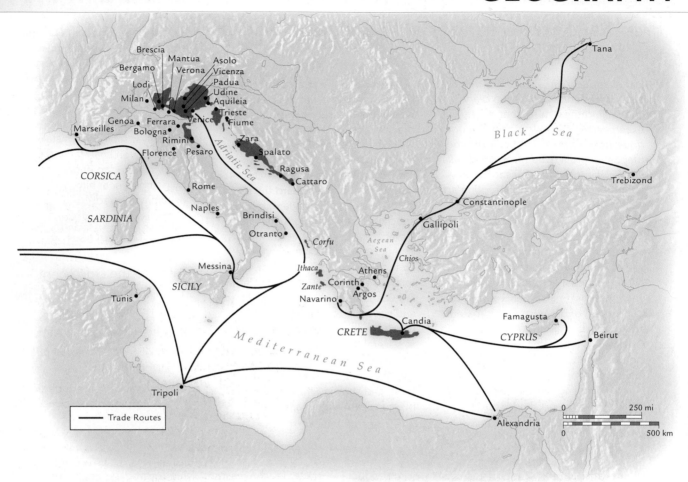

MAP 10.2

The Venetian Empire in the Fifteenth Century

This map shows the Venetian Empire, with the red lines indicating the main trade routes of Venice's prosperous commercial ventures.

Explore the Map

1. How would Venice's dominance of the Adriatic Sea and its control of Crete facilitate its ascendancy over the trade in the eastern Mediterranean?

2. Locate the Muslim cities of Tripoli, Tunis, Alexandria, and Beirut. How might Venetian trade with these centers have facilitated cross-cultural interactions?

Italian mainland—the city-state wanted to secure its food supply as well as its overland trade routes. **Map 10.2** shows the cities that became Venetian dependencies. Although this expansionist policy made sense to the Venetians, it understandably upset the neighboring states of Milan and Florence.

The Venetians perhaps should have looked more carefully at their maritime holdings, for Turkish expansion in the eastern Mediterranean (with the capture of Rhodes) seriously challenged Venetian supremacy in the seas. (See Chapter 11 for the subsequent confrontation.)

Through the Renaissance, however, this calm republic helped forward the progress of the new spirit. Its leaders wanted to grace their city with the magnificent new art, so their patronage brought talent to the fore, and their ships helped disseminate the new ideas along with the Italian trade goods.

Milan and Naples: Two Principalities

Milan's violent history mirrored that of Florence, but this city-state more quickly moved from a republican form of government to a hereditary principality.

During the thirteenth century, rival political factions in the city had constantly vied for power. In desperation, the commune invited a soldier from a family named Visconti to come in and keep the peace; he stayed on to rule as prince and established a dynasty that reigned in Milan from 1278 to 1447. The Visconti family recognized the volatility of Italian politics and focused on the military strength that had brought them to power in the first place. After fending off attempts to establish a republic, the Visconti established a principality that coveted the lands of the rest of northern Italy. Only the diplomatic and military talents of Florence, Venice, and its other neighbors kept this aggressive principality in check. Finally, in 1447, the Visconti dynasty ended when the prince died without an heir—the door was open for a new power struggle in Milan.

In 1450, another strong dynasty took power. The Sforza family kept the city-state's proud military tradition, yet also served as patrons of the arts to enhance their own political reputations. The Sforza continued to rule until the early sixteenth century, though always under the pressure of growing republican aspirations.

The Kingdom of Naples in the south was the only region of Italy that preserved a feudal form of government ruled by a hereditary monarchy. In the early fourteenth century, Naples was ruled by Angevin kings who were descendants of the king of France. Under these kings, the ideas of the Renaissance came to the feudal and rural south. Giotto (the shepherd-painter whose story opened this chapter) and Boccaccio (see Chapter 9) spent time in Naples under the patronage of King Robert (r. 1309–1343), and even Petrarch called Robert "the only king of our times who has been a friend of learning and of virtue." However, after Robert's rule, Naples became a battleground with claimants from the Angevins and the Spanish Aragonese competing for the throne.

| Naples |

In 1435, the king of Aragon, Alfonso the Magnanimous (r. 1435–1458), was able to reunite the crowns of Naples and Sicily. He worked to centralize his administration but was unable fully to subdue his barons, and Naples remained a feudal kingdom. Alfonso was a passionate devotee of Italian culture and served as a patron of the Renaissance. However, the dynastic claims on this throne by other kings in Europe would disrupt Italian politics in years to come.

The Papal States

The Great Schism ended in 1417, when some 400 churchmen gathered at the Council of Constance and elected a Roman cardinal to be Pope Martin V. When he returned to Rome after the papal sojourn in Avignon (see Chapter 9), Martin found traditional papal lands under the control of neighboring states, and the city in sad disrepair. How was he to restore papal prestige? Should he focus on spiritual or secular leadership? These were the weighty questions that confronted the new pope, and his responses would shape the history of the church.

Martin's first decision was to take political control over central Italy. As one supporter of papal rule said, "Virtue without power would be ridiculous." **Map 10.1** shows the extensive Papal States, which spanned the peninsula. As rulers of central Italy, the popes had a particular advantage in that their rule was a **theocracy** that derived its legitimacy from God (and election by the college of cardinals), so issues of republicanism and tyranny did not apply. However, their religious role also brought complications. For example, as worldly rulers in the Italian tradition, they were expected to improve the fortunes of their families, so they frequently (and accurately) fell prey to the charge of nepotism as they created positions for their relatives. The popes also looked backward to their medieval struggles with the Holy Roman Emperors to control Italy (see Chapter 8), so many felt they had a right—indeed, an obligation—to expand papal lands on the peninsula. All these factors helped propel the popes into the frequently violent sphere of Italian politics. But they also leaped into the exciting, brilliant world of Renaissance creativity.

Martin V determined that the city of Rome itself should be a place of beauty and a beacon of papal power. Just as the Italian princes used art to enhance their prestige, popes began an ambitious—and expensive—building program that would underscore their authority. The culmination of this effort was the construction of the new St. Peter's Church in the

| Papal patronage |

*Dates are for period of rule
RENAISSANCE RULERS

1364–1380	Charles V the Wise, France
1434–1464	Cosimo de' Medici, Florence
1461–1483	Louis XI the Spider, France
1469–1492	Lorenzo the Magnificent de' Medici, Florence
1490–1539	Isabella d'Este, Mantua
1492–1503	Pope Alexander VI
1503–1513	Pope Julius II
1509–1547	Henry VIII of England
1515–1547	Francis I of France
1558–1603	Elizabeth I of England

FIGURE 10.4 Melozzo da Forlí, *Sixtus IV Receives Platina, Keeper of the Vatican Library,* 1477 The popes were powerful patrons of the arts. This painting commemorates the founding of the Vatican library, which remains a major center of learning today.

Renaissance love of learning—as well as its penchant for nepotism and intrigue.

To increase (or even maintain) their secular power, the popes waded into the quagmire of Italian politics, and at the end of the Renaissance, a pope was elected from an influential family—the Borgia. The Borgia family

Like many other Renaissance princes, the Borgia pope Alexander VI (r. 1492–1503) tried to reclaim his lands from his acquisitive neighbors. Alexander also proved worldly in his personal life; gossips gleefully circulated accounts of his sexual escapades. He still upheld the tradition of Renaissance family life, however, favoring his illegitimate children by placing them in advantageous positions. The pope's warrior son, Cesare Borgia (ca. 1475–1507), seemed a candidate for uniting Italy under Alexander's authority. For his daughter Lucrezia, Alexander arranged three marriages designed to advance the family's dynastic aims. Isabella d'Este (featured in the Biography on page 314) arranged one of these marriages to protect the Este family's interests. All these manipulations came to nothing, however: Alexander died suddenly, and the family's ambitions failed. The reputation of the papacy as a spiritual authority also declined.

One of the most memorable of the Renaissance popes, Julius II (r. 1503–1513) embodied the ambitious values of the times, but without the scandals that had plagued Alexander. Julius was as perfect a Julius II Renaissance ruler as Florence's Lorenzo de' Medici. A patron of the arts he made Rome a cultural hub on a par with the greatness of Florence. He was also an experienced warrior, personally leading his armies into battle as he carried on Alexander's expansionist policies. Julius II summoned Michelangelo to Rome and commissioned him to decorate the ceiling of the Sistine Chapel (see **Figure 10.1**). Michelangelo also worked on the new St. Peter's Church in Rome that was being built at the time. Although Julius and Michelangelo had a stormy relationship, the patron helped his artist produce some of the most beautiful work of the Renaissance.

later 1400s. Money flowed from all over Europe to build the new Rome, a development that angered many northern Christians. With these contributions, the popes transformed Rome into one of Europe's major cultural centers. **Figure 10.4** shows Pope Sixtus IV (r. 1471–1484) seated in as much grandeur and surrounded by as much wealth as any king. His courtiers talk among themselves while the pope receives the humanist Platina (kneeling in the center). This painting commemorated the founding of the Vatican library, to be run by Platina. Even today, the library remains a major learning center. The cardinal standing in the center of the painting later became Pope Julius II. The courtiers on the left are Sixtus's nephews, who later participated in a plot to murder one of the Medicis. This painting depicts the

The Renaissance popes achieved their ambitious agenda: They were powerful earthly rulers living in a magnificent city. As the papacy proved to be a stronger institution than the church councils, efforts were ended to give supreme authority to bishops meeting in councils. However, over time, the popes' territorial power would undermine papal claims of universality, as many people began to question why Italian princes should have authority over lands outside Italy. As we will see in Chapter 11, these same people would begin to criticize the popes for what some called worldly extravagance.

The Art of Diplomacy

The wars, shifting alliances, and courtly intrigue of Italian politics sparked a new interest (and expertise) in the art of diplomacy. Not since the early Byzantine state had courtiers devoted such attention to the details of successful diplomacy. States exchanged ambassadors to facilitate official communication and sent spies to maintain advantages.

The most noted writer on political skill and diplomacy was Niccolò Machiavelli (1469–1527), whose book *The Prince* still influences many modern-day political thinkers. Machiavelli recognized the danger confronting Florence in the fifteenth century as
Machiavelli French armies threatened the independence of the city-states, and he wrote to offer advice about how to survive—indeed prevail—in these turbulent times. His was an eminently practical guide that looked at politics with a cold-blooded realism that had not been seen before. For Machiavelli, the most important element for a successful ruler (the prince) was his strength of will. He insisted that while princes might appear to have such traditional virtues as charity and generosity, they could not rely on these traits to hold power. They must actually be ruthless, expedient, strong, and clever if they were to maintain their rule. As he said, "It is better for a ruler to be feared than loved."

Machiavelli's blunt description of political power articulated a striking departure from medieval political ideals. During the Middle Ages, the perfect ruler was Louis IX of France (r. 1226–1270) (described in Chapter 8), who proved so virtuous that he was made a saint. With the Renaissance, men like Cosimo de' Medici and Cesare Borgia—self-made rulers who methodically cultivated their talents and grasped power boldly—took power. Machiavelli's book captured the new statecraft and showed that realistic politics often meant a brutal disregard for ethics. Indeed, many Europeans living during the Renaissance showed a social indifference and personal immorality that we might find dismaying today.

INDIVIDUALISM AS SELF-INTEREST: LIFE DURING THE RENAISSANCE

In spite of efforts to hone their diplomatic skills to a fine art, many Italians still resorted to brute force to get what they wanted. In all the city-states, some individuals came to power by stimulating social strife among competing factions or even using violence to vanquish their rivals. Taking part in politics could also get one in deep trouble. Petrarch's father, for example, like many other men of his time, made the mistake of supporting a losing political struggle in Florence, and the victors punished him by amputating his hand. Individuals struggling to better themselves politically and economically often did so at the expense of their neighbors.

Aside from offering the occasional opportunity to improve one's social position, Renaissance cities still had a clearly defined social hierarchy. The Florentines referred to these divisions as the "little people" and the "fat people." The "little people" consisted of merchants, artisans, and workers and made up about 60 percent of the population. Slaves and servants assumed even lower status, beneath the "little people." The "fat people" included well-to-do merchants and professionals and made up about 30 percent of the population. The wealthiest elite—bankers and merchants owning more than one-quarter of the city's wealth—made up only 1 percent of the population.

Whenever there is a great disparity between rich and poor in a situation of some social mobility, crime tends to run high. This was true throughout Renaissance Europe. One Florentine merchant, Luca Landucci, who kept a detailed diary of the events of his age, regularly wrote   Rising crime
of crime and punishment as he heard his neighbors gossip about the shocking misdeeds of the day. In one diary entry, he repeats news of a young woman who killed a child for the pearl necklace the girl was wearing. In another, he tells of the townspeople watching as a man was beheaded for "coining false money." Luca's dreary lists of crimes seem endless.

Many people blamed wanderers for the alarming rise in crime. According to such observers, soldiers discharged from mercenary armies, the poor fleeing poverty in cities and countryside, and other displaced persons made the highways more dangerous than ever. Italy and other states tried to control crime, but their methods were usually ineffective as well as misplaced. As in other times of rapid social change, rulers increased the regulation of social behavior. For example, in England in 1547 a new law stipulated that vagabonds be branded and enslaved for two years. The law tells us a great deal about Renaissance society's intense fear of crime and strangers.

Growing Intolerance

Renaissance governments enacted harsh legislation on people they found threatening, from prostitutes to paupers. This same impulse contributed to an increasing intolerance of other religions and cultures, as evidenced by an intensifying prejudice against Jews. In Italy, Christians passed laws against sexual relations between Christians and Jews, and authorities in Rome reputedly burned 50 Jewish prostitutes to death for having intercourse with Christian men. Laws also restricted Jews to certain parts of cities and required them to wear identifiable clothing. In some instances the clothing included colors that had been set aside for prostitutes. This cruel association left Jewish women open to ridicule, criticism, and sometimes abuse from non-Jewish neighbors.

Persecution of Jews existed during the Middle Ages—thirteenth-century kings of England and France had expelled Jews from their lands, and communities of Jews had experienced periodic violence. (As we saw in Chapter 9, Jews were subjected to particular violence in the wake of the bubonic plague.) However, increasing prejudice in the fifteenth century led to large-scale expulsions of Jewish communities from many cities and countries. Vienna began expelling Jews in 1421, and many other German cities followed. **Figure 10.5** is taken from a fifteenth-century Hebrew manuscript, and it shows Jews driven from a German town. The group was allowed to take their animals and a wagon for the women, children, and elderly as they headed down the hills seeking a new home. Most German Jews moved eastward into Poland and Russia, and the center of Judaism shifted from western Europe to the East.

Ferdinand and Isabella forced all of Spain's Jews to leave in 1492, causing one of the largest movements of peoples in the era. Portugal did the same in 1497. Many Iberian Jews fled to the Muslim lands in North Africa, and some people today still trace their ancestry back to this exodus. As a result of this intolerance, western Europe lost the talents of the many Jews who had inhabited these lands for centuries.

Economic Boom Times

The new ideas of the Renaissance (both good and bad) developed against the backdrop of the fourteenth century crises but were fostered in the fifteenth century by a vigorous economic life. Individualism was stimulated by the economic potential, and excess money made the all-important patronage possible. Growing commerce and industries brought money into Italy, stimulating the local economy and allowing wealthy people to indulge their desire for beauty and comfort.

Venice shone as the greatest merchant city in the world, importing tons of cotton, silk, and spices every year and exporting woolen cloth and mounds of silver coins to pay for their imports. As the sixteenth century opened, 1.5 million pounds of spices came through Venice alone every year. Venetians did not simply rest on their commercial wealth; some enterprising citizens developed and manufactured new products—most prominently, forks and windowpane glass—that would in time sweep through the world.

By contrast, Milan and Florence were craft-industrial cities. Florence, with its 270 workshops, led the way in wool cloth making. Renaissance Italy also profited from another new industry: silk. As early as the twelfth century, **Wool and silk** travelers had smuggled silkworms into Italy from China so that Italians could begin to produce the precious fabric locally. But the industry really blossomed after the thirteenth century, when the Chinese silk loom appeared in Italy. Italians powered the looms with waterwheels and produced large amounts of silk cloth. In the fourteenth century, one city had a silk mill employing 480 spindles rapidly spinning the precious silk. By the fifteenth century, Florence boasted eighty-three workshops devoted to silk production. The wealth let Florence take part in the thriving economy generated by the cloth trade network that connected countries like Italy and the Netherlands all the way to the New World. In the wake of this prosperous trade, even a shopkeeper in Florence wrote excitedly about his first taste of sugar brought in from overseas.

But the most profitable industry was banking. Throughout the Middle Ages, the development of banking and commerce had been impeded by the Christian belief in the immorality of usury, or charging interest, but **Banking** enterprising merchants found ways around the prohibition. Some people offered gifts in gratitude for a loan of money, thus effectively paying back more than they borrowed. However, the easiest way to collect interest was by changing money and making a profit on the exchange rate. By the thirteenth century, Christians all over Europe began to engage in the lucrative trade of money lending, but it was the Italian bankers of the Renaissance who really first perfected the art of using money to make money. In the process, many raked in fortunes—for example, the rich families in Florence purchased state-guaranteed government bonds that paid over 15 percent interest. It is not surprising that the "fat people" got even "fatter" as the Renaissance rolled on.

Slavery Revived

The booming economy of the Renaissance led to new institutional oppression—the revival of slavery in Europe. Why was slavery reintroduced precisely when even serfs were being freed from their bondage?

Some historians suggest that the labor shortage of the late fourteenth century caused by the bubonic plague drove people to look for fresh hands. However, this explanation is not satisfactory, because the new slaves were by and large not used in agriculture or industry. Instead, it seems that newly wealthy people trying to make their lives more comfortable looked to new sources for scarce domestic help.

Slavery had some complex facets. Renaissance families, for example, often considered slaves part of the household. One Florentine woman in 1469 wrote a letter to her husband asking him to acquire a slave girl to care for their young child or a "black boy" to become the child's playmate. Occasionally slaves bore children fathered by their owners, who sometimes raised them as legitimate heirs. **Figure 10.6** is a portrait of a slave named Katharina drawn by Albrecht Dürer (1471–1528), a popular engraver commissioned to render portraits of many famous people. Katharina was a slave of a Portuguese commercial agent living in Antwerp who became friends with Dürer in 1520. This portrait shows the high regard in which this owner held Katharina. She is well dressed, and the fact that she sat for a portrait shows that she was a valued member of the household.

The Venetians, positioned near the eastern Mediterranean, capitalized on this trade first, dealing mostly in Muslim and Greek Orthodox slaves obtained through warfare or simply taken captive. Between 1414 and 1423, Venetian traders sold about 10,000 slaves in their markets. Most of these slaves were young girls sold into service as domestic servants. The fall of Constantinople to the Turks in 1453 (see Chapter 9) led to a decline in slaves from Eastern lands, and Europeans began to look for new sources of captives. In the early fifteenth century, the Portuguese conquered the Canary Islands off the western coast of Africa, and what had been a trickle of African slaves into Europe swelled. In the following decades, Portuguese traders eager to compete with the wealthy Venetians brought some 140,000 sub-Saharan African slaves into Europe.

| Sources of slaves |

Many people questioned the reestablishment of slavery in Europe. The church disapproved of it, and numerous slaveowners considered it too expensive in the long run. Slavery gradually disappeared in Europe by the end of the Renaissance. However, the

FIGURE 10.5 Expulsion of Jews, ca. 1427 During the Renaissance, Jews were increasingly driven out of towns and countries. This image from a Hebrew manuscript depicts their expulsion from a German town.

precedent had been reestablished, and traders would later find a flourishing slave market in the New World (see Chapters 12 and 15).

Finding Comfort in Family

In the rugged world that emphasized individual achievement, the family assumed central importance as the one constant, dependable structure in Renaissance society. Men and women believed they could count on their kin when all else failed and highlighted these connections in art, literature, and the decisions they made in their daily lives. The emphasis on family loyalty was not limited to the upper classes. Artisan workshops, for example, were family affairs in which fathers trained sons and sons-in-law to carry on the family business.

Family ties also defined ethics in a world in which morality seemed relative. In a book about family written by Leon Battista Alberti (1404–1472), a Florentine architect, the author argued that whatever

| Marriage alliances |

FIGURE 10.6 Albrecht Dürer, *Portrait of Katharina,* **1520**
This etching was commissioned by a Portuguese commercial agent living in Antwerp and is silent testimony to the enslavement of peoples in the early modern period.

increased a man's power to help his family was good. Riches, however gained, fell into this category. Still, as Isabella d'Este proved, nothing beat a good marriage alliance for improving a family's standing.

Plans for such beneficial alliances began as early as the birth of a girl, when wealthy Florentine fathers would open an account with the public dowry fund, which paid as much as 21 percent interest. Family alliances depended on both parties bringing resources to the match. Wealthy families with sons wanted to be certain that their resources would not be diminished by marriage. Thus, parents of girls had to ensure that their daughters could bring enough money to an alliance to ensure a match with well-placed families. The dowry fund was implemented to guarantee that a girl had a sizable dowry when she reached marriageable age. Some Renaissance families could not afford dowries for all their daughters and encouraged some to enter convents (which required smaller dowries). Indeed, the number of convents in Florence increased from only five in 1350 to forty-seven in 1550.

Of course, all these efforts to secure important family alliances had an equal impact on men and women. In the literature and art of the period, too, both men and women appear, but here women play a strikingly different role than they did in real life. Frequently, following the medieval traditions of courtly love, women were given a prominent place as idealized beings who inspired men. Dante Alighieri (1265–1321) (discussed in Chapter 9), whose *Divine Comedy* stands at the cusp between the Middle Ages and the Renaissance, featured a young woman, Beatrice, as his guide into heaven. Petrarch devoted many sonnets to Laura, a young woman who served as his inspiration. Painters, too, portrayed numerous women, many of them nudes who represented idealized beauty and longing for perfection. Artists may have played with the notion of idealized women, but Renaissance men depended on real women to preside over the haven that was their family and their security for the future.

Children's Lives

Though idealized visions of women signaled the importance of the continuity that families provided, and Renaissance families wanted and loved their children, child-rearing practices undermined the hopes of many a proud parent. Privileged families of the Renaissance believed that it was unhealthy (and perhaps even unsavory) for women to breast-feed their infants. Therefore, they customarily sent their newborns to live with peasant women, who were paid to serve as wet nurses until the children were weaned. Some nurses took meticulous care of these infants; others were less attentive. Peasant mothers suffered from poor diets themselves and often had insufficient milk to nurse a fosterling along with her own infants. Foster babies faced other dangers in the villages as well: Criminal records tell horrifying stories of death in the countryside, such as that of a peasant man who murdered four children under the age of 8. Florentine city-dwellers hearing such tales sometimes worried about their children's safety in the countryside, but the force of custom sent infants away to depend on the kindness of strangers.

Wealthy urban parents reclaimed their children when they were weaned, at about 2 years old. These young strangers then had to fit into large households teeming with older children, stepchildren, and a host of other relatives. With busy parents and stepparents, children often formed their principal attachment with an older sibling or aunt or uncle. The artist Andrea Mantegna was commissioned to paint a cycle of frescoes for the Gonzaga family, who ruled the Duchy of Mantua, and **Figure 10.7** shows one portion of this magnificent work. Against the stunning background of the city, the painter shows a man with presumably three of his sons. The youngest, in the foreground, holds tightly to the eldest's hand, perhaps reflecting the situation in many crowded settings as older children cared for younger.

Childhood hardships

FIGURE 10.7 Andrea Mantegna, *The Cardinal Francesco Gonzaga Returning from Rome,* 1474 The painter was commissioned by the Marquis of Mantua to decorate a room with frescoes. The scenes show the marquis' family and are done with techniques of perspective that make the walls seem like windows on the world.

Child-rearing experts warned parents against pampering their offspring, and in general the parents obeyed. Ironically, in this culture of wealth and luxury, people raised their children with a degree of strictness that may seem extreme to us today. One writer (the Dominican Giovanni Dominici), for example, urged mothers to prepare children for hardship by making them sleep in the cold on a hard chest instead of a bed. To toughen them, parents fed children bitter-tasting objects such as peachstones and sometimes gave them "harmless" nausea-inducing herbs so as to accustom them to illness. A humanist (Filarete) writing about an ideal school recommended that children be fed only tough meat so they would learn to eat slowly. This same writer recommended that children eat standing up until they were 20 years old. Many parents let their children sleep only six to eight hours a night to keep them from getting lazy.

Within these strict guidelines, boys and girls were treated quite differently. One humanist (Paola da Certaldo) advised feeding and clothing boys well. For girls, he recommended: "Dress the girl well but as for eating, it doesn't matter as long as it keeps her alive; don't let her get fat."

At about 7 years old, middle-class boys were sent to school to learn reading and mathematics and to ready themselves for the complex world of Renaissance economics. As the boys prepared for careers, fathers arranged marriages for their young daughters. Girls were married relatively young—between 17 and 20 years old (although sometimes younger)—to bridegrooms in their 30s who had established their careers. (See Isabella d'Este's biography.) Many brides, still children themselves when they began having babies, did not survive the experience of giving birth. One Florentine man recorded in his memoirs that, between 1390 and 1431, he had four wives who gave him a total of 24 children. The first three wives died in childbirth.

The harshness of childhood took its toll on many boys and girls; mortality among children reached astonishing rates. In fifteenth-century Florence, 45 percent of children died before the age of 20, most of them girls. The 1427 census in Florence showed a surprising gender ratio: 100 women to every 110 men. This statistic reversed the situation that had prevailed through the High Middle Ages, when women outnumbered men.

AN AGE OF TALENT AND BEAUTY: RENAISSANCE CULTURE AND SCIENCE

Renaissance life had its unsavory side—as rich men struggled to get richer, powerful men worked for more power, and small children sometimes suffered. But at the same time, Renaissance society produced some astonishingly talented people whose works have transformed not only our ideas about beauty but also the very appearance of the world we live in today. During the Renaissance—as in classical Athens—people expected art to be a public thing, to be available to and appreciated by people as they strolled through the cities. Public art nurtured civic pride.

Artists and Artisans

During the Renaissance, many upper-class boys pursued humanistic literary studies to prepare for the day they would play a public role in city life, but their families generally discouraged them from following careers in the visual arts. Filippo Brunelleschi (1377–1446), for example, greatly displeased his father when he declared his interest in sculpting and architecture; his family had fully expected Filippo to become a physician or a notary.

Michelangelo's father dismissed his son's interest in art as "shameful." Peasant boys, too, had little chance at a career in the arts, for without family connections, there was little chance of entry into the art world. If a country boy was a talented artist, he would probably not have the good fortune to be discovered like the shepherd Giotto whose story opened this chapter.

The majority of Renaissance artists came from artisan families. As boys worked as apprentices in artisan workshops, masters recognized and supported genius. Botticelli, the great Florentine painter, was apprenticed at age 13, as was Michelangelo. These examples were typical—a boy entering adulthood had to learn to take his place in the world, and that place often began in the artisan workshops. As a young man developed his skill, people began to recognize that he was no longer a simple craftsman, an artisan, making goods, but instead an artist, a creator of beauty.

Women ordinarily were excluded from taking this path. Yet, in spite of this lack of official acceptance, a number of female artists won renown during the Renaissance. Two, in particular, were highly respected by their contemporaries. Sofonisba Anguissola (ca. 1532–1625) achieved fame as an artist through her skill and the support of her wealthy, aristocratic father. More typical was the case of Lavinia Fontana (1552–1614), the daughter of an artist who trained in her father's workshop. Despite these successes, the public role of artists precluded many women from active careers in art. For example, Anguissola delayed marriage until she was in her late 40s so she could paint—a privilege that most Renaissance fathers did not grant.

Late in the Renaissance, artists overall gained new respect—wealthy patrons stopped viewing them as simply manual laborers and began to recognize them as artists. Michelangelo even earned the title Il Divino, the Divine One. Europeans during the Renaissance valued genius, and these artistic geniuses obliged by creating magnificent works.

Architecture: Echoing the Human Form

The most expensive investment a patron of the arts could make was in architecture, and artists competed for these lucrative contracts. In the process, they designed innovative churches and other buildings that contributed to the prestige of their cities. Where did architects learn these new ideas? Part of the answer comes from the training of architects. Artisans did not consider architecture a separate craft, so there was no direct apprenticeship for this profession that rigidly inculcated old design ideas. Indeed, the greatest architects had all trained for other fields: Brunelleschi, for example, was a goldsmith, and Alberti a university-trained humanist. The Renaissance passion for the glory of classical Greece and Rome led would-be architects to look carefully at the old ruins that had

stood for so long; their love of the individual caused them to put humans at the center of their enterprise. The resulting architecture, while looking back to classical models, was strikingly and beautifully new.

Instead of creating soaring Gothic cathedrals dominated by vertical heights, architects followed classical models of balance and simplicity and combined circular forms with linear supports to break up the monotony of vertical lines. Instead of creating structures that made humans seem small and insignificant before God, they built to glorify the human form and proportions. The fifteenth-century architectural drawings pictured in **Figure 10.8** show the ideal of buildings designed along human proportions. The drawing on the left shows a front view of a building with a man standing to indicate the proper proportions, while the one on the right shows a floor plan with the man lying down in the building.

> Human architecture

The most influential architectural treatise, *On Building* by Alberti, dominated the field for centuries and expressed an architectural aesthetic that echoed that of the ancient Greeks. Alberti argued that buildings should mirror the human body in their supports and openings, and this sentiment is shown in **Figure 10.8.** Repeating the same principle, Michelangelo claimed that anyone who had not mastered anatomy and painting of the human form could not understand architecture. "The different parts of a building," he explained, "derive from human members." Thus, much of the architecture of the Renaissance was created in the image and likeness of the human form.

It is easy to miss the subtleties of human proportion within architecture as we look at the graceful buildings, but there is no overlooking one of the architects' debts to Rome—domes instead of Gothic spires now began to rise with more frequency over the skylines of Renaissance cities. **Figure 10.9** shows the cathedral of Florence, with its dome designed by Brunelleschi.

> Domes

The architect had admired the Pantheon dome in Rome (see Chapter 4), and he wanted to erect a massive dome to span the huge base of the new cathedral in Florence. However, Brunelleschi realized that the Roman dome was not suitable to the large space, so the architect creatively took the Gothic technique of using architectural ribs to create a magnificent new structure for the city. Brunelleschi designed the dome of the Florence cathedral with an inner and outer shell, both attached to the eight ribs of the octagonal structure. The drawing in **Figure 10.9** shows the structural design. Between the two shells the architect placed sixteen ribs to strengthen the dome. The two shells thus supported each other and shared the weight of the whole. Many Florentines predicted that the dome would collapse, yet Brunelleschi's handiwork continues to dominate the skyline of Florence.

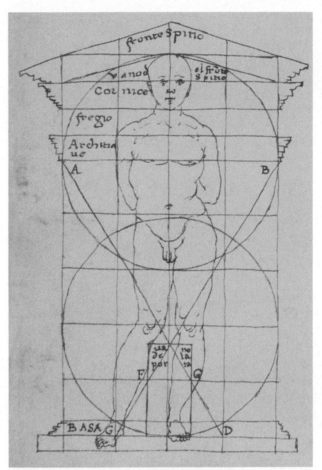
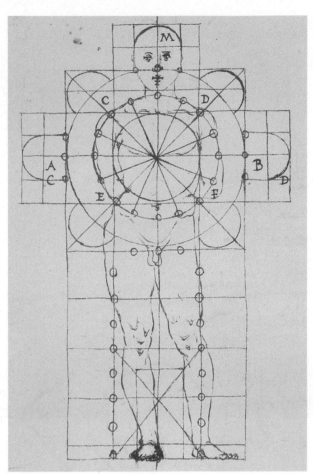

FIGURE 10.8 Francesco di Giorgio Martini, *Trattato di Architettura*, 1480 As theoreticians of architecture considered the best proportions for designing pleasing buildings, they looked to the human form to determine the proper ratios. These drawings show these ratios superimposed on the front and floor plan of buildings.

The Renaissance study of architecture also extended beyond individual buildings to town planning in general. In the fifteenth century, planners began to dream of laying out towns in the simple and logical grid pattern that characterizes our modern cities. Indeed, older European cities still feature a medieval center with curved and random streets surrounded by tidy, post-Renaissance grids. In Latin America, by contrast, towns founded by fifteenth-century Europeans were created in a grid pattern centered on the town square. On the peripheries of such towns, however, streets wove randomly in the tradition of the villages that predated the Renaissance town centers. All these new ideas about buildings and street planning reshaped the cities of the West.

> Town planning

Sculpture Comes into Its Own

Just as Brunelleschi's admiration of the ancients led him to re-create domed architecture, sculptors also drew from classical models. Italians, who had admired freestanding images from the ancient world, began to demand similar beauty for their cities. City communes and individuals commissioned life-size figures to stand free in the public spaces of cities.

Figure 10.10 shows Michelangelo's widely admired statue of David, the biblical figure who killed the giant Goliath. The statue stands more than 14 feet high and took the master three years to carve from a block of supposedly flawed marble. The work exhibits all the innovations of Renaissance sculpture: It is a huge, freestanding nude that depicts the classical ideal of repose, in which the subject rests his weight on one leg in a pose called ***contra posto.*** The figure exemplifies the confidence and the glorification of the human body that marked Renaissance pride.

> Michelangelo's *David*

Michelangelo's statue shows another hallmark of Renaissance spirit—an exuberant praise of realism; the sculptor knew anatomy and realistically portrayed the human body. Renaissance sculptors had to look at life carefully in order to reproduce it with such accuracy, and the audience, too, was led to an appreciation of realism through admiring the great sculptures that graced the public areas.

The statue also carried a political message, a common characteristic of the civic humanism of the day.

FIGURE 10.10 Michelangelo, *David*, 1504 This spectacular sculpture, more than 14 feet high, was in its day the largest marble nude created since antiquity. It was commissioned by Florence to symbolize how the Florentine republic would stand—like David the "giant killer"—against neighboring political giants.

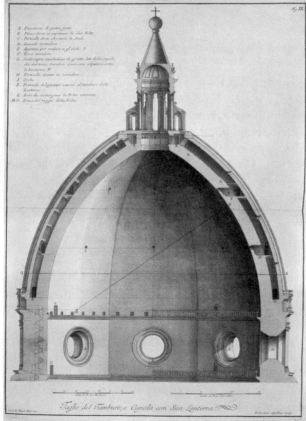

FIGURE 10.9 Florence Cathedral, 1420–1436 Brunelleschi's dome for the Cathedral of Florence was an architectural wonder. The drawing shows the ribbed structure that, despite Florentines' dire predictions that it would collapse, successfully held up the weight of the dome.

In 1494, when the French invasion of Florence caused a temporary fall of the Medici rule, the newly restored Republic of Florence commissioned Michelangelo to create a work with a patriotic theme—something that would celebrate the overthrow of the family that had dominated the city for so long. The sculptor chose David the "giant killer" to symbolize the republic's ousting of the goliath Medici. Michelangelo portrayed David before his fight with Goliath—the youth is confident and defiant, just as Florence saw itself confronting the rest of the world. In this masterpiece, art joined with politics in the best Renaissance tradition.

Painting from a New Perspective

The shepherd Giotto di Bondone (ca. 1267–1337), whose artistic talents were recognized by a Florentine master, was to revolutionize painting for Florence and the West. The young apprentice who fooled his master with a painting of a fly turned his talents to magnificent religious paintings, and he created realistic figures that showed a full range of human expression. For example, his images of the Virgin Mary were not done as remote queens of heaven, but instead painted as realistic young girls struggling to be caring mothers.

Figure 10.11 shows Giotto's fresco *Lamentation over Christ,* in which the faithful mourn the death of Christ. The painting looks back to medieval tradition with gold leaf on the halos and the theme of the painting. However, the painter points to the future with his three-dimensional figures and a new realistic portrayal of emotion. Giotto's talent was recognized during his lifetime, and his paintings were in great demand. Toward the end of his life, the city of Florence issued a proclamation that in part captures the painter's influence: "Many will profit from his knowledge and learning and the city's beauty will be enhanced." Painters following Giotto built on his techniques and further revolutionized this visual art.

Like architects and sculptors, Renaissance painters developed striking new techniques, including oil painting on canvas and the perfection of portraiture. However, perhaps their best-known innovation was **linear perspective,** which allowed painters to enhance the realism of paintings by creating the illusion of three-dimensional space on a two-dimensional surface.

> Linear perspective

The Florentines—and Brunelleschi in particular—proudly claimed to have invented this technique of painting. Whether they did or not is probably irrelevant; regardless of who invented linear perspective, the Florentines perfected it.

Before beginning to paint, Brunelleschi organized the painting around a central point and then drew a grid to place objects precisely in relation to each other. His real innovation, however, came when he calculated the mathematical ratios by which objects seem to get smaller as they recede from view. In this way, he knew exactly how big to paint each object in his grid to achieve a realistic illusion of receding space. In commenting on Brunelleschi's creations, Alberti asserted that a painting should be pleasing to the eye but also should appeal to the mind with optical and mathematical accuracy. And here is the essence of these complex works: They used all the intellectual skill of the artists to create images profoundly appealing to the senses.

Perspective also grew from and appealed to the Renaissance emphasis on the individual, for it assumed that a painting would be viewed from one single spot in front of the work. As one art critic wrote, "Every painting that used perspective proposed to the spectator that he was the unique center of the world." In other words, the painter designed the painting with the eye of the beholder in mind. For the next four

FIGURE 10.11 Giotto, *Lamentation over Christ,* ca. 1305
Although Giotto painted many medieval themes, his contemporaries believed that he introduced a new style that brought "light to the darkness," as Boccaccio wrote.

hundred years, Renaissance ideas of perspective and space set the standard for Western painting.

The painter Raphael (1483–1520) was widely regarded as one of Italy's best painters of the High Renaissance (the late fifteenth and early sixteenth centuries). During his lifetime, he was much acclaimed as an artist who could portray transcendent themes with all the realism of fifteenth-century Italian life,

> Raphael

and modern critics agree. His reputation gained him the coveted commission to paint a fresco for Pope Julius II's library, and **Figure 10.12** shows that fresco—*School of Athens.* Raphael created this fresco just as Michelangelo was painting the Sistine Chapel ceiling (see **Figure 10.1**).

Celestial Music of Human Emotions

Renaissance thinkers turned their attention to music in a quest to carry that art into the new age. Early humanists at first thought that music should imitate classical forms, but no one really knew what ancient Greek music sounded like. However, people did look to ancient mathematics to inform musical composition, for Pythagoras (ca. 569–475 B.C.E.) had postulated harmonious relationships among planets, and music intervals were supposed to echo the ratios of those relationships, creating what the ancients called a "music of the spheres." This search for heavenly music helped to standardize musical notation during the Renaissance and would continue into the seventeenth century.

FIGURE 10.12

Raphael, *School of Athens*, 1510–1511

Pope Julius II commissioned the painter Raphael to create a fresco for his library. The artist portrayed famous ancient philosophers, such as Euclid, Pythagoras, and Socrates, along with Plato and Aristotle in the center. Plato (looking remarkably like Leonardo da Vinci) is on the left, with his hand pointing in the air to remind viewers of the realm of ideas. He is speaking to Aristotle, whose hand presses downward, reminding viewers of his more earthly approach to knowledge. Raphael also included a self-portrait on the right (in the black hat) and a depiction of a brooding Michelangelo sitting in the center foreground, leaning his head on his hand.

Connecting Art & Society

1. Identify the following characteristics of the Renaissance in this image: individualism, appreciation of the classics, and perspective.

2. Why would the pope find the content of this fresco suitable subject matter for the papal library?

3. Why do you think Raphael included portraits of his artist contemporaries in the company of the philosophers?

On a practical level, composers drew from humanistic studies and put human feelings at the center of a piece so that the music itself would reflect the emotions of the lyrics. For example, if the lyric was sad, the pitch should descend and the tempo should slow down. Music also moved from the church to the courts in these centuries, and perhaps the best-known secular, emotional music was the **madrigals,** poetic songs usually about love. The attempt to link music, narrative, and emotion led to the invention of opera at the end of the sixteenth century.

Music became part of a well-rounded education. Castiglione, in his *Book of the Courtier,* wrote, "I am not pleased with the courtier if he be not also a musician." Music came into the households as well as the courts, and new instruments were developed to serve the home market. Noble households resonated with the sounds of instruments such as the viola da gamba (a bowed, stringed instrument), the whistle-like recorder, and the harpsichord (an instrument, like the piano, with strings that are plucked). The printing press helped to advance this popularization of music, as it allowed for the wide distribution of sheet music after the 1470s. Despite all the new instruments and the new technology of printing, however, the human voice, so expressive of human emotion, remained the central instrument of Renaissance music.

Science or Pseudoscience?

The Renaissance passion for direct observation and realistic assessment that led to such magnificent achievements in the visual, musical, and literary arts catalyzed a process that ultimately led to the scientific accomplishments of the seventeenth century. During the fourteenth and fifteenth centuries, however, much scientific inquiry was shaped by a desire to control as well as understand the world. This combination led to the pursuit of what we consider pseudoscientific studies.

As the Biography of Isabella d'Este indicated, astrology was extremely popular during these centuries. Even some popes hired their own astrologers. The bright appearance of Halley's comet in 1456 provoked a flurry of both dire and inspiring prophecies. For example, one humanist physician explained the outbreak of syphilis in Europe in terms of a conjunction of the planets Saturn, Jupiter, and Mars in the sign of Cancer. **Alchemy** was the early practice of chemistry, but the alchemists' interests were dramatically different from those of modern scientists. Their main goal was to find a "philosopher stone" that would turn base metals into gold. This science was perhaps even more popular than astrology.

Astrology and alchemy

Such pseudoscience aside, the Renaissance did succeed in combining visual arts with scientific observation. The study of linear perspective, for example, depended on an understanding of mathematics, and scholars spread the use of Arabic numerals to replace the Roman numerals that had previously dominated the West. The use of these numbers facilitated higher orders of calculations, like algebra, which was also learned from the Muslims. Musicians explored ratios and fractions to try to re-create celestial proportions. Realistic sculpture and painting required a study of anatomy, and this science also progressed. Amid these advancements, the Renaissance saw the birth of

Mathematics and anatomy

a man who came to represent the entire range and combination of talents that so defined this age.

Leonardo da Vinci: The "Renaissance Man"

Leonardo da Vinci (1452–1519) personifies the idea of the "Renaissance man"—the person who can supposedly do anything well. As a young man, he contributed to the architecture of Florence by helping to make the golden ball that topped Brunelleschi's dome (see **Figure 10.9**), but he excelled in much more than architecture and sculpture.

This multitalented Italian served in the courts of a number of patrons, from the Medici to the Sforza of Milan—even Isabella d'Este tried to woo him. At these courts, Leonardo painted magnificent portraits and beautiful religious works. **Figure 10.13** shows Leonardo's celebrated *Mona Lisa,* probably the most famous portrait from the Renaissance. Her famous hint of a smile and calm pose were strikingly original at the time and inspired many later portraits.

Painting

Although Leonardo's skill as a painter would have satisfied most men longing for greatness, he saw this medium only as a beginning, a means to a larger end. "Painting should increase the artist's knowledge of the physical world," he explained.

Leonardo left a collection of notebooks that showed his intense interest in the world. His drawings of plants revealed a skill and meticulousness that any botanist would envy, and his sketches of water in motion would have impressed the

Scientific notebooks

most accomplished of engineers. Leonardo's imagination seemed boundless—his sketches included tanks and other war machines, a submarine, textile machines, paddle boats, a "horseless carriage," and many other inventions that lay in the future.

Leonardo also took an interest in the inner workings of the human body. Although some medieval physicians conducted dissections, the practice was not common. During the Renaissance, however, physicians and scholars began to approach the study of the human body empirically by regularly dissecting cadavers. At the time, both artists and physicians saw dissection as a way to improve their portrayal of the human form. Like many other artists, Leonardo dissected cadavers to understand anatomy and thereby make his paintings as realistic as possible (as well as to satisfy his insatiable curiosity). **Figure 10.14a** shows Leonardo's sketches and descriptions of human shoulders and arms, including the bones of the left foot and lower leg. The image demonstrates how he drew from cadaver studies as it shows the intricate connections of the ligaments in the joint as well as the various parts of the muscles as they encase the arm bones.

FIGURE 10.13 Leonardo da Vinci, *Mona Lisa,* ca. 1504
Leonardo's most famous painting displays his genius at portrait painting as well as landscape perspective (in the background). Notice that the form of the aqueduct by the subject's left shoulder is echoed in the drapery over that shoulder. This is only one way in which the artist connected the sitter to her environment.

RENAISSANCE ARTISTS AND WRITERS

ca. 1267–1337	Giotto, Italy
1304–1374	Petrarch, Italy
ca. 1395–1441	Jan van Eyck, Flemish painter (Chapter 9)
1436	Brunelleschi completes dome of Florence cathedral
1452–1519	Leonardo da Vinci, Italy and France
ca. 1454	Johann Gutenberg begins printing books, Germany
1466–1536	Desiderius Erasmus, Holland
1475–1564	Michelangelo, Italy
1478–1535	Thomas More, England
1483–1520	Raphael, Italy
1513	Machiavelli, *The Prince,* Italy
1564–1616	William Shakespeare, England

Figure 10.14b, a depiction of a child in the womb, reveals the wide range of Leonardo's interests as well as his scientific curiosity. It is the oldest surviving illustration in the West of the actual position of an unborn child. To make this drawing, Leonardo secured a dispensation to dissect a deceased pregnant woman. In addition to capturing the correct positioning, the drawing explains the function of the placenta.

King Francis I of France (r. 1515–1547) once said of Leonardo, "No other man had been born who knew so much." Unfortunately for the future of science and engineering, Leonardo's voluminous notebooks were lost for centuries after his death. In retrospect, perhaps Leonardo's greatest achievement was that he showed how multitalented human beings could be. He proved the humanists' belief that an educated man could accomplish anything in all fields. Leonardo died at the court of Francis I, who had proudly served as his patron.

RENAISSANCE OF THE "NEW MONARCHIES" OF THE NORTH, 1453–1640

As we saw in Chapter 9, the medieval political structures of Europe began to fall apart under the pressures of the many disasters of the fourteenth century. The monarchies of the fifteenth century could no longer rely on feudal contracts and armies of mounted knights and began to search for new ways to rule their countries. To bypass their sometimes unreliable nobility, monarchs concentrated their royal authority by appointing bureaucrats who owed their status only to the will of the king or queen. As they looked for new sources of income to pay growing mercenary armies, kings and queens kept imposing new taxes and, in general, were receptive to new ideas to help them consolidate their power. Many hired Italians trained in the humanist tradition to work in their courts, and slowly and fitfully from the late thirteenth through the sixteenth century, the ideas of the Renaissance spread to northern European countries. As Renaissance notions traveled north and bore fruit in the courts of powerful rulers, the ideas were further transformed. This migration of ideas also accelerated the changes triggered by the disasters of the fourteenth century.

France: Under the Italian Influence

France offers a case study in how slowly and sporadically Renaissance ideas moved and how much this new spirit depended on the patronage of monarchs. The French king Charles V (r. 1364–1380), known as "the Wise," encouraged Renaissance learning among his subjects, gathering a circle of intellectuals around him. However, this early flowering of learning withered when his mentally unstable son, Charles VI (r. 1380–1422), took

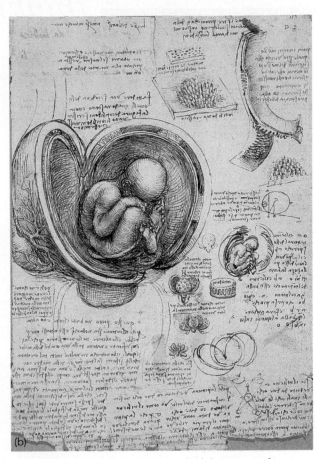

FIGURE 10.14 Leonardo's Notebooks, ca. 1510 Leonardo, like many other artists at the time, studied dissections of cadavers to learn about humans and in doing so forwarded science as well as art. Figure 10.14a shows his drawings of a shoulder and arm. Figure 10.14b is the oldest drawing in the West of a child in the womb.

power. Integration of Renaissance ideals in this northern court would have to wait until the end of the Hundred Years' War in 1453 (discussed in Chapter 9).

France eventually triumphed in the Hundred Years' War, but a new threat from the neighboring state of Burgundy immediately arose. As we saw in Chapter 9, Burgundy had allied with England to weaken France, and England's defeat did not weaken Burgundy's land hunger. As **Map 10.3** shows, the rulers of Burgundy were trying to forge a state between France and the Holy Roman Empire, and their hundred-year expansion represented a real threat to France. Instead of leading armies in the old chivalric manner, however, the French king Louis XI (r. 1461–1483) skillfully brought a new kind of diplomacy to bear in confronting this next challenge. His contemporaries called him "Louis the Spider" because he spun a complex web of intrigue and diplomatic machinations worthy of Machiavelli—bribing his allies and murdering his enemies. Louis subsidized Swiss mercenaries, who eventually defeated the Burgundian ruler. France then seized the Duchy of Burgundy and added the sizable new territory to its lands. (As **Map 10.3** shows, the Low Countries remained in the hands of Mary, the Duke of Burgundy's

Louis the Spider

daughter, and they later formed part of the inheritance of her grandson, Charles V, whose fortunes we will follow in Chapter 11.) Louis left France strong and prosperous and well placed to play a powerful political role in the coming centuries. Document 10.3 offers a contemporary's view of this complex king.

As **Map 10.3** shows, the French kings succeeded in slowly taking the lands from the nobles who had retained their holdings since the Middle Ages. With its increasing strength, France next began expanding across the Alps into Italy to assert dynastic claims in Naples, because, as we saw previously, the French royal family was related to the rulers in Naples. However, the French came back with much more than wealth. Nobles leading mercenary armies in the Italian campaigns of 1494 came in search of land and left feeling dazzled by the cultural accomplishments of the Italian Renaissance. In a letter to his courtiers back home, the French king Charles VIII (r. 1483–1498) gushed about discovering the "best artists" in Italy. He returned home with some 20 Italian workmen whom he instructed to build "in the Italian style." The aesthetic ideals of Italy thus moved north with the retreating French armies, and the early Renaissance spirit in France was reawakened.

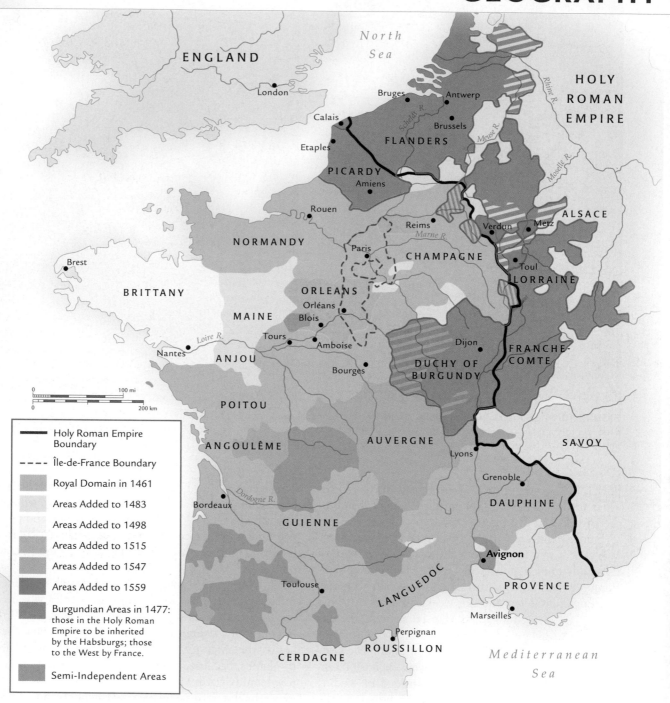

MAP 10.3

France in the Fifteenth and Sixteenth Centuries

This map shows the growth of the royal domain of the French kings from 1461 through 1559.

Explore the Map

1. Why did the Duchy of Burgundy pose a threat to the French kings?

2. Considering the location of Avignon, where the popes had lived so long, why did many in Europe accuse those popes of being pro-French?

DOCUMENT 10.3

A Courtier Describes a Suspicious King—Louis the Spider

Philippe de Commynes (ca. 1447–1511) served Louis XI and wrote an account of the king's reign shortly after Louis' death in 1483. Commynes had been raised at the court of Burgundy until he found it politically expedient to change sides and work for France. Thus, he was well placed to view the king with the eye of an outsider as well as a courtier.

The King had ordered several cruel prisons to be made; some were cages of iron, and some of wood, but all were covered with iron plates both within and without, with terrible locks, about eight feet wide and seven high. . . . I lay in one of them eight months together in the minority of our present King. . . . However, I have seen many eminent and deserving persons in these prisons, with these nets about their legs, who afterwards came forth with great joy and honor, and received great rewards from the King. . . .

It may be urged that other princes have been more given to suspicion than he, but it was not in our time; and, perhaps, their wisdom was not so eminent, nor were their subjects so good. They might too, probably, have been tyrants, and bloody-minded; but our king never did any person a mischief who had not offended him first, though I do not say all who offended him deserved death. I have not recorded these things merely to represent our

master as a suspicious and mistrustful prince; but . . . that those princes who may be his successors, may learn by his example to be more tender and indulgent to their subjects, and less severe in their punishments than our master had been: although I will not censure him, or say I ever saw a better prince; for though he oppressed his subjects himself, he would never see them injured by anybody else. . . .

I knew him, and was entertained in his service in the flower of his age, and at the height of his prosperity, yet I never saw him free from labor and care. Of all diversions he loved hunting and hawking in their seasons; but his chief delight was in dogs. As for ladies, he never meddled with any in my time; for about the time of my coming to his court he lost a son, at whose death he was extremely afflicted, and he made a vow to God in my presence never to have intercourse with any other woman but the queen; and though this was no more than what he was bound to do by the canons of the church, yet it was much that his self-command should be so great, that he should be able to persevere in his resolution so firmly, considering that the queen (though an excellent princess in other respects) was not a person in whom a man could take any great delight. . . .

He was involved [in warfare that] . . . lasted till his death, and many

brave men lost their lives in it, and his treasury was exhausted by it; so that he had but a little time during the whole year to spend in pleasure, and even then the fatigues he underwent were excessive. When his body was at rest his mind was at work, for he had affairs in several places at once, and would concern himself as much in those of his neighbors as in his own, putting officers of his own over all the great families, and endeavoring to divide their authority as much as possible. When he was at war he labored for a peace or a truce, and when he had obtained it, he was impatient for war again. He troubled himself with many trifles in his government, which he had better have let alone: but it was his temper, and he could not help it; besides, he had a prodigious memory, and he forgot nothing, but knew everybody, as well in other countries as in his own.

SOURCE: A.R. Scoble, trans. and annotator, *The Memories of Philip de Commines* (London: G. Bell & Sons, 1884), vol. II, pp. 75–81.

Analyze the Document

1. What qualities did Commynes value in the king and which did he criticize?

2. Would Machiavelli have considered Louis a good prince? Why or why not?

3. What qualities do you think made him a successful monarch?

Italian influence increased further with the substantial growth of the French court, which opened positions to Italian humanists and diplomats. France's kings employed more officials than any other state in Europe—one estimate places the number of bureaucrats at more than 4,000 during the reign of Francis I (r. 1515–1547). (Leonardo da Vinci was among those brought to France by this powerful and sophisticated patron.) Under Francis's rule, humanist literature flourished, and the new learning influenced university curricula from languages to mathematics to law. The king even ordered

Castiglione's *Book of the Courtier* to be translated into French and read to him nightly.

The French Renaissance did not merely copy the Italian movement. Indeed, many works by French artists and writers during this period show a unique blend of humorous skepticism and creative power. The imaginative humanist François Rabelais embodies this unmistakable French version of Renaissance ideals. His books *Pantagruel* and *Gargantua*—bawdy tales about giants with enormous appetites—are masterpieces of satire. Both stories continue to captivate modern readers. France had left its own mark on the Renaissance spirit.

Italians in France

English Humanism

When Henry VII (r. 1485–1509) became king in England after the Wars of the Roses (see Chapter 9), he succeeded in taming the rowdy and independent nobility and established a strong, centralized monarchy. Under the dynasty that he initiated, England again prospered. The English monarchs now turned their attention to the new spirit emanating from the south as they began to surround themselves with courtiers and art that served as the hallmarks of the courts of new monarchs. Delayed because of internal strife, the English Renaissance (1500–1640) gained momentum just as the Italian movement waned.

During the reign of Henry VII, English scholars intrigued by Renaissance thought traveled to Italy and studied under noted humanists. They frequented the newly established Vatican library and consulted with Platina, the papal librarian shown in **Figure 10.4,** and then returned home brimming with new ideas. By 1500, these scholars had so transformed the curriculum at Oxford that England could offer as fine a classical education as Italy. The forward-thinking English monarchs also brought back technological innovations. They embraced new artillery and set English engineers to work making gunpowder. Henry VII included a fireworks display at his wedding, in so doing importing this Italian skill into England and beginning a long tradition of English pyrotechnics. (See Thinking about Science & Technology in Chapter 11.)

Henry VIII (r. 1509–1547) proved an even more vigorous patron of Renaissance learning than his father. As we will see in Chapter 11, Henry met the French king Francis I and tried to outdo that Renaissance prince in splendor and patronage. The English king cultivated interest in astronomy, literature, and music—all the fields advocated by the humanists. Still, the talented monarch was outdone by his Lord Chancellor, Sir Thomas More (1478–1535).

More published a biography of the humanist Pico della Mirandola that revealed the author's debt to the Italian movement. The English scholar mastered classical learning and the humanist curriculum and applied his skills in public life in the best tradition of civic humanism. More's masterpiece, however, was *Utopia,* a work that commented on contemporary evils while offering a vision of a society free of poverty, crime, and corruption. More's work, with its visions of exploration and decidedly political orientation, points to distinct characteristics of the English Renaissance. More's studies gave him strong views on religion, which, as we will see in Chapter 11, led to a fatal conflict with his king.

Thomas More

Many Englishwomen also wrote during this Renaissance. The first wife of Henry VIII, Catherine of Aragon (1485–1536), had grown up with a love of the new learning encouraged by her mother, Isabella of Castile. When Catherine came to England, she stimulated interest among courtiers and scholars in the proper education of women. Consequently, Englishwomen wrote more publicly than their Italian counterparts. In fact, Italian travelers to England wrote disparagingly of the "brazen and violently assertive" Englishwomen. This tradition of education strongly influenced Queen Elizabeth I (r. 1558–1603), under whose rule England prospered and the Renaissance flowered.

Renaissance queens

Renaissance London: A Booming City

Sixteenth-century London—a vibrant city—scintillated during the English Renaissance, expanding physically and intellectually. Between 1560 and 1603, the population almost doubled, from 120,000 to more than 200,000, and travelers flocked there to see its wonders. **Figure 10.15** shows a 1616 painting of London by Claes von Visscher. In this cityscape, the great sailing ships that made London a bustling commercial hub waft by, along with small vessels that supplied the city's growing population. Rows of houses stand in front of St. Paul's cathedral, which dominates the skyline.

In the foreground of the painting is the south bank of the Thames, which had been a center of prostitution from the time of the Roman settlement of London. The south bank remained the unseemly quarter of the city, inhabited by criminals and prostitutes, and notorious for its violent forms of entertainment, such as bear baiting and dog fights. The south bank also housed private prisons, including the infamous "clink" that housed some of the fiercest criminals. Yet, the south bank was also home to the theaters where crowds gathered to watch the plays of the great Renaissance dramatists. The two tall, round structures in the foreground of **Figure 10.15** are examples of these theaters. The one on the right is inaccurately labeled "The Globe." Known as Shakespeare's theater, the building had burned down in 1613 because of sparks from fireworks set off as part of a play. This took place before Visscher painted his London scene. During the late sixteenth century, however, the Globe served as a backdrop for the work of the greatest writer England has ever produced, and crowds today gather to see plays performed in a newly rebuilt Gobe Theater on the south bank of the Thames.

The south bank

England's Pride: William Shakespeare

The new social mobility of the Renaissance permitted William Shakespeare (1564–1616) to rise to prominence. William's father, a modest glove maker,

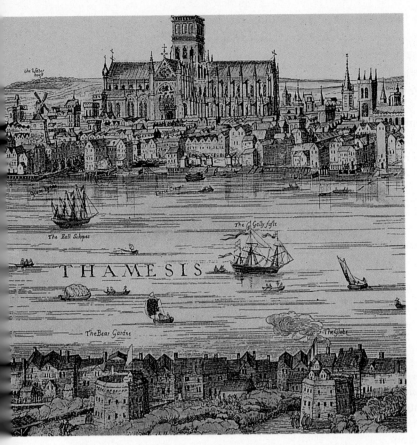

FIGURE 10.15 Claes von Visscher, *Map of London* (detail), 1616 The south bank of the Thames is shown in the foreground of the image. In this seedy part of town, patrons came to see bear baiting and dog fights. But also here, in the circular theaters, Shakespeare and other playwrights created masterworks of English drama that have come down to us through the ages.

a humanist education. At the age of 18, the young scholar married Anne Hathaway, about eight years his elder, who was pregnant with their first child. In 1592, William journeyed to London, where he worked as an actor and wrote comedies, histories, and tragedies.

This master of the English language articulated all the Renaissance ideals: Shakespeare's love of the classics showed in his use of Roman histories in his plays (*Julius Caesar*) and in his study of Roman playwrights that offered him models of theater. Furthermore, Hamlet's words "What a piece of work is man" expressed Renaissance optimism in human accomplishment; *Romeo and Juliet* re-created the story of "star-crossed lovers" (a reference to the Renaissance love of astrology) in the streets of Italy. *The Tempest* featured Renaissance magicians, and Shakespeare's histories described the fortunes of princes as surely as Machiavelli's analysis of history and politics had. His plays incorporated Renaissance music and modern warfare with cannons and fireworks. In Shakespeare's hands, the ideals of the Renaissance were given a new, enduring form—popular theater that reached the masses. However, some modern literary critics believe the great playwright accomplished much more than perfecting Renaissance ideas. Some claim that by expressing complex human emotions in magnificent language, Shakespeare created an understanding of humanity for the West. In this, perhaps, we can see the ideals of the Renaissance come full circle—the early humanists in Italy transformed themselves by the texts they read, and Shakespeare used the written word to shape our understanding of who we are. Western civilization was dramatically transformed.

married a woman above his station, the daughter of a wealthy landowner. Shakespeare probably attended the local school in Stratford-upon-Avon and received

LOOKING BACK & MOVING FORWARD

Summary In the crucible of the fourteenth century—in which plague, famine, warfare, and religious instability swirled—new ideas percolated in the turbulent Italian city-states. Scholars and statesmen alike resuscitated a pride in human dignity, a confidence in human activism, and a fascination with classical ideals, and they expressed these ideas primarily in the secular arena. Writers, painters, and politicians looked with new realism at the world around them and strove to exert an impact on it. Although all these ideas had a precedent in the Middle Ages, their prevalence and novel applications created a new spirit that historians call the Renaissance.

KEY TERMS

Renaissance, *p. 310*
humanists, *p. 312*
civic humanists, *p. 313*
Christian humanists, *p. 313*
condottieri, *p. 317*
doge, *p. 319*
theocracy, *p. 321*
contra posto, *p. 329*

This age of the Renaissance ushered in a period that had both great and shameful aspects. In booming economies, Italian city-states were able to support architects and artists who created masterpieces that have set Western standards of beauty for centuries. At the same time, many of these enterprising individualists turned a blind eye to social problems—increased crime, new slavery, and growing anti-Semitism.

The new ideas of the Renaissance flowed northward with humanist courtiers and talented artists and artisans. In the process, they helped transform the old feudal monarchies. At the same time, scholars in each country put their own stamp on the Renaissance spirit. For example, France gloried in court architecture and brilliant satire, and England most notably brought these ideas to the popular theater.

As we will see in Chapter 11, Spain and Germany, too, would mold the praise of individualism and literary criticism to their own interests. Like Savonarola in Florence, German humanists applied Renaissance ideas to spiritual matters. Their efforts would eventually bring about an upheaval in religion as great as the Renaissance revolution in art and ideas.

linear perspective, *p. 331*
madrigals, *p. 332*
alchemy, *p. 333*

REVIEW, ANALYZE, & CONNECT TO TODAY

REVIEW THE PREVIOUS CHAPTER

Chapter 9—"The West Struggles and Eastern Empires Flourish"—told of the disasters of the fourteenth century that contributed to the breakdown of medieval structures. It also told of the rise of empires in the East that would soon cast a long shadow on politics in the West.

1. Review the political order of northern Europe in the Middle Ages and contrast it with the political life of fourteenth-century Italy. How did the turbulent politics of Italy contribute to the growth of Renaissance thought?

2. Contrast medieval art, architecture, and literature with that of the Renaissance artists and humanists.

ANALYZE THIS CHAPTER

Chapter 10—"A New Spirit in the West"—considers the characteristics we have come to associate with the term *Renaissance*. It looks at the politics and social life of the Italian city-states that fostered these ideas and the magnificent accomplishments in the arts and science that accompanied them. It also follows the fortunes of the "new monarchies" of the north as Renaissance ideas spread.

1. Review the characteristics of the Renaissance and consider what contributed to the development.

2. One theme this chapter traces is the relationship between ideas—like individualism and realism—and actual events and accomplishments. Analyze some aspects of life and accomplishments of Renaissance Italy in light of these values, and consider how they were related.

3. How did Renaissance ideas spread northward, and how were they transformed in France and England?

CONNECT TO TODAY

Think about these key values of the Renaissance: individualism over community, realism over faith, and activism over passive obedience.

1. In what ways do contemporary U.S. society and culture also exhibit these values? In what ways are they expressed in public policy today?

2. Does the Western tradition of taking these values for granted prevent positive interactions with societies that do not share these values? Explain.

3. What examples can you cite from the world today wherein societies have censored religious criticism or suppressed individual liberties to strengthen the community? What do you think of such measures?

BEYOND THE CLASSROOM

A NEW SPIRIT EMERGES: INDIVIDUALISM, REALISM, AND ACTIVISM

Eisenstein, Elizabeth. *The Printing Revolution in Early Modern Europe*. New York: Cambridge University Press, 1983. Studies the shift from script to print and looks at the relationship between changes in communication and other developments.

Goldthwaite, Richard A. *Wealth and the Demand for Art in Italy, 1300–1600*. Baltimore: Johns Hopkins University Press, 1993. An original and important look at art in relation to the society and economy that produced it.

King, Margaret L., and Albert Rabil. *Her Immaculate Hand: Selected Works by and About the Women Humanists of Quattrocento Italy*. Asheville, NC: Pegasus Press, 1998. Presents writings of women humanists to illuminate an often-neglected side of the Renaissance.

Marek, G. *The Bed and the Throne: Isabelle d'Este*. New York: Harper & Row, 1976. A dazzling story of culture, art, and politics through the life of this talented ruler.

Naubert, Charles G. *Humanism and the Culture of Renaissance Europe*, 2nd ed. Cambridge: Cambridge University Press, 2006. A clear yet comprehensive description of the movement from its inception in Italy to its spread northward—definitely the place to begin.

THE POLITICS OF INDIVIDUAL EFFORT

Burckhardt, Jacob. *The Civilization of the Renaissance*. New York: Modern Library, 2002. A reissued edition of the nineteenth-century classic that began serious historical analysis of the Renaissance.

Femia, Joseph V. *Machiavelli Revisited*. Cardiff: University of Wales Press, 2002. Looks at the impact of Machiavelli's pivotal work, *The Prince*, while guiding the reader through the maze of contradictory interpretations.

Jones, P.J. *The Italian City-State: From Commune to Signoria*. Oxford: Clarendon Press, 1997. An impressive, scholarly study of the political history of the Italian city-states.

INDIVIDUALISM AS SELF-INTEREST: LIFE DURING THE RENAISSANCE

Brucker, Gene. *Florence: The Golden Age, 1138–1737*. Berkeley: University of California Press, 1998. A beautifully illustrated history by a prominent historian who brings the past vividly to life, including great families, common folk, wars, and artistic achievements.

Crum, Roger J., and John T. Paoletti, eds. *Renaissance Florence: A Social History*. Cambridge: Cambridge University Press, 2008. Comprehensive, accessible essays examining the social history of Florence and showing the ties between art and society.

Haas, Louis. *The Renaissance Man and His Children*. New York: St. Martin's Press, 1991. Sheds light on how Florentine parents (primarily fathers) viewed, reared, and cared for their children.

Katz, Dana E. *The Jew in the Art of the Italian Renaissance*. Philadelphia: University of Pennsylvania Press, 2008. A rigorous study of the portrayal of Jews in art, revealing animosity toward Jews even while some rulers upheld toleration legislation.

King, Margaret L. *Women of the Renaissance*. Chicago: University of Chicago Press, 1991. A short, accessible summary of women in the family, in the church, and participating in high culture.

McIntosh, Marjorie. *Controlling Misbehavior in England, 1370–1600*. Cambridge: Cambridge University Press, 2002. An in-depth study of the growing efforts of states to regulate behavior they deemed threatening to public order.

AN AGE OF TALENT AND BEAUTY: RENAISSANCE CULTURE AND SCIENCE

Baxandall, Michael. *Painting and Experience in Fifteenth-Century Italy: A Primer in the Social History of Pictorial Style*. Oxford: Oxford University Press, 1988. A brilliant work that shows the intersection between life in Florence and painters' expression of those experiences. A study of both painting and social history.

James, Frank A. *Renaissance and Revolution: Humanists, Scholars, Craftsmen and Natural Philosophers in Early Modern Europe*. New York: Cambridge University Press, 1994. A clear and engaging survey of the history of science and technology between 1400 and 1750.

RENAISSANCE OF THE "NEW MONARCHIES" OF THE NORTH: 1453–1640

Bloom, Harold. *Shakespeare: The Invention of the Human*. New York: Riverhead Books, 1998. A controversial but influential study of all Shakespeare's plays that argues that Shakespeare shaped the way we define ourselves.

Kendall, P.M. *Louis XI, the Universal Spider*. New York: W.W. Norton, 1971. A remarkable presentation of the French king Louis XI as one of the formidable personalities of Europe and one of the shapers of the modern world.

Martin, John J. *The Renaissance: Italy and Abroad*. New York: Routledge, 2002. A collection of essays that illustrates the current status of Renaissance studies, revealing its diversity and complexities.

Snyder, James, Larry Silver, and Henry Luttikhuizen. *Northern Renaissance Art*, 2nd ed. Upper Saddle River, NJ: Prentice Hall, 2004. Beautifully illustrated, comprehensive study of the artists and patrons who created the magnificent art of the northern Renaissance.

HANS HOLBEIN THE YOUNGER, *ERASMUS OF ROTTERDAM,* ca. 1523

As humanist ideas of scholarship and individualism spread north, they influenced a revolution in Christian thought, first led by the man portrayed here. Erasmus is shown resting his hands on a Greek book inscribed "The Labors of Herakles," a tribute to his Herculean task of revising biblical translations based on the study of ancient languages. He is placed in a room with hints of Renaissance design, reminding viewers of his debt to the Italian scholars. This quiet portrait reveals a pious man, seeking God alone. It does not reveal how this new approach to religion ripped at the social fabric as warfare and bloodshed tore through Europe.

"Alone Before God"

Religious Reform and Warfare, 1500–1648

"They used thumbscrews, which they cleverly made out of their pistols, to torture the peasants, as if they wanted to burn witches. . . . They put one of the captured peasants in the bake-oven and lighted a fire in it." This horrifying description of war in Germany (by a soldier, Jakob von Grimmelshausen) characterizes a period in European history when many innocents suffered horrible deaths. Rulers launched their armies at each other in an attempt to win new territory and enhance their power, and these armies fighting with new weapons unleashed untold misery.

At the same time, new ideas about how to worship God began to spread throughout Europe—religious reformers introduced an intellectual revolution that would not only alter how people viewed their relationship with God but also redefine their ideas about society, politics, and the very nature of human beings. However, as monarchs confronted the religious diversity boiling within their countries, they increased the violence: Civil wars over religion erupted and brought this period to a bloody close.

Out of this turmoil came a reform in religion that split the Christian body into many Christian churches. In the course of this reform, many men and women who were spared the bloodshed of warfare were killed for their beliefs. This religious reform also generated more subtle changes in society—ideas of love, marriage, education, and charity were transformed as some people rethought their relationship to God. The West was irrevocably changed.

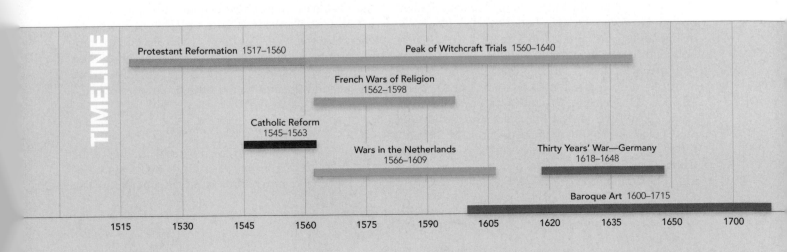

TIMELINE

Protestant Reformation 1517–1560

Peak of Witchcraft Trials 1560–1640

French Wars of Religion
1562–1598

Catholic Reform
1545–1563

Wars in the Netherlands
1566–1609

Thirty Years' War—Germany
1618–1648

Baroque Art 1600–1715

1515   1530   1545   1560   1575   1590   1605   1620   1635   1650   1700

PREVIEW

THE CLASH OF DYNASTIES,
1515–1555

In 1520, two of the most powerful kings in Europe met in France to hold a tournament and discuss matters of state. Francis I (r. 1515–1547) of France had invited Henry VIII (r. 1509–1547) of England to his court to seek an alliance against his powerful enemy the Holy Roman Emperor Charles V (r. 1519–1556). Francis hoped to impress Henry with his extravagant wealth, but the ostentatious display generated only more rivalry. Each king approached the meeting with as much state as he could muster. The kings, their followers, and even their horses wore clothing made of silver and gold thread. Silk and gold decorated the walls of the French palace and even the tents on the palace grounds that offered shade from the noonday sun. The meeting was dubbed the Field of the Cloth of Gold. All this opulence underscored the character of the sixteenth century—there was money to spend and kings thought excess bought power. However, Francis had offended Henry by outspending him, and he did not get the alliance he sought. Instead, much to Francis's dismay, Henry met with Charles V, who approached the king in a frugal and reserved manner—and received his alliance. The struggle for land and power between Francis I and the Holy Roman Emperor would not take place on a golden tournament field; instead, these kings opened a violent century by warfare, while Henry waited to see who would be left standing. The Italian city-states—too small to compete on fields of golden cloth—became the battleground in this bitter contest.

The kings of France and England ruled strong, unified states, but at the beginning of the sixteenth century, nation-states were not necessarily the ideal political form. Indeed, kings sought to extend their reach even further and acquire multinational empires like that held by the Holy Roman Emperor, Charles V. Ignoring considerations of common culture or the difficulties of holding large empires, each king believed simply that bigger was better.

Land-Hungry Monarchs

Charles V was the grandson of Ferdinand and Isabella of Spain (see page 360). Thanks to the prudent dynastic marriages of his ancestors, he had inherited a sprawling, multinational empire. **Map 11.1** shows the Habsburg lands of Charles V, which included the Netherlands, Spain, and lands in Austria, and highlights all the battles to indicate how warfare dominated Charles's reign. The map also shows the extensive empire of the Ottoman Turks, which threatened Charles in the East.

As we saw in Chapter 9, events in the eastern Mediterranean had complicated western European rivalry, for the empire of the Ottoman Turks had gained strength. After the Turks conquered Constantinople in 1453, they consolidated their rule and developed a | Turkish expansion | sophisticated administration and a well-trained military. Under Suleiman I the Magnificent (r. 1520–1566), the Turks began to advance again, this time toward the very heart of Europe. **Map 9.5,** on page 302, shows the sixteenth-century advance of the Ottoman Empire and indicates why western Europeans felt threatened by the growing power of the Muslims.

In 1521, the Turks marched up the Danube valley and seized Belgrade and Hungary, creating a panic throughout central Europe. By 1529, they were outside the walls of Vienna, the core of the Austrian Habsburg lands. At the same time, Turkish ships proved so effective in the eastern Mediterranean that all the western rulers wondered how long they could hold on to their share of the lucrative sea trade in that area. For Charles V in particular, however, the Ottoman Empire had become a major, distracting presence in the east as he struggled to extend his empire in the west. All these monarchs had to grapple with new complexities in their seemingly endless struggles with one another, for the scale of warfare was increasing, and the old rules no longer applied.

The Changing Rules of Warfare

As we saw in Chapter 9, the mounted knights of the Middle Ages were being replaced by infantry, and by the sixteenth century, that trend was complete. The

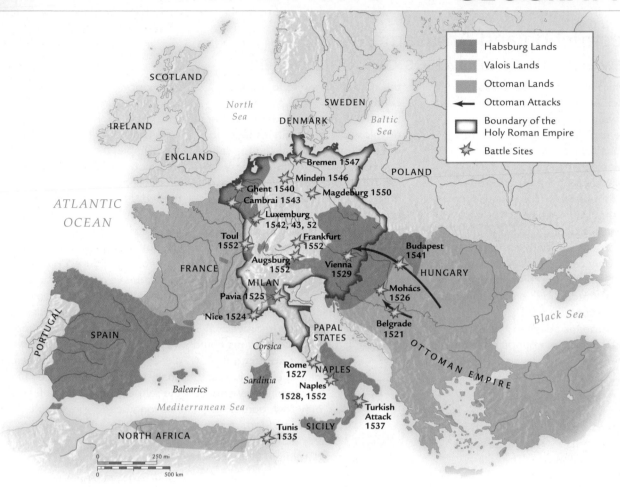

MAP 11.1

Europe in 1526— Habsburg-Valois Wars

This map illustrates the political division of Europe in 1526 and highlights the Habsburg lands inherited by Charles V. It also shows the Ottoman Empire on Charles's borders.

Explore the Map

1. Why did the French king feel threatened by his powerful neighbor?

2. Why was Charles so concerned about the proximity of the Ottoman Empire?

3. Notice all the battles Charles fought. What might have been the impact of this warfare both on the people and on the emperor's ability to rule?

---

primary reason for this change was military technology. By 1500, Europeans had improved on the unreliable early guns of the Hundred Years' War. Now, guns with 50-inch-long barrels gave marksmen a good deal of power and accuracy, and soon the Spanish developed the musket, a 6-foot-long gun that could shoot lead bullets up to 200 yards. Armed with these weapons, soldiers could do a great deal more damage. As one observer noted: "Often and frequently . . . a virile brave hero is killed by some forsaken knave with a gun." Indeed, warfare was now dramatically changed, and kings had to pay the price in men and materials

for new armies. See Thinking About Science & Technology to see how the changes in gunpowder facilitated its widespread use.

The new weapons dictated different military strategies. Now, captains arrayed their troops in a series of long, narrow lines. The infantrymen carried muskets and were backed by tight formations of pike-wielding foot soldiers. In this new kind of warfare, sheer numbers often determined a king's success, so monarchs strove to bolster the size of their armies. At the beginning of the century, most armies had fewer than 50,000 men;

> Growing armies

thinking about
SCIENCE & TECHNOLOGY

Destruction and Amusement: The Development and Uses of Gunpowder

By the tenth century, Chinese alchemists—recall that alchemy was the early practice of chemistry—were experimenting with mixing various substances for medicinal purposes. In the process, they invented an effective gunpowder. The formula was 75 percent saltpeter (potassium nitrate), which released chemically bound oxygen to support combustion; 15 percent charcoal to supply carbon to fuel the fire; and 10 percent sulfur to lower the temperature of ignition and speed up combustion.

Europeans adopted this recipe and began to use gunpowder on the battlefield in the fourteenth century. Then, in the fifteenth century, Western powder engineers developed a technique of binding the powder into small clumps called corned powder, which was easy to transport, to keep dry, and to load efficiently into guns and cannons. Importantly, the corned powder also was more stable; the corning technology prevented accidental dust explosions and detonation from static electricity and provided a more controlled burn rate. With the enhanced stability and transportability of the improved powder, large, mobile cannons could be brought into the battlefields, whereas previously they could only be mounted on ships and forts. From this moment on, battlefield violence increased dramatically, and foot soldiers faced devastating explosions as they charged. Gunpowder's impact would become starkly evident in the violence of the early modern wars and in the sea battles that would bring Europeans to power across the world.

People throughout history have found ways to adapt technological innovations for entertainment purposes, and this ingenuity was true for gunpowder. As early as the late fifteenth century in the West, gunpowder moved from wartime to peacetime uses as people set off gunpowder-powered fireworks to light up European night skies on special occasions. These displays were potentially hazardous, however; for example, the pyrotechnics that were lit during one of Shakespeare's productions ignited the fire that burned down the playwright's Globe Theatre in 1613. Even firemasters, individuals who made gunpowder, did not know exactly how gunpowder worked, and **Figure 11.1** shows the explosive results that often accompanied their experiments. This mystery stimulated scientific investigation for years to come, helping to move science from alchemy to chemistry as researchers finally identified the oxygen hidden in the saltpeter that fed the fires of what had long been believed to be a magic powder.

Remember the struggle for mastery of the chemistry of gunpowder so that when you learn about the Scientific Revolution in Chapter 14, you might consider again the relationship between practical utility and scientific theory.

FIGURE 11.1 Experimenting with gunpowder.

Connecting Science & Society

1. Trace how the scientific experimentation behind the development and improvement of gunpowder led to the application of gunpowder technology for various purposes.

2. How did advances in the stability and transportability of gunpowder transform warfare?

3. Cite some instances in your lifetime where inventions of practical items or techniques have been later adapted for entertainment purposes.

Charles V's forces boasted a whopping 148,000 (although they were widely dispersed through Charles's extensive lands).

To enlarge their armies, rulers had to resort to creative new ways to fill their ranks. In part, kings relied on mercenaries, hiring soldiers of fortune who offered their services to the highest bidder, but these were never sufficient. Traditionally, kings claimed the right to draft an army from among the able-bodied men of the land. Originally, these draftees were required to fight only on their home soil, but in 1544 Henry VIII sent his conscripts overseas. No one objected, and a useful precedent was set that helped kings boost their foreign armies. Sometimes men did not wait to be drafted into the growing armies, but instead volunteered. These soldiers joined up for various reasons— some wanted to escape poverty or the hardships of village life; others sought adventure. Martin Guerre, described in the Biography, was one such villager; he volunteered for the wars probably to escape the responsibilities of family life.

Not surprisingly, armies made up of poorly paid mercenaries, conscripts, and volunteers brought new problems to the art of making war. Officers repeatedly complained of soldiers' lack of discipline, and they imposed drilling and strict penalties for disobedience. Military leaders developed other strategies as well to manage their expanding forces. The Spanish evolved a complex military administration, which included the first battlefield hospitals. The Dutch introduced standardized-caliber weapons to help solve the problem of supplying larger numbers of infantrymen. Feeding and outfitting armies were still no easy matter, however. Wives, children, prostitutes, and servants trailed behind the lines to take advantage of the regular pay that the armies offered their men. These followers also needed to eat, of course, and at times they plundered the countryside through which the army moved.

Modernized warfare carried a high price. Heavy artillery was especially costly for both offensive and defensive forces. Not only did armies have to spend valuable currency to equip their armies with cannons, but rulers had to rebuild cities into massive fortresses with forts and gun emplacements to guard against opposing artillery. The new warfare also required larger navies, and ships, too, were expensive. Between 1542 and 1550, England spent more than twice its royal revenue on military campaigns. Other European powers also bankrupted themselves on these incessant wars. For example, between 1520 and 1532, Charles V borrowed an astounding 5.4 million gold coins from rich merchants to pay his troops— still, he could not compensate them completely.

FIGURE 11.2 Pieter Brueghel the Elder, *The Cripples,* 1568
This painting shows the tragic reality of modern warfare. Many combatants lost their limbs to gunfire and were relegated to a life of poverty.

At his death, Francis I owed bankers one full year's income of all the crown lands.

Winners and Losers

Kings were seldom able to deliver a decisive victory in this seemingly endless warfare, and small victories were soon avenged. Therefore, very few combatants "won" these military contests or profited at all. However, some individuals were able to gain a huge profit. Bankers who lent money to kings recklessly supplying ever-larger armies struck it rich. Guns and ammunition manufacturers, especially in the Netherlands, also profited hugely.

Overall, however, losers vastly outnumbered winners in these wars. As armies ballooned, so did casualties. With the increasing use of bullets and gunpowder, the nature of combat injuries also changed. In the Middle Ages, battlefield surgeons had been skilled at treating sword injuries; in the sixteenth century, | Casualties of war surgeons more often had to amputate limbs crushed by artillery shells (as happened to Martin Guerre; see the Biography). As one soldier wrote of the new guns: "Would to God that this unhappy weapon had never been invented." In **Figure 11.2,** a painting by the Dutch artist Pieter Brueghel the Elder (ca. 1525–1569), the wounded men's artificial limbs are depicted as particularly short. In this way, Brueghel emphasized the loss and disability that came with amputation. To survive, many legless or armless veterans resorted to begging in the towns and villages of Europe.

BIOGRAPHY

Martin Guerre
(1524–1594)

In 1527, a peasant family moved from their village in the Basque country, on the border between France and Spain, to a village in southern France. The Guerre family prospered in their new home and by the time their young son, Martin, was fourteen, his parents had contracted a promising marriage for him with the daughter of a relatively well-to-do peasant family nearby.

Peasant, Soldier, and Reluctant Family Man

Martin and his new bride, Bertrande, spent their wedding night in the Guerre household, where neighbor women gave them a heavily seasoned drink designed to stimulate their ardor and fertility. The potion failed. Martin remained impotent for eight years, while the village discussed whether he was under a spell and teased him mercilessly for not fulfilling his duty. Finally, an old woman told the young couple how to lift the spell through special prayers and cakes. The marriage was consummated, and Bertrande became pregnant immediately and bore a son. Martin, however, was not a happy young man. After quarreling with his father one day in 1548, the 24-year-old fled the village and was not heard from for years.

Martin traveled to Spain, where he served in the Spanish army in Flanders and France. During the fighting, he was shot in the leg; the limb then had to be amputated. Still, he sent no word to his village. In his absence, his parents died. Bertrande remained under the care of Martin's uncle Pierre as she raised their son and awaited the return of her husband.

Then, in 1556, a man strolled into the village and claimed to be Martin Guerre. He was actually an impostor, Arnaud du Tilh, who had left his own French village after a dissolute youth and joined the Spanish army fighting in Flanders. He had met Martin and learned about his life and marriage. Now, when Arnaud was ready to settle down into a new life, Martin's village seemed to offer that opportunity.

The village welcomed Arnaud as the lost Martin, and Bertrande took him in as her husband. If she had doubts about the newly passionate "Martin," she apparently set them aside. The couple harmoniously lived together for three years, during which Bertrande gave birth to two daughters.

Soon dissension arose in the village as Protestant ideas began to spread through the region. Bertrande's parents became Protestant, and Arnaud may have been drawn to Protestant ideas as well. As in so many villages throughout Europe, a split in religion caused tensions in previously unified villages, and these religious ideas may have exacerbated the suspicions that were growing in Bertrande's family. Arnaud and Martin's uncle increasingly began to quarrel over land and ideas, which caused Pierre to question Arnaud's very identity. Finally, Pierre had Arnaud arrested and charged him with impersonating his nephew. At Arnaud's trial, hundreds of villagers testified for both sides. Some were certain that Arnaud was the real Martin; others felt equally convinced that he was not. Most of them simply could not decide. The case went to appellate court, where the legal tide seemed about to turn in Arnaud's favor. However, one day during the appeal proceedings, the real Martin Guerre, outfitted with crutches and a peg leg, suddenly limped into the courtroom to reclaim his identity and his family.

The impostor was condemned to death, and Bertrande was judged an innocent victim of Arnaud's duplicity and returned to her husband. Over the coming years, Martin and Bertrande had two more sons. The historical records reveal nothing about Bertrande's response to Martin's return. In 1594, Martin died.

This extraordinary case was recorded by a contemporary witness, Jean de Coras, who was fascinated by the motivations of the various parties. Coras's account was widely circulated throughout France, although the author did not live long enough to enjoy the fame. The Protestant Coras was killed in the French wars of religion—a few months after the Saint Bartholomew's Day Massacre in 1572. Villagers related the tale of the impersonation of Martin Guerre for centuries.

Connecting People & Society

1. What does this biography tell you about how foreign wars disrupted families?

2. What does it reveal about changing religious ideas?

3. How does this life demonstrate the continuing belief in magic?

The wars of this period also contributed to inflation and ruined harvests, both of which tormented even noncombatants. Horrified contemporary witnesses repeatedly described the legions of poor, starving civilians who wandered the landscape in search of food and died along the way. One French writer told of "some thousands of poor people, . . . subdued like skeletons, the majority leaning on crutches and dragging themselves along as best they could to ask for a piece of bread." People weakened by hunger and traveling through the countryside also fell prey to all manner of diseases. In the sixteenth century, outbreaks of plague, typhoid fever, typhus, smallpox, and influenza took a terrible toll.

The Habsburg-Valois Wars, 1521–1544

All these costs of making war still did not deter kings from their drive for land and power, and the city-states of Italy—where both Francis I and Charles V had dynastic claims—became the battlefield. Thus began the Habsburg-Valois Wars, named after the ruling houses of Austria and France. These wars were fought sporadically for about twenty-five years.

The wars devastated the Italian city-states, demonstrating that only large states could successfully field large-enough armies for the new warfare. Charles also learned a hazard in using mercenary troops, for in 1527 the emperor was unable to pay them, and his enraged armies stormed Rome in search of booty to cover their pay.

Weary imperialists

Neither Charles nor Francis could win a decisive victory, so the two men finally negotiated a peace in 1544, and by its terms, Francis agreed to renounce his claim on Italy. Charles, too, wearied by all his problems, and in ill health, troubled by gout, decided to give up his imperial ambitions. He abdicated his various thrones between 1555 and 1556 and split his extensive holdings. He bestowed his Austrian and German lands on his brother Ferdinand I (r. 1558–1564) and the Low Countries, Spain, and Naples on his son Philip II (r. 1556–1598). Weary and disheartened, the ailing Charles V retired to a palace in Spain, where he died two years later. From this point on, these two branches of the Habsburg family went their separate ways.

During the wars, the kings had been willing to ally with unlikely partners. Sometimes Francis sought help from the Turks against Charles, and at times both Catholic kings courted critics of the church—"Lutherans"—to help against the other's Catholic forces. However, the treaty that ended the war attempted to present the Catholic kings as a united front against religious diversity that had flourished in their lands. Charles and Francis agreed to focus their energies on defeating "Muslims and Lutherans" who were threatening the Christian world. The Muslims had been a traditional enemy, but who were these Lutherans who appeared in the sixteenth century and who by 1544 seemed such a threat to the Christian kings?

A TIDE OF RELIGIOUS REFORM

The powerful medieval Christian church had called itself "Catholic," which meant "universal." In the hands of reformers, however, "Catholic" began to mean the traditional church, which even in the Middle Ages had come under criticism. Medieval critics had questioned some of the beliefs and practices of the church—its power, its wealth, and its insistence on obedience to the pope as necessary for spiritual salvation. The last point was central, because from the beginning, Christians had focused on salvation—everything from the best way to worship God to getting into heaven after death. As the sixteenth century opened, criticism began to intensify and many people wondered if their salvation was in good hands.

The Best Path to Salvation?

The church had promised Christians that the path to salvation lay in the hierarchy of the church and its sacramental system, which offered grace to the faithful through the seven **sacraments.** To further confirm this, the Fourth Lateran Council in 1215 (described in Chapter 8) had declared that there was no salvation outside the church. Churchmen also promised that the faithful would be supported by the community of Christians, including the Virgin Mary, all the saints, and the congregations on earth. No Catholic believer, the church claimed, would have to face God alone in the afterlife.

A new popular piety and personal mysticism, along with the spread of Renaissance ideas of individualism, began to raise questions about this path to salvation. Catholicism had emphasized the need for an ordained priest—a "father confessor"—to hear one's confession and offer absolution. This new sensibility of popular piety allowed individuals seeking God to seek Him directly through prayer, breaking the chain of mediators that had marked the Catholic church. Many men and women who called themselves the Brethren of the Common Life tried to create a devout personal relationship between themselves and Christ, to supplement the complex Catholic theology. This style of popular religion was called the ***devotio moderna*** (modern devotion), and it influenced many subsequent believers.

One pious follower of the *devotio moderna*, Thomas à Kempis (1380–1471), is reputed to be the author of the best articulation of their ideas, in *The Imitation of Christ* (1425). In this profoundly influential text, Thomas argued that personal piety and ethics were as important as religious dogma. In Thomas's view, individuals could work toward salvation by focusing on their own spiritual growth, and many agreed passionately with Thomas's assertion "Blessed is the soul which hears the Lord speak within it and receives consolation from his mouth." Many longed for this kind of personal contact with God that, as Thomas pointed out, would make society as a whole more spiritual. As devoted Christians began to experiment with new forms of a Christian life, intellectuals began to contemplate some of the more complicated aspects of Christian thought.

Desiderius Erasmus: "Prince of Humanists"

As humanism spread to northern Europe, scholars applied the techniques of humanist education to Christian thought. The greatest Christian humanist was Desiderius Erasmus (1466–1536), who became known as the "Prince of the Humanists." Erasmus (shown in the chapter-opening painting on page 342) knew firsthand that some elements of the church needed reform, because he was born in Holland as the illegitimate son of a supposedly celibate priest. He studied at a school that was the center of the Brethren of the Common Life and grew up imbued with the new devotion that called for people to approach God directly in their hearts. Erasmus became a priest and went to study in a traditional university in Paris, which he hated. He dropped out of school, complaining that the university offered "theology as stale as their eggs."

The young priest then went to England, where his intellect was awakened by the humanists in Henry VIII's London. Erasmus became great friends with Thomas More and began a course of study based on a humanist curriculum. His interests remained religious, however, and he turned the humanist emphasis on original texts to biblical studies. He learned Greek so he could immerse himself in the mental world of the New Testament, and like the Italian humanists, he insisted that language study had to be the starting point for any education: "Our first care must be to learn the three languages, Latin, Greek, and Hebrew, for it is plain that the mystery of all scripture is revealed in them." In this statement, we can see the literary work of the humanists applied to the highest Christian purpose.

Erasmus's greatest contribution to the intellectual life of the West was his critical edition of the New Testament. To approach this, Erasmus rejected the officially accepted version of the Bible—Jerome's (ca. 340–420) Latin translation, called the Vulgate—and returned to the Greek and Hebrew texts to create a new rendition. Erasmus even corrected portions of the Vulgate, and his edition became the basis for later translations of the Bible.

The humanist also criticized corruption in the church in many writings. For example, he wrote a satire, *Julius Excluded from Heaven* (1517), in which he showed the famous Renaissance warrior-pope Julius II (see Chapter 10) unable to enter heaven, even though popes had always

Religious satires claimed to hold its keys. His most famous satire, however, was *The Praise of Folly* (1511), in which he used his sharp wit to promote a greater spirituality in religion. In this book, his character, Folly, catalogs vices and in the process makes fun of the author himself, his friends, and the follies of everyday life. His attacks also probed deeply into many of the religious practices of the day, and as readers laughed at his attacks on people who "worshiped" the Virgin Mary over her son and popes who did not live like Jesus, their ideas on worship itself began to change.

Perhaps even more than his disappointment at church corruption, it was his humanist love of education that led him to propose a radically different approach to Christian life. Erasmus argued that Christians should read the Bible directly, rather than relying on priests to interpret it for them: "I would that even the lowliest women read the Gospels and the Pauline Epistles. And I would that they were translated into all languages." A scholar to the core, Erasmus did not advocate separation from the church, but a contemporary of his recognized the long-term impact of the humanist's thought, saying that "Erasmus laid the egg Luther hatched." Revolution in religious thinking had been planted, and the letters in Document 11.1 reveal the anger that served as fertile ground.

Luther's Revolution

Martin Luther (1483–1546), the intelligent son of an upwardly mobile family in Germany, was an improbable revolutionary. His father, a successful mine owner, expected him to further the family fortune by becoming a lawyer, but young Luther's life took a dramatically different turn. During a fierce thunderstorm, Luther was struck to the ground by a bolt of lightning. Frightened, Luther cried out to Saint Anne (the Virgin Mary's mother): "Help me and I will become a monk." He survived the storm and fulfilled his vow (much to his father's initial disapproval). Luther threw himself into his new calling—becoming a monk, priest, and doctor of theology—but he remained plagued with a deep sense of sin and a deep fear of damnation. He even believed he actually saw the devil during the torments of his conscience.

For all Luther's study, prayer, and attempts to live a Christian life, he still did not believe he could ever be worthy of salvation. Even the church's promise of grace in the sacraments and "good works" of the church brought him no comfort. Finally, he found peace in the Bible, especially its statement that the "just shall live by his faith" (Rom. 1:17). Luther interpreted this statement as meaning that people were saved only through God's mercy, not through their own efforts to live as good Christians. Faith alone—not ritual—would save their souls. For Luther, Christ's sacrifice had been complete and for all time, so humans did not have to do anything else for their own salvation. This central point of Luther's belief is called "**justification by faith.**"

Inflamed by his newfound belief, Luther challenged church doctrine over the issue of **indulgences.** Through the Middle Ages, the Catholic Church had

Germans Rage Against Papal Exploitation

These two documents, written in 1480 and 1503, reveal that some in Germany raged against what they saw as exploitation of Germans by a distant pope. These documents show that Luther's critique launched in 1517 would find fertile soil.

1. Critique of Church Wealth, ca. 1480. Author anonymous.

It is as clear as day that by means of smooth and crafty words the clergy have deprived us of our rightful possessions. For they blinded the eyes of our forefathers, and persuaded them to buy the kingdom of heaven with their lands and possessions. If you priests give the poor and the chosen children of God their paternal inheritance, which before God you owe them, God will perhaps grant you such grace that you will know yourselves. But so long as you spend your money on your dear harlots and profligates, instead of upon the children of God, you may be sure that God will reward you according to your merits. For you have angered and overburdened all the people of the empire. The time is coming when your possessions will be seized and divided as if they were the possessions of an enemy. As you have oppressed the people, they will rise up against you so that you will not know where to find a place to stay.

2. Against Abuses in Indulgences, Myconius, 1512

Anno 1512. Tetzel gained by his preaching in Germany an immense sum of money which he sent to Rome. A very large sum was collected at the new mining works at St. Annaberg, where I heard him for two years. It is incredible what this ignorant and impudent monk used to say. . . . He declared that if they contributed readily and bought grace and indulgence, all the hills of St. Annaberg would become pure massive silver. Also, that, as soon as the coin clinked in the chest, the soul for whom the money was paid would go straight to heaven. . . . The indulgence was so highly prized that when the agent came to a city the bull was carried on a satin or gold cloth, and all the priests and monks, the town council, schoolmaster, scholars, men, women, girls and children went out in procession to meet it with banners, candles, and songs. All the bells were rung and organs played. He was conducted into the church, a red cross was erected in the center of the church, and the pope's banner displayed. . . .

SOURCE: Oliver J. Thatcher and Edgar H. McNeal, *A Source Book for Mediaeval History* (New York: Charles Scribner's Sons, 1905), pp. 336–340.

Analyze the Document

1. What are the main criticisms of the church expressed in these documents?

2. How will the angry rhetorical style of the documents contribute to the coming of the Reformation? Does the rhetoric make it increasingly difficult to compromise? Explain.

---

developed a complex understanding of how people are forgiven for their sins, including confession, penance, and absolution. As part of **[Attack on indulgences]** this process, churchmen claimed that people had to perform certain "works"—like prayers, fastings, pilgrimages, or similar activities—to receive forgiveness for their sins. If people died before completing full repentance for their transgressions, they could expect to suffer for them in **purgatory** before they could enter heaven, and late-medieval people had come to believe it would be virtually impossible for anyone to do full penance for their sins before death.

In the Middle Ages, the pope had begun to alleviate some people's fears by offering an "indulgence," a remission of the need to do penance for sins. The pope claimed to control a "treasury of merit"—an infinite supply of good works that had been done by the saints and the Virgin Mary from which he could draw to remit sins. These remissions came in the form of "indulgences," documents that popes gave people in return for certain pious acts. Dating from the fourteenth century, a pious act might be a contribution of money to the church.

In 1517, Pope Leo X had issued a special indulgence to finance the construction of a new St. Peter's Church in Rome that would replace an old, smaller one. Johann Tetzel, a well-known Dominican friar, appeared to sell these indulgences to rich and poor alike in Germany and sent the money to Leo. Tetzel was reputed to have used the crude words: "As soon as the coin in the coffer rings, the soul from purgatory springs." Luther, horrified by this apparent trafficking in God's grace, wrote a series of statements decrying the selling of these indulgences and protesting the flow of money from Germany to Rome.

Tradition says that Luther tacked his list of arguments—the Ninety-five Theses—to the door of the church in Wittenberg, but he may well have simply sent it to his bishop. It seems that Luther merely wanted to engage a scholarly debate on the subject, but too many people **[Ninety-five Theses]** were profoundly interested in this topic. The inflammatory theses were soon translated into German and circulated even more widely than if they had been publicly posted on the church doors—they spread rapidly throughout Germany and beyond by way of the printing press. Their clearly drawn arguments and the passion that lay beneath them appealed to many intellectuals who criticized the church and to Germans who had begun to resent German money going to Italy. With Luther's strong words "It is foolish to think that papal indulgences . . . can absolve a man," the battle lines were drawn.

Luther's commitment to individual conscience over institutional obedience catalyzed major changes in his life that in turn shaped the emergence of the reformed church. It is somewhat ironic that within a generation, reformers would be enforcing institutional obedience with as much enthusiasm as the Catholics ever had. However, Luther himself pursued the logical consequences of his ideas. In Luther's new understanding, the monastic life made no religious sense; in the presence of God's grace, there was no need for heroic renunciations. Therefore, he left the monastery and married Katherina von Bora, a former nun, and wrote influential works on Christian marriage. He also composed moving hymns that transformed religious services. Furthermore, because he came to his understanding of religion through reading the Bible, he believed that it should be accessible to everyone, so he translated it into German. Indeed, this translation became his most influential legacy. Not only did it make the Bible available to an even wider group of readers; it also, through its popularity, helped shape the form of the developing German language.

Protestant Religious Ideas

Luther articulated a core of beliefs that subsequent religious groups would share, even as they departed from "Lutheranism." Christian churches (except the Roman Catholic and Eastern Orthodox) that share these beliefs today are called **Protestant.** The word derives from the protest of some German princes at the Diet (assembly) of Speier in 1529. Over the objection of the Lutheran princes, that body decided to protect the Catholic Church's right to offer services in Lutheran lands while denying the same privilege to Lutherans in Catholic lands. The name "Protestant" remained long after the issue had been resolved.

For Luther and subsequent Protestant reformers, at the heart of religious belief lay a faith in God's mercy that transcended the need for any good works. The Protestants thus conceived of a "priesthood of all believers," in which women and men were responsible for their own salvation. There was no need for an ordained priesthood to convey grace to believers by performing the sacraments.

Priesthood of all believers

Church leaders (whom Protestants called ministers, pastors, or preachers) could teach, preach, and guide Christian followers, but they could not help them achieve salvation. Each person stood alone before God throughout his or her life, and on judgment day prayers to saints and to the Virgin Mary were no more helpful than prayers offered by any other Christian. When people's spiritual quests combined with the Renaissance sense of individualism, it changed even the path to God.

With their emphasis on the individual's relationship to God, Protestants rejected many of the elements that had characterized the medieval church. No longer were the faithful to venerate saints or the Virgin Mary, so many claimed the relics of saints and martyrs that filled the churches of Europe were worthless. Protestant faithful would not become pilgrims traveling to the great cathedrals and saints' shrines in search of blessings or miracles. Indeed, the statues of the saints and other icons seemed to many Protestants to promote idolatry, and there was periodic Protestant **iconoclasm,** or destroying of the sacred images in the churches. (See **Figure 11.4.**)

Just as Protestants downplayed the importance of the priesthood and the intercession of saints, they restricted the significance and number of the sacraments. In the Middle Ages, Catholics had identified seven sacraments important for salvation (including marriage and the last rites at death). Most (but not all) Protestant reformers accepted only two sacraments—baptism and the Eucharist (the celebration of Christ's Last Supper before his Crucifixion). Furthermore, they rejected **transubstantiation,** which said that the bread and wine offered up at mass were turned into the actual body and blood of Christ—a transformation that only an ordained priest could perform. Although Protestants may have rejected transubstantiation, they held various views on how Christ was present in the Eucharist, but because the bread and wine were not transformed, any believer could celebrate the Last Supper. As other Protestant groups branched off from Luther's initial thinking, they would emphasize some points of this theology over others. However, all of them shared the same basic principles: salvation by faith, not works; the Bible as the sole authority; and a "priesthood" made up of all believers.

Sacraments

These ideas spread rapidly in large part because they offered a simple and elegant answer to the question that had plagued so many: "How do I know I am saved?" Printing presses produced pamphlets and flyers offering these notions to the literate of towns and manors, and popular preachers told peasants in villages about Luther's challenge. Luther's seeds of revolution disseminated widely and found fertile soil.

The Reformed Church Takes Root in Germany

Luther's attack on tradition and hierarchy could not go unnoticed. In July 1519, at the Leipzig Debate, the Catholic theologian Johann Eck forced Luther to look at the logical consequences of his stand on indulgences and actually to deny the authority of popes and councils. After this turning point, Luther was more and more ready to make a full break with Rome. Finally, in 1521, Luther was called to appear before Charles V at the Diet of Worms to defend his views. Though confronted with over a thousand years of tradition, Luther nevertheless adhered to his understanding of scripture, and he reputedly made the famous reply: "To go against conscience is neither right nor safe. Here I stand, I cannot do otherwise." During the Middle Ages, many men and women who had similarly stood by their beliefs had been executed for their stance. The political situation in Germany in the sixteenth century saved Luther from this fate—and turned his personal stance into a religious revolution.

Under pressure from Charles V to recant, Luther sought and received the protection of his prince, the powerful Frederick the Wise of Saxony. **Figure 11.3** shows Frederick surrounded by Protestant reformers under his protection. Frederick, at the center of the image, has an imposing presence, with his gold chains and richly embroidered clothing. The reformers gather behind him, Martin Luther at the prince's right arm. This painting suggests the degree to which the Reformation drew strength from the support of powerful local leaders.

In addition to reasons of conscience, German princes had other motives for supporting Luther's ideas. The reformer's call to stop sending German money to Rome suited princes who felt the sharp sting of inflation. Princes could also benefit from confiscating wealthy Catholic properties (like churches and monasteries) in the name of religion. Luther's call for a break with Rome also appealed to a growing sense of German nationalism as distinct from the international Christendom represented by the Catholic Church. Some princes may have hoped that any weakening of the pope's authority would also diminish the power of the Holy Roman Emperor Charles V, whose authority derived in part from papal support. A weakened emperor meant more opportunities for the princes to bolster their own power.

Many poor, too, rallied to Luther's banner of religious reform, and this support took a particularly violent form in Germany. Spurred on by fiery preachers, peasants who suffered from hunger, inflation, and skyrocketing manorial dues made Luther's attack on religious abuses part of their revolutionary program. In 1524, German peasants circulated the Twelve

Peasants' war

FIGURE 11.3 Lucas Cranach the Younger, *Martin Luther and the Wittenberg Reformers,* sixteenth century   The Reformation in Germany was not only a product of the skill and piety of Martin Luther, shown on the left. The movement and its leaders also drew strength from the protection and patronage of the powerful Prince Frederick the Wise of Saxony, center.

Articles, in which they demanded such things as a reduction of manorial dues and services and preservation of their rights to use meadows and woods. These wants dealt directly with the peasants' concerns, but they couched their demands in references to scripture—a direct consequence of Luther's call for people to conduct their lives in accordance with their biblical readings. The Twelve Articles claimed to "give a Christian reason for the disobedience or even the revolt of the entire peasantry" and further promised "[if any of] the articles here set forth should not be in agreement with the word of God . . . we will willingly recede from [it]." This widely circulated pamphlet linked Protestant theology directly with revolution, and Germany erupted.

In 1524, a violent peasant war broke out. As the peasants took up arms and stormed manor houses, they called for support from Luther's religious reformers. However, Luther was no John Ball (the religious leader who had led the peasant revolt in England in 1381). He advocated religious reform, not social revolution, for he believed the Bible called for people to obey secular rulers. Appalled by the violence in the countryside, Luther wrote a treatise called "Against the Robbing and Murdering Hordes of Peasants," in which he reprimanded peasants for defying legitimate government. He also urged those in power to "smite, slay and stab" rebellious peasants, but the nobility needed no urging from Luther to protect their privileges. The rebellion was brutally suppressed—more than 100,000 peasants were killed. The princes appreciated Luther's support of their repression and judged the movement perfectly consistent with their political needs. The Protestant Reformation thus found a warm welcome in the courts of many German princes.

By the time Charles V could turn his attention from the wars in Italy in the west and the Turkish threat in the east back to his German lands, the reformed church had taken firm root. At this point, Charles was in no position to uproot Lutheranism, which was supported by many of the great princes of the land. Furthermore, Charles's armies contained many Lutherans—as early as 1527, men among the rioting troops in Rome purportedly were calling for a silk rope to hang the pope. The emperor could not govern any longer without some accommodation.

Charles first tried to demand that his subjects come together under one religion. In 1530, he commanded all Lutherans to return to Catholicism or be arrested, but it was too late. Too many princes were willing to form a military alliance rather than obey. Then Charles tried compromise. In the 1540s, he encouraged talks between Lutherans and Catholics about the possibility of reconciliation, but these failed as well. By the 1550s, Lutheranism had captured about half the population of the empire.

In 1555, Charles's successor, Ferdinand, met with the German princes to negotiate a compromise to settle the religious turmoil. The resulting Peace of Augsburg established the Lutheran Church as a legitimate alternative to Catholicism in

Peace of Augsburg

Germany. By this treaty, each prince defined his principality as either Catholic or Lutheran. This compromise is known by the Latin phrase *cuius regio, eius religio,* which means "who rules determines the religion." Residents of any principality who did not agree with their prince's religious decision were free to move to a more congenial location. The Catholic emperor Ferdinand, the pope, and many churchmen did not like this concession to Lutheranism, which split the unity of the Christian church. However, they had no choice but to accept the compromise forced by the strong German princes.

The Augsburg treaty opened the door for the Reformation to fragment Christian Europe into a complex mix of different Christian sects. In addition, other monarchs and princes besides those in Germany saw the advantage in separating from Rome. Scandinavian kings, for instance, followed the example of German princes in supporting Lutheranism. These conversions left many problems unsolved—what about groups other than Lutherans? What about dissenting voices within either Catholic or Protestant principalities? What was the relationship between the state and religion? While these questions smoldered, the fire of religious reform continued to spread through Europe.

Bringing Reform to the States in Switzerland

While Luther's call for reform was the first to gain a large audience, his was not a solitary voice. Shortly after Luther's challenge, reformers in Switzerland successfully challenged old religious ideas. Switzerland consisted of a loose confederation of states (called cantons) in which many residents were ready for change, and the very independence of the cantons facilitated acceptance of new religious ideas. In addition, many of the young men from the Swiss cantons served as mercenaries in the seemingly insatiable armies of Europe, and service generated a growing disdain for the established order. Just as in Germany, dissatisfaction and growing national spirit combined with a desire for religious reform.

The first leader of the Reformation in Switzerland was Ulrich Zwingli (1484–1531), who lived in the northern canton of Zurich. Zwingli had been strongly influenced by   Zwingli   Erasmus's writings, and when he served as a chaplain with Swiss mercenaries, his longing for religious reform became joined with a desire to remove the Swiss confederation from the horrible wars.

In 1519 (a mere two years after Luther's challenge with his Ninety-five Theses), Zwingli became the priest of the main church in Zurich, and from there he began his own attack on traditional church practices. He believed Christians should practice only those things found in scripture, so his church in Zurich rejected such things as the veneration of saints, pilgrimages, purgatory, clerical celibacy, and most of the sacraments. In 1523, the city government in Zurich approved Zwingli's reforms, and Zurich became a Protestant city.

Zwingli and Luther shared many ideas, but would Protestants join together and form one church to oppose Catholicism? One German prince—Philip of Hesse—saw the advantages of consolidation and brought Luther and Zwingli together in 1529 at a meeting in Marburg to try to bring about an alliance. Although the two reformers agreed on virtually all points of doctrine, the meeting fell apart over their respective understanding of the nature of Christ's presence in the celebration of the Eucharist. Zwingli insisted the remembrance was symbolic, whereas Luther insisted that Christ's body was present as well as his spirit. As neither man could compromise with his conscience, there would be no united Protestant church or state. The new reformed churches would go their separate ways.

Just as in Germany, Protestantism came to the Swiss cantons with violence. In 1529, civil wars broke out between Protestant and Catholic cantons, and Zwingli himself died on the battlefield in 1531. The cantons reached a resolution similar to that of the later Peace of Augsburg in Germany—each canton would determine its own religion. However, the fires of reform stirred in more consciences and continued to spread, bringing both more hope and more violence.

Anabaptists: The Radical Reformers

The reforms of Luther and Zwingli appealed to many people but were implemented by princes or urban governments. However, many people saw power and religion as incompatible. New groups took a more radical turn in their efforts to reform the church and to keep it untainted by politics, and these reformers seemed threatening even to Protestants like Lutherans and Swiss reformers. Most members of these sects were referred to by their opponents as Anabaptists, meaning "rebaptizers" (although many of them preferred to be called simply Baptists), because they believed baptism should be reserved for adults, who could make a conscious choice to receive the grace of the sacrament. The radical sects drew heavily from peasants and artisans, especially those suffering from poverty and the relentless warfare of the period.

Confrontation between Anabaptists and the rest of society stemmed mainly from the Anabaptists' views on the relationship between church and state. Many radical reformers advocated a complete separation of these two institutions. They even argued that the "saved" (or the "elect") should not participate in government (including serving in the armies that were vigorously recruiting in the villages). One especially pacifist form of Anabaptism emerged in the Netherlands, developed by Menno Simons (1496–1561). Simons led his followers, the Mennonites, into Germany and Poland.

| Church vs. state |

While most Anabaptist groups were pacifists, others became revolutionaries fighting for what they believed was a religious cause—the ushering in of a biblically promised age of peace and prosperity during which the "meek shall inherit the earth." Some saw the horrors of war and famine in the sixteenth century as the expected biblical disasters and chose to take up arms to help fight against those who had previously oppressed the poor. In Germany in 1534, a fiery preacher named Melchior established a sect (called the Melchiorites) that gained political control of their city of Münster. They burned all books but the Bible, abolished private property, and introduced polygamy as they settled down to await the expected second coming of Christ. Lutherans and Catholics alike believed this was a threat to society, so they captured the city and massacred the Melchiorites. Thereafter, the radicals were persecuted by Catholics and other Protestants alike.

| Radical reformers |

Calvinism and the Growing Middle Class

As we have seen, the Swiss cantons with their prosperous middle class had voiced religious longings and aspirations under the guidance of Zwingli. In the mid-sixteenth century, another voice also appealed to many of these well-to-do people in cities throughout Europe. Many people found intellectual and spiritual satisfaction in the teachings of the brilliant French scholar John Calvin (1509–1564). While preparing for a career in law, Calvin had studied many humanist writings, and in about 1533, Calvin read some of Martin Luther's works. He experienced a profound calling to Protestant theology, as he said: "God by a sudden conversion subdued and brought my mind to a teachable frame." The new reformer soon experienced pressure from royal authorities who in the reign of Francis I began a periodic suppression of reformers. Calvin had to flee France to avoid persecution and found a safe haven in the Swiss city of Geneva, where he published the first edition of his masterwork, *The Institutes of the Christian Religion* (1536).

What was the nature of Calvin's vision that appealed particularly to the hardworking and often prosperous middle classes? Calvin accepted the basic elements of Protestant belief that Luther had articulated, but he added his own emphasis. Whereas Luther had focused on salvation as the goal of human struggle, Calvin urged people to recognize the majesty, power, and justice of God. Perhaps Calvin's greatest contribution to Reformation thought was to redirect theological speculation from individual salvation to a larger question of humans' place in the universe.

When he turned to the question of salvation, Calvin again emphasized the power of God, shown in **predestination,** the belief that God preordained who would be saved or damned, even before a person was born. Calvin explained that if God were *only* just, everyone would be damned, for all people were sinful.

| Predestination |

DOCUMENT 11.2

Marie Dentière Defends Reformation Women's Rights

In 1539, Marie Dentière (ca. 1495–1561) wrote a letter to Queen Marguerite of Navarre in which she defends the right of women to be active participants in the reformed churches. Selections from that letter appear below. Marie had been an abbess who left her monastery in the 1520s to come to Geneva and help bring about the Calvinist reform there. Within a few years, even the reformers in Geneva suppressed Dentière's work because it was written by a woman.

My very honored lady, since the true lovers of truth desire to know and understand how they ought to live in these very dangerous times, so too we women ought to know how to flee and to avoid all errors, heresies, and false doctrines, such as those of false Christians, Turks, infidels or others suspect in doctrine, as your writings have already very well demonstrated. . . .

I have not only wished, my lady, to write this letter for you but also to give courage to other women held in captivity, so that they will not fear exile from their countries, relatives, and friends, like I was, for the word of God. And principally I write for the poor little women, who desire to know and understand the truth; those who do not know which path, which way they ought to take, so that in the future they are not so tormented and afflicted within themselves, but rather they will rejoice, be consoled, and be moved to follow the truth, which is

the Gospel of Jesus Christ. And also [I write] to give courage to my little daughter, your god-daughter, to give the printers a small Hebrew grammar that she has written in French for the use and benefit of other little girls. . . . Because as you well know, the female sex is more shameful than the other, and not without reason. For until now, the scriptures have been hidden from them and no one dared say a word [about it], and it seemed that women should neither read nor hear anything of holy letters, which is the principal reason, my lady, that moved me to write to you, hoping in God that in the future women will no longer be so scorned as in the past. Because from day to day God changes the heart of his people for the better, which, I pray, will soon be so throughout the land. . . .

Not only would some slanderers and adversaries of the truth want to accuse us of too great audacity and boldness, but also some of the faithful say that women are too bold to write to one another about holy scripture. To them one can allowably respond that all those who have written and who have been named in holy scripture are not judged to be too bold, since several [women] are named and praised in holy scripture as much for their good morals, actions, behavior, and examples as for their faith and doctrine. . . .

Although there has been some imperfection in all women, nevertheless men have not been exempt from

it. Why is it so necessary to criticize women, seeing that a woman never sold or betrayed Jesus, but a man named Judas. Who are the ones, I ask you, who have invented and fabricated so many ceremonies, heresies, and false doctrines on earth, if not men? And the poor women have been seduced by them. Never was a woman found to be a false prophet, although they have been fooled by them. By this I do not wish to excuse the great malice of some women, which can surpass all measure, but there is no reason to make a general rule of it without any exception as some do daily. . . .

Therefore, if God has given grace to some good women, revealing something good and holy to them through his holy scriptures, will they dare not write, tell, or declare it to one another for the sake of the slanderers of the truth? Ah, it would be too impudent to wish to hinder them, and it would be too foolish to hide the talent that God has given us. He gives us grace to persevere until the end. Amen.

SOURCE: Marie Dentière, "A Very Useful Letter written and composed by a Christian woman from Tournai, sent to the Queen of Navarre, sister of the King of France, Against the Turks, Jews, Infidels, False Christians, Anabaptists, and Lutherans (Geneva, 1539)," trans. and ed. Elisabeth Wengler.

Analyze the Document

1. What does Marie say was the purpose of her writing? Notice she gives several reasons.

2. What arguments does she marshal in favor of women's studying and preaching?

3. Are her arguments consistent with the theology of the reformers?

4. Why do you think her writings were suppressed?

However, God tempered his justice with mercy, reaching down into the flames of damnation and plucking some souls out to share salvation. Calvin called these souls that were predestined to be saved the elect; the rest would experience eternal damnation. Many believers who, like Luther, felt that humans could do nothing to earn their salvation found comfort in the concept of predestination. Although predestination

was at the core of Calvin's beliefs, he never stressed it as much as his followers in subsequent generations did.

Many people seeking new paths to God were drawn to Geneva to join the exciting religious movement there. One such spiritual seeker was an ex-nun, Marie Dentière, who with her new husband was in the forefront of the reform movement in Geneva. Document 11.2, a letter from Marie to Queen

Marguerite of Navarre, reveals a tension that arose as part of the Reformers' theology: If all were responsible for their own salvation, did that mean women could preach and be leaders in the movement? Calvin, like Luther before him, rejected the idea that women should be leaders, but Marie expressed the ideas of many women—before and after her—that they, too, should be educated and preach the word of God.

As Calvinism took hold, Geneva became a vibrant center for Calvinist missionary work. Between 1555 and 1562, Calvin dispersed 100 preachers to the far-flung corners of Europe. Calvin had impressive organizational abilities, and he laid out directions for organizing congregations that explained how believers could establish underground groups to adopt Calvinism even where civil authorities were hostile. These techniques worked. The Netherlands were particularly receptive to Calvinist thought. In addition, many French cities soon amassed substantial Calvinist minorities, called **Huguenots.** German cities, too, began attracting Calvinist minorities—a problem because the Peace of Augsburg recognized only Lutheranism and Catholicism as acceptable religions. The Scot John Knox (1514–1572) was dazzled by Calvin in Geneva and returned to Scotland, where he established Calvinism as the predominant form of Protestantism. Like Knox, others from the British Isles were drawn to the exciting ideas of the reformers.

Spread of Calvinism

Protestant reliance on individual conscience made believers uncomfortable with much of the religious art that had dominated Christian worship in the West. In addition, many Protestants believed that religious art smacked of idol worship, drained precious resources better used on the poor, or simply distracted worshipers from focusing on the word of God. These concerns caused believers in many regions to attack religious art. Most of the Reformation leaders disapproved of such violence, but nevertheless, much religious art was destroyed in Protestant countries. This iconoclasm is reminiscent of the eighth-century conflict that had destroyed so much art in the eastern Orthodox lands. (See Chapter 6.) The engraving in Figure 11.4 shows people destroying religious art in the Netherlands. Statues are tumbled and precious windows broken while soldiers are unable (or unwilling) to stop the violence.

As a second-generation Protestant, Calvin moved the Reformation forward in important ways. In his

FIGURE 11.4 Destroying Images, 1566 Calvinists believed that the images that graced the churches were idolatry. This illustration from a work published in 1568 by Franz Hogenberg shows people in the Netherlands destroying these images in a riot.

writings and his life, he worked to establish a positive definition of Protestantism, that is, not simply as "not Catholic." In doing so, he articulated many of the theological principles that would define all Protestant churches. The passion for individualism and religious innovation kept Calvin (and anyone else) from uniting the various protest movements, but his intellect and strong faith made him an able advocate for Protestant thought.

Henry VIII and the English Church

In England in the 1520s, men with Protestant sympathies gathered to discuss some of Luther's writings that had been smuggled in. Perhaps even more exciting to the reformers was William Tyndale's English translation of the New Testament, which began to circulate in England in 1526. Protestant sympathies were growing on the island, but they would bear fruit from the actions of an unlikely ally—the king himself.

Henry VIII (r. 1509–1547), the proud king who appeared in state at the Field of the Cloth of Gold, was not initially a reformer. In fact, he had written an attack against Martin Luther in 1521 called the *Defense of the Seven Sacraments*, and Pope Leo X awarded him the title Defender of the Faith for his support. (Ironically, Protestant English monarchs still retain this title.) Although many English people wanted religious reform and some felt a strong antipathy toward the pope, it did not seem as if their king would lead them in a break with Rome. But Henry's desperate need for a male heir changed all this.

Remembering the devastating Wars of the Roses (Chapter 9) that had brought his Tudor dynasty to power, Henry believed he needed a male heir to secure the succession. His wife of eighteen years, Catherine of Aragon, had failed to produce one. Henry began to believe that God disapproved of this marriage, for he had married the widow of his brother (a practice normally forbidden) and had received special permission from the pope to do so. Henry also had fallen in love with a beautiful and bright young woman, Anne Boleyn. Anne did not want to become another of the king's mistresses, so she held off his amorous advances, insisting on a promise of marriage; first, Henry needed an annulment from the pope to end his first marriage.

Seeking a male heir

Ordinarily, such royal annulments were easy to obtain because the popes had traditionally acquiesced to royal wishes. However, just as Charles V's absence from Germany in the Italian Habsburg-Valois Wars allowed Lutheranism to take hold, it also facilitated religious reform in England. Henry wanted his divorce in 1527, just as Charles V's troops were sacking Rome and virtually holding Pope Clement VII prisoner. The pope needed the goodwill of Charles to restore order and Henry's queen, Catherine, was Charles V's aunt. The pope dragged his feet in granting Henry his annulment.

In 1533, Anne Boleyn, persuaded that the king would marry her, became pregnant. Now Henry was running out of time for his annulment, for he wanted Anne's child to be born legitimate. Henry's two principal advisors—Thomas Cranmer, archbishop of Canterbury, and Thomas Cromwell—devised a way for Henry to get his annulment. Parliament passed an act making the archbishop of Canterbury the highest ecclesiastical official in England (cutting off the pope's authority). Then Thomas Cranmer ruled that Henry's marriage to Catherine was "null and void," so Henry was free to marry Anne. He did so, and three months later, much to the king's dismay, she gave birth to a girl, the future Queen Elizabeth. (Henry finally had a male heir by his third wife, after Anne was beheaded for adultery, but the king would eventually marry six women in his quest for heirs and personal happiness.)

Henry's annulment

Henry had gotten his annulment, but the force of religious reform he had unleashed continued its momentum. Parliament passed a number of measures designed to control the Catholic clergy and finally passed the Act of Supremacy (1534) that declared the king the supreme head of the Church of England. This break with the papacy established the Church of England as a separate church (which later was also called Protestant), but not everyone in England

Church of England

welcomed this major reform. The most notable dissenter was the humanist Thomas More (1478–1535) (see Chapter 10), whose conscience would not allow him to obey a secular ruler in matters of faith, and he refused to swear an oath acknowledging the king's ecclesiastical supremacy. More was beheaded for his dissent, and this man of high integrity died blessing the king who had been his great friend, saying: "I die the king's good servant, but God's first."

Henry's position toward the reformers vacillated throughout his life. He did not support all the Protestant religious ideas—for example, he reaffirmed transubstantiation, which all the Protestants rejected. In fact, he considered himself a Catholic, although not a "Roman" Catholic. However, the powerful king readily implemented Reformation ideas that enriched his coffers and weakened the power of the Catholic Church. He shared the reformers' rejection of the monastic life and dissolved all the monasteries in England, confiscating their extensive lands and wealth. The king's treasury bulged from the confiscations, and many English religious reformers were satisfied with his new policies. However, the Church of England (also called the Anglican Church) really became Protestant under the reign of Henry's son.

Henry's third wife, Jane Seymour, finally bore him a son, Edward, in 1537. However, the boy was sickly when he took the throne upon Henry's death in 1547. Edward VI (r. 1547–1553) was a bright youth who was fond of Protestant theology, but he was young. Because of Edward's age, England was in fact ruled by a council of regents who wanted to solidify Protestantism in England.

Edward VI

The painting in **Figure 11.5** shows the young king at the center of the portrait, with his dying father on the left. The composition reveals the difficulties faced by the rule of a minor during these tumultuous times. The dying king, extending his right arm, transmits his blessing to rule, but the portrait includes many others with the father and son. On the right is the full Privy Council, which was to manage England during the boy king's minority. Seated next to Edward is his uncle, Edward Seymour, who served as the first Lord Protector of England. Seymour's successor, John Dudley, the Duke of Northumberland, is seated next to him. During Edward VI's brief six-year reign, both dukes would try to usurp power.

Beneath the young king in the painting, the pope and monks are crushed by the scriptures, while outside the window, iconoclastic Protestants destroy churches and images. Indeed, during the regency of the young king, Catholicism came under attack in England.

Archbishop Thomas Cranmer issued a Protestant manual of worship, *The Book of Common Prayer*, and Parliament issued the Act of Uniformity in 1549, making the prayer book's use mandatory for religious

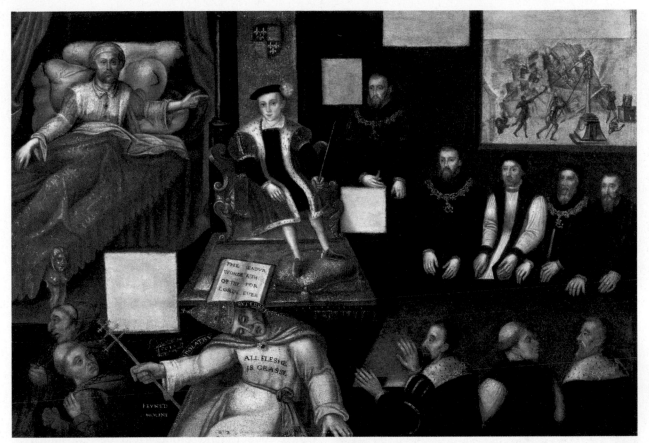

FIGURE 11.5 Anonymous, King *Edward VI* (1537–53) *and the Pope,* 1568–1571 This work commemorates—and tries to ensure—the successful reestablishment of the Church of England by the young King Edward VI.

service throughout the kingdom. It seemed as if the Church of England was securely established, but the English would suffer more upheavals before religious peace reigned.

The 16-year-old Edward died without an heir, and the kingdom next went to his elder sister, Mary (r. 1553–1558), daughter of Catherine of Aragon, Henry's first wife. A staunch Catholic, Mary promptly set about undoing the Protestant "Bloody Mary" reforms and returning England to the protective bosom of Rome. Although many prominent Protestants had fled to the Continent upon Mary's accession, the queen attempted to force remaining Protestants to renounce their beliefs. Bloody Mary ordered some 280 Protestants burned for "religious treason," including Archbishop Cranmer, who had originally granted Henry VIII his divorce. The English public was even more upset by her marriage to Charles V's son Philip II, the Catholic king of Spain. However, the marriage did not produce an heir who could continue her Catholic policies.

Upon Mary's death, the throne went to her half-sister, Anne Boleyn's daughter, Elizabeth I (r. 1558–1603), whose rule would earn her the affectionate nickname Good Queen Bess. Elizabeth (shown in **Figure 11.6**) proved a brilliant politician who skillfully positioned herself at the center of a contentious court. As the portrait in **Figure 11.6** shows, she portrayed herself as a haughty, yet gracious queen who cared deeply for her subjects. She also remained unmarried (the ermine on her left arm in the painting is the symbol of Elizabeth I virginity) and used that condition for her own diplomatic advantage by holding out the possibility of marrying into other European royal houses. Though arrogant and vain, Elizabeth was also a shrewd and frugal ruler who well deserved her people's grateful affection.

In matters of religion, Elizabeth did not worry about the fine points of theology. The young queen was appalled at the violence and destruction caused by the religious controversies, and she felt deeply responsible for maintaining peace in her realm while allowing people to follow their consciences. However, she was insistent on loyalty above all else, and she persecuted Catholics, who she felt had divided loyalties. She wanted to unify England around a Protestant core but also allow her loyal subjects latitude in religious practice and belief. For example, the prayer book that she instituted let people of differing convictions pray together in a national church. This moderate approach was effective: For a while, England basked in a time of peace that fostered an

FIGURE 11.6 Attributed to William Segan, *Portrait of Elizabeth I*, 1585 The shrewd Elizabeth brought a moderate approach to religious reform that allowed England to flourish. Her portraits both advertised her accomplishments and soothed her vanity.

intellectual flowering (see Chapter 10) and an era of international expansion (see Chapter 12).

Even as Elizabeth moved England toward moderation in religion, Scotland clung to the firm Calvinism preached by John Knox. In 1560, a Reformed Parliament gathered in Scotland and made a decisive break with Catholic France in favor of Protestant England. However, Scotland was to put its own mark on its church, which was established by the Scots Confession of 1560. Knox composed the church's liturgy, the *Book of Common Order*, which demonstrated how the Scottish church departed from the Anglican one. The Scots emphasized individual Christian conscience over ecclesiastical authority, and instead of placing bishops in authority, they established a Presbyterian form of organization that gave authority to pastors and elders of the congregations. The resulting Presbyterian congregations were more independent than the Episcopal congregations of the Anglican Church.

> Scotland's church

By the end of the seventeenth century, the old medieval notion of a Europe united under the protection of a uniform Christianity had evaporated.

Map 11.2 shows the religious diversity that characterized Christian Europe at the end of the sixteenth century. Lutheran and Anglican churches were accepted by princes and rulers. Calvinists formed a solid minority in many areas. Many rulers struggled to grapple with even this degree of diversity. Yet Protestantism, by its very nature, had the potential to yield even more divisions. Once the door had opened for individuals to define their own way to God, there was no limit to the paths that people might create. However, the Catholic Church could not ignore these theological controversies and cries for reform, and in the sixteenth century, Catholicism searched its own conscience.

> Europe divided

THE CATHOLIC REFORMATION

Even before Luther circulated his devastating criticism, many leaders in the Catholic Church were working to reform abuses and bring to Catholic worship new insights about textual criticism of Christian humanism. Girolamo Savonarola (1452–1498) in Florence, for example, had urged reform of the Renaissance papacy (see Chapter 10). His was not an isolated voice, though, for even popes in the early sixteenth century called councils and promulgated decrees aimed at reform. This movement of religious reform is called the Catholic Reformation by Catholics and the Counter-Reformation by Protestants, who saw these reforms as a response to the Protestant challenge. However, many of these religious reflections grew out of a continuing Catholic discussion that followed the Great Schism, the Conciliar movement, and the rule of the politically active Renaissance popes. Popes faced a tough challenge in implementing reforms at that time, because the Habsburg-Valois Wars occupied the attention of the Catholic kings Charles V and Francis I, who in normal times would have backed the papacy. These wars also carried a high financial price for the popes—during the sack of Rome in 1527, for example, imperial troops made off with mounds of gold coins from the papal treasury. To recover their losses, the popes stepped up the sort of fund-raising that had so incited Luther. Practical reform had to wait for peace.

The Stirring of Reform in Spain

In the fifteenth century, Spain emerged from its medieval decentralization and became a strong, unified kingdom. In 1469, Isabella (r. 1474–1504) and Ferdinand (r. 1479–1516) married, joining the kingdoms of Leon-Castile and Aragon (see **Map 8.5**). They immediately set about reducing the power of the nobility and establishing a centralized power. As part of their consolidation of royal authority, the two monarchs obtained permission from the pope to establish

MAP 11.2

Religions in Europe, ca. 1600

This map shows the distribution of the major centers of Catholics and Protestants in Europe at the end of the sixteenth century. Notice that there were strong Calvinist minorities in some countries.

Explore the Map

1. Where were Protestant minorities most likely to confront religious turmoil? Why?

2. Why might Catholics have felt threatened, even though Europe remained largely Catholic?

their own inquisition, directed against converted Jews and former Muslims who were suspected of secretly practicing their old faith. This newly established court brought great suffering to many of Spain's loyal citizens.

Ferdinand and Isabella became known as the "Catholic monarchs," emphasizing their faith and the degree to which they believed they carried the banner of an invigorated Catholicism. As part of their goal of a centralized and religiously homogenous Spain, they resumed the reconquest of the peninsula that had dominated the history of medieval Spain. The monarchs besieged Granada, the last Muslim stronghold in the south of Spain, and conquered it in 1492.

Ferdinand and Isabella

The religious zeal that grew out of the crusade against Granada continued after the fall of the city. In the same year, all Jews were expelled from Spain. Some 150,000 were given four months to leave. As we will see in Chapter 12, the same crusading zeal would extend across the Atlantic. By 1492, Spain was well placed to take the lead in fostering Catholicism against the forces of Protestantism.

As part of their dynastic aims, Ferdinand and Isabella had arranged marriages for their children to the leading families of Europe. Their daughter Joanna became the wife of the Habsburg archduke, and her son Charles V became heir to both Spain and the Habsburg lands. With such pious grandparents, it is not surprising that Charles V was so vigorous in his support of Catholicism.

The most influential religious figure in Spain during this time was Cardinal Ximénez de Cisneros 1436–1517). He was confessor to the queen, bishop of Toledo, Grand Inquisitor, and regent of Spain after Ferdinand's death. It was Ximénez who brought humanist ideas into Spain.

Ximénez was particularly impressed with Erasmus's emphasis on scholarly study of scripture and the works of the church fathers, and he wanted to strengthen this kind of education in Spain. In 1498, Ximénez received permission from the Borgia pope Alexander VI to found a new university at Alcalá de Henares that would feature humanist approaches to theological and ecclesiastical studies. The high quality of the scholarship at the school drew notice with the publication of the *Complutensian Polyglot Bible* (1520), an edition of the Bible written in three columns that compared the Hebrew, Greek, and Latin versions. This scholarship represented a high point in humanistic learning and new critical techniques in the study of the Bible.

Cardinal Ximénez

The Society of Jesus

Throughout its history, the Catholic Church had been reformed by monastic and mendicant orders that infused new life and ideas into the church. This pattern continued in the sixteenth century. Several new orders emerged, but the most influential was the Society of Jesus, whose members were called **Jesuits.**

The Society of Jesus was founded by Ignatius of Loyola (1491–1556), a soldier in the service of the Spanish monarch. In battle a cannonball shattered Loyola's legs, and he had a long and painful recovery—his legs had to be set and rebroken twice (without anesthesia) because they were healing crookedly. During his recuperation, Loyola read stories of Christian saints and decided to dedicate himself as a soldier of Christ. Loyola trained himself for a spiritual life with the same rigor that marked his military practice. In his quest, he was influenced by Thomas à Kempis's *Imitation of Christ* and wrote his own book that offered a Catholic version of the personal search for God. In the widely read work, *The Spiritual Exercises*, Loyola taught how spiritual discipline could satisfy people's desire to reach up to God while obeying the orders of the Catholic Church. Here was the perfect combination of Catholic orthodoxy and the longings expressed by Protestant reformers.

Jesuits established

In 1540, the pope established the Society of Jesus as a religious order, and the Jesuits, who vowed perfect obedience to the papacy, became the vanguard of reformed Catholicism. These men devoted themselves to education, sharing Cardinal Ximénez's belief that a Christian humanist education would combat the threat of Protestantism. Their schools became among the best in Europe, drawing even some Protestants who were willing to risk their children's conversion to Catholicism in exchange for the fine education. Document 11.3 contains a letter from Loyola that explains his recognition of the importance of education.

Jesuits also served as missionaries to bring Catholicism to the New World (see Chapter 12). However, in time the new shock troops of the papacy became controversial in their own right—the vigor with which they pursued their aims and the vehemence of their support of the papacy alienated some Catholics and Protestants alike. But there is no question that in the sixteenth century and beyond, the Jesuits would be a powerful force in the reformed Catholicism.

Figure 11.7, a painting by the Flemish artist Peter Paul Rubens (1577–1640), captures the spirit of reformed Catholicism. *The Miracles of St. Ignatius* was commissioned in 1620 to be placed in the Jesuits' first church in Antwerp in 1622 on the occasion of the canonization of Ignatius of Loyola. The painting shows the saint performing miracles: easing the pain of childbirth (on the right), reviving a suicide victim long enough for the dying man to take the last rites (in the foreground), and casting out demons (on the left). The image praises traditional Catholic doctrine, showing the efficacy of saints by representing them as

DOCUMENT 11.3

Ignatius Loyola Argues for Education as a Solution

In August 1554, Ignatius Loyola wrote a letter in which he reveals his desire to stop the growth of Protestantism. In this letter, he advocates education as the best way to stop Catholics from embracing the Protestant theology.

Seeing the progress which the heretics have made in a short time, spreading the poison of their evil teaching throughout so many countries and peoples . . . it would seem that our Society . . . should be solicitous to prepare the proper steps, such as are quickly applied and can be widely adopted, thus exerting itself to the utmost of its powers to preserve what is still sound and to restore what has fallen sick of the plague of heresy, especially in the northern nations.

The heretics have made their false theology popular and presented it in a way that is within the capacity of the common people. They preach it to the people and teach it in the schools, and scatter booklets which can be bought and understood by many, and make their influence felt by means of their writings when they cannot do so by their preaching. Their success is largely due to the negligence of those who should have shown some interest; and the bad example and the ignorance of Catholics, especially the clergy, have made such ravages in the vineyard of

the Lord. Hence it would seem that our Society should make use of the following means to put a stop and apply a remedy to the evils which have come upon the Church through these heretics.

In the first place, the sound theology which is taught in the universities and seeks its foundation in philosophy, and therefore requires a long time to acquire is adapted only to good and alert minds. . . . It would be good to make a summary of theology to deal with topics that are important but not controversial, and with great brevity. . . . In this way theologians could be produced in a short time who could take care of the preaching and teaching in many places. . . .

The principal conclusion of this theology, in the form of a short catechism [instructional manual] could be taught to children, as the Christian doctrine is now taught, and likewise to the common people who are not too infected or too capable of subtleties. This could also be done with the younger students in the lower classes, where they could learn it by heart. . . .

Another excellent means for helping the Church in this trial would be to multiply the colleges and schools of the Society in many lands, especially where a good attendance could be expected. . . .

The heretics write a large number of booklets and pamphlets, by means of which they aim at taking away all authority from the Catholics, and especially from the Society, and set up their false dogmas. It would seem expedient, therefore, that our Society here also write answers in pamphlet form, short and well written, so that they can be produced without delay and bought by many. In this way the harm that is being done by the pamphlets of the heretics can be remedied and sound teaching spread. These works should be modest, but lively. . . .

SOURCE: Ignatius Loyola, *Monumenta Ignatiana*, vol. 12 (Madrid, 1904), pp. 259–262, in Robert E. Van Voorst, *Readings in Christianity* (New York: Wadsworth Publishing, 1996), pp. 211–213.

Analyze the Document

1. What does Loyola argue are the main reasons for the spread of Protestant beliefs?

2. What solutions does he propose?

3. How effective do you think his suggestions will be?

4. What do you think will be other social effects of such an emphasis on education?

---

intermediaries between people and God. In the same way, Loyola is positioned in the vertical center of the painting. Rubens also affirms the importance of the sacrament of last rites (attacked by the Protestants) by depicting it as the occasion of a miracle. Finally, this work points out that, in less than a century, Loyola's accomplishments had earned him the status of sainthood and his Society of Jesus had become the army of the new Catholicism.

Rubens's painting is an example of a new style of painting (and the arts in general) called **baroque,** which also served to forward the ideas and spirit of reformed Catholicism. Baroque art was characterized by passion, drama, and awe and was designed to

Baroque art

involve the audience. Catholic patrons, in particular, spurred this art that spoke as eloquently of Catholic doctrine and passion as a Jesuit sermon. However, before either the new art style or the energetic order of Jesuits could be effective, the church had to agree on its doctrine in response to the Protestant critique.

The Council of Trent, 1545–1563

With the conclusion of the Habsburg-Valois Wars, the Catholic monarchs could focus on the divisive religious questions of the day. After the treaty of 1544 that ended the wars, church leaders from all over Europe

Reforming corruption

FIGURE 11.7 Peter Paul Rubens, *The Miracles of St. Ignatius*, 1620 Baroque artists portrayed the passions that accompanied the reformed Catholic faith. Here, Loyola, founder of the Society of Jesus, performs miracles as he stands as an intermediary between people and God.

church also affirmed the existence of purgatory and the power of prayer and even indulgences to free souls from their punishment.

These churchmen rejected Protestants by reaffirming their position that Christians needed both faith and good works to go to heaven. For Catholics, the sacraments by their very nature conveyed grace, so the council reaffirmed the existence of all seven rites. In further rejection of Protestant criticism, Catholics retained their idea of transubstantiation, by which priests presided over the transformation of the wine and host into the blood and body of Christ.

Like Rubens, the Spanish painter El Greco (the Greek) (1547–1614) was a baroque painter who reaffirmed Catholic theology. El Greco's painting *Burial of the Count of Orgaz* (**Figure 11.8**) is less about the burial of one man than about the theological stance of the Council of Trent. The dead count does not face his maker
El Greco
alone. Instead, he is buried with the full ceremony of the church presided over by the bishop. El Greco also shows saints Augustine and Stephen miraculously appearing and helping with the burial. The count's way to heaven is paved by the prayers of the living who surround the scene and the Virgin Mary, who sits between the dead man and Jesus as an intermediary for the count's soul. The painting depicts heaven as filled with saints and the souls of other saved individuals, who also pray for the count and help him enter their community. By all these means, the picture visually reaffirms the theology established at the Council of Trent.

While debating and refining their beliefs, the churchmen used principles that had guided previous councils and looked to two authorities— scripture and tradition. Armed with these pillars of Christian thought, they prepared to answer Luther and the other Protestants, who recognized only their own consciences and the complete authority of the Holy Book. Catholics, the Trent council argued, could draw strength from the body of practices that the faithful had
Scripture and tradition
accumulated over the course of a millennium. With its doctrine thus established, the Catholic Church showed a new strength and confidence. Dissenters had gone to other sects, leaving a vigorous corps of dedicated believers to challenge the Protestants head-on.

Catholics on the Offense

Throughout this period, as we have seen with baroque art, many Catholics expressed their faith with more passion and mystical emotion than they had shown

gathered in northern Italy at Trent, and the council met intermittently from 1545 to 1563. Charles wanted the council to concentrate on reforming abuses, and it confronted this thorny issue honestly, establishing stern measures to clean up clerical corruption, ignorance, and apathy. They even banned the selling of indulgences and the office of indulgence-seller. But the real work of the council took place when it confronted the theological debate that had driven the Protestants from the church. As these leaders clarified their beliefs, it became obvious that there would be no compromise with Protestant Christianity.

The Council of Trent determined that Catholics did *not* stand alone before God. Rather, it claimed, the community of the faithful, both
Affirming doctrine
living and dead, could help a Catholic to salvation. Thus prayers to the saints and to the Virgin Mary *did* matter. The

in centuries. Teresa of Avila, Spain (1515–1582), a sixteenth-century mystic who quickly became a saint, exemplified this newfound energy. The daughter of a converted Jew, Teresa entered a convent and experienced a series of visions. Not only a mystic, Teresa was an active reformer, establishing new convents for women as part of her dedication to a reinvigorated Catholicism. Her mystical writing, *Way of Perfection*, ensured her influence, for it inspired the pope to declare her a Doctor of the Church (which means that her writings were worthy of study). Soon she became the patron saint of Spain, replacing Saint James (Santiago), who had held that honor throughout the Middle Ages. The example of Teresa and other mystics offered the church a strong weapon to show skeptics the deep and passionate faith that came with Catholic worship. However, they also used stronger measures than the writings of gentle mystics.

Reinvigorated, and considering themselves at war with Protestants, the Catholics moved to repress opposition to their views. The Spanish Inquisition took a forceful role in this battle over religious diversity. (This court was separate from the papal inquisition that, as we saw in Chapter 8, had been introduced into Europe in the thirteenth century.) Inquisitors now added Lutherans and Calvinists to converted Jews and Muslims in their definition of suspect populations and launched a new round of public trials and executions. In 1542, the Inquisition was reestablished in Rome, as the popes also felt compelled to take extreme measures to protect Catholics themselves from incorrect ideas. In addition, the papacy began to publish an Index of Prohibited Books in 1557, which it updated and reissued regularly. (The index was finally abolished in 1966.)

| Spanish Inquisition |

While such measures aimed to control people's beliefs, the church looked to the Spanish king to champion the Catholic cause in the political and military arena. Philip II (r. 1556–1588), Charles V's heir to the kingdoms of Spain and the Netherlands, had an unparalleled zeal for both the Catholic religion and empire. Philip moved his capital from Toledo, a cramped medieval city, to the newly built city of Madrid, chosen because it was the geographic center of the Iberian Peninsula.

| Philip II |

Philip faced two dire threats to the Catholic faith: the Turks in the eastern Mediterranean and the Protestants in the north. In 1571, he assembled a league that included a number of Italian city-states and set out to challenge the Turks' supremacy in the Mediterranean. The Venetians, who had a large fleet and were highly motivated by their trading

FIGURE 11.8 El Greco, *Burial of the Count of Orgaz,* ca. 1586 Reformed Catholicism disagreed with Protestant views in asserting that the dead can be helped by the prayers of the living and by the intercession of the dead themselves. The famous Spanish painter el Greco illustrated these beliefs in this scene of the burial of a count.

* = Catholic

PROTESTANT AND CATHOLIC REFORMERS

ca. 1320–1384	John Wycliffe
1415	Jan Hus executed
1511	Erasmus, *Praise of Folly*
*1515–1582	Teresa of Avila
1517	Martin Luther, Ninety-Five Theses
1519	Zwingli's reform in Switzerland
*1520	Ximénez, *Complutensian Polyglot Bible*, Spain
1521	Luther at Diet of Worms
1534	Henry VIII's Act of Supremacy in England
1536	Calvin, *Institutes of Christian Religion*
*1540	Loyola founds Society of Jesus
*1545–1563	Council of Trent

KEY DATES

FIGURE 11.9 Anonymous, *The Battle of Lepanto*, 1571 This depiction of the famous Battle of Lepanto highlights the dramatic contrast between the old and the new warfare at sea. The Muslim ships' banks of oars are used to power the ramming of the enemy fleet, while the smoke of Spanish cannon fire from the high-hulled Spanish ships signals the naval combat of the future.

interests in the eastern Mediterranean, were particularly eager to join Philip's navy. Outfitted with 208 galleys—sleek warships rowed by slaves and armed with cannons—Philip's navy confronted the Turks' 230 warships at the Battle of Lepanto, off the coast of Greece. **Figure 11.9** depicts what the scene may have looked like. In this graphic image, cannons blaze and battering rams thrust forward as the galleys draw together.

When the smoke cleared after this spectacular battle, Philip's coalition had scored a decisive victory. The Turks lost two hundred warships, the Europeans only ten. Tens of thousands of men on both sides died in the fighting, and contemporary witnesses described the sea as running red with blood. Nevertheless, the success at Lepanto raised Catholics' spirits throughout the West. The navy had proved that Turkish power in the Mediterranean was not invincible after all. Indeed, some western Catholics began toying with the idea of invading the Ottoman Empire itself. But the Catholic monarchs had other adversaries in mind. Again, the kings of Europe went to war. This time, though, they marched against the Protestants in a series of battles that would drag on for a century and tear apart the soul of Europe.

EUROPE ERUPTS AGAIN: A CENTURY OF RELIGIOUS WARFARE,
1559–1648

The Reformation had done far more than just establish alternative Christian sects—it raised the possibility that individuals might follow their own consciences in matters of religion. In a society in which the church served as the central institution in people's lives, this radical new idea struck at the very foundation of European politics and social realities. From the time the Roman emperor Constantine supported the Catholic Church (see Chapter 5), people always assumed that there was an identity of belief between rulers and subjects. Political loyalty was considered a religious phenomenon; the Protestant Reformation questioned this assumption.

In fact, the wars of religion that scourged Europe from 1559 to 1648 involved much more than the proper way to worship God. They also centered on the question of what constituted a state—specifically, whether one state could encompass various religious expressions. Like the peasant wars in Germany in

1524, these new hostilities involved religion, but they had significant economic, political, and social dimensions as well.

French Wars of Religion, 1562–1598

By the 1550s, Calvinism had gained a good deal of strength in France among the peasants and in the towns of the south and southwest (including villages like that of Martin Guerre in the Biography). Although the French Calvinists (Huguenots) remained a minority—only about 7 percent of the population—they were well organized. Local congregations governed by ministers sent representatives to district assemblies that in turn coordinated their efforts with a national assembly and even mustered troops from local churches. This impressive minority even began to recruit members from the nobility—possibly 40 percent of French nobles had become Huguenots. Great noble families took the lead in forwarding their religious (and in turn political) interests—the Guises led the Catholics, and the Bourbons championed the Huguenots. By the mid-sixteenth century, French Protestantism was a force to be reckoned with and the French kings took notice.

Francis I (r. 1515–1547) and his heir, Henry II (r. 1547–1559), were both powerful kings who based their authority in part on a strong Catholic stance. However, this royal power was broken by a freak accident. King Henry was celebrating the wedding of his daughter by fighting in a joust (the war game still much beloved by the nobility), but during the last joust of the day, his opponent's lance shattered, gouging Henry's eye. Henry died of complications of this wound, leaving his widow, the Italian Catherine de' Medici, to rule as regent for her young sons from 1559 to 1589.

Catherine tried to preserve royal control, but her efforts were impeded by the struggle for power between the Guises and the Bourbons, both of whom had family ties to the monarchy and hoped to inherit the throne. Politics here intertwined with religion and the time was ripe for civil war. **Catholics vs. Huguenots** Fighting broke out in 1562, when the Duke of Guise massacred a Huguenot congregation, and it continued for about thirty-six years (with brief respites). The Huguenot forces, though outnumbered, were too well organized to be defeated. The most infamous point of these wars was the Saint Bartholomew's Day Massacre, which took place on August 23, 1572, just when peace seemed imminent.

A religious compromise seemed to be on the horizon with a marriage between Catherine's daughter and the Bourbon leader of the Huguenots, Henry of Navarre. However, the mutual suspicions and desire for revenge had not subsided—the Guise family persuaded the young king Charles IX (r. 1560–1574) that the Huguenot gathering for the wedding was a plot against the crown. The king then ordered his guard to kill all the Protestant leadership. On the morning of St. Bartholomew's Day, **Saint Bartholomew's Day Massacre** the soldiers unleashed a massacre against Protestants.

Although the young bridegroom escaped assassination, many others did not. Thousands were murdered, and the painting shown in **Figure 11.10** depicts a contemporary witness's memory of the slaughter. The massacre raged for six days, and as the image shows, it was particularly brutal. Women and infants were not spared, and the painting shows that even corpses were mutilated as religious fervor introduced a bloodbath. This violence did not end the wars, however. Civil war continued in France until King Henry III (r. 1574–1589) was assassinated, leaving no heir.

The next in line for the throne was Henry of Navarre—the Protestant bridegroom who survived the massacre. Recognizing that the overwhelmingly Catholic population would not accept a reformist king, he converted to Catholicism, reputedly **Peace in France** saying, "Paris is worth a mass." Sympathetic to both religions, the new king, Henry IV (r. 1589–1610), issued the Edict of Nantes (1598), which ended the religious wars and introduced religious toleration in France. However, a subsequent king (Louis XIV, discussed in Chapter 13) who believed that a nation was defined by loyalty to one religion would overturn Henry's policy. But for the time being at least, France gained a small respite from the violence of intolerance. The rest of Europe was not so lucky.

A "Council of Blood" in the Netherlands, 1566–1609

In addition to Spain, the Catholic king Philip II ruled over the Netherlands, which consisted of seventeen provinces. (Today these provinces are Netherlands, Belgium, and Luxembourg.) Trouble began when Philip began to exert more control over the provinces—he restructured the Catholic Church to weaken the local aristocracy, he insisted on billeting troops locally, and he levied new taxes, all of which offended the Dutch.

In response, riots broke out in 1566, and Dutch Protestants, though still a tiny minority, rebelled against their Spanish, Catholic overlords. In a spasm of violence, they destroyed Catholic Church property, smashing images of saints and desecrating the host. Philip was enraged. **Revolt breaks out** Vowing to silence the rebels, he sent the largest land army ever assembled into the Netherlands to crush the Protestants and bring the province

FIGURE 11.10 Françoise Dubois, *St. Bartholomew's Day Massacre,* **ca. 1576** A massacre of French Protestants began on St. Bartholomew's Day (August 24, 1572) and lasted six days. Even this violence did not end the brutal struggle for religious supremacy.

back under his Catholic rule. In 1572, organized revolt broke out and war officially began.

Philip's crackdown ignited a savage forty-year contest in which the Spanish general, the "iron duke of Alba," presided over a slaughter of thousands of Protestants in what he called a "Council of Troubles," but what the Protestants called the "Council of Blood." Calvinist preachers retaliated by giving their congregations complete license to kill the invaders. To protect themselves, the towns of the Netherlands even opened their dikes to flood their country rather than give in to Philip's armies. The Dutch found an able leader in William of Orange, a nobleman known for his wise counsel, who took charge in 1580. William was assassinated four years later, and the murderer was publicly tortured to death as blood continued to flow in the Netherlands.

The defiance of the Dutch cost Philip more than the loss of soldiers and huge amounts of gold to finance the wars. It also diverted his attention northward, away from his victory over the Turks at Lepanto in 1571. Preoccupied by events in the Netherlands, he failed to ride the wave of widespread Christian antipathy toward the Turks and launch a decisive campaign against the enemy in the eastern Mediterranean.

Philip also tried to "save" England from the Protestantism that Henry VIII had introduced. Philip had married Henry's Catholic daughter, Mary (r. 1553–1558), and when she died without an heir, the Spanish king proposed matrimony to her sister, Elizabeth I. But the Protestant Elizabeth refused his attentions and even dared support the Netherlands against him. Philip struck back by hurling the full force of his navy against England, sending a huge fleet across the English Channel in 1588. What happened next stood in stark contrast to Philip's triumph at Lepanto. Instead of scoring an easy victory, the Spanish Armada was wiped out by the well-armed English ships and the sudden onslaught of violent storms in the North Sea (what the English would later call a "Protestant wind").

Philip never succeeded in subduing the Protestants in the Netherlands; the conflict dragged on until the deaths of both Philip and Elizabeth. In 1609, the two sides finally drew up an agreement that gave the northern provinces virtual independence. The final recognition of an independent Netherlands would have to wait until the Peace of Westphalia in 1648. After the final settlement, Protestants in the southern provinces moved north to escape continuing Spanish rule in the south, so the two provinces became divided along religious lines. The northern provinces became the Protestant Dutch Republic,

Armada against England

Netherlands split

and the southern (and French-speaking) Spanish Netherlands (which later became Belgium) remained Catholic. But this solution still could not quell the religious tensions tearing at Europe. Instead, the wars shifted east, where they culminated in the bloodiest engagement of them all.

The Thirty Years' War, 1618–1648

The Peace of Augsburg had only temporarily answered the question of religious diversity in the Holy Roman Empire. For fifty years after Augsburg, pressure mounted as more and more people followed their consciences and as diverse spiritual beliefs proliferated in the principalities. These tensions reached the boiling point in 1618, when a Catholic prince took over Bohemia (in the modern Czech Republic) and set out to vanquish the substantial Protestant minority in his state. Protestant Bohemian nobles responded by throwing the prince's representatives out of the castle window in Prague. The hapless officials landed unhurt in a pile of manure, but the Catholic explanation was that their fall had been broken by angels. The two sides seemed to have irreconcilable points of view.

But the Holy Roman Empire's political structure contained a unique feature that made religious tensions much harder to resolve than by merely pushing bureaucrats out of windows. The essential problem was that Protestant and Catholic electors (princes who elected the Holy Roman Emperor) were roughly equal in number. If Bohemia went to a Protestant prince, the balance of power would shift away from the ruling Catholic Habsburgs. Fearing this possibility, the Holy Roman Emperor Ferdinand II (r. 1619–1637) went to war to reclaim Bohemia for Catholicism. His action provoked a civil war that began over the key issue of the authority of the emperor over the princes in Germany but that quickly turned international as Protestants and Catholics across the Holy Roman Empire faced each other in battle.

The first twelve years of the war were marked by the success of Emperor Ferdinand's forces, and it seemed as if the Catholic Habsburgs would be able to roll back the Protestant gains in the German lands. The powerful Catholic Maximilian of Bavaria put at Ferdinand's disposal an army that won a stunning victory over the Bohemians at the Battle of White Mountain in 1620 (shown on **Map 11.3**). The Bohemian rebels were killed or exiled, and it seemed as if the war was over. However, the Protestants continued their struggle, but with few gains.

In 1624, the emperor received considerable help when a soldier of fortune came to offer his services to the Catholic cause. Albrecht von Wallenstein, a minor Bohemian nobleman, recognized that the emperor needed a new army if he was to succeed, and Wallenstein offered to raise the force if he could billet it and raise its supplies wherever it happened to be stationed. Through these means, Wallenstein introduced a new way of funding wars.

Previously, warriors had been paid largely by the losers—that is, through the victors' plunder and sacking of defeated peoples. Wallenstein's innovative requirements served as a kind of war tax levied on all princes and cities who supported the emperor. Now wars would be funded by potential winners as well as losers. This strategy not only funded a large army but also made Wallenstein one of the richest men in the empire. By 1627, Wallenstein's army had begun to conquer the northern region of the empire—the center of Protestant strength. Ferdinand grew so confident that he issued the Edict of Restitution in 1629, ordering all territories lost to Protestants since 1552 to be restored to Catholics.

By 1630, the tide and nature of the war had begun to change. With help from abroad, Protestants made gains, but the war began to shift from a religious struggle to a purely political quest—to weaken the power of the Habsburgs; for example, the Catholic French king was willing to join Protestants in support of this cause. Protestant forces found a worthy champion in the Swedish king Gustavus Adolphus (r. 1611–1632), who was appalled by Ferdinand's treatment of Protestants. At the same time, he feared a Habsburg threat to Swedish lands around the Baltic Sea (see **Map 11.3**).

Gustavus had a clear vision of modern warfare: It would be dominated by gunpowder. He drilled his men incessantly on lining up in squares so that the front line could fire and then move backward to reload while others replaced them. This system, which required ironclad discipline, allowed for sustained firing—an essential tactic for weapons that were still inaccurate. Gustavus also introduced the idea that cannons could be used on the battlefield against men, and in doing so he created the first effective field artillery.

Arraying his new army, Gustavus fought a decisive battle against Wallenstein at Lutzen in 1632. Amid the blinding smoke of gunpowder, Gustavus's armies beat Wallenstein's forces, but in the heat of battle, Gustavus himself was killed by gunshots. The king's death prevented the Swedish forces from following up on the victory. Meanwhile, Wallenstein's loss sealed his fate: The German princes eventually compelled Ferdinand to turn on his enterprising and wealthy general, and the emperor had Wallenstein assassinated a few months later.

> War breaks out

> Wallenstein

> From religion to politics

MAP 11.3

The Thirty Years' War, 1618–1648

This map shows the major participants and the main battles of the Thirty Years' War, which took place on German territory.

Explore the Map

1. Based on geography, why did the king of Sweden become involved in this war?

2. Compare this map with **Map 11.2.** Which regions set aside their religious interests and fought primarily for political reasons?

3. Notice all the battles. How devastating was this war to the German people? Explain.

Gustavus's successes opened the final phase of the war (from 1632 to 1648), during which the emperor lost all his previous gains. The Protestant princes raised new armies, and by 1635, Ferdinand had to agree to suspend the Edict of Restitution and to grant amnesty to most of the Protestant princes. In return, the Protestants joined the imperial troops in driving the Swedes out of German lands. However, the Catholic French declared open war on Ferdinand in 1635, and for the next thirteen years, French and Swedish troops rampaged through the lands, causing destruction and devastation.

By the 1640s, the war had reached a stalemate. The kings and princes who had started the hostilities had all died, and their successors (as well as civilians) were exhausted. Both sides laid down their arms and took stock of their losses. This war

Devastation had raged with a violence that astonished even contemporary witnesses used to sixteenth-century battle methods, for armies on both sides had swept through villages and towns and laid to waste everything in their paths. The war had exacted a staggering price: Germany's population had plummeted (although historians do not agree on the figures, some suggest a population loss as high as 30 percent). The economy, too, was damaged. Spain had gone bankrupt and would never recover its standing as a leader on the European stage. France and Sweden emerged somewhat victorious gaining some land at the expense of the exhausted German states.

Peace at Westphalia

The series of agreements that ended the Thirty Years' War are collectively known as the Peace of Westphalia, named for the region of Germany where the agreements were drafted. German princes now had the freedom to choose their own religion, but the religious desires of individuals within the states were still not accepted. However, for the first time, Calvinism was included among the tolerated faiths. The religious landmark of Europe was roughly established along north-south lines. The northwest—England, Holland, Scandinavia, and the northern German states—was Protestant, whereas the south remained Catholic.

The war had marked political overtones at the end, and the treaty accordingly addressed issues of power beyond religious choice. The peace set the political geography of Europe for the next century and established a precedent for diplomacy

Political results that would shape the way nations resolved political problems in the coming centuries. **Map 11.4** outlines the aftermath of the Peace of Westphalia. The representatives at Westphalia conducted all these negotiations with an eye toward "balance of power," a relatively new principle that emerged in fifteenth-century Italy and was now applied to European politics. They believed that they could ensure peace by making all the European powers roughly as strong as their neighbors. This strategy would dominate European diplomacy for centuries.

LIFE AFTER THE REFORMATION

The early modern wars of religion were finally over. Christians with different beliefs would now have to learn to coexist. As the storms of religious rage subsided, Europeans began noticing the dramatic changes in other aspects of everyday life and thought that the Protestant Reformation had provoked.

New Definitions of Courtship and Marriage

When the Protestants excluded marriage as a sacrament, the institution changed in ways they could not have foreseen. After Martin Luther left the monastery and married Katherina, the couple formed a loving partnership and raised five children (along with caring for orphans). Luther explored this relationship in his writings and saw in marriage part of God's plan for humanity. Calvin, too, rejected the church fathers' "too superstitious admiration of celibacy" and extolled the benefits of conjugal partnerships. Although divorce was not easy in any of the Protestant groups, it was possible. With all these changes, the ideal of marriage shifted. Couples began to expect mutual love between man and wife, instead of simply duty that bound extended families together. The Catholic Church also was influenced by the new marital values, and in the late sixteenth century, church manuals began to use the word *love* to refer to conjugal relations.

POLITICS OF THE AGE OF REFORMATION	
1521–1544	Habsburg-Valois Wars
1524–1525	German peasants revolt
1529	Turks besiege Vienna
1555	Peace of Augsburg, Germany
1562–1598	French wars of religion
1566–1609	Wars in the Netherlands
1571	Battle of Lepanto
1572	Saint Bartholomew's Day Massacre, France
1588	Spanish Armada attacks England
1618–1648	Thirty Years' War
1648	Peace of Westphalia

KEY DATES

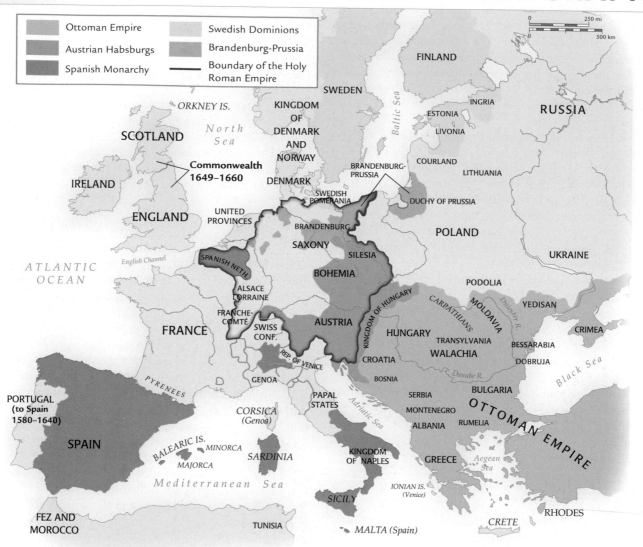

MAP 11.4

Europe, 1648

This map shows the political configuration of Europe after the Peace of Westphalia, which ended the Thirty Years' War.

Explore the Map

1. Which countries appear large and cohesive after the settlement of Westphalia?

2. Which countries control territories distant from their home center? Which of these remote areas might become centers of conflict in the future? Why?

People still did not marry just for love, however; instead, families continued to arrange suitable matches between young people. Arranged marriages were an essential and logical part of a view that valued family prosperity and continuity more than an individual's happiness. Individual's lives were seen as mere moments in the larger life of the family. Nevertheless, something new was going on in family relations. Although parents still negotiated a suitable match, prospective couples were allowed to consider their compatibility before marriage, and daughters had some

Courtship

say in vetoing disagreeable matches. Court-ship customs grew more complex, as men and women evaluated whether they would have a harmonious union. In **Figure 11.11,** a paint-ing titled *The Suitor's Visit,* a young man calls on a woman in one of many visits intended for the couple to get to know each other. Presum-ably, the suitor greets the young woman's mother, who will chaperone the courtship and approve the joining of the families that mar-riage still represented. The prospective bride is in the background playing her lute; young women in these years cultivated their skills at making music and clever conversation so as to beguile potential mates and convince them of their qualities as life partners.

Forging a Link Between Education and Work

The Christian humanists from Erasmus on urged everyone to learn to read. As we saw in Document 11.3, reformed Catholicism under the Jesuits also stressed education as central to a Christian life, and parochial schools and armies of nuns gave young children the rudiments of education. Protestants, too, urged study. As Luther and others emphasized Bible study as part of essential Christian behavior and translated the Bible into vernacular languages, the next logical step was to broaden literacy. Luther encouraged the cities and villages in Saxony to establish publicly funded schools, and many Protestants followed his call. A Bohemian reformer, Jan Amos Comenius (1592–1670), wrote: "All alike, boys and girls, both noble and ignoble, rich and poor, in all cities and towns, villages and hamlets, should be sent to school." This egalitarian notion would take centu-ries to implement, but it established a new educa-tional goal in the West.

The painter Jan Steen's depiction of an early-seventeenth-century classroom (shown in **Figure 11.12**) embodies the Protestant ideals of education. This is a village school where both boys and girls study. The strict schoolmaster slaps a boy's hand in reprimand for the poorly done assignment on the floor, while the boy cries. The girl on the boy's right smiles rather too gleefully at his distress. This scene must have played out repeatedly in the many small village schools that began to spring up as more chil-dren began to receive formal education.

Although education was intended primarily to help people study the Bible and learn to serve as their

Valuing literacy

FIGURE 11.11 Gerard Ter Borch, *The Suitor's Visit,* **1658** Many post-Reformation paintings captured the new courtship rituals—including conversations, letter writing, and musical performances—designed to ensure that married couples would be compatible.

own spiritual guides, it also had profound implications for the way people viewed work. In response to critics who complained about educating "rustics," the Bohemian educational reformer Comenius answered that universal education would help everyone avoid "that idleness which is so dangerous to flesh and blood." His words hinted at a new philosophy that stressed the value of work.

Valuing work

In the Middle Ages, "those who work" were rel-egated to the bottom of the social scale. The upper crust consisted of only those who could live off the income of their land and did not need to work to survive. The bourgeoisie—the middle class—that was becoming more and more prosperous since the Renaissance began to change that view and brought a new valuing of work into the consciousness of West-ern society. The Protestant reformers that appealed to many of the residents of these growing urban areas lent religious support to new ideas about work. In Luther's writings, even women were defined by the work they did. He described the ideal wife as fol-lows: "She likes working. . . . She girds her loins and stretches her arms, works with energy in the house."

FIGURE 11.12 Jan Steen, *The School Master*, ca. 1655 The Reformation stimulated the spread of literacy. The intent was to help everyone to read the Bible. The modern world was born in small village schools—like the one immortalized in this painting—where children struggled under sometimes harsh teachers.

Calvin, too, believed that men and women were called to work and that work itself was a virtuous activity. Centuries later, the German sociologist Max Weber, in *The Protestant Ethic and the Spirit of Capitalism* (1904), would argue that Calvinists' emphasis on work legitimized and therefore boosted the growth of capitalism in the West. Many Calvinists believed that hard work, efficiency, and frugality all indicated a person predestined to salvation. Not surprisingly, then, Protestants embraced what has come to be called the work ethic with fervor. Historians dispute the details of Weber's thesis, but his argument still offers us an insight into the way religious ideas shaped modern-day views of work in the West. In the Catholic Middle Ages, people had seen work as the curse of Adam laid on the damned; in the Protestant early modern period, work became God's gift to a saved humanity.

Anxiety and Spiritual Insecurity

The striking revolution in thought that the Protestant reformers introduced also prompted some spiritual anxiety and insecurity among Christians. In part, this unease stemmed from the hardship spawned by the relentless warfare of the period. The "community of the faithful" that Catholicism once represented had fragmented, and for Protestants encouraged to "stand alone before God," the new religious individualism often felt frightening.

The new mind-set began to raise questions about charitable institutions and their relationship with religious bodies. Where once the universal church had looked after the poor and widows and orphans, now separate congregations had to care for their own. The question of who was responsible for whom sometimes became quite murky, and a sense of individual responsibility for one's own plight slowly replaced a collective sense of charity. For example, civic authorities began to consider ways to help the needy, building workhouses for the poor and passing laws prohibiting begging. Such laws could never completely succeed, given the scale of need that we saw in the painting of the cripples in **Figure 11.2**. Yet, more and more societies tried designing institutional solutions to the problems of poverty.

Figure 11.13 depicts a girls' dining hall in a Protestant orphanage in Amsterdam. The painting emphasizes the institutional quality of charity

Charitable institutions

FIGURE 11.13 Jan Victors, *The Girls' Dining Hall on the Reformed Parish Orphanage*, ca. 1651 During the Reformation, the state began to take over the administration of charity from churches. This development gave rise to larger poorhouses, orphanages, and other such institutions.

in the early seventeenth century. The orphans are dressed alike, for example, and the girls in the foreground serve watery soup for dinner while the matrons watch.

As communities redivided themselves along religious loyalties, many people's sense of personal anxiety increased. The Catholic Church had also provided community support and at least the hope of miraculous cures for the sick and troubled. Men and women could themselves pray to saints or the Virgin Mary for help, and priests could say prayers for members of their congregation in need. The Catholic Church even turned a blind eye to "white" magic (like that described in the village of Martin Guerre in the Biography), but Protestants rejected saints and any forms of "magic." As village rituals split apart, it became harder to define "community." As changing times and beliefs generated anxieties, some people began looking for scapegoats.

Decline of "magic"

FIGURE 11.14 Salvator Rosa, _Witches at Their Incantations_ (detail), late seventeenth century Religious insecurity stimulated more witch trials during the early modern period than there had been in the Middle Ages. This painting shows witches engaging in some of their reputed practices, such as performing magic and making pacts with the devil.

Searching for Scapegoats: The Hunt for Witches

Catholics and Protestants alike shared a long-standing, deeply held belief in charms and potions that could affect people. These might be as benign as healing magical cures and love potions, or as harmful as spells to bring bad weather, illness, or crop failure. Traditionally, Catholic priests offered prayers and countercharms to combat the power of people—often, but not always, called witches—who had the knowledge to cast spells. Protestant preachers argued regularly against "superstitious magical practices," but some remained attached to charms and spells, and in England witchcraft accusations usually remained tied to spell-casting.

In the sixteenth century, especially on the Continent, some people began to link a fear of witches to diabolism, or the idea that magical powers came because of a pact with the devil. Martin Luther himself claimed to have confronted the devil several times and constantly remained alert to the presence of this evil being. Church authorities began to stress that witches were in league with the devil and performed mysterious ceremonies in his service. To stamp out the devil's assistants, many accused supposed witches, putting them on trial and executing them.

Fear of the devil

People in the sixteenth century were fascinated by the possibility of witchcraft. The best-known work on the subject was the _Malleus Maleficarum_ (the "Hammer of Witches"), which had been written in the late fifteenth century (before the start of the Reformation) for inquisitors to try witches. However, by 1669 it had been reissued in fourty editions and had become extraordinarily popular, appealing to Protestants and Catholics alike. In France alone, 345 books about witchcraft were published between 1550 and 1650.

There is no real evidence that any of the convicted "witches" engaged in pacts with the devil. Instead, many people were forced to "confess" under torture. Others may have thought they were confessing to using simple charms only to discover that they were convicted of diabolism.

Figure 11.14, a painting from the seventeenth century, reveals the characteristics of witches as imagined by many Europeans of this period. Those accused of witchcraft were predominantly female (90 percent of those executed for witchcraft were women), many of whom were old. In this picture, the witches prepare magic potions drawn from body parts taken from the corpse hanging on the left and the heart impaled on the sword in the center. At the right, a witch carries an infant who will be killed and whose body will be used for magical purposes. In the center is a broomstick. People believed that witches rode these and used them to apply hallucinogenic potions to their vaginas.

Catholics and Protestants alike persecuted witches, and the trials in Europe peaked between 1560 and 1640. Although precise numbers elude us, more than 100,000 people were executed for witchcraft, and 200,000 may have endured trials. These trials are probably the most disturbing indicator of the rampant anxiety stirred by the intellectual and social changes of the sixteenth century.

| Persecutions |

By the eighteenth century, the witchcraft panic had ebbed and the trials gradually ceased, as men and women adjusted to the religious diversity that had split their countries and their communities. However, the ideals of the Protestant Reformation—individualism, a desire for marital harmony, an emphasis on hard work, and a staunch reliance on conscience—left a permanent mark on European society.

LOOKING BACK & MOVING FORWARD

Summary

Through the sixteenth century, the monarchs of the unified states of Europe—England, France, Spain, and the Holy Roman Empire—struggled to snatch power, wealth, and land from one another. The wars that resulted accomplished little except to bankrupt some of the kings, leave the European countryside in ruins, and inflict misery on the people. Meanwhile, religious revolutionaries stepped up their criticism of the thousand-year history of Christian tradition. These Protestants effected a reformation that spurred century-long religious warfare and that split Christendom as people followed their own paths to God. The religious quest had political ramifications as well—kings involved themselves in the Catholics' and Protestants' conflict in part to try to exert religious hegemony over their own lands and to gain land from their neighbors.

When the century of religious wars in Europe ended, it left a legacy of economic devastation, social and political change, and an intellectual revolution that transformed Western culture. More boys and girls in village schools began to read and write, men and women hoped to find love in marriage, and people began to take more pride in work over leisure. Nevertheless, the Protestant revolution failed to stop the competition for Christian souls. In the centuries to come, Europeans would take the battle between Protestants and Catholics across the seas, as they discovered lands that were new to them.

KEY TERMS

sacraments, *p. 349*
devotio moderna, *p. 349*
justification by faith, *p. 350*
indulgences, *p. 350*
purgatory, *p. 351*
Protestant, *p. 352*
iconoclasm, *p. 352*
transubstantiation, *p. 352*
predestination, *p. 355*
Huguenots, *p. 357*
Jesuits, *p. 362*
baroque, *p. 363*

REVIEW, ANALYZE, & CONNECT TO TODAY

REVIEW THE PREVIOUS CHAPTER

Chapter 10—"A New Spirit in the West"—described the characteristics that we have come to identify with the Renaissance. In addition, Chapter 10 discussed the complex political structure of Italy that engaged popes as well as princes in power politics.

1. Which Renaissance characteristics also describe the ideas of the Protestant reformers? Consider how the Renaissance influenced the Protestant Reformation.

2. Review the policies of Renaissance popes as they strove to become political powers in Italy. How did those policies contribute to the Reformation?

ANALYZE THIS CHAPTER

Chapter 11—"Alone Before God"—follows the expansion of warfare until it engulfed all of Europe in the sixteenth century. It also looks at the new religious ideas that split the Catholic Church and brought about a change in life in the West.

1. Review the various religious beliefs of the different Protestant sects and consider the relationship of these ideas to the different social and economic groups who were attracted to them.

2. How did the differing appeal help lead to the century of religious warfare? What were the results of this warfare?

3. Review the reform movements of the Catholic Church. How did the church respond to the critique of the Protestants?

4. How did the Reformation help contribute to changing social and cultural patterns that marked seventeenth-century Europe?

CONNECT TO TODAY

Think about this chapter's discussion of the ways in which changing religious ideas led to warfare and suffering. Also consider how the new technology of warfare increased the human cost.

1. Many individuals thought that the violence of the Thirty Years' War would prevent people from fighting about religion ever again. That expectation has not been realized. In what countries or regions of the world does religious warfare continue today? Why do you think such warfare has not ended in these locations?

2. Is the technology of modern warfare further increasing the human cost? Explain. How might technology *decrease* the human toll of war?

BEYOND THE CLASSROOM

THE CLASH OF DYNASTIES, 1515–1555

Bonney, Richard. *The European Dynastic States, 1494–1660.* Oxford: Oxford University Press, 1991. A rich survey that includes eastern as well as western Europe and provides an excellent overview (although it does exclude England).

Davis, Natalie Zemon. *The Return of Martin Guerre.* Cambridge, MA: Harvard University Press, 1983. The classic study of Martin Guerre (the subject of the Chapter 11 Biography).

Kelly, Jack. *Gunpowder: Alchemy, Bombards, & Pyrotechnics: The History of the Explosive That Changed the World.* New York: Basic Books, 2004. An engaging, detailed account of the development and use of gunpowder in artillery and fireworks, from its beginnings in China through the nineteenth century.

MacCulloch, Diarmaid. *The Reformation.* New York: Penguin, 2005. A comprehensive and brilliant intellectual history analysis of the Reformation that goes beyond traditional accounts of the period's main reformers.

Maltby, William. *The Reign of Charles V.* New York: Palgrave Macmillan, 2004. A concise, accessible summary of this significant ruler that shows his influence in Latin America as well as Europe.

Parker, Geoffrey. *European Soldiers, 1550–1650.* New York: Cambridge University Press, 1997. A short, beautifully illustrated look into the lives of European soldiers.

Reston, James. *Defenders of the Faith: Charles V, Suleyman the Magnificent, and the Battle for Europe, 1520–1536.* New York: Penguin Press HC, 2009. A vibrant re-creation of a pivotal period in the confrontation between the West and Islam, illuminating the ideas that underlay this struggle.

A TIDE OF RELIGIOUS REFORM

Bainton, Roland H. *Here I Stand: A Life of Martin Luther.* New York: Meridian, 1995. First published in 1950, remains the best and most sensitive study of the man and his impact.

Baylor, Michael G. *The Radical Reformation.* New York: Cambridge University Press, 1991. Collects letters and other documents to illustrate the rich diversity and the fragile unity that existed in the political thinking of some of the major radical reformers in Germany.

Belloc, Hilaire. *How the Reformation Happened.* Rockford, IL: TAN Books, 2009. A Catholic perspective on the causes of the Reformation, offering a concise thesis for these causes.

Haigh, Christopher. *English Reformations: Religion, Politics, and Society Under the Tudors.* Oxford: Clarendon Press, 1993. A scholarly work that draws on a wealth of primary materials from catechisms to churchwardens' accounts to offer a full picture of the English Reformation.

Scribner, R.W. *The German Reformation,* 2nd ed. New York: Palgrave Macmillan, 2003. A brief and accessible analysis of the appeal of the Reformation to common people.

THE CATHOLIC REFORMATION

Ahlgren, Gillian. *Teresa of Avila and the Politics of Sanctity.* Ithaca, NY: Cornell University Press, 1996. Considers Teresa's struggle in the context of a world that did not always look kindly on an outspoken woman.

Birley, Robert. *The Refashioning of Catholicism, 1450–1700: A Reassessment of the Counter Reformation.* Washington, DC: Catholic University Press, 1999. Offers a comprehensive, balanced, historical view of the Catholic Reformation by a prominent historian of Catholicism. Its strength is placing these ideas into the context of the times.

O'Malley, John. *Trent and All That: Renaming Catholicism in the Early Modern Era*. Cambridge, MA: Harvard University Press, 2002. The best overview of early modern Catholicism that explains the intellectual and historical developments in an engaging way.

EUROPE ERUPTS AGAIN: A CENTURY OF RELIGIOUS WARFARE, 1559–1648

Holt, Mack P. *The French Wars of Religion, 1562–1629*, 2nd ed. Cambridge: Cambridge University Press, 2005. A brief, clear description of the events of these wars as well as an analysis of the issues that formed the backdrop of the warfare, clarifying a complex time.

MacCaffrey, Wallace. *Elizabeth I: War and Politics, 1588–1603*. Princeton, NJ: Princeton University Press, 1992. Recounts the conduct of the war with Spain and describes the diplomacy of alliances of the period.

Wedgwood, C.V. *The Thirty Years War*. New York: NYRB Classics, 2005. A comprehensive, scholarly, definitive account of this pivotal war that engagingly draws from a full range of sources.

LIFE AFTER THE REFORMATION

Harrington, Joel. *Reordering Marriage and Society in Reformation Germany*. Cambridge: Cambridge University Press, 1994. A provocative and sound interpretation.

Russell, Jeffrey B. *A History of Witchcraft*, 2nd ed. London: Thames and Hudson, 2007. Fully revised classic study that places the sixteenth-century witchcraft craze in its historical context while drawing comparisons with modern sorcery.

Weber, Max. *The Protestant Ethic and the Spirit of Capitalism*. Los Angeles: Roxbury Publishing, 1998. Originally published in 1904, this study of how the Reformation helped create the modern world has generated much controversy but has also shaped much of the historical thinking about the Reformation.

PORTRAIT OF DON FRANCISCO DE AROBÉ, DETAIL FROM *THE MULATTO GENTLEMEN OF ESMERALDAS,* BY ANDRÉS SÁNCHEZ GALLQUE, 1599

Globalization changed the world beginning in the fifteenth century as Europeans and Africans encountered native peoples in the New World. This portrait is part of a larger portrait of three men in Ecuador in the service of the Spanish king Philip III. The subject here, Francisco, was of mixed African descent, a Christian, and the governor of a settlement in Ecuador. He represents the new blending of peoples and cultures, and this portrait, the oldest surviving signed and dated painting from colonial South America, reveals the kind of changes that came about as people moved across the seas.

Faith, Fortune, and Fame

12

European Expansion, 1450–1700

"To serve God and the King, to give light to those who are in darkness, and to grow rich, as all men desire to do." With these words, the Portuguese explorer Bartholomeu Dias (1450–1500) explained purposes that drove men to sail their ships across uncharted oceans during the sixteenth and seventeenth centuries. At the same time that Italian Renaissance ideas spread and the Reformation created new martyrs, daring Europeans ventured where they had never gone before. Kings and queens sponsored these explorers in the hopes that the new territories and riches they promised would give monarchs an advantage over their dynastic rivals.

The adventurers traveled by ship east to China, Japan, and other places in the Pacific, and west to strange new islands and continents. As they journeyed, they met peoples living in great empires in the East and in the mountains and jungles of South and Central America. They traded with many others from tribes and kingdoms in sub-Saharan Africa, the Caribbean, and North America. The interactions among the many cultures prompted the emergence of new markets and the discovery of unusual products that whetted Europeans' appetites for yet more novelties. Some men, like Don Francisco, shown in the chapter-opening portrait, were able to prosper in the new global environment, but not all were so successful. Sadly, the commingling also led to the transmission of deadly new diseases and other hardships. Europeans were irrevocably altered by these cultural contacts, and so were the cultures they encountered.

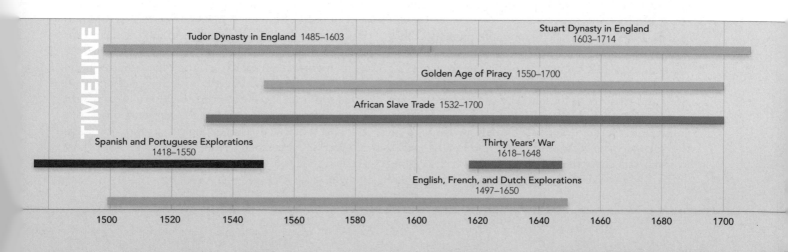

TIMELINE

Tudor Dynasty in England 1485–1603

Stuart Dynasty in England
1603–1714

Golden Age of Piracy 1550–1700

African Slave Trade 1532–1700

Spanish and Portuguese Explorations
1418–1550

Thirty Years' War
1618–1648

English, French, and Dutch Explorations
1497–1650

1500   1520   1540   1560   1580   1600   1620   1640   1660   1680   1700

THE WORLD IMAGINED

In 1498, four Portuguese ships led by Vasco da Gama sailed south from Europe and rounded the southern tip of Africa to reach India in the east. Gaspar Correa accompanied this journey, keeping a careful chronicle that told of the exciting, frightening voyage. In order to sail south with prevailing northwesterly winds, the navigators could not hug the shore but instead had to direct the ships southwest, tacking into the wind and going far away from the sight of land into the unknown sea. For two months, Vasco da Gama tacked out to sea to make sure that when they turned to shore, the ships would "double the cape," skirting the African continent. Correa wrote of the hardships of this venture into the Atlantic: "The fury of the sea [made] the ships seem every moment to be going to pieces. The crews grew sick with fear and hardship, . . . and all clamored for putting back to Portugal. . . . At times they met with such cold rains that the men could not prepare their food. All cried out to God for mercy upon their souls." Vasco da Gama finally ordered the ships about and they sailed southeast again. They circled the southern tip of Africa and with much celebration they headed northeast toward India.

The ships were to face much more hardship. They pulled into great rivers in Africa looking for food and for people to tell them where they were. They ate unknown fruits—one so toxic it made their gums swell and their teeth loosen. The captain ordered his ill men to rinse their mouths with urine to ease their gums, and the cure worked. Somehow, through all the adversity the crews carried on and finally docked in India at a city where citizens flocked to the shore, amazed at the Western ships. Correa succinctly and accurately described the confrontation between East and West: "All were much amazed at seeing what they had never before seen." Vasco da Gama's crew was not unique in the fifteenth century; brave sailors sailed east and west from Europe, and the world was transformed as Europeans and indigenous peoples almost everywhere were amazed at their new confrontation.

The Lure of the East

Western Europeans had long coveted goods from the East, which they generally considered China and India. When they used the name "China," they also meant Japan and the other lands of eastern Asia. When they referred to "India," they included southeast Asia and the many islands dotting the Pacific, and although Vasco da Gama reached the mainland of India, he would have been content to land on any of the Pacific islands. More than just a geographic entity, though, the East, in many Europeans' minds, was the source of valuable luxury goods.

Eastern trade

Since the Middle Ages, Europe had lusted after the silks, fine carpets, pottery, and precious jewels produced in the East. Europeans were so impressed by these exotic goods that they praised the Chinese as the finest craftsmen in the world. Yet it was the spices from the Orient that riveted Westerners' attention. European diets were bland, and those who depended only on local seasonings—garlic, saffron, and the ever-present salt—found the food tiresome. Recipes of the time and records showing commercial demand reveal that people clamored for cloves, cinnamon, coriander, and pepper in particular—all available only in the East. Throughout the Middle Ages, these products came overland through the Byzantine Empire into western Europe.

But after 1400, intensifying warfare in eastern Europe and Asia made overland travel difficult. (See Chapter 9 for the increased threat posed by the Turks.) Europeans began looking for new trade routes through the eastern Mediterranean to satisfy their appetite for spice. They revived centuries-old memories of journeys to the East by reading accounts like that of the Venetian explorer Marco Polo (1254–1324), who wrote detailed descriptions of his visits to China (see Chapter 9). These works were incorrect in much of their geography, however; for example, Marco Polo believed that Japan was 1,500 miles east of China. Furthermore, most of these older accounts contained exaggerated descriptions of botanical and biological features of Eastern lands. Nevertheless, no tale of the exotic East seemed too far-fetched to fifteenth-century European imaginations.

Imagined Peoples

Since the time of the Roman scholar Pliny the Elder (23–79), people had heard of unusual races of people who inhabited parts of the world outside the Mediterranean. Pliny's works had been read, copied, and embellished over the centuries, and by the fifteenth century, explorers expected to find beings as bizarre as dog-headed humans, headless people, one-legged "sciopods," and—south of the equator—"antipods," whose feet reportedly faced backward.

Figure 12.1 shows an illustration from a fifteenth-century manuscript about the travels of Marco Polo. Although Marco Polo never claimed to have seen such creatures, later Europeans imagined that he did. On the left of the illustration is a blemmyae, a headless man whose face is located on his chest. In the center is a sciopod, a one-legged creature believed to use his large foot as a parasol against the sun. These two beings are greeted by a cyclops approaching from the right.

A more plausible person the explorers expected to meet was Prester John, supposedly a rich and powerful Christian king reigning in the heart of Africa. By the Renaissance, Europeans hoped to enlist this king as an ally against the Muslims. However, the search for both Prester John and the fascinating creatures in Marco Polo's tales was stymied by an inaccurate geographic sense of the world that, like the descriptions of the monstrous races, the explorers had inherited from the ancients.

Ptolemy's Map

During the fifteenth century, western Europeans acquired the *Geography* of Ptolemy (ca. 100–ca. 178). This guide had been translated from Greek, reproduced by the new printing presses, and widely distributed. Now Renaissance explorers had a picture of the world that they could use to venture into the Atlantic, or the "green sea of darkness," as the Arabic commentators called it.

Ptolemy portrayed the world as a globe, divided into the familiar 360 degrees of longitude. **Figure 12.2,** from a 1482 edition of the *Geography*, shows Ptolemy's map of the world. This ancient geographer believed that the world consisted of three continents—Asia, Africa, and Europe—and two oceans—the Indian Ocean and the Western Ocean. The map is surrounded by figures representing the many winds so crucial to a sailing society. In addition to mistaking the number of continents, Ptolemy made two major errors: He underestimated the extent of the oceans, suggesting that land covered three-fourths of the earth's surface, and

FIGURE 12.1 Monstrous Races, fifteenth century Influenced by writings of medieval travelers, explorers expected to see strange creatures such as those pictured here: the blemmyae on the left, a sciopod in the center, and a cyclops on the right.

he miscalculated the earth as being one-sixth smaller than its true size. With only Ptolemy's map to guide them, later explorers understandably expected the journey east to be shorter than it really was. During this age of discovery, however, the theories of Ptolemy dissolved in the face of experience.

THE WORLD DISCOVERED

The explorers expected to capitalize on Europe's desire for Eastern goods and bring back wealth for themselves and their sovereigns. Sixteenth-century rulers were desperate for money to field their expensive armies, and the conquest of Constantinople by the Turks in 1453 increased the price of the valuable spices as they imposed steep taxes on the goods. This costly trade siphoned precious metals away from an already coin-poor western Europe, and monarchs were willing to reward anyone who hunted for new wealth. Brave, enterprising men eager for fame and fortune took up the challenge.

Fame, Fortune, and Faith: The Drive to Explore

Though the lure of wealth motivated explorers and the sovereigns who funded them, some adventurers had other incentives for embarking on these risky travels. As Bartholomeu Dias implied in the quotation that introduced this chapter, religion also served as a major impulse for Europeans to seek new worlds. Christians during the fifteenth and sixteenth centuries felt besieged by the Islamic empire of the Ottoman Turks that loomed on Europe's eastern border (see Chapter 11). Some voyages aimed to find

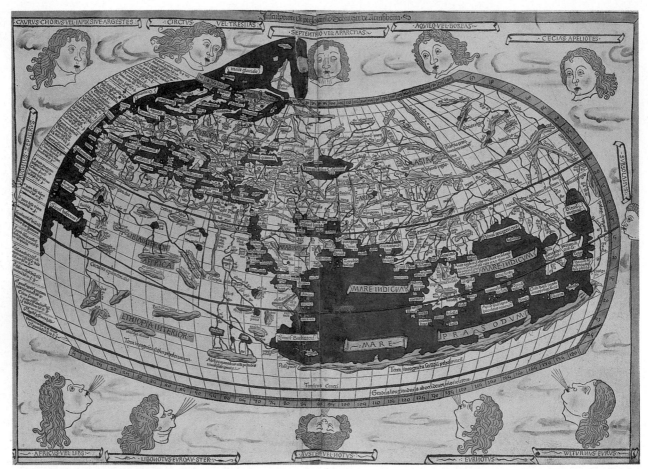

FIGURE 12.2 Ptolemy's Map The ancient map shows the world as the explorers expected it to be: largely land, with little sea, and Europe at the center. The four winds in the corners reminded sailors of their source of power.

allies against the Turks. The Reformation within Europe also stimulated explorations and migrations, as Catholics sought converts to Catholicism overseas and Protestants looked for new lands where they could practice their faith. Faith joined with fame and fortune to drive Europeans across the seas.

New Technologies and Travel

Europeans had a passion for adventure, but they also needed strong navigational tools and skills if they were to survive these hazardous journeys. Fortunately for them, sailors in the Middle Ages had perfected instruments to help them sail out of sight of land. One

> Navigation instruments

device, the **quadrant,** aligned with the fixed North Star at night to let navigators determine their latitude. However, this was not useful in the Southern Hemisphere, where the North Star was not visible. Sailors going south had to confront uncharted heavens as well as unmapped lands. During the day, sailors in both Northern and Southern hemispheres could check their calculations with the **astrolabe** (see **Figure 6.14**), which measured the height of the sun during the day or the altitude of a known star at night.

Finally, mapmakers had gained experience in charting the seas and lands and could graphically document their travels with some accuracy. Earlier skilled seafarers like the Vikings who first discovered North America lacked the cartography skills to allow them to reproduce their long sea voyages with as much certainty as did the sixteenth-century explorers. Navigators felt confident in their charts, and the newly discovered map of Ptolemy, though inaccurate, at least gave them a basic sense of direction.

Sailors lacked only the ships to carry them safely on long ventures. The galleys that had ruled the Mediterranean in the fourteenth century had large, square sails, but their locomotion came primarily from the many slaves who rowed the big ships. These ships were unsuitable for long distances and had little extra space left in their holds to store the provisions necessary for a lengthy sea voyage.

All this changed in the late fifteenth century, when the Portuguese built ships that marked the highest development of a long evolution of Mediterranean sailing ships. In the Middle Ages, shipbuilders had developed a new kind of sail rigging that allowed ships to maneuver near shore in uncertain winds. By

> Improved ships

the sixteenth century, shipbuilders had improved the mobility of the sails and the rigging of the ropes so that the sails could be moved readily. **Figure 12.3** shows a sixteenth-century watercolor of Portuguese caravels—the small (70 to 80 feet long) ships that conquered the great seas. The large square sails allowed the ships to move in the direction of the wind, or downwind. The real secret to long-distance sailing, however, was the lateen, a triangular, mobile sail at the rear (furled in **Figure 12.3**). This device not only let the ship sail faster but also allowed it to sail at an angle to the wind and thus progress upwind—a crucial advantage for traveling into the prevailing westerly winds of the Atlantic. This ship, with its absence of oar banks, stands in striking contrast to the Mediterranean galleys shown in **Figure 11.9**. The ships had to be heavy to withstand the storms of the Atlantic, and this weight gave the West an unforeseen advantage: They could support heavy cannons, giving them a military advantage over the lighter ships of the East that sailed the calmer Indian ocean. On these innovative vessels, the Portuguese set out on voyages of discovery that changed the world.

The Portuguese Race for the East, 1418–1600

As the chronicler of Vasco da Gama's voyage described in the account at the beginning of this chapter, the Portuguese explorers had an immediate goal in mind: to venture south around Africa to the Indian Ocean and trade directly with natives in India for spices and other luxury items. This route would eliminate the troublesome role of the Ottoman Turks as key players in the eastern Mediterranean trade network. Beginning in 1418, Prince Henry the Navigator (1394–1460) of Portugal sponsored annual expeditions down the west coast of Africa. Bartholomeu Dias continued Henry's work with great success, rounding the southern tip of Africa in 1488. King John II of Portugal (r. 1481–1495), expecting this route to yield the riches of the East, named the tip the Cape of Good Hope. But Dias never reached India. His frightened crew had experienced the storms and hardships that Correa described, but Dias did not maintain the iron control that Vasco da Gama would, and his crew mutinied as he sailed north along the eastern coast of Africa. He was forced to return home.

In 1498, his countryman Vasco da Gama (ca. 1460–1524) set out with four ships to complete Dias's ill-fated voyage to India. He succeeded and returned to Portugal with ships laden with spices worth sixty times the cost of the journey. On his first trip to India, da Gama carried casks of honey, hats, and other trifles to trade for the precious spices. On his second voyage four years later, the explorer brought a new trading item that would transform commerce in the Indian

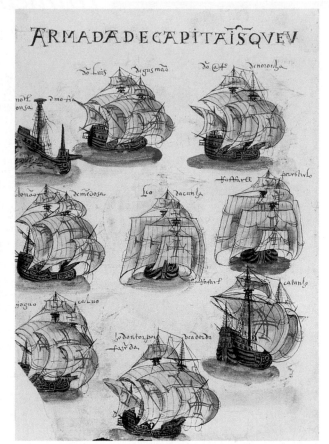

FIGURE 12.3 Portuguese Ships, sixteenth century
Portuguese caravels, the subject of this informative watercolor, were sturdily designed ships that sailed the great seas. Powered by huge sails, the ships did not need banks of oars, so they could be stocked with water and food for long voyages.

basin: His casks were now filled with gunpowder. Soldiers in India had long known the recipe for gunpowder, but when they saw its use in da Gama's deadly cannons, a new arms race would begin that would fuel escalating violence in the age of exploration.

Portuguese explorers scored spectacular successes in opening up the trade to the East. As one pleasant surprise, they discovered that India was not simply one location—it included the Moluccas, "spice islands," from which wafted the delightful aroma of cloves as the Portuguese ships approached. As **Map 12.1** shows, the Portuguese established a string of trading outposts throughout the East. In these small settlements, Europeans lived peacefully near native settlements in a mutually profitable relationship. Portugal's successful entry into the Indian Ocean trade struck a dramatic blow to the economy of the Muslims, who had previously held a monopoly on that trade. At the same time, their neighbors, the Spanish, took a quite different approach. Spain's explorers sailed westward in hopes of reaching the

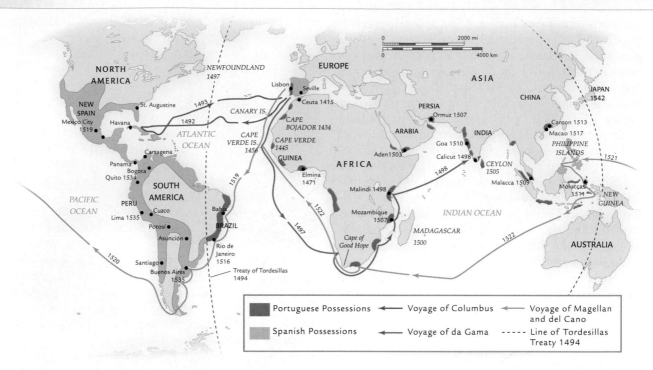

MAP 12.1

Exploration and Conquest, Fifteenth and Sixteenth Centuries

This map shows the routes and dates of the explorations of the fifteenth and sixteenth centuries, as well as the possessions claimed by the Spanish and Portuguese. It includes the Treaty of Tordesillas line, which divided the world between Portugal and Spain.

Explore the Map

1. What accounted for the differing settlement patterns in the Americas, Africa, and Asia?

2. How do you think the Treaty of Tordesillas influenced the differing settlement patterns of the Spanish and the Portuguese?

3. How were the small settlements around the coast of Africa useful for sailors and traders?

---

fabulous Orient, believing Ptolemy's claim that the land of plenty lay just over the horizon.

Spain's Westward Discoveries, 1492–1522

Christopher Columbus (1446–1506) perhaps best exemplifies Spain's travel ambitions. The son of an Italian (Genoese) weaver, Columbus traveled to Portugal in 1476 to learn about Portuguese shipbuilding and sailing. During his visit, he became captivated by the accounts of Marco Polo and the *Geography* of Ptolemy. Inflamed by images of glory and wealth, he asked the Portuguese king to sponsor him on a trip west to Asia. The king rejected him; like many others, he dismissed Columbus as a vague dreamer. Columbus then presented his idea to the Spanish monarchs

Ferdinand and Isabella. The queen, impressed with Columbus's proposal, made him an admiral in 1492 and financed his expedition.

Columbus embarked on his journey with three ships, the *Niña*, the *Pinta*, and the *Santa María*. In October, the small fleet landed on an island in the Caribbean Sea. According to the admiral's account, as he stepped ashore, Columbus "claimed all the lands for their Highnesses, by proclamation and with the royal standard displayed." According to Columbus, the many islanders who watched him did not object to his claims, so he accepted this as their tacit agreement—ignoring the language barrier that separated them. Subsequent explorers followed his lead, claiming ownership of already inhabited lands.

> Columbus's discoveries

FIGURE 12.4 Columbus's Discoveries This contemporary woodcut shows the New World as Columbus wanted to portray it: populated by beautiful, naked peoples; lush with exotic plants; and all under the control of the Spanish king on the left.

Figure 12.4 is a contemporary woodcut that was intended to capture this incident, and it shows all the essential elements: The king of Spain, on the left, gives Columbus the authority for his voyage. The three ships are featured in the center, and Columbus is shown landing on an island to claim it for the king. The island is depicted as a place as fanciful as any in the literature of imaginative travel, with exotic trees and beautiful, naked natives. The reality of the landing proved much less idyllic.

Columbus made four voyages between 1492 and 1502, during which he established settlements on several more Caribbean islands and visited the northern coast of South America and Central America. On his third voyage, he brought women from Spain to ensure the permanence of the settlements. The explorer was not a good administrator, and when Spain sent a judge to look into a revolt in the new lands, Columbus was brought back to Spain in chains. Though he was later released and made a final fourth voyage to the New World, Columbus never received the riches and acclaim he sought. Throughout these years, the Italian adventurer apparently felt sure that he had found Asian islands. He even referred to the natives as Indians because he was certain he was in the general region of India. Columbus never realized that he had discovered a world unknown by virtually all Europeans. Instead, he clung to the image of the world he had imagined. His continued misconceptions encouraged other voyagers, who would soon prove him wrong.

As the Spanish and Portuguese both raced to claim lands on their way east, they inevitably came into conflict. The Catholic sovereigns of Spain and Portugal appealed to the pope to divide the world into two spheres of influence. In the 1494 Treaty of Tordesillas (shown on **Map 12.1**), the Spanish received exclusive rights to the lands west of a line drawn 370 leagues (about 1,200 miles) west of the Cape Verde Islands off the west coast of Africa, and the Portuguese received rights to the lands east of the line. This agreement (which was virtually ignored by the other European monarchs) was one of many attempts to apportion the world without regard for the opinions of indigenous residents.

> **Treaty of Tordesillas**

Soon, subsequent travelers convinced Europeans that Columbus was wrong and that a great new landmass had been found. The most influential of these explorers was Amerigo Vespucci (1451–1512), an educated "Renaissance man" who worked for the Medici family of Florence (discussed in Chapter 10). In 1499, Vespucci set off on a voyage of discovery that took him westward from Spain and across the vast ocean to South America. During his voyage, he took careful navigational measurements and wrote colorful letters to his Medici patron, which were widely circulated. In the introduction to these works, Amerigo's publisher even suggested that Vespucci's name be given to the Mundus Novus (the New World) he had popularized with his maps and vivid tales of a continent across the ocean. The suggestion caught on, and the name "America" became attached to the western landmass that newly captured the European imagination. See Document 12.1 for an example of one of Vespucci's vivid descriptions.

After Vespucci's voyages, people set out purposefully to visit the new continent. For example, the Spanish adventurer Vasco Núñez de Balboa (1475–1517) trekked across the Isthmus of Panama, eventually reaching the Pacific Ocean on the other side. Besides adding to the evidence that a new continent existed, Balboa's discovery intensified the race to the riches of the East. New men with even bigger dreams of wealth joined the rush.

> **Circumnavigating the globe**

Ferdinand Magellan (ca. 1480–1521) was one of these men. A Portuguese explorer in the service of Spain, Magellan began the first expedition that succeeded in encircling the world. He sailed west from Spain in 1519 with three ships and discovered (and named) the Straits of Magellan at the southern tip of South America. The straits gave him access to the Pacific Ocean (which he also named). He and his crew braved the huge expanses of ocean and withstood mutinies. In 1521, Magellan was killed while interfering in a local war in the Philippines. His navigator, Sevastian Elcano (ca. 1476–1526), finished the

Amerigo Vespucci Describes the New World

In 1499, the naval astronomer Amerigo Vespucci wrote a letter to Lorenzo de' Medici of Florence (see Chapter 10) describing his travels. The letter serves as a valuable early source for European impressions of the new lands. It was particularly influential because of Vespucci's engaging style and sharp observations.

It appears to me, most excellent Lorenzo, that by this voyage most of those philosophers are controverted who say that the torrid zone cannot be inhabited on account of the great heat. I have found the case to be quite the contrary. I have found that the air is fresher and more temperate in that region than beyond it, and that the inhabitants are also more numerous here than they are in the other zones, for reasons which will be given below. Thus it is certain that practice is of more value than theory.

Thus far I have related the navigation I accomplished in the south and west. It now remains for me to inform you of the appearance of the country we discovered, the nature of the inhabitants, and their customs, the animals we saw, and of many other things worthy of remembrance which fell under my observation. After we turned our course to the north, the first land we found to be inhabited was an island at ten degrees distant from the equinoctial line. When we arrived at it we saw on the sea-shore a great many people, who stood looking at us with astonishment. We anchored within about a mile of the land, fitted out the boats, and twenty-two men, well armed, made for land. The people, when they saw us landing, and perceived that we were different from themselves—because they have no beard and wear no clothing of any description, being also of a different color, they being brown and we white—began to be afraid of us, and all ran into the woods. With great exertion, by means of signs, we reassured them and negotiated with them. We found that they were of a race called cannibals, the greater part or all of whom live on human flesh.

Your excellency may rest assured of this fact. They do not eat one another, but, navigating with certain barks which they call "canoes," they bring their prey from the neighboring islands or countries inhabited by those who are enemies or of a different tribe from their own. They never eat any women, unless they consider them outcasts. These things we verified in many places where we found similar people. We often saw the bones and heads of those who had been eaten, and they who had made the repast admitted the fact, and said that their enemies always stood in much greater fear on that account.

Still they are a people of gentle disposition and beautiful stature. They go entirely naked, and the arms which they carry are bows and arrows and shields. They are a people of great activity and much courage. They are very excellent marksmen. . . .

Nearly half the trees of this island are dye-wood, as good as that of the East. We went from this island to another in the vicinity, at ten leagues' distance, and found a very large village, the houses of which were built over the sea, like Venice, with much ingenuity. While we were struck with admiration at this circumstance, we determined to go and see them; and as we went to their houses, they attempted to prevent our entering. They found out at last the manner in which the sword cuts, and thought it best to let us enter. We found their houses filled with the finest cotton, and the beams of their dwellings were made of dye-wood. We took a quantity of their cotton and some dye-wood and returned to the ships.

Your excellency must know that in all parts where we landed we found a great quantity of cotton, and the country filled with cotton-trees, so that all the vessels in the world might be loaded in these parts with cotton and dye-wood.

SOURCE: Amerigo Vespucci, "Letter to Lorenzo de' Medici," in *The Great Events by Famous Historians*, vol. VIII, ed. Rossiter Johnson (The National Alumni, 1905), pp. 351–356.

Analyze the Document

1. How did Vespucci's observations foster a scientific attitude?

2. How might this narrative have persuaded people that there would be profits to be made in the New World?

3. How might Vespucci's descriptions of the native peoples influence future interactions between them and the Europeans?

---

journey to Asia and through the Indian Ocean back to Spain. Elcano's voyage took three years and he returned home with only one ship. But that ship was packed with enough spices not only to pay for the cost of the expedition but also to make the crew very rich.

Magellan and Elcano's successful circumnavigation of the globe revealed not that the world was round (they knew that), but its true size. It also demonstrated the impracticality of sailing to the Orient by way of the Pacific. The Spanish would have to search for new sources of wealth—this time in the New World.

The Northern Europeans Join the Race, 1497–1650

England, France, and the Netherlands came late to the race for the riches of the New World. Understandably, they were unwilling to accept the terms of the

Treaty of Tordesillas. Instead, they began their own explorations. They started by looking for a "northwest passage" to the East that would parallel the southern route around South America. In about 1497, the Genoese captain John Cabot (1450–1498) and his son Sebastian (1476–1557), who both had settled in England, received a letter from the English king Henry VII (r. 1485–1509) authorizing them to take possession for England of any new lands unclaimed by any Christian nation. So empowered, father and son sailed across the North Atlantic to Newfoundland and Maine. They found codfish so plentiful that their ships could not pass through the thick schools of fish. However, the voyage was immediately disappointing because they neither reached Asia nor returned laden with spices.

The French also hunted for a northwest passage to the East. In 1534, Jacques Cartier led three voyages that explored the St. Lawrence River in what is today

Settlements in Canada

Canada. He and his crew got as far as Montreal, but the great waterway led only inland, not out to the Pacific Northwest. An early settlement effort in the region of Quebec in 1541 failed, owing to the harsh winter and indigenes' hostility. In about 1600, Samuel de Champlain (ca. 1567–1635) made another try at establishing a settlement in North America. He founded Quebec, signing treaties with the natives to secure the settlement. Canadian settlements remained small in both size and number through the seventeenth century, but their existence ensured the continuous presence of European traders and missionaries in this northern land.

When the much-sought-after northwest passage proved elusive, northern Europeans shifted their journeys of discovery farther south and began to confront the Iberians directly. The Dutch established trading

Dutch colonies

posts in the Spice Islands, and Dutch warships proved their superiority and expelled the Portuguese from the islands that we now know as Indonesia. The Dutch also redesigned their ships to haul more cargo than the small Portuguese caravels that had first mastered the oceans. They then dominated the lucrative spice trade, founding colonies in strategic locations to protect their growing trade empire. As one example, they colonized the tip of South Africa to facilitate their Eastern trade and planted colonies in North America (most famously on Manhattan Island) and in the Caribbean.

The English, for their part, began to install settlements along the North American Atlantic seaboard in the seventeenth century: By

English colonies

1700, about 250,000 colonists lived along the coast. Many of these people moved there to escape the religious persecution that swept Europe in the seventeenth century. For this reason, they traveled west with their entire families, with the intent to stay. Their presence irrevocably altered the face of North America. **Map 12.2** shows the status of the European colonization in about 1700, and it illustrates how the northern European countries had joined the Spanish and Portuguese in their race around the world.

CONFRONTATION OF CULTURES

When the Europeans arrived in the New World, it was already abundantly populated by peoples who had lived there in resilient societies for millennia. From as early as 35,000 B.C.E., small groups of people walked from Asia northward across a land bridge from Siberia to Alaska. Slowly, over tens of thousands of years, families, clans, and tribes moved southward and settled throughout North, Central, and South America. At first, all these tribes pursued a highly effective hunting-and-gathering existence, with devastating consequences for their future development. As the hunters came through North America, they confronted great herds of large mammals—horses, elephants, camels, and giant ground sloths. Within a few centuries of human arrival, all those large mammals were extinct, probably because of effective hunting. However, this meant that there were no more large animals in North America for domestication—this would represent a fatal disadvantage when the Amerindians confronted Europeans millennia later.

The Original Americans South of the Rio Grande

In about 5500 B.C.E., tribes in central Mexico first developed agriculture, which, as we saw in Chapter 1, allowed large settled populations to become established. These civilizations would become tempting, wealthy targets for European explorers. Agriculture

Agriculture

spread north and south from there, but very slowly. The differing latitudes and varied growing seasons of the large American continents caused agriculture to diffuse more slowly in the Americas than it had in Europe and Asia, where crops spread primarily within similar latitudes. In the Americas, for example, it took about 3,500 years for maize (what we usually call corn) and beans to spread 700 miles from Mexico to the southern farmlands of the modern United States, but spread they did.

With the early use of agriculture in Central America and the western mountains of South America, populations grew large and elaborate empires—the Maya, Aztec, Inca, and others—developed. These civilizations thrived mainly through the cultivation of maize. This highly nutritious, versatile crop originally grew wild in the New World but had been

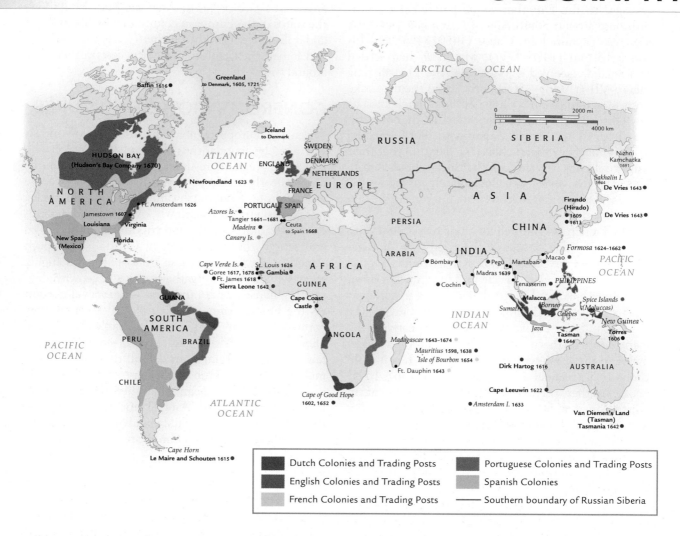

MAP 12.2

European Expansion, ca. 1700

This map shows the world around 1700, when Europeans had expanded around the globe. Notice where the people from the various countries settled, and compare the different settlement patterns of the Americas, Africa, and Asia.

Explore the Map

1. What might account for the differences in settlement patterns?

2. Compare this map with **Map 12.1.** What are the major differences between the maps, and what caused these differences?

3. Why was North America so heavily settled compared to Africa?

---

cultivated for so long that it no longer grew without human help. Maize offered high yields with very little effort. Cultivators worked only about fifty days a year to produce an abundant crop that could be eaten even before it was ripe. In these maize-growing societies, men cut and burned brush to clear the land to plant the grain, and women ground the hard kernels into flour to make tortillas, or flat bread.

The Incas, a people living in the Andes Mountains of South America, also cultivated a crop indigenous to that region—potatoes. An excellent alternative to maize, which did not grow in the high country, this hardy vegetable grew easily in the adverse conditions and high altitudes of mountain ranges and provided a hearty food supply. Once planted, potatoes required little work to harvest and prepare. Incas living in the mountains dried potatoes for long-term storage.

The small amount of time required to cultivate and harvest maize and potatoes left many days free for other work, and the great Central and South American empires developed a religious and aristocratic culture that demanded human labor for immense building projects. The Maya, Aztecs, and Incas built magnificent cities and roads and imposing pyramids. These constructions seem even more remarkable when we realize that they were built with Stone Age technology and without use of the wheel and (in most places) without the help of powerful, domesticated animals. Among these civilizations, only the Incas had domesticated the llama and alpaca as beasts of burden; throughout the rest of North and South America, people raised only dogs and fowl.

| Empire building |

Map 12.3 shows the locations of the large South American empires as they existed when the Europeans arrived in the fifteenth century. The illustration shows the narrow Isthmus of Panama, which formed an effective geographic barrier between the two major empires, and which also served to disadvantage the Amerindians in developing increasingly complex societies. For example, the Aztecs in Mexico invented a wheel, but because they lacked draft animals, the wheel remained a children's toy. The Incas had domesticated the llama but had no wheel to convert this animal into an effective beast of burden.

In Mexico, the Aztecs had located their capital at the great city of Tenochtitlán, built on a lake and accessible only by boat or causeway. (Tenochtitlán is the site of present-day Mexico City.) The Aztecs called themselves Meshica, from which we get the word *Mexico*. The Aztecs had conquered all the surrounding local tribes and claimed tribute from the vanquished, including humans sacrificed to the demanding Aztec gods, who people believed claimed human blood to delay an inevitable destruction of Aztec society. Much of the visual information we have on the South American tribes comes from manuscripts written in the sixteenth century after the Spanish conquests. Authors included drawings within these books—many created by the Amerindians themselves. From these drawings, we can gain information about life before and after the Spanish invasions. **Figure 12.5** is one such drawing, which shows the ritual human sacrifice. In the sacrificial ceremony, victims were forced to the top of a pyramid and stretched over a stone. A priest then used a sharp stone knife to cut out the victim's heart and offer it—still beating—to the god. The voracious demand for

| Aztec Empire |

FIGURE 12.5 Aztec Human Sacrifice from the *Codex Magliabecchiano*, ca. 1570 Spanish conquerors took advantage of internal warfare among the tribes that generated human sacrifices such as that documented in this Aztec manuscript. The priest at the top removes the heart of the victims.

such tribute from the subject peoples catalyzed resentment among them—a force that the new conquerors from Europe would find useful in overpowering the Aztecs.

The Original Northern Americans

The spread of maize led to large, settled agricultural communities in North America. In the American Southwest, Pueblo and Navajo peoples adapted to their dry lands by irrigating crops of maize, beans, and squashes. They built permanent adobe buildings, and their populations grew. Farther north and east, Amerindians shaped their environments in different ways. They made extensive use of fire to burn underbrush in forests and, probably more significantly, to burn the great plains and prairies. In doing so, they created a huge pastureland for game, and their populations grew as well. **Map 12.3** shows the general patterns of the North American settlements.

The largest settled populations north of the Rio Grande spread along the Mississippi valley with the mound-building cultures. The largest surviving mound, at Cahokia near St. Louis, Illinois, is an astonishing structure, 100 feet high and 1,000 feet long. There were more than a hundred smaller mounds nearby. By 1250 C.E., the settlement surrounding these mounds probably reached between 15,000 and 38,000 inhabitants. These people grew prosperous from long-distance trade along the Missouri and Mississippi rivers, which brought seashells from Florida,

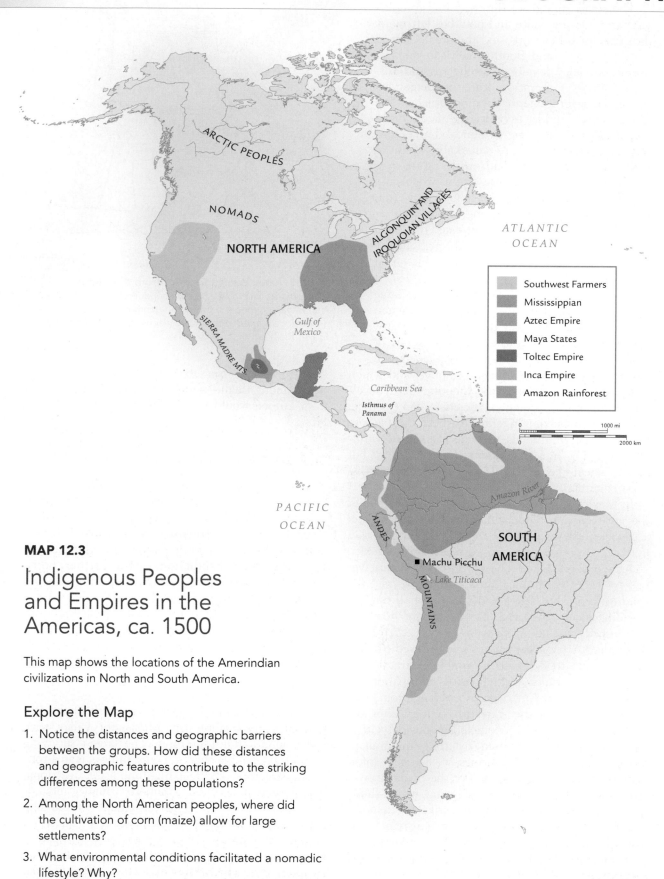

MAP 12.3

Indigenous Peoples and Empires in the Americas, ca. 1500

This map shows the locations of the Amerindian civilizations in North and South America.

Explore the Map

1. Notice the distances and geographic barriers between the groups. How did these distances and geographic features contribute to the striking differences among these populations?

2. Among the North American peoples, where did the cultivation of corn (maize) allow for large settlements?

3. What environmental conditions facilitated a nomadic lifestyle? Why?

Map legend:

- Southwest Farmers
- Mississippian
- Aztec Empire
- Maya States
- Toltec Empire
- Inca Empire
- Amazon Rainforest

copper from the Great Lakes, and other goods from all over the continent. The rise of Cahokia coincided with the spread of maize into the eastern part of the continent, a development that allowed the native populations to grow even more.

Fortunately, we have a visual record of the prosperity that eastern tribes of Amerindians enjoyed before their contact with Europeans, for an artist, John White, accompanied three voyages to the colony of Roanoke. White's detailed watercolors, copied by an engraver in the Netherlands and published in 1590, remain an excellent source of information about the lives and livelihoods of some North American tribes. The village White portrays in **Figure 12.6** is prosperous and orderly and has abundant food available. In the upper left of the etching, Amerindians hunt deer. In the hut at the upper right, a watchman makes "continual cries and noise" to frighten animals and birds from the fields, where maize and pumpkins (on the right) and tobacco (in the circular field on the left) grow. Villagers celebrate the abundance by dancing (lower right) and feasting (center).

There is much controversy over the size of these indigenous populations in North America, but certainly millions of people prospered in the American North. These flourishing cultures would be drastically affected by the arrival of Europeans.

Early Contacts

Christopher Columbus set the tone for the relationship between the original Americans and Europeans when he claimed land in the New World for the Spanish monarchs and when he treated the people as sources of revenue for the Spanish crown. With few exceptions, subsequent European explorers viewed the native peoples in the same way. Sometimes they traded with them; other times they used them as labor. Still other times, they killed or enslaved the men and women they found living in the new lands.

Explorers of the New World believed they had encountered a major problem: These lands lacked the spices and luxury goods of the East that had brought so much immediate wealth to merchants. These new explorers had to find other forms of riches to bring home. Sometimes they enslaved natives, but this was not particularly lucrative. Instead, they searched for silver and gold to take back to Europe. According to one contemporary observer, when an Amerindian asked a Spaniard what Europeans ate, the Spaniard responded, "Gold and silver." (We do not know whether this exchange actually took place, but the anecdote testifies to the insatiable European appetite for precious metals.) For the Europeans, all the early contacts involved questions of profit; for the Amerindians, such contacts brought suffering.

FIGURE 12.6 Amerindian Village from Theodore DeBry, _Grands et Petits Voyages_, 1590 This watercolor shows a well-ordered village in North America. Tribes grow tobacco, corn, and pumpkins.

Conquest of the Great Empires, 1520–1550

While in the Caribbean, the Spanish explorer Hernando Cortés (1485–1547) heard of a fabulously rich society to the west. Their curiosity aroused, he and 600 men sailed across the Gulf of Mexico in search of gold and glory. These Spanish soldiers of fortune were known as **conquistadors.** When Cortés landed on the Yucatán peninsula in southeast Mexico, the people he met there told him of a wealthy civilization in the interior (the Aztecs). As Cortés moved inland, he acquired a gift that proved more valuable to his quest than anything else—the slave woman Malinche.

Cortés's explorations

According to later Spanish sources, Malinche was a princess whose father had died when she was young. The girl's mother gave her to local slave traders when the mother remarried, and the traders included the young woman in their gifts to Cortés. Malinche spoke four Amerindian languages, including the Nahuatl of the Aztecs, and she easily learned Spanish. She converted to Christianity and took the baptismal name

FIGURE 12.7 Cortés and Montezuma, from *Lecuzo de Tlaxcala*, sixteenth century, copied in eighteenth century Cortés is accompanied by his translator Malinche as he negotiates with the Aztec ruler Montezuma.

of Marina. Malinche was constantly at Cortés's side, interpreting and advising him on matters of policy and customs as he made his way west. The various peoples they encountered on their journey recognized her importance, calling Cortés "Malinche's Captain."

Eventually, Cortés's group marched 250 miles into the interior of Mexico and reached the Aztec capital of Tenochtitlán. There, Cortés and Malinche met with Montezuma II (1502–1520), the Aztec emperor. **Figure 12.7** depicts this meeting. This drawing was

Confronting the Aztecs

taken from a valuable cloth that was painted in the mid-sixteenth century by a Mexican tribe that helped Cortés conquer the Aztecs. (Unfortunately, the original cloth has disappeared, but a copy was made in Mexico in the eighteenth century.)

By skilled use of images, the painter emphasized the role of Malinche in the conquest. In the illustration, Cortés and Malinche use the same gesture, showing that they speak with one voice. Montezuma sits in state, his nobles standing behind him. The Aztecs have gathered gifts for Cortés, drawn at the bottom of the page. The illustration foreshadows the coming European conquest: In the center of the picture, the Aztec royal headdress moves toward Cortés; in the upper-right corner, the hand of God reaches down to bless the proceedings.

Cortés knew that to transport the riches of the Aztecs back to Spain, he first had to vanquish this mighty civilization. With the help of Malinche, he garnered the support of nearly 100,000 people from neighboring tribes who were eager to throw off the Aztec yoke. Even with the advantage of gunpowder, armor, horses, and fierce dogs, it took him nearly a year to subdue the empire, and contemporary witnesses captured the violence of the struggle. Bernal Díaz del Castillo described the cap-

Aztecs conquered

ture of the last stronghold: "I have read of the destruction of Jerusalem, but I know not if that slaughter was more fearful than this—the earth, the lagoons, and the buttresses were full of corpses and the stench was more than any man could bear." In 1522, Cortés proclaimed the Aztec Empire "New Spain," and he prepared to rule. Although he had fathered a son with Malinche, he gave her as a bride to one of his soldiers and presented her with expensive estates to thank her for her help.

The Inca Empire fell to another conquistador, Francisco Pizarro (ca. 1475–1541). In 1532, Pizarro landed on the west coast of South America and began to march to Cuzco, the Incan capital. (See Global Connections.) The Inca rulers had

Incas conquered

just endured a five-year civil war over a disputed succession, and the newly victorious ruler, Atahualpa, apparently underestimated the Spanish. Atahualpa came unguarded to meet with Pizarro, and he was promptly captured. He offered a roomful of gold as his ransom, which the Spanish accepted. After collecting the ransom, they killed their hostage. The Incas fought fiercely for a few years after the fall of their leader, but they were unable to overcome the Spanish technical advantages. A new order arose in South America.

How did these small numbers of Europeans manage to conquer the impressive Amerindian empires? They gained a clear advantage from their steel weapons, horses, and high organization (including writing, which allowed

Germs

them to communicate effectively). However, in the long run, their greatest weapon was biological—germs they brought from Europe. When previously isolated populations mingle, it is common for epidemics to break out, but the confrontation between Europeans and Amerindians was particularly devastating because the New World had no history of interaction with domesticated animals. The most devastating acute diseases that Eurasians faced came initially from their animals: measles, tuberculosis, flu, whooping cough, and, perhaps most deadly, smallpox. With thousands of years of exposure to these diseases, Europeans had developed immunities. Amerindians had not. In what turned out to be a biological tragedy that clinched the European conquest, disease and death followed the colonists everywhere they ventured. As one Huron woman said of the Jesuit missionaries, "They set themselves up in a village where everyone is feeling fine; no sooner are they there but everyone dies except for three or four people. They move to another place, and the same thing happens."

The Inca Empire Falls

Ten years after Hernando Cortés had sailed from Spain and conquered the Aztec Empire in Mexico in 1521, another conquistador, Francisco Pizarro, set off to seek his own fortune in the New World. He landed on the west coast of South America—which included the 2,500-mile border of the mountainous Inca Empire. (See **Map 12.3.**) The Inca ruler used a hierarchic bureaucracy to govern a population of about 11.5 million peasants.

Before Pizarro even landed in South America, the great Inca Empire had endured deep troubles. Powerful earthquakes accompanied by giant waves had pounded the coast. Lightning had struck the palace of Huayna Capac. Messengers had also told Huayna that strange beings with beards had landed on the coast. In the midst of these disasters, the ruler remembered a prophecy claiming that during the reign of the twelfth ruler, strange men would invade and destroy the empire. Huayna was the eleventh. On his deathbed, he purportedly advised his subjects to submit to the newcomers, who would surely arrive soon in fulfillment of the prophecy.

But the empire's ruling house had suffered other problems as well. Civil war between two half brothers over the succession erupted after the death of Huayna Capac. Atahualpa, Huayna's illegitimate son, challenged Huascar,

the legitimate heir. In 1533, Atahualpa captured Huascar, but resistance to Atahualpa's rule continued in the region of Cuzco. At this volatile moment, Pizarro arrived. Some of Huascar's supporters claimed that their god, Viracochas, had sent the armed men to place Huascar on the throne. This account of Inca beliefs on the eve of Pizarro's conquest was recorded in the early sixteenth century by the conquerors themselves. Historians have used it in part to explain how Pizarro—with a force of only 62 mounted men and 106 foot soldiers—could overwhelm between 100,000 and 400,000 armed Incas. Yet, it was neither their fatalism nor Pizarro's temporary alliance with Huascar that gave the Spanish the advantage; it was their technological superiority.

In the sixteenth century, warfare had honed both the weapons and the tactical skills of the Spanish. Their horses made a huge difference, adding power and reach to the mounted soldier. Pizarro wrote that the horsemen "did all the fighting, because the . . . Indians hold the footsoldiers in slight account." Furthermore, the Spanish fighters' steel swords, spears, and pikes so outmatched the Incas' most effective weapon, the sling, that the armored invaders could engage many Indians without much fear of injury themselves. Yet, even with these

advantages, the Spanish took seven years to fully conquer the extensive empire. Despite the Incas' lack of advanced weaponry, they quickly assessed the Spanish tactics and bravely exploited what weaknesses they could find.

Due to the cultural and technological chasm between the Spanish and the Incas, the conquest took on unprecedented brutality. One conquistador wrote, "I can bear witness that this is the most dreadful and cruel war in the world. For between Christians and Muslims there is some well-feeling. . . . But in this Indian war there is no such feeling on either side. They give each other the cruelest deaths they can imagine." After finally crushing the Incas, the Spanish had little inclination to treat their captives with any humanity. The early Spanish rule—with its forced labor programs—proved as brutal as the conquest itself.

Making Connections

1. How did technological differences between the Incas and the Spanish contribute to the brutality of the Spanish rule?

2. How did internal problems and Spanish military technology lead to the Incas' defeat?

North American Contacts

The fortunes of the northern Amerindians in the wake of Europeans' arrival are more difficult to recount because the first contacts between the Europeans and the northern tribes were indirect. Direct contacts in the north did not occur until twenty-five to one hundred years later than the South and Central American contacts. Thus we do not have as many eyewitness accounts for the early period in the north. Yet the effects of the Europeans' arrival were still powerfully felt there, because European

germs were able to spread to North America, where they brought diseases to the people and destroyed their societies on a large scale. Thus, when the first accounts of the northern contact were written, the authors described societies that had already been severely disrupted.

One example of the ravages of disease in the north following European contact came in the wake of the Spaniard Hernando de Soto's (ca. 1496/97–1542) landing in Florida in 1539. For four years, de Soto's small force wandered through Florida and Georgia and elsewhere in the South looking for gold. De Soto's band killed many Indians in the course of their travels, but the explorer eventually succumbed to fever and died. Many of de Soto's pigs remained to roam in the woods. As we have seen, domestic animals often served as sources of disease in early modern times, just as they do in the world today, as we are periodically confronted by animal-borne diseases such as swine flu and avian flu. De Soto's pigs similarly brought disease that spread widely through the human population. By the time the next Europeans traveled through the Mississippi valley a century later, the population had fallen steeply, by perhaps as much as 96 percent. Disease had emptied this rich land of its peoples.

Across the continent in southwestern North America, a shipwreck stranded another Spaniard, Álvar Núñez Cabeza de Vaca (ca. 1490–ca. 1560), with his three companions, who included an African slave. Cabeza de Vaca created a valuable account that told of a society already damaged by earlier contacts. For eight years, the travelers roved among the southern nomadic tribes until they encountered a Spanish colony in 1536. De Vaca wrote of hunger, hospitality, and warfare among the Amerindians, and his narratives shaped many Europeans' views of the native North Americans.

Some scholars believe that the rich environmental and animal resources the North American colonists found, from the fertile Great Plains to the innumerable buffalo herds, existed because the native peoples who had tended the land had died off, primarily from imported diseases. The North American world was transformed by the European arrival as surely as was the Southern Hemisphere.

Life and Death Under European Rule, 1550–1700

The goal of the newly established European colonial empires was to enrich the home countries. To meet this aim, the colonists exploited natural resources and Amerindian peoples to their fullest. The Spanish crown divided up the lands, placing viceroys in charge of each section. These royal representatives were responsible for delivering to the crown the profits taken from the new lands. The crown claimed one-fifth of all gold and silver mined in the New World, and the treasure ships departed the coasts of the Americas heavily laden.

To get the human labor he needed to search and mine for precious metals, Christopher Columbus proposed enslaving the native peoples. Queen Isabella rejected the plan, for she considered the New World peoples her subjects. Instead, the Spanish developed a new structure, called the **encomienda** system, to provide the conquerors with labor. Under this system, the

Enforced labor

crown would grant an encomienda, which gave conquistadors and their successors the right to the labor of a certain number of Amerindians. Theoretically, in exchange for labor, the Spanish owed the natives protection and an introduction to the Christian faith.

The encomiendas lasted only through the sixteenth century, but this system was replaced by other forms of labor servitude, like the *repartimiento*, which required adult males to devote a certain number of days of labor annually to Spanish economic enterprises, such as plantations (called **haciendas**) or mines. Sometimes these contracts stipulated a lifetime of labor (though the subject peoples remained personally free); other times, the Amerindians had to work for the Spanish for a fixed number of years. Life under these contracts proved extremely harsh— with hard labor and a shortage of food—and many laborers died while working for their new overseers.

For the Spanish, the arrangement yielded untold wealth, exemplified by the silver mine in Bolivia—the Potosí—shown in the painting in **Figure 12.8**. In the background of this picture, workers and pack-trains climb steep peaks that lead to the veins of ore. The workers' homes are shown in the middle of the painting. In the foreground, other local Amerindians process the ore. First they watch a hydraulic wheel crush the raw ore; then they pound the ore with large hammers until it is reduced to powder. The waterwheel is fed by long canals that convey melting snow and rainwater from the mountain. The last step in the process was to mix the ore with mercury and convert it into a paste. This technique, brought from Europe in 1557, increased silver production tenfold. From 1580 to 1620, the great age of Spanish imperialism was financed by the silver extracted primarily from the Potosí mine.

Figure 12.8 also hints at the amount of work necessary to run sixteenth-century mines and the reason that the mine owners saw the enforced labor of the locals as essential. The Spanish crown gave the owners of the Potosí mine the conscripted labor of 13,300 Amerindians. These workers had to report to the mine on Monday morning and toil underground until Saturday evening. The mine owners did not provide meals; throughout the workweek, the men's wives had to bring them food. Many workers perished under the inhumane conditions.

Not everyone accepted this colonial brutality as a natural consequence of the need for silver. The most severe critic among these was the Dominican friar Bartolomé de Las Casas (1474–1566). In his book *The Tears of the Indians*, Las Casas wrote: "There is nothing more detestable or more cruel, than the tyranny which the Spaniards use toward the Indian." Historians have disagreed about the exact number of lives lost in the Spanish

Amerindian mortality

domination of Central and South America, but all the estimates are shocking. Diseases, overwork, and warfare took a terrible toll on indigenous people everywhere in the New World. When Columbus landed in 1492, for example, the population of the Caribbean Islands was about 6,000,000, and fifty years later, it numbered only a few thousand. The native population of Peru fell from about 1,250,000 in 1570 to just 500,000 in 1620. Mexico fared worse: About 24 million native individuals died between 1519 and 1605. Many fell victim to diseases, overwork, and the abuse that Las Casas had described. Some Europeans abhorred this destruction, but many saw it as merely a source of worry about where to get enough labor to work their mines and the plantations.

In another tragic turn of events, Las Casas proposed a solution that he thought might free the native workers from their burden of labor. He suggested that the king of Spain offer Spanish men and women a license to settle in the New World. In addition to land, each license would give permission for the holder to import a dozen African slaves to the Americas. In his old age, Las Casas recognized the problems with this policy. To his regret, the plan brought a shameful new injustice to the New World: the African slave trade.

FIGURE 12.8 Potosí Silver Mine, ca. 1584 This mine in Bolivia, worked by more than 13,000 conscripted Amerindians, supplied huge amounts of silver at great cost. The process used mercury, which polluted the waterways.

The African Slave Trade

By the beginning of the seventeenth century, the new rulers in the Americas were facing alarming labor shortages. The original Americans had died in huge numbers just as colonists stepped up the need for labor in their profitable enterprises. As we saw earlier, mining required countless workers. The sprawling plantations built to exploit demand for new crops also desperately depended on large numbers of ill-paid workers.

Sugar is the overriding example. Although sugarcane grew in Egypt and North Africa, it remained scarce and expensive. Europeans discovered that the cane flourished in the New World and began to cultivate it avidly in hopes of satisfying the intense European craving for its sweet flavor. Sugar also fueled a new vice—the alcoholic beverages (like rum) that it helped make. Throughout the Caribbean and in Brazil, colonists established grand sugar plantations and began using African slaves to work them. On the plantations, like the one in Barbados shown in **Figure 12.9,** workers tended the sugarcane and harvested it with large, sharp knives—a practice that often led to serious injuries. Then the cane had to be crushed to extract its juice. In this illustration, the cane is crushed in the background with grindstones.

Sugar plantations

In the center, the crushed cane is cooked in vats to produce molasses, and then the product is distilled into rum (in the lower left). The whole process was guided by overseers like the one in the foreground holding his stick to beat any recalcitrant slaves.

Sugar and other plantations (for example, cotton in North America) were designed to produce enough of their specified crop to satisfy a world market. Plantation owners took a consuming interest in the success of these endeavors. Indeed, the German naturalist Maria Merian (see the Biography on page 405) wrote that she was ridiculed in the colony of Surinam, in South America, because she was interested in things other than sugar. This monoculture, or focus on a single crop, forced the plantations to trade with the rest of the world for all their remaining necessities, including labor.

As we saw in Chapter 10, slavery on a small scale began to be reintroduced into Europe during the Renaissance, and the sixteenth-century warfare escalating between Christians and Muslims stimulated even more enslavements in North Africa. For example, in 1627 Muslim pirates from the Mediterranean raided distant Iceland and enslaved nearly 400 descendants of the Vikings. Current studies suggest that between 1580 and 1680, some 850,000 Christian captives were enslaved in Muslim North Africa. Some of these captives who escaped or were ransomed engaged in their own slaving raids against Muslims as a form of revenge.

This growth of slavery between Christians and Muslims likely suggested to Europeans a solution for

FIGURE 12.9 Sugar Plantation, 1667 Sugar was the crop that brought the most wealth to plantation owners. Originally from Egypt, sugar was transplanted wherever it would grow, to satisfy soaring European tastes for sugar and rum. Slaves were brought to work the fields and the processing plants.

the labor shortages in the New World. In 1532, the first slave shipments departed from Africa to transport slaves directly across the Atlantic to the plantations of the West Indies and Brazil. Before 1650, only about 7,000 slaves annually crossed the Atlantic, but the figure doubled to about 14,000 between 1650 and 1675. Before the 1680s, the Atlantic slave trade almost exclusively provided slaves for these sugar plantations. During the seventeenth century, blacks brought to North America came from the Caribbean, not directly from Africa—many had European surnames and knew a European language. A significant fraction of these early "servants for life" in North America became free, and some appear in the early records of the colonies (even in the South) as freeholders and voters. By the eighteenth century, the rise in plantations in North America caused slaves to be imported directly from Africa in large numbers (see Chapter 15).

African slaves

The slave trade generated huge profits, not only for the Europeans, but also for African chiefs who supplied slaves to the traders. Because of long, but periodic, contact with Europe for millennia, Africans had substantial resistance to European diseases, so they survived in larger numbers than the Amerindians had. Slavery had always been part of African warfare, and as early as the seventh century, Muslims profited from

Impact in Africa

slaves brought across the Sahara Desert. However, in the sixteenth century the huge profits created a new scale of trade—chiefs traded slaves to the Europeans in exchange for guns to gain advantage over their traditional rivals. Some tribes (such as the Congo in central Africa) were initially opposed to the trade but became heavily involved to stay competitive with their neighbors.

The political consequences of the trade in Africa varied. In the kingdom of the Congo, the Portuguese quest for slaves weakened the monarchy and led to local warfare and a decentralization of power. In the military kingdom of Dahomey on the west coast of Africa, kings made the slave trade a royal monopoly and profited enormously. When the trade ended, however, the resulting economic depression in Dahomey led to severe political disturbance. Although this discussion shows it is possible to treat the slave trade as one more manifestation of the growing world economy, one cannot ignore the fact that the trade of human beings rendered incalculable costs in human misery.

By 1700, traders were delivering about 30,000 slaves each year, and that number continued to escalate into the late eighteenth century. Packed tightly into the holds of ships and subjected to lack of food, water, and sanitary facilities, as many as 25 percent of these human beings died in transit. Anyone who survived the trip then faced new horrors: starvation and overwork and sometimes harsh physical discipline by their owners.

Some slaves ran away. In Brazil, in particular, many escapees fled into the forest and founded their own communities. The largest of the settlements was Palmares, which the Portuguese attacked in 1692 and destroyed three years later.

Slave rebellions Although it is impossible to get exact figures, it seems the community consisted of perhaps 10,000 fugitives who had formed a kingdom and designated a king and a council of elders. Other slaves devised more subtle forms of rebellion, including slow labor. In one interesting instance, an African woman in Surinam told the naturalist Maria Merian that the slaves practiced birth control to avoid bringing children into slavery. Although we know that Africans practiced some birth control in Africa, we cannot know for sure that it took a new purpose under slavery, but it may have.

Gathering Souls in the New Lands

Early explorers were partially motivated to travel by their desire to spread the Christian faith, and this desire only increased as Europeans found so many "heathens" around the world. Cultures all over the world became exposed to the Christian message. Many missionaries worked to alleviate the misery caused by the conquests, but others traveled from Europe with the zeal of crusaders and with the dogged insensitivity of the conquistadors. Some of them baptized natives in large groups, with no concern for their spiritual inclinations. Columbus and other early explorers, ignorant of native culture, wrote that the indigenous peoples had no religious sensibilities and thus should be easily converted. As a result, subsequent missionaries believed they were offering the benefits of religion to people who had none.

This attitude led to even further ill treatment of native peoples. In 1543, for example, the archbishop of New Spain (Mexico) tried 131 people for heresy, including 13 Aztecs, who he (rightly) believed practiced old forms of piety. In 1555, the Council of Mexico resolved not to ordain anyone of Indian, African, or mixed background—the priesthood was to be reserved for those of European descent. The suspicion extended even to churchmen sympathetic to native peoples. The Spanish crown had banned the writings of Bartolomé de Las Casas that decried Iberian treatment of Amerindians, and the Spanish Inquisition included them on its list of forbidden books.

A significant turning point in the conversion of the indigenous peoples of Mexico came in 1531, when a native convert named Juan Diego claimed to have seen the Virgin Mary. As Virgin of Diego explained it, Mary had commanded him to build a church in Guadalupe her honor, and when he needed proof of this command, the Virgin ordered him to gather roses within his cloak and take them to the bishop. Although it was not the season for the flower, Diego claimed to have found them and when he unfolded his cloak in the presence of the bishop, all claimed to see a miraculously formed image of the Virgin Mary left on the cloak. The Virgin of Guadalupe (named for the region near Mexico City where she reportedly appeared) became the patroness of Mexico, and Juan Diego's cloak with the Virgin's image remains in her shrine, where pilgrims gather to see it. **Figure 12.10** shows an eighteenth-century reproduction of the image on the cloak painted on wood. For many Mexicans, she lent credence to their belief that Christianity did not belong only to Europeans. Her shrine remains a major pilgrimage site today, and reproductions of the image have been widely circulated. Juan Diego, too, remained a venerated figure, and in 2002, he was declared a saint.

Some missionaries to the Americas proved acutely sensitive to the needs of the new converts and accommodated Christian practice to local religious ways. Las Casas was one such missionary; another was Marie de Missionaries l'Incarnation (1599–ca. 1669), a French nun who founded a convent in Quebec to teach native Canadian girls. Marie not only cared for the young women who came to her convent but also learned the Algonquin language and translated some religious writings into that language to make them accessible to the Algonquin-speaking peoples.

Missionaries generally paid more attention to the spiritual salvation of New World natives than to that of the African slaves brought to the Americas. A striking exception to this rule was the Portuguese missionary Pedro Claver (1580–1654), who has now been declared a Catholic saint. Claver settled in Colombia in 1610 and was horrified by the plight of the slaves who worked the plantations. From then on, whenever he signed his name, he added the vow "forever a servant to Africans." He lived up to that vow, converting many Africans to Christianity while caring for their physical needs. He even built and worked in a leper colony, caring for sick, neglected Africans.

Elsewhere across the world, European missionary work took on decidedly different forms than it did in the Americas. In Asia, the missionaries succeeded in their aims only after they acknowledged the validity and strengths of the local cultures. For example, some Jesuit priests in Japan adopted the status of Zen Buddhist priests and strictly observed Japanese etiquette. The Japanese were quite receptive to the missionaries, and by 1580, Jesuits claimed over 100,000 conversions in Japan. The goodwill ended in about 1600, when trade disputes unleashed a Japanese persecution of Christians that was so brutal it virtually stamped out Christianity on the

FIGURE 12.10 Virgin of Guadalupe In 1531, the Virgin Mary was said to have appeared to Juan Diego, a native convert in Mexico. This miracle was instrumental in bringing Christianity to the New World. This illustration of the Virgin of Guadalupe is by Pedro Antonio Fresquis, ca. 1790.

island. The Jesuit Roberto de Nobili in 1605 carried this policy of religious accommodation to its logical extreme in India by dressing in the robes of an Indian holy man, studying Sanskrit, and refusing all contact with fellow Europeans.

The Chinese proved more suspicious of the Westerners, at first denying them entry to their country. Nevertheless, a Jesuit—Matteo Ricci (1552–1610)—approached them with Western gifts (such as a mechanical clock) and gained admission to the court of the Ming emperor Wan-li (r. 1573–1620). While practicing his faith at the Chinese court, Ricci adopted much that was Chinese. He dressed as a Confucian scholar, for example, and preached the Christian message in terms consistent with Chinese ethics. By 1605, 17 missionaries were working in China. Not all the missionaries working in China were as tolerant as Ricci, and many condemned Confucianism as paganism.

As Christianity spread around the world, Christian practice changed as it accommodated the needs of new converts. Mexican Christians, for example, venerated the dark-skinned image of the Virgin of Guadalupe with a vigor unappreciated in Europe. Brazilian and Haitian converts worshiped in the Christian tradition, all the while acknowledging spiritual customs brought from Africa. Chinese Christians continued their practice of venerating ancestors, much to the chagrin of some European priests. In all these cases, the Catholic Church was itself transformed even as it transformed those around it. In time, Protestant worship, too, would be affected—the use of African rhythms in gospel music in modern North American churches offers one vivid example.

> Christianity transformed

THE WORLD MARKET AND COMMERCIAL REVOLUTION

Europeans had long traded over extensive distances; after all, it was the spices and silks of the Far East that had first lured them across the Atlantic. During the twelfth and thirteenth centuries, Europeans had enjoyed a growing commerce (see Chapter 8), creating northern and southern trade routes that brought goods through the Middle East from the farthest reaches of Asia. These centuries introduced a commercial revolution that greatly expanded the opportunities for many in the growing towns of the Middle Ages. However, the disasters of the fourteenth century (see Chapter 9) put the brakes on this growth, and this commercial contraction lasted almost until the middle of the sixteenth century. Now, the navigation of the seas and the exploration of new lands reopened and reshaped this pattern of production and commerce. By the end of the sixteenth century, Europeans were trading in a world market, on a scale larger than they had ever before experienced.

High Prices and Profits: Trading on the World Stage

In **Figure 12.11,** the Dutch artist Jan Vermeer (1632–1676) captures some of the themes of this new commercial age. Vermeer painted many everyday scenes praising the tranquillity and order of the prosperous Netherlands. However, these serene images also testify to the bustling world market that made middle-class townspeople so wealthy. Indeed, the lifestyle hinted at in this painting would have been unimaginable in the Middle Ages. Vermeer depicts a young woman gently grasping a water pitcher. The pitcher is made of silver, possibly from the Potosí mine in Bolivia (see **Figure 12.8**). The jewel box to the right of the pitcher lies open, revealing pearls, probably from the Orient. Both objects are set on a tablecloth of tapestry from India. The woman's clothing is made of oriental silk—an unusual luxury for everyday dress. Even the woman's movement to open a window suggests wealth, for expensive, leaded glass windows originally had been used only in churches. Vermeer completes this picture of prosperity with a leather map of the world hanging on the wall—a fitting symbol of the new global commerce.

What exactly stepped up the global demand for luxury goods? In part, the demand was fueled by population growth in the sixteenth and seventeenth centuries. During the sixteenth century, the number of Europeans expanded from about 80 million to 105 million as Europe recovered from the devastation of the Black Death. These increases continued. As the population steadily rose, goods became scarce. Demand intensified and drove prices up. In the sixteenth century, cereal prices escalated about fivefold, and the price of manufactured goods tripled. Contemporary witnesses repeatedly expressed shock at the inflation. As one sixteenth-century Spaniard lamented, "Today a pound of mutton costs as much as a whole sheep used to." People complained, but no one had concrete solutions to the problem.

> Inflation

At mid-century, some Europeans began blaming the influx of precious metals from the New World for their inflation woes. Their frustration was understandable. The Potosí mine alone yielded millions of Spanish coins a year, which poured unchecked into the European economy, moving rapidly from one country to the next. As just one example of the interconnected economy, the massive Spanish ships that transported silver across the Atlantic depended on French canvas for their sails. Silver coins from the New World paid for those sails. As one French author wrote, "They may have the ships, but we have their wings." Economists can trace Spanish silver from Europe to as far as China, where European merchants snapped up the silks and spices that initially inspired the explorations. Yet the flood of coins into Europe was only part of the picture. In truth, the price revolution stemmed from a combination of the new money, a surge in population growth, and unprecedented appetites for new goods.

The Rise of Commercial Capitalism

Inflation always hurts those with fixed incomes, but high prices also provide incentives for enterprising people to make a profit. The energetic sixteenth-

FIGURE 12.11 Jan Vermeer, *Young Woman with a Water Pitcher,* ca. 1664   The global trade brought wealth to new merchant classes. They could then afford beautiful art that celebrated their new acquisitions, such as glass windows, silver pitchers, woven tapestries, and even a world map for the wall.

century pursuit of trade stimulated new forms of production and economic concepts that together have been called the commercial revolution, but might more accurately be termed a commercial acceleration, during which trading practices developed in the Middle Ages spread and flourished. During this vital era, a set of business practices (and perceptions) arose that we know as capitalism. The word *capitalism* was actually not used until the nineteenth century. By the mid-seventeenth century, however, some individuals were called **capitalists,** a word indicating how they handled money. Capitalists were people who chose to invest their funds in business activities in order to make more money (capital). For these **entrepreneurs,** the most lucrative business opportunity was the growing world trade. Document 12.2 presents a seventeenth-century testimonial on the benefits of this long-distance trade.

Dutch entrepreneurs led the way in implementing capitalist ideas as they engaged in worldwide trade. For example, merchants in Amsterdam built huge warehouses to store goods so that they could control

Thomas Mun Praises Trade

Thomas Mun (1571–1641) was a director in the East India Company, and in 1630 he wrote "Discourse on England's Treasure by Foreign Trade," which was published in 1664. In this excerpt, Mun shows that he shared the mercantilist view that trade could enrich the kingdom.

Although a Kingdom may be enriched by gifts received, or by purchase taken from some other Nations, yet these are things uncertain and of small consideration when they happen. The ordinary means therefore to increase our wealth and treasure is by Foreign Trade, wherein we must ever observe this rule: to sell more to strangers yearly than we consume of theirs in value. For suppose that when this Kingdom is plentifully served with the Cloth, Lead, Tin, Iron, Fish and other native commodities, we do yearly export the overplus to foreign countries to the value of twenty-two hundred thousand pounds; by which means we are enabled beyond the Seas to buy and bring in foreign wares for our use and Consumptions, to the value of twenty hundred thousand pounds: By this order duly kept in our trading, we may rest assured that the kingdom shall be enriched yearly two hundred thousand pounds, which must be brought to us in so much Treasure; because that part of our stock which is not returned to us in wares must necessarily be brought home in treasure. . . .

Let Princes oppress, Lawyers extort, Usurers bite, Prodigals wast, and lastly let Merchants carry out what money they shall have occasion to use in traffique. Yet all these actions can work no other effects in the course of trade than is declared in this discourse. For so much Treasure only will be brought in or carried out of a Commonwealth, as the foreign Trade doth over or under balance in value. And this must come to pass by a Necessity beyond all resistance. So that all other courses (which tend not to this end) howsoever they may seem to force money into a Kingdom for a time, yet are they (in the end) not only fruitless but also hurtful; they are like to violent flouds which bear down their banks, and suddenly remain dry again for want of waters.

Behold then the true form and worth of foreign trade, which is *The great Revenue of the King. The honour of the Kingdom. The Noble profession of the Merchant. The School of our Arts. The supply of our wants. The employment of our poor. The improvement of our Lands. The Nursery of our Mariners. The walls of the Kingdoms. The means of our Treasure. The Sinnews of our wars. The terror of our Enemies.* For all which great and weighty reasons, do so many well-governed States highly countenance the profession, and carefully cherish the action, not only with Policy to increase it, but also with power to protect it from all foreign injuries; because they know it is a Principal in Reason of State to maintain and defend that which doth support them and their estates.

SOURCE: Thomas Mun, from *England's Treasure By Forraign Trade*, 1664, in *Modern History Sourcebook*, www.fordham.edu/halsall/mod/1664mun-engtrade.html.

Analyze the Document

1. What benefits does Mun say will accompany a vigorous foreign trade?

2. What does he consider a favorable balance of trade? How are these views consistent with mercantilist thought, and how do they differ from your understanding of modern economic life?

---

supplies and keep prices high. Through new strategies like this and through individual initiative (rather than through government policy), the Netherlands became the leading commercial center in Europe in the sixteenth century. Indeed, it was this very success that generated the wealth depicted in the households painted by Vermeer.

> **Capitalist ideas**

Capitalist initiative gave rise to fluctuations in demand for goods. We can follow an early example of this economic cycle in the tulip industry. Tulips originally were imported into the Netherlands from Turkey, in the sixteenth century. A Dutch botanist discovered how to grow the many varied colors of this versatile flower. By 1634, buyers not only in the Netherlands but also all over Europe were so enthralled by the exotic and beautiful plants that one rare tulip bulb sold for 1,000 pounds of cheese, four oxen, eight pigs, twelve sheep, a bed, and a suit of clothes. Investors rushed to take advantage of the lucrative tulip market and the supply of the bulbs ballooned. Three years later, however, the increased supply drove down the price, ruining many who had gambled on the rare flower. Novice capitalists learned the hard way about the cruel whims of the market economy.

People with moderate means also yearned to participate in promising financial ventures. To accommodate them, businesses built upon medieval concepts of trading partnerships and developed an innovative entity called the **joint-stock company.** This new economic structure allowed ordinary investors to buy shares in commercial ventures that were run by boards of directors. With successes in such investments, modest capitalists might generate enough money to set out on their own and gamble on higher-risk opportunities. These joint-stock companies made

> **Joint-stock companies**

it easier to raise enough capital for trading ventures around the world. Amsterdam was the site of the first stock exchange, and enterprising people in the colony of New York began trading shares at a tree at the end of Wall Street.

In the seventeenth century, English and Dutch merchants formed exceptionally efficient joint-stock companies that helped them dominate trade in Asia: the English East India Company, founded in 1600, and the Dutch United East India Company, known by its initials VOC (Vereenigde Oost-Indische Compagnie), founded in 1602. Although both companies enjoyed government support, they were privately owned by merchant investors. Their charters granted them remarkable powers—they could buy, sell, and even wage war in the companies' interests. These companies immediately generated huge profits, and both contributed to the early formation of a global network of trade.

Mercantilism: Controlling the Balance of Trade

With so much money at stake, western European governments attempted centralized regulation of their economies—**mercantilism**—to profit from the expanded global trade. Mercantilism was based on the assumption that the amount of worldwide wealth was fixed, so countries competed to get a larger piece of the pie. This was essentially economic nationalism, in which governments controlled their economies to increase their acquisition of hard currency. The simple principle "buy low, sell high" led these governments to discourage imports, particularly expensive ones, and encourage exports. In 1586, one Spanish bureaucrat asked King Philip II to forbid the import of candles, glass trinkets, jewelry, cutlery, and other such items, because these sorts of "useless" luxuries drained away precious Spanish gold. Such policies aimed to create a favorable balance of trade and fill bank vaults with gold.

| Economic nationalism |

Mercantilist governments passed laws to ensure a favorable trade balance. They imposed tariffs on imports and discouraged manufacturing in their colonies to force them to buy exports from the home country. Thus, hard currency would flow from the colonies to enrich royal treasuries in Europe. In fact, mercantilist policy encouraged the founding of new colonies to create new markets to purchase European exports. When other things failed, governments debased their coins to try to maintain a favorable balance.

| Economic regulations |

Some governments even tried to keep wages low so that citizens would have little discretionary income with which to buy expensive imports. All these efforts were meant to enrich the states, not the fortunes of wealthy citizens. Mercantilist policies placed the state before the individual. They achieved their goal, vastly enriching the powerful monarchies of western Europe. Sadly, they also financed the destructive wars that swept over Europe through the mid-seventeenth century (discussed in Chapter 11). Mercantilist economic policy would continue to shape government policy into the eighteenth century (as we will see in Chapter 15).

The Growth of Banking

Neither private capitalism nor mercantilism could have succeeded without innovations in banking practices. Medieval ideas that forbad charging interest and that kept royal treasuries locked in chests in royal bedrooms had become obsolete. In this new age, people needed easier access to a lot of money, and they refined banking techniques that had been developed in the late Middle Ages in the Italian cities of the Renaissance. Medieval bankers had developed bills of exchange and complex account books to facilitate commerce, but in the late fifteenth century, bankers added checks, bank drafts, and sophisticated double-entry bookkeeping to their skills, all of which made commercial ventures easier than ever.

Through the sixteenth century, private bankers handled most financial transactions. The Fuggers of Germany were the most successful at this profession, taking over a role that the Medicis in Florence had dominated in the fifteenth century. The Fugger family became so wealthy that they even lent money to Emperor Charles V. With the emergence of mercantilist ideas about economics serving the state, this kind of practice waned. Instead, government banks developed that controlled profits going to individuals. The Bank of Amsterdam was founded in 1609, followed by the Bank of Sweden in 1657, and the Bank of England in 1694. However, new banking policies could not ensure that even mercantilist governments would grow rich.

| State banks |

The Danger of Overspending: Spain Learns a Lesson

At first, Europeans believed that the wealth flowing into Europe from the New World was the primary payoff from their explorations. Entire countries became rich, and imperial powers grew in previously unheard-of ways. Spain immediately capitalized on the new wealth, its treasure ships offering unlimited prosperity and power to the monarchs. Yet, the vast influx of silver was deceiving, and the Spanish king spent it wastefully on the incessant wars that dominated the sixteenth and early seventeenth centuries.

Consequently, the Spanish crown had to declare bankruptcy several times in the course of the sixteenth and seventeenth centuries. Spain's financial troubles hurt merchants in Germany and Italy, but the real burden fell on the Spanish taxpayers, who were soon saddled with debt. Instead of relieving their debt burdens, the politics of empire only added to them. Domination of the New World passed to the governments of other countries (notably Holland and England) that proved more efficient in fiscal matters.

Ultimately, much of the gold and silver that motivated the expansionist countries did not even end up in Europe. A large percentage of this currency eventually flowed to the East for the purchase of luxury items. As Spain discovered, these precious metals were not enough to keep profligate governments in power.

Redefining Work Roles

The commercial revolution both enlarged the scale of business and redefined the way people viewed their work. While most people still worked the land, in the cities, which served as the nerve centers of the new economies, people experienced the most remarkable shifts in how they made their living. As the middle class rose to economic power on the dual waves of trade and hard work, the lives of urban women in particular diverged dramatically from earlier times. In the early Middle Ages, women had labored in the stores and workshops of Europe's cities. They dominated trades that they had controlled in the home—textile making and brewing, for example. Women had such a presence in these fields that feminine forms of certain words (ending in *ster*) derived from these jobs—for instance, *webster* (from *weaver*) and *brewster* (from *brewer*)—arose and even became common surnames. Women also owned taverns in such numbers that an instruction manual written for merchants in 1515 assumed that the innkeeper would be a woman and gave instructions on "how to ask the *hostess* how much one has spent."

Still, women's access to the workforce came primarily through their families. Daughters, like most sons, mastered trades in the family workshops, just as Maria Merian (in the Biography on page 405) learned printing from her stepfather. Wives worked with their husbands, and widows frequently ran businesses and took their husbands' place in the guilds. During the late Middle Ages, men slowly began to replace women in some of the most lucrative jobs, like cloth making, and just as in banking and commercial enterprises, this late-medieval trend accelerated in the early modern period.

> **Women's work**

Into the sixteenth century, as work generated more capital and power, it began losing its association with the family and became more linked to the public political arena. Many people (women and men alike) believed that public work and control of money were more appropriately managed by men than women. Late in the sixteenth century, cities accordingly began to issue ordinances restricting women's entry into guilds, which had taken on markedly political overtones. For example, a ruling in France in 1583 limited silk-making apprentices (who had previously been predominantly female) to only two males per master. In another example, a 1508 ordinance in the Netherlands referred to a "brotherhood and sisterhood" of a guild, but the reissued ordinance in 1552 mentioned only a "brotherhood of trimmers." By 1563, when the ordinances were again revised, even widows' rights had been omitted.

> **Leaving the workforce**

Similar examples emerged at local levels throughout Europe. As the commercial revolution spread and urban merchants grew powerful, the old divisions of those who worked and those who did not began to blur. Instead, the growing middle class began to divide the world between those who worked outside the home in the public, political arena and those who worked inside the home. Urban women, relegated increasingly to the domestic sphere, lost much of their visibility in the public arena.

Piracy: Banditry on a World Scale, 1550–1700

The expansion of trade into the Atlantic and Pacific brought with it another nettlesome problem: a rise in piracy. Piracy was as old as Mediterranean shipping, when seagoing robbers had preyed mercilessly on the ponderous merchant roundships that moved goods through the inland sea. As the pace of the world economy quickened, pirates moved to take advantage. From about 1550 to about 1700, a "pirate belt" developed that stretched from the West Indies to East Asia. The new entrepreneurial raiding coincided with the weakening of the great Turkish, Spanish, and Chinese empires that we saw in Chapter 11, because these navies could no longer effectively patrol their territorial waters.

Piracy as a way of life actually had a somewhat benign origin—monarchs had often issued licenses for people to steal from other countries in unofficial warfare. Before the seventeenth century, the word *pirate* rarely appeared. Instead, seagoing raiders were called **privateers** or corsairs, terms meaning that they had the authorization of formal commissions from their rulers. Even as late as the eighteenth century, the

> **Early privateers**

BIOGRAPHY

Maria Sibylla Merian
(1647–1717)

Maria Sibylla was born in Frankfurt, Germany, the daughter of a well-known engraver and publisher and his second wife, Johanna. Maria's father also had a keen interest in the explorations of the age. He published editions of *Grands et Petits Voyages*, which contained accounts of journeys to the New World (including the illustration shown in **Figure 12.6**). Although he died in 1650 when Maria was only 3 years old, she grew up to excel in the same fields that had so captivated her father. Maria's mother married a painter and art dealer, and the young girl cultivated her artistic interests and skills in her stepfather's workshop.

In her later years, Maria remembered acquiring an additional passion: "I have been concerned with the study of insects. This led me to collect all the caterpillars I could find in order to study their metamorphoses . . . and to work at my painter's art so that I could sketch them from life and represent them in lifelike colors."

FIGURE 12.12 Maria Sibylla Merian
Frontispiece to Merian, *Der Rupsen*, 1717.

Maria married Johann Andreas Graff, an artist and publisher, in 1665, and the couple had two daughters. Ten years later, she published her first book of copperplate engravings. This work consisted solely of illustrations of flowers and some insects. It contained no text but was used to provide patterns for artists and embroiderers, who preferred to work from an illustration rather than from life. This work established Merian's reputation as an artist and naturalist, and she was included in a contemporary book on German art.

A few years later, she published *Wonderful Transformation and Singular Flower-Food of Caterpillars.* This work contained her detailed observations and commentaries on the habits of caterpillars and was hailed as "amazing."

Yet Merian's scientific work was soon interrupted by dramatic changes in her personal life. In 1685, she was consumed with a fervor for religious renewal. With her elderly mother and two daughters, she joined a radical Protestant sect, the Labadists, in the Netherlands. The group established a community of the "elect," who held their property in common and lived in isolation from what they saw as a sinful world. When Merian's husband pleaded with her to return to him and bring home their daughters, she refused. He acquired a divorce and remarried.

After some years, the closed Labadist community must have felt too confining to the talented, curious Merian. She and her daughters left the group and settled in Amsterdam, the thriving port city that bustled with exotic goods and hummed with exciting tales of travel.

Recognized for her previous work, Merian was welcomed into the circle of naturalists in Amsterdam.

Despite the attractions of her new life, Merian continued to find fascination in insects. In 1699, she and her daughter Dorothea sailed from Amsterdam to Surinam, the Dutch colony on the northern shore of South America. The Labadists had established a community there, but it had failed due to the hardships of the tropics. Merian might well have heard about Surinam during her earlier stay with the Labadists and decided to go there to study tropical insects, butterflies, and plants.

The devoted naturalist lived in Surinam for two years. With the help of Amerindians and African slaves, she collected thousands of specimens and made hundreds of drawings of plant and insect species unknown in Europe. In 1701, she returned to Amsterdam, and several years later she published *Metamorphosis of the Insects of Surinam* in both Dutch and Latin. Her drawings were praised as "the most beautiful work ever painted in America" (see **Figure 12.15**). Merian lived the rest of her days in Amsterdam, consulted by other naturalists and continuing to seek out interesting new caterpillar specimens. Merian died in 1717, and in that year her daughter published a collection of her mother's work, including the image shown in **Figure 12.12.** Merian's books remained widely read by naturalists well into the next century.

Naturalist, Artist, and Traveler

Connecting People & Society

1. How did the Reformation and the age of exploration open up opportunities for Merian?

2. What evidence does this life offer about a growing scientific curiosity about the West?

3. What does this account tell us about the position of and opportunities for women?

United States Constitution gave Congress the right to issue letters of marque and reprisal, essentially to hire pirate ships. Privateers earned their profits from captured booty, and in the freewheeling raids that took place on the open seas, it was impossible to distinguish them from pirates acting on their own. The ships that were robbed probably did not draw any distinction between the two.

The difficulties of discerning pirate from privateer may be seen in the case of the famous early English privateers, particularly Francis Drake (ca. 1540–1596). By 1571, Drake had become a major force in the Caribbean, and this champion of the British was considered a ruthless pirate by the Spanish. Drake had numerous bases on land and gained the admiration and support of unconquered Amerindians and Spanish-hating escaped slaves. With the backing and affection of Queen Elizabeth I (r. 1558–1603), Drake and his fellow privateers relentlessly harassed the Spanish ships they found sailing in the Caribbean.

The fortunes of Drake's compatriot Walter Raleigh (ca. 1554–1618) showed how fragile royal support of these independent captains could be. Elizabeth backed Raleigh in his flamboyant enterprises, even knighting her champion. However, her successor, James I (r. 1603–1625) found the privateer less useful. As James began to have political difficulties with English Protestants, he sought an alliance with Spain (as we will see in Chapter 13). As a token of goodwill to Spain, James imprisoned Raleigh in the Tower of London and executed him in 1618.

Pirates included many Africans who had been captured as slaves, because after seizing wealthy slave-trading ships, pirates frequently gave the slaves the choice to continue on their way or join the pirate band. The eighteenth-century trial records of a pirate on the ship Whydah indicate that about 30 to 50 of the men on his ship were African and 1 was an Amerindian. The freedom of the pirate life drew many who had few choices elsewhere.

Pirate life

With all its hazards—from fickle royal supporters to war on the high seas—the pirate life could bring amazing riches even for those without a royal patron. Pirate cities sprang up based solely on the illicit trade. For example, Algiers in North Africa became a prosperous Muslim pirate city, and Malta in the Mediterranean was its Christian counterpart. Other pirate cities dotted the Caribbean from the coast of the Yucatán to the islands of the West Indies. These cities served as havens for the violent, reckless sea raiders and their families. They also were places where talented outsiders could rise to positions of considerable power. For example, a poor North African shepherd boy rose through the pirate ranks to become "king" of Algiers in 1569. During the eighteenth century, several women even took command of pirate ships.

By the mid-eighteenth century, however, governments had begun expanding their navies and set out to suppress the buccaneers. The British admiralty discouraged privateering because it lured sailors away from serving in the navy. The age of informal warfare came to a close and accounts of the bandits' careers retreated to literary works that romanticized their lives. For example, literary pirates made their victims walk the plank; real pirates would not have wasted time on such rituals. If they wanted to kill their captives, they unceremoniously threw them overboard.

THE WORLD TRANSFORMED

The booming world market that stimulated the movement of goods and the enterprise of pirates also served to spread other aspects of European culture around the world. During the sixteenth century, more than 200,000 Spanish people, 10 percent of them women, migrated to Latin America. In the next century, comparable numbers of English, French, and Dutch settled in North America. These immigrants became a new ruling class that transfused much of European culture into the New World. They built cities featuring the grid pattern that marked Renaissance urban planning and placed their churches in the city centers.

European Culture Spreads

The new immigrants brought their languages and religions, but also unique livestock, tools, plants, and other goods that transformed the lives of native peoples. When European horses escaped (or were stolen), for example, some indigenous peoples took them into their midst. The Plains Indians in the southwest of North America soon made horses central to their way of life. In time, guns, liquor, and many other goods also found their way into the many native cultures.

Plants from Europe, some of them intentionally cultivated, made their mark on the New World as well. For example, Europeans brought wheat to make the bread that had long served as their dietary staple. Along with their domesticated plants, they transported their traditional farming Plants methods. **Figure 12.13** shows Amerindians cultivating wheat on a Spanish plantation. The laborers use the same kinds of tools, including the overburdened donkey in the lower-left corner, that their European peasant counterparts had employed.

Europeans unwittingly altered the ecology of the New World in many other ways. As we have seen, they brought diseases that ravaged native populations. Less destructive but equally ubiquitous, plants transported to the New World spread with vigor. A sixteenth-century Inca observer (Garcilaso de la Vega) described how quickly the ecology of Peru had been transformed by invasive plants: "Some of them are becoming mischievous, such as the mustard, mint, and camomile, which have spread . . . [and] the first endives and spinach multiplied in such a way that a horse could not force its way through them." Inadvertent transportation of weed seeds also displaced native species. Dandelions are a particularly apt example of a European weed that spread accidentally as people, plants, and animals moved across the sea.

Europeans traveling and trading in Africa and Asia took New World plants to other regions of the world, transforming local consumption habits and economies. Africa, for example, received sweet potatoes and maize in the sixteenth century. In the Congo, the Portuguese introduced maize, although at first the tribes dismissed the vegetable as more suitable for pigs than human beings. In time, these plants became so central to the local culture that people no longer remembered that they were once strange imports. Because the societies of east Asia kept most Europeans at arm's length, they were less influenced by European culture than were the peoples of North and South America, and it would take several more centuries for European trade to exert its full impact in that region.

FIGURE 12.13 New Plants and Animals The spread of Europeans reshaped the New World's ecology. This image shows one such change as Amerindians plant wheat, a European crop, with metal tools, aided by an imported donkey.

Finally, the populations themselves mixed as immigrants settled among native societies. Because European men greatly outnumbered women from their home continent, many of them married native and slave women or Population mixing kept them as concubines. Generations of children born of mixed background, called *mestizos*, preserved aspects of both their parents' cultures. These generations ultimately made the Americas vastly different from Europe in spite of common languages, religions, and political structures.

Figure 12.14 reveals much about the cultural blending that marked the Americas.

European Culture Transformed

Europeans were as much transformed by contact with the New World as the original Americans were by their European conquerors. In one of the less savory examples of this exchange, the earliest explorers to the New World probably brought back a virulent form of syphilis. New archaeological excavations have revealed that some form of syphilis existed in Europe from classical times, but this new strain of the sexually transmitted disease ravaged Europe until the twentieth century, when the advent of penicillin offered a cure. The disease never took the kind of toll on Europeans that plagues such as smallpox and

thinking about
ART

FIGURE 12.14

Festival Scene Painted on a Screen, Mexico, ca. 1650

Many artists have a talent for portraying life at a particular time and documenting its distinguishing aspects. This painting by an unknown artist captures the blending of cultures that took place in the villages of Mexico in the seventeenth century. Notice the mestizos spinning on a pole in a traditional Amerindian celebration, and the hazy, dreamlike Spanish castles in the background.

Connecting Art & Society

1. What clothing do the participants wear? How is this evidence of cultural blending?

2. What other festival features can you identify, and how might such celebrations have served to join the community together?

3. What might the artist have intended by placing the castles of his homeland in this picture?

4. What conclusions can you draw about the blending of cultures in Mexico from this painting?

measles imposed on native populations. Nevertheless, its presence caused much misery and made some people more cautious about sexual activity.

New foods changed Europeans' diets and even the landscape. It is difficult to imagine Ireland without the hardy, nutritious potatoes that flourish today in that rocky land, but until the conquest of the Incas, the population of Ireland had to struggle to sustain **New foods** itself. The tomato—a New World fruit that people first rejected as poisonous—was eventually embraced as an aphrodisiac and became an often-used ingredient in European cuisine. Maize spread more slowly, for Europeans, like the Africans, did not initially view it as a food fit for humans. However, as early as 1500, it began thriving in Spain, from where it soon spread to Italy (near Venice) and eventually to the rest of Europe. Maize had immediate use as animal feed and peasant fare and allowed farming families to sell their more expensive wheat.

In addition to new staples, certain food stimulants from the Americas proved enormously popular in Europe. Chocolate, for example, came to Spain from Aztec Mexico in about 1520 in the form of loaves and tablets that were **New stimulants** boiled into a drink. A luxury at first, chocolate had become a common beverage by the eighteenth century. Tea, too, had been a rare treat in the Middle Ages, when some traders brought small amounts from China. Over time, more and more Europeans developed an unquenchable thirst for tea, making the East India Company rich in the process.

Coffee appeared in Europe for the first time in the early seventeenth century and replaced tea and chocolate as the most popular stimulant drink. Coffee seems to have first come from Africa and then spread to the Muslim lands—it was in Mecca by 1511, and Istanbul in 1517. By 1615, coffee had reached Venice, and merchants spread the product rapidly through Europe from there. Physicians praised the drink as medicinal for many ailments, from heart disease to "short breath, colds which attack the lungs, and worms." By the eighteenth century, coffee was so central to European society that even the social life of the West began to be centered at coffee shops.

But it was tobacco that made the biggest impression on European culture. Columbus saw Amerindians smoking it and brought the plant back home as an object of curiosity. Europeans cultivated tobacco at first for medicinal purposes—one sixteenth-century Parisian claimed **Tobacco** that it cured all ills—and the plant then spread rapidly all over the world. By the mid-seventeenth century, it had reached as far as China, where virtually the entire population took up the smoking habit. The difficulties of planting tobacco also stimulated settlement expansion. Because the crop rapidly depletes the soil, in an age without chemical fertilizers colonists seeking to profit from the lucrative crop constantly had to annex and cultivate new lands.

The New World's reshaping of European culture unfolded slowly. New products became available gradually, whetting appetites for yet more novelties. The commercial revolution stimulated the movement of goods all over the world, creating more and more demand, which fueled further explorations and commerce. Ironically, the demand for spices, and particularly pepper, that had originally served as the main force behind the voyages of exploration waned by the eighteenth century. Europeans had found other, more intriguing products to satisfy their restless desire for culinary novelties.

A New Worldview

When Europeans first set off across the seas, they had a false, though highly imaginative, view of what they would find. The world proved larger and far more diverse than they had ever imagined, and travelers began to study and write about the new reality. Amerigo Vespucci, the Italian mapmaker and chronicler we met earlier, wrote with awe in 1499 about New World flora: "The trees were so beautiful and so fragrant that we thought we were in a terrestrial paradise. Not one of those trees or its fruit was like those in our part of the globe." Such early descriptions were followed by systematic studies in the seventeenth century. For example, in 1648 a Dutch prince sponsored an expedition that published the *Natural History of Brazil*, followed by many other books by naturalists cataloging the wonders of the Americas.

Figure 12.15 shows an illustration from *Metamorphosis of the Insects of Surinam* by Maria Sibylla Merian (1647–1717) (see Biography). In this painstakingly rendered illustration, one can see both the detail that marked these kinds of studies and the artist's fascination with the exotic. Merian drew a guava tree (one of the fruits that Vespucci had found so strange) populated with spiders and ants. In the drawing, most of the spiders are eating ants. One of them, however, is shown attacking a nest of hummingbird eggs. Here Merian was illustrating a story told to her by the Surinam locals. (In fact, spider attacks on birds' nests are extremely rare.) This illustration, with its blend of careful attention to detail and elements of fantasy, typifies the European fascination with the newly discovered world.

The new maps created as explorers traveled the global coastlines and great rivers were almost as

Scientific observations

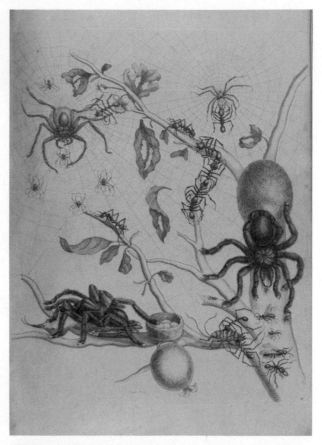

FIGURE 12.15 "Spiders and Ants on a Guava Tree," *Metamorphosis*, **plate 18, ca. 1705** Maria Sibylla Merian's careful study and drawings of New World plants and animals generated excitement and awakened scientific curiosity in Europe. She was just one of many such observers.

precise as the naturalists' drawings. These representations offered a much more realistic picture of the world than Ptolemy's map that guided Columbus. The map in **Figure 12.16** shows the globe flattened out. This projection method, which let sailors plot straight-line courses, was developed by the Flemish cartographer Gerhard Mercator (1512–1594), who first published it in 1569. Many modern European maps are still based on this technique.

Mercator maps

The **Mercator projection** was a huge step forward in mapmaking, but it still allowed for some measure of geographic illusion. By flattening out the map and placing Europe in the center, mapmakers could not help distorting their graphic representation of the world. Greenland, for example, appears much larger than it is, India becomes smaller, and Asia is divided, thus seeming to have less mass than it really does. Not surprisingly, the Mercator map encouraged the illusion that Europeans occupied the center of the world. This idea shaped Europeans' future mapmaking techniques and their attitudes and actions toward the rest of the globe.

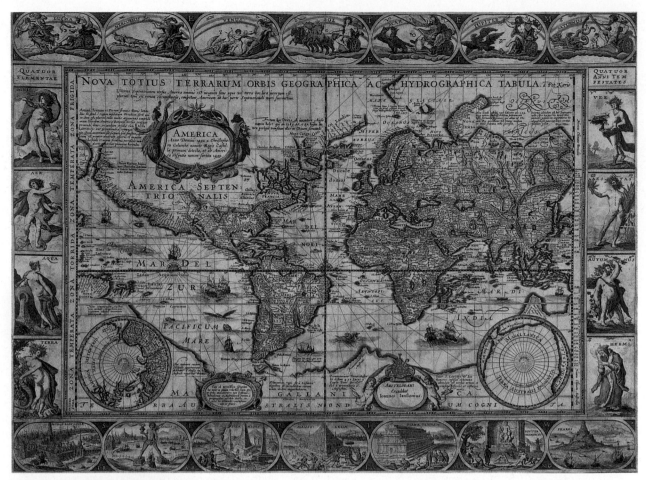

FIGURE 12.16 Mercator Map, 1608 The explorers mapped the world and in doing so replaced Ptolemy's vision, shown in Figure 12.2. However, the popular Mercator map kept Europe in the center and skewed the perspective of the rest of the world.

LOOKING BACK *&* MOVING FORWARD

Summary By the early sixteenth century, Western culture was no longer contained within Europe. Lured by faith, fame, and fortune, Europeans sailed all over the world. They also settled in the newfound lands, conquering and colonizing the Americas and establishing trading posts in the East. Merchants and entrepreneurs followed the explorers and established a world market that stimulated the growth of commercial capitalism, new banking techniques, and widespread popular interest in economic opportunity. Some governments began to set economic policy and tried to control the flow of money to and from their countries.

In this great movement of peoples and confrontation of cultures, Europeans generated enormous wealth—and equally unprecedented misery. Native populations were virtually eliminated by warfare, disease, and abuse, and hundreds of thousands of Africans were enslaved and taken by force from their homelands. The resultant blending of peoples, ideas, and goods profoundly affected the entire world and whetted European appetites for yet more exploration and conquest.

KEY TERMS

quadrant, *p. 384*
astrolabe, *p. 384*
conquistadors, *p. 393*
encomienda, *p. 396*
haciendas, *p. 396*
capitalists, *p. 401*
entrepreneurs, *p. 401*
joint-stock company, *p. 402*
mercantilism, *p. 403*
privateers, *p. 404*
Mercator projection, *p. 409*

REVIEW, ANALYZE, & CONNECT TO TODAY

REVIEW THE PREVIOUS CHAPTERS

Chapter 10—"A New Spirit in the West"—analyzed the revolution in thought that we have come to call the Renaissance, and in Chapter 11—"Alone Before God"—we saw how the new ideas were put into practice in religion. Chapter 11 also told the story of the struggles of European states as they competed with one another to claim superiority.

1. Review the characteristics of Renaissance thought and consider how they contributed to the sixteenth-century interest in discovering previously unknown areas of the world.

2. Review the Chapter 11 discussion of sixteenth-century European warfare and religious reforms. How did these wars and reforms affect the global exploration that was occurring at the same time?

ANALYZE THIS CHAPTER

Chapter 12—"Faith, Fortune, and Fame"—describes and analyzes the European explorations and conquests that spread Western culture around the world and, in turn, transformed Europe.

1. Review the areas of Spanish and Portuguese exploration, and consider where these early efforts forced England, France, and the Netherlands to focus their attention. Which areas turned out to be most profitable in the long run? Why?

2. Consider the complex relationship between technology, commercial exchange, and the lure of exploration and conquest, and review how this relationship was expressed in this chapter.

3. What advantages did the Spanish have in their conquests in the New World? How did the Spanish perceptions of the natives shape their treatment of them?

CONNECT TO TODAY

Think about the ways in which the medieval world was changed through sudden globalization—the movement and spread of peoples, ideas, religions, and goods.

1. Have the high levels of global trade and immigration in contemporary times led to a similarly escalated global transformation? Explain.

2. Which of the transformations described in this chapter has had the largest influence on today's world? Why?

BEYOND THE CLASSROOM

THE WORLD IMAGINED

Friedman, John Block. *The Monstrous Races in Medieval Art and Thought.* Cambridge, MA: Harvard University Press, 1981. The best study on this subject—scholarly, fascinating, and well illustrated.

Russell, Jeffrey B. *Inventing the Flat Earth: Columbus and Modern Historians.* Westport, CT: Greenwood, 1991. Studies the origin of the myth that only Columbus believed the earth was round.

THE WORLD DISCOVERED

Greenhill, Basil. *The Evolution of the Sailing Ship, 1250–1589.* Annapolis, MD: Naval Institute Press, 1996. A clear explanation of the technology of sailing ships that does not get bogged down in unduly technical language.

Subrahmanyam, Sanjay. *The Portuguese Empire in Asia, 1500–1700: A Political and Economic History.* New York: Longman, 1993. A comprehensive look at the economic and diplomatic history of the whole Portuguese Asian empire.

CONFRONTATION OF CULTURES

Benjamin, Thomas. *The Atlantic World: Europeans, Africans, Indians, and Their Shared History, 1400–1900.* Cambridge: Cambridge University Press, 2009. Comprehensive, smart, and clearly written account of the human interactions that transformed the world.

Berlin, Ira. *Many Thousands Gone.* Cambridge, MA: Harvard University Press, 1998. A sensitive study of the changing nature of the history of African-American slavery in mainland North America.

Diamond, Jared. *Guns, Germs, and Steel.* New York: W.W. Norton, 1997. A Pulitzer Prize–winning analysis of the interactions of cultures around the world that is utterly riveting.

Fagan, Brian M. *Clash of Cultures.* New York: W.H. Freeman, 1984. Concentrates on the first period of European exploration and settlement beginning in 1488.

Fritze, Ronald H. *New Worlds: The Great Voyages of Discovery, 1400–1600.* Westport, CT: Praeger, 2003. A balanced history of European expansion showing the historical roots of the explorations and detailing the voyages of Henry the Navigator, Columbus, da Gama, and Cabot.

Karlen, Arno. *Men and Microbes: Diseases and Plagues in History and Modern Times.* New York: Touchstone, 1996. A detailed look at the history of diseases, demonstrating how infections are always part of the changing natural and social human environment. Particularly strong on modern times.

Standard, David E. *American Holocaust: Columbus and the Conquest of the New World.* New York: Oxford University Press, 1993. Describes in horrible detail the mass destruction of the New World societies in the wake of European contact.

GLOBAL CONNECTIONS

Rostworowski de Diez Canseco, Maria. *History of the Inca Realm.* Cambridge: Cambridge University Press, 1999. A thorough and readable account drawing from the latest scholarship.

Wachtgel, Nathan. *The Vision of the Vanquished: The Spanish Conquest of Peru Through Indian Eyes, 1530–1570.* New York: Barnes and Noble, 1971. A comprehensive, readable account sensitively drawn from the few sources giving the Indian point of view.

THE WORLD MARKET AND COMMERCIAL REVOLUTION

Braudel, Fernand. *Civilization and Capitalism, 15th to 18th Centuries,* 3 vols. Translated by S. Reynolds.

New York: Harper & Row, 1981. A celebrated author's detailed economic history that analyzes patterns in European and world economy—particularly rich in details.

Magnusson, Lars. *Mercantilism: The Shaping of an Economic Language.* New York: Routledge, 1994. A book that directly deals with how nations could increase their wealth specifically through international trade.

Omrod, David. *The Rise of Commercial Empires: England and the Netherlands in the Age of Mercantilism, 1650–1770.* Cambridge: Cambridge University Press, 2008. Scholarly contribution to the field of global economics that emphasizes the important connections that make up the webs of trade.

THE WORLD TRANSFORMED

Crosby, A.W. *Ecological Imperialism: The Biological Expansion of Europe, 900–1900,* 2nd ed. Cambridge: Cambridge University Press, 2009. Discusses the expansion of Europeans and the animals, weeds, and pathogens that accompanied them.

Davis, Natalie Zemon. *Women on the Margins: Three Seventeenth-Century Lives.* Cambridge, MA: Harvard University Press, 1997. Explores seventeenth-century culture through the lives of three women—a Catholic missionary, a Jewish storyteller, and the Protestant Merian (described in the chapter's Biography).

Fuentes, Carlos. *The Buried Mirror: Reflections on Spain and the New World.* Boston: Houghton Mifflin, 1992. A fascinating essay by one of Mexico's greatest writers on the blending of cultures of Spain and the New World.

CHARLES LEBRUN, *CHANCELLOR SEGUIER,* ca. 1670

Chancellor Pierre Seguier (1588–1672) was an ambitious courtier to the French king Louis XIV and a member of France's new nobility that earned position by service to the crown, the *noblesse de robe.* In this painting, Seguier's office is symbolized by the formal robes he wears, rather than by arms. Several well-dressed pages surround him, one holding an umbrella over his head as if he were a minor monarch. His face conveys a sense of pleased assurance with the position he has gained. Charles Lebrun (1619–1690), like several other leading artists of the day, served as painter to Louis XIV and for eighteen years created decorations for the king's Versailles palace.

The Struggle for Survival and Sovereignty

13

Europe's Social and Political Order, 1600–1715

"This poor country is a horrible sight," wrote the abbess of a French town in January 1649. "[I]t is stripped of everything. The soldiers take possession of the farms . . . there are no more horses . . . the peasants are reduced to sleeping in the woods . . . and if they only had enough bread to half satisfy their hunger, they would indeed count themselves happy." France had just emerged a victor from the Thirty Years' War (discussed in Chapter 11), only to find itself embroiled in a series of internal revolts. These revolts, like many others erupting throughout Europe, signaled new strains on European society from the bottom to the top of the traditional order.

For the vast majority—peasants who worked the fields—pressures came from powers outside their control. The landowning aristocracy required service and obedience; governmental officials demanded ever more taxes and military service; and the impersonal forces that most people attributed to luck, fate, or God brought bad weather, failed harvests, and plagues. Sometimes peasants fled their aristocratic masters or turned violently against isolated governmental officials. However, against the fates and well-armed soldiers, they were powerless.

For those at the top of society, the pressures came from central governments and monarchs. Kings, struggling with the increasingly heavy burdens of war and governance, chipped away at aristocratic independence year after year. They argued that "the royal power is absolute. . . . The prince [king] need render account of his acts to no one." Elites insisted that "our privileges and liberties are our right and due inheritance, no less than our very lands and goods." This contention between monarch and aristocrat sometimes broke out in violence, at other times led to compromises, and often severely strained the elite order.

These two struggles—the first faced by the vast majority on the bottom, the second by the dominant elites on top—colored the West's social and political life during the seventeenth and early eighteenth centuries. This chapter follows these intertwined conflicts in four areas—France, eastern Europe, England, and the Netherlands—where the story took different turns.

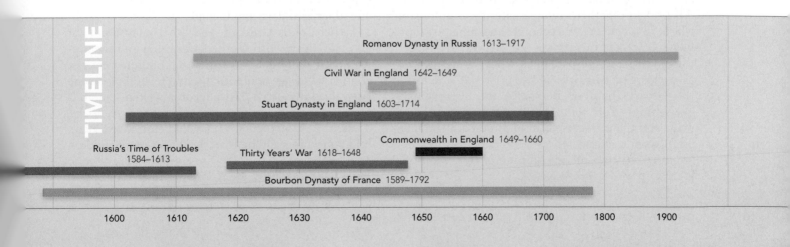

TIMELINE

Romanov Dynasty in Russia 1613–1917

Civil War in England 1642–1649

Stuart Dynasty in England 1603–1714

Commonwealth in England 1649–1660

Russia's Time of Troubles 1584–1613

Thirty Years' War 1618–1648

Bourbon Dynasty of France 1589–1792

1600   1610   1620   1630   1640   1650   1660   1700   1800   1900

PREVIEW

STRESSES IN TRADITIONAL SOCIETY

"It is necessary that some command and others obey," explained a French judge and legal scholar in 1610. "Sovereign lords address their commands to the great; the great to the middling, the middling to the small, and the small to the people." This description captures the traditional social order that reigned in the West during the seventeenth century. Indeed, people took this order for granted. The structure was based on a hierarchy of ranks, and each rank, from nobility to peasantry, had its set status and occupations. Within each rank were subranks. For example, a hierarchy of titles and offices determined position among the nobility. Artisans divided themselves into masters, journeymen, and apprentices. Within the peasantry, landholders stood above laborers, and all looked down on serfs. Each rank distinguished itself through conventions, dress, duties, and etiquette. Finally, within all these ranks, position went hand in hand with family, itself ranked with men at the top, followed by women, and then children at the bottom.

Together the ranks made up the "body politic," with kings and nobles serving as the head and arms, and artisans and peasants as hands and feet. All worked together to perpetuate life as an organic whole. Everywhere, the church and religious sentiments sanctified this organic social hierarchy. Indeed, the social structure paralleled what Westerners saw as the larger, hierarchical order of the universe—the **Great Chain of Being.** In the Great Chain, everything—from God to the angels, humans, animals, and plants—existed in an ordered, permanent arrangement. During the seventeenth century, new forces tested the smooth running of this traditional society.

Mounting Demands on Rural Life

Facing new demands from many quarters, rural life declined. At the beginning of the century, life for most Europeans typically centered on small, self-sufficient villages that contained a few to a hundred families. A church or manor served as the center of communal activities. Strangers attracted intense scrutiny, and most authorities were local people whom everyone knew. When bad harvests, plagues, or war struck, the villagers received little help from the outside.

The majority of people lived in crowded one-room houses made of timber, thatch, and mud, with one or two narrow windows. At one end of the house stood a stone hearth used for light, cooking, and heat. Wood and peat, which fired the stove, were often in short supply, and the villagers struggled to stay warm during the winters. Grain, in the form of black bread and porridge, made up most meals, though in some areas meat, vegetables, fruits, and dairy products supplemented diets. A few treasured pots, pans, and utensils served all.

In **Figure 13.1,** Louis le Nain (1593–1648), a French artist known for his realistic paintings of peasant life, shows a farmyard scene in rural France. The faces of these people express a grimness; clearly they have known hard times and would endure difficulties again and again. Many seventeenth-century Europeans were poorer even than those in this painting. According to one observer in 1696, "They suffer from exposure: winter and summer, three-fourths of them are dressed in nothing but half-rotting tattered linen, and wear throughout the year wooden shoes and no other covering for the foot."

As in past centuries, the family functioned as both a social and an economic unit. Women and men married for practical as well as sentimental reasons. The land, wealth, skills, and position one held counted **The family** for much in a potential marriage partner. Husband, wife, and children lived together, and most marriages, whether happy or not, lasted until death. At various times, relatives, domestics, and laborers might live for a while in the household. Finally, although everyone worked together in the fields, men generally did the heaviest work, while women gardened, raised poultry, and supervised dairy producing.

Fathers, older children, and other relatives might also participate with mothers in raising and socializing young children. Nevertheless, children were not considered at the center of family life, and girls were less valued than boys. Indeed, parents often sent children away to other households to work as apprentices, domestics, or laborers if they could earn more there. Infant mortality ran high; of the five or more children to whom a woman was likely to give birth, only two or three lived beyond 5 years. Parents valued and cared for their children, but in a time of grinding poverty, it is not surprising that parents also viewed children as either assets or liabilities in the struggle for survival; great emotional entanglements with them were risky.

The stresses on these common people are strikingly revealed by the population decreases that occurred during the first half of the seventeenth century. The devastation from the seemingly endless wars took many lives, especially in German lands. The old enemies—poverty, disease, and famine—also roared through these decades. Unusually severe winters—advancing glaciers marked the 1600s as part of the "little ice age"—froze rivers and fields, and wet summers destroyed crops. Suffering, malnutrition, illness, and, too often, death followed. "The staple dish here consists of mice, which the inhabitants hunt, so desperate are they from hunger," reported provincial officials in northern France in 1651. "They devour roots which the animals cannot eat . . . not a day passes but at least 200 people die of famine in the two provinces."

Population changes

Bad times also meant postponed marriages, fewer births, and an increase in the number of deaths among infants and children. Europeans already married late compared to the rest of the world. On average, men waited until their late 20s to wed; women, until their mid-20s. Sometimes so many people died, wandered away in search of food, or fled to the cities that whole villages were abandoned. Conditions improved a bit during the second half of the century, though only enough for the European population to maintain itself and perhaps grow slightly. Life expectancy, which varied by social class and region, was probably less than 30 years (in part because of high infant mortality).

New demands from central governments cut into traditional patterns of rural life. With every new outbreak of war, governmental officials intruded more and more into villages in search of army conscripts. People resisted, and for good reason. Military service took men out of the fields, increasing the burden on the women, children, and elderly who had to shoulder the men's share of the labor. Soldiers embroiled in nearby battles plundered what they could from the villages they passed.

Officials also came with new tax assessments, even though peasants already owed much to those above them. Traditional taxes to the government, tithes to the church, and rents to large landowners used up more than half of the already scant wealth peasants produced. **Figure 13.2,** a mid-seventeenth-century print, caustically depicts some of the peasants' grievances. On the left, the well-dressed noble sits authoritatively on his padded chair to receive the peasant ("thin as the noble's terrier"), who is bringing money in his right hand, fruits and vegetables in his left hand, and a sack

FIGURE 13.1

Louis le Nain, *The Cart*, 1641

This painting by Louis le Nain provides a glimpse of everyday life in rural France during the mid-seventeenth century. Here, women and children of varying ages stand on a cart or tend a few animals. One woman sits with her baby on the ground; another has slung a large pot over her back, perhaps in preparation for gathering water. In the background stands a modest house.

Connecting Art & Society

1. What does this painting reveal about how these people spend their time?

2. What roles do women and children play in this rural economy?

3. Considering his portrayal of the figures and details in this painting, what impression of rural life do you think the artist wanted to convey to viewers?

of wheat at his feet. Above the noble are a spider and a fly caught in its web. As the caption on the lower left states, "The noble is the spider and the peasant the fly." The noble says, "You must pay or serve." The peasant can only reply, "To all masters, all honors."

Peasants avoided collectors and hid what assets they could. In countless incidents, peasants and city dwellers across Europe rose against increasing taxes and attacked the hated collectors. In the 1630s, for example, French peasants rose against tax increases

Tax revolts

FIGURE 13.2 The Noble and the Peasant, seventeenth century This print starkly laments the lot of the poor peasant. Here he brings money and the fruits of his hard labor to the rich noble, who sits arrogantly in a padded chair.

and forced temporary concessions from local officials, only to have those victories reversed by the state. Farther south, in 1647, women demanding more bread led riots that swept through the city of Palermo in Spanish-occupied Italy. Rebels in the city chanted, "Down with taxes!" As in France, government forces eventually reversed early victories and crushed the revolt.

Other intrusions further eroded the traditional isolation that characterized rural life. Officials and merchants ventured more and more often to the countryside to buy grain for cities, creating food shortages in rural villages. Moreover, as members of the local nobility departed for capital cities and the king's court, new officials appeared and began administering affairs and rendering judgments in courts. For good or ill, villagers found themselves increasingly drawn into the web of national affairs.

Pressures on the Upper Orders

Monarchs faced pressures of their own, especially the demands of war. In the competition for territory and status, kings won by fielding ever-larger armies and mustering the resources needed to support them. During the seventeenth century, armies doubled and redoubled in size, as did the central governments that supported them (see Chapter 11). The costs of making war and supporting government increased accordingly. Governments devoted half or more of their income to the military, and monarchs desperate for money levied more and more taxes just to stay even. The ability to collect taxes could make or break a ruler. More than anything else, a king's unrelenting demands for more taxes sparked widespread resistance to his rule.

Competing centers of power added to the kings' problems. Independent town officials, church leaders, and provincial officials tried to hold on to their authority over local matters. Religious dissidents, for their part, guarded what independence they could. Finally, those who resented the royal tax collectors resisted the crown's reach. But the greatest threat to monarchical power came from aristocrats, who tried to retain as much of their social and economic dominance as possible. These nobles often challenged royal policies and decried royal "tyranny" as a violation of divine law. They guarded their traditional rights and local authority, and many of them refused to give up their tax exemptions. Should the crown falter, they stood ready to take back any powers they might have lost.

Competing centers of power

Monarchs argued with, fought, and schemed against these forms of opposition. They justified their power as a divine right, because they represented God on earth, and surrounded themselves with compliant advisors and admirers. As Document 13.1 reveals, their favored supporters, such as France's court preacher and royal tutor Bishop Jacques-Bénigne Bossuet (1627–1704), backed them. Bossuet declared, "The whole state is included in him [the monarch], the will of all the people is enclosed within his own."

Yet the kings used more than words and "yes-men" in this power struggle. Bypassing representative institutions, they sent their royal law courts into the provinces as a way to extend their authority. Sometimes they appointed new local leaders to gain allies. Other times, they attracted aristocrats from the provinces to the royal court, thereby creating a power vacuum that they then filled with their own men. When great nobles resisted being turned into obedient officials, rulers often turned to the lesser nobility or members of the wealthy middle class—men such as Chancellor Seguier, whom we met in the opening of this chapter. Such royal servants received titles or land and were elevated to high office as compensation for their loyalty.

Women also became entwined in these struggles between monarchs and aristocrats. With the royal courts growing in size, many women became important friends and unofficial advisors to kings and influential aristocrats. They used their intelligence, wit, services, and advice to gain privileged positions in royal courts. There they won titles, offices, lands, money, and advantageous marriages for themselves and their families. Mothers encouraged their daughters

Bishop Bossuet Justifies Monarchical Absolutism

In their efforts to acquire as much power as possible, European monarchs and their supporters sought justifications for monarchical rights. One of the most explicit and influential justifications was written and preached by Jacques-Bénigne Bossuet (1627–1704), a French bishop and tutor to the son of Louis XIV. In the following excerpt from his Politics Drawn from the Very Words of Holy Scripture, *Bossuet argues for the divine right of kings.*

Article I

There are four characters or qualities essential to royal authority: First, royal authority is sacred; second, it is paternal; third, it is absolute; fourth, it is ruled by reason. . . .

Article II

Royal authority is sacred.

Proposition 1

God established kings as his ministers and rules peoples by them.

We have already seen that all power comes from God. "The prince," St. Paul adds, "is the minister of God to thee for good. But if thou do that which is evil, be afraid; for he beareth not the sword in vain; for he is the minister of God, a revenger to execute wrath upon him that doeth evil."

Thus princes act as ministers of God, and as his lieutenants on earth. It is by them that he exercises his rule. . . .

Proposition 2

The person of kings is sacred.

It thus appears that the person of kings is sacred and that to make an attempt on their lives is a sacrilege. . . .

The title of Christ is given to kings; and they are everywhere called christs, or the anointed of the lord. . . .

Proposition 3

The prince must provide for the needs of the people.

It is a royal right to provide for the needs of the people. He who undertakes it at the expense of the prince undertakes royalty: this is why it has been established. The obligation to care for the people is the foundation of all the rights that sovereigns have over their subjects. . . .

Article III

The royal authority is absolute.

. . . The prince is by his office the father of his people; he is placed by his grandeur above all petty interests; even more: all his grandeur and his natural interests are that the people shall be conserved, for

once the people fail him he is no longer prince. There is thus nothing better than to give all the power of the state to him who has the greatest interest in the conservation and greatness of the state itself. . . .

Proposition 4

Kings are not by this above the laws. . . .

Kings therefore are subject like any others to the equity of the laws both because they must be just and because they owe to the people the example of protecting justice; but they are not subject to the penalties of the laws; or, as theology puts it, they are subject to the laws, not in terms of its coactive power but in terms of its directive power.

SOURCE: J.B. Bossuet, *Politics Drawn from the Very Words of Holy Scripture* (1709), in *Western Societies, A Documentary History,* vol. II, eds. Brian Tierney and Joan Scott (New York: McGraw-Hill, 1984), pp. 11–13.

Analyze the Document

1. What, according to Bossuet, are the nature and properties of royal authority?

2. How does Bossuet justify the various qualities of royal authority?

3. How absolute is the power of kings?

not to let good marriage opportunities pass by. "It is true that [the proposed groom] is some fifteen years older than you," wrote one aristocratic mother in 1622. "[B]ut . . . you are going to marry a man . . . who has spent his life honorably at court and at the wars and has been granted considerable payments by the king." Royal mistresses also achieved important positions in the king's household. Françoise d'Aubigné (Marquise de Maintenon), mistress (and, secretly, wife) of France's King Louis XIV, influenced court appointments and founded a royal school for the daughters of impoverished nobles in 1686. Some mistresses even persuaded kings to acknowledge their children as "royal bastards" and grant them titles and privileges.

This system of elevated royal authority has been called **royal absolutism** because the kings of the day commanded more loyalty, control, and resources than their predecessors had, and because they justified their right to rule as an absolute. However, no monarch gained true absolute power. Most people understood that even the strongest ruler, divinely ordained, was vaguely subject to tradition and law. As one seventeenth-century French jurist explained, the king's power "seems to place him above the law, . . . [but] his rank obliges him to subordinate his personal interests to the general good of the state." Further, with so many local centers of power, with scores of nobles who persisted in their independent

Royal absolutism

ways, and with too much information to control, no king in this era could hope to dominate everything. Some monarchs even found themselves on losing ends of internal battles for power.

ROYAL ABSOLUTISM IN FRANCE

In western Europe, the efforts of French kings to maximize their power exemplified the development of royal absolutism. Building upon the work of predecessors who had enhanced the power of the monarchy, Louis XIV (r. 1643–1715) took personal control of the French monarchy in 1661. By then, France had supplanted Spain as the most powerful nation in Europe. Under Louis' long rule, royal absolutism reached its peak and inspired other monarchs to emulate his style.

Henry IV Secures the Monarchy

French absolutism had its immediate roots in the reign of Henry IV (r. 1589–1610). When Henry IV ascended the French throne in 1589, his country had endured several decades of wars between Protestants and Catholics, combined with conflicts between different political factions. Law and order had broken down, and powerful nobles had reasserted their authority. The finances of the central government lay in disarray, and French prestige abroad had sunk to a low level.

The talented, witty Henry, in his prime at 36, set out to change all this. He defused the religious turmoil by issuing the Edict of Nantes (see Chapter 11), which granted to Huguenots (French Protestants) religious toleration and control of some two hundred fortified cities and towns as a guarantee against future oppression. He appealed to the traditional nobility by developing an image as a cultured warrior-king who could be trusted to enforce the law. He catered to rich lawyers, merchants, and landowners by selling new governmental offices, which often came with ennoblement as well as prestige. This growing elite became known as the nobility of the robe because their robes of office, rather than the arms borne by the traditional nobility of the sword, represented their power (see p. 414). Many of these nobles gladly paid annual fees for the right to pass their offices on to heirs. For the peasantry, Henry suggested that prosperity should bring "a chicken in the pot of every peasant for Sunday dinner." Not surprisingly, Henry's authority and popularity soared.

With the help of his able, methodical administrator, the Duke of Sully (1560–1641), Henry also launched a comprehensive program of economic reconstruction. Agriculture and commerce benefited from the increased security of life and property brought by better law enforcement; from improved transportation facilitated by the repair of roads, bridges, and harbors; and from the freeing of trade, thanks to lower internal tariff barriers. The monarchy even subsidized and protected new industries that produced luxuries such as glass, porcelain, lace, silk, tapestries, fine leather, and textiles. Sully's efficient collection of taxes and administration of expenditures produced a rare budget surplus.

Henry also dreamed of making France secure from ambitious foreign states and of ensuring his country a supreme position in all of Europe. However, the powerful Spanish and Austrian Habsburgs on France's borders stood in his way. In 1610, he prepared to join his armies for a campaign against his rivals. Yet before he could set out, he was assassinated by a fanatic, and his plans died with him.

Richelieu Elevates Royal Authority

For several years after Henry's death, his Italian wife, Marie de Médicis (1573–1642), ruled as regent for their son, the young Louis XIII (r. 1610–1643). Marie kept opponents at arm's length but made little headway in strengthening the position of the monarchy. Then in 1624, one of her favorite advisors, Cardinal Richelieu (1585–1642), became chief minister and began exercising power from behind the throne. Having come from a minor noble family and possessing a keen intellect, the arrogant and calculating Richelieu handled the young king deftly and controlled others through a skillful blend of patronage and punishment. His twofold policy was to make royal power supreme in France and to maneuver France into a position of dominance in Europe. To Louis XIII, Richelieu promised "to ruin the Huguenot party, to abase the pride of the nobles, to bring back all your subjects to their duty, and to elevate your name among foreign nations to the point where it belongs."

With the royal army at his disposal, Richelieu boldly destroyed the castles of nobles who opposed the king; he disbanded their private armies and executed a number of the most recalcitrant among them. When Huguenot nobles in the southwest rebelled, Richelieu sent in the army and stripped the Huguenots of the special military and political privileges that Henry IV had granted them. Only their religious liberties remained intact. To dilute local centers of political power, the dynamic minister divided France into some thirty administrative districts, placing each under the control of a powerful *intendant*, who was an agent of the crown. He chose these *intendants* from the ranks of the middle class and recently ennobled people and shifted them around frequently, lest they become too sympathetic with their localities. Finally, Richelieu plunged France into the Thirty Years' War in Germany (see Chapter 11). His purpose was to weaken the Habsburgs, chief rivals of the French monarchs for European supremacy.

By the time of his death in 1642, Richelieu had firmly secured royal power in France and elevated France's position in Europe. Nevertheless, the imperious cardinal, having more than doubled taxes to promote his policies, had gained few friends. Far more French subjects rejoiced in his death than mourned his passing.

Mazarin Overcomes the Opposition

Richelieu was succeeded by his protégé, Cardinal Jules Mazarin (1602–1661). Louis XIII's death in 1643, a few months after that of his great minister, left the throne to Louis XIV, a child of 5. Mazarin, who began his career as a gambler and diplomat, played the same role in the early reign of Louis XIV and his regent, Anne of Austria (1601–1666), that Richelieu had played during the reign of Louis XIII.

Early on, Mazarin, Anne, and the child-king faced a series of wide-ranging, uncoordinated revolts that forced them to flee Paris. Known collectively as the **Fronde** (the name of a child's slingshot game, which implied that the participants were childish), these revolts stemmed primarily from French subjects' objections to high taxes and increasing royal power. Between 1648 and 1653, ambitious nobles, footloose soldiers returning from war, urban artisans, and even some peasants fought the monarchy and its supporters in what amounted to a civil war at times. Bad harvests added to the chaos and suffering: "People massacre each other daily with every sort of cruelty," wrote an observer in 1652. "The soldiers steal from one another when they have denuded everyone else . . . all the armies are equally undisciplined and vie with one

The Fronde

another in lawlessness." Nobles conspired and shifted alliances for their own gains, resulting in growing disillusionment with their cause. Gaining support from city dwellers and peasants longing for peace, and shrewdly buying off one noble after another, Mazarin quashed the revolts by 1653. The crown gradually reasserted itself as the basis for order in France.

The Fronde was paralleled by other revolts during the 1640s in Spain, the Italian states, and, much more seriously, England. In each case, the catalysts included new taxes, the demand for more men and supplies for the military, and monarchies' efforts to acquire more power. In the Spanish provinces of Catalonia and Portugal, as well as in the Italian states of Naples and Sicily, rebels murdered tax officials, peasants took up arms, and local nobles joined the fray. Localities demanded and sometimes got concessions, but many of these victories proved short-lived when the crown reasserted its authority. As we will see, matters grew much worse in England. Taken together, these midcentury rebellions served as a warning to monarchs not to push unpopular policies too far—and to the aristocracy not to underestimate the power of the crown.

The Sun King Rises

Upon Mazarin's death in 1661, the 23-year-old Louis XIV finally stepped forward to rule in his own right. "Up to this moment I have been pleased to entrust the government of my affairs to the late Cardinal," he announced. "It is now time that I govern them myself." With his regal bearing and stolid build, young Louis fit the part well. His lack of intellectual brilliance was offset by a sharp memory, a sense of responsibility, and a capacity for tedious work. "One reigns only by dint of hard work," he warned his own son. Haunted by childhood memories of fleeing in terror across the tiled rooftops of Paris during the Fronde revolts, he remained determined to prevent further challenges from rebellious aristocrats. By his mother, Mazarin, and a succession of tutors, Louis had been convinced that he was God's appointed deputy for France. Supporting him was the most famous exponent of royal absolutism, Bishop Bossuet, who argued that the monarchy "is sacred, it is paternal, it is absolute, and it is subject to reason . . . the royal throne is not that of a man but the throne of God Himself." As Document 13.2 indicates, Louis XIV learned these lessons well. In words commonly attributed to Louis, "*L'état, c'est moi*" (I am the state).

However, Louis could not possibly perform all the functions of government personally. The great bulk of the details were handled by a series of councils and bureaus and administered locally by the *intendants*. Distrusting the traditional nobility, Louis instead usually appointed members of modest noble backgrounds

DOCUMENT 13.2

Louis XIV Describes Monarchical Rights and Duties

For many, France's Louis XIV embodied the nearly all-powerful king—at least in his glorious appearance and style, if not always in his deeds. Louis XIV probably wielded more power than any other seventeenth-century European monarch. In the following excerpts from his writings, he describes his view of kingship to his son.

Homage is due to kings, and they do whatever they like. It certainly must be agreed that, however bad a prince may be, it is always a heinous crime for his subjects to rebel against him. He who gave men kings willed that they should be respected as His lieutenants, and reserved to Himself the right to question their conduct. It is His will that everyone who is born a subject should obey without qualification. This law, as clear as it is universal, was not made only for the sake of princes: it is also for the good of the people themselves. It is therefore the duty of kings to sustain by their own example the religion upon which they rely; and they must realize that, if their subjects see them plunged in vice or violence, they can hardly render to their person the respect due to their office, or recognize in them the living image of Him who is all-holy as well as almighty.

It is a fine thing, a noble and enjoyable thing, to be a king. But it is not without its pains, its fatigues, and its troubles. One must work hard to reign. In working for the state, a king is working for himself. The good of the one is the glory of the other. When the state is prosperous, famous, and powerful, the king who is the cause of it is glorious; and he ought in consequence to have a larger share than others do of all that is most agreeable in life.

SOURCE: J.M. Thompson, *Lectures on Foreign History, 1494–1789* (Oxford: Blackwell, 1956), pp. 172–174.

Analyze the Document

1. In what ways, according to Louis XIV, should a king take steps to maintain his authority?

2. How does Louis justify the obedience owed to kings?

3. In what ways do these views support an alliance between church and state?

---

to the important offices of his government. Well supervised by the industrious king, the administrative machinery hummed along.

To raise his stature, Louis XIV initiated massive public-works projects that glorified him, his government, and his reign. His greatest architectural project was a new palace. Hating the tumult of Paris, with its streets teeming with commoners, he selected Versailles, 11 miles southwest of the city, as the new seat of government. There, as many as 35,000 workmen toiled for more than forty years to turn marshes and sand into Europe's most splendid palace and grounds.

Figure 13.3 shows Versailles in 1668. Over the next forty-three years, successive teams of workers added rear gardens and more than doubled the size of the buildings. This painting, which shows the roads, paths, and gardens of Versailles geometrically laid out, gives a sense of the scale of the project. In the foreground to the right, the royal coach, with its train of followers, arrives at the front gates. The exterior of Versailles was designed in long, horizontal, classic lines. The interior boasted a lavish baroque style with richly colored marbles, mosaics, inlaid woods, gilt, silver, silk, velvet, and brocade. Ceiling-to-floor windows and mirrors and crystal chandeliers holding thousands of candles illuminated the salons and halls. In terms of sheer capacity, the palace could

house 5,000 people and serve thousands more visitors each day. It faced hundreds of acres of groves, walks, canals, pools, terraces, fountains, statues, flower beds, and clipped shrubs—all laid out in formal geometric patterns symbolizing the triumph of engineering over nature. So dazzling was this hallmark of royal absolutism that other European monarchs soon attempted to copy it.

Louis used Versailles, images of himself, and symbols to enhance his authority among the nobility and everyone else. "The peoples over whom we reign, being unable to apprehend the basic reality of things, usually derive their opinions from what they can see with their eyes," he explained. **Figure 13.4,** a painting by an anonymous seventeenth-century artist, shows Louis—in the center astride a white horse—as he rides into the gardens at Versailles. His favored courtiers throng around him, hoping to be seen by him and others more than to see him. Servants mingle in the crowd as well. Above is the king's chosen symbol, the sun, with its light radiating out. As Louis put it, "The symbol that I have adopted and that you see all around you represents the duties of a Prince . . . endlessly promoting life, joy and growth." It is "the most dazzling and most beautiful image of the monarch."

The Sun King finally moved to Versailles in 1682. Once established there, he lured the men and women of the nobility away from their local centers

FIGURE 13.3 Pierre Patel the Elder, View of Versailles, 1668 A royal procession enters the grounds of Versailles in this aerial view. The new geometrically ordered palace and grounds became a monument to Louis XIV's reign and French royal absolutism.

of power where they might make trouble and turned them into domesticated court "butterflies." He subjected them to a complex system of etiquette and favoritism that made every aspect of Louis' daily life the center of their concern. Court became a theater where those already in favor, as well as aspiring favorites, had to scheme for gifts, patronage, and position. Winners might secure lucrative rewards, and losers might spend themselves broke trying to stay in the race.

Despite the grandeur of Versailles, this glittering monument to royal absolutism had its critics. In her novel *The Princess of Clèves* (1678), the Countess de Lafayette complained that at Versailles "everybody was busily trying to better their position by pleasing, by helping, or by hindering somebody else." The court reportedly seethed with gossip, scandal, and intrigue. Critics such as Pierre Jurieu, a French Calvinist pastor who fled to Holland, lamented that the king "is the idol to which are sacrificed princes, great men and small, families, provinces, cities, finances and generally everything." Resentful nobles once proudly drawing high status from their lands

Versailles' critics

and lineage came to depend on the approval of and service to the king as the primary route to power. Many hard-toiling, heavily taxed French commoners also grumbled about living in the reflected glory of a pretentious monarch.

To enhance the glory of his court, Louis XIV subsidized and attracted to Versailles leading French artists and literary figures. The elegance, the sense of order, and the formalism of royalty all found expression in much of the literature of this **classical style** in French culture. Pierre Corneille (1606–1684), for example, wrote elegant plays modeled on the ancient Greek tragedies. Human beings' conflicts with their own nature and with the workings of fate and the universe furnished the plots. Even more exquisite were the perfectly rhymed and metered couplets of Jean Racine's (1639–1699) dramas. Finally, in his profound comedies, Jean-Baptiste Molière (1622–1673) satirized pompous scholars, social climbers, false priests, and quack physicians. Louis and his court had little to fear from this literature. On the contrary, they appreciated its formal order and laughed along with other audiences at its satire, which was

Classical literature

FIGURE 13.4 Louis XIV at Versailles, seventeenth century In this painting by an unknown artist, Louis sits on a white horse surrounded by his courtiers at his Versailles palace. Above him radiates his adopted symbol, the sun.

aimed at humankind in general rather than at specific ruling regimes.

At court and elsewhere, many members of the elite also read historical romances. Perhaps the most popular of these was *Grand Cyrus* by Madeleine de Scudéry (1608–1701), a writer who rose from an impoverished background. The fact that this book was published under the name of the author's brother, Georges, hints at the difficulties women faced in expressing their cultural talents. Other forms of literature included letters and memoirs. The courtier Madame de Sévigné (1626–1696), for example, wrote almost two thousand letters to her daughter that reported what the king said and did as well as news of marriages, deaths, gossip, fads, and conspiracies that marked life at the court of Louis XIV. The Duke of Saint-Simon (1675–1755), who like many nobles felt slighted and grew to resent the king, chronicled life at Versailles in his forty-volume *Memoirs*.

While the literature of the seventeenth century amused monarchs, the visual arts of the period positively glorified them. Kings and aristocrats still favored the baroque style of painting and architecture (see Chapter 11). As they saw it, the baroque's swirling forms and massive, ornamental elegance perfectly

| Visual arts |

reflected their wealth and power. Yet during the second half of the seventeenth century, classicism, with its emphasis on control and restraint, began to gain favor. The appealing paintings of French artists Claude Lorraine (1600–1682) and Nicolas Poussin (1594–1665) helped classicism win official approval in France. Both men spent much time in Italy, studying the Renaissance masters and the Italian landscape. **Figure 13.5** embodies their style. In this painting, Lorraine has framed the foreground figures with trees under a radiant sky. The Italian landscape is geometrically balanced, the figures are in classic dress, and the scene exudes calm and discipline. Here is an idyllic vision, a scene designed to elevate the minds of viewers. Compared to the baroque, the classical style shows a logic that echoed the sense of order pervading the Versailles court of the Sun King.

Versailles, the arts, and all other aspects of government cost money. Louis assigned the talented Jean-Baptiste Colbert (1619–1683) to manage his finances. An engine of efficiency, Colbert toiled endlessly, supervising the details of the French economy while also promoting culture by founding the Royal Academy of Sciences in 1666 and subsidizing the arts. In keeping with his bourgeois origins, he chose service to the king as his means of advancement. His family shared in his success, becoming ministers, gaining high offices in the church, marrying well, and securing top positions in the military.

| Colbert |

Promoting mercantilistic economic policies (see Chapter 12), Colbert protected industries with high tariffs while subsidizing exports and new industries. To encourage France's growing empire and the commerce it generated, he built a large navy. Finally, Colbert worked to ensure a worldwide reputation for the uniformly high quality of French products. He subjected manufacturing to the most minute regulation and supervision: So many threads of such and such quality and color must go into every inch of this textile and that lace. Although Colbert's restrictive mercantilistic controls in the long run stifled initiative and economic change, French products earned wide acclaim for their quality. By his death in 1683, Colbert had balanced the budget and promoted relative prosperity despite Louis XIV's lavish expenditures.

During the following decades, however, Louis embarked on policies that undermined much of what Colbert had accomplished. The king's demands for religious conformity and his military ambitions ranked among the most destructive of these policies. Huguenots (French Protestants) paid the highest price for his religious intolerance. In 1685,

| Revocation of the Edict of Nantes |

Louis revoked the Edict of Nantes, which in 1598 had granted tolerance to the Protestant minority. Then he outlawed Protestantism and ordered Protestant churches demolished. The Duke of Saint-Simon lamented that the "ultimate results [of the reversal] were the depopulation of a fourth part of the kingdom and the ruin of our commerce . . . the country was given over to the authorized ravages of dragoons [armed troops], which caused the death of, literally, thousands of innocent people of all ages and both sexes." Although Huguenots were forbidden to emigrate, perhaps as many as 200,000 did, taking their wealth and skills with them to Protestant-friendly areas in Europe and America, "enriching them and causing their cities to flourish at the expense of France," according to Saint-Simon. Up to a million Huguenots who remained in France went underground.

Nor was Louis content to rule in peace as the leader of Europe's most powerful nation. During the last four decades of his 72-year reign, he fought four wars of aggression. The same old reasons prompted him to lead France into battle: more territory, more glory, and more wealth. He set his sights on the Spanish and Austrian Habsburg lands on France's eastern borders and on the Dutch, France's most powerful commercial rivals on the Continent. He put his war minister, the Marquis of Louvois (1639–1691), in charge of organizing France's huge military establishment on the model of a complex business, replete with supply depots and hospitals. While Louvois introduced strict discipline, uniforms, and promotions based on merit, Sébastien de Vauban (1633–1707) designed sturdy fortifications and brilliant siege operations. It was a common saying that whereas a city defended by Vauban was safe, one besieged by Vauban was doomed.

Louis initiated his foreign adventures in the War of Devolution (1667–1668), waged against Spain for French claims in the Spanish Netherlands and Franche-Comté (Burgundy). When victory seemed within reach, the United Provinces, England, and Sweden joined Spain to prevent France from upsetting the balance of power. The Treaty of Aix-la-Chapelle (1668) brought Louis only minor gains (see **Map 13.1**). In 1672, Louis turned against the Dutch, whom he blamed for organizing the alliance against him and who were France's chief trade competitors. The Dutch stopped the invading French only by opening the dikes and flooding the land. Dutch diplomacy brought Spain, Sweden, Brandenburg, and the Holy Roman Empire into an alliance against the French. Louis fought them to a standstill and gained some valuable territories in the Peace of Nijmegen (1679). In the following

Wars of aggression

FIGURE 13.5 Claude Lorraine, *The Marriage of Isaac and Rebekah (The Mill)*, 1640 This calm, balanced Italian landscape by a leading French artist exemplifies seventeenth-century classicism with its emphasis on control and restraint.

years, Louis made enemies of the Austrians by refusing to help in their war against the Turks, and he alienated Europe's Protestants by turning against the Huguenots. Fearful that he intended to upset the balance of power and dominate the Continent, much of Europe formed the Grand Alliance against him. The eight-year War of the League of Augsburg (1689–1697) gained France little territory at the cost of much bloodshed and misery. Louis' final struggle, the War of the Spanish Succession, was fought over French claims to the Spanish throne and the partition of Spanish holdings in the Netherlands and Italy. The war lasted eleven years (1702–1713), and the Grand Alliance defeated French and Spanish forces in a series of battles. Beaten, impoverished, and facing revolts fueled by despair and opposition to taxation, Louis XIV was forced to accept the Peace of Utrecht (1713), which ended Louis' ambitions to create a partnership of Bourbon monarchs in France and Spain—with France the senior partner. **Map 13.1** depicts France in 1661, when Louis XIV took control of the monarchy, and the territories he eventually acquired. In the end, he possessed little more than what he had started with some fifty years earlier, and he had even fewer holdings in North America.

Louis XIV died only two years after the Peace of Utrecht. He had long outlived his popularity. One widely circulated letter from an aristocratic critic, Archbishop Fénélon, complained that "for thirty years, your principal ministers have . . . overthrown all the ancient maxims of the state in order to increase your authority beyond all bounds. . . . For the sake of

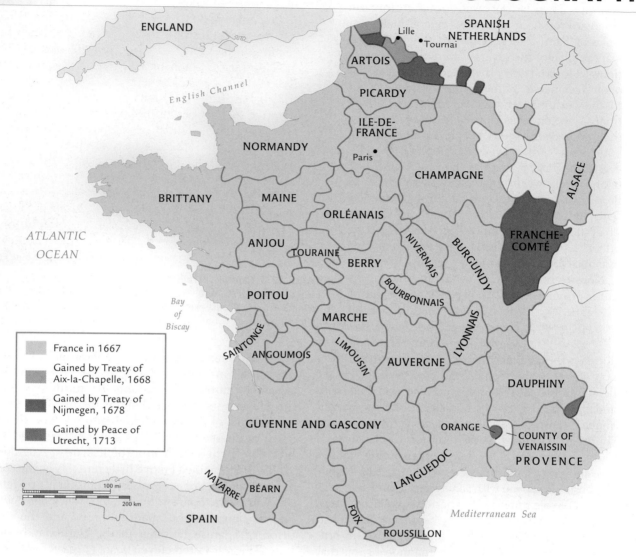

MAP 13.1

France Under Louis XIV, 1661–1715

This map shows France's provinces and the territorial gains the state made during the reign of Louis XIV. In four wars between 1667 and 1713, France fought against various rivals and coalitions of states to the south, north, and east.

Explore the Map

1. Notice that most of Louis' gains came from Spanish lands and German states on France's eastern border. What might this pattern imply about vulnerable areas of Europe and changing power relationships at the time?

2. Consider how small France's gains were despite the almost endless, costly wars the state waged. What were the wars' likely consequences for France's finances and the popularity of its monarch?

getting and keeping vain conquests abroad, you have destroyed half the real strength of your own state." As the coffin carrying Louis XIV's body was drawn through the streets of Paris, some of his abused subjects cursed his name.

The Sun King had built the French state into the envy of Europe, and his glittering court at Versailles outshone all others. His success relied on knowing how to use the old system, modified by preceding state-builders such as Richelieu, to his advantage. He tamed rather than fought the nobility, who at the same time remained the crown's most important ally and potent competitor. Clearly, strong central governments enjoyed advantages, and none were stronger than France's under Louis XIV. For many monarchs, France under Louis XIV became the model of absolutism. However, his expenditures and wars created unprecedented misery for most commoners saddled with relentlessly rising taxes, more military service, and famines. Recognizing that the continued power of the state required some support of the people, Louis' successors would try to avoid his mistakes and ameliorate the worst threats to the lives of French people.

Assessing Louis XIV

THE STRUGGLE FOR SOVEREIGNTY IN EASTERN EUROPE

In eastern Europe, people struggled just as fiercely to survive and to define sovereignty as they did in the west. However, the two regions differed sharply, and those differences affected the outcomes of battles over these issues. States east of the Elbe River (see **Map 13.2**) were less commercially developed than those in western Europe. Instead of farms worked by legally free and mobile peasants, estate agriculture (large landed estates owned by lords and worked by their serfs) dominated those economies. By the sixteenth century, the nobles who owned these estates had reversed the medieval trends toward greater freedom for the peasantry and the growth of towns. Most people who worked the fields sank into serfdom, bound to the land and owing ever-increasing services to their lords. The middle classes in the towns also declined, failing to gain in numbers and wealth like their counterparts in western Europe. Finally, most central governments at the beginning of the seventeenth century proved weaker than those in western European states, as powerful nobles retained much independence. Despite all this, several monarchs decided to change things in their own favor.

Centralizing the State in Brandenburg-Prussia

In Brandenburg-Prussia, the "Great Elector" Frederick William (r. 1640–1688) inherited a scattered patchwork of poorly managed lands weakened by years of war and population decline. He faced a number of other problems as well. His army was tiny—too weak to keep foreign forces out of his lands or to discipline internal opponents. His nobles, or Junkers, had an independent streak and had found ways to avoid

most taxes. Finally, his cities remained uncooperative, asserting their long-established political and economic independence.

Frederick William set out to correct the situation. He believed that the key was to strengthen his standing army. Only then could he gain control of his lands and make Brandenburg-Prussia a desired ally in international affairs. During the 1640s, he more than tripled the size of his army. This new strength and effective diplomacy won him several new territories at the end of the Thirty Years' War (see **Map 13.2**). With energy and skill, he next centralized and administered the governments of his fragmented holdings— while continuing to boost the size of his army. He prevailed over the **Estates**—the representative assemblies of the realm—and acquired the crucial authority to collect taxes. He then used his newly powerful army to enforce tax payments and organize state resources. In a pivotal compromise with landed aristocrats, he allowed them complete control over their serfs in return for support and service in his bureaucracy and army. Through mercantilistic policies, he protected industries, improved communications, and promoted agriculture. Though Frederick William could not afford a lavish court like that of Louis XIV, his policies ratcheted up his power. "Hold fast to the eminence of your superior position . . . [and] rely on your own strength," he advised his son. At the Great Elector's death in 1688, Brandenburg-Prussia was well on the road to becoming a major player in European politics. He also left a legacy of military values and reliance on armed might that would influence much of Prussia's subsequent history.

In 1701, his son, Frederick I (r. 1688–1713), increased the dynasty's status by acquiring the title of King of Prussia in return for helping the Holy Roman Emperor in a war against France. He used state revenues to turn his Berlin court into a great social and cultural center. By his death in 1713, Brandenburg-Prussia had become a respected force in eastern Europe.

Austria Confronts the Ottomans and Expands Its Control

Austria's Leopold I (r. 1657–1705), facing extreme local, language, and ethnic differences within his diverse lands, could not hope to acquire the same power as that enjoyed by Louis XIV in France or even Frederick William in Prussia. Localities retained considerable autonomy, especially in matters of taxation. The practical Leopold focused on securing his own Habsburg lands, rather than cementing the minimal control he had over the Holy Roman Empire, and allied himself closely with the Catholic Church. He gained the allegiance of the nobles by making them his chief advisors and granting them rights to

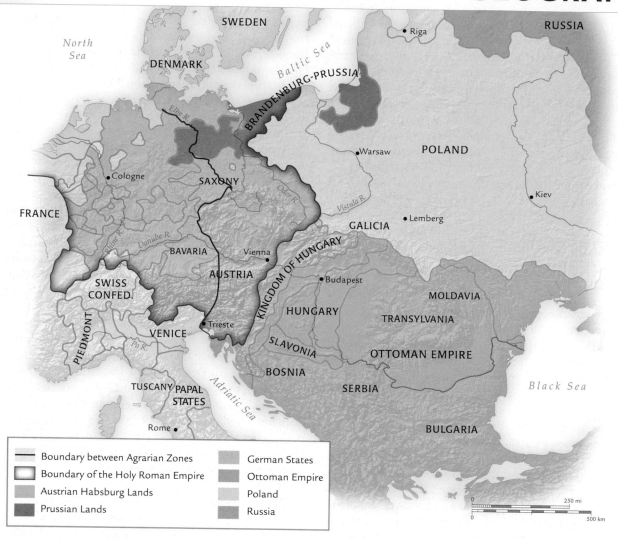

MAP 13.2

Central and Eastern Europe, 1648

This map shows the border between the western and eastern agrarian zones, running from the mouth of the Elbe River south to Trieste on the Adriatic Sea.

Explore the Map

1. Which states lay to the east of this border?

2. What did this dividing line imply about social differences between eastern and western European states at the time?

3. What problems did these differences pose for eastern European states such as Austria and Brandenburg-Prussia, which controlled provinces to the west of this line?

exploit lands and the peasants on them. Some peasants revolted, but as elsewhere in Europe, they did not pose a serious challenge to authorities. With the help of Poland's king, Jan Sobieski (r. 1674–1696), Leopold also fought the Ottoman Turks, who controlled most of Hungary as part of their large and still-powerful empire.

During the fifteenth and first half of the sixteenth century, the Ottomans had enjoyed great power and relative prosperity. The sultans in Istanbul, wielding secular and religious authority, ran a strong autocratic state that could **The Ottomans** compete with any European power. Increasingly, they struggled to maintain authority in the face of competition from bandit armies, mutinous army officers, and squabbling elites, but seventeenth-century Ottoman rulers managed to maintain control. In 1683, Ottoman armies pushed into Austrian lands and laid siege to the capital, Vienna. Leopold and Sobieski's forces saved the city, however, and then brought most of Hungary under Austrian control (see **Map 13.3**). The loss shocked Ottoman elites, and for good reason. From that point on, the empire ceased to expand, and during the following decades, the Ottomans' sources of wealth dried up. Moreover, the military weaponry and tactics of Ottoman armies and navies lagged behind those of their European foes. Ottoman power and imperial leadership would deteriorate further as weakened rulers struggled against political corruption, provincial revolts, and military insubordination.

After his victory in Vienna, the Austrian king tried to install his own nobility in Hungarian lands and ally himself with powerful Hungarian nobles at the expense of the peasantry. He succeeded only partially, and the still-independent Hungarian nobles remained a thorn in the side of the Austrian monarchy. Facing west, Leopold helped build a coalition that stood against Louis XIV. By the Austrian king's death in 1705, the Habsburg state had become one of the most powerful in Europe.

Russia and Its Tsars Gain Prominence

Even farther east, the Russian monarchy slowly rose to prominence. Already in the sixteenth century, Ivan IV ("the Terrible") (r. 1533–1584) had added both to the authority of the Russian tsars (caesars, or emperors) and to the span of territories over which they ruled. He destroyed the remaining power of the Mongols in southeastern Russia and annexed most of their territory. Next, he began Russia's conquest of Siberia. Within his expanding state, Ivan ruled as a ruthless autocrat, creating his own service gentry to bypass powerful nobles and using torture and terror to silence all he saw as his opponents.

A difficult period known as the Time of Troubles (1584–1613) followed Ivan IV's death. Ivan's feeble-minded son Fyodor ruled ineffec-

The Romanovs tively and left no successor upon his death in 1598. Great nobles vied for power among themselves and against weak tsars. To end the political chaos, a group of leading nobles in 1613 chose the 17-year-old Michael Romanov (r. 1613–1645) to rule as tsar. He began a dynasty that ruled Russia for over three hundred years.

Despite the political stability Michael and his immediate successors brought, discontent among those below the tsar and the nobility mounted during the century as the authorities increasingly restricted the freedom of the masses. The notorious Law Code of

1649, for example, merged peasants and slaves into a class of serfs and gave the landowning nobility the power to treat them as property. In a spate of uprisings between the late 1640s and early 1670s, the lower classes rebelled against landowners and officials by killing them and looting or burning their estates. The discontent reached a climax in the late 1660s and early 1670s with the revolts of Cossacks (free warriors) in south Russia led by Stenka Razin. A shrewd, seasoned warrior, Razin claimed to "fight only the boyars and the wealthy lords. As for the poor and the plain folk, I shall treat them as brothers." His rebel army marched north, and many towns opened their gates to welcome Razin's forces, now swelling with the addition of discontented peasants and the urban poor. Russian soldiers finally caught, tortured, and executed Razin, and the uprisings tapered off.

By the final decades of the seventeenth century, the Romanov tsars had shored up the government's central administration and extended their authority throughout the country. Lured by visions of wealth from access to **Russian expansion** Siberian furs, Russians had driven eastward into Asia, establishing fortified settlements, bringing indigenous peoples under their control (in the process decimating them with raids and diseases such as smallpox), and planting their flag on the shores of the Pacific. Moreover, through increased trade and travel, Russia's commercial and cultural contacts with the West expanded, bringing new European goods and ideas into the country. The stage was set for a dynamic tsar to propel Russia more fully into European affairs.

This new, energetic emperor came in the person of Peter I ("the Great") (r. 1689–1725). Standing nearly seven feet tall, Peter seemed born to rule. At the age of 17, he seized the **Peter the Great** reins of government from his elder sister. He soon concluded that the best way to bolster his own political and military power was to copy Western practices. To this end, he traveled to western Europe and learned as much as he could about Western politics, customs, and technology.

Back home, Peter took decisive steps to solidify his authority. In 1698, he crushed a revolt of his bodyguards and silenced critics with a ruthlessness that cowed all potential troublemakers. "Every day was deemed fit and lawful for torturing," wrote an observer. He also made five years of education away from home and state service requirements for the nobility and allowed movement within the ranks only through merit. Peter applied the bureaucratic system of western European monarchs to both central and local government to secure his rule. He also brought Western technicians to Russia in large numbers and protected new industries with mercantilistic policies. Western social customs were introduced to the upper

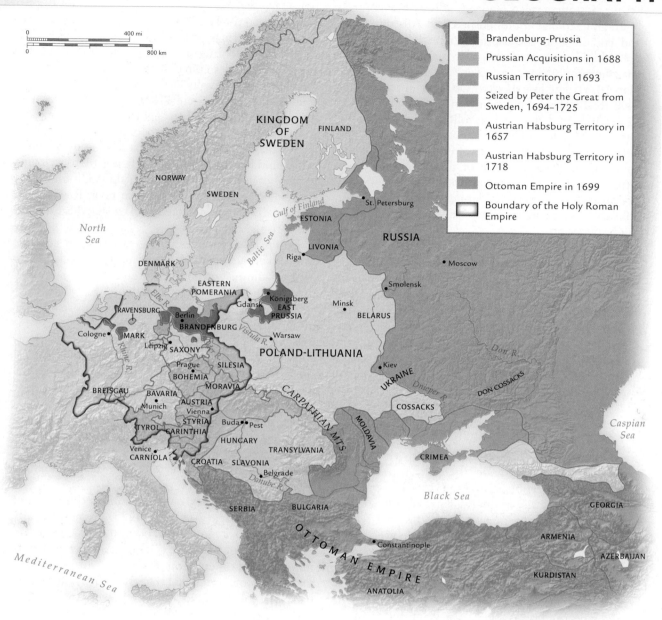

MAP 13.3

Central and Eastern Europe, 1640–1725

This map shows the changing political landscape in central and eastern Europe during the seventeenth and early eighteenth centuries.

Explore the Map

1. Notice how Russia's expansion to the west increased its contacts with European commerce and affairs. How might these widening interactions alter the balance of power in Europe?

2. Consider the gains made by the Austrian Habsburgs against the Ottomans. What did the declining fortunes of the Ottoman Empire imply for the future of this part of the Western world?

3. Locate Poland-Lithuania. What problems did this country face, hemmed in as it was by three growing powers?

and middle classes of Russian society, such as bringing Russian women out of seclusion to appear in Western dresses at official dinners and social gatherings. In addition, Peter banned the long beards and flowing Oriental robes that Russian men traditionally wore. When the patriarch of the Russian Orthodox Church opposed the tsar's authority and some of his Westernizing policies, Peter took control of the church and confiscated much of its wealth. Henceforth, the Orthodox Church served as a powerful instrument of the Russian government.

All these reforms left the peasantry in even worse straits than before. Peasants made up 97 percent of Russia's population during Peter's reign, and they became tied down in a system of serfdom bordering on slavery. The taxes they were forced to pay ballooned by a whopping 500 percent, and their feudal obligations and military service increased. Nowhere was peasant life harsher than in Russia, and Peter's efforts to Westernize the nobility only widened the gap between the educated elites and the enserfed peasantry. "The peasants are perfect slaves, subject to the arbitrary power of their lords," wrote a British envoy to Peter's court. They are usually "transferred with goods and chattels; they can call nothing their own."

| Russia's military establishments |

To keep Russia in step with the West and support his ambitions for territorial expansion, Peter devoted particular attention to his military establishment. He built a navy and patterned his expanded and modernized conscript army on the model of Prussia. Recruits were drafted for life and even branded with a cross on their left hand to deter desertion. Officials arbitrarily assigned serfs to work in mines and manufacturing establishments to supply the military with equipment and arms.

Peter meant to use his new military might. **Figure 13.6** depicts the clean-shaven tsar Peter the Great in heroic military pose. Clad in armor and carrying a sword, Peter asserts his authority over all potential rivals, who offer him their swords. Beneath the feet of his horse lies a defeated dragon. Above, an angel crowns Peter with divine authority. The tsar waged numerous military campaigns over his long reign, and he designed many of his great reforms to strengthen and modernize his armed forces. In the background of the painting, his troops surge to victory in a mighty battle.

Lacking warm-water access to the West, Peter tried to seize lands bordering the Black Sea that the Ottoman Turks held. Though they had weakened during the seventeenth century, the Ottoman Turks

FIGURE 13.6 Anonymous, *The Apotheosis of Tsar Peter I the Great* The painter portrayed the Russian tsar as a heroic, all-conquering military figure who is blessed with divine authority.

remained a formidable obstacle, and Peter's armies could not dislodge them. Frustrated, Peter turned northwest toward Sweden, which controlled lands bordering the Baltic Sea. Under King Gustavus Adolphus (r. 1611–1632), this Nordic country had become the dominant military power in northeastern Europe in the early seventeenth century (see Chapter 11). At the opening of the eighteenth century, Sweden held large areas east and south of the Baltic in addition to the homeland, and it ranked second only to Russia in size. Much of its success and the power of its monarchs came from the almost constant wars it fought during the seventeenth century. However, it lacked the population and resources to hold its far-flung territories for very long. Though Peter initially lost battle after battle to his brilliant Swedish adversary, Charles XII (r. 1697–1718), his persistence finally paid off. In the Battle of Poltava (1709), the Russians destroyed the Swedish army and managed to wound Charles.

| Conflict with Sweden |

The Rise and Fall of the Mughal Empire in India

While monarchs in Europe struggled to consolidate their authority during the seventeenth century, powerful rulers rose in the Asian states. These emperors would become strong enough to rival the Western powers and control relations with European traders. The Asian leaders had a proud history. During the sixteenth century, the Mughals (Moguls), a fierce Islamic Turkish tribe, had swept into the Indian subcontinent and established a flourishing realm ruled by able emperors such as Babur (1483–1530) and Akbar (1542–1605).

In 1605, the 38-year-old Jahangir succeeded the great Mughal leader Akbar and assumed the title of "the world-subduing emperor." In his memoir, he described the lavish ceremonies accompanying his crowning. During the festivities, the high officials of the empire, "covered from head to foot in gold and jewels, and shoulder to shoulder, stood round in brilliant array, also waiting for the commands of their sovereign."

By that time, the Portuguese had already established a flourishing trading base on the west Indian coast. As the seventeenth century unfolded, the Mughals also allowed the English, French, and Dutch to establish trading bases in India, but without power to be of any concern. The Mughals themselves paid little attention to foreign trade but welcomed the revenues from the commerce into their treasuries.

Though Jahangir wielded power arbitrarily, he also felt compelled to follow certain traditions and laws. In his view, to bring "prompt punishment to the man who violates the laws of his country is an alternative with which no person entrusted with the reins of power is authorized to dispense." Jahangir also struggled to bring unruly sections of his empire more firmly under his control, at one time ordering a bloody campaign against rebellious Afghans. The Mughal emperor recorded how prisoners from one battle were paraded before him "yoked together, with the heads of the seventeen thousand slain in the battle suspended from their necks." Reflecting on the burdens of office, Jahangir lamented, "There is no pain or anxiety equal to that which attends the possession of sovereign power, for to the possessor there is not in this world a moment's rest." Nevertheless, the emperor gave his wife, Nur Jahan, a major role in running the government. He also managed to find time to support and enjoy sports, literature, and art as well as to smoke opium regularly. He completed his *Memoirs* before his death in 1627.

An eventual successor, Aurangzeb, became Mughal emperor in 1658 and held power for almost fifty years. One of his chroniclers, Bakhta'war Khan, claimed it was "a great object with this Emperor that all Muslims should follow the principles of the religion." The biographer also boasted that his emperor "has learned the Qur'an by heart."

But Aurangzeb's reign marked both the apex of Mughal power and the beginning of its end. By the time of his death in 1707, reckless spending, endless military campaigns, and persecution of Hindus and Sikhs had weakened the regime. Widespread rebellions broke out, which Aurangzeb's weaker successors failed to overcome. In the 1720s, one observer, Khafi Khan, reported that many townships "have been so far ruined and devastated that they have become forests infested by tigers and lions, and the villages are so utterly ruined and desolate that there is no sign of habitation on the routes."

As the Mughal empire disintegrated, rivals quickly took power. European traders also gained influence—especially the British and French, who were competing for the Indian trade in textiles, spices, and sugar. By the mid-eighteenth century, the land controlled by Aurangzeb's successors had dwindled to Delhi. Meanwhile, the British and French forged strategic political alliances with Indian states and jockeyed for a dominant position on the subcontinent.

Making Connections

1. What were the similarities between the European and Mughal monarchs, particularly Louis XIV of France and Aurangzeb of India?

2. What policies weakened their respective states?

Through the Treaty of Nystad in 1721, Russia received the Swedish Baltic provinces and some Polish territories (see **Map 13.3**). On the shores of the Baltic Sea, Peter triumphantly built a modern capital, St. Petersburg, that faced west. Reigning from this new court, he emulated the cultured, royal ways of the West to enhance his personal authority. At his death in 1725, Russia had taken its place as a major player on the European stage.

The Victory of the Nobility in Poland

Not all the eastern European states drifted toward monarchical absolutism. In Poland, the competition between the monarchy and the nobility took a different turn—with severe consequences for the nation. In the sixteenth and seventeenth centuries, Poland seemed poised to become a major power. Taking advantage of Russia's Time of Troubles (1584–1613), the Poles had captured Moscow for a few years until the Russians finally drove them out in 1613. In reality, however, the Polish nation, which included Lithuania in a dual kingdom, was far from strong. Sprawling over a large area between Russia and the German states, it had no natural, protective boundaries either to the east or to the west. Ethnic and religious divisions undermined the Polish rulers' hopes for unity, and the economy stumbled. In the late Middle Ages, a sizable overland commerce between the Black and Baltic seas had flowed across Poland. However, with the shifting of commercial routes and centers to the west in the sixteenth century, Poland's commerce withered. Worse, the Polish nobility, protective of its own power and fearful of an alliance between merchants and the king, deliberately penalized merchants by passing legislation to restrict trade. The great mass of the Polish people remained serfs, bound to the estates of the powerful nobility.

In the face of such forces, only a strong central government could have ensured stability for Poland. Yet this was precisely where Poland proved weakest. For many years, Poland's nobles had been gaining the upper hand, and they closely guarded their power to elect the king. When King Sigismund II died in 1572, ending the long-ruling Jagellon dynasty, the nobles saw to it that no strong king ascended the throne. They monopolized the legislative body (the Diet) and, to safeguard their rights, required a unanimous vote to pass any measure. This system guaranteed political anarchy in which, in the words of a mid-seventeenth-century observer, "there is no order in the state," and "everybody who is stronger thinks to have the right to oppress the weaker."

Over the course of the seventeenth century, revolts by Ukrainian Cossack warriors and wars with Russia, Sweden, and Brandenburg-Prussia resulted in the loss of Polish territories. Rivalries among the Polish nobles worsened the chaos. Moreover, Tatar slave raiders carried off many people. Incursions and internal wars destroyed towns, and the once-thriving Jewish populations were pushed from their homes and often slaughtered. Tens of thousands of Jews were murdered in the pogroms (organized persecutions) that swept through Poland between 1648 and 1658. Protestants also suffered at the hands of the Catholic majority. Not surprisingly, Poland's population declined sharply in these years. By the beginning of the eighteenth century, it lay vulnerable to surrounding powers that boasted stronger central governments.

THE TRIUMPH OF CONSTITUTIONALISM

As the tendency toward absolutism intensified in central Europe, another major struggle began to unfold in a small island nation far to the west. Kings desiring absolute power in England faced a situation significantly different from that in France. In France, the nobility had little history of common action between classes and lost their solitary struggle against absolutism. In England, however, there had been a tradition of joint parliamentary action by nobles and commoners who owned land, and this helped contribute to a different outcome in the struggle for sovereignty. Instead of government residing in the person of an absolute monarch, it rested in written law—constitutions, not kings, would come to rule.

The Nobility Loses Respect

For over one thousand years, the English had taken for granted the idea of separate social classes. Peasants and members of the middle classes showed the high nobility an unmistakable deference, turning out to greet them when they emerged, gazing downward and holding their hats respectfully in their hands. Even upwardly mobile landowners with some wealth (the gentry) knew that they ranked well below the peers (the old nobility). In England, there were only about four hundred noble families, and they jealously guarded their exclusive position. Commentators wrote that "nobility is a precious gift" and accepted this privilege as the natural order of things: "Men naturally favor nobility."

At the beginning of the seventeenth century, several disturbing incidents pointed to ominous cracks in the wall of privilege. One member of the gentry actually jostled and swore at an earl as the two passed in a narrow passageway, and some tenant farmers neglected to turn out, hats in hand, to welcome passing noblemen. Later, a Protestant sect, the Quakers, enacted a religious policy that forbad members to take off their hats to men in authority. Something had changed and nobles no longer seemed so essential or so noble.

What explained this apparent loss of respect for the English upper crust? We can find a partial answer in the shifting role of money. In the early modern world, the old wealth of the nobility had declined relative to the "new money" of merchants and other enterprising individuals. Furthermore, the medieval base of noble power, the military, had also declined. No longer were nobles in charge of defending the realm; mercenary armies made up of commoners now took care of these matters. England had a relatively large sector of independent craftsmen compared to other countries, and noblemen depended

New wealth

more on "free labor"—that is, on wage laborers who could enter into contracts for their labor. These differences led commoners increasingly to feel they could control their own lives rather than defer to their "betters." In addition, education had become the key to upward mobility. More and more, knowledge and service, rather than birth, seemed the measure of a man.

The members of the nobility did not relinquish their traditional place easily. Indeed, critics complained that noblemen were becoming more arrogant than ever in exerting their privileges. Sometimes, nobles even exceeded the bounds of propriety. In 1635, the Earl of Arundel lost his temper when the mayor of a city did not turn out to greet him in the traditional way. The earl sought out the mayor, grabbed his staff of office, and proceeded to beat him with it, shouting, "I will teach you to . . . attend Peers of the Realm!"

As early as the sixteenth century, laws throughout Europe had begun to supplement tradition in keeping the social classes separate, and the situation in England was no different. Governments issued **sumptuary laws** to regulate what kinds of clothing were appropriate for members of each social class. For example, an individual could not wear velvet unless he had an independent income of over 100 pounds a year, and laborers could not wear cloth costing more than 2 shillings a yard. These laws were supposed to preserve social distinction, but the newly rich recognized that the path to gaining social respect lay in part in *looking* noble. Thus, men and women insisted on purchasing luxurious clothing to rival that of the highest classes. In 1714, a Sicilian traveler observed: "Nothing makes noble persons despise the gilded costume so much as to see it on the bodies of the lowest men in the world." Now, it seemed, there was no visual marker of a person's noble status.

Sumptuary laws

The nobles had more success in guarding their property rights than their fashion privileges. In 1671, Parliament passed game laws giving the nobility the exclusive prerogative to hunt on their own lands. The new mandates even allowed them to set lethal trapguns to kill poachers. Not surprisingly, these laws only exacerbated the common people's anger, as the poor continued to poach simply to survive in times of hunger. Still, many members of the nobility tried to hang on to their privilege while others pressed to undo them.

The portrait of James Stuart, a member of the royal family, shown in **Figure 13.7** captures the arrogance and complacency of the typical English nobleman of 1630, who was oblivious to the gathering social storm that would soon disrupt his idyllic world. James stands proudly dressed in the opulent clothing of the nobility that the sumptuary laws carefully tried to preserve.

FIGURE 13.7 Anthony Van Dyck, *James Stuart, Duke of Richmond and Lennox,* ca. 1630 The English nobility worked to set themselves apart from lesser folk in their appearance and privileges. Here, James Stuart is shown in the lavish clothing that only the noble could wear, accompanied by the giant dog that accompanied him in the hunt, another privilege reserved for the nobility.

His stockings are made of the finest silk, and the lace at his throat is expensive and handcrafted. Adorning his jacket sleeve is a sun image embroidered in silver thread—an early forerunner of Louis XIV's trademark symbol. The painting portrays James with his huge hunting dog, again proclaiming his privileged position through his hunting rights. The dog gazes up adoringly at his master with the kind of deference that James had come to expect. Sadly for members of the nobility, they would receive fewer and fewer admiring glances from their fellow humans.

Protestantism Revitalized

A good deal of social criticism also came from Protestants, many of whom believed that the implementation of Reformation ideas in England had not gone far enough. Because many Protestants were involved in the increasingly lucrative commerce, their wealth helped make their concerns more visible. For many, the compromise of Elizabeth I (discussed in Chapter 11) that allowed worshipers of many beliefs to share one Church of England was unacceptable. These critics believed that the Church of England (the Anglican Church) should be "purified"—that is, trimmed of any practice that lacked biblical precedent or smacked of Catholicism. They especially objected to priestly garments and the elaborate rituals of the Anglican Church. Some wanted to eliminate bishops altogether, preferring rule by church elders instead. (This was the practice common in Scotland, where Protestant churches came to be called Presbyterian—"ruled by elders.")

In their zeal, many Protestants became increasingly anti-Catholic, and their political actions were shaped by this prejudice. Other Protestants even wanted to purify daily life, objecting to theater, cockfights, and other seemingly frivolous activities. Although individuals disagreed among themselves on exactly how they wanted the Church of England purified, they all concurred that change was essential. Many members of this loose group of critics, called **Puritans,** became influential members of Parliament.

Puritans in England reconsidered the political relationship between monarchs and their subjects, wondering about competing loyalties between law and conscience, for example. These questions formed the backdrop of a struggle for sovereignty that dominated the seventeenth century. As early as 1561, the Scottish reformer John Knox warned Queen Mary of Scotland that monarchs were responsible to their subjects: "If their princes exceed their bounds, Madam, no doubt they may be resisted, even by power." This was tantamount to a call to revolution. As Puritans gathered to discuss the purification of the church, they could not help but consider the possibility of political action.

James I Invokes the Divine Right of Kings

Because Queen Elizabeth I had died childless, the throne went to her cousin, the king of Scotland, who became King James I of England (r. 1603–1625). As soon as James heard of Elizabeth's death, he rushed to England brimming with great plans. He made promises to many who greeted him on his way south to London, rapidly knighted thousands of gentry, and even ordered an accused thief hanged without a trial—assuming incorrectly that as king he had the right to do so. Many of his subjects turned out to see their affable new monarch, but, unfortunately for him, he would not prove as popular, or as politically shrewd, as Good Queen Bess.

The honeymoon of the new monarch and his people faded rather quickly, for unlike his predecessor, he was unable to mollify the varying religious beliefs of his people. He was a Calvinist, yet he favored Anglicanism, and his most enduring heritage was the translation of the Bible he commissioned, the King James Bible, which remains widely admired as both religion and beautiful literature. However, the king managed to offend his subjects who hoped for his support for religious change. At the beginning of his reign, Calvinists approached the king, hoping to eliminate the Anglican episcopal system and bring it in line with the Presbyterian Scottish practice with which the king was familiar. They were sadly disappointed, for James threatened to "harry them out of the land" if they did not conform to Anglicanism.

> **Religious problems**

James also offended his Catholic subjects, banning Jesuits and seminary priests. In 1605, a conspiracy of Catholics planned to blow up Parliament while it was in session. The plot failed and the conspirators were executed. Yet, the "gunpowder plot," as it came to be known, increased the anti-Catholic feelings in the country, which were exacerbated when James planned a political marriage between his son and a Catholic Spanish princess. Although the marriage negotiations fell through, the attempt alienated Calvinists and Anglicans alike.

Thus by 1610, there was much animosity between the king and many of his subjects. James thought the English ungrateful, and they found him arbitrary and arrogant. Unlike Elizabeth before him, James was disinclined to compromise his theoretical notions of divine right monarchy. Even before he ascended the throne, James had written two treatises in which he asserted the divine right of kings, and in 1610 he presented this position to a skeptical Parliament. As he put it, "Kings have power of . . . life and death; [they are] judges over all their subjects and in all causes, and yet accountable to none but God." This position was consistent with his hasty execution of the accused thief, but it offended many Puritans in the House of Commons, as well as many lords who viewed the king as subject to the law of the land.

> **Divine right**

During James's rule, the English colonies in North America grew. In part, the attention to the New World stemmed from James's financial difficulties: The first permanent English colony, named Jamestown after the monarch, was founded in Virginia in 1607. James hoped to generate new income from the Virginia colonies, which in 1619 had imported slaves from Africa to grow tobacco, an increasingly popular crop. Colonial settlement was also forwarded by James's high-handed attitude toward religious dissidents. When the king threatened to harry nonconformists out of the land, some took him literally and emigrated to North America to establish colonies.

> **Colonies**

They avoided Jamestown, which was sympathetic to the Church of England, and instead landed farther north, founding their first colony in Plymouth, Massachusetts, in 1620. The New World was not to be the solution to either James's religious or fiscal problems. He died leaving a shortage of money and an oversupply of ill will among both Parliament and Protestants.

Charles I Alienates Parliament

James's son, Charles I (r. 1625–1649), inherited both his father's rule and his policies. This sober monarch, continuing to invoke the divine right of kings, considered himself answerable only to God, not Parliament. His relationship with his subjects deteriorated rapidly. He approached Parliament in the same way his father had—calling it when he needed money and disbanding it when the members demanded concessions.

Showing a remarkable insensitivity to his Protestant subjects, Charles married a sister of the Catholic king Louis XIII of France. Soon after his wedding, Charles granted concessions to English Catholics, even allowing the queen and her entourage to practice Catholic rituals in the court itself. English Protestants were horrified at what they saw as outrageous behavior by the family of the titular head of the Church of England. Charles responded to critics by persecuting Puritans, whom he viewed as disloyal. More Puritans fled to North America, settling so many colonies in the northeast that the region came to be called New England. Meanwhile, the situation in old England grew more desperate.

Concessions to Catholics

As we saw in Chapter 11, warfare had become extremely expensive, and Charles's costly and fruitless wars with Spain and France had so strained his finances that he even tried to pawn the crown jewels. The king called Parliament several times in the 1620s, only to disband it repeatedly. Things came to a head in 1640, when the Scots, who also objected to the king's high-handed religious policies, invaded the north of England. To raise the army and funds he needed to fight the Scots, Charles called Parliament again. This time, Parliament forced him to agree that he could not disband it without the members' consent. The first crack in Charles's armor of divine right had appeared. The Long Parliament, as it came to be called, continued to meet from 1640 to 1653. Over time, it acquired a measure of power and established protections for the religious freedom of Anglicans and Puritans alike.

Parliament gains power

However, the temporary compromise between the king and Parliament came to an end when troubles in Ireland caused both to agree to send troops. However, their alliance ended there. The question of

who would command the army remained. Parliament did not trust the king to suppress his religious sympathies to fight the Catholic Irish, and the king did not trust Parliament to share control of any army it raised. In the end, Parliament appointed officers to raise an army, and Charles withdrew from London to raise an army of his own. The Irish no longer seemed the immediate enemy for either side.

"God Made Men and the Devil Made Kings": Civil War, 1642–1649

As **Map 13.4** shows, the alignments in the English civil war show some divisions in English life. The rural areas were more likely to support the king, and the Puritan strongholds in the cities followed the forces of Parliament. In response to Charles's call for support, noblemen, cavalry officers, and Irish Catholics rallied to his banner. His royalist supporters were called Cavaliers, or horsemen, as a reference to medieval knights who fought for their kings. Back in London, Parliament recruited an army 13,000 strong, drawn from the commoners, merchants, a few noblemen, Scots, and Puritans. All these generalizations, however, are drawn in broad strokes, and frequently the choice to support one side or another derived from private decisions, based sometimes on religion and sometimes on long-standing personal grudges against neighbors.

The strength of the parliamentary forces, called **Roundheads** for their short haircuts, stemmed mainly from their skilled infantry, the support of major sections of the navy, and their religious conviction. Parliament's forces also benefited from the leadership of Oliver Cromwell, a Puritan who not only forwarded the cause of revolutionary change in Parliament but also took charge of the army and forged it into a formidable force called the New Model Army. The royalists had more experience in battles and more skilled generals. The lines were drawn—the royalist forces led by the king fought a civil war against the forces led by Cromwell.

By 1646, Parliament forces had won a series of victories, and Charles surrendered to the Scots, who later turned him over to Parliament in exchange for their back military pay. While the king was moved from prison to prison as royalists conspired to free him, leaders of Parliament confronted new challenges: a series of social upheavals as more and more people were drawn into the turbulent events of the 1640s.

Charles captured

Women from all social groups participated in unprecedented numbers in the English civil war. In their husbands' absence, a number of noblewomen defended their fortified castles against parliamentary

Women in war

forces, inspiring many accounts of great heroics considered surprising in the "weaker sex." Working women disguised as men also passed themselves off as Roundhead soldiers. In 1643, Charles issued a proclamation intending to prevent women from joining the army: "Let no woman presume to counterfeit her sex by wearing man's apparel under pain of the severest punishment which law shall inflict." However, the king was in no position to enforce this edict, and women continued to serve as soldiers. It is impossible to know exactly how many women fought for their cause, but the fact that Charles tried to legislate their exclusion suggests that at least he and his advisors thought the numbers significant.

Women were well suited as spies, because people expected them to be noncombatants. One such woman, Jane Whorwood, dedicated herself fiercely to the king's cause. The tall redhead repeatedly tried to free Charles during his imprisonment after 1646. She smuggled money to him and once brought in acid to weaken the metal bars so that he could break free. One of Charles's aides described Whorwood as "the most loyal person to King Charles I in his miseries."

Other previously uninvolved members of society also jumped into the fray. After 1646, radicals, both men and women, raised new | Levellers | demands for social justice. Their complaints stemmed mostly from the severe economic problems that had hamstrung England in the 1640s. A series of bad harvests caused food shortages and rising prices, and disabled soldiers returning home discovered they could no longer earn a living. Crime increased as people stole to feed their families, and the social order deteriorated. One contemporary observed: "Necessity dissolves all laws and government, and hunger will break through stone walls." From these difficult circumstances, groups of radical Protestants arose. Known as **Levellers,** they insisted that social justice become part of Parliament's agenda. A pamphlet sympathetic to their cause claimed that "God made men and the Devil made kings."

Levellers were as varied a group as the Puritans, encompassing people with a broad array of agendas. In general, however, they harked back to a tradition of English religious radicals like John Ball (see Chapter 9) and espoused as their goal to level social differences. To that end, they advocated some reforms of Parliament. For example, they believed Parliament should be chosen by the vote of all male heads of households, which would represent a dramatic broadening of the vote. Furthermore, they wanted members of Parliament to be paid, so that even those with no independent income could serve. Although these ideas may seem natural to us, they posed a major threat to those who believed that only property brought privilege.

MAP 13.4

The English Civil War, 1642–1649

This map shows England during the civil war years, identifies the locations of the parliamentarian and royalist supporters, and pinpoints the major battles.

Explore the Map

1. Notice the scale of the map. How did the distances affect the progress of the war?

2. Why might the royalists have drawn from rural rather than urban centers?

3. Based only on the information on the map, does it seem possible for the royalists to have won without help from abroad? Explain.

The King Laid Low

In the midst of these controversies, the civil war broke out again in 1648 as Charles encouraged his supporters to rise up to free him. Cromwell's forces promptly crushed the uprisings, and some army leaders concluded that they would never come to peaceful terms with the king. With Cromwell's support, they demanded that Charles be tried for treason. The majority of Parliament members refused to take this extreme step, but in December 1648 invading soldiers purged Parliament of the cautious. The remaining members, scornfully called the Rump Parliament by opponents and historians, brought the king to trial.

The Rump Parliament tried Charles as a king, rather than deposing him first and then trying him as a private citizen. In other words, they wanted to find the *king*, not just the man, guilty. This bold act represented a direct clash between two theories of government—one claiming that the king stood above Parliament, the other declaring that he must answer to it. This unprecedented, highly public trial became the first in history to receive full press coverage. Newspapers had initially emerged in England in 1641, on the eve of the civil war; by 1649, six licensed newspapers recorded the testimony in the trial and provided differing opinions on the proceedings.

Charles was accused of claiming to rule by divine right: He who had been "trusted with a limited power to govern . . . had conceived a wicked design to . . . uphold in himself an unlimited and tyrannical power to rule according to his will. . . ." Though he genuinely believed in divine right, Charles refused to answer this or any other charge. Instead, he claimed that Parliament had no right to bring charges against him at all. He gained much popular support over the few days of the trial as he consistently reiterated his position, rising above a stutter that had plagued him all his life in order to express his views firmly and with dignity. He challenged Parliament to justify "by what power I am called hither." Both sides

clearly understood the magnitude of the trial's central question: Who had sovereignty? Charles claimed that God had sovereignty and had delegated it to the king; the Puritans in Parliament claimed that they had sovereignty. There was no room for compromise, and neither side gave way. Charles was found guilty and sentenced to die.

On January 30, 1649, the condemned king was led to a scaffold erected in front of Whitehall Palace. His public execution inspired a rash of etchings and paintings. **Figure 13.8** depicts the crowds who gathered to watch, including women, whose interest in the execution seemed remarkable to contemporary commentators. Many in the crowd were sympathetic to their king. Jane Whorwood, for example, who had worked tirelessly to free Charles, ran forward to greet the king as he walked to the scaffold. **Figure 13.8** shows some of these sympathizers; note the old man in the foreground, leaning on his cane and crying, and the woman fainting in the center.

Charles executed

Charles bravely addressed the few people near him on the scaffold and repeated his views on sovereignty: "I must tell you that the liberty and freedom [of the people] consists in having a government. . . . It is not for having a share in government. Sir, that is nothing pertaining to them. A subject and a sovereign are clear different things." Charles then laid his head on the block, and the executioner severed it cleanly with one blow. The man on the side of the platform in **Figure 13.8** holds the king's head up to show the crowd. The monarchy had ended, and a new form of

FIGURE 13.8 Weesop, *Execution of Charles I*, 1649 During the English civil war, King Charles I was put to death. This image documents the shocking event and shows how the audience was both attracted to and repelled by this act.

government arose to take its place: a republic in which sovereignty rested with representatives of those who owned property. England called its new republic the Commonwealth.

A Puritan Republic Is Born: The Commonwealth, 1649–1660

As the Rump Parliament began to rule the republic, chaos erupted throughout the realm. The new commonwealth faced warfare outside its borders and dissension within. Fortunately, Parliament had an able champion in Oliver Cromwell (1599–1658). While Parliament ruled, Cromwell with his army controlled the policies.

Rebellions broke out in Catholic Ireland and Protestant Scotland, and Cromwell led his army to those lands, putting down the revolts so brutally that the Irish still remember his invasion with anger. However, Cromwell was effective and brought Scotland and Ireland tightly under English rule. Yet Parliament had more to worry about than just these expensive wars.

Within England, Levellers continued to agitate for social reform, and many of their leaders were imprisoned. Then, in 1649, a gathering of women entered the House of Commons bringing a petition asking for "those rights and freedoms of the nation that you promised us." One member of Parliament taunted the women, saying their public stance was "strange," to which a petitioner responded, "It was strange that you cut off the king's head." These were odd times indeed, and many wondered whether Parliament's victory in the civil war had created more disorder than it had resolved.

| Domestic distress |

The 1649 cartoon in **Figure 13.9** expresses the fears of royalists and moderates alike during this difficult era and serves to illustrate the tumultuous times of the Commonwealth. In this complex image, ax-wielding men (representing the Roundheads) chop down the Royal Oak of Britain, England's longtime symbol of authority and tradition. The oak teeters, threatening to fall and take with it the Bible, the Magna Carta, and the traditional rule of law. Soldiers assist the woodsmen in destroying the tree and the order it represents. The pigs in the center symbolize the common people, being "fattened for the slaughter." Oliver Cromwell stands at the left, supervising the destruction. Below his feet is hell, although he is oblivious to how close he is to damnation. While this cartoon clearly vilifies Cromwell and all he embodied, it also reveals the disorder that had torn at England since the civil war began. Could the parliamentary forces under Oliver Cromwell resolve these fears and tensions?

FIGURE 13.9 *The Royal Oak of Britain, 1649* Royalists and moderates feared that the civil war would destroy England and its traditions. This cartoon captures these fears as it shows revolutionaries chopping down the oak, symbol of Britain, and bringing down with it religion, the Magna Carta, and other texts hanging from the tree.

Parliament seemed incapable of uniting the various constituents that demanded action after Charles's death. In 1653, when the House of Commons considered a proposal to dismantle Cromwell's large army, the general lost patience. He disbanded Parliament altogether, named himself Lord Protector of the Commonwealth of England, Scotland, and Ireland, and established a military dictatorship—the republic remained only as an ideal. Cromwell faced the same problems that had confronted Parliament and the king—foreign wars and religious struggles. A pious Puritan, Cromwell set out to make England the model of a Protestant land, banning horse races, cockfights, and even theater. He ultimately proved as intolerant of Anglicans as they had been of Puritans, and he alienated most of the population with his intrusive policies. The brief experiment with a rule purely by Parliament had failed, and a military dictatorship could not be popular in a land with such a tradition of participatory government.

| Lord Protector |

Who Has the Power to Rule?

Charles's trial and execution, and the disorder that followed, did not resolve the issue of who had the ultimate power in England. In 1651, the English philosopher Thomas Hobbes (1588–1679) wrote a political treatise, *The Leviathan*, that offered an answer to this question in the form of a new theory of government.

| Thomas Hobbes |

Perhaps shaken by the chaos of the civil war, Hobbes harbored a pessimistic view of human nature. He claimed that everyone was driven by a quest for power and that given the chance, people would try to exercise their power at the expense of their neighbors—even if it meant taking their property and their lives. In this state of nature where there was no controlling authority, Hobbes described human life as "solitary, poor, nasty, brutish and short." However, he held out a ray of hope: Humans, he explained, recognized their inability to live peacefully, so they created a social contract by which they erected a ruler above them. By this contract, subjects willingly surrendered their sovereignty to a ruler who, in turn, agreed to rule over them absolutely.

With this explanation, Hobbes reconciled the Protestant views of sovereignty—in which the people held the right to rule—with absolute monarchy, where the ruler (the king or Lord Protector) possessed sole sovereignty. In the famous frontispiece of *The Leviathan*, shown in **Figure 13.10**, Hobbes visually portrayed the benefits of his system. The ruler is shown at the top wielding the sword and scepter of absolute power. Even more significant, he comprises all the people of the land—he is the body politic. The king derives his power from his subjects, without whom he would not exist. However, with this delegated power, he presides over an orderly and peaceful countryside and village. Church, state, the army, and Parliament are all neatly ordered along the sides of the page. This tidy, comforting vision stands in stark contrast to the chaos shown in **Figure 13.9** and reveals Hobbes's hope that absolute monarchy would guarantee peace in the land.

Hobbes omitted a key point in his thesis: Absolute rule is only as effective as the ruler. Although Cromwell preserved order (albeit while offending many), he failed to develop an institution that could maintain the Puritan republic. When he died in 1658, he named his son Richard his successor. However, the young man could not lead with the same energy and fervor that his father had shown. Under pressure from members of Parliament, Richard resigned, and the right to govern again returned to the people's representatives.

The Monarchy Restored, 1660–1688

Sobered by the chaos that had followed Charles's execution, Parliament decided to reinstate the monarchy. It invited Charles II (r. 1660–1685), son of the executed king, to resume the throne. Ships sailed from England to Holland to escort the king home from his place of exile. Among those in attendance when the king returned was Samuel Pepys (see Biography on pages 442–443), an English diarist who became noted

FIGURE 13.10 Thomas Hobbes, Frontispiece of His Work *The Leviathan*, 1651 Thomas Hobbes warned that only an absolute monarchy would save people from violence, a life he famously called "nasty, brutish, and short."

for the detailed accounts he kept of events from 1660 to 1669. According to Pepys, the people of England greeted their new king with much fanfare and excitement. Charles II came home to a restored monarchy that had all the luxury that his father had enjoyed—and all the problems that had plagued this troubled institution.

Samuel Pepys devoted several pages of his diary to Charles's coronation in 1661. "So glorious was the show with gold and silver," he wrote, "that we were not able to look at it, our eyes at last being so much overcome with it." Like most of his countrymen, Pepys drank ale with wild abandon during the celebration—the years of Puritan temperance seemed to melt away in a haze of drunkenness.

Yet, not everyone got caught up in the celebration. Former Cromwell supporters saw the Restoration in a very different light. John Bunyan (1628–1688), for example, who had fought with Cromwell, was imprisoned in 1660 for preaching against the Restoration. His original sentence of three months was extended to twelve years because he refused to stop preaching.

John Bunyan

After his release in 1672, he continued to preach, and he wrote his masterpiece, *Pilgrim's Progress*, in 1678. Probably the most widely read book by an English author, *Pilgrim's Progress* tells of a hero named Christian and his search for salvation through an allegorical world. This tale of hope and confidence in the human power to prevail through times of tribulation was balanced by Bunyan's lesser-known work, *The Life and Death of Mr. Badman* (1680). In this allegory, Bunyan criticized the loose life of Restoration England by describing the journey of a man who goes straight to hell. Bunyan's works strongly suggested that the Restoration had definitely not solved the political struggles of England.

Charles II grappled with the same fiscal problems that had plagued James I and Charles I, but he had to face a Parliament that had proven its strength during the civil wars. The king was

Fiscal problems bound by law to call Parliament at least every three years, and the members of Parliament had severely curtailed royal power over taxation. Like his predecessors, Charles needed money, and to buttress his revenues without the restrictions Parliament imposed, the new king tried to exert more control over the colonies in North America. He increased the customs duties permitted by the Navigation Acts (imposed in 1651) and fought a war with the Dutch in 1665. This conflict ended in a treaty that gave the English New York in exchange for Dutch control of Surinam in South America.

Charles's international dealings were hampered by disasters at home. In 1665, England

Plague and fire experienced a plague of frightening intensity—70,000 people died in London alone. The following year, a devastating fire broke out in London, engulfing the city and destroying 13,000 dwellings and 87 churches, including the venerable St. Paul's Cathedral. After the fire had died out, Charles ordered the city rebuilt and hired the skilled architect Sir Christopher Wren to redesign the main buildings. Wren's masterpiece, the new St. Paul's Cathedral, still marks the London skyline.

In addition to these disasters, the issue of religion again came to the fore. Charles had Catholic sympathies, and to circumvent Parliament, he had several times turned to the Catholic king Louis XIV of France for help and money. The Protestant Parliament, wary of Charles's granting concessions to Catholics, passed the Test Act in 1673. The law required an oath of Protestant loyalties to prevent Catholics from holding public offices, but legislation could not affect the king's conscience, or alleviate Parliament's fears of Catholicism. In 1685, Charles died after converting to Roman Catholicism on his deathbed.

Charles's successor, his brother James II (r. 1685–1688), was not able to avoid direct confrontation with the Protestant Parliament. A Catholic, James demanded in vain that Parliament repeal the Test Act, and he proceeded to place Catholics in high office in violation of Parliament's law. Many English feared that James would adopt Louis XIV's policies against Protestants and even try to institute absolute rule. They may well have been right, but the members of Parliament were not going to wait and see. In 1688, when James's Catholic wife produced a Catholic heir to the throne of England, leading members of Parliament took action.

The Glorious Revolution

To preempt James, parliamentary leaders turned to the king's eldest daughter, Mary, a Protestant and the wife of William of Orange of the Netherlands. William staunchly opposed the policies of the Catholic **William and Mary** Louis XIV, so both his politics and his religion suited the English Protestants. William gathered a fleet and an army of 14,000 men and landed in England in November 1688. He marched slowly and peacefully toward London, while most of the English population rallied to his side. Recalling Charles I's fate, James decided to flee to France "for the security of my person." Louis XIV received his Catholic counterpart with kindness.

The Irish Catholics did not welcome the new Protestant king. Indeed, they thought of James II as a Catholic hero, and Irish leaders conspired with James to help him retake his throne while the French king helped fund this enterprise. Early in his reign, William led an army into Ireland and ruthlessly suppressed what he saw as Catholic treason. Abandoning both Ireland and his claim to the throne, James lived out his life in lavish exile in France, leaving the Irish to bear the brunt of William's wrath. The new king

ENGLISH CIVIL WAR

1625	Charles I becomes king
1629	Charles dissolves Parliament
1642	Outbreak of civil war
1649	Charles I executed
1649–1660	Commonwealth in England
1651	Hobbes, *The Leviathan*
1660	Restoration of monarchy with Charles II
1685	James II becomes king
1688	Glorious Revolution
1689	William and Mary become monarchs
1690	Locke, *Second Treatise of Government*

KEY DATES

BIOGRAPHY

Samuel Pepys
(1633–1703)

Enterprising Clerk, Member of Parliament, and Diarist

Samuel Pepys was born in London on February 23, 1633, the fifth of eleven children. Only he and two of his siblings survived childhood. Samuel's father was a relatively modest tailor and his mother was the sister of a butcher. Nevertheless, the family had relatives who included landed gentry, lawyers, and a physician. The Pepyses were Puritans, and although Samuel uncharitably recalled his mother as "quarrelsome and feebleminded" and his father as "always needing some kind of aid," the family did provide him with the educational opportunities he needed to succeed.

As a young boy, Pepys was sent to live with an uncle and attend the same grammar school where the young Oliver Cromwell had been educated. Samuel must have seemed a promising student, for when he was about 13 he returned to London to attend St. Paul's School, a stronghold of Puritanism and classical learning. He won scholarships to attend Cambridge University and received his bachelor's degree in 1654. After graduating, he found a job as secretary to a distant relative who had taken an important position in Cromwell's new Commonwealth.

A year later, Pepys married Elizabeth, the 15-year-old daughter of a French Protestant refugee. She brought no dowry to the marriage, though Samuel was probably drawn to her beauty—throughout his diary, he repeatedly made notes about attractive women. His domestic life proved stormy, but he wrote often about being pleased with his marriage during the more harmonious times in his household. Pepys complained that Elizabeth was untidy and that she mismanaged the household. For his part, Samuel was no model husband; he always kept his wife short of money and was relentlessly unfaithful to her. He recorded the details of his infidelities and of Elizabeth's pained reactions to them. Elizabeth died young and childless in 1669, and Samuel never remarried.

Through the late seventeenth century, Pepys was an active participant and a careful chronicler of the major events of the era. While still at Cambridge, he witnessed the execution of Charles I and supported the Commonwealth as a clerk. However, he must have harbored royalist sympathies, for his political career blossomed in 1660 with the Restoration. Pepys accompanied the fleet that escorted the new monarch back to England, and his contacts on that journey ensured him a position suited to his many talents.

Pepys began his diary in 1660 and for nine years detailed the events of his times, both great and small. In this extraordinary text, we have an eyewitness account of the devastating plague that scourged London in 1665, followed by the great fire the year after. Pepys juxtaposed historical events with the most intimate details of his daily life, from the food he ate

---

reduced Ireland to colonial status and offered new opportunity for English landlords to take possession of Irish Catholic lands. Irish anger toward the English festered and would grow, but William's victory was cheered in England.

William and Parliament turned to the immediate task of establishing the legitimacy of his kingship. Parliament decided that James's flight from England constituted an abdication of the throne. The sovereignty that, according to Hobbes, the people had surrendered to their king had been returned to Parliament, who now had the right to install a new monarch. Parliament determined to clarify its relationship with the king, and in 1689 it passed a Bill of Rights firmly stating that kings were subject to the laws of the land, thus creating a constitutional monarchy—the triumph of **constitutionalism.** Within the Bill of Rights, William agreed to "deliver this kingdom from

> **England's Bill of Rights**

popery [Catholicism] and arbitrary power" and to preserve freedom of speech, election, and the rule of law. The bill secured the position of Protestantism in England by ruling that "no person embracing Catholicism or married to a Catholic is eligible to succeed to the throne." Through this bloodless **Glorious Revolution,** Parliament had finally demonstrated that the power to rule rested with the people through their representatives, rather than absolutely with the king. After this, Parliament began to meet annually, which was a practical way to secure its authority.

Royalism Reconsidered: John Locke

Many English men and women were proud of their bloodless "revolution" that so peacefully changed their monarch, but others were uncertain about the legality of this step. The English philosopher John Locke (1623–1704) wrote an influential political

FIGURE 13.11 J. Hayls, *Samuel Pepys,* 1666

royal patronage under the reigns of Charles II and James II, but the Glorious Revolution of 1688 caused his fortunes to change. He lost the parliamentary election in 1689, and in the following year he was arrested on suspicion that he supported the deposed James II. Pepys had always been more interested in observing political events than in engaging passionately in them, and when he was released from prison he removed himself from political life. He spent the rest of his years reading, playing music, and exchanging letters with friends, including such eminent scholars as Isaac Newton. His last years were devoted to building a substantial library, which he bequeathed at his death to his alma mater, where it still remains intact and unaltered. He died peacefully in 1703.

Pepys wrote his diary in a shorthand that was used by clerks in the seventeenth century; Newton used the same shorthand for taking his notes. The four-volume, handwritten, leatherbound diary written in a forgotten code lay ignored on the library shelves until the nineteenth century. Then, an undergraduate of the college took on the gigantic task of transcribing the diary (omitting the erotic passages) and it became an instant success. Modern editions of the complete diary continue to engage readers with its direct picture of seventeenth-century England. It has ensured that Samuel Pepys will not be forgotten.

Connecting People & Society

1. How does Pepys's life reveal the impact of the Glorious Revolution and the growing power of Parliament on the individual?

2. What does this example show about the importance of educational opportunities in the seventeenth century?

to the arguments he had with his wife. He stopped keeping his diary in 1669 because his eyesight was failing him.

Pepys took an active role in political life by working in the naval office. In 1685, he was even elected to the House of Commons. He continued to receive the benefits of

---

tract—*The Second Treatise of Government* (1690)—to justify "to the world [and] the people of England" the Revolution of 1688 and proclaim the legitimacy of William. Locke did much more—he articulated a new relationship between king and subjects that provided a theoretical framework for constitutional forms of government. Like Hobbes, Locke believed that power originally rested with the people and that citizens themselves established a monarchy to keep order. However, whereas Hobbes had said that the people turned over their sovereignty completely to the monarch, Locke claimed that they retained it but created a contract of mutual obligations with their ruler. Locke argued that if the king broke the contract, the people had the right to depose him and install a new monarch, just as Parliament had done during the Glorious Revolution.

Locke's political theories were not intended to support full democracies—in his time, the "people" meant only those who owned property. He did not intend for individuals, such as the landless Levellers, to threaten property owners. Nor did he view women as sharing in the popular sovereignty of the privileged social order. Locke's highly influential rhetoric, in which he claimed natural rights of life, liberty, and property, actually applied to relatively few people in 1690. However, in time, his theory would broaden to form the basis for democracy as well as constitutional monarchy.

Parliament soon had the opportunity to exert its king-making authority once again. William and Mary died without an heir, so the crown went to James II's Protestant daughter, Anne. Queen Anne (r. 1701–1714) also died without an heir, whereby the Protestant Stuart dynasty evaporated. Parliament then passed the crown to George I (r. 1714–1727), a great-grandson of James I, who ruled the German principality of Hanover, introducing the Hanoverian dynasty

Hanover dynasty

thinking about GEOGRAPHY

Legend:
- United Provinces in 1609
- Spanish Netherlands
- ···· Linguistic Boundary (French/Flemish)
- — Boundary of the Holy Roman Empire

MAP 13.5

The United Provinces and the Spanish Netherlands, 1609

This map shows the location of the Netherlands in Europe and its division into two separate states. Notice the scale of the map and consider how small the United Provinces were.

Explore the Map

1. How did the location of these states contribute to their wealth and importance in the seventeenth century?

2. How might the Catholic Spanish Netherlands have served as a buffer between Catholic France and Protestant United Provinces?

to England. This peaceful transition demonstrated once and for all that the struggle for sovereignty in England was over—Parliament ruled.

The Netherlands Maintain a Republic

The English nobles asserted their rights over the king by exercising their authority through a parliament that ruled over a highly centralized government. This

struggle created a strong constitutional monarchy that preserved popular sovereignty while creating a state that would prove highly stable. Another way for people to preserve their sovereignty was to resist a strong central government in order to strengthen local institutions. In the seventeenth century, the Netherlands developed this political structure, which also gave power to the people instead of to absolute rulers. They instituted another form of constitutionalism that structured the government around consent of the propertied.

When the Low Countries split in 1609, the southern Catholic regions remained subject to the absolutist monarch, Philip III of Spain. **Map 13.5** shows the division of the Low Countries in 1609. The Spanish Netherlands of the south (now Belgium) formed a buffer between the United Provinces of the north and the divine right monarchy of France. In the United Provinces, which became largely Calvinist after the wars with Catholic Spain, a Protestant state developed that successfully resisted any attempts at royal absolutism.

> **The United Provinces**

The United Provinces—also known as the Dutch Republic—was the only major European power to maintain a republican form of government throughout the seventeenth century. Each province was governed locally by an assembly (called the State) made up of delegates from cities and rural areas. In reality, the States were dominated by an oligarchy of wealthy merchants. The union of the provinces was only a loose confederation, with each province sending deputies to the States General, a national assembly that implemented provincial assembly decisions.

Executive power at the local level was vested in governors (Stadholders) of each province. At the national level, executive power was given to the Council of State, made up of deputies drawn from the provinces.

This remarkable decentralization worked effectively for local issues but had some drawbacks for implementing foreign policy. During the 1650s, Holland—the largest province—began to take an informal lead in directing the state's foreign policy in the first two wars against England. After 1672, William III, a prince of the hereditary house of Orange, became the captain-general of the republic's military forces against France. The House of Orange had a permanent vote in the States General and served as a unifying point. However, William of Orange exercised more power once he became king of England in 1689 than he ever had in the Netherlands. Document 13.3 provides a description of the governmental structure of the Dutch Republic. The 1648 Treaty of Westphalia, which ended the Thirty Years' War (see Chapter 11), formally recognized the Republic of the United Provinces.

DOCUMENT 13.3

An Ambassador Describes the Dutch Government

Sir William Temple (1628–1699) was an English diplomat who served as ambassador to the Netherlands in 1668 and again in 1674. He negotiated the marriage of William of Orange to Princess Mary of England. This political insider was an acute observer of the government of the United Provinces of the Netherlands as shown in this account.

In the first constitution of this government, after the revolt from Spain, all the power and rights of Prince William of Orange, as Governor of the Provinces, seem to have been carefully reserved. But those which remained inherent in the Sovereign, were devolved upon the assembly of the States-General, so as in them remained the power of making peace and war, and all foreign alliances, and of raising and coining of monies: in the Prince, the command of all land and sea forces, as Captain-general and Admiral, and thereby the disposition of all military commands, the power of pardoning the penalty of crimes, the chusing of magistrates upon the

nomination of the towns; for they presented three to the Prince, who elected one out of that number. Originally the States-General were convoked by the council of State, where the Prince had the greatest influence: nor, since that change, have the States used to resolve any important matter without his advice. Besides all this, as the States-General represented the sovereignty, so did the Prince of Orange the dignity, of this State, by public guards, and the attendance of all military officers; by the application of all foreign ministers, and all pretenders at home; by the splendor of his court and magnificence of his expence; supported not only by the pensions and rights of his several charges and commands, but by a mighty patrimonial revenue in lands and sovereign principalities and lordships, as well in France, Germany, and Burgundy, as in thy several parts of the Seventeen Provinces; so as Prince Henry was used to answer some that would have flattered him into the designs of a more arbitrary

power, that he had as much as any wise Prince would desire in that State; since he wanted none indeed, besides that of punishing men, and raising money; whereas he had rather the envy of the first should lie upon the forms of the government, and he knew the other could never be supported, without the consent of the people, to that degree which was necessary for the defense of so small a State against so mighty Princes as their neighbors.

SOURCE: *The Works of Sir William Temple,* vol. I (London, 1814), pp. 118–119 in *Modern History Sourcebook,* www.fordham.edu/halsall/mod/17dutch.html.

Analyze the Document

1. Which powers remained in the hands of the prince and which in the assembly of the States General?

2. How does this division of rights compare with the governmental forms described in Document 13.1?

3. What might be the strengths and weaknesses of this form of government?

What were the special circumstances that led the Netherlands to develop and maintain this strong sense of local sovereignty when other areas of Europe were moving to centralized governments? In large part, such political independence was facilitated by prosperity. The seventeenth century has been called the golden age of the United Provinces, for this small region was a tremendous European and colonial power. Amsterdam became the commercial and financial center of Europe as ships brought huge quantities of herring from the North Sea, as well as sugar, tobacco, glass, and many other items from around the world, through the bustling port.

Dutch prosperity

In addition to commerce, the Dutch prospered through skilled shipbuilding that was the wonder of Europe. Not only did they design remarkable ships that could sail with fewer crew members than more traditional ships; they also built them quickly and cheaply. They obtained timber, pitch, and rigging from the

nearby Baltic regions, and they used the most modern technology for the assembly: mechanical saws, hoists for masts, and the manufacture of interchangeable parts. Contemporary witnesses were amazed to report that given two months' notice, Dutch shipbuilders could turn out a warship every week for the rest of the year. **Figure 13.12** shows an engraving of a Dutch shipyard that was the envy of the rest of Europe. It is no wonder that silver from the New World found its way into the coffers of Dutch builders.

The Dutch also grew rich from their activities as major slave traders in the New World. The population of Amsterdam grew from about 30,000 people in 1570 to 200,000 by 1660, and the growth was testimony to the wealth and opportunities people saw there. Its financial importance was secured in 1609 by the foundation of the Exchange Bank of Amsterdam, the greatest public bank in northern Europe. Europeans were astonished by the prosperity and enterprise of the Dutch.

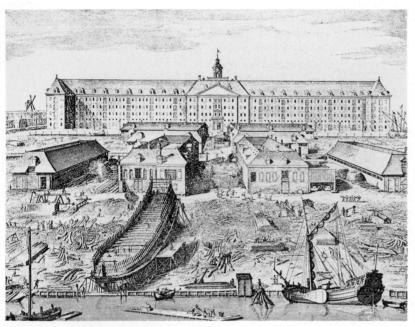

FIGURE 13.12 Dutch Shipyard Even small states such as the Netherlands could become rich in the new global marketplace. Dutch shipbuilding was the wonder of Europe, and it was proudly depicted in many images, including this anonymous engraving.

FIGURE 13.13 Rembrandt van Rijn, *Syndics of the Cloth Guild,* **ca. 1661** The painter Rembrandt had good reason to depict these wealthy merchants, for they had given him coal to heat his house when he had fallen on hard times.

The Dutch had other elements that contributed to their resistance of absolutism. The Dutch aristocracy was not as wealthy as that of England or France, for example. Their wealth lay more in commerce than in land, so the aristocracy had more in common with the merchants of their land than they did with the landed gentry in England or with the nobility at the

court of Versailles. Furthermore, in the United Provinces, the Protestant faith cultivated an ideology of moderation—rather than the aristocratic excess that marked the nobility of other states. That is not to say that the seventeenth-century United Provinces espoused notions of egalitarian democracy—the nobility were as interested in trying to increase their power as those of other countries. They were just not able to exert much centralized control over the prosperous, Protestant residents that were the wonder of Europe.

Overall, the Dutch exhibited an unusual degree of religious toleration for their time. They even allowed Catholics and Jews to practice their religions, | Religious toleration | a policy that encouraged religious refugees to flock to the Netherlands from all over Europe. These refugees greatly enriched the cultural and economic life of the republic. Not only did the United Provinces attract intellectuals, such as René Descartes from France and John Locke from England, but the open-minded assemblies stimulated the spread of ideas through the press. The United Provinces became a leading center for book publishing and transmitted ideas, even revolutionary ones, all over Europe. In 1649, for example, an anonymous pamphlet published in the Netherlands attacked Cromwell's government for not supporting the ideas of the Levellers. The pamphlet called for an "equality of goods and lands" and condemned the government that "hangs a poor man if he do steal, when they have wrongfully taken from him all his maintenance."

The refugees streaming into the Netherlands included some destitute travelers and in some ways burdened the small country. The Dutch, however, generously assisted the needy, who never sank to the same depths of hardship that faced the poor in many other European cities. In his brief stay in the Netherlands, Samuel Pepys recorded in his diary the provisions the Dutch made for the poor. He observed a guesthouse, "where it was very pleasant to see what neat preparation there is for the poor." He further noted that there were special entertainment taxes to raise money for the needy.

The wealthy middle classes treated themselves well also. For example, they commissioned paintings that depicted their unique way of life. The Dutch artist Jan Vermeer (see Chapter 12) was one of several whose talents flourished in the free Dutch environment. Even more celebrated was the Dutch artist

Rembrandt van Rijn (1606–1669), whose brilliant use of light and forceful expressiveness made him among the greatest of western European painters.

In the painting *Syndics of the Cloth Guild* (**Figure 13.13**), Rembrandt portrays the serious, successful merchants who had been chosen to manage the wealthy guild. The artist captures the proud intensity with which they work over a book on the table. In the uniformity in their clothing, they stand in striking contrast to the man in **Figure 13.7,** on page 434, who boasts luxurious designs and fabrics that set him apart from people precisely like these successful syndics. Rembrandt offered this painting to the cloth guild in thanks for their charity—the painter, who had fallen on hard times, needed coal to heat his house for the winter, and the cloth guild had provided it.

The preeminence of the Dutch began to wane by the beginning of the eighteenth century. The economies of England and France had gathered strength both in Europe and abroad and encroached on the commercial empire forged by the Dutch. Yet the two geographically small countries of England and the Netherlands had contributed much to the political development of the West. Both established the sovereignty of the people through constitutionalism—England through Parliament, and the Netherlands through local autonomy. For all their tremendous impact for the future, at the opening of the eighteenth century both nations seemed hardly whispers in a Europe dominated by strong monarchs proclaiming a divine right to rule.

LOOKING BACK & MOVING FORWARD

Summary   For upper-crust members of Western societies, the seventeenth century was a period of both comfort and struggle. The comfort came from these elites' continued dominance. From the beginning to the end of the century, they held most of the riches, status, and power. Those below them sometimes revolted, but the real threats came from competing colleagues and the monarch above. The efforts by monarchs to increase their power, to become "absolute" in both theory and practice, sparked intense struggles within states. In some places, such as France, Prussia, and Russia, strong monarchs offering order and stability won. In other places, such as Poland, England, and the Netherlands, powerful nobles—sometimes allied with commoners—overcame kings.

For the vast majority who toiled in the fields, the period offered struggle without much comfort. In western Europe, demands from expanding central governments for taxes and conscripts only aggravated the hardships wrought by unusually bad harvests and disease. In eastern Europe, landowning nobles added to these problems by burdening peasants under an increasingly heavy yoke of serfdom.

Thus the structure of this hierarchical society may have loosened enough for some people in western Europe to improve their lot. However, that structure only tightened in eastern Europe. For all of Europe, war, revolt, and even revolution shook societies without breaking the traditional hierarchies. Nevertheless, some traditions started to crumble. Important changes in science and thought were already afoot that would soon transform the intellectual foundations of Western society.

KEY TERMS

Great Chain of Being,   p. 416
royal absolutism,   p. 419
Fronde,   p. 421
classical style,   p. 423
Estates,   p. 427
sumptuary laws,   p. 434
Puritans,   p. 435
Roundheads,   p. 436
Levellers,   p. 437
constitutionalism,   p. 442
Glorious Revolution,   p. 442

REVIEW, ANALYZE, & CONNECT TO TODAY

REVIEW THE PREVIOUS CHAPTERS

Chapter 11—"Alone Before God"—examines the Reformation, which shattered the unity of western Christendom, and the entwined religious and dynastic wars that followed. Chapter 12—"Faith, Fortune, and Fame"—told how several European powers expanded overseas during this same period and grew rich from the commerce developed in their colonies.

1. Analyze how the religious divisions and wars of the sixteenth and seventeenth centuries laid the groundwork for both the growth of absolutism in France and central Europe and the struggle against it in England and the Netherlands.

2. In what ways might the competition for overseas empires and the commerce that resulted have affected the power of central governments and their responsibilities? How might the Netherlands' political structure have contributed to its commercial expansion?

ANALYZE THIS CHAPTER

Chapter 13—"The Struggle for Survival and Sovereignty"—describes how kings and nobles battled for power, the resolutions of those struggles, and their impact on the millions of people outside the elites.

1. Analyze the ways monarchs tried to increase their power.

2. What groups opposed the increase in monarchical power, and what political theories were developed to support their positions?

3. In what ways might the term *absolutism* also apply to the Mughal emperors?

4. How do you explain why in some areas monarchs won the battle for sovereignty, whereas in others they lost?

5. Describe the struggles peasants throughout Europe faced during the seventeenth century. How did their conditions differ in western and eastern Europe?

CONNECT TO TODAY

Think about this chapter's account of the struggles for power between rulers and various groups, and consider the political theories that those in power developed to justify their positions.

1. Why might some people in today's world still find the idea of monarchy appealing?

2. Why would most people in the West today oppose monarchical rule? How might they justify their views?

3. What lessons from this chapter might today's political leaders do well to apply?

BEYOND THE CLASSROOM

STRESSES IN TRADITIONAL SOCIETY

Braudel, Fernand. *Civilization and Capitalism: The Structures of Everyday Life*. New York: Harper & Row, 1981. An excellent survey by an important historian that details the transformations in economic and social history.

Chartier, Roger, ed. *A History of Private Life, Vol. III: Passions of the Renaissance*. Cambridge, MA: Harvard University Press, 1989. Part of a fine series that describes the creation of the sphere of private life.

Gottlieb, Beatrice. *The Family in the Western World from the Black Death to the Industrial Age*. Oxford: Oxford University Press, 1994. A thorough survey of the transformations in family life.

Sturdy, D.J. *Fractured Europe: 1600–1721*. London: Wiley/Blackwell, 2002. A comprehensive introduction, nicely organized around regions.

ROYAL ABSOLUTISM IN FRANCE

Bercé, Yves-Marie. *The Birth of Absolutism*. London: Macmillan, 1996. A solid examination of French absolutism from the reign of Louis XIV to 1789.

Phillips, Henry. *Church and Culture in Seventeenth-Century France*. Cambridge: Cambridge University Press, 2002. Excellent analysis of French culture and its connections with the Catholic Church.

Treasure, Geoffrey. *Louis XIV*. London: Longman, 2001. A well-written study of the king and his times.

THE STRUGGLE FOR SOVEREIGNTY IN EASTERN EUROPE

Goffman, Daniel. *The Ottoman Empire and Early Modern Europe*. Cambridge: Cambridge University Press, 2002. An informative survey of the topic.

Hughes, Lindsey. *Russia in the Age of Peter the Great.* New Haven, CT: Yale University Press, 1998. A recent study of this important figure.

Kirby, David G. *Northern Europe in the Early Modern Period: The Baltic World, 1492–1772.* London: Longman, 1990. A good survey of the region during this period.

Wilson, Peter H. *Absolutism in Central Europe.* London: Routledge, 2000. A good comparative study of absolutism in Prussia and Austria.

GLOBAL CONNECTIONS

Richards, John F. *The Mughal Empire.* Cambridge: Cambridge University Press, 1993. A solid, useful survey of Mughal history.

THE TRIUMPH OF CONSTITUTIONALISM

Braddick, Michael. *God's Fury, England's Fire: A New History of the English Civil Wars.* New York: Penguin Global, 2009. A splendid history of the civil wars that details events and people from the earliest rebellions through the execution of Charles. Gives careful attention to all parts of the United Kingdom.

Cust, Richard. *Charles I.* Harlow, UK: Pearson, 2007. Balanced exploration of this complex man whose reign spawned the civil war.

Fraser, Antonia. *The Weaker Vessel.* New York: Knopf, 1984. A detailed, illustrated, and comprehensive study of women in seventeenth-century England.

Gaunt, Peter. *Oliver Cromwell.* Cambridge, MA: Blackwell, 1995. A good study on the life and career of the Lord Protector.

Geyl, Pieter. *History of the Dutch-Speaking Peoples 1555–1648.* Phoenix, AZ: Phoenix Press, 2001. A fine historical summary that illuminates questions of national identity and the problems of a small country functioning in the shadows of great powers.

Hill, Christopher. *A Nation of Change and Novelty: Radical Politics, Religion, and Literature in Seventeenth-Century England.* London: Routledge, 1990. A history of the revolution by an eminent historian.

Miller, John. *Restoration and the England of Charles II,* 2nd ed. White Plains, NY: Longman, 1997. Clarifies the complex issues of the major political and religious themes surrounding the Restoration.

Purkiss, Diane. *The English Civil War: Papists, Gentlewomen, Soldiers, and Witchfinders in the Birth of Modern Britain.* New York: Basic Books, 2007. Vividly illuminates the details of everyday life and the personalities of the participants in the English civil war.

Sharpe, Kevin. *Culture and Politics in Early Stuart England.* Stanford, CA: Stanford University Press, 1994. A revisionist look at the culture and politics in England at this time.

van Deursen, A.Th. *Plain Lives in a Golden Age: Popular Culture, Religion, and Society in Seventeenth-Century Holland.* Translated by M. Ultree. New York: Cambridge University Press, 1991. A fascinating analysis of how laborers, peasants, and sailors made their living.

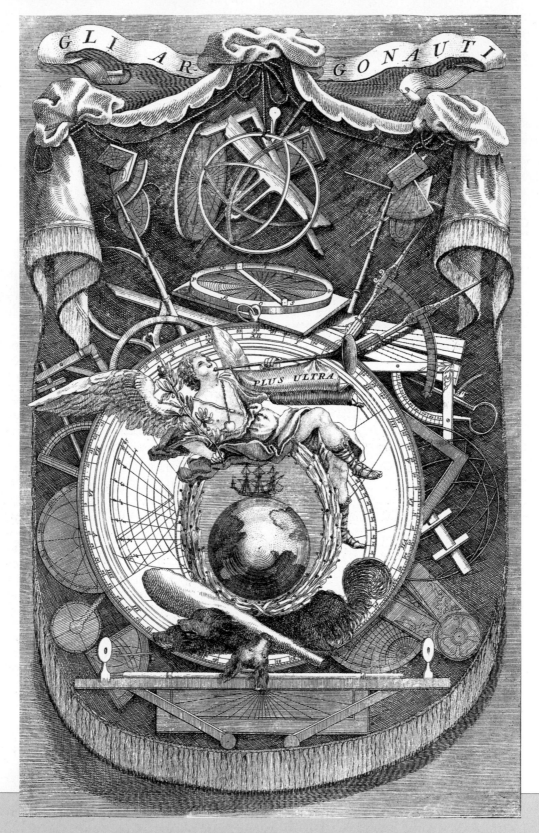

FRONTISPIECE TO MARCO VINCENZO CORONELLI'S ATLAS, 1691

In this frontispiece from an atlas, a globe and ship occupy center stage and represent the West's exploration of the world. Just above, the banner of a trumpeting angel reads, "Yet farther"— words that contrast sharply with the traditional medieval expression "No farther." Drawings of the numerous instruments that characterized the new age of exploration and science occupy the periphery of the image.

A New World of Reason and Reform

14

The Scientific Revolution and the Enlightenment, 1600–1800

I n 1655, French scientist Blaise Pascal (1623–1662) retired from his studies and began recording his thoughts in writing. "Man is but a reed, the most feeble thing in nature; but he is a thinking reed," he wrote. "All our dignity consists, then, in thought . . . by thought I comprehend the world." Pascal's words hint at the changes emerging in scholars' thinking about ideas, the world, and the place of humans in it.

We can detect more clues about these changes in the artwork on page 450. The 1691 world atlas itself, published by the accomplished Venetian mapmaker and mathematician Marco Coronelli (1650–1718), echoes the overseas expansion of Europe, already two centuries old. It also reveals the underlying culture of the Renaissance, which stressed learning and exploration through reading and art. Coronelli chose this illustration to open his new atlas. With the images of a ship, the earth, and scientific instruments and the provocative phrasing "Yet farther," he declared the end of limits to the search for knowledge. The entire illustration suggests a people proudly using science to fuel their growing power—over other peoples as well as nature itself.

Buoyed by the accumulation of scientific discoveries, this optimism about the power of thought and the search for knowledge grew and spread throughout the West during the eighteenth century. Widening circles of intellectuals and the reading public learned about the new ways of thinking being applied to all fields, from politics and religion to economics and criminology. Despite resistance from church and state, this dawning of what became known as the Age of Reason would gather strength, filter down through the ranks of society, and form the intellectual foundation for life in the modern West. Certainly the West was not unique in reasoning about the world. In the centuries preceding Europe's Renaissance, the Chinese had made many scholarly and scientific advances. The Arabs not only had prized learning and science but also had provided Europeans with tools such as translations of Greek science and Arabic numerals that were essential for Europe's scientists. On the other hand, by the sixteenth century most European scientists had university educations, whereas non-Western civilizations lacked institutions comparable to the medieval universities in places such as Bologna, Paris, and Oxford. Moreover, during the seventeenth and eighteenth centuries, the Islamic, Chinese, Japanese, and other civilizations of the world declined to question their traditional ways. Only Westerners challenged the standard assumptions of their civilization. The power and attitudes that the West gained from this intellectual exploration helped redefine Western civilization and distinguish it from the non-Western world.

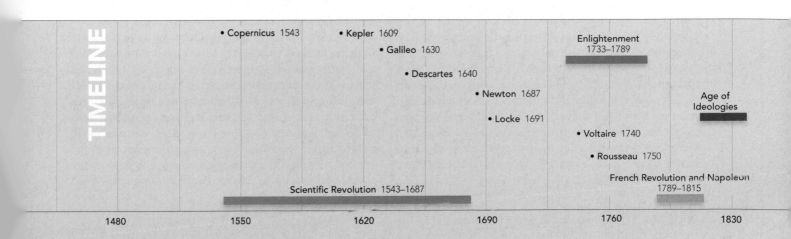

TIMELINE

- Copernicus 1543
- Kepler 1609
- Galileo 1630
- Descartes 1640
- Newton 1687
- Locke 1691

Enlightenment
1733–1789

Age of Ideologies

- Voltaire 1740
- Rousseau 1750

French Revolution and Napoleon
1789–1815

Scientific Revolution 1543–1687

1480   1550   1620   1690   1760   1830

PREVIEW

QUESTIONING TRUTH AND AUTHORITY

On June 22, 1633, the well-known Italian scientist Galileo Galilei (1564–1642) knelt in a Roman convent before the cardinals who served as judges of the Inquisition. The cardinals informed Galileo that he was "vehemently suspected of heresy." They also showed him the customary instruments of torture, though they did not use them. Next, they ordered him to deny "the false opinion that the sun is the center of the universe and immovable, and that the earth is not the center of the same"—views that Galileo had supported in a book he published the previous year. Threatened with being tried and burned as a heretic, Galileo had to denounce his views as heresy. The court and papacy sentenced Galileo to house arrest in Florence for the rest of his life and forbad him to publish on the topic again. Nevertheless, Galileo would not change his mind. The sequence of events leading to Galileo's trial and conviction is a story of its own, but the conflict lay at the core of a major development of the age: the Scientific Revolution.

The Old View

Until the sixteenth century, most European scholars shared the standard medieval understanding of the physical nature of the earth and the universe. This understanding was based on a long legacy stretching back to the views of the fourth-century B.C.E. Greek philosopher Aristotle. His ideas had been modified in the second century C.E. by Ptolemy of Alexandria and then passed on through Byzantine and Arab scholars to medieval European thinkers. After the thirteenth century, Europeans translated Aristotle's works into Latin and merged his thinking with Christian ideas about the universe.

*Hic canet errantē Lunam, Solisq; labores
Arēturūq;, pluuiasq; hyad.gēmosq; triōes*

FIGURE 14.1 The Medieval View of the Universe, 1559
This woodcut shows the earth at the center of a stable, finite universe. A band with signs of the zodiac suggests the importance of astrology within this Christian understanding.

According to this Christian medieval understanding, illustrated in the woodcut in **Figure 14.1,** the earth rested at the center of an unchanging universe. Around it in ascending order rose the perfect spheres of air, fire, the sun, the planets, and the stars (the firmament), with God (the prime mover) just beyond. The signs of the zodiac are recorded on one band in the illustration, revealing the importance of astrology. Westerners accounted for the succession of day and night by explaining that this finite universe rotated in precise circles around the earth once every twenty-four hours. The heavenly abode of angels consisted of pure matter, and the earthly home of humans was made of changeable, corrupt matter. This universe was clear, finite, and satisfyingly focused on the earthly center of God's concern.

Common sense supported this worldview. A glance at the sky confirmed that the sun and stars indeed circled around the earth each day. Under foot, the earth felt motionless. To careful observers, the motion of planets, whose position often changed, was more perplexing. To explain this mystery, Ptolemy and others had modified their theories, concluding that planets moved in small, individual orbits as they traveled

> The earth-centered universe

predictably around the earth. People had lived by the wisdom of the ancients and authoritative interpretations of the Bible for centuries. Accordingly, investigation of the physical universe generally consisted of making deductions from these long-accepted guides.

Undermining the Old View

During the fifteenth and sixteenth centuries, new problems began undermining this traditional view. Authorities of all kinds—including Aristotle—came into question during the Renaissance. Some of this questioning stemmed from the Renaissance search for classical writings, which led scholars to discover and read the works of Greek authorities who contradicted Aristotle. **Neoplatonism,** based on the ideas of Plato, stressed the belief that one should search beyond appearances for true knowledge; truth about both nature and God could be found in abstract reasoning and be best expressed by mathematics. Neoplatonic **Hermetic doctrine** provided especially powerful alternatives to Aristotelian thought.

According to Hermetic doctrine, based on writings mistakenly attributed to Hermes Trismegistus (supposedly an ancient Egyptian priest), all matter contained the divine spirit, which humans ought to seek to understand. Among many scholars, this doctrine stimulated intense interest in botany, chemistry, metallurgy, and other studies that promised to help people unlock the secrets of nature. The Hermetic approach also held that mathematical harmonies helped explain the divine spirit and represented a crucial pathway to understanding God's physical world. This approach encouraged scholars to use mathematics and to measure, map, and quantify nature. Moreover, Hermetic doctrine also held that the sun was the most important agency for transmission of the divine spirit and thus rightly occupied the center of the universe. Finally, these beliefs fostered the idea of the natural magician who could unleash the powers of nature through alchemy (the study of how to purify and transform metals, such as turning common minerals into gold), astrology (the study of how stars affect people), and magic. Scholars often saw no distinction between seeking to understand the harmony, oneness, and spiritual aspects of the natural world and what we would call scientific observation and experimentation. Although Hermetic doctrine often proved not useful, all these ideas encouraged investigators to question traditionally accepted knowledge.

Figure 14.2, an illustration from a book on alchemy by the German Heinrich Khunrath, shows these close connections between spiritual beliefs and

Hermetic doctrine

FIGURE 14.2 Heinrich Khunrath, *The Laboratory and the Chapel,* 1609 Amid the tools of his trade, an alchemist prays in a small chapel. This seventeenth-century illustration reveals the close connections between spiritual beliefs and alchemy.

the "science" or "Hermetic art" of alchemy. At the left, the author prays in a small chapel. Lettering on the drapery of the chapel states, "When we attend strictly to our work, God himself will help us." At the center, musical instruments and a pair of scales rest on a table, representing the links among music, harmony, and numbers so characteristic in alchemy. The inscription on the table reads, "Sacred music disperses sadness in evil spirits." On the floor lie containers and other apparatus used to mix materials, and at the upper right are flasks and other storage containers.

In addition to new ideas and beliefs, geographic exploration during the Renaissance also upset traditional assumptions. The discovery of the New World, for example, disproved Ptolemaic geography. Furthermore, overseas voyages stimulated demand for new instruments and precise measurements for navigation. This demand, in turn, encouraged research, especially in astronomy and mathematics.

Exploration

Finally, the recently invented printing press enabled even out-of-favor scholars to publish their findings, which spread new ideas and discoveries even further. Renaissance rulers supported all these efforts in hopes of gaining prestige as well as practical tools for war, construction, and mining. Church authorities did the same at times, especially backing

The printing press

research in astronomy in the hopes of improving the calendar to date Easter more accurately.

Like the Renaissance, the Reformation unleashed forces that provoked the questioning of long-held views. Most researchers had religious motives for their work, though those motives were not necessarily grounded in tradition. In particular, they yearned for insights into the perfection of God's universe. As we read in Chapter 11, the Reformation shattered confidence in religious authorities. By upsetting hallowed certainties, sixteenth- and seventeenth-century scholars hoped to establish new, even sounder certainties and thereby regain a sense of mastery over nature.

DEVELOPING A MODERN SCIENTIFIC VIEW

Even with these rumblings of change, no sudden breakthrough cleared away the centuries-old understanding of nature. Most scientific work still proceeded slowly, as did scholarly and public acceptance of its findings. Investigators had to demonstrate the effectiveness of their new methods again and again to convince even their colleagues. Indeed, few scholars suggested a wholesale rejection of traditional authorities; most simply chipped away at old notions. By the end of the seventeenth century, however, an entirely new scientific view of reality, initiated by just a handful of scholars, had replaced the traditional view. To understand this startling shift, we need to trace developments in astronomy, physics, and scientific methodology.

Astronomy and Physics: From Copernicus to Newton

During the sixteenth and seventeenth centuries, astronomy and physics attracted the most systematic attention from scholars. Researchers in these fields became particularly dissatisfied with the inability of Aristotelian theory to explain, simply and efficiently, careful observations and mathematical calculations of the stars. The Ptolemaic system for predicting planetary movements seemed overly complex and cumbersome to these scholars. Their findings would dramatically alter Westerners' perceptions of nature and of the earth's place in the universe. As the English poet John Donne complained in 1611, "New philosophy calls all in doubt."

Nicolaus Copernicus (1473–1543), a Polish clergyman with an interest in astronomy, astrology, mathematics, and church law, took the first steps in this intellectual adventure. Like so many other northern European scholars, he crossed the Alps to study in an Italian university. There he became influenced by the rediscovery of Greek scholarship, Neoplatonism, and the Hermetic doctrine.

> Nicolaus Copernicus

FIGURE 14.3 Andrea Cellarius, *The Copernican System*, 1661 This page from Cellarius's *Celestian Atlas* shows the "Copernican System of Planets," with the sun at the center of the universe and the planets circling around it.

Copernicus sought a simpler mathematical formulation to explain how the universe operated. His search convinced him that the earth was *not* at the center of the universe. Instead, he believed that the sun "sits upon a royal throne" in that location, "ruling his children, the planets which circle around him." Moreover, Copernicus concluded that the earth was not stationary: "What appears to be a motion of the sun is in truth a motion of the earth." According to Copernicus, the earth moved in perfect, "divine" circles around the sun, as did other bodies in the universe. Day passed into night because the earth turned on its axis. **Figure 14.3** shows this view of the universe. At the center is the sun, circled by the earth (showing night and day) and the other planets, (note Jupiter and its moons on the right). The signs of the zodiac are on the outer band, suggesting continuing beliefs in astrology. The figure on the lower right, holding a globe and a scientific instrument, is Copernicus. This change from an earth-centered (geocentric) to a sun-centered (heliocentric) universe would become known as the **Copernican revolution.**

Copernicus worked on his **heliocentric model** of the universe for almost twenty-five years. However, fearing ridicule and disapproval from the clergy, he waited until 1543—what became the year of his death—to publish it. Few people outside a limited circle of scholars knew of his views, and even fewer accepted them. Nevertheless, Catholic and Protestant authorities who were wedded to the earth-centered system soon recognized the threat to the Christian conception of the universe that these ideas represented. They denounced the Copernican system as illogical, unbiblical, and unsettling to the Christian faith. One Protestant associate of Martin Luther complained that "certain men . . . have concluded that the earth moves. . . . It is want of honesty and decency to assert such notions publicly. . . . It is part of a good mind to accept the truth as revealed by God and to acquiesce in it."

Still, Copernicus's thinking had some supporters. An Italian monk, Giordano Bruno (1548–1600), tested Catholic authorities by openly teaching and extending Copernican thought, arguing that "the universe is entirely infinite because it has neither edge, limit, nor surfaces." Bruno also professed a series of unusual religious notions. Outraged, the Catholic Inquisition burned Bruno at the stake. Nevertheless, Copernicus's views began to influence other scholars who were investigating the physical nature of the universe.

The Danish aristocrat Tycho Brahe (1546–1601) did not share Copernicus's belief in a heliocentric universe, nor did he grasp the | Tycho Brahe | sophisticated mathematics of the day. Still, he became the next most important astronomer of the sixteenth century. He persuaded the king of Denmark to build for him the most advanced astronomy laboratory in Europe. There he recorded thousands of unusually accurate, detailed observations about the planets and stars over a period of twenty years—all without a telescope. His discoveries of a new star in 1572 and a comet in 1577 undermined the Aristotelian belief in a sky of fixed, unalterable stars moving in crystalline spheres. Although Brahe mistakenly concluded that some planets revolved around the sun, which itself moved around the earth, other astronomers with better understandings of mathematics would use his observations to draw very different conclusions.

Tycho Brahe's assistant, Johannes Kepler (1571–1630), built on Brahe's observations to support the Copernican heliocentric theory. | Johannes Kepler | A German Lutheran from an aristocratic family, Kepler—like other Hermetic scholars—believed in an underlying mathematical harmony of mystical significance to the physical universe. He sought one harmony that would fit with Brahe's observations. Between 1609 and 1619, he announced his most important findings: the three laws of planetary motion. After determining the first law—which stated that the planets moved in ellipses around the sun—he excitedly wrote, "It was as if I had awakened from a sleep." The second law declared that the planets' velocity varied according to their distance from the sun. The third law concluded that the physical relationship between the moving planets could be expressed mathematically. Kepler thus showed "that the celestial machine . . . is the likeness of [a] clock," further undermining the Aristotelian view and extending the Copernican revolution.

Document 14.1 reveals that in 1597, Kepler responded to a letter from Galileo Galilei, the Italian astronomer, physicist, and mathematician discussed at the beginning of this chapter. Although Galileo expressed a reluctance to publicize his beliefs in Copernican ideas, Kepler encouraged him to take the risk. "Be of good | Galileo Galilei | cheer, Galileo, and appear in public. If I am not mistaken there are only a few among the distinguished mathematicians of Europe who would dissociate themselves from us. So great is the power of truth."

Galileo already believed that the world could be described in purely mathematical terms. "Philosophy," he wrote, "is written in this grand book, the universe, which stands continually open to our gaze. . . . It is written in the language of mathematics, and its characters are triangles, circles, and other geometric figures without which it is humanly impossible to understand a single word of it. . . ." Galileo also felt that harmonies could be discovered through experimentation and mathematics. By conducting controlled experiments such as rolling balls down inclines, he demonstrated how motion could be described mathematically. He rejected the old view that objects in their natural state were at rest and that all motion needed a purpose. Instead, he formulated the principle of inertia, showing that bodies, once set into motion, will tend to stay in motion. He thus overturned Aristotelian ideas and established rules for experimental physics.

Galileo, hearing about the recent invention of the telescope, then studied the skies through a telescope that he built in 1609 out of a long tube and magnifying lenses. He saw that the moon's surface, instead of being a perfect heavenly body, was rugged (like the earth's), with craters and mountains indicated by lines and shading. The telescope also revealed that Jupiter had moons and that the sun had spots. These observations confirmed the view that other heavenly bodies besides the earth were imperfect and further convinced him of the validity of Copernicus's hypothesis. For years, Galileo had feared the disapproval of the Catholic Church. Now, however, he was ready to publicly argue that "in discussions of physical problems we ought to begin not from the authority of scriptural passages, but from sense-experiences and necessary demonstrations." Galileo published his findings in 1610.

Six years later, the church attacked his proposition that "the earth is not the center of the world nor immovable, but moves as a whole, and also with a daily motion." This statement, the church said, was "foolish and absurd philosophically, and formally heretical." To back up its claim, the church cited the authority of both the Bible and itself. For the next several years, Galileo kept his thoughts to himself. In 1632, believing that the church might be more open, he decided again to present his views. To avoid challenging the church, he submitted his book to the official church censors and agreed to some changes they demanded.

DOCUMENT 14.1

Kepler and Galileo Exchange Letters About Science

Many leading European scholars of the Scientific Revolution feared publishing their views, which were often unpopular with religious authorities. Such scholars sometimes turned to each other for support, as the following late-sixteenth-century letters between Kepler and Galileo suggest. Here the two men discuss their beliefs in Copernican theory.

Galileo to Kepler: "Like you, I accepted the Copernican position several years ago. I have written up many reasons on the subject, but have not dared until now to bring them into the open. I would dare publish my thoughts if there were many like you; but, since there are not. I shall forbear."

Kepler's Reply: "I could only have wished that you, who have so profound an insight, would choose another way. You advise us to retreat before the general ignorance and not to expose ourselves to the violent attacks of the mob of scholars. But after a tremendous task has been begun in our time, first by Copernicus and then by many very learned mathematicians, and when the assertion that the Earth moves can no longer be considered something new, would it not be much better to pull the wagon to its goal by our joint efforts, now that we have got it under way, and gradually, with powerful voices, to shout down the common herd? Be of good cheer, Galileo, and come out publicly! If I judge correctly, there are only a few of the distinguished mathematicians of Europe who would part company with us, so great is the power of truth. If Italy seems a less favorable place for your publication, perhaps Germany will allow us this freedom."

SOURCE: Giorgio de Santillana, *The Crime of Galileo* (Chicago: University of Chicago Press, 1955), pp. 11, 14–15.

Analyze the Document

1. Why is Galileo reluctant to publish his views on the Copernican position?

2. How does Kepler respond to Galileo's concerns?

3. In what ways does Kepler's reply suggest that the Scientific Revolution was already a growing movement by the end of the sixteenth century?

Finally he published his *Dialogue on the Two Chief Systems of the World*—in Italian rather than the less-accessible Latin. This text advocated Copernicanism, portrayed opponents of the Copernican system (such as the Jesuits) as simpletons, and brought Galileo directly into public conflict with conservative forces in the Catholic Church. Because Galileo could show that his book had already been approved by church officials, prosecutors had to use questionable evidence against him. **Figure 14.4,** painted by an anonymous artist, shows Galileo, wearing a black suit and hat, sitting alone facing church officials. Behind him a man records the trial, while surrounding them are observers—some members of the clergy, others laypeople. In the lower left, two men discuss or argue the issues being decided within; above them some members of the audience look out toward the viewers and the greater world. As we saw at the beginning of the chapter, the Roman Inquisition ultimately forced Galileo to renounce his views.

News of Galileo's sensational trial spread throughout Europe, as did fear of publishing other radical views. Soon, however, his book was translated and published elsewhere in Europe, and his views began to win acceptance by other scientists. Even though Galileo admitted that the new science was beyond the grasp of "the shallow minds of the common people," he effectively communicated its ideas to his peers. By the time

FIGURE 14.4 Anonymous, *Trial of Galileo Before the Inquisition* In 1632, Galileo came into conflict with conservative forces in the Catholic Church over his Copernican views. In this painting by an anonymous artist, Galileo sits facing the church officials who will judge him.

DOCUMENT 14.2

Isaac Newton: God in a Scientific Universe

Like Galileo and Descartes, Newton was well aware that his ideas had profound implications for theology. His views, he realized, might even be considered contrary to religious doctrine. Yet Newton was a deeply spiritual man and took pains to distinguish the appropriate realms of science and religion. In the following selection from Opticks *(1704), his analysis of light, Newton emphasizes that his ideas and systems still allow room for God in the universe.*

All these things being consider'd, it seems probable to me, that God in the Beginning form'd Matter in solid, massy, hard, impenetrable moveable Particles, of such Sizes and Figures, and with such other Properties, and in such Proportion to Space, as most conduced to the End for which he form'd them; and that these primitive Particles being Solids, are incomparably harder than any porous Bodies compounded of them; even so very hard, as never to wear or break in pieces; no ordinary Power being able to divide what God himself made one in the first Creation. . . .

It seems to me farther, that these Particles have not only a *Vis inertiae*, accompanied with such passive Laws of Motion as naturally result from that Force, but also that they are moved by certain active Principles, such as is that of Gravity, and that which cause Fermentation, and the Cohesion of Bodies. These Principles I consider, not as occult Qualities, supposed to result from the specifick Forms of Things, but as general Laws of Nature, by which the Things themselves are form'd; their Truth appearing to us by Phaenomena, though their Causes be not yet discover'd. . . .

Now by the help of these Principles, all material Things seem to have been composed of the hard and solid Particles abovemention'd, variously associated in the first Creation by the Counsel of an intelligent Agent. For it became him who created them to set them in order. And if he did not, it's unphilosophical to seek for any other Origin of the World, or to pretend that it might arise out of a Chaos by the mere Laws of Nature; though being once form'd, it may continue by those Laws for many Ages.

SOURCE: Sir Isaac Newton, *Opticks*, 4th ed. (London, 1730), pp. 400–402.

Analyze the Document

1. What is Newton's view of God's role in the universe?

2. What objections might scientists today have to these ideas?

3. What does Newton mean by "Principles" and "Laws"?

---

of his death in 1642, Europe's intellectual elite had begun to embrace the Copernican outlook.

In England, Isaac Newton (1642–1727) picked up the trail blazed by Copernicus, Brahe, Kepler, and Galileo. Late in life, Newton described his career modestly: "I do not know what I may appear to the world; but to myself I seem to have been only like a boy playing on the sea-shore, and diverting myself in now and then finding a smoother pebble or a prettier shell than ordinary, while the great ocean of truth lay all undiscovered before me." Newton may have held himself in humble regard, but his accomplishments were astonishing.

In 1661, Newton entered Cambridge University, where he studied the ideas of Copernicus and Galileo as well as the advantages of scientific investigation. He distinguished himself enough in mathematics to be chosen to stay on as a professor after his graduation. Like most other figures of the Scientific Revolution, Newton was profoundly religious and, as indicated by Document 14.2, hoped to harmonize his Christian beliefs with the principles of science. He also believed in alchemy and elements of Hermeticism.

Starting in his early 20s, Newton made some of the most important discoveries in the history of science. He developed calculus and investigated the nature of light; he also formulated and mathematically described three laws of motion: inertia, acceleration, and action/reaction. Yet he is best known for discovering the law of universal attraction, or gravitation. After working on the concept for years, he finally published it in 1687 in his great work *Principia* (*The Mathematical Principles of Natural Knowledge*). In the book, he stated the law with simplicity and precision: "Every particle of matter in the universe attracts every other particle with a force varying inversely as the square of the distance between them and directly proportional to the product of their masses." In his view, this law applied equally to all objects, from the most massive planet to a small apple falling from a tree.

Newton had managed to synthesize the new findings in astronomy and physics into a systematic explanation of physical laws that applied to the earth as well as the heavens. This Newtonian universe was infinite and had no center. Uniform and mathematically describable, it was held together by explainable forces and was atomic in nature. Essentially, everything in the universe consisted of only one thing: matter in motion.

Isaac Newton

Newton's *Principia*

The Revolution Spreads: Medicine, Anatomy, and Chemistry

Although astronomy and physics led the way in dramatic scientific findings, researchers in other fields made important discoveries as well. Many of these advances also had roots in the sixteenth century. For example, several scholars developed new ideas in the related fields of medicine, anatomy, and chemistry.

In medicine, a flamboyant Swiss alchemist-physician known as Paracelsus (1493–1541) strongly influenced the healing arts. A believer in Hermetic doctrine, Paracelsus openly opposed medical orthodoxy and taught that healers should look for truth not in libraries ("the more learned, the more perverted," he warned) but in the Book of Nature. "I have not been ashamed to learn from tramps, butchers, and barbers," he boasted. As a teacher and wandering practitioner, he treated patients, experimented with chemicals, recorded his observations, and developed new theories. Paracelsus concluded that all matter was composed of salt, sulfur, and mercury—not the traditional earth, water, fire, and air. Rejecting the standard view that an imbalance in the humors of the body caused disease, he instead looked to specific chemical imbalances to explain what caused each illness. He also encouraged research and experimentation to find natural remedies for bodily disorders, such as administering mercury or arsenic at astrologically correct moments. Though rejected by most established physicians, Paracelsus's ideas became particularly popular among common practitioners and would later influence the study of chemistry.

| Paracelsus |

Other researchers founded the modern science of anatomy. In the sixteenth century, Andreas Vesalius (1514–1564), a Fleming living in Italy, wrote the first comprehensive textbook on the structure of the human body based on careful observation. **Figure 14.5** shows the 28-year-old Vesalius displaying one of his studies on human anatomy from his 1543 treatise, *On the Fabric of the Human Body*. This figure is one of more than two hundred woodcut illustrations showing the composition of the body, stage by stage. Vesalius himself dissected cadavers, as suggested by the scalpel resting on the table. A notable aspect of this illustration is that Vesalius boldly looks the viewer in the eye, perhaps to challenge directly the old, authoritative assumptions about human anatomy. Nevertheless, his dissections of human bodies brought him into conflict with traditional physicians and scholars. Disgusted, he finally gave up his scientific studies and became the personal physician to Emperor Charles V.

| Andreas Vesalius |

Despite relentless criticism, other scholars continued anatomical research. A line from a poem written for the opening of the Amsterdam Anatomical Theatre

ANDREÆ VESALII.

FIGURE 14.5 Andreas Vesalius, from *On the Fabric of the Human Body*, 1543   Vesalius looks boldly out at the viewer while displaying one of his studies of human anatomy.

in the early seventeenth century reflects the sense that this research needed special justification: "Evil doers who while living have done damage are of benefit after their death." In other words, the body parts of criminals "afford a lesson to you, the Living." The most important of these researchers was William Harvey (1578–1657), an Englishman who, like Vesalius, studied at the University of Padua in Italy. Harvey dissected hundreds of animals, including dogs, pigs, lobsters, shrimp, and snakes. He discovered that the human heart worked like a pump, with valves that allowed blood to circulate through the body: "The movement of the blood occurs constantly in a circular manner and is the result of the beating of the heart." Yet, despite this mechanistic view, he also considered the heart the physical and spiritual center of life—in his words, "the sovereign of everything."

| William Harvey |

By the seventeenth century, anatomists and others benefited from several newly invented scientific instruments, such as the microscope. Anton van Leeuwenhoek (1632–1723), a Dutchman, became the chief pioneer in the use of this instrument.

In observations during the 1670s, he described seeing "little animals or animalcules" in water from a lake. "It was wonderful to see: and I judge that some of these little creatures were above a thousand times smaller than the smallest ones I have ever yet seen, upon the rind of cheese, in wheaten flour, mould and the like." Leeuwenhoek discovered what would later be identified as bacteria in his own saliva: "little eels or worms, lying all huddled up together and wriggling. . . . This was for me, among all the marvels that I have discovered in nature, the most marvellous of all."

Anton van Leeuwenhoek

Around this same time, Robert Boyle (1627–1691), an Irish nobleman particularly interested in medical chemistry, helped lay the foundations for modern chemistry. Drawing inspiration from Paracelsus, Boyle attacked many assumptions inherited from the ancients and began a systematic search for the basic elements of matter. Relying on the experimental method and using new instruments, he argued that all matter was composed of indestructible atoms that behaved in predictable ways. Boyle also discovered a law—which still bears his name—that governs the pressure of gases. His exacting procedures set a standard for the scientific practice of chemistry.

Robert Boyle

The Methodology of Science Emerges

The scientists who challenged traditional views in their fields also used new methods of discovery—of uncovering how things worked and of determining "truth." Indeed, this innovative methodology lay at the heart of the Scientific Revolution. Earlier techniques for ascertaining the truth—by referring to long-trusted authorities and making deductions from their propositions—became unacceptable to the new scientists. They instead emphasized systematic skepticism, experimentation, and reasoning based solely on observed facts and mathematical laws. The two most important philosophers of this methodology were Francis Bacon and René Descartes.

Francis Bacon (1561–1626), an English politician who was once lord chancellor of England under James I, took a passionate interest in the new science. He rejected reliance on ancient authorities and advocated the collection of data without preconceived notions. From such data, he explained, scientific conclusions could be reached through inductive reasoning—drawing general conclusions from particular concrete observations. "Deriv[ing] axioms from . . . particulars, rising by gradual and unbroken ascent, so that it arrives at the most general axioms of all. This is the true way," he proclaimed. In addition, Bacon argued that scientific knowledge would

Francis Bacon

be useful knowledge: "I am laboring to lay the foundation not of any sect or doctrine, but of human utility and power." He believed that science would benefit commerce and industry and improve the human condition by giving people unprecedented power over their environment.

Figure 14.6, the title page from Bacon's 1620 book, *New Instrument,* graphically depicts these views. The illustration shows a ship of discovery sailing out from the western end of the Mediterranean Sea into the unknown. Below is the quotation "Many shall venture forth and science shall be increased." Here is an optimistic assertion that knowledge is limitless and that science constitutes a voyage of discovery—a view that would be echoed again and again, as we saw in the picture at the beginning of this chapter. As **Figure 14.6** suggests, Bacon thus became a noted propagandist for the new science as well as a proponent of the **empirical method.**

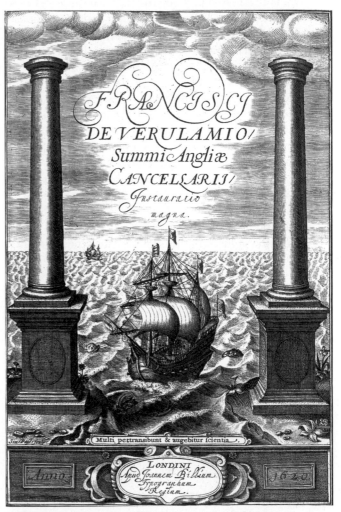

FIGURE 14.6 The New Science The title page of Francis Bacon's book *New Instrument* (1620) asserts optimistically that science is like a voyage of discovery with almost limitless potential.

Despite his brilliance, Bacon did not have a thorough understanding of mathematics and the role it could play in the new science. His contemporary René Descartes (1596–1650) would be the one to excel in this arena. Born in France, Descartes received training in scholastic philosophy and mathematics at one of France's best Jesuit schools and took a degree in law. He entered military service and served during the Thirty Years' War. During his travels, he met a Dutch mathematician and became interested in the new science. An ecstatic experience in 1619 convinced him to commit to a life of the mind. He spent his most productive years as a mathematician, physicist, and metaphysical philosopher in Holland. In 1637, he published his philosophy and scientific methodology in the *Discourse on Method*—in French, not Latin. The book presented an eloquent defense of skepticism and of abstract **deductive reasoning**—deriving conclusions that logically flowed from a premise. "Inquiries should be directed, not to what others have thought, nor to what we ourselves conjecture, but to what we can clearly and perspicuously behold and with certainty deduce; for knowledge is not won in any other way."

René Descartes

Descartes questioned all forms of authority, no matter how venerable—be it Aristotle or even the Bible. He tried to remove systematically all assumptions about knowledge and advocated doubting the senses, which he claimed could be deceptive. Taken to its logical conclusion, his argument left him with one God-given experiential fact—that he was thinking. "I think, therefore I am" became his starting point. From there he followed a rigorous process of deductive reasoning to draw a variety of conclusions, including the existence of God and the physical world. He argued that there were two kinds of reality: mind, or subjective thinking and experiencing; and body, or objective physical matter. According to this philosophy, known as **Cartesian dualism,** the objective physical universe could be understood in terms of extension (matter occupying space) and motion (matter in motion). "Give me extension and motion," vowed Descartes, "and I will create the universe." He considered the body nothing more than "an earthen machine." In his opinion, only the mind was exempt from mechanical laws.

Descartes emphasized the power of the detached, reasoning individual mind to discover truths about nature. Unlike Bacon, he put his faith in mathematical reasoning, not in empirical investigation. By challenging all established authority, by accepting as truth only what could be known by reason, and by assuming a purely mechanical physical universe, Descartes established a philosophy and methodology that became the core of the new science.

SUPPORTING AND SPREADING SCIENCE

Only a small group of people actually participated in the **Scientific Revolution.** Of these, a handful of women managed to overcome barriers to take part as patrons for scientists or as scientists themselves. Men ignored or discounted their work, and scientific societies usually excluded them. The few women engaged in science, such as the naturalist Maria Sibylla Merian (see Biography, page 405) and the Germany astronomer Maria Winkelmann (1647–1717), had to rely on their own resources or work in collaboration with their husbands.

Few scientific scholars—whether male or female—got far without calling on a network of peers and soliciting the support of wealthy patrons. To spread their ideas, these scientists needed to publish their works, interact with like-minded colleagues, and gain the backing of prestigious elites. Fortunately for them, these elites were eager to comply.

Courts and Salons

Governments and wealthy aristocrats served as benefactors and employers of scientists. Kepler, for example, received help from the imperial court, serving in Bohemia as Rudolf II's official mathematician. Galileo became court mathematician to Cosimo de' Medici in Tuscany. Vesalius served as physician to Holy Roman Emperor Charles V, and Harvey as royal physician in England.

Queen Christina of Sweden, like several other monarchs, invited scholars and artists to her court. **Figure 14.7** shows her in 1649 with the French philosopher and mathematician René Descartes (on the

KEY DATES

THE SCIENTIFIC REVOLUTION

1543	Copernicus's heliocentric model published
1543	Vesalius, *Fabric of the Human Body*
1609–1619	Kepler, three laws of planetary motion
1620	Bacon, *New Instrument*
1633	Trial of Galileo
1637	Descartes, *Discourse on Method*
1662	English Royal Society founded
1687	Newton, *Principia*
1690	Locke, *Essay Concerning Human Understanding*
1697	Bayle, *Historical and Critical Dictionary*

right, pointing to papers). Books, papers, and instruments attest to the importance of the new science at this meeting. In this Protestant country, the religious figure on the far right seems to indicate that there is little conflict between science and religion. The artist portrays Christina, a deeply religious person (who would later become a Catholic), as an interested and gracious benefactor helping to bring to light scientific findings.

Rulers had their own motives—namely, practicality and prestige—for assisting scholars and scientists. Royals especially hoped that scholarship and scientific inquiry would yield discoveries that would enhance the strength and prosperity of the state. For example, they sought experts in building projects, armaments, mapmaking, navigation, and mining. They also tried to burnish their own reputations as powerful, educated people by patronizing scholarship, science, and the arts. In this way, support of science became a supposed hallmark of good government. Enticed by this assistance, learned people gathered at royal courts, which gradually filled rooms with new tools, machines, exotic plants and animals, and books.

Beyond the court, people formed private salons and local academies where those interested in science could meet. In the 1540s, the first academy for scientific study was established, in Naples. Women ran several important salons where scientists discussed their findings along with literature, art, and politics. Some scientists even found benefactors at these meetings.

FIGURE 14.7 Queen Christina and Descartes The Swedish queen Christina displays her support of science in this depiction of a 1649 meeting with the French philosopher René Descartes.

The Rise of Royal Societies

During the second half of the seventeenth century, central governments stepped up their support of scientific experimentation, publications, and academies. In 1662, for example, Charles II chartered the Royal Society in England; four years later, Louis XIV's finance minister, Jean-Baptiste Colbert, founded the Académie des Sciences in France. These organizations, and others patterned after them, furnished laboratories, granted subsidies, brought scientists together to exchange ideas, published their findings, and honored scientific achievements. This governmental support of science added to the growing prestige of science and the scientific community.

Religion and the New Science

Religious organizations played a mixed role in the spread of the new science. Traditionally, the Catholic Church supported scholarship and learning in general, including, in natural science. Moreover, religious orders staffed most universities, and many key figures of the Scientific Revolution held university positions. Numerous leading scholars also felt a profound sense of spirituality. Copernicus, for example, who dedicated his work to the pope, was a cleric, as were many other natural scientists. Although we may be tempted to assume that the skepticism inherent in the scientific method would lead to atheism, the great scientists attacked neither faith nor established religion. Nor were they dispassionate investigators holding themselves apart from the spiritual nature of their age. They often believed in magic, ghosts, and witchcraft and typically considered alchemy, astrology, and numerology (predicting events from numbers) valuable components of natural science. Galileo, though he later decried his trial as the triumph of "ignorance, impiety, fraud and deceit," remained a believing Catholic. Even Robert Boyle, who like others came to think of the universe as a machine, attributed its origin to God: "God, indeed, gave motion to matter . . . and established those rules of motion, and that order amongst things . . . which we call the laws of nature." Newton agreed: "This most beautiful system of the sun, planets, and comets, could only proceed from the counsel and dominion of an intelligent and powerful Being. . . . He endures forever, and is everywhere present. . . ."

Nevertheless, the new science did challenge certain tenets of faith and the traditional Christian conception of God's place in the ordering of the world. Neither Protestant nor Catholic leaders welcomed Copernican ideas and the implications of the new science. The Catholic Church, itself ordered in a hierarchy that paralleled the old view of the universe, stayed particularly committed to established authorities. Moreover, the church's condemnation of Galileo in 1633 discouraged scientific investigations throughout much of Catholic Europe. Descartes was not alone in deciding not to publish ideas incorporating Copernican assumptions. As he explained in 1634, "It is not my temperament to set sail against the wind. . . . I want to be able to live in peace . . . out of sight." Although the French government would actively promote science, after the mid-seventeenth century most scientific work and publishing took place in Protestant areas—particularly in England and the Netherlands.

The New Worldview

By the end of the seventeenth century, the accumulation of convincing scientific findings and the support for those findings among the educated elites had broken the Aristotelian-medieval worldview and replaced it with the Copernican-Newtonian paradigm. According to the new view, the earth, along with the planets, moved around the sun in an infinite universe of other similar bodies. The natural order consisted of matter in motion, acting according to mathematically expressible laws. Scientific truths came from observing, measuring, experimenting, and making reasoned conclusions through the use of sophisticated mathematics. Religious truths still had their place, and the orderliness of nature reflected God's design (see Document 14.2, on page 457). However, science now claimed precedence in explaining the material world.

In the sixteenth and early seventeenth centuries, great thinkers such as Copernicus and Galileo had been ridiculed and persecuted for their ideas. By the late seventeenth and early eighteenth centuries, Isaac Newton's fate revealed the acceptance of the new paradigm among educated elites. Famous and popular, Newton became a member of Parliament, served for many years as director of the Royal Mint, and was knighted by Queen Anne.

| The Copernican-Newtonian paradigm |

LAYING THE FOUNDATIONS FOR THE ENLIGHTENMENT

In the course of the eighteenth century, the ideas of the Scientific Revolution spread widely and were applied in stunning new ways. With this broadening, the eighteenth century witnessed the birth of a major cultural movement known as the **Enlightenment.** At the heart of this movement lay the firm conviction—especially among intellectuals—that human reason should determine understanding of the world and the rules of social life. "[H]ave the courage to use your own intelligence," and leave your "self-caused immaturity," exhorted the German philosopher Immanuel Kant (1724–1804). "All that is required for this enlightenment is freedom, and particularly . . . the freedom for man to make public use of his reason in all matters."

The Enlightenment hit its full stride in the middle decades of the eighteenth century, when it particularly influenced literate elites of Europe and North America. Yet, its roots stretched back to the end of the seventeenth century. At that time, the thinking that would characterize the Enlightenment emerged in the writings of people who popularized science, applied a skeptical attitude toward religious standards of truth, and criticized accepted traditions and authorities.

Science Popularized

Unevenly educated and facing challenging findings, members of scientific societies often struggled to understand one another's work. For the nonscientific public, the problem of communicating new, complex ideas was even worse. Late in the seventeenth century, several talented writers, nonscientists themselves but believing that science had established a new standard of truth, began explaining in clear language the meaning of science to the literate public. For example, the French writer Bernard de Fontenelle (1657–1757) enjoyed a long, brilliant career as a popularizer of science. In *Conversations on the Plurality of Worlds* (1686), he presented the Copernican view of the universe in a series of conversations between an aristocratic woman and her lover under starry skies. The English essayist and publisher Joseph Addison (1672–1719), in the March 12, 1711, issue of his newspaper, *The Spectator*, said that he hoped to bring "philosophy out of closets and libraries, schools and colleges, to dwell in clubs and assemblies, at tea-tables and in coffee-houses." He aimed his daily paper not only at men but at women "of a more elevated life and conversation, that move in an exalted sphere of knowledge and virtue, that join all the beauties of the mind to the ornaments of dress, and inspire a kind of awe and respect, as well as love, in their male beholders." Other writers also targeted women. In 1737, for example, *Newtonianism for Women* was published in Naples and was soon translated into English. Writings such as these helped make science fashionable in elite circles.

In the mid-eighteenth century, this popularization of science merged with another foundation of Enlightenment thinking: the belief that

Teaching science

every educated man and woman should be familiar with the nature and methods of science. **Figure 14.8,** an illustration from a British book on the arts and sciences, depicts this connection between science and education. Here a teacher instructs three young men in the principles of astronomy by demonstrating the planetary movements on a new machine—the orrery. The stuffed animals hanging from the ceiling underscore the importance of natural history. Atop the bookcase and on the floor are seminal instruments of science—an air pump, a microscope, a telescope, and a globe. A human skeleton hangs in the closet.

Soon scientific ideas were being taught to children of the middle and upper classes. For example, the year 1761 saw the publication of *The Newtonian System of Philosophy, Adapted to the Capacities of Young Gentlemen and Ladies*, a book engagingly advertised as the "Philosophy of Tops and Balls." In it, a fictional boy named Tom Telescope gave lectures on science topics to children while also teaching the virtues of good manners and citizenship. The book proved immensely popular, going through many editions in Britain and in other countries.

Many of these books emphasized Newton—and for understandable reasons. Enlightenment thinkers saw this brilliant Englishman as the great

Glorifying Newton: reason and nature

synthesizer of the Scientific Revolution, an astute observer who rightly described the universe as ordered, mechanical, material, and set into motion by God. From Newton, they concluded that reason and nature were compatible: Nature functioned logically and discernibly; therefore, what was natural was also reasonable. Many writers of the day agreed with the spirit of a poem written for Newton by the English author Alexander Pope upon the scientist's death in 1727:

Nature and Nature's Laws lay hid in Night.
God said, "Let Newton be," and all was Light.

In simple terms, Newton had become a European cultural hero, as **Figure 14.9** suggests. At the left center of this allegorical painting, a great urn "wherein is supposed to be deposited the Remains of the deceased Hero" is displayed. Above the urn shines a beam

FIGURE 14.8 Science, Education, and Enlightenment, 1759
Surrounded by scientific instruments and objects, a teacher instructs three students. This illustration reveals the growing sense during the Enlightenment that an educated person should be familiar with science.

of light, broken into the colors of the spectrum by a prism—a bow to Newton's famous prism experiments. At the right are pages filled with mathematical calculations; below them, a globe and measuring instruments. Various figures in classical dress admire these objects and perhaps discuss Newton's ideas. The entire painting glorifies not only Newton but all of science.

Enlightenment thinkers also admired the ideas of Newton's compatriot John Locke (1632–1704), who applied scientific thinking to human psychology. This English philosopher did not hold the mind exempt from the mechanical laws of the material universe. In his *Essay Concerning Human Understanding* (1690), Locke pictured the human brain at birth as a blank sheet of paper that sensory perception and reason filled as a person aged.

The psychology of John Locke

FIGURE 14.9 Giovanni Battista Pittori, *Allegorical Monument to Isaac Newton*, 1727–1730 This celebratory painting pays homage to Isaac Newton by glorifying the urn that stores his remains and highlighting his scientific discoveries.

"Our observation, employed either about external sensible objects or about the internal operations of our minds perceived and reflected on by ourselves, is that which supplies our understanding with all the materials of thinking." Locke's empirical psychology rejected the notion that human beings were born with innate ideas or that revelation was a reliable source of truth. What we become, he argued, depends solely on our experiences—on the information received through the senses. Schools and social institutions should therefore play a major role in molding the individual from childhood to adulthood. These ideas, like those of Newton and the Scientific Revolution, also set the stage for the skeptical questioning of received wisdom.

Skepticism and Religion

Locke's ideas, along with those of Newton and the Scientific Revolution, set the stage for the questioning of established wisdom that came to define the Enlightenment. Among several writers, skepticism—or doubts about religious dogmas—mounted. Pierre Bayle (1647–1706), a French Huguenot forced to flee to the Dutch Republic because of Louis XIV's religious persecutions, became the leading proponent of skepticism in the late seventeenth century. In his *News from the Republic of Letters* (1684), Bayle bitterly attacked the intolerance of the French monarchy and the Catholic Church. In most of Europe, where religious principles shared by ruler and ruled underlay all political systems, nonconformity was a major challenge. Therefore, the book earned him condemnation in Paris and Rome. Eventually, however, Bayle would have the last word. In 1697 he published the *Historical and Critical Dictionary*, which contained a list of religious views and beliefs that Bayle maintained did not stand up to criticism. Bayle cited human reason and common sense as his standard of criticism: "Any particular dogma, whatever it may be, whether it is advanced on the authority of the Scriptures, or whatever else may be its origins, is to be regarded as false if it clashes with the clear and definite conclusions of the natural understanding." Bayle also argued that "morals and religion, far from being inseparable, are completely independent of each other." For Bayle, a person's moral behavior had little to do with any particular religious doctrine or creed. With these stands, Bayle pushed much harder than Galileo in challenging the Catholic Church and other religious beliefs. He became recognized as an international authority on religious toleration and skeptical criticism of the Bible.

New information and arguments added weight to Bayle's criticism of biblical authority. For example, geological discoveries suggested that life on Earth had actually begun earlier than biblical accounts claimed. Investigators also began casting doubt on reports of miracles and prophecies. David Hume (1711–1776), a first-rate Scottish philosopher and historian, carried the skeptical argument even further. In *An Essay Concerning Human Understanding* (1748), he insisted that nothing—not even the existence of God or our own existence—could be known

> Pierre Bayle

> David Hume

for sure. Reality consisted only of human perceptions. To Hume, established religions were based on nothing but hope and fear. Reason demanded that people live with skeptical uncertainty rather than dogmatic faith.

Broadening Criticism of Authority and Tradition

Travel writing had a long history, and by the eighteenth century many Enlightenment thinkers had read explanations of China's lucid Confucian traditions as well as accounts of customs and beliefs in Islamic, Buddhist, and Hindu lands. Several writers—among them the Baron de Montesquieu (1689–1755), a wealthy judge in a provincial French court, and the French author Voltaire (1694–1778)—used comparisons of place and time to criticize authority and tradition during the early decades of the eighteenth century. Journeying abroad and writing about their experiences gave such people a new perspective on their home societies. Montesquieu and Voltaire, for their part, chastised European customs in general and French institutions in particular for being contrary to reason and good ethics.

> Travel writings of Montesquieu and Voltaire

Both presented the traveler as an objective observer. In his best-selling book *Persian Letters* (1721), Montesquieu bitingly satirized the customs, morals, and practices of Europeans from the point of view of two Persian travelers. Through this comparative perspective, Montesquieu painted the French as lacking in both good morals and effective government. Voltaire, in his widely read *Letters Concerning the English Nation* (1733), similarly criticized French politics and Catholic intolerance. In the island nation, "one thinks freely and nobly without being held back by any servile fear." Like many people, Voltaire idealized England because it allowed greater individual freedom, religious differences, and political reform than most other countries, especially France. England was also enviably prosperous and was the home of Newton and Locke, so admired in France. Many French intellectuals wanted for their own country what the English already seemed to have.

Other writers took a new historical perspective to criticize tradition and trumpet rapid change. For them, the tools of science and reason enabled people to surpass their historical predecessors, even the admired Greeks and Romans of antiquity. History became a story of relentless human progress, and people living in the eighteenth century stood on the brink of unprecedented historical achievements. Some people, such as the American scientist and philosopher Benjamin Franklin (1706–1790), embraced the idea of progress with an almost religious

> History and progress

fervor: "The rapid Progress of *true* Science now occasions my regretting sometimes that I was born so soon. It is impossible to imagine the Height to which may be carried . . . the Power of Man over Matter, . . . all diseases may by sure means be prevented, . . . and our lives lengthened at pleasure."

THE ENLIGHTENMENT IN FULL STRIDE

Building on the foundations of science, skepticism, and criticism, Western intellectuals systematically investigated the ethical, political, social, and economic implications of science after the 1730s. For them, nature—with its laws, order, simplicity, and rationality—served as a guide for human thought and society. "The source of man's unhappiness is his ignorance of Nature," claimed France's influential Baron d'Holbach (1723–1789). The Marquis de Condorcet argued, "The time will therefore come when the sun will shine only on free men who know no other master but their reason" (see Document 14.3). These optimistic intellectuals pushed for reform and change, using critical and empirical reasoning to back up their arguments. Specifically, they urged people to shrug off the shackles of tradition and custom and to participate in the accelerating progress of civilization. The spark of reason would soon dispel ignorance and enlighten all human understanding. Indeed, it was this image that lent the Enlightenment its name.

The *Philosophes*

Although Enlightenment ideas bubbled up throughout Europe and North America, France was the true heart of the movement. There Enlightenment thinkers came to be called **philosophes,** the French term for "philosophers." In a sense, the questions these thinkers grappled with were philosophical: How do we discover truth? How should we live our lives? Yet the *philosophes* were not traditional philosophers. Coming from both noble and middle-class origins, they were intellectuals—though often not formally trained by or associated with a university. They tended to extend, apply, or propagandize others' ideas rather than initiate new concepts themselves. They also wrote more plays, satires, histories, novels, encyclopedia entries, and short pamphlets than formal philosophical treatises. Finally, they considered themselves part of a common intellectual culture, an international "republic of letters" held together by literature, correspondence, and private gatherings. In the eyes of leading *philosophes* such as Jean Le Rond d'Alembert (1717–1783), this republic of letters should "establish the laws of philosophy and taste for the rest of the nation."

Condorcet Lauds the Power of Reason

No one lauded the power of reason and the Enlightenment, or had more hope for the future—thanks to the Enlightenment—than the French mathematician and philosophe the Marquis de Condorcet (1743–1794). The following is an excerpt from his Sketch of the Progress of the Human Mind, a book tracing human "progress" over time, which he completed in 1794.

Our hopes for the future condition of the human race can be subsumed under three important heads: the abolition of inequality between nations, the progress of equality within each nation, and the true perfection of mankind. Will all nations one day attain that state of civilization which the most enlightened, the freest and the least burdened by prejudices, such as the French and the Anglo-Americans, have attained already? Will the vast gulf that separates these peoples from the slavery of nations under the rule of monarchs, from the barbarism of African tribes, from the ignorance of savages, little by little disappear? . . .

In answering these three questions we shall find in the experience of the past, in the observation of the progress that the sciences and civilization have already made, in the analysis of the progress of the human mind and of the development of its faculties, the strongest reasons for believing that nature has set no limit to the realization of our hopes.

If we glance at the state of the world today we see first of all that in Europe the principles of the French constitution are already those of all enlightened men. We see them too widely propagated, too seriously professed, for priests and despots to prevent their gradual penetration even into the hovels of their slaves; there they will soon awaken in these slaves the remnants of their common sense and inspire them with that smoldering indignation which not even constant humiliation and fear can smother in the soul of the oppressed. . . .

The time will therefore come when the sun will shine only on free men who know no other master but their reason; when tyrants and slaves, priests and their stupid or hypocritical instruments will exist only in works of history and on the stage; and when we shall think of them only to pity their victims and their dupes; to maintain ourselves in a state of vigilance by thinking on their excesses; and to learn how to recognize and so to destroy, by force of reason, the first seeds of tyranny and superstition, should they ever dare to reappear amongst us.

SOURCE: Jean Antoine Nicholas Caritat, Marquis de Condorcet, *Sketch for a Historical Picture on the Progress of the Human Mind*, trans. June Barraclough (London: Weidenfeld and Nicolson [Orion Books], 1955), pp. 236–237, 244.

Analyze the Document

1. What "hopes" does Condorcet have for the future of humanity?

2. According to Condorcet, what will open the door to such great progress?

3. In Condorcet's opinion, why are the French and the Anglo-Americans the most "enlightened" peoples?

The witty, versatile François Arouet, who took the pen name Voltaire (1694–1778), best represented the *philosophes*. The son of a Parisian lawyer, Voltaire received a fine classical education from the Jesuits and soon denounced their religious doctrine. He became the idol of French intellectuals while only in his 20s, and the enemy of many others. He soon ran afoul of state authorities, who imprisoned him in the Bastille for writing verses that criticized the crown. Released, he became embroiled in a dangerous conflict with a prominent nobleman and again landed in the Bastille. By promising to leave the country, he gained his freedom. In England, he encountered the ideas of Newton and Locke and came to admire English parliamentary government and the nation's religious tolerance. As we saw, he popularized Newton's and Locke's ideas and extolled the virtues of English society in his writings.

Slipping back into France, Voltaire hid for a time under the protection of Émilie du Châtelet (1706–1749), a wealthy woman who became his lover and match. Châtelet had already shown brilliance as a child. By the age of 12, she could speak four languages and had already translated Greek and Latin texts. Her mother worried that she would not find a mate because she "flaunts her mind, and frightens away the suitors her other excesses have not driven off." In 1733, she insisted on joining a group of male intellectuals who met regularly at a Parisian coffeehouse, donning men's clothes after the management refused to admit her because of her gender. Voltaire lived openly with Châtelet and her husband. In the great hall of their country chateau, she hung rods, pipes, and balls from the ceiling for her experiments in physics. She made her reputation by publishing a three-volume work on the German mathematician and philosopher Leibnitz and translating Newton's *Principles of Mathematics*. A *philosophe*, accomplished scientist, and leading proponent of Newtonian thought in her own right, Châtelet helped Voltaire gain a better understanding of the sciences and their significance. When she died in childbirth in 1749, the despondent Voltaire accepted

Voltaire

Émilie du Châtelet

an invitation from King Frederick II of Prussia to join his court. However, they soon argued, and Voltaire returned to France.

Having made both a fortune in financial speculations and a rich network of friends and acquaintances, Voltaire was not without resources. He wrote poetry, drama, history, essays, letters, and scientific treatises—ninety volumes in all. The novel *Candide* (1759) became his best-known work. In this dark satire, Voltaire created the epitome of the "ivory-tower" intellectual, ridiculed the pretensions of the nobility and clergy, and skewered the naïveté of optimists who believed that "this is the best of all possible worlds and all things turn out for the best." He aimed his cynical wit especially at the Catholic Church and Christian institutions. His *Philosophical Dictionary* became the most famous, wide-ranging attack on supernatural religion and churches. Voltaire mounted several campaigns for religious toleration, coming to the defense of individuals attacked by prejudice. In his *Treatise on Tolerance* (1763), he attacked the mentality that led to the torture and murder of a Protestant merchant, Jean Calas, on the false charges of murdering his son for threatening to convert to Catholicism. "Christians ought to tolerate one another. I will go even further and say that we ought to look upon all men as our brothers. What! call a Turk, a Jew, a Siamese, my brother? Yes, of course, for are we not all children of the same father, and the creatures of the same God?" Voltaire was celebrated as a national hero and lionized internationally, and his popularity reveals the widespread acceptance of Enlightenment thought throughout the West by the late eighteenth century.

The *Encyclopedia*

No work better summarizes the philosophy of the Enlightenment than the *Encyclopedia*, a collaborative effort by many *philosophes* under the editorship of Denis Diderot (1713–1774) and Jean Le Rond d'Alembert. In the preface, the editors stated their aim: "to overturn the barriers that reason never erected" and "contribute to the certitude and progress of human knowledge." The *Encyclopedia* embodied the notion that reason alone could be used to discover, understand, or clarify almost anything. This massive work explored the complete spectrum of knowledge, offering articles on subjects ranging from music to machinery interpreted through the lens of the *philosophes'* criticism and empiricism. The authors wrote with supreme self-importance: "I can assure you," said d'Alembert in a 1752 letter, "that while writing this work I had posterity before my eyes at every line."

The first volume of the *Encyclopedia* was published in 1751. **Figure 14.10** shows one of its many

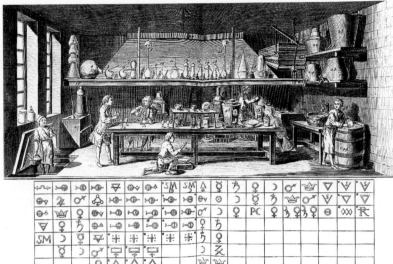

FIGURE 14.10 The *Encyclopedia*, 1751 This page from the *Encyclopedia* shows a chemical laboratory and a table with symbols for each chemical substance.

illustrations. In this image of a chemical laboratory, two chemists and their assistants work. Each piece of equipment is numbered in the illustration and labeled in the text. At the bottom of the picture is a "table of affinities," a system used to organize and symbolize each chemical substance. The illustration conveys a sense of both the practicality of chemistry and its ordered progress. Although the study of chemistry and the hundreds of other topics covered in the *Encyclopedia* at first glance may appear innocent enough, they were saturated with the philosophy of the Enlightenment. Church authorities and their governmental allies therefore saw the *Encyclopedia* as a direct threat to the status quo. They censored it, halted its publication, and harassed its editors. Thanks in great part to the persistence of Diderot, who fought the authorities and managed a difficult group of contributing authors, the project was finally completed in 1772.

Battling the Church

Diderot's struggle to publish the *Encyclopedia* was part of a wider conflict between the *philosophes* and the church. Both sides spent much time and effort attacking each other. In countries such as France and Italy, where clerics were strongly entrenched in government, officials censored the writings of the *philosophes* and threatened to imprison or exile them. Governmental censorship was usually more nominal than real. However, Diderot and others trying to publish "offensive" books constantly worried about these threats: "How many times did we awake uncertain if . . . we would be torn from our families, our friends, our fellow citizens. . . ." French authors often sent their works to Holland or Switzerland for publication, and private companies then made a business of smuggling the books back into France across Swiss or Dutch borders.

Sometimes the *philosophes'* "crime" was promoting toleration of religious minorities, whether Christian or otherwise. Montesquieu and Voltaire, in France, were among several who attacked discrimination against Jews, for example. These views were particularly controversial because religious tolerance—formal and informal—was not the rule. Most governments maintained a state religion, rooted in law and viewed as the custodian of received views, that discriminated against nonmembers. For example, Denmark barred Catholic priests from entering the country, and the Catholic Inquisition remained active in Spain.

Some *philosophes*, such as the Baron d'Holbach and David Hume, verged on atheism in their attacks on organized religion. "The Christian religion not only was at first attended by miracles, but even now cannot be believed by any reasonable person without one," Hume claimed. However, few Enlightenment thinkers pushed matters that far. Most believed in some form of deism—that an impersonal, infinite Divine Being created the universe but did not interfere with the world of human affairs. The prominent author and political philosopher Thomas Paine (1737–1809) stated, "I believe in one God, and no more; and I hope for happiness beyond this life. . . . I do not believe in the creed professed by the Jewish church, by the Roman church, by the Greek church, by the Turkish church, by the Protestant church, nor by any church that I know of. My own mind is my own church." These ideas, like other ideas of the Enlightenment, gained momentum over the course of the eighteenth century. In the long run, the church probably lost more supporters among the upper and middle classes than it gained by so ardently attacking the *philosophes* and their ideas.

Deism

Reforming Society

The *philosophes* thought long and hard about reforming society. They wrote and argued about the relationship between the individual and society and reevaluated the functioning of traditional social institutions. Applying their critical reasoning to fields from government to education, they generated influential ideas for reform.

Political thought: Montesquieu and Rousseau

The most important political thinkers of the Enlightenment—Montesquieu and the Swiss-born writer Jean-Jacques Rousseau (1712–1778)—built on John Locke's work. Locke had pleaded eloquently for the "natural rights"—life, liberty, and property—of

human beings. In his *Second Treatise on Civil Government* (1690), Locke had argued that to safeguard these rights, individuals agree to surrender a certain amount of their sovereignty to government. However, the powers of the government, whether it be monarchical or popular, were strictly limited. No government was allowed to violate the individual's right to life, liberty, and property. If it did, the people who set it up could and should overthrow it—something the English had done in their Glorious Revolution, according to Locke.

An admirer of Locke and the English system of government, the Baron de Montesquieu analyzed political systems from a relativistic perspective. In his widely acclaimed political masterpiece, *The Spirit of the Laws* (1748), Montesquieu argued that political institutions should conform to the climate, customs, beliefs, and economy of a particular country. For instance, limited monarchy is most appropriate for countries of moderate size, like France; and republics for small states, like Venice or ancient Athens. Each form of government had its virtues and vices.

Not only did Montesquieu approve of Locke's doctrine of limited sovereignty, but he specified how it could best be secured—by a separation of powers and a system of checks and balances. The alternative, he warned, was tyranny and an end to liberty: "There would be an end to everything, were the same man or the same body, whether of the nobles or of the people, to exercise those three powers, that of enacting laws, that of executing the public resolutions, and of trying the causes of individuals." This theory, equally applicable to monarchies and to democracies, became Montesquieu's greatest practical contribution to political thought. In North America, framers of the U.S. Constitution incorporated his ideas into their structuring of the United States government, creating separate executive, judicial, and legislative branches of government.

Rousseau offered a more radical political theory than Montesquieu's (see Biography). In his *Discourse on the Origin of Inequality* (1755), Rousseau argued that people in the "primitive" state of "noble savagery" were free, equal, and relatively happy. Only when some of them began marking off plots of ground, claiming them as their own and thereby founding civil society, did the troubles begin. Private property created inequality and the need for laws and governments to protect people from crime and wars. In *The Social Contract* (1762), Rousseau began by challenging his contemporaries: "Man is born free; and everywhere he is in chains." He then offered a solution to this conflict between individual freedom and social restrictions. In an ideal state, he argued, people entered into a compact with one another, agreeing to surrender their individual liberty, which was driven by self-interest, to the whole society. In return, the individual gained freedom by virtue of being part of the society's "general will," which was driven by the common good. "This means nothing less than that [the individual] will be forced to be free," explained Rousseau. Although Rousseau never made it clear just how the general will operated in practice, he believed that the people themselves—rather than a monarch or a parliamentary body—should make laws. His controversial ideas would powerfully influence the development of democratic theory over the next two centuries. For some, *The Social Contract* would support participatory democracy, whereas for others, Rousseau's emphasis on conforming to the general will would justify authoritarian political systems.

Although critical and combative, neither Rousseau, Montesquieu, nor the other *philosophes* were political or social revolutionaries. They did not champion the lower classes, whom they dismissed as ignorant, prone to violence, and, in Voltaire's words, "inaccessible to the progress of reason and over whom fanaticism maintains its atrocious hold." Diderot, of humble parents, admitted that he wrote "only for those with whom I should enjoy conversing . . . the philosophers; so far as I am concerned, there is no one else in the world." Most *philosophes* hoped for painless change from above rather than a revolutionary transfer of power to the still-unenlightened masses. Many shared Voltaire's belief that enlightened absolutism—rule by a well-educated, enlightened monarch—offered the best chance for the enactment of Enlightenment reforms such as religious toleration, rule subject to impartial laws, and freedom of speech (see Chapter 15).

If the functioning of the universe and politics could be described by understandable, rational laws, why should the same not hold true for economic activity? Several Enlightenment thinkers turned their thoughts to this question and attacked mercantilism, the system of regulated national economics that still operated throughout much of Europe. A group of French thinkers known as Physiocrats, led by François Quesnay, personal physician to Louis XV, began to teach that economics had its own set of natural laws. The Physiocrats believed that the most basic of these laws was that of supply and demand, and that these laws operated best under only minimal governmental regulation of private economic activity. This doctrine, which became known as *laissez-faire* (noninterference), favored free trade and enterprise. In France, the Physiocrats saw land and agriculture as the main source of national wealth. Other economists would build on their ideas and apply them to different settings.

In 1776, Adam Smith (1723–1790), a Scottish professor of philosophy who associated with the Physiocrats while traveling in France, published

Economic ideas: the Physiocrats and Adam Smith

Wealth of Nations. The book became the bible of laissez-faire economics. By nature, Smith argued, individuals who were allowed to pursue rationally their own economic self-interest would benefit society as well as themselves. Focusing on Britain's economy, Smith emphasized commerce, manufacturing, and labor rather than agriculture as the primary sources of national wealth. Anticipating the industrial age that would first emerge in Britain, he concluded that "the greatest improvement in the productive powers of labor . . . have been the effects of the division of labor." For Smith as well as the Physiocrats, laissez-faire economics held the key to national wealth—whether a nation was built on agriculture or industry.

What Smith and the Physiocrats did for economics, the Italian Cesare Beccaria (1738–1794) did for criminology and penology. Beccaria wrote *On Crimes and Punishments* (1764), an international best-seller, to protest "the cruelty of punishments and the irregularities of criminal procedures, . . . to demolish the accumulated errors of centuries." He argued that criminal laws and punishments, like all other aspects of life, should incorporate reason and natural law. Good laws, he explained, promoted "the greatest happiness divided among the greatest number." Criminal law should strive to deter crime and rehabilitate criminals rather than merely punish wrongdoers. In Beccaria's view, torture and capital punishment made no sense; indeed, only new penal institutions that mirrored natural law could transform convicted criminals.

Criminology, penology, and slavery

Other Enlightenment thinkers used similar arguments to denounce slavery. Abbé Guillaume Raynal (1713–1796), an outspoken and widely read critic of slavery, argued that this institution and many other practices of European and American colonists were irrational and inhumane. In the name of natural

THE ENLIGHTENMENT

1733	Voltaire, *Letters Concerning the English Nation*
1748	Montesquieu, *The Spirit of the Laws*
1751	The *Encyclopedia*
1759	Voltaire, *Candide*
1762	Rousseau, *The Social Contract*
1764	Beccaria, *On Crimes and Punishments*
1776	Smith, *Wealth of Nations*
1792	Wollstonecraft, *Vindication of the Rights of Women*

KEY DATES

Jean-Jacques Rousseau
(1712–1778)

Jean-Jacques Rousseau described himself as a "singular soul, strange, and to say it all, a man of paradoxes." A celebrity both admired and hated in his own time, he wrote more deeply on a wide range of subjects than any of his contemporaries.

"My birth was my first misfortune," Rousseau once stated wryly. His mother died shortly after he was born in 1712 in the Republic of Geneva. His father, a watchmaker, raised him to the age of 10 and then abandoned him to a series of homes where he served unhappily as an apprentice. One day in 1728, returning late from walking in the countryside, he found the gates of Geneva closed. Anticipating punishment from his master for his tardiness, he turned around and set off on the first of a series of wanderings that would mark the rest of his life.

Singular Soul, Controversial Thinker

He lived for much of the next ten years as the guest and lover of a baroness, Madame de Warens. In his own words, Rousseau became her "piece of work, student, friend. . . ." Rousseau addressed Madame de Warens as "Momma," and she referred to him as "my little one." This was the first of Rousseau's numerous relationships, many of them with older women. Yet he also lived as a recluse for long stretches of time during which he educated himself.

In 1742 the shy Rousseau arrived in Paris. He would often live there, though he harbored "a secret disgust for life in the capital," with its "dirty stinking little streets, ugly black houses, . . . poverty, [and] beggars." He first gained attention in Paris by writing about music and by joining the cultural circles. He also earned a modest income by serving as secretary to aristocratic patrons and by copying music. In 1745, Thérèse Levasseur, a young laundress, became his lifelong companion and ultimately his wife. The couple would have four children and abandon them all to a foundling hospital for adoption.

In 1749, Rousseau entered an essay contest that abruptly changed his life. He won the competition by arguing that progress in the arts and sciences corrupted rather than improved human conduct. Suddenly he was controversial and famous. "No longer [was I] that timid man, more ashamed than modest. . . . All Paris repeated [my] sharp and biting sarcasms. . . ." Buoyed by his newfound fame, he contributed several articles on music and political economy to the *Encyclopedia*, edited by his close friend Denis Diderot. He came to know and eventually quarrel with most of the leading figures of the Enlightenment.

Rousseau went on to publish several critical and widely circulated books, including *Discourse on the Origin of Inequality* (1755), *Julie, or*

rights, he called for a slave rebellion. An article in the authoritative *Encyclopedia* asserted similar views, declaring that all enslaved individuals "have the right to be declared free. . . ." These arguments, like the ideas of Beccaria and, in politics, of Montesquieu and Rousseau, would resound again and again through eighteenth-century Western society.

Becoming enlightened required education. Diderot claimed that the *Encyclopedia* was written so "that our children, by becoming more educated, may at the same time become more virtuous and happier. . . ." Many Enlightenment thinkers based their ideas on the psychological ideas of John Locke, which emphasized the power of education to mold the child into the adult. These thinkers often attacked organized religion in particular for controlling education.

Education

Rousseau became the outstanding critic of traditional education. In *Émile*, he argued that teachers should appeal to children's natural interests and goodness rather than impose discipline and punishment. "Hold childhood in reverence," he counseled. "Give nature time to work." He also pushed for less "artificial" schools, maintaining that nature and experience were better guides to independent thinking and practical knowledge—at least for males. "I hate books," he pointed out. "They only teach us to talk about things we know nothing about." By emphasizing practical education, learning by doing, and motivating rather than requiring the child to learn, Rousseau's *Émile* became one of the most influential works on modern education. His ideas on the education of females, however, were not so modern. Like most men of his time (enlightened or not), he believed that girls should be educated to fulfill their traditional domestic roles as wives and mothers.

In theory at least, the Enlightenment emphasis on individualism opened the door to the idea of equality between men and women. Several intellectuals explored this controversial issue. Early in the period, some challenging books on the "woman question" were published by female authors. In one of the best known of these, *A Serious Proposal to the Ladies* (1694), the English writer Mary Astell (1666–1731) argued that women should be educated

The "woman question"

The New Heloise (1761), Émile (1762), and The Social Contract (1762). These writings inspired not only learned responses but ardent mail from ordinary readers. One reader of The New Heloise, a novel focusing on the conflict between social demands and personal feelings, wrote, "Ever since I read your blessed book I have burned with love of virtue. . . . Feeling has taken over once again." Yet the books also inspired scorn. Peasants once stoned Rousseau's house, for example, after a pastor attacked him from the pulpit. Authorities issued more serious threats. In 1762, Parisian officials ordered The Social Contract burned and Rousseau arrested. He fled to Geneva, only to discover that officials there were also seeking his arrest. Again he escaped, moving from place to place and finding shelter with friends whom he quickly lost after bitter arguments. **Figure 14.11** shows him in the distinctive fur hat and collar he often wore during this period, when he was a guest of the English philosopher David Hume.

In the last fifteen years of his life, Rousseau felt persecuted and

FIGURE 14.11 Allan Ramsay, *Jean-Jacques Rousseau*, 1766

depressed. "I appear," he wrote, "as the enemy of the Nation." He published stunning, often exaggerated self-revelations in his *Confessions*, disclosing his affairs, lies, and quarrels.

A difficult man and a tortured soul, Rousseau was also a superb writer whose *New Heloise* became the most widely read novel of his age. He counts among the most important educational theorists in history and became an accomplished composer and musical theorist. Author of one of the most striking autobiographical works ever written, he also proved an extremely influential philosopher and political theorist. "I am different," he wrote, "alone on earth. . . . Whether nature did well or ill to break the mould in which she formed me, this is something one can only judge after reading me." Sixteen years after Rousseau's death in 1778, France's revolutionary government moved his body to a place of honor near Voltaire's burial site in Paris.

Connecting People & Society

1. What were Rousseau's early life experiences, and how might they have colored the ideas in his writings?

2. What do authorities' and ordinary people's harsh reactions to Rousseau's socially critical works reveal about eighteenth-century society?

3. How did Rousseau's work and life reflect the ideas and efforts of other Enlightenment thinkers?

according to the ideas of the new science—reason and debate—rather than tradition. Later, she explained that men seem to know more than women because "boys have much time and pains, care and cost bestowed on their education, girls have little or none. The former are early initiated in the sciences" and "have all imaginable encouragement" while "the latter are restrained, frowned upon, and beaten." In other writings, she questioned the inequality of men's and women's roles: "If all Men are born Free, how is it that all Women are born Slaves?" Later in the eighteenth century, the British author Mary Wollstonecraft (1759–1797) published *Vindication of the Rights of Women* (1792), in which she analyzed the condition of women and argued forcefully for equal rights for all human beings. Like Astell, Wollstonecraft stressed the need to educate women: "If she be not prepared by education to become the companion of man, she will stop the progress of knowledge and virtue; for truth must be common to all, or it will be inefficacious with respect to its influence on general practice."

Few male writers went that far. Although some men supported better education for women, most held the traditional view that women were weaker than men and best suited for domestic rather than public affairs. According to Immanuel Kant, who spoke so optimistically and eloquently about education and enlightenment, "laborious learning or painful pondering, even if a woman should greatly succeed in it, destroy the merits that are proper to her sex." The editors of the *Encyclopedia* also ignored contributions from women, instead praising those who remained at home. Some of Rousseau's writings were particularly influential among women, primarily because they glorified child rearing, maternalism, and emotional life. Rousseau never suggested that women were independent beings equal to men. For him, "Woman is made to please and to be subjugated to man."

The Culture and Spread of the Enlightenment

The Enlightenment glittered especially in Paris, and salon meetings became the chief social setting for this intellectual culture. These meetings were hosted by wealthy Parisian patrons, usually women of the aristocracy or upper-middle class. In an environment lush with art, music, and wealth, the *philosophes*,

Salon meetings

powerful nobles, diplomats, statesmen, artists, and well-educated conversationalists gathered regularly to read, listen to, and debate the ideas of the Enlightenment. They also discussed—and sometimes influenced—economic policies, wars, and the king's choice of ministers. The German critic Friedrich Grimm (1723–1807), who published a private newsletter on Parisian life, described the salons of Julie de Lespinasse, who lived openly with the *philosophe* d'Alembert: "Her circle met daily from five o'clock until nine in the evening. There we were sure to find choice men of all orders in the State, the Church, the Court—military men, foreigners, and the most distinguished men of letters. Politics, religion, philosophy, anecdotes, news, nothing was excluded from the conversation." These salon meetings became self-conscious forums for arbitrating and molding public opinion through the open use of reason.

As leaders, patrons, and intellectual contributors to these gatherings, women played a particularly important role in the Enlightenment. Independent, witty, powerful women governed the potentially unruly meetings and discussions by enforcing rules of polite conversation. One of the most famous of these patrons was Madame Marie-Thérèse Geoffrin (1699–1777), a rich middle-class widow who served as a model and mentor for other women leaders of salons. **Figure 14.12,** a painting by Anicet Charles Lemonnier, shows a salon meeting at her home in 1755. Madame Geoffrin, wearing a blue dress and looking at the viewer, sits at the left next to Bernard de Fontenelle, 98-year-old popularizer of science. Above is a bust of Voltaire, the Enlightenment hero living in exile at the time. Women with the right intellectual and social qualifications attended this and other salons, but the star invitees were usually men.

Smaller meetings in other French and foreign cities, from Berlin to Philadelphia, paralleled the Parisian salon meetings. Moreover, all these meetings went hand in hand with an extensive international correspondence carried out by participants. For some, letter writing, like good conversation in the salons, was an art. People also read and discussed Enlightenment ideas in local academies, Freemason lodges, societies, libraries, and coffeehouses. In addition, most municipalities had clubs where the social and intellectual elites could mingle.

Even bookstores, where people could purchase books or pay small fees to read recent works, became hotbeds of Enlightenment ideas. **Figure 14.13** shows

FIGURE 14.12 Anicet Charles Lemonnier, *An Evening at Madame Geoffrin's in 1755,* 1812 *Philosophes,* nobles, statesmen, and well-educated conversationalists often gathered in Enlightenment-age salons led by women such as Madame Geoffrin, shown here sitting on the right in a blue dress.

thinking about
ART

FIGURE 14.13

Léonard Defrance, *At the Shield of Minerva*, 1781

In this painting, French artist Léonard Defrance depicts a street scene in front of a bookstore in France. Notice the reference in the store's name to Minerva, the Roman goddess of poetry and wisdom. Also note the mix of people and the prominence of the clergyman (in white robes) among them.

Connecting Art & Society

1. What might the packages of books bound for, or being delivered from, Spain, Portugal, Rome, and Naples suggest about the spread of Enlightenment ideas throughout Europe?

2. In what ways does this painting imply that people of all classes were being touched by books—and perhaps by Enlightenment ideas?

3. Why do you think the artist included a member of the clergy in such a central place in this painting?

an eighteenth-century bookstore. In the doorway stand two women, reading books. Just outside are packages of books being delivered from or to Spain, Portugal, Rome, and Naples. In the street, apparently drawn to the bookstore, are people of all classes, from a peasant with his scythe at the left to a cleric

Bookstores

in his white robes at the center. The name of the bookstore, "The Shield of Minerva," refers to the Roman goddess of wisdom. In a growing number of bookstores such as this, all sorts of works became increasingly available, from religious tracts and chivalric tales to new novels and Enlightenment literature.

These gatherings and interchanges spread the ideas of the Enlightenment throughout society and enhanced the social respectability of intellectuals. They also helped create a common intellectual culture that crossed class lines and political borders and that contributed to an informed body of public opinion. People who participated in these interchanges came to sense that they could freely express ideas as well as debate political and social issues. By the last quarter of the eighteenth century, Enlightenment ideas could be heard even in the camps of the *philosophes'* traditional opponents—the clergy, governmental officials, and monarchs. As we will see, these ideas pushed some monarchs to enact "enlightened" reforms and encouraged many other people to demand revolutionary change.

LOOKING BACK & MOVING FORWARD

Summary   The great intellectual revolution of the seventeenth and eighteenth centuries was fueled by advances in science. Brimming with new scientific ideas and discoveries, Western civilization relinquished its medieval assumptions and embarked on an innovative journey unique among the cultures of the world. This change in direction became one of the main forces behind the power and dynamism that came to characterize the West. Through science, Westerners hoped to gain greater control over the material world and nature.

Enlightenment thinkers carried these daring aspirations further, self-consciously leading a mission of reform and freedom from the shackles of tradition. By striking the match of reason, they believed, people could at last dispel the darkness of the past and liberate themselves as never before. Thus enlightened, humanity as a whole could move from childhood to adulthood. As the *philosophe* Baron d'Holbach proclaimed, "The *enlightened man*, is man in his maturity, in his perfection; who is capable of pursuing his own happiness; because he has learned to examine, to think for himself, and not to take that for truth upon the authority of others."

Many participants in Enlightenment circles have since been criticized as self-concerned dilettantes reluctant to take on the risks of real reform. Most historians, however, see the *philosophes* as thoughtful, sincere, and sometimes brilliant thinkers. The *philosophes* clearly left a mark on Western culture. Their ideas, like those of the seventeenth-century scientists, threatened the traditional order, especially the church. As their primary legacy, they widened the gap between religiously influenced doctrines and accepted scholarly thought. Equally significant, they set the intellectual stage for a series of revolutions that would soon sweep America and Europe. Above all, their way of thinking—stressing reason, individualism, and progress—would form the intellectual foundation of modern Western society and further distinguish this civilization from its non-Western counterparts.

KEY TERMS

Neoplatonism, *p. 453*
Hermetic doctrine, *p. 453*
Copernican revolution, *p. 454*
heliocentric model, *p. 454*
empirical method, *p. 459*
deductive reasoning, *p. 460*
Cartesian dualism, *p. 460*
Scientific Revolution, *p. 460*
Enlightenment, *p. 462*
philosophes, *p. 465*

REVIEW, ANALYZE, & CONNECT TO TODAY

REVIEW THE PREVIOUS CHAPTERS

Chapter 12—"Faith, Fortune, and Fame"—told how several European powers expanded overseas during the fifteenth, sixteenth, and seventeenth centuries and grew rich from the commerce. Chapter 13—"The Struggle for Survival and Sovereignty"—focused on how kings and nobles battled for power, the resolutions of those struggles, and their impact on the millions of people outside the elite.

1. Analyze how the expansion of Europe might have stimulated scientific research.

2. In what ways did the effort of monarchs to increase their power and create stability relate to the promotion of science and the desire for greater intellectual certainty?

ANALYZE THIS CHAPTER

Chapter 14—"A New World of Reason and Reform"—examines the changing intellectual foundations of the West.

1. List and analyze the differences between the new scientific views of the world and traditional medieval views.

How did standards for ascertaining the "truth" differ between these two perspectives?

2. Analyze the beliefs and motives of three central figures in the Scientific Revolution. What barriers did they have to overcome to present their views?

3. Do you think the Enlightenment merely popularized the Scientific Revolution, or did it accomplish something more?

4. In what ways did the Enlightenment threaten traditional views and authorities?

CONNECT TO TODAY

Think about the meaning of the Scientific Revolution and the values underlying the Enlightenment.

1. In what ways are our present-day assumptions about the physical universe and the workings of nature based on the ideas and discoveries of the Scientific Revolution?

2. What aspects of world politics today reflect Enlightenment values? What aspects of present-day global politics seem to be opposed to those values?

BEYOND THE CLASSROOM

QUESTIONING TRUTH AND AUTHORITY

Kuhn, Thomas S. *The Structure of Scientific Revolutions*, 2nd ed. Chicago: University of Chicago Press, 1970. A landmark analysis of the nature, causes, and consequences of transformations in scientific concepts.

Mandrou, Robert. *From Humanism to Science*. Atlantic Highlands, NJ: Humanities Press, 1979. A description of how the role of intellectuals changed between 1480 and 1700.

Teresi, Dick. *Lost Discoveries: The Ancient Roots of Modern Science—From the Babylonians to the Maya*. New York: Simon & Schuster, 2003. Focuses on discoveries from non-Western societies that predated Europe's Scientific Revolution.

DEVELOPING A MODERN SCIENTIFIC VIEW

Cohen, H.F. *The Scientific Revolution*. Chicago: University of Chicago Press, 1994. An analysis of when and where modern science began.

Dear, Peter. *Revolutionizing the Sciences: European Knowledge and Its Ambitions, 1500–1700*. Princeton, NJ: Princeton University Press, 2001. A survey of the main ideas of science and its new institutions.

Feingold, Mordechai. *The Newtonian Moment: Isaac Newton and the Making of Modern Culture*. New York: Oxford University Press, 2004. A well-illustrated book that focuses on Newton and how his ideas affected eighteenth-century culture.

Hall, Rupert A. *The Revolution in Science, 1500–1750*. London: Longman, 1983. A useful introduction to the developments in science during this period.

Schiebinger, Londa. *The Mind Has No Sex? Women in the Origins of Modern Science*. Cambridge, MA: Harvard University Press, 1990. An examination of the participation of women in science; stresses how science reflected male biases.

Shapin, Steven. *The Scientific Revolution*. Chicago: University of Chicago Press, 1996. A concise, new interpretation questioning whether there was a "scientific revolution."

Westfall, Richard. *The Construction of Modern Science: Mechanisms and Mechanics*. New York: Cambridge University Press, 1977. A good survey of scientific developments during the seventeenth century that emphasizes the importance of mathematics and mechanics.

SUPPORTING AND SPREADING SCIENCE

Jacob, Margaret C. *The Cultural Meaning of the Scientific Revolution*. New York: Knopf, 1988. Examines the evolution of science within its political, social, and cultural context.

Moran, Bruce T., ed. *Patronage and Institutions: Science, Technology and Medicine at the European Court, 1500–1750*. Rochester, NY: Boydell Press, 1991. Examines the role of royal courts in supporting and shaping science during this period.

LAYING THE FOUNDATIONS FOR THE ENLIGHTENMENT

Outram, Dorinda. *The Enlightenment*. Cambridge: Cambridge University Press, 2005. Presents the various interpretations of the Enlightenment.

Porter, Roy. *The Enlightenment*, 2nd ed. London: Palgrave, 2001. A solid, well-written survey of eighteenth-century intellectual life.

Sklar, Judith. *Montesquieu*. Oxford: Oxford University Press, 1987. A concise, well-written study of Montesquieu and his ideas.

THE ENLIGHTENMENT IN FULL STRIDE

Besterman, Theodore. *Voltaire*, 3rd ed. Chicago: University of Chicago Press, 1976. A useful biography of this major Enlightenment figure.

Darton, Robert. *The Business of Enlightenment: A Publishing History of the* Encyclopedia, *1775–1800*. Cambridge, MA: Belknap Press, 1979. A well-written social history and analysis of the publication of the *Encyclopedia*.

Gay, Peter. *The Enlightenment: An Interpretation*, 2 vols. New York: Knopf, 1966–1969. A classic study, exhaustive, but with a strong point of view.

Goodman, Dena. *The Republic of Letters: A Cultural History of the French Enlightenment*. Ithaca, NY: Cornell University Press, 1994. A study of the cultural and intellectual life of eighteenth-century France that concentrates on the role played by the salons.

Lougee, Carolyn. *Le Paradis des Femmes. Women, Salons, and Social Stratification in Seventeenth-Century France*. Princeton, NJ: Princeton University Press, 1976. Analyzes the foundations and importance of the French salons, emphasizing the role played by women in them.

Melton, J.V.H. *The Rise of the Public in Enlightenment Europe*. Cambridge: Cambridge University Press, 2001. Connects publishing and the reading public during the Enlightenment.

Note to users: Terms that are foreign or difficult to pronounce are transcribed in parentheses directly after the term itself. The transcriptions are based on the rules of English spelling; that is, they are similar to the transcriptions employed in the *Webster* dictionaries. Each word's most heavily stressed syllable is marked by an acute accent.

A

Absolute monarch (máh-nark) A seventeenth- or eighteenth-century European monarch claiming complete political authority.

Absolutism (áb-suh-loo-tism) (Royal) A government in which all power is vested in the ruler.

Abstract expressionism (ex-présh-un-ism) A twentieth-century painting style infusing nonrepresentational art with strong personal feelings.

Acropolis (uh-króp-uh-liss) The hill at the center of Athens on which the magnificent temples—including the Parthenon—that made the architecture of ancient Athens famous are built.

Act of Union Formal unification of England and Scotland in 1707.

Afrikaners Afrikaans-speaking South Africans of Dutch and other European ancestry.

Age of Reason The eighteenth-century Enlightenment; sometimes includes seventeenth-century science and philosophy.

Agora In ancient Greece, the marketplace or place of public assembly.

Agricultural revolution Neolithic discovery of agriculture; agricultural transformations that began in eighteenth-century western Europe.

Ahura Mazda In Zoroastrianism, the beneficial god of light.

Ahriman In Zoroastrianism, the evil god of darkness.

Akkadian (uh-káy-dee-un) A Semitic language of a region of ancient Mesopotamia.

Albigensians (al-buh-jén-see-unz) A medieval French heretical sect that believed in two gods—an evil and a good principle—that was destroyed in a crusade in the thirteenth century; also called Cathars.

Alchemy (ál-kuh-mee) The medieval study and practice of chemistry, primarily concerned with changing metals into gold and finding a universal remedy for diseases. It was much practiced from the thirteenth to the seventeenth century.

Allies (ál-eyes) The two alliances against Germany and its partners in World War I and World War II.

Al-Qaeda A global terrorist network headed by Osama bin Laden.

Anarchists (ánn-ar-kissts) Those advocating or promoting anarchy, or an absence of government. In the late nineteenth and early twentieth centuries, anarchism arose as an ideology and movement against all governmental authority and private property.

Ancien régime (áwn-syáwn ráy-zhéem) The traditional political and social order in Europe before the French Revolution.

Antigonids (ann-tíg-un-idz) Hellenistic dynasty that ruled in Macedonia from about 300 B.C.E. to about 150 B.C.E.

Anti-Semitism (ann-tye-sém-i-tism) Prejudice against Jews.

Apartheid "Separation" in the Afrikaans language. A policy to rigidly segregate people by color in South Africa, 1948–1989.

Appeasement Attempting to satisfy potential aggressors in order to avoid war.

Aramaic (air-uh-máy-ik) A northwest Semitic language that spread throughout the region. It was the language that Jesus spoke.

Archon (áhr-kahn) A chief magistrate in ancient Athens.

Areopagus (air-ee-áh-pa-gus) A prestigious governing council of ancient Athens.

Arête (ah-ray-táy) Greek term for the valued virtues of manliness, courage, and excellence.

Arianism (áir-ee-un-ism) A fourth-century Christian heresy that taught that Jesus was not of the same substance as God the father, and thus had been created.

Assemblies, Roman Institutions in the Roman Republic that functioned as the legislative branch of government.

Assignats (ah-seen-yáh) Paper money issued in the National Assembly during the French Revolution.

Astrolabe (áss-tro-leyb) Medieval instrument used to determine the altitudes of celestial bodies.

Augury (áh-gur-ee) The art or practice of foretelling events though signs or omens.

Autocracy (au-tóc-ra-cee) Government under the rule of an authoritarian ruler.

Autocrat (áuto-crat) An authoritarian ruler.

Axis World War II alliance whose main members were Germany, Italy, and Japan.

B

Baby boom The increase in births following World War II.

Babylonian Captivity Period during the fourteenth century in which seven popes chose to reside in Avignon instead of Rome. Critics called this period the "Babylonian Captivity" of the papacy.

Bailiffs Medieval French salaried officials hired by the king to collect taxes and represent his interests.

Balance of power Distribution of power among states, or the policy of creating alliances to control powerful states.

Balkans States in the Balkan Peninsula, including Albania, Bulgaria, Greece, Romania, and Yugoslavia.

Baroque (ba-róak) An artistic style of the sixteenth and seventeenth centuries stressing rich ornamentation and dynamic movement; in music, a style marked by strict forms and elaborate ornamentation.

Bastard feudalism (feúd-a-lism) Late medieval corruption of the feudal system replacing feudal loyalty with cash payments.

Bastille (bas-téel) The royal prison symbolizing the old regime that was destroyed in the French Revolution.

Bauhaus (bóugh-house) An influential school of art emphasizing clean, functional lines founded in Germany by the architect Walter Gropius just after World War I.

Bedouin (béd-oh-in) An Arab of any of the nomadic tribes of the deserts of North Africa, Arabia, and Syria.

Berlin airlift The airborne military operation organized to supply Berlin's Western-occupied sectors during the Soviet Union's 1948 Berlin blockage.

Berlin Wall The wall erected in 1961 to divide East and West Berlin.

Bessemer (béss-uh-mer) **process** A method for removing impurities from molten iron.

Black Death Name given the epidemic that swept Europe beginning in 1348. Most historians agree that the main disease was bubonic plague, but the Black Death may have incorporated many other diseases.

Blackshirts Mussolini's black-uniformed Fascist paramilitary forces in the 1920s and 1930s.

Blitzkrieg (blíts-kreeg) "Lightning war," a rapid air and land military assault used by the Germans in World War II.

Boers (boars) Dutch settlers in south Africa.

Bolshevik (bówl-shuh-vick) "Majority faction," the Leninist wing of the Russian Marxist Party; after 1917, the Communist Party.

Bourgeoisie (boor-zhwa-zée) The middle class.

Boxers A nineteenth-century Chinese secret society that believed in the spiritual power of the martial arts and fought against Chinese Christians and foreigners in China.

Boyar A Russian noble.

Brezhnev (bréhzh-nyeff) **Doctrine** Policy that justified Soviet intervention in order to ensure the survival of socialism in another state, initiated by USSR leader Brezhnev in 1968.

Brownshirts Hitler's brown-uniformed paramilitary force in the 1920s and 1930s.

Burschenschaften (bóor-shen-sháhf-ten) Liberal nationalist German student unions during the early nineteenth century.

C

Cabinet system Government by a prime minister and heads of governmental bureaus developed by Britain during the eighteenth century.

Caesaropapism (see-zer-oh-pápe-ism) The practice of having the same person rule both the state and the church.

Cahiers (kye-yéah) Lists of public grievances sent to the French Estates General in 1789.

Caliph (káy-liff) A title meaning "successor to the Prophet" given to Muslim rulers who combined political authority with religious power.

Capitalists Those promoting an economic system characterized by freedom of the market with private and corporate ownership of the means of production and distribution that are operated for profit.

Capitularies (ka-pít-chew-làir-eez) Royal laws issued by Charlemagne and the Carolingians.

Caravel (care-uh-véll) A small, light sailing ship of the kind used by the Spanish and Portuguese in the fifteenth and sixteenth centuries.

Carbonari (car-bun-áh-ree) A secret society of revolutionaries in nineteenth-century Italy.

Cartel (car-téll) An alliance of corporations designed to control the marketplace.

Cartesian (car-tée-zhen) **dualism** A philosophy developed by René Descartes in the seventeenth century that defines two kinds of reality: the mind, or subjective thinking, and the body, or objective physical matter.

Catacombs Underground burial places. The term originally referred to the early Christian burial locations in Rome and elsewhere.

Cathars (cáth-arz) A medieval French dualist heretical sect; also called Albigensians.

Central Powers World War I alliance, primarily of Germany, Austria, and the Ottoman Empire.

Centuriate (sen-chúr-ee-ate) **Assembly** An aristocratic ruling body in ancient Rome that made the laws.

Chancellor A high-ranking official—in Germany, the prime minister.

Chartists English reformers of the 1830s and 1840s who demanded political and social rights for the lower classes.

Checks and balances A balanced division of governmental power among different institutions.

Chivalry (shív-el-ree) Code of performance and ethics for medieval knights. It can also refer to the demonstration of knightly virtues.

Christian humanists During the fifteenth and sixteenth centuries, experts in Greek, Latin, and Hebrew who studied the Bible and other Christian writings in order to understand the correct meaning of early Christian texts.

Civil Constitution of the Clergy New rules nationalizing and governing the clergy enacted during the French Revolution.

Civic humanists Those practicing a branch of humanism that promoted the value of responsible citizenship in which people work to improve their city-states.

Classical style A seventeenth- and eighteenth-century cultural style emphasizing restraint and balance, and following models from ancient Greece and Rome.

Cold War The global struggle between alliances headed by the United States and the Soviet Union during the second half of the twentieth century.

Collectivization The Soviet policy of taking agricultural lands and decisions away from individual owners and placing them in the hands of elected managers and party officials.

Comecon (cómm-ee-con) The economic organization of communist eastern European states during the Cold War.

Committee of Public Safety Ruling committee of twelve leaders during the French Revolutionary period of the Terror.

Common law Laws that arise from customary use rather than from legislation.

Common market The European Economic Community, a union of Western European nations initiated in 1957 to promote common economic policies.

Commonwealth of Independent States A loose confederation of several former republics of the disintegrated Soviet Union founded in 1991.

Commune (cómm-yune) A medieval or early modern town; a semi-independent city government or socialistic community in the nineteenth and twentieth centuries.

Communist Manifesto A short, popular treatise written by Karl Marx and Friedrich Engels in 1848 that contained the fundamentals of their "scientific socialism."

Complutensian Polyglot (comm-plue-tén-see-an pólly-glàht) **Bible** An edition of the Bible written in 1520 that had three columns that compared the Hebrew, Greek, and Latin versions.

Compurgation (comm-pur-gáy-shun) A Germanic legal oath taken by twelve men testifying to the character of the accused.

Concert of Europe The alliance of powers after 1815 created to maintain the status quo and coordinate international relations.

Conciliar (conn-síll-ee-ar) **movement** The belief that the Catholic Church should be led by councils of cardinals rather than popes.

Concordat (conn-córe-dat) A formal agreement, especially between the pope and a government, for the regulation of church affairs.

condottieri (conn-duh-tyáy-ree) From the fourteenth to the sixteenth century, captains of bands of mercenary soldiers, influential in Renaissance Italy.

Congress of Vienna The peace conference held between 1814 and 1815 in Vienna after the defeat of Napoleon.

Conquistadors (conn-kéy-stah-doors) Spanish adventurers in the sixteenth century who went to South and Central America to conquer indigenous peoples and claim their lands.

Conservatism An ideology stressing order and traditional values.

Constitutionalism The idea that political authority rests in written law, not in the person of an absolute monarch.

Constitutional monarchy Government in which the monarch's powers are limited by a set of fundamental laws.

Consuls (cónn-sul) The appointed chief executive officers of the Roman Republic.

Containment The Cold War strategy of the United States to limit the expansion and influence of the Soviet Union.

Continental System Napoleon's policy of preventing trade between continental Europe and Great Britain.

Contra posto (cón-tra páh-sto) A stance of the human body in which one leg bears weight, while the other is relaxed. Also known as counterpoise, it was popular in Renaissance sculpture.

Copernican (co-pér-nick-an) **revolution** The change from an earth-centered to a sun-centered universe initiated by Copernicus in the sixteenth century.

Corinthian order One of three architectural systems developed by the Greeks to decorate their buildings. The Corinthian order is marked by the capitals of columns decorated with acanthus leaves.

Corn Laws British laws that imposed tariffs on grain imports.

Corporate state Mussolini's economic and political machinery to manage the Italian economy and settle issues between labor and management.

Corsair A swift pirate ship.

Cossacks The "free warriors" of southern Russia, noted as cavalrymen.

Cottage industry Handicraft manufacturing usually organized by merchants and performed by rural people in their cottages.

Coup d'état (coo-day-táh) A sudden taking of power that violates constitutional forms by a group of persons in authority.

Creoles (crée-ohlz) People of European descent born in the West Indies or Spanish America, often of mixed ancestry.

Crusades From the late eleventh century through the thirteenth century, Europeans sent a number of military operations to take the Holy Land (Jerusalem and its surrounding territory) from the Muslims. These military ventures in the name of Christendom are collectively called the Crusades.

Cult of sensibility The eighteenth-century emphasis on emotion and nature forwarded by several European artists and authors.

Cuneiform (cue-née-uh-form) A writing system using wedge-shaped characters developed in ancient Mesopotamia.

Curia Regis (kóo-ree-uh régg-ees) A medieval king's advisory body made up of his major vassals.

Cynicism (sín-uh-sism) A Hellenistic philosophy that locates the search for virtue in an utter indifference to worldly needs.

Cyrillic (suh-ríll-ik) **alphabet** An old Slavic alphabet presently used in modified form for Russian and other languages.

D

Dada (dáh-dah) An early twentieth-century artistic movement that attacked traditional cultural styles and stressed the absence of purpose in life.

Dauphin (dough-fán) Heir to the French throne. The title was used from 1349 to 1830.

D-Day The day of the Allied invasion of Normandy in World War II—June 6, 1944.

Decembrists (dee-sém-brists) Russian army officers who briefly rebelled against Tsar Nicholas I in December 1925.

Decolonization The loss of colonies by imperial powers during the years following World War II.

Declaration of the Rights of Man and Citizen France's revolutionary 1789 declaration of rights stressing liberty, equality, and fraternity.

Deductive reasoning Deriving conclusions that logically flow from a premise, reasoning from basic or known truths.

Deism (dée-iz-um) Belief in a God who created the universe and its natural laws but does not intervene further; gained popularity during the Enlightenment.

Demotic A form of ancient Egyptian writing used for ordinary life. A simplified form of hieratic script.

Détente (day-táhnt) The period of relative cooperation between Cold War adversaries during the 1960s and 1970s.

Devotio moderno (day-vóh-tee-oh moh-dáir-noh) A medieval religious movement that emphasized internal spirituality over ritual practices.

Diaspora The dispersion of the Jews after the Babylonian conquest in the sixth century B.C.E. The term comes from the Greek word meaning "to scatter."

Diet The general legislative assembly of certain countries, such as Poland.

Directory The relatively conservative government during the last years of the French Revolution before Napoleon gained power.

Division of labor The division of work in the modern process of industrial production into separate tasks.

Doge (dóhj) The chief magistrate of the Republic of Venice during the Middle Ages and Renaissance.

Domesday (dóomz-day) **Book** A record of all the property and holdings in England, commissioned by William the Conqueror in 1066 so that he could determine the extent of his lands and wealth.

Doric order One of three architectural systems developed by the Greeks to decorate their buildings. The Doric order may be recognized by its columns, which include a wide shaft with a plain capital on the top.

Drachma (dróck-mah) Hellenistic coin containing either 4.3 grams (Alexander's) or 3.5 grams (Egypt's) of silver.

Dreyfus (dry'-fuss) **affair** The political upheaval in France accompanying the unjust 1894 conviction of Jewish army officer Alfred Dreyfus as a German spy that marked the importance of anti-Semitism in France.

Dual Monarchy The Austro-Hungarian Empire; the Habsburg monarchy after the 1867 reform that granted Hungary equality with Austria.

Il Duce (ill dóoch-ay) "The Leader," Mussolini's title as head of the Italian Fascist Party.

Duma Russia's legislative assembly in the years prior to 1917.

E

Ecclesia (ek-cláy-zee-uh) The popular assembly in ancient Athens made up of all male citizens over 18.

Edict of Nantes (náwnt) Edict issued by French king Henry IV in 1598 granting rights to Protestants, later revoked by Louis XIV.

Émigrés (em-ee-gráy) People, mostly aristocrats, who fled France during the French Revolution.

Emir (em-éar) A Muslim ruler, prince, or military commander.

Empirical method The use of observation and experiments based on sensory evidence to come to ideas or conclusions about nature.

Ems (Em's) **Dispatch** Telegram from Prussia's head of state to the French government, edited by Bismarck to look like an insult, that helped cause the Franco-Prussian War.

Enclosure Combining separate parcels of farmland and enclosing them with fences and walls to create large farms or pastures that produced for commerce.

encomienda (en-koh-mee-én-da) A form of economic and social organization established in sixteenth-century Spanish settlements in South and Central America. The encomienda system consisted of a royal grant that allowed Spanish settlers to compel indigenous peoples to work for them. In return, Spanish overseers were to look after their workers' welfare and encourage their conversion to Christianity. In reality, it was a brutal system of enforced labor.

Enlightened absolutism (áb-suh-loo-tism) Rule by a strong, "enlightened" ruler applying Enlightenment ideas to government.

Enlightenment An eighteenth-century cultural movement based on the ideas of the Scientific Revolution and that supported the notion that human reason should determine understanding of the world and the rules of social life.

Entente Cordiale (on-táhnt core-dee-áhl) The series of understandings, or agreements, between France and Britain that led to their alliance in World War I.

Entrepreneur (on-truh-pren-óor) A person who organizes and operates business ventures, especially in commerce and industry.

Epic (épp-ik) A long narrative poem celebrating episodes of a people's heroic tradition.

Epicureanism (epp-uh-cúre-ee-an-ism) A Hellenistic philosophy that held that the goal of life should be to live a life of pleasure regulated by moderation.

Equestrians (ee-quést-ree-ans) A social class in ancient Rome who had enough money to begin to challenge the power of the patricians.

Essenes (Ess-éenz) Members of a Jewish sect of ascetics from the second century B.C.E. to the second century C.E.

Estates Representative assemblies, typically made up of either the clergy, the nobility, the commoners, or all three meeting separately.

Estates General The legislature of France from the Middle Ages to 1789. Each of the three Estates—clergy, nobility, and bourgeoisie—sent representatives.

Ethnic cleansing The policy of brutally driving an ethnic group from their homes and from a certain territory, particularly prominent during the civil wars in the Balkans during the 1990s.

Eugenics (you-génn-iks) The study of hereditary improvement.

Euro (yóu-roe) The common currency of many European states, established in 1999.

Eurocommunism The policy of Western European Communist parties of supporting moderate policies and cooperating with other Leftist parties during the 1970s and 1980s.

European Economic Community The E.E.C., or Common Market, founded in 1957 to eliminate tariff barriers and begin to integrate the economies of western European nations.

European Union (EU) The community of European nations that continued to take steps toward the full economic union of much of Europe during the late twentieth century.

Evolution Darwin's theory of biological development through adaptation.

Existentialism (ekk-siss-ténn-sha-lism) A twentieth-century philosophy asserting that individuals are responsible for their own values and meanings in an indifferent universe.

Expressionism A late-nineteenth- and early-twentieth-century artistic style that emphasized the objective expression of inner experience through the use of conventional characters and symbols.

F

Fabian (fáy-bee-an) **Society** A late-nineteenth-century group of British intellectuals that advocated the adoption of socialist policies through politics rather than revolution.

Factory system Many workers producing goods in a repetitive series of steps and specialized tasks using powerful machines.

Falange (fa-láhn-hey) A Spanish fascist party that supported Francisco Franco during the Spanish civil war.

Fascism (fáh-shism) A philosophy or system of government that advocates a dictatorship of the extreme right together with an ideology of belligerent nationalism.

Fealty (fée-al-tee) In the feudal system, a promise made by vassals and lords to do no harm to each other.

Federates In the late Roman Empire, treaties established with many Gothic tribes allowed these tribes to settle within the Empire. The tribes then became "federates," or allies of Rome.

Fibula (pl. fibulae) An ornamented clasp or brooch, favored by the ancient Germanic tribes to hold their great cloaks closed.

Fief (feef) In the feudal system, the portion—usually land—given by lords to vassals to provide for their maintenance in return for their service.

Five-Year Plan The rapid, massive industrialization of the nation under the direction of the state initiated in the Soviet Union in the late 1920s.

Forum The central public place in ancient Rome which served as a meeting place, marketplace, law court, and political arena.

Fourteen Points U.S. President Wilson's plan to settle World War I and guarantee the peace.

Frankfurt Assembly Convention of liberals and nationalists from several German states that met in 1848 to try to form a unified government for Germany.

Free companies Mercenary soldiers in the Middle Ages and Renaissance who would fight for whoever paid them. They were called "free" to distinguish them from warriors who were bound by feudal ties to a lord.

Free Corps (core) Post–World War I German right-wing paramilitary groups made up mostly of veterans.

Free trade International trade of goods without tariffs, or customs duties.

Fresco A technique of painting on the plaster surface of a wall or ceiling while it is still damp so that the colors become fused with the plaster as it dries, making the image part of the building's surface.

Fronde (frawnd) Mid-seventeenth-century upheavals in France that threatened the royal government.

Fundamentalists Those who believe in an extremely conservative interpretation of a religion.

G

Galley A large medieval ship propelled by sails and oars.

General will Rousseau's notion that rules governing society should be based on the best conscience of the people.

Gentry People of "good birth" and superior social position.

Geocentric Earth-centered.

Gerousia (gay-róo-see-uh) Ruling body in ancient Sparta made up of male citizens over age 60.

Gestapo (guh-stóp-po) Nazi secret police in Hitler's Germany.

Girondins (zhee-roan-dán) Moderate political faction among leaders of the French Revolution.

Glasnost (gláz-nost) Soviet leader Gorbachev's policy of political and cultural openness in the 1980s.

Globalization Twentieth-century tendency for cultural and historical development to become increasingly worldwide in scope.

Global warming The heating of the earth's atmosphere in recent decades, caused in part by the buildup of carbon dioxide and other "greenhouse gases" produced by burning fossil fuels.

Glorious Revolution In 1688, English Parliament offered the crown of England to the Protestant William of Orange and his wife Mary, replacing James II. This change in rule was accomplished peacefully and clarified the precedent that England was a constitutional monarchy with power resting in Parliament.

Gosplan The Soviet State Planning Commission, charged with achieving ambitious economic goals.

Gothic (góth-ik) A style of architecture, usually associated with churches, that originated in France and flourished from the twelfth to the sixteenth century. Gothic architecture is identified by pointed arches, ribbed vaults, stained-glass windows, and flying buttresses.

Grand tour An educational travel taken by the wealthy to certain cities and sites, particularly during the seventeenth and eighteenth centuries.

Great Chain of Being A traditional Western-Christian vision of the hierarchical order of the universe.

Great Depression The global economic depression of the 1930s.

Great fear Panic caused by rumors that bands of brigands were on the loose in the French countryside during the summer of 1789.

Great Purges The long period of Communist Party purges in the Soviet Union during the 1930s, marked by terror, house arrests, show-trials, torture, imprisonments, and executions.

Great Reforms Reforms instituted by Russia's tsar Alexander II in 1861 that included freeing Russia's serfs.

Great Schism (skíz-um) Period in the late Middle Ages from 1378 to 1417 when there were two (and at times three) rival popes.

Greek fire A Byzantine naval weapon made of combustible oil that was launched with a catapult or pumped through tubes to set fire to enemy ships.

Guild An association of persons of the same trade united for the furtherance of some purpose.

Guillotine (ghée-oh-teen) A device for executing the condemned used during the French Revolution.

H

Hacienda (ha-see-én-da) Large landed estates in Spanish America that replaced encomiendas as the dominant economic and social structure.

Haj (hodge) The Muslim annual pilgrimage to Mecca, Medina, and other holy sites.

Hasidim (hah-see-déem) Sect of Jewish mystics founded in Poland in the eighteenth century in opposition to the formalistic Judaism and ritual laxity of the period.

Heliocentric (hee-lee-oh-sén-trick) Pertaining to the theory that the sun is the center of the universe.

Hellenes (Héll-eenz) The name ancient Greeks assigned to themselves, based on their belief that they were descended from a mythical King Hellen.

Hellenistic Of or related to the period between the fourth century B.C.E. and the first century B.C.E.

Helot (héll-ots) A serf in ancient Sparta.

Heresy A religious belief that is considered wrong by orthodox church leaders.

Hermetic doctrine Notion popular in the sixteenth and seventeenth centuries that all matter contains the divine spirit.

Hieratic (high-rát-ick) A form of ancient Egyptian writing consisting of abridged forms of hieroglyphics, used by the priests in keeping records.

Hieroglyph (hígh-roe-gliff) A picture or symbol used in the ancient Egyptian writing system—means "sacred writing."

Hijra (hídge-rah) (also *Hegira*) Muhammad's flight from Mecca to Medina in 622 B.C.E.

Holocaust (hóll-o-cost) The extermination of some six million Jews by the Nazis during World War II.

Holy Alliance Alliance of Russia, Austria, and Prussia to safeguard the principles of Christianity and maintain the international status quo after the Napoleonic Wars.

Homeopathy (home-ee-áh-pa-thee) Medical treatment emphasizing the use of herbal drugs and natural remedies.

Hoplites (hóp-lights) Ancient Greek infantrymen equipped with large round shields and long thrusting spears.

Hubris Excessive pride, which for the ancient Greeks brought punishment from the gods.

Huguenots (húgh-guh-nots) French Protestants of the sixteenth, seventeenth, and eighteenth centuries.

Humanists Students of an intellectual movement based on a deep study of classical culture and an emphasis on the humanities (literature, history, and philosophy) as a means for self-improvement.

Hundred Years' War A series of wars between England and France from 1337 to 1453. France won and England lost its lands in France, thus centralizing and solidifying French power.

I

Icon (éye-con) A sacred image of Jesus, Mary, or the saints that early Christians believed contained religious power.

Iconoclasm (eye-cónn-o-claz-um) A term literally meaning "icon breaking" that refers to an eighth-century religious controversy in Byzantium that argued that people should not venerate icons.

Ideogram (eye-dée-o-gram) A hieroglyph symbol expressing an abstract idea associated with the object it portrays.

Ideograph A written symbol that represents an idea instead of expressing the sound of a word.

Ideology (eye-dee-áh-lo-gee) A set of beliefs about the world and how it should be, often formalized into a political, social, or cultural theory.

Imam Muslim spiritual leader, believed by Shi'ites to be a spiritual descendant of Muhammad who should also be a temporal leader.

Imperialism The policy of extending a nation's authority by territorial acquisition or by the establishment of economic and political control over other nations or peoples.

Impressionism A nineteenth-century school of painting originating in France that emphasized capturing on canvas light as the eye sees it.

Indo-European Belonging to or constituting a family of languages that includes the Germanic, Celtic, Italic, Baltic, Slavic, Greek, Armenian, Iranian, and Indic groups.

Inductive reasoning Drawing general conclusions from particular concrete observations.

Indulgence A certificate issued by the papacy that gave people atonement for their sins and reduced their time in purgatory. Usually indulgences were issued for performing a pious act, but during the Reformation, critics accused the popes of selling indulgences to raise money.

Industrial revolution The rapid emergence of modern industrial production during the late eighteenth and nineteenth centuries.

Information revolution A rapid increase in the ability to store and manipulate information accompanying the development of computers during the second half of the twentieth century.

Inquisition A religious court established in the thirteenth century designed to root out heresy by questioning and torture.

Intendant (ann-tawn-dáunt) A French official sent by the royal government to assert the will of the monarch.

Internationalism The principle of cooperation among nations for their common good.

Ionia (eye-ówn-ee-uh) Ancient district in what is now Turkey that comprised the central portion of the west coast of Asia Minor, together with the adjacent islands.

Ionic order One of three architectural systems developed by the Greeks to decorate their buildings. The Ionic order may be recognized by its columns, which are taller and thinner than the Doric columns and capped with scroll-shaped capitals.

Iron Curtain The dividing line between Eastern and Western Europe during the Cold War.

Islamic fundamentalism A movement within Islam calling for a return to traditional ways and a rejection of alien ideologies that gained strength during the second half of the twentieth century.

J

Jacobins (jáck-o-bins) A radical political organization or club during the French Revolution.

Jacquerie (zhak-rée) The name given to the peasant revolt in France during the fourteenth century.

Jansenism A religious movement among French Catholics stressing the emotional experience of religious belief.

Jesuits (jéh-zu-it) Members of the Catholic religious order the Society of Jesus, founded by Ignatius Loyola in 1534.

Jihad (jée-hod) Islamic holy war in which believers feel they have the authority to fight to defend the faith.

Joint-stock company A business firm that is owned by stockholders who may sell or transfer their shares individually.

Journeyman A worker in a craft who has served his or her apprenticeship.

Joust A medieval contest in which two mounted knights combat with lances.

Junkers (yóong-kers) Prussian aristocracy.

Justification by faith The belief that faith alone—not good works—is needed for salvation. This belief lies at the heart of Protestantism.

K

Kamikaze (kah-mih-káh-zee) Usually refers to suicidal attacks on Allied ships by Japanese pilots during World War II.

Kore (kóh-ray) (pl. *korai*) Greek word for maiden that refers to an ancient Greek statue of a standing female, usually clothed.

Kouros (kóo-ross) (pl. *kouroi*) Greek word for a young man that refers to an ancient Greek statue of a standing nude young man.

Kristallnacht (kriss-táhl-nahkt) The "night of the broken glass"—a Nazi attack on German Jewish homes and businesses in 1938.

Kulak (kóo-lock) A relatively wealthy Russian peasant labeled by Stalin during the period of collectivization as a "class enemy."

Kulturkampf (kool-tóur-kahmpf) Bismarck's fight against the Catholic Church in Germany during the 1870s.

L

Laissez-faire (léss-say-fair) "Hands-off." An economic doctrine opposing governmental regulation of most economic affairs.

Laudanum (láud-a-numb) Opium dissolved in alcohol, used as a medicine in the eighteenth and nineteenth centuries.

League of Nations A post–World War I association of countries to deal with international tensions and conflicts.

Lebensraum (láy-benz-rowm) "Living space." Hitler's policy of expanding his empire to the east to gain more land for Germans.

Legume (lég-yoom) A pod, such as that of a pea or bean, used as food.

Levée en masse (le-váy awn máhss) General call-up of all men, women, and children to serve the nation during the French Revolution.

Levellers Revolutionaries who tried to "level" the social hierarchy during the English civil war.

Liberalism A nineteenth- and twentieth-century ideology supporting individualism, political freedom, constitutional government, and (in the nineteenth century) laissez-faire economic policies.

Liege (léezh) **lord** In the feudal system, a lord who has many vassals, but owes allegiance to no one.

Linear perspective An artistic technique used to represent three-dimensional space convincingly on a flat surface.

Lollards Followers of the English church reformer John Wycliffe who were found heretical.

Long March An arduous Chinese communist retreat from south China to north China in 1934 and 1935.

Luddism The smashing of machines that took jobs away from workers in the first half of the nineteenth century.

M

Ma'at (máh-aht) An Egyptian spiritual precept that conveyed the idea of truth and justice, or, as the Egyptians put it, right order and harmony.

Maccabean (mack-uh-bée-en) **Revolt** Successful Jewish revolt led by Judas Maccabeus in the mid-second century B.C.E. against Hellenistic Seleucid rulers.

Madrigal Musical composition set to a short poem usually about love, written for several voices. Common in Renaissance music.

Magi (máyj-eye) Ancient Persian astrologers or "wise men."

Maginot (máh-zhin-oh) **Line** A string of defensive fortresses on the French/German border that France began building in the late 1920s.

Magna Carta The Great Charter that English barons forced King John of England to sign in 1215 that guaranteed certain rights to the English people. Seen as one of the bases for constitutional law.

Marshall Plan A package of massive economic aid to European nations offered in 1947 to strengthen them and tie them to American influence.

Marxism A variety of socialism propounded by Karl Marx stressing economic determinism and class struggle—"scientific socialism."

Megalith An archaeological term for a stone of great size used in ancient monuments.

Meiji (máy-jee) **Restoration** The reorganizing of Japanese society along modern Western lines; initiated in 1868.

Mendicant orders Members of a religious order, such as the Dominicans or Franciscans, who wandered from city to city begging for alms rather than residing in a monastery.

Mercantilism (mírr-kan-till-ism) Early modern governmental economic policies seeking to control and develop the national economy and bring wealth into the national treasury.

Mercator projection (mer-káy-ter) A method of making maps in which the earth's surface is shown as a rectangle with Europe at the center, causing distortion toward the poles.

Mesolithic Of or pertaining to the period of human culture from about 15,000 years ago to about 7000 B.C.E. characterized by complex stone tools and greater social organization. "Middle Stone Age."

Methodism A Protestant sect founded in the eighteenth century that emphasized piety and emotional worship.

Metics (métt-iks) Foreign residents of Athens.

Miasma (my-ázz-ma) Fumes from waste and marshes blamed for carrying diseases during the eighteenth and the first half of the nineteenth centuries.

Middle Passage The long sea voyage between the African coast and the Americas endured by newly captured slaves.

Minoan (mínn-oh-an) A civilization that lived on the island of Crete from 2800 to 1450 B.C.E.

Mir (mere) Russian village commune.

Missi dominici (mée-see do-min-ée-kee) Royal officials under Charlemagne who traveled around the country to enforce the king's laws.

Mithraism (míth-ra-ism) A Hellenistic mystery religion that appealed to soldiers and involved the worship of the god Mithra.

Mughals (móe-gulls) Islamic rulers of much of India in the sixteenth, seventeenth, and eighteenth centuries.

Munich Conference The 1938 conference where Britain and France attempted to appease Hitler by allowing him to dismantle Czechoslovakia.

Mycenean (my-sen-ée-an) A civilization on the Greek peninsula that reached its high point between 1400 and 1200 B.C.E.

Mystery religions Ancient religions that encouraged believers to cultivate a deep connection with their deity. Initiates swore not to reveal the insights they had gained during rites and ceremonies; the shroud of secrecy resulted in the name "mystery" religions.

N

Napoleonic (na-po-lee-ón-ik) **Code** The legal code introduced in France by Napoleon Bonaparte.

Nationalism A nineteenth- and twentieth-century ideology stressing the importance of national identity and the nation-state.

Natural law Understandable, rational laws of nature that apply to the physical and human world.

Nazi Party Hitler's German National Socialist Party.

Neolithic (nee-oh-líth-ik) Of or denoting a period of human culture beginning around 7000 B.C.E. in the Middle East and later elsewhere, characterized by the invention of farming and the making of technically advanced stone implements. "New Stone Age."

Neoplatonism (nee-oh-pláy-ton-ism) Views based on the ideas of Plato that one should search beyond appearances for true knowledge; stressed abstract reasoning.

New Economic Policy (NEP) Lenin's compromise economic and social policy for the USSR during the 1920s.

New imperialism The second wave of Western imperialism, particularly between 1880 and 1914.

Night of August 4 Surrender of most privileges by the French aristocracy at a meeting held on August 1, 1789.

Nominalism (nóm-in-al-ism) A popular late medieval philosophy based on the doctrine that the universal, or general, has no objective existence or validity, being merely a name expressing the qualities of various objects resembling one another in certain respects. Also called New Nominalism.

North American Free Trade Agreement (NAFTA) The 1994 agreement between the United States, Mexico, and Canada to create a free trade zone.

North Atlantic Treaty Organization (NATO) A military alliance against the Soviet Union initiated in 1949.

Nuremberg Laws Hitler's anti-Jewish laws of 1935.

O

Ockham's razor A principle that states that between alternative explanations for the same phenomenon, the simplest is always to be preferred.

October Revolution The 1917 Bolshevik revolt and seizure of power in Russia.

Old Regime (re-zhéem) European society before the French Revolution.

Oligarchy (áh-luh-gar-kee) Rule by a small group or by a particular social class—often wealthy middle classes, as in ancient Greek or medieval European cities.

Operation Barbarossa (bar-bar-óh-ssa) The German invasion of the USSR during World War II.

Optimates (ahp-tuh-máht-ays) The nobility of the Roman Empire. Also refers to the political party that supported the nobility. Contrast with the *populares*.

Ordeal An ancient form of trial in which the accused was exposed to physical dangers that were presumed to be harmless if the accused was innocent. Ordeals might include grasping hot pokers, trial by battle, immersion in water, and other similar challenges.

Organization of Petroleum Exporting Countries (OPEC) An Arab-dominated organization of Middle Eastern oil-producing states that became effective during and after the 1970s.

Ostracism (áhs-tra-sism) A political technique of ancient Greece by which people believed to be threats to the city-state were chosen for exile by popular vote.

P

Paleolithic (pay-lee-oh-líth-ik) Of or pertaining to the period of human culture beginning with the earliest chipped stone tools, about 750,000 years ago, until the beginning of the Mesolithic, about 15,000 years ago. "Old Stone Age."

Pantheon (pán-thee-on) A great temple in Rome built in 27 B.C.E. and dedicated to all the gods. In 609 C.E., it was rededicated as a Christian church called Santa Maria Rotunda.

Paris Commune The revolutionary government of the city of Paris, first in the 1790s and then in 1871.

Parlement (parl-máwn) A French court of law during the Old Regime.

Parliament Britain's legislature, including the House of Commons and House of Lords.

Parthenon (párth-uh-non) A famous Doric temple of Athena on the Acropolis in ancient Athens.

Patricians The ancient Roman aristocracy who populated the Senate and were particularly powerful during the Republic.

Pax Romana ("pocks" or "packs" row-máhn-ah) Literally, "Roman Peace." Two hundred years of relative, internal peace within the Roman Empire beginning with the rule of Caesar Augustus.

Peace of Paris The 1919 peace settlement after World War I.

Peers Members of the House of Lords in England.

Perestroika (pair-ess-trói-ka) Gorbachev's policy of "restructuring" the Soviet economy during the 1980s.

Petrine (pée-tryn) **doctrine** The belief that the popes, bishops of Rome, should lead the church because they are the successors of Peter, who many claim was the first bishop of Rome.

Phalanstery (fa-láns-ter-ee) The model commune envisioned by the French utopian socialist Fourier.

Phalanx (fáy-langks) An ancient Greek formation of foot soldiers carrying overlapping shields and long spears.

Pharaoh The title of the rulers of ancient Egypt. Also refers to the household and administration of the rulers.

Pharisees (fáir-uh-sees) Members of an ancient Jewish sect that rigidly observed purity laws, including dietary rules. They also believed in the resurrection of the just and the existence of angels.

Philosophes (fee-low-zóff) Leading French intellectuals of the Enlightenment.

Phonogram A character or symbol used to represent a speech sound used in ancient writing.

Physiocrats (fízz-ee-oh-crats) Eighteenth-century French economic thinkers who stressed the importance of agriculture and favored free trade.

Pictogram A picture representing an idea used in ancient writing.

Pietism (píe-uh-tism) An eighteenth-century Protestant movement stressing an emotional commitment to religion.

Plebeians (pleb-ée-an) The members of the urban lower classes in ancient Rome.

Plebiscite (pléb-uh-sight) A direct vote that allows the people to either accept or reject a proposed measure.

Pogrom ('puh-grúhm'; also 'póe-grom') An organized persecution or massacre of Jews, especially in eastern Europe.

Polis (póe-liss) (pl. *poleis* [póe-lease]) An ancient Greek city-state.

Poor Laws Eighteenth- and nineteenth-century British laws enacted to deal with the poor.

Populares (pop-you-lahr-ays) In Roman history, the political party of the common people. Also refers to the people themselves. Contrast with the *optimates*.

Popular Front The political partnership of parties of the Left, particularly in France and Spain, during the 1930s.

positivism A mid-nineteenth-century theory of sociology holding that scientific investigation could discover useful fundamental truths about humans and their societies.

Postindustrial societies Late-twentieth-century societies that moved from manufacturing to services led by professionals, managers, and financiers.

Postmodernism A late-twentieth-century approach to the arts stressing relativism and multiple interpretations.

Pragmatic Sanction The international agreement secured by the Habsburg emperor in the 1730s to ensure that his daughter would succeed him without question.

Prague Spring The brief period of democratic reforms and cultural freedom in Czechoslovakia during 1968.

Predestination Doctrine claiming that since God is all-knowing and all-powerful, he must know in advance who is saved or damned. Therefore, the salvation of any individual is predetermined. This doctrine is emphasized by Calvinists.

Preemptive War War initiated by one side on the justification that another side was on the verge of attack.

Prefect Powerful agents of the central government stationed in France's departments.

Preventive war War initiated by one side on the justification that another side might attack sometime in the future.

Principate (prínce-a-pate) The governmental system of the Roman Empire founded by Octavian (also known as Caesar Augustus).

Privateer An armed private vessel commissioned by a government to attack enemy ships.

Protestant Of or pertaining to any branch of the Christian church excluding Roman Catholicism and Eastern Orthodox.

Psychoanalysis Pioneered by Sigmund Freud, a method of investigating human psychological development and treating emotional disorders.

Ptolemaic (ptah-luh-máy-ik) **system** The traditional medieval earth-centered universe and system of planetary movements.

Ptolemies (ptáh-luh-meez) Hellenistic dynasty that ruled in Egypt from about 300 B.C.E. to about 30 B.C.E.

Purgatory In Roman Catholic theology, a state or place in which those who have died in the grace of God expiate their sins by suffering before they can enter heaven.

Purge Expelling or executing political party members suspected of inefficiency or opposition to party policy.

Puritans In the sixteenth and seventeenth centuries, those who wanted to reform the Church of England by removing all elaborate ceremonies and forms. Many Puritans faced persecution and were forced to flee to the American colonies.

Q

Quadrant An instrument for taking altitude of heavenly bodies.

Quadrivium (quad-rív-ee-um) The medieval school curriculum that studied arithmetic, music, geometry, and astronomy after completion of the trivium.

Quadruple (quad-róo-pull) **Alliance** Alliance of Austria, Prussia, Russia, and France in the years after the Napoleonic Wars to maintain the status quo.

Quietism (quíet-ism) A movement among seventeenth-century Spanish Catholics that emphasized the emotional experience of religious belief.

Qur'an (also Koran) The Muslim holy book recorded in the early seventh century by the prophet Muhammad.

R

Racism Belief that racial differences are important and that some races are superior to others.

Raison d'état (ráy-zawn day-táh) "Reason of state." An eighteenth- and nineteenth-century principle justifying arbitrary or aggressive international behavior.

Rationalism The belief that, through reason, humans can understand the world and solve problems.

Realism A medieval Platonist philosophy that believed that the individual objects we perceive are not real, but merely reflections of universal ideas existing in the mind of God. In the nineteenth century, this referred to a cultural style rejecting romanticism and attempting to examine society as it is.

Realpolitik (ray-áhl-po-lee-teek) The pragmatic politics of power; often a self-interested foreign policy associated with Bismarck.

Redshirts Garibaldi's troops used in the unification of Italy.

Reform Bill of 1832 English electoral reform extending the vote to the middle classes of the new industrial cities.

Reichstag (ríkes-tahg) German legislative assembly.

Reign of Terror The violent period of the French Revolution between 1792 and 1794.

Relativity Einstein's theory that all aspects of the physical universe must be defined in relative terms.

Relics In the Roman Catholic and Greek Orthodox churches, valued remnants of saints or other religious figures. Relics usually are parts of bodies but may also include objects that had touched sacred bodies or that were associated with Jesus or Mary, such as remnants of the True Cross.

Renaissance Literally, "rebirth." The term was coined in Italy in the early fourteenth century to refer to the rebirth of the appreciation of classical (Greek and Roman) literature and values. It also refers to the culture that was born in Italy during that century that ultimately spread throughout Europe.

Resistance movements Underground opposition to occupation forces, especially to German troops in conquered European countries during World War II.

Restoration The conservative regimes in power after the defeat of Napoleon in 1815 that hoped to hold back the forces of change or even turn back the clock to prerevolutionary days.

Risorgimento (ree-sor-jee-mén-toe) A nineteenth-century Italian unification movement.

Rococo (roe-coe-cóe) A style of art developed from the baroque that originated in France during the eighteenth century that emphasized elaborate designs to produce a delicate effect.

Romanesque (Roman-ésk) A style of architecture usually associated with churches built in the eleventh and twelfth centuries and that was inspired by Roman architectural features. Romanesque buildings were massive, with round arches, barrel vaulted ceilings, and dark interiors.

Romanticism A cultural ideology during the first half of the nineteenth century stressing feeling over reason.

Rosetta Stone A tablet of black basalt found in 1799 at Rosetta, Egypt, that contains parallel inscriptions in Greek, ancient Egyptian demotic script, and hieroglyphic characters. The stone provided the key to deciphering ancient Egyptian writing.

Rostra The speaker's platform in the Forum of ancient Rome.

Roundheads Members or supporters of the Parliamentary or Puritan party in England during the English civil war (1642).

Royal absolutism The seventeenth- and eighteenth-century system of elevated royal authority.

S

Sacraments In Christianity, rites that were to bring the individual grace or closeness to God. In Roman Catholicism and Greek Orthodoxy there are seven sacraments: baptism, confirmation, the Eucharist, penance, extreme unction, holy orders, and matrimony. Protestants in general acknowledge only two sacraments: baptism and the Lord's Supper.

Sadducees (sád-juh-sees) Members of an ancient Jewish sect that emphasized worship at the Temple in Jerusalem. They rejected new ideas such as resurrection, insisting on only those ideas that could be found in the Torah.

Saga A medieval Scandinavian story of battles, customs, and legends, narrated in prose and generally telling the traditional history of an important Norse family.

Salon (suh-láhn) Seventeenth- and eighteenth-century social and cultural gatherings of members of the upper and middle classes.

Sans-culottes (sawn-key-lóht) Working-class people of Paris during the French Revolution.

Sarcophagus (sar-kóff-a-gus) A stone coffin.

Satellite states Eastern European states under the control of the Soviet Union during the Cold War.

Satrap (sát-trap) An ancient Persian governor in charge of provinces called "satrapies."

Schlieffen (shléaf-en) **Plan** German military strategy in World War I that called for a holding action against Russia while German forces moved through Belgium to knock out France.

Scholasticism The dominant medieval philosophical and theological movement that applied logic from Aristotle to help understand God's plan. It also refers to the desire to join faith with reason.

Scientific Revolution The new sixteenth- and seventeenth-century methods of investigation and discoveries about nature based on observation and reason rather than tradition and authority.

Scutage (skyóot-ij) Medieval payment in lieu of military service.

Seleucids (se-lóo-sids) Hellenistic dynasty that ruled in Asia from about 300 B.C.E. to about 64 B.C.E.

Semitic (sem-ít-ik) Of or pertaining to any of a group of Caucasoid peoples, chiefly Jews and Arabs, of the eastern Mediterranean area.

Senate, Roman The deliberative body and influential governing council of Rome during the Republic and Empire. Composed of ex-magistrates with lifetime membership, the Senate did not legislate, but conducted foreign policy and warfare and authorized public expenditures.

Septuagint (sep-tu-eh-jint) A Greek translation of the Hebrew scriptures (the Old Testament), so named because it was said to be the work of 72 Palestinian Jews in the third century B.C.E., who completed the work in seventy days.

Serfs Medieval peasants who were personally free, but bound to the land. They owed labor obligations as well as fees.

Shi'ite (shée-ite) **Muslims** Those who accepted only the descendants of 'Ali, Muhammad's son-in-law, as the true rulers. It was not the majority party in Islam but did prevail in some of the Muslim countries.

Shire An English county.

Sinn Fein (shín féign) "Ourselves Alone." An extremist twentieth-century Irish nationalist organization.

Skepticism (skép-ti-cism) The systematic doubting of accepted authorities—especially religious authorities.

Second Reich (rike) German regime founded in 1871 and lasting until the end of World War I.

Sepoy (sée-poy) **Mutiny** The 1857 uprising of Indians against British rule.

Social Darwinism The effort to apply Darwin's biological ideas to social ideas stressing competition and "survival of the fittest."

Socialists Those promoting or practicing the nineteenth- and twentieth-century ideology of socialism, stressing cooperation, community, and public ownership of the means of production.

Socratic method The method of arriving at truth by questioning and disputation.

Solidarity A Polish noncommunist union that became the core of resistance to the communist regime during the 1980s.

Sophists (sóff-ists) Fifth-century B.C.E. Greek philosophers who were condemned for using tricky logic to prove that all things are relative and success alone is important.

Sovereignty (sóv-rin-tee) The source of authority exercised by a state; complete independence and self-government.

Soviet A workers' council during the 1905 and 1917 Russian revolutions and part of the structure of government in the Soviet Union.

SS The Schutzstaffel, Hitler's elite party troops of the 1930s and 1940s.

Stadholder (stáhd-holder) A governor of provinces in the Dutch United Provinces.

Statutory law Laws established by a king or legislative body. Contrast with common law.

Stoicism (stów-i-cism) A Hellenistic philosophy that advocated detachment from the material world and an indifference to pain.

Strategoi (stra-táy-goy) Generals in ancient Athens who eventually took a great deal of political power.

Struggle of the Orders The political strife between patrician and plebeian Romans beginning in the fifth century B.C.E. The plebeians gradually won political rights as a result of the struggle.

Sturm und drang (shtúrm unt dráhng) "Storm and stress." A literary movement in late eighteenth-century Germany.

Sumptuary (súmp-chew-air-ee) **laws** Laws restricting or regulating extravagance (for example, in food or dress), often used to maintain separation of social classes.

Sunna (sóon-a) A collection of sayings and traditions of the prophet Muhammad that delineates the customs adhered to by Muslims.

Supply and demand Adam Smith's liberal economic doctrine that demand for goods and services will stimulate production (supply) in a free-market system.

Surrealism (sur-rée-a-lism) A twentieth-century literary and artistic style stressing images from the unconscious mind.

Symphony A long sonata for orchestra.

Syncretism (sín-cre-tism) The attempt or tendency to combine or reconcile differing beliefs, as in philosophy or religion.

Syndicalism (sín-di-cal-ism) A late-nineteenth-century anarchist ideology envisioning labor unions as the center of a free and just society.

T

Taliban The strict, fundamentalist Islamic regime that ruled most of Afghanistan from 1996 to 2001.

Tennis Court Oath Oath taken by members of the French Estates General not to dissolve until they had created a constitution for France.

Tetradrachma (tet-ra-drák-ma) Hellenistic coin worth four drachmas.

Tetrarchy (tét-rar-key) The governmental system of the Roman Empire founded by Diocletian that divided the empire into four administrative units.

Theocracy (thee-áh-kruh-see) Government by priests claiming to rule by divine authority.

Theme A division for the purpose of provincial administration in the Byzantine Empire.

Thermidorian (ther-mi-dór-ee-an) **Reaction** The overthrow of Robespierre and the radicals in July 1794, during the French Revolution.

Third Estate Commoners, or all people except the nobility and clergy, in early modern European society.

Third French Republic The republican government established in 1871 and lasting until Germany's defeat of France in 1940.

Torah (tór-uh) The first five books of the Jewish sacred scriptures, comprising Genesis, Exodus, Leviticus, Numbers, and Deuteronomy.

Tories A conservative British political party during the eighteenth and nineteenth centuries.

Totalitarianism A twentieth-century form of authoritarian government using force, technology, and bureaucracy to effect rule by a single party and controlling most aspects of the lives of the population.

Total war A form of warfare in which all the forces and segments of society are mobilized for a long, all-out struggle.

Transubstantiation (trán-sub-stan-chee-áy-shun) In the Roman Catholic and Greek Orthodox churches, the belief that the bread and wine of the Eucharist were transformed into the actual body and blood of Christ.

Trench warfare An almost stagnant form of defensive warfare fought from trenches.

Triangular trade Trade pattern between European nations and their colonies by which European manufactured goods were traded for raw materials (such as agricultural products) from the Americas or slaves from Africa.

Tribune An official of ancient Rome chosen by the common people to protect their rights.

Triple Alliance Alliance of Germany, Austria-Hungary, and Italy in the years before World War I.

Triumvirate (try-úm-vir-ate) A group of three men sharing civil authority, as in ancient Rome.

Trivium (trív-ee-um) The basic medieval curriculum that studied grammar, rhetoric, and logic; after completion, students could proceed to the quadrivium.

Troubadour (tróo-buh-door) Poets from the late twelfth and early thirteenth centuries who wrote love poems, meant to be sung to music, that reflected the new sensibility of courtly love, which claimed that lovers were ennobled.

Truman Doctrine U.S. policy initiated in 1947 that offered military and economic aid to countries threatened by a communist takeover with the intention of creating a military ring of containment around the Soviet Union and its satellite states.

Tsar The emperor of Russia.

Twelve Tables According to ancient Roman tradition, popular pressure in the fifth century B.C.E. led to the writing down of traditional laws to put an end to patrician monopoly of the laws. The resulting compilation—the Twelve Tables—was seen as the starting point for the tradition of Roman law.

U

Ultra-royalism The nineteenth-century belief in rule by a monarch and that everything about the French Revolution and Enlightenment was contrary to religion, order, and civilization.

Unconscious According to Freud, that part of the mind of which we are not aware; home of basic drives.

Unilateralism Actions or policies taken by one nation in its own interests regardless of the views and interests of its allies.

United Nations (UN) An international organization founded in 1945 to promote peace and cooperation.

Universal A metaphysical entity that does not change, but that describes particular things on earth—for example, "justice" or "beauty." Explained by the ancient Greeks and examined by subsequent philosophers. (Also called "forms" or "ideas.")

Utilitarianism (you-till-a-táre-ee-an-ism) A nineteenth-century liberal philosophy that evaluated institutions on the basis of social usefulness to achieve "the greatest happiness of the greatest number."

Utopian (you-tópe-ee-an) **socialism** A form of early nineteenth-century socialism urging cooperation and communes rather than competition and individualism.

V

Vassal In the feudal system, a noble who binds himself to his lord in return for maintenance.

Versailles (ver-sígh) **treaty** Peace treaty between the Allies and Germany following World War I.

Victorian Referring to the period of Queen Victoria's reign in Britain, 1837–1901.

Vulgate (vúll-gate) A version of the Latin Bible, primarily translated from Hebrew and Greek by Jerome.

W

Wahhabism (wuh-háh-biz-uhm) An Islamic reform movement founded in the eighteenth century that stressed a strict, literal interpretation of the Qur'an.

War guilt clause Article 231 of the Treaty of Versailles that places all blame on Germany for causing World War I.

Warsaw Pact A military alliance in Eastern Europe controlled by the Soviet Union and initiated in 1955.

Waterloo Site in Belgium of a decisive defeat of Napoleon in 1815.

Weimar (wy'e-mar) **Republic** The liberal German government established at the end of World War I and destroyed by Hitler in the 1930s.

Welfare state Governmental programs to protect citizens from severe economic hardships and to provide basic social needs.

Wergeld (véhr-gelt) In Germanic law, the relative price of individuals that established the fee for compensation in case of injury.

Whigs A British political party during the eighteenth and nineteenth centuries.

Witan The ancient Anglo-Saxon men who participated in the Witenagemot.

Witenagemot (wí-ten-uh-guh-mote) Ancient Anglo-Saxon assembly of nobles.

Z

Zealots (zéll-ets) An ancient Jewish sect arising in Palestine in about 6 C.E. that militantly opposed Roman rule and desired to establish an independent Jewish state. The sect was wiped out when the Romans destroyed Jerusalem in 70 C.E.

Zemstva (zémst-fah) Municipal councils established in Russia in the second half of the nineteenth century.

Ziggurat (zíg-gur-raht) A pyramid-shaped Mesopotamian temple.

Zionism A late-nineteenth- and twentieth-century Jewish nationalist movement to create an independent state for Jews in Palestine.

Zollverein (tsóll-ver-rhine) Nineteenth-century German customs union headed by Prussia.

Zoroastrianism (zorro-áss-tree-an-ism) An ancient Persian religion that had a belief in two gods: a god of light named Ahura Mazda and an evil god named Ahriman.

Chapter 1

p. 2: Scala/Art Resource, NY; p. 5: Marijan Murat/ dpa/Corbis; p. 6: PhotoDisc/Getty Images; p. 9: World Religions Photo Library/The Bridgeman Art Library; p. 11: The Iraq Museum, Baghdad, Iraq/Erich Lessing/Art Resource, NY; p. 11(inset): University of Pennsylvania Museum of Archaeology and Anthropology; p. 12: The Louvre Museum, Paris, France/Bridgeman-Giraudon/Art Resource, NY; p. 13: Ashmolean Museum, Oxford, UK/ Bridgeman Art Library; p. 16: Gianni Dagli Orti/ Corbis; p. 19: Egyptian Museum, Cairo, Egypt/ Werner Forman/Art Resource, NY; p. 20T: Fred J. Maroon/Photo Researchers, Inc.; p. 20B: Corbis; p. 21: British Museum, London, UK/ Bridgeman Art Library; p. 22: Private Collection/ The Bridgeman Art Library; p. 23: M. Busing/ Bildarchiv Preussischer Kulturbesitz/Art Resource; p. 25: Aegyptisches Museum, Staatliche Museen zu Berlin, Germany/Erich Lessing/Art Resource, NY; p. 32: Erich Lessing/Art Resource, NY; p. 38: Roine Magnusson/Getty Images.

Chapter 2

p. 40: Metropolitan Government of Nashville/ Gary Layda. Alan Lequire creator and sculptor; p. 44: Archaeological Museum, Heraklion, Crete, Greece/Erich Lessing/Art Resource, NY; p. 48L: National Archaeological Museum, Piraeus, Greece/ Nimatallah/Art Resource, NY; p. 48R: Acropolis Museum, Athens, Greece/Nimatallah/Art Resource, NY; p. 49: Photo: Johannes Laurentius. Photo Credit: Bildarchiv Preussischer Kulturbesitz/ Art Resource, NY; p. 52: Archives Charmet/The Bridgeman Art Library; p. 55: Attributed to The Bryn Mawr Painter. Red-figure Plate with Woman Playing Kottabos, 480 BC. Terracotta; actual: 2.5 × 21.8 cm (1 × 8 9/16 in.). Harvard Art Museums, Arthur M. Sackler Museum, Bequest of David M. Robinson, 1960.350. Photo: Michael Nedzweski © President and Fellows of Harvard College; p. 57: Agora Museum, Athens, Greece/Scala/Art Resource, NY; p. 58: National Archaeological Museum, Athens, Greece/Erich Lessing/Art Resource, NY; p. 63: Scala/Art Resource; p. 64B: British Museum, London, UK/Bridgeman Art Library; p. 64T: Acropolis Museum, Athens, Greece/Nimatallah/Art Resource, NY; p. 70: Museo Gregoriano Etrusco, Vatican Museums, Vatican State/Scala/Art Resource, NY.

Chapter 3

p. 76: The Metropolitan Museum of Art, Rogers Fund, 1909. (09.39) Photograph © 1997 The Metropolitan Museum of Art/Art Resource, NY.; p. 82: Archaeological Museum, Istanbul, Turkey/ Erich Lessing/Art Resource, NY; p. 87L: Erich Lessing/Art Resource, NY; p. 87R: Image copyright © The Metropolitan Museum of Art/Art Resource, NY; p. 88: The British Museum, London, England/ Art Resource, NY; p. 89B: © The Trustees of the British Museum/Art Resource, NY; p. 89T: Hermitage, St. Petersburg, Russia/Bridgeman Art Library; p. 89T: Hermitage, St. Petersburg, Russia/ Bridgeman Art Library; p. 90: The Louvre Museum, Paris, France/Scala/Art Resource, NY; p. 92: Bibliotheque Nationale, Paris, France/Bridgeman-Giraudon/Art Resource, NY; p. 95: Bildarchiv Preussischer Kulturbesitz/Art Resource; p. 96: Museo Nazionale Romano delle Terme/Scala/Art Resource, NY; p. 99: Museo di Villa Albani, Rome,

Italy/Alinari/Art Resource, NY; p. 101: Staatliche Antikensammlungen und Glyptothek Muenchen. Foto by Christa Koppermann.

Chapter 4

p. 106: Museo Archeologico, Florence, Italy/Scala/ Art Resource, NY; p. 108: Musei Capitolini, Rome, Italy/Scala/Art Resource, NY; p. 109: The Louvre Museum, Paris, France/Erich Lessing/Art Resource, NY; p. 116: Galleria Nazionale d'Arte Antica (Pal. Barberini-Corsini), Rome, Italy/Alinari/Art Resource, NY; p. 117: Museo Chiaramonti, Vatican Museums, Vatican State/Scala/Art Resource, NY; p. 118: Cubiculum (bedroom) from the Villa of P. Fannius Synistor at Boscoreale, ca. 50–40 BCE. Fresco, Room: 8 ft. 8 1/2 in. × 10 ft. 11 1/2 in. × 19 ft. 7 1/8 in. (265.4 × 334 × 583.9 cm). Rogers Fund, 1903 (03.14.13a-g).The Metropolitan Museum of Art, New York, NY, U.S.A. Image copyright © The Metropolitan Museum of Art/Art Resource, NY; p. 119L: Mansell Collection/Alinari/ Art Resource, NY; p. 119R: Scala/Art Resource, NY; p. 120: Museo Pio Clementino/Vatican Museums, Vatican State/Scala/Art Resource, NY; p. 127: © Apply Pictures/Alamy; p. 128: Scala/ Art Resource, NY; p. 131: Museo Archeologico Nazionale, Naples, Italy/Scala/Art Resource, NY; p. 133: The British Museum.

Chapter 5

p. 136: Erich Lessing/Art Resource, NY; p. 138: British Museum, London, UK/Ancient Art and Architecture Collection Ltd./The Bridgeman Art Library; p. 141: Braccio Nuovo/Vatican Museums, Vatican State/Scala/Art Resource, NY; p. 143: Photo:Hermann Buresch.Bildarchiv Preussischer Kulturbesitz/Art Resource, NY; p. 148: Joyce Salisbury; p. 149: R. Balsley; p. 150: Scala/Art Resource NY; p. 151L: Corbis; p. 151R: Corbis; p. 152: Deutsches Archäologisches Institut, Rome, Italy; p. 154: Alinari/Art Resource, NY; p. 158:Villa of the Mysteries, Pompeii, Italy/ Scala/Art Resource, NY; p. 162: David H. Wells/ Corbis; p. 163: Arch of Titus, Rome, Italy/Scala/ Art Resource, NY; p. 165: Rough Guides/Alamy; p. 167: Museo Pio Cristiano, Vatican Museums, Vatican State/Scala/Art Resource, NY; p. 168: Mausoleum of Galla Placidia, Ravenna, Italy/ Scala/Art Resource, NY; p. 170: Courtesy of the Orthodox Church in America; p. 175: Robert Harding Picture Library Ltd/Alamy.

Chapter 6

p. 176: Scala/Art Resource; p. 179: Heribert Proepper/AP Images; p. 180: Victoria & Albert Museum, London, England/Art Resource, NY; p. 184: The Board of Trinity College, Dublin, Ireland/Bridgeman Art Library; p. 185: Bibliotheque nationale de France/Art Resource, NY; p. 187: Real Monasterio del Escorial Spain/Granger Collection/ Art Archive; p. 188: Bayerische Staatsbibliothek, Muenchen, Germany, Clm 4452, fol.152v; p. 190B: Tibor Bognár/Corbis; p. 190T: John A. Rizzo/Getty Images; p. 192L: S. Vitale, Ravenna, Italy/Scala/Art Resource, NY; p. 192R: S. Vitale, Ravenna, Italy/Scala/Art Resource, NY; p. 195: Prado, Madrid, Spain/The Bridgeman Art Library; p. 198: Pergamon Museum, Berlin, Germany/The Bridgeman Art Library; p. 204: Real Monasterio del Escorial Spain/Granger Collection/Art Archive; p. 207B: Private Collection/The Bridgeman Art Library; p. 207T: Courtesy of National Library of Medicine.

Chapter 7

p. 212: Art Resource, NY; p. 218: British Library, London, UK/© British Library Board. All Rights Reserved/The Bridgeman Art Library; p. 220: The Louvre Museum, Paris, France/Erich Lessing/Art Resource, NY; p. 222: S. Giovanni in Laterano, Rome, Italy/Alinari/Art Resource, NY; p. 226B: Courtesy of HistoryofScience.com; p. 226T: Reproduced by kind permission of the Syndics of Cambridge University Library; p. 227: Private Collection/The Bridgeman Art Library; p. 231: Viking Ship Museum, Bygdoy, Norway/ Werner Forman/Art Resource, NY; p. 234: Viking Ship Museum, Oslo, Norway/Giraudon/The Bridgeman Art Library; p. 236: Ruprecht-Karls Universitaatsbibliothek Heidelberg.

Chapter 8

p. 242: The Pierpont Morgan Library, New York, N.Y./Art Resource, NY; p. 245: Fitzwilliam Museum, University of Cambridge/Bridgeman Art Library; p. 246L: Corbis; p. 246R: Christie's Images/Corbis; p. 250: Snark/Art Resource, NY; p. 251L: Ste. Madeleine, Vézelay, France/Scala/Art Resource, NY; p. 251R: Amiens Cathedral, France/ Scala/Art Resource, NY; p. 252: Sainte Chapelle, Paris, France/Bridgeman-Giraudon/Art Resource, NY; p. 255: Photo: Joerg P. Anders.Bildarchiv Preussischer Kulturbesitz/Art Resource, NY; p. 256: TTL Images/Alamy Images; p. 259: CADW: Welsh Historic Monuments; p. 260: University Library Heidelberg/Gianni Dagli Orti/The Art Archive; p. 261: Universitaatsbibliothek/Staatliche Museen zu Berlin Preussischer Kulturbesitz Kunstbibliothek/ Lipp Cc18. Foto: Knud Petersen/Bildarchiv Preussischer Kulturbesitz; p. 265: Bibliotheque nationale de France/Bridgeman Art Library; p. 268: Bildarchiv Preussischer Kulturbesitz/Art Resource, NY; p. 275: British Library/HIP/Art Resource, NY.

Chapter 9

p. 280: Erich Lessing/Art Resource, NY; p. 285L: Jean-Loup Charmet/Photo Researchers, Inc.; p. 285R: Les Belles Heures de Jean, Duc de Berry by Pol, Jean and Herman de Limbourg (active ca. 1400–1416). Folio 74v: Procession of Flagellants. Tempera and gold leaf on parchment. Accession #54.1.1. The Metropolitan Museum of Art, The Cloisters Collection, 1954. (54.1.1) Photograph © 1987 The Metropolitan Museum of Art/ Art Resource; p. 286: British Library, London, UK/Bridgeman Art Library; p. 287: Fundacion Coleccion Thyssen-Bornemisza, Madrid, Spain/ Erich Lessing/Art Resource, NY; p. 292: Erich Lessing/Art Resource, NY; p. 295: Duomo, Florence, Italy/Scala/Art Resource, NY; p. 296: Photo: R.G. Ojeda. Musée Condé, Chantilly, France/Réunion des Musées Nationaux/Art Resource, NY; p. 297: National Gallery, London/ Art Resource, NY; p. 301: The Marsden Archive, UK/The Bridgeman Art Library International; p. 304: Bibliotheque nationale de France.

Chapter 10

p. 308: Galleria Nazionale delle Marche, Urbino, Italy/Scala/Art Resource, NY; p. 312: The Sistine Chapel, Vatican Palace, Vatican State/ Scala/Art Resource, NY; p. 314: Erich Lessing/ Art Resource, NY; p. 316: Accademia, Venice, Italy/Erich Lessing/Art Resource, NY; p. 322: Pinacoteca, Vatican Museums, Vatican State/ Scala/Art Resource, NY; p. 325: Staats-und. Universitätsbibliothek Hamburg; p. 326: Gabinetto dei Disegni e delle Stampe, Uffizi, Florence, Italy/Scala/Art Resource, NY; p. 327: Camera degli Sposi, Palazzo Ducale, Mantua, Italy/Scala/Art Resource, NY; p. 329L: Biblioteca Nazionale Centrale di Firenze; p. 329R: Biblioteca Nazionale Centrale di Firenze; p. 330BL: Scala/Art Resource, NY; p. 330R: Corbis; p. 330TL: Duomo, Florence, Italy/Scala/Art Resource, NY; p. 331: Scrovegni Chapel, Padua, Italy/Alinari/Art Resource, NY; p. 332: Stanza della Segnatura, Stanze di Raffaello, Vatican Palace, Vatican State/Scala/Art Resource, NY; p. 334: The Louvre Museum, Paris, France/Bridgeman-Giraudon/Art Resource, NY; p. 335L: Bettmann/Corbis; p. 335R: Ann Ronan Picture Library/HIP/Art Resource, NY; p. 339: The Granger Collection.

Chapter 11

p. 342: On loan to the National Gallery, London from the collection of the Earl of Radnor/Bridgeman Art Library; p. 346: Oxford Science Archive/HIP/Art Resource, NY; p. 347: The Louvre Museum, Paris, France/Scala/Art Resource, NY; p. 353: Lucas Cranach the Younger (German, 1515–1586), *Martin Luther and the Wittenberg Reformers*, ca. 1543. (1926.55), oil on wood panel, 72.8 × 39.7 cm, Toledo Museum of Art, Purchased with funds from the Libbey Endowment, Gift of Edward Drummond Libbey; p. 357: The Granger Collection, NY; p. 359: National Portrait Gallery, London, UK/The Bridgeman Art Library; p. 360: Courtesy, The Marquess of Salisbury, Hatfield House/Fotomas Index/Topfoto/The Image Works; p. 364: Kunsthistorisches Museum, Vienna, Austria/Erich Lessing/Art Resource, NY; p. 365: S. Tome, Toledo, Spain/Bridgeman-Giraudon/Art Resource, NY; p. 366: Erich Lessing/Art Resource, NY; p. 368: Musée des Beaux Arts Lausanne/Gianni Dagli Orti/The Art Archive; p. 373: *The Suitor's Visit*, 1658 by Gerard ter Borch II. (137.1.58. (58)/PA). c. 1658, oil on canvas, framed: 43 5/8 × 41 3/4 × 5". #1937.1.58., Andrew W. Mellon Collection, © 1999 Board of Trustees, National Gallery of Art, Washington, DC; p. 374B: Amsterdams Historisch Museum on loan from Protestanse Diaconie Amsterdam; p. 374T: Giraudon/The Bridgeman Art Library International; p. 375: National Gallery, London/Art Resource, NY.

Chapter 12

p. 380: Museo de América en Madrid; p. 383: Bibliotheque Nationale, Paris, France/The Bridgeman Art Library; p. 384: Royal Geographical Society, London, UK/Bridgeman Art Library; p. 385: The Pierpont Morgan Library/Art Resource, NY; p. 387: Private Collection/The Bridgeman Art Library; p. 391: Biblioteca Nazionale, Firenze/Fotomas/Bridgeman Art Library; p. 393: The Granger Collection; p. 394: © British Library Board. All Rights Reserved/The Bridgeman Art Library; p. 397: Library of the Hispanic Society of America, New York; p. 398: SSPL/Science Museum/Art Resource, NY; p. 400: Smithsonian American Art Museum, Washington, DC/Art Resource, NY; p. 401: *Young Woman with a Water Pitcher*. Ca. 1662. Oil on canvas, 18 × 16 in.

(45.7 × 40.6 cm). Vermeer (van Delft), Jan (1632–1675). The Metropolitan Museum of Art, Marquand Collection, Gift of Henry G. Marquand, 1889. (89.15.21). Photograph © 1993 The Metropolitan Museum of Art/Art Resource, NY; p. 405: Typ 732.18.567, Department of Printing and Graphic Arts, Houghton Library, Harvard College Library; p. 407: Institut Amatller D'Art Hispanic (MAS); p. 408: Museo de América en Madrid; p. 409: Special Collections, Lehigh University Library; p. 410: Royal Geographical Society, London, UK/Bridgeman Art Library.

Chapter 13

p. 414: The Louvre Museum, Paris, France/Scala/Art Resource, NY; p. 417: Erich Lessing/Art Resource, NY; p. 418: Bibliotheque nationale de France; p. 423: Réunion des Musées Nationaux/Art Resource, NY; p. 424: Erich Lessing/Art Resource, NY; p. 425: © National Gallery, London/Art Resource, NY; p. 431: Russian Historical Museum Moscow/Alfredo Dagli Orti/The Art Archive; p. 434: Dyck, Anthony van (1599–1641) *James Stuart (1612–1655), Duke of Richmond and Lennox*. ca. 1634–35. Oil on canvas, 85 × 50 1/4 in. The Metropolitan Museum of Art, Marquand Collection, Gift of Henry G. Marquand, 1889. (89.15.16). Photograph © 1998 The Metropolitan Museum of Art/Art Resource, NY; p. 438: The Granger Collection; p. 439: British Library, London, UK/Bridgeman Art Library; p. 440: British Library/HIP/Art Resource, NY; p. 443: National Portrait Gallery, London, UK/The Bridgeman Art Library; p. 446B: Bildarchiv Preussischer Kulturbesitz/Art Resource, NY; p. 446T: The Granger Collection, New York.

Chapter 14

p. 450: Houghton Library, Harvard University; p. 453: Charles Walker/Topfoto/The Image Works; p. 454: V&A Images, London/Art Resource, NY; p. 456: Erich Lessing/Art Resource, NY; p. 458: Snark/Art Resource, NY; p. 459: Image Select/Art Resource, NY; p. 461: Réunion des Musées Nationaux/Art Resource, NY; p. 463: Houghton Library, Harvard University; p. 464: Fitzwilliam Museum, University of Cambridge/Bridgeman Art Library; p. 467: Private Collection/The Stapleton Collection/The Bridgeman Art Library; p. 471: Chateau, Coppet, Switzerland/Bridgeman-Giraudon/Art Resource, NY; p. 472: Réunion des Musées Nationaux/Art Resource, NY; p. 473: Musee des Beaux-Arts, Dijon, France/Erich Lessing/Art Resource, NY.

TEXT CREDITS